Towards World Constitutionalism

Towards World Constitutionalism

Issues in the Legal Ordering of the World Community

Compiled and Edited by

Ronald St. John Macdonald and Douglas M. Johnston

MARTINUS NIJHOFF PUBLISHERS

LEIDEN • BOSTON

A C.I.P. Catalogue record for this book is available from the Library of Congress.

Printed on acid-free paper.

ISBN 90 04 14612 1
Typeset by *jules guldenmund layout & text*, The Hague

Printed and bound in The Netherlands.

Table of Contents

Foreword   ix
Introduction   xiii

Part 1   **1**
Foundations of the International Legal Community

1. World Constitutionalism in the Theory of International Law   3
    Douglas M. Johnston
2. Multilateralism in the Age of US Hegemony   31
    Christian Tomuschat
3. American Unilateralism and the Rule of Law   77
    Robert F. Turner
4. International Democratic Constitutionalism   103
    Brun-Otto Bryde

Part 2   **127**
Uniformity and Diversity in International Law

5. The Globalisation of Philosophy and the Philosophy of Globalisation   129
    Philip Allott
6. A Transcivilizational Perspective on Global Legal Order in the
    Twenty-first Century: A Way to Overcome West-centric and
    Judiciary-centric Deficits in International Legal Thoughts   151
    Onuma Yasuaki
7. International Law as a Cultural Perspective: Towards a Convergence
    of Civilizations: Contributions of Developing Countries to the
    Formation and Application of International Law   191
    Saeid Mirzaee-Yengejeh
8. Fragmentation of International Law? A View from Russia   223
    Roman A. Kolodkin

9.   Centrifugal and Centripetal Tendencies in the International System:
     Some Reflections   241
     V.S. Mani

10. Universalism, Regionalism and Localism in the Age of Globalization   255
     Władysław Czapliński

11. The Search for Universal Justice   273
     Eric Wyler and Alain Papaux

Part 3   **303**
Geopolitics, Values and the Clash of Civilizations

12. Contributions of Islam to the Development of a Global Community
     Based on Rules of International Law   305
     Ahmed Abou-el-Wafa

13. Developing Countries in the Group of 77: A Journey in Multilateral
     Diplomacy, 1964 to 2004   355
     Awni Behnam

14. America's Doctrines: The Monroe and Bush Doctrines Compared   381
     Alfred P. Rubin

Part 4   **399**
The Historical Development of International Legal Institutions

15. Basic Principles of UN Charter Law   401
     Karl Zemanek

16. The Legislative Powers of the United Nations Security Council   431
     Munir Akram and Syed Haider Shah

17. Legislative Powers of the Security Council   457
     Axel Marschik

18. Contribution of the General Assembly to the Constitutional
     Development and Interpretation of the United Nations Charter   493
     Manuel Rama-Montaldo

19. The Relevance of International Adjudication Revisited: Reflections
     on the Need and Quest for International Compulsory Jurisdiction   515
     Antonio Augusto Cançado Trindade

20. The Legal Ordering of International Trade: From GATT to the WTO   543
     Donald M. McRae

21. The Legal Ordering of Environmental Protection   567
     Alexandre Kiss

22. Accountability of International Organizations – A Critical View   585
     Gerhard Hafner

23. Forging a Multilayered System of Global Governance   631
     Charlotte Ku

Part 5   **653**
Confrontations with Established Principles of International Law

24. Security Concerns and National Sovereignty in the Age of
     World-Wide Terrorism   655
     Vaughan Lowe

25. Terrorism and Non-state Organizations   681
     Bertrand G. Ramcharan

26. The Doctrine of "Just War" and Contemporary International Law   705
     Benedetto Conforti

27. *Hostes Humani Generis*: Piracy, Territory and the Concept of
     Universal Jurisdiction   715
     Hilario G. Davide, Jr.

28. Sovereign Equality of States and the Legitimacy of "Leader States"   737
     Sienho Yee

Part 6   **773**
Idealism and the Arena: International Law under Stress

29. Solidarity as a Constitutional Principle: Its Expanding Role and
     Inherent Limitations   775
     Karel Wellens

30. Straddling Law and Politics: Judicial Review in International Law   809
     Jan Klabbers

31. The Meaning of International Constitutional Law   837
     Bardo Fassbender

32. The International Community as a Legal Community   853
     Ronald St. John Macdonald

33. The United Nations and New Threats, Challenges and Change:
     The Report of the High-Level Panel   911
     Bertrand G. Ramcharan

About the Contributors   927
Index   939

Foreword

I wish to begin by thanking the co-editors of this important book, Judge Ronald Macdonald and Professor Douglas Johnston, for inviting me to write this foreword. I have known and admired them for over 20 years. In 1982, after the conclusion of the Third UN Conference on the Law of the Sea, another distinguished friend and colleague from Dalhousie University, the late Professor Elizabeth Mann Borgese, invited me to spend the summer at Halifax, Nova Scotia, to direct a workshop on ocean law and policy for young scholars and officials from developing countries. My wife and I look back on that summer with many happy memories.

One of the happy discoveries of that summer was the depth and diversity of talent of the faculties at Dalhousie. Apart from Ronald Macdonald, Douglas Johnston, Elizabeth Mann Borgese, I also met with Professor Gilbert Winham and Professor Arthur Hanson. I wish to use this opportunity to salute all of them. I wish, however, to pay a special tribute to the two co-editors who have done so much to promote the cause of international law in the world.

This is an important and timely work. Why is it timely? It is timely because the consensus of the last 60 years, that we should work for a world ruled by law, seems to be under attack. Paradoxically, the attack is not coming from the non-Western world which had, in the past, questioned the legitimacy and universality of customary international law because of its European origin. The attack is coming from some influential voices in the United States. This book will make a solid contribution to that debate.

This is an important book because it contains contributions from 33 leading scholars from all parts of the world, from every civilisation and from every point of view. It is also a very ambitious book, containing six chapters, on the foundations of the international community; uniformity and diversity in international law; geopolitics, values and clash of civilisations; the historical development of international legal institutions; confrontations with established principles of international law; and idealism and the arena. Although the book has tried to be fair and balanced by including contributions from all points of view, this does not mean that the co-editors do not have a point of view of their own. They are certainly not neutral in this debate.

I have asked them three questions. *First*, what is the inspiration or provocation which led the two of them to conceive of co-editing this volume of essays?

Judge Macdonald replied that they wished to contribute positively to the current debate about the shaping of the international legal order at this juncture in the history of the development of the UN. They wished to argue that international is more, not less, important than previously, and that the structural organisation of global society needed to be built through continuous contributions of international jurists from all parts of the world.

I agree with the co-editors that international law is more important today than it was previously. It is more important partly because of globalisation, partly because of technology and partly because of increased human solidarity. Globalization and technology have shrunk the world, increased the interactions among economies and peoples across borders and made us more dependent on one another. This has resulted in the growing importance of international law governing, for example, banking and financial transactions, trade, telecommunications, intellectual property rights, the environment, etc. At the same time, there is an enhanced sense of solidarity of the human family. Thus, it is no longer permissible for a government to oppress its people and take shelter behind Article 2, paragraph 7 of the UN Charter. For example, there is growing support for the concept of the duty to protect when faced with the drama of massive human suffering or deprivation. I share the editors' vision of building an international order based on the rule of law.

Second, what erroneous views do the editors wish to dispute? Judge Macdonald replied that they wished to dispute the view advocated by some influential American officials that international law was not binding; that the global system, especially in the economic domain, should be allowed to grow like topsy; that the strengthening of international institutions was to be resisted; and that the pursuit of distributive justice was illusory.

I support the editors in disputing those propositions. The rhetoric and conduct of the United States, in the recent past, have caused grave disquiet throughout the world. Friends and admirers of the United States could not understand why the country which had, in the past, championed international law and the rule of law in the world, should turn its back against the International Criminal Court, the Kyoto Protocol, the UN Convention on the Law of the Sea, the Convention on Biological Diversity, etc. They could not believe their eyes when they read statements by US officials claiming that the US was not bound by international law because it was above the law. The United States clearly has a major credibility problem. It is in danger of squandering the goodwill which it had earned from 1945 until about the end of the Cold War.

Recently, the new Secretary of State of the United States, Dr Condoleezza Rice, spoke to the American Society of International Law, at its annual meeting. Dr Rice said:

> ... the time for diplomacy is now. One of the pillars of that diplomacy is our strong belief that international law is vital and a powerful force in the search for freedom. The United States has been and will continue to be the world's strongest voice for the development and defense of international legal norms.

America is a country of laws. When we observe our treaty and other international commitments, our country – other countries are more willing to cooperate with us and we have a better chance of persuading them to live up to their own commitments. And so when we respect our international legal obligations and support an international system based on the rule of law, we do the work of making the world a better place, but also a safer and more secure place for America.

When I first read that statement, I was tempted to say, "Amen". Dr Rice has made an important policy statement. We should take the statement seriously and not dismiss it out of hand. I do not know whether we will see a different approach by the US Administration towards international law, in the President's second term. Let us wait and see whether Dr Rice's good words will be matched by deeds. As a friend of America, I wish her well.

Third, what propositions or theses do the editors wish to advance through this book? To paraphrase the editors, I think they wish to use this book to marshal the best minds from all regions of the world to address the constitutionalism of international law. They wish to promote both the rule of law and human dignity in world affairs. Their vision is a lofty one, to improve the international system for the six billion people of planet Earth.

In September this year, the UN General Assembly will hold a very important session. The session will discuss the UN's Millennium Development Goals; the Report of the High-Level Panel entitled, "Threats, Challenges and Change"; and the Secretary-General's report entitled "In Larger Freedom". The debate is, in essence, a debate about the future of the UN. An unwritten item on that agenda is the relationship between the UN and the world's only superpower. It is clear to me that the UN needs the US and the US needs the UN. An UN without the US will likely become increasingly irrelevant, like the League of Nations. There are some people in the US who believe that the US does not need the UN. They are wrong. No country, not even the US, powerful as it is, can succeed in solving all her problems without the cooperation and support of other countries. There are some in the US who dream of establishing an American Empire. Neither the American people nor the rest of the world will accept such an empire. Nor is retreating into Fortress America a viable option. It is America's destiny to lead the world into the 21st Century. The question is whether we will have the good fortune to see the emergence of another generation of American leaders, like the one which emerged after the Second World War, who will have the vision, strength and wisdom to translate American power into a new moral consensus in the world.

Tommy Koh

Ambassador-At-Large, Ministry of Foreign Affairs, Singapore
Chairman, Institute of Policy Studies
President, Third UN Conference on the Law of the Sea
Chairman, Main Committee, UNCED
Chairman, Preparatory Committee, UNCED

Introduction

The system of public international law is not of modern origin. Early evidence of principles and practices that we would regard as "legal" and "international" can be discovered as far back as the third millennium B.C. Many rulers of neighboring territories in the age of primitive antiquity resorted occasionally to a rudimentary form of treaty-making for certain purposes and usually recognized the need to afford special privileges to one another's envoys. Some major civilizations produced idealists who envisaged a future in which all people would eventually be brought under a single system of world law.

By the 16th century AD Europe took the lead in developing the concept of state sovereignty at a time in history when the major countries of the continent were beginning to organize systems of rule that jelled around firmly established central authority. Although it is somewhat controversial in contemporary literature, many international lawyers still perceive the Treaty of Westphalia (1648) as the beginning of a totally new mode of inter-state relations, which placed on international lawyers the role of developing legal norms protective of state interests. By the end of the 19th century a corpus of international rules had evolved in accordance with a "classical" conception of international law framed around the rights and duties of sovereign states. This "transactional" period of international law was dominated by the bilateral relationships of states accepted as being equal and qualified to negotiate with each other on the basis of reciprocity or mutual benefit. This classical period of international law, wholly statist in orientation, evolved with only modest acknowledgment of the rights of individuals and groups below the level of the nation state.

A major advancement took place after the First World War with the creation of the League of Nations and the Permanent Court of International Justice. For the first time, world society had the benefit of a global framework of "constitutional" character that could be considered analogous with the structure of the nation state. In the 1920s and 1930s it was assumed that development within this new "organizational" framework would involve the filling of institutional gaps in the new order. With the creation of the United Nations in 1945 a new surge of optimism swept through the international law community as more and more countries acquired independence and brought the world closer to universal membership in an organization that was mandated more clearly than the League to work toward the completion of the global system. However, the problems of institutional development were complicated by East-West antagonisms and North-South tensions.

With the collapse of communism in Europe and most of Asia in the late 1980s, renewed optimism inspired plans for more ambitious international legal planning. In particular, it seemed politically possible now for serious efforts to be undertaken to strengthen the United Nations system, partly through reform of the United Nations Charter. In the 1990s the apparent prevalence of capitalism as the globally shared ideology of most of the world's major economies seemed to sustain new hopes for cooperation not only in the international trade sector but in many other non-economic sectors as well.

However, the international law community since the early 1990s has seen the emergence of the United States as the world's only superpower. The presence of colossal hegemonial power has introduced new concerns regarding the role of international law within a community of states possessing the formal appearance, if not the political reality, of equality. Moreover, a world that might have been expected to become safer with the end of Cold War threats and hostilities has in fact become imperilled by new eruptions of violence associated mostly with non-state terrorist organizations. Perhaps inevitably, the superpower and its allies have become increasingly the targets of these new threats and assaults.

Moreover, the very structure of international society has been transformed, as corporate entities with global capabilities have come to dominate the world economy. The largest of these wealth-producing enterprises have acquired greater resources and capabilities than all but a dozen or so of the richest and most capable of states. The new world in which we find ourselves today is no longer governable entirely by resort to the classical system of international law that had developed to a level of sophistication for purely inter-state cooperation by the end of the 19th century.

Even more seriously, it now appears that the purposes and principles of the United Nations Charter are no longer being served sufficiently in light of new concerns. The text adopted in 1945 does not convey the image of a world tormented by terrorists. Nor does it reflect the most pressing commitments of our time: to democratic governance, to environmental responsibility, and to a freer and more equitable system of world trade. Increasingly the international law community acknowledges the need to set new priorities in the development of international law. To that end it seems timely to reconsider the case for strengthening the constitutional framework of norms and institutions that seemed to offer the promise of fulfilment in the second half of the 20th century. The post-Cold War euphoria of the 1990s has virtually evaporated under the stress of new concerns at a time when the states comprising the UN system are no longer capable of addressing these challenges.

Recent international events have demonstrated the fragility of constitutional order at the global level. It might be conceded that no constitutional order, at any level of authority, can be expected to operate without a degree of friction. Sometimes it is necessary, for the best of reasons, to find a way of circumventing the rigidities of constitutional structure through cost-sharing, power-sharing or other cooperative arrangements. Most constitutional lawyers agree on the need for flexibility in the interpretation, application, and occasional finessing of an aging constitutional text that no longer reflects accurately the values and priorities of the society it serves. Yet the case for constitutional flexibility must be guarded: deviations from constitutional text and normal constitutional practice must be justified in light of the values most critically at stake.

The concept of constitutional order in world affairs is more vulnerable than in national affairs. The obligation to comply is often resisted, particularly by power-holding elites, by invoking considerations of "vital national interest". Within a "collateral" system like that of international law and diplomacy it is unrealistic to suppose that the most powerful sovereign states can be prevented from "contracting out" of an established decision-making process, if it is honestly believed that compliance imperils the security and welfare of their people.

Analysis of the "constitutional crisis" in world affairs should take account of the various "models" of international law, each of which represents a cluster of associated values that have to be served by international (or world) law. It seems best to assume, at the level of abstraction, that no one model should have ascendancy over all the others. In any specific context, it is a matter of judgement how to weigh the values and principles associated with each.

In no particular order of priority, twelve models of international law can be suggested in "functionalist" terms: (i) state autonomy; (ii) world constitutionalism; (iii) civic benevolence; (iv) fairness; (v) order; (vi) regulation; (vii) war prevention and management; (viii) peaceful conflict resolution; (ix) national development; (x) environmental protection; (xi) cooperation; and (xii) convergence of legal systems. Each tends to reinforce several of the others, but some are clearly competitive with two or more other models.

Within this conceptual framework, the world constitutionalism model of international law might be expected to find support, in most contexts, from the state autonomy, order, war prevention and management, and peaceful conflict resolution models. However, the interventionist role of the UN Security Council, "validated" by the world constitutionalism model, represents a direct challenge to the state autonomy model, which pivots on such norms as sovereign entitlement, sovereign immunity, state equality, and the principle of non-interference. Above all, the Council is authorized by the world community to impose *order* in dangerous situations. This authority was designed to transcend the pacifist ethic inherent in *war prevention*, which, in world popular opinion, currently diminishes the Council's moral authority behind the coercive elements of its *war management* mandate.

Six of these models – state autonomy, world constitutionalism, order, regulation, war prevention and management, and peaceful conflict resolution – were in collision during the decade-long debate in the Security Council on how to deal with Iraq in the aftermath of the Gulf War. With a view to the central ("scripted") problem of weapons proliferation, the majority and minority in the Council seemed to differ on the efficacy of the established *regulatory* processes and on the immediacy of the need to impose *order*. Outside the "script" of the Security Council, the minority began to invoke another model, that *of civic benevolence*, to justify extra-constitutional intervention on humanitarian grounds.

Against the background of this recent controversy, the international law community is trying to come to grips with difficult and fundamental issues. Pre-eminent among these is the question how the values and principles of world constitutionalism can be protected and promoted more effectively. The core of the problem resides within the United Nations. No-one suggests that the Security Council reflects the fairest way of representing the system of member states, but all proposals for UN Charter reform have fallen like seed on barren soil.

Even with reforms affecting the Security Council, the UN system as a whole would remain a statist organization that cannot be truly representative of world society. By this view, the *constitutional* model of international law, derived from the ideal of constitutional democracy, requires more radical innovation in service to the modern goal of "global governance". It can be argued, for example, that even a reformed statist model of the United Nations needs to be counter-balanced with a more directly accountable, more democratic, institution, such as a Peoples' World Assembly.

Furthermore, world society might be ready to experiment more boldly with the concept of constitutional authority at the regional level, at least for certain purposes, beyond what was envisaged by the drafters of the UN Charter. Certain national governments in certain regions might prove more willing to accept responsibility for *civic benevolence* deficiencies if they were answerable more directly to their own region, and not merely to the distant world community. Innovative thinking about constitutionalism at the regional level may be an important part of the debate on the future of world constitutionalism.

In the past some have argued that international agreements can be likened to contracts. Indeed the codification of the law of treaties, through such instruments as the 1969 Vienna Convention on the Law of Treaties, is based to a considerable extent on a suggested treaty-contract analogy. The reality is, however, that only a limited number of bilateral agreements that fall into the domain of public international law can be treated confidently in that manner. Most multilateral agreements are clearly not contract-like. Some function more like legislation than contract, particularly if they are designed to govern an international regime or organization. Instruments of this kind may be characterized as "constitutive" in nature and purpose.

The Charter of the United Nations is surely the most basic of all constitutive instruments. It has been described as a "sacred text" and might be considered as having residence at the apex of the hierarchy of international agreements. For practical purposes, it is often treated as the "constitution" of the organized world community, or at least as "quasi-constitutional" in function.

Some constitutionalists argue that the UN Charter, because of its unique status, should be extremely difficult to revise, given ever-present political temptations to undertake revision for special-interest rather than common-interest reasons. Others argue, on the contrary, that precisely because of its basic constitutive status, the Charter should be subject to periodic, or at least occasional, review, so that it remains viable as a "living constitution". Numerous proposals for Charter revision have been submitted over the years, but all have failed to clear the political or bureaucratic hurdles erected along the course.

The depiction of the organized world community as a "constitutional order" goes far beyond the present reality of the United Nations and its Charter. Yet certain specialized areas of international law have been developed systematically to the point of having permanent global mechanisms with rule-making, executive, administrative, and judicial roles. At the global level, certain fields of international law provide conspicuous examples of specialized sectors that can be regarded as evolving along the lines of constitutional development.

In the case of the law of the sea, for example, the 1982 UN Convention on the Law of the Sea (UNCLOS), as subsequently re-negotiated, stands as the "constitution of the oceans". The Convention sets out the "allocation of powers" to coastal states and prescribes a system of special enforcement jurisdiction for flag states, coastal states, and port states for certain pollution control purposes. Although the Convention does not create the full institutional apparatus associated with a constitutional order, the Meeting of Contracting Parties is available to serve as a rule-making and rule-amending institution; the Department of Ocean Affairs and the Law of the Sea (DOALAS) Office of the UN Secretariat has day-to-day administrative responsibilities; and the International Tribunal for the Law of the Sea (ITLOS) is one of the principal mechanisms within a comprehensive system for judicial settlement. To conduct and regulate future mining activities in the submarine International Area beyond limits of national jurisdiction, the International Seabed Authority (ISA) is at the centre of what seems close to a complete "constitutive" system of principles and procedures for these activities. Substantially, the oceans of the world are regulated, more than ever before, through an evolving system of constitutional order.

In normal times – if we could discern "normality" in international affairs – it might be objected that devoting a substantial collection of essays to the goal of world constitutionalism promotes dangerously seductive "over-expectations". Very clearly, however, there is nothing at all normal about the first decade of the 21st century. Since this book was first conceived and our distinguished contributors were first approached, criticisms of the UN system have grown in intensity. Even those most faithful to the purposes and principles enunciated in the Charter have had to admit to concerns about the management of certain sectors of the organization; and most concede the unrepresentative character of the powerful Security Council granted legal supremacy as the enforcer of international peace and security. Many go further and complain of unconscionable political bias in the General Assembly and in certain, overly politicized, agencies.

During the gestation of this work, the call for reform of the United Nations has become more insistent than at any time in its 60-year history. At the time of writing (May 2005), the report of the Secretary-General's High-Level Panel on Threats, Challenges and Change (*A More Secure World: Our Shared Responsibility*) has identified a wide range of institutional and political issues that need to be addressed. On behalf of our contributors, and perhaps of many others in the international law community, we would like to suggest that the current world-wide debate on the strengthening of the United Nations must also include a principled, professional review of the *normative provisions* of the UN Charter and of other constitutive instruments that form the conceptual infrastructure of the organized world community. We believe that the "invisible college" of international and constitutional lawyers should have a visible – and audible – role to play in the re-thinking of world order.

In the meantime, we hope this collective treatment of the case for a more "constitutionalized" system of international law and diplomacy will be seen as a useful contribution to that larger, and even more urgent, debate.

Ronald St.John Macdonald
Douglas M. Johnston

Part 1

Foundations of the International Legal Community

1. World Constitutionalism in the Theory of International Law

Douglas M. Johnston

1. Controversy Within the International Law Community

More than ever, the international law community today is aboil with controversies. Sometimes the disputes are so heated, the factions so fractious, that it is hard to detect firm common ground. Some of the rifts opening up may even be cultural in origin, but the chief source of controversy is the jurisprudential division that now separates so many international jurists. Given the ethical dimensions of contemporary world law, it is a division that can be likened to a "moral divide".

Many international lawyers, especially those trained on the continent of Europe, are educated in a tradition, grounded in Roman law, which insists on the scientific nature of the "discipline" and therefore on the need for technical "rigour". The discipline is advanced through *centripetal* progression into its core. The highest values are *juridical* values: precision, clarity, consistency, and predictability. Logic follows the course prescribed by legal *form*. Pride is taken in excluding law, as completely as possible, from the cognate – but sometimes competing – normative domains of religion, ethics, custom, conventional morality, and above all politics. At the risk of rewarding inflexibility, law so conceived is promoted as the paramount normative presence in human affairs. International lawyers who give priority to values such as these are generally comfortable with the constraints of *legal formalism*.

Others, especially those most strongly influenced by exposure to the intellectual and social values of North America, tend to look at law as *social process*. For them, international law is a "field" that can never be unified and perfected, because it must always be sensitive to the need for change. Law so regarded is advanced through *centrifugal* progression to the periphery, where legal specialists can interact fruitfully with specialists in other relevant disciplines. The quest is for a kind of intellectual "sophistication" that is assumed to be unattainable without a conscious effort to keep in mind the social and other purposes of a legal system. For such lawyers, law functions best when it is balanced against the claims of ethics and the realities of political life: it is always important to maintain the credibility of a legal system as fair and effective within the larger social context. The prevailing values to

Ronald St. John Macdonald & Douglas M. Johnston (eds.), Towards World Constitutionalism, *pp. 3-29.*
© *2005 Koninklijke Brill NV. Printed in The Netherlands. ISBN 90 04 14612 1.*

be served are *human welfare* values such as individual dignity, communal cohesion, social utility, and civic benevolence. Flexibility is believed to be a necessary condition of experimentation in the tradition of *legal realism*.

Not all international lawyers will see themselves as totally committed to either of these philosophies. Many lawyers operate almost exclusively in a purely juridical mode, juxtaposing doctrine, engaged in textual analysis or interpretation, committed to professional tasks without much regard for philosophical allegiance. But when truly fundamental issues have to be confronted, technicality merely indicates the weapons to be used.

Commonly, legal realists criticize the narrowness and "artificiality" of legal formalism, and formalists deplore the "indeterminacy" of open-ended legal realist scholarship that looks to extra-legal ends and values. Formalists are sometimes denigrated as abstractionists and utopianists; realists as relativists and accommodationists. Yet whatever the choice of path to follow, it may be possible for jurists to agree that the history of modern international law has been a constant alternation between conflicting modes of idealism and realism. Some favour might be given to the position that the international law system is sufficiently distinct from other legal systems to need large measures of both for its healthy development. But to the extent the global legal system is always at risk of subversion by the intrusion of too much "reality", it is important to give full weight to the modes of idealism that have animated international law throughout world history. Constitutionalism is one kind of idealism for world society, but it must compete for priority – or even parity – with other modes.

2.   Twelve Idealistic Models of International Law

Within a purposive, teleological framework of legal theory, at least twelve "functional" models of idealism in international law might be distinguished. Each model represents a cluster of related values, principles, and aspirations.

A.   Order. One of the most conspicuously recurrent themes in the modern literature of international law is the remedial function of the legal system in an "anarchic" world of sovereign nation-states.[1] The rise of the concept of national sovereignty was, of course, a reflection of the growing intensity of nationalist sentiment in the early modern era and of the increasingly prevalent role of national interest in governmental decision-making. In a world society perceived to be internationally structured and divided among competing nation-states, international law has been the cement needed to keep the world together as an orderly system of global cohabitation.

---

[1]   Bull, Hedley, *The Anarchical Society: A Study of Order in World Politics* (London: Macmillan, 1977). The early history of international law is perhaps best treated as more-or-less disjointed pursuits of "world order". Bozeman, Adda B., *Politics and Culture in International History* (Princeton, NJ: Princeton University Press, 1960).

The preservation of order is the most basic of all functions of government in human society. Formal legal systems emerged, and became increasingly crucial to social development, in direct response to the necessity for order. For thousands of years – while technology was still too modest to pose the challenge of "chaos" – it was "anarchy" that was seen to present the greatest threat to social cohesion. Today the threat of global anarchy is heightened by the spread of terrorism as a political and religious weapon in the hands of (mostly non-state) extremists and by the availability of highly dangerous modes of war-making technology.

In ancient China, formal law was developed in penal form by a control-minded imperial bureaucracy.[2] In the history of Western and Central Europe, the relationship between bureaucracy and formal legal development became more complicated: the idea of law as an instrument of social control had to co-exist with the idea of law as an agency of justice.

The paramountcy of state sovereignty in the early modern Western world gave birth to the notion that all states, being independent, had the right, equally, to withhold their consent to international laws intended to govern them. To that extent at least, world society is in a chronic state of "anarchy". Hence the idealized perception of international law as the principal institutionalized form of *control over the forces of anarchy inherent in international society.*

B.   Regulation. In modern times, science has accelerated the process of human transformation, enlightening our understanding of the universe and of the roles that we might inherit. Knowledge has expanded into technical skills that have altered the face of the earth. In the early 19th century, as the quality of life improved for the possessors of modern technology, the idea of progress became associated with material welfare. The new complexity of modern society created the need for problem-solving skills at the service of rulers and ruling elites.

The 19th century witnessed the development of modern regulatory arrangements designed for a widening variety of purposes. As it became accepted that national government was responsible for *regulating activities in the public interest*, it became possible to extend regulatory controls beyond national boundaries, first to neighboring states and then to the international community at large. Europe led the way in both bilateral and sub-regional experiments to regulate the uses of shared areas and resources, such as lakes, rivers, canals and ocean fisheries.[3]

---

2   Bodde, Derk, and Clarence Morris, *Law in Imperial China: Exemplified by 190 Ch'ing Dynasty Cases.* Trans. from the Hsing-an hui-lan. Philadelphia: University of Pennsylvania Press, 1973.

3   See, for example, Kunz, Josef L., "The Danube Regime and the Belgrade Conference", 43 *American Journal of International Law* 104 (1949); Baxter, Richard R., *The Law of International Waterways, with Particular Regard to Interoceanic Canals* (Cambridge, Mass.: Harvard University Press, 1964); and Johnston, Douglas M., *The International Law of Fisheries: A Framework for Policy-Oriented Inquiries* (New Haven, Conn: Yale University Press, 1965).

In the era of global institutionalization, when the international legal system became "organizational" as well as "transactional' in orientation, the operational life of the system became routinized through hundreds of international regulatory agencies. For over a century, the norms of international law have been applied, on a day-to-day basis, within a vast and constantly expanding network of cooperative *regimes* designed to regulate governmental, industrial and commercial activities over a broad spectrum of sectors.[4]

C.   Autonomy. On the other hand, there are still many who characterize international law as *a system of sovereign state entitlements designed primarily to protect the weak from the strong.* To political realists, the history of international relations is essentially a history of power-holding, in which small or relatively weak nations have always been at a disadvantage *vis-à-vis* the major military, economic and political powers. By this reasoning, states cooperate with one another only when it serves their national interest to do so. Diplomatic success in negotiating cooperative arrangements is limited by the will of the most capable and resourceful players. Consequently, the most vulnerable states need legal rules that can be invoked as a constraint on the misuse of power.

The idea of international law as a shield had been a constant motif of world history for hundreds of years, but it has had to endure the scepticism of the ages. During the period of Western imperialism, many nations or territories were denied the status of legally sovereign and politically independent states. As colonies or dependencies, they had no standing as subjects of international law.[5] Any privileges they enjoyed in the international community derived not from any legal entitlement but from the favor of the pervasive colonial power. Since they lacked autonomy, they had no direct access to the emerging institutions of the imperial world community. Relief from exploitation, if it came at all, came from the benevolence of the patron state.

The autonomy model of international law today holds out the prospect, if not the guarantee, that the norms and institutions of world order will prevent the recurrence of imperial exploitation in the post-colonial era. The concepts of state

---

4   See, for example, Shelton, Dinah (ed.), *Commitment and Compliance: The Role of Non-Binding Norms in the International Legal System* (Oxford: Oxford University Press, 2000). The spread of international regulatory regimes for multiple purposes creates difficulties for legal formalists, who tend to be more troubled than legal functionalists by this phenomenon. More often than not, these regimes have (or acquire) informal/non-binding as well as formal/binding characteristics. There is no clear evidence that effectiveness is highly correlated with formal bindingness within those environmental or resource management contexts that attract "mixed" regime-building experiments. Miles, Edward L., and others, *Environmental Regime Effectiveness: Confronting Theory with Evidence* (Cambridge, Mass.: M.I.T. Press, 2002).

5   For a modern evaluation of this restriction, see Broms, Bengt, "Subjects: Entitlement in the International Legal System", in Macdonald, Ronald St. J., and Douglas M. Johnston (eds.), *The Structure and Process of International Law: Essays in Legal Philosophy, Doctrine and Theory* (Dordrecht: Martinus Nijhoff Publishers, 1986), pp. 383-423.

sovereignty and territoriality, and related constructs and doctrines, are seen to be necessary to protect the weak. However, sovereignty was never as absolute as lesser powers today might wish it to be. The paradox of international organization is that only autonomous states can participate as members, but the fact of participation increases the member's dependency on others. Global systems such as the United Nations, the World Bank, and the World Trade Organization pay daily lip-service to the autonomy of their members, and yet function primarily through a vast network of obligations that make the weaker members increasingly dependent on them. Cynics argue that since these systems are largely controlled by the United States and other major powers, the weak are still subject to the will of the strong, although less obviously so than in the age of formal imperialism. Egalitarians deplore what they perceive to be a system of "informal" or "indirect" imperialism. Realists respond by suggesting that the state, in today's changing world, is a concept that needs to be re-designed.[6]

D. Benevolence. International law can also be conceptualized as the evolving system of "world law", intended eventually not for the benefit of states but of society in general. By this view of things, the system is just beginning to break out of its early obsession with the nation-state and its preoccupation with legal values elevated to protect the "sanctity of the state". Developments in the second half of the 20th century suggest that international law is evolving into a transnational phenomenon to be *an extension of early efforts to achieve civic enlightenment through cross-cultural policies of benevolence to all members of world society.*

From this perspective, international law has its origin in primitive antiquity in those distant, imperfectly recorded, efforts by a few enlightened rulers to deal benevolently with their subjects and with neighboring rulers and their peoples.[7] Law,

---

6   The counter-statist literature gives weight to a number of relatively new "realities" that need to be accommodated within any contemporary theoretical framework of international law. For example, it is agreed that recognition must be given to: (i) the accumulation of enormous wealth, and therefore power, by the largest transnational corporations, exceeding the wealth and power possessed by all but the dozen or so most influential nation-states; (ii) the growing political influence of indigenous peoples and other non-corporate non-state institutions as actors within the world community: (iii) the "ethicization" of international law in human rights, environmental and humanitarian sectors of concern, in which the right of the international community to intervene in a state's "domestic" affairs, in certain circumstances, is strongly argued; (iv) the electronic networking of the "transnational ethical community", which initiates and sustains well-informed critiques of global institutions that purport to make decisions on behalf of "world society" despite their lack of democratic credentials; (v) the artificiability of the doctrine of state equality; and (vi) the limitations of the national-government level as the traditional approach to problems of human welfare.

7   A list of the most enlightened rulers of classical antiquity might include progressivists such as Asoka the Great of India (c. 274-232 B.C.); and the meritorious Roman ("Flavian") emperors such as Nerva (c.38-98 A.D.), Trajan (c. 53-117 A.D.), Hadrian (766-138 A.D.), Antonius Pius (86-161 A.D.) and Marcus Aurelius (120-180 A.D.). Payne,

by this model, begins with values and sentiments rather than rules. The concept of "civic benevolence" might be construed broadly enough to include that of "order", since some rulers of the distant past who must be accepted as "enlightened" or "civilized" by the standards of the day, such as Alexander the Great, are remembered by posterity for their ability to impose order as much as by their acceptance of enlightened rule as a moral commitment.[8] A conqueror even today might be considered "civilized" or "benevolent" if sufficient evidence is shown of genuine concern for the welfare of society. Along with David Hume, we might regard the "moral sense" as more directly influential on human welfare than either ideology or law.

The benevolence model puts a premium on considerations of individual and social justice. It gives weight to recent advances in the development of *human rights* and the promotion of *humanitarian and environmental concerns* at the international level. It endows international law with a "moral core", and leans to the tradition of natural law values that transcend the prerogative of state authorities to grant or withhold consent. It challenges established statist principles such as sovereignty and the duty not to interfere in the domestic affairs of another state. Autonomy and majoritarianism are suspect norms in a world perceived as insufficiently benevolent.

E.   Fairness. The "classical" conception of international law that emerged in Europe in the 19th century conveys a different picture: that of a statist order intended originally to provide a system–maintenance purpose. The European nation-state system jelled before the convergence of common civic policies and practices that could be described as benevolent. Civic benevolence in any modern sense was not a precondition of membership of the club of "civilized states". Barbarities were not uncommon in the treatment of foreign peoples and rulers deemed to fall outside the prescribed limits of "civilization".

Yet within those limits, *the statist purposes served by classical international law could be interpreted as equitable in nature, intended to ensure fair dealing.*[9] Fairness within the system requires that all member states be treated as equal in law. The doctrine of formal equality emphasizes that all states, being sovereign, have the same legal entitlements and prerogatives, and should be accorded the same courtesies. In the "classical" age down to1919, when the system of international law was essentially designed as the legal infrastructure for *bilateral* inter-state relationships, fairness typically assumed the transactional form of *reciprocity*.[10] But

---

Robert, *Ancient Rome* (New York: Horizon, 2001). In more modern times we might wish to include Peter the Great of Russia and Frederick the Great of Prussia among the enlightened monarchs, but several others could also be regarded as candidates. Braun, Geoffrey, *The Enlightened Despots* (New York: Henry Holt, 1924).

8   Fox, Robin Lane, *Alexander the Great* (London: Allen Lane, 1973).

9   Franck, Thomas M., *Fairness in International Law and Institutions* (Oxford: Clarendon Press, 1995).

10   Simma, Bruno, "Reciprocity", in *Encyclopedia of Public International Law* (ed. Bernhardt), Vol. 7 (Amsterdam: North-Holland, 1984), pp. 400-404.

reciprocity reflects fairness only if the larger law-making process is accepted by all participants as "legitimate".[11]

The fairness model is still uppermost in the minds of most practitioners of international law who are officially responsible for the day-to-day maintenance of bilateral sectors of diplomacy, such as trade, extradition, cross-boundary relations, and most kinds of routine treaty-making. It is also of high relevance to the process of third party adjudication, which deals with the problem of transactional breakdown that periodically afflicts bilateral inter-state relationships and may even threaten to render them dysfunctional during a period of stress. Today, of course, questions of fairness and reciprocity are treatable also within multilateral or even global institutions such as the World Trade Organization. However, some contemporary scholars associated with the fairness model no longer envisage the goal of fairness within an exclusively statist framework. In arguing instead for a broader conception of international law that places at its center the moral imperative to pursue the betterment of human welfare through liberal democracy and justice, some writers come close to combining the models of fairness and benevolence.

F.   National Development. The sixth model of international law is related to the autonomy model, and yet is distinguishable from it. For most of the first half-century of its existence, the United Nations gave highest priority to the nation-building needs of its developing members. Since the end of the Second World War the more affluent national economies have grown enormously, widening the disparity between the richest and poorest nations. Although the process of decolonization was virtually completed in the early 1970s, the UN General Assembly, the Economic and Social Council (ECOSOC), the specialized agencies of the United Nations, and other key institutions such as the United Nations Development Programme (UNDP)) have continued to view international law within the nation-state framework chiefly as the *ethical and institutional apparatus for the promotion of national economic and social development.*

In the 1970s and 1980s a sustained effort was made by the developing countries to use their combined strength as UN member states to put national developmental ethos firmly in place at the moral center of the international legal order. In specific sectors considerable gains were achieved. At the Third UN Conference on the Law of the Sea (UNCLOS III), for example, the extension of coastal state jurisdiction was considered a major gain for many developing countries. These beneficiaries gained not only in legal autonomy but, more specifically, in the acquisition of natural resources within coastal areas that had now become an extension of their land economy. During those years similar efforts were devoted to national development needs, chiefly under the aegis of the New International Economic Order

---

11   According to Thomas Franck, fairness is the rubic under which the tension between substantive distributive justice and procedural right process is "discursively managed". Simpson, Gerry J. ,"Is International Law Fair?", 17 *Michigan Journal of International Law* 615 (1995-96).

(NIEO).[12] Advantage was taken of leverage opportunities created by the rivalries between the two dominant superpowers, but, with the demise of world communism as a counterweight against world capitalism, the NIEO movement became a spent force.[13]

Since the early 1990s, the development model of international law has become less dependent on UN General Assembly programs and more anthropocentric in orientation. Specialists in "international development law" now move more frequently within the vast and ever-growing network of non-state institutions, where considerable resources – especially human resources – can be made available in local situations where social distress is most acute. "Bottom-up" strategies often offer the best hope in many developing countries for direct improvements in the welfare of the populations, especially in rural communities at a distance from the center of their political system.[14]

G.   Environment. International environmental law is a relatively new sector of specialization. Its ethical attraction is widely apparent. In many cultures it has acquired a spiritual force akin to religion, but it has developed most rapidly as a linkage among secular humanists. The environmental movement today is an intensely ethical compartment of international law that commands the most committed loyalists. For many transnational ethicists, international law maintains credibility as a normative system only to the extent it is framed around the *obligation to preserve the vitality and variety of the planetary environment.*

The environmental (or ecological) model of international law looks forward to an imagined future rather than back to a remembered past. No one knows how bleak the future might be, but most citizens around the world are convinced that the global environment is under strain and that stricter controls on human activities are an important task for international diplomats and lawyers. The general public may be confused by differences within the scientific community regarding such matters as the causes of climate change: many are uncertain whether the Kyoto Protocol represents the best approach to the mitigation of future harms. Yet there is surely a growing realization that, as certain environmental problems become

---

12   Franck, Thomas M., and Mark M. Munansangu, *The New International Economic Order: International Law in the Making* (New York: UN Institute for Training and Research, Policy and Efficacy Studies No. 6, 1982).

13   The failure of the NIEO movement may be explained in two ways: by reference to unsuccessful efforts to convert hortatory norms in "hard-law" instruments (such as the UN Convention on the Law of the Sea) into operationally significant commitments in subsequent implementation processes; and to the failure to convert soft-law instruments into obligatory "hard-law" form. But the UN General Assembly and other bodies continue to press the need for reducing disputes among rich and poor nations. The tendency in recent years has been to focus more sharply on specific types and areas of poverty.

14   See, for example, Stone, Roger D., and Eve Hamilton, *Global Economies and the Environment Towards Sustainable Rural Development in the Third World* (New York: Council on Foreign Relations Press, 1991).

more critical, it is important to find a more effective way of inducing compliance with well-considered environmental treaty regimes. Non-compliance with the basic principles of international law may not be the daily problem that critics sometimes suggest, but regime-compliance and capacity-building are surely two of the major challenges that need to be addressed by the international system at large.

Environmental ethos has had to find a *modus vivendi* with developmental ethic. Since the Brundtland Commission's report,[15] a synthesis has been offered to the world community: the concept of *sustainable development*, or more precisely the ethic of "sustainability".[16] Yet semantic neatness should not conceal the difficulties that continue to complicate the formation of public policy in numerous resource use and management contexts. Moreover, international lawyers of a pragmatic, problem-solving disposition are chary of newly emergent principles of environmental law accorded transcendent status as "governing" norms that would limit the scope of multi-factoral decision-making, but accept them as important "guides" to sound policy and planning.

H.   Cooperation. Other international lawyers look upon development and environment as only two – albeit two of the most urgent – reasons for building a "cooperative ethic" in the world community. Given the dangers of conflict through excessive competitiveness, and the selfishness and greed sometimes associated with the building of national autonomy, the case can be made that the central concern of the world legal order is the *development of cooperative arrangements for the effective treatment of the most complex problems and the most fundamental issues in modern society*. In behavioral terms, the central task of international law and diplomacy is to facilitate cooperative action as a constraint on *competitive* and *autonomous* behavior among states and other international actors that is seen to be dangerous or at least selfish.

The cooperative model of international law is optimistic. It assumes, against some evidence to the contrary, that state representatives, directly or through international organizations, can succeed in overcoming their normal preference for autonomous or competitive behavior. After almost a century of experience with international organizations, some lessons have been learned. For example, normally there must be strong inducements in place – either effective "negative sanctions" (sticks) or seductive "positive sanctions" (carrots) – if member states are to sacrifice autonomy as a matter of national interest. Like-mindedness in a *fundamental issue* context may sometimes be unattainable due to cultural disparity. On the other hand, agreement on a common approach to a *highly complex problem* that appears not to be culturally constrained may be amenable to effective implementa-

---

15   World Commission on Environment and Development, *Our Common Future* (Oxford: Oxford University Press, 1987).

16   For a recent discussion of suggested principles, see Seggier, Marie-Claire Cordonier, and others, *Weaving the Rules for our Common Future: Principles, Practice and Prospects for International Sustainable Development Law* (Montreal: Centre for International Sustainable Development Law, 2002).

tion, if disadvantaged governments have access to capacity-building opportunities. Recent experience suggests, at least in certain circumstances, that successful capacity-building depends on "civil society coalitions" consisting of goodwill partnerships of state and non-state institutions.

The "functionalist logic" of the cooperative model of international law asks the analyst to keep in mind the strengths and weaknesses of the area of international law in question. International environmental law is framed around ethical constructs that may be better suited to govern the treatment of fundamental issues than of complex problems. The transition to sophisticated environmental problem-solving is just beginning. The law of outer space, seen originally in terms of fundamental "commons" issues, is also just beginning to enter a more technically sophisticated stage of human development as new space technology permits progress toward a more effective regulatory order. The same is surely true of weapons control. On the other hand, significant progress in the international law of human rights seems more difficult to achieve in an age of increased religious and cultural fundamentalism.[17]

I.   War Prevention and Management. World public opinion has become increasingly pacifist in recent years. The younger generation in many, mostly Western, countries has sensed in the end of bipolar world politics an opportunity to renounce the use of force except in the case of self-defence against actual, impending, or foreseeable physical attack. Unlike the older generation, who lived through the terrors of state aggression, most Western citizens born after the Second World War are pacifists, who look to international law, above all, as a morally prescribed order responsible for the maintenance of peace.

For advocates of the war-prevention-and-management model, the UN Charter has peremptory status chiefly because of its emphasis on the role of the Security Council as the sole possessor of *mandatory world authority in the regulation of force*. Some pacifist ethicists are reluctant to concede even the occasional need to "manage" disorder through the use of collective force as long as there remains a reasonable case for continuing UN diplomacy, even in the most provocative or dangerous circumstances. Yet unconsented intervention in a failed, divided or "culprit" state is often the only potentially effective option available to the Security Council, if it is politically prepared to deal with problems of international insecurity or fundamental violations of the international law of human rights.

In most contexts that seem to invite UN intervention, the decision to intervene is complicated, and often sharply politicized, by the collision of several models of international law: the models of order, regulation, autonomy, benevolence, and cooperation, as well as war prevention and management.[18] The process of in-

---

17   For arguments that religion has been a positive contribution to the evolution of international law, see Janis, Mark J., *The Influence of Religion on the Development of International Law* (Dordrecht: Martinus Nijhoff Publishers, 1991).

18   Most of these dilemmas are captured in UN Commission on Intervention and State Sovereignty, *The Responsibility to Protect* (Ottawa: International Development Re-

tervention by the Security Council is almost always slow, usually contentious, and often ineffective. The role of the United States has been particularly controversial.[19] The role of force in international relations continues to be a challenge of unusual complexity in the international law community.

J.   Conflict Resolution. There are many international lawyers who concentrate on the existence of disputes in inter-state relations and look to international law as *the world system that provides resolutive norms, institutions and procedures.* The principle of international arbitration was widely invoked, and occasionally applied, during the period of the Greek city-states, and even earlier.[20] Although the practice fell into desuetude for two millennia, it re-emerged in the 19th century and became increasingly common in the 20th, especially in the context of trade, boundary and related disputes. The creation of a standing World Court, first under the League and then under the United Nations, gave unprecedented credence to the conflict resolution model of international law.

Not all cultures, however, elevate the judicial tradition to the same extent as the Western civil law and common law countries. Most governments still display reluctance to refer important disputes with other states to an international court, or even to an *ad hoc* tribunal, trusting rather to the diplomatic process which remains within the disputants' control. Some regard the Western institutional model of third party adjudication as overly formal and ill-suited to the production of an amicable outcome. Accordingly, recent global treaty initiatives to accommodate diverse cultural traditions and preferences have resulted in dispute settlement systems based on *choice*: fact-finding, mediation and conciliation, for example, as well as binding third party adjudication. The maximal degree of choice was designed into the system created at UNCLOS III for the settlement of disputes arising from the new law of the sea, and later carried into the regime for parties to the 1995 UN Agreement for the Implementation of the Provisions of the United Nations Convention on the Law of the Sea Relating to the Conservation and Management of

---

search Centre, 2001). See also: Mackay, Stephen, and Alison M. Rohe (eds.), *Reflections on Humanitarian Action: Principles, Ethics and Contradictions* (London: Pluto Press, 2001). Failed UN intervention is analyzed in numerous writings: for example, Adelman, Howard, and Astri Suhrke (eds.), *The Path of a Genocide: The Rwanda Crisis from Uganda to Zaire* (New Brunswick, N.J.: Transnational Publishers, 1999; Mayall, James (ed.), *The New Interventionism: United Nations Experience in Cambodia, Former Yugoslavia and Somalia* (New York: Cambridge University Press, 1996); and United Nations, *The United Nations and Somalia, 1992-1996* (New York: United Nations, Department of Public Information, 1996).

19   On the interventionist role of the United States, see Brune, Lester H., *The United States and Post-War Interventions: Bush and Clinton in Somalia, Haiti, and Bosnia, 1992-1998* (Claremont, Calif.: Regina Books, 1999). On the diversity of opinion on these issues within the American international law community, see recent articles in the American Journal of International Law, such as Volume 97 (2003), pp. 553-642 and pp. 803-872.

20   Ralston, Jackson H., *International Arbitration from Athens to Locarno* (Stanford University Press, 1929).

Straddling Fish Stocks and Highly Migratory Stocks.[21] It is too early to predict any pattern of choice within these systems.

From the perspective of the conflict resolution model, considerable progress has been achieved in the development of international law since the late 1980s. Several of these mechanisms are not yet fully operational, much less highly active, but there is now a greater frequency of resort to the International Court of Justice. Moreover, several new global and regional tribunals have been created since the early 1990s. International lawyers have better reason now than ever before for optimism about the future of international litigation.

K.   System Convergence. As we survey recent and contemporary trends in legal development around the world, it is realistic to hold out the prospect of *convergence among national legal systems*, at least in certain sectors that seem to reflect the convergence of national interest. The idea of a single uniform system of world law was envisaged by Alexander the Great, admittedly in his capacity as aspirant to world rule but also as a cross-cultural idealist. Later, Cicero wrote compellingly of a golden future, when the entire world would enjoy the protection of the same public laws and concepts of justice , under an improved version of Roman law and government. Seneca followed in this same mode of universalist legal idealism.

Today we have the advantage over Alexander, Cicero, and Seneca. Behind us we survey an impressive modern history of successful transnational exercises in the unification[22] and codification[23] of laws, both national and international. From

---

21   McDorman, Ted L., "The Dispute Settlement Regime of he Straddling and Highly Migratory Fish Stocks Convention", 35 *Canadian Yearbook of International Law* 57 (1997). See also McDorman, Ted L., "An Overview of International Fisheries Disputes and the International Tribunal for the Law of the Sea", 40 *Canadian Yearbook of International Law* 119 (2002).

22   Efforts to promote the unification of *private law* became an organized activity in 1924 when the Assembly of the League of Nations accepted an offer by the Italian government to establish in Rome an institute devoted to that goal. In 1928 such a body came into existence. Early difficulties forced reorganization upon the International Institute for the Unification of Private Law, but work progressed outside the League in a number of commercial and property law sectors such as the sale of goods (corporeal movables), patrimonial questions, the liability of innkeepers, compulsory automobile insurance, commercial arbitration, international enforcement of family maintenance obligations, and international loans. In collaboration with other organizations, the Institute also undertook early studies of unification possibilities in such areas as bills of exchange, copyright, and the legal status of women. Numerous unification projects have been undertaken since then, as described in the *Unidroit Yearbook* (1926-1973) and the *Uniform Law Review* (1971 to date).

Fundamental disagreements persist on the merits of formal legal unification. One specialist has distinguished three types of arguments on both sides of the debate. "*Substantively*, the argument for unification says that we should find the best solution to any problem and unify accordingly. The counter-argument is that different contexts, groups, or societies require different solutions and that unification makes this impossible. *Formally*, the pro argument says that unification, irrespective of content, enhances

the late 19th century, generations of comparative lawyers, mostly Europeans, have concentrated on description of the differences and similarities among the major legal systems of the world: the typical and atypical versions of the civil law and common law systems. More recently, comparatists have found it more useful to prescribe merger or adaptation in sectors of potentially common interest.

Since the 1970s significant advances have been made in the internationalization of national laws under UN and other auspices. The sectors of common interest that lend themselves to the processes of unification and codification (or "harmonization") are mostly those of economic or commercial orientation. At least in theory, the concept of common interest is expanding in the absence of cultural, economic, or educational barriers.[24] In contemporary perspective, international law is becoming an agency of cross-systemic globalization.

L.   Constitutional Authority. Finally, modern international law can be envisaged idealistically, in ethical and institutional terms, as *a collective effort to achieve universal order through the development of constitutional structure and procedure among nations.* Although the institutional experiment in world constitutionalism did not begin until the League of Nations era, such a goal has been a dream of idealists down the ages, at least since the time of Cicero.

The modern constitutional model of international law has been assembled out of various Western cultural modes of civic idealization: British rule-of-law

---

predictability, lowers transaction costs, and enables equal treatment of like situations. The counter-argument is that it ossifies what may be suboptimal solutions and prevents competition between legal orders. *Institutional* arguments focus on the institutions required to unify and to safeguard uniform application. Proponents of unification tend to argue that centralized administration of (legislative and adjudicative) justice is more efficient, while opponents argue for subsidiary and local regulation." Michaels, Ralf, "Three Paradigms of Legal Unification: National, International, Transnational", *Proceedings of the 96th Annual Meeting of the American Society of International Law* (March 13-16, 2002), pp. 333-36 at pp. 333-34.

23   The idea of codifying *public international law* was first put forward by Jeremy Bentham (1748-1832) in his *Principles of International Law* (1786-1789). Only a systematic code, he felt, could cure the uncertainties inherent in the law of nations, which he attributed to the vagueness of its cognate, the law of nature. Initial private efforts at codification were made by individuals such as Johann Caspar Bluntschli (1808-1881), David Dudley Field (1805-1894), and Pasquale Fiore (1837-1914), and various private organizations. The codification process was brought under inter-governmental auspices initially through the Hague Peace Conferences of 1899 and 1907, then the International Naval Conference (1908-09), and subsequently, of course, the League of Nations and the International Law Commission of the United Nations. The arguments for and against the codification of public international law are somewhat similar to those for and against unification of private law.

24   Ferguson, Gerry, and Douglas M. Johnston, "Conclusion: Reflections on the Convergence and Divergence of Legal Systems,: in Johnston, Douglas M., and Gerry Ferguson (eds.), *Asia-Pacific Legal Development* (Vancouver: UBC Press, 1998), pp. 548-594.

ideology; the German concept of the *Rechtsstaat*; American and Dutch experiments in federalism; the Western bill-of-rights tradition; and, more recently, spectacular success in regional integration under the aegis of the European Union. In some other, non-Western, regions of the world constitutionalism may be seen as the most presumptuously intrusive of the twelve models of international law. Even within the Western system of civilization that gave it birth, constitutionalism is an ideal that expresses itself differently in different legal cultures. Among Western international lawyers the constitutionalist vision invites controversy especially between the proponents of legal formalism and legal realism.

3.   The Concept of Constitutionalism

Constitutionalism is a concept derived from the theory of the state. It can be treated semi-ironically as "the name given to the trust which men repose in the power of words engrossed on parchment to keep a government in order".[25] If it arises from a distrust of power-holders, then constitutionalism rests on a widely shared sentiment. On the other hand, it is "neither clearly prescriptive nor clearly descriptive; its contours are difficult to discern; its historical roots are diverse and uncertain."[26]

The theory of the state extends far back into the classical antiquity of Greece, India, and China, and no doubt other systems of civilization,[27] but it is common to elevate Cicero as the first true constitutionalist in any modern sense. It was in light of the Athenian model of democracy that the Romans of the republican era insisted upon – or conceded – the right of the common people (the plebeians) to grant or withhold consent to laws intended to bind the entire community, but it was Romans such as Cicero who first developed the idea of democracy as a constitutional right.[28] Even at the end of the Republic, Augustus made a cunning show

---

25   Hamilton, Walton H., "Constitutionalism", *Encyclopedia of the Social Sciences*, Vol. II (190), at p. 255.

26   Casper, Gerhard, "Constitutionalism", *Occasional Papers from the Law School of the University of Chicago*, No. 22 (Buffalo, N.Y.: William S. Hein, 1987), at p. 3.

27   None of the early literature on the theory of the state, East or West, captures the constitutionalist ethic of the modern era. On the ancient Greek conception of constitutionalism, for example, see McIlwain, Charles H., *Constitutionalism Ancient and Modern* (Ithaca, N.Y.: Cornell University Press, 1940), pp. 25-42.

28   *Ibid.*, pp. 43-68. Cicero's most recent biographer attributes the famous lawyer-orator's political failure not to "lack of talent but to a surplus of principle". He declined to join Julius Caesar, Pompey and Crassius in their political alliance because "it would have betrayed his commitment to the Roman constitution and the rule of law...He failed to understand the reasons for the crisis that tore apart the Roman Republic. Julius Caesar, with the pitiless insight of genius, understood that the constitution with its endless checks and balances prevented effective government, but like so many of his contemporaries Cicero regarded politics in personal rather than structural terms. For Caesar the solution lay in a completely new system of government; for Cicero it lay in finding better men to run the government and better laws to keep them in order".

of declining the offer of extraordinary powers, even in circumstances of public emergency,[29] on grounds that today we recognize as constitutional. In later Roman usage, the term *constitutio* came to be applied to imperial legislation that transcended all other law.

As the concept of *constitutio* evolved, it took on many "evocative and persuasive connotations, which, though "cloudy" in analytic and descriptive content, "at once enrich and confuse political discourse".[30] Its complexity is reflected in numerous, heterogeneous propositions, such as these:

(i)   a constitution is fundamental law;
(ii)   a constitutional amendment requires special, rather onerous, legislative procedures;
(iii)   "true" constitutional principles cannot be cobbled together in a made-up document, but must be seen to reflect the customary "living law" of the people;
(iv)   modern constitutionalism is derived, above all, from the sovereignty of the people;
(v)   a constitution is presumed to acquire its ultimate legitimacy from a primordial "social contract";
(vi)   the ethical core of constitutionalism is a bill of rights that guarantees legal protection to individuals and minorities from the threat of tyrannical rulers, elites, and majorities;
(vii)   constitutionalism rests on a "separation of powers" (i.e. limitative checks and balances) among the organs of the state;
(viii) in a healthy constitutional system, the judiciary should be authorized to review and, if necessary, invalidate "ordinary" legislation that is seen to depart from the core norms of the constitution;

Everitt, Anthony, *Cicero: The Life and Times of Rome's Greatest Politician* (New York: Random House, 2005), at pp. 321-22.

Yet it is Cicero's constitutionalist principles that have endured, not his reputation for political judgment. Since the fall of the famous empire, most would agree, all the states of Western Europe, and many beyond, have "remained indebted to the Roman idea of law as supreme over men ... When the framers of the United States Constitution created what they termed 'a government of laws, not men', they were in effect reasserting Rome's better self". Payne, *supra* note 7, at pp. 277-78.

29   Mindful of the reasons for Caesar's assassination, Augustus "understood that the nobles would only tolerate his autocracy if he concealed it behind acceptable republican traditions. For the first eight years after his victory at Actium, the constitutional basis of his power remained a continuous succession of consulships. But in the middle of this period, in 27 BC, he pronounced 'the transfer of the state to the free disposal of the Senate and the people', thereby earning the misleading, though outwardly plausible, reputation of the restorer of the *res publica*, or ancestral system". Grant, Michael, *The History of Rome* (London: Faber and Faber, 1979), at p. 203.

30   Gray, Thomas C., "Constitutionalism: An Analytic Framework", in Pennock, J. Roland, and John W. Chapman (eds.), *Constitutionalism* (New York: New York University Press, 1979), 189-209 at p. 189.

(ix) in exercising the power of judicial review, the courts may invoke the "common law" of the land to invalidate legislation inconsistent with it; and

(x) in a federal state especially, constitutionalism requires an agreed-upon system for allocating powers to the different levels of government.

Several, but not all, of these propositions would be insisted upon by all as central to the notion of constitutionalism. But which? In modern times, the multifaceted concept of constitutionalism has become difficult to disentangle from the ideals of democracy and the rule of law. So other strands of political theory might be added to the ten suggested above.

Even if we restrict the concept of constitutionalism to these ten elements, the "constitutional model" of international law will be seen to be seriously incomplete in comparison with domestic models operative in the most highly "constitutionalized" national societies. Certain of these ten propositioins are not applicable to international law: for example, the third ("living law"), fourth ("popular sovereignty"), and fifth ("social contract") propositions offer theories that cannot fit the social reality of the highly heterogeneous "world society". The "world government" system is not yet sufficiently developed to be evaluated by reference to the seventh ("separation of powers") criterion. Since the International Court of Justice lacks the power of "judicial review" over international "legislation" – however that might be defined – the eighth determinant drops out of the international model. Since international lawyers would have difficulty agreeing on universally shared norms that could be considered the foundation of a global constitution, the ninth ("common law") element is of doubtful relevance. At the global level of political organization, no system exists to reflect the tenth ("allocation of powers") function of constitutionalism.

Accordingly, current international law reflects only three of these suggested features of constitutionalism: the admittedly paramount legal status of the UN Charter (i); the difficulty (or near-impossibility) of achieving significant amendment of the Charter (ii); and the existence of an ethical core in the system by virtue of a "bill of rights" nucleus of civil rights principles, covenants, and supportive instruments (vi).

To the extent that a "model" of law reflects aspiration as much as reality, it is important to work toward the incorporation of additional constitutional elements in order to develop the system as a whole. There is surely no questioning the importance of constitutionalism as a work-in-progress within the international order. It is a struggle that must be seen as both "juridical" and "operational" in significance.[31] Even counter-statist ethicists, who look to international law in its "societal"

---

31   From a functionalist perspective, it is useful to distinguish the "juridical" or "litigational" domain, where international law is characterized as a distinct science or discipline, from the "operational" or "diplomatic" domain, where international law is seen to be a field, in which juridical considerations compete with political, economic, environmental, ethical and other values and factors. In certain situations it is possible to limit analysis to purely juridical concepts and arguments, as in adjudication by an international tribunal, but within the daily diplomatic "arena", a balancing of some kind is usually dictated by various pressures.

mode[32] as the chief hope for an international public morality in today's world, may be prepared to concede the need for a constitutional core within the inter-state system in order to elevate the human welfare social development responsibilities of governments across all societies in accordance with the *Sozialrechtsstaat* ideal at the national level. Trends toward the constitutional model of international law are clearly visible: for example, in the fields of human rights, international trade law, and international criminal law and in the phenomenon of "judicial globalization".[33]

Promotion of the constitutional model of international law may be condemned as "utopian" – and therefore obstructed by "realists" – unless the promoters take stock of the various kinds of resistance they are likely to encounter. Why should anyone challenge the legitimacy of this kind of idealism in the theory of international law?

4.   Resistance to World Constitutionalism

The goal of world constitutionalism may be perceived to be threatening for a variety of reasons: jurisprudential, ethical, cultural, social and political. Realization of this kind of idealism for world society will require a high degree of persistence on the part of its adherents.

Jurisprudential resistance is offered mostly by legal realists, whose conception of a healthy constitutional order at the national level places a premium on common civic values and strong institutions directly accountable to the people they serve:

---

32   Since the establishment of the UN Charter, international law has acquired a moral core of considerable societal value, so that international law is now also perceived to occupy an "ethical" or "societal" domain. For a discussion of these three domains – juridical, operational and societal – see Johnston, Douglas M., *Consent and Commitment in the World Community: The Classification and Analyses of International Instruments* (Irvington-on-Hudson, N.Y.: Transnational Publishers, 1997), at 81-95.

33   The international law of human rights is the ethical core of world constitutionalism. It is now the focus of numerous monitoring organizations around the world and of several international tribunals. Despite this attention, dozens of national governments continue to be suspected as persistent human rights offenders. The establishment of the World Trade Organization has led to a major restructuring of the global economy. This development has been recognized as a significant "constitutionalization" in the prescriptive (legislative), bureaucratic (executive), and resolutive (judicial) sectors of "world government". Jackson, John H., *The World Trading System: Law and Policy of International Economic Relations*. 2nd ed. (Cambridge Mass.: MIT Press, 1987). The emergence of several international criminal tribunals give hope of flushing out war criminals and similar individuals from behind the barriers of state immunity. Increasing resort to cross-reference and "dialogues" among national judges on "bill of rights" and other constitutional issues present new opportunities for enhancing awareness of internationally shared constitutional standards. Baudenbacher, Carl, "Judicial Globalization: New Development or Old Wine in New Bottles?", 38 *Texas International Law Journal* 505 (2003). It is still uncertain whether this progress is real or merely apparent. Young, Ernest A. "The Trouble with Global Constitutionalism," 38 *Texas International Law Journal* 527 (2003).

"democratic constitutionalism". The kind of constitutionalism associated with legal formalism is suspected of being too inflexible, controllable by a judicial elite trained to give the greatest weight to strict adherence to constitutional text. In short, legal realists fear that an excess of constitutionalist ideology in international law will raise the level of *textualism* within the professional community.

Jurisprudential resistance to the constitutional model of international law is reinforced by *ethical* concerns about the unrepresentative status of international judges who would be called upon to adjudicate disputes over the interpretation of constitutional text. Especially in North America but also elsewhere, many contemporary ethicists are distrustful of legalists, who are seen to be servants – consciously or unconsciously – of corporate and state power-holders. The ethical trend in contemporary world society is to more open, participatory, democratic modes of *governance* at all levels: local, regional, national and global.

There is also a *cultural* issue at the core of the constitutional model of international law. Culturalists unite around the ideal of *human diversity*. Concerns about the uni-civilizational (Eurocentric) bias built into international law would be compounded by Western or European pressures to move the system decisively toward a kind of constitutional legalism seen to be alien to many non-Western legal cultures. Promotional efforts to that end might risk further erosion of the universalist ideal, which is still emotionally essential to most endeavors in global diplomacy and treaty-making.

Cultural and ethical opponents to world constitutionalism are likely to find allies in the cognate sector of *social* activists, who champion the cause of local communities seen to be vulnerable to the exploitative or insensitive practices of central state authority and large-scale corporate power. Anti-statist/anti-corporate advocates are in open rebellion against wholly statist responses to the problems of *civil society*. The constitutional model of international law is likely to be a target for international governance scholars and supporters, unless great care is taken in the design or re-design of global institutions assigned the key roles in constitutional system maintenance.

Not least, promoters of global reform along constitutionalist lines should be aware of a range of *political* objections to such a priority. Current enthusiasm for world constitutionalism is strongest in Europe, where resentment against the dominance of the United States is prevalent in many arenas, especially in those associated with the European Union. Rivalry between Europe and the United States is expected to become an increasingly conflictual feature of international geopolitics. To the extent that Europeans would be expected to acquire disproportionate leverage on the workings of a more highly "constitutionalized" global system, the constitutional model of international law is unlikely to command American allegiance, especially if it is promoted as the paramount ethic of the global community. It is probable also that China, as an emergent great power, would be equally reluctant to concede the primacy of a constitutional ethos for the world of the 21st century, reflecting a continuing cultural discomfort with the political consequences of state equality. Nor is it clear how countries such as Russia and Japan, and even India, would respond to constitutionalist proposals that might seem to strengthen further the European Union's hand at the table of world diplomacy.

5.   Exceptionalism in World Politics and Diplomacy

It is difficult to imagine a politically acceptable version of world constitutionalism that would depart radically and explicitly from the embedded principle of *state equality*.[34] This is a legal fiction that cannot be jettisoned on the call of political realists without threatening to undermine the political foundations of international law. Within the United Nations, as well as outside, numerous ways have admittedly been found to soften the logical rigour of the equal-state principle, but if the system were further "constitutionalized" the occasional, crisis-driven need for circumvention would be aggravated, adding to the strains between legal text and political reality.

The United States is not the only power that would be tempted on occasion to invoke national interest (*raison d'etat*) for departure from constitutional text. However, over the last two decades or more, the United States has shown a particularly dispiriting pattern of reluctance to ratify, or even sign, a number of important global treaties, even instruments which US government delegations have played a central role in shaping in the conference arena. Its flouting of the ethic of "multilateralism" in global diplomacy has convinced most observers that the United States is unlikely to favour a brand of world constitutionalism that would limit the prerogatives that it considers politically essential to its status as the pre-eminent superpower in the international community and to protect its citizens and interests around the world.

It might be protested in fairness that since 1945 no power, or grouping of states, has come close to matching the role that the United States has played in the advancement of the international community. Almost all the important global institutions that we have come to depend upon, within and beyond the UN system, have been heavily influenced by enlightened, albeit mostly self-interested, US foreign policy initiatives and investments. Indeed the UN Charter and most other major global instruments of constitutional stature were the work, in large part, of American drafters representing the internationalist stream of the US foreign policy establishment.

On the other hand, it is commonly acknowledged that growing opposition to the United States within the UN system has turned a large proportion of the

---

34   The doctrine of state equality is derived from the Western democratic ideal of the Enlightenment that individuals are equal under the law. State equality is also associated with the 17th century theory of state sovereignty: if an entity is "sovereign", it cannot be inferior to another. Alternatively, sovereignty can simply be equated with independence. Yet, however rationalized, the legal concept of state equality has had to yield to the existence of superior status granted to certain powers under the UN Charter, which itself is generally conceded to have at least quasi-constitutional status. Castro Rial, J.M., "States, Sovereign Equality", in *Encyclopedia of Public International Law* (ed. Bernardt), Vol. 10 (Amsterdam: North-Holland, 1987), pp. 477-481.

American people against the "international community". Since the 1970's, when the United States lost "control" over the UN General Assembly, more and more Americans have come to regard that body as a hostile chamber. Even many of the most knowledgeable American critics of the UN system have yielded to the temptation to focus on the evidence of internal corruption, waste, and incompetence. Cynicism has become the mark of American sophistication.

At the back of this welling up of American cynicism, we find not only the persistent tradition of American isolationism, which has always had a strong presence in the halls of the US Congress, but also the shock of ordinary Americans that they have become unpopular in so many countries, even those that should be aware of the merits and virtues of the American civic tradition. It seems unlikely that world constitutionalism can be advanced unless the psycho-cultural gaps between the United Nations and the American people can be bridged. For many observers, the difficulty resides in US exceptionalism: the conviction of many Americans that their historical experience has been unique, creating civic values, ideals and institutions that place their nation above the level of all others.

In American culture, "exceptionalism" denotes the belief that the United States is "an extraordinary nation with a special role to play in human history; not only unique but also superior among nations".[35] Although this belief might be traced back to the early colonial period of American self-justification,[36] it did not have the status of *idée fixe* until it was described famously by Alexis de Tocqueville in his *Democracy in America* (1835-40) as a core element of the American national identity. In addition to the usual range of factors influencing the making and implementing of foreign policy everywhere, US foreign policy has always been molded by the myth of exceptionalism.

Arguably, there are two strands of US exceptionalism. First, there is the traditional idea of America as the *examplar nation*. False dealings will result in the withdrawal of divine favour and notoriety throughout the world. In the words of the early American settler, John Winthrop (1588-1649), the nation is "a city upon a hill"; or, in the words of Abraham Lincoln, an "almost chosen nation". Second, America has been idealized as *a missionary nation*. It is called to fulfil its "manifest destiny", most recently as "leader of the free world". Its self-image of uniqueness and national greatness has received set-backs, not least in the Vietnam War, but the myth persists as a "civil religion". American nationalism is "not built on the usual elements of nationhood such as shared language, culture, common descent or historical territory, but on 'an idea which singled out the new nation among the nations of the earth.'"[37] As the leader of progress in virtually every domain, it is not destined to rise and then fall like other nations.

---

35   McCrisken, Trevor B., *American Exceptionalism and the Legacy of Vietnam: U.S. Foreign Policy Since 1974.* (Basingstoke: Palgrave Macmillan, 2003), at p. 1.

36   Greene, Jack P., *The Intellectual Construction of America: Exceptionalism and Identity from 1492 to 1800* (Chapel Hill, Car.: University of North Carolina Press, 1993).

37   McCrisken, *supra* note 35, at p. 7.

Adherents to the exemplary branch of US exceptionalism have always believed that the United States should maintain a distance from other states, content to lead by example without interference in the political affairs of others. This was the philosophy of George Washington,[38] and in a more sophisticated way by Thomas Jefferson., who advocated avoidance of "entangling alliances". Adherents to the missionary strand of the myth believe that the United States has a moral duty to proselytize American values overseas through a foreign policy supporting intervention in appropriate circumstances. The most influential proponent of America's mission to civilize the world was Woodrow Wilson, an international lawyer at Princeton University – perhaps the principal American vehicle for the dissemination of the ideas of the French and Scottish Enlightenment in the formative period in the late 18th century.[39] Interventionism is justified by many American idealists on the ground that the United States has consistently refrained from the establishment of colonies overseas, being itself the successor to a colonized people.

The emotional appeal of US exceptionalism has, of course, been greatly strengthened by the searing events of 9/11. Few Americans doubt the seriousness of terrorist threats to their country posed by Islamist extremists, even though they disagree quite sharply on the limits of appropriate response. Around the world,

---

38   In his famous Farewell Address of 1796 Washington warned his fellow citizens against the dangers of allowing foreign events or ideas to affect the indigenous development of American republican government. It might be suggested that the American "enemy", no longer the monarchists, has been transposed to a succession of later subversionists: socialists, anarchists, communists, and now Islamic terrorists. The Americans are "deeply suspicious of other peoples – other states – that have not experienced the American liberal revolution and have not yet achieved the level of historical progress that the United States has". Cohen, H. Grant, "The American Challenge to International Law: A Tentative Framework for Debate", 28 *Yale Journal of International Law* 551 (2003) at p. 562.

39   On the special importance of the Scottish contribution to the political, social and economic development of the United States, see Herman, Arthur, *How the Scots Invented the Modern World* (New York: Crown Publishers, 2001). The actual influence of the French *philosophes* on the American Founding Fathers is more questionable, since only a few American intellectuals could read the famous works of Voltaire, Rousseau, Montesquieu and their contemporaries in the original French. It has been observed that the presence of French books in a private library may indicate *interest*, but not necessarily *influence*. Spurlin, Paul M., *The French Enlightenment in America: Essays on the Times of the Founding Fathers* (Athens, Geo.: University of Georgia Press, 1984). George Washington could not speak, read or understand French. Benjamin Franklin could read French easily, but he did not write much in the language of the country where he practiced diplomacy for several years. Nor could he speak French grammatically or pronounce it well. Jefferson, similarly, was uncomfortable with spoken French, and did not write it, though he could read it easily. Madison learned French with a Scottish accent. Rush, Hamilton and Morris, on the other hand, were fluent in French. Many American historians today give much more weight to the influence of the English common law heritage of liberty and judicial independence, especially among those many Founding Fathers who were lawyers.

most observers seem to accept that such a direct and massive assault on the home-land of the world hegemon is bound to change the dynamics of power diplomacy, in an age when the target states have no alternative but to assign a new, war-like, priority to national security. It is a difficult time in world history to convince most Americans that their foreign policy should be further constrained by global con-stitutional norms and procedures that are likely to be applied against them by un-friendly foreigners.

6.   The Roman Precedent

Exceptionalism is not an American invention. Many of the earliest civilizations were exceptionalist in the sense that their superiority was directly linked to their unique association with the gods of their own imagination. The first system of civilization to base an enduring exceptionalist ethos on its estimation of its own human worth was probably China. But that phenomenon occurred far beyond the periphery of Western experience, and indeed long before the formation of the "Western world". The record of early Chinese imperial history, such as it is, provides no evidence of any special regard for the notion of state equality, despite pre-imperial accounts of a coexistence of several quasi-sovereign states prepared to accept certain recipro-cal rights and courtesies.[40]

Classical Greece was also a culture strongly imbued with a sense of its own merit. In the eye of posterity, the Athenians in particular perceived themselves as the leader of the only truly advanced system of civilization, one that was clearly superior to its competitors. It has been argued by some classicists that the Greek inter-city alliances were impressive antecedents of the European system of nation-states that emerged 2,000 years later in Western Europe. However, others, pointing to the religious rites performed by these leagues, have questioned their political significance and underlined their role as reflector of the Greek sense of ethnic su-periority shared by all the city-states.[41]

---

[40]   Sinologists speculate on the "Spring-and-Autumn" period (722-481 BC), when 170 or so "states" or principalities co-existed throughout the region of Northeast and Central China. Each of these realms was controlled by an aristocratic family ensconced within its walled capital. There seems to have existed for over two centuries a "system" of cooperation, held together by alliances and leagues and animated by the spirit of reci-procity, until it was succeeded by the era of Warring States (403-221 BC) and eventu-ally the imperial triumph of the Ch'in (Qin). Latourette, Kenneth S., *The Chinese: Their History and Culture* (New York: Macmillan, 1934), pp. 36-43.

[41]   In early times the Greek word *barbaros* simply meant "foreigner", without any hostile connotation. Homer presents the Trojans as the cultural equals of the Greeks, never as inferiors because of their alien status. The overseas Greeks of the 7th and 6th centuries were not too proud to learn refinements from their Lydian neighbours. But after the horrific encounters of the Persian Wars, the Greek view of foreigners hardened. "It was felt that foreigners, being without liberty, had at the best the morality of slaves and might all too easily indulge in acts of violence fit only for brutes. Just as freedom was what the Greeks valued most highly in their own traditions, so what they most

In Western history, however, the most famous example of an exceptionalist ideology was, of course, ancient Rome. So it is tempting to compare and contrast the Romans of antiquity with the Americans of our own age.[42] First, of course, there are some rather obvious differences. By the mid-1st century AD, the territorial limits of the Roman Empire had become clearly defined. Within those expansive domains, Roman law by then had become the definitive system of formal secular law, subject to one regime of central public administration based in Rome. Throughout its huge captive territories, the authority of Rome was unquestioned. No imperial power before it had matched the *depth* of Roman *control*. After Nero's suicide in AD 68 – and his succession by the popular plebeian soldier Vespasian – a "relative peace" descended on most of Europe and Western Asia and much of Northern Africa. It created a 200-year era of unprecedented stability and prosperity. Most of the institutions of Western civilization flourished under the conditions of the *pax Romana*. They did so within a system of rule that placed faith in its own indigenous legal tradition and saw only the occasional tactical need to enter into treaty relations with other peoples.[43]

On the other hand, America's undeclared, "informal" world-empire has no definable territorial limits. American law participates within a world-wide framework of evolving national legal systems that are formally independent of one another, though mostly variants of the same original civil-law or common-law model. The possibilities of centralizing public administration rest with a proliferating array of global and regional sectoral arrangements, which often make it politically costly for the United States to evade its duties to cooperate with others. No one before has ever matched the *extent* of American *influence* internationally, but today we do not have a world of "relative peace". America's leadership role in the Western world is now being challenged by the enlarged membership of the European Union, especially in the context of international constitutionalism. America also looks uneasily to the East, as China begins to catch up as a future world power.

---

deplored in alien peoples was their tendency to behave below the level of free and responsible men". Bowra, C. Maurice, *The Greek Experience* (London: Cardinal, 1973), at p. 25.

42   For a recent re-evaluation of the Roman Republic, see Holland, Tom, *Rubicon: The Triumph and Tragedy of the Roman Republic* (London: Little, Brown, 2003).

43   Alliances and treaties of peace had, of course, been a common feature of the early republican period of Roman history, when the rising nation was vying for ascendancy over its rivals in the Western Mediterranean. The choice between war and diplomacy was frequently in debate between the hawks and doves of the Senate, even in the context of Rome's relations with Carthage, the most bitter and most formidable of its traditional enemies. However, as they became accustomed to the advantages of military (and non-military) superiority, the Romans had gradually lost interest in the "soft-power" alternative to a policy of conquest and the practice of imposing settlements on client-kings. By the time of Claudius I (10 BC – 54 AD) the Empire had developed a central civil service large enough to sustain a system of direct rule throughout most of its extensive colonial territories. See, generally, Grant, *supra* note 29.

There are also a number of arresting similarities. Both Rome and America, in their own very different time and place, have set higher standards than anyone else in virtually all sectors of wealth-production, knowledge and skill. The same kind of practical virtuosity has enabled both empires to extract the maximum benefits from the international economy, which they have shaped in their own interest. Continuing pre-eminence for both "hyperpowers" has depended upon a perception by others that their material welfare is most likely to be enhanced through collaboration. Both have cultivated highly litigious societies for the settlement of *domestic* disputes, but in the public domain of international diplomacy neither has been comfortable with the principle of third party adjudication.

Since the late 18th century, American intellectuals have made remarkably seminal contributions to the Roman rule-of-law ideal articulated by Cicero, the first great constitutionalist of antiquity, and to the institutionalization of Athenian democracy. Building on the more modern traditions of civil and individual rights pioneered by the British and French, Americans have been at the centre of most recent efforts to develop an international system of human rights. If world constitutionalism consisted mostly of that moral core, there might be little reason to question the depth of American commitment to that model of international law.

In its primitive form as natural law, a sort of "international law test" was frequently applied by Rome before it committed itself to the use of military force. For early Romans, it was necessary to know that the impending war was favored by the gods.[44] For later sophisticates such as Cicero, it was essential to know in one's heart that the cause for Roman wars was "just". Patriotism was the civic energy needed to maintain the state and its institutions. In times of stress, patriotism fused with religiosity to convince all but the cynics and satirists that Rome was in the right. Unnecessary butchery in battle was felt to be unworthy of the Romans' superior civilization, excusable only if provoked by the barbarities of an inferior people that had chosen to challenge Rome.

Like ancient Rome, modern America usually acts decisively under stress. Its actions are clearly visible to an attentive and critical world. It is a highly "constitutionalized" state, in some ways more so than any other. The calibre of its leadership usually bears comparison with that of other major states, but the citizens of America and their populist leaders do not always support the internationally-oriented senators and other patricians who counsel moderation and cooperation.[45]

---

44   The Romans in the early republican era used the gods to legitimize their declarations of war. Their deities were brought in as adjudicators to declare the lawfulness, the justness, of their resort to hostilities. Watson, Alan, *International Law in Archaic Rome: War and Religion* (Baltimore: Johns Hopkins University Press, 1993).

45   The extreme version of US exceptionalism tends to be associated with the Republican Party. Under President Eisenhower the Rockefeller internationalists maintained a relatively moderate orientation in foreign policy, and President Nixon was certainly "pragmatic" in his dealings with the international community. A more "hostile", confrontational phase of US foreign policy *vis-à-vis* the United Nations became conspicuous in the Reagan years (1980-1988).

Further comparison might suggest a similar conjunction of religiosity and chauvinism in the popular and political cultures of ancient Rome and modern America. The plebeian tendency to reject the civic values of other peoples has regular operational significance for the possessor of global hegemony, if its own political ideology requires that the people's bias should be reflected in the workings of foreign policy. The role of the intellectual community as a moderator is greatly complicated in a society that rejects the concept of an intelligentsia.[46]

7.   Prospects for World Constitutionalism

Advancing the cause of world constitutionalism – or any other mode of international utopianism – requires a combination of political realism and intellectual imagination. The outline of a transnational, cross-cultural project along these lines is suggested in the introduction to this collection of essays.

The political reality is that such a project, to be useful, must be shared across all regions, so that allegations of cultural bias in the field of international law can be confronted. The goals of legal uniformity and universality may have to be reconciled with the value of cultural diversity. Moreover, a world constitutionalism project cannot realistically be restricted to state or inter-state actors, since they themselves are the chief object of study. Trust would have to be placed in an open-ended coalition of state and non-state institutions, so that the voices of civil society can be heard within the chambers of the power-holders.

Whether such a coalition could be assembled depends on the persuasiveness of the argument for the constitutionalization of world society. The credibility of such a vision is impaired by the intellectual vagueness of the concept of "constitution". For some, what needs to be advocated is a convergence of juridical elite opinions on what constitute the *basic norms* of international law: perhaps a combination of human rights principles[47] and infrastructural concepts.[48] Legal formalists might prefer to

---

46   It is true in all cultures that discussions regarding the applicability of international law to issues of the day tend to be the preoccupation of a tiny intellectual elite. Very seldom is the general public given an opportunity to examine contemporary political developments from the international law perspective. References to "violations of international law" in the media are rarely accompanied by an informed commentary on the exchange of relevant arguments and counter-arguments exchanged within the professional community. In North America a great deal of *political* debate erupted in the television media after the 2003 US intervention in Iraq, but academic comment on the legal issues involved was almost entirely lacking.

47   The concept of "human rights constitutionalism" invites attention to the late 20th century expansion of "human welfare" beyond the sector of civil and political rights to that of economic, social and cultural rights, and indeed to the even wider context of "human needs". Macdonald, Ronald St. J., Douglas M. Johnston, and Gerald L. Morris (eds.), *The International Law and Policy of Human Welfare* (Alphen aan den Rijn: Sijthoff & Noordhoff, 1978). Through a series of recommendations by the UN Human Rights Commission and unanimous resolutions adopted by the UN General Assembly, a "right to democracy" might now be said to have become an important civic compo-

stress the need for *sacred text*: not only a strengthening of the constitutional credentials of the United Nations Charter[49] but also an integration of other "constitutive"
instruments.[50] A third road to world constitutionalism would take us over the difficult terrain of *organizational reform*: a journey that might begin with a re-evaluation of the League of Nations[51] before a more detailed analysis of the institutional
and procedural strengths and deficiencies of the United Nations.[52] A fourth channel

nent of "human rights" in the early years of the 21st century. Franck, Thomas M., "The
Emerging Right of Democratic Governance", 86 *American Journal of International Law*
46 (1992). For the most comprehensive vision of "human dignity", se McDougal, Myres
S., Harold D. Lasswell, and Lung-chu Chen, *Human Rights and World Public Order*
(New Haven, Conn.: Yale University Press, 1980). Admittedly, there are many conceptions of "democracy" in world culture, but boiling it down to the universal minimum
does not seem to serve the highest aspirations of humanity.

48   The 19th century witnessed the construction of a dozen or so fundamental statist concepts as the infrastructure of international law: subjects, sovereignty, equality, consent,
custom, jurisdiction, responsibility, recognition, and other constructs – all Latin terms
that reflect the Roman law foundations of the classical model. See Macdonald and
Johnston, *supra* note 5, pp. 381-712. The tension between these statist concepts and the
more modern claims to human welfare is the dominant ethical motif in the literature
of international law, and the principal motivation for calls to restructure the field.

49   Macdonald, Ronald St. J., "The Charter of the United Nations in Constitutional Perspective", 20 *Australian Yearbook of International Law* 205 (1999); and Fassbender,
Bardo, "The United Nations Charter as Constitution of the International Community",
36 *Columbia Journal of International Law* 529 (1998).

50   Despite its "non-binding" status, in a formalistic sense under the law of treaties, the
Universal Declaration of Human Rights has parental status within the family of human
rights instruments. Some human rights lawyers over the years, especially in the cold
war years of ideological struggle, have questioned whether the International Covenant
on Economic, Social and Cultural Rights has acquired "sacred text" status comparable
to that of the International Covenant on Civil and Political Rights. With the demise of
the Marxist-Leninist champions of collective rights and the apparent triumph of capitalism, some writers now argue in favour of inducting the freedom of contract and other
property rights into the hall of vested human rights. Compare Petersmann, Ernst-Ulrich,
"Time for a United Nations 'Global Concept' for Integrating Human Rights into the Law
of Worldwide Organizations: Lessons from European Integration", 13 *European Journal
of International Law* 621 (2002), with Howse, Robert, "Human Rights in the W.T.O.:
Whose Rights, What Humanity?", 13 *European Journal of International Law* 651 (2002).

51   The League of Nations emerged out of meetings that began, arguably, with a discussion
of academics held at the Century Club in New York on 25th January, 1915. The League
"remained essentially an Anglo-Saxon affair". Northedge, Frederick S., *The League of Nations: Its Life and Times (1920-1949)* (Leicester: Leicester University Press, 1986), at p. 26.

52   There have been numerous evaluations of the UN system, and numerous proposals
for its reform. For recent studies, see, for example, Knight, W. Andy, *Changing Unit-
ed Nations: Multilateral Evolution and the Quest for Global Governance* (New York:
Palgrave, 2000); and Reinicke, Wolfgang H., and Francis Deng, *Critical Choices: The
United Nations, Networks, and the Future of Global Governance* (Ottawa: International
Development Research Centre, 2000).

of inquiry might concentrate on the need for integration among the most highly constitutionalized *systems of transnational law*: United Nations law, World Trade Organization law, and European Union law.[53] Other points of departure include the premise that international law cannot be constitutionalized in any truly democratic sense until it passes the test of *domestication*: that is, until at least some of the basic norms of "world law" become incorporated as fundamental norms of national law through legislative enactment and judicial acknowledgement.[54] Conversely, we might think "out of the box" – the international law box – that world constitutional law should evolve out of the core elements of *national* constitutional law.[55] For still others, of course, constitutionalism is essentially a *political symbol*, a manifold construct intended to mobilize popular sentiment in support of the key institutional structures and procedures of a political community.[56]

Skeptics might conclude that such a multi-faceted concept means too many things to too many people to serve as a focus of concerted action. Yet to many of us in the international law community, the future of "world law" rests on a common willingness to go down these paths together.

---

53   This approach has been supported especially by European jurists who envisage the European Union as a model for constitutional experimentation at the global level. For example, see Petersmann, *supra* note 50.

54   On the need for "internalization" of international law, se Koh, Harold H., "Why Do Nations Obey International Law?", 106 *Yale Law Journal* 2599 (1997).

55   For a major work in the distinct discipline of comparative constitutional law, see Beer, Lawrence W. (ed.), *Constitutional Systems in Late Twentieth Century Asia* (Seattle: University of Washington Press, 1992). This kind of descriptive scholarship is important for international lawyers seeking to prescribe a global constitutional order based on common, or widely shared, principles and mechanisms of constitutionalism at the national level.

56   The more emphasis given to constitutionalism as a symbol of political solidarity, the more questionable it becomes as a governing construct for the heterogeneous "world community".

2. Multilateralism in the Age of US Hegemony

Christian Tomuschat

Shortly after the the invasion of Iraq by the troops of the Anglo-American Coalition, *Michael J. Glennon* wrote an article in Foreign Affairs[1] which sounded like the trumpets of Jericho. According to his views, the fate of the Security Council had now been definitively sealed, and the regime of non-use of force ushered in by the UN Charter (henceforth: Charter) had collapsed. Instead of expressing any kind of regret, *Glennon* disclosed his satisfaction with this development, stating that this meant at the same time the end of "one particularly pernicious outgrowth of natural law ... the idea that states are sovereign equals". The title above seems to give credit to his assertion, but this contribution rather proceeds from the traditional premises of the international legal order, attempting to find out whether indeed some dramatic change, a revolution, has occurred in the structures of the edifice of international law.

1. Introduction

A. *Sovereign Equality*

According to a well-established proposition, sovereign equality constitutes the cornerstone of the current world order. It is not by accident that this principle has been set forth as the first of the basic principles listed in Article 2 (1) of the Charter. In fact, sovereign equality provides the conceptual basis of a system which does not acknowledge any natural authority above individual States.[2] Even the United Na-

---

[1]   "Why the Security Council Failed", *Foreign Affairs* 82 (May/June 2003), p. 16-35.

[2]   Whoever denies sovereign equality as one of the founding axioms of international law tears down the whole edifice of international law; see for instance H. Grant Cohen, "The American Challenge to International Law", *The Yale Journal of International Law* 28 (2003), p. 551, at 569; see also pessimistic conclusions by N. Krisch, "More equal than the rest? Hierarchy, equality and US predominance in international law", in: M. Byers and G. Nolte (eds.), *United States Hegemony and the Foundations of International Law*, Cambridge 2003, p. 135, at 174.

Ronald St. John Macdonald & Douglas M. Johnston (eds.), Towards World Constitutionalism, *pp. 31-75.*
© 2005 *Koninklijke Brill NV. Printed in The Netherlands.* ISBN 90 04 14612 1.

tions was established by virtue of a multilateral treaty which States were – and are – free either to accept or reject. Should a State wish to "go it alone", it could not be prevented from so doing. Such freedom of choice does not amount to a discretionary power to dismiss the requirements deriving from the existence of an international legal order. Sovereign equality constitutes a legal position which is granted to States by virtue of that order and which, hence, confines the sovereign powers enjoyed by one State by the sovereign powers of every other State. As a logical corollary, the prohibition of intervention and the principle of non-use of force provide complementary legal protection to sovereign equality.[3] States are possessed with individual decision-making jurisdiction only with regard to their own matters, defined primarily *ratione territorii*, but also *ratione personae* and *ratione materiae*. However, today few matters can be squeezed into neatly defined boxes of domestic jurisdiction. Most of the vital challenges humankind has to cope with today transcend national boundaries. The global scope of these challenges, on the one hand, and the confined nature of national sovereignty, on the other, continually generate tensions for which solutions must be found which may oscillate between unilateralism and multilateralism.

B.   *Multilateralism and International Cooperation*

In such instances, which *de facto* have rather become the rule than the exception, international cooperation becomes a necessity. Cooperation is largely a synonym of multilateralism. When speaking of cooperation, reference is made primarily to the factual conduct of States acting in concert with one another, as suggested by the elaboration of the principle in the Declaration on Principles of International Law concerning Friendly Relations and Co-operation among States in accordance with the Charter of the United Nations (hereinafter: Friendly Relations Declaration).[4] On the other hand, multilateralism connotes more the legal and organizational framework underlying international cooperation. The United Nations constitutes the most tangible expression of multilateralism and, concomitantly, the clearest rejection of unilateralism in trying to resolve international problems that affect the international community as a whole.

Logically, hence, the international community is the third of the key concepts that fall to be defined in the context of this section. Although the international community is mentioned in a number of international treaties, above all in Articles 53 and 64 of the Vienna Convention on the Law of Treaties (VCTL) as the legitimizing authority of *jus cogens* and more particularly in numerous resolutions of the UN General Assembly, it lacks a constitutive act determining its identity and setting out its procedures and tools of action. In fact, the concept of international community may be described as a synthetic abstraction derived from a number

---

3   However, it would appear rather naïve simply to prohibit hegemonism as done by the UN General Assembly in Resolution 34/103, 14 December 1979, on "Inadmissibility of the policy of hegemonism in international relations".

4   Annex to GA Resolution 2625 (XXV), 24 October 1970.

of elements suggesting that, notwithstanding the principle of sovereign equality, humankind constitutes a unity which is held together by many ties, both of a factual and a legal character.[5] First and foremost, it is (almost) uncontested today that all of the nations of the world live under the overarching roof of a common legal order. Proceeding from the premise of the existence of an international community with a large array of common interests,[6] one cannot but conclude that cooperation based on multilateral structures corresponds in a perfect manner to these empirical foundations.

C. *Hegemony*

Since it is incumbent on this contribution to analyze multilateralism "in the age of US hegemony", it has first to be asked what hegemony means. It is no legal term of art. Nowhere do international treaties or other legal instruments explicitly provide for "hegemony" or "hegemonic powers".[7] In his seminal work *Die Hegemonie. Ein Buch von führenden Staaten,*[8] *Heinrich Triepel* struggles at length with an appropriate definition. According to his view, hegemony, although not a legal concept and largely based on sociological criteria, has a foundation in legal data which the observer must assess in their interrelationship in order to grasp the leadership function which hegemony encapsulates. This contribution shares the views expounded by *Triepel*. In fact, hegemony should not be equated with a pure factual situation of power dominance which might change on the spur of the moment and which, in any event, is not set in stone, given the ongoing competition among nations.[9] Newspapers provide information on the actual distribution of might in international society. Neither should hegemony be taken to mean the absence of any rules which are binding on its champion.[10] If the term is meant to have any

---

5   For recent attempts to grasp the essence of the term "international community" see D. Kritsiotis, "Imagining the International Community", *EJIL* 13 (2002), p. 961-992; E. Kwakwa, "The international community, international law, and the United States: Three in one, two against one, or one and the same?", in: *United States Hegemony, op. cit.* (note 2), p. 25, at 27-35; A. Paulus, *Die internationale Gemeinschaft im Völkerrecht*, München 2001; id., "The influence of the United States on the concept of the "international community", in: *United States Hegemony, op. cit.* (note 2), p. 57-90; C. Tomuschat, "International Law: Ensuring the Survival of Mankind on the Eve of a New Century", *Recueil des cours* 281 (1999), p. 72-90.

6   See S. Kadelbach, "Ethik des Völkerrechts unter Bedingungen der Globalisierung", *HJIL* 64 (2004), p. 1, at 11.

7   By contrast, hegemony was ruled out in Article II of the Treaty of Peace and Friendship between China and Japan, 12 August 1978, *ILM* 17 (1978), p. 1054, and condemned by General Assembly Resolution 34/103, 14 December 1979.

8   (*The Hegemony. A Book of Leading States*), first ed. 1938, 2nd ed. Stuttgart 1943.

9   See, for instance, J.F. Hoge, "A Global Power Shift in the Making", *Foreign Affairs* 83 (July/August 2004), p. 2-7.

10   This is the dream propagated by J.R. Bolton, "Is There Really 'Law' in International Affairs?", *Transnational Law and Contemporary Problems* 10 (2000), p. 1 *et seq.*; for a

significant meaning for political and legal analysis, it should be taken to connote a consolidated position of leadership which essentially rests on factual elements, but which is supplemented by an additional element of recognition by those who are placed under the hegemonic regime and at the same time reap the benefits of that regime.[11] Consequently, hegemony is founded on a relationship of reciprocity, it cannot be brought about in international relations just by unilateral action of a mighty State. A hegemon enjoys a privileged position, but it must as a corollary be prepared to assume specific obligations which an ordinary State does not have to shoulder.[12] Privilege and burden thus constitute an indivisible whole. Otherwise, one should not speak of hegemony.

In his opening speech to the Conference on International Organization, which drafted the Charter from April to June 1945, President Truman expressed in clear terms how he saw, after the expected end of hostilities, the role of the Allied Powers which had carried the main weight of the fight against the Axis Powers. He said:

> "The responsibility of great states is to serve, and not to dominate the peoples of the world",[13]

and he added in his concluding speech in which he congratulated the participants on their success in finalizing the Charter:

> "It is ... the duty of those powerful nations to assume the responsibility for leadership towards world peace".[14]

Thus, in a few simple sentences, he captured the essence of hegemony which is nothing else than responsible leadership.

It is with this understanding that hegemony can find a place in a world the basic axiom of which is sovereign equality. Equality does not belong to the class of rules of *jus cogens*. It is common ground in international organizations that the rights and obligations of the parties may and should be differentiated according to their specific contributions to the discharge of the functions of the organization concerned. Thus, for instance, Monaco, as a tax-free annex of France, would neither qualify as a permanent member of the Security Council, nor does it qualify as

---

forceful rejection of this vision see D.F. Vagts, "Hegemonic International Law", *AJIL* 95 (2001), p. 843 *et seq.*

11   Triepel, *op. cit.* (note 8), p. 141, 144, 148.; K. Ginther, "Hegemony", in: *Encyclopedia of Public International Law*, Vol. II, Amsterdam *et al.* 1995, p. 685. It must be acknowledged that the choice of terminology is to some extent a semantic problem. Hegemony can also be equated with pure factual predominance. But then it loses any specific contours.

12   Triepel, *op. cit.* (note 8), p. 222-239, devotes an entire chapter of his book to the means which a hegemon should use in order to stabilize his position.

13   Speech of 25 April 1945, *UNCIO* I, p. 1 (3).

14   Speech of 27 June 1945, *ibid.*, p. 679 (682).

a non-permanent member. Such differentiations cannot be imposed by the powerful nations on the poor and weak nations. Hegemonic structures may be warranted by valid reasons.[15] But these reasons must be explained, and eventually the status of inequality must be accepted by all concerned.

2. The United States in International Relations

As far as the factual side of the concept of hegemony is concerned, one cannot deny that currently the United States is the most powerful actor in the international arena. It is not the most populous nation of the globe, but in terms of population it ranges in third position after China and India. Assessed by territorial size, it occupies also the third place, but this time after Russia and Canada. Concerning its economic performance, it comes first among all of the large States, distancing by far not only China and India, but also being ahead of the other big industrial powers like France, Germany, and the United Kingdom, only Japan remaining roughly at a par with it. In the military sector, the country has an even more impressive edge over its competitors. Regarding its military spending, it has overtaken all the other nations. Per annum, it currently devotes about 400 billion dollars to its armed forces,[16] thereby affording between 40 and 50% of the world's military expenditure. In other words, assessed in terms of factual power, the United States is not only "second to none", but has undoubtedly assumed the leading role in the world.

Factual strength should not be equated with invulnerability. A high standard of living goes evidently hand in hand with a high level of consumption. In order to maintain the current levels of well-being for its population, the United States must ensure an unimpeded flow of commodities from other continents to its shores. Like Western Europe, the United States is highly dependent on the supply of oil to satisfy its ever-growing energy needs in all sectors of life, in particular for industrial purposes, in the traffic sector, and for home consumption. Any interruption of the continuous flow of that commodity would entail disastrous consequences for its economic system. In this perspective, the United States – like all of the countries of Western Europe – is conspicuously weak, a fact which is well known to all of its enemies, in particular to the fundamentalist terrorists organized in the network of Al Qaeda.

Does the unique position which the United States has reached after the demise of the socialist systems in central and eastern Europe make it a hegemon in the international legal order? To be sure, pursuant to concepts as they are currently used in political science one may well speak today of US hegemony. But, as explained above, this inquiry does not focus solely on the factual aspects as borne out by the figures just referred to. The question needs to be asked – and answered

---

15   Krisch, *loc. cit.* (note 2), p. 151-152, is seriously mistaken in criticizing the privileges of the permanent Security Council members from the viewpoint of sovereign equality.

16   See <http://www.globalissues.org/Geopolitics/ArmsTrade/Spending.asp#WorldMilitarySpending>, visited 26 June 2004.

– whether the United States is "more equal" than the other nations of this globe, whether it enjoys *de lege* and/or by political consensus certain privileges in derogation from the basic principle of sovereign equality of States.

In the past, the United States did claim a privileged position on the American continent by virtue of the *Monroe* doctrine. This doctrine, proclaimed in 1823, not only purported to exclude the European powers from the whole of the Western hemisphere, but also served in later decades (from 1890 to 1930) as the basis for interventionist policies of the United States particularly in the Caribbean area.[17] All such claims of legal preponderance have become obsolete under the impact of the Charter, although the actual practice of intervention was not forestalled by it.[18]

3.   Multilateralism in Action

Since under general international law all States are juridically equal, multilateral treaties and the regimes brought into existence by them are the most appropriate ground for any inquiry into hegemonic elements in present-day international law. It stands to reason that solely a number of these regimes, to the extent that they reflect contemporary trends, can be appraised with a view to eliciting the answers which may satisfy the central question of this contribution. Consequently, our focus will be mainly, but not exclusively, on international organizations and/or multilateral treaty regimes.

Generally, international organizations, which by definition are based on multilateral treaties, may be characterized as common agencies for the discharge of tasks which cannot be successfully performed by States acting individually. The United Nations encapsulates the concept of multilateral cooperation in the most exemplary fashion. Having emerged from the ashes of World War II, the "Peoples of the United Nations" decided in 1945 to "save succeeding generations from the scourge of war" (Charter, Preamble). To ban the prospect of war was indeed the primary goal of the World Organization when it was founded in 1945. Besides, the Preamble of the Charter and its Article 1 outline a vast program of economic and social reforms designed to bring about peaceful conditions within nations in order also to secure peacefulness in their external relations.

It stands to reason that the principle of equality of States has its limits when certain tasks are tackled by the international community. Equality is focused on the matters for which each State bears individual responsibility. At home, every State is its own master. Any multilateral framework, however, is a collective undertaking which depends on the contributions of its members. Large States which make

---

17   For a more detailed assessment see D.W. Dent, *The Legacy of the Monroe Doctrine. A Reference Guide to U.S. Involvement in Latin America and the Caribbean*, Westport, Connecticut, and London 1999; W.G. Grewe, *The Epochs of International Law*, Berlin and New York 2000, p. 433, 476; P. Malanczuk, "Monroe Doctrine", *Encyclopedia of Public International Law*, Vol. III, Amsterdam *et al.* 1997, p. 460-464.

18   One needs only recall the toppling of the democratic Government of Guatemala with all the disastrous consequences flowing therefrom.

more substantial contributions than the other members can legitimately expect to have a greater say in running the relevant organization than small or tiny States.[19] Insisting on the unrestricted application of sovereign equality also in this context may almost amount to heresy. Above all, it falls to the larger States to take the necessary initiatives which may serve as a blueprint for the policies of the organization concerned. Some differentiation in the rights and duties corresponds, therefore, to functional necessities.

A.   Security

No State is in a position to guarantee its security exclusively by its own means. Even the United States depends for its external security on the solidarity of its neighbors and allies. In this regard, two different pathways were outlined at the end of World War II. On the one hand, the United States, the driving force behind the reorganization of the international legal order after the havoc caused by that War, engaged its best efforts for the establishment of a system of collective security through the United Nations, bringing into existence a system open to all States of this globe. In Chapter VII of the Charter, the necessary instruments for the maintenance of international peace and security are provided for. On the other hand, when the ideological divide between itself and the Soviet Union deepened, the United States had to acknowledge that it was manifestly illusory to expect the necessary assistance against any threats from the main responsible institution, the Security Council. As was confirmed by the historical experiences in the following decades, the Security Council was of no avail in international conflicts that resulted from or affected the structural rivalry between the two superpowers, given the right of veto which every permanent member of that body enjoys under Article 27 (3) of the Charter. For that reason, the United States in 1949 formed an alliance with its Western partners, the North Atlantic Treaty Organization (NATO).[20] NATO is predicated on Article 51 of the Charter, which grants to every State member of the United Nations the right of "individual or collective self-defence".

The NATO Treaty does not provide for a privileged position of the United States. The Organization is founded, according to the most traditional thinking, on sovereign equality of its members. No vote by majority is foreseen. In the practice of the Organization, however, it was always considered self-evident that the United States had to assume the main responsibilities deriving from the Alliance. The procedural arrangement presented many advantages for the United States. For its part, it could never be overruled. The other members were much more dependent for their security on it than *vice versa*. Consequently, the United States could be fairly sure that its political strategies would almost automatically be endorsed by its partners.

---

19   See M. Cosnard, "Sovereign equality – 'the *Wimbledon* sails on'", in: *United States Hegemony, op. cit.* (note 2), p. 117, at 122.

20   34 *UNTS* 243.

In no other region of the world does a similarly integrated system of collective self-defence exist. The Inter-American Treaty of Reciprocal Assistance (Rio Pact) of 2 September 1947[21] contains also a clause (Article 3) according to which any "armed attack by any State against an American State shall be considered as an attack against all the American States". But it has never been possible to translate that pledge of joint defence into common institutions comprising forces under a unified command earmarked for purposes of collective self-defence. During the regime of socialism in central and eastern Europe, the Warsaw Pact, signed on 14 May 1955,[22] provided a system of collective self-defence counter-balancing the western military alliance. Understandably, however, the demise of the socialist ideology also brought to an end the Warsaw Pact organization.[23] Africa totally lacks a common defence system, and Asia is much too diverse to permit even envisioning such a system that might include all of the States of the region. Therefore, States have generally turned to sub-regional associations. In any event, governments are generally aware of the fact that the Security Council is an unreliable institution which, in a crisis situation, may or may not provide the necessary assistance. In sum, the concept of collective security at world-wide level has taken shape, but it lacks the requisite effectiveness. No nation can trust that its security will under all circumstances be guaranteed by the United Nations.

B.   The Oceans

As far as the oceans of the globe are concerned, the United Nations Convention on the Law of the Sea of 1982 (UNCLOS)[24] has ushered in a comprehensive regime that regulates all aspects related to human use of this major resource of the entire international community. Whereas the four law of the sea conventions adopted at the first Conference on the Law of the Sea held in Geneva in 1958 confined themselves to setting forth rules on the well-known traditional issues, UNCLOS purported to deal also with the consequences of the most recent technological developments. Thus, in particular, protection and preservation of the marine environment and marine scientific research became topics that were included in the new instrument. Although the negotiations on UNCLOS had lasted for an entire decade and although the provisions on its most objectionable element, Part XI on mining on the ocean floor, were largely suspended by virtue of an Agreement of 28 July 1994[25] adopted before its actual entry into force,[26] universality has not yet been reached. Now, almost a quarter of a century after its adoption, UNCLOS still has a

---

21   OAS Treaty Series, No. 8.

22   219 *UNTS*.

23   It was formally dissolved on 1 July 1991.

24   1833 *UNTS* 3.

25   Agreement relating to the implementation of Part XI of the Convention, *ILM* 33 (1994), p. 1309.

26   16 November 1994.

limited circle of States parties (145 according to data provided by the UN in August 2004). In particular, the United States remains aloof from the instrument although its main concerns were largely satisfied by the Agreement of 28 July 1994.[27]

C. Environment

It is clear also that the most serious environmental problems affecting other media can be resolved only by concerted multilateral action. From among the "commons of mankind", the gas layers surrounding the globe determine in the most direct fashion the possibility of plant life, animal life and human life. Should the protective ozone layer be destroyed by chlorofluorocarbons, halons and other obnoxious substances, any kind of organic life could be irreparably harmed. There is no remedy by which the ozone layer could be restored once it would have disappeared. Consequently, all nations should have a vital interest in seeing the harmful substances definitively banned. In fact, the international community succeeded in establishing a complex legal regime which comprises the 1985 Vienna Convention for the Protection of the Ozone Layer[28] as well as the 1987 Montreal Protocol on Substances that Deplete the Ozone Layer.[29] In this case, the efforts of a number of nations could become futile if other nations just continued on their course of using the banned substances without any hindrance. Multilateralism in the form of universality was therefore not just a desirable aim, but a practical necessity. Consequently, the drafters established an ingenious system of, on the one hand, control measures, including prohibitions on production and consumption, and, on the other hand, incentives for poorer countries through a Financial Mechanism fed by a Multilateral Fund.[30] Here, the United States was one of the first nations to subscribe to the two instruments. Universality has almost been reached. While the Vienna Convention counts 188 States parties, the Montreal Protocol has by now been ratified by 187 States. None of the most populous nations is absent. Among the participants are China and Russia, India and Indonesia, Brazil and Mexico. The regime for the protection of the ozone layer may be recorded as a major success story of cooperative multilateralism.

Climate change is another one of the core concerns of the international community. There is no need in the present context to dwell at large on the harmful effects of the greenhouse phenomenon, which are all but too well known. The 1992 UN Framework Convention on Climate Change[31] seeks to put a brake on developments that may lead to a progressive warming up of the earths's atmosphere. For that purpose, in particular, a ceiling must be set on the emission of

---

27   China ratified UNCLOS on 7 June 1996, Russia did so on 12 March 1997.

28   Of 22 March 1985, *ILM* 26 (1987), p. 1529; 1513 *UNTS* 293.

29   Of 16 September 1987, *ILM* 26 (1987), p. 1550; 1522 *UNTS* 3.

30   For details see P. Sands, *Principles of International Environmental Law*, 2nd ed. 2003, pp. 342-357.

31   Of 9 May 1992, 1771 *UNTS* 107.

certain gases with a potential to contribute to the greenhouse effect. Details were determined in the Kyoto Protocol to the Climate Change Convention. While the Climate Change Convention itself does not impose any actual obligations on States and has attracted a membership of 189 States, the Kyoto Protocol specifies concrete obligations for States, which affect in particular the entire energy sector. This has deterred many States, among them, in particular, Russia and the United States.[32] Since Article 25 of the Kyoto Protocol requires participation of States accounting for 55 per cent of the total carbon emissions for 1990, the Kyoto Protocol has not yet entered into force although it currently counts not less than 121 parties. This is a case where multilateralism based on treaty making shows all of its weaknesses. The United States and Russia are of the view that to put a cap on their carbon dioxide emissions could seriously harm their economies. Therefore, although the harmful effects of greenhouse gases can hardly be challenged any longer, the two countries have placed their specific interests over the interests of humankind in general. To date, the international community lacks institutions and mechanisms that could cope with such situations.[33]

D.   International Trade

International trade has also been given a multilateral framework through the WTO rules which encompass, in particular, GATT 1994 and GATS, the General Agreement on Trade in Services.[34] Here, treaty-making has been fairly successful. All of the world's leading trading nations have become members of the WTO (June 2004: 147 States). After many years of negotiations, China was also admitted to the WTO in December 2001. Obviously, large as well as small States see great benefits in WTO membership. For small States it is vital to enjoy the advantages that derive from progressive elimination of trade barriers through the mechanisms of GATT. The United States, on the other hand, has a paramount interest in the protection of the intellectual property rights of its nationals, which is secured on the basis of the Agreement on Trade-Related Aspects of Intellectual Property Rights, an integral part of the entire WTO package. On the other hand, the WTO procedures provide effective guarantees against any unfair practices in contravention of the agreed regime. Thus, on balance, the United States has seen fit to accept the whole package, including the Understanding on Rules and Procedures Governing the Settlement of Disputes. It is certainly not unreasonable to conclude that the United States, more than any other State, carefully examines the pros and cons of participation in a multilateral framework of binding legal rules and has come to the result in the case

---

32   Australia and Indonesia are also among the absentees like the oil producers Iran, Iraq, Kuwait and Saudi Arabia.

33   Of 11 December 1997, ILM 37 (1998), p. 32. After ratification by Russia, the Protocol entered into force on 16 February 2005.

34   Reprinted in: WTO (ed.), *The Legal Texts. The Results of the Uruguay Round of Multilateral Trade Negotiations*, Cambridge 1999.

of WTO that the balance sheet is outright positive although it has not been able to secure for itself any special rights, setting it apart from the other members.[35]

E. *Terrorism*

It is a truism to state that the fight against international terrorism can be won only on the basis of tight international cooperation. After 9/11, that fight has gained paramount importance for the United States. Multilateral efforts to combat terrorism were launched many decades ago when seizure of aircraft became a dangerous habit of political extremists. The first relevant instrument was the 1963 Convention on Offences and Certain Other Acts Committed on Board Aircraft,[36] which was followed by other, more specific instruments in the following years. Progressively, in a piece-meal approach, other dangers were identified which the entire international community, regardless of its political orientation, found unacceptable. Only a few years before the tragic events of 9/11, two instruments with a wide scope of application were adopted, the 1997 International Convention for the Suppression of Terrorist Bombings[37] and the 1999 International Convention for the Suppression of the Financing of Terrorism.[38] Although the international community has unanimously voiced its condemnation of all "acts, methods and practices of terrorism, as criminal and unjustifiable, wherever and by whomever committed",[39] this principled stance has not had any direct effect on the preparedness of States to endorse the relevant international treaties. Thus, the International Convention against the Taking of Hostages, which was adopted in 1979,[40] has today, more than a quarter of a century later, no more than 138 States parties. The 1997 International Convention for the Suppression of Terrorist Bombings remains at a level of 123 States parties notwithstanding 9/11,[41] and the 1999 International Convention for the Suppression of the Financing of Terrorism has to date attracted no more than 117 ratifications.[42] A general convention designed to fight terrorism in all its forms is pending for many years already in the UN General Assembly. Its adoption is impeded by lack of consensus on whether State terrorism should be included in its scope *ratione materiae*. There is no real hope that this divergence of opinions can be overcome soon.

This slow process of acceptance *vis-à-vis* the threatening phenomenon of terrorism highlights quite drastically the cumbersome nature of the traditional pro-

---

35   For a recent assessment see S. Esserman and R. Howse, "The WTO on Trial", *Foreign Affairs* 82 (January/February 2003), p. 130-140.

36   704 *UNTS*, No. 10106.

37   Adopted by GA Resolution 52/164, 15 December 1997.

38   Adopted by GA Resolution 54/109, 9 December 1999.

39   GA Resolution 49/60, 9 December 1994.

40   GA Resolution 34/146, 17 December 1979.

41   It is interesting to note that the United States deposited its instrument of ratification only after 9/11, on 26 June 2002.

42   The same observation applies as in note 41.

cess of law-making. Multilateral institutions and mechanisms must first of all be put into place. Once they have been established, they may operate quite effectively, but the founding stage is one of great difficulties. Recognizing that there was an urgent need to prevent the transfer of funds to persons preparing terrorist attacks along the lines drawn by the Convention for the Suppression of the Financing of Terrorism, the Security Council adopted on 28 September 2001, a few days after the attacks on the Twin Towers in New York and the Pentagon, Resolution 1373 (2001) on "Threats to international peace and security caused by terrorist acts". This resolution enjoins all States, on the basis of the authority of the Security Council under Chapter VII of the Charter, to prevent and suppress the financing of terrorist acts, thereby translating large parts of the earlier Convention into a binding act of secondary legislation. Many authors have challenged the claim of the Security Council thus to exercise the powers of a world legislative body.[43] Whatever the outcome of that debate may be: the effectiveness of multilateralism in a world-wide framework would be greatly enhanced if at the UN level there existed an authority entitled to wield legislative powers at least with regard to key issues of international peace and security. It is obvious that the United States as a permanent member of the Security Council has much to gain from an expansive interpretation of Chapter VII of the Charter.

F.   Human Rights

Whereas according to the preceding observations adherence to multilateral regimes depends essentially on an easily understandable assessment of the advantages which the State concerned may derive from such a step, the establishment of international regimes for the promotion and protection of human rights is predicated on more subtle considerations. In a direct sense, no State can gain any tangible benefits from submitting to international control mechanisms which monitor its conduct as to their conformity with the commitments undertaken. The rationale behind the decision to join the circle of States parties varies greatly. For a State like the Federal Republic of Germany, it was necessary in the decades subsequent to World War II to show to the outside world that the new democratic regime, which had emerged from a criminal dictatorship, had nothing to do with that criminal past and that it was fully prepared to accept any kind of international review of its conduct. Hence, to become a party to the European Convention on Human Rights or to the International Covenant on Civil and Political Rights (CCPR) amounted

---

43   See, for instance, A. Zimmermann and B. Elberling, "Grenzen der Legislativbefugnisse des Sicherheitsrats", *Vereinte Nationen* 2004, p. 71-77; for a positive approach to the issue see C. Tomuschat, "Obligations Arising for States Without or Against Their Will", *Recueil des cours* 241 (1993-IV), p. 199, at 344-346; J.-D. Aston, "Die Bekämpfung abstrakter Gefahren für den Weltfrieden durch legislative Maßnahmen des Sicherheitsrats – Resolution 1373 (2001) im Kontext", *HJIL* 62 (2002), p. 257, at 280-289; P.C. Szasz, "The Security Council Starts Legislating", *AJIL* 96 (2002), p. 901-905.

to a demonstrative showing of a new identity under the rule of law. Some States, although believing that they themselves had such complete systems of review of governmental action that there was no need for an additional layer of monitoring, wished to expand the human rights regime by submitting to international control and thus inspiring other nations to follow their example. Governments are not unaware of the basic truth that countries where human rights and the rule of law are respected will generally conduct peaceful foreign policies. As far as, in particular, the CCPR was concerned, several countries saw the necessity of upholding Western values in the interpretation and application of that key instrument of human rights protection, given its widespread ratification by socialist States, a fact which aroused fears of a "kidnapping" of that key element of the International Bill of Rights by those States. Lastly, it is a matter of international reputation to be seen as a nation that values human rights and fundamental freedoms. Whoever shies away from joining the group that has embraced the main United Nations instruments in the field of human rights falls prey to the suspicion that he has something to hide in the domestic arena.

G.   *International Legislation?*

There are many other fields where the necessity of international cooperation through multilateral institutions is evident in that the natural foundations of human life are in issue. It would be highly desirable to be able to resort to an international legislative authority for the regulation of human activities in those fields. To date, however, at world-wide level the international community has shied away from establishing institutions with true law-making powers. Multilateralism must therefore rely on the traditional procedures of treaty-making. Under the applicable rules of general international law, no State is under an obligation to ratify an international treaty, not even when such treaty serves to protect fundamental interests of humankind. Only in the European Union has decision-making by majority vote gained considerable ground. Regulations and directives may be enacted in most fields of jurisdiction of the European Union by a qualified majority in the Council, complemented, as specified in more detail by the relevant treaty stipulations, by an affirmative vote in the European Parliament. By contrast, treaty-making within the framework of the United Nations requires active consent by each and every individual State. Thus, even a small State is legally in a position to distance itself from a project of far-reaching importance for the future of humankind, although the political costs of choosing the position of an outsider may be high. Big powers, on the other hand, enjoy mostly true freedom of choice. Nobody can compel China, Russia or the United States to join an international treaty of which they consider that the advantages accruing to them do not outweigh the disadvantages of being enmeshed in an internationally binding regime.

3.   Hegemony in International Multilateralism

A.   *Historical Recollection*

At its origins, the modern international society did not acknowledge any kind of superiority of a single State. During the 19th century in Europe, the principle of sovereign equality of States was formally proclaimed, but on the other hand the leading role of the great powers – Austria, Great Britain, France, Prussia and Russia – was tacitly admitted.[44] After the Vienna Peace Conference of 1815, Austria, Prussia and Russia had first formed the "Holy Alliance".[45] Two months later, these three powers together with Great Britain established the so-called "Quadruple Alliance"[46] which, after the admission of France ("Quintuple Alliance") in 1818, became the "Concert of Europe". It was by these five powers, acting through diplomatic contacts and conferences at irregular intervals, that the European history was shaped in the following decades until the middle of the century. Later, Turkey (1856) and Italy (1867) were admitted into the group. The "Concert of Europe" claimed for itself the right to act as a directorate that enjoyed the legitimate authority to settle any major disputes in the whole of Europe.[47]

After the Franco-German war of 1870/71, as a result of which the German Empire took the place of Prussia, the Concert of Europe progressively lost its leading role. In the face of rising political tensions, it was unable to safeguard peace and security among its members. But it still succeeded in settling a number of disputes at the margins or outside of Europe. Thus, the Treaty of Berlin of 1878[48] reorganized the political landscape of the Balkans, and the General Act of the Berlin Conference of 1885[49] made determinations on the boundaries of the colonial territories in Africa which still today constitute binding law for the States that gained their independence almost 80 years later. The Hague Peace Conferences of 1899 and 1907 cannot be counted as a continuation of the Concert since they refrained from imposing any solutions on third States, but confined themselves to elaborating treaties which each and every interested State was meant to ratify by its own free will. In any event, however, there has never been in Europe a single hegemon. The

---

44   See, for instance, B. Kingsbury, "Sovereignty and Inequality", in: A. Hurrell and N. Woods (eds.), *Inequality, Globalization, and World Politics*, Oxford 1999, p. 66, at 72-76.

45   Proclamation of 14/26 September 1815, reprinted in: W.G. Grewe (ed.), *Fontes Historiae Iuris Gentium*, Vol. 3/1, Berlin and New York 1992, p. 107; for a comment see Stephan Verosta, "Holy Alliance", in: *Encyclopedia of Public International Law*, Vol.II, 1995, p. 861.

46   Treaty of 20 November 1818, reprinted in: Grewe, *op. cit.* (note 45), p. 100.

47   See Grewe, *The Epochs* (note 17), p. 434-435; H. Mosler, *Die Grossmachtstellung im Völkerrecht*, Heidelberg 1949, p. 13-17.

48   Reprinted in: Grewe, *op. cit.* (note 45), p. 38.

49   Reprinted in: Grewe, *ibid.*, p. 297.

hegemonic structures of the 19th century were based on collective mechanisms that included all of the leading powers of the epoch.

The League of Nations confirmed this tendency. Established in 1919 after the horrors of World War I, it constituted the first universal organization the aim of which was to secure international peace and security through permanent institutions within a multilateral framework. The Council was entrusted with settling any question "affecting the peace of the world". It was composed of representatives of the "Principal Allied and Associated Powers"[50] together with originally four[51] non-permanent members. As a rule, decisions of the Council required unanimity. It had again be felt that a distinction should be made between the leading nations, which enjoyed the factual power necessary to be respected by other States in matters of peace and war, and those other nations that legally were placed on a level of parity, but which in terms of real might were light weights. Generally speaking, the Council of the League of Nations had too large a membership. It was hampered in its dealings by the requirement of unanimity although in a dispute the vote of the parties directly involved was not to be counted. Additionally, the absence of the United States, which had failed to ratify the Covenant, made it a body which lacked the most powerful actor in world politics. Consequently, the Council remained an institution hardly in a position to live up to its task. When Germany decided to leave the League of Nations in 1933 and Russia was excluded from the Organization in 1939, the fate of the League was sealed. It could not any longer plausibly justify its claim for universality, which in any event was rather hollow given the fact that the colonial powers still held most of Africa and large parts of Asia under their rule.

B.   The Security Council

Currently, the most conspicuous example of collective hegemony[52] is provided by the Security Council of the United Nations. The five nations that hold permanent seats (China, France, Russia, United Kingdom, United States) do not muster a majority of the fifteen votes. For a decision to be adopted, an affirmative vote of nine members is required. But through the veto power which is granted to them ("an affirmative vote of nine members including the concurring votes of the permanent members"), the permanent members are able to exert a decisive influence on the decision-making process in the Security Council. Their interests and concerns have to be accommodated by the non-permanent members since otherwise any draft resolution will remain stuck, mostly at some early stage during the delib-

---

50   This terminology becomes understandable only against the background of the fact that the Covenant was an integral part of the Treaty of Versailles, the 1919 Peace Treaty with Germany.

51   The number of non-permanent members was progressively increased: six as from 1922, nine as from 1926, eleven as from 1934.

52   A concept also relied upon by S. Sur, "Le Conseil de sécurité : blocage, renouveau et avenir", *Pouvoirs – Revue française d'études constitutionnelles et politiques* 109 (2004), p. 61, at 65.

erations: if it is obvious that a draft resolution is unable to receive the support of the five permanent members, the sponsors will normally abstain from formally putting the text to a vote. Although juridically all five permanent members are equal regarding the right of veto, it is much more difficult for smaller powers like France and the United Kingdom to actually make use of it. A legal entitlement like the veto power must be used with great circumspection by nations the privileged position of which within the framework of the United Nations is not uncontested any longer. In that regard, factual might backs and strengthens the formal position. For countries like China, Russia and the United States, the choice between "yes" and "no" constitutes a real alternative where they can choose without too many external constraints solutions best suited to their interests. And among this group of three, the United States is currently the most influential actor. Via the Security Council, it is able to a large extent to shape the policies of the Security Council, thereby covering its national policy aims with the veneer of legitimacy provided by the United Nations.[53]

And yet, it remains true that the Security Council remains an institution of collective and not of individual hegemony. The United States cannot command or order, it is compelled to win the approval not only of the other permanent members, but also of at least four non-permanent members. For the first time, this scenario revealed itself fully when in the spring of 2003 the United States sought the agreement of the other members of the Security Council for a resolution authorizing an armed attack against Iraq. Knowing that it could not overrule France, which was opposed to a war without prior completion of the search for weapons of mass destruction on Iraqi soil, it tried to win over to its position at least eight other members of the Security Council in order to be able to denounce France as a nation that irrresponsibly stood in the way of a necessary resolution that was supported by a broad majority in the Council. This attempt failed. The United States could not be sure that a draft formally put to the vote by it would receive at least nine affirmative votes, and it therefore decided to go it alone, renouncing to press its way through the Council. This example clearly shows that in legal terms the United States does not enjoy a hegemonic position and that, in order to realize it political aims, it is dependent on close cooperation with the other members of the Security Council.

C.   The Non-Proliferation Treaty

The Treaty on the Non-Proliferation of Nuclear Weapons of 1968[54] provides another example of a treaty regime which acknowledges two classes of parties, those which are holders of nuclear weapons – all the permanent members of the Security Council – and those which do not possess such weapons.[55] The Treaty takes

---

53   J.E. Alvarez, "Hegemonic International Law Revisited", *AJIL* 97 (2003), p. 873, *passim*, denounces the almost boundless power which the United States can wield through the Security Council.

54   Adopted by UN General Assembly Resolution 2373 (XXII), 12 June 1968.

55   The legal position was frozen as of that date.

as a fact of life this uneven distribution of nuclear power, seeking to stop the arms race by enjoining the nuclear-weapon States to refrain from any transfer of nuclear explosive devices and making it incumbent on the non-nuclear-weapon States to renounce receiving any such transfer. The sole obligation of the nuclear-weapon States consists of a duty to pursue in good faith negotiations for nuclear disarmament. For more than 36 years now, these negotiations had made no significant headway.[56] There is no escaping the conclusion that this inequality amounts to a collective hegemony of the privileged nations.

D.   The World Financial Institutions

In the world financial institutions, the International Monetary Fund (IMF) and the World Bank (IBRD), voting power is determined by the assigned quota (IMF) or the number of shares which a country has subscribed (IBRD). This capitalist principle ensures the United States, together with its Western Allies, a clear predominance in the two institutions.[57] In the IMF, it holds 17.14% of the quotas, and in the IBRD its percentage is a little bit lower, standing at 16.41%. This special voting pattern entails policies which may run counter to strategies pursued by the UN General Assembly. Thus, during the epoch of apartheid in South Africa, the General Assembly continually attempted to align the Washington institutions with its aim to isolate South Africa, denying it any loans from international sources. These efforts essentially failed. The two institutions insisted on their autonomy, claiming that they were committed to respecting the rules and principles enshrined in their statutes, which prohibited any discrimination of members.

4.   The Challenge to Multilateralism by the United States

The world of the Security Council, of the Non-Proliferation Treaty and of the world financial institutions is the playground most appreciated by the United States. However, in many other fora it just has to play according to the general rules as they are applicable to any other member. Such ordinary status may sometimes be hard to accept for the most powerful nation. Gulliver must feel frustrated by being barred from making use of its real might in military, economic and financial terms.[58] Obviously, the law has a different meaning for small States, on the one hand, and large States, even super-powers, on the other. Whereas the entire existence of a small State depends on its being respected by its neighbors as a partner

---

56   See ICJ, *Legality of the Threat or Use of Nuclear Weapons, Advisory Opinion, ICJ Reports* 1996, p. 226, at 267: "There exists an obligation to pursue in good faith and bring to a conclusion negotiations leading to nuclear disarmament in all its aspects under strict and effective international control", conclusion reached unanimously by the judges.

57   See also Krisch, *loc. cit.* (note 2), p. 157.

58   The warning not to get enmeshed in such frustrating constraints is the main message of R. Kagan, *Of Paradise and Power*, New York 2003.

whose legal entitlements, in particular its protection against the use of force by virtue of Article 2 (4) of the Charter, are to be taken seriously, the fate of a nation like the United States does not depend on the safeguards by which the rules and principles of international surround it. A powerful State even knows that if it commits a serious breach of international law no serious sanctions are to be expected, given the weakness of the relevant mechanisms of the international community. Of course, any violation of international rules of conduct has some political costs. Even a superpower cannot ignore the negative responses to its straying from the track defined by the law in force among nations. And yet, a superpower may even hope that its deviant behavior will become the law of tomorrow, that its interpretation and application of the law in force will eventually be acknowledged willy-nilly by the other nations as a fact of life which simply has to be reckoned with as a reality.

Not infrequently an essential distinction is overlooked. On the one hand, the United States can refuse to play the desirable role of a world leader in multilateral frameworks designed to protect community interests. In particular, when refusing to ratify world order treaties it creates disappointment within the international community; in such instances, the treaty concerned may even be doomed because United States participation is considered indispensable. But to stay away from international treaty regimes is an option open to every State. A different matter altogether are instances when the United States ignores existing obligations under international law, which derive either from customary law or which it has accepted by a formal act of ratification as binding upon it.

A.   *Distancing from World Order Treaties*

Regarding non-ratification of major world order treaties, an impressive list can be drawn up. The United States has failed to ratify the United Nations Convention on the Law of the Sea (UNCLOS), the Kyoto Protocol, the Convention Banning Anti-Personnel Mines, and the Rome Statute for the International Criminal Court. Likewise, it has refrained from accepting the UN Comprehensive Nuclear-Test-Ban Treaty.[59] All these are instruments which establish the foundations of a peaceful world order based on mutual rights and obligations. Likewise, its record regarding human rights treaties is significantly poor.

a)   Non-ratification of UNCLOS by the United States has been a major disappointment for the international community. Originally, the resistance of the United States was motivated by well-justified opposition against the planned top-heavy bureaucracy for deep-sea mining in the "Area". However, after the suspension of most of Part XI of UNCLOS little remains that may be called truly objectionable on grounds of distributive fairness. It can be assumed that currently it is the principle of compulsory third-party settlement of disputes (Article 286 UNCLOS) which acts as a deterrent for the United States. Given the number of opportunities where

---

59   Adopted by UN General Assembly Resolution 50/245, 10 September 1996.

it has lost a case before the International Court of Justice (ICJ) in recent years, it may feel that it should reject, as a matter of principle, judicial settlement of its differences with other nations. On the other hand, as far as the substantive law of UNCLOS is concerned, one can hardly assume that the United States is in a position to carve out for itself a niche where the general rules of international law do not apply. Even though it has not accepted UNCLOS, it cannot prevent the rules of UNCLOS from progressively crystallizing as customary law.

In order to distance itself from the modern law of the sea regime as it was ushered in by UNCLOS, it would have needed the support of the doctrine of the persistent objector.[60] This doctrine, however, has long since fallen into obsolescence. It is precisely the growth of modern concepts in the law of the sea which has made clear that no single State can halt the progression of rules designed to find universal application.[61] Thus, the breadth of the law of the sea stands now at 12 miles – alike for States parties to UNCLOS and non-parties. Similarly, and even more importantly, the exclusive economic zone (EEZ) with its extension of 200 miles into the sea has gained general approval. No State could have stopped this marine extension of the coastal States – and no State has attempted to do so, except for the United States itself when still in the 1980s it claimed that tuna fish in the EEZ zone did not belong to the reserved resources of the Pacific States concerned.[62] The ICJ has also distanced itself[63] from its earlier *obiter dicta* in the 1950 *Asylum* case[64] and the 1951 *Norwegian Fisheries* case,[65] a fact which has not been perceived by all those authors who still today staunchly defend the concept of persistent objector.

Clearly, the United States has not been successful in attempting to win for itself a position as a privileged outsider who can exclusively act as deemed politically advantageous by it. To remain aloof from UNCLOS was and still is its sovereign right, but that decision has not greatly improved its position inasmuch as it remains bound by the general rules of international law which progressively tend to become identical to the provisions laid down in UNCLOS. The only "advantage" which the United States enjoys is the fact that it finds itself outside the judicial mechanisms of dispute settlement which Part XV of UNCLOS has introduced. However, as a corollary the United States lacks the opportunity to commence proceedings against any other State that might violate its own rights. No matter how

---

60   Set out, for instance, as applicable international law by the American Law Institute's *Restatement of the Law Third. The Foreign Relations Law of the United States*, Vol. 1, St. Paul 1987, p. 26, comment d.

61   The failure of US policies in invoking the persistent-objector rule are exposed by S. Toope, "Powerful but unpersuasive? The role of the United States in the evolution of customary international law", in: *United States Hegemony, op. cit.* (note 2), p. 287, at 308-313.

62   This practice came to an end in 1990 when the United States claimed for itself the right to harvest the resources found in its EEZ.

63   Particularly relevant is the *Fisheries Jurisdiction* case, *ICJ Reports* 1974, p. 3, at 24.

64   *ICJ Reports* 1950, p. 266, at 277-278.

65   *ICJ Reports* 1951, p. 116, at 131.

on balance one calculates the benefits of this configuration, it should be obvious that one can hardly speak of a hegemonic position of the United States concerning the law of the sea.[66] In any event, regarding UNCLOS the international community has shown that it can go forward even without the United States, which could not realize its claim to be the "indispensable nation".

b)   In the field of security, the United States has shown great reluctance to submit to multilateral arms control and disarmament conventions. However, in that regard it does not stand alone. The UN Comprehensive Nuclear-Test-Ban Treaty was adopted on 10 September 1996 by an overwhelming vote of 138 to 3,[67] with 5 abstentions. According to its Article XIV, its entry into force requires that all of the 44 States specifically listed in Annex 2 to the Treaty have deposited their instruments of ratification. From those 44 States, 32 have indeed accepted the Treaty (August 2004). But among the 12 remaining ones one finds not only the United States, but also China, Israel and Egypt, India, Iran and Pakistan.[68] It stands to reason that the absence of these States constitutes a tremendous threat to world security. Under these circumstances, it is understandable that the United States does not wish to go ahead while other nuclear powers keep an unfettered right of testing. World leadership is not tantamount to self-sacrifice.

Similar considerations apply to the Convention on the Prohibition of the Use, Stockpiling, Production and Transfer of Anti-Personnel Mines and on their Destruction of 1997.[69] The United States has until now refused to ratify this Treaty, but many other military powers have likewise refrained from curtailing their national defence, among them China, India and Iran, Israel, the two Korean States, Poland and Russia. Although the Convention has by now (August 2004) 143 parties, the absence of roughly 50 States, many of which being in a situation of potential armed conflict with their neighbors, seriously hampers the effectiveness of the Convention. In any event, however, given the complex security configuration, where many States wish to maintain full command over their defence arsenal, it would be wholly unjustified to reproach the United States with not fulfilling a moral responsibility to secure conditions where nobody risks to lose life and limb by an anti-personnel mine.

One will also have to note that the United States stood in the way of enhancing the effectiveness of the Convention on the Prohibition of the Development,

---

66   Indeed, recently the US Commission on Ocean Policy has recommended ratification of UNCLOS, arguing that the United States must be a full participant "to ensure that its interests as a maritime power and coastal state are protected", see *AJIL* 98 (2004), p. 590; this is in line with an earlier statement of Department of State Legal Adviser W.H. Taft IV of 21 October 2003, *ibid.*, p. 174.

67   The three States were Bhutan, India, and Libya.

68   As far as the other permanent members of the Security Council are concerned, one can note the ratifications by France, Russia and the United Kingdom.

69   Adopted at Oslo, 18 September 1997, opened for signature in Ottawa, 3 December 1997, *ILM* 36 (1997), p. 1509.

Production, and Stockpiling of Bacteriological (Biological) and Toxin Weapons and on Their Destruction of 1972.[70] This Convention establishes a fairly complete set of substantive rules, but lacks any appropriate mechanism of control and supervision. At the Fifth Review Conference of the States parties to the Convention in November 2002 it was the resistance of the United States which impeded the adoption of an additional protocol designed to fill that lacuna. The draft protocol did not provide for a special position of any of the major military powers; such treatment as an ordinary party was apparently not to the liking of the United States.

c)   Even a quarter of a century after their adoption, the United States has not seen fit to ratify the two Additional Protocols to the Geneva Conventions of 1949. These Protocols have by now been almost universally accepted. While France entertained reservations for more than two decades, it decided in 2001 to join the mainstream. The Protocols constitute major achievements in the quest to improve the minimum standards of civilization that should be maintained even during armed conflict. It is significant that the United States finds itself now in the position of an isolated outsider who cannot even prevent the rules enunciated in the Protocols from crystallizing as customary law.

d)   Examples of a chronic reluctance of the United States to submit to international review of its conduct also abound in the field of human rights. In this regard, the most significant element is its half-hearted ratification of the CCPR. To be sure, in principle it is to be welcomed that Washington finally decided to join all of the other nations that had preceded it. Its instrument of ratification was deposited on 8 June 1992. However, this was not a straightforward act of acceptance of the Covenant.[71] The United States Government attached to it a number of "Reservations, declarations and understandings",[72] the most important of which being the declaration that "the provisions of Articles 1 through 27 of the covenant are not self-executing". By virtue of that declaration, the entire American judiciary was enjoined never to apply the Covenant directly.[73] To be sure, such a declaration is lawful. It does not constitute a reservation proper since a reservation purports to modify the scope of obligation under an international treaty, which is not the case here. The United States made known that the Covenant as such cannot be invoked

---

70   *ILM* 11 (1972), p. 309.

71   For a fuller discussion see L. Henkin, "U.S. Ratification of Human Rights Conventions: The Ghost of Senator Bricker", *AJIL* 89 (1995), p. 341-350.C. Redgwell, "US reservations to human rights treaties: all for one and none for all?", in: *United States Hegemony, op. cit.* (note 2), p. 392-415.

72   Reprinted in: H. Hannum and D. Fischer (eds.), *United States Ratification of the International Covenants on Human Rights*, Irvington-on-Hudson 1993, p. 327.

73   See US Supreme Court, *Sosa v. Alvarez Machain*, 29 June 2004: "Although the Covenant does bind the United States as a matter of international law, the United States ratified the Covenant on the express understanding that it was not self-executing and so did not itself create obligations enforceable in the federal courts."

before its domestic courts and tribunals. According to general international law, it is indeed left to the sovereign discretion of any State to make determinations on the modalities of internal implementation of a treaty which it has entered into. On the other hand, however, it is obvious that the real impact of a human rights treaty discarded from any actual dispute between governmental agencies and the citizens under their authority finds itself downgraded to an almost irrelevant minimum. Additionally, the United States took care not to ratify the [First] Optional Protocol to the Covenant, which permits individual "communications" (complaints) to be addressed to the Human Rights Committee, the monitoring body of the Covenant. On the other hand, a certain degree of seriousness of its commitment is shown by its declaration under Article 41 of the Covenant, by which it submitted to the procedure of inter-State communication.[74] On the whole, however, it is disturbing to note that a human rights instrument is denied any kind of domestic applicability. Such a declaration has a crippling effect on the effectiveness of the instrument concerned. In fact, in the debate about the condition of the prisoners at the US military base at Guantánamo the commitments of the United States under the CCPR have invariably been overlooked.

Concerning a number of other human rights treaties, the United States has also shown a remarkable reluctance to bind itself. It has refrained from accepting the Convention on the Elimination of All Forms of Discrimination against Women[75] and it has stayed away from the Convention on the Rights of the Child,[76] an instrument from which by now only two States are absent, Somalia and the United States. For unknown reasons, the United States fought a bitter battle against the Optional Protocol to the Convention against Torture and Other Cruel, Inhuman or Degrading Treatment or Punishment,[77] which provides for a right of inspection of all places where human beings are held under governmental authority against their will. This opposition against an instrument which seeks to give teeth to the classical principle of *habeas corpus* constitutes perhaps the most intriguing act of defiance *vis-à-vis* mainstream tendencies in the international community.

This is not the true profile of a hegemon. As explained above, a hegemon in the political sense claims for itself specific rights which other nations cannot aspire to. But it also assumes responsibilities which are too burdensome for smaller nations. In the field of human rights the United States has continually wished to play a leading role. It was among the most active States when in the Commission on Human Rights immediately after the establishment of the United Nations the different elements of the International Bill of Rights were drawn up. Human rights belongs also to the leitmotivs of American foreign policy. However, by denying the internal applicability of the Covenant the United States has not lived up to its self-proclaimed ideals. Legally, no reproach can be formulated against it. However,

---

74   To date, not a single communication has been brought under Article 41 of the Covenant.

75   Of 18 December 1979, 1249 *UNTS* 13.

76   Of 20 November 1989, 1577 *UNTS* 3.

77   Of 18 December 2002, not yet in force.

a nation which does not spare its criticisms of other countries in the field of human rights and which is keen on being granted a quasi-permanent seat on the Commission on Human Rights[78] should not relegate the CCPR, the centerpiece of the International Bill of Human Rights, to an almost irrelevant position within its domestic legal order.

e)   Lastly, among the occurrences reflecting an attitude that distances itself from basic aspirations of the international community one should mention the confrontation between the United States and the international community with regard to the Rome Statute of the International Criminal Court. Adopted in July 1998, the Rome Statute translates into hard law political objectives which have always been pursued by an active group of States since the Nürnberg trial of the major war criminals of Nazi Germany in 1945/46. At Nürnberg, the concept that individuals may directly incur criminal responsibility under international law was for the first time transformed into a concrete procedural mechanism. For many decades thereafter, in particular during the Cold War, the concept lay dormant since almost everybody believed that the establishment of an international criminal court would mean starting a new round in the ongoing rivalry between the superpowers. Eventually, after the demise of the socialist regimes in central and eastern Europe, the ideal of a world court was resuscitated by Resolution 827 (1993) of the Security Council which established the International Criminal Tribunal for the Former Yugoslavia. One year later, by Resolution 955 (1994), the International Criminal Tribunal for Rwanda was brought into existence. Under the impact of these decisions, it was almost inevitable to envision the creation of a criminal court the jurisdiction of which would not be confined *ratione territorii* or *ratione temporis*, but would extend to any serious offence under international law, wherever committed.

It is common knowledge that this undertaking was successfully performed at a Conference in Rome from 15 June to 17 July 1998. When the text of the Rome Statute was formally adopted on 17 June 1998, the United States voted against it together with six other nations, while 21 States abstained. Although the United States had initially been one of the most fervent proponents of the International Criminal Court (ICC), it changed to its most determined opponent once it had become clear that the Rome Conference would not be prepared to accept all of the United States' wishes. In particular, it had been one of the aims of the United States to grant a monopoly of seizure of the ICC to the Security Council. This suggestion raised an issue of principle. It was tantamount to stating that no American citizen could ever be prosecuted before the ICC against the will of the United States, and the same would have been true for the nationals of all the other permanent members of the Security Council. Such a procedural mechanism, which rides roughshod over the principle of equality before the law, could not possibly be accepted by the world

---

[78]   The United States held a seat on the UN Commission on Human Rights constantly from 1947 to 2001, when it was voted off the Commission for one year in a secret ballot in the Economic and Social Council; it was re-elected to a three-year term on 29 April 2002, see *AJIL* 96 (2002), p. 718. On this issue see Kwakwa, *loc. cit.* (note 5), p. 41.

at large, those nations which are "ordinary" members of the international community.

Notwithstanding its principled opposition to the Rome Statute, the United States first signed the Statute on the last day of President Clinton's term of office on 31 December 2000. This move was designed to ensure American presence in the preparatory bodies which had been entrusted with drawing up the ancillary documents needed for the working of the judicial machinery once the Rome Statute would enter into force. President Bush, however, did not stick with this decision. His Administration "unsigned" the Statute by a letter of 27 April 2002[79] in order to win a free hand regarding its strategy to prevent any potential threat for United States nationals from the actual operation of the ICC. Indeed, Article 18 VCLT enjoins signatory States to refrain from any action that would "defeat the object and purpose" of the treaty concerned. Thus, the United States had to distance itself from the Rome Statute in order to get rid of any legal constraints. To "unsign" a treaty is certainly an unusual step, rarely encountered in diplomatic practice, but in legal terms it is perfectly unobjectionable, precisely in view of the limitations which Article 18 VCLT imposes on the freedom of action of a State which, by signing a treaty, has manifested its intent to initiate at home the requisite process of parliamentary approval.

Several strategies were employed by the United States to combat the new institution although its Government had participated in establishing the International Military Tribunal in Nürnberg as well as the International Criminal Tribunal for the Former Yugoslavia and the International Criminal Tribunal for Rwanda. First of all, it contended that to prosecute an American citizen on the basis of the consent to the jurisdiction of the ICC by the State on the territory of which the alleged crime had been committed was contrary to the principle of *pacta tertiis non nocent* as laid down in Article 35 VCLT. This contention is untenable since every State is entitled to prosecute persons who have perpetrated offences in its territory. If a right of criminal prosecution exists, such right can also be delegated to an institution of the international community. It would be almost absurd to maintain that the State concerned must in that regard act individually, without having recourse to the procedures and mechanisms which have been created by international cooperation specifically in view of offences with a political background.

However, in order to show that its objections were meant seriously, the United States President Bush signed into law on 2 August 2002 the so-called American Servicemembers' Protection Act, a congressional statute which prohibits all relevant authorities of the United States from cooperating with the ICC and which, at the same time, authorizes the American Armed Forces to liberate, if need be by force, any American citizen put on trial before the ICC. The threat inherent in that statute was considered to be so serious by the Netherlands, the host State of the ICC, that its Ambassador to the United States publicly expressed his dismay.[80] To date, all this seems to be almost ridiculous since the Prosecutor of the ICC will

---

79 *ILM* 41 (2002), p. 1014.

quite naturally endeavour to steer a course which does not hurt the interests of any of the big powers. Yet, the attitude of the United States gives indeed rise to concern in that the ICC constitutes one of the core elements of the institutionalized international community.

With a view further to eliminating the danger that American citizens might one day be indicted before the ICC, the United States has additionally begun concluding bilateral non-extradition treaties with other States, parties and non-parties to the Rome Statute alike. By virtue of these treaties, the two sides pledge not to surrender nationals of the other party to the ICC. For States having ratified the Rome Statute to enter into such a commitment constitutes a clear breach of their main obligation under the Statute, namely to cooperate with the ICC. Article 98 (2) of the Statute, which takes indeed into account treaties concluded by a State party with a third State, is not meant to permit new derogations from obligations which have been validly assumed.[81] Hence, the United States is again attempting to take the gist out of the Rome Statute.

Lastly, the United States has used the Security Council in order to obtain complete immunity from international prosecution for its nationals. After the entry into force of the Rome Statute on 1 July 2002, it threatened not only to deny its support to any future UN-sponsored military action, but also to block any proposed operation if no determination was made that the nationals of non-parties to the Rome Statute, participating in a UN-established or authorized operation, would under no circumstances be prosecuted by the ICC. In 2002, the Security Council adopted indeed a resolution which requested the ICC to refrain from investigating or prosecuting such persons,[82] and in 2003 this request was reiterated.[83] Although the United States had hoped that this request had by then become a matter of routine, it turned out, after the mistreatment of detainees in Iraqi prisons by American personnel had become known to the outside world, that no government represented on the Security Council was ready any longer to provide cover for American actions which were clearly in violation of human rights and international humanitarian law. Recognizing this dilemma, in 2004 the United States Government abandoned after a while its attempt to obtain a renewal of immunity for personnel contributed to a UN operation.

The particular configuration of the deliberative process in the Security Council in 2004 makes again clear that the United States is not a hegemonic power which enjoys a superior authority of command. Rather, it remains enmeshed in the network of the United Nations where the Security Council is the pivotal institution which can justify and legitimize any action in the vast field of international peace and security. Notwithstanding its immense influence in the Council, where it can act by persuasion and by threat, the United States is not able totally to domi-

---

80   See *AJIL* 96 (2002), p. 976.

81   See P. Mori, "Gli accordi di esenzione *ex* art. 98 dello Statuto della Corte penale internazionale", *Rivista italiana di diritto internazionale* 86 (2003), p. 1000, at 1034-1037.

82   Resolution 1422 (2002), 12 July 2002.

83   Resolution 1487 (2003), 12 June 2003.

nate the other members, and this is a most welcome observation. Without taking into account the interests and concerns of the other members of the Council, the United States is not able to enforce its political will. When issues of principle are in issue, the members of the Council will normally remain attached to their publicly declared goals.

The ICC has thus become a test case for the United States. Its merciless opposition to a project promoted by almost the entire international community has cost it many sympathies with world public opinion. In legal terms, however, the United States has in most regards behaved in consonance with the imperatives of international law, except for the threat possibly to invade the Netherlands should ever an American citizen be prosecuted before the ICC in The Hague. On the other hand, its vain effort to shape the ICC according to its specific wishes has shown that multilateral institutions can be set up even against the wishes of the most powerful State. The sole fact that the ICC has come into being evinces that the international legal order is not placed under the command of the only remaining superpower.

The fact remains, however, that the effectiveness of the ICC is severely hampered by the absence of the United States, which has also prompted other big powers like India, Russia and China to stay away from the Rome Statute. It stands to reason that an international judicial body like the ICC needs a strong backing from the international community. As long as such support is lacking, the ICC will be able only to act in the interstices of the zones of influence of the great powers, where none of them has any tangible interest. The Darfur crisis in Sudan provides a primary example of the stalemate which negatively impacts the work of the ICC. The Security Council approached the situation with great reluctance, and nothing was heard of any attempt by the ICC to investigate the charges brought against the Arab forces responsible for the plight of the black population. Thus, it can be concluded that the refusal of the United States to assume a role of true leader in international relations entails utterly negative consequences for the entire international community.

f)   For a powerful nation, staying aloof from a multilateral treaty regime is a real option, as demonstrated by the examples described above. On the other hand, by choosing that avenue, the United States inevitably isolates itself. It must acknowledge that the international community tries to go its way alone, without the assistance of the sole superpower. On balance, playing the isolationist card is probable more burdensome than profitable. Above all, the United States risks losing its influence in treaty negotiations if one can forecast at the very outset that the United States, even if its partners grant it substantial concessions, will eventually not be prepared to submit to the planned conventional regime.[84]

---

84   For a lucid analysis see P. Klein, "The effects of US predominance on the elaboration of treaty regimes and on the evolution of the law of treaties", in: *United States Hegemony, op. cit.* (note 2), p. 363, at 371-376.

B.   *Violation of Binding Rules of International Law*

Much more worrying are the instances in which the United States has publicly announced its intention not to abide by established rules of international law or where it has actually breached such rules. No State is always in full compliance with the obligations which it has to live up to under the rules of international law applicable to it. But again a distinction should be made. Overt defiance of rules of international law stands apart from violations which are due to negligence or lack of capabilities and resources. Sometimes, it may even be open to doubt whether a violation pure and simple has occurred or whether the door has been opened towards a new practice which everyone desires but which no one had the courage to embrace first. Of course, a leading power has a much greater potential to try to revamp or overhaul certain rules of international law deemed outdated by it than a smaller nation that just has to stick with the vast array of international law it is confronted with. States that do not agree with such attempts at introducing changes that suit the powerful actor behind them should not be oblivious to their right to raise protests in order to forestall the new practice to crystallyze as customary law.[85]

a)   Among the manifestations of a clear will to depart from the legally defined paths of good conduct the National Security Strategy, proclaimed by the United States on 17 September 2002, roughly one year after 9/11, stands out as the most blatant challenge against a fundamental rule of international law, the principle of non-use of force.[86] According to Article 2 (4) of the Charter, any threat or use of force against another State is prohibited, and Article 51 of the Charter allows for measures of self-defence only "if an armed attack occurs". Following a literal interpretation of Article 51, one would have to conclude that any kind of preventive or preemptive action is unlawful. This may be too rigid a construction of Article 51. Many authors rightly point out that no State can be expected to remain passive in the face of a military build-up by a neighboring State at its borders; consequently, they are of the view that anticipatory self-defence must be permissible in circumstances where the enemy strike would follow as an automatic consequence from the preparatory measures already taken. In order verbally to illustrate this idea, the Israeli author *Yoram Dinstein* has coined the term "interceptive strike", where a military operation already commenced in the territory of the potential enemy can be averted at the last minute.[87]

In all of the writings on the issue of self-defence, the concept of "imminence" occupies a key position, which also corresponds to the views expressed in the dip-

---

85   Rightly recalled by M. Byers, "Terrorism, the Use of Force and International Law After 11 September", *ICLQ* 51 (2002), p. 401, at 411.

86   For the political background see B.R. Roth, "Bending the law, breaking it, or developing it? The United States and the humanitarian use of force in the post-Cold War era", in: *United States Hegemony, op. cit.* (note 2), p. 232-263.

87   Y. Dinstein, *War, Aggression and Self-Defence*, 3rd ed., Cambridge 2001, p. 172.

lomatic correspondence on the *Caroline* case, pursuant to which self-defence is permissible in situations where its necessity is "instant, overwhelming and leaving no choice of means and no moment for deliberation".[88] However, such preemptive action must be clearly confined to extreme circumstances where the threat of armed attack is imminent in a tangible sense. There must exist a real need to take defensive measures before irreparable harm will be caused. Whenever a longer-term strategy may be required to combat future threats to international peace and security, the Security Council is called upon to take care of the matter. According to Article 39 of the Charter, its authority extends far beyond the eventuality of a breach of the peace or an act of aggression to include also "threat(s) to the peace".

The United States National Security Strategy considerably departs from the determinations by the Charter. It states in unequivocal terms:

> "The United States has long maintained the option of preemptive actions to counter a sufficient threat to our national security. The greater the threat, the greater is the risk of inaction – and the more compelling the case for taking anticipatory action to defend ourselves, even if uncertainty remains as to the time and place of the enemy's attack. To forestall or prevent such hostile acts by our adversaries, the United States will, if necessary, act preemptively.
>
> The United States will not use force in all cases to preempt emerging threats, nor should nations use preemption as a pretext for aggression. Yet in an age where the enemies of civilization openly and actively seek the world's most destructive technologies, the United States cannot remain idle while dangers gather. We will always proceed deliberately, weighing the consequences of our actions."[89]

Through these lines, the United States makes clear that it will act whenever it should perceive a threat to its national security, no matter how close or how remote that threat may be.[90] It is significant that no mention is made of the Security Council and the system of collective security of which the Council is the main arm. Quite obviously, the National Security Strategy has served as a blue-print for the Anglo-American invasion of Iraq which, 18 months later, has definitively lost its alleged legitimacy by the involuntary recognition that the (evil) regime of Sadam Hussein had no weapons of mass destruction at its disposal. The tragic events unfolding in

---

88   Secretary of State Webster, in: J.B. Moore, *Digest of International Law*, vol. II, Washington 1906, p. 412.

89   The National Security Strategy of the United States of America, September 2002, p. 15.

90   Rightly, W.M. Reisman, "Assessing Claims to Revise the Laws of War", *AJIL* 97 (2003), p. 82, at 87, calls pre-emptive self-defence a "nip in the bud strategy" to arrest "an incipient development that is not yet operational, hence not yet *directly* threatening"; in a similar sense E. Sciso, "La risoluzione 1511 del Consiglio di sicurezza: verso una 'sanatoria' dell'intervento contra l'Iraq?", *Rivista italiana di diritto internazionale* 87 (2004), p. 171, at 176, speaks of defence against "*attacchi futuri meramente ipotetici*". This is precisely the crux of the matter.

Iraq, which have not ceased at the time of writing this contribution (August 2004), illustrate the dangers inherent in hasty unilateral action, not sanctioned by the Security Council.[91]

For a world devoted to tackling its vital issues through multilateral cooperation, the principle of non-use of force constitutes one of its cornerstones. In particular, the rule enunciated in Article 2 (4) of the Charter protects the sovereign equality of States. If States had no guarantee of that kind, their sovereignty, ceremonially proclaimed in Article 2 (1) of the Charter, would remain a hollow dream. They would feel the pressure of the big powers much more intensely than currently against the backdrop of the prevailing factual conditions. Nobody ignores that the principle of non-use of force cannot be considered a watertight guarantee. But for smaller States it would be fatal to be dependent, as far as their external security is concerned, on the materials gathered by the intelligence services of the United States (or other big powers). The Iraq war has amply demonstrated to what extent intelligence reports may manipulate or mislead those whose action they are designed to orient. The principle of non-use of force constitutes a necessary safeguard in a world which is based on such elementary concepts as self-determination of peoples and concomitant sovereignty of nations. It would be utterly unreasonable to lay the decision on war and peace into the hands of just one State, which would indeed be a hegemon if its claim to superiority met with approval. But this is

---

91   There is almost universal consensus that the Bush doctrine is much too broadly framed, see, *e.g.*, from Austria H. Neuhold, "Law and Force in International Relations – European and American Positions", *Heidelberg Journal of International Law* 64 (2004), p. 263, at 273; France: T. Christakis, "Vers une reconnaissance de la notion de guerre préventive?", in: *L'intervention en Irak et le droit international*, Paris 2004, p. 11-48; F. Nguyen-Rouault, "L'intervention armée en Irak et son occupation au regard du droit international", *Revue générale de droit international public* 107 (2003), p. 835, at 851; A. Pellet, "L'agression", *Le Monde*, 22 March 2003; from Germany: M. Bothe, "Terrorism and the Legality of Pre-emptive Force", *EJIL* 14 (2003), p. 227, at 229-230; R. Hofmann, "International Law and the Use of Military force Against Iraq", *GYIL* 45 (2002), p. 9, at 33; D. Murswiek, "Die amerikanische Präventivkriegsstrategie und das Völkerrecht", *Neue Juristische Wochenschrift* 2003, p. 1014, at 116-1017; G. Seidel, "Quo vadis Völkerrecht?", *Archiv des Völkerrechts* 41 (2003), p. 449, at 476; C. Stahn, "Enforcement of the Collective Will After Iraq", *AJIL* 97 (2003), p. 804, at 820, and, from a philosophical viewpoint, J. Habermas, "Hat die Konstitutionalisierung des Völkerrechts noch eine Chance?", in: id., *Der gespaltene Westen*, Frankfurt/Main 2004, p. 113, at 181; from Spain: M. Pérez González, "La legítima defensa puesta en su sitio: observaciones críticas sobre la doctrina Bush de la acción preventiva", *Revista española de derecho internacional* 55 (2003), p. 187, at 198-203; from Switzerland: R. Kolb, "Self-Defence and Preventive War at the Beginning of the Millennium", *Austrian Journal of Public and International Law* 59 (2004), p. 111, at 121-134 (with ample references in note 25 at p. 119); D. Thürer, "Irak-Krise: Anstoß zu einem Neuüberdenken der völkerrechtlichen Quellenlehre?", *Archiv des Völkerrechts* 41 (2003), p. 314, at 317; from the United Kingdom: V. Lowe, "The Iraq Crisis: What Now?", *ICLQ* 52 (2003), p. 859, at 865; from the United States: T.M. Franck, "What Happens Now? The United Nations After Iraq", *AJIL* 97 (2003), p. 607, at 619.

not the case. The response of the international community to the invasion of Iraq has been overwhelmingly negative. Even American lawyers have for the most part recognized that the operation undertaken by their Government did not meet the test of lawfulness. We note, in particular, the voice of Anne-Marie Slaughter, the president of the American Society of International Law, who at the crucial moment expressed some understanding for the invasion[92] but who, one year after the event, unequivocally stated that the operation could not be justified, neither on moral nor on legal grounds.[93] On the occasion of the Agora organized by the American Journal of International Law on the issue, all the writers, with the exception of those who held an official position with the Government[94] or were close to it as advisers,[95] took a clear stance against the extreme expansion of self-defence under the Bush doctrine.[96]

It should also be emphasized that the Security Council has refrained from passing judgment on the attack on Iraq by the Anglo-American coalition. None of the relevant resolutions addresses the lawfulness of the operation, which means that any notion of confirmation must be discarded. Already in its first decision on the situation as it existed after the end of hostilities, Resolution 1483 of 22 May 2003, the Security Council affirmed as a priority the "sovereignty and territorial integrity of Iraq".[97] This line was continued by the later decisions, Resolution 1511 of 16 October 2003 and Resolution 1546 of 8 June 2004. Instead of looking back, the Security Council deliberately confined itself to making determinations on what had to be determined after the actual occupation of the country by the troops of the coalition. At first glance, it may look as an absurdity to acknowledge the powers and responsibilities in Iraqui territory of a military coalition which flagrantly breached the law by its actions. On closer reflection, however, the realism of international humanitarian law should be applauded. Once the governmental and administrative structures in a foreign country have been destroyed by an occupant force, that force is under an obligation to do everything in its power to restore a viable framework of public institutions that may take over the relevant govern-

---

92   *New York Times*, 18 March 2003, p. A33.

93   *American Society of International Law Newsletter*, March/April 2004, p. 2.

94   W.H. Taft IV and T.F. Buchwald, "Preemption, Iraq, and International Law", *AJIL* 97 (2003), p. 557, at 563; J. Yoo, "International Law and the War in Iraq", *ibid.*, p. 563, at 571-574. None of these authors was, however, as drastic as shortly before the war A.D. Sofaer, "On the Necessity of Pre-emption", *EJIL* 14 (2003), p. 209, at 212: "... the rigid and limited view of the propriety of pre-emptive action has no valid historical basis, and is unsound, artificial and futile in attempting to restrict resort to the use of force".

95   R. Wedgwood, "Preemptive Self-Defense", *AJIL* 97 (2003), p. 576, at 582-585.

96   R. Gardner, "Neither Bush nor the 'Jurisprudes'", *AJIL* 97 (2003), p. 585, at 588; R.A. Falk, "What Future for the UN Charter System of War Prevention?", *ibid.*, p. 590, at 598; M. Sapiro, "Iraq: The Shifting Sands of Preemptive Self-Defense", *ibid.*, p. 599, at 603; Franck, *loc cit.* (note 91), p. 608, 610;

97   Second preambular paragraph.

mental responsibilities.[98] If in a rigid form the general rules on State responsibility were applied, entailing an obligation for the occupant to immediately withdraw its troops, the final result would be utter chaos. In other words, the Security Council acted in accordance with the requirements of international humanitarian law.[99] Its silence on the issue of the invasion, its lack of criticism can in no event be interpreted as constituting approval of the operation of the coalition forces.[100] On the other hand, the recourse of the United States to the Security Council after the end of the armed conflict shows convincingly that the legitimacy which a resolution of the authoritative UN body can provide carries far more weight than sheer military power.[101]

In concluding the argument, one simply has to note that the first test to which the new security doctrine of the United States was submitted has revealed fatal flaws of that doctrine. And it is indeed almost impossible to accept a legal proposition according to which individual (powerful) States should have an unfettered right to invade the territory of any other State on the basis of no more than suspicions that one day the targeted State might pose a serious threat to their national security.[102] The Iraqi adventure cannot but strengthen the conviction that international peace and security must remain entrusted to collective bodies of the international community, the Security Council playing a pivotal role in that regard. It is true that the Security Council cannot be deemed to be an absolutely reliable institution, given the fact that national interest is never absent when an international crisis is gauged. During the Cold War, it was paralyzed for decades regarding major confrontational issues in the East-West relationship. However, a body charged with maintaining international peace and security will never breathe in the sterile atmosphere of a scientific laboratory. It would be futile to expect that the Security Council might one day take its decisions pursuant exclusively to strict legal criteria. On the other hand, in situations which pose an actual, concrete threat to the international community at large the Security Council will normally be prepared

---

98   See Article 43 of the 1907 Hague Regulations Respecting the Laws and Customs of War on Land, reprinted in: A. Roberts and R. Guelf, *Documents on the Laws of War*, 3rd ed. Oxford 2000, p. 73.

99   See Stahn, *loc. cit.* (note 91), p. 818-819.

100 See M.P. Andrés Saénz de Santa María, "El Consejo de Seguridad en la guerra contra Irak: ONG privilegiada, convalidadora complaciente u órgano primordial?", *Revista española de derecho internacional* 55 (2003), p. 205, at 214, 219, 222; Sciso, *loc. cit.* (note 90); Falk, *loc. cit.* (note 96), p. 596; at 817-818; Stahn, *loc. cit.* (note 91), p. 817-818; Sur, *loc. cit.* (note 52), p. 72; C. Tomuschat, "Iraq – Demise of International Law?", *Die Friedenswarte – Journal of International Peace and Organization* 78 (2003), p. 141, at 152-153.

101 Persuasively underlined by Shashi Tharoor, "Why America Still Needs the United Nations", *Foreign Affairs* 82 (September/October 2003), p. 67, at 68, 73. R. Kagan, "America's Crisis of Legitimacy", *Foreign Affairs* 83 (March/April 2004), p. 65, at 73-74, is right only in asserting that the Security Council is not the only source of legitimacy.

102 The most drastic comments on the unfortunate consequences of the Bush doctrine see Franck, *loc. cit.* (note 91), *passim*, and Kolb, *loc. cit.* (note 91), *passim*.

to act. To show helpless passivity towards attempts on the part of extremist groups to terrorize the world by weapons of mass destruction cannot be in the interest of any one of the five veto powers. In fact, the events preceding the Anglo-American invasion of Iraq show that there was a genuine will on the part of the members of the Security Council other than the United Kingdom and the United States to seriously investigate all the sites in Iraq where such weapons could be hidden. France, as the main voice of the opposition to the United States, wished to see a clear factual record before rushing into a dubious military adventure[103] whereas the United States was keen on commencing military operations as soon as possible, holding that sufficient evidence had already been obtained.

No easy solutions can be suggested for the purpose of overcoming such clashes of views in the Security Council. Without any difficulty, one can state on the level of substantive law the principle which should guide all members of the Security Council in their actions, namely the principle of institutional responsibility.[104] In fact, the Security Council is an organ of the United Nations entrusted with the "primary responsibility for the maintenance of international peace and security" (Charter, Article 24 (1)). Every individual member, including the permanent members, must be aware of the fact that it is not called upon exclusively to pursue its individual interests, but that its seat on the Security Council constitutes a public trust which it has to discharge in the interest of the entire membership of the world organization. This applies also to the permanent members. Their position is not a "natural" one, which predates the establishment of the United Nations, but rests on the Charter and thereby on the will of all of the 191 member States.

Though simple and straightforward and hardly challengeable, the concept of institutional responsibility cannot easily be translated into procedural mechanisms. It has been suggested that permanent members making use of their veto power should be under an obligation to justify their conduct by indicating the reasons which have prompted them to reject the draft which they have prevented from being adopted. Obviously, such justification should be presented to the General Assembly as the main organ of the United Nations. It is clear, however, that the proposed scheme provides no panacea. Any State can easily invoke reasons which sound legitimate but which rather hide its true motivation. These difficulties of practical implementation do not discredit in general the concept of institutional responsibility. Imaginative suggestions are required which it should be possible to identify in the current process of elaborating proposals for the United Nations of tomorrow. On the other hand, it must be acknowledged that precisely in the field of war and peace borderline situations may arise where the law loses it guiding force. It is common knowledge that in its opinion on the *Threat or Use of Nuclear Weapons* the ICJ stated in its *dispositif*:

---

103   Rightly observed by Franck, *loc. cit.* (note 91), p. 616; for more detailed references see P. Weckel, "L'usage déraisonnable de la force", *Revue générale de droit international public* 107 (2003), p. 377, at 383-384.

104   J.E. Stromseth, "Law and Force After Iraq: A Transitional Moment", *AJIL* 97 (2003), p. 628, at 640, postulates for the Security Council a role as an instrument for forging consensus.

" ... the Court cannot conclude definitively whether the threat or use of nuclear weapons would be lawful or unlawful in an extreme circumstance of self-defence, in which the very survival of a State would be at stake."[105]

b)   In connection with respect for the principle of sovereign equality of States, the question arises also whether it is in conformity with international law to label certain States "rogue States", which is a synonym for "criminal" States.[106] The United States does not hesitate to use this term almost in a routine fashion. It can not only be found in political speeches, but has also been included in formal governmental documents such as the National Security Strategy.[107] *Inter alia*, Iran, Libya (before the re-orientation of its policies), North Korea, and Syria have been subjected to such negative judgment. The classification as a "rogue State" has entailed numerous constraints for its citizens. Travelling with a passport of a "rogue State" can become a nightmare, and economic relations with such outsiders have been severely curtailed.

A century ago any classification of a State as a "rogue State" would have been considered a violation of its dignity as inherent in its international personality.[108] In the world of today, which is permeated by a much greater degree of realism, the concept of freedom of speech, although essentially an individual human right, has also gained ground in inter-State relations. Leading governmental representatives do not feel inhibited any longer to call a spade a spade, and from the second half of the last century to our time not a single legal instrument or judicial decision is known that would have mentioned the right to respect for dignity or noted that similar statements constitute an internationally wrongful act. In principle, the opening of the arena of political dialogue for clear language is to be welcomed. However, the limits of what may be legally defensible are reached when the term "rogue State" is combined with the assumption that such States are placed *hors la loi* and that the use of force against them is lawful at any time. No State member of the United Nations can *a priori* be downscaled to the status of an outcast. In particular, the principle of non-use of force protects all of them, even non-members of the world organization.[109] Thus, the conclusion is that the use of the term "rogue

---

105   *ICJ Reports* 1996, p. 226, at 266.

106   It should also be recalled that in an address of 29 January 2002 President Bush spoke of an "axis of evil", referring to North Korea, Iran, and Iraq, see <http://www.whitehouse.gov/news/releases/2002/01/20020129-11.html>.

107   See the exhaustive study by P. Minnerop, "The Classification of States and the Creation of Status within the International Community", *Max Planck UNYB* 7 (2003), 79 *et seq.*

108   For a discussion see L. Oppenheim and H. Lauterpacht, *International Law*, Vol. I, 8th ed. London 1955, p. 282-285.

109   In this regard, the conclusions drawn by Yoo, *loc. cit.* (note 94), p. 576, are most alarming. In fact, the establishment of the no-fly zones in Iraq, which could not be supported by the authority of any Security Council resolution, smacked of a doctrine according to which with regard to a rogue State any violation of its territorial sovereignty is lawful, if committed "for a good cause". It is remarkable that this measure drew almost no international criticism. Against such tendencies L. Condorelli, "Vers une reconnaissance

State" runs the risk of trespassing upon forbidden territory but that it cannot be considered unlawful *per se*.[110]

c)   State immunity is another field where the United States has attempted to carve out for itself a hegemonic position in derogation from general rules of international law. There is no need to recount in detail that the earlier doctrine of absolute immunity of States in judicial proceedings has given way to a more flexible doctrine which distinguishes between *acta jure imperii*, on the one hand, and *acta jure gestionis* (or commercial activities), on the other. The great change was brought about by the Taft letter of 1952,[111] and to date it is almost universally recognized that in business matters foreign States can be sued before domestic courts. However, the United States went one important step further in amending its Foreign Sovereign Immunity Act of 1976[112] by the Antiterrorism and Effective Death Penalty Act of 1996.[113] According to this new legislation, any State certified by the US Department of State as practising terrorism can be sued before US tribunals by the victims if they were subjected to torture, extrajudicial killing, aircraft sabotage, or hostage taking. On the basis of this amendment, judgments with miraculous amounts of reparation were rendered against Cuba, Iran, Libya, and Syria,[114] almost none of which could be enforced since the defendants in such cases are simply unwilling to pay the amounts granted by juries which have lost any contact with realities.[115]

Tribunals from two other countries have followed suit. In Greece, the Areopag, the highest court in civil matters, held in a suit brought against Germany on account of atrocities committed by German troops at the end of World War II that Germany could not invoke immunity which was a defence to well-behaving States only (*Distomo* case),[116] and in March 2004 the Italian Court of Cassation embraced

---

d'un droit d'ingérence à l'encontre des "Etats voyous"?, in: *L'intervention en Irak et le droit international*, Paris 2004, p. 49-60.

110   See also the conclusions drawn by Minnerop, *loc. cit.* (note 107), p. 180-182; Krisch, *loc. cit.* (note 2), p. 146.

111   *Department of State Bulletin* 26 (1952), p. 984.

112   *ILM* 15 (1976), p. 1388.

113   *ILM* 36 (1997), p. 759, Subtitle B: Jurisdiction for Lawsuits Against Terrorist States.

114   For an overview of the relevant cases in 2002 see *AJIL* 96 (2002), p. 964-967. In the *Hegna* case the family of a US citizen killed by hijackers in Tehran obtained an award of 375 million US-dollars in compensatory and punitive damages against Iran, see *AJIL* 97 (2003), p. 187.

115   K. Reece Thomas and J. Small, "Human Rights and State Immunity: Is There Immunity from Civil Liability for Torture?", *Netherlands International Law Review* 50 (2003), p. 1, at 27, note 110, contends that in the *Flatow* case (see *AJIL* 93 [1999], p. 181), where an amount of 247 million US dollars had been granted in the final judgment, the plaintiffs were able to collect 61 million dollars.

116   Judgment of 4 May 2000, short summary in *AJIL* 95 (2001), p. 198, with comment by M. Gavouneli, *ibid.*, p. 201.

the same doctrine of forfeiture.[117] However, in Greece the Areopag was rebuked by the highest specialized tribunal under the Constitution which pointed out that the principle of sovereign immunity did not yield even in instances of serious crimes under international law.[118] No similar precedents are known from other countries.

No justification for the derogation from the established standards, which derive from the principle of sovereign immunity (*par in parem non habet imperium*), can be found in customary law.[119] Except for two isolated decisions in *Letelier v. Chile*[120] and *Liu v. Republic of China*,[121] no evidence is available in national case law from any country before the adoption of the Antiterrorism and Effective Death Penalty Act of 1996, for the proposition that in (alleged) instances of grave human rights violations the principle of State immunity must yield.[122] In two decisions of 21 November 2001, the European Court of Human Rights has explicitly recognized that no breach of the guarantee of judicial protection for civil rights (Article 6 of the European Convention on Human Rights) is committed by a State the courts of which refuse to entertain suits against foreign States.[123] Nor can the derogation be justified by the paramount importance of rules of *jus cogens*. *Jus cogens* rules as primary rules define conduct which is contrary to the very foundations of the international community. But it is far too simplistic to argue that on the level of secondary rules any breach of a *jus cogens* norm entails consequences that do not fit into the general schemes determining such consequences.[124] In each and every instance, it must be examined with great care whether it seems to be warranted to

---

117   Judgment of 11 March 2004, *Rivista di diritto internazionale* 87, (2004), p. 539.

118   Judgment of 17 September 2002, not yet published.

119   The article by L.M. Caplan, "State Immunity, Human Rights, and Jus Cogens: A Critique of the Normative Hierarchy Theory", *AJIL* 97 (2003), p. 741-781, is predicated on the untenable assumption that there exists no customary rule prescribing judicial immunity for civil suits against foreign States.

120   748 F.2d 790 (2d Cir. 1984).

121   892 F.2d 1419 (1989). In both cases, isolated acts of criminal violence had been committed by governmental agents to the detriments of opponents of that government living in the United States.

122   In the *Bouzari* case, the Ontario Superior Court of Justice recently confirmed by a judgment of 1 May 2002, *ILR* 124, p. 427, at 443, the traditional legal position with regard to an alleged case of torture.

123   *Al-Adsani v. United Kingdom, Human Rights Law Journal* 23 (2002), p. 39; *McElhinney v. Ireland, ibid.*, p. 57, with critical comment by I. Pingel, "Droit d'accès aux tribunaux et exception d'immunité: La Cour de Strasbourg persiste", *Revue générale de droit international public* 106 (2002), p. 893-906. See also D. Lloyd Jones, "Article 6 ECHR and Immunities Arising in Public International Law", *ICLQ* 52 (2003), p. 463, at 468-472.

124   This is the logical error committed by A. Bianchi, "L'immunité des Etats et les violations graves des droits de l'homme", *Revue générale de droit international public* 108 (2004), p. 63, at 95 ; Pingel, *loc. cit.* (note 123), p. 905; Reece Thomas and Small, *loc. cit.* (note 115), at 19 *et seq.*

establish a special regime.[125] The disastrous effects of armed conflict, in particular, where more often than not human rights and international humanitarian law are trampled underfoot, can be settled only through inter-State agreements that provide for global reparation amounts to the benefit of the victim State(s).[126] Thus, for instance, the invasion of Iraq by the Anglo-American Coalition will require a comprehensive settlement. If before Iraqi courts – should they exist – thousands of individual claims were brought by civilian victims, nobody's interests would be satisfied. By winning their claims, the Iraqi plaintiffs would misled into false hopes since it would appear to be crystal clear from the very outset that neither the United States Government nor the United Kingdom Government would comply with such judgments. On the other hand, it appears also to be extremely doubtful whether the United States would honour a judgment handed down against it by the courts of a third country, e.g. the courts of Guatemala or Afghanistan.

In other words, the United States arrogates to itself a role of world judicial authority regarding situations which are truly international in character and which call for determinations according to the usual inter-State mechanisms. By so doing, the United States implicitly asserts to be superior to those nations regarding which it asserts to enjoy jurisdiction *ratione personae*.[127]

d) This claim of superiority manifests itself even more explicitly in the Alien Tort Claims Act, a statute enacted in 1789, which permits aliens to bring suits in the United States against anyone who has allegedly violated the "law of nations". After this statute had lain dormant for more than 170 years, it was re-discovered in 1979 in the case of *Filártiga v. Peña Irala*,[128] where the family members of a youth tortured to death in Paraguay successfully sued the torturer whose presence in the United States they had found out. The judgment was a moral victory only, the defendant leaving the United States even before his judicial defeat. In recent years, the ATCA has been used to bring claims against corporate bodies, in particular transnational corporations.

---

125 In that regard, E. Voyiakis, "Access to Court v. State Immunity", *ICLQ* 52 (2003), p. 297, at 320-331, is on the right track but misses important elements for consideration. A. Orakhelashvili, "State Immunity and International Public Order", *GYIL* 45 (2002), p. 227, at 257-258, also finds the right approach, but again fails to appraise the issue in its true complexity: a breach of a *jus cogens* rule does not mean the end of international law. Pertinent arguments by W. Cremer, "Entschädigungsklagen wegen schwerer Menschenrechtsverletzungen und Staatsimmunität vor nationaler Zivilgerichtsbarkeit", *Archiv des Völkerrechts* 41 (2003), p. 137, at 158 *et seq.* The multi-faceted character of the issue is also recognized by A. Skordas, "Hegemonic custom?", in: *United States Hegemony, op. cit.* (note 2), p. 317, at 341-344.

126 Rightly, therefore, the German Federal Supreme Court, judgment of 26 June 2003, *ILM* 42 (2003), p. 1030, did not recognize the Greek judgments awarding damages to the plaintiffs in the *Distomo* case.

127 Assessment shared by Krisch, *loc. cit.* (note 2), p. 144-145.

128 Final judgment: 630 F.2d 876 (2d Cir. 1980).

The objectionable feature of the ATCA is the claim of the United States which it represents to exercise the jurisdiction of its courts over occurrences anywhere in the world, also in instances which have nothing to do with the United States.[129] In fact, the ATCA must be seen as an expression of universal jurisdiction in matters of private law. Again, the question arises what consequences may be drawn from a breach of a paramount rule of international law which is classified as a *jus cogens* rule. In the field of criminal law, as shown above, the United States is strictly opposed to any power of prosecution by the courts of third countries without any tangible contact with the crime, or by the ICC. Obviously, this is an inconsistency which calls for careful consideration. Maybe the necessary process is already underway as a consequence of the judgment of the Supreme Court in *Sosa v. Alvarez Machain*,[130] where the judges held that the ATCA does not provide a cause of action but simply defines the jurisdiction of the United States federal courts. In the case reviewed, the issue of extraterritorial jurisdiction was of no relevance since the plaintiff, Alvarez Machaín, had been kidnapped from Mexico to the United States on behalf of United States authorities. Thus, the case had a genuine link with United States territory and United States governmental action. However, on the basis of all the briefs submitted to them, the judges were clearly conscious of the complex issues related to the extraterritorial scope of the ATCA. They implicitly stated that on later occasions they would carefully examine those aspects which they had been able to leave aside in the case at hand.[131] Hence, it would seem as if the extraterritorial reach of the ATCA has already been blunted.[132]

e)   In many other instances, too, the United States has not felt inhibited to issue regulations producing extraterritorial effects with regard to occurrences lacking any reasonable link with its constitutive elements, its territory and its people. Such regulations have become a major bone of contention in its relationship with the European Union. One may recall the attempt to prevent the building of a gas pipeline from Siberia to western Europe[133] or more recently the enactment of the

---

129   Critical Assessment also by Krisch, *loc. cit.* (note 2), p. 163.

130   Judgment of 29 June 2004.

131   "It is one thing for American courts to enforce constitutional limits on our own State and Federal Governments' power, but quite another to consider suits under rules that would go so far as to claim a limit on the power of foreign governments over their own citizens, and to hold that a foreign government or its agent has transgressed those limits". Along similar lines, Justice Breyer said in his individual opinion: "Since enforcement of an international norm by one nation's courts implies that other nations' courts may do the same, I would ask whether the exercise of jurisdiction under the ATS is consistent with those notions of comity that lead each nation to respect the sovereign rights of other nations by limiting the reach of its laws and their enforcement."

132   In the case *Hoffman-La Roche v. Empagran*, judgment of 14 June 2004, the Supreme Court showed indeed remarkable restraint regarding the lawful exercise of extraterritorial jurisdiction.

133   See, e.g., the memorandum of the Commission of the European Communities, *ILM* 21 (1982), p. 891.

Cuban Liberty and Democratic Solidarity (Libertad) Act, more generally known as the Helms-Burton-Act.[134] This Act seeks to protect former US property in Cuba by permitting the former UN owners to bring compensation suits, involving punitive damages, against buyers who have purchased any items from the Cuban Government. Clearly, this legislation has no basis in the general rules on jurisdiction to prescribe.[135] However, recognizing that it has gone too far, the United States Government has provisionally suspended the effect of the legislation so that no actual infringement of international law has occurred. One certainly does not err in assuming that this caution was mainly due to the existence of an economic countervailing power, the European Union.

f)   Within the context of this contribution, our aim cannot and should not be to establish a complete balance sheet of all of the instances where the United States has failed to honour its obligations under international law. America bashing has no place in a sober assessment. However, one particular aspect deserves to be mentioned in any event because it discloses again a certain sense of disdain for international commitments validly undertaken. Reference is made to the United States' financial obligations towards the United Nations. According to Article 17 (2) of the Charter, "the expenses of the Organization shall be borne by the Members as apportioned by the General Assembly". There can be no doubt, hence, that the relevant budgetary resolutions of the General Assembly are truly binding for all of the member States. Notwithstanding this legal position, the United States has made it a habit never to pay in full and in due time its assessed contributions. For decades now, it has an outstanding debt that amounts to several hundred million dollars.[136] Currently (31 July 2004), the share of the United States of the budgetary arrears of the entire membership of the United Nations stands at 57%.[137] Care is taken only to avoid coming within the scope of applicability of Article 19 of the Charter, which provides for forfeiture of a State's the right to vote in the General Assembly "if the amount of its arrears equals or exceeds the amount of the contributions due from it for the preceding two full years". In this way, the United States, which bears 22.00% of the total expenditure of the regular budget,[138] has a powerful weapon to

---

134   *ILM* 35 (1996), p. 357. For a contextual description see S.V. Scott, "The impact on international law of US noncompliance", in: *United States Hegemony, op. cit.* (note 2), p. 427, at 429-431.

135   Tomuschat, *op. cit.* (note 5), p. 198-200; P.-T. Stoll, "Compliance: multilateral achievements and predominant powers", in: *United States Hegemony, op. cit.* (note 2), p. 456, at 470; see also D.F. Vagts, "Extraterritoriality and the Corporate Governance Law", *AJIL* 97 (2003), p. 289, at 291.

136   For an overview covering the years from 1995 to 2003 see <http://www.globalpolicy.org/finance/info/usdebt.htm>.

137   <http://www.globalpolicy.org/finance/tables/index.htm>.

138   A different scale of assessment applies to the costs of peacekeeping operations, where the permanent Security Council members bear a higher share.

put the world Organization under pressure.[139] This policy is not a sign of mature leadership, but a strategy that considerably harms the Organization in which the permanent members of the Security Council should provide an example of perfect compliance with the Charter. It need not be underlined specifically that the size of the amounts owed to the United Nations, as such, causes no problem whatsoever to the United States. The contributions due constitute just an infinitesimal part of its budget. Obviously, therefore, the permanent delays are the reflection of a deliberate strategy. For the outside observer, it does not matter that the responsibility lies mainly with Congress and much less with the Administration.

g) The relationship between the United States and the ICJ requires a short comment as well. The judicial mechanisms brought into being by the Charter, no matter how embryonic, constitute a precious asset of the international community. Their potential should not be squandered. Logically, therefore, the Charter provides that it is one of the duties of every member State to comply with the decisions of the ICJ in any case to which it is a party (Article 94). In this regard, the balance sheet of the United States is far from stainless. In the *Nicaragua* case, the United States withdrew from the proceedings after the Court had rejected its preliminary objections,[140] claiming that nonetheless the Court lacked "jurisdiction and competence". In the *LaGrand* case, the United States did not heed the order issued by the ICJ on 3 March 1999, enjoining it to "take all measures at its disposal to ensure that Walter LaGrand is not executed pending the final decision" in the proceedings.[141] However, it should not be overlooked that the ICJ itself had contributed to the misunderstanding in the minds of the responsible US authorities by framing its request in soft terms ("should") which did not openly disclose the fact that the Court had indeed pronounced a binding decision. That the indication of provisional measures under Article 41 of the ICJ Statute has a binding character was definitively clarified by the ICJ only in its judgment on the merits of 27 June 2001.[142] However, according to reliable sources insufficient attention has been given by the United States to the findings of the ICJ that went beyond the specific case at hand.[143] Likewise, in the recent *Avena* case, introduced by Mexico against the United States, the judgment of 31 March 2004, which concluded that Mexico's rights under the Vienna Convention on Consular Relations as well as the individual rights of 51 (49)

---

139   See also Scott, *loc. cit.* (note 134), p. 435-437.

140   *Military and Paramilitary Acrtivities in and against Nicaragua, ICJ Reports* 1984, p. 392.

141   *ICJ Reports* 1999, p. 9, at 16.

142   *ICJ Reports* 2001, p. 466, at 506.

143   Now documented by C. Paulson, "Compliance With Final Judgments of the International Court of Justice Since 1987", *AJIL* 98 (2004), p. 434, at 444-449. But see the case of Mexican citizen Gerardo Valdez Maltos on death row in Oklahoma, *AJIL* 96 (2002), p. 461 (Comment by C. Hoss, *Revue générale de droit international public* 107 [2003], p. 401-414), as well as the case of the Polish citizen Gregory Madej, *AJIL* 97 (2003), p. 180, AJIL 98 (2004), p. 446.

Mexican nationals had been breached by lack of information, had to overcome serious obstacles before being recognized as truly binding by the State authorities that bear responsibility for jails and other places of incarceration. Originally, some Governors had manifested their rejection of the judgment, arguing that the ICJ had no authority in a US State. No precise information on the state of implementation of the judgment is currently available to an outsider.[144] In any event, however, the impression cannot be escaped that respect for the commands of international law is not too well guaranteed in the United States.

h)   The situation in the United States military base of Guantánamo is also of relevance in the present context. There is no need to dwell at length on the factual and legal details of that situation, which has been commented upon by many authors. It can hardly be disputed that the Taliban fighters were combatants according to Article 4 of Geneva Convention III of 1949 relative to the Treatment of Prisoners of War.[145] Regarding alleged members of the terror network Al Qaeda, in any event the provisions of the CCPR had to be respected.[146] Under both instruments, persons under detention have a right that their status be reviewed by an independent judge, the conventional provisions reflecting the venerable principle of habeas corpus which is also part and parcel of the American domestic system.[147] In a lamentable failure to uphold that cherished heritage of the culture of human rights, the federal courts first seized with applications by or on behalf of the prisoners denied their jurisdiction, thus confirming the Administration's policy not to allow the prisoners any contacts with the outside world, neither with their families, nor with legal counsel, nor with judicial bodies. Eventually, the honour of United States as a nation having embraced the rule of law was partly re-established by the judgment of the Supreme Court in *Rasul v. Bush*.[148] Curiously enough, however, this decision does not mention at all the international commitments of the United States, but confines its *rationes decidendi* exclusively to considerations drawn from

---

144   But see official report by the Mexican Embassy in Washington about a case in Oklahoma (Osvaldo Torres) where the *Avena* judgment was taken into account by State authorities: <http://portal.sre.gob.mx/usa/index.php?option=displaypage&Itemid=88&op=page&SubMenu>, now also documented in *AJIL* 98 (2004), p. 581-584, with comment by J.H. Carter, "Avena in an Oklahoma Court", *ASIL Newsletter*, August/October 2004, p. 1, at 5.

145   The most impartial witness of this assessment is G.H. Aldrich, "The Taliban, Al Qaeda, and the Determination of Illegal Combatants", *AJIL* 96 (2002), p. 891, at 894.

146   In its advisory opinion of 9 July on the *Legal Consequences of the Construction of a Wall in the Occupied Palestinian Territory*, the ICJ has now confirmed that the Covenant finds application outside the national territory of its individual parties if a State performs acts in the exercise of its jurisdiction (para. 110).

147   By a decision of 12 March 2002, *AJIL* 96 (2002), p. 730, *HRLJ* 23 (2002), p. 15, the Inter-American Commission on Human Rights issued a decision on "precautionary measures" in order to protect the relevant rights under the Inter-American system.

148   Judgment of 28 June 2004.

United States domestic law. It is true that the declaration made in connection with the ratification of the CCPR prevented the Supreme Court from directly applying that instrument. But the judges could at least have had recourse to it in construing the relevant provisions of the applicable statute law. It should also be noted that the plight of the prisoners is not yet over. Proceedings are just beginning (August 2004), and according to many critics the military commissions established to hear the complaints of the prisoners do not provide the required guarantees of fair trial.[149]

Guantánamo remains a dark stain on the record of the United States.[150] The practices pursued by the Bush Administration do not so much reflect a will to arrogate to itself hegemonic positions, but rather the state of mind of a nation deeply traumatized by the events of 9/11 and erroneously believing that the traditional rules of international law are inappropriate in combating the new terrorist threats as they manifested themselves in New York and Washington. National psychology contains many mysteries. But governments are there to lead and not to bow to the slightest wind of media pressures. It is clear in this regard that the world at large is by no means persuaded by the grounds advanced for justifying the complete isolation of human beings for a span of more than two and a half years. It is impossible to demonstrate that the security of the United States depends on the treatment of the detainees in the United States military base in Cuba. Thus, Guantánamo cannot be seen as the first step in a process of thorough review of the law as it stands, but rather as a blatant breach which lacks legitimacy even in a perspective of legal policy.

C.   *Tentative Conclusions*

A tentative assessment of the United States' conduct *vis-à-vis* multilateral frameworks leads to the conclusion that the United States does not reject multilateralism as a matter of principle. Its active participation not only in the United Nations, but also in a vast array of other multilateral agencies provides ample proof for its preparedness to cooperate with other nations. However, it is noteworthy that the

---

149   See J. Fitzpatrick, "Jurisdiction of Military Commissions and the Ambiguous War on Terrorism", *AJIL* 96 (2002), p. 345, at 352; H.H. Koh, "The Case Against Military Commissions", *ibid.*, p. 337, at 338-342; D.A. Mundis, "The Use of Military Commissions to Prosecute Individuals Accused of Terrorist Acts", *ibid.*, p. 320 *et seq.*, at 328; for a defence of the lawfulness of the military commissions entrusted with trying Taleban and Al Qaeda fighters see R. Wedgwood, "Al Qaeda, Terrorism, and Military Commissions", *ibid.*, p. 328, at 332-336.

150   See also criticism by E. Sciso, "La condizione dei detenuti di Guantanamo fra diritto umanitario e garanzie dei diritti umani fondamentali", *Rivista italiana di diritto internazionale* 86 (2003), p. 111-128; J. Steyn, "Guantanamo Bay: The Legal Black Hole", *ICLQ* 53 (2004), p. 1-15; C. Tomuschat, "Menschenrecht und die Gefangenen in Guantánamo", *Anwaltsblatt* 2004, p. 397-400; P. Weckel, "Le statut incertain des détenus sur la base américaine de Guantanamo", *Revue générale de droit international public* 106 (2002), p. 357-369.

United States is extremely reluctant to submit to procedures where it would have to accept binding majority decisions. In that regard, the Security Council constitutes for the United States an almost ideal institution inasmuch as in that body nothing of importance can happen against its will. Significantly enough, the United States has not accepted a single one of the UN procedures allowing for individual complaints ("communications") to be brought to the attention of international bodies, and the same attitude of cautious distance characterizes its relationship with the Inter-American system for the protection of human rights: to date, is has refrained from ratifying the American Convention on Human Rights. The only mechanism of third-party settlement to which in recent years the United States has submitted of its own free will is that of WTO, where the Understanding on Rules and Procedures Governing the Settlement of Disputes constitutes an integral part of the entire framework of legal regulation, which cannot be departed from by way of a reservation. A general assessment of the experiences won with the implementation of that mechanism reveals a mixed picture. In many instances, the United States and the European Union have been at loggerheads with one another, and implementation has encountered many obstacles.[151] In any event, however, the United States has been able to learn within WTO to hold the position of an ordinary member that enjoys no special prerogatives.

D.   *The Importance of Independent Institutions*

Given the factual might of the United States, which makes it impossible to impose any sanctions on it in case of a breach of its obligations, independent institutions gain primary importance. For the purposes of maintaining and upholding international law on issues of principle, the ICJ still occupies the first place. The United States is related to the ICJ by virtue of its being a member of the United Nations. Since the ICJ is "the principal judicial organ of the United Nations" (Article 92 Charter), every member of the World Organization acknowledges the institution as such, even without submitting to its jurisdiction. Shortly after the establishment of the ICJ (14 August 1946), the United States made a declaration under Article 36 (2) ICJ Statute accepting the jurisdiction of ICJ, with the restrictive proviso, however, that the declaration did not encompass disputes over "matters which are essentially within the domestic jurisdiction of the United States of America as determined by the United States of America".[152] After it had emerged in the *Nicaragua* case that this proviso was not able to protect it against unwanted applications, the United States first terminated its declaration to a limited extent by a notification

---

151   For a quantitative analysis of the wins and losses in the relationship between the two largest trading partners see R.H. Steinberg, "Judicial Lawmaking at the WTO: Discursive, Constitutional, and Political Constraints", *AJIL* 98 (2004), p. 247, at 268-273; for two case studies see S. Princen, "EC Compliance with WTO Law: The Interplay of Law and Politics", *EJIL* 15 (2004), p. 555-574.

152   Connally amendment, see M.M. Whiteman, *Digest of International Law*, Vol. 12, Washington 1971, p. 1304.

of 6 April 1984 and thereafter (letter of 4 October 1985,[153] notified 7 October 1985) withdrew it completely. Consequently, as from 7 April 1986 applications could be brought against the United States only on the basis of Article 36 (1) ICJ Statute, i.e. mainly by virtue of compromissory clauses contained in treaties in force. On that narrow ground alone, the United States has been the defendant in a considerable number of cases.[154] Its record is a fairly mixed one. In particular, the United States succeeded in settling three difficult cases (*Aerial Incident of 3 July 1989*, *Lockerbie* case and *Breard* case) by negotiations with the applicant State so that the proceedings could be discontinued on the basis of mutual consent of the parties. In the *LaGrand* and *Avena* cases, where the treatment of arrested persons with regard to the Consular Convention was in issue, the United States lost and had to realize that its internal procedures were subject to international review to the extent that international rules apply to the facts at hand.

Of even greater importance are the advisory opinions which the ICJ can give at the request of the General Assembly (Article 96).[155] Such opinions may be sought with a view to counteracting the policies of the Security Council and thereby also to counteracting the influence of the United States in the World Organization. Indeed, when the General Assembly requested the ICJ to express itself on the legal aspects of the use of nuclear weapons it was clearly aiming at the permanent members of the Security Council who all hold stocks of nuclear weapons. Likewise, the advisory opinion of the ICJ on *Legal Consequences of the Construction of a Wall in the Occupied Palestinian Territory*[156] has as its background the dissatisfaction of the great majority of nations with the leniency of the Security Council – and implicitly the United States – regarding the occupation of Palestinian territories by Israel. Although advisory opinions, as their name indicates, are not binding in a true sense, they state the law, and even for the United States it is extremely difficult to discard such a statement to which it has indirectly contributed not only through its membership in the United Nations, but also through the person of the judge nominated by it for that post. In many instances, parties to a dispute may argue that there exists no legal rule or that the law is so indeterminate as to permit almost any

---

153   See explanatory statement, *AJIL* 80 (1986), p. 164.

154   *Elettronica Sicula (United States v. Italy)*, judgment of 20 July 1989, *ICJ Reports* 1989, p. 15; *Aerial Incident of 3 July 1989 (Iran v. United States)*, case discontinued in 1996, *ICJ Reports* 1996, p. 9; *Lockerbie* case *(Libya v. United States)*, case discontinued in 2003; *Oil Platforms* case *(Iran v. United States)*, judgment of 6 November 2003; *Vienna Convention on Consular Relations* (Breard) case *(Paraguay v. United States)*, case discontinued in 1998, *ICJ Reports* 1998, p. 426; *LaGrand* case *(Germany v. United States)*, judgment of 27 June 2001, *ICJ Reports* 2001, p. 466; *Legality of Use of Force (Yugoslavia v. United States)*, judgment of 2 June 1999, *ICJ Reports* 1999, p. 916; *Avena* case *(Mexico v. United States)*, judgment of 31 March 2004.

155   Only in exceptional circumstances does the Security Council request an advisory opinion. The only relevant instance is the opinion on the status of *Namibia*, *ICJ Reports* 1971, p. 16.

156   Issued on 9 July 2004.

interpretation. After the ICJ has rendered a judgment or given an advisory opinion, such a situation of openness or boundless interpretation does not exist any longer. In that regard, the importance of the ICJ for protecting international law against arbitrariness is invaluable. It is extremely difficult for a State to oppose views expressed by the ICJ.[157] Being aware of the normative power which thus it enjoys, the ICJ is usually extremely cautious in framing its considerations on a given case. However, the sole fact that the Court is composed of 15 judges who all enjoy the same power of vote speaks convincingly against any notion of individual hegemony – as opposed to collective hegemony which is one of the defining features of the Charter.

5.   Concluding Observations

There can be no doubt that the United States enjoys a unique position in the world of today. Its factual power surpasses the power of any other nation, although it is not boundless, as the aftermath of the military victory in Iraq has brought to light. Thus, United States predominance in international relations is a fact of life. Should the United States therefore be labelled as a "hegemon" – over and beyond displaying the features of an empire? Acknowledging that the choice of terminology is to some extent a question of semantics, our review of the multilateral structures taken into consideration has not been able to confirm that the United States has succeeded in carving out for itself a leadership role truly consolidated by legal instruments. Undeniably, through the Security Council a collective hegemony has been created, where the United States participates as an actor at the highest level. But the United States must share this privilege with other nations, not being able unilaterally to impose its will on the entire international community. This scheme is attractive to any constitutional lawyer who knows that constitutional processes require effective checks and balances. Propositions which have stood the test of time at the national level are quite appropriate also for building a viable international system of governance.

Even a tight network of legal rules does not resist a deliberate move of a powerful nation to get rid of such constraints. Violating rules deemed too onerous is always a political option. But open challenge to the existing legal order entails considerable costs in a globalized world where also the individual members of civil society have an interest in seeing the legal rules for transnational transactions respected. More often than not, political scientists, brooding over drawing boards of strategic games, overlook this vital interest in stability and order. Yes, states of emergeny do exist. But contrary to Carl Schmitt, we do not interpret the interna-

---

157   In any event, formally to voice disagreement is the only way in which it can be attempted to check such views: In this regard, see paper by Department of State Legal Advisor W.H. Taft IV, *AJIL* 98 (2004), p. 598, challenging the interpretation of the limits on self-defence specified by the ICJ in the *Oil Platforms* case, judgment of 6 November 2003, paras. 51-78.

tional legal order in terms of the *Ausnahmezustand*,[158] but from the viewpoint of normalcy which most of the time prevails in international relations.

---

158 C. Schmitt, *Politische Theologie. Vier Kapitel zur Lehre von der Souveränität*, München and Leipzig 1922, p. 9: "Souverän ist, wer über den Ausnahmezustand entscheidet" ("Sovereign is he who decides on an emergency situation").

3. American Unilateralism and the Rule of Law

Robert F. Turner

Even among its closest traditional friends and allies, there is a great deal of frustration today over America's behavior on many fronts. The United States has withdrawn from the 1972 ABM Treaty[1] and has refused to become a party to a variety of new treaties of great importance to the world community dealing with the prohibition of land mines[2] and other aspects of the law of armed conflict,[3] environmental protection,[4] and the International Criminal Court.[5] The US Senate has still not consented to the ratification of the 1982 Law of the Sea Convention[6] more than a decade after key provisions were renegotiated to satisfy American concerns.

More importantly, in the eyes of many, our "cowboy" President claims a right to use military force to "preempt" States we don't like, and when we don't get our way in the Security Council we charge off on our own and invade another sover-

---

1 Treaty Between the United States of America and the Union of Soviet Socialist Republics on the Limitation of Anti-Ballistic Missile Systems, Signed at Moscow 26 May 1972, entered into force 3 October 1972. President Bush's public statement on the occasion of announcing the US decision to withdraw from this treaty can be found at <http://www.whitehouse.gov/news/releases/2001/12/20011213-4.html> (last visited 19 January 2005).

2 Convention on the Prohibition of the Use, Stockpiling, Production and Transfer of Anti-Personnel Mines and on their Destruction, adopted 18 September 1997, entered into force 1 March 1999, 36 *ILM* 1509.

3 Protocol Additional to the Geneva Conventions of 12 August 1949, and relating to the Protection of Victims of International Armed Conflicts (Protocol I), 8 June 1977, entered into force 7 December 1979.

4 Kyoto Protocol to the United Nations Framework Convention on Climate Change, adopted 11 December 1997, entered into force, 16 February 2005, 37 *ILM* 32.

5 United Nations Diplomatic Conference of Plenipotentiaries on the Establishment of an International Criminal Court, Rome Statute of the International Criminal Court, 17 July 1998, U.N. Doc. A/CONF/189/9, 37 *ILM* 999.

6 United Nations Convention on the Law of the Sea. Concluded at Montego Bay, Jamaica, on 10 December 1982, entered into force 16 November 1994, UN Doc A/CONF. 62/122 (1982); 21 *ILM* 1261.

Ronald St. John Macdonald & Douglas M. Johnston (eds.), Towards World Constitutionalism, *pp. 77-101.*
© 2005 *Koninklijke Brill NV. Printed in The Netherlands. ISBN 90 04 14612 1.*

eign State in the absence even of clear evidence that an attack against the United States (or any other country) was imminent. Because of our vast military power, it seems to many, Americans now think the rules no longer apply to them and they may do as they please without regard to the rule of law. The United States, many fear, has become a major threat to world peace.

As an American international lawyer who vividly recalls seeing remnants of the destruction from World War II while living in Europe where my father was assigned to NATO during that organization's infancy more than half-a-century ago, who later saw the horrors of war first-hand during my own military service in Vietnam and subsequent visits to war-torn areas of Central America in the early 1980s, I have a passionate hatred for war, an abiding love for peace, and a conviction that international law has an important role to play in promoting perpetual peace for all humankind. And while I certainly understand the anger, concern, and in some cases genuine *fear* that my country's behavior has instilled in many people of good will around the world, I believe that much of the criticism is unwarranted and premised upon a failure to understand the American character and the motivation for much of the behavior at issue.

My goal in this chapter is not to persuade readers that America has been "right" in what it has done, but rather to try to help readers understand *why* some American international lawyers who share fundamental values with our colleagues around the world believe many of these policies to be defensible. (Which is not to suggest that I am in full accord with or willing to defend *everything* my country has done over the years.[7])

First of all, it is important to distinguish policy decisions that are not even arguably contrary to the obligations of international law – such as the American decisions to withdraw from the 1972 ABM Treaty pursuant to its clear terms[8] and not to become a party to various new treaties – from those that many believe are in fact contrary to America's legal obligations. There is no duty to accept every proposed new treaty.[9]

---

7   Among other things, I was a strong critic of America's refusal to pay its UN dues in 1997. *See, e.g.*, Robert F. Turner, "U.S. and U.N.: The Ties that Bind", *Wall Street Journal*, 1 December 1997 at A 23. I was also unhappy with the 1989 decision to intervene in Panama (although I think the outcome of restoring the democratically-elected Endora-Ford government was on balance a good thing, and the principle of military intervention to restore democracy seemed implicit in the subsequent Security Council Resolution 940 on Haiti – which reaffirmed that "the goal of the international community remains the restoration of democracy in Haiti," declared the situation there to be a "threat to the peace," and authorized the use of military force under Chapter VII to bring about "the prompt return of the legitimately elected President" in Haiti).

8   *See* Robert F. Turner, *The ABM Treaty and the Senate*, 98 (1999).

9   Nearly two decades ago I was invited by the *Atlantic Community Quarterly* to take part in an exchange of views on international law with a very distinguished British legal scholar, Professor (now International Court of Justice Judge) Rosalyn Higgins. In her quite excellent piece that called the United States to task for not ratifying key human rights treaties, Judge Higgins wrote: "In the West the picture is mixed. The

1. "Entangling Alliances" and the Rule of Law

One of the characteristics of American foreign policy from the days of George Washington until the relatively modern era was a reluctance to become involved in "entangling alliances,"[10] and many Americans continue to believe that it has been our tradition of limited government and individual freedom that has provided us with a high standard of living. Domestic legislative proposals to expand the role of government over the lives of our people often face high hurdles in this country, and much of our reluctance to join in new treaty regimes may stem from similar caution about "too much government regulation." I'm not saying this is "right" or "wrong," just trying to explain the thinking of some of our people.

For the past seventeen years, it has been my great honor to teach and do scholarly research at a university designed and founded by Thomas Jefferson. As our first Secretary of State, in 1791 Jefferson wrote to William Short, who had succeeded him as US Minister to Paris: "If there be one principle more deeply rooted than any other in the mind of every American, it is, that we should have nothing to do with conquest."[11] Eighteen years later Jefferson advised his successor as Presi-

---

United States, whose domestic human rights record is second to none, is party to few of the leading human rights instruments .... It makes no reports; its procedures are subject to no international scrutiny." *See* Rosalyn Higgins, Robert Turner, "Two Contrasting Views of International World Order", *Atl. Com. Q.* 145, 153 (Summer 1987). While serving as Acting Assistant Secretary of State for Legislative Affairs in 1984-85, I was given special responsibilities for obtaining Senate consent to ratification of the 1948 Genocide Convention, which had been held up in the Senate for decades. During the debate, on which we ultimately prevailed, no one suggested that the right of Americans to commit genocide ought to be protected, any more than current opponents of the International Criminal Court want to immunize American war criminals. The concern has always been that foreign tyrants or other anti-American forces around the world might misuse such treaties to go after American leaders and soldiers on false charges.

10   In his farewell address to the nation, which was published in several newspapers but never actually delivered as a speech, President George Washington wrote: "It is our true policy to steer clear of permanent alliances with any portion of the foreign world; so far, I mean, as we are now at liberty to do it; for let me not be understood as capable of patronizing infidelity to existing engagements. I hold the maxim no less applicable to public than to private affairs, that honesty is always the best policy. I repeat it, therefore, let those engagements be observed in their genuine sense. But, in my opinion, it is unnecessary and would be unwise to extend them." Washington, "Farewell Address to the People of the United States", *The Independent Chronicle*, September 26, 1796, available on line at <http://earlyamerica.com/earlyamerica/milestones/farewell/>. Although often attributed to Washington, the expression that America should avoid "entangling alliances" actually came from President Jefferson's inaugural address of 4 March 1801: "Equal and exact justice to all men, of whatever state or persuasion, religious or political; peace, commerce, and honest friendship, with all nations – entangling alliances with none ...." 3 *Writings of Thomas Jefferson* 317, 321 (Mem. ed. 1903).

11   "Jefferson to Short", 28 July 1791, in 8 *Writings of Thomas Jefferson* 216, 219 (Mem. Ed. 1903).

dent, James Madison: "it has a great effect on the opinion of our people and the world to have the moral right on our side."[12] Both principles, I believe, continue to characterize the thinking of an overwhelming majority of Americans. And it pains us a great deal when friends around the globe perceive our behavior to be immoral or motivated by a covetous interest in the territory or resources of other nations.

Jefferson was a great champion of the law of nations, and even in the absence of effective means of compulsory international dispute resolution he believed that the new nation ought to be respectful of its treaty obligations. When called upon by President Washington to provide advice on whether the United States was obligated to carry out its commitments under the treaty with France during the French Revolution, the Secretary of State responded that: "Compacts ... between nation and nation are obligatory on them by the same moral law which obliges individuals to observe their compacts." In both instances, he said, obligations may be excused if performance becomes *impossible*, and also if it becomes "*self-destructive* to the party," because "the law of self-preservation overrules the law of obligation in others."[13]

But Jefferson drew a distinction between treaty obligations that were truly "self-destructive" and those that were merely "dangerous, useless, or disagreeable." And in assessing this risk, he noted:

> Of these, it is true, that nations are to be judges for themselves; since no one nation has a right to sit in judgment over another, but the tribunal of our conscience remains, and that also of the opinion of the world. These will revise the sentence we pass in our own case, and as we respect these, we must see that in judging ourselves we have honestly done the part of impartial and rigorous judges.[14]

Yet Jefferson also understood that the law was but a means to an end, and not the ultimate end in itself. And he recognized that:

> A strict observance of the written laws is doubtless *one* of the high duties of a good citizen, but it is not *the highest*. The laws of necessity, of self-preservation, of saving our country when in danger, are of higher obligation. To lose our country by a scrupulous adherence to written law, would be to lose the law itself, with life, liberty, property and all those who are enjoying them with us; thus absurdly sacrificing the end to the means."[15]

On October 24, 1823, an eighty-year-old Jefferson sent a letter to President James Monroe embracing the proposed new "Monroe Doctrine"[16] prohibiting European

---

12   "Jefferson to Madison", 19 April 1809, in 12 *id*. 273, 274.

13   Jefferson, "Opinion on the question whether the United States have a right to renounce their treaties with France, or to hold them suspended till the government of that country shall be established", 28 April 1793, in 3 *id*. 226, 228.

14   *Id*. at 229.

15   "Jefferson to John Colvin", 20 September 1810, in 12 *id*. 418 (emphasis in original).

16   The "Monroe Doctrine" is viewed by many today as an early example of American exceptionalism and unilateralism, as during the early twentieth century is was repeatedly

colonization of American republics. Jefferson argued that America should "make our hemisphere that of freedom," adding: "Nor is the occasion to be slighted which this proposition offers, of declaring our protest against the atrocious violations of the rights of nations, by the interference of any one in the internal affairs of another ...."[17] One hundred and twenty-two years later to the day, the UN Charter entered into force. In Article 2(4) of that illustrious document, the world community finally codified Jefferson's non-intervention principle as binding international law[18] – arguably the most important single rule of law today save perhaps for *pacta sunt servanda*.[19]

2.   Peace Through Strength

Like the overwhelming majority of Americans throughout our history, Jefferson was very much a man of peace. Few intelligent men or women have any fondness for war. As Jefferson explained to Monroe in 1793: "I believe that through all America there has been but a single sentiment on the subject of peace and war, which was in favor of the former.... We have differed perhaps as to the tone of conduct exactly adapted to the securing it."[20] And *this* is in my view the core of the discord between

used to justify military interventions in Latin America that produced a legacy of resentment that continues to this day. Space does not permit a full discussion of this doctrine, but originally it was intended merely to protect the western hemisphere from European colonialism and exploitation and was warmly received by Latin American democrats. During the presidency of Theodore Roosevelt a century ago, Great Britain complained that several Latin American states had defaulted on treaty obligations which under international law at the time Britain was entitled to enforce by the threat or use of armed force. Roosevelt was told that the United States must elect between abandoning the Monroe Doctrine – so Britain and other European states could enforce their legal rights through measures of self-help – or assume the responsibility for ensuring that the beneficiaries of that doctrine would abide by their treaty obligations. On its face, it was hardly an unreasonable demand. From the start the doctrine was dependent upon the widespread belief that the powerful British navy would assist America to protect this hemisphere from colonialism, and British compliance with the doctrine was always premised upon good will. Ultimately, the United States lacked the power to challenge the British navy. So Roosevelt concluded that assuming the role of regional "policeman" was preferable to seeing the region opened to colonial exploitation from Europe. But the subsequent military interventions authorized by Roosevelt and his successors in the early twentieth century were understandably resented by America's neighbors to the south and were certainly not an element of Monroe's original plan.

17 "Jefferson to Monroe", 24 October 1823, in 15 *Writings of Thomas Jefferson* 477, 478 (Mem. ed. 1904).

18 "All Members shall refrain in their international relations from the threat or use of force against the territorial integrity or political independence of any state, or in any other manner inconsistent with the Purposes of the United Nations." *UN Charter*, Art. 2(4).

19 "Treaties are to be obeyed." Obviously, if there is no duty to obey treaty obligations the content of those obligations becomes less important.

20 "Jefferson to Monroe", 28 June 1793, in 26 *Papers of Thomas Jefferson* 392 (John Catanzariti *et al.*, eds, 1995).

America and much of the world: we *all* want a peaceful world, but we disagree about the "tone of conduct" best calculated to promoting that end. Americans tend to believe that peace can best be preserved in the long run if tyrants do not perceive that they will benefit from breaking the law – particularly when the violations involve threats or uses of force or egregious violations of the dignity and rights of large numbers of human beings. So, as much as we hate war – indeed, *because* we so hate war – many of us embrace the maxim "peace through strength." Yet our determination to keep Weapons of Mass Destruction (WMD) out of the hands of "repeat offenders"[21] like Iraq, Iran, Syria, Libya, and North Korea are seen by many as the greatest threat to world peace today.

The genesis of an American policy of "peace through strength" can be traced back to Thomas Jefferson's days as Minister to Paris even before America had a Constitution. In a letter to John Jay, at the time Secretary of Foreign Affairs for the Continental Congress, Jefferson embraced what might be termed a doctrine of "peace through justice and strength":

> Justice ... on our part, will save us from those wars which would have been produced by a contrary disposition. But how to prevent those produced by the wrongs of other nations? By putting ourselves in a condition to punish them. Weakness provokes insult and injury, while a condition to punish it often prevents it .... I think it to our interest to punish the first insult: because an insult unpunished is the parent of many others.[22]

3.   Dealing with Islamic Terrorists

While in Paris, Jefferson proposed and won broad international support for the concept of a mutual security treaty in which the victims of Barbary piracy would combine their naval assets to "compel the piratical States to perpetual peace, without price, and to guarantee that peace to each other."[23] Lacking the power to compel the American states to furnish money or naval forces, however, the Continental Congress concluded that it would not be able with any certainty to fulfill such an

---

21   Iraq and North Korea have long histories of supporting international terrorism and each have been condemned in the past by the Security Council for major acts of international armed aggression. Iran, Syria, and Libya have long histories of both open and covert support for international terrorism. In apparent response to the coalition intervention in Iraq, Libya appears to have now renounced both its quest for WMD and its support for terrorism.

22   "Jefferson to Jay", 23 August 1785, in 8 *id.* 427. *See also,* "Jefferson to Edward Rutledge", 24 June 1797, 9 *Writings of Thomas Jefferson* 408, 410-11 ("We must make the interest of every nation stand surety for their justice, and their own loss to follow injury to us, as effect follows its cause. As to everything except commerce, we ought to divorce ourselves from them all.").

23   Thomas Jefferson, "Proposals for Concerted Operation Among the Powers at War With the Piratical States of Barbary", November 1786, reprinted in 17 *Writings of Thomas Jefferson* 145, 146 (Mem. ed.).

obligation. Later, after the Constitution was ratified, both Washington and Adams decided to follow the European practice in dealing with the terrorists of their day and simply paid annual tribute to protect American seamen.[24]

When he became President in 1801 Jefferson put his theory of peace through strength into practice by confronting the Barbary Pirates who were preying upon American merchant ships and enslaving our citizens. Jefferson found the Federalist policy of appeasement both objectionable in principle and unwise as a matter of sound policy, and at his very first cabinet meeting – with the approval of such wise advisers as Madison and Albert Gallatin – he decided to dispatch two-thirds of the new American Navy to the Mediterranean under the command of Commodore Richard Dale with instructions to distribute his forces "so as best to protect our commerce & chastise their insolence – by sinking, burning or destroying their ships & Vessels wherever you shall find them."[25]

America ultimately succeeded in this endeavor and paved the way for an end to Barbary piracy, in part by relying upon a covert operation engineered by a former Army Captain named William Eaton, who had served as US Consul at Tunis from 1798 until 1803. (Like Jefferson a believer in peace through strength, Eaton had become so enraged over the negotiating instructions he had received from the Adams Administration at one point that he wrote back: "[I]f we will have peace at such a price, recall me, and send a *slave*, accustomed to abasement, to represent the nation."[26])

Eaton led a party of American Marines – in civilian clothes and pretending to be on leave – to Alexandria, Egypt, to track down and recruit a man named Hamet, who was the elder brother of the Bey of Tripoli. With covert American financing, Eaton and Hamet assembled a motley army of several hundred Arab and Greek mercenaries and launched a 500-mile trek across the Western Desert to Tripoli. After learning that his brother Hamet with American support had won a quick victory seizing Tripoli's second largest town of Dern, the Bey quickly agreed to sign a new treaty without provision for annual tribute and promising severe punishment for any of his officers who abused Americans in the future. The Bey's only proposed addition to the American treaty was a promise that US support for Hamet's army would be terminated and the Americans with him would withdraw.

Shortly thereafter, Jefferson sent Commodore Stephen Decatur with a squadron of ships to Algiers to demand peace without price. When the Bey of Algiers

---

24   I have elaborated on this history at greater length in Robert F. Turner, "State Responsibility and the War on Terror: The Legacy of Thomas Jefferson and the Barbary Pirates", 4 *Chicago Journal of International Law* 121 (2003).

25   Instructions from Navy Secretary Samuel Smith to Commodore Richard Dale, May 20, 1801, reprinted in 1 *Naval Documents related to the United States Wars With the Barbary Powers* 465, 467 (Claude A. Swanson, ed., 1939). These instructions were premised upon a determination by Dale that Tripoli had breached the existing treaty and declared war against the United States, as had been anticipated and had actually occurred.

26   Donald Barr Chidsey, *The Wars in Barbary: Arab Piracy and the Birth of the United States Navy* 68 (1971).

sought a few days, or at least a few hours, to consider the demand, Decatur responded: "Not a minute." The American treaty was accepted, and other Barbary States soon agreed as well. Emboldened by the American example, European leaders quickly announced their own refusal to continue paying tribute, and centuries of terror on the high seas soon came to an end.[27]

I believe both that Jefferson was right in recognizing the importance of strength and a willingness to act in response to threats to the peace and that a foreign policy founded on moral principles that eschew "conquest" continues to command the allegiance of an overwhelming majority of Americans. These are lessons not only drawn from Jefferson's early examples, but as well from painful mistakes of the twentieth century.

4.   The Consequences of Unforced International Law

To America's credit, President Woodrow Wilson played a prominent role during World War I in building a broad international consensus that aggressive war was no longer an acceptable instrument of national policy. Without his leadership, there might never have been a League of Nations. But – in part because of America's traditional aversion to "entangling alliances" – the United States then refused to join the League once it was established. I believe America must accept a share of responsibility for the failure of the League to achieve Wilson's dream, although in candor I don't think many other States had the will to give real "teeth" to the new organization either.

In 1927, French Foreign Minister Aristide Briand proposed that France and the United States enter into a bilateral treaty renouncing the use of military force between them. American Secretary of State Frank Kellogg responded by proposing instead a multinational convention in which *all* countries would be invited to renounce war as an instrument of national policy. Kellogg and Briand shared the Nobel Peace Prize for the treaty signed the following year to which more than sixty nations ultimately became parties. But the treaty contained no provisions for enforcement, and when Japan invaded Manchuria in 1931, and Italy invaded Abyssinia (Ethiopia) four years later, neither the parties to the Pact of Paris nor the League of Nations had the will to do more than make speeches, issue reports, and pass resolutions.[28]

Yale University Professor Donald Kagan, among the world's leading authorities on these issues, eloquently captures the reality in his superb volume, *On the Origins of War*:

> Within the British government there was little sentiment for a strong stand against Italy, but a considerable feeling that the League could not be abandoned. Yet there was great reluctance to antagonize the Italians and risk driving them to the side of Germany and an unwillingness to resist Mussolini without French support. There was also a keen sense of Britain's military weakness .... The French could not understand

---

27   *See* Turner, *supra* note 24 at 132-37 and sources cited therein.
28   See generally on this period, Robert H. Ferrell, *Peace in Their Time* (1952).

Britain's enthusiasm for collective security to defend a backward African nation that still practiced slavery, at the cost of alienating Italy .... .

In the end, ... the League and collective security were finished. Britain's prestige was damaged badly, and Italy was alienated, shortly to join forces with Hitler. The democracies seemed weak, indecisive, and cowardly, and their failure and inaction gave courage to their enemies.[29]

In the months that followed, Europe quickly moved closer and closer to war. Professor Kagan observes:

Few took the League of Nations seriously. It served chiefly as a form of self-delusion or an excuse for inaction. Whenever tested it proved the emptiness of the concept of "collective security" when not led by one or more responsible states with the will and the means to resist aggression.

In Britain pacifism, isolationism, and other forms of wishful thinking were widespread and contributed to the mood favoring disarmament and concession. The idea of maintaining peace through strength was not in fashion ....

The French, much less influenced by the intellectual currents so powerful in Britain and America, were psychologically crippled by the memory of the slaughters of 1914-18, when excessive reliance on the offensive had led to disaster. French military and political leaders were dominated by that one historical analogy only. They built the Maginot Line and tried to hide behind it ....[30]

The United States might have made a difference had it been willing to play a leadership role in the cause of peace, but a powerful spirit of isolationism led the US Congress to pass a series of "neutrality" and "war powers" laws restricting President Roosevelt's ability to act to assist threatened democracies. At Munich at the end of September 1938, British Prime Minister Neville Chamberlain thought he had purchased "peace for our time" by appeasing Hitler and permitting the conquest of Czechoslovakia's Sudetenland. A year later, on the eve of the Nazi invasion of Poland, when Hitler's generals warned him that the correlation of forces was not yet adequate to risk offending France and England, the Fuhrer replied: "I saw them at Munich. They are little worms."[31]

When World War II finally ended, tens of millions of people around the globe were dead. Because it was geographically more isolated from the conflict than most, the United States emerged from the conflict with the least-damaged military and industrial infrastructure of any major power – and with a monopoly on the atomic bomb. Some countries might have sought to use that position of military power to claim territory or demand political or economic concessions. I believe to its credit, America took the lead in promoting the establishment of the United Nations, helped rebuild Germany and Japan as great world democracies, and es-

---

29   Donald Kagan, *On the Origins of War and the Preservation of Peace* 347-51 (1995).

30   *Id.* at 414.

31   *Id.* at 412.

tablished the Marshall Plan to help our European allies recover from the economic destruction they had experienced during that tragic conflict.

5.   The Security Council Responds to Aggression in Korea

In June 1950, the first major military challenge to the United Nations occurred as North Korea invaded its southern neighbor. A few months earlier, there had been widespread accord within the American military and foreign policy establishments that Korea was not a strategically vital territory, and the United States probably contributed to undermining deterrence by withdrawing most of its forces from South Korea by early 1950 and making public statements about Korea being outside the American 'defensive perimeter.' Yet, following the invasion, American support for defending South Korea was overwhelming. The issue had become not whether South Korea was strategically critical, but rather whether it was important to uphold the Charter prohibition on the aggressive use of force. And working through the Security Council, America took the lead in resisting that aggression under the UN flag. When the shooting and shelling had stopped, the United States had suffered more than 150,000 casualties, losing more than twice as many troops as all other UN forces combined. This was not because the Charter or the safety of the Republic of Korea were more important to Americans than they were to others, but because, following two world wars, the United States was firmly committed to doing more than its "fair share" in upholding the rule of law and resisting threats to the peace.

6.   Security Council Impotence and US Unilateralism during the Cold War

 Foiled by a US-led United Nations in Korea, Mao and later Castro began supporting Communist insurgency movements in the Third World. America's post-Korea reliance upon the threat of nuclear retaliation to keep the peace was not well structured to deal with low-intensity guerrilla wars, and new challenges to the Charter and the rule of law soon emerged.

A.   *Vietnam*

In May 1959, the *Lao Dong* ("Workers" or Communist) Party of the Democratic Republic of [North] Vietnam made a decision to liberate South Vietnam by armed force and began secretly sending tens of thousands of troops and tons of supplies south via the Ho Chi Minh Trail to overthrow the Republic of [South] Vietnam. This was just as much a violation of the Charter as had been North Korea's 1950 decision to "liberate" South Korea by force. But North Vietnam (with strong support from the Soviet Union and China) concealed its role, and persuaded much of the world through a brilliant propaganda offensive that the United States was not "resisting Communist aggression" but was instead trying to impose a puppet dictatorship on South Vietnam against the will of its people. Hanoi's actual role was a major point of dispute during the war, as anti-war protesters around the world accused the US State Department of lying. But after the war, Hanoi readily acknowledged its 1959 decision to initiate the war and also that the "National Liberation Front" (NLF) set up in South Vietnam the following year was created and controlled by Hanoi as a tool for misleading the west.[32]

The threat of a Soviet veto would have precluded the UN from taking effective action in Indochina even if a majority of its members had possessed the will to act. So President Kennedy concluded that if the principles of the Charter were to be upheld, America would have to take the lead outside the Charter framework. With the help of troops committed by Australia, New Zealand, Thailand, South Korea, and the Philippines – at their peak nearly 70,000 strong, far in excess of those who were committed to fight alongside the United States in Korea under the UN flag – and various types of financial and other support from more than thirty other UN members, the United States sent nearly three million young men over a period of more than a dozen years to fight a war against a foe that did not directly threaten US territory. More than 58,000 of those men gave their lives in that effort, hundreds of thousands more were wounded, and, adjusted for inflation, in terms of 2005 dollars the US financial contribution was nearly $500 billion.

In the beginning, Americans overwhelmingly supported that war. We thought we were doing our international duty by helping to enforce the non-aggression provisions of the UN Charter. But millions of angry anti-American protesters around the world (including in our own cities) denounced America as an "aggressor" and accused our State Department of lying when it said the NLF was in reality a tool of Hanoi. The Soviet Union poured resources into a propaganda offensive that very effectively persuaded much of the world that the United States was a force for evil.

This is not the occasion to renew the old Vietnam debates,[33] but a few observations are nevertheless pertinent. After the American Congress succumbed to pressure from the "peace movement" and made it unlawful to spend money on combat operations in North Vietnam, South Vietnam, Laos or Cambodia (essentially "snatching defeat from the jaws of victory" in the eyes of many experts), North

---

32   Anyone who seriously looked at the evidence could not have been fooled by either of these myths, which I disposed of readily in a book published three decades ago. *See* Robert F. Turner, *Vietnamese Communism: Its Origins and Development* 180-82, 228-29, 234 (1975). For postwar admissions by Communist Vietnam, *see*: William Duiker, "Foreword: The History of the People's Army", in *Victory in Vietnam: The Official History of the People's Army of Vietnam, 1954-1975* at xvi (2002). *See also*, Truong Nhu Tang, *A Viet Cong Memoir: An Inside Account of the Vietnam War and Its Aftermath* 240 (1986); and "How North Vietnam Won the War," *Wall Street Journal*, August 3, 1995, p. 8.

33   This is not to say that a reconsideration of the Vietnam War is not very much in order. In April 2000, on the occasion of the 25th anniversary of the fall of Saigon, our Center held a major conference reexamining many of the arguments both factual and legal that had so divided our country during the war. None of the leading legal scholars who had opposed the war were even willing to defend their old positions, and the debate that did occur demonstrated how little of the old case against the war could still be sustained. See John Norton Moore & Robert F. Turner (eds.), *The* Real *Lessons of the Vietnam War* 99-143 (2002).

Vietnam sent almost its entire Army and conquered its neighbors in a blatant act of international aggression. Sadly, the United Nations and its members did nothing. Virtually the entire world seemed delighted that the Americans had finally ceased their interference in Indochina.

In the three years that followed, the new Communist regimes in Indochina slaughtered an estimated three million human beings[34] – far more people than had died in combat during the previous fourteen years – and tens of millions of other good people were consigned to a Communist tyranny that continues to rank among the "worst of the worst" human rights violators.[35] Yet few today pay attention to developments in Indochina, and for much of the world "Vietnam" continues to bring to mind visions of wrongful American intervention.

B.   Grenada and Nicaragua

The anti-Americanism that thrived during the Vietnam War continued to surface in the years that followed. When American troops landed in Grenada in October 1983 at the request of Governor General Sir Paul Scoon,[36] it was alleged by some critics that the goal was conquest. But within three months the United States had helped organize an internationally supervised free election and withdrawn its troops. Today, the Castroites who had murdered the Prime Minister and seized control in 1983 are gone and Grenada is a free country with a multi-party, democratically elected government as free as Costa Rica.[37]

Also during the 1980s, angry Europeans and Americans alike rushed to the barricades because of President Ronald Reagan's efforts to resist Leninist aggression by the Sandinistas against Nicaragua's neighbors. I was in charge of intelligence oversight in the White House at the time and was thus privy to sensitive intelligence information that left absolutely no doubt in my mind that unlawful in-

---

34   Stéphane Courtois, "Introduction: The Crimes of Communism", *The Black Book of Communism* 1. 4 (Stéphane Courtois *et al.*, eds. 1999). For more details, *see* Jean-Louis Margolin, "Vietnam and Laos: The Impasse of War Communism", *id.* at 565-76; and Jean-Louis Margolin, "Cambodia: The Country of Disconcerting Crimes", *id.* at 577-635.

35   Freedom House, "World's Worst Regimes Unveiled," 2 April 2004, available on line at <http://www.freedomhouse.org/media/pressrel/040204.htm>.

36   Originally the fact that the intervention was at the invitation of the lawful authority in Grenada was not disclosed, because the Governor General was still very much in danger on the island when the justification was presented. Subsequently, he has publicly confirmed the fact that he requested the military intervention by the United States and Organization of Eastern Caribbean States. *See, e.g.*, the interview with his publisher in connection with publication of his autobiography, available on line at at <http://www.macmillan-caribbean.com/Aboutus/pscoonint.htm> (last visited 21 January 2005).

37   *See, e.g., Freedom House, Freedom in the World 2004: The Annual Survey of Political Rights and Civil Liberties* 231-33 (2004) (ranking Grenada a '1' in Political Rights and a '2' in Civil Liberties, putting it in a tie with Costa Rica and several other states for fifth place in all of Latin America and the Caribbean).

ternational aggression was taking place. Indeed, after reviewing some of this same material, even the President's political opponents on the House Permanent Select Committee on Intelligence unanimously acknowledged that the evidence showed "with certainty" that – working closely with Cuba – Nicaragua was engaged in a wide range of activities supporting Communist guerrillas in El Salvador and other Central American countries, providing arms, training, money, intelligence, facilities, and the like.[38]

The Leninist character of the Sandinista Front for National Liberation was hardly a great secret. It was founded in 1961 by Carlos Fonseca Amador and other radicals who resigned from the Moscow-line "Socialist Party of Nicaragua" (PSN) to pursue a more revolutionary line following the path of Fidel Castro (at a time when Moscow was instructing its parties in the region to forego "armed struggle"), and its official program called for supporting "national liberation" movements in Latin America, Africa, and Asia.[39]

It was, after all, President Jimmy Carter who, at the end of his term, ended US assistance to the Sandinista regime and began giving military assistance to El Salvador to help it resist the Nicaraguan intervention. But when President Reagan stepped up efforts to help protect El Salvador and other targets of Sandinista covert aggression, the world community largely united against America. My colleague Professor John Norton Moore noted that it was as if the world community had been struck with the AIDS virus, turning its immunity system against the defensive response to covert aggression.[40] Sadly, the International Court of Justice did not distinguish itself when called upon to pass judgment upon the issue.

In May 1984, while working for the Department of State, I accompanied a delegation of election observers sent by President Reagan to San Salvador to monitor the run-off presidential election. Following the delegation's meeting with President Alvaro Magana Borja, the outgoing Salvadorian leader confirmed in my presence that El Salvador had requested military assistance from the United States pursuant to Article 51 of the UN Charter in order to end the Nicaraguan aggression. And when Nicaragua later brought a suit against the United States before the International Court of Justice, El Salvador formally confirmed the American declaration that it was acting pursuant to a request for assistance in collective self-defense against Sandinista efforts to overthrow the government of El Salvador by force. Yet, shockingly, a majority of the World Court ignored both sworn declarations (the only relevant evidence before it on the issue from States with actual knowledge of this fact) and decided that no such request had ever been made.[41] As the most vocal opponent within the State Department at the time to the US decision to withdraw

---

38   *See*, Robert F. Turner, *Nicaragua v. United States: A Look at the Facts* 84-85 (1987).

39   *Id*. at 27-30.

40   For an excellent legal analysis of this issue, *see* John Norton Moore, *The Secret War in Central America: Sandinista Assault on World Order* (1987).

41   See Robert F. Turner, "Peace and the World Court", 20 *Vanderbilt Journal of Transnational Law* 53, 76-78 (1987).

Article 36(2) jurisdiction from the World Court,[42] I was both appalled and deeply saddened by the *Paramilitary Activities* Case, in part because I thought an injustice had been done but as well because I realized it would undermine American confidence in international judicial institutions for the future.

On May 23, 1993, an explosion in a secret underground arms depot in Managua led to the discovery of numerous similar facilities around Nicaragua and in neighboring countries containing millions of rounds of ammunition, thousands of rifles, grenades, C-4 explosives, and anti-aircraft missiles earmarked for the use of Salvadoran guerrillas of the Farabundo Marti National Liberation Front (FMLN) in violation of solemn assurances given to the United Nations by FMLN leaders. Also found following the explosion were hundreds of fake passports from twenty-one countries with stolen immigrations stamps, and documents tying the Sandinistas to international kidnapping rings and to terrorist groups like the Colombian M-19, the Italian Red Brigade, the Spanish ETA, and the PLO. These disclosures helped even some former critics of US actions realize that President Reagan's concerns about what was going on in Nicaragua had been valid. The *Washington Post* finally acknowledged following the 1993 explosion: "For most of the 1980s, the FMLN received substantial arms support from Nicaragua's Marxist-oriented Sandinista government, and the weapons caches are believed to date from that period."[43] The following month, the *Post* added in a related article: "Following the triumph of their revolution in 1979, the Sandinistas developed, with the help of Soviet bloc and Cuban advisers, the most sophisticated intelligence operation in Central America. The Sandinista Front also hosted groups from the PLO, Italian Red Brigades, ETA and Libya."[44]

For those who might argue that the Sandinista's heavy involvement with international terrorism was none of America's business, I might add that Ibraham Elgabrowny, one of the Islamic terrorists convicted for the February 26, 1993, bombing of the World Trade Center in New York, was found in possession of several fake Nicaraguan passports, birth certificates, and driver's licenses when he was arrested. For many Americans, Washington's and Jefferson's fear of "entangling alliances" must now be tempered by the reality that what happens in far off places like Sarajevo, Managua, and Afghanistan can have a serious impact upon American security.

---

42   As by far the most vocal dissenter in the interagency group that ultimately recommended that the United States withdraw its acceptance of compulsory jurisdiction under Article 36(2) of the ICJ Statute, I argued that we had a legal and moral obligation to permit the Court to hear the case and expressed confidence that we would receive a fair hearing. I noted we had recently won a unanimous case in the Court against Iran over the seizure of our diplomats as hostages. Being well acquainted with the facts of the case, I was very dismayed over the Court's ultimate decision.

43   John M. Goshko, "Salvadorans Accused of Hiding Arms; Guerrilla Cache Said to Be in Nicaragua", *Wash. Post*, 17 June 1993 at A37.

44   Douglas Farah, "Managua Blasts Expose Arms Nest, Kidnap Ring Links to NY Bomb, El Salvador Plot Explored", *Washington Post*, 14 July 1993 at A1.

C. Libya

The United States was again denounced for violating international law when on April 14, 1986, it launched air attacks against military targets in Libya. Few people outside the US government knew the details – that Muammar Khadafi had ordered his agents around the world to initiate terrorist attacks designed to "cause maximum casualties to United States citizens,"[45] and that several Libyan attacks in Lebanon, Turkey, and France had already been foiled in cooperation with those governments or had failed.[46] On April 4 a message had been intercepted from the Libyan "People's Bureau" (embassy) in East Berlin informing Tripoli that an attack against a West Berlin nightclub frequented by American soldiers would take place the following night.[47] The next night more than 230 people, including more than 50 Americans, were killed or injured by a blast at the *La Belle* discotheque in West Berlin. A few hours later, Tripoli was notified that the operation had been a great success.

I argued at the time,[48] and continue to believe, that the American air attacks against Tripoli were fully justified as necessary and proportional measures of self-defense under Article 51 of the Charter. And I believe that the subsequent reduction in Libyan terrorism – and the more recent Libyan decision to terminate its nuclear weapons development program and accept IAEA inspections[49] – were a direct consequence of military actions taken by the United States outside the purview of the UN Security Council. My strong preference remains to work through the Security Council where possible, but when a threatened veto prevents the Council from functioning we must retain the inherent right of self-defense as recognized by Article 51 of the Charter.

D. The Defense of Kuwait

Shortly after Iraq invaded Kuwait in August 1990, my colleague John Norton Moore and I published an article in the *International Herald Tribune*[50] that called, *inter alia*, for the Security Council to impose various measures on the government of Saddam Hussein. In addition to calling for reparations and international controls over Iraq's poison gas and nuclear weapons programs, we may have been the first to recommend that Saddam Hussein be tried as a war criminal.[51] After

---

45 Robert F. Turner, "International Law, the Use of Force, and Reciprocity: A Comment on Professor Higgins' Overview", *Atl. Com. Q.* 160, 165 (Summer 1987).

46 *Id.*

47 *Id.* at 166.

48 *Id.* at 165-67.

49 *See, e.g., U.S. Dep't State, Patters of Global Terrorism 2003* at 85, 91 (2004).

50 John Norton Moore & Robert F. Turner, "Apply the Rules of Law", *International Herald Tribune*, 12 September 1990 at 12.

51 "One important possibility is that the Security Council has authority under Articles 39 and 41 of the UN Charter to establish an ad hoc international tribunal to hear 'war crime' charges against Mr Hussein and his chief lieutenants." *Id.* This article was ini-

the war, in my capacity as Chairman of the American Bar Association's Standing Committee on Law and National Security, I wrote the first resolution and report ever approved by the ABA House of Delegates calling for a war crimes trial. When the idea of establishing an international criminal court was first proposed, I was most enthusiastic. But when reports came back from Rome that the negotiations were being rushed through under pressure from vocally anti-American NGOs – in what was described to me by one observer as "an anti-American feeding frenzy" – I remembered the *Paramilitary Activities* case and ultimately shared some of the reservations expressed by ICC critics. (Which is not to say that I would not still like to see the United States became a party to an international criminal court if adequate safeguards could be included to address some of the concerns that have been expressed by the American military.[52])

7.   Reagan's "Peace Through Strength" Approach

The current international atmosphere of anti-Americanism brings to mind fears expressed by some very able and intelligent European experts when President Reagan sought to impose serious verification requirements before concluding further arms control agreements with Moscow. Over the shouts of angry protesters, President Reagan persuaded NATO to deploy US Ground Launched Cruise Missiles (GLCMs) and *Pershing II* Intermediate Range Ballistic Missiles in Western Europe as an incentive to persuade the Soviets to agree to constraints on its own IRBM assets. Even prominent American experts said the demand was proof that Reagan was not serious about arms control and predicted that the unprecedented demands

---

tially submitted to the *New York Times* and was initially written within days of the invasion. When the *Times* did not publish it we submitted it to the *Tribune* around the end of August.

52   As a former American military officer who continues to work closely with military professionals in several capacities, I can assure the reader that the overwhelming majority of American men and women in uniform are outraged when they learn of incidents like the Abu Gharib Prison abuses that made front pages around the world. They understand that effective international legal prohibitions against war crimes might protect their own lives and dignity during combat and want to see all true war criminals brought to justice. The only serious opposition I hear to the ICC does not concern the prosecution of true war criminals, but rather the possibility that an "out of control" prosecutor might bring false charges against American pilots or other servicemen (or American leaders, as has often been suggested by critics of the United States with respect to former Secretary of State Henry Kissinger). What I believe to be unfounded international allegations against the United States for our sacrifices in places like Indochina and Grenada make me a bit wary as well of submitting to an international tribunal – and the World Court's handling of the Paramilitary Activities Case only strengthens my concern. Yet, had I been responsible for bringing Lt. William Calley and the others responsible for the 1968 My Lai massacre in Vietnam – which was a horrible war crime – I would have demanded the maximum possible sentence. Like most soldiers, I was outraged that they had disgraced their uniforms by such conduct.

would doom further negotiations to failure. But history shows that Reagan's strategy proved brilliant and more serious progress on meaningful arms control was made during his presidency than had been made during the previous decade.

Hundreds of thousands of protesters marched through the streets of major European cities denouncing the "war-mongering" American president; and when Ronald Reagan called the Soviet Union an "evil empire" and demanded that Mikhail Gorbachev tear down the Berlin Wall, critics on both sides of the Atlantic and throughout much of the rest of the world were outraged. But history shows again that Ronald Reagan's "peace through strength" approach ultimately worked – just as had Thomas Jefferson's nearly two centuries earlier – and because of his policies the cause of world peace was furthered and millions of human beings had at least a chance to live in human freedom.

During the early 1970s and again in the 1980s, one aspect of US foreign policy that clearly offended many intellectuals around the world was its anti-Communism. But surely, anyone who has read the *Black Book of Communism* must now realize that resisting international Communism was indeed a purpose every bit as noble as standing up to Adolf Hitler. During the twentieth century, the *Black Book* informs us, Communism in its various forms killed between eighty-five and one-hundred million human beings[53] – roughly four times the deaths attributable to Hitler[54] – and other reputable sources give even higher estimates.[55] I think most Americans are now proud of the role our country played in helping others to resist Communist aggression and ultimately bringing about the emancipation of much of the Communist world. And when we hear that our "hard line" policies have, once again, upset friends and allies around the world – while we are both concerned and saddened by that reality – we remember that many of the same critics who currently denounce George W. Bush as the enemy of peace were also outraged over the policies of President Reagan.

8.   Fears of "Unchecked Power" and American "Preemption"

As I listen to some of America's critics today, I sense that there are really several factors at work in the growing spirit of anti-Americanism around the globe. Few people seem genuinely upset that Saddam Hussein has been removed from power or that the people of Iraq have at least some chance of organizing a democratic government and having a future of peace and freedom. Rather, the concern is, first of all, that America has this vast "unchecked" power that might well be used to undermine the interests of others; and, more specifically, that the Bush Administration has asserted this new "preemption" doctrine claiming a right to use military force unilaterally virtually at will.

It is obviously true that, in military terms, the United States currently has a great deal of power – power that for the foreseeable future is not likely to be

---

53   *Black Book of Communism, supra* note 34 at x.

54   *Id.* at 15.

55   *See especially*, R. J. Rummel, *Death by Government* 10 (1994).

matched by any other country. Part of the explanation, of course, is that many of America's friends found it convenient to rely upon the United States to defend them during the Cold War, and for that purpose we found it necessary to invest vast sums of our money while other countries were expending their own resources to improve their economies or address more immediate needs of their people. Many Americans would have much preferred to have seen more burden sharing during the Cold War, even if that produced a much stronger military capability in Europe, Canada, and among our other friends and allies around the world. We don't tend to fret much about the fact that France and Great Britain have nuclear weapons capable of attacking New York and Washington, DC, because we are persuaded that democracies have powerful incentives to live in peace and we view these countries as our friends.

The most thoughtful Americans of my acquaintance don't believe that wars "just happen" or that they are caused by the mere existence of weapons or imbalances in power.[56] The United States certainly has a much more powerful military capability than Canada, yet the two countries have lived in peace with an unguarded boarder for close to two centuries; and, presumably, few Canadians go to sleep at night worrying about the dangers of an American military invasion.

The reality is there is not a vast sum of "unchecked" power in America. It may well be true that our military potential is currently superior to that of any other country. But those who draw the conclusion from that reality that America is a major threat to world peace fail to understand either the American political system or the character of the American people. If an American president or Secretary of Defense decided it was in the nation's self-interest to invade a foreign country to seize land, steal oil or other valuable resources, or for any other illegitimate reason, the Security Council would not need to respond because the American people would quickly bring the enterprise to an end.

If an example is needed to illustrate this reality (beyond the example of America's behavior during the years immediately following World War II when it had a monopoly on atomic weapons), consider Vietnam. I have argued – and after decades of studying and teaching about the war I very firmly believe – that Vietnam was as noble and honorable a war as any in which the United States has ever been involved. Our goal was to prevent Communist North Vietnam from conquering its neighbor to the south by armed force – just as in World War II we attempted to protect other victims of armed international aggression. But Hanoi and its allies succeeded through a brilliant political warfare (propaganda) campaign in persuading a lot of people that the United States' motive was evil – that we were propping up dictators and standing in the way of self-determination and human rights. And as a result, angry citizens persuaded Congress to deny funding to prosecute the war. And the same thing will happen anytime an American president forgets that the American people have never had a stomach for conquest and retain the ultimate sovereign authority in a democracy. American presidents know that there are

---

56   For a superb discussion of some of the finest American thinking about the causes of war, *see* John Norton Moore, *Solving the War Puzzle* (2004).

numerous institutions – not the least of which are the Congress and the news media – that are watching their behavior and that have the power to rally the American people in the event of an egregious abuse of power.

That still leaves us with the problem of "preemption." And the first thing we must do is understand that it is a very narrow doctrine that potentially involves terrorist groups and a very small number of "rogue States." These countries have a history of involvement with international terrorism and are, or have been, engaged in unlawful efforts to acquire Weapons of Mass Destruction. As announced in the 2002 *National Security Strategy of the United States*, the new doctrine provides: "We must be prepared to stop rogue states and their terrorist clients before they are able to threaten or use weapons of mass destruction against the United States and our allies and friends."[57] This is a narrow doctrine that does not threaten Canada, France, Russia, or any other country that is not actively involved in promoting international terrorism and seeking illegally to acquire Weapons of Mass Destruction.

The concept of preemptive attack (often termed "anticipatory self-defense") is hardly a new one, and despite its potential for abuse (like the power of self-defense itself[58]) has been embraced by scholars for centuries.[59] Two hundred and fifty years ago, the great Swiss international lawyer Emerich de Vattel wrote:

> [T]here is no question but that if that formidable prince is clearly entertaining designs of oppression and conquest ... [o]ther Nations have a right to check him .... [This right of nations] is still more evident against a sovereign who is always ready to take up arms without cause and without plausible pretext, and who is thus a constant disturber of the public peace.[60]

In 1837, upon learning that anti-British American nationals were outfitting a steamer named the *Caroline* to be used to transport volunteers and supplies to support an insurrection in Canada, British agents crossed the Niagara River into US territory and burned the vessel before it had legally violated their rights. American citizens on board the *Caroline* were killed in the struggle. The United States protested to Great Britain, and during the diplomatic exchanges Secretary of State Daniel Webster enunciated a standard for anticipatory self-defense that met with widespread acceptance. Webster argued there must be "a necessity of self-defence, instant, overwhelming, leaving no choice of means and no moment for delibera-

---

57   The White House, *National Security Strategy of the United States*, Part V, available on line at <http://www.whitehouse.gov/nsc/nss.html>.

58   Keep in mind that when Hitler invaded Poland in 1939 and Kim Il Song invaded South Korea in 1950 they portrayed their actions as "self-defense" responses to attacks on their own territory.

59   *See, e.g.*, George K. Walker, "Anticipatory Collective Self-Defense in the Charter Era", 31 *Cornell International Law Journal* 321, 322 (1998).

60   Emerich de Vattel, 3 *The Law of Nations* 252 (James Brown Scott, ed., Charles G. Fenwick, trans., William S. Hein & Co., 1995) (1758).

tion," and the defensive action must involve "nothing unreasonable or excessive, since the act justified by the necessity of self-defence must be limited to that necessity and kept clearly within it."[61]

This has been a useful rule, and Webster's declaration helped make customary international law just as the UN Charter contributed to the conventional law governing the use of armed force more than a century later. But lawmaking is an evolutionary process in which the scales of justice must from time to time be rebalanced to address new realities. It made great sense in the early twentieth century to set a very high bar before any country claiming a right to preemptively attack a neighbor in the name of self-defense, because the costs of waiting until the first tank crossed the border was usually minimal. And requiring States to wait until aggression had actually begun deprived aggressors of the legal cover that they "had to attack first" in order to protect themselves.

But the advent of Weapons of Mass Destruction greatly alters the equation. Even without using WMD, *al Qaeda* has repeatedly demonstrated that coordinated attacks in several countries or against multiple targets that are hundreds of miles apart can produce devastating results. Particularly when we are dealing with a "repeat offender" who has already demonstrated a propensity for unprovoked aggression and a willingness to use WMD – and has time and again been branded a "threat to the peace" by the Security Council – we must ask whether it is *reasonable* to tell potential victims they must sit idly by and permit him yet another "free kick" that may involve multiple WMD attacks that could endanger tens of thousands, hundreds of thousands, or conceivably even *millions* of lives? Keep in mind that the United States waited patiently for more than a decade trying to work through the Security Council while Saddam Hussein ignored more than a dozen legally binding directives to comply with his legal obligations.

This is not a new issue. In 1962, President John F. Kennedy threatened to use armed force to prevent Soviet ballistic missiles believed to be armed with nuclear warheads from being delivered to Cuba. As Kennedy explained in his October 22, 1962, address to the American people: "We no longer live in a world where only the actual firing of weapons represents a sufficient challenge to a nation's security to constitute maximum peril," adding that "any substantial increased possibility of their use" constituted a "threat to the peace." That, I submit, is the same reasoning that led the Bush Administration to speak of acting "preemptively" in "self-defense" against terrorists and the rogue States that support them.[62]

One might add that an underlying goal of announcing the possibility of preemptive action if rogue States continued supporting terrorism and developing WMD was obviously *deterrence*. As Sun Tzu observed 2,500 years ago, the "acme of skill" is not to win one hundred victories in one hundred battles, but to subdue the enemy "without fighting."[63] And at its core, the UN Charter is similarly based

---

61   *See, e.g.*, J. L. Brierly, *The Law of Nations* 405-06 (6th ed. 1963).

62   *See* Robert Turner, "What's So New About Pre-Emption?", *Washington Times*, 29 November 2003 at A 2.

63   Sun Tzu, *The Art of War* 77 (Samuel B. Griffith trans., 1963).

upon the goal of deterrence and the doctrine of preemption. Members pledge not just to maintain the peace by *responding* to acts of aggression or breaches of the peace, but also "to take effective collective measures for the *prevention* and *removal* of *threats* to the peace ...."[64]

9.   Operation Iraqi Freedom

Few American foreign policy initiatives have been more strongly criticized around the world by those who were once viewed as among America's strongest allies than "Operation Iraqi Freedom," and history may well ultimately show that it was a terrible mistake. But it must be considered in context. Saddam Hussein had already committed flagrant and massive acts of international aggression against Iran and Kuwait that had cost an estimated one million human lives, and he had committed lesser acts of aggression against Saudi Arabia, Israel, and the United States. He had not only unlawfully procured Weapons of Mass Destruction, he had actually used them to slaughter his neighbors and his own people – something that not even Adolf Hitler did. When the United States and its coalition partners entered Iraq to remove Saddam Hussein from power and promote a democratic election, it was in the context of more than a decade of futile efforts by the world community to compel his regime to abide by its legal obligations, during which the Security Council passed more than a dozen resolutions declaring his regime to be a "threat to the peace." The first "purpose" set forth in the Charter was to act collectively to "remove" threats to the peace, but the Security Council ultimately proved unwilling to do more than pass new resolutions demanding that Iraq comply with earlier resolutions – emulating the worst traditions of the League of Nations.

Did the United States have clear evidence that Saddam was planning an imminent attack against the United States that would satisfy the *Caroline* test? Certainly not. Russian President Vladimir Putin has confirmed publicly that President Bush was repeatedly warned prior to the war that Russian intelligence had confirmed that Saddam Hussein was planning terrorist attacks both within the United States and against American targets abroad,[65] and there was a broad consensus among intelligence services that Saddam was continuing his quest for new Weapons of Mass Destruction.[66] General Tommy Franks, Commander of US Central Command, has noted that in January 2003 King Abdullah of Jordan personally told him Jordanian intelligence had determined that Saddam had biological and chemical weapons

---

64   UN Charter, Art. 1(1) (emphasis added). ("The Purposes of the United Nations are: 1. To maintain international peace and security, and to that end: to take effective collective measures for the prevention and removal of threats to the peace, and for the suppression of acts of aggression or other breaches of the peace ....")

65   "Putin claims Bush was personally informed", *Pravda*, 18 June 2004, 16:30 hrs, available on line at <http://english.pravda.ru/main/18/88/350/13132_Putin.html> (last checked 26 January 2005).

66   *See, e.g.*, Robert F. Turner, "Operation Iraqi Freedom: Legal and Policy Considerations", 27 *Harvard Journal of Law and Public Policy* 781-91 (2004).

and that Egyptian President Hosni Mubarak provided a similar account.[67] But there was no evidence that a specific attack on a date certain against a particular target was planned – and little reason to believe that had such an attack been planned the United States would have been able to learn about it in advance.

I believe we must ask whether the *Caroline* test makes any sense in the twenty-first century when dealing with a repeat offender who had been identified by the Security Council as a "threat to the peace," who is honestly believed by most of the world to possess illegal WMDs and to be developing still others, and who had repeatedly demonstrated a willingness to use them? The prospects for penetrating Saddam's brutal dictatorship to gain the kind of reliable intelligence that would disclose details of a specific planned attack were minimal, as anyone even suspected of disloyalty was routinely executed. If Saddam had possessed WMD stockpiles that could be shared with *al Qaeda* or other terrorist groups or covertly delivered by Iraqi agents themselves – perhaps simultaneous anthrax, smallpox, or plague dispersals in Washington, New York, Los Angeles, London and Tokyo, putting at risk the lives of millions of innocent people – how could the scales of justice be balanced to justify a legal rule that this established "threat to the peace" was entitled to yet another "free kick" and that his potential victims had no right to protect themselves?

I would add that I believe a strong case can be made that Operation Iraqi Freedom was also justified by the doctrine of humanitarian intervention.[68] What many of the critics of Operation Iraqi Freedom seem to ignore is the reality of what was going on inside Iraq while the Security Council continued to make insincere threats of decisive enforcement action. Despite reports by Amnesty International and the United Nations on the humanitarian crisis in Saddam's Iraq, few critics of the US intervention seem aware that *hundreds of thousands* of innocent small children paid with their lives, through starvation and disease, as Saddam withheld humanitarian supplies in an effort to blackmail the Security Council into lifting

---

67   *Id.* at 785.

68   *See* Robert F. Turner, "Was Operation Iraqi Freedom Legal?", in Laurie Mylroie, *Bush Vs. The Beltway* 164 (2003). While there is a great deal of disagreement among international lawyers about the legitimacy of "humanitarian intervention," in my view if international law protects an Adolf Hitler so he may slaughter millions of Jews, gypsies, or other "undesirables," or a Stalin so he can slaughter "class enemies" with impunity, then international law has become part of the problem and is not worthy of our support. Obviously, external intervention can only be justified in extreme cases and ought ideally to be conducted through the Security Council or (in the event Security Council action is blocked by a veto) through other international organizations (such as the NATO intervention in Kosovo). But the case for intervention in Iraq was a compelling one in my view even absent the concern about WMD and a decade of violating Security Council resolutions. (One might add that when the Security Council acts under Chapter VII and demands compliance from a "threat to the peace" and then ignores a dozen years of refusal to comply, it undermines the entire Charter system and signals tyrants around the world that the United Nations is not to be taken seriously.)

its sanctions.[69] An honorable option of continuing to do nothing but pass more resolutions demanding compliance and issuing further toothless ultimatums – undermining the credibility of the Security Council around the world as more and more children perished and their parents were raped and tortured – simply did not exist. As I saw it at the time, the viable options were either to enforce the Charter by removing the "threat to the peace" or to terminate the sanctions and accept the reality that international law was no more effective in saving succeeding generations "from the scourge of war"[70] in the twenty-first century than it had been in the 1930s.

10. Conclusions

As I noted in the beginning, it is not my goal to persuade readers that the United States made the right decision by intervening in places like Vietnam, Grenada, Central America, or Iraq, or when it terminated the ABM Treaty and refused to sign or ratify a variety of important new treaties. Americans themselves are very much divided on all of these issues, and none of us has a monopoly on the truth. My goal, instead, is to try to help people of good will understand some of the thinking – and some of the historic national traditions – that contributed to each of these decisions. In none of these cases was the United States trying to seize territory, acquire colonies, or enrich itself from another nation's natural resources. Each of the interventions I have discussed – and I might add as well several more recent instances where American forces went into harm's way to protect the lives and rights of Muslims in places like Kuwait, Somalia, and the Former Yugoslavia – a key purpose was to try to uphold the rule of law and deter further wrongful uses of armed force.

America and its people are far – very far – from perfect, and as we condemn the past colonialism of European powers we at the same time recall our own legacy of slavery and abusive treatment of those who lived here when the first whites arrived from Europe. Any American who travels widely around the globe must

---

69   *See, e.g.,* Amnesty International, "IRAQ: Systematic torture of political prisoners", 15 August 2001, at 2, available on line at <http://web.amnesty.org/library/Index/engMD E140082001?OpenDocument&of=COUNTRIES%5CIRAQ?OpenDocument&of=CO UNTRIES%5CIRAQ>; and UN Commission on Human Rights, *Situation of Human Rights in Iraq*, Gen. Assembly Doc. A/54/466, 14 October 1999 at 5. This report notes that an August 1999 report by the United Nations Children's Fund (UNICEF) concluded that Saddam Hussein's refusal to cooperate with the UN in the oil-for-food program resulted in "serious and prolonged suffering" by "millions of innocent people," and reported "children under five are dying at more than twice the rate they were ten years ago ...." *Id.* para. 31. *See also, id.* paras. 26-28. *See also,* Human Rights Watch, *Report on Iraq for 1999*, available on line at <http://www.unhchr.ch/Huridocda/Huridoca. nsf/TestFrame/a7cebod6cd8b23bd80256820005404cf?Opendocument>.

70   UN Charter, Preamble ("We the people of the United Nations determined to save succeeding generations from the scourge of war ... have resolved to combine our efforts to accomplish these aims ....").

recognize the relative brevity of our own history as a nation and our cultural in-debtedness to civilizations that existed for thousands of years before we became a nation and from which we have drawn ideas and, more importantly, people who have helped make us what we are today.

The motto on America's Great Seal is *e pluribus unum* – "out of many, one" – referring to the joining together of thirteen separate colonies into one new na-tion. But in another sense it also captures the demographic character of America, whose people trace their roots around the globe to every region and probably ev-ery country. Some of our ancestors came here centuries ago fleeing tyranny and searching for human freedom. Others have arrived within this millennium. When they obtain their citizenship, they become every bit as much an "American" as those of us who had the good fortune of being born here.

The idea of American "exceptionalism" may trace back to Thomas Jefferson's vision of a just and enlightened America standing as a beacon of freedom for all the world to emulate. Of many examples, consider this comment from an 1816 letter Jefferson wrote to his good friend John Adams:

> We are destined to be a barrier against the return of ignorance and barbarism. Old Europe will have to lean on our shoulders, and to hobble along by our side, under the monkish trammels of priests and kings, as she can. What a colossus shall we be when the southern continent comes up to our mark! What a stand will it secure as a ralliance for the reason and freedom of the globe.[71]

Five years later, in another letter to Adams, the seventy-eight-year-old former Pres-ident wrote even more eloquently:

> And even should the cloud of barbarism and despotism again obscure the science and liberties of Europe, this country remains to preserve and restore light and liberty to them. In short, the flames kindled on the 4th of July, 1776, have spread over too much of the globe to be extinguished by the feeble engines of despotism; on the contrary, they will consume these engines and all who work them ....[72]

Many Americans hope that vision proves true, and that the blessings of liberty Jefferson and his contemporaries bequeathed to America will one day be shared by men, women, and children around the globe. If we sometimes act like we feel "special," it is from a sense of feeling more *fortunate* rather than a belief that we are somehow superior to others. Many Americans, I suspect, would not know the League of Nations or the Kellogg-Briand Treaty from the *Magna Carta* – recalling all of them, perhaps, as terms mentioned at one point during high school history classes. But there are others of us who do know about that part of our history, and

---

71   "Jefferson to Adams", 1 August 1816, in 15 *Writings of Thomas Jefferson* 56, 58-59 (Mem. ed. 1903).

72   *Id*. at 333, 334.

who regret that our own country did not play a more active role in helping the world guard against the scourge of war seven decades ago.

Since the days of Thomas Jefferson it has been our strong desire to live in peace and friendship with all nations where possible. And after 150 years of blissful isolation, during which our ocean boundaries protected us from much of the world's strife, the painful lessons of World War II taught us that we have certain duties to our neighbors and others in the world that, if neglected, may jeopardize our own lives and freedom. We also learned from the twentieth century that *wanting* to live in peace is not enough, and that ignoring threats to the peace in far off places like Sarajevo, Baghdad, and Afghanistan cannot be done without a serious risk of peril.

Americans watched in frustration for more than a decade following the successful conclusion of the 1991 Gulf War as the Security Council seemed to emulate the League of Nations, passing resolution after resolution declaring Saddam Hussein's Iraq to be a "threat to the peace" and demanding immediate compliance with the law. And from our perspective, the world should be criticizing the leaders of France and Russia – who after voting to give Iraq a "final opportunity" to comply with its legal obligations, announced they would veto any effective "collective measures" to remove what they had time and again recognized to be a "threat to the peace." And the subsequent revelations that Saddam Hussein was secretly diverting money from the Oil for Food Program to reward French, Russian, UN, and other officials and their close associates[73] left us all the more confused about the growing anti-American climate around the globe.

After bearing most of the costs paid by the international community in places like Korea and Indochina during the Cold War and taking the lead in upholding the principles of the Charter as the Cold War came to an end and Iraq invaded Kuwait, we hoped that the Security Council would finally fulfill the critically important role envisioned for it when the Charter was negotiated sixty years ago and international law would finally achieve its potential as a force for world peace. The dream remains, and it might some day be realized. But, in the meantime – especially in an era of WMD and international terrorism – many Americans remain wary of any interpretation of international law that might leave our national security subject to the whims of the leaders of France, Russia, China, or any other foreign country.

---

73   *See, e.g.*, Scott Shane, "The Issue of War: Corruption; Report Says Iraq Misused U.N. Oil Plan", *New York Times*, 7 October 2004 at A28; William Safire, "U.N. Obstructs Justice", *id.*, 15 November 2004 at A21; and Judith Miller, "The Oil-For-Food Program: Panel Pegs Illicit Iraq Earnings at $21.3 billion", *id.*, 16 November 2004 at A13.

4. International Democratic Constitutionalism*

Brun-Otto Bryde

1. International Law in a Globalised World Society

In the age of globalisation, international law has to meet unprecedented challenges. Historians may point out that the phenomenon we call globalisation today started in the 15th century.[1] But such glances into history should not make us overlook that in today's world society human beings everywhere are dependent on economic and social processes everywhere in a way unknown to earlier periods.[2] Today, not a single major social problem can be solved within the boundaries of the nation state.[3]

The internationalised economy has to a large extent evaded the regulatory power of the nation state. Security is endangered by international terrorism and international organised crime. Neither water nor air takes notice of borders so that the fight for an ecologically sustainable future (if not already lost as a result of the sabotage of even modest programs like the Kyoto-protocol by powerful, but short-sighted interests) can only be an international one. In the education of our children, parents and national curricula have to compete with limited success against global media monopolies. The picture of the global village[4] often used for this situation is much too idyllic: we are not living in a global village but a global megalopolis of the sort that we know from the third world: with a few upper class districts, heavily guarded but by no means secure, some middle class areas and a lot of slums and no-go areas.

---

* During preparation of this chapter I received comments, assistance and support from Alexander Hanebeck, Astrid Wallrabenstein, Joerg Mohr, Johannes Bryde and Sibylle Duennes.

1 Wallerstein (1974); Kurth, *IESBS* 6248 *et seq.*; de Sousa Santos, *IESBS* 6277, at 6278; O'Brien, *IESBS* 6237 at 6239: "nothing particular new".

2 Early and seminal Niklas Luhmann's concept of a 'Weltgesellschaft' (Luhmann, 1971).

3 Held *et al.* (1999).

4 Mac Luhan (1968).

Ronald St. John Macdonald & Douglas M. Johnston (eds.), Towards World Constitutionalism, *pp. 103-125.*
© *2005 Koninklijke Brill NV. Printed in The Netherlands. ISBN 90 04 14612 1.*

The process of globalisation has far reaching consequences for international law. We need much more international law because all these problems can only be addressed on an international level, and at the same time international law becomes more demanding.

Traditional international law was primitive and modest. It did not expect much from a law-abiding actor. A legal system that allows war and does not restrict the behaviour of states in their *domaine réservé* is easy to comply with. For this reason, classical international law did not need differentiated structures of lawmaking and law enforcement. Today, the international legal system cannot content itself with regulating the coexistence of a small number of actors (50 states when the UN was founded) in restricted fields of action. Instead, it has to provide for a vast and complex mass of rules for all areas of life. Such a legal system has to develop an adequate level of internal differentiation. This is the most basic fact at the heart of the constitutionalisation of international law. The more demanding international law becomes, the greater are the demands on the capabilities of its lawmaking and law enforcement structures. But in addition, the question of legitimacy arises: When important decisions (for many people the most important ones) are made outside of the boundaries of their home state (for Argentineans by the IMF) the demand for the legitimacy of international law is increased. International systems of government have to be controlled under the rule of law and the interests of those who are affected by their decisions have to be represented: we need a democratic constitutionalist world order.

2.   International Constitutionalism and Its Critics

That international law undergoes a process of constitutionalisation is widely recognised,[5] but this observation also draws criticism.

Some critics attempt to reserve the concept of constitution to the nation-state.[6] Regularly, their understanding of a (national) constitution is very value loaded and based on an idealised picture of a constitution. The creation of a constitution is linked to exceptional conditions, a specific constitutional moment or revolution. A constitution is expected to fulfil formal (a consolidated document) and substantive (the constitution as the assertion of the identity of a nation) requirements before a legal order can be called a constitution. This idealised version of a constitution is then compared with a realist picture of the imperfect international legal order. This way the foregone conclusion that a constitution is not possible beyond the nation state is easily reached. While both idealism and realism are legitimate approaches

---

5   Tomuschat (1993), 209-240; Simma (1994), 217-384; Dupuy (1997), 1-33; Tomuschat (1997), 37 *et seq.*; Fassbender (1998), 529-619; Macdonald (1999), 205-231; Frowein (2000), 427 *et seq.*; Uerpmann (2001), 565-573; Petersmann (2002), 291-313; Cottier/ Hertig (2003), 261-328; Bryde (2003), 61 *et seq.*; Fischer-Lescano (2003), 717 *et seq.*; Habermas (2004), 113 *et seq.*; Peters (2004).

6   Rubenfeld (2003), 28 *et seq*; Grimm (1995), 282 *et seq.*; Haltern (2003), 511-556.

to our problem, comparing a realistically drawn international situation with an idealised national one is not.

Such a narrow concept of constitution is not even supported by comparative
constitutional law in view of the abundant variety of different constitutional systems.[7] Constitutions can be laid down in an unorganised mass of different sources,
they may be technocratic reform projects or octrois of colonial powers or occupation forces. Often they are rather weak compromises than self-confident assertions
of the national will, and yet they have been adopted by the people as a foundation
for a constitutionalist system.[8]

If we turn to international law, such a critique from the perspective of national
constitutional law misses the point because the position of international constitutionalists is much more modest than the critics assume.

Especially if we adopt a weak reading of international constitutionalism, the
existence of a "constitution" in international law is hardly debatable. In this reading international constitutionalism means not more than that a differentiated legal
system needs a differentiated structure. It must comprise not only a sum of substantive legal norms but also basic (constitutional) principles and secondary rules[9]
about norm-creation, norm-application and adjudication. By identifying such rules
and principles one can descriptively construct a constitution of the international
legal order. In this sense, the claim that the international legal order has a constitution is not very exiting: every developed legal order has a constitution in this sense.
Speaking of a "constitution" of the international order has therefore a long and
legitimate tradition.[10]

It would be somewhat dishonest, however, if I based my defence of international constitutionalism only on such a week reading of international constitutionalism because my own concept is not that modest. Together with most international constitutionalists I neither search for the constitution of a world state nor try
to introduce the complete tradition of western constitutionalism to international
law: The international community has no "constitution" in the "emphatic"[11] sense of

---

7   Peters (2001), 93 *et seq.*

8   The popularity of a purely national concept of constitutionalism in Germany is espe-
     cially astonishing given the creation of the Basic Law in 1949. It was not even consid-
     ered a constitution in the proper sense at that time but only a basis for the provisional
     organisation of part of occupied Germany; it was drafted under the tutelary oversight
     of the occupation powers and with little popular input. Yet it became the most legiti-
     mate and accepted constitution Germany ever had. Post-war Germany is therefore an
     excellent example for the proposition that a constitution is not a historical document
     but a process, a plebiscite *de tous les jours*, and constitutionalism is possible on the
     basis of a constitution that has none of the assumed prerequisites of an ideal-typical
     constitution.

9   In the sense of Hart (1997).

10   Seminal Verdross (1926); Mosler (1980); Tomuschat (1993), 209, at 216 *et seq.*; Simma
     (1994), 217, at 259 *et seq.*; good English resumé Fassbender (1998), 529, at 541.

11   Peters (2004).

Art. 16 of the French Declaration of Human Rights.[12] But the case of international constitutionalism I am going to argue does indeed draw on the normative idea of constitutionalism. The ratio of constitutionalism is the restriction of the lawmaker's omnipotence. The lawmaker is bound to general principles of higher law. In international law the place of lawmaker is taken by the states and international organisations. A constitutionalist concept of international law tries to bind these actors not only to procedural rules about lawmaking and adjudication but also to substantive constitutional principles, especially the rule of law and human rights.

The challenge of this programme can be seen when we compare it with Westphalian international law.

Classical international law organised a well-ordered anarchy. International law was created by sovereign states through treaties or common practice. It was a horizontal legal system which knew no common interest beyond the sum of interests of individual states, no hierarchy of norms, no higher authority than the states themselves. With the help of international law the states regulated their international affairs, but the regulation of their own affairs ("domaine réservé") knew no restrictions. This horizontal concept of international law was formulated forcefully at the twilight of the old order in the Lotus-decision of the Permanent Court of International Justice.[13]

The contrasting model of a constitutionalist system of international law, on the other hand, is not horizontal but verticalised. It recognises a source of legitimacy that is higher than the individual states, a hierarchy of norms in which ordinary legal rules have to be reviewed against constitutional principles, and it employs constitutionalist methods of interpretation.

This constitutionalist model of international law does not have to be defended against those who reserve constitutionalism to the nation-state. But it has to be defended against a possible argument that this model is merely wishful thinking that does not adequately reflect the present state of international law.

The process of constitutionalisation of international law is indeed neither complete nor systematic. But it has started and made greater progress than often assumed, even if there is still a long way to go.

On the normative and conceptual level a set of basic changes even have found general acceptance (sub3). Other changes are more controversial but can be shown to be logical consequences of these developments (sub 4). On the institutional level the onstitutionalization of international law is developing much more slowly (sub 5).The biggest problem where we will be discussing policy rather than *lex lata* to a certain extent is the question how the legitimacy of this new order can be institutionalized (sub 6).

---

12   See Article 16: "Any society in which no provision is made for guaranteeing rights or for the separation of powers, has no Constitution."; cf. Peters (2004); Tomuschat (1993), 209, at 232 *et seq.*

13   Lotus, PCIJ, series A, No. 9, 18: "The rules of law binding upon states ... emanate from their own free will as expressed in conventions or by usages generally accepted as expressing principles of law."

3. Consensual Basis of Constitutionalisation

A. *Common Interests of Mankind*

The core of a constitutionalised international law is the general acceptance of a common interest of mankind that transcends the sum of individual state interests.[14] This acceptance has materialised in very different areas of international law.

An important step in this process was the recognition of goods that are legally protected not in the interest of individual states but in the interest of mankind as a whole. After tentative beginnings in Antarctica[15] and the treaty about space and celestial bodies,[16] the most advanced discussion of this concept was undertaken during the Law of Seas conference with the result of the designation of the high sea and ocean floor as common heritage of mankind.[17]

Similarly, in the development of an international law of environmental protection it became soon apparent that the problem could not be solved on the basis of classical rules about transboundary delicts. The destruction of the environment and its dramatic consequences require a concept of international law in which the interests of the states are subordinated to the interest of mankind as a whole.[18]

Even more relevant for our subject is the development of international human rights law. Human rights do not fit into the classical model of international law as a horizontal system of mutual obligations: they do not create a system of rights and duties between states but duties of the states towards human beings, duties derived from common values and the interests of mankind as a whole.[19] Protection of human rights in international law, therefore, has meaning only if we recognize it as a system of obligations of states owed to an authority different from the states themselves.

The recognition of common interests of mankind is of fundamental importance. The challenges facing mankind cannot be solved by balancing the interests between individual states. Solutions can only be found if common interests of mankind are recognised as paramount and all actors of international law are obliged to pursue a global policy program.

---

14   Simma (1994), 217, at 229 *et seq.*

15   The Antarctic Treaty 1959, UNTS Vol. 402 p. 71.

16   Treaty on Principles Governing the Activities of States in the Exploration and Use of Outer Space, including the Moon and other Celestial Bodies 1967, UNTS Vol. 610 p. 205.

17   Preamble to the Law of the Sea Convention 1982, UNTS Vol. 1833 p. 3; seminal Pardo (1968), 2166 *et seq.*; see also Macdonald (1995), 153 *et seq.*; Wolfrum (1992), 692 *et seq.*; Simma (1994), 217, at 240 *et seq.*

18   Simma (1994), 217, at 238 *et seq.*; Bryde (1997 a), 75 *et seq.*

19   ICJ, Case concerning the Barcelona Traction, Light and Power Company, ICJ Reports (1970), p. 3, para. 32; Advisory Opinion concerning the Reservations to the Convention on the Prevention and Punishment of the Crime of Genocide, ICJ Reports (1951), p. 23: "In such a convention the contracting States do not have any interest of their own; they merely have, one and all, a common interest."; Bryde (1994 a), 165-190, Engl. summary at 189 *et seq.*

Such a program is outlined in the UN Charter: peace in an international order defined by social justice and human rights. This program has been concretized especially in the human rights treaties. The three sets of human rights contained in the universal human rights convenants – liberties, social rights and non-discrimination principles – define a demanding picture of a humane international society. The demand for international social justice is not merely a political aim of the critics of globalisation but the result of a thorough interpretation of human rights treaties that are binding under international law.[20]

Because the foundation for the constitution of the international community including human rights and social justice has been laid in the UN Charter one can argue that the charter itself should be seen as the constitution of the international community.[21] While the constitutionalisation of international law goes beyond the text of the charter,[22] the charter can indeed be used as the basic document informing and organising the process of constitutionalisation.

B.   *Verticalisation of International Law*

Another important – though not necessary – feature of a constitutionalised system, a hierarchy of norms, has also been achieved. International law is no longer governed by a positivist concept of the omnipotence of the lawmaking states. In creating law, states are bound by constitutional principles. The existence of *jus cogens* from which states cannot depart even if they agree has been generally recognized.[23] This is not only true for treaty law because of the explicit provision in Art. 53 Vienna Convention on the Law of Treaties, but also for customary law.[24] Thereby, the "higher law" concept of constitutionalism has been transferred to international law.

International *jus cogens* comprises not only the basic principles of international relations, especially the "sovereign" equality of states and the prohibition of the use of force,[25] but in addition the core of human rights.[26]

With the recognition of *jus cogens* constitutionalisation of international law ceases to be a vague idea of idealist scholars and their wishful thinking but has become an accepted feature of positive international law.[27]

---

20   Bryde (1989), 73-83.

21   Fassbender (1998), 529 *et seq.*; Verdross/Simma (1984), 69 *et seq.*

22   Tomuschat (1993), 209, at 219; Petersmann (2002), 291-313 *et seq.*; Peters (2004).

23   Kadelbach (1992); Hannikainen (1988); Fischer-Lescano (2003), 717, at 743 *et seq.* with further references.

24   ICTY, Case IT-95-17/1-T, *Prosecutor v. Furundzija*, 38 ILM (1999), 317, para. 153; ECHR, *Al-Adsani v. Great Britain*, judgment of 21 November 2001, 23 *HRLJ* (2002), 39, sep. op. Rozakis et al., para. 3.

25   ICJ, Case concerning the military and paramilitary activities in and against Nicaragua (Nicaragua v. USA), ICJ Reports (1986), para. 112, at 114.

26   Kadelbach (1992), 284 *et seq.*; Sieghart (1988), 64 *et seq.*; Hannikainen (1988), 425 *et seq.*

27   Fischer-Lescano (2003), 717 *et seq.*; Peters (2004).

4.   Consequences

A.   *Constitutional Methodology*

An important consequence of the constitutionalisation of international law is the change in methodology.[28] Such a change can already be observed and it is also necessary.

Methodologically, the point of reference for classical international law has been private contract law. The commanding inspiration for interpretation is the parties' intent. In an international law in which state sovereignty is paramount this methodology is important in order to avoid creating obligations of the states' without their consent.[29] With a changed structure of international law in which the interest of mankind is paramount and in which lawmaking is subjected to constitutional principles, the methodology, too, can be and must be constitutionalised.

Interpretation of international law must be directed towards the attainment of the constitutional principles. These constitutional principles are much more open textured and therefore much more adaptable to new circumstances and to a reception of normative arguments, especially the results of a human rights discourse. This way international legal development can be made more dynamic and responsive. At the same time, such a new methodology is not without dangers. The balancing of principles typical for constitutional law can also be used for ideological agendas. This problem will have to be solved by the creation of adequate institutions.

B.   *Mankind as the Source of Legitimacy of International Law*

With the recognition of obligations of states towards human beings and of common interests of mankind a conception of international law as a horizontal system of mutual obligations between states has to be abandoned. The states are no longer the sovereign authority in the international legal system, neither alone nor together. If we substitute the international community[30] for the states as ultimate authority, this is a huge advance but still falls short of international law's new quality if we take it to mean a community of states. The international community is no longer restricted to states[31] and state interests are no longer paramount.

There is no sovereign in international law. The central role of human rights in this legal system as well as the recognition of an ever expanding concept of "Heritage of Mankind" point to the nature of international law's new source of

---

28   Alvarez (2001), 104-154; Ress, in Simma (ed.), *The Charter of the United Nations*, 2002, "Interpretation"; Fassbender (1998), 529, at 595 *et seq.*

29   Arangio-Ruiz (1997), 1, at 26.

30   Mosler (1980); Tomuschat (1993), 209 *et seq.*; Simma (1994), 217 *et seq.*; Paulus (2001), 225 *et seq.*

31   Schreuer (1993), 447, at 453 *et seq.*

legitimacy: not the ensemble of states but mankind. International law has to derive from the people.[32]

5.   Institutional Constitutionalisation

While the constitutionalisation of international law has made huge advances on the normative and conceptual level, its institutional arrangements are still in need of a readjustment to the new international law.

A.   *Costs of (Incomplete) Constitutionalisation*

Binding international lawmaking to constitutional principles has its price. Despite the scepticism among non-internationalists about the efficacy of international law, classical international law was very effective, but this claim holds true only because international law was so undemanding as a result of the close connection between international law and actual state practice. A law that allows war obviously is broken less often than a law that forbids the use of force; and no state complies all the time with all of the obligations that arise under human rights law.

In addition, a constitutionalist interpretation has to resolve conflicts between constitutional principles and is therefore potentially much more divisive than the interpretation of an international law in which the historical intent of the states is controlling the interpretation. The constitutional balancing between different sets of principles can easily be abused, the employment of human rights argumentation for unilateral military intervention being the most obvious case in point.

International law that has been constitutionalised on the conceptual level, therefore, can no longer rely on its implementation through the interests of state actors and must overcome a decentralised interpretation. The recognition of the common interests of mankind as paramount requires fora where these interests are defined. Compliance of the political actors with open textured constitutional principles asks for institutions and procedures which define, expound and enforce such principles.

The underpinning of normative constitutionalisation with adequate institutions has begun but is far from complete. International law has advanced on the normative level faster than its institutions can follow. But ironically, criticism of this development[33] is less realist than it claims to be. While international law has failed to fully adjust its institutional arrangements to its normative principles, a regressive adjustment of its principles to its institutional capacities is no longer possible. International society would not accept an international law not bound by these principles.

---

32   Allott (1990), 254 *et seq.*; Dupuy (1997), 1-33; Bryde (2003), 61 *et seq.*; Kunig (2003), 327 *et seq.*

33   Weil (1983), 413 *et seq.*

B. *International Governance*

International law since the Second World War has not only restructured its normative order but also created new institutions. The most remarkable development is
the rise of international organisations, especially the United Nations. Despite the
textbooks' continuing insistence on a hierarchy between states as original subjects
of international law and international organisations as merely partial subjects, in
today's international law international organisations are central actors. This is especially true for the UN system and regional organisations. International organisations have become the main fora for international law making. Even though in
these fora state representatives are negotiating, the quality of the process is deeply
affected by its international setting. In this respect, too, the traditional concept of
an international law centred on states and their sovereignty has to be abandoned.
The international community is no longer an ordered anarchy, but it is a community with a high level of organisation.[34]

In the sociology of international law an important aspect of international organisations is the creation of support structures for community interests. International civil servants and office-holders join international organisations as representatives of national interests, but regularly, sooner rather than later, they develop a
competing identification with the organisation's mandate.

In addition, organised international society provides a framework for law-
making, adjudication and law enforcement that is much more effective than the
mechanisms of classical international law (though by no means adequate for the
challenges that lie ahead).

The potential of international organisation is exemplified by the development
of the European Union. Here we find an organisation of states with democratic
law-making structures, the acceptance of the precedence of community law in all
member states, interpretation and application of this law by an independent international court, mechanisms to enforce compliance in the member states. In Europe
it is common to draw a sharp line between supra-national European law and international law,[35] and from a jurisprudential perspective this is perfectly sensible. But
in a global international law perspective the importance of the European Union
lies in its role as a model: it shows that independent nation states can organise
themselves in a transnational organisation based on the rule of law, democracy and
social justice for the people in all member states. Such an organisation will not be
possible on a global level for some years to come, but other regions might profit
from the European example.

---

34   Simma (1994), 217, at 256 *et seq.*: "Institutionalization of the International Commu-
     nity".

35   Following the seminal decisions of the ECJ, Judgement of the Court of 5 February
     1963,van Gend en Loos/Netherlands Inland Revenue Administration, Case 26-62, ECJ
     Reports 1963, 1; Judgement of the Court of 15 July 1964, Costa/ENEL, Case 6-64, ECJ
     Reports 1964, 585; cf. Oppermann (1999), 73 *et seq.*

Not only regional organisation but also functionally specialized international organisations (WTO, WHO, regimes for international seas and rivers) have developed highly effective legislative, judicial and administrative instruments that constitute a considerable improvement compared to classical international law.[36] They are no longer adequately conceptualised as treaty-systems: they are international systems of government.

Highlighting such progress does not mean that the institutional arrangements necessary for international law in a globalised world society are already in place. The capacity of international organisations is distributed very unevenly. Organisations of rich countries are more capable than those of poor countries, and organisations that serve powerful economic interests like WTO or IMF have more advanced mechanisms of control than those with a social or ecological agenda. Such differences in the constitutionalisation of different policy areas are therefore in danger of increasing the imbalance of power in the international community rather than decreasing it.

The institutional effectiveness of a normatively constitutionalised international law will have to prove itself especially in the fields where its principles are most in conflict with state interests: human rights and the prohibition of the use of force.

C.   *Constitutional Protection of Human Rights*

In the international protection of human rights the greatest progress has been achieved on the regional level. The regional human rights courts, most notably the European Court of Human Rights, are the most advanced examples of a constitutionalised international law. Regional systems have a constitutional order including a bill of rights and a constitutional court to protect them.

But the global structures for the protection of human rights should not be underestimated (as they often are). The committees created to monitor the compliance with the UN human rights treaties[37] play an important role in the constitutionalisation process. While their instruments to enforce human rights are modest, their methodology is clearly constitutionalist. They take the treaties, ratified by the states often more for propaganda reasons than with a real commitment to their content, by their word and expound their meaning far beyond what the drafters imagined them to contain.[38] In a continuing discussion process with the states they have managed to achieve substantial progress in the guarantee of human rights world wide. For this purpose they have created their own specific instruments which appear to be very well adapted to their tasks. Whether at the present state of the international community a world human rights court would be preferable[39] is highly debatable. The more flexible combination of monitoring, expressing concern

---

36   Simma (1994), 217, at 322 *et seq.*
37   Klein (1998); Bayefsky (2000); Alston/Crawford (2000).
38   Cf. for CERD Banton (1996), 140 *et seq.*
39   Buergenthal (2000), 299 *et seq.*

and advising undertaken by the committees has its own functionality. An international court would have to show much more restraint in pursuing international protection of human rights.

Under present conditions, however, the limitations of international human rights law become apparent when states stubbornly refuse to honour their obligations. The international community can monitor breaches, it can criticise and even apply sanctions, but only in extreme circumstances it can enforce human rights against the will of a regime that flouts them.

D.   *The Constitutionalisation of the Use of Force*

The international legal regime for the use of force is both the most constitutionally advanced in theory and the most defective in practice.

If we wrote a history of the constitutionalisation of international law since the Second World War, the prohibition of force in the UN Charter could mark the beginning of the story.[40] At least in theory, the charter's system of collective security with the power of the Security Council to enforce peace with military means, if necessary, against aggressive states was the decisive break with state sovereignty and the first "supra-national" element of international law. It has suffered, however, from a structural deficit. Quite realistically the charter assumes that peace can only be enforced with the help of the major powers, not against them, and therefore they were awarded veto powers in the Security Council. This means that the Security Council cannot enforce the prohibition of force against them. During the cold war this meant that not only these veto powers but also its allies and clients (and in the bipolar world of the time this comprised more or less all states with the exception of some outlaws – Rhodesia,[41] South Africa[42]) were immune against sanctions by the Security Council. Therefore, there have been repeated breaches of the prohibition of force by the states thus privileged during the last 50 years. In this respect, the Iraq War is – unfortunately – nothing new. International law remains weak in its most central place. After the end of the cold war, prospects for a consensual use of the mechanisms of collective security appeared to be possible.[43] But the system could not stop the USA and its allies from starting war in Iraq in clear breach of international law. The positive news was that Security Council and international community were strong enough to withstand the enormous pressure of the super power and refuse to give legitimacy to an illegitimate use of force. Resistance against the breach of international law has grown stronger, international public opinion is more robust in condemning such breaches than was the case in the cold war era when the aggressor could be certain of the support of half of the world. The political costs of unilateralism have grown and it can only be hoped that

---

40   Frowein (2000), 427, at 432 *et seq.*

41   SC Res. 217, Nov. 20, 1965; 221, Apr. 9, 1966.

42   SC Res. 418, Nov. 4, 1977.

43   Frowein (1998), 97 *et seq.*

this will be recognised in the US, too. Still, the open defiance of countries on whom the support of a growing recognition of an international rule of law very much depends has seriously affected the future of international law.[44]

Despite this central weakness, the UN system of collective security remains a central corner stone of a constitutionalised international law. The ineffectiveness of chapter VII due to the use of veto power has given rise to a constitutionalist interpretation of the UN peace keeping system to meet new challenges. The most prominent examples are the peace keeping instruments under chapter "6 ½".[45] The Security Council has used its competence to secure peace to create ad hoc courts for war crimes and crimes against humanity[46] and thereby opened a new chapter of the enforcement of international law. The substitution of these ad hoc courts by the new International Criminal Court is an even more important innovation – despite the exaggerated opposition of the US against it. Another important new instrument is the administrative system the UN has created to handle the consequences in the aftermath of war and civil war.[47]

Another result of a constitutionalist interpretation is the understanding of the concept "threat to peace" by the Security Council to extend to massive human rights' violations, especially genocide.[48] Thereby international law is in theory equipped to deal with such extreme cases.

Inefficiency of the system of collective security during the Cold War and frustration about the fact that even the most urgent actions where hindered by the use of the permanent members' veto power have given rise to a lot of attempts to weaken the absolute prohibition of Art. 2 IV to justify the use of force without a UN mandate.[49] None of these attempts, with the possible exception of a humanitarian intervention in the case of stopping imminent genocide, is convincing, none has found the general acceptance necessary for the creation of customary law. Quite the opposite, international consensus that exceptional use of force for humanitarian purposes needs a UN mandate to be lawful and may never be unilateral has been confirmed in the world wide condemnation of the USA's unilateral action in Iraq. The results of this war, which was not only illegal but counterproductive in every

---

44   Fassbender (1998), 529 *et seq.*

45   Bothe, in Simma (ed.), *The Charter of the United Nations*, 2002, MN 83-92, "Peace-keeping".

46   SC Res. 827, May 25, 1993 on the International Tribunal for the former Yugoslavia; Res. 955, Nov. 8, 1994 on the International Tribunal for Rwanda.

47   Successfully in East-Timor on the basis of SC Res. 1264, Sep. 15, 1999 and SC Res. 1272, Oct. 25, 1999; at least avoiding a complete catastrophe in Kosovo on the basis of SC Res. 1244, June 10, 1999.

48   SC Res. 794, Dec. 3, 1992, on Somalia; Res. 929, June 22, 1994, on Rwanda; Res. 1078, Nov. 9, 1996 on Zaire; later on reaffirmed by the SC for human rights law in the situation of armed conflicts, see Res. 1296, Apr. 19, 2000 and Res. 1214, Aug. 11, 2000.

49   See the references in Randelzhofer, in Simma (ed.), *The Charter of the United Nations*, 2002, Article 2 (4) MN 49-60.

possible perspective (especially that of fighting terrorism[50]), should have taught the correctness of this position also to the USA and its coalition of the willing.

6.   Legitimacy

The more comprehensive the regulatory reach of international law and the more effective its implementation structures become, the more the question of legitimacy arises.[51] International governance needs control under the rule of law and it must be democratic.

A.   The Control of International Governance

In the past, the main object of international constitutionalism has been to bind states to the constitutional principles of the international community. From this point of view, international organisations and bureaucracies are perceived as support structures for international law, and therefore the internationalist has a natural tendency to welcome every increase of the capacities of international organisations and organs.

That has to change with the increasing ability of international systems of governance of effective decision-making. Constitutionalism requires that they, too, are bound to the constitutional principles. The international system of justice (with the exception of the European Union) is not too well prepared for this task. The International Court of Justice, for instance, can only deliver advisory opinions for UN organs, not binding decisions.[52]

Even in exercising this function the Court is much more concerned with strengthening international decision-making than controlling it.[53] Therefore, judicial review of *ultra vires* acts in the UN system is not guaranteed. In light of the increase of binding decisions of the Security Council, this state of the law appears no longer acceptable.[54]

Equally unsatisfactory is the state of the law concerning the binding force of human rights for international organisations. In international law, human rights

---

50   According to conservative estimates the war has swelled the ranks of Al-Quida from 2000 to 18000.

51   See contributions in Coicaud/Heiskanen (2001).

52   UN Charter, Art. 96.

53   ICJ, Certain Expenses of the United Nations (1961-1962), ICJ Reports, 1962, p. 157, at 168; Case on the Legal Consequences for States of the Continued Presence of South Africa in Namibia (South West Africa) notwithstanding Security Council Resolution 276 (1970) (1970-1971), ICJ Reports, 1971, pp. 16, at 45; The Lockerbie Decision (Case Concerning Questions of Interpretation and Application of the 1971 Montreal Convention Arising from the Aerial Incident at Lockerbie, *Libya v. UK*, ICJ Reports, 1992, p. 3) might signal a change: Dugard (2001), 83 *et seq.*

54   Dugard (2001), 83 *et seq.*; see Fitzmaurice dissenting in the Namibia Case, ICJ Reports, 1971, p. 440.

are protected by treaties which sociologically are bills of rights of the international community,[55] but legally these treaties are binding for most but not all states. International organisations are no parties to these treaties. Because of the overlapping but not completely identical membership it is difficult to construe their binding nature for international organisations. It is, however, of crucial importance to guarantee that international organisations are bound by human rights. UN sanctions,[56] decisions of the WTO,[57] or decisions of IMF or World Bank[58] must comply with international human rights standards. This is obvious for those human rights that form part of customary international law and even more for those rules that are *jus cogens* and have *erga omnes* application. For the UN family Art. 55 can be used as an additional argument.[59] But this falls short of an application of the ensemble of human rights treaties which should also be possible. The doctrinal legal framework for such a binding force has been developed by the European Court of Justice. It recognized that an international organisation that has the power to directly affect the lives of the citizens in the member countries has to be bound by human rights. As the treaties establishing the European Communities did not contain a bill of rights, the court developed them from the common heritage of human rights in the constitutional systems of the member states.[60] With a comparable argument, it should be possible to hold international organisations to the human rights standards that the vast majority of their members have subscribed to and that have been formulated and are controlled in their organisational framework.[61]

B.   International Democracy

i.   The Democratic Imperative

The search for transnational democracy faces doctrinal and semantic problems. In English, "people" is both a singular and a plural so that when we speak of "government by the people" we are not in danger to lose sight of the manyness of the people, of human beings. In the oldest constitutional text containing a formulation of the basic democratic principle that power derives from the people, the Virginia Declaration of Rights of 1776, we read:

---

55   Kälin (1993), 9 *et seq.*, Eng. summary at 47 *et seq.*; Bryde (1994 a), 165 *et seq.*

56   Clapham (2001)131 *et seq*; Bossuyt, E/CN.4/Sub.2/2000/33; Frowein (2003), 121, at 126 *et seq.*

57   Petersmann (2002), 291, at 307 *et seq.*

58   Suchsland-Maser (1999), 127 *et seq.*

59   Bossuyt, E/CN.4/Sub.2/2000/33.

60   ECJ, Judgement of the Court of 17 December 1970, Internationale Handelsgesellschaft/ Einfuhr- und Vorratsstelle, Case 11-70, ECJ Reports 1970, 1125, at 1135; Judgement of the Court of 14 May 1974, Nold/Kommission, Case 4-73, ECJ Reports 1974, 491, at 507 et seq.; Judgement of the Court of 13 December 1979, Hauer/Land Rheinland-Pfalz, Case 44-79, ECJ Reports 1979, 3727.

61   Petersmann (2002), 291, at 304 *et seq.*

That all power is vested in, and consequently derived from, the people; that magistrates are their trustees and servants and at all times amenable to them." Such an understanding of people as a plural is more than a peculiarity of the English Language. For Hannah Arendt it is the essence of the American republic: "(The people) never became a singular to the founders. The word "people" retained for them the meaning of manyness, of the endless variety of a multitude whose majesty resided in its very plurality.[62]

In many languages the semantics (or socio-linguistics) are rather different. "*Peuple*", "*popolo*", "*Volk*" are widely, though not necessarily, perceived in the sense of "a people", a collective above human beings.[63] From this arises an understanding of the sentence "the power derives form the people", which binds democracy to the existence of a concrete people, a demos. This theory, which has been criticised as the no-demos thesis[64] or "container"-theory, excludes democracy categorically beyond the nation state.[65]

A more radical version of this theory excludes any lawful possibility to ever transcend the nation-state. Where national constitutional law locates the ultimate source of power in "the people", this is translated as meaning sovereignty of the concrete nation (*Deutsches Volk, le peuple française*). In this reading no higher earthly authority is ever possible. All powers below or above have to be derived from this concrete people. Classical international law, which knows no higher power than the state-components of the international legal order, is compatible with this view; constitutionalised international law and supra-national government is not.

A softer version would link democracy to "a" people endowed with the same attributes that define "the people" in the national constitutional doctrine but accept, at least in theory, the possibility that such "a" people might one future day materialize on the regional level (e.g. in Europe) but never on a world level.

The contrasting approach by those who see democracy not based on a collective but rather on human beings has no problems with transnational democracy. Democracy is a form of governance based on self-determination of equals.[66] All those affected by a decision should take part in decision-making. When under the conditions of globalisation human beings are affected by decisions of international government systems, their interests should be represented in these systems.[67]

---

62   Arendt (1963), 1990, p. 93: But Americans are not immune against national conceptions of constitutionalism; Rubenfeld (2003), 28 *et seq.*

63   See references in Bryde (1997 b), 251 *et seq.*

64   Weiler (1996), 91 *et seq.*

65   On the view of the nation-state as "container" of democracy cf. (critically) Marks (2001), 47 *et seq.*; for a critique Bryde (1994 b), 305 *et seq.* with further references.

66   Bryde (2003), 61 *et seq.*; with further references Dahl (1990), 49; Held (1995), 141 *et seq.*; Marks (2001), 47 *et seq.*; von Bogdandy (2003), 853 *et seq.*; Volkmann (2002), 575 *et seq.*

67   Dahl (1989), 83 *et seq.*; Held (1995), 141 *et seq.*; Tully (1995); Bryde (1994 b), 305 *et seq.*, at 321; Häberle (2004), 317 *et seq.*; von Bogdandy (2003), 853 *et seq.*

Without enfranchising the people in the process of international law making the new construction of its normative foundations that centres on the common interests of mankind remains theoretical. The obligation of states towards a common interest is difficult to enforce against parochial interests as long as state governments monopolise international decision-making.

This is even more so because interests tend to be translated into "national" interests as soon as there is a border between the different interests (as e.g. in transborder pollution[68]). The same interests would be regarded as mere particular interests to be weighed against competing particular interests (economic interests of emitting industry against health and economic of those affected by pollution) within nation states.

A transnational democratic organisation is therefore necessary to organise and to give voice to transnational common interests.

ii.   International Civil Society

An important first step is the creation of an international democratic civil society. This has begun.

The tragedy of the Iraq-war is remarkable in this respect. Pessimists will notice only that the millions demonstrating around the globe could not prevent the war. Optimists will notice that these millions demonstrated – perhaps for the first time in history – for the international rule of law. In the past, anti-war demonstrations have been influenced either by partisanship for one side (on anti-Vietnam demonstrations in Europe you could hear chants for Ho-Tschi-Min, there have been none for Saddam Hussein), by the threat of the draft, or by pacifism. This time the outrage was directed against the blatant breach of international law. International law is acquiring support in the international civil society.

The Anti-Globalisation protests, too, have an international law agenda,[69] much more than comparable protest movements in the past.

Central actors of the international civil society are NGOs.[70] Especially in the international protection of human rights and in the fight against poverty and for the environment they have played an increasingly important role.

International organisations have recognized this role of NGOs by awarding them a formal observer position in international negotiating processes following the UN Charter's far-sighted provisions in Art. 71.[71] This is important as it gives voice to the international civil society. It is perhaps even more important because NGOs provide support for the less well endowed international concerns; UNEP could hardly function without the support of the NGOs in the environmental field;[72] the UN human rights committees would be helpless in their monitoring

---

68   Bryde (1997 a), 75 *et seq.*

69   Kahn (2001), 323 *et seq.*

70   Weiss et al. (1996); Willetts (1996); Peters (2004); Kahn (2001), 323, at 336 *et seq.*

71   Lagoni/Chaitidou, in Simma (ed.), *The Charter of the United Nations*, 2002, Art. 71 MN 19 *et seq.*

72   Bryde (1997 a), 75 *et seq.*

role without the assistance of human rights organisations. The reporting system has become effective only after the bilateral relation between reporting state and committee has been transformed into a triangular discourse in which the civil society has assumed a major role.[73]

Because legal development in international law is to a large extent an ongoing process in which legally not binding but influential documents (soft law) play an important role, the distinction between governmental law making and NGOS in a mere advisory role is much more flexible than in states. So NGOs help to create world pluralism and a global civil society.

iii.   Transnational Democratic Institutions

The next step should be transnational elected bodies participating in international law-making. Obviously this is extremely difficult to envisage for the time being. Many members of the international community are no democracies, and the election of international assemblies by peoples that are not allowed to elect their national parliaments is – while not impossible[74] – not a realistic perspective. To democratise itself the international community has to help its members to develop democracy. After the end of the cold war, the notion that democratic rights are a natural component of international human rights law has gained wide acceptance.[75] While a right for military unilateral pro-democratic intervention[76] has not found wider acceptance and the attempt to bomb people into democracy is counterproductive anyhow, working for an international human rights system, whose open and pluralist program for social organisation in its consequence leads to political democracy, is a legitimate concern of the international community.

It would be wrong, however, to see the aim of international democratisation only in creating national democracies. The aim has to be the democratic representation of transnational interests. National democracy cannot thrive in a sea of international non-democracy.[77] Democratisation of international society cannot wait until the last member of the international community has developed a functioning democracy. Membership in a community ruled by democratic principles can help to support and to safeguard national democratic reforms.

That transnational democracy is possible not only in theory but also in practice is again shown by the example of the European Union. Within Europe there are many discussions about the deficiencies of the European parliament, but in a global perspective it has to be recognized as a breakthrough for transnational democracy.[78]

---

73   Banton (1996), 140 *et seq.*; Bryde (2002), 61 *et seq.*; contributions by Clapham, Miller, Grant, Thomson, Dandan in Bayefsky (2000).

74   In Imperial Germany under the Constitution of 1871 the Federal Parliament was elected democratically (universal male suffrage) while the electoral systems in many member states were clearly undemocratic.

75   Fox (2000), 48 *et seq.*

76   Reismann (1984), 642.

77   Marks (2001), 47, at 51.

78   Held (1995); Bryde (2003), 61 *et seq.*

On such a regional level international democratization has to start. The management of international natural resources could certainly be improved if decision making in organisations responsible for an international river or (semi-)enclosed seas was not restricted to conferences of state parties and secretariats but included parliamentary assemblies in which the interests of those inhabiting the banks and shores were represented.[79] The subject asks for and allows innovative thinking.

7.   The Internationalisation of Constitutional Law

The constitutionalisation of international law is no one-way street. While constitutionalist concepts and methods borrowed form constitutional law discourse have helped to change international law, at the same time international law has influenced national constitutions,[80] especially human rights. By encouraging the reception of international human rights law, international law has transformed national constitutional law and helped to create a world wide human rights discourse, which in turn has aided the constitutionalisation of international law.

This development started after World War II with the creation of the major instruments of international human rights law, the European Convention of Human Rights of 1950 and the international covenants of 1966.

In drafting bills of rights after these dates, especially in the worldwide process of reform and democratisation in the 1980s and 90s, international human rights treaties provided the main source of inspiration. In Europe the new democracies tried to avoid any possible conflict between their new constitutional law and European human rights law by integrating the Strasbourg law and jurisprudence into their own constitutional texts. On other continents the UN treaties were of major importance.[81]

International human rights law influences national constitutional law not only by serving as a textual model. In constitutional systems without a bill of rights the international treaties are sometimes treated as constitutional law to fill this gap in the legal order. An obvious example is Austria, where the constitutional protection of human rights is guaranteed through the ECHR. But we find examples for the incorporation of international human rights law on all continents. In Tanzania, e.g., the courts gave legal force to the invocation of the international human rights treaties in the constitution, which in the view of the drafters probably was mere rhetoric.[82]

Another way in which international human rights law influences national law is the interpretation of national law in conformity with international law. This method is especially popular in Common Law jurisdictions where conferences of high judges approved the Bangalore principles to this effect.[83] This way of incorpo-

---

79   Bryde (1997 a), 75, at 82 *et seq.*

80   Peters (2004).

81   Kabudi (1995), 25 *et seq.*; Dugard (1995), 193 *et seq.*; Bryde (2001), 203, at 212 *et seq.*

82   Kabudi (1995), 33, 94 *et seq.*

83   Kabudi (1995), 28 *et seq.*

ration by interpretation has now been put into written law in the British Human Rights Act.[84]

In this family of constitutions whose constitutional law has been influenced by the reception of international human rights law the interpretation of constitutional law is internationalised. Legal doctrine and courts borrow freely from other countries. It is not unusual to cite case law from international courts or from other jurisdictions.

International human rights law influences national law not only as a model but also because national courts have to take the possibility into account that international courts will declare their judgments unlawful if they deviate from international human rights standards. Especially for the highest tribunals it is an unfamiliar situation no longer to be the highest authority.

This fact has influenced the development of constitutional control in countries without a tradition of judicial review. Obviously, the incorporation of the ECHR in Britain through the human rights act was heavily influenced by the wish to stop those cases from reaching Strasbourg. Also in Scandinavia we find the strengthening of constitutional control through the courts to be a result of a dialogue with international courts.[85]

This international process of receiving international human rights law has in return influenced international law. In many countries constitutional texts that are identical or very similar to the international texts are now the law of the land. That helps to strengthen international law because this way a body of case law and interpretative scholarship is created that could never have arisen on the international level alone. And national courts have become support structures for the enforcement of international human rights law that in many countries are more efficient than international tribunals.[86]

Thus, constitutionalisation of international law and internationalisation of national constitutional laws work together to create a world constitutionalist law based on human rights and the rule of law.

---

84   Lord Irvine of Lairg (1998), 221, 232 *et seq.*

85   Mors (2002), 98 *et seq.*

86   Lamer (2000), 305 *et seq.*

Bibliography

Allott, Philip, *Eunomia*, Oxford: Oxford University Press, 1990.

Alston, Philip/Crawford, James (eds.), *The Future of UN Human Rights Treaty Monitoring*, Cambridge: Cambridge University Press, 2000.

Alvarez, Jose E., "Constitutional interpretation in international organizations", in: Jean-Marc Coicaud/Veijo Heiskanen (eds.), *The legitimacy of international organizations*, United Nations University Press, 2001, pp. 104-154.

Arangio-Ruiz, Gaetano, "The 'Federal Analogy' and UN Charter Interpretation: A Crucial Issue", 8 *European Journal of International Law* (1997), pp. 1-28.

Arendt, Hannah, *On Revolution (1963)*, New York: Viking Press, 1990.

Banton, Michael, *International Action against Racial Discrimination*, Oxford 1996.

Bayefsky, Anne F. (ed.), *The Human Rights Treaty System in the 21st Century*, The Hague: Kluwer Law International, 2000.

Bossuyt, Marc, "The Adverse Consequences of Economic Sanctions on the Enjoyment of Human Rights", The Bossuyt Report of 21 June 2000, Economic and Social Council, E/CN.4/Sub.2/2000/33.

Bryde, Brun-Otto, "Menschenrechte und Entwicklung", in Ekkehart Stein/Heiko Faber (eds.), *Auf einem dritten Weg (Festschrift für Helmut Ridder zum siebzigsten Geburtstag)*, Neuwied 1989, pp. 73-83.

Bryde, Brun-Otto, "Verpflichtungen Erga Omnes aus Menschenrechten", 33 *Berichte der Deutschen Gesellschaft für Völkerrecht* (1994 a), p. 165-190, engl. summary at 189 *et seq.*

Bryde, Brun-Otto, "Die bundesrepublikanische Volksdemokratie als Irrweg der Demokratietheorie", *Staatswissenschaften und Staatspraxis* (1994 b), pp. 305 *et seq.*

Bryde, Brun-Otto, "Grenzüberschreitende Umweltverantwortung und ökologische Leistungsfähigkeit der Demokratie", in Klaus Lange (ed.), *Gesamtverantwortung statt Verantwortungsparzellierung im Umweltrecht*, Baden-Baden (1997 a), pp. 75 *et seq.*

Bryde, Brun-Otto, "Le Peuple Européen and the European People", in Andreas Auer/ Jean-François Flauss (eds.), *Le Referendum Européen*, Bruylant Bruxelles (1997 b), pp. 251-274.

Bryde, Brun-Otto, "Der Verfassungsstaat in Afrika", in Martin Morlok (ed.) *Die Welt des Verfassungsstaates (Kolloquium zum 65. Geburtstag von P. Häberle)*, Baden-Baden 2001, pp. 203 *et seq.*

Bryde, Brun-Otto, "Die Tätigkeit des Ausschusses gegen jede Form der Rassendiskriminierung (CERD)", in Eckart Klein, *Rassische Diskriminierung – Erscheinungformen und Bekämpfungsmöglichkeiten*, Berlin 2002, pp. 61 *et seq.*

Bryde, Brun-Otto, "Konstitutionalisierung des Völkerrechts und Internationalisierung des Verfassungsrechts", 42 *Der Staat 2003*, pp. 61-76.

Buergenthal, Thomas, "A Court and Two Consolidated Treaty Bodies", in Bayefsky (ed.), *The Human Rights Treaty System in the 21st Century*, The Hague: Kluwer Law International, 2000, pp.299 *et seq.*

Clapham, Andrew, "Sanctions and Economic, Social and Cultural Rights" in Vera Gowlland-Debbas (ed.), *United Nations Sanctions and International Law*, The Hague: Kluwer International Law 2001.

Cottier, Thomas/Hertig, Maya, "The Prospects of 21st Century Constitutionalism", 7 *Max Planck UNYB* (2003) 261-328.

Dahl, Robert A., *Democracy and its critics*, New Haven, Yale University Press 1989.

Dahl, Robert A., *After the Revolution*, New Haven, Yale University Press 1990.

de Sousa Santos, Boaventura, "Globalization: Legal Aspects", *IESBS* 2001, 6277 *et seq.*

Dugard, John, "International Human Rights", in: Dawid van Wyk/John Dugard/Bertus de Villiers/Dennis Davis, *Rights and Constitutionalism: the New South African Legal Order*, Oxford: Clarendon Press 1995.

Dugard, John., "Judicial Review of Sanctions", in Vera Gowlland-Debbas (ed.), *United Nations Sanctions and International Law*, The Hague: Kluwer International Law 2001, pp. 83-91.

Dupuy, Pierre-Marie, "The Constitutional Dimension of the Charter of the United Nations Revisited", 1 *Max Planck UNYB* (1997) 1-33.

Fassbender, Bardo, "The United Nations Charter as Constitution of the International Community," Vol. 36 *Columbia Journal of Transnational Law* (1998) 529-619.

Fischer-Lescano, Andreas, "Die Emergenz der Globalverfassung", 63 *Zeitschrift für ausländisches öffentliches Recht und Völkerrecht* (2003), pp. 717 *et seq.*

Fox, Gregory H., "The right to political participation in international law", in Gregory H. Fox/Brad R. Roth (ed.), *Democratic Governance in International Law*, Cambridge: Cambridge University Press 2000.

Frowein, Jochen A., "Unilateral Interpretation of Security Council Resolutions – a Threat to Collective Security?", in Volkmar Götz/ Peter Selmer/Rüdiger Wolfrum (eds.), *Liber amicorum Günter Jaenicke – Zum 85. Geburtstag*, Berlin: Springer 1998, pp. 97-112.

Frowein, Jochen A., "Konstitutionalisierung des Völkerrechts", in *Völkerrecht und internationales Privatrecht in einem sich globalisierenden internationalen System*, 40 *Berichte der deutschen Gesellschaft für Völkerrecht*, Heidelberg 2000, pp. 427-447.

Frowein, Jochen A., "Issues of Legitimacy around the United Nations Security Council", in: Jochen A. Frowein/Klaus Scharioth/Ingo Winkelmann/Rüdiger Wolfrum, *Verhandeln für den Frieden – Negotiating for peace, Liber Amicorum Tono Eitel*, Berlin: Springer, 2003., pp. 121-139.

Grimm, Dieter, "Does Europe need a Constitution?", 1 *European Law Journal* (1995) 282 *et seq.*

Habermas, Jürgen, "Der gespaltene Westen", Frankfurt am Main 2004.

Häberle, Peter "Die Menschenwürde als Grundlage der staatlichen Gemeinschaft", in: Josef Isensee/Paul Kirchhof (eds.), *Handbuch des Staatsrechts II*, 3rd ed. Heidelberg 2004, pp. 317 *et seq.*

Haltern, Ulrich, "Internationales Verfassungsrecht", 128 *Archiv des öffentlichen Rechts* (2003) 511-556.

Hannikainen, Lauri, *Peremtory Norms (Jus Cogens) in International Law*, Helsinki 1988.

Hart, Herbert L.A., *The concept of law*, Oxford: Clarendon Press 1997.

Held, David, *Democracy and the Global Order*, Cambridge: Polity Press 1995.

Held, David et.al., *Global Transformations*, Cambridge: Polity Press 1999.

Kabudi, Palamagamba J., "Human Rights Jurisprudence in East Africa", 15 *Verfassungsrecht in Übersee, Beihefte* (1995), Baden-Baden, pp. 25 *et seq.*

Kadelbach, Stefan, *Zwingendes Völkerrecht*, Berlin 1992.

Kahn, Ramatullah, "The Anti-Globalization Protests: Side-show of Global Governance or Lawmaking on the Streets?", 61 *Zeitschrift für ausländisches öffentliches Recht und Völkerrecht* (2001), pp. 323 *et seq.*

Kälin, Walter, "Menschenrechtsverträge als Gewährleistung einer objektiven Ordnung", 33 *Berichte der Deutschen Gesellschaft für Völkerrecht* (1994), pp. 9-48, eng. summary at 47 *et seq.*

Klein, Eckart (ed.), *The Monitoring System of Human Rights Treaty Obligations*, Berlin 1998.

Kunig, Philip, "Das Völkerrecht als Recht der Weltbevölkerung", 41 *Archiv des öffentlichen Rechts (2003)*, pp. 327-335.

Kurth, James, "Globalization: Political Aspects", *IESBS* 2001, 6284 *et seq.*

Lamer, Antonio, "Enforcing International Human Rights Law: The treaty System in the 21st Century" ,in Bayefsky, Anne F. (ed.), *The Human Rights Treaty System in the 21ˢᵗ Century*, The Hague: Kluwer Law International, 2000. pp. 305 *et seq.*

Lord Irvine of Lairg, "The Development of Human Rights in Britain under an Incorporated Convention on Human Rights", *Public Law 1998*, pp. 221 *et seq.*

Luhmann, Niklas, "Die Weltgesellschaft", 57, *Archiv für Rechts- und Sozialphilosophie* (1971), pp. 1 *et seq.*

Mac Luhan, Marshall, *War and Peace in the Global Village*, New York: Bentam Books 1968.

Macdonald, R.St. J., "The Common Heritage of Mankind", in Ulrich Beyerlin (ed.), *Recht zwischen Umbruch und Bewahrung: Völkerrecht, Europarecht, Staatsrecht, Festschrift für Rudolf Bernhardt*, Berlin 1995, pp. 153 *et seq.*

Macdonald, Ronald, "The Charter of the United Nations in Constitutional Perspective", 20 *The Australian Yearbook of International Law* (1999) 205-231.

Marks, Susan, "Democracy and international Gouvernance", in Jean-Marc. Coicaud/Veijo Heiskanen (eds.), *The legitimacy of international organizations*, United Nations University Press 2001, pp. 47-68.

Mors, Wolff-Michael, *Verfassungsgerichtsbarkeit in Dänemark*, Baden-Baden 2002.

Mosler, Hermann, *The International Society as a Legal community*, Alphen aan den Rijn/ Germantown, Sijthoff & Noordhoff 1980.

O'Brien, Patrick K., "Global History", *IESBS* 2001, 6237 *et seq.*

Oppermann, Thomas, *Europarecht*, 2nd ed., München 1999.

Pardo, Arvid, "Whose is the Bed of the Sea?", 62 *American Society of International Law Proceedings* (1968) 2166 *et seq.*

Paulus, Andreas L., *Die internationale Gemeinschaft im Völkerrecht*, München 2001.

Peters, Anne, "Elemente einer Theorie der Verfassung Europas", Berlin 2001.

Peters, Anne, "Global Constitutionalism Revisited", 5 *European Journal of International Law* (2004) forthcoming.

Petersmann, Ernst-Ulrich, "Constitutionalism, International Law and 'We the Poeples of the United Nations'" in Hans-Joachim Cremer/Thomas Giegerich/Dagmar Richter/ Andreas Zimmermann (eds.), *Tradition und Weltoffenheit des Rechts (Festschrift für Helmut Steinberger)*, Berlin: Springer 2002, pp. 291-313.

Reismann, W. Michael, "Coercion and Self-Determination: Construing Charter Art. 2(4)", 78 *American Journal of International Law* (1984), pp. 642 *et seq.*

Rubenfeld, Jed, "The Two World Orders", 27 *The Wilson Quarterly* (2003) 28 *et seq.*

Scholler, Heinrich "Die neue äthiopische Verfassung und der Schutz der Menschenrechte", 30 *Verfassungsrecht in Übersee* (1997) pp. 166-181.

Schreuer, Christoph, "The Waning of the Souvereign State: Towards a New Paradigm for International Law?", 4 *European Journal of International Law* (1993) 447-471.

Sieghart, Paul, *The lawful Rights of Mankind*, Kehl am Rhein 1988.

Simma, Bruno, "From Bilaterism to Community Interests", 250 *Recueil des Cours* (1994), pp. 217-384.

Simma, Bruno (ed.) in collaboration with Hermann Mosler, Albrecht Randelzhofer, Christian Tomuschat und Rüdiger Wolfrum, *The Charter of the United Nations. A Commentary*, 2nd ed., Oxford, Oxford University Press 2002.

Suchsland-Maser, Ulrike, *Menschenrechte und die Politik multilateraler Finanzinstitute*, Frankfurt am Main 1999.

Tomuschat, Christian, "Obligations Arising for States without or against their will", 241 *Recueil des Cours* (1993), pp. 209-240.

Tomuschat, Christian, "International Law as the Constitution of Mankind", in: United Nations (ed.), *International Law at the Eve of the Twenty-first Century, Views from the International Law Commission*, New York 1997, pp. 37-50.

Tully, James, *Strange multiplicity*, Cambridge: Cambridge University Press 1995.

Uerpmann, Robert, "Internationales Verfassungsrecht", 11 *Juristen-Zeitung* (2001) 565-573.

Verdross, Alfred, *Die Verfassung der Völkerrechtsgemeinschaft*, Wien: Springer 1926.

Verdross, Alfred/Simma, Bruno, *Universelles Völkerrecht*, 3rd ed., Berlin 1984.

Volkmann, Uwe, "Setzt Demokratie den Staat voraus?", 127 *Archiv des öffentlichen Rechts* (2002), pp. 575-611.

von Bogdandy, Armin, "Demokratie, Globalisierung, Zukunft des Völkerrechts – eine Bestandsaufnahme", 61 *Zeitschrift für ausländisches öffentliches Recht und Völkerrecht* (2003), pp. 853-877.

Wallerstein, Immanuel M., *The Modern World-System*, San Diego: Academic Press 1974.

Weil, Prosper, "Towards Relative Normativity in International Law", 77 *American Journal of International Law* (1983), pp. 413-442.

Weiler, Joseph H.H., "Der Staat 'über alles'", 44 *Jahrbuch des öffentlichen Rechts der Gegenwart* (1996) pp. 91-135.

Weiss, Thomas *et al.* (eds.), *NGO's, the UN and Global Governance*, Lynne Rienner Publications, 1996.

Willetts, Peter (ed.), *The Conscience of The World: The Influence of Non-Governmental Organisations in the UN-System*, London : Hurst, 1996.

Wolfrum, Rüdiger, *Encyclopedia of Public International Law* 1992, pp. 692 *et seq.*

Part 2

Uniformity and Diversity in International Law

5. The Globalisation of Philosophy and the Philosophy of Globalisation

Philip Allott

'A new science of politics is needed for a new world.'

A. de Tocqueville, Democracy in America.[1]

1. The Intellectual Challenge of the Twenty-first Century

History is the self-consciousness of the self-constituting of human societies. The time has come to change the course of human history. The time has come to actualise an ancient potentiality – the history of the self-constituting of the society of all-humanity, the society of all human societies. It will be the beginning of universal human history.[2]

The nature of human beings is formed by the societies to which they belong. The time has come to change human nature. Revolutionary social transformation is a re-forming of human nature.[3] The revolutionary transformation of the society of all-humanity, the society of all human societies, will change human nature at the level of the human species. Developments in the social conditions of the co-existence of subordinate human societies are producing a new form of international

---

1   A. de Tocqueville, *Democracy in America*, vol. I (1835), Introduction (tr., H. Reeve, F. Bowen & P. Bradley; London, David Campbell (Everyman's Library); 1994), 7.

2   The idea of the possibility of a history of all-humanity (universal history) has its own history. It has been inspired at different times by: the Stoic idea of the moral identity and equality of all human beings (*humanitas, homonoia*); the Christian idea (Augustine) of the human world (the City of Man) and the Kingdom (the City of God); the idea of a history of humanity as an instrument of human enlightenment and empowerment (Raleigh, Bossuet, Voltaire, Vico); the idea of all-human history as a predictive and prescriptive instrument (Condorcet, Kant, Herder, Hegel, Comte, Marx, Toynbee).

3   'He who dares to undertake the making of a people's institutions ought to feel himself capable, so to speak, of changing human nature ... .' (J.-J. Rousseau, *Social Contract* (1762), bk. II, chap. VII, in J.-J. Rousseau, *The Social Contract and Discourses* (tr., G.D.H. Cole; London, J.M. Dent & Sons; 1915/1973), 194. For the English poet, William Wordsworth, such was, indeed, the ideal effect of the French Revolution: 'And human nature seeming born again.' W. Wordsworth, *The Prelude* (1805 version), bk. VI, line 354 (1850 version: bk. VI, line 341).

Ronald St. John Macdonald & Douglas M. Johnston (eds.), Towards World Constitutionalism, *pp. 129-150.*
© 2005 *Koninklijke Brill NV. Printed in The Netherlands.* ISBN 90 04 14612 1.

society. History's new beginning will be the end of the pre-history of the human species.[4]

The history of the twentieth century contains the pre-history of revolutionary global social transformation. Global war, global economy, global public order, global consciousness, global climate change, global crime, and global government (legislative, executive, and judicial) were the outward signs of deep-structural processes of transformation in the social conditions of the co-existence of human beings at the global level. It was obvious, even to the least philosophically inclined observer, that the socialising phenomena at the global level were related to, or at least analogous to, familiar socialising phenomena in the history of subordinate societies, including tribes, nations and states. In particular, familiar patterns of social development seemed to be reproducing themselves at the global level. Familiar patterns of the distribution of social power – political, economic and cultural – seemed to be escaping from the internal life of subordinate societies to meet and interact in an obscure and formless realm formed from the externalising of those very patterns. The hypothetical realm of so-called international relations familiar from past centuries, dominated by the rudimentary social processes of diplomacy and war, was being transformed into a new kind of hypothetical realm formed from the practical co-existence of self-externalising transnational social phenomena.

At the subordinate social level, human history has been characterised not only by a bewildering diversity of social forms and processes but also by a striking diversity in patterns of social change, with some societies demonstrating patterns of continuous, even frenzied, social change, while others have been capable of resisting social change for very long periods of time. These overwhelming diversities in the self-constituting of societies at the subordinate level led some people to suppose that, at the global level, there will not be, or even cannot be, anything which could be seen, even analogously, as a process of social self-constituting. It has led others to suppose that social self-constituting at the global level would be radically different in kind. On this view, analogies with, and extrapolation from, social processes at subordinate social levels would be inappropriate and inadequate and could be misleading.

A society constitutes itself not only in day-to-day political and economic struggle (*real* self-constituting) and in the day-to-day functioning of its legal system (*legal* self-constituting), but also in the form of ideas (*ideal* self-constituting), ideas which condition, and are conditioned by, its real and legal self-constituting.[5] In its

---

4   The idea that the end of the mere co-existence of competing national societies is the beginning of universal human history is intended to recall Karl Marx's idea that the end of antagonistic social relations would be the end of the prehistory of human society in general. K. Marx, 'A Contribution to a Critique of Political Economy', Preface, in K. Marx & F. Engels, *Selected Works* (Moscow, Progress Publishers; 1969), vol. I, 502-6, at 504. (Only a first part of the work, including the preface, was published (1859), the substance of the remainder being included in Marx's *Capital*).

5   For further discussion of the three dimensions of a society's constitution, see P. Allott, *Eunomia. New Order for a New World* (Oxford, Oxford University Press; 1990/2001) (hereafter referred to as *Eunomia*), ch. 9.

theory[6] a society accumulates a constantly evolving set of ideas capable of explaining and justifying to itself its distribution of political, economic and cultural power. Revolutionary social transformation, whatever its real and legal causes and effects, includes, above all, a transformation of ideas, a re-thinking of a society's theory.

In the French Revolution, the paradigm case of revolution in the modern world, the part played by ideas has been variously assessed, but ideas certainly played a significant part.[7] As a revolution in the mind of France, and not merely in the streets of Paris and Versailles, it was more like the religious revolutions which had, in earlier centuries, re-formed the mind of Europe.[8] The revolutionary re-constituting of international society in the twenty-first century will be a revolution in the species-mind of the human species.

The revolutionary transformation of international society, the society of all societies, necessarily entails a transformation of all subordinate social forms and processes, a re-constituting of all human societies, a re-constituting not only in their social forms and social processes but also in the theories which explain and justify those forms and processes. The re-forming of international society is also a re-forming of all social philosophy.

So it is that the great intellectual challenge of the twenty-first century can be stated with relative clarity. The globalising of social phenomena is taking place in a philosophical vacuum, with social forms and processes crudely separated from their philosophical foundations and left to develop, if at all, in a waste land of rational and ethical nihilism. Is the self-consciousness of the self-constituting of a true international society to be dominated by accident and force because the human species is unable to re-constitute itself by reflection and choice?[9] What is to

---

6   For further discussion of a society's theory, see *Eunomia*, ch. 2.

7   Hegel is among those who take the view that 'the Revolution received its first impulse from Philosophy'. 'The conception, the idea of Right asserted its authority *all at once*, and the old framework of injustice could offer no resistance to its onslaught. A constitution, therefore, was established in harmony with the conception of Right, and on this foundation all future legislation was to be based. Never since the sun had stood in the firmament and the planets revolved around him [*sic*] had it been perceived that man's existence centres in his head, *i.e.* in Thought, inspired by which he builds up the world of reality.' G.W.F. Hegel, *The Philosophy of History* (tr., J. Sibree; New York, Dover Publications; 1956), 446, 447.

8   '*It is a revolution of doctrine and theoretic dogma*. It has a much greater resemblance to those changes which have been made upon religious grounds ... The last revolution of doctrine and theory which has happened in Europe is the Reformation.' E. Burke, *Thoughts on French Affairs* (1791), in E. Burke, *Reflections on the Revolution in France* (London, Dent (Everyman's Library); 1910), 285-330, at 288 (emphasis in original). 'Thus the French Revolution, though ostensibly political in origin, functioned on the lines, and assumed many of the aspects, of a religious revolution.' A. de Tocqueville, *The Old Regime and the French Revolution* (1856) (tr., S. Gilbert; Garden City, Doubleday Anchor Books; 1955), 11.

9   'It has been frequently remarked that it seems to have been reserved to the people of this country [the United States of America], by their conduct and example, to decide

be the philosophy of revolutionary social transformation at the global level? What is the social function of philosophy? What is philosophy?

2.   Unphilosophy

The response to the intellectual challenge of the twenty-first century could have been relatively straightforward.[10] The philosophy of global revolutionary social transformation is *idealism*. The social function of philosophy is *the self-perfecting of society*. Philosophy is *the self-perfecting of the human mind*.

Such a response is readily available in the great tradition of philosophy. But the actualising of that response has been made immeasurably more difficult by two circumstances which are the product of certain historical contingencies in the self-constituting of certain human societies. (1) The great tradition of philosophy has produced from within itself something which we must call *unphilosophy* – philosophy's self-denying, a denial of the possibility of philosophy in the form in which it had been inherited from the great tradition. (2) The mental superstructure of the social forms known as democracy and capitalism, itself full of ideas produced within the great tradition of philosophy, is acting as a default pseudo-philosophy within the general globalising of social phenomena.

To speak the language of human self-perfecting seems quaint and old-fashioned to those for whom the great tradition of philosophy has no continuing reality. Such things can surely only be said by those for whom twentieth-century philosophy did not happen, for whom the twentieth century in general did not happen. Surely the Spirit of the Time has decreed that to use essentialist language or, still worse, transcendentalist language is to talk nonsense[11] or, still worse, to talk ideology.[12]

True philosophy is found wherever human beings have communicated and collected their thinking about the nature of humanity's existence as a self-con-

---

the important question, whether societies of men are really capable or not of establishing good government from reflection and choice, or whether they are forever destined to depend for their political constitutions on accident and force.' *The Federalist Papers* (1787), No. 1 (A. Hamilton) (New York, Mentor Books); 1961), 33.

10   *Challenge and response* is a leading concept used by Arnold Toynbee in analysing the success and failure of particular civilisations. A Toynbee, *A Study of History* (London, Oxford University Press; 12 vols., 1934-61).

11   'While Xenophon was writing his History and Euclid teaching Geometry, Socrates and Plato were talking nonsense, on pretence of teaching wisdom and morality.' J. Bentham, *Deontology* (1834) (ed., A. Goldworth; Oxford, Clarendon Press; 1983), 135. (Euclid was not a contemporary of Socrates or Plato).

12   Karl Marx's influential formulation of the idea that consciousness is a product of assignable social causes and can take effect as a form of social power (ideology) was used to demonstrate that idealist philosophy must be condemned because it had been at the root of disastrous twentieth-century ideologies. For a thoroughgoing rejection of the central thread of the great tradition, see K. Popper, *The Open Society and its Enemies* (London, Routledge & Kegan Paul Ltd.; 1945).

scious presence in a universe which immeasurably transcends human existence. The human mind found itself capable of responding to the human situation in ways which have formed and transformed the conduct of human life. In the mental activity which came to be known as philosophy, a particular form of collective self-consciousness has been an active presence in the theoretical self-constituting of whole societies for more than twenty-six centuries. And then, at a particular period in the history of those societies, philosophy in this great tradition was rejected. In the nineteenth century, the great tradition of philosophy simply come to an end, like a great highway stopping in the middle of nowhere. The human mind chose to disable and disown one of its most remarkable capacities.

Philosophy in the great tradition has always contained a dialectical moment. It is as if creative thinking is intrinsically a binary process.[13] Philosophy typically contains the presence of affirmation through negation. In the Socratic tradition, the capacity of the mind to think contrasting and even contradictory ideas is a powerful means of generating other ideas, a surpassing and an enriching of thought.[14] A philosopher typically reviews and re-thinks some part of the thinking of one or more predecessors and, in so doing, finds a new way of thinking.[15] The great tradition has also always included a tradition of philosophical scepticism, a long story of self-doubting about the status, purpose and methods of philosophy.[16] But, over the last two centuries, the oppositional thinking and self-doubting of the great

---

13   'Nature has set us so exactly in the middle that if we alter one side of the scales we alter the other as well…This leads me to believe that there are certain mechanisms in our head so arranged that we cannot touch one without touching its opposite.' B. Pascal (1623-62), *Pensées* (published posthumously) (tr., A. Krailsheimer; London, Penguin Books; 1966), 213. In his discussion of the education of the philosopher, Plato identified *dialectic* as the route to true knowledge: ' … we have set dialectic above all other studies to be as it were the coping stone – and … no other higher kind of study could rightly be placed above it …' *Republic*, Bk. VII, 534e (tr., P. Shorey; in eds., E. Hamilton & H. Cairns, *The Collected Dialogues of Plato*; Princeton, Princeton University Press; 1961), 766.

14   Hegel used the German verb *aufheben*, with its substantive form *Aufhebung*, to express his version of the process of dialectical thought. For his interpretation of the word (as meaning to set aside, to preserve, and to surpass), see *Hegel's Logic, being part one of the Encyclopaedia of the Philosophical Sciences* (1830), §96 (tr., W. Wallace; Oxford, Clarendon Press; 1975), 142. At §81, he distinguishes 'mere Scepticism'. 'The sceptic mistakes the true value of his result, when he supposes it to be no more than a negation pure and simple. For the negative which emerges, as the result of dialectic is, because a result, at the same time positive: it contains what it results from, absorbed within itself, and made part of its own nature.' (119). Hegel's querulous epigone, Karl Marx, used a materialist version of the concept to explain the general historical process of social transformation.

15   Thus Socrates-Plato negated the Sophists and the Materialists; Aristotle negated Plato; Bacon negated Aquinas; Locke negated Hobbes; Descartes negated Locke; Hume negated Locke; Kant negated Hume; Hegel negated Kant; Marx negated Hegel; Schopenhauer negated Hegel.

16   For example: sophism, pyrrhonism, scepticism (Carneades), Epicureanism, empiricism, nominalism, materialism.

tradition gave way to something new, something which was not a self-surpassing but a self-destroying. *Aufhebung* became *Vernichtung*. Philosophy denied its own possibility. Society's ideal self-constituting would thereafter contain, alongside the continuing social effects of the old philosophy, a ferment of forms of its own self-denying, a litany of philosophical despair, a philosophy of unphilosophy.[17]

Unphilosophy became an ideology. Denying the possibility of one idea being better than another, of one activity of the mind being better than another, still less of one thinker being better than another, it became tendentiously associated with the ideology of freedom, egalitarianism, and populism in a spurious democratising of the social activity of the human mind.[18] Nonchalantly abandoning the ideals of truth and value, it surrendered the self-transcending of the human mind to the processes of public power, to those who have power over the public mind through the exercise of political, economic and cultural power.[19] The outcome occurred which cultural observers in the nineteenth century had predicted. The new masters of the democratic public mind borrowed a traditional attribute of the masters of absolutism. The public mind became its own philosopher.

The new ideology of unphilosophy served well the new masters of public power, and not only in democratic societies. We practise philosophy when we live the ideas that philosophy produces. The nineteenth century did philosophy in countless half-revolutions and failed revolutions and sporadic wars. The twentieth century did philosophy in the gas-chamber and the Gulag and the killing fields of four continents. Bad philosophy is a form of human evil. It is one of the worst forms of human evil, because it can corrupt and destroy human beings, could now be on the point of corrupting and destroying all-humanity.

How did the self-destruction of philosophy come about? Why did the human mind abandon a tradition of human self-perfecting? To attempt to answer those questions we may bring together three Hegelian ideas:

---

17   The many-headed unphilosophy has many names: realism, relativism, nihilism, positivism, utilitarianism, naturalism, reductionism, hermeneutics, pragmatism, logical positivism, phenomenology, existentialism, analytical and linguistic philosophy, structuralism, neo-pragmatism, postmodernism, deconstructionism, professional philosophy.

18   Bentham classed the fine arts, including music and poetry, among 'the arts and sciences of amusement'. 'Prejudice apart, the game of push-pin is of equal value with the arts and sciences of music and poetry. If the game of push-pin furnish more pleasure, it is more valuable than either.' J. Bentham, 'The Rationale of Reward', in ed., J. Bowring, *The Works of Jeremy Bentham* (Edinburgh, William Tait; 1843), Vol. 2, 253.

19   'Many people in our time have so ill understood the doctrine of liberty, that in some of the most active circles in society they now count you a bigot if you hold any proposition to be decidedly and unmistakably more true than any other.' J. Morley *On Compromise* (London, Macmillan & Co.; 1874/1886), 106. Morley discussed what he called 'the slow transformation now at work of the whole spiritual basis of thought' and 'the discredit of abstract theory and general reasoning among us, in all that relates to politics, morals, and religion.' He referred to 'the newspaper press, that huge instrument for keeping discussion on a low level.' (at 36, 22, 32).

- philosophy is the self-consciousness of consciousness;[20]
- philosophy is a gradual accumulation of consciousness over the course of time;[21]
- the state of philosophy at any particular time reflects social conditions at that time.[22]

Putting these ideas together, we may say that something in the particular conditions of nineteenth-century European society changed the course of the history of the self-consciousness of the human mind. If we can identify those conditions and the nature of that change we may also be able to form a view of the possible development of human self-consciousness at the global level at the beginning of the twenty-first century.

There seem to have been five main social factors involved in the rise of unphilosphy and the defeat of philosophy in the great tradition.

(1)   The rise of the intellectual activities variously called the 'human sciences' or the 'social sciences' or the 'mind sciences' (*Geisteswissenschaften*), especially sociology, historiography and psychology took up the aspiration of eighteenth-century rationalism to find empirically-based solutions to problems traditionally dealt with by philosophy. Especially as theoretically supported by the *utilitarianism* of Bentham and James Mill and the *positivism* of August Comte and his followers, the human sciences claimed to offer a form of 'truth' analogous to, but obviously distinct from, the 'truth' of the natural sciences.[23]

---

20   Hegel referred to philosophy as 'the Thinking of Thinking', in *The Philosophy of History*, Introduction (fn. 7 above), 69.

21   ' ... the study of the history of Philosophy is the study of Philosophy itself, for, indeed, it can be nothing else.' 'Such knowledge is thus not learning merely, or a knowledge of what is dead, buried and corrupt: the history of Philosophy has not to do with what is gone, but with the living present.' G.W.F. Hegel, *Lectures on the History of Philosophy* (1825-6), Vol I (tr., E.S. Haldane; London, Kegan Paul, Trench, Trübner & Co.; 1892), 30, 39.

22   'Whatever happens, every individual is a child of his time; so philosophy too is its own time apprehended in thoughts.' *Hegel's Philosophy of Right* (tr., T. Knox; London Oxford University Press; 1952/1967), 11. But, compare Nietzsche : 'More and more it seems to me that the philosopher, being *of necessity* a man of tomorrow and the day after tomorrow, has always found himself, and *had* to find himself in contradiction to his today: his enemy was ever the ideal of today. So far all these extraordinary furtherers of man whom one calls philosophers, though they themselves have rarely felt like friends of wisdom but rather like disagreeable fools and dangerous question marks, have found their task, their hard, unwanted, inescapable task, but also the greatness of their task, in being the bad conscience of their time.' F. Nietzsche, *Beyond Good and Evil. Prelude to a Philosophy of the Future* (1886), §212 (tr., W. Kaufmann; New York, Vintage Books; 1946),137 (emphasis in original).

23   The last part of G.H. Lewes, *A Biographical History of Philosophy* (1845-6) is entitled 'Philosophy finally relinquishing its place in favour of positive science.' Cited in W.E. Houghton's absorbing account of the early Victorian collective neurosis, *The Victorian Frame of Mind 1830-1870* (New Haven, Yale University Press; 1957), 33-4. Lewes was a characteristic member of the Victorian intellectual class – biographer of Goethe,

(2)   The natural sciences, pure and applied, developed dramatically after 1780. Although the Industrial Revolution had been the product of technology rather than of theoretical science, the Baconian promise – unlimited human power over the natural world – seemed to be vindicated by the remarkable achievements of a way of thinking whose great merit, for Bacon, was precisely that it was not the way of thinking of the old philosophy. Human science and natural science had become a new version of 'double truth', in which the last word would be with natural science.[24] Apparently the old philosophy had simply become otiose, and philosophers were marginalised as professional philosophers, talking to each other in an obscure corner of the academic grove or acting as lackeys of the currently dominant social class.[25]

(3)   The religious crisis of the nineteenth century caused a deep trauma in social and personal consciousness. It is now difficult, in post-Christian Europe, to imagine the mental torment caused to thinking people in the nineteenth century by the collapse of the structures of religious faith which they had inherited.[26] Developments in the human sciences tended to re-conceive faith in terms of illusion and delusion and historical contingency. Developments in the natural sciences (especially geology and evolutionary biology) tended to undermine a spiritual conception of the universe in general and of the human condition in particular. A believer beset by doubt found no solace in old philosophy in the face of the new self-confidence of the apostles of scepticism, atheism and agnosticism.[27]

expounder of the ideas of Comte for an English audience, writer on physiology, long-term partner of George Eliot (pen-name of novelist Mary Ann Evans, herself the translator of Feuerbach's devastating *Essence of Christianity*).

24   In the theory of *double truth* (faith and philosophy) in Christian scholastic theology (from the 13th century), faith was privileged over philosophy.

25   'It is admitted, on all sides, that the Metaphysical and Moral Sciences are falling into decay, while the Physical are engrossing, every day, more respect and attention. In most of the European nations there is now no such thing as a Science of Mind ... ' T. Carlyle, 'Signs of the Times' (1829), in T. Carlyle, *Critical and Miscellaneous Essays* (London, Chapman & Hall; 1888), Vol. II, 236. ' ... in other European countries [other than Germany], where the natural sciences and the cultivation of the scientific intellect have been pursued with enthusiasm and respect, philosophy, except in name, has disappeared without trace, even from memory.' Hegel's Inaugural Lecture at Heidelberg (1816), in G.W.F. Hegel, *Introduction to the Lectures on the History of Philosophy* (tr., T. Knox & A. Miller; Oxford, Clarendon Press; 1985), 2. Hegel discussed the new 'contempt for philosophy' in bitter terms in the Preface to his *Philosophy of Right* (fn. 22 above). Perhaps he was referring to J.W. von Goethe (1749-1832), a contemporary of Professors Kant and Hegel, who drew on his mesmerising celebrity, his supposed belief in the reasons of the heart, his calculated nonchalance, and his penchant for the natural sciences, to fuel his disdain for *Kathederphilosophie* (professors' philosophy).

26   Carlyle spoke of an age 'fallen into spiritual languor, destitute of belief, yet terrified at Scepticism.' T. Carlyle, 'Sir Walter Scott' (1838), in *Essays* (fn. 25 above), Vol. VI, 52.

27   T.H. Huxley (1825-95), who coined the word 'agnostic', was the tireless apostle of Darwinism and the prophet of the triumph of science over religion. His many writings on religion are best summarised in some aphorisms not published in his lifetime. 'Religions rise

(4)   The mental crisis caused by the rise of industrial capitalism and popular democracy. After 1789, what seemed to be a collapse of an inherited social order
and the annihilation of inherited high values created a prolonged and profound disturbance in the minds of thinking people in one European country
after another.[28] The thinking class staged a passionate and articulate dialectic
concerning the meaning of the fundamental social transformation that they
were experiencing. For some, it was a mental revolution, an overdue liberation
of the human mind, allowing it to apply itself at last to the pursuit of useful
knowledge.[29] For others, the materialism and philistinism of the newly dominant bourgeois class was nothing less than the decline and fall of a laboriously
constructed, centuries-old civilisation.[30] For both sides, the purpose of educa-

---

because they satisfy the many and fall because they cease to satisfy the few. They have
been the day dreams of mankind and each in time has become a nightmare from which a
gleam of knowledge has waked the dreamer. The religion which will endure is such a day
dream as may still be dreamed in the noon tide [sic] of the glare of science.' C. Bibby, The
Essence of T.H. Huxley. Selections from his Writings (London, Macmillan; 1967), 110.

28   'There is one great fact, characteristic of this our nineteenth century, a fact which no
party dares deny. On the one hand, there have started into life industrial and scientific
forces, which no epoch of the former human history had ever suspected. On the other
hand, there exist symptoms of decay, far surpassing the horrors recorded of the later
times of the Roman empire …. All our invention and progress seem to result in endowing material forces with intellectual life, and in stultifying human life into a material
force.' K. Marx, Speech at the anniversary of the People's Paper (1856), in K. Marx & F.
Engels, Selected Works (fn. 4 above), vol. I, 500.

29   'At length the time arrived when the barren philosophy which had, during so many
ages, employed the faculties of the ablest men, was destined to fall. It had worn many
shapes. It had mingled itself with many creeds. It had survived revolutions in which
empires, religions, languages, races had perished … Words, and more, words, and nothing but words, had been all the fruit of all the toil of all the most renowned sages of sixty generations. But the days of this sterile exuberance were numbered.' T.B. Macaulay,
'Lord Bacon' (1837), in Lord Macaulay's Essays (London, Longmans, Green, and Co.;
1885), 346-414, at 393. Macaulay presented the sixteenth-century Francis Bacon as the
prophet of a new intellectual crusade under the very nineteenth-century banner of
'Utility and Progress'. They had both been undergraduates, evidently of the recalcitrant
sort, at Trinity College, Cambridge.

30   For Matthew Arnold, Macaulay was 'the great apostle of the Philistines'. M. Arnold,
'Joubert' , in Essays in Criticism. First Series (1875) (ed., T.M. Hoctor; Chicago, University of Chicago Press; 1968), 159-182, at 181. For Arnold, a 'philistine' was a sort of
intellectual barbarian within the civilised world – 'the enemy of the children of light,
or servants of the idea'. M. Arnold, Culture and Anarchy: An Essay in Political and
Social Criticism (London, Smith, Elder and Co.; 1869), 98. Arnold carried the banner
for 'culture', presenting the ancient Greeks as the fons et origo of true civilisation. 'The
whole scope of the essay is to recommend culture as the great help out of our present
difficulties; culture being a pursuit of our total perfection by means of getting to know,
on all the matters which most concern us, the best which has been thought and said
in the world, and, through this knowledge, turning a stream of fresh and free thought
upon our stock notions and habits … ' (Preface, viii).

tion – should it be liberal or practical? – was a central issue.[31] For both sides also, a central obsession was the coming of a new kind of society dominated by the majority, by the masses. Then the educated class itself and its anguished debates about the meaning of civilization would simply be swept aside.

(5)   There remains the possibility that philosophy in the great tradition contained the seed of its own overcoming and betrayed itself. Nietzsche suggested the interesting idea that the long history of Christianity had prepared the way for the end of Christianity.[32] By enforcing an absolutist conception of belief, Christianity inspired a negation which had to be absolute unbelief, a belief in Christianity's unbelievability. Similarly, it might be said that, when traditional philosophy was presented, or presented itself, as the search for 'truth', it gave the ground for an inevitable negation, that the truth of philosophy was its essential untruth or, at least, that its claim to truth was spurious.[33]

The perennial dialectical search for world-transforming ideas had produced, over the course of three centuries, Voltaire and Rousseau (reason and romanticism),

---

31   'If we were asked for what end, above all others, endowed universities exist, or ought to exist, we should answer – To keep philosophy alive.' J.S. Mill, 'Professor Sedgwick's Discourse on the Studies of the University of Cambridge' (1835), in J.S. Mill, *Dissertations and Discussions. Political, Philosophical, and Historical,* Vol. I (London, J.W. Parker & Son; 1859), 95. In the Rome of the first century CE, Seneca took issue with Cicero's view on essentially the same issue: education as a preparation for life or the liberal arts as an education in *humanitas* ('the humanities'). Rome's preference for the Ciceronian view determined the nature of higher education in Europe until the reform of the universities in the nineteenth century.

32   'Thus Christianity as dogma perished by its own ethics, and in the same way Christianity as ethics must perish; we are standing on the threshold of this event … .Christian truthfulness must now draw its strongest conclusion, the one by which it shall do away with itself … It is by this dawning self-consciousness of the will to truth that ethics must now perish. This is the great spectacle of a hundred acts that will occupy Europe for the next two centuries, the most terrible and problematical but also the most hopeful of spectacles.' F. Nietzsche, *The Genealogy of Morals* (1887), XXVII (tr., F. Golffing; New York; Doubleday Anchor Books;1956), 298. We might return the compliment and say that Nietzsche's own life's work could be read as a cry of despair at humanity's self-destroying despair. *Desperare desperandum* might have been his motto.

33   'Do you see, then, said I, that we were not wrong in saying that the very qualities that make up the philosophical nature do, in fact, become, when the environment and nurture are bad, in some sense the cause of its backsliding … ?' Plato, *Republic*, Bk. VI, 495a (fn. 13 above), 731. 'This misapprehension of philosophic method has veiled the very considerable success of philosophy in providing generic notions which add lucidity to our apprehension of the facts of experience. The depositions of Plato, Aristotle, Thomas Aquinas, Descartes, Spinoza, Leibniz, Locke, Berkeley, Hume, Kant, Hegel, merely mean that ideas that were introduced into the philosophic tradition must be construed with limitations, adaptations, and inversions, either unknown to them or even repudiated by them.' A.N. Whitehead, *Process and Reality: an Essay in Cosmology* (Cambridge, Cambridge University Press; 1929), 14.

Hegel and Huxley (idealism and scientism), Comte and Marx (reform and revolution), and, finally, Freud and Wittgenstein (irrationalism and unrationalism). The proclamation of the end of philosophy in the great tradition and the triumph of the philosophy of unphilosophy had been products of a particular state of social self-consciousness produced by a particular process of revolutionary social transformation, a state and a process which are a source of our own social self-consciousness within a new process of revolutionary social transformation at the beginning of the twenty-first century.

3.   The Dimensions of Revolution

Is it possible to make any useful generalisations drawn from the historical experience of revolutionary social transformation?[34] Is it possible to postulate a theory of the causation of revolutionary social transformation? Is it possible, at least, to detect repeated patterns in epochs of revolutionary social transformation?

A particular form of history-writing, which came to be called historicism, tended to answer these questions in the affirmative.[35] Even if it might be difficult to demonstrate that there are iron laws of history which not only explain the past but allow us to predict the future with relative certainty, it seemed obvious to such historians that the human past must have some more or less coherent meaning which the human mind can recover, not least because human history can only be the history of what the human mind itself has caused.

From the chaos of human history and the contradictions of historiography, it is possible to extract four mildly historicist generalisations. (1) Chance and accident have played major roles in the making of human history.[36] (2) World-historical individuals have played a major role.[37] (3) Social forms, and changes in social forms,

---

34   'Everything tells us that we are now close upon one of the great revolutions of the human race. If we wish to learn what to expect from it and to procure a certain guide to lead us in the midst of its vicissitudes, what could be more suitable than to have some picture of the revolutions that have gone before it and prepared its way?' Marquis de Condorcet, *Sketch for a Historical Picture of the Progress of the Human Mind* (1793), in M.J.A.de Condorcet, *Selected Writings* (ed., K. Baker; Indianapolis, Indianapolis University Press; 1976), 217-8.

35   For further discussion of the history of historiography, see P. Allott, 'International law and the idea of history', 1 *Journal of the History of International Law* (1999), 1-21; and P. Allott, *The Health of Nations. Society and Law beyond the State* (Cambridge, Cambridge University Press; 2002) (hereafter *Health of Nations*), ch. 11.

36   For discussion of their role in the making of what has been called 'war', see P. Allott, *Towards the Internatioal Rule of the Law. Essays in Integrated Constitutional Theory* (Cameron May Ltd., forthcoming), ch. 12.

37   Hegel spoke of world-historical individuals who are agents of the World Spirit within Universal History. 'Such individuals had no consciousness of the general Idea they were unfolding ...; on the contrary, they were practical, political men. But at the same time they were thinking men, who had an insight into the requirements of the time – *what was ripe for development.* This was the very Truth for their age, for their world;

are intimately related to the economic conditions, and changes in the economic conditions, of a given society.[38] (4) The history of ideas is as significant as the history of events. A revolution in the streets is also a revolution in the mind.[39] We should expect revolutions to exhibit all four of these aspects.

More speculative is the possibility of identifying epochs within the apparent formlessness of history. From the very beginning of history-writing historians have identified historical epochs and, for so long also, certain epochs have been identified as 'revolutions' – religious, political, social, economic, intellectual or artistic. Revolutions seem to have a generic character – an abrupt and profound change in social phenomena which may be apparent to those living through it or may be isolated retrospectively by historians. But each revolution is, of course, unique in its nature and purposes within its given historical context. All revolutions are the same. Each revolution is unique. Similarly, the succession of epochs is a function of unique sets of historical circumstances, but some historians have been inclined to see a pattern even in the succession of epochs. Most interesting among these patterns is the idea of an alternating pattern, a cycle of 'bearing and barrenness' (Plato),[40] of 'organic and critical' periods (Saint-Simon),[41] of periods of 'belief and

---

the species next in order, so to speak, and which was already formed in the womb of time.' He mentioned Alexander, Caesar and Napoleon as examples. G.W.F. Hegel, *Philosophy of History* (fn. 7 above), Introduction, 30 (emphasis in the original). Thomas Carlyle spoke of them as heroes sent into the world to be 'the modellers, patterns, and in a wide sense creators, of whatsoever the general mass of men contrived to do or to attain.' T. Carlyle, *On Heroes, Hero-Worship, and the Heroic in History* (1841) (London, Chapman & Hall; 1888), 1.

38   Karl Marx was certainly not the discoverer of this ancient truth. 'In the opinion of some, the regulation of property is the chief point of all, that being the question upon which all revolutions turn.' Aristotle, *Politics*, II.7 (tr., B. Jowitt; Oxford, Clarendon Press; 1905), 72.

39   For the French historian, Charles Guizot, whose historiography influenced Mill and de Tocqueville and Marx, revolutionary change is not only in social forms but also in the human mind. ' ... the inward is reformed by the outward, as the outward by the inward.' C. Guizot, *The History of Civilization in Europe* (1828) (tr., W. Hazilitt; London. Penguin Books (Penguin Classics); 1997), 22. See also Editor's Introduction, vii.

40   *Republic*, Bk. VIII, 546a (fn. 13 above), 775.

41   In his autobiography, J.S. Mill recalls how impressed he had been by the writings of the followers of the French social philosopher, the Comte de Saint-Simon (1760-1825): ' ... especially their division of all history into organic periods and critical periods. During the organic periods (they said) mankind accepted with firm conviction some positive creed, claiming jurisdiction over all their actions, and containing more or less of truth and adaptation to the needs of humanity. Under its influence they make all the progress compatible with the creed, and finally outgrow it; when a period follows of criticism and negation, in which mankind loses their old convictions without acquiring any new ones, of a general or authoritative character, except the conviction that the old are false.' J.S. Mill, *Autobiography* (London, Longmans, Green, Reader & Dyer; 1873), 163-4.

unbelief' (Carlyle).[42] Such a phenomenon suggests that the public mind of a society[43] reflects upon itself, upon its own nature and history and current condition in a way analogous to the way in which the mind of the human individual reflects on itself, re-imagining its own identity and its own potentiality.[44] A qualitative change in self-consciousness may be the result of such reflexive thinking in a society as in an individual human being.

Yet another speculation would be that the nature of revolutions reflects the hypothetical pattern of the self-constituting of society mentioned above.[45] We might extend that hypothesis to suggest that revolutions can occur in all or any of the three dimensions of a society's self-constituting – the real, the ideal, and the legal. A revolution (*metastasis*) may be a change in the structure of power, a 'real' revolution (*metarchia*), a 'legal' revolution, a change of institutional structures and fundamental laws (*metanomia*), an 'ideal' revolution, a revolution in the realm of ideas, in a society's theory of itself (*metanoia*).[46] It might be possible to make sense of the remarkable diversity of actual revolutions within the generic uniformity of revolutions by analysing the story of a revolution in one or more of these dimensions. It might even be possible to understand the potentiality of global revolution in the same way.

The Meiji Revolution in Japan (1868-9), the October Revolution in Russia (1917), and the Chinese Revolution (1949) are surely examples of three-dimensional revolutions in which all aspects of society, including its 'theory' of itself, were changed as a result of a physical struggle for power in the 'real' constitution. The French Revolution (from 1789) is an example of a revolution which eventually emerged, many years later, as a three-dimensional revolution but whose first phase was largely a metanoia, as France reconceived itself as nation which, in turn, had consequences on its understanding of itself as legal system.

Similarly, the Roman Revolution (from about 60BCE), which eventually transformed Rome from a 'republic' into an 'empire', began as a struggle for power within the real constitution (more or less decided by Octavian's victory over Antony at the battle of Actium in 31BCE), but which, at first almost imperceptibly, gradually allowed a virtual constitutional monarch under the republican system to become an emperor within an empire conceived as such, but with many aspects of the ideal and legal constitutions remaining unchanged.

---

42 'The fever of Scepticism must needs burn itself out, and burn out thereby the Impurities that caused it; then again will there be clearness, health.' T. Carlyle, 'Characteristics', in *Essays* (fn. 25 above), Vol. IV, 35.

43 For the concept of 'public mind' – a society's collective consciousness which flows from and to the private consciousness of society-members – see *Health of Nations*, §§3.6 ff.

44 It is notable that Plato himself lived during a vigorous power-struggle in Athens which no doubt inspired both him and his pupil, Aristotle, to consider the nature and causes of revolution.

45 Text at fn. 5 above.

46 These Greek terms are either invented or adapted for the present context.

The English Civil War (1640-49) has generated a whole series of conflicting interpretations. Was it a class struggle within the real constitution? Or was it a 'Puritan revolution' against a supposed revival of Catholicism in England and hence a struggle about the ideas which would dominate the unfolding of the real and legal constitutions? Eventually, after the republican interregnum (1649-60), not much had changed in any constitutional dimension. The so-called Glorious Revolution (1688/89) was primarily a transformation in the legal constitution, as the monarchy was given an explicit parliamentary foundation, leading to somewhat exalted new theorising about the theory of society and government. Similarly, the American Revolution (from 1776) might be seen as almost exclusively a metanomia, changing the legal basis of public power in the former colonies, but leaving the distribution of power in the real constitution almost unchanged, and the theory of government hardly changed from its English seventeenth-century bases.

Colonising empires (the Roman Empire, the European empires from the sixteenth to the twentieth centuries) are intrinsically three-dimensional. Federative empires – the leagues of ancient Greece, the Holy Roman Empire (ninth to nineteenth centuries), and the European Union of today – are a form of self-colonising and have a more uncertain effect on the self-constituting of their members. The Holy Roman Empire did not produce a general *metarchia* to realise Dante's vision of a *monarchia* (unified transnational government). The EU, Europe's half-revolution, is precarious and problematic in all three of its constitutional dimensions.[47]

For anyone considering the revolutionary effects of globalisation, revolutions in the dimension of ideas are of particular interest, not least for their long-term consequences on the other dimensions of the constitution – the movement of Buddhism from India into China and Japan, the extension of Christianity into the Roman Empire, the development of science in ancient China and ancient Greece, the development of mathematics and astronomy in the countries of the Middle East, the impact of Greek culture within the Roman Republic and Empire, European contact with Arab culture in the European 'Middle Ages', the movement of Greek-speaking scholars into Italy from Constantinople after the fall of that city in 1453, the scientific revolutions in Europe (from the thirteenth century, but especially in the seventeenth century), the diffusion of the idea of representative democracy from Britain after 1689, the various 'enlightenments' which spread from one European country to another,[48] the technological revolutions in agriculture and manufacturing (especially in the later eighteenth century), the diffusion of the idea of republican constitutionalism from France after 1789, the diffusion of various strains of 'socialism' from about 1800 ....

In difficult times, history reassures us with the thought that things change, that things can be changed, and that some things get better.

---

47   For discussion of the constitutional problem of the EU, see *Health of Nations*, Part II.

48   For the hypothesis that Western Europe, after the end of the Roman Empire in the West in the 5th century CE, has generated periods of 'enlightenment' at three-century intervals, the last having been in the eighteenth century, see *Health of Nations*, §3.18.

4. True Philosophy

Facing the challenge of the three-dimensional revolution of globalisation, can the human mind recover its capacity of self-perfecting, self-transforming, self-transcending, self-creating? Can humanity change the direction of its unfolding history and leave behind an epoch dominated by self-doubting and self-destroying? Can *Yang* re-assert itself in relation to *Yin* in the dialectic of the human mind?[49] If true philosophy in the great tradition were to be resumed, how might it respond to the fundamental social transformation of international society?

We may postulate five relevant principles of a perennial ideal philosophy.

A. First Principle: World-making

The human mind makes a human world, the world where humans live, a second habitat. We make the world out of ideas. We can change the world by means of ideas. New ideas, new world. New world, new ideas. New ideas, new powers.

Every 'is' statement is a philosophical statement, because the verb 'to be' is something that the human mind does to all that it thinks about. The real is also an idea. The human mind is a mirror of nature, but it is a *speculum spectans*, a mirror that sees, a mirror that thinks, and, in thinking, is always also thinking about itself.

B. Second Principle: Philosophy's Moral Imperative

True philosophy is ruled by a *moral imperative*. Pure reason is also practical reason. The mind can think anything, capriciously and randomly. It has a natural freedom, an apparently unlimited capacity to make worlds from ideas. But the rational mind is a self-ordering mind, thinking about itself in accordance with an imperative. The rational mind is the mind trying to think *well*. *Rationality*, that is to say, good philosophising, is a sub-set of goodness in general, a form of virtue, to use the word 'virtue' in both of its Aristotelian senses – a virtuous mental *disposition* on the part of the philosopher and virtuous *behaviour* in the act of philosophising. In philosophy, we think about what others have thought when they were trying to think well, and we try to think *better*.

So true philosophy is a moral activity. It is the human mind seeking to perfect itself. The dialectical struggle of ideas within philosophy is a struggle of human self-redeeming. Even philosophy's self-doubting and self-denial may be the dark night of the human mind when we experience emptiness and nothingness and despair, in

---

49   In Chinese philosophy *yin* and *yang* express the intrinsic duality of reality, a structural and dynamic dialectic. 'The perfect *yin* is majestically passive. The perfect *yang* is powerfully active ... The interaction of the two forms a harmony from which things are produced.' A quotation from ch. 21 of the Taoist *Chuang-tzŭ*, in Fung Yu-Lan, *A History of Chinese Philosophy*, Vol. I (tr., D. Bode; Princeton, Princeton University Press; 1952/1983), 179.

order to rediscover fullness and hope and, in due course, the joy of thinking better, the joy of becoming something better.

C.   Third Principle: Universalism

The great post-Socratic philosophical tradition of philosophy is not a philosophy of the *Western* mind. It is a philosophy of the *human* mind. It originated in a *particular* cultural contingency but it spoke to *universal* self-consciousness.

The ancient Greeks themselves were exceptionally conscious of cultural diversity, not only diversity within the Greek-speaking world but also the cultural diversity of other civilisations and other peoples, some of them much more ancient and more complex than Greek civilisation. It was, perhaps, the sense of cultural diversity which sowed the seed of philosophy as a universalising activity.

Universalist philosophy was created to occupy an intellectual territory situated between the other universalising, but culturally determined, territories of mythology and religion, on the one hand, and scientific enquiry, on the other hand. And philosophy would be a mental activity which would be distinct from the other great powers of the human mind – feeling, imagination, and belief. As a universalising activity of the mind, philosophy's closest relatives are mathematics and art. Rationality is the mathematics of philosophy. Moral purpose is the beauty of philosophising.

D.   Fourth Principle: The Idea of the Ideal

The greatest benefit which philosophy has bestowed on the human race is the idea of the *ideal*. It has been the traditional role of religion to enable human beings to aim at a target which transcends them. Within the religious mind-world, the existential target – enlightenment, nirvana, eternal life, paradise, rebirth – derives its meaning and its compelling force from a reality which is conceived as not itself being a mere product of the activity of the human mind.

By contrast, the philosophical idea of the ideal is a form of human *self*-transcending. It is a combined product of various capacities of the mind – the capacities to construct possible realities, to order that construction by means of rationality, to desire to actualise such possibilities, to will that those possibilities should be actualised. It is a universal capacity of the human mind to judge the actual in terms of the possible, the good in terms of the better and, having done so, to choose to actualise the possible. For human beings, whose species-being combines thought and desire, the ideal is the *logos* of the *libido*.

The possible ideas of reality made by philosophy, like the models made by the natural sciences, are structures for human habitation. The world-making human mind – the private mind of the human individual and the public mind of human societies – can think of a *better world* as a world which human beings can chose to make into a place to live. And the mind that can think a better world can also *will* a better world. For individuals and for societies, the *idea* of a better world and the capacity to *will* a better world are a potentiality of human self-perfecting. The ideas that we call *ideals*, even in everyday speech – the ideas of justice, truth, beauty, goodness – are the targets at which we aim but can never reach, since their function is to judge the actual and to inspire the possible.

For the great tradition of philosophy which derives from Plato, the task of philosophy is to perfect the human mind in terms of the mind's ideal potentiality with a view to perfecting human society in terms of society's ideal potentiality. The function of philosophy is not to discover truths but to speak truly. The attribution to philosophy of the task of discovering truths was a tragic misunderstanding or misrepresentation of philosophy's task and may have played a part in the conquest of philosophy by unphilosophy in the nineteenth century.[50] Platonism, like Taoism and Buddhism and early Christianity, is a path and a destination, not a truth.[51]

E.   Fifth Principle: Public Enlightenment

Philosophy in the great tradition is a social activity. True philosophy is a communicated, collective, co-operative enterprise, but also its reason-for-being is as a message of human self-redeeming through human self-perfecting, a message which would have no meaning or value if it were not disseminated as widely as possible. Accordingly, it matters greatly what ideas people have in their minds. The ideas that we have in our minds come from within our own mind – including the unconscious mind – but they come also from outside our mind, from other people's minds, and from society. The collected consciousness of the public mind of society is something we are born into, to which we may contribute, and which will continue after we are gone, and which dominates our minds for every moment of our waking lives.

We are what we think. And that is true of whole societies as well as of individual human beings. Societies are what they think. The human mind is a political mind. The *zōon politikon* has a *nous politikos*. True philosophy in the post-Socratic tradition is humanity's collective self-educating.[52]

---

50   See text at fn. 32 above. 'The safest general characterization of the European philosophical tradition is that it consists of a series of footnotes to Plato.' A.N. Whitehead, *Process and Reality* (fn. 33 above), 53. But some footnotes are better than others.

51   In discussing Plato's concept of 'ideas', Kant wondered whether Plato himself had understood his own thought. 'I need only remark that it is by no means unusual, upon comparing the thoughts which an author has expressed in regard to his subject, whether in ordinary conversation or in writing, to find that we understand him better than he has understood himself.' I. Kant, *Critique of Pure Reason* (1780/1787) (tr., N. Kemp Smith; London, Macmillan; 1929), 310. But, whatever the many subsequent 'Platonisms' may have suggested, Plato's works make clear that he understood that the 'knowledge' and 'truth' that were the aim of philosophical enlightenment were certainly not everyday truths about human nature or human society, but rather a self-transforming of the human mind which enhances its capacity for individual and social self-perfecting.

52   Plato was almost obsessively concerned with both things – contemplation *and* education. 'If you wish to know what is meant by public education, read Plato's *Republic*.

Bad thinking is also a social activity. The human mind is capable of thinking otherwise than in pursuit of the ideal. The human mind is capable of thinking in a disordered way, in a formless confusion of emotions and ideas. The human mind is capable of corrupting itself and damaging itself. The human mind is even capable of rationalising the pursuit of evil. And what is possible for the mind of the human individual is possible also for the collective mind of human societies. The public minds of societies are capable of bad thinking and of enacting and enforcing bad thinking in social practice. The essential social value of philosophy necessarily co-exists with the possibility of its abuse.

One thing is certain. The human mind cannot, by thinking, prove the impossibility of a particular mode of thinking.[53] It may pass judgment on the utility or desirability of a particular form of philosophy in a particular human context. It cannot extinguish its possibility.

5.   The Philosophy of Democracy-Capitalism

Never has good philosophy in the great tradition been more appropriate or more necessary or more challenging than it is in the human world of the early twenty-first century. What is called 'globalisation' is a form of fundamental social transformation in three modes – (1) the flow of transnational social effects across frontiers, especially economic effects; (2) the emergence of social structures and systems at the global level; (3) the tendency of the structures and systems of national social systems to converge, especially through the adoption of the structures and systems of democracy-capitalism.

None of these developments is a linear or regular progression, an orderly march towards a new international social order. On the contrary, they display a large measure of the random and the accidental, and they meet many kinds of political and cultural resistance, and they interact with many countervailing forces, including the sheer inertia of traditional social forms, the more or less corrupt self-interest of ruling-classes, and the constant threats to national and international public order in the form of the statal and non-statal use of armed force.

However, a linking factor in all three modes of globalisation is the social phenomenon of democracy-capitalism. (1) Social flows from countries with a democratic-capitalist system dominate the transnational social process. (2) Political and economic actors from democratic-capitalist countries, including economic and

---

Those who merely judge books by their titles take this for a treatise on politics, but it is the finest treatise on education ever written.' (J.-J. Rousseau, *Émile* (1762), Bk. I (tr., B. Foxlet; London, Dent (Everyman's Library); 1911/1974), 8.

53   This may be seen, at least analogously, as a Gödel limit of undecidability. See *Health of Nations*, §1.52, fn.70. 'Therefore is the mind too strait to contain itself.' St Augustine (354-430 CE), *Confessions*, Bk. X (tr., E. Pusey; London, Dent (Everyman's Library; 1907), 212. 'Man transcends man. Let us then concede to the sceptics what they have so often proclaimed, that truth lies beyond our scope and is an unattainable quarry.' B. Pascal, *Pensées* (fn. 13 above), 64.

other non-governmental actors, dominate the constitutionalising of international society. (3) Democracy-capitalism is playing a leading role in the fundamental
social transformation of national social systems. In short, democracy-capitalism
is at the heart of the revolutionary transformation of international society as the
society of all societies. It is possible that the philosophy of democracy-capitalism
will become, as it were by default, the philosophy of globalisation. To understand
democracy-capitalism as an evolutionary process, with a future as well as a past, is
a formidable challenge for philosophy in the twenty-first century.

Democracy-capitalism is *actualised philosophy*. It is a system of actualised philosophy as much as it is an institutional system. It contains genetic material acquired
from every period of the great philosophical tradition – from Plato, Aristotle, Cicero,
Augustine, Aquinas, the humanism of the Italian Renaissance, More, Grotius, Hobbes, Locke, Hume, Rousseau, the Scottish and French Enlightenments, Jefferson, the
Federalist Papers, nineteenth-century Liberalism and Socialism and Positivism and
Political Economy – to name only its most substantial progenitors. Without them it
would not be what it is. It contains also the historical circumstances inhabited by all
its progenitors, together with the social circumstances in which it succeeded or failed
in the revolutionary transformation of national societies. Without them it would not
be what it is. To install and to operate the institutional systems of democracy-capitalism is to give effect to its embedded philosophy and its embedded history.

The evolution from church-and-state to nation-and-state to democracy-capitalism is a story of the adaptation of totalitarianism and absolutism to changing
social circumstances. Seen within the dialectical tradition, democracy-capitalism
contains totalitarianism and absolutism in a surpassed form. *Totalitarianism* is the
total dominance by social systems over every aspect of human life in society, including mental life. Democracy-capitalism has proved to be totalitarian in principle: nothing is beyond the control of public power, including power enacted in law.
Absolutism is the explanation and justification of social power by the fact of social
power. Democracy-capitalism has proved to be absolutist in principle: it contains
within itself the whole explanation and justification of public power.

Both democracy and capitalism have achieved their success by means of their
respective naturalist theories. The General Will and the Market are God and King
depersonalised, omniscient and omnipotent. Their activity is meta-rational and
meta-ethical and hence meta-cultural. By this means their social systems are de-
transcendentalised, isolated from religion or philosophy. The General Will produces the law that society needs. The Market produces the things that people desire.
Together they produce the Good Life. The goods they produce are supposed to be
good, because they are produced by systems that are not themselves moral actors,
systems that are beyond good and evil.[54] It is for these reasons, that democracy-

---

54   In his third Critique, Immanuel Kant, self-proclaimed admirer of Rousseau, the proph-
      et of the General Will, analysed the 'natural purpose' of an organic system produced by
      the formal integration of its integral parts and which is a purpose of the whole system,
      not of its parts. I. Kant, *Critique of Judgment* (1790), §65 (tr., W. Pluhar; Indianapolis,
      Hackett Publishing Company; 1987), 251ff.

capitalism is thought to be readily exportable, to be, in principle, universal, even if it naturally adapts itself to the different circumstances of different national societies.

Because the General Will and the Market are seen as systems for processing consciousness, democracy-capitalism contains its own negating within the very structure and functioning of its systems. Democracy-capitalism negates the possibility of its own negation. This means that, in its own terms, it is not denied or disproved by the fact that, in its day-to-day practice, it is capable of producing real-world phenomena which are vivid aspects of the Bad Life – social oppression and exploitation, legally enforced inequality of every kind, crime, corruption, violence, cultural and moral degeneration, the cult of collective irrationality and collective fantasy, public and private pathologies, social and personal evil of every kind familiar from the darker side of human history.[55] Democracy-capitalism is, in practice, compatible with human misery and the depression of the human spirit. But its naturalist theory explains such things as unfortunate incidents on the way to the Good Life, since, in principle, democratic-capitalist society is always capable of redeeming itself by the natural functioning of the social processes which produce both the Good Life and the Bad Life.

It is for these reasons that democracy-capitalism is a close ally of the End of Philosophy rather than the messenger of the End of History. It is its own religion and its own philosophy. It does not proscribe either religion or philosophy, so long as they are practised in the conditions, and within the limits, set by law. It is no accident that democracy-capitalism and totalitarian fascism and communism co-existed under the aegis of the End of Philosophy in the twentieth century. A particular society may seek to exclude from its own theory and its own public mind the consciousness which transcends actual social forms, including philosophy in the great tradition. But, in so doing, it surrenders its self-creating, self-evolving freedom to the tyranny of the actual and, in particular, to the tyranny of those who actually have exceptional power over social structures and systems, including power over society's public mind, over the self-creating consciousness which flows to and from the minds of the citizens.[56]

---

55   Pascal said that Plato and Aristotle, who were by nature cheerful, only wrote seriously about politics 'to lay down rules for a madhouse. And if they pretended to treat it as something really important it was because they knew that the madmen they were talking to believed themselves to be kings and emperors.' B. Pascal, *Pensées* (fn. 13 above), 217.

56   It is unlikely that Hegel, whose ideas are invoked in the name of a theory of democracy-capitalism as 'the end of history', would have shared that view, given that it might be said, on the contrary, that his Rousseauesque ideals of 'the self-awareness of freedom' and the mutual construction of the self within society are actualised in democracy-capitalism as a sense of the almost total unfreedom of the citizen whose self-recognition is the tragic sense of a residual and derivative individuality within 'the lonely crowd'. See D. Riesman, with R. Denney & N. Glazer, *The Lonely Crowd* (New Haven, Yale University Press; 1952/2001).

6.   New World

'The whole book that is here offered to the public has been written under the influence of a kind of religious awe produced in the author's mind by the view of the irresistible revolution which has advanced for centuries in spite of every obstacle and which is still advancing in the midst of the ruins it has caused ... . A new science of politics is needed for a new world.'[57]

'The change which is thus in progress, and to a great extent consummated, is the greatest ever recorded in social affairs; the most complete, the most fruitful in consequences, and the most irrevocable. Whoever can meditate on it, and not see that so great a revolution vitiates all existing rules of government and policy, and renders all practice and all predictions grounded only on prior experience worthless, is wanting in the very first and most elementary principle of statesmanship in these times. "Il faut," as M. de Tocqueville has said, "une science politique nouvelle à un monde tout nouveau."'[58]

Such was the revolutionary self-consciousness of the nineteenth century. Of the specific aspects of that consciousness which led to the temporary *Vernichtung* of true philosophy,[59] we can now say the following, speaking from the perspective of the beginning of the twenty-first century. (1) The human sciences have revealed not one single incontrovertible truth about humanity. They have shown themselves to be, at their best, the continuation of philosophy by other means, respecting a particular set of intellectual conventions. (2) The natural sciences, especially neurology and microbiology, will continue to reveal more and more about the physical basis of the human mind, but will not, in the foreseeable future, remove the necessity for human beings to think, and to think about their thinking. We also understand better now, as Bacon and Newton already knew, that the natural sciences are themselves, not the revelation of an ultimate truth, but another form of philosophy, respecting yet another set of intellectual conventions.[60] (3) A resurrected Voltaire or Huxley might be saddened, but not surprised, to find that religions and their social effects show no signs of evaporating in the foreseeable future. The phenomenon of religion continues to be a formidable and urgent challenge facing philosophy in all its forms. (4) The theory of democracy-capitalism is seen by many as a possible philosophy of globalisation. But the mental crisis caused by the endemic co-existence of the Good Life and the Bad Life within the theory and the reality of democracy-capitalism has deepened. It is the most difficult challenge facing the self-transcending potentiality of philosophy in the great tradition. (5) Philosophy itself, in all its forms, not least philosophy in the great tradition, can be enriched, in

---

57   A. de Tocqueville, *Democracy in America* (fn. 1 above), 6-7.

58   J.S. Mill, 'Civilization', in *Dissertations* (fn. 31 above), 160-205, at 172.

59   Text beginning at fn. 22 above.

60   See *Health of Nations*, §§3.13 fn.8, 9.29.

sophistication and utility, by all that it has learned from its prolonged and profound self-examination and self-doubting.

We are living a new revolution. Philosophy in the great tradition remains as a permanent possibility of human self-evolving and self-perfecting through self-transcending. Yet again, a new human world needs the help of the old philosophical tradition, as a self-redeeming possibility within the three-dimensional global revolution of the twenty-first century, a revolution that is the beginning of a new kind of history of a new kind of human nature.

6. A Transcivilizational Perspective on Global Legal Order in the Twenty-first Century: A Way to Overcome West-centric and Judiciary-centric Deficits in International Legal Thoughts*

Onuma Yasuaki

1. Introduction

When we conceive of global legal order in the 21st century, we must consider two elements without which it would be impossible to conceive of the very idea of legal order. The first element is legitimacy[1] or justice, and the second is power, which is often expressed as effectiveness in international law. If the order of a society is perceived as illegitimate, unfair or unjust by a large number of its members, it would be difficult for the rules underpinning such an order to be positively obeyed or observed. The order would have to be maintained by the constant threat of negative sanctions against such non-obedient members, which would be too costly for the order. Such an order would be constantly challenged by those who regard it as illegitimate by various means including violence. It would be difficult for this order to guarantee security to its society members. If the primary *raison d'être* of order in a society is to provide security to its members, such an order does not deserve the name of "order".

---

* This paper is based on some of my earlier works. A number of references are therefore made to my own writings. For further references, please refer to the pages of my writings indicated in the footnotes.

1 Although international legal studies have always dealt with the problem of legitimacy in various forms and in various ways, the pioneering work dealing with the problem of legitimacy characterizing it as a core question in international law is that of Thomas Franck, *The Power of Legitimacy among Nations*, Oxford Univ. Press, 1990. However, the definition of legitimacy adopted in this book is so narrow that even Franck himself changed his position in his following work, *Fairness in International Law and Institutions*, Oxford Univ. Press, 1995. In this paper, the term "legitimacy" is used according to a general usage of the term, *i.e.*, the state of affairs that is characterized as fair, righteous and justifiable. See also Kelly, J. P., "The Twilight of Customary International Law", *Virginia Journal of International Law*, vol.40(2000), pp. 449-543; Chigara, B., *Legitimacy Deficit in Custom*, Ashigate, 2001.

Ronald St. John Macdonald & Douglas M. Johnston (eds.), Towards World Constitutionalism, *pp. 151-189.*
© 2005 *Koninklijke Brill NV. Printed in The Netherlands.* ISBN 90 04 14612 1.

If, on the other hand, the global order lacks support by powerful nations, such an order would remain just wishful thinking with little possibility of being realized. The so-called "New International Economic Order" in the 1970s is a good example. This "order" was vehemently advocated by developing countries and a certain number of experts, and was adopted in the form of UNGA resolutions. But it remained basically on paper. It lacked support from most developed countries, which possessed various kinds of power.

However, the power itself needs to be legitimized. Even the greatest power in the world cannot disregard the element of legitimacy or justice for a long period of time. International law generally embodies legitimacy because of its shared perception as "law", which is associated with the notion of justice.[2] Behavior of a powerful nation that disregards important rules or principles of international law would be not only resisted by other nations but also checked by domestic mechanisms including criticism by voters.[3] They may at the beginning support such "powerful" or "macho" policies. But later they change their minds, realizing that they have to pay too much if they continue disregarding legitimacy and inviting increasing resistance from other nations.[4]

This chapter deals with this crucially important problem of legitimacy in the global legal order. It seeks to demonstrate the need for and significance of what I call a transcivilizational perspective[5] in conceiving of and constructing the legitimate global legal order in the 21st century. Section 2 elaborates the idea of transcivilizational perspective in comparison with the predominant perspectives dealing with transboundary issues: the international perspective and the transnational perspective. Section 3 elucidates how civilizational factors have been preserved in the sovereign states system and why problems of civilizations came to be discussed vocally after the end of the Cold War. Section 4 deals with the problem of general international law, which underlies global legal order, from the viewpoint of global legitimacy. It will be shown that contemporary theory and practice of equating

---

2   Onuma, Y., "International Law in and with International Politics: The Functions of International Law in International Society", *European Journal of International Law*, vol.14-1(2003), p. 123.

3   *Ibid.*, pp. 119-120.

4   The policy of the Bush Jr administration on the Iraq War of 2003 is a good example. At first, the Bush administration started the war with little regard to the perceived legitimacy of its policy. Disregarding international law and paying little attention to the UN Security Council apparently demonstrates this attitude. However, as the US continued to face strong resistance including terrorist attacks from Iraqi people on its occupation policies, the administration suffered not only from international criticism but also domestic criticism. They thus had to change their policies and paid more regard and respect at least as a lip service to international law and the UN in order to mitigate harsh criticism due to the lack of legitimacy of their policies.

5   The term "transcivilizational" is a neology. I first used the term "intercivilizational", which is also a neology, in 1981 when I gave a paper at the 75th anniversary convocation of the American Society of International Law. See Onuma, Y., "Remarks", *Proc. ASIL*, vol. 77(1983), pp. 163-70.

general international law with customary international law must be rectified in order that the global legal order may satisfy the fundamental requirements of international, transnational and transcivilizational legitimacy.

2. Transcivilizational Perspectives as Compared with International and Transnational Perspectives

A.   Problems of the 21st Century World

The inauguration of the 21st century revealed a world characterized by great schisms and serious conflicts. These schisms and conflicts exist in various forms. The most serious ones exist between a military, economic and informational superpower with universalistic preconceptions yet little understanding of "others", and a far greater number of those who share desperate resentment and frustrations against the existing regimes, whether they are international or domestic. September 11th was symbolic of these schisms and conflicts. Humanity must make every effort to bridge such schisms and resolve or mitigate the incidence of such conflicts.

Some of those who resort to terrorism or acquiesce to it believe that there is no other way but to resort to violence because their voices and claims are not heard by those who control global affairs. Seeking to secure opportunities for discourse and argumentation to those who believe that they are not heard and are victimized by the present regimes may contribute to such resolution or mitigation. It may also help to find a clue to identify certain values and virtues of a high degree of legitimacy, shared by peoples on the globe, regardless of religions, cultures and diverse ways of thinking. This identification of global values and virtues transcending national, cultural, religious and civilizational boundaries is a prerequisite for conceiving of the legitimate global legal order in the 21st century. The transcivilizational perspective constitutes an important way of understanding transboundary problems, and can contribute to this important task.

The transcivilizational perspective is a perspective from which we see, recognize, interpret, assess, and seek to propose solutions to problems transcending national boundaries by developing a cognitive and evaluative framework based on the recognition of plurality of civilizations that have long existed in human history.[6] It is a theoretical device by which we can recognize and appreciate various ways of thinking of diverse peoples and seek to identify values and virtues that are perceived as legitimate by as many people as possible. This perspective is particularly useful in that it can demonstrate that predominant views, ideas and understanding in globally influential discourse are often based on West-centric perspectives, shared by less than 20% of the human species, and are alien in many respects to the rest of the global population.

---

6   See generally Onuma, Y., *Jinken, kokka, bunmei*, Chikuma Shobo, 1998, pp. 13-36, 332-337, 345-347. See also Onuma, Y.,"Towards an Intercivilizational Approach to Human Rights", *Asian Yearbook of International Law*, vol. 7 (2001), pp. 22-31.

Any ideas or discourses without critical examination of the presumptions and preoccupations of these West-centric perspectives can hardly be conducive to a global legal order that would be appreciated by more than 80% of the human species as legitimate. If these people are to accept those ways of thinking characterized as "universal" or "general", those ways of thinking must be critically reconceptualized so that these people find them more comfortable and more akin to their own ways of thinking. The notion of human rights is a typical example that requires such critical reconceptualization.[7]

On the other hand, the transcivilizational perspective is a perspective that has already been tacitly and unconsciously adopted by those who see, evaluate and seek to solve the problems transcending national boundaries. When unconsciously adopted, however, the transcivilizational perspective tends to distinguish "we" and "they" according to the preconceived, substantive and monolithic notion of civilization. This substantive notion of civilization is often associated with preoccupations, biases and superiority complexes. Cultures or civilizations are not a substantive entity that a person or society exclusively belongs to. A person generally senses, thinks and behaves according to plural cultures and civilizations simultaneously. Also, cultures and civilizations change over the period of time, influencing each other. However, many people tend to believe that they belong to a certain civilization in an exclusive and unchangeable manner. They tend to stick to a particular interpretation of this substantive and exclusive notion of civilization, if they take a transcivilizational perspective in an unconscious manner.

It is important, therefore, to make people aware of the flaws originating from this substantive and exclusive notion of civilization that has been unconsciously adopted. Considering the problem of civilizations is of crucial importance to conceive of legitimate legal order in the 21st century world, because a number of seri-

---

7   Human rights is characterized as one of the globally legitimate values in today's world, shared by people all over the globe, regardless of religion, culture, and diverse ways of thought and behavior in general. It has become one of the most important notions that guide and shape the spirit of the time in the latter half of the 20th century. Recognition of the universal value of human rights is one of the most important indices that distinguish postwar international society from prewar international society. After humanity witnessed the Holocaust, the most serious and massive violation of human rights, the status of human rights has continuously been elevated. Human rights has established its status as a "trump" in almost all areas of human life. Together with global environmental concerns, human rights will most likely maintain such a preeminent status at least during the former half of the 21st century. Human rights thus constitutes one of the most important elements of the *ordre public* in the 21st century global community. However, even this human rights value must be critically reexamined, re-construed and reconstructed through this transcivilizational perspective in order to be perceived as legitimate by a large number of human species whose way of thinking may not be necessarily familiar with the ideas and ways of thinking that underlie human rights. See generally Onuma, *supra* note 6 [*Jinken, kokka, bunmei*]. See also Onuma, Y., "In Quest of Intercivilizational Human Rights", Warner, D. (ed.), *Human Rights and Humanitarian Law*, Kluwer Law International, 1997, pp. 72-78.

ous problems threatening the global order will likely take a form of "clash of civilizations". We must thus liberate ourselves from the exclusive, substantive notion of civilization, and reconstruct it from a functional perspective in order to overcome conflicts associated with the substantive and exclusive perception of civilizations. The first step for understanding the nature, meaning and significance of the transcivilizational perspective is to understand other predominant perspectives from which we unconsciously view problems transcending national boundaries. They are international and transnational perspectives.[8] By comparing with those predominant perspectives, we can see characteristic features and functions of the transcivilizational perspective.

B.   The International Perspective

The international perspective is the predominant perspective from which we see, recognize, interpret, assess, and seek to propose solutions to, problems that transcend national boundaries. This perspective is a product of the globalization of a European perception that grasps the world as an international society composed of sovereign states. This is a novel image in human history. Until the 17th century, such an image was not held even by Europeans. For them, the world was basically composed of Christians and pagans. Even for the "fathers" of international law, the international perspective was not so familiar. For example, Grotius did not see problems arising from conflicting interests between independent entities as problems between *states*. He used various terms such as *potestas publica*, *maxime summa*, *summa potestas*, *magistratus*, *populus* in addition to *civitas*, to express subjects of law and interests, and to explain phenomena and problems which today's people would usually classify as "international" questions.[9]

In other regions, the situation was similar. For Muslims, who dominated vast areas in Central and South Asia[s] as well as in the Mediterranean, the world was divided into the abode of Islam and the abode of War. The former is the area where Muslims reigned, while the latter is the area where non-Muslims reigned.[10] The fictitious notion of the unity of the Islamic world was maintained although the Islamic world was actually divided by a number of competing dynasties. Like Europeans, Muslims adopted a kind of inter-religious perspective for grasping problems

---

8   In order to conceive of global order in the 21st century, we also need to think of transgender legitimacy and trans-generational legitimacy. Because of the lack of space, these problems will not be discussed here.

9   Grotius, H., *De jure belli ac pacis libri tres*, 1646 ed., vol. I, i, 1; vol. I, iv-v; vol. II, xxv-xxvi. See Onuma, Y., "War", Onuma, Y.(ed.), *A Normative Approach to War*, Clarendon Press, 1993, pp. 98-121; *id.*, "Conclusion", *id.*, pp. 334-338.

10   For a classical view of this Islamic perception, see Khadduri, M., *War and Peace in the Law of Islam*, Johns Hopkins Press, 1979. See also Khadduri, M., *The Islamic Law of Nations*, Johns Hopkins Press, 1966, and Suzuki, T., *Isuramu no ie kara baberu no to e*, Libro Port, 1993.

transcending boundaries of entities within which the life of a certain people was organized, governed, regulated and administered.

For those who lived in East Asia, the world was composed of the civilized and the barbarians.[11] This Sino-centric view of the world was shared not only by the Chinese but also by people in East Asia in general. It was only when the Quing Dynasty recognized that Korea was an independent nation in Article 1 of the Peace Treaty of 1895 between China and Japan that China finally gave up the Sino-centric view, which grasped the world as composed of civilized and barbarians. For China, to recognize Korea, which had been the most faithful tribute state, as an independent state meant the decisive renunciation of the Sino-centric view of the world, which had already deteriorated since the defeat in the Opium War of 1840-42.[12]

In all these cases, no perception of the world as composed of sovereign states existed. Hence there existed no notion of the "international" as it is conceived of today. It is only after European powers established hegemony on a global scale around the end of the 19th century that the image of the world as composed of nation states, which was first held by modern Europeans, came to be shared by people all over the world.[13] With the globalization of this image of the world, the international perspective came to be predominant. When non-European societies attempted to assert themselves in the international arena, they sought to become independent nation-states. The European model of the nation-state was thus universalized.

The idea of the "international" has often been equated with the "interstate" or the "intergovernmental". Until recently, this was only natural. People came to perceive the world from an international perspective because the power of nation-states overwhelmed that of other entities or agents, such as churches, temples, cities and feudal lords, and because this power is represented and exercised by national governments. International agreements have basically been interstate agreements made by national governments. International organizations have basically been intergovernmental organizations.[14] The United Nations was established by states, that is, by national governments, and has been run by states, again by national governments. The 20th century was the era of nation-states *par excellence.*

The international perspective has most typically been adopted by those who decide and carry out policies of the national governments. It has also been adopted by international lawyers, international relations scholars, other experts, officials of international organizations, business people, journalists and ordinary citizens.

---

11   See Fairbank, J. (ed.), *The Chinese World Order*, Harvard Univ. Press, 1968; Hamashita, T., *Kindai chugoku no kokusaiteki keiki*, Tokyo Univ. Press, 1990. See also Onuma, Y., "When was the Law of International Society Born?", *Journal of the History of International Law*, vol. 2 (2000), pp. 27-54 and references cited therein.

12   *Ibid.,* pp. 51-54.

13   *Ibid.,* pp. 27-54.

14   Since the late 20th century, the term "international organization" has sometimes been used as including non-governmental organizations, reflecting the emerging importance of NGOs.

Whenever they consider problems transcending national boundaries, they have unconsciously been inclined to take this international perspective. It is symbolic that Oppenheim's treatise of international law, which established international legal theory based on the definition of international law as law among nations in the most sophisticated manner, was prevalent through the 20th century. Some international lawyers sought to establish a theory of international law regarding the world as composed of individuals rather than nations,[15] but this attempt was rejected by most experts.

As will be demonstrated later, multinational enterprises and NGOs have played, are playing, and will play, an important role in addressing trans-boundary issues. However, they cannot have the legitimacy of life and death. Few would die for the cause of multinational enterprises or NGOs. None would accept the death penalty or even imprisonment sentenced by them. Moreover, for most of the developing countries that are home to about 80% of the world's population, the task of nation-building began only after World War II. For the overwhelming majority of humanity, the 21st century will be the period of nation-states. At least for the first half of the 21st century, the international perspective will continue to be the most important perspective from which human beings see, recognize, interpret, assess, and seek to propose solutions to, problems beyond the reach of a single nation-state.[16]

C.   *The Transnational Perspective*

Even in modern times when the power of a nation state became preeminent, however, human activities are not always driven by, represented by, or associated with nation states. Especially in the latter half of the 20th century, the scale of private activities transcending national boundaries became enormous. Major agents of these activities are multinational enterprises and global NGOs. They all assume non-state characteristic features. It is difficult to grasp their critical aspects from the international perspective alone, because this perspective tends to pay attention mainly to phenomena associated with national governments.

The term "international" has been used not only to refer to phenomena associated with nation-states or national governments, but to refer to a wider range of problems transcending national boundaries, including arts, sports, literature, movies and the like. Such usages as "international sports" or "international music" are typical examples. A major reason for this general usage of the term "international" is that the notion of international is so predominant that people use it unconsciously even when they refer to phenomena not directly associated with nation-states or national governments. Yet, as long as the term "international" is

---

15   Scelle, G., *Précis de droit des gens*, I, Recueil Sirey, 1932, p. 14 *et passim*; Scelle, G., *Précis de droit des gens*, II, Recueil Sirey, 1934, p. 10 *et passim* ; Scelle, G., "Le phénomène juridique du dédoublement fonctionnel", *Rechtsfragen der Internationalen Organisation: Festschrift für Hans Wehberg*, Vittorio Klostermann, 1956, p. 333.

16   See Onuma, *supra* note 6 [*Jinken, kokka, bunmei*], pp. 15-16.

adopted, there remains a tendency to unconsciously think of something related to states or national governments even when it would be more appropriate to think of non-state actors or their activities. This is why a transnational perspective, which is centered on non-state actors and their activities, was needed and has actually been used in an influential manner. Transnationalism is both a cause and a consequence of increasing criticism of state-centrism.

The transnational perspective has established itself as an important perspective since the 1950s. Philip Jessup published a book titled *Transnational Law* as early as 1956.[17] Although the transnational perspective was first adopted explicitly by Jessup, an eminent international lawyer, it has been more consciously and explicitly adopted and emphasized by experts of international relations. Not only those who use the term "transnational" in phrases such as "transnational law" or "transnational legal process", but also those who emphasize the significance of (1) transnational flow of capital and information, (2) interdependence of nations, (3) the role of NGOs and international institutions in various trans-boundary areas, (4) global governance, and (5) global civil society, have represented and applied the transnational perspective in their own ways. Through these theories and advocacies, the transnational perspective came to be well accepted in various forms by ordinary citizens in developed societies by the end of the 20th century.

Because so many different advocates have adopted the transnational perspective in a diverse manner, it is difficult to define it in an unequivocal manner. Generally speaking it has been understood as implying the following factors: (1) Attention is paid to non-state or non-governmental actors, especially those enterprises and/ or NGOs that are engaged in trans-boundary activities; (2) It is generally assumed that such non-state actors are characterized by modernistic features such as those pursuing capitalist profits or modernistic values of civil society; (3) It is also generally assumed that when this perspective is adopted as a normative framework, the values and virtues to be pursued are Western-oriented modernistic ones, such as democracy, human rights, and market economy.

The transnational perspective is useful as a tool to complement and modify the international perspective, which tends to be state-centric and to overlook the activities of non-state actors. For example, those who pay attention to transnational activities of enterprises have advocated that agreements and standards between enterprises or industrial associations have been creating legal regulatory systems that are neither domestic nor international law. Enterprises, which did not have means to pursue responsibility of states under international law when their rights were violated, are today entitled to claim reparations or compensations directly under international law in the ICSID mechanism and other arbitration tribunals. Multinational enterprises and the United Nations have worked together in such a way as to regulate the formers' behavior by means of the Global Compact in the fields of human rights, environment, labor conditions and the like.

---

17   Jessup published *A Modern Law of Nations*, which contained basic ideas on transnational perspective already in 1952.

The significance of NGOs has also tremendously been enhanced. NGOs have been heavily involved in the creative process of international law. In the fields of human rights and environment, it is unthinkable today to draft major international instruments without consultations with NGOs. Even in the field of international security, NGOs were heavily involved in the creation of the Landmine Ban Treaty of 1997. In the application of international law and other normative instruments too, the role of the NGO is significant. The UN Human Rights Committee, its subcommittee, and all monitoring bodies of human rights instruments have been heavily dependent upon the information, knowledge and advice of NGOs when they carry out their mandates. Not only huge international NGOs, such as Amnesty International and Human Rights Watch, but also a number of local NGOs have played a critical role for international organizations and monitoring bodies to redress human rights violations. NGOs in the fields of economic cooperation and development, as well as environment, have also played important roles and have contributed towards the proper functioning of the treaty system in each field. In this way, the significance of the transnational perspective has been widely recognized since the late 20th century, when the issues generated by the global market economy, human rights and the global environment came to be perceived as major global issues.[18]

D.   Problems of Transnational Perspectives

Is the combination of international and transnational perspectives sufficient to see, understand and seek to solve the global problems in the 21st century? My answer to this question is "no". Why? Because it cannot fully address, recognize and respond to the aspirations, expectations, frustrations and resentments held by the overwhelming majority of humanity: the people in the non-Western world, who comprise more than 80% of the human species. We can see this problematic feature by turning our attention to the major agent of transnational perspectives.

Major agents of non-state transnational activities, exerting a great influence on the creation and realization of international law, diplomacy of national governments and behavior of international organizations, are multinational enterprises and NGOs: Microsoft, Citibank, Amnesty International, Greenpeace and so on. Although they have a global character in their compositions, activities and influences, their West-centric preconceptions and propensities are apparent. In the case of multinational enterprises, their transnational activities are motivated by the sprit of capitalism, which is essentially a product of modern Western society. Most influential enterprises are owned and run by Western elites, except for Japanese companies and a few Korean companies. Some of the international normative instruments mainly advocated and generated by organizations representing interests of global enterprises have been harshly criticized by a number of developing countries. The failure of MAI is a good example.

---

18   See, *e.g.*, Teubner, G., *Global Law Without a State*, Dartmouth, 1997; Koh, H., "Transnational Legal Process", *Nebraska Law Review*, vol.75(1996), pp.181-207; Koh, H., "Why Do Nations Obey International Law?", *Yale Law Journal*, vol.106(1997), pp.2599-2659.

In the case of NGOs, the situation is more complicated. Some NGOs have sought to work for the people in the South in the spirit of solidarity. This is particularly true for those NGOs that are engaged in economic and social development of developing countries and humanitarian assistance to them. Many of these NGOs have made serious efforts to overcome their West-centric preconceptions. Even Western NGOs engaged in human rights activities, many of whom are critical of human rights violations in developing countries, and are often criticized for their West-centric preoccupations and arrogance, are critical of their own Western governments.

However, it cannot be denied that most of them are based, administered and financed in Western societies. Many of the leaders have Western educational and cultural backgrounds, and communicate with each other in English without any reservations, as if it is a matter of course. Their basic assumptions, ways of thinking and cultural propensities are undeniably, and understandably, West-centric.[19] NGOs in Asia and Africa are far less influential. To make matters worse, some Asian and African NGOs are even more West-centric than their Western counterparts because of their members' educational backgrounds in the West, their inferiority complex towards Western society, and their elitist status in their own societies.[20]

Thus, they have failed to sufficiently represent voices, aspirations and desperations of the poor, suppressed, and frustrated massive populations in the non-Western world. Some of their frustrations and resentment have taken a violent form: terrorist attacks on the US, Americans, Israel and Western society in general. There also exist negative perceptions shared not only by the governments, but also by the ordinary people against West-centric NGOs, regarding them as aggressive, arrogant and imposing. These facts suggest that merely modifying and complementing the international perspective with the transnational perspective is not sufficient. Although the state-centric nature of the international perspective may be rectified by the transnational perspective, the modernistic and West-centric nature of the international perspective cannot be rectified by the transnational perspective. In order to address the critical problems such as those of terrorism and human rights that will likely continue in the 21st century, we need a perspective from which we can grasp problems that cannot be addressed either by the international or the transnational perspective or a combination of the two together.

Here, we should recognize that non-state actors are not limited to private enterprises and NGOs as they are generally and vaguely considered to be in the predominant discourses. Non-state actors may comprise various entities or groups such as indigenous peoples, ethnic minorities, churches, temples, Islamic communities, trans-boundary global or regional networks of Christians, Buddhists, or Muslims and other entities or groups based on various types of links. Moreover,

---

19   As to problematic features of West-centrism in the major human rights NGOs, see Onuma, *supra* note 6 [Towards an Intercivilizational Approach to Human Rights], pp. 38-46.

20   See Onuma, *supra* note 6 [*Jinken, kokka, bunmei*], pp. 151-179.

values and virtues humans or groups of humans pursue are not limited to national interests, capitalistic economic interests or modernistic civil interests. Humans are associated or connected with each other by a variety of bonds such as religious, cultural, linguistic, and/or pre-modernistic social features. They sense, think and behave according to these common standards or frameworks. These thoughts and behaviors are not always appreciated by state-centric international perspectives, or modernistic and West-centric transnational perspectives. In order to appreciate these various thoughts and behaviors we need some other perspectives.

E.   The Transcivilizational Perspective

The 20th century was the era when the international perspective was predominant and the transnational perspective complemented it. However, there existed perspectives through which people sought to see other aspects of the world that were overlooked by these major perspectives. They are the perspectives of "developing countries" or the "Third World". These perspectives are most useful when we seek to grasp the problems in terms of economic inequality between nations, famines, hunger and poverty on a global scale. Some international lawyers developed theories dividing nations into three groups – First, Second and Third Worlds – and required a consensus among these groups for the validity of general international law.[21] These theories enjoyed a certain degree of reality until the end of the Cold War.

However, by the end of the 20th century, these perspectives and theories lost their relevance to realities in a number of respects. First, these perspectives are mainly concerned with economic aspects of humanity. As far as economic development is concerned, however, it came to be more and more difficult to talk about the Third World as a single group. A small number of countries such as Singapore, South Korea, Malaysia and Thailand underwent significant economic development, but a far larger number of countries in Africa became even more miserable in economic terms than they used to be. In the multinational treaty-making process, such as that of the UN Convention on Climate Change, and multilateral negotiations involving economic interests of various governments, producers, consumers and others such as those of WTO conferences, the Third World nations no longer act as a single group. Moreover, the end of the Cold War meant the disappearance of the major part of the Second World, the Soviet bloc. It would be difficult to talk about the First, Second and Third Worlds in the 21st century.

More fundamentally, although many problems have their causes in economic poverty and inequality, humans are not driven solely by economic factors. Take the example of terrorism. Terrorism does not originate from poverty alone. It has a political dimension. If a suppressive and corrupt regime is regarded as closely connected with some powerful foreign nation regarded as arrogant and aggressive, a desperate frustration due to the suppression and corruption may take the form of a terrorist attack against the latter. Terrorism has religious dimensions as well.

---

21   カセーセ、レーリンク.

The extremist interpretation of an influential religion, coupled with economic and political resentment, may produce terrorism. Also a memory of a massacre of an ethnic group committed by other ethnic groups may be a cause of terrorism against the latter.

Thus, we need a perspective that pays attention not only to economic factors but to more comprehensive factors including political, social, cultural, religious and historical ones. A transcivilizational perspective is such a comprehensive perspective. It is a perspective from which we may be able to grasp important aspects of human activities that transcend national boundaries and yet may be overlooked if seen from international and transnational perspectives alone. However, the term "civilization" is notoriously equivocal. It may also remind people of the notorious argument of Samuel Huntington's "Clash of Civilizations."[22] It is necessary to elaborate on the notion of civilization.

I agree with the preceding theories on civilization such as those advocated by Arnold Toynbee, Oswald Spengler and Samuel Huntington in that we should adopt a perspective from which we can we see, recognize, interpret, assess, and seek to propose solutions to global problems with the comprehensive notion of civilization in mind. However, I cannot agree with them insofar as they view humans as belonging exclusively to a particular civilization. In my view, excluding the possibility of a human thinking and behaving according to plural civilizations is theoretically wrong. In most cases human beings sense, think and behave according to plural civilizations simultaneously.[23]

For example, contemporary British people behave according to modern European civilization, which is basically secular in its constitution. However, albeit unconsciously and implicitly, most of them also think and behave according to Christian civilization, which originates in the pre-modern period. They further spend their daily life by adopting a lifestyle of mass production, mass consumption and mass waste, typically formulated as the "American way of life." This way of life, which is a contemporary civilization on a global scale, has been accepted not only by people in the US, but also by most people in developed societies. In this way, British people behave according to plural civilizations simultaneously. They do not exclusively "belong to" British or (modern) European civilization. For other people, whether they are Japanese, Indians, and Cubans, the situation is basically the same.

Defining the notion of civilization as excluding the possibility of multilayered "belonging" to plural civilizations is practically inappropriate as well. People are generally proud of their own civilizations. If the contemporary life of a particular people is miserable, then they tend to glorify the mystified civilization to which they believe they belong. They are inclined to disclaim other civilizations. If we

---

22   Huntington, S., "Clash of Civilizations?", *Foreign Affairs* (Aug 1993). See also Huntington, S., *Clash of Civilizations and the Remaking of World Order*, Simon and Schuster, 1996.

23   See Onuma, *supra* note 6 [Towards an Intercivilizational Approach to Human Rights], pp. 30-31.

define civilization as allowing humans to belong to only one civilization, such an exclusive notion of civilization will certainly contribute to the glorification of a particular civilization at the cost of other civilizations, thus inviting the conclusion of a "clash of civilizations".

We should therefore define the concept of civilization as a functional term that allows humans to behave according to plural civilizations simultaneously. People usually refer to civilizations when they talk about common ways of thinking and behavior that geographically extend beyond a single nation and historically last for at least several centuries. In some languages and sometimes the term civilization is understood as centering on material aspects of human life, in contrast to the concept of culture understood as centering on the spiritual aspects of life. In Germany, this tends to be the case. In other languages and at other times, the term civilization is understood as synonymous to culture, to be used to characterize a national characteristic features as well. In France, for example, when they refer to French culture, they say "*la civilisation française*" rather than "*la culture française*". Such equivocal usage of the term cannot be avoided because the term civilization is a word that is used in ordinary life as an ordinary word.[24] The polysemy of the term "civilization" should be understood as a sign of fruitfulness, rather than weakness, of the term.

Although the term "transcivilizational" sounds new, transboundary phenomena have actually long been seen and interpreted from various transcivilizational perspectives in an unconscious manner. The important task for us is to make explicit this actual adoption of the transcivilizational perspectives and to liberate them from an exclusive and substantive notion of civilization, *re-characterizing* it as a functional notion. We shall first explore the relationship between civilizations and global society from this functional perspective of civilizations. How has the modern international system characterized and treated various civilizations? Why did people begin to talk about civilizations with the end of the Cold War? How should we introduce the concept of civilization into the international legal discourse?

3.   Civilizational Factors and Perspectives in International Law and International Relations

A.   *Civilizational Factors as Preserved within the Framework of the Sovereign States System: The Significance of the Non-Intervention Principle*

As described earlier, the international perspective became predominant when the modern European states system (*die europaische Staatensystem*) became global. The predominance of the international perspective, however, does not mean the end of the cognizance or understanding of the world from various civilizational perspectives. In fact, the sovereign states system and international law that came

---

24   As to the equivocal usage of the terms civilization and culture, see classical works of Febre, L. *et al., Civilisation: Le mot et l'idee*, Paris, 1930; Kroeber, A. and Kluckhorn, C., *Culture: A Critical Review of Concepts and Definitions*,Cambridge, Mass., 1952.

to be globally valid were heavily characterized by a Eurocentric perspective of civilization. From the late 19th to the early 20th century, international law was often defined as the law among civilized nations.[25] Here, the term "civilization" meant no other than European civilization. Other great civilizations were simply not regarded as civilizations.

Yet this Eurocentric civilization was a modern, secular civilization based on modern sciences and technologies. Christianity, the preeminent characteristic feature of the European civilization for a long time, was not a requirement of civilization. The capacity to abide by the rules and principles of international law established by the European nations was the critical requirement for recognition as a civilized nation.[26] In this way, a particular Eurocentric perspective of civilization was tacitly adopted in the definition and treatment of international law from the late 19th to the early 20th century.

The most famous use of the term "civilization" in international law is in Article 38 of the Statute of the International Court of Justice. It provides that "the general principles of law recognized by civilized nations" is one of the norms that the ICJ shall apply. When this provision was first adopted in 1919, the term "civilized" implied European civilization, reflecting the self-confidence of the aggressive and arrogant Europeans at that time. Today, the term "civilized" is generally ignored. Why? Because the term was abused by Western powers to rationalize colonization of Asia and Africa, as well as discriminatory treatment against Afro-Asians, and therefore is now regarded as connoting inappropriate Western arrogance.

However, there is another, structural reason why the term "civilization" has not been used explicitly in international law and international relations. The sovereign states system is a fundamental principle of ordering the world that was adopted by modern Europeans and was later imposed on, or accepted by, non-Europeans. One of the basic principles of this sovereign states system is the principle of non-intervention. Each nation is sovereign. It can decide its own rules, economic system,

---

[25]   See Kunz, J., "Zum Begriff der 'nation civilisée' im modernen Völkerrecht", *Zeitschrift für öffentliches Recht*, vol.7(1927-28), S. 89; Schwarzenberger, G., "The Standard of Civilization in International Law", *Current Legal Problems*, vol. 8 (1955), pp. 220; Gong, G., *The Standard of 'Civilization' in International Society*, Oxford Univ. Press, 1984, pp. 45-53, 76-81 *et passim*.

[26]   It was the Western powers who were to judge whether a certain nation was civilized or not. Japan, a non-Christian nation, made serious efforts to modernize (=Westernize) its society and to be recognized as a civilized nation by them. Its main purpose was to revise the unequal treaties it was forced to conclude when it started to have substantial foreign relations with them in the 19th century. Japan was so recognized when it demonstrated that it could comply with the law of war in the Sino-Japanese War in 1894-5 and the Russo-Japanese War in 1904-5. Japan succeeded in revising the unequal treaty with Great Britain in 1902. Other Western powers followed the example of Britain and revised their unequal treaties with Japan in the early 20th century. Other Afro-Asian nations suffered from unequal treaties much longer. Japan itself, as a newly emerging imperial power, imposed unequal treaties on other weaker Asian nations such as Korea.

culture and religion within its territory. Various civilizations including non-Western civilizations survived within territorial boundaries under the non-intervention principle. Naturally, these civilizations took slightly different forms in different territorial settings according to different national cultures as well as political, economic and social systems. However, this intra-civilizational diversity was inherent in any civilizations. The Euro-centric sovereign states system merely accepted and maintained this intra-civilizational diversity.

Even when the European powers established global hegemony, they did not require non-European nations to adopt either Christianity, or a European political, economic, social and cultural system. More precisely, European powers, although they were far superior to Asian rulers in their military powers, could not require non-Europeans to adopt the European way of life in terms of political and economic system, religion, culture and language. They reorganized the administrative structure to rule colonies according to their ways, but they could not penetrate into the life of ordinary people in the colonies. The European imperial powers did not possess effective means to change the way of thinking and behavior of massive populations in Asia and Africa.[27] The lifestyle of ordinary people in the non-European world was basically preserved intact[28] except for economic influences that were exerted on local life by the global capitalist economy conducted by mainly Europeans and Americans.

As long as governments of the non-European nations protected the rights of aliens and conducted their foreign affairs in accordance with Eurocentric international law and diplomacy, the European powers were basically content. Eurocentric international law has not been concerned with what kind of religion, culture or social customs each nation has. Civilizational diversity was thus preserved within the sovereign nation-states system as domestic matters not regulated by international law. The principle of non-intervention has protected the civilizational diversity within national boundaries, although it was sometimes violated by powerful nations. Afro-Asian and Latin American nations regarded the non-intervention principle as an important means to protect them from various forms of intervention by imperialist powers, and were eager to strengthen it.

After World War II, when Afro-Asian nations attained independence and formed a majority in international society, this principle was thus further strengthened. The principle of non-intervention provided in the Declaration on the Principles of International Law concerning Friendly Relations and Co-operation among States of 1970 is a typical example of this strengthened principle of non-interven-

---

27 The situation was different in South and Central America, where active propagation of Christianity was conducted. Christianity penetrated deep into the daily life of ordinary people. There were also a substantial number of intermarriages between the European settlers and original inhabitants.

28 This makes a contrast with the 20th century US hegemony. The US hegemony has been characterized by its mass culture, represented by Hollywood movies and other forms of soft power resources. Therefore, US culture penetrated deep into the daily lives of ordinary people of non-US areas.

tion.[29] The ICJ, in its judgment in the Nicaragua Case of 1986, recognized the non-intervention principle in this Declaration as an indication of the *opinio juris* as to customary international law.[30] There are other international normative instruments that embody this strengthened principle of non-intervention.[31]

B.   Decline of the Non-Intervention Principle

Toward the end of the 20th century, however, the non-intervention principle gradually deteriorated. From a substantive perspective, the global market economy and the global flow of information gradually undermined the non-intervention principle. Economic, social, cultural and informational activities have transcended national boundaries. Sovereign states came to find it more and more difficult to control these activities through national regulations. On the other hand, the US, the largest beneficiary from private transnational activities, has enacted extraterritorial laws that are in conflict with the traditional principle of non-intervention. Although the US faced resistance from various nations, it has gradually transformed the system of sovereign states to its own liking. In the fields of foreign exchange and investment too, huge forces of the market economy overwhelm national regulations of most countries. Substantive bases underlying the non-intervention principle came to be seriously undermined.

In addition, problems relating to human rights and the global environment quickly caused concern in a large number of people, especially those in influential developed countries. These problems, once characterized as matters falling within a domestic jurisdiction of a state, came to be characterized as matters of international concern. Nations can no longer claim that they can deal with these issues as they like. Afro-Asian nations, which had been the major supporter of the principle, sought to deny it *vis-à-vis* South Africa, because South Africa had tried to defend its apartheid policy by invoking the non-intervention principle. However, by denying the non-intervention principle *vis-à-vis* South Africa, Afro-Asian nations themselves had to accept certain limitations on the principle. Thus, serious violations of human rights that are characterized as matters of international concern

---

29   The Declaration provides, as the principle concerning the duty not to intervene in matters within the domestic jurisdiction of any State, that "No State or group of States has the right to intervene, directly or indirectly, for any reason whatever, in the internal or external affairs of any other State. Consequently, armed intervention and all other forms of interference or attempted threats against the personality of the State or against its political, economic and cultural elements, are in violation of international law." UNGA Res. 2625 (XXV), UN GAOR, 25th Sess., Supp. No. 28, at 121, UN Doc. A/8028 (1971), adopted by consensus on October 24, 1970.

30   Case Concerning Military and Paramilitary Activities in and against Nicaragua, *ICJ Reports*, 1986, para.191. See also *ibid.*, paras.202-203.

31   G.A.Res.2131,UNGAOR, 20th Sess., Supp.No.14, UN Doc. A/6014(1965); G.A.Res.2625, UNGAOR, 25th Sess., Supp.No.28, UN Doc. A/8028(1970); G.A.Res.36/103, UNGAOR, 36th Sess., Supp.No.51, UN Doc. A/36/51(1981).

could not be protected by the shield of the non-intervention principle.[32] In the field of the protection of global environment, we can see a similar development.

The deterioration of the non-intervention principle proceeded only gradually, but the end of the Cold War radically changed the situation. The US and Western European powers regarded it as the victory of their system as a whole, represented by market economy, democracy, human rights and rule of law. Also, this "victory" was realized in the midst of the emergence of powerful NGOs based in the West. Triumphant voices questioning the legitimacy of the state or the government in general worked further against the principle of non-intervention. The principle now came to be regarded as a protective shield of a corrupt government in developing countries Moreover, people witnessed a number of large-scale atrocities in the former Yugoslavia, Sudan, Rwanda and many other places due to the malfunctioning of a state.

By the end of the 20th century, a number of political, social and intellectual elites in the Western nations raised their voices against the non-intervention principle and state sovereignty in various ways. Their claims are far more vocal than those of the rest of the world because of the power and influence of global media institutions in the West. These claims include furthering projects dealing with "the global market economy", "the universality of human rights", "global civil society", "humanitarian interventions" and others. Diverse civilizational factors, which had been preserved within national boundaries under the non-intervention principle, came to be attacked for various reasons. Violations of human rights based on long-standing interpretations of religions, social practices, customs or cultures in non-Western societies are leading examples.

There have been a large number of serious human rights violations in those countries, including even genocides. Western NGOs, which were flourishing in the 1980s and 1990s, have played a crucial role in criticizing these human rights violations all over the world. Many of the claims critical of state sovereignty were, ironically, adopted and executed as *governmental policies* by the Western *states*. Although Western states themselves are not immune from criticisms, it is mostly the state in the developing countries that has been criticized and whose domestic jurisdiction has become more and more restricted.[33] This has naturally elicited

---

32   See Onuma, *supra* note 6 [*Jinken, kokka, bunmei*], pp. 91-100. See also Onuma, *supra* note 6 [Towards an Intercivilzational Approach to Human Rights], pp. 61-63.

33   Major Western states, which find it necessary to respond to mounting pressures from human rights NGOs, have taken a far harsher attitude toward those countries whose record of human rights violation is conspicuous. International organizations whose mandates are directly or indirectly related with the promotion or protection of human rights have also come to take a more severe attitude towards human rights violations in developing countries. The UN Human Rights Commission and its Subcommittee as well as monitoring bodies of major human rights treaties came to be an arena where human rights violations in developing countries are discussed and criticized as well as where calls for an end to such violations are made. Major developed countries and the international financial institutions such as the World Bank and the IMF came to impose conditions relating to human rights on the recipient nations.

harsh reactions from Afro-Asian nations. Assertions of "Asian values" or "Asian human rights," which are critical of West-centric discourses and policies of human rights in the early 1990s, are some examples of such reactions.[34]

The formidable power of globalization penetrating the national boundaries involved the destruction and criticism of various forms of civilizations and cultures that had been preserved in non-Western societies. Thus, reactions from the latter inevitably assumed the character of *repercussions in terms of civilizations or cultures*. This is why the conflicts between the West-centric globalizing forces undermining the non-intervention principle and the repercussions from various developing countries have given the impression of a "clash of civilizations". Terrorist attacks from various sectors of Afro-Asian nations have many causes, but many people have been inclined to understand them in the context of "clash of civilizations." The September 11th Event is symbolic of this understanding.

Many Western governments and commentators have been aware of the danger of such an understanding. They have therefore argued that the war against terrorism is not a clash of civilizations nor should it be. However, this argument can hardly persuade those who dare to resort to terrorism and a far larger number of people who may not commit terrorism by themselves yet support or acquiesce to it. Those who characterize attacks against Israel and the US as *jihad* believe that their civilizations *have already been attacked by the Western civilizations*, whether it is a Judeo-Christian, or modern, secular and capitalist one. According to this perception, their religion, cultures, and social practices have not been respected by Western people but have been threatened by various means involving military, economic and ideological ones. They thus justify their acts of violence as *jihad*, characterizing them as defensive acts or counter-attacks against the aggressive Western powers or civilization, regarding Western civilization as the civilization of power.[35]

Here, we can see a strong tendency to understand civilizations as substantive entities to which a human belong in an exclusive manner. Also, we must take into consideration that the very space or arena where thoughts, ideas, claims and arguments are exchanged is overwhelmingly West-centric and that there is little space for the non-Western discourses. However loudly they shout, however sophisticatedly they argue, their voices and arguments are not heard by Western elites who can exert influence on the global decision-making process. They have been desperate that their arguments cannot be understood or even heard by those who control affairs in Israel, the Middle East, Iraq, and all over the world. If their voices are not heard there is no other way but to resort to violence. Whether one likes such reasoning or not, this is the way they tend to think.

---

34   Onuma, *supra* note 7, pp. 47-52. See also Inoue, T., "Liberal Democracy and Asian Orientalism," Bauer, J. and Bell, D. (eds.), *The East Asian Challenge for Human Rights*, Cambridge Univ. Press, 1999, pp. 27-59.

35   See Onuma, Y., "Bunmei wa shototsu shite inainoka?", *Asahi Newspaper* (Nov. 30, 2001), p. 17.

Unless people can liberate themselves from a substantive and exclusive notion of civilization, it is natural that transcivilizational perspectives tend to lead them to the negative conclusion of a clash of civilizations. Unless the overwhelmingly West-centric space of perception and argumentation on a global scale is changed, and those who make arguments that are critical of West-centric discourses can feel that their arguments are sufficiently heard and fairly understood, it would be difficult to persuade those desperate peoples to refrain from resorting to violence. These are fundamental challenges for the legitimate global order in the 21st century.

C.   *Transcivilzational Perspectives Tacitly Adopted and Crucially Needed in Transboundary Relations*

The transcivilizational perspective is a theoretical device to meet such challenges. On the other hand, transcivilizational perspectives in the wider sense of the term have already been adopted by various people in a number of occasions albeit in an unconscious manner. What we need today is to recognize this undeniable fact, and to reconceptualize the notion of civilization as a functional concept. This reconceptualization is important so that ways of understanding the transboundary issues may not lead people to consider problems involving civilizational factors as a clash of civilizations, which are understood in a substantive and exclusive manner.

As the foregoing analyses suggest, civilizational factors were not lost even after the sovereign states system became global. Civilizational factors, whether natural, religious, linguistic, cultural, political, or economic, produced civilizational diversity for more than four millennia. They could not be lost in a few centuries of West-centric modernity. Confucian civilization survived, although in the weaker form of social customs, maxims or aphorisms that guide people in an unconscious manner in their daily lives.[36] Buddhist civilization survived, actively in some areas such as in Thailand, or in the weaker form of ceremonies, maxims and proverbs, guiding people unconsciously, as is the case with Japan. In Africa and in West, Central, South and Southeast Asia, Islamic civilization survived with great intra-civilizational diversity.

Because diverse civilizational factors were until recently preserved as domestic matters, they were not conspicuous in international relations. However, policymakers have been well aware of their importance in international relations. They have taken these factors into account when they conduct foreign policies. The US policy in the Gulf War of 1991 is a good example. In carrying out campaigns against Iraq, the US made serious efforts to have Muslim and Arab nations on its side. A major reason for this attitude was the concern with the perceived legitimacy or the "image" of the campaigns. The US government wanted to avoid giving the impression that its military actions were against Muslims or Arabs in general.

---

36   The depth and strength of Confucianism varies from country to country, with Korea being the strongest.

Likewise, after the events of September 11th, the Western powers emphasized that their campaigns against Al-Qaeda and the Taliban regime were not a war against Muslims. They stressed that their military campaigns should not be interpreted as a clash of civilizations. When the US and the UK governments carried out war in Iraq in 2003, they held a similar attitude. The Bush Jr administration was far less concerned with the perceptions held by others, yet even this Bush administration paid a certain degree of attention to civilizational factors. After President Bush was severely criticized for referring to the crusade, the administration made serious efforts to avoid the impression that their campaign against Iraq was interpreted as a clash of civilizations. In all these cases, they knew well that they needed transcivilzational legitimacy or at least an appearance of it in conducting military campaigns. That is why they made serious efforts to establish a coalition that includes Muslim and Arab nations, transcending civilizational boundaries.

Yet, their military actions were often interpreted as "Western" or "Judeo-Christian" campaigns against Muslim nations by a large number of Muslims and other peoples all over the world. Still today, this interpretation and perception is highly influential in Muslim nations. The persistence and further resurgence of the intercivilizational or transcivilizational perspective, understood in a substantive and exclusive manner, is obvious. The above three events are just a few examples where such an understanding is preeminent. There are a number of other issues of the same sort.

The above examples demonstrate that the transcivilizational perspective in the wider sense of the term has been adopted to complement international and transnational perspectives albeit tacitly and unconsciously. At the same time, "civilizations" as understood from this kind of transcivilizational perspective have been basically those perceived in a substantive and exclusive manner. These perceptions have tended to invite people to the negative perception of conflicts between civilizations. This sort of substantive and exclusive understanding of civilizations in global affairs must be replaced by a functional or relational understanding of civilizations. The predominant understanding of global affairs from international and transnational perspectives must be modified and complemented by this functional or relational understanding of transcivilizational relations.

The issue of human rights is another outstanding example. In any ideas and discourses on human rights that transcend national boundaries, the need for transcivilzational legitimacy is evident.[37] Human rights policies of a government are now scrutinized by international organizations, other governments, NGOs and media institutions. Social customs and institutions that are based on religious, cultural, political and economic factors in national societies and have lasted for centuries are now openly criticized by outsiders. These outsiders claim that some of these customs or institutions violate human rights, and call for their change or

---

37   See Onuma, *supra* note 6 [*Jinken, kokka, bunmei*] and Onuma, *supra* note 6 [Towards an Intercivilizational Approach to Human Rights]. See also An-Na'im, A., *Human Rights in Cross Cultural Perspective: A Quest for Consensus*, University of Pennsylvania Press, 1992.

abolition.[38] These demands have elicited harsh reactions from sectors of the targeted nations that believe that their customs or institutions must be respected and preserved. The controversies over the universality *vs.* relativity or particularity of human rights have revealed that the universalization of human rights involves civilizational dimensions. They have demonstrated that we need a transcivilzational perspective to fully understand and to solve the problems accompanying the universalization of human rights.

The transcivilzational perspective enables us to see, understand and construe the problems not merely as an issue of conflicting national interests, nor merely from a West-centric transnational perspective of "global civil society". It assumes, rather, the plural existence of long-lasting and diverse civilizations, and urges us to see those problems as connoting civilizational conflicts. At the same time, however, the functional or relational understanding of transcivilizational affairs enables us to liberate ourselves from the preconception that we belong to only one civilization. It thus enables us to avoid a glorification of "our" civilization at the cost of "their" civilizations.

Further, the transcivilizational perspective suggests us that civilizations have influenced each other, and have transformed themselves through these mutual influences. Thus, the transcivilizational perspective enables us to understand that even a rigid interpretation of a certain religion or culture conflicting with today's human rights norms may change over time. We can also understand that human rights themselves are, like many other ideas and institutions, historical products of West-centric modern civilization with universalizable features. As such, they may also change themselves in the very process of universalization.[39]

As the above examples demonstrate, the transcivilizational perspective is an essential tool to conceive of any transboundary issues affecting nations and people, particularly issues relating to global validity and legitimacy. The legitimacy as seen from this perspective, together with the legitimacy as seen from international and transnational perspectives, must be an important element of global legal order in the 21st century. In the following section, we will seek to elucidate its place and functions in conceiving the problem of international law with universal validity, which underlies the global legal order.

---

38   The status of women in Islamic and Confucian civilizations and certain kinds of punishment administered by certain Muslim nations are typical examples of these customs and institutions under attack.

39   Onuma, *supra* note 7, pp. 69-78; Onuma, *supra* note 6 [Towards an Intercivilizational Approach to Human Rights], pp. 61-81.

4.   Status and Functions of General International Law as Seen from International, Transnational and Transcivilizational Perspectives

A.   *Theoretical Flaws of the Equation of General International Law with Customary International Law*[40]

When conceiving of the problem of the global legal order in the 21st century, it is highly important to assess the status and function of general (or universal) international law applicable to all members in international society.[41] Other important notions in the global constitutionalism and legal order, such as *jus cogens*, obligations *erga omnes* and hierarchy of norms in international law, all presuppose the notion of international law with universal validity. How and to what extent can norms of general international law assert universal validity, transcending national, regional, cultural, religious and civilizational boundaries? How can they be realized in international society where power, interests and value judgments of its members are so diverse? These constitute crucial problems in the deliberation of global legal order in the 21st century.

The ICJ has often used the notion of customary international law when it is necessary to refer to international law that obligates all states in international society. A large number of international lawyers have resorted to the same method. Although a number of international lawyers have argued that some other instruments such as multilateral treaties and the UNGA resolutions can generate international law with universal validity, most of them have sought to demonstrate that these norms can be characterized as customary international law, and *consequently*, be characterized as general international law. A major reason for such reasoning is that they have regarded Article 38 of the ICJ Statute as indicating the "sources" of international law. It has been explicitly or implicitly assumed that because Article

---

40   This chapter is based on my argument[s] in Onuma, Y., "The ICJ: An Emperor Without Clothes?", N. Ando *et al.*, (eds.), *Liber Amicorum Judge Shigeru Oda*, vol 1, Kluwer Law International, 2002, pp. 191-212.

41   If seen from a purely academic viewpoint, it may be better to distinguish between universal international law, which is valid to all members in the international society, and general international law, which is valid to most members in the international society. However, it is impossible to demonstrate the truly universal validity of law by empirical means. Even if one defines universal international law as international law that is valid to all subjects of international law, one may be asked who those subjects are. Is Taiwan a subject of international law? To some it is, but to others, it is not. The answer may be different according to the area of international law as well. And how can one demonstrate this universal validity by empirical means? There are many other difficult issues involved in this universality "in the true sense of the term". On the other hand, actual problems occur where one party argues that some norm is universally or generally valid, and therefore the opposing party must be bound by this norm, whereas the opposing party negates such a claim. Whether a norm is truly universal or not from a strictly academic viewpoint does not matter. From the perspective of concrete forms and functions of international law in the actual world, the distinction is not so crucial.

38 of the ICJ Statute provides for binding norms of international law, any binding norms of international law must be located in one of the categories of this article.

However, this assumption must be scrutinized in many respects. First, even as norms to be applied by the ICJ, Article 38 may not exhaustively enumerate such binding norms. It may provide applicable norms only as an examplary enumeration.[42] If so, even from the viewpoint of norms of adjudication, there may be norms to be applied by the ICJ other than those stipulated in Article 38 of the ICJ Statute.

Second, it is theoretically questionable to assume that all binding norms of international law are enumerated in Article 38, which basically stipulates *norms to be applied by the ICJ*. When rules and principles of international law are actually referred to, discussed, and used in various forums in international or domestic society, they are assumed to be *norms regulating conducts of states*. This means international law is mainly discussed and dealt with as norms of conduct. Some of them may certainly function as norms of adjudication and be applied by the court, but not all of them.[43] Thus, it is highly questionable why we should always refer to Article 38 of the ICJ Statute when we discuss binding norms of international law in general. The tacit equation of norms of conduct with norms of adjudication must be critically scrutinized. It may not be necessary for general international law to be characterized as customary international law. As far as norms of conduct are concerned, there may be other grounds than those enumerated in Article 38 that can generate norms of international law with universal validity.[44]

Third, from the viewpoint of global legitimacy, it may not be appropriate for international law with universal validity to be characterized as customary interna-

---

42   See Danilenko, G.M., *Law-Making in the International Community*, Kluwer Law International, 1993, pp. 30-43.

43   For the notions of "norms of conduct" and "norms of adjudication", see E. Ehrlich, *Grundlegung der Soziologie des Rechts*, 3. Aufl., 1967, 10, 97 *et passim*. Ehrlich's famous concepts of *Handlungsregel* and *Entscheidungsnorm* are translated into a "rule of conduct" and a "norm for decision", respectively (*Fundamental Principles of the Sociology of Law*, translation by W. L. Moll, 1962, pp. 10, 121 *et passim*.). Ehrlich's concept of *Entscheidungsnorm* is slightly different from my concept of norms of adjudication. First, the former covers not only norms to be applied by the judicial court, but other organs whose mandate is to settle disputes in general including courts of honor, courts of societies etc. (*Ibid.*, p. 122). Second, it can mean various kinds of legal and non-legal norms to be applied by such organs of dispute settlement (*Ibid.*, pp. 123 *et seq.*). In contrast, norms of adjudication signify norms to be permanently and consistently applied by the judicial court as an institution of dispute settlement. Also, Ehrlich defines the *Handlungsregel* as a rule including both elements of customarily regulating human conduct and a rule designating for the addressees how they ought to conduct themselves (*Ibid.*, pp. 11 *et passim*.). It seems more appropriate, however, at least in the case of international law, to distinguish between the validity and the efficacy of the norms. Thus, my notion of the norms of conduct simply means norms prescribing specific conduct to the addressees as law. The efficacy or effectiveness of such norms is another question.

44   Onuma, *supra* note 40, pp. 195-212.

tional law. There may be other norms creating mechanisms that are more legitimate than the traditional customary law-creating process. Although the latter may be effective, it may not satisfy the requirement of global legitimacy.

The following part deals with the first and second problems, the theoretical flaws of the equation of general international law with customary international law. The third problem will be dealt with in the following sections.

First, as far as the ICJ is concerned, the equation of general international law with customary international law may be understandable, though not justifiable. The ICJ is bound to identify the binding norms *within the framework of* Article 38 of the ICJ Statute. According to the predominant theory of international law, the principle *pacta tertiis nec nocent nec prosunt* has been rigidly interpreted, and the treaty has been regarded as *lex specialis*, lacking universal validity. If the ICJ is required to apply *only* norms enumerated in Article 38 of the ICJ Statute, it has to apply either norms of "customary" international law or those of "general principles of law recognized by civilized nations", when it needs to apply norms with universal validity.

The ICJ has sought to avoid resorting to the notion of general principles of law recognized by civilized nations because this notion has many problems.[45] The ICJ has hardly ever resorted to the notion of the general principles of law explicitly, even when it actually appeared to rely on it. The ICJ has sought to give norms universal validity in terms of customary law even in a situation where it is difficult to do so according to the traditional, "rigid"[46] theory of customary law. The ICJ has sought to *re*-characterize the concept of customary law so as *to apply norms of general international law under the name of customary international law.*[47]

However, from a theoretical perspective, this is not persuasive. The category of customary law is concerned with the cognitive or existential form of law. The category of general international law is concerned with the range of validity or applicability of law. They are different categories. Simply demonstrating that a certain norm is customary law does not guarantee its universal validity at all.[48] In fact, there are norms of special customary law which lack universal validity. The ICJ is naturally aware of the distinction between general customary law and special customary law.[49] Yet, the ICJ and most international lawyers have characterized a cer-

---

45   See p.13 of the text. There have also been long debates whether the "general principles" are those of domestic laws, of international law, or of both. There are other problems as well.

46   It will be shown soon that the traditional theory of customary law is not as rigid as it has been claimed to be. It might be rigid in some requirements but not at all rigid in other requirements such as the generality of state practice and *opinio juris.*

47   As to problematic features from this artificial reasoning, see Chigara, *supra* note 1.

48   See Komori, T., "Joyaku no daisansha koryoku to kanshuho no riron (The Effect of Treaties upon Third States and the Theory of Customary Law)", (1)(2)(3), *Chiba Daigaku Hokei Ronshu*, vol. 9 (1980), pp. 53 *et seq.*, vol. 10 (1981), pp. 79 *et seq.*, vol. 12 (1982), pp. 43 *et seq.*

49   See Haggenmacher, P., "La doctrine des deux éléments du droit coutumier dans la pratique de la Cour Internationale", *RGDIP*, vol. 90 (1986), pp. 5 *et seq.*, esp. 32-104.

tain norm as customary international law when they have sought to demonstrate the universal validity of the norm.[50]

On the other hand, the ICJ sometimes referred to general rules of international law without characterizing them as customary norms.[51] Thus, it might be possible to argue that the ICJ has tacitly applied rules which do not fall within the category of Article 38 (1) (a)-(d). This may suggest that the ICJ has interpreted Article 38 not as an exhaustive enumeration but as an exemplary enumeration of the applicable rules. If this is the case, we might be able to argue that even the ICJ, which is required to apply norms of adjudication, has actually abandoned the idea that *all* binding norms of international law should be found in Article 38 of the ICJ Statute.

Second, we must distinguish the positions of the ICJ and international lawyers in general. It may be understandable for the ICJ to resort to the equation between general international law and customary international law because the ICJ must apply norms that are provided in Article 38. They are no more and no less than norms to be applied by the ICJ. It is natural for the ICJ to think and behave within the framework of Article 38 of the ICJ Statute. However, international lawyers in general are not required to think and behave within the framework of Article 38 of the ICJ Statute. They could, and they should, think independently of the ICJ Statute, although the Statute is an important treaty that they should take into consideration when they consider the problem of cognitive bases or existential forms of international law.[52]

When international lawyers deal with problems of international law, what they have in mind are primarily rules and principles of international law that are supposed to *regulate the conduct of states* and other subjects of international law.

---

50 Even Chigara, who criticizes the mystical theory of customary international law, does not seem to doubt this equation between general international law and customary international law. See Chigara, *supra* note 1.

51 See, *e.g.*, North Sea Continental Shelf Cases, *ICJ Reports*, 1969, p. 42. The ICJ has also blurred the distinction between state practice and *opinio juris* in demonstrating norms of (general) customary international law, and relaxed the time requirement in the formation of general international law (customary international law). Further, it has become more inclined to rely on the UNGA declarations and resolutions as well as multilateral treaties for demonstrating the customary rules and principles of general international law (see Case Concerning Military and Paramilitary Activities in and against Nicaragua, ICJ Reports, 1986, pp. 99-100). These tendencies might be characterized as a tacit sign of the *de facto* deviation of the ICJ from the traditional theory of customary international law, which equates general international law with customary international law.

52 As early as 1966, Falk wrote that "Such an approach [to associate the creation of international law with "the sources of international law" contained in Article 38 of the ICJ Statute] distorts inquiry by conceiving of law-creation exclusively from the perspective of the rules applicable in this one centralized, judicial institution" Falk, R., "On the Quasi-Legislative Competence of the General Assembly," *American Journal of International Law*, vol. 60 (1966), p. 782.

What they have in mind are norms of conduct in international law. Therefore, when they have discussed the problem of "sources" of international law, they could, and they should, have thought of them independently of Article 38, which stipulates norms of adjudication. Even if norms of adjudication can provide a *useful clue* to the problem of cognitive bases or existential forms of law in general, they do not necessarily provide *all* forms of norms of conduct. Their failure to find "sources" of international law independently of Article 38 has produced many problems. It helped prolong the prevalence of the mythical theory of customary law beyond its proper lifespan. The most awkward example of this failure is the concept of "instant" customary international law.[53]

Bin Cheng was right when he pointed out that there may be norms of general international law regulating the conduct of states in outer space and claimed that such norms might be created almost instantly because of the shared legal consciousness of the members of international society. However, he sought to explain this *new phenomenon* within the traditional framework of Article 38 of the ICJ Statute. Thus he was compelled to invent a term which he himself did not particularly like: instant customary law.[54] The term itself is, of course, a contradiction. It clearly reveals how inappropriate and outdated it is to think of general international law within the framework of Article 38. Cheng himself was aware of this fact.[55]

Jennings wrote, already in 1982, that "The time has surely come to recognise boldly that it [most of the non-treaty international law of today] is not custom at all, and never was."[56] He even went on to say that "To use Article 38 as it stands, as we constantly do still, for the purpose of analysing and explaining the elements and categories of the law today, has a strong element of absurdity."[57] Jennings was perfectly right. From the viewpoint of norms of conduct in international law, there are sufficient reasons to believe that there are norms of general international law that are not necessarily provided in Article 38 of the ICJ Statute. We should further consider this problem from the viewpoint of global legitimacy that is required for international law to regulate the behavior of states and other actors, overcoming national, regional and civilizational differences.

B.   The Legitimacy Deficit of the Traditional Theory of Customary International Law: Liberation of the Concept of General International Law from the Mystical Theory of Customary International Law

In the 21st century world, the importance of non-governmental actors is highly regarded, and the overcoming of West-centrism and the appreciation of multi-cul-

---

53   B. Cheng, "United Nations Resolutions on Outer Space: 'Instant' Customary Law?", *Indian JIL*, vol. 5 (1965), pp. 23 *et seq.*

54   Cheng, B., "On the Nature and Sources of International Law", Cheng, B. (ed.), *International Law*, Stevens, 1982, p. 223.

55   *Ibid.*

56   Jennings, R.Y., "The Identification of International Law", in Cheng, *supra* note 54, pp. 1, 6.

57   *Ibid.*, p. 9.

tures and plural civilizations is a great task to be fulfilled. The norms of international law with universal validity must satisfy the highest degree of legitimacy in order to be accepted or at least acquiesced by all members in international society. The rules and principles of general international law must thus satisfy international, transnational and transcivilizational legitimacy. Seen from this perspective, reliance on the "customary" norms when identifying norms with universal validity has a number of deficiencies. Comparatively speaking, multilateral treaties and UNGA declarations have more advantages in terms of global legitimacy than mystical rules and principles of "customary" international law. Here, a brief analysis of the UN resolutions in comparison with *opinio juris* and state practice in "customary" international law in the norm creating process of general international law is in order.[58]

As is well known, debates over the normative nature of the UNGA resolutions and declarations have a long history. A number of prominent international lawyers have argued for resorting to the UNGA declarations as a means to identify international legal norms with universal validity. However, this argument has been criticized in many respects. It has to overcome many obstacles.

First, it has been pointed out that the UNGA resolutions are not enumerated in Article 38. However, this argument has already been settled above. Even from the viewpoint of norms of adjudication, Article 38 does not necessarily enumerate *all* applicable norms of adjudication in an exhaustive manner. Further, the fact whether particular rules or principles of international law can be applied by the ICJ provides only *a useful clue,* not *a decisive test,* to the question whether they are legal norms in international law. Even if they are not applied by the ICJ, still they can be norms of international law, which can perform a number of functions as international law. They can regulate behaviors of states and induce compliance with international legal rules and principles as norms of conduct. They can fulfill an important role of communicative function as a means of peaceful communication between states with diverse interests, values and propensities. They can embody common understanding of international society in an explicit and relatively determinate manner. They can legitimize behaviors of states as compatible with norms of international law.[59] In this way, although certain rules and principles that are not necessarily expected to be applied by the ICJ, yet they are perceived as international law and actually function as such.[60]

---

58   Because of the lack of space and preparation, the problem of multilateral treaties is not discussed here.

59   As to various functions of international law other than providing a useful means for settling disputes, see Onuma *supra* note 2, pp. 130 *et seq.*

60   During the Cold War period, no one would have expected that either the US or the Soviet Union would resort to the ICJ when they had a conflict in interpreting arms control treaties. Yet, these treaties were perfectly regarded as international law, and actually functioned as international law. One might argue that even in this case, the "shadow of the court" worked. It will soon be demonstrated that this argument cannot hold, due to the structural differences between Western societies and international society.

It has also been argued that UNGA resolutions have other problems. It has been asserted that it is impossible to identify the legal consciousness or the intention to be bound of a state from voting in the adoption of an UNGA declaration. Voting is a political act of a state, not a juridical one. In many cases, had the state known that the resolution would be binding, it would not have voted in the affirmative. Because states know that the UNGA resolution or declaration has only hortatory force, they would vote in the affirmative.[61] If the fact whether states regard certain norms binding upon them as juridical norms or not provides a decisive test whether they are legal norms or not, these arguments certainly sound persuasive.

However, the traditional notion of state practice does share similar defects from the viewpoint of the distinction between what is political and what is legal. Many international lawyers have regarded statements or declarations by the executive organ such as the president, prime minister and foreign minister as an expression of state practice and/or *opinio juris*.[62] Yet, they are typically political acts. Even a non-verbal act by an executive organ of a state is not a purely juridical act. Most of the concrete executive acts are discretionary and have political aspects as well as juridical aspects. If one argues that the act of the executive is constrained by law and therefore should be characterized as juridical, then the same argument should apply to the voting in the UNGA.

Representatives of states do not vote independently from the laws of their states. Although they have a certain degree of discretionary competence, they act within the framework of their domestic laws. In this respect, there is no difference whether a concrete act of a state is performed in the international organization or elsewhere. Unless concrete acts to be used as indicating the "state practice" and *opinio juris* are limited to domestic laws and judgments of the domestic courts, one cannot be sure whether the state agent in question really acts with the sense of law, or the sense of "hortatory force", or some other sense. It is *only through an interpretation by international lawyers or courts* that certain elements within the concrete

---

61   See Schwebel, S., "The Effect of Resolutions of the U.N. General Assembly on Customary International Law", *Proc. ASIL*, vol. 73 (1979), pp. 301-309; Wolfke, K., *Custom in Present International Law*, 2nd ed., Martinus Nijhoff, 1993, p.84; Danilenko, *supra* note 42, pp. 203-210.

62   Some international lawyers such as D'Amato and Judge Read assert only acts, not statements, of states constitute state practice. However, a large number of international lawyers and many judgments of the ICJ treat statements, official views and proclamations by executive organs as state practice and/or an expression of the *opinio juris*. If one denies this view, one would have to conclude that for a state to claim a new norm as law, it has to violate the existing law in order to demonstrate its practice and *opinio juris*. This would be absurd and dangerous for a peaceful change of law. Such a conclusion would also actually deprive smaller states of claiming the change of law, for only a limited number of stronger states could safely violate the existing international law without being "punished". See Akehurst, M., "Custom as a Source of International Law", *BYBIL*, vol. 47 (1974-75), pp. 1-8; Byers, M., *Custom, Power and the Power of Rules*, Cambridge Univ. Press, 1999, p. 134; Gunning, I., "Expanding the International Definition of Refugee: A Multicultural View", *Fordham International Law Journal*, vol. 13 (1989-90), p. 158.

act of state should be characterized as juridical. No act of state is inherently purely political or purely juridical.

Once this common nature of acts of states including verbal acts such as statements and declarations is recognized, then the comparative advantages of relying on the UNGA declarations as basing an important element of the general international law creating process become evident. Advocates for the comparative advantages of the UNGA resolutions do not argue that all resolutions and declarations adopted by the UNGA should be used as evidence or an element of the process which creates general international law. Only those limited number of important declarations that can be construed as expressing the norms of general international law by their wording and by the voting pattern should be used. They are far clearer and more elaborate in articulating the normative consciousness of states than verbal or non-verbal acts of political organs of individual states that have been used in the traditional doctrine of customary law. Most importantly, the UNGA process of adopting resolutions or declarations can satisfy the requirement of quasi-universal participation of states for the creation of general international law far more concretely and explicitly than the traditional theory of customary law.

In the traditional theory of customary international law, most "customary" norms have been provided by leading international lawyers of great powers in their treatises or textbooks. These international lawyers have sought to identify acts and statements of the executive branch of the government, domestic laws, and domestic court decisions as major materials of state practice.[63] However, it is impossible to identify these materials of all states. They have thus identified the practice of a few, yet powerful and influential Western states, and have regarded it tacitly or explicitly as representative of general practice.

Oscar Schachter frankly admits that "As a historical fact, the great body of customary international law was made by remarkably few States."[64] Rules and prin-

---

63   Basically the same materials have been used as the evidence of *opinio juris*. According to the established view on customary international law, a customary law must be demonstrated by two standards: state practice and the *opinio juris*. As to the latter, however, there have always been criticisms on various grounds. Particularly, the criticism to the effect that a state as a fictitious entity cannot have an *opinio juris* is a pertinent one, which urges many international lawyers to search for more concrete agents of the *opinio juris*, *i.e.*, various organs of the state. Since these organs are so diverse, ranging from the head of the state to a soldier engaged in warfare, many international lawyers and the ICJ have come to argue that the *opinio juris* can be induced from external acts, *i.e.*, state practice.

64   Schachter, O., "New Custom: Power, Opinio Juris and Contrary Practice", Makarczyk, J. (ed.), *Theory of International Law at the Threshold of the 21st Century*, Kluwer International, 1996, p. 531. See also de Visscher, C., *Théories et réalités en droit international public*, 4 éd., A. Pedone, 1970, p. 170; Stern, B., "La coutume au coeur du droit international: Quelques reflections", *Mélanges offerts à Paul Reuter*, A. Pedone, 1981, pp. 492-4; Kelly, J. P., "The Twilight of Customary International Law", *Virginia Journal of International Law*, vol. 40 (2000), pp. 519-522; Roberts, A., "Traditional and Modern Approaches to Customary International Law: A Reconciliation", *American Journal of International Law*, vol. 95 (2001), pp. 767-768.

ciples characterized as customary through this method have usually enjoyed a high degree of effectiveness, precisely because they have been formulated on the basis of the practice of the great powers. *This effectiveness of the "customary" law has actually eclipsed its lack of generality.* This may be a blatant admission of the crude fact in the history of international law, which has reflected the power structure in international society. Seen from the viewpoint of global legitimacy that is required for norms with universal validity in the 21st century, however, this is a serious flaw.[65] It must be rectified.

Effectiveness is certainly an important element of international law. Even if a certain normative idea is accepted by all states, it cannot be a law if it totally lacks a possibility of being enforced. However, the element of effectiveness or power must be discussed separately from the element of legitimacy and generality. If the principle of effectiveness eclipses the lack of generality, then it becomes a sugar-coated expression of camouflaging the ideological and discriminatory nature of international law as the hand-maiden of great powers. This lack of legitimacy would certainly exasperate a large number of peoples who have already felt that they have been ignored, despised and even attacked by predominant forces of a few powerful Western nations. We must rectify this fundamental flaw of "general" international law as formulated in the form of customary international law.

Because the study of international law has been overwhelmingly West-centric, lack of state practice and *opinio juris* of a large number of non-Western nations has not been seriously considered. The fact that the latter occupy the overwhelming majority of the human species has been ignored, first by the argument that they were not subjects of international law, and then, after the attainment of their independence, by the continued preeminence of the mythical theory of customary international law.[66] Theoretically, the notions of acquiescence and tacit (or inferred) consent have often been used to camouflage the lack of generality.[67] However, because there was no international forum through which states can know

---

65   A number of international lawyers have criticized this flawed aspect of customary international law as general international law. See, e.g., Charney, J., "Universal International Law," *American Journal of International Law*, 87 (1993), p. 537; Kelly, *supra* note 64, pp. 519-522; Roberts, *supra* note 64, pp. 767-768.

66   Most of the leading international lawyers have been citizens of developed countries, where democracy is highly valued. However, they do not seem to have been much concerned with the democratic principle in international society. They do not seem to have been particularly bothered when they have continued ignoring the state practice and the *opinio juris* of the majority members of the international society and concentrating their attention on those of a limited number of Western powers in international society. It is true that many non-Western nations have problems of democracy in their domestic regimes. However, this is a separate problem, which should not be used as an excuse to ignore the participation of the overwhelming majority of humans in the norm-creating process of general international law.

67   For those who do not adhere to the voluntarist-positivist construction of international law, either "natural law" or some other form of "objective" idea played a similar camouflaging role (Stern, *supra* note 64, pp. 493-94).

that a certain legislative process was going on, both acquiescence and tacit consent inevitably assume a highly fictitious character.

In contrast, in the case of the UNGA norm-creating process, this fictitious character can be minimized. This process is far more centralized and transparent through the organizational mechanism of the UN than in the traditional "customary" process. Because the UNGA is an organ composed of virtually all states, its norm-creating process satisfies the requirement of a global participation far better than the traditional "customary" international law-making process does.[68]

In addition, in the UNGA norm-creating process, voices of transnational actors such as NGOs are much more explicitly heard than in the mystical process of "customary international law", which is basically a process that cannot be explicitly identified.[69] Further, from the transcivilizational perspective, the UNGA norm-creating process can provide a far more equitable forum than the traditional norm creating process of "customary international law", because states with diverse civilizational backgrounds participate in the norm- creating process of the UN.[70] Thus, they can claim a much higher degree of legitimacy in terms of global participation, introduction of various transnational actors, and the possibility of arguments and debates from various transcivilizational perspectives than the traditional norm-creating process of "customary international law". This relative superiority is tremendously important for norms with universal applicability in the 21st century.[71]

C.   *Recognizing Norms with Universal Validity in International Law: Liberation from Excessive Judicial-centrism in International Law*

As the above analysis shows, most international lawyers have conceived of general international law only in the form of customary international law. They have ignored a difference between two categories: one of general or partial validity of law and the other of cognitive bases or existential forms of law. But why have they taken

---

68   Even in terms of the traditional doctrine respecting the sovereign will of individual states, the UNGA norm-creating process is far more legitimate in that it actually gives an opportunity to all members of the UNGA whether they agree or disagree with the proposed norms.

69   It is true that the present structure of the UN including the General Assembly is state-centric and has a number of flaws from the transnational perspectives. Still, if compared with the mystical norm- creating process of customary international law, the UNGA norm-creating process is relatively better, or at least less flawed.

70   Here again, the UN General Assembly is flawed in that it is too state-centric to be transcivilizational. The argument in the text is merely from a comparative perspective with the traditional norm-creating process of general international law based on the mystical theory of customary international law.

71   Although the UNGA declarations have these merits, they do not necessarily possess the element of effectiveness. They must therefore be followed and completed by more concrete behavior[s] of states including influential powers. The adoption of the UNGA declaration *per se* does not generally create a norm of general international law, even if adopted unanimously or by consensus.

such an attitude? In most of their actual analyses of international legal affairs, they have dealt with international legal norms that are supposed to regulate the actual conduct of states. Yet, when they refer to the "sources" of international law, they have concentrated their attention on Article 38 of the ICJ Statute, which stipulates norms of conduct. What explains this apparent difference, or even contradiction?

A number of factors may be enumerated. The deeply rooted West-centric, or power (or effectiveness)-centric way of thinking as mentioned earlier certainly contributes to ignoring the lack of the participation of most members in international society in the elaboration of customary international law, which should reflect general practice and *opinion juris* shared by a large number of states in international society. Predominance of excessive formalism or positivism of international legal studies in the 20th century may be another factor.[72]

The most problematic feature, however, seems to be excessive judiciary-centrism, which reflects the domestic model (of Western society) thinking shared by international lawyers. Most international lawyers have actually dealt with various problems of international law mainly in terms of norms of conduct. But once they think of "sources" of international law, they unconsciously consider the problem in terms of the norms of adjudication. It is true that international law has functioned as norms of adjudication both internationally and domestically. Adjudication is certainly an important means to redress violations of international law, to settle disputes between states and to realize norms of international law. In the fields of human rights, international criminal law, the WTO and others, judicialization in the wider sense of the term has been in progress. This trend has been highly appreciated by most international lawyers, and with good reasons.[73]

Moreover, many leading international lawyers are not only academics but also practicing lawyers. There have actually been increasing demands for leading international lawyers to deal with international law in the judicial setting as practitioners. Their writings based on these activities and experiences have been highly influential. Finally, most international lawyers have adopted a domestic model approach in their theories. In most cases they have unconsciously, or sometimes consciously, regarded the *domestic legal system of "Western democracies"* as the *model* of the international legal system. In Western democratic societies, judiciaries functions effectively as an important means of rule of law. They generally regard legal norms

---

72   Most international lawyers have, either consciously or unconsciously, sought to identify some "positive" source of general international law. They have wanted some explicit provisions in treaties or statements in jurisprudence. Article 38 of the ICJ Statute provides such "positive" sources, which make many international lawyers feel comfortable. And as long as they rely on Article 38, the only feasible candidate for general international law would be customary international law. All norms which claim universal validity must therefore take the form of customary international law. Thus equation of general international law with customary international law has prevailed.

73   One of the reasons why not only international lawyers but also international relations studies have begun to pay attention to "legalization" of international relations is that in the area of the WTO the "judicialization" of the dispute settlement developed.

as norms to be applied by the court.[74] Thus, it is natural for many international lawyers to conceive of norms of international law in terms of norms of adjudication and to seek to find their "sources" in Article 38 of the ICJ Statute, which is the most conspicuous provision to enumerate the norms of adjudication.

However, not all norms of international law function as norms of adjudication. Not all norms of international law regulating conduct of states are norms to be applied by the ICJ. This is evident if we consider concrete situations where international law actually works or is dealt with.[75] When an organ of state A, such as the executive, the legislative, or the judiciary, wants to take an action which involves some norms of international law, it usually considers whether its action is compatible with these norms. It generally acts in accordance with norms of international law. However, in certain cases, it acts in violation of international law, or in such a way that its compliance with international law is dubious. In those cases, however, the state organ seldom publicly admits that it is acting in violation of international law. On the other hand, many actors would argue that the state A has acted illegally under international law. It is here that rules and principles of international law are actually resorted to, discussed, and utilized.

There are various actors who may participate in the argumentative process where international law as norms of conduct is discussed: (1) other states (actually governments) who claim that their rights are violated by the alleged illegal act of state A;[76] (2) political rivals in the ruling party or opposition parties in state A, who seek to use any inappropriate acts by the government as a means to criticize the present government; (3) NGOs, media institutions and activists, either in the state A or elsewhere, who regard the observance of the norm in question as important and are ready to criticize any government who violates it; (4) governments which are demanded by the agents of (3) to take a tough position with respect to state A; (5) international organizations whose mandate includes securing compliance with the norm in question; and, (6) individuals who claim that their rights are violated by the act of state A.

Among these cases, only (1) is generally concerned with international law as norms of adjudication to be applied by the ICJ.[77] However, even in the case (1), if state A does not accept the jurisdiction of the ICJ on the issue in question, the argument as to the lawfulness of the act of state A cannot be settled by the ICJ. Because only 63 out of some 190 states accept the compulsory jurisdiction of the ICJ, and most of them accept it with a wide range of reservations and qualifications, the

---

74   Onuma, Y., "Kokusaihougaku no kokunai moderu shiko", Hirobe, Tanaka, T. (eds.), *Kokusaiho to kokunaiho*, Yuhikaku, 19. See also Suganami, Domestic Model Analogy.

75   The following argument is based on Onuma, *supra* note 40, pp. 210-211.

76   International organizations are also possible claimants.

77   If *actio popularis* is recognized in international law, (4) can be concerned with international law as the norms of adjudication. However, this possibility is low, given the past jurisprudence of the ICJ. In case (6), international law may function as norms of adjudication, but not in the ICJ but basically in domestic courts.

possibility that the norms of adjudication play a substantive role is very low. Under these circumstances, the shadow of the court[78] can hardly play an important role in the argumentative or bargaining process between state A and other states.

It is thus evident that in most cases, forums where international law as norms of conduct is discussed are outside the ICJ. Arguments on the lawfulness of the act of state A center on the interpretation of international law as the norm of conduct. Governments, political rivals, opposition parties, NGOs, media institutions and activists resort to various sources of interpretation of the norm of conduct in question in order to secure an interpretation favorable to them. These sources range widely: provisions of treaties; judgments and advisory opinions of the ICJ; arbitral awards; judgments of international courts other than the ICJ; resolutions or declarations of the UNGA; decisions of the UN Security Council; reports of the panels and the appellate body of the WTO; views, opinions and recommendations of the monitoring bodies of various multilateral treaties; resolutions of various international organizations and important international conferences; judgments of municipal courts; views of the leading international lawyers, and so on. If there is a judgment or advisory opinion that gives a decisive interpretation of the norm in question, this interpretation has a high degree of authority and persuasive power. However, such a case is not a rule, but rather an exception, as indicated above.

In this way, the situation where international law as the norms of conduct is taken up and actually discussed is the argumentative process where it is resorted to by parties to a dispute. In such a process, a rule of international law is generally used by both parties as a means of justifying their claims.[79] This is common to the rule of international law used by the parties before the ICJ. However, arguments made in forums other than the judiciary do not end in the form of a judgment by a court. Without a judiciary with compulsory jurisdiction, argumentation between parties to a dispute does not proceed under the shadow of the court. Under such circumstances, the argumentation concerning the binding force of law tends to assume the character of the degree of persuasiveness.[80] It involves the argument concerning the procedural and participatory legitimacy in the promulgation of the rule, intergovernmental, transnational and intercivilizational substantive legitimacy, relative strength in terms of effective realization of the rule in question, and so on.

Seen from this perspective, the persuasive power of the traditional theory of customary international law is not as great as it appears to be. Neither "state practice" nor "*opinio juris*" advocated by the traditional theory of customary in-

---

78   In Western domestic societies, particularly in the US, most negotiations are carried out under the shadow of the court, because of their adjudication-oriented culture. This is one of the reasons why many leading international lawyers, most of whom are Westerners who have been accustomed to such culture, have excessively emphasized the importance of adjudication in international society.

79   Onuma, *supra* note 2, pp. 136-8.

80   See Sorensen, M., "Theory and Reality in International Law", *Proc. ASIL*, vol. 75 (1981), pp. 140, 148.

ternational law can provide more convincing evidence of the sufficiently general and wide coverage of states than, for example, multinational treaties of a universal nature or the UNGA resolutions and declarations adopted unanimously or by consensus. Multinational treaties of a universal nature such as the Geneva Convention of 1949, the UN Charter and the Convention of the Rights of the Child can provide a far more explicit and transparent evidence of the commitment of the overwhelming number of states than the fictitious notion of "state practice" nor "*opinio juris*" advocated by the traditional theory of customary international law. The legitimacy of "customary" law in terms of global participation of states in the creation of global norms, transparency and identification of sovereign will of nations, is far inferior to that of the norm-creating process based on multinational treaties of a universal nature or the UN declarations.

Naturally, neither multilateral treaties nor the UNGA resolutions are immune from defects as the evidence of the norm of universal validity. In the former case, how to assess the normative consciousness of the states which do not ratify or accede to the treaty creates a difficult question.[81] Likewise, the whole process of follow-up measures must be examined. In the case of the UNGA declarations or resolutions, whether they are phrased in a form either declaring or elaborating the existing or emerging law must be closely examined.

However, the critical point is that these are problems of degree in comparison with "general" rules formulated as "customary" rules of international law under the traditional doctrine. It is not fair at all to allow camouflaging the lack of generality by the abuse of "tacit (or inferred) consent", "acquiescence" and other fictitious notions for the traditional theory of customary international law on the one hand, and, to set an excessively high threshold for an alternate theory seeking to formulate the notion of general international law on the basis of the actual norms of conduct among nations, on the other. Such a double standard is a product of the myth that the "sources" of international law should be found in Article 38 of the ICJ Statute and nowhere else.[82]

---

81 One might be able to say that because the overwhelming majority of states express their commitment either in the form of ratification, accession or signature, the flaw of inferred consent is minimized, at least if compared with the traditional doctrine on customary law. However, if there is a powerful state persistently objecting to some rules in the treaty or the UN declaration, this factor must be seriously considered. The "persistent objector" rule has been argued and discussed in relation with customary international law. However, the crucial problem is not an existential category of law, but the universal validity of law. Thus, we could, and should, consider the problem of persistent objection whenever we deal with the problem of international law with universal validity, whether it derives its universal validity from a general custom, a general treaty or a UN resolution or declaration.

82 I fully admit the views expressed in the text are not elaborate and sophisticated. It is not my intention to develop a detailed theory that can take the place of the traditional theory of customary law in identifying general international law. The latter has a long history and is highly sophisticated. Many attempts to "save" the doctrine relying on "customary" international law are technically even more sophisticated. Roberts' article

D.   Identification of Global Norms of Conduct with International, Transnational and Transcivilizational Legitimacy

When we conceive of the global legal order in the 21st century, we must think of general norms of international law that can effectively regulate behaviors of states and other international actors. Some of these norms of conduct in general international law might not be able to make all states including the US, the only superpower at present, comply with specific norms strictly defined and interpreted in international courts. However, they can at least demonstrate the shared goals and understandings of international society, guide the behavior of states including the hegemonic state, and induce convergence of various behaviors of diverse states with different interests and value judgments. They can carry out various functions as law in international society.[83]

In order to identify such general norms of conduct in international law, we need to identify actual situations where rules and principles of international law are actually involved, resorted to, and utilized. We also need to identify actual actors who are involved in the process where rules and principles of international law are discussed, drafted, formulated, applied, utilized to justify or criticize certain claims or interests of various subjects, violated by some actors, enforced and finally realized. By paying attention to such concrete realities through not only international, but also transnational and transcivilizational perspectives, we can liberate ourselves from excessive state-centrism, positivism and judicial-centrism, as well as deeply rooted West-centrism.

We can see that a large number of non-state actors are heavily involved in such a process where international law is involved, invoked and utilized. They are enterprises, NGOs, international lawyers and other experts, various kinds of activists, media institutions, ethnic minorities, indigenous peoples, churches, independent priests, Buddhist monks, ayatollahs, victims of human rights violations and all others. They resort to international law in order to justify their claims and interests, and to negate the legitimacy of the claims made by their opponents. Through such "political" use of international law, international law contributes to various socially useful functions including legitimation through the process of conflicting justification.[84]

Forums where these justification and legitimation is carried out are not limited to judiciaries. They include (1) bilateral negotiations between national gov-

---

(*supra* note 65) is one of such examples. However, it seems to me that it is useless to revive the theory equating the fictitious notion of customary international law with general international law, which has been dead for many years. The theory has outlived its proper lifespan. It would be far more constructive to make efforts to elaborate a theory based on the recognition that ordinary norms of conduct in international law can be identified independently of Article 38 of the ICJ Statute, although the latter can provide a useful clue to such identification.

83   Onuma, *supra* note 2, pp. 130-138.

84   *Ibid.*, pp. 136-8.

ernments; (2) various organs in international organizations such as UNGA, UN Human Rights Commission and UN Security Council; (3) national parliaments; (4) media institutions such as op-ed pages of leading newspapers; and (5) bilateral negotiations between private persons, enterprises, ethnic minorities and national governments. The ICJ and other judiciaries occupy just a minor place in these diverse argumentative processes. In order to identify these diverse actors who are involved in the various processes where rules and principles of international law function as an important tool of justification and legitimation, we need to observe and assess these actors not only through international perspectives, but also through transnational and transcivilizational perspectives. By adopting these non-state-centric and non-West-centric perspectives, we can identify many functions and much usefulness of international law as well as its nature as a tool of a few powerful states in a more explicit and more balanced way.

As far as the transnational perspective is concerned, its importance has been more and more recognized. A number of international lawyers have either consciously or unconsciously adopted this perspective, and have made arguments based on it. A leading example is the area of human rights, but even in the field of security, one can see conspicuous examples including the case of the creation of the Landmine Ban Treaty of 1997. In the problem of customary international law, some authors argue that the international community is composed not only by states but also by non-state actors and that *opinion juris* of the international community must be identified in such a community consciousness including NGOs and media institutions.[85] Although I do not necessarily agree with those views because they tend to overemphasize the importance of West-centric non-state actors, I do believe that this move must be encouraged in order to widen our perspectives.

Unfortunately, however, a similar kind of development has seldom seen as far as the transcivilizational perspective is concerned. We must deliberately encourage and enhance the move to invite our attention to the importance of this third perspective, transcivilizational one. In order to conceive of any problems involving international law, including the problem of terrorism, the problem of a huge gap between the developed and developing countries, the problem of human rights and global environment, where various ways of life, *i.e.*, cultures and civilizations, are at issue, the transcivilizational perspective is desperately needed.

Finally, it is important to pay attention to the aspect where international law works not as a means of settling conspicuous conflicts, but as an important means to help realize people's ordinary life in a tacit and peaceful manner. International law generally works in a far more quiet and invisible manner than in the cases where it is required to justify conflicting claims, and to settle actual conflicts in a conspicuous manner. Rules and principles of international law function as an important means for various actors whose political and economic systems, cultures, religions and civilizations are diverse to communicate with each other, and help them to negotiate and settle various issues of conflict on a daily basis. They

---

85   Byers, M., Nolte, G. eds., *United States Hegemony and the Foundations of International Law*, Cambridge Univ. Press, 2003.

contribute to the well functioning of the international system without necessarily being recognized of its importance.

As Rosalyn Higgins wrote at the very beginning of her excellent book *Problems & Process*, "If a legal system works well, then disputes are in large part avoided. The identification of required norms of behavior, and the techniques to secure routine compliance with them, play an important part …. Of course, sometimes dispute-resolution will be needed; or even norms to limit the parameters of conduct when normal friendly relations have broken down and dispute resolution failed. But these last elements are only a small part of the overall picture."[86] H. L. A. Hart expressed the same idea in the following way: "The principal functions of the law as a means of social control are not to be seen in private litigation or prosecutions, which represent vital but still ancillary provisions for the failures of the system. It is to be seen in the diverse ways in which the law is used to control, guide, and plan life out of court."[87]

Again, however, this crucially important role of international law can be possible only where its legitimacy is recognized by its society members either explicitly or implicitly. The global legal order is based on the shared perception of global legitimacy. Even the power of the most powerful nation, which may at some moment be able to violate norms of international law and ignore values of diverse cultures and civilizations without being punished, will be eroded in the long run. Such a power that pays little attention to the perception shared by others as to international, transnational and transcivilizational legitimacy will not be supported by domestic voters, who constantly see, hear and feel negative assessments of their government's behavior in a global society. Although the only superpower may not be constrained by other states, *i.e.*, governments, alone, it may be constrained by transnational networks of media institutions that can reach to domestic voters of that power.

It is true that there exist serious problems of West-centric or US-centric structures of global information, which reflect the overall power structure of the present world. In order that the global "market of ideas" in terms of international law functions well, it is necessary for international society to guarantee equality of those who introduce arguments of international law to the market. Present international society certainly lacks this precondition. It has a huge asymmetry between those who can introduce their voices and arguments far more easily and effectively through powerful public relations facilities of the government and media institutions, and those who lack such powerful means of expressing their ideas. If we think of influential media institutions that shape "public opinions" in the world and in the US, we can immediately see the problematic features of the above argument. From CNN, Fox News to academic publications such as the *American Journal of International Law*, almost all media are either US centric, or West-centric, at most.

---

86   Higgins, R., *Problems and Process: International Law and How We Use It*, Clarendon Press, 1994, p. 1.

87   Hart, H.L.A., *The Concept of Law* (2nd ed.), Clarendon Press, 1997, p. 39.

Still, we should not be too pessimistic. Even in this area of global information or cognitive space, where the influence of West-centric discourse has been overwhelming, we may be able to expect that there will be more multi-cultural and multi-civilizational media institutions and academic spaces that may rectify this excessively West-centric global informational structure. Activities of small, yet highly visible reports by the Aljazeera in the Iraq war and other events have demonstrated that this expectation is not without grounds. The transcivilizational perspective can help people to understand that such various efforts to rectify the excessively West-centric discourse must be highly appreciated. These efforts are extremely important in order to establish and maintain a more equitable and legitimate international order in the 21st century.

7. International Law as a Cultural Perspective: Towards a Convergence of Civilizations
Contributions of Developing Countries[1] to the Formation and Application of International Law

Saeid Mirzaee-Yengejeh[2]

1. Introduction

A review of the contemporary literature relevant to law-making at the international level, as well as the appraisal of the legal issues on the agenda of international bodies, indicates that the debate over "Euro-centric"[3] or "universal" international law, "old"[4] or "new" international law, and "classical" or "modern" international law has faded away.[5] That debate was vigorously pursued, *inter alia*, by the newly inde-

---

1   The expression "developing countries" is a general term, which refers to the countries that are not developed. In this chapter, the term is used to cover the Asian, African and Latin American countries, a majority of which became independent in the post World War II era. The above countries have coordinated their positions on political subjects in the framework of the Non-Aligned Movement and on economic matters in the Group of 77. Nonetheless, coordination among these countries on international issues has not always been steady and without stumbling blocks, mainly, due to their large number, lack of an all embracing and efficient organization, as well as, because of their declining common international interests in a mounting competitive world.

2   The views expressed in this chapter are those of the author and do not represent any government's or organisation's position.

3   For hundreds of years, the State system was centered in Europe and its politics were the politics of the European powers. International law, too, therefore was inevitably Euro-centric. The core of customary international law was mainly created and developed by the practice of the European powers, and then of their offspring in the western hemisphere. As a result of colonialism, that law applied to much of Asia and Africa.

4   Debate on this issue had been focussed on the problem of the claims to the legitimacy and continued application today of legal principles and rules manifestly developed in an era now past.

5   Elias observed, for instance, that international law has ceased to be European law and that its institutions were now worldwide. (T.O. Elias, *Africa and the Development of International Law*, Leiden: Sijthof, 1972, p.82). Anand referred to the "expansion of international law from the law of European Christendom to the law applicable to the universal community of nations. (R.P.Anand, *New States and International Law* (Delhi: Vikas, 1972, p. 7).

Ronald St. John Macdonald & Douglas M. Johnston (eds.), Towards World Constitutionalism, *pp. 191-221.*
© 2005 *Koninklijke Brill NV. Printed in The Netherlands.* ISBN 90 04 14612 1.

pendent countries from the colonial rule ("the new States"), in the 1950s and 1960s. The new States, tied by the bonds of common colonial experience, challenged the prevailing international law as European, Christian, and Colonial, which had been developed in an era prior to their independence. They pursued this policy because they had not contributed to the formation of the basic rules governing relations among nations at the time. These challenges to the legitimacy of international law lost their relevance by adherence of the new States to the Charter of the United Nations, through reaffirmation of the basic principles of international law by General Assembly resolutions, by developing new rules with the participation of developing countries, and by their contribution to the application of international law.

Following the liberation of the new States from colonial rule, they enthusiastically sought membership in the United Nations and its specialized agencies. As a prerequisite to the membership in the State-club, they acceded to the Charter, the founding instrument of the United Nations, which embodied the basic principles of the so-called "Euro-centric international law". As a result, the new States did not press for radical changes in the norms and principles governing relations among nations; instead they sought the re-examination and codification of these principles while asserting their right to participate in the process of law-making in order to dissociate themselves from the history of customary international law. The General Assembly approved the Declaration on Principles of International Law Concerning Friendly Relations and Cooperation Among States in accordance with the Charter of the United Nations ("the friendly relations declaration"), in 1970.[6] Approval of this Declaration clearly demonstrated the manner in which the new States contributed, in practice, to the reaffirmation of the principles of international law enshrined in the Charter of the United Nations.

In addition, the increased membership in the United Nations marked the exerted efforts on the part of the new States to confirm in law, the principles that had already been politically established. For instance, rapid and near-total decolonisation confirmed that self-determination had become an established principle of international politics. Consequently, the new members of the United Nations fervently sought its inclusion in various international instruments adopted within and outside the United Nations.[7] Similarly, the ongoing struggle against racial discrimination and apartheid regimes gained legitimacy and renewed strength by its inclusion in several international instruments that were adopted under the auspices of the Organization. Likewise, the desire of these States to emphasise their sovereignty over natural resources met the approval of the General Assembly in accordance with its Resolution 1803[8] of 1962, and its reaffirmation by way of the

---

6   General Assembly Resolution 2625 (XXV) dated 24 October 1970.

7   The General Assembly by approving the declaration on the granting of independence to colonial countries, declared that the subjection of people to alien subjugation constituted "a denial of fundamental human rights" and was "contrary to the Charter of the United Nations". See A/RES/1514 dated 14 December 1960.

8   The General Assembly adopted Resolution 1803, entitled "permanent sovereignty over natural resources", during its 17th session in 1962.

adoption by the General Assembly of the Declaration on New International Economic Order, in 1974.[9]

The developing countries actively participated in the international conferences, convened under the auspices of the United Nations in 1970s, 1980s, and 1990s, in which several international instruments were prepared to regulate new areas of inter-State relationship. Enthusiastic participation of the third-world countries in the third United Nations conference on the law of the sea was the beginning of an era, which was marked by the active involvement of the developing world in making the law among nations and continued until the end of the twentieth century.

The developing countries also played a tangible role in the application of the norms and principles of international law. Resort to the International Court of Justice for the settlement of disputes by many developing countries, and their initiative on the proclamation of the period 1990-1999 as the United Nations Decade of International Law demonstrated the willingness of the new States to apply norms and principles of international law, and to oppose the violation of these norms by the actors of the international arena.

In this chapter, an attempt will be made to give an overall view of the role of the developing countries in the law-making process following the foundation of the United Nations. This task will be carried out by organising the chapter in the following sections.

2.   Accession to the United Nations

The Charter of the United Nations was drafted by the representatives of fifty-one States, who participated in the San Francisco Conference in 1945. The Charter established a new world order in the post World War II era with the aim of preserving the succeeding generations from the scourge of war. It incorporated several basic customary norms and principles to govern relations among its Member States. It also included a number of new rules to be applicable in the inter-State relationship. The Charter further provided for the mechanisms for the peaceful settlement of disputes between States[10] in conformity with justice and international law. The Security Council was empowered, in accordance with Chapter VII of the Charter, to take action with respect to threats to peace, breaches of peace, and acts of aggression.

Moreover, the Charter laid down the necessary foundations for the liberation and self-determination of the former colonies. It embodied extensive rules on the administration of non-self-governing territories[11] and established an international trusteeship system[12] for supervising the administration of such territories, with a view to promoting their progressive development towards self-government and

---

9   General Assembly Resolution 3281, dated 12 December 1974, on the Charter of Economic Rights and Duties of States.

10   See Article 33 of the Charter.

11   See Chapter XI of the Charter entitled "declaration regarding non-self-governing-territories".

12   See Chapter XII of the Charter entitled "international trusteeship system".

independence.[13]Additionally, it established the Trusteeship Council under the authority of the General Assembly to assist the Assembly in carrying out the functions under the trusteeship system. With this legal groundwork and the prevailing favourable political clout, decolonisation was reinvigorated and the former colonies were swiftly liberated and achieved their independence in almost a quarter of a century following the foundation of the United Nations.

Though critical of customary international law, as Colonial and Western, the new States freely chose to accede to the Charter, which embodied several appealing principles, such as, sovereign equality of States, peaceful settlement of disputes, non-use of force in international relations, and equal rights and self-determination of peoples. By becoming parties to the Charter, the new States conceded to abide by the customary norms and principles enshrined in the Charter, and to fulfil, in good faith, their obligations under these rules.

The new States felt that by joining the State-club, they would be in a better position to pursue their past grievances, including the re-examination of the norms and principles developed by Western nations and the wisdom of their continued applications in international relations. They demonstrated in practice their determination to actively participate in the process of law- making at international level. The establishment of the Asian Legal Consultative Committee, in 1956, which was expanded later to incorporate African countries as well,[14] was the first practical step taken by the Asian and African countries towards the realisation of the desire of these nations to re-evaluate the existing norms governing relations among nations.[15] Thus, the members of the Asian African Consultative Organization ("AALCO") succeeded in taking a number of positive steps in the General Assembly, to reaffirm in writing the principles which had already been politically established, and in codification of the existing norms

3.   Reaffirmation of the Basic Principles of International Law

As mentioned earlier, the membership of the United Nations increased significantly as a result of decolonisation.[16] Hence, developing countries enjoyed a clear

---

13   Article 76 (b) of the Charter.

14   The Asian Legal Consultative Committee, as it was originally known, was founded on 15 November 1956 as an outcome of the historic Bandung Conference in April 1955, by seven Asian States Burma, India, Indonesia, Iraq, Japan, Ceylon and the United Arab Republic. Later, in April 1958, its name was changed to Asian-African Legal Consultative Committee so as to admit African States as members. The Committee transformed itself into an organisation and was named the Asian-African Legal Consultative Organisation (AALCO) in 1998.

15   The Statute of the AALCO, which entered into force on 12 January 1987, stipulated the purpose and objective of the organisation, *inter alia*, "[to] serve as an advisory body to its Member States in the field of international law and as a forum for Asian-African co-operation in legal matters of common concern", <http://www.aalco.org/Statutes>.

16   The Member States of the United Nations increased from 51, in 1945, to 127 States in 1970, and to 159 in 1990. The current number of the States members of the United Na-

majority in the General Assembly, and were able to easily pursue their policies, and actively participate in and influence the law-making process in the United Nations. In the prevailing environment, the General Assembly adopted a number of declarations, which reaffirmed, with the participation of the new States, several principles of customary international law that had already been incorporated in the Charter. Among several declarations and resolutions adopted by the General Assembly, with law-declaring characteristics, the following could be mentioned as examples:

–   The approval of the **friendly relations declaration** by consensus, in 1970, was a significant step in the process of assertion of the basic principles of international law.[17] This Declaration contained seven "basic principles of international law" applicable to "all States in their international conducts".[18] It identified the following principles applicable to the friendly relations and cooperation among States in accordance with the Charter of the United Nations: *non-use of force in international relations; peaceful settlement of disputes; non-intervention in the internal affairs of other States; the duty of States to co-operate with one another in accordance with the Charter; equal rights and self-determination of peoples; sovereign equality of States; fulfilment of obligations under the Charter in good faith.*

The merits of the Declaration are manifold. It represents the authoritative interpretation of the principles enshrined in the Charter; it reaffirms that the fundamental principles contained in the Charter are binding to the entire membership of the Organization in their international relations; and, above all, it is indicative of the conviction of the new States that adherence to the said principles, without regard to their original formation, could better

---

tions is 192. See Growth in the United Nations Membership at: <http://www.un.org/Overview/growth.html>.

17   The importance of this declaration had been emphasised by several of the participants in the work of the Ad Hoc Committee, which prepared the declaration. For instance, Rosenstock, a US representative, describes the declaration as "the text represents a very substantial contribution to clarification of the key concepts of international law", cited by Ian Sinclair in "The Significance of the Friendly Relations Declaration", p. 6, *The United Nations and the Principles of International Law*, Vaughan Lowe and Colin Warbrick, editors. According to Jimenez de Arechaga, "[a]doption in these terms and without a dissenting vote, it constitutes an authoritative expression of the views held by the totality of the parties to the Charter as to these basic principles and certain corollaries resulting from them." In his view, the legal weight and authority of the declaration lied both in "recognising what the Members themselves believe constitute rules of customary law and as an interpretation of the Charter by the subsequent agreement and the subsequent practice of all its members." *Ibid*, p. 8. In the view of Oscar Schachter, "it recognizes that interpretations and declarations of the law by the Assembly are official expression by the governments concerned and consequently are relevant and entitled to be given weight in determinations of the law in question.", *Ibid*. p. 9.

18   A/RES/25/2625, last paragraph.

serve the interests of all States, including those of the former colonies.[19] In the view of the International Court of Justice the adoption of the friendly relations declaration by States was "an indication of their *opinio juris* as to customary international law on the question."[20]

The far-reaching effects of this Declaration in the process of codification and development of international law is palpable from the references made to it in almost all subsequent declarations adopted by the General Assembly,[21] as well as, from frequent references made to it in official statements delivered on behalf of governments and in documents issued by them. Some of the principles mentioned in the Declaration were the subject of subsequent declarations, which further developed the principles contained in the friendly relations declaration.

– The General Assembly by the adoption of its Resolution 3314,[22] on **the definition of aggression**,[23] laid down another milestone on the codification of international law and its progressive development. It was an attempt undertaken to fill the lacuna left behind by the authors of the Charter, who did not provide for the definition of aggression. The definition was intended to serve as a guide[24] to the Security Council in fulfilling the mandate entrusted to it under Article 39 of the Charter on the determination of acts of aggression. It also offered a guide by which States could regulate their international conduct and

---

19   Sinclair noted in this respect "the work of the Special Committee on Friendly Relations provided an ideal opportunity for the representatives of some newly independent States to flex their muscles in the international arena, and to pursue their quest for a 'new' international law which would be responsive to their needs and which would be freed from constrains of what they perceived to be outmoded , Eurocentric and inevitably 'colonialist' concepts." *Op cit.*, p. 28.

20   ICJ reports, case concerning military and paramilitary activities in and against Nicaragua, 1986, p. 101.

21   A/RES/43/51, annex, preambular paragraph 6; A/RES/37/10, annex, preambular paragraph 8; A/RES/42/22, annex, preambular paragraph 3; A/RES/3314 (XXIX), annex, preambular paragraph 8; A/RES/46/59, preambular paragraph 1; A/RES/49/57, annex, operative paragraph 11.

22   Adopted on 14 December 1974.

23   As a result of compromise, the definition of aggression is both abstract and enumerative. It contains a preamble, recalling and reaffirming the fundamental principles on which it is based, followed by 8 articles. Article 3 enumerates aggressive acts, and Article 4 provides that the list is not exclusive. The legal consequences of aggression are contained in Article 5. Articles 6 and 7 ensure that the definition does not alter Charter provisions concerning self-defence and right of peoples to self-determination. Article 8 provides that any interpretation of any article should be construed in the context of other articles.

24   See Paragraph 9 of the Preamble of General Assembly Resolution 3314 of 14 December 1947.

a deterrent to potential aggressors who would undermine the goals of Articles 2 (3) and 2(4) of the Charter.

The historical significance[25] of the Resolution cannot be overestimated. It represented a desire of the entire membership of the United Nations to work on the basis of the principles provided for in the Charter of the United Nations. The adoption of the definition also reflected the rising power of smaller nations in the General Assembly and the increasing reluctance of major powers to confront them, at least on such theoretical issues as the definition of aggression.

As regards the impact of the definition of aggression on the development of international law, it must be pointed out that it has been cited in the subsequent documents adopted in the United Nations.[26] States also frequently referred to it in their statements and documents, as an expression of the prevailing international law.[27] Moreover, the International Court of Justice has referred to it as reflecting customary international law.[28]

During the United Nations Diplomatic Conference of Plenipotentiaries on the Establishment of an International Criminal Court, in 1998,[29] upon the initiative of the Non-Aligned Movement, the crime of aggression was included among the core crimes within the jurisdiction of the Court.[30] However, in spite of the efforts of the members of the Movement, the conference could not

---

25   The United Nations interests in the definition of aggression grew out of the efforts of the League of Nations to prevent war by outlawing it. The formal goal of outlawing war was achieved in 1928 by the pact of Paris. The Soviet Union proposed a definition of aggression in 1933. These efforts were continued by Latin American nations, but it was not until 1945 that the issue was again discussed by a widely representative group. The San Francisco Conference rejected two draft definitions to allow the Security Council maximum flexibility in determining acts of aggression. Thereafter efforts to define aggression continued in the General Assembly. See "The Definition of Aggression", *Harvard International Law Journal*, Vol. 16, pp. 589-510.

26   A/RES/48/59 B; A/RES/49/60; A/RES/42/22, annex, preambular paragraph 3.

27   A/C.6/43/SR. 33; A/C.6/43/SR. 35; A/C.6/43/SR. 37; A/C.6/43/SR. 39; A/C.6/44/SR. 40; A/C.6/43/SR. 43; A/C.6/44/SR. 28; A/C.6/44/SR. 29; A/C.6/44/SR. 38; A/C.6/54/ ;SR. A/C.6/50/SR. 22; A/C.6/50/SR.25; A/C.6/50/SR.28; A/C.6/50/SR.31;A/C.6/51/SR.12; A/C.6/51/SR. 27; A/C.6/51/SR. 31; A/C.6/51/SR.32; A/C.6/51/SR.33; A/C.6/55/SR. 11; A/C.6/54/SR.12; A/C.6/54/SR.13; A/C.6/55/SR. 14; A/C.6/55/SR. 9;A/C.6/55/SR.11; A/C.6/55/SR. 12; A/C.6/55/SR. 15; A/41/282; A/40/854; A/42/766; A/45/430; A/44/476; A/46/372; A/53/499; A/53/PV. 22; A/53/PV.95;S/18392; S/18065; S/20363; S/20704; S/22625; S/1994/586; S/1995/201; S/1995/506; S/1998/ 827; S/1998/1130; S/1999/45; S/1999/205; S/1999/733; S/1999/742; S/2001/1014; S/2001/ 1026 ; S/2001/1027; S/PV.3314; S/PV.3988; S/PV.3653; S/PV. 2874; S/PV. 2875.

28   ICJ Reports, Case concerning Military and Paramilitary Activities in and against Nicaragua, 1986, p. 103, paragraph 191.

29   The United Nations Conference of Plenipotentiaries on the Establishment of an International Criminal Court was convened from 15 June to 17 July 1998, in Rome, Italy.

30   Rome Statute of the International Criminal Court, Article 5.

agree on the definition of aggression, nor did the Preparatory Commission on the Establishment of the International Criminal Court succeed in fulfilling the mandate[31] entrusted to it on the definition of the crime of aggression.[32]

–   Adoption of the **Manila Declaration on the Peaceful Settlement of International Disputes** by the General Assembly,[33] in 1982, was another important step towards the reaffirmation of this basic principle, which had already been incorporated in the Charter. The Declaration does not add any new mechanism to the existing methods of the settlement of disputes enshrined in Chapter VI of the Charter. It rather elaborates on the obligation of States to act in good faith and in conformity with the purposes and principles of the Charter with a view to avoiding disputes among themselves, and on their obligation to settle their existing or future disputes exclusively by pacific means, including, in particular, by way of resort to the means provided for in Article 33 of the Charter. The free choice of means of the settlement of disputes has also been underlined in a number of paragraphs of the Declaration. Furthermore, States have been encouraged to include in their bilateral agreements and multilateral conventions effective provisions for peaceful settlement of disputes relating to the interpretation or application of the treaty in question.[34]

Formulation and inclusion of an agreed text relating to the referral of disputes to the International Court of Justice in the Declaration was a significant achievement. In this regard, the Declaration reaffirmed the Charter provision that, "legal disputes as a general rule be referred by the parties to the International Court of Justice, in accordance with the provisions of the Statute of the Court."[35] It encouraged States to insert, in treaties concluded between or among them, clauses providing for submission of disputes to the ICJ, and to study the possibility of accepting the compulsory jurisdiction of the Court in accordance with Article 36 of its Statute. This provision reflected a significant policy shift on the part of many developing States, who previously had doubts about the settlement of disputes by way of referral to the ICJ. Following the adoption of the Declaration, the number of cases submitted to the ICJ, in particular, by developing countries, increased considerably.[36]

---

31   The Final Act of the United Nations Diplomatic Conference of Plenipotentiaries on the Establishment of an International Criminal Court, Resolution F, paragraph 7.

32   During the Rome Conference a number of proposals, based on General Assembly Resolution 3314, were presented to the Conference. Similar proposals were also made in the course of the discussion of the subject in the Preparatory Commission on the establishment of the ICC. For further discussion of the subject see section 5 of this chapter, and for the text of the proposals consult: <http://www.un.org/law/icc>.

33   A/RES/37/10.

34   A/RES/37/10, paragraph 9 of the annex.

35   Article 36(3) of the Charter.

36   For further discussion of the subject, see section 62 on Application of International Law by Developing Countries of this chapter.

It was also important for the new States to be involved in the drafting of the Declaration and in the proclamation of the continued legitimacy of this fundamental rule following their admission to the United Nations. Many members of the NAM actively participated in the negotiations, and expressed their satisfaction after the adoption of the Declaration.[37] This Declaration has been referred to in numerous statements made on behalf of the Movement and has been re-emphasized in the subsequent resolutions and declaration adopted by the General Assembly.[38]

–   The Declaration on **the enhancement of the effectiveness of the principle of refraining from threat or use of force in international relations**, adopted by the General Assembly,[39] in 1987, affirmed among others, the obligation of all States not to use or threaten to use force in their international relations, as enshrined in the Charter of the United Nations.

The initiative that led to the adoption of the Declaration was taken by the former Soviet Union in 1976, which had originally proposed the adoption of a treaty on the non-use of force in international relations. However, a group of western States, who had opposed the idea, were of the opinion that it was unnecessary to repeat the United Nations Charter provisions, that it would be dangerous to depart from those provisions, and that interpretation of that principle beyond what is contained in the friendly relations declaration and the declaration on the definition of aggression would detract from its coherence.[40] The proposal by the Non-Aligned Movement, in 1985, to work on a draft declaration on non-use of force broke the stalemate[41] in the Special Committee on Enhancing the Effectiveness of the Principle of Non-Use of Force in International Relations and led to the adoption, without a vote, of the Declaration by the General Assembly.

Since the Declaration reproduces several provisions of the Charter of the United Nations, the friendly relations declaration and the resolution on the definition of aggression, the question of the added value of the Declaration was the subject of discussions.[42] For many States, however, including in particular

---

37   Bengt Broms, "The Declaration on the Peaceful Settlement of International Disputes", *Essays in International Law in Honor of Judge Manfred Lachs*, Martinus Nijhoff Publishers,1984, p. 353.

38   A/RES/43/51, annex, preambular paragraph 6; A/RES/42/22, annex, preambular paragraph 3; A/RES/46/59, preambular paragraph 1; A/RES/49/57, annex, operative paragraph 11.

39   A/RES/42/22, dated 18 November 1987.

40   Christine Gray, "The principle of non-use of force", *The United Nations and the Principles of International Law*, FN. No 17, pp. 39-40.

41   See the report of the Chairman of the Special Committee to the Sixth Committee during the forty-second session of the General Assembly, A/C. 6/42/SR. 16, p.2, paragraph 2.

42   *Ibid*, pp. 37-38.

developing States, the Declaration has a symbolic value. It is a unanimous expression of the continued validity of a number of important international law principles, contained in the instruments adopted on previous occasions, in particular the Charter of the United Nations. This Declaration is among the chain of declarations adopted by the General Assembly, which has been referred to in subsequent resolutions and declarations of the Assembly.[43]

– The General Assembly adopted three additional declarations, in the following years, which reaffirm the previous declarations of the Assembly, but do not add any new rule to those enshrined in the Charter and the previously mentioned declarations. These declarations elaborated on ways and means of implementing the norms and principles of international law as contained in the said instruments and the employment of the existing mechanisms as provided for in the said documents.

The first of these declarations, namely, the **Declaration on the Prevention and Removal of Disputes and Situations Which May Threaten International Peace and Security and on the Role of the United Nations in This Field**, was approved in 1988.[44] This Declaration mainly provides, in detail, ways and means of preventing international disputes and their removal at early stages. It primarily recommends to States and the United Nations competent organs to make full use of the mechanisms provided for in the Charter, at early stages of disputes, so that they cannot be escalated to the level that might threaten international peace and security.

The **Declaration on Fact-finding by the United Nations in the Field of the Maintenance of International Peace and Security**,[45] adopted in 1991, seeks to promote and strengthen the role of the United Nations in the maintenance of international peace and security, peaceful settlement of disputes and prevention and removal of disputes, by way of full use of the fact-finding capabilities of the United Nations.[46] The Declaration encourages the Security Council, the General Assembly and the Secretary-General to undertake fact-finding, in the context of their responsibilities in accordance with the Charter. It also provides for, in detail, the modalities of the operation of the fact-finding activities.

The **Declaration on the Enhancement of Cooperation between the United Nations and Regional Arrangements or Agencies in the Maintenance of International Peace and Security**,[47] adopted in 1994, was intended to strengthen the cooperation between the United Nations and regional ar-

---

43   A/RES/43/51, annex, preambular paragraph 6; A/RES/46/59, preambular paragraph 1; A/RES/49/57, annex, operative paragraph 1.

44   A/RES/43/51, dated 5 December 1988.

45   A/RES/46/59.

46   *Ibid*, preambular paragraph 3.

47   A/RES/49/57.

rangements or agencies in the maintenance of international peace and security in accordance with the provisions of Chapter VIII of the Charter, as well as, to enhance the role of regional arrangements and organisations in the prevention and peaceful settlement of disputes. This Declaration was referred to in the Statements made on behalf of governments, and also in the resolutions and declarations adopted by the Assembly in subsequent years.[48]

◆   ◆   ◆

The significance of the above declarations and their added values has been the subject of different interpretations and analysis. Although some have doubts on the law-making competences of the General Assembly, there is no controversy, however, over the authority of the Assembly in identifying and declaring customary norms of international law. In the view of the author, the importance of these declarations lies in the participation of the new States in the reaffirmation of the essential norms of a peaceful world as foreseen by the authors of the Charter, and also in the clarification of the point that they are binding on each and every nation irrespective of their participation in the original formation of these principles.

4.   Codification of New Norms of International Law

The increased membership in the United Nations was marked by exerted efforts on the part of the new States to confirm in law the principles that had already been politically recognised. For instance, rapid and near-total decolonisation confirmed that self-determination had become an established principle of international relations. Consequently, the new members of the United Nations fervently sought its inclusion in various international instruments adopted within and outside the United Nations.[49] Similarly, the ongoing struggle against racial discrimination and apartheid regimes gained legitimacy and renewed strength by its inclusion in several international instruments that were adopted in or by support of the Organization. Likewise, the desire of these States to reiterate their sovereignty over their natural resources met with the approval of the General Assembly, in accordance with its Resolution 1803[50] of 1962, and reaffirmed by way of the adoption by the General Assembly of the declaration on the new international economic order, in 1974. The following instruments are viewed as achievements of Third World countries in the post World War II era.

---

48   A/RES/49/57, annex, operative paragraph 11.

49   The General Assembly by approving the declaration on the granting of independence to colonial countries, declared that the subjection of people to alien subjugation constituted "a denial of fundamental human rights" and was "contrary to the Charter of the United Nations". See A/RES/1514 dated 14 December 1960.

50   General Assembly Resolution 1803, entitled "Permanent sovereignty over natural resources", adopted during its 17th session in 1962.

—   The United Nations Charter had laid down main principles of the **self-determination of peoples**. Under Chapter XI of the Charter, all Member States with the responsibility of the administration of non-self-governing territories accepted the basic principle that the interests of the inhabitants of these territories had paramount importance and regarded the obligation "to promote their well-being" as a sacred trust. To achieve this objective, they undertook to assist the peoples of these territories to develop their political institutions with a view to enabling them to attain self-governing as rapidly as their conditions would permit.

The Trusteeship System established under Chapters XII and XIII of the Charter, was mandated to promote the political, economic and social advancement of the Trust Territories towards eventual independence and self-government. The Trusteeship Council, which is one of the principal organs of the United Nations, was entrusted with the responsibility for the operation of the system. As a result, dozens of non-self-governing territories achieved their independence, in the years after the United Nations foundation.

Nonetheless, upon the initiative of Afro-Asian countries,[51] the General Assembly by its historic Resolution[52] of 14 December 1960, entitled "Declaration on the Granting of Independence to Colonial Countries and Peoples", stressed the necessity for the speedy and unconditional termination of colonialism in all its forms. In accordance with the Resolution, "the subjugation of peoples to alien subjugation and exploitation" constituted a denial of fundamental human rights, was contrary to the Charter of the United Nations and was an impediment to the promotion of world peace and co-operation. It affirmed that all peoples had the right to self-determination, and consequently, they were entitled to freely determine their political status and freely pursue their economic, social and cultural development.

Subsequently, the right to self-determination was included in many resolutions and declarations of the General Assembly.[53] The friendly relations declaration, for example, provided that every State had "the duty to promote, through joint and separate action, realization of the principle of equal rights and self-determination of peoples." The Declaration further provided that,

---

51   The draft resolution was presented to the General Assembly by 43 Afro-Asian countries.

52   A/RES/1514 (XV).

53   A/RES/2625, dated 24 October 1970, annex, *The principles of equal rights and self-determination of peoples*; A/RES/3314, dated 14 December 1974, annex on the definition of aggression, Article 7; A/RES/37/10,5 November 1982, annex entitled "Manila Declaration on the Peaceful settlement of disputes between States", penultimate paragraph; A/RES/42/22, 18 November 1987, Declaration on the Enhancement of the Effectiveness of the Principle of Refraining from the Threat or Use of Force in International Relations, penultimate paragraph; A/RES/43/51,5 December 1988, Declaration on the Prevention and Removal of Disputes and Situations Which May Threaten International Peace and Security and on the Role of the United Nations in this Field, last paragraph.

every State had the duty "to refrain from any forcible action which deprives peoples in the elaboration of the principle of their right to self-determination and freedom and independence", and that "peoples who act against and resist such forcible action in the pursuit of exercise of their right to self-determination" were entitled to seek and receive support.

This principle was also incorporated in several international conventions, which have entered into force and have become legally binding to its parties. For instance, both the international covenants on civil and political rights and social and economic rights stipulated that, "All peoples have the right of self-determination. By virtue of that right they freely determine their political status and freely pursue their economic, social and cultural development."[54]

–   Practices of **apartheid**[55] by the South African regime, then, definitely constituted a violation of fundamental principles of international law and human rights law as enshrined in the Charter and Human Rights Declaration of 1948.[56] The struggle of the South African people against the apartheid regime of that country enjoyed unreserved support of the developing countries. The support of the international community culminated, *inter alia*, in developing a body of international norms aimed at opposing racial discrimination and apartheid.

The General Assembly approved, in 1963, the declaration on the elimination of all forms of racial discrimination.[57] Subsequently, it adopted an international convention bearing the same title, in 1963.[58] Those two documents directly addressed apartheid, which the General Assembly considered as a violation of the principles of international law enunciated in the Charter and other international instruments. The first article of the declaration condemns racial discrimination as:

> an offence to human dignity … [which] shall be condemned as a denial of the principles of the Charter of the United Nations, as a violation of the human rights

---

54   Article 1 of the International Convenant on Civil and Political Rights, and Article 1 of the International Convenant on Economic and Social Rights.

55   Apartheid is an Afrikaans word, which literally translated into English, means "apartness". This term is used to describe a body of law enacted by the South African government to bring about legal separation among white, black and African peoples of South Africa.

56   "Promotion and encouraging respect for human rights and for fundamental freedoms for all without distinction as to race, sex, or religion" is among the principles of the United Nations Charter (Article 1, paragraph 3). Moreover, the United Nations is under an obligation in accordance with the Charter to promote "universal respect for, and observance of, human rights and fundamental freedoms for all without distinction as to race, sex, language, or religion." (Article 56 (c)). These principles were enunciated with greater specificity in the 1948 Universal Declaration of Human Rights (Article 2).

57   A/RES/1904 (XVIII), 20 November 1963.

58   A/RES/2106 (XX), 21 December 1965.

and fundamental freedoms proclaimed in the Universal Declaration of Human Rights, as an obstacle to friendly and peaceful relations among nations and as a fact capable of disturbing peace and security among peoples.

The International Convention on the Elimination of All Forms of Racial Discrimination, adopted two years later,[59] reaffirmed the provisions of the earlier declaration. Article III of the Convention elaborated on the declaration's apartheid provision by requiring that: "States Parties particularly condemn racial segregation and apartheid and undertake to prevent, prohibit and eradicate all practices of this nature in territories under their jurisdiction."

This specific commitment to eradicate apartheid, wherever present in territories governed by signatories of the Convention, was followed in 1968 by the Convention on the Non-Applicability of Statutory Limitations to War Crimes against Humanity.[60] That Convention listed apartheid as a crime against humanity, to which "no statutory limitation shall apply ... irrespective of the date of ... commission."[61]

Four years later, the General Assembly adopted the International Convention on the Suppression and Punishment of the Crime of Apartheid.[62] That Convention declared that *apartheid* was "a crime against humanity and that inhuman acts resulting from the policies and practices of apartheid and similar policies and practices of racial segregation and discrimination" were crimes violating the principles of international law, in particular the purposes and principles of the Charter.[63]

Following entry into force of the Apartheid Convention, several other international instruments were developed, which reiterated the basic principles contained in the Convention and elaborated on the instruments mentioned earlier.[64] Most notably, apartheid was placed among the crimes against humanity in the Rome Statute of the International Criminal Court.[65]

---

59   The Convention was adopted by the General Assembly of the United Nations in accordance with Resolution 2106 (XX), on 7 March 1966, in New York.

60   754 U.N.T.S. 74 (1970).

61   *Ibid*, Article 1 (b).

62   A/RES/3068 (XXVIII), dated 30 November 1973, annex.

63   *Ibid*, paragraph 1 of the annex.

64   List and texts of anti-apartheid instruments could be found in the following document: Compendium of international and regional standards against racism, racial discrimination, xenophobia and related intolerance, E/CN.4/2004/WG.21/5.

65   Rome Statute of the International Criminal Court, Article 7 (1) (j). The Rome Statute defines apartheid as follows: "The crime of apartheid means inhumane acts of a character similar to those referred to in paragraph 1, committed in the context of an institutionalised regime of systematic oppression and domination by one racial group over any other racial group or groups and committed with the intention of maintaining that regime", see Article 7 (2) (h).

–   It was through the efforts of the third world countries that **the principle of permanent sovereignty over natural resources** gained universal recognition. As early as in 1952, the General Assembly passed a resolution recognising that all States have the right to freely use and exploit "their natural wealth and resources", an intrinsic part of their sovereignty, for their own progress and development.[66]

Later, in 1962, the Assembly approved the declaration on the permanent sovereignty over natural resources, by which it declared that "[t]he right of peoples and nations to permanent sovereignty over their natural wealth and resources must be exercised in the interest of their national development and of the well-being of the people of the State concerned".[67] Furthermore, the declaration acknowledged that nationalisation and expropriation on "grounds or reasons of public utility, security or national interest", which were overriding purely individual or private interests, both domestic and foreign.[68] The declaration pronounced that the violation of the right of the peoples and nations to sovereignty over their natural resources was contrary to the spirit and the principles of the Charter.[69]

Subsequently, the Assembly approved the Charter of Economic Rights and Duties of States, in 1974, which re-emphasized and elaborated on the principle of permanent sovereignty of States over natural resources.[70] In accordance with this Charter, the principle of permanent sovereignty over natural resources included "possession, use and disposal, over all its wealth, natural resources and economic activities."[71] Preparation of regulations on foreign investment, and on the activities of transactional corporations and their implementation within national jurisdictions, became an integral part of the said principle.[72]

The above-mentioned instruments summarise the policies pursued by and achievements of the new States following their independence. These instruments also laid the ground work for the cooperation among third world countries in the law-making conferences, which will be considered in the next section of this chapter.

5.   Contribution to the Law-making Conferences

The advent of the new States and their membership in the United Nations was followed by the convening of dozens of international conferences to codify the

---

66   A/RES/626 (VII), paragraph 1.

67   A/RES/1803 (XVII), paragraph 1.

68   *Ibid*, paragraph 4.

69   *Ibid*, paragraph 7.

70   A/RES/3281 (XXIX), Article 2.

71   *Ibid.*

72   *Ibid.*

existing norms and to develop new rules to be applied to the new aspects of international relations. Asian and African States, which were critical of the history of international law, ardently participated in these conferences to safeguard the common interests of the developing countries. They succeeded in influencing the negotiations process mainly because of their majority and coordinated positions in the course of a number of conferences. The developing countries made sensible contributions to many of these conferences, out of which their role in the Third United Nation Conference on the Law of the Sea and 1998 United Nations Conference on the Establishment of the International Criminal Court will be discussed as examples.

A.   Third United Nations Conference on the Law of the Sea[73]

The third world countries led the General Assembly, in 1970, to declare, *inter alia*, that the area of the sea-bed and ocean floor and the subsoil thereof, beyond the limits of national jurisdiction ("the Area"), as well as its resources, were the common heritage of mankind, and that the exploration and exploitation of which should be carried out for the benefit of mankind as a whole.[74] Subsequently, third world countries piloted the efforts to expand the scope of the item on the agenda of the United Nations to cover all matters relating to the law of the sea, and to convene the Third United Nations Conference on the Law of the Sea. Moreover, the developing countries zealously engaged in the negotiations and persistently followed their common interests during the entire period of the Conference, which resulted in meeting their concerns in many respects. During the negotiations, the Group of 77 ("G77")[75] emerged as a single negotiation team, which mainly defended the

---

73   Third United Nations Conference on the Law of the Sea, convened in accordance with General Assembly Resolution 2750 C (XXV), with the mandate "to adopt a convention dealing with all matters relating to the law of the Sea"(see paragraph 3 of the resolution 3067 (XXVIII) of 16 November 1973). The conference after working for 12 sessions produced the draft United Nations Convention on the Law of the Sea, which was adopted on 30 April 1982, and was opened for signature in Montego Bay, Jamaica, on 12 December 1982.

74   S/RES/2749 (XXV) of 17 December 1970, entitled declaration of principles governing the sea-bed and ocean floor, and the subsoil thereof, beyond the limits of national jurisdiction.

75   The Group of 77 (G77) was established on 15 June 1964 by 77 developing countries signatories of the "Joint Declaration of the Seventy Seven Countries" issued at the end of the first session of the United Nations Conference on Trade and Development (UNCTAD) in Geneva in 1964. Although the membership of the G77 has increased to 132 countries, the original name was retained because of its historic significance. G77 is the largest third world group in the United Nations, which provides the necessary means for the developing countries to articulate and promote its collective economic interests, and enhances its negotiating capacity on all major economic issues in the United Nations system. For further information consult: <http://www.g77.org/main/main.htm>.

common economic interests of the developing countries. G77 conducted regular consultations, in advance and during the sessions of the Conference on issues of common concern, and formulated common positions on many points, which were the subject of negotiations.[76]

The AALCO[77] also made substantive contribution to the negotiations on several concepts of common interest to its member States. The main concerns of the member States of AALCO were, *inter alia*, concepts of the exclusive economic zone,[78] exclusive fisheries zone, archipelagic States,[79] the accommodation of the interests of the land-locked Sates,[80] and different aspects of the regime and of the international machinery for the exploration and exploitation of the resources deposited in the sea-bed, which were the subjects of discussions in several sessions of AALCO.[81]

The adoption of the Law of the Sea Convention, in 1982, was generally welcomed by the developing countries, because it embodied a number of provisions, which were viewed by the third world countries as steps towards the realisation of the NIEO, proclaimed by the United Nations in 1974.[82] The text of Article 320 of the Convention, for instance, reflected the desire of the developing world, which pronounced that:

1.   Activities in the Area shall, [...] be carried out for the benefit of mankind as a whole, irrespective of the geographical location of States, whether coastal or land-locked, and taking into particular consideration the interests and needs of developing States and of the peoples who have not attained full independence or other self-governing status [...].

2.   The Authority shall provide for the equitable sharing and other economic benefits from activities in the Area through any appropriate mechanism, on a non-discriminatory basis [...].

---

76   A.O. Adede , "Law of the Sea-Developing Countries Contribution to the Development of the Industrial Arrangements for the International Sea-Bed Authority", *Brooklyn Journal of International Law*, Vol. IV, pp.1-42.

77   See footnote nr. 14.

78   Major coastal states of Asia, including China, India, Sri Lanka, Myanmar, and the Asian Pacific Islands, along with Latin American and African countries supported the inclusion of 200 miles Exclusive Economic Zone (EEZ), in the 1982 United Nations Convention on the Law of the Sea.

79   Fiji, Indonesia, and the Philipines were the promoters of the concept of archipelagic States.

80   Nepal and Afghanistan insisted on the recognition of their rights to have access to and from the sea.

81   S.P. Jagota, "Asia and the Development of the Law of the Sea: 1983-1992", *Essays in Honour of Wang Tieya*, edited by Ronald St. John Macdonald, Martinus Nijhoff Publishers, 1993.

82   T.O. Elias, *Africa and the Development of International Law*, Martinus Nijhoff Publishers, p. 266.

As indicated in section 3, by introducing the NIEO, developing countries were seeking the reformulation of the international economic order that would ensure greater third world participation and reward in the areas of trade, finance, aid and commodities.[83] In their view, the provisions of the Law of the Sea Convention relating to the activities in the sea-bed were an attempt "to restructure a significant part of the international economic system on an equitable basis in an acceptable legal regime."[84] Moreover, the provisions of the Convention pertaining to the transfer of technology by developed countries to the Authority and to the developing countries were of the utmost importance to the third world States.[85]

As regards the institutional arrangements for exploration and exploitation from the sea-bed, the developing countries had expressed their preference for the establishment of the Seabed Authority, composed of five principal organs, which would have the responsibility to deal with all activities relating to the exploration and exploitation of the common heritage of mankind. In the course of negotiations, they followed three basic elements on the establishment of the Authority. First, they advocated, as a matter of principle, the application of the equitable geographical representation in all organs of the Authority. Secondly, they expressed their opposition to the introduction of veto or any other form of weighted vote in the decision making process in the Authority. Thirdly, they favoured the exploitation of the resources of the Area exclusively by the Enterprise.

The developing nations, however, moved from their original positions and accepted compromised formulations in the course of negotiations on a number of issues. For instance, they accepted the idea of representation of "special interests" in the council of the Authority in addition to representation on the basis of equitable geographical distribution.[86]

The Enterprise was considered by the developing countries to be the organ through which the Authority would explore and exploit the resources of the Seabed Area. During the negotiations, G77 accepted the inclusion of State enterprise and States themselves, among the entities with which the Authority could enter into appropriate contractual arrangements for the purpose of conducting activities in the Area.[87]

It was recognised, in the course of negotiations, that a "free market" regime could adversely affect the interests of land-based mineral producers, particularly those of Zaire, Gabon, Zimbabwe and Zambia. Therefore, a mechanism for production control was set up by the Convention, and provisions were included therein for the compensation to the land-based mineral producers to ease the economic hardships, which might ensue from ocean-based mining.[88]

---

83   *Ibid*, p. 267.
84   *Ibid*, p. 268.
85   UNCLOS, Article 144.
86   UNCLOS, Article 161 (7).
87   UNCLOS, Article 151.
88   UNCLOS, Article 150 (h).

The developing countries supported the 200 miles Exclusive Economic Zone[89] ("EEZ") for the coastal States. In their view, the coastal States claims over the resources in the EEZ were an aspect of "economic-self-determination" and in line with the permanent sovereignty over natural resources.

The above points demonstrate that the achievements of the developing countries during the Law of the Sea Conference were substantial by all means. They were made possible essentially due to their concerted efforts in articulating and harmonising their common positions in the framework of G77. Their endeavours in safeguarding the achievements of the conference continued in the course of the negotiations in the Preparatory Commission on the Establishment of the Sea-bed Authority and the Law of the Sea Tribunal.

The Preparatory Commission had been established "to take all possible measures to ensure the entry into effective operation without undue delay of the Authority and the Tribunal."[90]

In spite of the endeavours of G77, the negotiations in the Preparatory Commission were prolonged,[91] and the developed countries did not ratify the Law of the Sea Convention, mainly due to their objections to certain provisions of part XI of the Convention, relating to the exploration and exploitation of the sea-bed. As a result, the Convention was not ratified by the required number of States[92] to enter into force.

In order to facilitate the entry into force of the Convention, the Secretary-General of the United Nations took the initiative of convening informal consultations aimed at universal participation in the Convention, from 1990 to 1994, which culminated in the preparation and adoption of the agreement amending part XI of the Convention, by the resumed session of the forty-eighth session of the General Assembly, on 28 July 1994.[93]

In accordance with the agreement, the States Parties to it undertook to implement part XI of the Convention, relating to the exploration and exploration from the area, in accordance the provisions of the agreement and its annex.[94] The annex provided for three major changes on part XI of the Convention. **First**, at the initial

---

89   S.P. Jagota, *op. cit*, p. 370.

90   See Resolution I, adopted by the Third United Nations Conference on the Law of the Sea.

91   The Preparatory Commission on the Establishment of the Seabed Authority and Law of the Sea Tribunal, was convened by the Secretary-General in accordance with General Assembly Resolution 37/66, in 1983, and ceased to exist at the conclusion of the first meeting of the Assembly of States Parties to the Law of the Sea Convention, which was convened in New York on 21 and 22 November 1994, immediately following the entry into force of the Convention.

92   The Convention entered into force on 16 November 1994, 12 months after the date of deposit of the 60th instrument of accession.

93   A/RES/48/263.

94   Agreement relating to the implementation of part XI of the Convention, 1994, Article 1.

stages of the operation of the Seabed Authority, the enterprise shall not operate independently and shall carry out its functions by joints ventures. Its independent operations have become subject to a decision of the Council of the Authority.[95] **Second,** another major change was related to the decision-making in the Council of the Authority, in which a collective veto system was introduced. In accordance with the provisions of the annex, decisions in the Council on questions of substance shall be taken by a two-thirds majority of members present and voting, provided that such decisions are not opposed by a majority in any one of the chambers referred to in paragraph 9.[96] **Third,** the obligations of developed States in respect of the transfer of technology would be limited to training and technical assistance and scientific cooperation programmes in marine science and technology. The developing States wishing to obtain deep sea-bed mining technology shall seek to obtain such technology on the open market, or through joint-venture arrangements.[97]

❖ ❖ ❖

One might view the developments relating to the Law of the Sea Convention from different perspectives. A pessimistic viewpoint might consider these developments as a setback to the developing countries; because there earlier achievements could not hold and were later modified in favour of industrialised countries. However, a realistic view should take into consideration the fact that part XI provisions were not customary law, but contractual in nature. Therefore, adherence to these provisions depended on the free will of States. Consequently, without expression of consent by the developed countries to be bound by the said provisions, they could not be binding on these States.

In analysing the developments relating to the law of the sea a number of factors should be taken into consideration. There can be no doubt that political and economic changes in the international arena played a significant role in the above developments. By changes in international politics and the collapse of the bipolar system, the Non-Aligned Movement is in need of a new strategy for active involvement in international affairs. Likewise, the expansion of liberalisation and competitive economies has questioned the viability of the exploration and exploration of the sea-bed area by the Enterprise. Moreover, the minerals projected to be extracted from the sea-bed are not in immediate demand as previously thought. Thus, it seems that in the near future their production from the sea-bed will be less profitable than from land based resources.

---

95   Annex to the Agreement relating to the implementation of part XI of the Convention, section 2, Article 2.

96   *Ibid.* section 3, Article 5.

97   *Ibid.* section 5, Article 1 (a).

B   Establishment of an International Criminal Court

The international community has endeavoured to establish an international criminal court since the end of World War I.[98] The matter was pursued on a number of occasions in the United Nations after its foundation. The International Law Commission while considering its agenda item entitled "Code of Crimes Against Peace and Security of Mankind", in its thirty-fifth session, in 1983, requested the General Assembly "to indicate whether the Commission's mandate extended to the preparation of the statute of a competent international jurisdiction for individuals;"[99]and repeated the query in its subsequent reports to the Assembly.[100] In spite of the positive reaction of the developing countries, including in particular the African countries, the Assembly could not come up with a decision in this regard until its forty-seventh session in 1992. In that session, the Assembly requested the Commission to continue its work on the question of an international criminal jurisdiction, "by undertaking the project for the elaboration of a draft statute for an international criminal court as a matter of priority".[101]

Despite general support of the developing countries, their positions with regard to many issues relating to the establishment of the Court were not unified. In May 1998, in advance of the convening of the Rome Conference, the NAM adopted a ministerial statement on the establishment of the ICC, in which it highlighted its positions in respect of a number of issues that were the subject of consideration in the Conference. Three main elements contained in the NAM statement were as follows:
- NAM preferred an independent court, which should be aloof from interference of political bodies, including, in particular, the Security Council.
- NAM supported the inclusion of the crime of aggression within the jurisdiction of the Court.
- NAM favoured the inclusion of the use or threat of use of nuclear weapons among war crimes in the Rome Statute.[102]

In spite of the preference of the NAM countries for having a court to be aloof from the interference of political organs, three indispensable issues relating to the relationship between the Security Council and ICC were discussed in the course of negotiations.

---

98   Cherif Bassiouni, "Historical Survey: 1919-1998", *The Statute of the International Criminal Court*, 1998, pp. 1-38.

99   Yearbook of the International Law Commission, 1983, vol. II (Part Two), p. 16, document A/38/10.

100   Report of the International Law Commission on the work of its thirty-ninth session (1987), supplement No. 10 (A/42/10), p. 32.

101   A/RES/47/33, paragraph 6.

102   Statement issued by the Ministerial Meeting of the NAM on the Establishment of the International Criminal Court, 20 May 1998, Cartagena, Colombia.

The **first issue** was the authorisation of the Security Council to refer situations, in which crimes under the jurisdiction of the Court appear to have been committed, to the ICC. In the negotiations, it was clear that States would be authorised to refer such situations to the Court. However, the question of referral by the Security Council was the subject of discussion. In this regard, an argument was advanced that where individual States were authorised to refer cases to the Court, there could be no convincing reason against collective referral of cases by States. Consequently, the Security Council was authorised to refer the situations, in accordance with a decision under Chapter VII of the Charter, to the Court.[103]

The **second issue** was the inclusion of a provision in the Statute to authorise the Security Council to defer proceedings in respect of a case before the Court. It was argued in this regard, that the Security Council bears the primary responsibility regarding the maintenance of international peace and security.[104] Accordingly, if the Council decides that the continuation of a proceeding before the Court was not in the interest of the maintenance of international peace and security, the Council by making a decision under Chapter VII may request the Court to defer a case before it for twelve months, which may be renewed. The argument went on to say that in accordance with Article 103 of the Charter, in cases of conflict between obligations of States under the Charter and their obligations under any other international agreement, their obligations under the Charter shall prevail.

Although this provision has been the subject of criticism,[105] the compromise formula was part and parcel of a package deal on the relationship between the Council and the Court.

The **third issue** was the relationship between the Council and the Court concerning the definition of the crime of aggression and the role that the Council should play in this regard. The developing countries insisted on the inclusion of the crime of aggression among the crimes within the jurisdiction of the Court, and argued that the exclusion of this crime from the scope of competences of the Court would be retrogression in comparison to the Charters of the Tokyo and Nuremberg tribunals. On the other hand, many States in the western group stated that in the short time left until the end of the Conference an agreement on the definition of the crime and on the role of the Security Council would not be possible. Thus, the discussions in the Rome Conference did not bring delegations closer to a consensus on this matter.

Therefore, on 14 July 1998, the NAM proposed that the crime of aggression be included in the Statute, but the elaboration of its definition be left to a later stage. In accordance with the proposal the Court would not exercise its jurisdiction over the crime until a definition was agreed and conditions under which the Court

---

103   See Article 13 (b) of the Rome Statute.

104   Article 24 of the Charter of the United Nations.

105   Elaraby, for instance, observed that, "[t]he role assigned to the Council cast shadows on the credibility of the ICC as an independent Court of Law." See *The Rome Statute of the International Criminal Court: A Challenge to Impunity*, edited by Mauru Politi and Giuseppe Nesi, 2001, p. 43.

should exercise its jurisdiction be defined.[106] This proposal constituted a basis for a compromise on the inclusion of the crime of aggression in the Statute. However, the Bureau of the Preparatory Commission added a sentence to the NAM proposal at the end of Article 5(2), providing that the definition "shall be consistent with the relevant provisions of the Charter of the United Nations".[107]

As a result of the compromise, Resolution F, annexed to the Final Act of the Rome Conference, provided for the continuity of work on the crime of aggression in the Preparatory Commission.[108] Subsequently, the non-aligned countries pursued the question of definition of the crime of aggression in the Preparatory Commission. A working group on the crime of aggression was established and considered several proposals submitted to it by some members of NAM, and also by some countries from the western group.[109] However, the Commission could not complete its mandate with respect to the crime of aggression, mainly due to the complexity of issues involved, the workload of the Commission and early entry into force of the Statute.[110]

In the new circumstances, the NAM countries were concerned that many of its members might not be able to become parties to the Statute in the early years of activities of the Assembly of States Parties to the Rome Statute, and consequently, they may not be in a position to make a meaningful contribution to the activities of the Assembly in this regard. Therefore, they, again, presented a draft resolution on the continuity of work regarding the crime of aggression in the context of the Assembly of States Parties, which was adopted by the Preparatory Commission in 2002.[111] In accordance with the resolution, a special working group on the crime of aggression, open on equal footing to all States members of the United Nations or members of the specialised agencies or of the International Atomic Energy Agency, was established to elaborate proposals for a provision on aggression in accordance with paragraph 2 of Article 5 of the Rome Statute and paragraph 7 of Resolution F adopted by the Rome Conference in 1998.[112]

---

106   Amendments submitted by the Non-Aligned Movement contained in document: A/ CONF. 183/C.1/L.75.

107   Herman von Hebel and Darryl Robinson, "Crimes within the jurisdiction of the Court", in *The International Criminal Court: The Making of the Rome Statute*, ed. Roy S. Lee, Kluwer Law International, 1999, p.84.

108   Paragraph 7 of Resolution F, adopted by the Rome Conference stipulates: "The Commission shall prepare proposals for a provision on aggression, including the definition and Elements of Crimes of aggression and the conditions under which the International Criminal Court shall exercise its jurisdiction with regard to this crime".

109   See U.N. Doc, PCNICC/1999/L.5/Rev.1 (Dec. 22, 1999).

110   Having acquired sixty ratifications the Rome Statute of the International Criminal Court entered into force as of 1 July 2002. For full analysis of the discussion of the definition of the crime of aggression in the Preparatory Commission see: Silvia A. Fernandez de Gurmendi, "An Insider's View", in *The International Criminal Court and the Crime of Aggression*, edited by Mauro Politi and Giuseppe Nesi, 2004, pp. 180-188.

111   ICC-ASP/1/Res. 1.

112   *Ibid.*, paragraph 2.

The inclusion of the use of nuclear weapons among war crimes in the Statute was another issue, which was strongly supported by the NAM countries, including India and Pakistan, who had undertaken nuclear tests at the time. They argued that a prohibition on such weapons already existed in customary international law, and that all weapons of mass destruction, including nuclear, biological and chemical weapons, should be treated equally, and that all of them should be included in the Statute. However, the addition of nuclear weapons was vehemently opposed by the Permanent Members of the Security Council, as well as by a number of members of the North Atlantic Treaty Organization. They argued that unlike chemical and biological weapons, no explicit prohibition of nuclear weapons existed under conventional or customary law. As a result, the weapons provisions were restricted to those weapons which have plainly been banned; now appearing in paragraphs (xvii) to (xix) of Article 8 of the Statute. The inflexible debate on weapons of mass destruction was deferred to a review conference, in accordance with paragraph (xx) of Article 8. The provision allows further expansion of the list of weapons through amendment procedure to the Statute.[113]

❖ ❖ ❖

The ICC has entered into an operational stage and has begun investigation of two cases submitted to it by States Parties.[114] However, the developing countries have not followed a unified policy towards ratification of the ICC Statute. There are many countries, including a number of developing countries, which are closely monitoring the performance of the ICC in practice and may modify their positions with regard to the ICC on that basis. Obviously, proper functioning of the ICC as a universal and independent judicial body will persuade many developing countries to consider ratifying the ICC Statute. Developing countries are particularly interested in the definition of the crime of aggression by the special working group of the Assembly of States Parties and its adoption by the review conference, so that the Court could exercise its jurisdiction with regard to this crime.

6.   Application of International Law by Developing Countries

Although no general conclusion can be made as to the consistency of conduct of States with international norms and principles, however, it can be argued, in general, that small States are more prone to rely on law than big powers, in defense of their sovereignty, independence and territorial integrity. With this logic in mind, and having actively participated in the law-making process for a few decades, the developing countries increasingly supported the rule of law in international relations. They referred a good number of disputes to the ICJ, in the 1980s and 1990s. Moreover, upon the initiative of the NAM, the General Assembly pronounced the

---

113   Herman von Hebel and Darryl Robinson, FN. 107, p. 116.

114   The situation in the Democratic Republic of Congo and the situation in Uganda have been referred to the ICC by the said States.

period 1990-1999 as the United Nations Decade of International Law ("Decade"), which was aimed at promoting the rule of law worldwide.

A.   Resort to the International Court of Justice

The infrequent resort to the International Court of Justice for the settlement of disputes had been a matter of concern for a number of States in the early decades of its establishment.[115] The matter was the subject of consideration by the General Assembly on a number of occasions. In 1947, the Assembly recommended to the competent organs of the United Nations and specialised agencies to refer the important points of law to the Court for an advisory opinion.[116] The Assembly also recommended to States to submit, as a general rule, their legal disputes to the Court for adjudication.[117] In 1974, the Assembly, while repeating its earlier recommendations on the recourse to the Court, reaffirmed that, "recourse to judicial settlement of legal disputes, particularly referral to the International Court of Justice, should not be considered as an unfriendly act between States."[118]

As stated previously, the adoption of the Manila Declaration on the Peaceful Settlement of Disputes by the General Assembly, in 1982, containing a consensus language, stronger than previous recommendations, on the referral of disputes to the ICJ, was a turning point.[119] It reflected an increasing willingness and confidence of States in submitting their differences to the Court. In practical terms, more cases were brought before the Court, in particular by developing countries, in the years following the adoption of the Manila Declaration. Fifty-five contentious cases were brought before the ICJ since the adoption of the Declaration, a considerable number of which were disputes between developing countries mainly on boundary differences and demarcation. Other types of disputes also brought before the Court, in which the Court's adjudication covered important aspects of international law.[120]

Requests for advisory opinions by the General Assembly on a number of important questions before it, was another sign of the growing confidence of developing countries in the Court. The following advisory opinions were requested of the Court upon the initiative of developing countries: Legal Consequences for States of

---

115   During twenty four years between 1947 and 1970, when the Court's functioning was again the subject of concern in the United Nations, fifty-one cases were filed with the Court, which delivered thirty judgments. At the same period, there were thirteen requests for advisory opinions. Leo Gross, "Underutilization of the International Court of Justice", *Harvard International Law Journal*, Vol. 27, p. 573.

116   A/RES/171 (II) A.

117   A/RES/171 (II) C, paragraph 3.

118   A/RES/3232 (XXIX), paragraph 6.

119   A/RES/37/10, paragraph 5.

120   See, for instance: Military and Paramilitary Activities in and against Nicaragua (Nicaragua v. United States of America) (1984-1991); Oil Platforms (Islamic Republic of Iran v. United States of America) (1992-2003).

the Continued Presence of South Africa in Namibia (South West Africa); Western Sahara (1974-1975); Legality of the Threat or Use of Nuclear Weapons (1994-1996); Legal Consequences of the Construction of a Wall in the Occupied Palestinian Territory (2003-2004). Evidently, the impact of the above opinions, as authoritative expressions of existing international law, on the development of international law cannot be underestimated.

Frequent resorts to the ICJ also meant that parties to disputes no longer questioned the basic norms and principles of international law, which would be the basis for the judgements of the Court. Claimants and defendants before the Court, including developing countries, extensively relied on the basic norms and principles, which had their origins in the period prior to their independence.

B.   United Nations Decade of International Law

As indicated, the General Assembly approved the proposal[121] submitted by the NAM,[122] in 1989, and declared the period 1990-1999 as the United Nations Decade of International Law. The resolution of the Assembly did not contain a plan of action to be carried out during the Decade. Instead, it defined the main purposes of the Decade which were, *inter alia*: (a) To promote acceptance of and respect for the principles of international law; (b) To promote means and methods for the peaceful settlement of disputes between States, including resort to and full respect for the International Court of Justice; (c) To encourage the progressive development of international law and its codification; (d) To encourage the teaching, study, dissemination and wider appreciation of international law.[123] In short, the main purpose of the Decade was to enhance and solidify the rule of law in international relations.

A working group of the Sixth Committee was entrusted to prepare a plan of activities for the Decade. The working group prepared a general plan to be commenced in the period 1991-1992, and updated it three times, to cover all activities of the Decade.[124] Moreover, the working group acted as the coordinating body of the activities of the Decade, and requested States, international organisations and

---

121   A/44/L.41, A/44/L.41/Add. 1.

122   The proposal on the United Nations Decade of International Law was originally made in the Conference of Ministers of the Movement, in Nicosia, in September 1988. Subsequently, it was elaborated in the NAM meeting on Peace and International Law, in The Hague, in 1989, and endorsed by the Summit meeting of the NAM in the same year.

123   A/44/23 of 17 November 1989.

124   Programme for activities to be commenced during the first term (1990-1992) of the United Nations Decade of International Law, A/RES/45/40; Programme for activities to be commenced during the second term (1993-1994) of the United Nations Decade of International Law, A/RES/47/32; Programme for activities for the third term (1995-1996) of the United Nations Decade of International Law, A/RES/49/50; Programme for activities for the term (1997-1999) of the United Nations Decade of International Law, A/RES/51/157.

non-governmental organisations to disseminate the purposes and main ideas of the Decade and to contribute to its activities.

The program was divided into four sections, which carried the same titles as the purposes of the Decade. It contained, *inter alia*, the following main elements:

–   It called upon States "to act in accordance with international law, and in particular the Charter of the United Nations", and encouraged "States and international organizations to promote the acceptance of and respect for the principles of international law."[125]
–   It further invited States "to consider, if they have not done so, becoming parties to existing multilateral treaties, in particular those relevant to the progressive development of international law and its codification."[126]
–   Peaceful settlement of disputes had a prominent place in the program of activities of the Decade. In this regard, it encouraged the wider use of the International Court of Justice by States in the peaceful settlement of their disputes.[127]
–   Particular emphasis was placed, in the program, on the dissemination and wider appreciation of international law. To this end, States were encouraged to introduce and expand courses in international law for students of law, political sciences, social sciences and other relevant disciplines. The United Nations and regional organisations were requested to conduct seminars, symposia and lectures on different aspects of international law.

Annual reports of the Secretary-General presented to the General Assembly contain an account of a range of activities carried out during the Decade that reported to him.[128] Out of various relevant activities,[129] a number of important events require particular reference. The establishment of two Ah Hoc Criminal Tribunals for the Former Yugoslavia and Rwanda, in 1993 and 1994, respectively, the establishment of the Law of the Sea Tribunal in 1996, and the adoption of the Rome Statute on the establishment of the International Criminal Court, in 1998, were among the major achievements of the international community during the Decade.

There was general agreement, in the working group of the Sixth Committee, that the activities of Decade should not be limited to holding some closed doors

---

125   A/RES/45/40, annex, section I, paragraph 1; A/RES/47/32, annex, section I, paragraph 1; A/RES/49/50, annex, section I, paragraph 1 ; A/RES/51/157, annex, section I, paragraph 1.

126   A/RES/45/40, annex, section I, paragraph 2; A/RES/47/32, annex, section I, paragraph 2; A/RES/49/50, annex, section I, paragraph 2 ; A/RES/51/157, annex, section I, paragraph 2.

127   A/RES/45/40, annex, section II, paragraph 3; A/RES/47/32, annex, section II, paragraph 3; A/RES/49/50, annex, section II, paragraph 3 ; A/RES/51/157, annex, section II, paragraph 3.

128   A/54/632, and its addendum 1; A/51/278 and addendum.1; A/50/368, and its addenda 1 to 3; A/49/323, and its addenda 1 and 2; A/48/312; A/46/372; A/45/430.

129   General Assembly Resolution 54/28 refers to the main activities carried out during the Decade.

meetings in the United Nations, but that participation of NGOs and academia in the activities of the Decade should be encouraged in order to spread the purposes of the Decade throughout of the world. To this end, several important events were organised in different parts of the world, of which particular references should be made to the convening of the United Nations Congress on Public International Law, in 1995,[130] and events in The Hague, in 1999, to commemorate the centennial of the first International Peace Conference and the closing of the United Nations Decade of International Law.[131]

The initiative of the NAM countries in the proclamation of the Decade should be viewed in the light of evolving positions of the new States with respect to international law principles. It was indicative of the conviction of these States that in our independent world everyone's interests are best served by adherence to and respect for the principles and norms of international law. States from different regions embraced this initiative,[132] supported the objectives of the decade – the promotion of the rule of law in international relations – and contributed to the implementation of the program of the Decade. In the course of events of the Decade everyone agreed that a peaceful world can only be achieved through an orderly world based on law. The General Assembly reaffirmed, at the end of the Decade, "the continued validity of the main objectives of the Decade" and declared that the fulfillment of these objectives were "essential to achieve the purposes of the United Nations."[133]

7.   International law as Convergence of Civilizations

The examination of the role of the developing countries in the law-making at international level, as discussed in the previous sections, was mainly based on the experiences gained by the author in two major international law-making events. It is needless to point out that a comprehensive evaluation of the role of the third world countries also requires an assessment of their participation in other important global negotiations, such as: the 1992 United Nations Conferences on the Environment and Development, the negotiations that led to the drafting of 1993

---

130   In 1992, two States, namely, the Islamic Republic of Iran and Mexico, proposed the convening of the United Nations congress on public international law within the program of activities of the Decade, and also for the commemoration of the fiftieth anniversary of the United Nations. After two years of negotiations, and following the approval by the General Assembly, the congress convened from 13 to 17 March 1995, in the United Nations headquarters, at New York. A five-day long congress devoted one day for the discussion of each one of the four purposes of the Decade, and in the fifth and final day it discussed further actions that needed to be taken in the remaining period of the Decade. The proceedings of the congress and articles presented therein were published by the United Nations (A/CONF. 176).

131   A/RES/53/99; A/RES/54/27.

132   More than eighty States from different regions of the world co-sponsored the draft resolution on the proclamation of the Decade.

133   A/RES/54/28, paragraph 3.

Convention on the Prohibition of the Use of Chemical Weapons and on their Destruction, and the negotiations that culminated in the establishment of the World Trade Organization. Nonetheless, from the analysis presented in the previous pages the following general conclusions could be made on the accomplishments of the third world countries.

First and foremost, in the new world order, based on the norms and principles enshrined in the Charter of the United Nations, the developing countries had the opportunity to participate in the negotiations on international standard setting with equal rights and opportunities. They were parties to a process, in which the fundamental international law principles were reaffirmed in a number of consensus declarations approved by the General Assembly. The third world countries also succeeded to write, into law, the principles that had already been politically accepted as norms of international relations. In the post-colonial era, the decolonisation and rejection of apartheid were successfully incorporated in many international treaties and resolutions of the General Assembly.

In addition, the developing States influenced the negotiation processes in a number of international conferences, including in particular, the Third United Nations Conference on the Law of the Sea, mainly due to their shared interests and common positions, coordinated through the G77 and the NAM.

However, third world States had limited success in standard setting in a number of other areas. Their aspirations to establish a new international economic order did not materialize. Likewise, their endeavours for total disarmament bore limited results. Additionally, their achievements in the law of the sea conference were subject to a later revision, in which considerable concessions were made to industrialised countries regarding exploration in the sea-bed area.

In this respect, it should be clarified, however, that law-making has always been an instrument of politics, both at the national and international levels. Law-making at global level is, in particular, a multifaceted process and the product of interplay among political actors through negotiations, in which several factors are involved. The forces that exert general influence on the political system have the potential of doing so in the course of making the law as well. Group commitments certainly play a significant role in the law-making process. In addition, States are subject to persuasion and other forms of influence in their international behaviour, which includes standard setting as well.

Still, the application of the principle of unanimity in making the law provides leverage to all States, irrespective of their size and power, to be used in support of formation of a balanced law. Setting realistic objectives, finding a place in group settings, and familiarity with techniques of negotiations can definitely help the utilization of this power in pursuit of national interests of States.

Setting **realistic objectives** in the negotiations is highly important. Setting goals, which are impossible to achieve, may end up nowhere. Accordingly, attempts to change the basic principles that govern an orderly system may run the risk of achieving the impossible. For instance, in spite of general support of States for the increase in the membership of the Security Council, lengthy negotiations on the reform of Council have yet to arrive at an agreement.[134] The same is true with respect to the unsuccessful attempts made in the Rome Conference to include the use of nuclear weapons among the crimes within the jurisdiction of the International Criminal Court.

Identifying **common group positions** is extremely helpful. As indicated earlier, the new States that were linked with historical common bonds effectively fought for a number of shared objectives in the post-colonial era. There is no reason to believe that this type of coordination cannot continue among developing countries in pursuit of their common interests in the future. Yet, the interests of States and groups of States are subject to change in different periods of time. For instance, the interests and policies of India, now a nuclear weapon State, which has become an undeniable trade and technological partner of a number of industrialised countries, may not be the same as those of a pioneer member of the NAM in the post-colonial era. The Non-Aligned Movement itself, a coordinating forum for developing countries, which was the product of the Cold War era, has yet to define a new role for itself in the age of globalisation. The latter phenomenon has transformed States groupings and States policies to a great deal. Therefore, it is essential for States, especially for developing countries, to find or set up a proper forum for group coordination in the competitive era of globalisation.

The **emergence of new global issues**, caused by technological advancement and ever-increasing interdependency among States, requires participation of all States, big or small, developing or developed, south or north, to cope with them. For instance, the protection of the Ozone layer, curbing and elimination of life-threatening viruses, the fight against terrorism, suppressing drug and human trafficking, and preventing computer-generated crimes are examples of mounting global menaces. In the prevailing conditions, no State can be immune from the adverse effects of the new problems facing the international community.

Management of the new global issues and confronting new menaces to the rule of law in international relations require a joint and coordinated approach of the international community as whole. In these circumstances, the repetition of the historic differences over the origins of international law can only weaken the rule of law in the world. Such claims, if there are any, are not commensurate with the activities pertaining to the codification and progressive development of international law that has been carried out under the auspices of the United Nations.

Obviously, the achievements of the international community in the field of law-making are the results of collective endeavours of the members of the community as whole. As was explained, all nations, including developing countries, have contributed to the formation of a body of norms and principles that govern relations among nations. This body of law is indeed the convergence of the political will of the world's civilisations in setting international standards, which needs to be safeguarded by each and every nation, irrespective of its size, wealth and power.

---

134   For the latest report of the working group on the "question of equitable representation and increase in the membership of the Security Council and related matters", see: UN Document A/58/47.

It is, therefore, incumbent on all nations to respect and ensure reverence for these norms and principles. Implementation of obligations, undertaken by each member of the community of nations, would certainly help maintain law and order in the world, a necessity for the maintenance of international peace and security. Equally important is the opposition of peace-loving nations to the violations of the accepted norms and principles. There are established legal and political mechanisms to protest and to take appropriate measures against violators of international norms. Certainly, appropriate reaction against States that infringe the basic norms will enhance the promotion of the rule of law in international relations. Conversely, applying double standards, either in the fulfilment of international obligations, or in rejection of breaches of international norms, is not in the interest of the promotion of the rule of law in international relations; thus, it should be avoided.

8. Fragmentation of International Law? A View from Russia[1]

Roman A. Kolodkin

Since the early 90s of the last century the so-called "fragmentation of international law" has been widely discussed by international law specialists. This issue has come to be the topic of scientific research; it is under consideration in the United Nations International Law Commission (ILC) and in the 6th Committee of the UN General Assembly.[2]

---

1   The author's views stated in this article may differ from Russia's stance on the issues in question. The author would like to thank Ms. S. Sarenkova for her kind assistance in preparation of this chapter.

2   See, for example: Brownlie I., Problems concerning the unity of international law. In: *Le droit a l' heure de sa codification. Etudes en l'honneur de Roberto Ago*, vol. I (Universita di Genova, Instituto di Diritto Internazionale e della Navigazione della Facolta di Guirisprudenza, Giuffre Milano, ed. 1987), pp. 153-162; Wellens K.C., Diversity in secondary rules and the unity of international law: some reflections on current trends. In: 25, *Netherlands Yearbook of International Law* (1994), pp. 3-57; Sur S., The State between Fragmentation and Globalization. In: 3, European Journal of International Law (1997), pp. 421-434; Treves T., Recent trends in the settlement of international disputes. In: *Cursos Euromediterraneos Bancaja de Derecho Internacional*, vol. I, 1997, pp. 395-436; Charney J.I., International Law and Multiple International Tribunals, *Recueil des Cours*, Academie de Droit International, 271 (1998), pp. 101-382; Symposium on "Proliferation of International Tribunals: Piecing Together the Puzzle", New York Journal of International Law and Politics, vol. 31, No.4 (1999), pp. 679-970; Dupuy P-M., Multiplication des jurisdictions internationals et dangers de fragmentation de l'ordre juridique international. In: *CEBDI*, vol. III, 1999, pp. 265-281; Casanovas O., *Unity and Diversity in Public International Law*, Martinus Nijhoff Publ., The Hague/New York/London, 2001; ASIL, Proceedings of the 96th Annual Meeting, March 13-16, 2002, pp. 368-380; for more bibliography see: Koskenniemi M. & Leino P., Fragmentation of International Law? Postmodern Anxieties, 15(3) Leiden Journal of International Law (2002), pp. 553-579; Brown C., Review Essay "The Proliferation of International Courts and Tribunals: Finding Your Way through the Maze", Melbourne Journal of International Law, vol. 3, 2002, pp. 453-475. See also speeches by G. Guillaume, President of the International Court of Justice, to the General Assembly of the United Nations of 26 Oct. 2000 and

Ronald St. John Macdonald & Douglas M. Johnston (eds.), Towards World Constitutionalism, *pp. 223-240.*
© *2005 Koninklijke Brill NV. Printed in The Netherlands.* ISBN *90 04 14612 1.*

Unfortunately, the Russian scholars' views on this issue were not presented at the scientific debates leaving the gap this article tries to fill, to some extent at least.

"Fragment" is a piece broken off; a small portion of anything; a detached, isolated, or incomplete part.[3] As applied to the system of international law, proceeding from the fact that it really exists, fragmentation, i.e. a breaking or separation of a whole into fragmented, disconnected parts, seems to be a negative phenomenon. However, the representatives of several States in the 6th Committee of the General Assembly also highlighted that the ILC should take into account both negative and positive aspects of fragmentation.[4] The same was said in the Study Group established by the ILC to consider the fragmentation issue. The Group came to the conclusion that "the title of the topic, 'Risks Ensuing from Fragmentation of International Law [that the ILC started considering – R.K.] was not entirely adequate because it depicted the phenomena described by the term 'fragmentation' in too negative a light". It was decided to replace this title with a less alarmist one such as "Fragmentation of International Law: Difficulties Arising from the Diversification and Expansion of International Law".[5]

What is meant by fragmentation of international law? Fragmentation or, at least, its threat is seen as proliferation of international legal rules and institutions, the autonomous character of some international legal regimes and expansion of international law in those areas of relations that were not considered fit for international legal regulation before. Fragmentation is also seen in the regionalization and specialization of international law, in particular, in such areas as human rights and international trade, in the establishment of international courts and other bodies that apply and interpret international law and have competence to decide the same or partially the same issues. It is noted that this results in conflicts between rules and regimes, interpretation and application of the same rules in different situations, disintegration of the holistic and homogeneous system of international law.[6] Or that

---

of 30 Oct. 2001 and to the Sixth Committee of the General Assembly of 27 Oct. 2000 and of 31 Oct. 2001, <www.icj-cij.org/icjwww/ipresscom/SPEECHES/iSpeechPresident_Guillaume>. To summarize the discussions in the Sixth Committee of the UN General Assembly see: United Nations Doc. A/CN.4/513, paras. 379-380; UN Doc. A/CN.4/529, paras. 215-229; UN Doc. A/CN.4/537, paras. 218-231.

3   See, for example., *The Shorter Oxford English Dictionary*, ed. by C.T. Onions, Claredon Press, 1964, p. 745.

4   UN Doc. A/CN.4/529, para. 218-220; UN Doc. A/CN.4/537, para. 220.

5   United Nations General Assembly, Official Records, Fifty-seventh session, Supplement No. 10 (A/57/10), paras. 494, 498, 500.

6   UN Doc. A/CN.4/529, paras. 216-217. As M. Koskenniemi writes about fragmentation: "… the emergence and consolidation of special regimes and technical sub-disciplines: human rights law, environmental law, trade law, the use of force, and so on. In each of such realms, particular interests and standards are projected as universal ones, resulting in normative and jurisdictional conflicts." Koskenniemi M., What Is International Law For? In: *International Law*. Ed. by M.D. Evans, Oxford Univ. Press, 2003, p. 109.

"the system of international law consists of erratic parts and elements which are differently structured so that one can hardly speak of a homogeneous nature of international law".[7]

They speak about the danger of institutional fragmentation that is expressed in non-uniform, inhomogeneous activities of the increasing number of international judicial and arbitrary bodies as well as about the threat of material fragmentation associated with conflicts between the rules of international law.

The following situations are mostly drawn as examples demonstrating the fragmentation of international law.

Speaking about proliferation of international courts, differences in judgments between the International Court of Justice (ICJ) on Military and Paramilitary Activities in and against Nicaragua of 1986 and the International Criminal Tribunal for the Former Yugoslavia (ITFY) in the Tadic case of 1996 are pointed at. The ICJ stated that a State is responsible for operations of paramilitary formations in the territory of another State if it exercises an "effective control" over those operations. In addition, the Court emphasized the importance of the degree of control.[8] The ICTY decided that for attribution of responsibility it is enough for a State to exercise only "overall control".[9] Therefore, the conclusion is made that the two Courts interpreted and applied the same rule of international law differently.

Speaking about diversification of international law and the rapid development of its human rights branch, the problem of reservations to international treaties on human rights is pointed at. To be more precise, the question is that the regime of reservations and objections to them stipulated by the 1969 Vienna Convention on the Law of Treaties does not apply when we deal with international treaties on human rights. In connection with the reservations, the stance of the bodies established under those treaties is mentioned. Thus, the General Comment No. 24 of the Committee on Human Rights implies that this body considers itself competent to invalidate the reservation made by a State while undertaking obligations under the International Covenant on Civil and Political Rights of 1966. If the Committee does so, the State will be completely bound by the provisions of this treaty without benefitting from the reservation.[10]

Another example is the activities of the European Court of Human Rights (ECHR). For instance, in the Belilos case of 1988 the ECHR decided in its jurisdiction to determine the validity of a reservation or of an interpretative declaration to the European Convention on Human Rights and admitted that the interpretative declaration (the validity of which the Court actually examined, as if it was a res-

---

7   Hafner G., Risks ensuing from fragmentation of international law. United Nations General Assembly, Official Records, Fifty-fifth session, Supplement No.10 (A/55/10), p. 321.

8   Military and Paramilitary Activities in and against Nicaragua (*Nicaragua v. United States of America*), Merits, Judgment, I.C.J. Reports, 1986, p. 14, at pp. 52, 54-55, paras. 109, 115.

9   ICTY: *Prosecutor v. Tadic*, 38 I.L.M. 1518 (1999), pp. 154-159, paras. 117-162.

10   UN Doc. CCPR/C/21/Rev. 1/Add. 6, 11 November 1994.

ervation) made by Switzerland was invalid and that Switzerland was bound by the Convention irrespective of the validity of the declaration.[11]

As to the evidence of the loss of integrity by international law, reference is made to the appearance of the so-called self-contained regimes. One of the examples of such a regime is the regime of reservations to treaties on human rights. Another one is the WTO legal system. In particular, it is noted that the documents of this organization, as well as decisions of its Dispute Settlement Body do not reflect enough the rules of general international law.

They also speak about the so-called parallel settlement of the same questions on the universal and regional level. For example, there are two Conventions on non-navigational uses of international watercourses: the universal Convention on the Law of the Non-navigational Uses of International Watercourses which was adopted by the UN in 1997, and the regional European Convention on International Watercourses of 1992.[12]

Does all this really testify to the inevitable fragmentation of international law? Can we speak about international law as an integral system? Provided that international law is a system, is it complete and comprehensive? Or do we deal with a fragmentary phenomenon and does international law only regulate some aspects of relations without any system, leaving without control others whereby its rules are often in conflict with one another and these conflicts cannot be settled?

Approximately since the mid-sixties of the last century the major opinion in the Soviet and then Russian international legal doctrine evolved, according to which international law is, first of all, a system of rules.[13] Almost all modern definitions of international law in Russian doctrine point at this fact with minor differences.[14]

---

11   ECHR, Belilos judgment of 29 April 1988, Series A no 132, pp. 24-28, paras. 50-60.

12   For these and other examples of "fragmentation" see: Hafner G., *Op. cit.*; Report of the ILC Study Group on the topic of fragmentation, United Nations General Assembly, Official Records, Fifty-eighth session, Supplement No. 10(A/58/10), para. 419.

13   To study the history of the system approach in the Soviet international law doctrine see: Kurs mezhdunarodnogo prava. In 7 volumes. Vol. 1. *Ponyatie, predmet i sistema mezhdunarodnogo prava*. Ed. by Y. Baskin, N. Crylov, D. Levin and others, M, Nauka, 1989, pp. 253-256.

        S. Chernichenko notes that the words "first of all" should be used in this context because the notion of international law does not amount to the system of rules only. See: Chernichenko S., Teoriya mezhdunarodnogo prava. In 2 volumes. Vol. 1: *Sovremennye teoriticheskie problemy*. M.: "NIMP", 1999, p. 15.

14   See, for example.: *Mezhdunarodnoe pravo*. Ed. by V. Kuznetsov, M.: Yurist, 2001, p. 27; *Mezhdunarodnoye pravo*. Ed. by G. Ignatenko and O. Tiuonov, 3-rd ed., M.: Norma 2003, p. 6; *Mezhdunarodnoye pravo*. Ed. by Y. Usenko, G. Shinkaretskaya, M.: Yurist, 2003, p. 17; *Mezhdunarodnoye pravo*. Ed. by Y. Kolossov and E. Krivchikova, M., Mezhdunarodnye otnosheniya, 2001, p. 15; *Mezhdunarodnoye pravo*. 2-nd ed., M.: Yurist, 2001, pp. 10-15; *Mezhdunarodnoye pravo*. Ed. by G. Tunkin, M.: Yuridicheskaya literatura, 1994, p. 10; Lukashuk I., *Mezhdunarodnoye pravo*. Obschaya chast, M.: BEK, 1996, pp. 1, 98-101; Feldman D., *Sistema mezhdunarodnogo prava*. Kazan: Kazan Univ. Publ., 1983.

Russian doctrine proceeds from the structural, hierarchic nature of the system of international law where the leading role is assigned to its basic principles, which constitute the platform and the ideological, normative and legal framework of this system.[15] It is considered that the fundamental principles are the most important, fundamental, generally recognized rules of international law having the superior legal authority.[16]

Most Russian scholars think that fundamental principles of international law are the *jus cogens* rules and all other rules of international law shall comply with them.[17] At the same time, as G. Tunkin wrote, "No sufficient research has been made to prove whether all fundamental principles are peremptory or as it may be supposed some of them are only partially peremptory".[18] (For instance, R.Mullerson who previously worked in the USSR and works in Great Britain now wrote on the partially peremptory nature of all fundamental principles or, at least, of some of them.[19] However, he noted that be it as it may with the *jus cogens* nature of fundamental principles, the very existence of international law as a coherent normative system would indeed be in doubt without them.[20])

As fundamental principles of international law are usually considered those of the Charter of the United Nations, the essence of which is stated in the Declaration on Principles of International Law concerning Friendly Relations and Cooperation among States in accordance with the Charter of the United Nations adopted by the UN General Assembly in 1970 and in the Declaration on Principles of the Final Act of the CSCE Conference on Security and Cooperation in Europe of 1975 (the principle of sovereign equality, non-interference in domestic affairs, non-use of force and the threat of force, pacific settlement of disputes etc.).[21]

We can hardly speak about a comprehensive list of fundamental principles of international law. For example, besides the abovementioned principles, there is the principle of responsibility of a State for internationally wrongful acts[22] or the

---

15   *Kurs mezhdunarodnogo prava.* Vol. 1, p. 261. I. Loukashuk thinks that judicial, moral and political factors that form the system include not only principles but the objectives of international law as well. See Loukashuk I. *Op. cit,* pp. 98-101, 116-120.

16   *Mezhdunarodnoye pravo.* Ed. by Y. Usenko and G. Shinkaretskaya, p. 41.

17   Kurs mezhdunarodnogo prava. Vol. 1, p. 261. See also: *Mezhdunarodnoye pravo.* Ed. by G. Ignatenko and O. Tiuonov, p. 99; *Mezhdunarodnoye pravo.* Ed. by V. Kouznetsov, p. 124; *Mezhdunarodnoye pravo.* Ed. by Y. Kolossov and E. Krivchikova, pp. 41-42, 47-48.

18   Tunkin G. International Law in the International System, *Recueil des Cours,* Academie de Droit International, IV, 147 (1975), p. 98.

19   Mullerson R. *Ordering Anarchy. International Law in International Society.* Martinus Nijhoff Publ., The Hague/Boston/London, 2000, pp. 156-159. See there also the analysis of western doctrine about the fundamental principles of international law.

20   *Ibid.,* p. 159.

21   See, for ex.: *Mezhdunarodnoye pravo.* Ed by Y. Usenko and G. Shinkaretskaya, p. 42.

22   I. Lukashuk notes that the responsibility "first of all, is a principle of international law in accordance with which any wrongful act leads to the responsibility of a subject accused under international law". Lukashuk I., *Op. cit.,* p. 179.

principle connected with that of sovereign equality under which the limitations of sovereignty in international law cannot be presumed and, as a result, the State's behavior which is not restricted by international law is lawful.

Besides fundamental principles, Russian scholars point at the so-called branch principles of international law, that is, rules which are most general and important for each of its branches.[23] It is essential that the branch principles are often derived from the fundamental principles and in any case may not contradict them.

Such a systematic approach to international law, which the author of this chapter shares, does not mean that international law is a static homogenious phenomenon. International law progresses along with the public relations it regulates. It reflects the whole variety of such relations. Along with the few fundamental rules which protect basic values of the mankind and have peremptory character there are numerous dispositive rules. These rules, unlike peremptory ones can be eluded by States in agreements they conclude. This is the way special rules appear and co-exist with general ones, whereas particular and local rules co-exist with universal ones. Today, new universal and particular, general and special rules exist in one international legal system developing and completing it.

It is generally recognized that the area which international law regulates is constantly developing. International law extends in those areas which were closed for international cooperation before (for example, environmental protection). It regulates those relations which used to be related to a State's internal affairs exclusively and were regulated only by national law (for example, human rights). It deals with subjects whose activities were not directly related to it (individuals and other non-state actors). We always see the appearance of new international legal rules. However, this does not mean that the existing international law is fragmentary and, therefore, abounds with gaps.

Certainly, not all particular relations between States are regulated by particular international legal rules. In this context, one can speak about certain gaps that exist in the international law. However, it is difficult to agree with the opinion of some experts who deny the systematic comprehensive nature of international law,

---

23   For example, as applied to international air law, the principle of the State's sovereignty over its air space, the principle of the permissive procedure of international flights and transportations in the sovereign air space and the principle of free flights outside the State's territory are referred to. The branch principles of internationals economic law are the principle of economic cooperation, sovereignty of States over natural resources, mutual interest, economic non-discrimination as well as the principle of the most favorable nation and of providing national regime. As the branch principle of environmental international law, the principle is mentioned in accordance with which a State should not, as a result of activities within its jurisdiction or control, damage to the environment of other States or regions outside its national jurisdiction. In international environmental law as well as in international economic law the principle of the State's sovereignty over its national natural resources is mentioned; as a principle under formation (or have formed already, as some authors note) Russian scholars speak about the branch principle of cautious approach or the precautionary principle and some other principles.

according to which, international order has numerous "lacunae".[24] In fact, we can use principles of international law to assess the behavior of any State as lawful or not. This is possible because, as G.Tunkin noted, fundamental principles of international law embrace all areas of relations between States.[25]

In any case, the lawfulness of a State's behavior can be determined with the help of the principle according to which the behavior which is not prohibited under international law is lawful. Considering the question of the legality of the use of nuclear weapons in the ICJ, a number of States noted that "States are free to threaten or use nuclear weapons unless it can be shown that they are bound not to do so by reference to a prohibition in either treaty law or customary international law".[26] In the Lotus case, the Permanent Court of International Justice stated that "restrictions upon the independence of States cannot ... be presumed" and that international law grants the States "a wide measure of discretion which is only limited ... by prohibitive rules".[27] In this very context, the ICJ in Military and Paramilitary Activities in and against the Nicaragua Case noted: "... in the international law there are no rules, other than such rules as may be accepted by the State concerned, by treaty or otherwise, whereby the level of armaments of a sovereign State can be limited, and this principle is valid for all States without exception".[28]

---

24   See for ex.: Carreau D., *Droit international public.* 7-e édition, Paris, ed. A. Pedone, 2001, pp. 35-36.

25   *Mezhdunarodnoye pravo.* Ed. by G. Tunkin, M.: Yuridicheskaya literatura, 1994, p. 51.

26   Legality of the Threat or Use of Nuclear Weapons, I.C.J. Rep., 1996, p. 226, at p. 238, para. 21.

27   P.C.I.J., Series A, No. 10, Sept. 7th, 1927, Collection of judgments, The case of the S.S. "Lotus", pp. 18 and 19.

28   Military and Paramilitary Activities in and against Nicaragua (*Nicaragua v. United States of America*), Merits, Judgment, I.C.J. Reports, 1986, p. 14, para. 269. It would be appropriate to quote O. Casanovas here: "It is said that a lacunae exists when it is considered that the legal system does not contain a rule which would be worth having. In this case the lacunae is not so much a lacunae as a criticism of current law and the proposal of a new rule *de lege ferenda;* we could call them lacunae *de lege ferenda.* The term lacunae is used, in another sense, to indicate the non-existence of specific rules dealing with certain matters. They are the so-called 'technical lacunae'. The absence of rules regulating activities in space at a certain stage was 'the lacunae of the rules, but not of the law because there is the possibility of applying other more general precepts of law which might adequately resolve a problem not specifically regulated'. In addition, it is said that a lacuna exists when, in spite of the existence of rules to deal with the question in Court, they neither take exceptional cases into account, nor any limitations which may be considered necessary. There are 'inappropriate lacunae' or 'hidden lacunae' ". He goes further saying that "all legal systems tend to avoid or limit the existence of lacunae. ... Applied to the problem of the completeness of law, this principle [limitations to the independence of States cannot be presumed – R.K] would amount in international law to say that everything which is not expressly prohibited is permitted." But, he adds, "it probably cannot be sustained that this principle applies in all cases relating to the international legal system." He continues: "The advisory opinion of the International Court of Justice in The legality of the threat or use of nuclear weapons case illustrates the dif-

At the same time, it is clear that efficient international legal regulation requires not only fundamental and branch rules, but also specific ones.[29]

International law is multiform or diverse by definition. Its rules are the product of the interaction between States with different levels of economic and political development, interests, ideologies, traditions, cultures, law schools, etc. This situation is enhanced by the mainly, but not completely, horizontal character of the international system and the presence of different regional and specialized branches or subsystems in it. At the same time, we cannot deny that even in the time of the most striking ideological, political, value and economic disjunction of the modern world, that is, in the time of Cold War and the global confrontation of two systems – capitalist and socialist – general, universal international law lived out the time of rapid development.

During that period, pessimistic views were also spread concerning the possibility of the existence of general international law in the conflict of two systems and the appearance of new independent States after decolonization, a lot was spoken about prospects of failure of the existing universality of international law.[30] Such views seemed to have sufficient grounds. Groups of States united by geographic location, economy, shared ideology, values, political ambitions, etc., not only created and developed their regional legal subsystems as it was before. Socialist countries insisted that beside general international law, there was a specific "socialist international law", as for its contents, ideological and political basis. According to socialist States, the rules of "socialist international law", based on the principles of "socialist internationalism", regulated relations between them, substituting the principles of general international law. These principles of socialist legality in the relations between socialist States were considered to be *"lex specialis* to the norms of general international law."[31]

However, at that very moment general international law saw rapid development. The principles of non-use of force and the threat of force, peaceful settlement of disputes, respect for human rights, self-determination, territorial integrity,

---

ficulties which may arise due to the lack of applicable rules. ... The absence of specific rules concerning the threat or use of nuclear weapons does not produce a legal vacuum which cannot be substituted by rules and principles of general character, such as provisions of the Charter of the United Nations concerning legitimate self-defense and the principles of humanitarian international law." O. Casanovas, *Op. cit*, pp. 92-96.

29   See also: *Mezhdunarodnoye pravo*. Ed. by G. Tunkin, M.: Yuridicheskaya literatura, 1994, p. 51.

30   For detailed information on these views, see: G. Tunkin, *Teoriya mezhdunarodnogo prava*. M.: Mezhdunarodnye otnosheniya. 1970, pp. 24-40.

31   I. Scobbie, Some common heresies about international law. In: *International Law*. Ed. by M.D. Evans, p. 75. However, G. Tunkin wrote that as far as basic principles of general international law are of *jus cogens* character, the principles of socialist internationalism cannot contradict them. Correspondingly, they do not dominate principles of general international law but develop and complete them, and that is why, being special rules, they replace common rules of international law in the relations between socialist States. See G. Tunkin, *Teoriya mezhdunarodnogo prava*, pp. 503-506.

i.e. those fundamental rules which determine the framework and system of international law came to be generally recognized. This very period became the "gold era" of codification and the progressive development of international law: law of the sea, law of treaties, diplomatic and consular law, law of human rights, humanitarian law, law of international security, space law etc. This became possible mainly because, despite all the differences, States remained tied by certain top values such as, first of all, peace and security. It is important that States realize the necessity to strengthen these values in generally binding legal rules.

The dissolution of the "socialist camp", the end of the global confrontation of two ideologies and, correspondingly, of the Cold War, along with the globalization phenomenon created objective conditions for further universalization of international law, for the development of its system and the deepening of the transnational character of its influence. The global challenges which are sometimes called factors causing fragmentation of international law demand, in fact, the search for primarily global international legal answers. But whether the international community will be able to work them out is open to question.

When there are no global international law solutions for global issues, they are looked for on other levels. A characteristic example is the elaboration of anti-terrorist treaties on the regional level in a situation when talks on the UN Comprehensive Convention on Terrorism have been in a deadlock for several years already.

It is obvious that many differences between States still exist and will lead to the appearance and existence of new regional, bilateral and other non-universal legal rules. However, if all the problems associated with the confrontation of the two systems did not interfere with the establishment of the international law system and did not break its integrity, then we can hardly consider fragmentation as a real threat to the international law system in the globalization era. In any case, there seem to be no objective reasons for the fragmentation of the international law system now. We should also take into account that it is finally States that set up and preserve international law. Judging by the discussion in the 6th Committee of the UN General Assembly and by the reaction of States to the activity of different international judicial bodies, the WTO and other international institutions, States do not consider this activity as really threatening the integrity of the international legal system so far. In this connection, the abovementioned evolution of the fragmentation issue in the ILC is also logical.

As for methodology, the ILC seems to have been right in deciding to consider what is called fragmentation from the point of view of the approaches to conflicts between different rules of international law.[32] Nevertheless, as I think, at least in ac-

---

32   The following topics were included in the work program of the ILC Study Group in 2002: (a) The function and scope of the *lex specialis* rule and the question of "self-contained regimes"; (b) The interpretation of treaties in the light of " relevant rules of international law applicable in the relations between the parties" (art. 31 (3) (c) of the Vienna Convention on the Law of Treaties), in the context of general developments in international law and concerns of the international community; (c) The application of successive treaties relating to the same subject matter (art. 30 of the Vienna Con-

ademic analysis beyond the framework of the Commission, such a static approach, when conflicts between existing rules are considered, should be expanded.

The activity of different international institutions that are engaged in applying and interpreting international law, establishment of regional and other particular international law rules should be considered in the context of the existing international legal system and its fundamental principles. It is important to take into consideration that this system is constantly developing following the changes occurring in the world, and also the fact that it is States that set up rules of international law. Dispute settlement international bodies themselves do not establish international law rules (unless they are vested with this right by States, of course). That is why the activity of international bodies that apply and interpret international law (here we speak about bodies where judges or experts in person are represented but not States) should be considered and assessed taking into account the States' reaction to it, their practices and *opinio juris* following the decisions of that bodies.

In addition, we should bear in mind that the establishment of international law rules, the substitution by new rules of the old ones is a process that can be controversial. The States' behavior may sometimes seem to be violating the existing legal rule, and we find out only later that it was actually the beginning of the formation of a new rule. Furthermore, when there is no specific international legal rule or when its substance is not entirely clear, the decisions of international bodies on approximately similar cases may differ. It requires time and clarification of the stances on the point of not only international bodies, but rather and primarily, of States, for the substance of a certain rule being formed to become clear. Thus, the issue of fragmentation should also be regarded in terms of shaping the customary rules of international law and their interrelation with the treaties.[33]

Let us analyze the abovementioned examples of fragmentation from the point of view of the established principles of resolving conflicts between legal rules (general/special; subsequent/former; peremptory/dispositive) as well as in the context of the system of international law, taking into account that developing a rule is a process in which States play the key role.

In the decision of the ICJ in the Military and Paramilitary Activities case[34] and the ICTY decision in the Tadic case[35] in their respective parts concerning the

---

vention on the Law of Treaties); (d) The modification of multilateral treaties between certain parties only (art. 41 of the Vienna Convention on the Law of Treaties); (e) Hierarchy of international law: *jus cogens*, obligations *erga omnes*, Article 103 of the UN Charter as conflict rules. (UN General Assembly, Official Records, Fifty-eighth session, Suppl. No. 10 (A/58/10), para. 413.)

33   See the analysis of the modification process of the existing rules of international law during the appearance of new customary rules, proposed by R. Higgins. (Higgins R. *Problems & Progress. International Law and How We Use It*. Oxford Univ. Press, 1995, pp. 18-22, 28-32.)

34   Military and Paramilitary Activities in and against Nicaragua (*Nicaragua v. United States of America*), Merits, pp. 62, 64-65, paras. 109, 115.

35   ICTY: *Prosecutor v. Tadic*, 38 I.L.M.1518 (1999), pp. 1541-1549, paras. 117-162.

issue of State control over the activities of a person or a group of persons so as to attribute their activities to this State there is no question of a conflict between different rules. These decisions may be regarded as indications of an existing or developing rule under which the activities of a person, group of persons or of non-governmental formations are attributed to a State if it controls these persons or formations in performing such activities. This assertion is confirmed by the provisions of Article 8 of the draft articles on State responsibility for internationally wrongful acts, drafted by the ILC and the Commission's commentary on this Article.[36] At the same time, the assumption of the ICJ that for the attribution of responsibility to a State it is necessary that such control be effective was supported by neither ICTY nor ILC. The Commission did not include the control degree criterion in the said Article 8. Noting that the cases differed "both *de jure* and *de facto*", the ILC indicated: "In any event it is a matter for appreciation in each case whether particular conduct was or was not carried out under control of a State, to such an extent that the conduct controlled should be attributed to it."[37] The differences in the stances of the ICJ and the ICTY are not an example of international law fragmentation, but elements of the process of forming of a customary rule which was defined also by the ILC in the draft articles on State responsibility. It follows from the text of the abovementioned Article 8 that the control degree is not an element of this rule. However, its existence *de lege lata* can be a definite question only as soon as the attitude of States towards it is clarified.

The abovementioned interpretation by the ECHR of the reservations regime, as applied to the European Convention on Human Rights and Fundamental Freedoms in the Belilos case, was later reaffirmed by the Court in the Loizidou case.[38] Firstly, the ECHR *inter alia* confirmed its right to consider the matter of validity of reservations related to the European Convention on Human Rights whereas under the general rule of the law of treaties it is the prerogative of the States Parties of a certain treaty. Secondly, in both the Loizidou and Belilos cases, the Court resolved substantively the problem of "territorial restrictions" attached to Turkey's Articles 25 and 46 declarations under the Convention: these "restrictions" (restrictive declarations) were held invalid and Turkey was considered bound by corresponding provisions of the Convention without any limitations provided by its declarations (in fact, as it was with the Belilos case, the issue of the validity of statements was considered by the Court as that of the validity of reservations).[39] This conclusion clearly differs from the reservations regime provided by the Vienna Convention on the Law of Treaties

---

36   United Nations General Assembly, Official Records, Fifty-sixth session, Supplement №
     10 (A/56/10), pp. 103-109. Article 8 says: "The conduct of a person or group of persons
     shall be considered an act of a State under international law if the person or group of
     persons is in fact acting on the instructions of, or under the direction or control of that
     State in carrying out the conduct."

37   *Ibid.*, p. 106-107.

38   ECHR, *Loizidou v. Turkey*, (Preliminary objections) judgment of 23 March 1995, Ser. A
     no 310, p. 31, para. 94.

39   *Ibid.*, paras. 68 f.

of 1969.[40] The ECHR itself generally substantiated its actions and conclusions by the specific character of the regime established by the European Convention and, respectively, by the differences between its practice as a specialized court from that of the ICJ which is a free-standing international tribunal that has no links to a stand-ard-setting treaty such as the European Convention.[41] It is worth noting that the ILC Study Group actually agreed with the ECHR's opinion. It qualified the situation as a collision caused due to the fact that in this case special law was applicable.[42]

In this connection the following should be noted. Firstly, this collision is re-solved in favor of a special regime that appeared later. In this case the special re-gime is the regional customary regime of reservations. Secondly, this regime has formed (or, is forming) not only as the result of the ECHR's activity, but also due to the attitude of the European States to this activity. The members of the Council of Europe do not object to such a position of the Court, though over a number of years already, the reservations issue has been a disputed question at the Ad Hoc Committee of Legal Advisers on Public International Law of the Council of Europe (CAHDI). Moreover, the Committee set up a special group of experts on reserva-tions to international treaties in the early 90s. The discussion in the Group and then in the CAHDI proved that the practice on the matters of restrictions has some specific features within the Council of Europe.[43] In the Recommendations to the answers on inadmissible reservations worked out by this Group, approved by CAHDI and then adopted in the Committee of Ministers of the Council of Europe, it was noted in particular that "when the Vienna Convention on the Law of Trea-ties was adopted, subsequent developments were not envisaged, in particular the formulation of reservations of a general character and the increasing role of the monitoring bodies provided for by certain treaties".[44]

The rules of general international law in the field of the law of treaties stated in the Vienna Convention on the Law of Treaties of 1969 have a dispositive character and may be modified by agreement between some participants of the Convention. As a result of establishing the regional customary *lex specialis* regime working in the relations between the Council of Europe member States, a change of the treaty

---

40   Article 21(3) of the Vienna Convention: "When a State objecting to a reservation has not opposed the entry into force of the treaty between itself and the reserving State, the provisions to which the reservation relates do not apply as between the two States to the extent of the reservation."

41   ECHR, *Loizidou v. Turkey*, (Preliminary objections), judgment of 23 March 1995, Ser. A no. 310, pp. 26-27, paras. 68, 70-71, 84-85.

42   United Nations General Assembly, Official Records, Fifty-eighth session, Supplement no. 10 (A/58/10), para. 419.

43   See *Ad Hoc* Committee of Legal Advisers on Public International Law (CAHDI), Group of Experts on Reservations to International Treaties (Di-e-rit), Meeting Report, Di-e-rit (99) 6, Strasbourg,16/08/99; *Ad Hoc* Committee of Legal Advisers on Public Interna-tional Law (CAHDI), Meeting Report, CAHDI (99) 15, Strasbourg, 04/05/99, pp. 9-10.

44   Council of Europe Committee of Ministers, Recommendation no. R (99) 13, adopted on 18 May 1999.

regime stated in the Vienna Convention occurred in Europe as far as reservations are concerned.

Another situation is seen in the activity of the Committee on Human Rights functioning under the International Covenant on Civil and Political Rights of 1966. The abovementioned General Comment No. 24 aroused objections of some States, particularly the USA, Great Britain and France.[45] J.A. Frowein notes that "this shows that on the worldwide level there is still a great reluctance by States to adopt the line now established within the system of the European Convention on Human Rights".[46] A. Aust analyzed the outcomes of the discussion in 1997 on the report of the ILC in the 6th Committee of the General Assembly and came to the conclusion that almost all 47 representatives of States who spoke at the discussion "reaffirmed that the [Vienna – R.K.] Convention regime applied to all treaties, and disagreed in varying degrees with the view that treaty-monitoring bodies were competent to make authoritative determinations [on the validity or admissibility of reservations – R.K.]".[47] So, at least now it is early to speak about the establishment of a universal common *lex specialis* rule within the framework of the International Covenant on Civil and Political Rights, which would be similar to the rule established in Europe as well as about deviation from the regime stipulated by general international law on the universal level.[48] However, it should not be excluded that we are witnessing a gradual crystallization of such a rule. Everything seems to depend on the future reaction of States to the activity of the treaty bodies in this field. As for the Committee on Human Rights, it confirmed the stance stated in the General Comment No. 24 when considering the Kennedy case.[49]

---

45   Observations on General Comment 24, 16 Human Rights Law Journal (1995) at pp. 422-426. See the analysis of the States' reaction in: B. Simma, Reservations to Human Rights Treaties – Some Recent Developments. In: G. Hafner, G. Loibl, A. Rest, L. Sucharipa-Behrmann and K. Zemanek (eds.), *Liber Amicorum Professor Seidl-Hohenveldern – in honor of his 80th birthday*, 1998, Kluwer Law Int., pp. 674-675; Y. Tyagi, The conflict of law and policy on reservations to human rights treaties. In: 71 *British Yearbook of International Law* (2000), pp. 245-246.

46   Frowein J.A., Reservations and the International public order. In: *Theory of International Law at the Threshold of the 21st Century, Essays in Honor of Krsysztof Skubiszewski*. Ed. By J. Makarczyk, Kluwer Law Int., 1996, p. 408.

47   Aust A., *Modern Treaty Law and Practice*. Cambridge University Press, 2000, p. 124.

48   Y. Tyagi states that, as a result of the activity of the Committee on the basis of the Covenant concerning reservations, we see the establishment of the *lex specialis* regime, nevertheless he notes that the Committee's comments "are not part of the hard law on reservations".(Y. Tyagi, *Op. cit.*, p. 246.) B.Simma points out that *de lege ferenda*, the UN human rights treaty bodies need – and deserve – to be made competent to render legally binding decisions on admissibility and severability of reservations to human rights treaties (B. Simma, *Op. cit.*, p. 680).

49   The Committee stated: "The normal assumption will be that the ratification or accession is dependant on the acceptability of the reservation and the unacceptability of the reservation will not vitiate the reserving State's reserving State's agreement to becoming party to the Covenant is dependant on the acceptability of the reservation. The

The regime of reservations to treaties (regional and universal) on human rights is sometimes called an autonomous or self-contained one.[50] Leaving alone the discussion over the concept of an "autonomous" or "self-contained regime" itself and its right to existence,[51] I would like to note that neither the practice of the ECHR, nor the practice of the bodies established under universal treaties testifies to their autonomous and self-sufficient character or deviation from common international law. The said General Comment No. 24 contains numerous references to the Vienna Convention of 1969 and to the general international law expressed in it, and it also applies its provisions and concepts.[52] The ECHR also bases its decisions on the universal international law rules in the abovementioned Belilos and Loizidou cases.[53] The same is true with respect to other instances which are referred to as autonomous or self-contained regimes and in particular to the WTO.

Analyzing the practice of the WTO Dispute Settlement Body, J. Jackson notes that "... the Appellate Body has made it reasonably clear that general international law is relevant and applies in the case of WTO and its treaty annexes, including GATT. In the past there has been some question about this, with certain parties arguing that the GATT was a 'separate regime,' in some way insulated from the general body of international law. The Appellate Body has made it quite clear that this is not the case and has made references to general international law principles, particularly as embodied in the Vienna Convention on the Law of Treaties, which the Appellate Body calls upon for principles of treaty interpretation."[54]

---

same applies with reservations to the Optional Protocol." *Rawle Kennedy v. Trinidad and Tobago*, Comm. No. 845/1999, Decision, 2 November 1999, UN Doc. A/55/40, vol. II. Annex XI, A.

50   Wellens K.C., *Op. cit.*, p. 27.

51   See *Ibid.*, Simma B., Self-contained regimes, 16 NYIL (1985); L.A.N.M. Barnhoorn, Diplomatic Law and Unilateral Remedies, 25 *Netherlands Yearbook of International Law* (1994), pp. 30-81. P.-M. Dupuy, for example, calls the doctrine of "self-contained regimes" "misleading" (P.-M.Dupuy, The danger of fragmentation or unification of the international legal system and the International Court of Justice, International Law and Politics, vol.31:753, 1999, p. 797).

52   UN Doc. HRI/GEN/1/Rev.4, pp. 118-124.

53   E.g. ECHR, Belilos judgement, paras. 42, 46; ECHR, *Loizidou v. Turkey* (Preliminary objections), paras. 67, 90. References to general international law are frequent in ECHR case-law, see e.g. *McElhinney v. Ireland* [GC], no. 31253/96, para. 38, ECHR 2001-XI; *Al-Adsani v. The United Kingdom* [GC], no. 35763/97, paras. 54-55, 60-66, ECHR 2001-XI; *Fogarty v. The United Kingdom* [GC], no. 37112/97, paras. 37-38, ECHR 2001-XI; *Streletz, Kessler and Krenz v. Germany*, nos. 34044/96, 35532/97 and 44801/98, paras. 90 f., ECHR 2001-II; *Bancovich and others v. Belgium and others*, no. 52207/99, paras. 55-59, 73, ECHR 2001-XII.

54   Jackson J., *The jurisprudence of GATT and the WTO.*, Cambridge Univ. Press, 2000, p. 181. Jackson comes to an even more general conclusion. International economic law, he says, "cannot be separated or compartmentalized from general international law. The activities and cases relating to IEL contain much practice which is relevant to general principles of international law, especially concerning treaty law and practice." *Ibid.*, p. 11.

The analysis of the important role of international law and, in particular, of general international law in the WTO made by J.Puawelyn is, I believe, highly convincing.[55]

M. Koskenniemi and P. Leino think that fully self-contained regimes may seem to pose a lesser threat than semi-autonomous ones that apply concepts of general international law but do this from a special perspective. Here, they write, perhaps "is the core of the problem: not so much in the emergence of new sub-systems but in the use of general law by new bodies representing interests or views that are not identical with those represented in old ones".[56]

In my view, however, that we are dealing not with autonomous or semi-autonomous regimes, but with those rules/regimes that quite naturally appear in the international legal system as special ones with respect to general dispositive rules/regimes. There may be also formation of rules/regimes which are not special, as there are no general dispositive international legal rules in the corresponding field, with respect to which these new rules would be special. But in this case, new rules all the same appear on the basis of the international law principles they cannot contradict. This is important, in particular, for the formation of regional international law rules.

The above drawn example of the parallel existence of the universal (1997) and regional (1992) Conventions on Non-navigational Uses of International Watercourses cannot be considered as fragmentation of international law. In fact it is an example of co-existence of a universal dispositive regime and a special regional one, given that the latter appeared earlier than the former. Which rule is applied in the situation when two States concerned are parties to both treaties should be decided first of all with reference to Article 3(1) of the 1997 Convention. It says: "In the absence of an agreement to the contrary, nothing in the present Convention shall affect the rights or obligations of a watercourse State arising from agreements in force for it on the date on which it became a party to the present Convention."[57] Thus, the priority is given to special rules which are in force for those States at the moment of their joining the 1997 Convention, though it is a *lex posteriori* for such rules.[58]

In situations which are analogous to the just described, regional agreement is a starting point to the establishment of universal rules. And *vice versa*. Universal treaties similar to the Convention of 1997 become framework regimes for the later regional agreements.[59]

---

55   Pauwelyn J., The Role of Public International Law in the WTO: How Far Can We Go? 95 AJIL 535, 2001.

56   Koskenniemi M. & Leino P, *Fragmentation of international law? Postmodern anxieties*, p. 561.

57   U.N. Doc. A/51/869.

58   Article 3(2) of the Convention invites States to harmonize special agreements with its basic principles: "Notwithstanding the provisions of paragraph 1, parties to agreements referred to in paragraph 1 may, where necessary, consider harmonizing such agreements with the basic principles of the present Convention."

59   Article 3 (3) of the 1997 Convention says: "Watercourse States may enter into one or more agreements ... which apply and adjust the provisions of the present Conven-

The situation is more complicated when attempts to agree upon universal rules on universally important issues fail *inter alia* because of the differences between the stances of States of different regions, and States start concluding regional agreements in this field that do not coincide with one another. This is the case, for instance, with the suppression of terrorism.

Attempts to work out a universal definition of terrorism for the purposes of the so-called Comprehensive Convention for the Suppression of Terrorism, which would allow finishing the work on that Convention in the UN, have brought no positive results so far. A number of regional agreements have been concluded using different definitions of terrorism. In the League of Arab States, The Arab Convention on the Suppression of Terrorism was concluded in 1998.[60] In 1999 the Treaty on Co-operation among the States Members of the Commonwealth of Independent States in Combating Terrorism, the Convention of the Organization of the Islamic Conference on Combating International Terrorism and the Organization of African Unity Convention on the Prevention and Combating of Terrorism were adopted,[61] all containing rather different definitions of this crime. In the 2002 Inter-American Convention against Terrorism[62] such a definition is absent. In Europe the idea to conclude a comprehensive regional anti-terrorist treaty has not been successful so far.[63] This regional diversity in approaches to the definition of terrorism interferes with reaching an agreement on the universal level. This reality obviously influences the rulemaking process on the universal level not only with respect to the suppression of terrorism but also in other fields. As J.Crawford says, "the underlying diversity of nations and the tendency to regionalism ... raises significant tensions for international law and may even call in question its claim to "universality."[64]

At the same time, it is also obvious that the more quick formation of international law rules on the regional level plays a positive part for the establishment of universal rules. It was mentioned above that regional rules become a model, or basis, for universal ones. In any case, the appearance of regional rules gives an impetus to the universal negotiations process, contributes to it. For regionalism to play such a part, it is necessary that the problem itself require not only a regional

---

tion to the characteristics and uses of a particular international watercourse or part thereof."

60   International instruments related to the Prevention and Suppression of International Terrorism, New York 2001, p. 152.

61   *Ibid.*, pp. 174, 187, 220.

62   *Ibid.*, p. 210.

63   The existing European Convention on the Suppression of Terrorism adopted in 1977 deals basically with issues of extradition. (ETS No. 90). However, a number of Member States of the Council of Europe where a new "comprehensive" regional treaty was discussed believe that it could be counterproductive to the universal UN effort.

64   Crawford J. Universalism and regionalism from the perspective of the work of the International law commission. In: *International Law on the Eve of the Twenty-first Century. Views from the International Law Commission*, UN, New York, 1997, p. 102.

solution but also a universal one. Terrorism is an example of such a problem.[65] It is not an accident that this problem is dealt with not only in the UN but also in almost all regions of the world. It is important that regional conventions are based, for one thing, on the fundamental principles of international law (respect of the sovereignty of states, pacific settlement of disputes, non-use of force, respect of human rights, cooperation between states, etc.), and for another thing, on the universal, so-called anti-terrorist conventions currently in force. So, despite the regional diversity and the absence of progress in the UN talks at the moment, the conclusion of a universal comprehensive anti-terrorist convention is a question of time. I suppose that the regional activity will prove to be a positive factor for establishing a universal regime in the long run. Let me refer once again to J.Crawford who, analyzing the relationship between universalism and regionalism, writes: "The ideal of universality could only be achieved on the basis of some allowance for disagreement on particulars."[66]

The foregoing allows us to draw the following conclusions. The threat of fragmentation of international law (if we see fragmentation as a disintegration of the international legal system to different parts not associated with one another) is hardly real. There are no objective grounds for fragmentation. On the contrary, despite the individual, group, regional diversity of States, globalization imposes the necessity of working out new rules to settle new issues, and the end of confrontation between two world systems provides favorable conditions for that.

International law is a comprehensive system in the sense that, at least on the level of its most general fundamental principles, it covers all relations that are the object of international legal regulation. New rules that fill up certain gaps are formed based on fundamental and branch principles of international law, within the international law system.[67] This system is constantly developing, along with the relations it regulates. The certain concrete gaps are filled up, and at the same time the rules in force are changing. Such changes often begin with the appearance of special universal or regional rules. It is possible when the rule in force has a dispositive character.

The international law system allows settling conflicts arising from the formation of new international law rules, between the old and new ones. One of the ways

---

65   The evidence is the resolutions of the UN General Assembly and Security Council on terrorism (e.g., General Assembly Resolutions 49/60 of 9 Dec.1994; 51/210 of 17 Dec.1996; 52/165 of 15 Dec.1997; 53/108 of 8 Dec.1998; 54/110 of 9 Dec.1999; 55/158 of 12 Dec.2000; 56/1 of 12 Sept. 2001; 57/27 of 19 Nov. 2002; 58/81 of 9 Dec. 2004; Security Council Resolutions 1368 (2001) of 12 Sept. 2001; 1373 (2001) of 28 Sept. 2001; 1377 (2001) of 12 Nov. 2001).

66   Crawford J., *Op. cit.*, p. 119.

67   J. Pauwelyn writes that "states, in their treaty relations, can contract out of one, more, or, in theory, all rules of general international law (other than *jus cogens*), but they cannot contract out of the system of international law. As soon as states contract with one another, they do so automatically and necessarily within the system of international law." Pauwelyn J., *Op. cit.*, p. 539. It deems that the same is true with respect to the formation of customary rules of international law.

of settling such a conflict is to apply the legal technique rules common for all legal systems, such as that a special rule prevails over a general one, the subsequent prevails over the previous one.

The decisive word in those processes is after States. The activity of dispute settlement international bodies or of other treaty bodies interpreting and applying international law rules, whatever its significance, does not itself lead to establishing new international law rules or changing the existing ones. Important is the stance of States on that activity and their further practice. Different decisions of international courts in similar situations may be a sign of the certain international law rule to regulate such situations being only formed. Its contents will depend, first of all, on the stance of States in this respect.

At the same time, the speculative character of the threat of fragmentation does not mean that States should not pay any attention to this issue. It is important for States to follow the activity of international bodies applying and interpreting international law, particularly in the context of their activity in the international law system, and to react to that in appropriate cases. States should encourage those bodies to get to know one another's activity and to be mindful of it. In some cases, the establishment of mechanisms providing harmonization of the activity of such bodies should not be excluded. (For instance, the UN Security Council found it feasible for the Tribunals for Rwanda and for the Former Yugoslavia to have a common chamber of appeal.)

It may also be of use if provisions are included into international treaties clearly pointing at their interrelation with other international law rules in the field they regulate.

It is important that the task of studying this issue was given to the International Law Commission that could offer to the States certain guidelines for ensuring the further harmonious development of international law.

However, it is States in the long run that bear responsibility for keeping the integrity of the international law system and using the advantageous conditions for its further development that we see at the turn of the 20th and 21st centuries.

9. Centrifugal and Centripetal Tendencies in the International System: Some Reflections

V.S. Mani

Constitutionalism is generally identified with a pyramidal normative and institutional, usually formal, structure of governance. The structure might have evolved over time corresponding to the demands of a community that was in search of a system of governance mandated to provide it and its individual members with relative safety and security from forces inside and outside it. Soon, even as such communities continued to subsist, or changed and regrouped, seeking to find some common identity of their respective members, such as nationhood, the mandate of the structure of governance transformed – it now focused on human welfare through social welfare. This dominant expectation of welfare from governance caused havoc in most communities. Monarchies and dictatorships were overturned and some communities began to practice democracies.[1] Over time, states expanded territorially, broke up, regrouped, often gave way to new states, new forms of governance.

Political theory tells us that the foundation of the modern state is an adhesive force usually identified as nationhood. But what constitutes nationhood? In a country like India, it is very difficult to pinpoint, with its so patently apparent diversity that one comes across through the length and breadth of the country. Is it the language (an ancient, now dead, language like Sanskrit provides an undercurrent of oneness of roots of most Indian languages); is it the history of the land (for at no point in time was the entire Indian subcontinent under one rule, not even under the British rule); is it race or ethnicity; or is it religion? None of these, but perhaps it is the cultural consciousness or cultural identity shared by the bulk of the people. The Indian nation has been and still is subjected to serious threats of

---

[1] In some ancient civilisations, such as the Indian, it is difficult to say whether the transformation took place precisely in this order. There is evidence to show that even during the Vedic period, powerful kingdoms coexisted with independent republican states (or at least communities) some of which appear to have enjoyed some degree of democratic governance. See, i.e., A.S. Altekar, *State and Government in Ancient India* (Motilal Banarsidass Pub, Delhi, 1949, 1997 reprint), Chp. VI, "Republics," at pp. 109-138.

Ronald St. John Macdonald & Douglas M. Johnston (eds.), Towards World Constitutionalism, *pp. 241-254.*
© *2005 Koninklijke Brill NV. Printed in The Netherlands. ISBN 90 04 14612 1.*

dismemberment. Yet the people seem to have resolved to stay together, as they are firmly bound together by one culture, one composite culture.

Basic to the staying together of a community is the collective decision to pursue consensually selected common goals through a consensually evolved system of governance that by and large recognises the right of self-determination of the people. The bulk of the individuals recognise that the right of self-determination of each of them must be subsumed in the collective right of the community. The integrity of the process and institutions of governance is a function of that recognition. It is a function of the faith of the individuals in the achievement of their right of self-determination through the achievement of collective good.

However, there is an operational gap between the normative and institutional structure of governance and the social and human welfare resulting from this structure. There is an on-going tension between the norm and its realisation at the ground level. Should the process of tension cross a threshold point, the trust of the individuals in the community institutions and norms breaks down, and 'chaos' follows, regrouping of individuals takes place, another attempt at establishing a new normative and institutional order of governance takes shape. The process goes on.

What are these centripetal and centrifugal tendencies in a community that play havoc with the normative and institutional structures of governance? At the outset, it must be recognised that it is difficult to characterise any tendency as 'unifying' or 'divisive' *per se*. A feature of federalism, for instance, could preserve the integrity of a nation at one point in time, but could contribute to its breakdown at another.

The above thesis is more easily demonstrable in terms of an overview of the nature and functioning of international institutions, whether intergovernmental or non-governmental. It is important to note that all international institutions, both intergovernmental and non-governmental, reflect a level of crystallisation of the forces in the international community that promote creation of varied levels of formal institutional frameworks. The progression from informal set up to a formal institutional mechanism is typified by the Commonwealth which in 1965 decided to set up some token of administrative set up giving it some semblance of an institutional form. This has been the case with SAARC. Such institutions illustrate the pronounced hesitation of national communities to evolve formal institutional mechanisms to steer their operational projects. Indeed, all this represents a stage in the process of international organisation, a process whereby certain goal values commonly shared by the members of the international community dictate expression through formal institutionalism. Quite possibly, the present state system must have undergone a similar, if not the same, process of consolidation – or at least coincidence of interests of individuals and groups over millennia. The loosely knit 13 colonies eventually became the United States, in spite of the fact that some of the participants at the 1789 constitutional convention at Philadelphia did at that time find that they were in a 'strange land.' The progress of constitutionalism in America further integrated the country giving American nationalism a new identity and the traumatic experience of the Civil War further cemented the inter-individual and inter-State bonds.

1. Intergovernmental International Organisations[2]

The prime example of an international intergovernmental institution is indeed the United Nations. Christened by President F. D. Roosevelt of the United States as 'The United Nations Organisation' at its inception, it lost the last word, 'Organisation,' soon thereafter. Did this anticipate what was to come over the years? Did the UN end up being merely a 'standing conference of states,' now only to be a 'plaything' at the hands of the powerful? In which case, what 'advance' did it make, except having acquired some fixed assets in Geneva, Vienna, Bangkok and such other places, besides of course New York? Or is it an organisation that 'now you see and now you don't'? Indeed, it a mix of realism and idealism at once. It is an association of states whose ruling elites may or may not represent the vast majority of the people in their respective nations. Article 1 (4) of the UN Charter ('the Constitution for the international community'?) perceives its role to pre-eminently lie in being a centre for harmonisation of national action. Has it been able to fulfil this 'minimalist' role? The answers perhaps lie in understanding the nature of the United Nations.

A.   The UN Charter: A Mix of Idealism and 'Realism'

On the opening day of the San Francisco Conference on International Organisation on April 25, 1945, President Harry S. Truman of the United States reminded the participating national delegations of their mission:

> You members of this Conference are to be the architects of the better world. In your hands rests our future. By your labors at this Conference, we shall know if suffering humanity is to achieve a just and lasting peace.
>
> We must make certain, by your work here, that another war will be impossible.
>
> …
>
> With ever-increasing brutality and destruction, modern warfare, if unchecked, would ultimately crush all civilization. We still have a choice between the alternatives: the continuation of international chaos or the establishment of a world organization for the enforcement of peace.
>
>   It is not the purpose of this Conference to draft a treaty of peace in the old sense of that term. It is not our assignment to settle specific questions of territories, boundaries, citizenship and reparations.
>
>   This Conference will devote its energies and its labors exclusively to the single problem of setting up the essential organization to keep the peace. You are to write the fundamental charter.[3]

The leader of the mightiest nation then said:

---

2   Some of the materials used for this Part are drawn from V. S. Mani, "Six Decades of the United Nations – An Indian Perception," Indian Journal of International Law, vol. 44 (2004), pp. 1-74, at pp. 2-9.

3   <http://www.trumanlibrary.org/whis…/large/sf_conference/un_sf7-1.htm>.

While these great states ["which had to muster the force necessary to defeat the conspiracy of the axis powers to dominate the world"] have a special responsibility to enforce the peace, their responsibility is based upon the obligations resting upon all states, large and small, not to use force in international relations, except in the defense of the law. The responsibility of the great states is to serve, and not to dominate the peoples of the world."

...

The essence of our problem here is to provide sensible machinery for the settlement of disputes among nations. Without this, peace cannot exist. We can no longer permit any nation, or group of nations, to attempt to settle their arguments with bombs and bayonets.

The presidential Proclamation of the United Nations Charter and Statute of the International Court of Justice issued by Truman on 31 October 1945 proclaimed and made public the UN Charter and the ICJ Statute "to the end that the same and every article and clause thereof may be observed and fulfilled with good faith, on and from" 24 October 1945, "by the United States of America and by the citizens of the United States of America and all other persons subject to the jurisdiction thereof."[4]

Addressing the inaugural plenary meeting of the UN General Assembly in London, British Prime Minister Clement Atlee, emphasised the rule of law in world affairs and asserted:

The United Nations Organisation must become the over-riding factor in foreign policy.
... [G]reat nobles and their retainers used to practice private war in disregard of the authority of the central government. The time came when private armies were abolished, when the rule of law was established throughout the length and breadth of this island. What has been done in Britain and in other countries on a small scale has now to be effected throughout the whole world.[5]

Atlee also underscored the fact that "the constitution of the new Organization is essentially realist in that it provides for the sanction of force to support the rule of law."[6]

However, the drafting of the UN Charter was pre-eminently an exercise of down-to-earth people wedded to the national interests they represented. Thus, although "[t]he United Nations took birth on a note of high idealism embodied in the noble wording of the Charter," Pundit Jawaharlal Nehru, Independent India's first Prime Minister, remarked on the floor of the General Assembly in 1960: "there was also a realization of the state of the postwar world as it was. Therefore, provision was

---

4   Available at the Yale Avelon Project, "A Decade of American Policy," <http://www.yale.edu/lawweb/avalon/decade/decad029.htm>.

5   GAOR, 1st Plenary Mtg, London, Thursday, 10 January 1946, at pp. 40-41.

6   *Ibid.*, p. 42.

made in the structure of the organization to balance certain conflicting urges. There were permanent members of the Security Council and there was provision for unanimity amongst the great powers. All this was not very logical. But it represented certain realities of the world as it was and because of this, we accepted them."[7]

Although India is recognised as a founding member of the United Nations, the Indian delegation that participated in the San Francisco Conference on International Organisation (UNCIO) did not represent the voice of the independent India – independence came only in 1947.[8] In fact, the world representation in the UNCIO was still lopsided. Of its original 50 members, 17 were from Europe, North America and Oceania, 20 were Latin American countries, 9 Asian and 4 from Africa (one of which from the White minority government). Did the UN Charter evolved in 1945, truly reflect the aims and aspirations of the vast unrepresented multitudes of peoples of Asia and Africa then under the colonial yoke?

Yet, many of the ideals embodied in the UN Charter were largely shared by the people of India and the rest of the developing world – freedom and human dignity, peace, international co-operation, and an equitable international economic and social order of human welfare. Making his first radio broadcast, as the Vice-President of the Interim Government of India, Jawaharlal Nehru, the architect of the independent India's foreign policy, proclaimed:

> We believe that peace and freedom are indivisible and the denial of freedom anywhere must endanger freedom elsewhere and lead to conflict and war. We are particularly interested in the emancipation of colonial and dependent territories and peoples and in the recognition in theory and practice of equal opportunities for all peoples... We seek no domination over others and we claim no privileged position over other peoples... The world, in spite of its rivalries and hatreds and inner conflicts, moves inevitably towards closer co-operation of free peoples and no call or group exploits another.[9]

More as a pragmatist than an idealist,[10] Nehru emphasised the role of international law and of the United Nations to facilitate it. An important goal of international

---

7   Prime Minister Nehru at the UN General Assembly, October 3, 1960. Available at <http://www.indianembassy.org/policy/Disarmament/disarm4.htm>.

8   More on this, see M. S. Rajan, "India and The Making of the UN Charter," International Studies (New Delhi), vol. 12 (1973), pp. 430-461, at pp. 434-435. Mrs. Vijayalakshmi Pundit (Nehru's sister, and a future – 1953 – President of the General Assembly) denounced the British-appointed Indian delegation at the venue of the Conference as lacking "the slightest representative capacity." Rajan, id. Professor Rajan also wrote a sequel to this essay. See his "India and the Making of the UN Charter-II," International Studies, vol. 36 (1999). pp. 3-16.

9   Jawaharlal Nehru's speech on the All India Radio, 7 September 1946, The Hindu (Madras), 9 September 1946.

10   There are many in India who describe Nehru as an idealist, and hence blame him for taking the Kashmir issue to the UN Security Council in 1947, without adequately assessing the implications of Cold War politics that bedevilled the functioning of the Council at that time.

law, according to him, was to promote "understanding of peace between nations," friendly relations among nations, elimination of war, peaceful settlement of disputes and international co-operation.[11] He was concerned that while international law had considerably expanded, its effectiveness had not in equal measure. It was a function of commitment to and acceptance of rule of law by all nations, big and small – a function of disarmament and an acceptable international order and international authority.[12] "There is not much of a choice left between some international order, international authority, and the ever present danger of a major war between nations,"[13] Nehru said.

The United Nations, in Nehru's perception, reflected "a very noble attempt to bring the world into some scheme of international law. The Charter of the United Nations is a very fine and inspiring document – I mean the objectives and ideals that it sets before itself."[14] Responding to the criticism that the UN had not lived up to its ideals, he remarked:

> That criticism is both justified and unjustified – justified because it is true and unjustified because the United Nations has only to function in the world as it is. It cannot function in some rarefied atmosphere, which is away from the world … Nevertheless, here is something, which keeps this ideal of some kind of world order, the international law applied to the world before us. It is true that in practice it is not applied, in the opinion of many, as justly and as equitably as it ought to be. Great interests pull the United Nations, this way or that… groups of nations pull it in various directions. It may be so, but the ideal is there and that itself is a great gain.[15]

Now, forty-four years later, is our assessment of the United Nations any different, even after the two wars of the 21st century?

---

11   Nehru's inaugural address at the establishment of the Indian Society of International Law on 29 August 1959, reprinted in Indian Journal of International Law, vol. 1 (1960-1961), pp. 509, ff..

12   Nehru, *Proceedings of the Annual Conference of the Indian Society of International Law, 1963*, pp. 4 ff, at pp. 4-5.

13   *Ibid.*, at p. 5.

14   Note. 12, at p. 7.

15   *Ibid.*, at p. 8. Nehru echoed these views when he addressed the UN General Assembly on October 3, 1960. He said: - "During these past fifteen years, the United Nations has often been criticised for its structure and for some of its activities. There criticisms have some justification behind them. But, looking at the broad picture, I think we can definitely say that the United Nations has amply justified its existence and repeatedly prevented the recurrent crises from developing into war. It has played a great role, and it is a little difficult now to think of this troubled world without the UN. If it had defects, they lay in the world situation itself which inevitably it mirrored. If there had been no United Nations today, our first task would be to create something of that kind. I should like, therefore, to pay my tribute to United Nations as a whole, even though I might criticize some aspects of it from time to time." <http://www.indianembassy.org/policy/Disarmament/disarm4.htm>.

B.   'Autonomy' of the UN and World Order

The above perception of the performance of the United Nations as a global international organisation evidently underscores in a large measure the nature and structure of the international 'community' and the problems it faces in evolving generally agreed world order goals, and the institutional frameworks through which it seeks to achieve those goals. At least three points of perspective may be made here.

First, in a world of sovereign states, neither the United Nations (or for that matter any international organisation) nor the regulatory framework it seeks to implement can truly be autonomous. Sovereign equality, peaceful co-existence, good faith and international co-operation, are no doubt at the foundation of international law and organisation. In a generally understood legal order, legal norms prompt compliance and behavioural restraint on the part of the subjects mainly in two ways: one, by a sense of duty to comply, or, two, by a cost-benefit (expectation of advantage or the detriment of punishment) analysis of compliance/non-compliance. As a general rule, both forms of restraints are rudimentary among the members of the international community. And they are as good as absent in situations of self-defined vital interests of members, particularly those of the more powerful ones.[16] Thus the nature and effectiveness of both international law and organisation are a function of coincidence of wills of states, Gregory Tunkin said long ago at the thick of the Cold War. There is no guarantee for the strength and stability of this state of coincidence. This conditions not only the legendary gap between the normative order (the promise) and ultimate compliance (the voluntary performance) – a phenomenon obtaining in all legal order – but also the 'tentative' nature of 'agreement' on both the form and substance of the international normative order itself. States remain the final individual arbiters, at any point in time, to determine how much of power of restraint they consider themselves to have conceded to the world order. After all, they retain the vital functions of global governance, including 'enforcement' of international norms they 'agree' on.

Second, while state sovereignty has suddenly become a much maligned term in the West since 1990's, the current Western debate points to only a partial story of absolutism and expansionism of the historically evolved concept of sovereignty

---

16   As Hoffmann asserts, "The trouble with international law [and, we may add, with international organisation] is, each time the more important interests of the members are in play 1) that the nature of the group rules out the first form of constraint, for ...the international milieu cannot practice the ethics of law alone; it has, at best, to find a compromise between those ethics and the ethics of combat, between Kant and Machiavelli. Only a group in which violence is effectively outlawed can afford to be guided by Kant alone; 2) that the second form of constraint ...does not always coincide with the imperatives of international law [and organisation], i.e., calculations of power and commands of law, instead of converging, tend to live on separate planes; 3) that coercion – through "self-help" – again has often nothing to do with the enforcement of law." See Stanley Hoffmann, "International Law and the Control of Force," in Karl W. Deutsch and Stanley Hoffmann, eds., *The Relevance of International Law: Essays in Honor of Leo Gross* (Schenkman Publishing, Cambridge, Mass., 1968), pp. 21-46, at 25-26.

in terms of abuse of state authority resulting in gross violations of human rights, particularly in small states (the prevalent human rights deprivations in some of the great countries are, of course, not considered 'gross' enough to render their sovereignty abhorrent[17]), yet claiming protection under an absolutist concept of sovereignty. Without taking away the human rights thrust of the debate (as there is some truth in it: the very functional justification for a state's claim to sovereignty is its responsibility to strive for the welfare of its people), it must be pointed out that the question is not simply whether the Westphalian concept of absolute sovereignty should cease to be acceptable. In fact, the so-called absolute sovereignty of small or weak countries ceased to be operational ages ago, ever since the Concert of Europe, ever since the great powers decided to run world affairs the way they wanted, with little or no regard for what the small states said or felt. In other words, the sovereignty of the latter never mattered, whereas the sovereignty of the great powers subsumed and transcended that of the small countries in every situation in which the two came into direct conflict. It is logical – even if, indeed, highly inequitable – that the transnational interests of the dominant groups in a powerful state should persuade those ruling groups to utilise all the power available with the state machinery to prevail over other states.[18] "The sovereignty of the great state today," wrote Laski during the 1930's, "is a technique for the protection of its imperialism. That imperialism is the outcome of its own internal relations which, given the distribution of effective demand within its boundaries, is driven to the competitive search for markets abroad in order to realise profit. Its sovereignty is the protective

---

17   See the Amnesty International Report of 1998 (*United States of American Rights for All 1998*, pp. 2-3) castigating the United States for "a persistent and widespread pattern of human rights violations." The report has been noted in Sean D. Murphy, "Contemporary Practice of the United States Relating to International Law," American Journal of International Law, vol. 99 (1999), pp. 657-659. In its first ever campaign against a Western country, the AI claims that the US authorities, notes Murphy, "failed to prevent repeated violations of basic human rights: the right to freedom from torture and cruel, inhuman or degrading treatment, the right to life and the right to freedom from arbitrary detention." AI says the majority of the victims of custodial crimes "have been members of racial or ethnic minorities ..." "US authorities persistently violate the fundamental human rights of people who have been forced by persecution to leave their countries and seek asylum." IA report further says: "International human rights standards exist for the protection of all people throughout the world, and the USA has been centrally involved in their development. ... While successive US governments have used these international human rights standards as a yardstick by which to judge other countries, they have not consistently applied those same standards at home."
     For a critique of the first US report to the Human Rights Committee, see Upendra Baxi, " 'A Work in Progress?' – The United State Report to the United Nations Human Rights Committee," Indian Journal of International Law, vol. 36, (1996), pp. 34-53.

18   Laski: "The State has sovereign rights; and those who manipulate it will too often cause it to be used for the protection of existing rights. The two get identified; the dead hand of effete ancestralism falls with a resounding thud on the living hopes of to-day." Harold J. Laski, *Studies in the Problem of Sovereignty* (First pub. 1917, 1997 reprint published by Routeledge, London/NY), Chapter I on "Sovereignty of the State," at p. 22.

armament of that adventure. The international law [and the international organisation, one might add] it recognises is, therefore, always hampered and frustrated by the logical requirements of imperialism. It cannot part with the control of any vital function, the scale of its armament, the right to make war, its hold on colonies and spheres of influence, its power over tariffs, currency, migration, labour conditions, because to do so is to threaten, internally, the relations of production its sovereignty exists to maintain."[19] Thus the sovereignty of the great powers is one of "creeping" character, transcending their political or territorial boundaries, but dictated by the interests of the dominant groups in those countries.[20] It asserts itself, holding the entire world of small powers to ransom. The small powers today hold their sovereignty rather zealously for several reasons. One, most of them have emerged independent after a sustained, often bloody, freedom struggle. Two, now that they have won their political independence, they still have to continue fighting for their economic independence,[21] including protection from the "creeping," expansionist economic sovereignty of the great countries. Three, this struggle coupled with the urgency of economic development demands international cooperation, not predatory interference, from the developed countries, including the great powers.

Third, the small countries well realise that the modern concept of sovereignty is issue-based. Hence their dependence on international law and organisation, not just for their own security, but more importantly because they need them as instruments conditioning and catalysing their development through international cooperation. In fact, the relevance of or dependence on international law and organisation are inversely proportionate to the military and economic might of a state. The less powerful a state is, the more is its reliance on international law and

---

19   Harold J. Laski, *A Grammar of Politics* (3rd. edn. 1934, 1997 reprint, Routledge, London/NY), p. xxi.

20   Hence the propensity of the United States, the sole super power, to unilateralism. A recent (yet pre-Iraq war of 20 March 2003) study identifies the following issue areas in respect of which "US predilections for unilateral behaviour" are the strongest over the years: international law, the United Nations, nuclear policy, international monetary coordination, and the environment. On the issue of peacekeeping, the US "vacillates between multilateral and unilateral strategies. In the area of human rights, the US is a party to many multilateral human rights regimes, "although the US Senate qualified US commitments by attaching reservations." "Moreover the United States remains outside several important human rights regimes." See David M. Malone and Yuen Foong Khong, eds., *Unilateralism and US Foreign Policy: International Perspectives* (Lynne Rienner, Boulder/London, 2003), p. 422.

21   Speaking at a joint session of the US Congress on 13 October 1949, India's Prime Minister Jawaharlal Nehru said: "We have achieved political freedom but our revolution is not yet complete and is still in progress, for political freedom without the assurance of the right to live and to pursue happiness, which economic progress alone can bring, can never satisfy a people. Therefore, our immediate task is to raise the living standards of our people, to remove all that comes in the way of the economic growth of the nation." Available at <http://www.indianembassy.org/indu...us/nehru_congress_Oct_13_1949.htm>.

organisation. As Dag Hammarskjold said in 1960, it is the small powers which need the United Nations, not the great ones. In an interface between multilateralism and unilateralism, the unilateralism of the great powers holds sway, unless of course they decide to pursue a course of enlightened unilateralism. Some of the small countries may have failed to live up to the demands of good governance and realisation of human rights, both of which require considerable economic resources. However, the 'more fortunate' members of the international community have for their part grossly failed to live up to their commitments of international cooperation (Articles 55 & 56 of the UN Charter). Their failure to promote international transfer of resources has been one of the contributory factors to occurrence of the phenomenon of 'failed states' in the 'developing' parts of the world. Having patently failed to live up to their Charter commitments, these powerful states now resort to unilateral use of force on grounds of 'humanitarianism'. Indeed, the label of 'humanitarian intervention' has become a convenient façade for the powerful to pursue their hegemonic goals in gay abandon. Thus, the sovereignty of the powerful subsumes and is far greater than that of the weak.

An international organisation founded on the vortex of the dynamic clash of sovereignties of great powers is also expected to plough through it, often surrendering itself to their mercy. Very clearly, as Inis Claude Jr. remarked some time ago, it is a rudderless ship thrown into the troubled waters of history, commanded by a succession of men, each of whom has his own idea of where to go. This is the principal phenomenon that conditions the transience of coincidence of state sovereignties, and often leads to a perception of 'fragmentation' of the international system – the so-called 'fragmentation' of international law and international organisation.

C.   The UN: A Functionalist View

Paradoxically, however, the UN as an international entity does perform some useful role, even if in fits and starts. As a phenomenon currently representing the crest of multilateralism,[22] the United Nations performs a variety of functions. It is a standing international conference highlighting world problems – bilateral, regional, and global – and often evolving global policies for states to implement, and even providing a "centre for harmonising actions of nations."[23] At best, the UN presents a framework for coordination of national action on global problems. It provides fora where conflicts get aired, with the disputant parties letting their steam off, and at times, in the process, getting issues clarified and eventually helping themselves to find resolution. It offers a range of dispute settlement mechanisms that the parties to a dispute could utilise, should they be so inclined or suitably persuaded. It serves

---

22   This does not mean that the UN cannot be manipulated by a great power to achieve its unilateral goals. In a given context, a UN action could subserve these unilateral goals, with unilateralism subsuming multilateralism. Yet on rare occasions – such as the case of US-UK invasion of Iraq in March 2003 – it could resolutely refuse to give its stamp of approval, it could refuse to bow down before the sole surviving super power!

23   Article 1(4) of the UN Charter.

as a focal point of interactions amongst states on all issues that bother them. It helps to highlight and spread awareness on many global problems.

Viewed in terms of its Charter, the United Nations performs two categories of functions, namely, international norm-setting and operational activities pursuant to the Purposes and Principles of the UN Charter. On both counts, the performance of the United Nations has been a mixed bag, although in the realm of norm setting, its successes have been more noteworthy. This reflects the desire of the international community to forge and share some common values for the common good of its teeming millions, yet a failure of the international ruling elites to live up to them, often for fear of losing their respective positions of power. A case in point is the gap between human rights norms and national implementation of these norms.

3.   Non-governmental International Organisations

The non-governmental international organisations (INGO's) more broadly represent what Myres S. MacDougal used to call, the "world constitutive process." They highlight the vibrant existence and operationality of transnational pluralism. Pluralism in itself recognises the existence of multiplicity and diversity of interests of individuals and groups. In view of their non-recognition or inadequate recognition, the need for more effective realisation of these interests motivates individuals and groups to come together and even transnationally organise into NGOs visible and operational at the international level. They often function either transnationally following up their respective mandates or as international pressure groups on governments, and intergovernmental organisations, or indeed, both. Some develop their focus and orientations as their members' mandate. Thus, Amnesty International focuses on transnational protection of civil and political rights – "prisoners of conscience." Until recently, it consistently resisted recognising the importance of promotion of economic and social rights, as also of the role of non-state entities in causing human rights deprivations. In view of widespread criticism, a rectification/reorientation process has recently been under way. The exclusive preoccupation with some of these INGO's is understandable – this is a 'locational hazard.' There has been an undue emphasis in the West on civil rights, almost to the exclusion of economic, social and cultural rights. (We in India are glad that our Supreme Court has so far sought to make a fair balance between the various categories of rights while interpreting the constitutional "right to life and personal liberty.")

There are INGO's with a partisan role of largely promoting private industry – international dredgers association, international chamber of commerce, and the various international guilds. There are also INGO's subserving the cause of some governments, because of their capacity to achieve transnational penetration to reach out to the people, often without the state machinery in the target state being aware of such penetration. In such cases, these INGO's play a dysfunctional role for the process of international organisation. They render any neat functional distinction between them and IGO's nearly impossible.

With the concept of 'civil society,' an interactive space is being created between the IGO's and INGO's, although one would object to the term 'civil society' being exclusively, and perhaps wrongly applied to INGO's. The term 'civil society' must refer to true representatives of a people, not these voluntary 'clubs,' some good, some bad, and many indifferent. This notwithstanding, one hopes that this development would further strengthen the process of international organisation.

4.   'Fragmentation' of the International System

The conceptual insistence on universality and universal application of the normative framework of the international system is more popular among international lawyers than among any other tribe. To many of them, it is a religion, unquestioned and unquestionable. Such a 'fundamentalist' approach to the international system ignores the reality of pluralistic tendencies in that system, as also such tendencies within each nation which over time find affinity in similar group interests outside the nation transcending the political and territorial boundaries. Very often these tendencies find expression in transnational groups, as well as in the concept of state sovereignty itself, which, as seen earlier, often represents the interests of the dominant groups within a nation now occupying the seat of power. In the political relations between a powerful state and a weaker state, the zealous and emphatic assertion of sovereignty by the latter against the former is as much an effective use of sovereignty as a legal and moral shield, as the assertion of an inclusive interest by the former in justification of its interventionist policies vis-à-vis the latter. The powerful state in seeking to penetrate/subsume the sovereignty of the weaker state is in fact seeking to claim a more expansive use of its sovereign power to the detriment of the latter's interest.

This being the reality, the principle of sovereign equality enshrined in Article 2(1) of the UN Charter gets eroded all the time. The Charter is not of course operationally equipped to promote the principle. The explicit recognition of the P5's power of veto under Article 27 stands in the way. The principle of supremacy of Charter obligations embodied in Article 103 deals a further severe blow to sovereign equality. Politically at least, it tends to legitimize and blindly seeks to establish the superior binding effect of Security Council decisions adopted at the instance of or with the connivance of the P5. Thus there is a normative framework for the non-P5 countries, and there is another for the P5. This is duality of normative frameworks based on power-political relations. Indeed, this situation runs all through the Charter system. Maybe, this is why we say that the UN only mirrors the world at large! This is fragmentation based on power relations.

'Fragmentation' has traditionally resulted from the freedom of action enjoyed by states by virtue of their sovereignty, despite the reining in by the International Court of Justice in the *Anglo-Norwegian Fisheries* case (1951).[24] Thus a multilateral

---

24   In this case, the Court's ruling has had the effect of casting the burden of proof of legitimacy and validity on the state committing a unilateral act that has international consequences. *ICJ Reports 1951*, p. 116, at p. 132.

treaty does not normally lead to establishment of one single legal framework, but a series of interlapping bilateral subsystems, thanks to the facility of reservations. The situation has not improved even after the onset of the famous 'compatibility' require imposed by the Vienna Convention on the Law of Treaties, 1969. The system of reservations even following Articles 19 and 20 of the Conventions retains the freedom of states to create multiplicity of regimes even while being parties to a multilateral treaty.

Then of course there is the maze of legal webs within webs represented by the phenomenon known as international customary law. It is by now recognised and judicially noted that there can be customary law in existence at three levels – universal,[25] regional[26] and local (bilateral)![27] The situation arising from the 'general principles of law' is no better. Despite the historical divide between the Anglo-Saxon system and the Continental system, even within each of these systems, there is a diversity of subsystems.

However, as luck would have it, there arose one important normative development that would contribute to universal constitutionalism in the realm of evolution of a truly global legal framework. This was the emergence of the concept of *Jus Cogens* or the peremptory norms of international law. A valuable contribution of the International Law Commission, the concept now embodied in Article 53 of the Vienna Convention on the Law of Treaties envisions a framework of international law presided over by a set of peremptory norms, whose validity derives from the bedrock of the general acceptance of their special 'higher' status by the international community of states. Although Article 53 limits their applicability only to determine the validity or nullity of treaty provisions militating against these peremptory norms, it can *a priori* be argued that since treaties represent joint or coordinate acts of states, by the underlying logic of Article 53, *Jus Cogens* shall determine the validity or otherwise of all acts of states, whether collective, or unilateral. They shall equally determine the validity of the conduct of all subjects of international law, the international organisations, NGO's, and TNC's included. Perhaps, *Jus Cogens* are the first stepping-stones towards an eventual build-up of international constitutionalism. To say this is not to ignore the formidably gigantic boulders that lie along the path. There are many questions that remain to be answered by the international community in a definitive manner, questions that the ILC shunned to answer, or did not gather enough courage even to attempt to answer. How does one identify *Jus Cogens*? How are they different from lesser principles, and still lesser rules – should their birth tend to give us a feeling of rearrangement of the various rules and principles into a pyramidal structure? What are the *Jus Cogens* of each branch of international law, such as human rights law, humanitarian law, the law of international organisation, the law of international transport, international trade law, international economic law, the law of dispute settlement, international space law, international environmental law, and so on? To what extent do the UN Char-

25   *North Sea Continental Cases, ICJ Reports 1969*, p. 3.
26   The *Asylum* case, *ICJ Reports 1950*, pp. 276-77.
27   The *Rights of Passage over Indian Territory* case, *ICJ Reports 1960*, p. 6.

ter principles, the principles of Friendly Relations,[28] etc contribute to the making of *Jus Cogens*, and of international constitutionalism? Are *Jus Cogens* any different from principles and rules imposing on subjects of international law, obligations *erga omnes?*

5.   Concluding Remarks

In the final analysis, the intense and constant transnational interpenetration of social forces, whether governmental or non-governmental or even a mixed variety, makes it impossible to identify any force or set of forces to be continually contributing to the 'world constitutive process' – except perhaps the general yearning for peace and for cooperative endeavours for furtherance of human welfare. The latter goal values remain the chief driving force for the creation and sustenance of international frameworks for the promotion and harmonisation of action amongst states and amongst transnationally operating groups of individuals.

There can be a broad convergence of interests that permits evolution of a normative framework at the international and regional levels. The emergence of the concept of *Jus Cogens* may represent such a process of building-up of world constitutionalism brick by brick. But the chances of implementation of such a normative order on the ground are riddled with fissiparous tendencies and unilateralist attitudes on the part of states. Thus, constitutionalism remains a largely misleading description of a process of norm creation detached from a definitive framework of implementation that is nearly non-existent. While the major wars such as the First and the Second World Wars have led to experiments at world constitutionalism, such as the League of Nations and the United Nations, the currents and cross-currents of centrifugal and centripetal forces have made it almost impossible for the international community – unlike the national communities – to evolve a sure mechanism and methodology for translating the normative framework into a framework for community institutional action. The task remains a far cry, but the lure of the idea shall remain intensely seductive.

---

28   See UN General Assembly Resolution 2625 (xxv) of 24 October 1970.

10. Universalism, Regionalism and Localism in the Age of Globalization

Władysław Czapliński

Universal application of international law seemed to be a dream of statesmen and international lawyers for centuries. The idea of a global community governed by a uniform legal system was fascinating and it could bring order in international relations. Interestingly, a few authors only wholly rejected the idea of universalism, indicating as important factors of decentralization: some trends towards an autonomous development of regional international order in the New World (which started in the end of 19th century), the formula of civilized nations applied in Article 36 of the Statute of the PCIJ[1] and subsequently adopted also in the Statute of the ICJ, or the development of the communist system in Europe, leading allegedly to the establishment of a new socialist international law.

The idea of world government was present in the period of the League of Nations, which was in fact the first attempt to organize the whole of the international community. It is remarkable that the League was not reluctant to promote the development of regional norms of international law except specific regulations in the field of international commercial law. This is clearly visible from the documents relating to relations between the League and regional organizations. At the same time, however, multilateral conventions can be found which include dispositions providing for possible derogations by particular (regional) arrangements.

As the experiment of the League failed, it was replaced by the new order of the United Nations, which was expected to become a new system of collective security. Unfortunately, the competition between the two political, economic, and social systems (Western democracy *versus* communism) led to inefficiency of the system. Moreover, the UN, including the Security Council, constituted an important field of confrontation, characterized by the abuse of the power of veto by the permanent members. Even during the period of the Cold War and the subsequent period of détente in international relations (which have been commonly called an era of

---

1   In fact, the notion of "civilised nations" appeared in international relations during the Berlin congress in 1885, to enable the partition of colonial territories in Africa. The issue was discussed also at the Lausanne session of the IDI in 1888.

Ronald St. John Macdonald & Douglas M. Johnston (eds.), Towards World Constitutionalism, *pp. 255-271.*
© *2005 Koninklijke Brill NV. Printed in The Netherlands.* ISBN 90 04 14612 1.

peaceful coexistence), the international community created certain mechanisms to respect the unity of fundamental principles of the international legal order. Their expression can be found in Resolution 2625(XXV) of the UNGA[2] and in the Final Act of the CSCE of 1 July 1975.[3]

1.   The Notion of Regional Norms in International Law: Issues of Law-Making

The vast majority of authors dealing with the structure of the international legal order construct their ideas referring to a dichotomy between universal and particular norms. As H. Kelsen explained, universal law means the set of norms that are binding upon all States, while particular norms are binding upon a certain limited number of States only.[4] There is no unanimity as to whether universal norms can be identified with general ones, and in particular with regional ones; for the purpose of this chapter such identification has been adopted. Certain authors indicate that the international legal system consists of the norms situated on more than two levels, adding also local norms. The latter category encompasses plurilateral (i.e. multilateral of limited scope) and bilateral norms. In any case, regional norms are not synonymous with special norms of international law, which constitute exceptions to the universal ones and apply to a limited number of subjects of international law.

Usually the expression the regional norms of international law is used in connection with the set of norms binding upon the group of States situated in the same geographical region and constituting a compact and cohesive structure. The geographical classification can be combined with political and social factors, what allows the inclusion into the specific regional groups the States which are relatively far away from the geographical region but represent the same political system or level of economic model. Such understanding of regionalism can be identified in the practice of the UN, e.g. in the composition of the Security Council and ICJ.

According to a traditional concept, mostly treaties create regional international law. The right to conclude international agreements has always belonged to the prerogatives of the States and has never been seriously denied; the Final Act of the CSCE, also with respect to particular international instruments, has expressly confirmed it. However, the question has sometimes been raised in the context of regional international law which treaties can be classified as regional ones. We agree with the view expressed *inter alia* by P. de Visscher within the IDI[5] accord-

---

2   Declaration on Principles of International Law Concerning Friendly Relations and Co-operation among States in Accordance with the Charter of the United Nations, 24 October 1970.

3   See on that topic e.g. P. van Dijk, The Helsinki Final Act – Basis for a pan-European system?, *NethYBIL* 11(1980), p. 97 ff, and authors quoted there.

4   H. Kelsen, *Principles of International Law*, New York etc. 1966 (2nd ed.), at 228-229.

5   AIDI 1961, at 223, 283. Cf. also G. Tunkin, *Teorya mezhdunarodnogo prava*, Moscow 1970, at 107-108.

ing to which the category of regional agreements covers exclusively treaties, which are open for accession to all the States of the specific region (of multilateral rather than plurilateral nature). Regional treaties should also be distinguished from local (subregional) and bilateral agreements, although some writers seemed to put them on similar footing[6] because of a comparable structure and limited number of parties. This opinion is not correct, as the formation of custom is always much more complicated than that of treaties, and the fact that the number of parties bound by the norms is similar is not sufficient to create identity of both notions.

It is universally accepted (and confirmed by the jurisprudence of the World Courts[7]) that customary rules can exist not only on universal, but also on regional level. The formation and existence of particular (regional, special etc.) customs should be ascertained in a similar way to universal customary law, i.e. both constant, State practice and *opinio iuris* must be evaluated. Stronger evidence of the binding force of the regional customs is required, including an active participation by all the States concerned.[8] Examples of regional customary norms are: diplomatic asylum, Calvo clause, *uti possidetis* principle in relation to Africa[9] etc. In the *Western Sahara* case the ICJ indicated that the life of the local population was governed by "local norms belonging to Arab and Islamic system", but it did not refer to any specific norm. In that context we can quote also the customary rules in EC law, like the right of the State to be represented within the Council of the UE by the State Secretary instead of the Minister, or direct effect of directives. In the context of the preceding observations one can remark only that it is disputable whether EC law can be treated as a regional system, as it is closed for accession for third States without the consent of all the Member States. Finally, the CSCE/OSCE process and its importance for the customary law-making process must be mentioned. The prevailing view is that the Helsinki Act of 1975 is a political instrument, but it constitutes an important step towards the codification of customary law. The principles embodied in the Act refer in fact to general international law and correspond mostly with the principles of the UN Charter and Declaration on Principles

---

6   A. D'Amato, *The Concept of Custom in International Law*, Ithaca-London 1971, at 250; compare also M. Soerensen, Principes de droit international public, *RCADI* 101(1960), at 43, in the context of similarities between particular treaties and customary law. This opinion is not correct, as the formation of custom is always much more complicated than that of treaties, and the fact that the number of parties bound by the norms is similar is not sufficient to create identity of both notions.

7   See in particular V.D. Degan, *Sources of International Law*, The Hague-Boston-London 1997, pp. 243 ff, and K. Wolfke, *Custom in Present International Law*, Dordrecht-Boston-London 1993, pp. 88 ff.

8   The ICJ in the Asylum case, ICJ Rep. 1950, at 276, proposed the traditional test. However, we could suggest that it should be liberalized and acquiescence could be sufficient to impose the binding force of the specific customary norms upon the States not directly participating in the law-creating practice but not manifestly opposing to them. Such a proposal is even more probable in case of regional custom (in the meaning of geographical proximity) than in case of other particular norms based upon political, social, religious or economic factors.

(Resolution 2625) of 1970. The Act gives also a new interpretation of the principles, which allows the development of the set of regional European norms.

It is disputable whether the regional norms can be of peremptory nature. The definition formulated in Article 53 of the Vienna Convention on the Law of Treaties suggests that *jus cogens* is composed exclusively of norms of general international law which are accepted and recognized by the international community of States as a whole. However, the wording of the provision indicates that the definition has been drafted exclusively for the purposes of the said Convention. The notion of peremptory norms developed since that time and acquired new dimension. Theoretically we could accept the existence of regional *jus cogens*. The examples *in statu nascendi* of such norms could be constitutional instruments of the Council of Europe including in particular the European Convention for the Protection of Human Rights and Fundamental Freedoms of 1950, and a customary principle of democracy and rule of law which acquires the status superior to other norms in Euro-Atlantic legal space. However, the acceptance of those norms is not really general even on regional level. The European Convention allows reservations (although no restrictions can be imposed upon the core human rights embodied in it) and limitations on specific rights if the State interest so requires. The right to democracy and rule of law is relatively widespread over the region, but is has not been implemented effectively and consistently – the example of Belarus is certainly the most instructive, but we could also quote the position of the European Union towards such States responsible for grave breaches of human rights as China or Cuba.

Treaties and custom remain the principal sources of regional law, exactly like in the case of universal international law. However, it seems that under contemporary international law other sources of regional law can be found, in particular general principles and acts of international regional organizations.

2.   Practical Consequences of Regional and Particular Norms in the International System: Conflict of Norms

The problem of hierarchy of international legal norms is interesting and controversial.[10] It is generally admitted that – contrary to domestic law – all the international norms have the same importance and legal force. We have to discuss therefore

---

9   Although the ICJ in the Burkina *Faso/Mali* case (ICJ Rep. 1986, at 565) referred to that principle as universal, it was difficult to find its application in practice outside Africa before the Yugoslav crisis. Then it was applied in the opinions of the Badinter Committee Nos.2 and 3, and finally in the Lithuanian declaration of independence, in connection with the Wilna region. Cf. W. Czapliński, International Legal Aspects of the Relations of Poland with Neighboring States, AVR 36(1998), p. 437-438.

10   Cf. our stance on the problem expressed in W. Czaplinski, G. Danilenko, Conflicts of Norms in International Law, *NethYBIL* 21(1990), p. 3 ff; see also Ph. Weckel, *La concurrence des traités dans l'ordre international*, Paris 1990; S.A. Sadat-Akhavi, *Methods of Resolving Conflicts between Treaties*, Leiden-Boston 2004; E. Roucounas, Engagements parallèles et contradictories, *RCADI* 206(1987), p. 13 ff.

whether and to what extent the same rules can be applied to resolve conflicts between different sources and norms of international law, including conflicts between
universal and regional instruments. It seems to us that neither clear rules establishing or confirming a general practice as a constituting element of custom can be
formulated, nor convincing evidence of *opinio iuris* can be found for cases in which
no conflict rule is included in the agreement concerned.

The situation is clear if the conflict rules are contained in the agreements
themselves. Regional agreements, in particular the ones relating to regional security, often contain special provisions concerning their relationship to the UN
Charter, in accordance with Article 103. The model provisions are Articles 1, 4 and
20 of the OAS Charter, and Article 1 of the NATO Pact.[11] They establish also their
priority over other regional arrangements. Other treaties dispose that they do not
alter the rights and obligations of the parties arising from other agreements (bilateral or regional), which are compatible with the treaties concerned. In some cases
more detailed regulations can be proposed. The best example is Article 311.2 of
the UNCLOS. The same Convention provides for the parties a possibility to conclude special agreements dealing with the protection of the marine environment
(Article 237). The said goal can probably be achieved in the best way through the
concluding of regional instruments. The agreements of that kind will enjoy priority
over the general treaty; however, in that case the basis for the solution proposed is
the *lex specialis* principle. Some multilateral treaties provide for the possibility of
concluding special agreements between their parties, which are intended to keep
in force specific regimes existing between some of the parties to the main treaty
or can by their very nature better realize the goals of the agreement. Examples can
be found *inter alia.* in the conventions concluded in the framework of the Hague
Conference on Private International Law or in two conventions concluded in the
framework of the International Atomic Energy Agency: the 1986 Convention on
Early Notification of a Nuclear Accident and the 1986 Convention on Assistance
in the Case of a Nuclear Accident or radiological Emergency.[12] Finally, there is also
an option to conclude inter se agreements, including the ones on regional level,
that modify the universal treaty in the relations between the parties to that special
agreement. The example of the provision concerning such a special agreement can
be found in Article 311.3 of the UNCLOS. The special agreement in question must
be compatible at least with the object and purpose of the UNCLOS, cannot affect
the position of other parties to the Convention nor affect the fundamentals of the
law of the sea.

The rules governing the conflicts between treaties formulated in Article 30 of
the Vienna Convention on the Law of Treaties do not draw any distinction whether
the treaties concerned are universal or particular; it might be however disputable

---

11   Interestingly, the provisions of Art. 1 of the Warsaw Pact and Art. IIe of the Charter
     of the OAU – now abrogated – contained corresponding clauses, while Art. 3 of the
     Constitutive Act of the African Union of 11 July 2000 refers only to taking due account
     of the Charter of the United Nations and the Universal Declaration of Human Rights.

12   UNTS 1439, p. 276, and 1457, p. 134, respectively.

whether they cover all the possible situations. In particular they do not provide specific guidelines for the state agencies how to decide in the cases of conflicting treaties if none of them contain any disposition on the matter. Modern international law rejects the absolute and unconditional application of the principle of the priority of the earlier treaty, as the States are free to establish and to shape their mutual relations. We could favour the *lex specialis* rule, which has often been applied by the Hague Courts. However, different solution can be adopted with respect to the situation of a later plurilateral agreement modifying the provision of the earlier one. Generally the conclusion of such a special agreement will be possible if the main treaty allows this, and if the new agreement does not infringe on the position of the other party to that treaty. Two distinct hypotheses can be considered. According to the first one, several (but not all) parties to the multilateral treaty conclude an agreement to facilitate the application of the earlier treaty. Such agreement would certainly be acceptable. The latter one consists of the conclusion of the agreement that is in fact *contra* the earlier multilateral treaty. The international legal authors classify such an act as a violation (breach) of that treaty with all the consequences arising from international law. If so, we do not think that the *lex specialis* rule should be universally applied in case of conflicts between special and universal international law.

It seems also that the same conflict rules embodied in the Vienna Convention apply to the conflicts between two regional agreements concerning the same topic, as most of them are also multilateral. In the case of two subsequent treaties concerning the same subject matter, a later treaty supersedes an earlier one; however, we can also suppose that the arguments can be found in favour of another solution: in case of the overlapping agreements, a later treaty will not affect earlier ones. This means that in practice the decision resolving the possible conflict will be taken on the basis of evaluation of the effectiveness and the real needs of the parties.

As to the conflicts between customary rules, they should be resolved in accordance with the *lex specialis* rule which means that special customary rules (in particular regional ones) have priority over general/universal ones.[13] Special customary rules require special proof of acceptance, stricter than universal ones, and so also must changes to such rules. We can easily consider the possibility of emergence of special customary rules as the exception to the general rules. However, they can bind exclusively among the group of States that are bound by special ties or relationships. The possibility of creating of such regional/particular customs is limited in the domains, which from their very nature call for a universal solution, e.g. limiting the freedom of the high seas or of outer space. The resolving of conflicts between customary laws is more difficult than those relating to concurring treaties, and requires more detailed analysis. We must consider the existence

---

13   The ICJ in the Right of Passage case, ICJ Rep.1960 at 43, took the same position, where the Court ascertained the existence of the local customary rule in favor of Portugal, and then declined to consider the possible content of the universal customary rules. As to the writers, cf. K. Wolfke, Custom, p. 95; M. Akehurst, Custom as a Source of International Law, *BYBIL* 47(1974-75), p. 29.

of State practice and *opinio iuris*, and subsequently we must define the temporal scope of application of the new norm, as it develops within a certain time. In the case of treaties we can pinpoint the moment of their entry into force. The same is not always true with respect to customary rules. Because of that reason the role of the principle of non-retroactivity of customary law is less important than in the case of international agreements. Finally, one must consider whether the specific special rule is opposable to the specific State.

We do not see any reason as well why treaties could not be modified by customary rules, including a possible amendments or changes of multilateral conventions by particular practice. That would require the emergence of practice within a clearly defined group of States linked by regional or other – similar – special relations. The modification is possible – in analogy to the law of treaties – if it does not affect the position of the other parties to the convention in question, and it does not destroy the object and purpose of the treaty as a whole. There are no obstacles to elaborate special customs *infra legem*, in order to facilitate the implementation of the treaty or to fill the possible gaps.

We can conclude here that the status of universal, regional, subregional and local norms has not changed in the recent period. No revolutionary changes in the law-making process, sources of law and approach to the relationship between universal and particular law can be noticed. Contemporary international legal writers have not devoted much attention to the issue. We turn now to the question of substantive norms on regional level, addressing two issues: decentralisation of the use of force and the role of regional arrangements in that respect and protection of human rights.

3.   Use of Force[14]

The end of the Cold War introduced a number of important changes into international law. The regulation of the use of force in international relations certainly belongs to domains widely influenced and modified by those changes. The problem is even more acute nowadays, when the tendency towards decentralization of the use of force in international relations is present. This poses important question

---

14   As the issue is currently of great importance, the number of publications is still growing. We can quote here e.g. Ch. Walter, *Vereinte Nationen und Regionalorganisationen*, Springer Berlin a.o. 1996; C. Schmolinsky, *Friedenssicherung durch regionale Systeme kollektiver Sicherheit*, Berlin 2000; D. Geyrhalter, *Friedenssicherung durch Regionalorganisationen ohne Beschluss des Sicherheitsrates*, Münster 2002; H. Kühne, *Friedenssicherung durch regionale Organisationen in Europa*, Frankfurt/M. 1998; D. Sarooshi, *The United Nations and the Development of the Development of Collective Security : The Delegation by the UN Security Council of its Chapter VII Powers*, Oxford 1999; A. Abass, *Regional Organisations and the Development of Collective Security*, Oxford-Portland 2004; E. de Wet, *The Chapter VII Powers of the United Nations Security Council*, Oxford-Portland 2004, pp. 256 ff; J. Frowein, R. Wolfrum, Security Council Control over Regional Action, *MPYBUNL* 1(1997), p. 129; Ch. Walter, Security Council Control over Regional Action, *MPYBUNL* 1(1997), p. 1.

about the relationship between the universal regulation of the UN Charter and other regulations including customary international law.

The rule formulated in Article 2.4 of the UN Charter is clear and unequivocal: States should refrain from the use of force in their mutual relations, except in two situations: when force is necessary to resist to an armed attack (Article 51 of the Charter – self-defence), and when the UN Security Council recommended or at least accepted the use of force on the basis of Chapter VII of the Charter. We leave aside here a dispute as to the meaning of the disposition that the ban on the use of force should concern exclusively the use in the manner contrary to the aims of the Charter, as from our perspective this dispute is of secondary importance. The said provisions seem to set up a monopoly of decision on the possible use of force in the hands of the UNSC. There is, however, one more provision dealing with the use of force: Chapter VIII conferred some powers in that respect to regional organizations.

According to their role in international relations, regional organizations can be divided into three categories:[15] regional organizations *sensu stricto* within the meaning of Chapter VIII of the UN Charter; regional organizations *sensu lato*, including bodies dealing with political, economic, social and cultural cooperation; and regional organizations as arrangements of a subsystem of international law.

The basic characteristics of regional organizations are: they are established on the basis of regional multilateral agreements, they initiate or directly elaborate international instruments enabling international cooperation; they initiate or implement regional processes of codification, harmonization, and unification of law, both on the domestic and international plan; their practice constitutes important element of establishing of customary law; they can enact regional norms on the basis of their law-making powers, creating therefore particular international legal norms.[16]

Chapter VIII of the UN Charter details certain requirements which should be fulfilled by the regional organizations serving as subsystems of the collective security systems: the object of their activity should be defined as matters relating to the maintenance of international peace and security; the competence should be limited to the specific region; their fundamental functions should encompass the pacific settlement of international disputes (between the States of the region); the organizations should act conform to the aims and principles of the UN Charter. The organizations fulfilling those criteria can be found in all the regions of the world; Article of the OAS Charter is the only disposition stating that the OAS is the regional organization in the framework of the UN. In fact, however, no organization strictly corresponds with all the criteria set up in Chapter VIII.

There are several possibilities of taking action by regional organizations. Firstly, they can act on the basis of an agreement concluded by them with the Security Council, granting them an *a priori* consent to react to all the violations and threats

---

15   R. Yakemtchouk, Le régionalisme et l'ONU, *RGDIP* 59(1955), at 406.

16   T. Jasudowicz, *Normy regionalne w prawie międzynarodowym*, Toruń 1983, at 55.

to peace and security in the region. Secondly, the organization can act with a prior consent of the UNSC given in the particular cases. Thirdly, it can take action without any consent of the UNSC, and seek for such acceptance after the military action.

While considering the position of the regional organizations entitled to use armed force, the following aspects should be addressed:

(a)   Whether the regional organizations can act independently of the decisions of the UNSC, or their powers are strictly limited to the implementation of their decisions;

(b)   Whether the decision to act can be taken by the statutory bodies of the respective international organization prior to the decision of the UNSC, or a posterior acceptance by the latter is also possible;

(c)   What are the criteria of the decision-making by the regional organization;

(d)   Who bears international responsibility for illegal acts of the organization? What is the scope of possible reparation by those member States, which participated in those activities?

(e)   How should the notion of "regional arrangements or agencies" in Article 52 of the Charter be interpreted? Does it cover "the coalition of the willing" acting in the First Gulf War of 1990-1991, and in the current Iraq conflict, or should it be interpreted narrowly to cover formal organizations only?

Contemporary practice with respect to the use of force by regional organizations can be limited to two cases: the intervention of the NATO in Kosovo, and the intervention of the ECOWAS in the conflicts in Liberia and Sierra Leone. In the case of West Africa, where the operations by the ECOWAS were aimed at the elimination of the military governments and termination of mass persecutions of the civilian populations, the UNSC accepted a posteriori the intervention of the ECOMOG in Liberia in Resolutions 788(1992) and 866(1993), thanking the Community for its role in the peaceful solution of the conflict and establishing the observance mission. The intervention in Sierra Leone was much less transparent. In the most important Resolution 1132(1997) the SC supported the efforts of the ECOWAS to restore peace and to strengthen the constitutional order; the following resolutions were much less enthusiastic, their evaluation is neither clear nor univocal. However, in all the resolutions concerning West Africa the ECOWAS activities were appreciated and none of them condemn the Community. In the contrary, there was a strong opposition by two of the permanent members of the UNSC against the action of NATO against Yugoslav forces in Kosovo.[17] The action was taken in response to the activities of the Yugoslav Army against the civilian population of Albanian origin, which included also the destruction of villages and mass expulsion of local population. After nearly one year (the hostilities started in March 1997, and the bombings of the Yugoslav troops in late March 1998, after Yugoslavia had

---

17   See on different legal aspects of the intervention Ch. Tomuschat (ed.), *Kosovo and the International community. A Legal Assessment*, Kluwer Law International 2002, *passim*.

rejected the proposals towards autonomy of Kosovo and deployment of international peace-keepers) NATO started military operations. They were justified by the NATO members, the Arab and Islamic States, because of the humanitarian needs of the local population; and strongly contested by three States including Russia, China and Namibia. However, the draft resolution sponsored by Russia condemning the bombings was rejected by the UNSC by 12 votes to three. The mediation brought both parties of the conflict to the conclusion of the so-called Kumanovo Agreement. The UNSC passed Resolution 1244(1999) welcoming the agreement, endorsing its general principles and invoking its powers under Chapter VII to ensure the implementation of the Agreement. Notwithstanding some similarities, we must notice a number of differences between the two interventions, the most important being that Liberia and Sierra Leone were both members of ECOWAS while Yugoslavia was not a member of NATO. The action taken by the NATO was an attempt towards the international law enforcement outside the territories of the member States.

We are in favour of the recognition of power of regional organizations to intervene in armed conflicts of different kinds, including civil war; we also accept an obligation of those organizations to intervene on humanitarian reasons. The advantages of such competence are clear. The regional groupings are much more flexible as far as decision-making is concerned. They have much better knowledge of the real situation, political, economic and social relations in the region. Usually they enjoy also much more confidence among the States of the region than the remaining States.

On the other hand, the history of international law and international law show that regional arrangements were often treated as an instrument ensuring the domination of one (super) power. This was particularly true in the case of the Warsaw Pact, which in fact was a tool of the implementation of imperial policy of the USSR. In order to avoid such a situation, particularly sensible, the legal and political instruments of such arrangements should be analysed from the perspective of their conformity with general international law.

The decision on the use of force by the regional organization should be based on two sets of premises: legality and legitimacy. The issue of legality has been addressed above, but the legitimacy needs an explanation. They can be formulated by reference to the same criteria applied by the UNSC: seriousness of threat, proper purpose of the military action, last resort, proportional means, balance of consequences. All the criteria should be applied to all kinds of action, including collective self-defence, counteraction to aggression, but also humanitarian intervention and other sorts of action against mass and grave violations of human rights. We could ask only whether in case of the collective self-defence in the framework of the regional organization a necessity of special declaration by the State attacked is still needed, as the current threats are different than those, which were present at the time of formation of the customary law of self-defence. If we look at the reaction of the US after 9/11 (the US Government declared that it was under attack, and requested its Allies from NATO to support its action against the terrorists), we

conclude that the view expressed by the ICJ in the *Nicaragua* case as to the requirement of declaration is still valid under present international law.

The issue of responsibility for the acts of regional organizations connected
with the possibly of the illegal use of force is worthy of a short analysis. A first
consequence thereof directly connected with the responsibility of States is the issue of control over the action. The Security Council executes political control, but
the possibility of a judicial control over that action is desirable. There is no judicial
organ, which would be competent in this respect. Neither the ICJ, nor any regional
court on human rights has any power in relation to international organizations. We
could therefore consider a possibility of invoking the responsibility of the member
States. According to a traditional stance, member States are not responsible for the
acts of the international organization, nor vice versa. This position has been to a
certain extent modified by the jurisprudence of the two international courts: the
International Court of Justice and the European Court of Human Rights, in two
cases concerning the NATO attacks against Yugoslavia. If the classical approach
had been observed, both courts should have rejected both claims brought against
the group of NATO member States by Yugoslavia and group of Yugoslav nationals, respectively. The Court of Strasbourg decided that it had no jurisdiction in the
case as the bombings by NATO took place outside the territorial sovereignty of
the member States (which certainly was not very convincing). On the other hand,
the Hague judges rejected the claim against the US and Spain, as the ICJ had no
jurisdiction in respect of the two States because of the limited scope of their declarations on the acceptance of the jurisdiction. The World Court, however, was ready
to admit the claims against the remaining eight States and continued to proceed
with the jurisdictional phase.

As the principle of non-use of force is an *erga omnes* obligation, and it could
even be suggested that it is one of the very rare (if any) peremptory norms in current international law, a right to bring claims against the regional organization and
possibly also against its member States should be granted to every State in accordance with the ILC Draft Articles on State Responsibility, as well as to the UNSC.
That right certainly should not be limited to the States located in the same region
as the (directly) injured State. However, it does not mean that every State could
bring a case before the ICJ, as the rules confirmed in the *East Timor* case must be
observed.

Finally, we would to like to discuss the extremely delicate problem of the qualification of the coalitions of the willing as regional arrangements within the meaning of Chapter VIII of the UN Charter.[18] In international legal practice there was
one case only that involved the participation of the international organization in
the action undertaken by the coalition of that kind – the case of the common action
of the UNPROFOR and NATO in Bosnia and Croatia on the basis of Resolutions

---

18   We do not intend to discuss here international legal issues connected with the war in
     Iraq. Our critical opinion can be found in W. Czapliński, Intervention in Iraq from the
     Point of View of International Law, *The Polish Foreign Affairs Digest* 4(2004), No. 1 (10),
     p. 32.

836(1993) and 958(1994). In particular para 10 of Resolution 836 entitled the member States [of the United Nations] acting nationally or through regional organizations and arrangements [sic!] to take under the authority of the UNSC and in cooperation with the UNSG and UNPROFOR all necessary measures [...] to support UNPROFOR in the performance of its mandate. All the other cases that concerned the coalitions of the willing and were accepted by the UNSC involved either individual States or groupings of States not limited to one geographical region.

It is certainly beyond any doubt that if regional organizations can sometimes be dominated by one State (such a situation can be observed e.g. in the case of ECOWAS which is influenced by Nigeria), such a situation is nearly certain in respect of the said coalitions. We suggest therefore that the coalition of the willing can be treated as the regional arrangement exclusively if the participating States come mostly from the same geographical region as the State concerned. The political affiliation of the States is also important. We suggest a distinction between self-defence and humanitarian intervention (or, more generally speaking, any form of intervention in civil war or internal conflict). It is hard to imagine that the State representing a totally different position towards fundamental problems of the contemporary world, or belonging to another political block, will be accepted as a member of the coalition intervening in the civil war. Such participation could be evaluated as an intention to enlarge the zone of influence of that State. Finally, the position of the intervening States towards the use of force in general should be considered. That can be evaluated e.g. on the basis of the voting of the particular States on the specific resolutions of the political organs of the UN, attitude towards the ILC draft articles on state responsibility and towards the Statute of the International Criminal Court.

From the local perspective, however, a problem of unilateral use of force remains disputable. There are two options for the evaluation of such situations. Firstly, armed force can be used in individual self-defence in reaction to an armed attack, such reaction being perfectly legal. Secondly, States can refer to armed force as a countermeasure. There is a general consensus mirrored in the 2001 ILC Draft Articles on State Responsibility that forcible countermeasures should be forbidden. Some States including the US (under the Republican administration), Israel and Russia (under President Putin) seem to accept a possibility of recourse to military countermeasures. As to the former, they could eventually be considered as persistent objectors if such a stance could be accepted with respect to a peremptory norm of international law. The position of South Africa towards apartheid and the reaction thereto by the UN, including the imposing of sanctions by the Security Council, suggest that there can be no justification for any rejection of the peremptory norms of international law. On the other hand, however, the definition of Article 53 of the Vienna Convention states expressly that the norm of *jus cogens* must be accepted as such by the international community as a whole. As usual, it will be difficult to find a compromise between the two opposite opinions.

4.   Human Rights[19]

Protection of human rights is another aspect of international law where interactions between universal and particular norms are clearly visible and important.

The UN Charter reaffirms in the preamble "the faith in fundamental human rights, in the dignity and worth of the human person, in the equal rights of men and women and of nations large and small", as well as establishes "the achieving international co-operation in solving international problems of an economic, social, cultural or humanitarian character, and in promoting and encouraging respect for human rights and for fundamental freedoms for all without distinction as to race, sex, language, or religion" as one of the purposes of the Organization. The ideas of the Charter were implemented by the Universal Declaration of Human Rights of 10 December 1948. Based on the concept of individual protection, it formulated a number of important rights and freedoms accepted by the liberal democracies. That was the reason for abstention by a number of States: Saudi Arabia, South Africa, the USSR and five communist States during the voting within the UNGA (all of them except Saudi Arabia withdrew their reservations in the 1990s).

The Universal Declaration has become a cornerstone of all instruments dealing with human rights, both of universal and regional dimensions. It was followed by a number of different multilateral treaties elaborated in the framework of the UN, ILO, UNESCO, but also conventions on international humanitarian law. Finally, two international Covenants on Human Rights have been adopted by the UNGA that completed the system. The characteristic feature of all the six conventions constituting the system is the establishing of the control organs. Their tasks are: the identification of violations of those treaties, adopting of recommendations and general comments interpreting the conventions, accepting of State reports and individual petitions, promoting of the idea of human rights. Two measures provided for in the conventions deserve particular attention: reports and petitions. Unfortunately, they are not as effective as they could be because of long lasting procedures before the human rights agencies, infringements of procedures by governments, inefficiency of the committee staff etc. There is a general consensus that the said instruments require modification and amendment.

Further instruments developed the idea of human rights into a universal concept; e.g. the Convention on Elimination of All Forms of Discrimination of Women obtained – as for 2003 – 165 ratifications, the Convention on the Elimination of Racial Discrimination – 161, and the Convention on the Rights of the Child – 191.

---

19   See *e.g.* J. Donnelly, *International Human Rights* (1998); B.G. Ramcharan, *The Concept and Present Status of the International Protection of Human Rights*, Dordrecht 1987; Ph. Alston (ed.), *Human Rights Law*, Darmouth 1996; L. Doswald-Beck, R. Kolb, *Judicial Process and Human Rights. United Nations, European, American and African Systems*, Kehl-Strasbourg-Arlington 2003; *La protection des droits de l'homme et l'evolution du droit international*, Colloque de Strasbourg SFDI, Paris 1998; A.A. Cançado-Trinidade, Coexistence and Coordination of Mechanisms of International Protection of Human Rights (at Global and Regional Levels), *RCADI* 202(1987), p. 9.

A lot of treaty obligations in that field transformed subsequently into customary norms.[20] This was confirmed by the ICJ in *Barcelona Traction* (stating that certain fundamental human rights including protection against slavery and racial discrimination result from general international law) and *Tehran Hostages* (the privation of liberty of the hostages was contrary to the principles of the UN Charter and fundamental idea of the Universal Declaration of 1948) cases; other human rights of universal nature include, according to the ICJ, the right to life, ban on racial discrimination and prohibition of cruel and inhuman treatment. The Hague judges were not willing to guarantee a complete protection of those rights, and to grant the *actio popularis* and universal jurisdiction in cases of the violations of obligations *erga omnes*. Surprisingly, other international bodies including the Badinter Committee, Inter-American Committee on Human Rights and Human Rights Committee tend to recognize the peremptory and *erga omnes* nature of at least "core" human rights. Those statements should be evaluated with certain caution, as those agencies rarely analysed thoroughly both state practice and human rights.

The protection of human rights on the regional plane was introduced later – with the exception of the European system, which is based on the European Convention on the Protection of Human Rights and Fundamental Freedoms of 4 November 1950. The ECHR expressed the idea that the protection of human rights was not the matter of exclusive domestic competence of the particular States any more. It was divided into two parts, concerning the regulation of specific individual rights and the enforcement the judicial mechanism, and it was completed by additional protocols amending the rights and modifying the procedure in order to increase the effectiveness of the system. Obligations created for the member States of the Council of Europe were always treated as an objective and not based upon reciprocity; they constituted an important element of the European public order; they are also applicable within the domestic legal system and should be taken into account by the courts of the state parties. The Council of Europe elaborated also further instruments of protection of human rights that included the European Social Charter, European Convention for the Prevention of Torture, and Framework Convention on the Protection of Minorities. This system was developed by the instruments of the CSCE/OSCE. Those acts constituted an important element of ideological struggle between the Soviet Block and Western democracies. The so-called human dimension of the CSCE not only covered human rights but also promoted such values as democracy, rule of law, free elections, political pluralism, civil society etc. Standards elaborated under the auspices of the OSCE often serve as a point of reference for numerous conventions and other binding legal acts. The ICJ also took them into account in its jurisprudence (notably in the *Nicaragua* case).[21] As the OSCE process is not limited to European States, its influence is present in the whole Northern hemisphere, from Vancouver to Vladivostok. Finally, the

---

20   See on that topic Th. Meron, *Human Rights and Humanitarian Norms as Customary Law*, Oxford 1989; B. Simma, International Human Rights Law and General International Law; A Comparative Analysis, *RCADE* 1993, vol. 4, Part Two, p. 213 ff.

21   ICJ Rep. 1986, p. 100.

EU elaborated a special subsystem of protection of human rights. Because of formal reasons, the Union could not accede to the European Convention on Human Rights, although the European Court of Justice often applied the Convention in its practice. Because of the lack of political will among the member States that were not eager to accept the control of the Community acts by the Strasbourg Court,[22] the founding treaties were not amended during the 1997 IGC but a system of political reaction to possible violations of the principles of democracy, human rights and rule of law was introduced (Article 6-7 EU). That system was amended by the Treaty of Nice, which contained the Charter of Fundamental Rights. Although not binding, it granted an additional factor of protection.

The system of protection of human rights on the regional (European) plane can create important problems. Let us discuss the problem of protection of refugees. In Europe, at least four different levels of protection: the Geneva Convention of 1951, the system of recommendations elaborated by the Council of Europe, the system introduced by the European Union based upon the Schengen agreements of 1985 and 1990, and subsequently replaced by the Community instruments, and finally the provisions of national regulations. The former levels are relatively liberal and directed towards a wide scope of protection, while the EU system is much more restrictive and limits the possibility of obtaining refugee status. It has also been suggested that the EU regulations are incompatible with the Geneva Convention, although the Treaty on the European Union contains special provisions declaring the conformity of the solutions adopted with the European Convention on Human Rights and the Geneva Convention.

Other systems of protection were created in America, Africa and the Arab States. The American system was based upon the Declaration of Rights and Duties of the Man of 1948, adopted initially as a non-binding instrument. The approach to the Declaration changed after the establishment of the Inter-American Commission of Human Rights, initially a consultative body that was subsequently granted with a number of important powers in the implementation process of the American Convention on Human Rights of 1969. The system of implementation of the convention is a little different from the European one. An acceptance of the system based upon the individual claims is mandatory while that of state claims is facultative. The Commission after having considered the claim formulates recommendations for the government concerned, and if necessary it can submit the claim to the Inter-American Court. The problem is that the States accepting the jurisdiction of the Court are not very numerous, although we can suppose it will increase together with the gradual democratisation of Latin America. The African system is founded upon the African Charter on Human and People's Rights (the Banjul Charter) of 1981. That act well reflects the specific approach of the African States towards human rights. In the field of substantive law, the Charter endorses certain rights and freedoms only, permitting the deviation from the others if national law and tradition so require. The social and economic rights, as well as collective rights including the self-determination and sovereignty over national resources are em-

---

22   See Opinion 1/94 of the ECJ, ECJ Rep. 1996, p. I-1759.

phasized. There was no judicial enforcement of the rights – first in 1998 the parties to the Charter agreed to establish the court. The state parties present reports that are considered by the Commission. If we look at the modern history of Africa, we realize that human rights do not play an important role in the life of that continent. Even worse, the mass and grave violations of core human rights and humanitarian law during the numerous armed conflicts in Africa, including civil wars and States governed by bloody dictators, did not meet any reaction on the part of the OAU. As to Islamic States, the specificity of their political and social systems meant that human rights did not draw their attention too much. The Arab Charter of Human Rights repeated the provisions of the Universal Declaration, including the principle of equality of men and women, but excluding the ban on slavery and lack of religious freedom. The Committee supervising the implementation of the Charter is an expert body, deprived of any power to evaluate the human rights situation in the signatory States.

There are numerous interactions between the universal and regional systems of protection.[23] All of them are directed towards maximum protection of human rights. There are numerous convergences between different international instruments in the domain. On the legislative plane, the convergences are visible in the stage of elaboration of the texts of the conventions. The American Convention of 1969 was modelled on the European Convention of 1950 and UN Covenants of 1966. The practice of law enforcement agencies shows that they use specific techniques of interpretation based upon referring to other international agreements on human rights in order to increase the level of protection under the specific agreement. The European Court of Human Rights, interpreting the Convention in the light of, has often applied that method, invoking the International Covenants, but also the American Convention on Human Rights.[24] On the other hand, the bodies responsible for the application of other human rights instruments followed the European Convention and decisions of the enforcement agencies.

We can conclude that as far as the protection of human rights is concerned, the action on regional level is much more effective than the universal one if we look at the European practice; the situation in America and in particular in Africa is much worse, to say nothing about Asia. The closer cooperation between the States concerned is the more advanced and sophisticated methods of protection of individuals. International judicial protection was possible on the basis of regional ar-

---

23   See Ch. Tomuschat, The Interaction between Different Systems for the Protection of Human Rights, [in:] R. Bieber a.o. (Ed.), *Un nom des peoples européens, un catalogue des droits fondamentaux de l'Union européenne*, Baden Baden 1995, p. 30 ff; B. Conforti, Les interactions entre les norms internationals relatives à la protection des droits de l'homme, [in:] *La protection des droits de l'homme et l'evolution du droit international*, Colloque de Strasbourg SFDI, Paris 1998, p. 121 ff; H. Gros-Espiell, La convention americaine des droits de l'homme et la convention européenne des droits de l'homme, *RCADI* 218(1989), p. 167 ff.

24   Cf. judgments of 25 March 1993, *Costello-Roberts v. UK*, Series A, No 247C; and of 7 July 1989 *Soering*, Series A, No 161, and others.

rangements only. This is an important political factor that influences many people from different regions where the standards of protection are lower. It is also worth mentioning that individuals have found their way to the (supra)national organs of protection and that the number of claims is still increasing. On the other hand, the regional instruments contain important guarantees for States and governments, including the power to make reservations, emergency clauses and the possibility to restrict certain rights if public interest so requires.

5.   Summing up

Our present time is often called "A period of globalization"; the development of the "global village" has influenced international law in the same way as the world economy. However, if economic processes tend to facilitate a transfer of capital, goods and technology all over the world, regional norms still play an important or even – in some aspects – growing role within international law, democratic principles and the rule of law. Even if there is a tendency towards the universal application of international law, and the body of multilateral treaties is still growing, this does not lead automatically to an increasing respect of the rules. Regional norms can be more effective in protecting certain rights and interests including peace and security, but also human rights. Regional treaty bodies – in particular in Europe and in America – can replace the ineffective universal organizations in fulfilling their tasks.

11. The Search for Universal Justice

Eric Wyler and Alain Papaux*

1. Introduction: What Is Justice?

Whoever ponders the notion of *justice* finds himself immediately plunged into profound bewilderment given how polysemic the concept appears to be. As with all basic notions of *Geisteswissenschaften* ("human sciences"), it does not lack "emotional shading", which implies that "agreement on the conceptual meaning is only reached to a very limited degree."[1]

A modest consensus seems to have been reached with Aristotle's statement, ever so contemporary in resonance, that the determination of justice requires *a certain resemblance* between the beings it means to compare and measure, which presumes a correlation of *otherness* between them. Thus they must display a certain commensurability, a "same" measure, which makes them equal. The whole debate about justice deals with the development of this "com-mensurability" and the criteria for its construction (formal equality, material equality, equal opportunity, etc.).

In order to delimit the themes of this book, which deals with international law, one must begin by distinguishing, within practical philosophy, as opposed to theoretical philosophy or philosophy of nature, between politics, ethics and law. If Ricoeur is right, modern Western philosophers have primarily dealt with relationships between ethics and politics but have neglected the specificity of the legal realm.[2]

This omission by the moderns is all the more problematic since the philosophers who actually devoted some of their thinking to the subject were not jurists.[3]

---

*   The challenge of expressing our ideas in English would not have been overcome without the extraordinary cleverness and culture of Iwan and Rémi Samson from Ottawa. We remain exclusively responsible for any ambiguous passages.

1   Ch. Perelman, *Ethique et droit*, Editions de l'Université de Bruxelles, Bruxelles, 1990, 16.

2   P. Ricoeur, *Le Juste*, Editions Esprit, Paris 1995, 8.

3   Ricoeur quite rightly notes that this omission is all the more surprising as it is recent. As a reminder, he adds that tradition labelled Plato's *Republic* with the subtitle of 'Justice', a notion to which Aristotle in turn devotes a number of lengthy passages in his *Nicomachean Ethics*.

Ronald St. John Macdonald & Douglas M. Johnston (eds.), Towards World Constitutionalism, *pp. 273-302.*
© *2005 Koninklijke Brill NV. Printed in The Netherlands. ISBN 90 04 14612 1.*

Not that one necessarily has to be a jurist to offer relevant opinions or comments on law, but the model traditionally adopted has skewed the analyses. Criminal law is frequently the chosen model, as it corroborates in the clearest of ways the verticality of law, which stems from the notion of *command* and develops into that of *imposition* of some behaviour or other, of *public force* or *public power,* and more emblematic still, into that of *sanction.* Criminal law is also the place of the idea that law, resorting to the threat of sanction, can guarantee public order and civil peace. Furthermore, the basic taboos posited by criminal law are known and shared by all citizens. These taboos reflect the most fundamental tendencies of Western moral doctrine, which are tautological in reality because the rules make up the secularized version of the principles of the Decalogue, a sort of Law of laws, laid down through the incontestable verticality of a top-down approach. Their simplicity, their legally evident and binding character, result more from a tradition that everyone co-opts than from any scholarly approach all citizens should take, even those who can neither read nor write: "ignorance of the law is not an excuse". Everyone, through their upbringing, has sufficient experience of these laws to ensure "social cohesion".

From the criminal model, and by taking the part for the whole, it was easy to infer the requirement of the separation between legal and other areas also permeated by normativity, such as politics, ethics and religion: only law boasts institutionalized sanction, which is combined with resort to public force.

For those who break with the criminal law model, sanctions are far from representing the keystone of any legal system, as evidenced by the absence here of a constitutional court, by the lack there of control over compliance of national laws with international treaties, by arbitration without institutionalized sanction, by custom, by commercial practices, and so forth. This reality is as valid for domestic as for international law, which in the latter case invalidates Austin's famous *"law improperly so called."* It is not a question of denying a difference of degree between both types of law: "Compared to the model provided by State law, international law mixes elements of adherence and constraint in inverse proportions, the former being predominant."[4]

If order is the essence of law, command appears to be only a *means*, next to, for instance, negotiation-contractualization or incitement, such as the granting of fiscal benefits. The ultimate *end* of law is social peace, a dynamic reality that requires continuous reconstruction through, notably, judicial decisions. "The short-term finality of this act [of judging] is to settle a conflict – that is, to put an end to uncertainty –, its long-term finality is to contribute to social peace, *i.e.* ultimately to consolidating society as a cooperative enterprise, owing to trials of acceptability which go beyond the court room and bring into play the universal audience so often referred to by Ch. Perelman."[5] In this light, it is not difficult to understand the

---

4   F. Rigaux, *Loi des juges*, Odile Jacob, Paris, 1997, 18. We shall come back at length to this specificity of international law.

5   Ricoeur, *op. cit.*, 10. He warns in this passage against reducing law to the judiciary, which leads to the distinction, despite their irrefutable link, between justice as judicial practice and justice as social practice. This chapter deals with the latter premise.

spirit of the General Courses taught during the first half of the 20th century at the Academy of International Law in The Hague titled precisely "Law of Peace". "*War* is the nagging theme of political philosophy, *peace* is the theme of legal philosophy."[6]

Bent on achieving and maintaining peace, legal thought must at the very least articulate two themes revolving around *commensurability* or the development of a common measure required by the presence of the Other. These themes are *acceptability* of norms and decisions, and *recognition* of a certain resemblance *in* otherness.

The first theme reflects induction, the second horizontality. The thinking on justice becomes eminently practical, and hence "*relative to*" in the sense of a requirement to accept the other concretely. In other words, law is conceived of as a *relationship* between two subjects, as a defining of shares. This perspective is undoubtedly more familiar to the jurist than the philosopher. In order to take the specificity of the legal realm into account, legal philosophy must not forget this initial and ultimate orientation of law toward the *concrete*. Which is why, by taking into account the *concrete* in international relations, the theme of universal justice will be experienced as an authentic *search* rather than an imposed *a priori* principle.

On the other hand, conceiving of justice in the abstract, namely, *a priori*, more precisely *a priori causa*, hence without cause,[7] which is the perspective taken by the various idealisms, is by definition to refuse the incarnation of otherness, opting for an Other without depth, without flesh, relying on concepts such as the individual, the atom of society, at the root of the social contract (Section 2A), the Human Being at the heart of human rights (Section 2B), or the Being without Belonging, which plagues any form of aculturalism (Section 2C). This perspective reveals a polar conception of law, for the presence of the other, even disincarnated, is not required to think about the law; any individual, by virtue of his membership in the human family, enjoys fundamental rights, even if he is the last person on Earth or outside any State.

The contents of Parts 2 and 3 of this chapter are in conflict as regards the commensurability of people, cultures, and nationals. Part 2 on utopian universal justice, leads to artificialism, to utopia, which is sufficient for political philosophy but hardly acceptable for the jurist who must find applicable principles. In Part 3, on a realistic universal justice, the approach does not reject ideals but treats them as background horizons against which discussions aimed at action take place, discussions which assume reachable and acceptable ends. This second part is therefore more complete than the first and also more modest. The aim of the chapter is to use the language of law, of constitutionalism, not of lyric poetry. We will contrast the idealist universal, correlatively *utopian universal justice*, with the *a posteriori* universal, which is analogical, to be elaborated, and in this sense pragmatic, along with its *realistic universal justice*.

---

6   *Ibidem.* Need we remind ourselves that the "goal of goals" of the UN Charter is peace, and that it constitutes its "historic goal" according to Molotov (*UNCIO*, vol. 1, 154)?

7   Note that in Latin *causa* means "cause" but also "thing", which reveals an eminently practical or pragmatic mindframe (*pragmata* in Greek denotes concrete things).

Before tackling the three most important theories and the alternative of a universal justice searching for itself, a serious difficulty must be flagged: it has been known since 1977 at least that the United States embraced the human rights cause on the international stage not out of humanist conviction but out of strategic calculation,[8] a Trojan horse of sorts to overthrow, notably, communist regimes. If law becomes a stake in the international policy of states, what becomes of justice? This question is all the more serious since the seminal notions of the idea of international justice, such as *jus cogens* or *world heritage,* were from the outset instruments of ideological offensives led in this case by non-Western states,[9] to the point where their claim to universality no longer seems to involve a community spirit: "law, in a conflictual and divided society, is no longer the settler of conflicts, but the stake and core even of rivalries."[10]

If law is merely ideology, would justice not be reduced, to the point of contradicting itself, to the disastrous "law of the strongest", the lowest degree of commensurability arrived at through the domination of the other, who becomes homogeneous or at the very least stripped of any otherness through his subjection? Hence we admit that ideology does not sum up the legal phenomenon and that which is just (*jus, justitia)* involves the attempt by heterogeneous parties to reach a "good social cohesion".

Underneath this last characterization lies a type of synthetic description of the most traditional meanings of the notion of justice that can be found in a dictionary of philosophy. Considering this book's theme of world constitutionalism, we have given thought more broadly to the justice called "general justice", as opposed to "specific justice", a "community" virtue whose end is the common good, of which international peace is a natural part.

Various understandings of "general justice" reveal common generic features which will orient our analyses. Since general justice cannot be reduced to a purely internal disposition (virtue), since it necessarily concerns others, otherness is therefore a component of the notion, which calls for a process of commensurability that enables the players of international law to recognize[11] each other. These features are decisive in a society as profoundly multicultural as international society. A last feature particularly fitting with this fact is the relativity of the requirement for justice. It is not an absolutely perfect virtue, but a "merely" incarnated, pragmatic one, that is, a virtue relative to the ethico-political state of society to which the considered player belongs: the virtue of a "good citizen", not the perfect person, both of which are identical only in a society governed by an ideal constitution.

---

8   See O. Schachter, "Les aspects juridiques de la politique américaine en matière de droits de l'homme", *Annuaire français de droit international,* 1977, 53.

9   P.-M. Dupuy, "Le droit international dans un monde pluriculturel", *Revue internationale de droit comparé,* 2-1986, 593.

10   *Idem,* 596.

11   In the broad philosophical sense, and not in the technical sense given by international law. On this philosophical meaning, see notably P. Ricoeur, *Parcours de la reconnaissance,* Stock, Paris, 2004.

From these different characteristics, we can see that general justice never involves a person alone, the modern *subject* isolated in his solipsism, a pole around which all reality is articulated, but that it *seeks* to take into account the constituent (social) relationship of any political player. In sum, otherness asserts itself as much at the heart of *justice* as at the heart of the *international community*, a reality that is so troubling that people often prefer to ignore its constituent tension: "in international community, the other is no longer the complete other; he becomes a brother, but a rival brother whose conversion is hoped for more than his death."[12]

2.   A Utopian Universal Justice

International justice, and the quest for it, will only start to be realized when the concept of justice reflects the reality of the world for which the concept is designed.

The major characteristic of international relations lies undeniably in multiculturalism. Refusing to embrace multiculturalism by placing oneself immediately in an already harmonized, even homogeneous world, is an indication of a utopian approach, a more or less probable anticipation of reality. Utopia has been defined by S. Sur, without any negative connotation whatsoever: "As a method, utopia consists of defining an ideal object toward which conscious actions must converge. Therein lies its originality, and its mystery, since utopia gives up indicating a specific method of achievement. It rests more on a vague aspiration to a conversion than on a plan or programme requiring that given milestones be progressively passed."[13]

The symbolic value of social contract theory and of human rights theory is indisputable, with the following proviso evident to all who are used to "legal otherness":[14] far from being universal, the meaning of the symbol is dependent upon the axiology from which it is drawn. As for acultural universal justice, it replaces any axiological option through so-called neutral, formal, procedures which are derived from distinctive conceptions of the good (cloaked under the pureness of Reason, for instance), as Rawls himself concedes in his *Theory of Justice*.[15]

However, these three "models" – social contract, human rights, and acultural universal justice – fail in their attempts to establish a universal justice, as much on the level of *justice* as on the level of *universality*. As for universality, suffice

---

12   R.-J. Dupuy, "Communauté internationale et disparités de développement", in *Recueil des Cours de l'Académie de Droit International de La Haye* (RCADI), 1979, IV, 9 ss. (226).

13   S. Sur, "Système juridique international et utopie", in *Le droit international, Archives de philosophie du droit*, Sirey, Paris, 1987, 35 ss. (36).

14   Such as legal sociologists and anthropologists, comparatists, private international law experts, critical legal studies scholars, etc.

15   Compare the conclusion to his *Theory of Justice*, declared valid for any rational being, and his *Dewey Lectures* (587), in which he only means to illustrate the implicit principles of common sense in a democratic society (in practice, Western societies, if not US society).

it to mention the relativity of notions as central as *secularism* in France and the United States, the two emblematic homelands of fundamental freedoms, and the virtual absence of the meaning of secularism in the Jewish, Muslim[16] and fundamentalist Christian traditions. As for *justice*, these three doctrines to which we have just referred postulate a homogeneity of principle, a non-otherness between "their" subjects. They take for granted precisely what needs to be constructed and elaborated: the co-optees of the social contract and individuals in the doctrines of human rights are intrinsically the "same", "homo-geneous", despite their multiple belongings and their dependence on cultures and traditions that are different from each other. Their various types of belonging are viewed as cloaks that the rational being can take off at will without his identity being changed. In this respect, acultural universal justice is tied to social contract and theories of human rights, which certainly operate within cultures but without the co-opting individual or individual-Person ever being intrinsically linked or involved: the rational being is by definition disincarnate.

Thus no commensurabilty need be constructed between rational beings, no pertinent otherness stands to divide the monolithically "same" (homogeneous) type, and therefore no recognition is required: everyone ignores everyone else and, in theory, others are not perceived as being intrinsically necessary to *self*-actualization, to the identity of *I*, of the *cogito*.

It is in reference to these last aspects that we now undertake to assess the three typical theories referred to above.

A.   *The Social Contract Model*

For the moderns, the main model of the constitution of the state is the social contract. That is why social contract is frequently used to explain international law. However, a triple error must be brought to light in this attempt: an error of legal philosophy, an error of political philosophy and, lastly, an error of general philosophy.

First there is the "internist" error of selecting the domestic law system of Western *States* as a model for international law. A double fallacy emerges at this stage. On the one hand, to conceive of international law on the model of domestic law is to deny its international law specificity. The horizontal nature of international law and thus its logic of co-existence (co-ordination and co-operation), rarely of integration and almost never of imposition, is sufficient evidence of its originality. Whereas domestic public law, by virtue of its initial verticality, ignores the logic of opposability, it is precisely that logic which constitutes the most powerful workings of international law. It is in that way that the ambivalence of the notion of *potestas* (power) is substantiated. Seen from the point of view of the individual, the legal system operates vertically and according to a logic of validity;[17] seen from the point

---

16   See Michel Rosenfeld's works, for example, on the problem of civilizations and cultures.

17   In a famous article, "Logique de la validité contre logique de l'opposabilité dans la convention de Vienne sur le droit des traités", in *Mélanges M. Virally*, Pédone, Paris, 1991,

of view of states, the legal system operates horizontally and according to a logic of opposability. The point of view of the individual is therefore not to be confused with that of the state.

The second fallacy is to use a model developed to account for relationships of justice in a society made up of *individuals*, who are said to be rational, to analyze and even found relationships in a society primarily comprising states.

The second error, a classic in political philosophy, lies in the paralogism at the root of the social contract, which may be summed up as follows: how can the social *contract* found political order that precedes the legal order when its obligatory character stems from the legal order? Since theories of social contract are developed in a linear way of thinking, the reality of a legal order simultaneously existing prior and subsequent to the contract is inconceivable. Social contract theorists often mock jurists who accuse them of deforming the figure of the contract. They say they do not mean "contract" in the strict legal sense. On this basis, the requisites and consequences of legal logic associated with this figure are not valid: the contract does not require everyone individually to accept it, which allows the explanation to dodge any historical influence and existence, and, by the same token, the aforementioned paralogism. It would be impossible to maintain the contrary without turning once again to the paralogism of a legal order with *stems* from the social contract and yet which precedes it, at least according to *pacta sunt servanda*, since legal order establishes it as a contract. Be this as it may, how do we explain that social contract advocates, perhaps without realizing it, use *legal* devices and the benefits of *legal* figure of contract? In order to prevent the questioning of the given word, *pacta sunt servanda* constitutes a legal (possibly moral) pretence, but not necessarily a practical, pragmatic, utilitarian or even rational explanation.[18] A political agreement for purposes of governing can be broken at any moment.

From the point of view of political philosophy, social contract carries out the passage from a political ontology founded on the citizen (or political animal, *zoon politikon*, tending by nature to live with others) to an ontology founded on the individual. Forming the political and the legal by using the individual as the atom of society, social contract doctrine confuses the establishment of the *political regime* in any given society with the *existence of the political and the juridical* regimes that are always already present and established: everyone is born into an already consti-

---

195 ss., J. Combacau characterizes the logic of validity as an "objectivist" way of thinking (196): an objective status (attributed to a treaty or to legal situations, for example) makes it possible "to say that the treaty *is* valid, that it *is* expired or null, that a given State *is* a party or a third party, that a ratification *is* forbidden [...]" By contrast, the logic of opposability assumes that legal beings and legal situations cannot enjoy objective status, as they do in domestic law, since they remain dependent upon the evaluation States makes of them, which makes their existence contingent on "the concordance of acts by which, through their mutual relations, States accept to recognize this existence" (196).

18   *E.g.* the *clausula rebus sic stantibus* or even, the philosopher's example, the *strict* prohibition to lie (Kant), even if it leads to death or the arrest of innocent people.

tuted society and into a tradition that surrounds them, which they can nevertheless change. In the end, social contract emerges as the tautological expression of the need for collective bonds. From this basis, social contract is not the inaugurator of the *political*, only a method of choosing a *political regime*.

Now, in international law ("inter-state" law), it is no longer a question of establishing (or constructing *ex nihilo*) a legal order that is supranational, nor is it a question of choosing one regime or another, because such questions have no meaning in a forum where *community-based* or even merely centralized political reality is absent. The international forum is a sort of no man's land where the plinth of the *zoon politikon* disappears, where a logic of opposability and a kind of minimal agreement on disagreement prevails. Is this not an ideal realm for socio-political constructivism? Precisely not, on the decisive grounds that international law admits a customary foundation to its juridico-political reality. The weight of history, of tradition, of culture, of repetition dissolves the constructivist illusion. In such a context, the figure of instantaneousness, that is to say, disincarnation, as in the situation of Rawls' veil of ignorance, unveils its whole artifice, exposing the cognitive and ethical feat performed under the disguise of Reason: if ethos still exist in great diversity, they are only in the form of objective facts which sum up the knowledge one can have about the society to be governed, without personally involving those who put them into practice on a daily basis and are supposed to ignore their effective position in the socio-politcal system.

And if idealism has a role to play in law, notably in the form of regulating ideas, it has yet to be assigned its proper place. Though its symbolic dimension is of the utmost importance, idealism must be resolutely rejected as a sign of the incommensurability of this ideal and "idealized" law with the ethos of the players of international society, particularly states in their practice of international law. In fact, by refusing from this angle to address the central question of justice, namely, the development of commensurability between international law players, and to run off to a brighter future, idealism could not for long hold the attention of the jurist who is asked to act and think without losing sight of the achievable, of what Aristotle said about Politics: "the good we are presently seeking is something within our reach."[19] From this perspective, soft law is of great interest.

The third error, one of general philosophy, is at the basis of all the others and is linked to *modern* ontology, particularly its inclination for dualism.[20] This error hinges on the presupposition of purity or homogeneity, as opposed to hybrids, mixes, and compenetrations, in the reality of the national and world situations.

The modern version of the social contract described by Rawls illustrates the homogeneous conception of reality. The emblematic figure of the veil of ignorance provides both the total transparency of the possible social positions in a given so-

---

19   Aristotle, *Nicomachean Ethics*, I, 4 (1096 b 34).

20   Among others, *res cogitans* soul *vs* *res extensa* body; natural science *vs* social science; in the legal realm: science of law *vs* law, formal sources *vs* material sources, fact *vs* law; procedure *vs* substance; private law *vs* public law; domestic law *vs* international law; etc.

ciety and the total ignorance of the effective positions, which renders all the co-op-tees perfectly homogeneous among themselves, regardless of their initial position.

The homogenizing function of social contract is by no means secondary or optional. It is to be found at the very basis of this doctrine, since the conclusion of the contract leads to the separation of two worlds: the worldly world of culture and the worldwide world of nature. The state, prior to its conclusion, is termed "state of nature"; at a subsequent stage it is called the "politico-legal order". Thus social contract emerges as a great purveyor of dualism: nature vs culture, individual vs citizen, natural philosophy vs political philosophy, anarchy vs state. One remains in the logic of pure reality,[21] any thing being *either* subject *or* object, *either* nature *or* society, a typically modern mindset culminating with the idealist constructivism of Kantian transcendental philosophy: is there not first the thing *per se* (noumenon), pure to the point of not being within the reach of human knowledge, and *then* the phenomenon mixed with concept and sensation?

Is it possible to rise above the fundamental paralogism of social contract by looking for pure entities, which alone are worthy of an ontology? Social contract doctrine suggests that the political is based on the legal – if only in the broader sense of setting a limit, a split between the state of nature and society – which in turn requires a certain conception of the polis, that is to say a policy. This circularity can only be understood if considered from the angle of an already formed society, namely, a hybrid or a mix. It is at this point that social contract reveals its nature as a Result,[22] and not as a Search for justice. In other words, social contract falls within the category of justification, not discovery or development, action or even praxis. From its place as a rhetorical constitution, it acquires an enormous symbolic value, inevitably impatient with the modesty of the steps of pragmatic justice, which is the kind of justice actually being done.

Where should this impatience come from if not from the abolishment of time, as evidenced by the figure of self-establishment, or simultaneousness of the individual and the collective, in the instantaneous transformation of individual wills into a general will?

Social contract theorists conceive the contract neither from a strictly histori-cal point of view, due to a lack of instances, nor from a strictly metaphysical point

---

21   On this *modern* logic as enterprise starting at one of the poles of pure "nature" or "subject/society" in order *then*, by multiplying the go-betweens, head toward the en-tity to be explained, which is at that point conceived as a mix, a hybrid involving both poles (*vs contemporary* thought, which starts with the hybrid, goes through a series of mediations and ultimately reaches the poles by construction, the process of selection, of purification emerging as a specific mediation and not a universally received and objective one), see naturally B. Latour, *Nous n'avons jamais été modernes*, La Décou-verte, Paris, 1991. *Modern* logic is prevalent in law in the shape of formalism notably: overdetermined formal sources in legalism, formal equality which everyone seeks, so that everyone may be treated alike, with the content becoming secondary.

22   *Normative* result, as far as it generally calls for changes to the current state of the so-ciety of which it claims to be theoretically independent since it is the fruit of Reason, valid everywhere and at all times.

of view, since the internal contradiction of the social *contract* is too obvious. It is at the epistemological level that social contract acquires its strongest influence, short of the "deforming" effects of its symbolism. It has perhaps hardly been studied from this perspective. This is where the contradictions disappear, the simultaneousness of the individual and the collective, of synchrony and diachrony. That being the case, the figure of the social contract, from an epistemological point of view, does not express a synallagmatic logic but rather more a reticular logic specific to the *network*, which conjugates from any of its points (nodes or poles) the before *and* the after, the top *and* the bottom, without any discernible absolute hierarchy.

Merely stopping at the simple description of bilateral connections, whose juxtaposition rather mysteriously generate a qualitative leap toward a new entity that is more than the simple sum of its parts, does not explain *pacta sunt servanda*, the ultimate device of contract theories, any more than it does the politico-legal system – in the strong sense of "wholly organic" – which is supposed to result from this/ these agreement(s) of individual wills.

In light of these brief arguments, two initial deficiencies of social contract theory become clear with respect to justice, particularly as regards justice in the international order.

First, the reductionism of all rationalism in political philosophy becomes evident: it throws back the pre-existing network of connections, which fashion the identity of the citizen, onto the individual, who is given inordinate power to create everything from "I" alone, following the example of the Cartisian *cogito*. That is, it folds back diachrony on a pure synchrony and, consequently, loses all notion of *process* and hence *proceedings*, of development in time, of quest or search.

Second, social contrat, as far as it establishes a politico-legal *order*, namely, a situation of stability, is equivalent to the constitution of, and adherence to, a *status* or *regime*, which are operations that cannot be philosophically or conceptually instantaneous, since a status always results from a sedimentation, hence a process, such as a body of ties, of laws, and of institutions. In this sense, social contract turns out to be an intrisically contradictory concept: diachrony is not to be found in synchrony, no more than verticality can be obtained from horizontality alone or strict synallagmaticity. Borrowing from conventional vocabulary, *commutative justice* only makes sense once the shares are proclaimed and the goods and duties divided, thus only *after distributive justice* has spoken.

Consequently, the approach to the notion of universal justice through the concept of social contract brings very little heuristic value *to the jurist* and therefore to the constitutionalist, even if the political philosopher may be seduced.

Even so, international law should eliminate any illusion. To be sure, nowhere else are the lines of social contract more pronounced than in the international legal order. The almost total absence of a logic of validity demonstrates that the logic of social contract applied on the basis of societal atoms is unable to establish verticality, the absence of which is so often and maliciously invoked by the advocates of the state-law or "internist" model. In truth, only the latter is misleading: if the social contract of domestic law seems to work, is it not because society precedes the co-opting individuals? In other words, social contract is never *constituent*, only *justifi-*

catory: the polis being there already, we make believe that we discovered verticality as deduced from the consent of the co-optees.

Alas, international law does not have such a community, at least not preceding it. The absence of community on the inter-state level is such that social contract doctrine reveals its artificialism by pretending to establish an order in the strong sense, that is, a verticality (logic of validity) that can inflict itself on any state: we are of course speaking about "inter-state" law, if not "inter-governmental", and not superstate or supranational law.

B.   The Human Rights Model

From the perspective of legal philosophy, the human rights model immediately raises a question of commensurability: we seek to define a "general justice", universal in scope, whereas the human rights model, for its part, involves the specificity of the "human" subject in international law. The singularity of *human rights* in relation to the logic of consent – a subjective logic based on the self-appreciation of legal situations by states – which is prevalent in international law is notorious and can be described by the following attributes: objectivity (application not subject to reciprocity), elimination of the distinction domestic/international (when human rights are of immediate application), opposability to any state, including within its own sphere of competence.

A problem of political philosophy arises from this singularity: to base the entirety of general justice on the specificity of human rights entails a double deficiency in the acceptance of otherness. To begin with, the absorbing figure of the "same" patently overlooked the Other, otherness. All the more so once it was extended universally, while considering too quickly the varied instantiations of the so-called universal principles as being mere accidents (or secondary facts), principles whose nobility is otherwise indisputable. Dealing with the question of the "reasserted value" of international law through human rights, P.M. Dupuy stressed as early as 1986 that it had to necessarily lead in the name of cultural differences to "the abandonment of the apparent unanimous consensus with respect to the true universality of the conception of man, which had dictated the Universal Declaration of Human Rights of 1948."[23]

Is all lost then? Absolutely for anyone who thinks that universal justice refers to that ideal situation where individuals enjoy identical rights, regardless of where (and when) they live. This dream of perfect equality, which unfortunately often translates into hardly more than formal equality,[24] corresponds to a univocal universal, the omnipresence of the "same", and the absence (or irrelevance) of other-

---

23   P.-M. Dupuy, *op. cit.*, 591. The author simply sees in it the end of the myth of the ideological neutrality of the foundations of international law, which Western countries had believed to be real with respect to the common conception within an international society reduced to a happy few.

24   Which only represents one of the dimensions of justice, as we have seen.

ness. What better than human rights to ensure such homogeneity of reality? To be sure, one is never *more or less* human.

Today the positivist sees from the outset the multiplicity and diversity of the universal, regional and religious declarations of human rights. These declarations express an anthropological truism, which is that "humankind is characterized by cultural variation, for *in order to forge his identity, Man produces difference*. We only exist in relation to others, positioned on a continuum ranging from similar to alien."[25]

Consequently, by means of a paradoxal reversal caused by the abandonment of a substantialist and deductivist conception of Man, the plurality of declarations about the same object, which happens to be the most prominent in legal thought, namely Man, constitutes a positive element which orients the thinking on universal justice toward the necessary acceptance of otherness as a starting point, thereby giving way to the challenges of commensurability and recognition, and thus to the necessity of an intercultural dialogue. From this perspective, enough cannot be said about the importance of the United Nations and the debates within it, which reveal the cultural differences and otherness to be acknowledged.[26] The awareness of the need for intercultural dialogue could hardly have developed in the context of the Western ethnocentricity and statocentricity of the last century. The unilateralist notion of "sacred trust" (UN Charter art. 73, the famous "*mission sacrée*" *de civilisation*, The Covenant of the League of Nations art. 22) ended up sanctioning this "mono-logism" (*vs* "dia-logos"). Times have changed.

Secondly, the logic of human rights initially developed only in the vertical dimension, against the usually all-powerful state. However important this dimension may be, such logic leads only to a partial view of justice. True, the individual is afforded a certain number of freedoms that represent powers or types of non-collapsible spheres within which he can exercise them *freely*, but the state is the only otherness taken into account, and theoretically at that: it is exclusively a matter of powers or prerogatives, that is, efficient causes or *potestas*, hence of the same kind: "homo-geneous". The state prevails simply from a quantitative point of view; it enjoys power bordering on a monopoly of public power but does not exhibit in this logic any qualitative difference with respect to the power itself.

More importantly, the connections between those who make up society remain unexplored, as though the spheres were impermeable monads.[27] This gap has not escaped the defenders of human rights, who are determined to introduce *human duties*, in order to find a horizontal dimension or otherness. This irreplaceable

---

25   N. Rouland, *Anthropologie juridique*, PUF, Paris, 1988, 12. The author notes that while the State is expected to protect human rights – they themselves directed against the State! –, they can only multiply. A justice based on these rights will therefore not escape the State logic nor, thereby, actual interstate considerations.

26   "To be a centre for harmonizing the actions of nations in the attainment of these common ends." (Ch. 1, art.1, par. 4, Charter of the United Nations).

27   According to the canonical formula or its analogues: "My freedom stops where the freedom of others begins."

presence of society in its concretion[28] and of "others" does not necessarily sentence legal orders to insurmountable distance or a kind of overdevelopment of dissimilarities. Anthropology, on the contrary, explains relevant similarities for whoever examines institutions beyond their structures and their differences to get at their functions. Private international law experts are familiar with this "ana-logical" reasoning, that is, where a "same logos" can be distinguished, such as "polygamous marriage (or repudiation) is to Algerian law from what monogamous marriage (or divorce respectively) is to French law, from the point of view of the basic social function", which favours similarities and thus paves the way for the international recognition in France of these polygamous marriages (or repudiations), a recognition often rejected today.

In other words, the necessary mediation of a collective does not conflict with the universality of human rights but shifts its understanding and makes it more complex, in the direction of the meaning given here to justice, that is, otherness: univocal universality is replaced by analogical universality *developed* in reference to the function, a search which leads us back to a pragmatic (bottom-up) and transcultural approach (Part 3).

Even if it means admitting that values can have meaning outside any cultural system, one has to acknowledge that the naked *individual*, stripped of all concrete existence, disincarnate, cannot constitute the referential of justice, as illustrated by Robinson Crusoe alone on his island, equipped with a catalogue of human rights which the absence of "others" renders formal, that is, *form* or *eidos* (idea) in Greek, namely, the Platonic Idea: one is clearly in the world of Ideas. How then, from this point of view, do we rethink international law as a whole, a legal order of coexistence, of coordination and cooperation, and sometimes of integration, in other words, a law in which otherness is an explicit constituent?

However, let us not forget the increasingly firmer and more rousing demand surrounding the concept of the "right to peace", which manages to fuse the two chief ideas of the UN Charter: international peace and security, on the one hand, and human rights, on the other.

C. The Acultural Universal Justice Model

This model is associated with the idea of global or world governance, which is specific to the spirit of the doctrine known as "cosmopolitanism". Without necessarily aiming to eliminate states, cosmopolitanism seeks to establish above inter-state relationships they create its own agnostic space which is neutral with respect to both political systems and cultures, and thus to establish a possibly universal justice. Perhaps one should see in this model the contemporary manifestation of the myth of progress drawing on Reason progressively achieving progress in the manner of the philosophies of History, for which politics would not be able to go beyond the "local" and culture beyond the irrational.

---

28   As a significant example, Inuit tradition has winter law (relatively focused on bonding) and summer law (relatively focused on splitting).

And in order to ensure the equal sovereignty of states, that is, formal equality with reference to which the international legal order can claim homogeneity, international law asserts its agnosticism as much regarding differences of political regimes as regarding those of culture. Meeting the first neutrality, the UN General Assembly adopted Resolution 2625 (XXV) of November 4, 1970 on friendly relations and cooperation among states to foster "irrespective of their political, economic or social systems or the levels of their development." (Preamble). In order to meet the second neutrality, international law left problems relating to culture to the domestic domain, thus singing the same tune of development of international law as "the great story of slow and checkered progress of law against power, of reason against ideology, of the international against the national, and of order against chaos."[29] In the spirit of cosmopolitanism, since politics are naturally imbued with nationalism and culture with irrationalism, both appear contrary to their rationalist and universalist approach.

In terms of political philosophy, this agnosticism ties in with procedural theories of justice and, emblematically, with the theory of Rawls, which is entirely based on the claim that it imposes no particular conception of the good, thereby presenting itself as acceptable for any subject exercising Reason. Whatever the interest of this theory, we know, notably through P. Ricoeur, that its fundamental claim to axiological neutrality is wrong. In this respect, it is worth noting a more complete argument developed by H.-G. Gadamer against the philosophy of the Enlightenment, which cosmopolitanism claims as its own: namely, its claim to objectivity-rationality-universality (they are all one from the point of view of Reason), which weakens its critical power: the bias of believing oneself to be free of all bias. Such a bias prevents us from being aware of the bias that is within us. Pretending to be free of bias must, in all fairness, be advanced as an *argument* – and not imposed as a *given* – in a dialogue where the *other* can also put forward a different *reason*. That is when an authentic discussion can proceed, one which is often lacking in international law because the "mainstream has generally misinterpreted the emergence of culture. Where traditional discourse sees nationalism springing from everywhere, the idea of the modern secular and rational movement ignores the extent to which cosmopolitanism is itself a culture and does not oppose culture."[30] This return of the cultural, in universalist forms, such as in altermondialism or certain types of Islamism, heralds the problem of multiple allegiances, as much supported by the "right to difference" as fought against by the prohibition of discrimination. In any event, *otherness* is once again at the heart of the debate about justice. It is clear how threatening the acceptance of multiple belongings can be for the homogeneity of traditional international law, which even manages to make the very notion of rationality-objectivity-universality relative.

We see then that the acultural version of universal justice also displays an insufficient consideration – even absence – of the *other*, of otherness. Where does

---

29   D. Kennedy, "Droit international et politique", in *Droit international 4*, Institut des Hautes Etudes internationales de Paris, Pedone, Paris, 1999/2000, 93.

30   *Idem*, 127.

this denial come from? It stems perfectly and consistently from the philosophical choice at the root of modern rationalism, namely, an aprioristic philosophy which allows knowledge of the world in its principles to exist outside of or prior to any practical, concrete and incarnate experience. Everything is linked to subjects, if not to a single Subject, termed *transcendental*, according to whom all possibilities of knowledge are determined. Objects are cognitively inert, serving only to fill out concepts that are already there. The Subject can thus deduce everything from (universal) Reason. In short, otherness is in no way constituent of theoretical or practical knowledge. This brings us back to the same problem as that of Robinson on his island.

The irrelevance of otherness is expressed in political philosophy by the rejection of all tradition – here again we have the negation of the mediation of culture in any knowledge whatsoever – by means of the two complementary figures of the *tabula rasa* and of self-establishment or self-transcendence. Believing to have found the ultimate origin of all thought, the modern subject rejects any influence of tradition and only relies on the discovered origin-point, from which, like the Cartesian *cogito* or the Kantian transcendental Subject, he professes to be able to reconstruct the world in an objective and scientific manner. Everyone is familiar with the example, a most abstract one at that, of the Rawlsian "veil of ignorance", which allows diachrony to be abolished while preserving all the knowledge contained by culture, with players being unaware only of their social position. Such an approach is emblematic of "social engineering", also a belief derived from the Enlightenment, according to which the collective may be reconstructed using philosophical concepts and abstract procedures without taking into account the ethos and mores as they are personally lived out within the society under consideration.[31]

Refusal to acknowledge the difficult question of commensurability also results from viewing human beings according to a homogeneity of principle included in the premise of Reason, whose claims to universality and objectivity are challenged by the emergence of cultures on the international stage.[32] Warnings by internationalists against these clever and abstract constructions are legitimated by the practice of international institutions. R.-J. Dupuy criticizes the utopia aspect of these ideas, which "the builders of miracle systems are guilty of and from which they expect the

---

31   This abstract conception of the politic is contrary to the pragmatic conception which views man as he is and not as one wishes him to be, a conception that runs into the problem of commensurability and which can be summed up by the formula of Isidore of Seville (*Etymologies*, book 2, chapter 10) "The law must be possible and according to nature and according to the country's custom", quoted by Thomas Aquinas, *Summa Theologiae*, Ia IIae, quaest. 96, art. 2. For further elaboration on this conception, see Part 3.

32   To be noted as well that the challenge also comes from the legal systems of the Western world, namely common law in particular, especially the British system, and for which the top-down approach or deduction from Reason is a purely theoretical view. The post-modern philosophies of law, more critical legal studies, call for a revision of the classic legalist model.

happiness of society: they consider themselves as inventors of perfect institutions, of international organizations whose mechanisms will, by themselves, guarantee peace and prosperity between nations."[33]

These last considerations allow us to see the philosophical device common to the three models we have outlined: freedom equals power or *potestas*, the universal quality of efficiency (in the philosophical sense of efficient cause), by means of which the homogeneity of reality is ensured, with the problem of commensurability remaining unexplored. As far as freedom-power (prerogatives) is concerned, everyone from the perspective of their dignity is equally endowed with it, cultural belonging being irrelevant at this "ontological" level.

D.   Conclusion

Despite its rationalist label, modern practical philosophy is based more on will than on reason. With its thought focused on the individual, it could not embrace this individual in its peculiarity other than by overweighing will, among human faculties, as reason (or Reason better yet) is by definition "universal-*impersonal*". In order to avoid the determinism which seemed to burden the *free* man in philosophies which assert the existence of natural ends, modern philosophy developed on the principle of an "in-finite" will, i.e. not naturally finalized for a particular end (good), hence *absolute*.[34] That is why culture represents a threat: culture is where axiological choices are sedimented and passed on to its members. As for human rights, *absolute* freedom constitutes nothing less than its foundation. Finally, regarding the social contract, it accomplishes precisely the self-finalization of the will of co-optees, who accept to limit it in order to survive.

If belonging to – not being absorbed into – a group that is more or less large but bears an identity for the political animal that is man (*zoon politikon*) appears last in the three doctrinal currents, this is not only in accordance with a solipsist original position but, more fundamentally still, by virtue of the nature of the will afforded to man: an infinite will from which flows a power that is absolute, less in the sense of all-mighty than of being non-constituted in its principle by the presence of others. Otherness thus seems secondary, accidental.

Law that is sensitive to cultures and the multiplicity of allegiances, sometimes defined as post-modern, will need to revisit this notion of "infinite will" because it conceals and even annihilates any presence of others and any recognition; it allows social life to be experienced only in the mode of juxtaposition, of a weighing of interests and forces.

---

33   In J.-P. Cot / A. Pellet (dir.), *La Charte des Nations Unies*, Economica, Paris, 1991, comm. art.1, §4.

34   *Cf.* the typically *modern* theme of voluntary slavery which runs from Suarez to Burlamaqui and which can be found in the doctrines of the social contract when it is thought as definitive, with no possible renegociation and with no political obligation from the established sovereign with respect to "his" people.

3.   A Realistic ("Ana-logical") Universal Justice in a Multicultural World

A.   Introduction

One of the features common to various notions of "justice" relates to its breeding ground: unless one disregards reality, justice applies in and for an imperfect world.

This modesty, conveyed by Aristotle and Thomas Aquinas, is expressed today in international law by M. Koskenniemi, for example, who insists on staying clear of apologistic and utopian positions. In other words, justice is to be thought of *from* a certain state of society, even if it aims at going towards an ideal or utopian model. Utopia, which reflects the absence of means, shows how essential is this intermediate stage of considering society and man as they actually are in order to proceed to *probable* and not merely *desirable* horizons of justice. How could it be otherwise in an eminently heterogeneous and decentralized society, where the primary subjects, states, act by virtue of a self-appreciation of situations and where players multiply, a society set between (at least) two fundamental tendencies, relational and institutional: "It's just that the international community is conflictual by nature. The couple, the family, the city, the province, the nation are shaped by tensions. How could the most heterogeneous community not be?"[35] For anyone who accepts this finding, how can he or she not subscribe to this conception, modest to be sure, but faithful to international law's constituent tension of a justice continuously in the making, hence a search?

B.   The Philosophical Meaning of "Search"

If the problem of otherness represents the core of the notion of justice, the substitution of a "logic" (*logos*: reason, thought, discourse) of commensurability for a logic of homogeneity, which is conceivable only within an idealist philosophical line of thought, where any singularity is erased, should come as no surprise to anyone. Nothing in these apriorist philosophies guarantees the correspondence (commensurability) of the model with the pragmatic reality it is supposed to apprehend: "*a priori*" summarizes an "*a priori causa*", outside of and prior to any cause (thing), namely, prior to any pragmatic experience, to any practice. By thinking exclusively at the level of principles, it is easy to understand the inclination towards utopia (in the sense described here).

The terms "search" and "uniformity and diversity" (Part 2 of this book) indicate on the contrary an inductive, bottom-up line of thought, the only one capable of seeing otherness for what it is, or at the very least without reducing it immediately to the repetition of the "same".[36]

---

35   R.-J. Dupuy, *ibidem*.

36   For its part, inductive thought must keep from being only apologistic, that is from confirming "established facts", which often in international law reflect the "law of the strongest".

Furthermore, only an otherness-justice is capable of accepting the increasing complexity of international law, precisely because it is necessarily a search, and hence dynamic. The ability to evolve is indispensable in order to satisfy the endless developments of this branch of the law, notably its growing institutionalization as well as the emergence of cultures and multiple allegiances. The two tendencies might seem contradictory yet they both involve the spirit of democracy, which is plurality: more and more agoras to discuss and organize common actions, fora which accelerate the crystallization of the rules of general international law, and at the same time more and more active cultures as sources of identity, problematic though their articulation may be.

On the basis of this type of phenomena (including concepts such as "world heritage" and "the international community of states as a whole"), some critics think international law has gone from a "state-based" structure to a "community-based" structure. This new qualification seems to be more the fruit of the powerful effect of attraction and seduction which any utopia produces (and where commensurability finds itself by definition without means) than of contemporary social reality. Admittedly, new players, new fora, and new rules are rapidly emerging, but they are far from overthrowing the primacy of states, which remain primary subjects *and* unquestionably the most effective and the most efficient on the international stage.

Does this mean that everything depends on the goodwill of states, that no verticality can come into being, that international law is condemned to the logic of opposability exclusively, since all characteristics prevent the development of an international community, which would at best be a new mode of *their potestas*?

Many critics believe that this is so, which indicates that even *jus cogens*, the most promising beginning of a logic of validity, is reliant on the goodwill of the state: a standard of *jus cogens* never exists unless "accepted and recognized" by the community *of states* (Art. 53, Vienna Convention on the Law of Treaties). So the community-based approach may be not only a utopia but an outright illusion. However, the announcement of the victory of voluntarism only constitutes a paralogism, for only the adoption of an *exclusively* voluntarist conception makes objectivism look unrealistic. Conceiving the will and sovereignty of states as being absolute results from (idealistic) philosophical analyses, not from legal thought, which is not in the slightest condemned to having to be divided between advocates of voluntarism and supporters of objectivism. *Jus cogens* will teach us to move beyond this opposition toward a "state-based *and* community-finalized" structure of international law.

C.   Jus Cogens *as the Beginning of a "State-Based and Community-Finalized" International Law*

Thinking about *jus cogens* in a subdivision of this chapter devoted to *realistic* universal justice may be surprising, and rightly so, since it is acknowledged that *jus cogens* is miserably short of applications, of practical cases. Its content remains vague and undefined yet no one disputes its quality as positive law.

But what is positive law without practical application if not law in the books (as opposed to law in action), hence an abstract form of law, idealized but in any case not pragmatic in the least? However coherent it may be, this position still reduces the legal phenomenon, and the functioning of international relations, to a formalism governed by a binary logic, incapable of apprehending the realities gradually, on a "more or less" basis, by a method of apprehension which is in fact crucial in law, particularly in public international law, which is so heavily blended with politics.

To be sure, such a position becomes coherent only if one considers that law is not discourse. And yet if it is not only that, it is also precisely that, starting with its symbolic dimension. Undoubtedly the *linguistic turn* imperatives have not reached all legal minds, since many continue to believe that language is only the apparel of thought and that, once decoded, the text univocally transmits its message placed as though from time immemorial in the body of the text, regardless of who its reader, culture, or tradition may be. The consistent jurist should therefore abandon any jurisprudence and any rule of precedent since both serve to show that any text is insufficient in having meaning on its own.

Additionally, the positivist cannot ignore the phenomenon of differential and gradual normativity which is so pronounced in international law: normativity is not a homogeneous or monolithic quality. The absolute (binary) distinction between law and non-law is too cut-and-dried to reflect practice, hence a pragmatic point of view based on the "more or less". The same is true for soft law ("more or less" compelling obligations), particularly recommendations and resolutions adopted by international organizations; for the legal value of preambles, of common declarations and other joint final releases; for the "instant custom" (*coutume instantanée* in French). Besides, discourses are far from being reducible to mere rhetorical or esthetic exercises; they even become determining in a culturalist approach to international relations notably taking into account international public opinion, which is almost instantaneously made by the modern media.

Jus cogens is one of the eminent figures of differential normativity, since it refers to "norms with fortified authority" or "superlaw."[37] As already mentioned, numerous critics see in the "accepted and recognized" a sign of voluntarism, which is the inescapable plinth of international law, even if such norms are considered to be peremptory, that is, surpassing the all-mighty will of the state after the state has accepted and recognized them, mind you. This is where the modern theme of voluntary alienation[38] can be seen, explored and adopted to dismiss the paralogism of the social contract, where it is also known that one is a prisoner of the alternative *voluntarism vs objectivism*.

The voluntarist statement according to which imperative law only exists if decreed by states is too radical and monological to account for the complexity of reality. Who will dispute *in principle* the non-decreed imperativeness of *pacta sunt*

---

37   P. Weil, "Le droit international en quête de son identité", in *Recueil des Cours de l'Académie de Droit International de La Haye* (RCADI), 1992, VI, 261 ss. (237).

38   *Supra* footnote 34.

servanda, the sovereignty and equality of states, the prohibition of genocide? The jurisprudence of the International Court of Justice is unambiguous about the matter, with its statements becoming increasingly explicit, as in its advisory opinion of 8 July 1996 on whether the threat of use of nuclear weapons is permitted under international law. There the Court qualified as "intransgressible principles of international customary law" the fundamental rules of humanitarian law, to which states are therefore subject "whether or not they have ratified the conventions that contain them."[39]

If some of these principles can be seen as *structural*, it is still advisable not to overestimate this determination: structural nature does not refer to any necessity. To be sure, for law, ethics or politics to be able to surface, there still needs to be some *choice* for man: the possibility even of being transgressed provides a criterion of differentiation between nature and culture, without the distinction being absolute.

Conversely, if certain principles appear to be the result of voluntary choices, they are not an indication of an infinite will, that is, of a discretionary choice to be understood as being *arbitrary* (i.e. without *reasons* or arguments attributable to them, hence "un-reasonable", "ir-rational"). An authentic choice occurs only where all the terms of the alternative are not of equal merit, except to fall into relativism: any one of them will do, when all is said and done, since none is in a position to fulfill metaphysically the author of the choice more than the others, it is as if all the interpretations of a text are of equal merit ("equi-vocity"), in which case none wins the conviction and the selected one is purely accidental (in the philosophical sense), due only to chance, which is the very denial of choice.

If everyone attaches very great value to principles such as *pacta sunt servanda* or the prohibition of torture, no one can deny that their application is not *absolute*, perfect, or flawless: law is only valid on the register of the "most often" and not of the "always"; the former features a pragmatic and prudent attitude, the latter features an idealist, aprioristic way of thinking, in the image of the strict prohibition against lying which Kant professes.

If the "most often" constitutes a mode of the "more or less", of the gradual, it reflects "freedom of adherence" *vs* "freedom of indifference": man feels more fulfilled *by adhering* to a certain value and therefore having a will aimed at a certain

---

39   *CIJ, Recueil 1996*, par.79. Without expressly coming back to the controversial question of custom in international law, let us simply note the same split within the doctrine between voluntarists and objectivists, a dualism which indicates a *modern* way of thinking. This dichotomy, reflected in the so-called theory of the two elements of custom, reveals the inadequacy of classic positivism in the face of mixed, hybrid realities which make up the concrete world, particularly that of praxis (human actions). It is this very inadequacy that P.-M. Dupuy addresses when he speaks of the "simplism" of this theory ("L'unité de l'ordre juridique international", in *Recueil des Cours de l'Académie de Droit International de La Haye* (RCADI), 2002, 165); he shows how "fact" (repetition of the same behaviours) and "law" (*opinio juris*) are intrinsically linked, and places us on the path of a paradigm of law thought of as a relation. See in the body of this chapter the development of this last point.

goal, than by following a path that is simply devoid of obstacles ("freedom" in the *modern* sense of the term), a path he feels indifferent about taking, since his will is not finalized toward any specific end: he is a sort of being without measure, a "man without qualities" because cut off from any culture, trapped in a solipsism.

It is indeed the spirit of measure, more specifically of "com-mensurability", that voluntarism theoretically ignores by claiming an infinite will, which manifests itself in the most striking manner, even to contradiction, in the notion of sovereignty: "Most certainly, if you give the sovereignty of the State an absolute meaning, if you define it according to a conception that is more philosophical than legal, such as the power to decide entirely freely, sovereignty becomes incompatible with the existence of international law. This abstract idea of sovereignty, developed out of the analysis of the notion in domestic law and especially of another myth, that of the limitless will of the State, leads to a total impasse in the international legal order."[40]

This *relativity* of fundamental notions is not surprising to the jurist who is sensitive to practice, since he proceeds inductively. For him, law only exists in *relationships* between human subjects. Law that is constituted by, and in the presence of, others finds its confirmation and its ultimate foundation in the notion of recognition. The voluntarist doctrine has not always been able to stay clear of the (philosophical) idealist vision of sovereignty and authority (power or *potestas*).

Can one therefore rely on objectivist doctrine? Not to any further extent. Objectivism also stems from modern dualist thought which separates the Subject and the Object in the act of knowing (theoretical as much as practical). Whereas voluntarism focuses only on the Subject in his all-mighty will (substituted by secularization for that of God), objectivism only considers the Object and forgets that it exists in its qualities only under the eye of a subject. Besides, this mediation is evident in the legal realm: not all facts constitute admissible evidence, for example, the procedural codes limiting the means of proof; a *selection* is made among the known facts, which can even go to the denial of biological truth, such as children whose mothers give them up at birth in French law (*accouchement sous X*), a legal regime in which the perfectly identified mother ("objective" fact) remains legally anonymous (legal fact). In short, law determines facts according to its own ends: it imbues them with legal existence.

The jurist is a stranger as much to pure observation as he is to pure disposal; he must work between a perfect objectivity which is valid at all times and places, refuted by contemporary science, and a totally available world, at the mercy of limitless and absolutely sovereign wills, namely, the arbitrary, which is the denial of any just law. In this "in-between", more precisely in the "inter-determination" ("co-determination") or intrinsic collaboration between Subject and Object in the act of knowing, one finds one of the central figures of post-modernism and one of the most productive perspectives to the approach to the phenomenon of culture. It occurs where this intimate collaboration takes place of man making culture as much as it makes him. This manner of "co-belonging" is part of the search for a universal justice aimed at articulating different legal cultures. It is not by denying

---

40   J.-A. Carrillo-Salcedo, "Droit international et souveraineté des Etats", in *Recueil des Cours de l'Académie de Droit International de La Haye* (RCADI), 1996, vol. 257, 59.

our entrenchment in a given culture[41] but rather by exploring its depths to see how it biases us, how it makes us up, and vice-versa, that we can tackle the pluricultural and conflictual problems inevitably attached to it with any clarity. In short, if universal justice as a search should proceed inductively and adopt a conception of international relations that is pragmatic and attentive to otherness, it can only start with cultures, more specifically with cultural entrenchment.

The first stage of this approach, which is still uncommon or at least poorly aware of itself, involves the abandonment of law thought of from *poles* and developed as a set of prerogatives, a realm of competence (freedom-power) of each Subject (mainly the state), which is in theory unlimited but in practice framed by equivalent peer rights. What is required instead, is a perspective in which law is thought of in terms of a *relationship* (between), as a *measure*, a good measure even, that is to say, a measure which suits a given group, hence "commensurability", from which an *entitlement* is then drawn, which in some way picks up and reflects this just measure. To assess and measure each person's place within a perpetually changing system requires a yardstick which is itself dynamic, evolving and yet consistently oriented in order to guarantee a certain continuity in international relations and in the judgements that law makes about them.

This is where *jus cogens*, one of the major contributions directing legal thinking to the relationship more so than onto the poles, is located. The classic positivist conception tends to essentialize law by claiming to deduce it from the nature of its subjects, the human person in one instance, the state in the other. The legal *relationship* thus becomes the attribute of two subjects freely accepting to be linked, that is, to finalize their will, to limit it according to the contract (each expecting a certain advantage). The "polar conception" of law or "law-pole" most certainly favours a contractualist reading of the legal phenomenon as evidenced by the doctrines of the social contract *contemporaneous* with the arrival of the individual in the political realm. And to the extent that the individual's freedom is theoretically limitless,[42] practically limited only through the exercise of freedom by others, nothing seems to be instrinsically unavailable, nothing stands in the way of the free determination of the subject up to, and including, his voluntary enslavement, at least on a theoretical-idealist level.

Jus cogens allows the idea of free determination to be overturned since it states the unavailability of a number of principles or "goods" (in the philosophical sense of the term).[43] It views the legal phenomenon *first and foremost* as a relationship and,

---

41   Which makes up the most deforming bias of the Enlightenment, according to H.-G. Gadamer, as we have seen, and which contemporary cosmopolitanism does not always elude. Here the sinister equation between equality and homogeneity comes into play.

42   As a reminder, on this topic and emblematically, the absolute character of property law as defined in the French Civil Code, Article 544: "right to enjoy and determine what to do with things in the most absolute of manners [...]".Not to be forgotten either is that the abuse of right (*abus de droit*) is the result of *recent* jurisprudence in the history of this code.

43   An assertion which on its principle is no longer disputed.

from there, considers the poles which the relationship helps define.[44] Yet, strictly thinking, the notion of "absolute relationship" is contradictory, since it constitutes an oxymoron: any relationship is by nature woven out of otherness, defining itself as "between", in-between (things designated as *poles*): the relationship is by essence *relative to*.

The theory of *jus cogens* may have seemed revolutionary, fascinating even, because critics, while seeing that it fractured the almost totally horizontal legal order which banned any hierarchy between norms, saw that not only did the theory not push us out of law, but on the contrary that it completed or concluded an essential dimension of law which voluntarist legal thought had not reached. How could it have been otherwise after the disaster of the Nazi regime, whose laws were formally valid but materially repulsive and scandalous? The denial of the other cannot in any way constitute law. And besides, that is why international law has a *jus in bello*: war is still a relation, the most frightening for sure since its quest is to homogenize the other and reduce any otherness into the *same*.

The unanimity of critics is apparent when it comes to the serious flaws of *jus cogens* at the very centre of treaty law and in its extension to the whole of international law (indetermination of obligations whose normativity is reinforced, absence of *actio popularis*, disappearance of the notion of "State crime", etc.). But this unity of doctrine is also valid as far as the foundation on which superlaw is concerned (*jus cogens*, *erga omnes* obligations, *omnium* obligations): the concept of international community. So the question is: has international law undergone a paradigm change, substituting a community-based legal order for a state-based legal order?

Put in those terms, the question is barely pertinent. Indeed, abandoning the "state-based" perspective is equivalent to ignoring the influence of one of the essential players of international law, perhaps the most powerful and "effective" player. Are we certain, for instance, that the growing development of institutions is occurring at the expense of the "classic" inter-state dimension? International organizations remain subject to the principle of functional specificity (*principe de spécialité* in French), and to the more or less regular payments by member states.

Reciprocally, an exclusively "state-based" perspective that would refuse to take into account efforts of cooperation and integration or the presence of new players with growing influence (non governmental organizations, international companies, altermondialist movements, miscellaneous informal meetings, public- and private-media facilitated "international opinion", etc.) would miss an entire side of contemporary international law, a side which is still poorly positioned and imperfectly set in the international landscape owing to the fact that it contributes to the

---

44   As it has been well established in cognitive sciences operating according to the paradigm of complexity or of the network, and according to the systemic approach to reality, where relationships and poles co-determine themselves through a dialectical process shaped by circular causalities or feedbacks. The choice between relationships and poles therefore does not rest on a logic of exclusion of one of the terms, but satisfies a cognitive primacy in the act of human knowing or what constitutes the primary object, relationship as an eminent path.

development of international law precisely by changing it. One point seems to have been recognized: the state is no longer the only ultimate end of international law.

In short, *jus cogens* involves more a *process* analysis of legal phenomenon than the observance of fixed or static legal regimes with precise outlines and uniform logic, if indeed any such regimes ever existed.

What matters is to hold the two bases by articulating them in order to stay realistic, *i.e.* to reflect the state of international relations not as a static photograph, but as a movement and direction toward community; the "finalized" expresses a process moving beyond the juxtaposition of states to achieve cooperation and even integration with other players in order to construct the *common,* but not necessarily the *uniform.* The choice of the end influences the content of *jus cogens.* If international law aimed at the survival solely of states, limiting itself to the "inter-state" approach taken literally, then the prohibition of genocide, for instance, notably perpetrated against one's own nationals, would not satisfy any "logical" necessity. And, in fact, that is what happened until the 20th century.

The "state-based" approach simply expresses the political minimum of the society of states, that is, coordination, without translating any *process* (which is why the static figure of social contract seemed sufficient), whereas a proper search indicates movement toward a goal that is "community-finalized". The term "state-based", taken by itself, refers to law-entitlement (as opposed to law-measure), leaving the legal system with no end or at least remaining silent about this end, or, more troublingly, making the state the sole model and even the ultimate end of this form of law. However beautiful law may be, it is never more than a *medium,* in the strict sense of the term, namely, that "which is located *between*". When the term "state-based" is completed by "*and* community-finalized" the general measure of law (law-measure) is rendered explicit: the end of international law is not (or no longer) the state. The conjunction "and" is meant to underscore both the inescapable character of the state on the international stage and the surpassing of it for some end other than itself, both considerations going hand in hand.

Furthermore, by making the "community-based" approach explicit, the "reasserted value" of international law raised by P.-M. Dupuy is recognized, thereby abandoning the myth of neutral law. And the return of values to the international stage simultaneously marks the return of cultures, since values do not exist in and of themselves, outside a given culture. Thus the "finalized" approach, an expression of the attraction of an objective, forces the realist internationalist to take culture out of the domestic realm to start thinking of it as a distinctive object of international law.

More immediately still, the "finalized" approach forces the realist to think about different legal cultures which represent so many prisms through which any norm said to be universal and univocal ("uni-voces" in Latin meaning one single voice) is diffracted, received and reappropriated in a *more or less analogous* manner by the various cultures under consideration, to such an extent that the assertion of *national practices of international law* become increasingly less marginal. This phenomenon affects even the most uncontested international obligations whose univocity and identical content appear to everyone to be perfectly universal. For example, no one could imagine that the obligation to repress the crime of genocide could be mediatized by a culture and undergo a form of "national" reappropriation at the moment it is applied, an occurrence even more inconceivable prior to any concrete application. Nevertheless, state legislation introducing this offence into various national systems interprets it very differently. Whereas French law makes the "concerted plan" a constituent element of the crime, found under the word "intention", United States legislation only requires a "specific" intent by the authors, without requiring the premeditation necessarily involved in the French requirement of a "concerted plan". As for the Genocide Convention itself, it merely stipulates "intent to destroy a group" (Art. 2), without specifying the explicit or tacit nature of it.

The European Union is also experiencing the phenomenon of differentiation, sometimes purposely sought. The Directives *vs* Regulations, which set the end for member states, leave them free to choose the means of implementation that are appropriate for their own legal-political structures. However, the Court of Justice of the European Communities has jurisdiction to level differences, an institutional centralization not known in international law, for which each state still remains largely judge and party, or judge of its own case. This does not take anything away from the awareness of the need for an effective articulation of legal cultures, as evidenced by the extraordinary development of comparative law research up to and including international law.[45] The latter is perfectly aware of this requirement, made concrete, for example, in the rules of procedure before the international criminal tribunals, which creatively mix procedures under civil law and common law.

The foregoing considerations show that the dimension of the *application* of law belongs at the forefront, giving the classic figures of legal modernity little credibility *for the jurist*: the *a priori* universal, the postulated homogeneity, the deductive approach. This is why universal justice cannot be established from a logic of uniformity. If we managed not to see this, despite noting a highly uncentralized, heterogeneous and conflictual society, it is because modern thought focused on the great principles, that is, on a high level of abstraction which, on many fronts, bore fruit, some of which is exquisite. Post-modern thought, marked by perpectivism[46] and infinitely more modest, abandons the position, or more precisely the postulation, of universals and the rather rigid formalism that often accompanies it. Such thought is more interested in the media, in the genuine sense, namely, in everything that mediatizes the relationship of man to the world, all of which is concealed by the *a priori* of Reason and the dualisms that go with it. Instead of studying the world under the postulate of a constituent homogeneity, it seeks convergences between phenomena initially perceived as disparate. The internationalist knows that a plurality of legal cultures exists, which, considered *per se*, are so many prisms

---

45   See, for instance, the Harvard School, with authors such as David Kennedy.
46   A conception of knowledge, according to which everything known about reality must always be tied to the perspective from which the act of knowing was carried out. Thus, the problems of scale assume the greatest importance, in accordance with the teachings of contemporary physics, as a matter of fact.

whose diffractive effects cannot be avoided by denying them or by ignoring the national or cultural reappropriation of the norms of international law when these fulfill their original destiny: becoming effective applied law.

This approach, far from being a trend, turns out to be adequate to the very structure of the international society just described: heterogeneous and conflictual, where adherence occupies a central place, quite specifically nodal. Hence the easy mistake of reducing *adherence* to consent, the most typical mark of contratualist logic, when in fact it is much more about *acceptability* as defined by Aristotle and taken up again by Umberto Eco: "Aristotle knew full well that the parameter of acceptability or unacceptability of a story does not reside in the story itself, but in the system of opinions which govern social life. In order to be acceptable, the story must therefore seem plausible, the plausible being nothing more than the subscription to a system of expectations usually shared by the audience."[47]

Is some inconsistency not reached by starting with *jus cogens*, a fascinating legal concept to be sure but of rare application, and ending up with the reassessment of application (and therefore of contextualization) considered to be the essential dimension, the ultimate value of *ars juris* as art?

The concept of *jus cogens* refers to a type of norm, more precisely to a certain expectation with regard to norms some of which are *then* endowed with exorbitant qualities with respect to the "normal" non-reinforced legal regime. It is not a norm *per se*, with any given content. Its scope is therefore much more epistemological in nature than normative, for its reinforced normativity does not *concretely* lead to any specificity from the point of view of application as we have seen. It should be seen rather as the mark of a paradigm, a sign of law-measure (as opposed to law-entitlement), which is the most immediate expression of law-relationship and engages thought to go beyond law-pole.

This going beyond occurs precisely by the finalization of "in-finite" wills toward a few "goods" or "unavailable" principles, *imperatives* (peremptories), namely, "rules that cannot be departed from without putting the very survival of that order [normative set]in peril,"[48] authentic beginnings of the overturning of the logic theoretically presiding over the modern conception of law. Not to be forgotten in this respect, *jus cogens* was born out of a dispute over the West, a "legal revisionism" according to S. Sur's strong words; only then followed by Westerners appropriating

---

47   U. Eco, *De Superman au Surhomme*, Grasset, Paris, 1993, 15. The growing importance of *narrativization* in law thus becomes clear, particularly in common law, which conceives law inductively (bottom-up approach), yet still poorly explored in civil law, which is always focused on the abstract principles, in theory at least. We shall come back in Section D to the notions of consent, of postulation of homogeneity and to those of adherence to an authority and of recognition of otherness and of "superiority".

48   Carrillo-Salcedo, *op. cit.*, 134. *Imperative* is taken here as "unavailable" for the individual will of each member of the group, material but also moral survival, in this pre-legal relationship that ensures that each member of the group can be considered, or *recognized*, as a peer. For developments regarding this philosophical meaning of *recognition*, see *infra*, Section D.

it for themselves, a notion which is consequently heightened by ideological stakes, which at least have the merit of restoring law to a dynamic logic by placing it *and maintaining it* (post-modern attitude) in a state of tension – hence in a relationship – between voluntarism and objectivism, between relational and institutional, between coordination and cooperation/integration.

The agreement in principle on the existence of *jus cogens* therefore takes on a huge significance in that it marks the awareness of going beyond the conception of "in-finite" wills and, thereby, absolute power-sovereignty: the focus can be shifted back to law-measure, which comes before law-entitlement, since entitlement begets its legitimacy from measure, more precisely from *recognized*, shared, and accepted measure. Although many critics have seen in *jus cogens* a reminiscence of natural law,[49] it is much more a return to the classical conception of justice (Plato and Aristotle) as that concept has been tested throughout centuries of legal experience, which modern doctrines, seeking to start with a clean slate, tried to reject without even studying its kernel of truth: *distributive justice* necessarily precedes *commutative justice* (here, in international law, contractualist logic) because in order to exchange, everyone's "legitimate" share, the share each one enjoys "freely" in view of the type of society in which they live, must be recognized first. It should come as no surprise then to see in recognition (in the philosophical sense) the *suum cuique tribuere* and, in this context, reciprocity before synallagmaticity.

D. At the Crux of a Universal Justice: Auctoritas (Authority), Reciprocity and Recognition

J. Basdevant captured in one phrase the general spirit, the "logic" (the Greek *logos*) of international law: "the full importance of relativism in international law is revealed only owing to the fact that the power of the latter stems, not from the authority of a legislator who, in this case, does not exist, but from the recognition which its rules receive."[50] The essential value of consent was almost naturally inferred from recognition, particularly in the voluntarist school. What prevailed then was a contractualist logic which, as such, stumbled against the same problems as those affecting the social contract. As a quick reminder, in order to make sense, the contract necessarily falls *within* the framework of some regime or status which surrounds it or encases it from all sides. That explains why consent must have certain qualities: it must originate from a person endowed with the capacity to discern, not be constrained in any way, not deal with just any object, etc. It is therefore never a question of naked consent, of a "yes" without a specific *legal* quality, otherwise there would be no need for the term *defects of consent*.

This means that the subject (pole) who enters into a contractual *relationship* does not do so through an absolute will authorizing him to exchange anything for

---

49   A statement that is riddled with ambiguity in so far as the concept of "natural law" is among the most ambivalent.

50   J. Basdevant, "Règles générales du droit de la paix", in *Recueil des Cours de l'Académie de Droit International de La Haye* (RCADI), 1936-IV, tome 58, 485.

everything and at any price. By stressing law-relationship in relation to law-pole, *jus cogens* is less intent on establishing a true verticality – which is shown to be utopian by the absence of definition of *jus cogens* and by the absence of real guarantees – than it is on placing back at the centre of internationalist thought the international society's distinctive regime or status, gathering the requisites of its survival, which ultimately ties in with finality, itself justifying the establishment of a certain hierarchy among norms. As Aristotle highlighted more than 23 centuries ago, the final cause infuses any praxis activity as any action is always carried out with some end in mind, other than power for the sake of power, since *potestas* itself is only actualized with the idea of a certain goal, which drives it.[51]

The goal therefore comes before the action, as a project in relation to which it orients itself during the course of its accomplishment and, once the action has been carried out, at its completion as its term. The goal thus encompasses the action, surrounds it, and makes up the centre within and from which it makes sense. Consequently, thoughts on power alone, that is to say on means, turn out to be insufficient. Modern political philosophy has all too often forgotten this by over-determining the effective causality, a type of scientism intended to transport the central figure of natural sciences, the *force* or the *power*, into thoughts on society. For anyone wishing today to think about "an international community worthy of that name, the main thing is to gradually regenerate the very vision of power. As Charles De Vischer once stressed, the secret to an effective international organization will never be in the technical arrangement of skills and procedures, in a form whose multiplicity and interchangeable nature would be enough to demonstrate the vanity of such a claim. It is rather in the very idea that men have of power, in their disposition to enclose the State's action within the limits of a functional conception, to order it for human purposes instead of devoting it to the indefinite extension of power."[52]

To regenerate the vision of power is necessary for a conception of international law of which *potestas* still often occupies the centre, on the basis of absolute sovereignty and its exercise – evidenced in contractualist logic, notably in the explanatory primacy of consent – when it is in fact a question of articulating it with some end in mind, which is what *jus cogens* is attempting to do, notably by indicating a measure or, correlatively, by pointing out immoderateness (hubris), in this case absolute will or sovereignty.[53] Except for the admission of power for power's sake or in terms of justice, the "law of the strongest", the regeneration of the conception of power finds dynamism in the change of paradigm from law-pole to

---

51   See the first sentence in Aristotle's *Nicomachean Ethics*.

52   Carillo-Salcedo, *op. cit.*, 219.

53   It is easier to realize how much thinking has changed since the 1950s by looking back, for instance, at these remarks by P. Guggenheim, taken from the renowned *Droit international public*, Georg, Geneva, vol 1, 1953, 57-58 : "The rules of international law are not imperative in character. International law thus contends that a treaty can have any content whatsoever … It is therefore wrong to claim that one can appreciate the validity of a convention based on the criteria of its morality."

law-relationship provoked by *jus cogens*, which leads to the question of the legiti-macy of power and hence of its finality. Starting from finality, it becomes possible to think and to develop some measure from which *entitlement* and the authority attached to it might flow.

Jus cogens therefore signals an authentic shift of perspective, in which *synal-lagmaticity*, the eminent form of consent, changes into *reciprocity* via the *authority* through which thought eludes the deadly repetition of the "same" or homogeneity. The search for a universal justice pushes us to further explain its key concepts of *authority* and *reciprocity*.

Jus cogens may be defined as a "reinforced authority norm". But authority means as much *potestas* (power) as *auctoritas* (authority due to wisdom, to a more "meas-ured" mind or attitude). From the perspective of *power*, authority is understood as force of command. From this angle, *jus cogens* represents a failure in international law because it is hardly more than an incantation, a utopian expectation at best. However, from the perspective of *auctoritas*, *jus cogens* marks a particular deference, a superiority recognized by practical or pragmatic reason (not Reason) which admits its finiteness, and therefore the constituent value of otherness, hence of heterogene-ity for its own identity, whereas *consent* is tied to the (Cartesian) attitude of control by the Subject and of availability of Objects, specific to the modern project.

In order to adequately grasp the scale of this change of perspective, we must briefly examine the roots of authority-*auctoritas*. The *Enlightenment* established a complete opposition, at least in theory, between reason and authority, the latter understood as being that "which is institutionally imposed, because of a superior position, notably hierarchical" as opposed to rationally, as in the expression "ar-gument of authority". This dichotomy and the negative connotation weighing on *authority* aimed at creating a definite rift with the past and the weight of tradition, of culture, of the ethos, in order to ensure a univocal Reason, a sort of origin-point from which all "scientific" knowledge flows. H.-G. Gadamer manages to go be-yond the exclusive opposition reason-authority by rediscovering the rational na-ture of *authority*: contrary to an abdication of reason, *auctoritas* exercises it in and through knowledge and recognition "that the other is superior in judgement and in astuteness, that his judgement prevails and has pre-eminence over ours[...] an act of reason itself which, aware of its limits, grants to others greater astuteness."[54] Article 38 al.1 lit. d. of the Statute of the International Court of Justice provides an example that is as much valuable as explicit of this renewed notion: "[...] the teach-ings of the most highly qualified publicists of the various nations [...]".

An analogous attitude is elicited by *jus cogens*, here regarding texts, which calls for a higher responsibility than what is negotiated, exchanged and hence paid for in a *do ut des*, a spirit of synallagmaticity for which the "other" – more exactly the co-optee – is only ever a peer, that is, a "same". This *quid pro quo* no longer op-erates in the framework of *jus cogens* or of so-called integral obligations.

The spirit of strict synallagmaticity prolongs "the mythic tale of the birth of political societies which is itself structured on the idea of a repudiation of the "state

---

54   H.-G. Gadamer, *Vérité et méthode*, Seuil, Paris, 1996, 300.

of nature" through the conclusion of a "social contract" between up-to-then antagonistic members of the same community."[55] It is the illusion given by essentialized law-pole, which, by placing all of law in its subjects and not in their reciprocal links, can think of social relationships only in terms of contract, with subjects agreeing to give up a portion of their sovereign power to create the collective, and forgetting that the subject without the collective would not even be endowed with language. In other words, unavailable "goods" (still in the philosophical sense of the word) exist because the relationship (more precisely the type of relationship discussed) precedes the poles eminently from a cognitive point of view and not necessarily a material one.

How could *consent* constitute the fundamental workings of the imperativity of reinforced authority rules when the definition of *jus cogens* is controversial and the identification of those rules themselves even more so? Consent is always supposed to be precise, particular, covering all the details to make the interests even, in accordance with the spirit of the contract, of the exchange. On the other hand, *reciprocity* links members who, *equal or not*, wish to "live well together", not just "live together", in a society that surpasses them, and in this respect is unavailable to them, if only as a matrix of the relationships they can build among themselves and by means of which they are and become authentic *subjects* of law: "reciprocity involves first the recognition of otherness but also the search for balance with the other. It is not only a matter of balance of interests or forces; reciprocity presents itself as an element of justice which corresponds to the classical definition of law – *suum cuisque tribuere*."[56]

And if we must *"give" to each his due*, it is because there is a place, a whole, in relation to which these different shares can be defined. In short, the *suum cuisque tribuere* is "community-finalized".

4.   Conclusion

Not only does reciprocity acknowledge otherness, that is, heterogeneity, but it also accepts it. Thus the parties in a relationship of reciprocity can be non-equals, which is a crucial characteristic of a relationship in which universal justice is realized. Universal justice needs to contain or more exactly "hold together", not only the primary subjects of international law but the new players as well, asymmetrical *vis-à-vis* the state, whose influence on international relations can no longer be considered negligeable for purposes of saving the logic of commutative (contractual) justice. To conceive of a justice between non-equals, in the sense of recognizing heterogeneity up front (as constituent of any society), is to regain, on the one hand, the primacy of distributive justice over commutative justice, and, on the other, justice as a movement or never-ending search. It is, in other words, to admit that homogeneity constitutes the product of a construct and not the starting point of a concrete "living together", nor a given which can solve the problem of commensurability raised by the presence of the Other, by denying him.

---

55   P.-M. Dupuy, *op.cit.* note 39, 77.

56   E. Decaux, *La réciprocité en droit international*, Paris, LGDJ, 1980, 344.

Part 3

Geopolitics, Values and the Clash of
Civilizations

12. Contributions of Islam to the Development of a Global Community Based on Rules of International Law

Ahmed Abou-el-Wafa

1. Introduction

Islam appeared in Arabia in the seventh century AD, approximately fourteen centuries ago. The messenger of Islam is Mohamed, peace be upon him (PBUH). The principles and rules of Islam are mainly embodied in the Quran, the holy book, and the Sunna of the Prophet. All Muslims are considered as one Ummah. The bond, which unites them, wherever they are, is their common faith. The Prophet says: "A believer must hold to another believer as one solid edifice, each part consolidating the other."

Since the dawn of human civilization, religions have played, and still are playing, a leading role in the formation of our global community. All religions are closely bound to particular cultures. For example, Islam "was a revolt against empty theological polemics."[1] It is "a religion and a civilization (culture), both interpreting each other to some extent."[2] Unfortunately, today we hear escalating accusations against Islam and Muslims relating, for example, to terrorism, human rights violations, war, the reduced status of woman, and so on. Allegations against Islam, since its advent or appearance until the current time, have been repeatedly circulated. Many in the East and the West, as well as the media and works of literature on the subject, continue to perpetuate such myths. Hence, in order to prove that Islam is totally innocent of such accusations, it is necessary to judge such matters in light of the sources of rules applicable in Islam (particularly the Quran and the Sunna) and not by the misbehaviour or wrong application by the ruled or the rulers. Moreover, some non-Muslim authors imagine and/or believe that the relationship between Islam and international law remains unsolved and even problematical. It is hoped that by reading this study such a view will change. This chapter will look at the

---

1   *Thomas Arnold*: The Preaching of Islam, p. 67.

2   *M. Hofmann*: Basic Cultural Factors of Muslim Society: A View from Without, in "Towards a Civilized Project for the Renaissance of the Muslim World," Eleventh General Conference of the Supreme Council for Islamic Affairs, Cairo, 1420-1999, p. 7.

Ronald St. John Macdonald & Douglas M. Johnston (eds.), Towards World Constitutionalism, *pp. 305-353.*
© 2005 *Koninklijke Brill NV. Printed in The Netherlands.* ISBN 90 04 14612 1.

influence of Islamic religion on international society, particularly on the establishment of a global community based on rules of international law, in order to prove that Islam is a good partner in the dialogue among civilizations and that Islam respects the other.

2.   Christian Origin of Contemporary International Law

International law originated in western Europe. This state of things lasted until 1856 when Turkey, an Islamic nation, was admitted into the international community of states. According to Oppenheim, "[t]he modern law of nations is a product of Christian civilization. It originally arose between the states of Christendom only, and for hundreds of years was confined to these states."[3] One non-Muslim author does not accept such a conclusion:

> Why all the repercussions in the field of international law, where for instance the Islamic world was not allowed to benefit from the law of nations, as it was put during the past century? ... For the next millennium, for the future of international normative system, it is impossible to maintain the entire ancient misunderstandings and grudges. The future world cannot afford such a state of affairs.[4]

In this context, another Western author writes: "The Shari'ah is a source the west must no longer overlook."[5] This is self-evident: *"[E]n effet, tandis que l'Europe était plongée dans les ténèbres de barbarie que perçaient à peine quelques faibles lueurs, une vive lumière de littérature, de philosophie, de science, d'arts, d'industrie, inondait toutes les capitales de l'islamisme".*[6]

3.   Islam Permits Dealings with Non-Muslims

Isolation is not a good policy, and, therefore, Islam permits Muslims to deal with non-Muslims, be they individuals or groups, provided that they do not transgress Muslims. In this context, the Quran states: "God does not forbid you, (as regards) the ones who have not fought you on account of the Religion, and have not driven you out of your homes that you should be benign to them, and be equitable towards them; surely God loves the equitable" (Al-Mumtahannah: 8). Al-Qurtubi, a Muslim exegist, explains: "This Verse is a license from God to deal with those who do not take Muslims as enemies or fight them, and to be benign to them and generous to them." It is the opinion of this author that the verse affirms the following rules:

---

3   *Oppenheim*: International Law – A Treatise, London, 8th ed., vol. 1, 49.

4   *Gohnson*: Changes in the Norms Guiding the International Legal System, R. Egyp. D.I., 1980, p. 13.

5   *David A. Schwartz*: International Terrorism and Islamic Law, Columbia Journal of Transnational Law, vol. 29, 1991, p. 652.

6   *V. Duruy*: Histoire Du Moyen Age, Libraire Hachette, Paris, 1884, p. 122-23.

1. Peaceful relations between Muslims and non-Muslims are always possible. This means averting clash, confrontation, tensions, and frictions.
2. Relations between Muslims and the "other" must be primarily based on justice.
3. The essential condition for dealings between Muslims and the "other" is that the later should not fight Muslims and should not drive them out of their homes.

4.   International Tribunals and Contributions of Islam to International Law

In some cases, international tribunals have highlighted various legal contributions of Islam. In the *Aramco* case, the tribunal affirmed:

> Muslim law does not distinguish between a treaty, a contract of civil or commercial law. All these types are viewed by Muslim jurists as agreements or pacts, which must be observed, since God is a witness to any contract entered into by individuals or collectivities. Under Muslim law any contract is obligatory in accordance with the principles of Islam and the law of God, as expressed in the Koran: "Be faithful to your pledge to God, when you enter into a pact."[7]

Moreover, the International Court of Justice (ICJ) pointed out: "The principle of the inviolability of the persons of diplomatic agents and the premises of diplomatic missions is one of the very foundations of this long established regime (of diplomatic law), to the evolution of which the traditions of Islam made a substantial contribution."[8] In his dissenting opinion, Judge El-Tarazi affirmed:

> I entirely concurred in the reasoning of the judgement on this point. I was pleased to note that the judgement took particular account of the traditions of Islam, which contributed along with others to the elaboration of customary rules of contemporary public international law on diplomatic and consular inviolability and immunity.[9]

Finally, in its arbitral award between Eritrea and Yemen, the tribunal stated:

> As it has been aptly put, in today's world, it remains true that the fundamental moralistic general principles of the Quran and the Sunna may validly be invoked for the consolidation and support of positive international law rules in their progressive development towards the goal of achieving justice and promoting the human dignity of all mankind.[10]

---

7   ILR, Vol. 117 (1963).
8   ICJ, Rep., 1980, p. 41.
9   *Ibid.*, p. 59.
10   Award of the Arbitral Tribunal in the Second Stage of the Proceedings (Maritime Delimitation), p. 28, para. 94.

5.   Impact of Islam on Western International Law

International law has not been made solely by one civilization *ut singuli*. Its *fons et origo* lies at the core of the interrelationship between different nations, groups, and states. It is, thus, the by-product and the common heritage of humanity in its entirety. For this reason, one can affirm that Islam, by its rules and *modus operandi*, has exerted a great impact on the development and evolution of international law. A Western author, Judge Weeramantry, affirms that it is untenable to say that international law is a Western creation, for the following reasons. First, the prior existence of a mature body of international law worked out by accomplished Islamic jurists in textbooks upon the subject is an incontrovertible fact. Second, the flow of knowledge in all departments of science and philosophy from the Islamic to the Western world, commencing from the eleventh century, is likewise an indisputable fact. Third, the fundamental rule of Western international law, *pacta sunt servanda*, which was worked out by Grotius in the seventeenth century is also the fundamental rule of Islamic international law, where it is based upon Qur'anic injunctions and the Sunna of the Prophet. Fourth, there has been contact between Christian and Islamic civilizations both in war and peace for many centuries dating back to the Crusades. The crusaders, encountering such monarchs as Saladin, saw their observance of principles of international law. Fifth, although there is no doubt that a great deal of original Western thought went into the elaboration of the current principles of international law, some of the original impetus both in regard to the general concept and to a number of specific ideas must clearly have come from the world of Islam. Sixth, Western scholars were not insular in their attitudes when they triggered the brilliant cultural and intellectual resurgence that led Europe to world supremacy. They built their humanistic, literary, and legal traditions on whatever foundations they could draw from the ancient classical civilizations of Greece and Rome. However, in relation to the vital discipline of international law, there was no literature from Greece and Rome comparable to their own literature in private law. There were no treatises dealing with such questions as the binding force and interpretation of treaties, the duties of combatants, the rights of non-combatants, or the disposal of enemy property. The only body of literature in this discipline was Islamic. Seventh, knowledge of Arabic was part of the literary understanding of the accomplished fifteenth- and sixteenth-century scholar, particularly in Spain and Italy. Arabic literature was not a great unknown in the days when the first seeds were being sown of what was to become Western international law.[11]

6.   Establishing a Global Community Is the *"ultima ratio"* of Islam

Islam is a world religion. More than one quarter of the world population, principally concentrated in Asia and Africa with some minorities in Europe, the Americas,

---

11   *C.G. Weeramantry*: Islamic Jurisprudence:An International Perspective, Macmillan Press, London, 1988, pp. 149-50. The same author speaks of possible impact upon Grotius (*Ibid.*, p. 150 et ss).

and Australia, adhere to the religion of Islam – it is truly an "extra-territorial and supra-national movement."[12] In fact, medieval Islam "[e]ncouraged international brotherhood rather than provincial nationalism."[13] This principle is in conformity with the *raison d'être* of the religion of Islam, as one sent to all mankind in every age, place, time, and generation. In short, the religion of Islam is destined to be a universal one. In this context, the Quran states: "We have not sent thee otherwise than as mercy unto all creatures … [a]nd we have sent thee to mankind at large to announce good news and to warn" and "Blessed be He who hath sent down Al-Furqan (the illumination) on his servant, that to all creatures he may be a warner … Islam has consistently emphasised the universal brotherhood of mankind."[14]

There are many verses in the Quran that confirm the concept of a global community – the most important of which are the following:

– "O men revere your lord who created you from a single soul and made out of it a peer and therefore brought multitudes of men and women; reverence Allah, through whom ye demand your mutual (rights), and (reverence) the wombs (that bore you): for Allah ever watches over you"(IV: I). With respect to this verse, one author explains: "The word 'wombs' is worthy of being interpreted in the broadest meaning of 'general human womb' so as to conform with the address 'O mankind' in the beginning and with the 'single person' from which Allah has created all humans, men and women."[15] *Prima facie*, this Quranic passage states that all human beings are from the same origin. Accordingly, they belong, according to their *fons et origo*, to a broader and all encompassing universe rather than to a single subdivision.
– "The Believers are but a single brotherhood" (LIX: 10).
– "Your nation is but one nation and I am your Lord, so worship me" (Al-Anbiy'a 92).
– "And hold fast all of you together, to the cable of God and do not separate. And remember God's favour unto you; how ye were enemies and he made friendship between your hearts" (III: 103).
– "O men, we have indeed created you of a male and a female, and have made you peoples and tribes that you might know one another, surely the most precious one amongst you is he who is godfearing. Indeed Allah is Omniscient, Cognizant" (Al-Hyjurat "Chambers": 13).

Accordingly, Islam, from the beginning, has laid stress on a global human community. In fact, the Islamic message has been universal ever since the beginning

---

12   *R. Kemal*: The Concept of Constitutional Law in Islam, Fasé Brothers, India, 1955, p. 72.

13   *B. Dodge*: The Significance of Religion in Arab Nationalism, in Islam and International Relations, Ed. Harris Proctor, Pall Mall Press, London, 1965, p. 97.

14   *C.G. Weeramantry*: Islamic Jurisprudence: An International Perspective, *op. cit.*, p. 133.

15   *Y. Al-Qaradawi*: General Characteristics of Islam, Islamic Inc. Publishing and Distribution, Cairo, 2002, p. 113.

– most of the verses revealed in Makkah begin by the saying of God: "O you mankind." For instance, the Quran says: "O, you mankind, the messenger has already come to you with the truth from your Lord; so believe; most charitable is it for you" (An-Nisâ': 179).

The Sunna also confirms this concept of global community. In reality, according to Islam, which is a universal religion, the Messenger of Allah was sent to humanity in its entirety. The very first time Mohamed proclaimed his message to the Arabs, he said: "I am the messenger of Allah to all mankind and to you in particular." He also states: "Every prophet was sent to his own people whereas I was sent to all mankind." The Prophet refers to this notion of global community by comparing it to a human body. He explains: "The true believers, in their love and compassion, look like a single living body in that if any organ is sick, the rest of the body will suffer as well the pains of fever and insomnia (sleeplessness)." Moreover, the Prophet (PBUH) says, "I have been given five (traits) that none of the messengers before me was given," and he then mentions among them: "A prophet used to be sent to his people, but I have been sent to mankind as a whole."

7.   Scheme of Research

It is not easy, in this limited study, to enumerate all of the principles, rules, and roles of Islam regarding the development of a global community based on international law and, particularly, on respect of the other, in order to promote and enhance dialogue among civilizations rather than war or confrontation. Thus, it is necessary to limit the discussion and speak, in brief, about only some of them. The chapter will be divided into the following sections:

Section A: Contributions of Islam in regard to the normative aspects of international law and relations (general principles of law);

Section B: Contributions of Islam that are related to the operative (*modus operandi*) aspects of international law and relations;

Section C: Contributions of Islam in regard to human rights;

Section D: Contributions of Islam concerning Jihad (war) and peace; and

Section E: Islam and the concept of the clash of civilizations as a threat to the global community.

A.   Contributions of Islam in Regard to the Normative Aspects of International Law and Relations (General Principles of Law)

Clearly, the general principles of law are of cardinal importance for the whole structure of international law. They constitute the measure and the extent of the respective obligations of subjects of international law. They may as well play a role in filling the gaps (*lacunae*) in the positive sources of international law in order to avoid *non liquet* decisions. The general principles of law in Islam fall under two categories: principles existing in other legal systems and principles specific to the Islamic legal system.

i.   Islamic General Principles of Law Existing in Other Legal Systems

a.   Prohibition of Cheating

Cheating is prohibited. The Prophet says: "He who cheats us, does not belong to Islam." Accordingly, deceit in one's conduct with others is forbidden in Islam.

b.   Acceptance of Good Deeds and the Prohibition of Bad Ones

Muslims must enjoin what is right and forbid what is wrong. The Quran says: "You are the best of peoples, envolved for mankind, enjoining what is right, forbidding what is wrong and believing in God" (2: 110). The Prophet states: "A Muslim who sees wrong must change it with his hands; if he cannot, with his tongue; if he cannot, with his heart and this last way is to be considered the weakest form of belief." He continues: "By God, you must order good deeds, prevent people from doing wrong deeds, fight the oppressor, or else God will cause you to lock each others hearts" (that is, against the right path). Under this heading, one can also add the principle by which "[i]t is allowed to follow a non-Muslim in good deeds," not bad ones. For similarity as regards what benefits human beings does not harm.

c.   No Harm and No Harming

Under a well-established principle of international as well as internal orders: "He who causes a harm must repair it." Accordingly, harm should be averted and repaired. In Islam, harm, even unintentional, should be averted, which is a simple application of the principle: "No harm and no harming" (that is, "no harm and no infliction of harm"). Furthermore, "[i]f necessary then the lighter harm is preferred to the heavier one," "the lesser harm is preferred to the more serious one," and the "avoidance of greater evil by choosing the lesser one."

Accordingly, a preson is forbidden from doing an act that is originally permitted for him, if, by his doing it, another person would be seriously harmed or a general harm would happen. Thus, Islam allows for conduct that either provides (1) an absolute benefit or (2) has benefits that are greater than its harm. Moreover, Islam forbids any conduct that (1) has an absolute harm or (2) is more harmful than it is useful.

d.   Non-Execution of Illegal Orders

In international law, superior orders do not completely relinquish criminal responsibility for war crimes: The commission of war crimes in the execution of an order by the government or by a superior does not relieve the perpetrator from responsibility. However, it may be considered to be a mitigating circumstance. Under the statute of the International Criminal Court (Article 33), the perpetrator may be relieved of criminal responsibility if:

–   he was under a legal obligation to obey the orders in question;
–   he did not know that the order was unlawful; or
–   the order was not manifestly unlawful (it is worth recalling that orders to commit genocide or crimes against humanity are manifestly unlawful).

The Prophet says that no-one is obliged to obey the ruler of any creature if the latter's orders amount to disobedience to the creator. Moreover, the prophet points out that "God ordered you to perform certain acts, do not waste them. He set out limits, do not cross them. He forbade you from certain things, do not commit them. He kept silence as regards certain things out of mercy do not look for them." The Prophet also states: "A believer should obey as long as he is not ordered to sin. If he is ordered to sin, then he should not listen or obey."

e.   Collective Security

In current international law, international organizations are a *forum conveniens* for the application of collective security. For example, the Security Council of the United Nations, acting under Chapter VII, may apply some military or non-military measures to restore international peace and security. Moreover, under the Pact of the League of Arab States (Article 6), the council may, if an aggression occurs against a member state, determine the measures necessary to repulse the aggression. The Quran highlights the fundamental law of collective security, mutual repulse or reciprocal self-defence, as follows: "And were Allah not to repel some people by another, the earth would have been utterly corrupted. But Allah is Bounteous to all mankind" (Al-Baqara "The Cow": 251). The Quran also states: "If two groups among the believers come to fight one another, promote peace between them, but if one of them transgresses beyond the bounds against the other, fight against the one that transgresses till it returns to God's order; But if it complies, then make peace between them with justice, and be fair: for God loves those who are fair and just (XLIX: 9). It is to be noted that, in his book *La sagesse de l'orient*, Edmond Briva comments after having read this verse: "Il mériteriat d'être inscrit sur le palais de Genève."[16]

It is believed that this verse lays down six fundamental principles, namely (1) the principle of the rule of law. (2) the principle of the prohibition of the illegal use of force; (3) the principle of the peaceful settlement of disputes; (4) the principle of the equitable and fair settlement of disputes; (5) the principle of a collective response to the aggressor (or that of a collective self defence); and (6) the principle of the application of a single criteria against the aggressor and the prohibition of a double standard in such a case. Moreover, Anas (a companion of the prophet) reports the Prophet as saying: "Give aid to your brother be he the oppressor or the oppressed." Anas states: "O Messenger of Allah, we give him aid when he is oppressed, but how can we give him aid if he is oppressing? The Prophet replies: "By stopping him." This dialogue means that an alliance to repel the oppressor is permitted, whereas granting assistance to him is prohibited.[17] Such a principle is justifiable. When the oppressor is sure that he will not be punished or that the op-

---

16   Quoted in, *A. Arabi*: L' Islam et la guerre à l'époque du prophète Mahomat, thèse, Lausanne, Ambilly, 1954, p. 48.

17   *Ibn Hagar Askalany*: Fath Al-Bari, Dar Al-Manar, Cairo, 1999, vol. 6, pp. 599-600 (in Arabic). The Quran also says: "Now the man of his own religion appealed to him against his foe and Moses struck him with his fist and killed him" (XXVIII: 15).

pressed will not have access to the ruler, he becomes even more oppressive and will transgress all bounds.

The principle of collective security is justifiable under another principle of Islamic law, whereby "[h]e who ignores the right is a silent devil." Furthermore, the Prophet says: "A Muslim is the brother to any other Muslim; he should not wrong him or leave him in troubles (by abstaining from helping him). He who helps his brother Allah will certainly help him."

The Prophet himself accepted the principle of collective security in what is known as the Hilf Al-Fudul (Alliance of Fudul), which was concluded for the following reason. The war of the "Fijjar," which was started by the murder of a member of the Hawazin tribe and which lasted for four years, led the Meccans to reflect on the results that lawlessness had brought upon them. Mohamed (the prophet of Islam) and the other leading members of his clan (Bani Hashim and Bani Al-Muttalib) and the leaders of the clans of Bani Zuhra and Bani Taym formed themselves into a league (that is, an alliance) and pledged to defend the weak and champion the oppressed and to vindicate their rights against tyranny and aggression. This league, which came to be known as Hilf Al-Fudul, exercised such efficient protection that for a long time the mere threat to apply it or to have recourse to it was sufficient to repress lawlessness and afford redress to the helpless or the defenceless. Mohamed was very proud of his membership in this alliance and used to say: "I would not have the riches of the earth in exchange for my membership of it."

f.   Avoidance of Negative Effects of Sanctions Related to the Civilian Population

It is well known that the imposition of sanctions against a state may entail certain negative effects concerning civilians. In such a case, Islam approves the removal of sanctions. With respect to this ruling, we have a decisive precedent from the time of the prophet when Thumamah-Ibn-Athal embraced Islam and informed the Meccans: "Not a grain of Yamamah will reach you unless the Messenger of God permit, otherwise." When the Meccans greatly suffered, they besought the Prophet to lift the ban on their foodstuffs and clothes, which was graciously and immediately approved by him. *Prima facie,* this decision of the Prophet is in conformity with what is set forth in UN General Assembly Resolution no. 51/242 (1997), which provides that "unintended adverse side effects of sanctions on the civilian population should be minimized" and "sanctions should be resorted to only with the utmost caution."

g.   Respect for Jurisdiction and Laws of Other States (Principle of Territoriality)

A state's jurisdiction extends to all persons – nationals or aliens – and things existing within its territory. The basis of jurisdiction is, *prima facie,* territorial. Accordingly, a state may not exercise its powers in the territory of another state. Muslim scholars have known the *fons et erigo* of the principle of territoriality. It suffices to mention, in this context, what Sarakhsy has stated:

If a Muslim enters the territory of non-Muslims by their permission, and lends or borrows from them money, or usurps their property or his property is usurped there, his case will not be heard (in the court of the Muslim territory), because they did that in a place outside Muslim jurisdiction. As for the Muslim who usurped their property after guaranteeing them not to do that, we hold this because he violated his pledge, not the pledge of the Muslim ruler. Nevertheless, jurisconsults will advise him to return the property though the Muslim court will not compel him to do that. And as for the foreigners in their homes, who usurped the property of the Muslim, we hold this because they violated their pledge in a place where they were not under the Muslim jurisdiction. So, if they kill him, they will not be held responsible. If they destroy his property or usurp it, the same holds good in a pre-eminent degree. All this because the Muslim took the risk and exposed himself to that when he quitted the Muslim resisting power (i.e., jurisdiction).[18]

With respect to the same idea, a Western author states: "Islamic law does not claim universal validity; it is binding for the Muslim to its full extent in the territory of the Islamic state, to a slightly lesser extent in enemy territory, and for the non-Muslim only to a limited extent in Islamic territory."[19] In our view, the principle of territoriality also has its origin in the holy Quran, demonstrated by the following passage: "And those who have believed, and have not immigrated (to you) – you are in no way to offer them patronage in any thing till they immigrate" (Al-Anfal: 72).

ii.   Principles Specific to the Islamic Legal System

There are some principles specific to Islam that do not totally exist, or that exist in a lesser degree, in other legal systems. It is common knowledge that in reality every system has its own imperatives and essentials. In this context, the following principles may be highlighted.

a.   Giving Aman

Giving Aman is a specific Islamic principle that does not exist in any other legal system. In describing it, one author explains: "Allowing foreigners to enter the country and according them the protection of Muslim state simply on the invitation of a Muslim citizen of this state, was a unique system and one that has no equivalent in present international law."[20] Quarter means the duty of every Muslim not to kill, injure, or capture non-Muslims, be they belligerents or not. Quarter may be given during hostilities or in time of peace, and it may be given by any Muslim (even the lowest one) or by a Muslim ruler. The following rules govern Aman in Islam:

–   Muslims should abide by the conditions of Aman. Thus, if the Aman "has been granted after a victory, the law forbids the killing of prisoners but they may

---

18   *Sarakhsy*: Mabsout, Vol. X, p. 95-97; *M. Hamidullah*: Muslim Conduct of State, *op. cit.*, pp. 105-6.

19   *J. Schacht*: An Introduction to Islamic Law, Clarendon Press, Oxford, 1991, p. 199.

20   *I. Shehata*: Islamic Law and the World Community, The Harvard I.L. Club Journal, Dec.1962, p. 108.

be reduced to slavery. If the Aman has been granted before victory, the lives of prisoners shall not merely be spared, but they shall also be granted their freedom."[21]

– Aman given by a Muslim, even the lowest one, is opposable to the totality of the Muslim state, and especially to the Caliph and Islamic authorities.

– If Aman is revoked by Muslims (for example, for spying by non-Muslims or committing criminal acts), the Musta'min should be returned to a place of safety of his own choice or to the same place where he was when the Aman was initially granted.

– Any violation, by a Muslim, of the conditions of Aman is punished under Islamic law.[22]

b.   Non-Abuse of Rights

In public international law, the non-abuse of rights is not considered to be one of the general principles of law. In fact, some legal systems hesitate to recognize this principle at all.[23] Whereas in Islam, and *ab initio,* the principle of non-abuse of rights is one of its fundamental principles.[24] A Western scholar explains: "Western law is slowly moving to a recognition that a right, however absolute, must not be abused ... There is now a belated but very incomplete recognition of this notion in the modern legal system." He adds: "The notion of good faith underlying Islamic law does not permit such an abuse of rights."[25]

c.   La Hissbah (l'actio popularis)

Hisbah is "one of the good deeds which repel the unlawful."[26] Under the system of Hissbah, a person may defend a general interest that is not necessarily his own – that is, not an individual interest. To put it differently, Hissbah means the right for any member of the community to take legal action in vindication of a public or general interest. The Quran states: "Let arise out of you a band of people inviting

---

21   *F.H. Ruxton*: Maliki Law, Huzac & Company, London, 1916, p. 77.

22   *Ahmed Abou-el-Wafa*: A Book on the Rules of International Law and Relations in Islamic Shari'a, *op. cit.*, vol. 2, pp. 202-4.

23   *Schwarzenberger and Brown*: A Manual of International Law, Professional Books Limited, London, 1979, p. 28, 85; *A. Ch. Kiss*: L'abus de droit en droit international, Paris, 1953; *Taylor*: The Content of the Rule Against Abuse of Rights in International Law, BYIL, 1972.

24   *M. Fathy*: La doctrine musulmane de l'abus des droits, Librairie des Facultés, Paris, 1913; *A. Abou-el-Wafa*: A Book on the Rules of International Law and Relations in Islamic Shari'a, *op. cit.*, vol. 1, pp. 74-75; *Souhaib*: Les origines coraniques de la théorie musulmane de l'abus de droit, R. de DI et de droit comparé, 2001, pp. 340-55.

25   *C.G. Weeramantry*: Islamic Jurisprudence an International Perspective, Macmillan Press, London, 1988, p. 72.

26   See: *A. Zidan* (translator): The Revitalisation of the Sciences of Religion, Al-Ghazali's Ihya'ulum Al-Din, abridged by A. Haroun, Islamic Inc. Publishing and Distribution, Cairo, 1418-1997, p. 280.

to all that is good, enjoining what is right, and forbidding what is wrong" (3: 104). *Prima facie*, this principle does not accord with the rule "no interest, no action" since we are in the presence of what Muslims call "the right of God," that is, a right that concerns the community as a whole.[27]

d.   Principle of "Being on a Par" (Being on Equal Terms)

Allah, the Almighty said: "If thou fearst treachery from any group, throw back (their covenant) to them so as to be on equal terms." A Muslim scholar explains: "It was stated upon its implication that truth and justice should be taken in consideration on waging wars against the enemies. This law is an Islamic privilege which does not exist in any previous religion."[28] It is worth noting that the Islamic principle "being on equal terms" has great advantage over the concept of anticipatory self-defence, which is, at present, adopted by Western scholars. In fact, anticipatory self-defence means that states do employ force in anticipation of an alleged armed attack, for

---

27   Whereas in contemporary international relations, the ICJ (speaking of *actio popularis*) said: "But although a right of this kind may be known to certain municipal systems of law, it is not known to international law as it stands at present; nor is the court able to regard it as imported by the general principles of law, referred to in article 38, paragraph 1 (c) of its statute" ICJ, Rep., 1966, p. 47. However, it had been maintained that the philosophy underlying the judgment of the ICJ, in the 1966 South Africa cases, that states could only act where their national interest was involved: "had been a blow to international law." See Report of the ILC, Supp. No. 10 (A/55/10), 2000, p. 114, para. 372. A western author affirms this concept in Islam and compares it with what happens in Western legal systems, as follows:

> Lord Atkin in the famous English case of *Donoghue v. Stevenson* [1932] AC 562, asked the question, "Am I my brother's keeper?" in highlighting the general aversion of the English law for interference in another's affairs, even for the latter's advantage. The English common law looks upon persons who interfere in the affairs of others even for the latter's advantage as being officious meddlers. It is for this reason that it is possible under the English law for a healthy man to pass by an old person who is drowning in a puddle of water without coming to that person's assistance, even though such actions would have caused no injury to the helper. Such conduct may be morally reprehensible but it involves no responsibility in law.
>
> Islamic law rejects this notion. "Unless you do this [protect each other] there would be tumult and oppression on earth and great mischief" (VIII: 73). Furthermore, the notion of Bidding unto Good (*al-amr bi al-ma'ruf*) renders it obligatory on Muslims to require their fellow Muslims to behave rightly and to restrain them from doing wrong. This Islamic ethic (known as the hisba) conflicts directly with the common law's notion of the officious meddler ...
>
> Allied to the doctrine of the Bidding unto Good, is the doctrine of the Rejecting of the Reprehensible (*al-nahi 'an al-munkar*) ... The underlying notion is that must as one must affirmatively lean towards the good one must, take affirmative action to correct that which is evil in society.

  C.G. Weeramantry: Islamic Jurisprudence : An International Perspective, *op. cit.*, p. 83-85.

28   *A. Ghoshah*: The Gihad Is the Way to Gain Victory, Fourth Conference of the Academy of Islamic Research, Cairo, 1970, p. 240.

example, Israel's strike on the United Arab Republic in June 1967. The justification for anticipatory self-defence can be reconciled with the obligation on United Nations member states to refrain from either "the threat or use of force." States that are threatened with the use of force may take appropriate anticipatory measures to repel such a threat.[29]

e.   The End Does Not Necessarily Justify the Means

In his book, *The Prince*, N. Machiavelli (1469–1532) adopted his well-known motto: "The end justifies the means." In explaining it, he says: "Let princes aim at conquering and maintaining the state, and the means will always be judged honourable and praised by everyone."[30] With respect to the necessity of possessing deceptive character, Machiavelli states: "It is necessary [for the prince] to know well how to disguise this characteristic and to be a great pretender and dissembler ... It is unnecessary for a prince to have all the good qualities ... But it is very necessary to appear to have them ... to appear merciful, faithful, humane, religious, upright, and to be so, but with a mind so framed that should you require not to be so, you may be able and know how to change to the opposite."[31] In Islam, the end does not necessarily justify the means. In fact, a good end necessitates a good means, which is the Islamic motto.

The Machiavellian philosophy is not accepted by Islam since:
–   Islam prohibits cheating;
–   Islam orders its followers to observe justice and equity;
–   Islam enjoins good deeds and prohibits bad ones; and
–   under an Islamic rule, "[w]hat leads to a prohibited thing is prohibited in itself." God says: "Making lawful for them the good things, and prohibiting for them the wicked things" (Al-A'araf: 157).

In other words, in Islam, whatever leads to the Haram is in itself Haram. In fact, if something is, *per se,* prohibited, then everything that leads to it is also prohibited.

---

29   *R. Wallance*: International Law, Sweet & Maxwell, London, 1997, p. 254; *M. Shaw*: International Law, Cambridge Univ. Press, 1998, p. 789-90. The above-mentioned view is wholly inadmissible for the following reasons: (1) In fact, to base anticipatory self-defence on the general obligation to refrain from either "the threat or use of force" is contrary to the specific provision laid down in Article 51, which limits self-defence to the occurrence of an "armed attack" against a member of the UN. Accordingly, in such a case: *lex specialis* (Art. 51) *derogat generalis* (Art. 2/4). Consequently, a special rule prevails over a general one; (2) Moreover, Article 51 constitutes an exception and it is well established that exceptions must be interpreted restrictively (*exceptiones sunt strictissimae interpretationis*); and (3) Finally, Israel's strike on the United Arab Republic (Egypt and Syria) in June 1967 was, according to UN resolutions, an illegal war waged by Israel contrary to the principles and purposes of the UN (*A. Abou-el-Wafa*: Public International Law, *op. cit.*, p. 629).

30   *Niccolo Machiavelli*, The Prince, translated by *W.K. Marriorr*, London; J.M. Dent and Sons Ltd., p. 144.

31   *Ibid.*, pp. 142-44.

Thus, Islam requires that the means and the end must be lawful and legitimate – that is, the lawful means does not justify the illegal end, and the lawful end does not justify the illegal means. This principle is primarily justified by the fact that "[e]nds and means are intricately connected; a good end can never be achieved through bad means."[32]

f.   No Jahilia (Nationalism or Chauvinism) in Islam

Islam forbids Muslims from reviving or inciting nationalism or chauvinism and considers it to be a kind of Jahilia (in other words, reviving the bad habits and usages of the pre-Islamic era). In this regard, the Prophet states: "He who calls others to group chauvinism does not belong to us; he who fights for the sake of group chauvinism does not belong to us; and he who dies upholding group chauvinism does not belong to us."[33] Moreover, when the Muhajirin (emigrants) called out aloud for help, by saying "O Emigrants," and the Ansaar (partisans) shouted: "O partisans," the prophet said "[T]hese are the practices of the Jahilia (the pre-Islamic era) despite the fact that I am among you." This Hadith means (1) that the prophet does not approve a call that might lead to conflicts, frictions, or tensions; and (2) that such a call is an uncivilized one – it is a kind of Jahilia. Accordingly, even enmity or hatred cannot justify any chauvinism in Islam. For the aim of Islam is justice in the proper sense of the word. The Quran states: "And do not let hatred of (other) people cause you to deviate from justice (V: 8). It continues: "O you who believe, be steadfast in justice, as witnesses for Allah, even though it be against yourselves or parents or kindred" (4: 135).

B.   Contributions of Islam that Are Related to the Operative (modus operandi) Aspects of International Law and Relations

There are various aspects relating to the *modus operandi* of international relations. The most important of which are:
- international treaties;
- diplomatic intercourse;
- combating international terrorism; and
- international responsibility.

i.   In the Field of the Law of International Treaties (pacta sunt servanda and ex consensu advenit vinculum)

a.   Prefatory Remarks

Islam affirms the necessity of the fulfillment of pledges and the respect for agreements. This principle is deeply rooted in the Islamic Shari'a. It is the motto adopted

---

32   A. An-Na'im: Islamic Ambivalence to Political Violence: Islamic Law and International Terrorism, GYIL, 1988, p. 335.

33   English version quoted in *Yusuf Al-Qaradawi*: The Lawful and the Prohibited in Islam, Cairo, p. 330. The Prophet also says that God dislikes he who follows in Islam the tradition of Jahilia (Fath Al-Bari Sharh Sahih Al-Bokhary, vol. 12, p. 244, in Arabic.)

by Islam from the very beginning and one that continues to be a constitution for its society. To keep one's word, therefore, is the basis on which international relationships between Muslims and non-Muslims depend. A treaty is not a game of chess, where a man can move his agreement, whenever he pleases, to another square on the board. In Islam, the rule is the bindingness of international treaties.[34] In this regard, the prophet states: "He who has concluded a pact with a nation should neither tie a knot nor open it until the time expires."

b.   Sayings of Non-Muslim Authors

Some Western scholars have pointed out the adherence of Islam to the sacrosanct character of treaties. With this notion in mind, H. Wehberg states: "For the Islamic peoples, the principle *Pacta sunt servanda,* has also religious basis."[35] Moreover, W. Jenks affirms: "The maxim 'Muslims must abide by their stipulations' is perhaps one of the best known of the traditional maxims of Islamic law."[36] In addition, D. Schwartz points out: "Significantly, the legitimate authority of treaties over every Islamic state is also sanctioned by the Shari'ah."[37] And M. Boisard explains: "*L'Islam a vraisemblablement donné une dimension nouvelle au concept du respect obligatoire des traités en rendant les clauses contraignantes sur une base religieuse.*"[38]

c.   Rules Governing the Bindingness of Treaties in Islam

There are some important rules that govern the bindingness of treaties in Islam, the most important of which are the following:

—   Power does not, *per se,* justify the violation of a treaty. In fact, Allah states: "Fulfil the Covenant of Allah when ye have entered into it, and break not your oaths after ye have confirmed them. Indeed ye have made God your surety. For God knoweth all that ye do. And be not like a woman who untwisted her spun thread, after it has become strong. Nor take your oaths to practise deception between yourselves, lest one party should be more numerous than another"(16:92). A non-Muslim author has made the assertion: "This verse indeed signals out one of the most sensitive issues in international law – the ability of the mere powerful nations to flout their contractual and other obligations towards the weaker."[39] Accordingly, God strongly recommends us not to use this pretext in order to breach a treaty, for this action could threaten the legal security of international legal relations.

---

34   *Ahmed Abou-el-Wafa*: A Book on the Rules of International Law and Relations in Islamic Shari'a, *op. cit.*, vol. 1, pp. 251-56.

35   *H. Wehberg*: Pacta Sunt Servanda, AJIL, 1959, p. 775.

36   *W. Jenks*: The Common Law of Mankind, Stevens and Sons, London, 1958, p. 143.

37   *D. Schwartz*: International Terrorism and Islamic Law, Columbia Journal of Transnational Law, vol. 29, 1991, p. 637.

38   *M. Boisard*: L'Islam et la morale internationale, thèse No. 298, Univ. de Genève, A. Michel, Paris, 1979, p. 228.

39   *G. Weeramantry*: Islamic Jurisprudence: An International Perspective, *op. cit.*, p. 131.

- A Muslim state must carry out its obligations under a treaty, so long as the other party keeps it and does not help enemies to fight Muslims. In this regard, God says: "But the treaties are not dissolved with those pagans with whom ye have entered into alliance and then they have not been deficient toward you in any thing, nor aided anyone against you. So fulfil your engagements with them to the end of their term: for God loveth the righteous" (Sura Tawba: verse 4).
- A Muslim state must abstain from helping other Muslims if it is bound by a treaty prohibiting such help (for example, a peace treaty, a non-aggressive agreement, or a binding decision adopted by an international organ under a constitutive instrument of an international organization to which the Muslim state is a party). It suffices to mention what God says: "Those who believed, and emigrated, and fought for the Faith, with their property and their persons, in the cause of God, as well as those who gave (them) asylum and aid – these are (all) allies, one of another. As to those who believed but did not emigrate, ye owe no duty of protection to them until they emigrate; but if they seek your aid in religion, it is your duty to help them, except against a people with whom ye have a treaty of mutual alliance. And (remember) God seeth all that ye do (Sura Al-Anfal: verse 72).
- In some cases, Muslims must not respond to treachery by using treachery. This principle is merely the application of a Hadith of the prophet "fulfilment (by Muslims) against treachery (of non-Muslims) is better than treachery by treachery."
- Islam also knows the principle of *non-adimpleti contractus,* which is well illustrated by the Quran: "How should the idolaters have a covenant with Allah and with His Messenger, excepting those with whom you made a Covenant at the Holy mosque so long as they go straight with you, go straight with them, for Allah loves the godfearing" (Al-Tawba "Repentance": 7).
- If the Imam perceives treachery on the part of the other parties, he has the right to repudiate the agreement, provided that he gives them notice. Thus, if Muslims feel that other parties have betrayed their covenant or notice any sign of betrayal through their deeds or words, the Imam has the right to terminate the treaty without any deception, treachery, or injustice. Muslim jurists affirm that this action may not occur unless the Muslim ruler informs the other party. The Quran thus reveals: "If thou fearest treachery from any group, throw back (their covenant) to them, so as to be on equal bar (on equal terms): For God loveth not the treacherous" (Anfal: 58). Sarakhsy explains that the expression "on a bar" "[m]eans that you and they are on a bar with regard to knowledge. Thus, it is not permissible to fight them before they know that we have terminated the treaty."[40]
- Islam also prevents Muslims from resorting to treachery. In this context, the prophet Mohamed says: "When Allah gathers together all the first and the last people on the Last Day, a flag will be hoisted up for every treacherous person. Then it is said 'It is the flag of the treachery of so-and-so.'" To illustrate

---

40   *Sarakhsy*: Al-Mabsout, vol. X, p. 87.

this point, it is worth mentioning the following example: There had been a convenant between Mo'awyah (a Muslim Caliph) and the Romans. When the period of the Covenant came to an end, Mo'awyah invaded them. Then a man riding on horseback cried out (Allah is the Great ... there should be fulfilment and no treachery). That man was Amr Ibn Anbasah. Mo'awyah asked him why he had cried out like that. He answered that he had heard the Prophet saying: "As long as there is a covenant between the Muslims and other people, the Muslims should not break it when its stated period comes to an end before notifying them of war." On hearing this tradition, Mo'awyah returned.

– A Muslim ruler must not go back on his word of honour, if it was given to, or concluded with, even the most hated of enemies or non-Muslims and in the most critical times and situations. In fact, under this principle of Islamic law, "the fulfilment of international treaties is imperative even when it is against Muslim state's interest."[41] Moreover, in Islam, "the sanctity of a pledge is above all other considerations, even, in certain cases, above the sanctity of the religion."[42] It suffices to mention the following example. Hothaifa Ibn Al Yaman said that he would not fight with the Muslims in the battle of Badr because, when some of the dis-believers of Quraish tribe had caught him with a fellow of his on their way to the Prophet, he had made a promise not to fight them and not to join the Muslim forces. When the Prophet of Allah knew of the promise, he said: *Do not fight, keep your promise, and God will help us.*

– Muslims must ascertain for themselves the breach that has been made by the other party to the treaty before drawing any consequences therefrom. This principle is an application of what the Quran says: "Ye who believe if a wicked person (Fassik) comes to you with any news, ascertain the truth, lest you harm people unwittingly (in ignorance) and afterwards be sorry for what ye have done" (XLIX: 6). The principle of ascertaining the breach of the treaty is justified by the following factors: (1) to be sure of the breach of the treaty; (2) to ensure the stability and security of international treaties, whereby the Prophet says: "Leave that which brings you doubt to that which makes you doubtless"; (3) to observe to the utmost the principles *pacta sunt scrvanda, ex consensu advenit vinculum,* and *solus consens est obligat*; and (4) to avert treachery, which is wholly inadmissible in Islam.

– A treaty is binding irrespective of the religion of the other party, which means that a treaty concluded by a Muslim state with a non-Muslim state has the same value as that concluded with another Muslim state. In this regard, Imam Al-Maqri says: "A contract with a non-Muslim is like a contract with a Muslim."[43] Moreover, under a well established Islamic rule: "[C]ontracts in Dar

---

41   *Ahmed Abou-el-Wafa*: A Book on the Rules of International Law and Relations in Islamic Shari'a, *op. cit*, vol. 1, p. 257-58.

42   *A. Azzam*: The Eternal Message of Muhammad, p. 141.

43   *Al-Maqri*: Ikhlas Al-Nawi, the Supreme Council for Islamic Affairs, Cairo, 1420 H-2000, Vol. 4, p. 241.

Al-Harb are as binding as those in Dar Al-Islam."[44]

ii.   In the Field of Diplomatic Intercourse

a.   Preliminary Remarks

The right to send and receive diplomatic agents and missions is one of the essential prerogatives and attributes of sovereignty. Rules governing diplomatic relations are the product of long-established practices of different nations, religions, and civilizations.[45] Nowadays, diplomatic intercourse is a necessity of life. In fact, from time immemorial, peoples of all nations have recognized the importance of diplomatic interchanges.

b.   Islam and Diplomatic Intercourse

The contributions of Islam in regard to the law of diplomatic relations are numerous. It suffices to mention the following:
–   From the beginning of the Islamic state, the Prophet sent ambassadors to kings and the heads of state of the neighbouring countries. Ibn Hishâm said that the Prophet sent some of his Companions Sahabah as envoys with letters to the kings, calling them to Islam. Ibn Hishâm also stated that Abû Bakr al Hudhalî said: "I heard that the Prophet (PBUH) went out one day after the 'Umrah which he had been refrained from performing on the Day of Al-Hudaybiyah, and said 'O people, Allah has surely sent me as a mercy to the whole (of mankind), so do not differ among yourselves about me as did the disciples of Îsâ ibn Maryam about him.'" The companions asked: "How was the disciples' difference, O Messenger of Allah?" He (PBUH) answered: 'He invited them to that which I have invited you to. Those who were sent on a near mission were pleased, while those who were sent on a far mission were displeased and showed hesitation. Îsâ complained to Allah, so every one of those who had showen hesitation woke up the next morning speaking the language of the people to whom they were sent." The Prophet (PBUH) sent the following envoys with letters to the following kings, calling them to Islam:
  –   Dihyah ibn Khalîfah al-Kalbî to Caesar, the Roman emperor;
  –   'Abduallâ ibn Hudhâfah to Chosroes, the king of Persia;
  –   'Amr ibn Umayyah ad-Damrî to Negus, the king of Abyssinia;
  –   Hâtib ibn Abî Balta'ah to Muqawqis, the king of Alexandria;
  –   'Amr. ibnul-'Âs as-Sahmî to Jayfar and 'Iyâdh, the sons of Al-Julandâ Al-Azdî, the two kings of 'Umân;
  –   Salît ibn 'Amr, one of the sons of 'Âmir ibn Lu'ayy, to Thumâmah ibn Uthâl and Hawdhah ibn 'Alî, from Banû Hanîfah, the two kings of Al-Yamâmah;
  –   Al-'Alâ' ibnul-Hadramî to Al-Mundhir ibn Sâwâ al-'Abdî, the king of Bahrain; and

---

44   *Ahmed Abou-el-Wafa*: A Book on the Rules of International Law and Relations in Islamic Shari'a, *op. cit.*, vol. 1, p. 238, vol. 15, p. 256.
45   *Ahmed Abou-el-wafa*: Public International Law, p. 370.

- Shujâ' ibn Wahb al-Asadî to Al-*H*ârith ibn Abî Shamir al-Ghassânî, the king of the Syrian borders.[46]
- All of the Muslim rulers who have succeeded the Prophet (PBUH) have, since then, followed the same conduct.[47]
- An ambassador or an envoy need not have an aman granted to him because his mission – that is, carrying diplomatic messages – automatically gives him protection and security. In such a case, he has the right to enter Dar Al-Islam unmolested as an official messenger. This rule has been affirmed by the ICJ[48] and by non-Muslim scholars. It suffices to say that *"[l]'institution de la sauvegarde … fournissant la sécurité aux envoyés étrangers en mission, elle fut à la base de l'activité diplomatique qui, très vite, s'établit entre l'Islam et les pays limitrophes."*[49]
- Islam respects the immunity and inviolability of foreign envoys and ambassadors. They must be respected and never maltreated, molested, or killed. It suffices to mention that, when two envoys committed a criminal act, the prophet said: "Had you not been envoys, I would have ordered you to be killed (beheaded). (But for the fact that ambassadors must not be killed I would have ordered you to be beheaded)." This is not the rule to be found in non-Islamic states, as one author points out: *"Le moyen le plus élémentaire pour entretenir des relations consiste à envoyer, en cas de besoin, des messagers ou des négociateurs temporaires … Dans l'absence de toute règle, ces missions étaient parfois dangereuses pour les envoyés. Nombre d'entre eux, à travers l'histoire, se firent massacrer simplement parce qu'ils apportaient des messages qui ne plaisaient pas au chef ou prince local."*[50] Accordingly, in Islam, envoys and messengers should never be killed or maltreated. The prophet also said to Abou-Rafi'a (an ambassador sent by Quraysh): "I do not breach pacts and I do not arrest ambassadors." Moreover, there is a well-established rule in Islamic law, under which "[d]ifferences in opinion with a diplomatic envoy does not impair his immunity."[51]
- Imam Ibn-Qudama says that "[a] Muslim ambassador who enters the territory of a non-Muslim state must not commit any act of cheating, for cheating constitutes a treachery, and treachery is not valid in our religion."[52] Accord-

---

46   *Sirat Ibn Hisham:* Biography of the Prophet, Cairo, pp. 272-73.

47   *Ahmed Abou-el-Wafa*: A Book on the Rules of International Law and Relations in Islamic Shari'a, Vol. 4: Islamic Diplomatic Law, Dar Al-Nahda Al-Arabia, Cairo, 1421-2001, 543 pp. (in Arabic).

48   *Vide supra.*

49   *M. Boisard*: L'Islam et la morale internationale, *op. cit.*, pp. 222-23; *Abdul-Rahman Arabi*: L'Islam et la guerre à l'époque du prophète Mahomet, thèse, Lausanne, Ambilly, 1954, pp. 38.

50   *J.B. Duroselle*: Tout empire périra-une vision théorique des relations Internationales, publications de la Sorbonne, Paris, 1981, p. 211.

51   *Ibid.*, p. 246.

52   *Ibn Qudama*: Al-Mughny, vol. 10, p. 565 (in Arabic).

ingly, a Muslim ambassador cannot use his status as a cover for cheating or treachery.

–   At present, the legal basis of diplomatic privileges and immunities is that which combines the two theories of "functional necessity" and of the "diplomatic agent's representative character" as the real rationale for the granting of diplomatic privileges and immunities.Thus, the preamble to the 1961 Convention on Diplomatic Relations provides that "the purpose of such privileges and immunities is not to benefit individuals but to ensure the efficient performance of the functions of diplomatic missions as representing states."[53] Islamic law has known this double basis for fourteen centuries:[54] One example is given by Hadith of the prophet: "Had you not been envoys, I would have ordered you to be killed," proves that Muslims know the "diplomatic agent's representative character" as a basis for the accordance of diplomatic privileges and immunities. Another example can be given as Muslim scholars adopt the theory of "functional necessity" as a basis for diplomatic privileges and immunities. Thus, Imam Ibn Qudama says: "It is permitted to give Aman to the ambassador and Musta'amin for it is necessary to do that, because if we kill their envoys they will kill ours, thus we lose the benefits of correspondence."[55] Imam Sarakhsy affirms this idea: "Ambassadors are immune in Jahiliya (i.e., pre-Islamic era) and Islam, for war and reconciliation is made by them, accordingly the Aman of ambassadors is imperative in order to arrive at what is wanted."[56]

–   In case the functions of an ambassador come to an end, the following rules are applicable:

    –   he must be permitted to leave Dar Al-Islam for a safe place, in which he can enjoy Aman;

    –   his family must be immune until they leave Dar-Al-Islam. In this respect, Imam Al-Nawawy says: "If a Harby (a military non-Muslim) enters our territory under an Aman, Dhimma or a message, and he broke his pledge, his sons must not be considered as slaves and must be permitted to arrive at a safe place";[57] and

    –   he must be allowed a reasonable time to leave Dar Al-Islam. In this context, Imam Shaybani says: "If a Muslim gave Aman to a non-Muslim (Harbi), and the Imam (caliph) disliked his residence in Dar Al-Islam, he (the caliph) has the right to ask him to leave, provided that the caliph:

        –   ensures that he will arrive at a safe place; and

---

53   See also: Preambles of the 1963 Vienna Convention on Consular Relations; of the 1969 Convention on Special Missions; of the 1975 Vienna Convention on Representation of States in Their Relations with International Organizations.

54   *Ahmed Abou-el-Wafa*: A Book on the Rules of International Law and Relations in Islamic Shari'a, op. cit., vol. 4, pp. 282-87.

55   *Ibn Qudama*: Al-Mughni Wal-Sharh Al-Kabeer, vol. 10, pp. 436-37 (in Arabic).

56   *Al-Sarakhsy*: Al-Mabsout, vol. 10, pp. 92-93 (in Arabic).

57   *Al-Nawawy*: Rawdat Al-Talibeen, vol. 10, p. 289 (in Arabic).

> – gives him a period which enables him to leave harmless (i.e. without any damage)."[58]

iii.   In the Field of Combating International Terrorism

We will refer first to the Western view of "terrorist Islam" and then to arguments that prove that the said view is ill-founded.

a.   Western View of "Terrorist Islam"

It is well known that acts of terrorism have existed *ab intiquo*. They have developed to the extent of constituting a severe menace to the life and safety of persons as well as the security of property. Such acts are increasing on an alarming scale. They are inadmissible under present international law. With respect to this phenomenon, one can safely say that Islam has no link with such terrorist acts. It has been well established that Islam[59] is a tolerant religion, which prohibits illegitimate violence, intimidation, and terror. However, in the western world, some writers make a *stricto sensu* relationship between Islam and terrorist acts that occur in Muslim and non-Muslim states. They think that Islam is responsible for these acts.[60] This notion is gaining currency among Europeans and other non-Muslims, without anyone caring to debate it or to judge of its impact or repercussions.

b.   Arguments Proving the Fallacy of the "Terrorist Islam" View

Prima facie, this tendency is untenable and ill-founded for the following reasons:
1.   Islam prohibits any unjustified or illegitimate violence. The following Hadiths are relevant: (1) "Kindness is preferable to Allah in all affairs"; (2) "Allah is Kind, and thus He likes kindness. He gives reward for kindness more than what He gives for hardness (harshness) or other acts"; (3) "Kindness decorates anything whenever existent, and it distorts everything, whenever removed;" and (4) "He who has been given his share of kindness is given his share of blessings (goodness) while those who are prevented from their share of kindness are deprived of their share of blessings" (goodness). Even Islam is consid-

---

58   Sharh Kitab Al-Siyar Al-Kabeer, Haidar Abad, Vol. 2, p. 106 (in Arabic).

59   In regard to Islam, it has been highlighted that "with regard to religious tolerance, Islam seems to have a better record than Christianity"(*H. Bielfldt*: Muslim Voices in the Human Rights Debate, Human Rights Quarterly, vol. 17, 1995, p. 597).

60   Thus, in: "Terrorism: How the West Can Win", *B. Netanyahu* ed. (1986), we can find the following articles: *M. Khadduri*: Political Terrorism in the Muslim World; Lewis: Islamic Terrorism; Vatikiotis: The Spread of Islamic Terrorism. See also: *An-Naim*: Islamic Ambivalence to Political Violence-Islamic Law and International Terrorism, German Y.I.L., 1988, pp. 307-336. Moreover, a writer speaks of "[t]he threat of Islamic fundamentalism" and of "the increasing and menacing threat posed by Islamic fundamentalists" (*M. Curtis*: International Law and the Territories, Harvard I.L.J., vol. 32, 1991, p. 467-68). Another writer says: "The term (Islamic revivalism) evokes various associations: antiwestern sentiment, terrorism, factional struggles, a return to traditions, the veil, the Koran (*K. Hamlin*: The Impact of Islamic Revivalism on Contract and Usury Law in Iran, Saudi Arabia and Egypt, Texas I.L.J., vol. 22, 1987, p. 352).

ered to be *a sine qua non instrumentum* to combat terrorism. In this respect, the concept of Islam is clear. On the one hand, it is forbidden to attack the life of others. Thus, the holy Quran says: "Take not life which God Hath made sacred, except by way of justice and law" (6/151). It also says: "Those who invoke not, with Allah, any other God, nor slay any other life as Allah has made Sacred, except for just cause, nor commit fornication; and any that does this (not only) meets punishment" (Al-Furqan: 68). On the other hand, according to the holy Quran, the protection of the lives of others (and vice versa) is a matter that belongs to humanity in its entirety. Thus, the Quran says: "That if any one slew a person – unless it be for murder or for spreading mischief in the land – it would be as if he slew the whole people: and if any one saved a life, it would be as if he saved the life of the whole people." This verse of the Quran connotes three consequences, namely (1) that terrorists are to be considered as *"hostis humane generis."* They must be reckoned as outside the pale of humanity. Their existence is considered injurious to all mankinds; (2) that this inevitably means that respect of human life, in Islam, is a duty *erga omnes,* not only a duty *si omnes*; (3) that the holy Quran considers homicide to be an attack against all mankind and saving a man's life as saving the lives of all mankind (that is, terrorism ought to be considered as a *delicta juris gentium).* In this regard, one can say: *"Bref, l'Islam a pour but la préservation de la valeur absolue de la vie, étant donné son caractère précieux: la vie humaine doit toujours être respectée et protégée dans tous les cas où aucune raison valable ne justifie le contraire. Elle est en effet un don qui intéresse l'humanité toute entière. Cela exige, toujours du point de vue de l'Islam, l'inviolabilité des corps humains afin de préserver la vie de l'individu et, par ce biais, de la collectivité humaine."*[61] Thus, Allah "equates the killing of an innocent person to that of annihilating the entire human kind."[62]

2.   Moreover, the Prophet says: "A Muslim is not permitted to frighten another Muslim"; "Do not frighten a Muslim. For the frightening of a Muslim is a flagrant transgression (injustice); "No one should point to his brother with a weapon. For, he would not know that Satan might drop it from his hands and he would fall in a ditch of the fire"; "The first cases to be judged between people on the Day of Resurrection will be those of bloodshed"; "When anyone is killed unjustly, a portion of the sin falls upon the elder son of Adam, for he was the first to commit murder"; and "I was sent to preach a merciful religion, a gracious religion." The prophet as well says: "Surely I have been sent forth only to perfect righteous morals" (Makarem Al-Akhlak).

3.   In this context, a Western author states: "An appeal to the Shari'ah doctrines might well provide an effective counter method to international terrorism." He

---

61   *Ahmed Abou-el-Wafa*: Le devoir de respecter le droit à la vie en droit international public, Revue Egyptienne de droit international, vol. 40, 1984, p. 69.

62   *Alhaji M. Maccido*: Promoting Religious Harmony in Plural Societies – the Perspective of Islam, in "The Truth about Islam in a Changing World," Fourteenth General Conference of the Supreme Council for Islamic Affairs, Cairo, 1423H.-2002G., p. 46.

adds that "Islamic law condemns terror-violence, and a terrorist who invokes that law may be legally wrong." This is mainly because "respect for human life and property is a fundamental principle of the Shari'ah." He concludes: "Islamic law coordinates, integrates and legislates against that which western jurists have so far failed to control. The Shari'ah is a resource the west must no longer overlook."[63]

4.   In Islam, terrorism is regarded as the most inhumane practice.[64] The offence is heavily punishable. The Quran says: "The punishment of those who wage war against God and His Apostle, and strive with might and main for mischief through the land is: execution, or crucifixion, or the cutting off of hands and feet from opposite sides, or exile from the land: that is their disgrace in this world, and a heavy punishment is theirs in the Hereafter" (V: 33). Moreover, in Islam, there is no impediment to the extradition of criminals. A classical example is that of the year 31 H (more than 1,400 years ago) when a pact was concluded whereby the King of the Nubians (Sudan) accepted the condition: "It will also be incumbent upon you to repulse towards the territory of Islam all fugitive slaves who come to you but who belong to Muslims. Further, you will repulse every Muslim combating Muslims and taking refuge with you. You shall return him from your territory towards the territory of the Muslims. You shall not incline to him nor protect him."[65] A leading scholar affirms: "Against western claims that Islamic fundamentalism feeds terrorism, one powerful paradox of the twentieth century is often overlooked. While Islam may generate more political violence than western culture, western culture generates more street violence than Islam. Islam does indeed produce a disproportionate share of mujahideen, but western culture produces a disproportionate share of muggers."[66]

iv.   In the Field of International Responsibility

The question of responsibility is increasingly placed on the international level, mainly because of the proliferation of organizations, officials, and agents.

a.   Concept of International Responsibility In Islam

Islam has played an important role in crystallizing legal responsibility in general and international responsibility in particular.[67] In fact, "[q]uestions of liability form

---

63   *D.A. Schwartz*: International Terrorism and Islam, Columbia J. of transnational law, vol. 29, 1991, pp. 630, 650-51, 652.

64   *Adh-dhahabi* considers the act of highwaymen who menace the road as one of the major sins in Islam (*Adh-dhahabi*: Major Sins, Cairo, pp. 125-27).

65   English version quoted in *M. Hamidullah*: Muslim Conduct of State, Ashraf, La Hore, 1945, p. 132.

66   *A. Mazuri*: Islamic and Western Values, Foreign Affairs, 1997, p. 130.

67   See: *Ahmed Abou-el-Wafa*: A Book on the Rules of International Law and Relations in Islamic Shari'a, vol. 8: International Responsibility in Islamic Shari'a, *op. cit.*, 271 pp; *El-Sanhoury*: La responsabilité civile et pénale en droit musulman, Revue de l'Union des Universités Arabes, 1995, pp. 549-570; *Jacque El-Hakim*: Le dommage de source

one of the most intricate subject-matters in the Islamic law of obligations."[68] One scholar explains: *"ce qu'il importe de relever dès maintenant, c'est le fait que nous nous trouvons dès le début du droit musulman en présence d'une théorie, moderne pour ainsi dire, de la responsabilité délictuelle. Elle est à base de faute."*[69] In Islamic jurisprudence, there are some rules that govern the question of responsibility, the most important of which are the following:

- Imam Kassani put a very concise rule concerning the origin of liability in Islamic doctrine, whereby "[l]iability in Shari'a is due to the breaking of an obligation or causing a destruction."[70]
- The basis of responsibility in Islam lies essentially in a Hadith of the Prophet, under which, in Islam, there is "no harm and no harming."[71] The rule "no harm and no harming" means:
- that the prohibition of causing harm or damage is a well-established rule in Islam;
- that responsibility is engaged *vis-à-vis* any perpetrator of the wrongful act, irrespective of the religion of the victim – that is, be he a Muslim or a non-Muslim;[72] and
- that the harm or damage must be removed or repaired.
- No-one can be held responsible for anyone else's guilt or actions (principle of personal liability) – that is, a person will be held responsible for his own deeds. The Quran states: "[N]o bearer of burden shall bear the burden of another" (LIII: 38); "Every soul will be (held) in pledge for its deeds" (LXXIV: 38); "[W]hoever works evil, will be requited accordingly" (IV: 123); "[T]hat was a people that hath passed away. They shall reap the fruit of what they did, and Ye of what you do and Ye are not responsible of what they were doing" (2: 134). Accordingly, vicarious liability is, in principle, forbidden in Islam.In this context, Imam Shawkani says that assets of persons are immune in Islam and that engaging the responsibility of a person whom the Shari'a does not consider responsible for the act is contrary to the fundamentals of Islam.[73]
- Under a well-established rule in Islamic Shari'a, "in case of doubt, reparation is forbidden" (*"dans le doute, la réparation n'est point due"*).[74]

---

délictuelle en droit musulman, LGDJ, Paris, 1964, 258 pp; *Ch. Chehata*: Essai d'une théorie générale de l'obligation en droit musulman, thèse, Faculté de Droit-Univerasité du Caire, 1936; *S.H. Amin*: Remedies for Breach of Contract in Islamic and Iranian Law, Royston Limited, Glasgow, 1984; *A. Kazmi*: L'Islam et la réparation du préjudice moral, Librairie Droz, Genève, 1990, 148 pp.

68   *J. Schact*: An Introduction to Islamic Law, p. 147.

69   *E. Tyan*: Le système de responsabilité en droit musulman, thèse, Lyon, 1926, p. 9, 201.

70   *Kassani*: Bada'e Al-Sana'ea, vol. 7, pp. 167-18 (in Arabic).

71   *Ahmed Abou-el-Wafa*: A Book on the Rules of International Law and Relations in Islamic Shari'a, vol. 8: Theory of International Responsibility in Islamic Shari'a, pp. 27ss.

72   *Ibid.*, pp. 31-32.

73   *Shawkani*: Al-Sayl Al-garar, vol. 3, p. 218.

74   *J. El-Hakim*: Le dommage de source délictuelle en droit musulman, *op. cit*, p. 153.

b.   Effects of International Responsibility in Islam

Reparation – that is, undoing the damage and eliminating the consequences that the breach of an international obligation had caused – is an outstanding principle of present international law. Reparation essentially has three forms, namely *restitutio in integrum,* compensation, and satisfaction. Islam knows the effects of responsibility, especially *restitutio in integrum*, compensation, and satisfaction:

Restitutio in integrum

Restitutio in integrum is established in Islam by the following verse: "God doth command you to render back your trusts to these to whom they are due" (IV: 58). Moreover, a Hadith of the Prophet says: "A hand (namely, a person) must render back what it (he) has taken." There are many examples proving that Muslims have adopted the principle of *restitutio in integrum* or the restitution of *status quo ante*, the most important of which are the following:

- It is related, that when Qutaiba ibn Muslim (a commander) conquered the city of Samarcand, without warning, the latter sent to the just Caliph Umar ibn Abdul-Aziz, complaining of what Qutaiba had done. The Caliph referred the complaint to his magistrate and told him to investigate the case. The magistrate's inquiry proved the charge to be true, so the soldiers were told to go back to their camp and the choice was offered to the people of Samarcand who preferred to make a covenant with the Muslims.
- When the Umayyad caliph Al-Walid ibn Yazid exiled the People of the Covenant from Cyprus and resettled them in Syria, the scholars of religion and law were furious with him and considered his action to be oppressive and hostile. When his son Yazid became the Caliph, the scholars addressed him about repatriating the Cypriots, because they knew him to be a just man. He agreed.
- At the time of the fourth Caliph Ali Bin Abi Taleb, Judge Shoraih ordered the Muslim army to evacuate an occupied city, for the army occupied it in contravention to the treaty of peace concluded with that city.

Compensation

Prima facie, the payment of compensation for loss caused is a general principle of law. The ICJ affirmed that "[i]t is a well-established rule of international law that an injured state is entitled to obtain compensation from the state which has committed an internationally wrongful act for the damage caused by it."[75] This principle is also true in Islam. It suffices to mention the following example. The prophet Mohamed sent Khaled Ibn Al-Waleed to Bani-Gothaymah to call them to Islam, not to fight them. However, Khaled killed some of them and took their weapons. After the prophet had known what Khaled did, his reaction was twofold, namely (1) the prophet said: "O! God I do not approve what Khalid did" and (2) the prophet told Ali Ibn Abi-Taleb to go to Bani-Bothaymah in order to examine their case and ordered him (a) to disregard what happened in Djahilia – that is, "ignorance" or the dark days of Arabia (the state of things that was prevailing before Islam (for exam-

---

75   ICJ, Rep., 1997, p. 69, para. 152.

ple, not to remember revenges or retaliations)); and (b) to compensate them for each damage suffered by them (for example, concerning their blood or assets and even dogs). Having finished, Ali asked them: "[W]as there any thing (blood or asset) which had not been compensated?" They replied: "No." Then Ali, still having a great sum of money, told them: "I give you as well what rests with me from the sum of money sent by the prophet, as a precaution for what we know or do not know of the damage suffered by you. When Ali came back, he told the prophet what he had done. The prophet said: "[Y]ou were right and you did a good thing." Then, the prophet said (three times): I do not approve what Khalid did."[76] This incident reveals three important principles, namely:

– The prophet did not follow what states follow now – that is, to cover errors of their armed forces. On the contrary, he did not approve them. This is in conformity with the obligation of non-repetition of the wrongful act, which was recently adopted by the international law commission in its 2001 draft articles on international responsibility (Article 30).[77]

– The prophet approved what Ali made, particularly paying more than what was necessary as a compensation. Needless to say, nowadays, lump-sum agreements concluded between states usually compensate a part, not all, of the damage.

– Al-Waquedi said that the prophet borrowed the sum of money sent to Bani-Gothaymah.[78] This proves that, in the eyes of the prophet, that compensating for the damage suffered must be made as soon as possible even in cases where there is a shortage of money. *Prima facie*, states do not usually apply this principle in present international relations.

Satisfaction

Satisfaction is usually made by the state that has committed the wrongful act, particularly, and not exclusively, for non-material injury (préjudice immatériel in French) that has been occasioned by that act. Satisfaction usually takes the form of expression of regret, an acknowledgment of the breach, formal apology, application of disciplinary measures or punishment against tortfeasors or responsible officials, the holding of an inquiry, the taking of measures to prevent the recurrence of the injury, damage, or the internationally worngful act, and so on. As an example of satisfaction in Islamic practice, one can mention the following incident. Muslims entred the territories of Jews and took some of what they had cultivated. The Jews complained to the prophet. The prophet, after having blessed God said: "The Jews complained that you entered their territory, we have given them Aman for their persons and assets and what they have in their territories, assets of Mua'ahideen is not Mubah except for a just reason."[79] Having heard this, the Muslims followed what the prophet said and did not take any thing from the Jews, save by buying it. In the final analysis, one can safely affirm that, in Islam, there is a well-established rule according to which "[a] Muslim is

---

76   *Ibn-Hisham*: Al-Syrah Al-Nabaweya, vol. 2, p. 428-13 (in Arabic).
77   General Assembly, off. Rec., supp. No. 49 (A/56/49), 2001, p. 503.
78   *Al-Waquedi*: Kitab Al-Maghazi, vol. 3, p. 882 (in Arabic).
79   *Al-Waquedi*: Al-Maghazi, *op. cit.*, vol. 2, pp. 690-91 (in Arabic).

forbidden from committing an internationally wrongful act."[80] This rule is a result of the fact that "his religion and reason prohibits him from committing illegal acts."[81]

C.   *Contributions of Islam in Regard to Human Rights*

Humanity is one of the characteristics of Islam.[82]

i.   Preliminaries

The codification of human rights and fundamental freedoms has been done in stages, from the British Magna Charta Libertatum (1215), habeas corpus act (1679), and Bill of Rights (1689), via the French human rights declaration (1789), to the universal declaration of human rights (1948), the United Kingdom Human Rights Act (1998), and the United States International Religious Freedom Act (1998),[83] and finally the other relevant pacts, decisions, covenants, resolutions, declarations, and treaties (including those that are related to the rights of woman, children, and so on). Islamic doctrine has made great contributions to the issue of human rights, in some cases, predating these aforementioned Western efforts.[84] In this context, a great Western scholar, Count Leon Ostrorog, explains:

> Those Eastern thinkers of the 7th Century laid down the principle of the Rights of Man in those very terms comprehending the rights of individual liberty and of inviolability of person and property; described the ruling power as based on a contract implying conditions of capacity and performance and subject to cancellation if the conditions under the contract were not fulfilled; elaborated a law of war the human and chivalrous prescriptions of which would have put to the blush belligerents in the Great War; and expounded a doctrine of tolerance on non-Muslim creeds so liberal that our West had to wait a thousand years before seeing equivalent principles adopted.[85]

ii.   *"Ratio Legis"* of Human Rights in Islam

Islam aims to maintain the five "universals"[86] ("fundamentals" or "essentials"), namely religion, life (the soul), reason (the brain, mind), descendants (pogency),

---

80   *Ahmed Abou-el-Wafa*: A Book on ..., vol. 8, *op. cit.*, p. 251.

81   *Ibid.*, vol. 14, p. 274.

82   *Y. Al-Qaradawy*: Introduction to Islam, Islamic Inc. Publishing and Distribution, Cairo, 1997, pp. 131-39.

83   ILM, 1999, p. 176, 464.

84   *M.A. Al-Midani*: Les apports Islamiques au développement du droit international des droits de l'homme, thèse, Strasbourg, 1987, 499 pp.

85   Quoted by *T. Mahmoud*: Civilizational Content of Islamic Teachings Relevance for 21st Century, in "Islam and the 21st Century," Tenth General Conference of the Supreme Council for Islamic Affairs, Cairo, 1419 H. – 1998G., p. 85.

86   This is, in my opinion, the best translation of the Arabic word: "Kuliaat." The translation is that of *Dr. R. Gilani*: The Reconstruction of Legal Thought in Islam, Idara Turjman Al-Quran, La Hore, 1977, p. 365.

and property (money, the wealth). In Islam, man is God's vicegerent on earth. This belief is well illustrated by the following verses of the Quran: "Behold, your Lord said to the angels: I will create a vicegerent on earth. They said: will You place therein one who will make mischief therein and shed blood? Whilst we do celebrate Your praises and glorify Your Holy (Name). He said, 'I know what you know not.' And He taught Adam the names of all things, then he placed them before the angels, and said: "Tell me the names of these if you are right," They said: "Glory be to You: of knowledge we have none, save what You have taught us: in truth it is You Who is perfect in knowledge and wisdom; He said: 'O, Adam, tell them their names.' When he had told them, God said, 'Did I not tell you that I know the secrets of heavens and earth, and I know what you reveal and what you conceal?' And behold, we said to the angels 'Bow down to Adam,' and they bowed down: not so Iblis, he refused and was haughty; he was of those who reject faith" (2: 30–34). In Islam, there are two principles according to which "[t]he inviolability of a Muslim is better than the inviolability of the territory (Dar)" and "[a] Muslim is not permitted to protect himself by sacrificing the soul of another person who is as inviolable as him."[87]

iii.   *"Fons et origo"* of Human Rights in Islam: Human Dignity

In its preamble, the universal declaration of human rights states that the "recognition of the inherent dignity ... is the foundation of freedom, justice and peace in the world."[88] Fourteen centuries before the universal declaration of human rights, Islam affirmed the same *"fons et origo"* of these rights. In fact, respect for human dignity is deep-rooted in Islam. It affirms that each human being enjoys his human dignity, irrespective of his race, colour, or religion. It suffices to mention that the holy Quran says: "And we have honoured the sons of Adam" (XVII: 70); "Surely, we have created man in the best stature" (XCV: 4); and "We have provided them (the human-beings) with transport on land and sea; given them for sustenance things good and pure; and conferred on them special favours above a great part of our Creation" (XVII: 70). Moreover, the prophet says that "[i]t is not permitted that believers humiliate themselves to others." The prophet also states: "You all come from Adam, and Adam was created from dust. An Arab has no merit over a non-Arab, as well a white has no merit over a black, except by piety." There are two Islamic rules: (1) "The human being is honoured even if he is non-Muslim (Kafir)" and (2) "The human being is the building of Allah, so it is forbidden to destroy the building of Allah."[89]

---

87   *Ahmed Abou-el-Wafa*: A Book on the Rules of International Law and Relations in Islamic Shari'a, *op. cit.*, vol. 5, p. 131; vol. 15, pp. 261; vol. 6, p. 343; vol. 15, pp. 265-66.

88   *Ahmed Abou-el-Wafa*: The International Protection of Human Rights, R. Egyptienne de Droit International, 1998, pp. 55-56.

89   *Ahmed Abou-el-Wafa*: A Book on the Rules of International Law and Relations in Islamic Shari'a, *op. cit.*, vol. 2, p. 209; vol. 15, pp. 257, 292; vol. 13, pp. 227.

iv.   Muslim Authors Have Known the International Protection of Human Rights for More than a Thousand Years

Muslim jurists have known the principle of the international protection of human rights for many centuries. Imam Sarakhsi (in his book Al-Mabsut) recognized the principle by saying:

> If the king of the dhimmis asked to be accorded full authority to rule his subjects: to kill and crucify whom he likes to be put to death, and to resort to other tyrannical measures which are inappropriate to be enforced in the land of Islam, his request should be wholly refused; since the recognition of injustice, while it is being possible to have it eradicated, is strictly Haram (Forbidden). This is also due to the fact that the dhimmi abides by the rules of Islam in his transactions. To stipulate any term that is contradictory to the covenant is null and void. If peace is made, together with the obligations accorded to dhimmis, terms included, proving to be contrary to the Islamic principles, cease to be effective; since the Prophet says, "Any condition or term, not explicitly mentioned in the Book of God (i.e., the Qur'an) is null and void."[90]

This verse means that (1) it is forbidden to have relationships with those who violate human rights and fundamental freedoms; (2) it is indispensable to adopt all possible measures to remove every violation of human rights and fundamental freedoms since such violations, in Sarakhsi's opinion, are Haram; (3) the criterion to be adopted, in this regard, is that of consistency or not of the act with the rules of Islamic law; (4) the protection of human rights and fundamental freedoms of non-Muslims must constitute one of the essential concerns of the Islamic state; (5) a treaty providing for, or allowing, violations of human rights is null and void; and (6) solidarity in regard to human rights is an Islamic principle. Moreover, Shaybani affirms: "It is a principle that the ruler of the Muslims is bound to protect foreigners as long as they are in our territory, and to do justice to them against those who do (them) wrong."[91]

v.   Non-Muslim Authors Have Admitted the Role of Islamic Doctrine in this Context

Thus, one author states: *"[L]es valeurs sur les droits de l'homme se retrouvent à quelques détails près dans le fonds Islamique."*[92] Judge Weeramantry explains: "It is indeed the reverse of the truth for western jurists to suggest that there was no doctrine of human rights in Islamic jurisprudence. In fact, the Islamic concepts took the doctrine of human rights well beyond their western formulation by reason of the more rounded and community-oriented attitudes of Islamic law."[93]

---

90   *See: Ahmed Abou-el-Wafa*: A Book on the Rules of International Law and Relations in Islamic Shari'a, vol. 6: Human Rights in Islamic Shari'a, *op. cit.*, pp. 580-81.

91   *Shaybani*: Sharh Kitab siyar Al-Kabir, vol. 4, p. 108 (in Arabic).

92   *R. Santucci*: Le regard de l'Islam, in Islam et droits de l'homme, librairie des libertés, Paris, 1984, p. 182.

93   *C.G. Weeramantry*: Islamic Jurisprudence an International Perspective, *op. cit.*, pp. 126-127.

vi.   Study of Some Human Rights in Islam

This section will examine, *inter alia*, the following three rights.

a.   *Rights of the Child*

Prima facie, having children is an instinctive desire for each human being. This desire preserves the human species and perpetuates the human turnover on our globe. There are some important rules governing the legal position of a child in Islam, namely:

–   At war, children that are taken are subject to a well-known principle in Islam: "The separation between a mother and her child is not permitted." This is a direct application of a saying of the prophet: "He who separates between a mother and a child shall be separated from his love one by Allah in the Hereafter." Accordingly, in Islam, the reunion of a family (and, particularly, of a child and his mother), who has been dispersed as a result of war, is an obligation incumbent upon Muslims. In this context, international law, fourteen centuries after the emittence of this verse, has evolved in the following way:

–   The fourth Geneva Convention (1949) provides for the possibility of members of families dispersed owing to war, to renew contact with one another and to meet (Article 26);

–   The Additional Protocol no. 1 (1977) to the 1949 Geneva Conventions states that "[t]he High contracting parties and the parties to the conflict shall facilitate in every possible way the reunion of families dispersed as a result of armed conflicts" (Article 74).

–   The Convention on the Rights of the Child, which was adopted by the UN General Assembly in 1989) has adopted one of the principles of Islamic law – that is, the kafalah (giving financial, material, and moral care) principle. In fact, in regard to the child who is temporarily or permanently deprived of his or her family, he or she is entitled to special care. Article 20, paragraph 3, of the convention adds: "Such care could include, inter alia, foster placement, kafalah of Islamic law, adoption or if necessary placement in suitable institutions for the care of children." Evidently, this proves that a principle of a certain legal system may be embodied in present positive international law.

–   Even, the unborn child is entitled, in Islam, to the protection of any harm. Thus, for example, abortion is absolutely prohibited in Islam, unless the mother's life is endangered. Another example is that the unborn child is entitled to inheritance. If his father dies before his birth, the inheritance is decided upon after the child's birth.

–   Children are to be treated with justice. Islam aims at realizing justice among the children of the same person. For this reason, a father or a mother is prohibited from giving more favours on one child than on others without any justifiable reasons to do so. Such actions may, *prima facie*, arouse tension, friction and jealousy, hatred and enmity among the children and may affect the right of, for example, their inheritance. In this context, the prophet says: "Do justice among your sons, and repeated it thrice." The story behind this hadith is that the wife of Bashir Ibn Said Al-Ansari requested her husband to give a gift of a garden or a slave to her son, Al-Nu'man Ibn Bashir. She asked Bashir to go to the Prophet (PBUH) and request him to be a witness. Bashir went to him, saying. "The daughter of such and such – meaning his wife – has asked me to give a slave to her son." "Does he have brothers?" the prophet (PBUH) asked. "Yes," he replied, "Did you give the same to each of them"? inquired the prophet (PBUH) "No" said Bashir. The prophet (PBUH) then said: "This is not correct, and I can never bear witness to other than what is just." Some other Hadiths in this regard include: "Do not ask me to be a witness to injustice. Your children have the right of receiving equal treatment, as you have the right that they should honor you" and "Fear Allah and treat your children with equal justice."[94]

b.   Women's Rights in Islam

Islam did a lot to change the reprehensible treatment of women. In 1993, the Prince of Wales (Prince Charles) said (during his visit to the Oxford Centre for Islamic Studies): "The rights of Muslim women to property and inheritance, to some protection if divorced, and to the conducting of business, were rights prescribed by the Qur'an fourteen centuries ago, even if they were not everywhere translated into practice, some of these rights were novel even to my grandmother's generation."[95] The following rules concern women's rights in Islam:

c.   Right to Life

During the pre-Islamic era, countless dehumanizing and barbarous acts were applied to brutalize the status of women on this earth. The shari'a, for example, prohibited the old pre-Islamic custom of burying females alive (female infanticide). In this regard, the Quran states: "When the female (infant) buried is questioned for what crime she was killed" (81/8–9).

d.   Prohibition of Al-Shighar

The prophet forbade Al-Shighar, which was a practice of marrying a daughter to a person and, then, in return the latter marries his daughter to the former without paying dowry.[96]

e.   Right of Property

In Islam, a woman has total economic independence. Assets and property remain her own, and she has the right to freely and solely manage and dispose of her property, money, and assets without her husband's permission. This rule dates back to as early as the beginning of Islam – that is, more than 1,400 years ago. Whereas,

---

94   English version quoted in *Yusuf Al-Qaradawi*: The Lawful and the Prohibited in Islam, *op. cit.*, p. 305.

95   See Islam and the West, Ninth General Conference of the Supreme Council for Islamic Affairs, Cairo, 1998-1419, p. 9.

96   See: *A. Marzouk* and *M.B. Salem*: Selections from Saheeh Al-Bukhary, The Supreme Council for Islamic Affairs, Cairo, 1414-1993, p. 110.

until the nineteenth century, other civilizations gave the husband the right to sell his wife's property against her will and without her permission and even prevented her from managing and disposing of her property without her husband's permission. In this context, one author argues: "Women before Islam were divested of all rights as human beings, as though they were beings without souls. Even in the sixties of this century in the province of Quebec, Canada, the husband could sell his wife's property without her knowledge nor with a power of attorney."[97] Moreover, Article 217 of the French Civil Code (Napoleonic Code) stated that "a married woman, even when her wedding was on the basis of separating between her property and that of her husband, may not give, transfer possession, mortgage, or possess through compensation or not, without the participation of her husband in the contract or his consent to it in writing."

f.   Right of Inheritance

Before the Islamic era, women were deprived of inheritance. They were even inherited as property, in the same way as cattle, goods, and assets. This practice was condemned by the holy Quran: "O, Ye who believe! You are not allowed to inherit women against their will" (4: 19). In this regard, a scholar asserts: "The interpreters said that Ous Ibn Thabet El Ansari died leaving a widow called 'Om Kahha' and three daughters. Two men called Souwayed and Arfaga who were the cousins of the deceased and his guardian, took his money giving nothing to his wife or daughters. In the Djahilia neither the Women nor the young even if the latter was a male did inherit the deceased. Only the adult men inherited him. It was said in the Djahilia: only he who fights mounting his horse and taking spoils, is entitled to inheritance. Om Kahha came to the prophet (PBUH) and said: 'Apostle of God, Ous Ibn Thabet has died leaving me three daughters. I am a woman and have nothing to give them. Their father has left a good fortune which is held by Sowayed and Arfaga. The two gave me nothing and the three daughters are with me. The two gave me neither to eat nor to drink, nor do they care about the children.' The prophet (PBUH) called the two. They said to God's Apostle, her offspring does not mount a horse nor wound a foe. Here the Apostle of God (PBUH) said: 'Go now until I see what is to be revealed to me for them.' They went away. God then revealed the verse, 'Unto the men belongth a share of that which parents and near kindred leave, and unto the women a share of that which parents and near kindred leave.'"[98] Another scholar writes: "British women, however, were granted the right to own property independent of their husbands, only in 1870, while Muslim woman have always had the right. Indeed, Islam is the only world religion founded by a businessman in commercial partnership with his wife. While in many western cultures daughters couldn't inherit anything if there were sons in the family, Islamic law has always al-

---

97   *Abu-Shabanah*: A Favourable Aspect of the Qur'an in Honouring the Woman, the Supreme Council for Islamic Affairs, Cairo, 1999-1420, p. 12.

98   *I. Al-labban*: The Qur'an and Society, Fourth Conference of the Academy of Islamic Research, Cairo, 1388-1968, p. 561.

located shares from every inheritance to both daughters and sons. Primogeniture has been illegal under the shari'a for 14 centuries."[99]

Some orientalists affirm that Islam treats women unjustly since men inherit twice as much of the inheritance as the women, according to the verse: "God directs you as regards your children's (inheritance): to the male a portion equal to that of two females" (4/11). However, if this verse is understood correctly, it would be acknowledged that there is no injustice for females. In fact, in Islam, a husband is under a duty to maintain and provide for his wife and children (as well as other members of his family), and his wife is not charged with any financial expenditure, however wealthy she may be. In Islam, a woman is not burdened with the up-keep of her family. Moreover, there are some cases in which Islam equalizes between male and female in bequest. For example, when there are two parents, a son with two daughters or more, the mother's share will be equal to that of the father's. Both will take one-sixth, according to God's saying: "And for his parents each will have a sixth of what he left behind if he has a son" (IV: 11). In case there are brothers and sisters of the mother, they all deserve one-third of the bequest, which will be divided among them equally unless there is a reason for not doing so. In this regard, God says: "If the man or woman whose inheritance is in question, has left neither ascendants nor descendants, but has left a brother or a sister, each one of the two gets a sixth, but if more than two, they share in a third" (Verse 12; Surat Al-Nisa-a).[100]

g.   Right of Equality

From the outset, Islam has recognized the foundations of the principle of equality. No-one is superior to another by reason of his or her creed, ancestry, lineage, national origin, gender, wealth, birth, colour, language, caste, and so on. The message, mission, and purpose of Islam are totally contrary to such an idea. Accordingly, there is: "[n]o racialism in Islam."[101] In fact, it is hard to find, and even to imagine, any system that can equal Islam in its respect of human dignity and its prohibition of any form based on racial elements. Islam "equalized between people in common human value."[102] Abdur Rahman Shad explains: "Islam is the only religion in the world which transcends all racial barriers and sweeps away all sorts of distinctions whatsoever from the Society. It guarantees equal status to all human beings. It brings all the people on equal footing declaring that the sole criterion of honour and superiority with Allah is not riches but piety."[103] Moreover, M. Watt states: "It is one of the noteworthy achievements of Islam that it has united in a great society men of different races and social traditions." He adds that Islam is "a great brother-

---

99   *A. Mazuri*: Islamic and Western Values, Foreign Affairs, vol. 76, Sept. 1997, p. 119.

100   *A.A. Wafi*: Human Rights in Islam, Riyadh, p. 124.

101   *M. A. Alkhuli*: The Need for Islam, Riyadh, 1987, p. 45.

102   *A. A. Wafi*: Human Rights in Islam, *op. cit.*, p. 13.

103   *Abdur Rahman Shad*: The Rights of Allah and Human Rights, Adam Publishers Distributers, Delhi, 1987, pp. 5-6.

hood including countless races and states."[104] Accordingly, one can safely say that *"[l]'Islam voit l'humanité comme un immense jardin, dont les fleurs sont de couleurs multiples, mais aucune couleur n'a priorité sur l'autre."*[105] Another author adds: "Islam reaches out to all classes and is not in favor of any group over others."[106] Let us now consider what the Quran, the Sunna, and the practice of Islamic states and other states have to say about equality.

h.   Quran

There are many verses in the Quran that illustrate the equality of all human beings. It suffices to cite the following: "The believers are but a single brotherhood" (49/10); "Mankind was but one nation, but differed later" (10/19); "O, Mankind! Reverence your Guardian-Lord who created you from a single person, created of like nature, his mate, and from them twain scattered (like seeds) countless men and women"(4/1); and "O, Mankind! We created you from a single (pair) of a male and a female, and made you into nations and tribes, that ye may know each other. Verily, the most honoured of you in the sight of God is (he who is) the most righteous of you" (49/13).

i.   Sunna

The Sunna also admits no difference between people and does not recognize any racism, discrimination, or xenophobia. It suffices to mention the following examples:

—   The prophet said: "People are as equal as the teeth of a comb."
—   It is related that Osama Ibn-zeid asked the prophet forgiveness for a woman who committed stealing. The prophet said: "You want to violate one of the God's rules; those before us perished because they left an influential man (dignitary or honorable) to go free if he stole, and if a weak (a common man) stole they punished him. By God, if my own daughter Fatma stole, I would cut her hand."
—   In his farewell speech, the prophet affirmed: "O people! Your God is one God and your father is one father, for you are all descendants of Adam, and Adam was created from dust (clay). The most honoured of you in the sight of God is the most righteous. No Arab is superior to a non-Arab and no non-Arab is superior to an Arab. No dark-skinned man is superior to a fair-skinned man, except by his piety."
—   On one occasion, the prophet (PBUH) heard Abou Tharr talking angrily with Bilal while arguing and saying to him, "you son of a black woman." The prophet was very angry. He said to Abou Tharr: "You are a man with jahilite attitude. You are all sons of Adam and are fully equal. The son of a white woman has no privilege over the son of a black woman except by righteousness or good

---

104   *W. Montgomery Watt*: Islam and the Integration of Society, *op. cit.*, pp. 87, 136.
105   *A. Kamil*: L'Islam et la question raciale, UNESCO, Paris, 1970, p. 30.
106   *Y. Al-Qaradawi*: General Characteristics of Islam, Islamic Inc. Publishing and Distribution, Cairo, 2002, p. 137.

deeds." This Hadith is good proof of the incorrectness of the following opinion: *"L'histoire nous montre que les musulmans de race non arabe (a'gâm) furent toujours maintenus par les conquérants dans une condition d'infériorité."*[107]

j.   In the Practice of Islamic States and Other States

Unlike some systems of law that declare that the king can do no wrong, Islamic law does not give this inviolability to the ruler for acts done in his private capacity. In such a case, he is as liable to be tried before an ordinary court as any other Muslim citizen commoner. Thus, authors of the biography of the prophet consecrated a chapter entitled "His Giving Retaliation (*lex talionis*) against His Own Person." The caliphs also heard cases against their proper persons.[108] In short, in Islam, there is no discrimination between the ruler and the ruled, the rich and the poor, the noble and the commoner, the conqueror and the subject, the weak and the strong, the black and the white. These sayings of Islam date back to fourteen centuries ago, whereas, until very recently, the legal rules of the United States discriminated between American white and black citizens. Thus, in an address to Howard University in 1965, the American president Lindon Johnson stated:

> To be a Black man in the United States is to be deprived economically, culturally, politically, socially, educationally. In far too many ways, American Negroes have been another nation deprived of freedom, crippled by hatred, the door of opportunity closed to hope ... Despite the Court orders and the law, despite the legislative victories and the speeches for them, the walls of segregation are rising and the gulf between the Blacks and Whites is widening ... Negroes may be equal in the eyes of the law in America but not always in the eyes of the law-enforcer.[109]

Additionally, it is only in the year 2000 that South Africa issued an act, calling for the "[p]romotion of equality and prevention of unfair discrimination Act."[110] Moreover, in a comparison between Islam and the attitude of Americans towards Blacks, H. Dunant said:

> *Quelle différence entre Cette conduite de la plupart des américains, et celle si humaine des sectateurs du koran envers les hommes de couleur! chez les Musulmans les lois ont été faites en faveur de l'esclave, tandis qu'en Amérique, dictées par l'avarice et l'égoisme, elles l'enserrent, de toutes parts, comme une prison aux murs de fer. Chez les premiers,*

---

107   *M.V. Berchem*: La propriété territoriale et l'impôt foncier sous les premiers califes, thèse, Genève, 1886, p. 35.

108   For more examples, see: *Ahmed Abou-el-Wafa*: A Book on the Rules of International Law and Relations in Islamic Shari'a, Vol. 6: Human Rights in Islamic Shari'a, *op. cit.*, pp. 123-32; *A.A. Wafi*: Human Rights in Islam, *op. cit.*, pp. 34-43.

109   Quoted by *Colin Legum*, "America's Colour crisis-1," The Pakistan Times (Lahore), December 4, 1967, p. 7, and cited by: *Z. Ahmad*: Islamic vs Western Approach Towards Human Rights, Umm Al-Qura University, 1414H; p. 211.

110   See: ILM, 2000, pp. 905 *et seq.*

non seulement le noir ou le mulâtre est traité avec ménagements et bonté, mais il est considéré par les moeurs et par la loi comme l'égal de l'homme blanc; aucun mépris ne pèse sur lui: en un mot, c'est un frère. [111]

D.   Contributions of Islam Concerning Jihad (War) and Peace

In international relations, the question of war and peace has been of great importance. It lies at the *fons et origo* of many legal rules governing relations between the subjects of international law. This section will first study the question of war and then turn to the notion of peace.

i.   Islam and Jihad (War)

Clearly, war holds a great place in history. The gravity of the phenomenon of wars and of the suffering that they cause are beyond any doubt.[112] For this reason, war is now prohibited. War is, *par excellence* and *per definitionem,* murderous and destructive. The sorrows and sufferings of war are well known. With respect to Jihad, a Muslim scholar explains: "Jihad in Arabic means the exerting of one's utmost power in repelling an enemy."[113] Accordingly, as far as its linguistic origins are concerned, Jihad is far from being an offensive war. Before and at the beginning of Islam there was no law but that of the powerful. The principle was that: "the strong swallow the weak."

The study of Jihad in Islam necessitates that we refer to: (1) the opinions of scholars; (2) the cases in which war is prohibited in Islam; and (3) the cases in which Jihad is permitted in Islam.

a.   Opinions of Scholars

There are two leading views. The first is that war is the basis of relations between Muslims and non-Muslims. Certain authors consider that relations between Islam and other states are primarily based on war. In fact, some Western scholars describe Islam as a "warrior religion." In this respect, L. Milliot affirms: "*Les relations extérieures de la communauté musulmane étant ainsi définies par la guerre.*"[114] Nys explains: "*La guerre sainte, le Djihad, doit être entreprise contre tous les infidèles qui ... refusent d'embarrasser l'Islamisme.*"[115] The second view is that peace is the

---

111   *H. Dunant*: L'esclavage chez les musulmans et aux Etats – Unis d'Amérique, Genève, imprimerie Jules – Guillaume Fick, 1863, pp. 43-44.

112   Thus, in regard to the use of force by the states members of NATO against Yugoslavia, the ICJ states that it is: "Profoundly concerned with the use of force in Yugoslavia." And that: "such use raises serious issues of international law" ICJ, Rep., 1999, *Case Concerning Legality of the Use of Force (Yugoslavia V. Belgium)*, para, 17.

113   *Al-Raghib Al-Asphahany*: Al-Mufradat fi Ghareeb Al-Qur'an (in Arabic).

114   *L. Milliot*: La conception de l'Etat et de l'ordre légal dans l'Islam, RCADI, Vol. 75, 1949, p. 602.

115   *Nys*: Le droit des gens dans les rapports des Arabes et des Byzantins, R. de DI et de législation comparée, 1894, p. 464; *G.H. Bousquent*: Du droit musulman et de son application effective dans le monde, imprimerie Nord-Africaine, Alger, 1949, p. 100.

basis of relations between Muslims and non-Muslims, while recourse to war is the exception. According to this ideology , in Islam, only "a war which meets the tests of Jihad, i.e., one which has its objective the preservation of Islamic faith and community, may be undertaken."[116] Moreover, D. Schwartz says: "Islamic law places strict limitations upon a state's exercise of military force. The western notion that Islam encourages or contributes to the current violent upheaval in the Middle East is absolutely inaccurate. The shariah does not counsel aggression."[117] This second view is the one that had now been adopted by the overwhelming majority of Muslim scholars. It is understood from the cases in which war is prohibited and those in which war may be waged.

b.   Cases in which War Is Prohibited in Islam

According to the jurist-philosopher Al-Farabi, there are four kinds of forbidden war, namely: (1) wars motivated by the ruler's personal advantage, such as lust for power, honour, or glory; (2) wars of conquest waged by the ruler for the subordination of peoples other than the people of the city over which he presides; (3) wars of retribution – the object of which can be achieved by means other than force; and (4) wars leading to the killing of innocent men for no reason other than the ruler's propensity or pleasure for killing.[118] To this list, one can add three other types of war, namely: (1) waging war in cases other than those mentioned below (that is, cases in which a recourse to Jihad is permitted); (2) waging war in violation of a treaty prohibiting the use of force to settle a dispute; and (3) waging war against neutral states.

c.   Cases in which Jihad is Permitted in Islam

Islam is not eager to wage war. The prophet says: "Do not be eager to meet enemy, and ask God for safety." In fact, when Allah sent His Apostle and ordered him to call all people to embrace his religion, Allah did not allow the prophet to fight until the believers were oppressed and tyrannized. At that very time, Allah permitted the Muslims to fight their enemies. In this context, the Quran says: "To those against whom war is made, permission is given (to fight), because they are wronged; and verily, God is the Most Powerful for their aid." This verse was the first to be revealed on the subject of fighting.This being so, war is legitimate in Islam only in the following cases:

–   In the event of an aggression against the Muslim state (self-defence). War in Islam is primarily of a defensive nature. It suffices to cite as an example Chapter 16: II of the holy Quran: "Fight in defence of the cause of God against those who attack you, but begin ye no hostilities. Verily, Good loveth not the ag-

---

116   *R. Algase*: Protection of Civilian Lives in Warfare: a Comparaison Between Islamic Law and Modern International Law Concerning the Conduct of Hostilities, Revue De Droit Pénal Militaire Et De Droit De La Guerre, 1977, p. 250.

117   *David A. Schwartz*: International Terrorism and Islamic Law, Columbia Journal of Transnational Law, vol. 29, 1991, p. 641.

118   *Khadduri*: The Islamic Conception of Justice, 1984, p. 172.

gressors. And if they (i.e. the enemies) incline towards peace, incline thou (the prophet) also to peace, and have trust in God." Moreover, the Quran states: "And fight for the cause of Allah those who fight you, but do not commit aggression, for Allah loves not the aggressors" (Al-Baqara "The Cow": 190). Accordingly, resorting to combat "[h]ad been decreed to ward off mischief, because if the wicked were left to perpetrate wanton destruction without any hindrance or deterrent, confusion and corruption would spread throughout land and sea."[119] It is worth recalling that, in case of a sudden attack by enemies on a Muslim country, the Muslims of that country must repel them. If they cannot, Muslims who are nearest to the enemy must help them. If all fail, it becomes incumbent upon all other Muslims to fight until the enemy is repulsed. Accordingly, self-defence in Islam may be individual or collective.

– To liberate occupied Islamic territory. Jihad becomes a Fard-Ain if Dar Al-Islam is occupied. In such a case, every Muslim, whether his own country is close to, or remote from, the occupied territory, should participate, in one way or another, in repulsing the aggression or the occupying authority. In this context, the Quran states: "And slay them and turn them out from where they have turned you out: for tumult and oppression are worse than slaughter; but fight them not at the Sacred Mosque, unless they (first) fight you there; but if they fight you, slay them." Even, war in Islam may be waged not only to protect Muslim mosques but also to save buildings pertaining to other religions – that is, churches, synagogues, and cloisters. In this regard, Chapter XXII, verse 40, of the holy Quran says: "Did not God check one set of people by means of another, they would surely have been pulled down monasteries, churches, synagogues, and mosques, in which the name of God is commemorated in abundant measure."

– Istinquath[120] (or saving Muslims abroad). Under a well-known theory – that is, that of humanitarian intervention – some states, for example, the United Kingdom, the United States, France, and Belgium resort to force in order to save or protect their nationals abroad from imminent danger. In this regard, for example, the United Kingdom affirms that force may be used in self-defence against threats to one's nationals, if (1) there is good evidence that the target attacked would otherwise continue to be used by the other state in support of terrorist attacks against one's nationals; (2) there is, effectively, no other way to forestall imminent further attacks on one's nationals; and (3) the force employed is proportionate to the threat.[121] The Istinquath, in Islam, is the equivalent of humanitarian intervention in contemporary international law. In fact, it may be applied in order to save the weakest men, women, and

---

119   *Abu Zahra*: The Jihad (Striving), Al-Azhar, Fourth Conference of the Academy of Islamic Research, Cairo, 1388-1968, p. 50.

120   See, *Ahmed Abou-el-Wafa*: A Book on the Rules of International Law and Relations in Islamic Shari'a, vol. 5, The Islamic Shari'a and the Theory of Non-Intervention in the Jurisdiction of Third Parties, pp. 77-186.

121   BYIL, 1993, p. 732.

children who, being powerless, have been victimized by tyrants and oppressed by them. The holy Quran says: "And why should you not fight in the cause of God and of those who, being weak, are ill-treated (and oppressed)? – Men, women, and children, whose cry is: 'Our Lord! rescue us from this village, whose people are oppressors; And raise for us from Thee one who will help and one who will make us win'" (IV: 75). Accordingly, the following conditions are necessary for a nation to intervene to protect oppressed people abroad: (1) the fight should be in the cause of God, which means that it must be just and fair (that is, necessary and proportionate). Otherwise, it will not be "in the cause of God"; (2) there must be the existence of some oppressed persons; (3) those people must be truly and seriously oppressed; (4) there must be in existence a treaty in force *vis-à-vis* the Muslim state that prohibits intervention. In fact, if there is a treaty that provides that the Muslim state should abide by the non-use of force, this treaty has precedence over the duty to protect Muslims abroad. This idea is highlighted by the holy Quran: "But if they seek your aid in religion, it is your duty to help them, except against a people with whom ye have a treaty" (VIII: 72).[122] Commenting on this verse, a Muslim scholar explains that the verse proves that fulfillment of a pact has priority even over "religious solidarity."[123] In a word, the Muslim state has not the right to intervene in favour of its co-religionists if it is bound by an agreement prohibiting such intervention.

– Use of force to defend an ally, victim of an aggression. The striking example, in this respect, is the truce of Al-Hudaybiyah, which was concluded between the prophet and Quraysh. The fourth condition of the truce permitted third parties to choose sides as they wished. Accordingly, the Banu-Bakr allied themselves with Quraysh, and the Khuza'ah tribe with the prophet. In the times of Jàhiliya, the Khuza'ah had been the allies of Abd-Al-Muttalib, and they sought to renew their pledge as given to the prophet's grandfather. The prophet reaffirmed the terms of the alliance and renewed the pledge, adding two conditions: first, not to aid the Khuza'ah if they turned oppressors and, second, to aid the Khuza'ah if they became oppressed. Two copies of the pact were then drawn up, and each party was handed one. At that time, the Khuza'ah had not been converted to Islam. They were still polytheistic in their beliefs.

ii.   Islam and Peace

After some prefatory remarks, reference will be made to the concept of peace in the Quran and the Sunna, arbitration as a peaceful means, and armed peace in Islam.

---

122   *Ahmed Abou-el-Wafa*: A Book on the Rules of International Law and Relations in Islamic Shari'a, Vol, 5: Islamic Shari'a and the Theory of Non Intervention in Third Parties' Affairs, Dar Al-Nahda Al-Arabia, Cairo, 1421-2001, pp. 132-47 (in Arabic).

123   *Mahmassani*: The Principles of International Law in the Light of Islamic Doctrine, RCADI, 1966, I. Vol. 117, p. 268.

a.   Prefatory Remarks

Contrary to what the overwhelming majority of non-Muslims think, Islam greatly believes in peace. The principle of peaceful settlement of international disputes has its *fons et origo* in Islam.[124] Usually, the prophet was "unwilling to take irrevocable action if anything could be gained by gentler means."[125] Muawiyah (a Muslim caliph) tells a well-known dictum: "I do not use my sword where my whip sould be sufficient, nor my whip when my tongue would suffice." Accordingly, peace has a pivotal position in Islamic teachings. Islam, moreover, means "[s]ubmission to God's will." Islam comes from the same linguistic root that produces "Salam" – that is, peace. This coincidence in etymology proves that there is a convergence and interrelationship between Islam and peace.

b.   Peace in the Holy Quran

The Quran prefers that Muslims accept peace if their enemy does so. It suffices to mention the following verses: "But if the enemy incline towards peace, do thou (also) incline towards, and trust in Allah: for he is the one that heareth and knoweth (all things)" (VIII: 61); "Therefore if they withdraw from you but fight you not, and (instead) sent you (guarantees of) peace, then Allah hath opened no way for you (to wage war against them)" (IV: 90); and "Ye who believe, enter all into peace" (2:208). Moreover, any attempt to disturb peace or create disorder is wholly condemned by the Quran. Witness the following verses: "Do not promote disorder in the earth after peace has been established" (7: 56–57); "Do not go about committing inequity in the earth and causing disorder" (8:75; II:86; 29:37); "They seek to create disorder, and Allah loves not those who create disorder" (5:65); "Seek not to create disorder in the earth. Verily, God loves not those who seek to create disorder" (28:78); and "There are those who talk glibly and plausibly on all subjects and call God to witness as to the sincerity of their motives and intentions, and yet they constantly promote dissension by their persistence in magnifying differences and disputes, and when they happen to wield authority they run about in the land seeking to create disorder, which destroys harvests and entails severe suffering and hardship upon men. Allah loves not such conduct" (2:205–206).

c.   Peace in the Sunna (Conclusion of Peace Treaties)

Prophet Mohamed preferred peace to waging war, in case the enemy had accepted to enter into peaceful relations.Thus, he concluded the Hodaibiyah treaty and abandoned fighting the infidels, despite the fact that he was prevented from performing one of the leading rituals of Islam – that is, the Umrah – and despite the fact that he had to extradite Muslims to the other contracting party, whereas the latter was not bound to do so since they had taken refuge on his territory. There are

---

124   *Ahmed Abou-el-Wafa*: A Book on the Rules of International Law and Relations in Islamic Shari'a, vol. 9: The Peaceful Settlement of International Disputes in Islamic Shari'a, P. 20.

125   *A. Zidan*: The Battles of the Prophet, Cairo, p. 54.

other examples of treaties of peace and alliance concluded by the prophet.[126] The treaty with Banu-Damrah reads:

> With the name of God, the Compassionate, the Merciful. This is the writ of Muhammad, the Messenger of God, in favour of the Banu-Damrah, assuring them the security of their persons and their properties; that they may count on (his) help if anybody takes aggressive action against them, except in case of fight in the name of religion. This assurance is valid so long as a sea wets the shells. Similarly, when the prophet requires it of them, they will help him; and they pledge for that God and His Messenger. To help them will depend upon their loyalty and piety.

The treaty with Ailah states: "In the name of God, the Compassionate, the Merciful. This is the writ of protection from God and Muhammad, the Prophet and Messenger of God, in favour of John son of Rubin and the people of Ailah. Their boats and their traders on land and sea shall have the protection of God and of Muhammad, the Prophet. This includes also the people of Syria, of Yaman, of countries beyond the seas who are with them (i.e., the people of Ailah)." It is worth recalling that a treaty of peace concluded by a Muslim state is governed by the following rule: "The treaty of Solh (reconciliation) with the enemies is valid *vis-à-vis* all Muslims" (principle of the validity *erga omnes*).[127]

E.   Islam and the Concept of the Clash of Civilizations

i.   Concept of the "Clash of Civilizations" and Islam

Some Western scholars hold the theory that there currently exists an unhealthy and dangerous situation, using such terms as "Islam, the new enemy"[128] and the "clash of civilizations."[129] In fact, S. Huntington has characterized the post-Cold War era as no longer a clash of states but rather a clash between civilizations, whereby he considers Islam as the great enemy of the democratic, secular, and scientific West.[130] Even Islam has been called the "green danger," following the collapse of the "red danger" (communism). In this context, one western scholar explains: "Now that the red communist peril has disappeared, we are often made to believe that it has been replaced by a green Muslim threat. This image is already being exploited to reinforce the feel-

---

126   *See*: *M. Hamidullah*: Muslim Conduct of State, *op. cit.*, p. 288.

127   *Ahmed Abou-el-Wafa*: A Book on the Rules of International Law and Relations in Islamic Shari'a, *op. cit.*, vol. 14, p. 140; vol. 15, p. 309.

128   *J. Nielson*: Can Islamic Studies Programmes in European and Muslim Universities Cooperate? in Islam and the 21st Century, the Tenth General Conference of the Supreme Council for Islamic Affairs, Cairo, 1998, p. 71.

129   It is worth recalling that the clash of cultures may occur even between professionals, *J.A. Raelin*: The Clash of Cultures-Managers Managing Professionals, Harvard Business School Press, Boston, 1991, 299 pp.

130   *S. Huntington*: The Clash of Civilization, Foreign Affairs, 72, 1993, pp. 22 et ss.

ing of European unity by depicting a scenario of uniform, fanatical Muslim masses preparing to storm the bastions of the West's welfare systems under the green banners of Islam, with scimitars in one hand and the Qur'an in the other."[131] Another author affirms: "We are living in an era in which a North-South clash in cultural or even military terms is anticipated (if not predicted or even desired) within both academic and military circles, including NATO headquarters."[132] We ought to know that there is no contradiction between Islam and other religions. *Per contra*, there is a co-existence, complementarity, and a kind of living together or standing "side by side." This perspective helps others to understand better Muslims' belief and, consequently, to eradicate foreover the mediaeval stereotypes, misapprehensions, and thoughts that have been built over the centuries and even recently (for example, the theory of "confrontation" or the "clash of civilizations" of Huntingtion).

Another western scholar asserts: "In viewing Islam itself, many Muslims refer to Islam in broad and convenient terms: that is, as a civilization. The writers who want to make politics dependent on Islam do this the most frequently, but I think this leads to a serious problem. Dealing with Islam at this level seems to invite a preoccupying comparison with the West and to distort both civilizations by pitting 'us' against 'them.'"[133] This opinion is also unacceptable: In fact, we must consider the duality as "us" and "them" (not "us" against "them") – as "complementarity" and not as "opposition or contradiction" and as "joint venture," not "mutual exclusion." This is well illustrated by the following verse of the Quran: "O, people of the Book, come to an equitable word between us and you" (3: 64).

ii.   Dangerous Consequences of the Concept

To adopt the concept "clash of civilizations" will inevitably lead to catastrophic consequences for the global community. In this context, the El-Mansoura declaration affirms: "The meaning of the conflict that some western theorists call for is not suitable at all for the relation between civilizations in the modern time for it has destructive results for the humanity."[134] The catastrophic consequences of the clash of civilizations lie, in my view, in the fact that such a clash:

–   leads, at best, to endless conflicts, crises, tensions, dissensions, and injustices;
–   threatens and disturbs, at worst, international peace and security;
–   creates fear and instability among individuals, groups, nations, and states;

---

131   *I. Karlsson*: The Muslim Immigrants – a Bridge Between Two Cultures, in "The Truth about Islam in a Changing World," Fourteenth General Conference of the Supreme Council for Islamic Affairs, Cairo, 1422-2002, p. 101.

132   *Murad Hofmann*: Solving Contemporary Problems through Cooperation Between Islam and Christianity, in Islam and the Future Dialogue Between Civilizations, the Eighth General Conference of the Supreme Council for Islamic Affairs, Cairo, 1996, p. 11.

133   *J. Piscatori*: Islam in the Political Process, Cambridge University Press, 1983, p. 8.

134   "Islam and the Dialogue of Civilizations," Islamic Universities League, Cairo, 1423-2002, p. 5.

- spreads the culture of hatred among civilizations;
- endangers mankind through such moods and lusts;
- eliminates cultural diversity, identity, heritage; and characteristics of all people. In fact, one cannot turn a blind eye to where this tendency may lead in our
  age. It is, so to speak, the modern "apocalypse" – a non-Muslim scholar says:
  "Reality demands that culture be protected against decay and vandalism";[135]
- paves the way for hegemony and the lust for expansion on account of the
  other;
- propagates the phenomenon of extremism, fanaticism, terrorism, and violence;
- destroys the universe and civilizations and the common heritage of mankind;
- entails the application of a double standard, double language, and *deux poids
  et deux mesures* (not single criteria) when dealing with events and problems
  facing the world;
- may lead to actions and reactions and to violence and counter-violence. The
  prophet says: "Love is inherited and enmity is inherited";[136] and
- constitutes a setback for the present global community and returns it to the
  age of "primitive culture," putting it outside "civilised culture."[137]

These catastrophic consequences lead us to ask the following question, namely
why a doctrinal tendency speaks of a clash among civilizations, whereas such a
clash inevitably leads to a dead end. This tendency should change our vision of
the question since the avoidance of any clash has *nolens volens* deep roots in every
human being. This *fons et origo* is a reflection of the intimate disposition (*fitra*) *per
se* of man.

iii.   Factors Indispensable for the Existence of a Global Community and the Avoidance of a "Clash of Civilizations" According to Islam

The indispensable factors for the existence of a global community include, *inter
alia*, the following.

a.   Recognition of the "Other" and of Diversity and Pluralism

To recognize the "other" is part of man's natural disposition – the innate nature (*al-
fitra*) of man. *Prima facie*, the acceptance of "difference," "diversity," and "pluralism"
is the cornerstone of understanding as well as the recognition of others. It must be
stressed that Islam admits diversity and pluralism. The Quran says: "If Allah had
willed, he would have made you one united nation" (Al-Ma'idah: 48). In fact, Islam

---

135   *P. Gurevich*: Dialogue of Cultures or Cultural Expansion, Progress Publishers, Moscow,
      1990, p. 7.

136   *Ahmed Abou-el-Wafa*: A Book on the Rules of International Law and Relations in Is-
      lamic Shari'a, op. cit., vol. 15, p. 227.

137   *Ibn Khaldun* in his Muqaddimmah adopted the same distinction between "umran bad-
      awi" and "umran hadari". See *A. Lambton*: State and Government in Medieval Islam,
      Oxford University Press, 1981, p. 158.

aims at setting up a global community based on pluralist and multicultural values or cultural diversity. This necessarily implies the "recognition of the "other,"[138] not the exclusion of others, and the respect of ideas, concepts, and particularities entertained by others. Moreover, it is well established that "[t]he Qur'an is a veritable manifesto of religious pluralism."[139] In fact, believing in other religions is a prerequisite for every true Muslim. The Quran says: "The Messenger has believed in what has been sent down to Him from His Lord, and the believers; everyone of them has believed in Allah, and His angels, and His Books, and His Messengers: we make no distinction as regards any of His Messengers" (The Cow: 285). Additionally, in Islam, a global community must be based on mutual understanding, respect, and reconciliation between the followers of different faiths. In this regard, the Quran states: "Surely those who believe and those who are Jews and the sabeans and the Christians whoever believes in Allah and the last Day and does good-they shall have no fear nor shall they grieve" (5: 69) and "O, people of the Book, come to an equitable word between us and you, that we shall serve non but Allah and that we shall not associate aught with Him, and that some of us shall not take others for lords besides Allah" (3: 64).

b.   Dialogue in Order that "You May Know Each Other" (Quran, 49:13)

Evidently, dialogue unites human beings, whereas confrontation separates them. This principle is a *sine qua non conditio* for the refoundation and the reconstruction of a new and improved international global community. We are sitting in the same boat. Consequently, relations among civilizations must be organized in a cohesive and well-founded manner, just like a building whose parts consolidate one another. What should be emphasizes is that such a dialogue must, to say the least, be based on acceptance, respect, and tolerance of others, not *"un dialogue des sourds."* The Quran highlighted the importance of dialogue for the establishment of a global community more than fourteen centuries ago. Witness, *inter alia*, the following verse: "O Mankind, we created you from a single pair of male and female and made you into nations and tribes, so that you may know each other. The best of you in the sight of Allah is he who is most conscious of Allah" (49: 13). The words "that you may know each other," in my view, mean:
- that relations between nations must be founded on peace and dialogue for only those two factors may lead to better knowing the other;
- that knowing each other is the best way for existence and co-existence, for ignorance breeds hatred, tension, friction, enmity, prejudice, fanaticism, and extremism. In this context, a wise voice from the west states: "Lack of infor-

---

138   See also *Mansur Escuedero*: Islam in the Face of Racism in the Social Project, in Islam and the 21st Century, Tenth General Conference of the Supreme Council for Islamic Affairs, Cairo, 1998, pp. 20-22.

139   *Murad W. Hofman*: The Protection of Religious Minorities in Islam, in Islam and the 21st Century, Tenth General Conference of the Supreme Council for Islamic Affairs, Cairo, 1418 H – 1998 G, p. 7.

mation leads to misunderstandings and prejudices which in their turn lead to bitterness. Out of bitterness come tensions, national and international";[140]
- that scientific knowledge is a common heritage of mankind;
- that the same *"fons et origo"* of human beings implies two consequences, namely
- equality; and
- cooperation in solving problems of societal life, be they internal or external;
- that knowing each other is an example of the way in which human beings can cooperate for the common good of humanity.
- that human beings, irrespective of their origin, race, language, wealth, and so on, must think in terms that unite them rather than in terms that separate them;
- that respect for the cultural and religious identity of others is necessary. So, one should not disdain or contempt the other;
- that "diversity," "difference," and pluralism are the most important cornerstones of the "knowledge" of the other – that is, through which we can be "acquainted" with the other;
- that living together, not in isolation, is a *sine qua non conditio* for our worldly life;
- that knowing each other presupposes the existence of a will to do so – that is, it is not, as dialogue itself, a simple motto; and
- that dialouge is a must and that we are obliged willy-nilly to proceed to dialogue in order that we know each other.

In short, as described earlier, the best solution is to proceed in a cross-cultural dialogue rather than in a cross-warrior clash. Everyone "acts relative to his perception of the world,"[141] and "consciousness is ontologically prior to action."[142]

c.   Violations of Rules of Islamic Shari'a by Some Muslims Must Not Justify a Clash between Civilizations

Some Muslims have violated the rules and principles of Islam. They have tried to misuse religion contrary to its clearly correct concepts. Looked at from this perspective, non-Muslims may understand this violation to be a plea against Islam. Evidently, this perspective is untenable. Any practices that do not reflect the true Islamic concepts must be considered to be odd and un-Islamic. In fact, events, acts, and deeds must be judged by the texts and not *vice versa*. *Prima facie*, if there are some violations of applicable Islamic rules, one "should not blame Islam as a whole

---

140   *C.G. Weeramantry*: Islamic Jurisprudence: An International Perspective, *op. cit.*, pp. XV-XVI.

141   *Dr. Ali Shariati*: Man and Islam, FILINC, Houston, 1981, p. 11.

142   *K. Litfin*: Towards an Integral Perspective on World Politics, Secularism, Sovereignty and the Challenge of Global Ecology, Millennium Journal of International Studies, vol. 32, 2003, pp. 29 et s.

for its being abused politically."[143] Such acts have not been done on the basis of any Islamic injunction.

d.   "Let Not Some People Mock at Other People" (Quran, 49: 11)

The Quran says: "Let not some people mock at other people, for they may be better than themselves" (49: 11). *Prima facie*, this verse means: (1) that respect of the other is a must; (2) that treating others with honesty should be ensured; (3) that avoiding any cause of clash or confrontation, even if it is a simple mockery, is an imperative Islamic principle; (4) that treating others justly is a *sine qua non conditio* of the Islamic religion; and (5) that a dialogue with the other, in a good manner, ought to be observed.

e.   Better to Argue with Each Other

Arguing with the other is governed, in my view, by the following rules according to Islam. First, dialogue requires arguing in a better way and with full respect to the other. This principle is affirmed by the Quran in the following verses: "And do not argue with the people of the scripture (i.e. Christians and Jews) except in a way that is best, except for those who commit injustice among them" (XXIX: 46); "Invite to the way of your Lord with wisdom and good preaching, and argue with them in a way that is best" (XVI: 125); and "And do not insult (revile) those who invoke other than Allah, lest they insult (revile) Allah in enmity without knowledge" (VI: 108). These verses mean:

- that dialouge should be conducted in peaceful ways;
- that mutual respect is a *sine qua non conditio* for the success of any dialogue;
- that using the best ways to arrive at a fruitful and positive dialogue must be observed by all parties concerned; and
- that arguing with non-Muslims in the best way possible is an Islamic principle.

Second, even when the other party in dialogue has transgressed all acceptable bounds, a Muslim must speak to him kindly. In other words, the evil of the other party or his bad behaviour should be repelled by a good reply. The Quran states: "Go, both of you, to Pharoah, for he has indeed transgressed all bounds. But speak to him mildly; perchance he may take warning or fear (God). These (Moses and Aaron) said: 'Our Lord! We fear lest he will hasten with insolence against us, or lest he will transgress all bounds'" (XX: 43–45); and "Repel, by means of what is best, their evil" (XXIII: 96). Third, dialogue with the other in Islam necessitates that a Muslim must not insult the other party. In this regard, the Quran says: "Revile not ye those whom they call upon besides God, lest they out of spite revile God in their ignorance. Thus have we made alluring to each people its own doings" (VI: 108).

Fourth, in dialogue, a Muslim must forgive the wrongdoings of the other party. The Quran states: "Hold to forgiveness; enjoin what is right, but turn away from the

---

143   *H. Bielefeldt*: Muslim Voices in the Human Rights Debate, Human Rights Quarterly, vol. 17, 1995, p. 595.

ignorant (VII: 199); "And the servants of God most Gracious are those who walk on the earth in humility, and when the ignorant address them, they say words of peace" (XXV: 63); and "Allah loves not the shouting of evil words in public speech except by one who has been wronged" (An-Nisa': 148). The prophet says: "The believer is not one who curses"; "Whoever speaks must say the right and good things; otherwise it is better for him to keep silent"; and "Fear Allah wherever you are, follow the evil deed with the good one so that it may erase it, and deal with people in a good manner." Fifth, Islam incites kindness in dialogue for its positive results – that is, enmity and/or hatred may become friendship. The Quran says: "Nor can goodness and evil be equal, Repel (evil) with what is better: Then will he between whom and thee was hatred become as it were thy friend and intimate" (XLI: 34).

f.   Prohibition of Any Attempt to Impose a Certain "mode de vie" on the Other

Apparently, some states have tried recently to impose a certain *"mode de vie"* on other states, hoping that the latter will imitate the former (for example, in their culture, policy, morals, and customs).

g.   Provocation of Evil Is Totally Prohibited in Islam

It is well known that, in present global community, there are some persons, states, or agencies whose sole task is to try to sow the seeds of instability, provoke evil or wrong among peoples, and spread chaos. Any of these actions are inadmissible according to the Shari'a. The Quran says: "Commit not evil in the land with intent to do mischief" (XI: 85). Moreover, in Islam, there is a rule that states: "We must not provoke wrong (evil) on the Muslim and non-Muslim."[144] The prophet says: "If you pass by wicked people say to them salam (peace be upon you)."[145] One Western author asserts that Islam is not a wicked religion:

> For ten centuries, however, Islam stood at the doorstep of the world of Christendom, sometimes knocking for entry, sometimes forcing open the door, but always an apparent threat to its religious ideology and power structure. It was no wonder therefore that in these ten centuries Islam was misrepresented as a force for evil by whatever media lay at the command of the age. Scholarly writing and religious preaching were the principal media available and the distortion and indoctrination continued for centuries through these media. Islam was represented as being wicked, blasphemous and opposed to all that civilisation stood for – although it stood for moral values, intellectual advancement and the rule of law. When the direct military threat ceased, around the sixteenth century, the same attitudes of prejudice continued, for Islam was still the world force which was a counterpoise to the world of Chistianity.[146]

---

144   *Ahmed Abou-el-Wafa*: A Book on the Rules of International Law and Relations in Islamic Shari'a, *op. cit.*, vol. 1, p. 427; vol. 15, p. 283.

145   *Ibid.*, vol. 15, p. 239.

146   *C.G. Weeramantry*: Islamic Jurisprudence: An International Perspective, *op. cit.*, pp. 128-29.

Undoubtedly, abstaining from provoking evil is an indispensable tool for a fruitful, positive, and cross-cultural dialogue.

h.   Observance of the Principle of Good Faith *(bona fides)*

This principle constitutes a *leit motif* of every legal system. The prophet outlines this principle as follows: "The signs of a hypocrite are three: whenever he speaks, he tells lies; whenever he promises, he breaks his promise, and whenever he is trusted, he proves to be dishonest." *Prima facie*, if this Hadith is followed by states, individuals, and nations that is, by telling the truth, keeping promises, and being honest), all the troubles of our world will disappear, and the seeds of any clash of civilizations in particular will be uprooted. Imam Al-Ghazali asserts *in externso* this principle:

> Know that the word truthfulness is applied in six ways: Truth in words, truth in intention or will, truth in strength, truth in fulfillment, truth in deeds and truth in achieving the pillars of the religion. Whoever is described as truthful in all these is strictly veracious. The first truthfulness: a true tongue. Whoever keeps his tongue away from giving any information contrary to what is true, he is truthful. The second truthfulness: Intention and will, this depends on sincerity. The third truthfulness: Truth in strength, when mankind intends to work he performs it with all his strength. The fourth truthfulness: Truth in fulfillment, God Almighty said: "men who have been true to their pledge to God" (Surah 33 verse 23). The fifth truthfulness: Truth in deeds. That is the one who strives to his utmost so that his external deeds do not differ from what is inside him. The sixth truthfulness: This is the highest grade: Truthfulness in achieving the pillars of the religion, such as truthfulness in fear and hope, gratitude and ascetism, contentment, dependance and love.

8.   Conclusion

Needless to say, without full respect for all the rules and principles of international law, including those of Islamic jurisprudence, all talk of a global community based on law will remain empty verbiage or nonsense, will increase friction and tension, and, accordingly, will lead to clashes as well as confrontation. Consequently, it is imperative for the contemporary global community to review, rearrange, and reconsider the application of rules governing present international relations. This necessity presupposes the existence of a will to do so: "Where there is a will, there is a way." The Quran highlights this rule in the following verse: "Surely Allah (God) does not change what is in a people, Until they change what is in themselves" (Al-Ra'ad : 11). It is essential to start, at least, step by step. In fact, that which cannot be achieved as a whole should not be abandoned as a whole. I hope that, through this study, I have exposed the true face, image, and role of Islam in the establishment of a global community based on the rules of international law. This image and role of Islam inevitably leads us to say that the *corpus juris gentium* has been considerably enriched, proving that Islam is a viable religion and civilization. It constitutes a lifestyle for the present global community and a well-balanced means for international relations. Accordingly, it is necessary:

–   not to disregard Islam and its contributions to the setting up of a global community based on the rules of international law;

–   to give practical effects and special attention to the rules and principles of Islam in the conduct of international relations, especially the principles specific to the Islamic system. In fact, each religion has its peculiarities. The holy Quran says: "To each among you have we prescribed a law and an open way (a method)" (V: 49); and

–   to consider that all violations of any rules or principles mentioned in this study are contrary to Islamic teachings. As a Muslim, I testify that they are condemned by the Shari'a and are totally foreign to it. In other words, they are Haram or Munkar. Respect for the imperative rules of Islamic Shari'a in general, and for those applicable to relations with non-Muslim states and individuals in particular, is, in my view, Fard Ayn (a binding obligation on all Muslims) incumbent upon every Muslim as well as the Ummah Islamiah (Islamic nation) as a whole.

13. Developing Countries in the Group of 77: A Journey in Multilateral Diplomacy, 1964 to 2004

*Awni Behnam**

1. The Group of 77

The Group of 77 (Group) appeared officially on the international scene in 1964 on the occasion of UNCTAD I. The founding father of both UNCTAD and the Group, Dr. Raul Prebisch,[1] who led the fledging UNCTAD secretariat, had laboured hard to bring about a historical coalition of a reluctant Latin America with Africa and Asia.

Prebisch had called at UNCTAD I for a new Trade Policy[2] for development, sixteen years after the failed world trade conference of Havana in 1949. The Group, conceived as a twin of UNCTAD was a manifestation of the political and economic dimension of the event itself that would forever change the nature of multilateral diplomacy – not only in the economic sector but in time, all sectors of human endeavour.

The emergence of the Group was hailed as one of the most significant political phenomena of the post Second World War era. It was recognized immediately as an indispensable instrument in securing much needed new attitudes and approaches in the international economic field. That was due primarily to opportune timing – developing countries, the majority of which were the exploited, ignored and the marginalized nations of the world, found a common voice and rallied around a common platform. It was thus that the group system came into being. During the 1960s developing countries were in search of political negotiating

---

*   The author is the President of the International Ocean Institute and Former Senior Advisor to the Secretary General of UNCTAD. The views expressed are those of the author. I am indebted to the contributions of Ambassador Muchkund Dubey, Dr. Branislav Gosovic of the South Centre and to Ambassador Anthony Hill. I also acknowledge with gratitude the editorial advice of Mr. John Pappas.

1   Raul Prebisch was the founder and first Secretary-General of the United Nations Conference on Trade and Development (UNCTAD).

2   "Towards a New Trade Policy for Development", reproduced in proceedings of UNCTAD Second Session, Vol. 11, UN Publications, Sales No. 64.11.B.12.

Ronald St. John Macdonald & Douglas M. Johnston (eds.), Towards World Constitutionalism, *pp. 355-380.*
© *2005 Koninklijke Brill NV. Printed in The Netherlands.* ISBN 90 04 14612 1.

power proportional and to their economic potential. They focused their collective action on changing the status quo and the inequitable world system with rules-of-the-game being drawn up in colonial and imperialist ethos. They sought to use the power of democratic decision-making, through the exercise of the vote, in order to advance new values and principles in pursuit of socio-economic development and to strengthen their support institutions in the UN system.

At its conception, the Group intended to adopt a positive approach to dealing with international economic issues. That approach was not to confront, but to cooperate – not to play the zero-sum game of seeking to acquire gains at the cost of others, but to play the positive-sum game in which all the players stood to gain. The Group was based on the principles of interdependence of nations, and the shared values and common destiny of humankind.

The leaders of developing countries and the Group as a whole strove for equity and justice in the world economic order, in the belief that this alone could build a solid foundation for world peace and make for a stable and prosperous world. In international trade, they wished to improve the terms of trade that was tilted heavily in favour of the North. They endeavoured to secure fair, remunerative and stable prices for their primary commodities on which they depended heavily for both their national incomes and export earnings. The Group sought affirmative action by way of non-reciprocal access to markets of developed countries for their manufactured and semi-manufactured products in order to transcend the handicaps inherent in the backward state of their economic and technological development. They called for enhanced inflow of foreign resources at favourable terms and conditions, in order to supplement their meagre resource base. Moreover, they demanded access to technology under affordable terms and conditions. They sought fair and competitive freight rates for the transport of their seaborne trade. In short, through the Group, the developing countries sought a rightful place for themselves in the world community.

This would not have been possible but for one important and even mysterious ingredient – unity, unity *vis-à-vis* the North and unity within the South.

At the conclusion of UNCTAD I in Geneva in 15 June 1964, the Group adopted its famous joint Declaration in which they stated:

> The developing countries regard their own unity, the unity of the seventy-five,[3] as the outstanding feature of this Conference. This unity has sprung out of the fact that facing the basic problems of development they have a common interest in a policy for international trade and development. They believe that it is this unity that has given clarity and coherence to the discussions of this Conference. Their solidarity has been tested in the course of the Conference and they have emerged from it with even greater unity and strength.
>
> The developing countries have a strong conviction that there is a vital need to maintain, and further strengthen, this unity in the years ahead. It is an indispensable

---

3   Joint Declaration at the conclusion of UNCTAD I, 15 June 1964, Trade and Development: Final Act and Report, Vol. I, page 68. Two additional countries joined at the adoption of the declaration. Today, the Group of 77 has 132 member countries.

instrument for securing the adoption of new attitudes and new approaches in the international economic field. This unity is also an instrument for enlarging the area of cooperation endeavour in the international field and for securing mutually beneficent relationships with the rest of the world. Finally, it is a necessary means for a cooperation amongst the developing countries themselves.

That formidable human experience of the coalition, of the larger part of humanity, was not an accident of history as neither was the creation of UNCTAD. It was part of a sweeping change as the yoke of colonialism was being shed and newly independent States were conceived in search of new identity with political as well as economic independence.

Julius Nyerere once described the Group as a political force, an ideology that could reverse a situation where developing countries "were not the prime movers of their own destiny."

2.   Unity in Diversity

The main strengths of the Group have been its unity, cohesion and solidarity. That newly found unity at the origin of the Group was its very "DNA". The Group as a coalition of developing countries was not a homogeneous product. It was a coalition of countries that differed in their historical experiences having different political, economic and social systems with vastly different cultural and religious identities. Some of the countries were just emerging from colonialism, others had already a significant social and economic structure of institutions, others were endowed with natural and mineral resources and still others were agricultural economies ranging from landlocked to island countries. However, the coalition found strength and unity in the sharing of a common perception – the inequitable nature of the existing economic order and the overriding need to change it and in the need for improved management and functioning of the world economy. The necessity to change inherited rules-of-the-game in international economic relations that, for example, determined the terms of trade to the detriment of commodity of producing developing countries, constituted a core of those common perceptions. While specific national interests varied, the countries were not seeking a universal value[4] system or equal gains. They bonded together in support of a common international

---

4   Murphy explains the lack of a uniform development ideology is important, because in fostering diversity, the alliance had a built-in, prior moral justification for the inevitable disagreements that the members of the broad alliance would, and did, have. Rather than resolving differences, the preservation of cultural diversity provided a cooperative way to accept those differences. To put it another way, national economic and political ideologies did not threaten the alliance because moral principles justified the differences themselves. Even when countries were aware that real differences were less cultural than ideological, cooperating governments could invoke the "right of States to choose their own development path". (Murphy, c. 1984). The emergence of NIEO ideology as quoted by Kathryn C. Lovelle, Ideas within the context of power. *The Journal of Modern African Studies*, Cambridge University Press 939, 1(2001).

economic platform that as a whole covered principal economic interest of every member country of the Group. The construct of that original platform at UNCTAD I was the brainchild of Dr. Raul Prebisch and his committed secretariat that insisted the ultimate responsibility for the development of developing countries was in the hands of the developing countries themselves emphasising the central responsibility of each Government and each people to rely on themselves.

For such a diverse and heterogeneous group to be able to overcome civilization prejudices, conflicting political ideologies and be able to work together fashioning consensus, on intricate and difficult economic issues that impacted on the daily life of their citizens, was deemed anything short of miraculous. In explaining how this was possible Anthony Hill,[5] surmised "that developing countries left their differences at the door step outside the meeting rooms as if they were personal baggage". Perhaps the Group experiment was a microcosm of humanity that designed the United Nations. The Group was as near a universal body of the underprivileged nations of the South. As such, it came to represent and act on behalf of that part of humanity and thus became the depository of universal values that overcome civilization prejudices.

However, that did not mean there were no underlying tensions at individual country levels and particularly at sub-regional levels. Nevertheless, overall collective interest for ending the division of the world into areas of affluence and "intolerable poverty", transcended individual interests of member States particularly in the formative years of the Group. Collectively the Group has always displayed pride in their unity while celebrating their diversity.

3.   The Early Drive

The first reward of the efforts of the Group was the establishment of UNCTAD as a permanent organ of the General Assembly with a wide-ranging mandate relating not only to trade but also trade in the context of development. Through UNCTAD, the developing countries were able to mobilize collective strength and launch dialogue with the North.

As the Group was conceived as a twin of UNCTAD, it therefore commenced with UNCTAD's agenda of trade and development. Subsequently, it brought its collective will to bear on the pursuit of common goals in the related fields of money, finance, external indebtedness, food, agriculture, industrialization, intellectual property rights, health, education, environment and sustainable development, and science and technology. There were thus Groups of 77 functioning in one form or the other, within the forums of FAO, UNIDO, WIPO, UNEP, WHO, ILO, UNESCO, IMF, World Bank and GATT.

For over a decade after its conception, the Group came to exercise significant influence in shaping the world economic order. Among its major achievements are contributions to the successful negotiation of the Generalized Scheme

---

5   Ambassador Anthony Hill was the Permanent Representative of Jamaica for some 15 years and was actively involved in the work of the Group of 77.

of Preferences (GSP), the Charter of Economic Rights and Duties, the Integrated Programme for Commodities including the Common Fund to buttress it and the International Development Strategies, which constituted the most comprehensive framework of international accountability. The Group also played a leading role in the clarification of concepts that imparted operational content to the targets for the transfer of resources to developing countries (0.7 ODA and IDS targets). Initiatives taken by the Group led to the creation of new institutions such as UNIDO and IFAD, as well as formulation of new rules, guidelines, norms, principles, and comprehensive frameworks of cooperation on a whole new range of economic and social issues. A solid landmark in this regard was the adoption by the United Nations General Assembly of the Declaration and Programme of Action for the Establishment of a New International Economic Order. The Group brought to light the inequities, imbalances and anomalies prevailing in the various components of the world economic system, particularly shipping,[6] insurance and other invisibles. Nevertheless, in spite of these inroads, it has since been an uphill struggle – to this day the battle for removing these and other imbalances and inequities have yet to be won. UNCTAD, which was the principal arena of the activities of the Group, pioneered a number of ideas, programmes and schemes which were subsequently adopted for building consensus of appropriate action, in other organizations of the United Nations family, including the IMF and the World Bank. These included supplementary financing, compensatory financing, external debt management and special drawing rights.

The Group functioned in tandem with the Non-Aligned Movement. Many of the ideas that the Group painstakingly pursued through the mechanism of the United Nations were first mooted in Non-Aligned fora – benefiting from the political weight of the Movement. However, the early achievements of the Group were dwarfed in relation to proposals put forward by developing countries for negotiations but more importantly, in relation to the massive extent of poverty and the poor prospect for reducing it.

4.   The Universality of the Group System and Multilateral Diplomacy

The Group has made a notable contribution to the effective functioning of the United Nations. The Group can legitimately claim a large part of the credit for the United Nations system moving toward a global governance system in the economic and social field during the decade 1964–1974. Thus, the Group has been a bulwark in the process of the evolution of multilateralism under the United Nations.

The Group was the offspring of the inherent dynamics of negotiations in the universal fora of the organizations of the United Nations system. The only practicable way of conducting negotiations in such large fora, is for countries sharing com-

---

6   During the existence of the shipping committee in UNCTAD, some five legally binding UN Conventions were adopted in the conferences prepared or convened by UNCTAD in the area of shipping and multimodal transport. See A. Behnam "Unfulfilled Promises of the Seventies", *Ocean Yearbook*, Vol. 18, Chicago University Press 2004.

mon interests and vision, to join together and negotiate collectively, setting aside their differences, particularly those of a political nature. This is true not only of developing countries, but also of developed countries. This inevitable group mechanism role was formally recognized in General Assembly Resolution 1995(XIX), setting out the procedures to be followed for election to the Trade and Development Board of UNCTAD. This resolution established the umbilical link between the United Nations and the Group.

The group system soon spread to all United Nations entities as the only meaningful instrument for dialogue and negotiations at intergovernmental fora.[7] The group system provided functionality as it facilitated dialogue and prior consultations, and thus provided a basis for collective negotiations that allowed for maturity of ideas.

5.   A Pendulum of Success and Setback

It is first and foremost an amazing phenomenon that the Group, a loose informal coalition of developing countries of the South survived as a functioning institution for forty years. (The Group celebrated its fortieth anniversary in Sao Paulo on the occasion of UNCTAD XI in June 2004).

The Group has never had a written constitution nor a legislative foundation or rules of procedure. It adopts decisions entirely by consensus and does not vote on substantive issues. It does not have a regular secretariat or permanent institutional support mechanism, nor does it enjoy the luxury of administrative services or maintain official records of its meetings. Its leadership is rotational, regionally based and diffused among the different chapters in Geneva, New York, Paris, Nairobi, Vienna, Rome and Washington with different cycles of country leadership. Despite these obvious administrative handicaps, it continues to function as the negotiating machinery of the developing countries. While the perseverance of the Group has been a manifestation of its strength, it is nevertheless part of its vulnerability.

From its conception the Group has had total reliance on the UNCTAD secretariat for the intellectual and substantive analysis required for policy formulation. In fact, during the leadership of the UNCTAD secretariat under Raul Prebisch, Sidney Dell, Malinowsky, B. Chidzero, one could not differentiate between the two identical twins – the Group and the UNCTAD secretariat. The depth of the commitment of the secretariat to development of developing countries was the dominant factor in pursuing the development agenda. The secretariat while claiming it was not biased to developing countries, was not impartial to development. Consequently, the Group considered the UNCTAD secretariat its own and in turn made excellent use of it. It was that organic link between the Group and an intellectually committed, competent secretariat, motivated by idealism that made possible the early success of a unique albeit short-lived partnership in multilateral diplomacy.

---

7   For details on the working methods, coordination and organization of the Group of 77, see A. Behnam; The Group System, *Multilateral Diplomacy*, Kluwer Law International, London, 1991, page 193.

6.   Confrontation and Accommodation

At the Centennial of Raul Prebisch (October 2001), Gamani Corea[8] recalled that Dr. Prebisch was very careful that UNCTAD with a developing country majority, united in the Group, should not be a forum for confrontation – sterile confrontation between various groups of countries. He wanted it to be a forum for dialogue and did not wish for decisions be steamrolled by majority vote but to provide for opportunity to think and interact to achieve results –not only creating a strong institution reflecting development issues but one which could interact with the world economy as a whole.

Of course this desire proved difficult to achieve. Inevitably the North had to face demands for concessions from the South. Negotiations[9] often took place in Geneva in an atmosphere of rich-poor confrontations dynamics. UNCTAD's *raison d'être* was to provide a forum for questioning basic assumptions underlying the then existing world economic order. However, the Group soon wanted to also be an effective instrument for international action. Extensive friendly persuasion evolved into accusation and recrimination in a North-South context – which was to be expected. This, primarily because the Group and UNCTAD were conceived out of deeply contested negotiations and against the wishes of most countries of the North who resisted vehemently the creation of UNCTAD and were particularly suspicious of the developing countries coalition in the Group.[10]

As Gosovitch[11] explained, UNCTAD, unlike other institutions, was born in controversy. Those who forced the Group's establishment wanted it to be a lever for achieving radical changes in the then existing world economic order – changes with far reaching economic and political consequences. It became the focus of hope of developing countries and the misgivings of the developed.

Nevertheless, there were also early successes. These successes can be credited to a number of factors including:

–   An intellectually independent and ideologically committed secretariat;
–   The state of the economy in the North that was enjoying growth and full employment in conjunction with sympathies for the colonies, (if not a guilt con-

---

8   Gamani Corea, Third Secretary-General of UNCTAD, UNCTAD archives, Raul Prebisch Lecture.

9   W.R. Malinowski described such confrontation as a "situation which the interest of various groups formulated either as demands or as defence of the status quo." Each participating group looks for ways and means to obtain total or at least partial satisfaction. Such situations may lead to deadlock, to unilateral action or to accommodation and reconciliation of interest through negotiations. Thus confrontation is the opening of the road to progress.

10   W.R. Manlinowski, "Shipping and the Third World," *Intereconomics*, No. 1, January 1971.

11   Branislav Gosovic, UNCTAD: North-South Encounter, *International Conciliation*, May 1968, No. 568.

sciousness) allowing for some accommodation to meet "reasonable" demands from developing countries;
– Policy makers in the North had a more pragmatic view of the future where interdependence played an important part – namely that growth in the South was good for the North as it provided the North with more market opportunities. The emergence of like-minded countries among the Group B is an example of this;
– The then existing East-West rivalry, with the communist bloc and capitalist countries vying for allies and clients, thus carrying favour in negotiations. The Group did not shy away from taking advantage of that rivalry to achieve their aims in negotiations.

However, in the earlier days there was a unique almost spiritual experiment in adherence to principles motivated by the newly found solidarity combined with the charisma of leaders emerging on the international stage and enjoying the newly discovered excitement of multilateral diplomacy in smoke filled conference rooms of the United Nations – the leaders of the Group in the 1960s and 1970s from the Secretary-Generals of UNCTAD, Prebisch, Perez Guerrero, Gamani Corea, deputies Rosen, Chidzero, Pronk and directors Dell, Arsenis to Permanent Representatives who lead the regional groupings in the Group. Those having experienced the early years of UNCTAD and of the Group will recall images of negotiators from capitals and Permanent Representatives such as Ambassadors Brillantes, Amir Jamal, Anthony Hill, David Soyza, Shukla, Pradhan, Battista and many many others who devoted all their energies and passion to the cause of the Group.

There was then the short lived impact of the oil crisis of the early 1970s and the fear it generated in the North that there could be a serious attempt by the developing countries to pool their resources particularly in the area of commodity trade and negotiate trade and development measures by placing oil and other commodities in the negotiating basket. The promise of the use of that oil power to provide leverage to assist developing countries to strengthen their bargaining power created apprehension in developed countries as well as a momentum for some accommodation.

In the earlier days of the creation of the Group, there was a healthy emotional almost passionate attachment to the Group for what it represented in terms of hope for the future. Consequently, there was considerable political will and serious follow-up in capitals on the issues placed on the negotiating agenda of trade and development. The Group, as an institution, managed to attract the attention of the policy-makers at highest levels in developing countries.

Finally the Group sought South-South cooperation as a tool to leverage their countervailing power *vis-à-vis* the North. By strengthening economic ties among themselves developing countries aimed at influencing policy decision-making and consequently increasing North-South cooperation. In fact that policy worked for a short period of time until it became evident to the North that players of collective self reliance and other forms of South-South cooperation did not enjoy real political will to implement on the ground those measures that found their way into multiple declarations by resolutions and programmes of action of developing countries.

7.   Crisis and Defiance

By the time UNCTAD V met in 1979 in Manila strains in the North-South dialogue were clearly evident. The momentum generated at UNCTAD I had considerably slowed. However, the Group had established itself as an irreversible and indispensable instrument in multilateral diplomacy and an outstanding characteristic of international negotiations. The group system soon spread to all other centres of the United Nations, particularly in New York. This was also in no small part due to the contribution of the group system to awareness creation in the mind of policy-makers dealing with issues of underdevelopment. The Group was a school that educated Governments and stakeholders in articulating problems faced by developing countries for pursuit of development and the possible demand formulations that could be made in seeking multilateral and binding solutions. The early successes of the Group in Geneva, particularly in UNCTAD' may have inadvertently contributed to the ensuing stalemate and rollback.

The developing countries began to seek redress to issues of development in other fora and in particular New York, the General Assembly and in conferences such as the CIEC in Paris, 1975-1977. This diverted the political focus from UNCTAD as the main arm of economic development of the United Nations, which the founding fathers had envisaged at its creation.[12] The vicious circle of lack of progress lead to frustration and frustration lead to the shift in centralizing activities to New York, ultimately resulting in fragmenting developing countries' focus and efforts in the negotiating process, allowing their detractors to use divisive tactics of institutional rivalry in weakening their solidarity.[13]

---

12   Unfortunately, the emergence of several UN bodies, the more so when those institutions are located in different places, complicated this formative period. It is arguable, for example, that to set up UNCTAD in Geneva, with its own technical, diplomatic and political constituency, was an historic mistake. Conflict and competition developed between the New York and Geneva economic arms of the UN, and the difficulties encountered by Governments in their efforts to coordinate their policies within these multilateral institutions reduced the effectiveness of the UN. Diego Cordovez, Diplomacy for Development, *Multilateral Diplomacy*, page 212, Kluwer Law International, The Netherlands, 1998.

13   The 1970s were heady years for the G77. It was then that the G77 in New York shifted its attention, more strongly than ever before, to economic matters that had, until then, been largely left to UNCTAD and the G77 in Geneva. The regular processes of UNCTAD and its global conferences were now supplemented by "committees of the Whole" of the General Assembly set up to give momentum to economic issues. The high watermark was the bid in 1979 – doomed to eventual failure – to launch "global negotiations" under the auspices of the General Assembly of the United Nations on all the key aspects of North-South relations. Thirty Years of the Group of 77, South Centre publication, Geneva 1994.

Perhaps the earliest sign of the vulnerability of the Group came in 1973 and again later in 1975. The Group failed to build on its momentum created earlier in relations with the developed countries when the oil crisis broke-out and when interdependence acquired a new meaning in international multilateral diplomacy.

As indicated earlier, the golden opportunity of translating rhetorical solidarity into action was to place oil in the basket of primary commodities, treating it as part of the integrated programme for commodities. However, short-term economic interest prevented collective self-reliance from delivering its potential. Unfortunately for the Group the oil producers had their own priorities. It was not cultural or civilization diversity, that was at the root cause of the setback, but classical human greed that defined the act. Instead of the oil crisis bringing together developing and developed countries in realizing common endeavours and mutual interdependence, it instead lead to a downward spiral of confrontation, antagonism and missed opportunity. With the shift to New York and the convening of the first session and special session of the General Assembly exclusively dealing with economic issues, UNCTAD was pre-empted from playing its intended role. When the Paris Conference on International Economic Cooperation was convened and failed, UNCTAD inherited the serious deadlock and legacy.[14]

The consequence of the second oil shock in 1975 was economic slowdown, collapse of commodity prices, mounting protectionism and dwindling resource flow leading to devastating debt crisis in developing countries. Furthermore, high rates of inflation and low growth combined with under-employed resources in many developed countries, the origin of which stemmed from structural rigidities and disequilibria in those countries, undermined sympathetic attention to the development crisis of developing countries.

Since the late 1970s and early 1980s, the Group was not able to play as dynamic a role as it did during the first decade after its advent on the world scene. The relative decline and weakening of the Group coincided with the decline and enfeebling of the multilateral system under the United Nations itself, due to a variety of factors, both autonomous and policy-induced. Simultaneously with the concerted attempt to weaken the United Nations system, efforts were mounted to also weaken and undermine the unity of the Group. At the intellectual level, the very notion of the unity of the developing countries was sought to be falsified on the ground of the prevalence and accentuation of differentiation among them. This, in spite of the fact that there is hardly any group of countries in the world which is not characterized by differentiation, including the counterpart of the Group – the members of Group B, (OECD countries) or later the European Community or even Group D, the ex-socialist countries of Eastern Europe.

The 1980s ushered a decade of crisis and momentous change for developing countries, starting with the weakening and the collapse of the socialist bloc. The developing countries soon discovered they no longer enjoyed an automatist of support on demands placed on the industrialized or free market economies. Soon following the fall of the Berlin Wall former Soviet Union countries began compet-

---

14   See Diego Cordovez (*op. cit*) page 223.

ing for international development assistance, including financial resources, thus distracting even more the attention of developed countries from the development needs of developing countries.

The developed countries were successfully able to refocus the debate from one concerning the need to change the (hostile) inequitable external economic environment to one focussing on the need for domestic policy and domestic reform in developing countries. The gap, in the perceptions and positions of developed and developing countries, widened further with the Group B countries dismissing proposals put forward as extreme and dirigiste.

The debate between efficiency and equity began to shift in favour of developed countries as developing countries themselves struggled with conditionalities imposed on them by the Bretton Woods institution which in addition to their crippling problem of debt accepted that painful measures were justified.

In 1984, at the Group's twentieth anniversary, the Ministers of Foreign Affairs of the Group, then representing some 122 countries, issued a declaration[15] of a litany of challenges facing the developing countries. The Ministers expressed "grave concern at the critical state of the world economy." While the economic recovery in developed countries remained uneven and its durability was in no way guaranteed, most developing countries continued to experience stagnant or declining growth rates. The developing countries continued to be confronted with an adverse external environment characterized by declining commodity prices, sharp exchange-rate fluctuations, deterioration in terms of trade, increased protectionism, very high real interest rates, crushing debt burdens, reverse transfer of financial resources, decline of official development assistance (ODA) in real terms and the resource crisis experienced by multilateral development financing institutions. The Ministers observed that the ever-widening gap between the developed and developing countries was a result of the inequities and inequalities inherent in the existing system, and that the crisis was not merely a cyclical phenomenon but the manifestation of deep-rooted structural imbalances and disequilibrium. They therefore observed that sustained and balanced growth of the international economy required "an equitable adjustment process."[16]

---

15   General Assembly document A/39/536, 20 October 1984.

16   The Ministers expressed their concern with the policies adopted by some developed countries and international financial institutions that affected the development prospects of developing countries, threatening to exacerbate the magnitude and scope of the present international economic crisis, with unpredictable consequences. They also deplored the continued impasse in international economic negotiations – resulting from the fact that some developed countries were not living up to their commitments. They particularly regretted attempts to erode the international consensus for development that had existed and attempts, in some areas, to deny such a consensus. In this regard, developed countries were called upon to renew a positive interest in development issues capable of transforming the sterile dialogues, through genuine political will, into serious negotiations to provide constructive and lasting solutions of development problems.

The Ministers, while asserting their traditional adherence to their guiding principles, indicated that as a whole the declaration showed that the North-South dialogue had come to total standstill.

At the policy level, various measures were adopted to undermine the unity of the Group. These included the policy of graduation, temptations of technical assistance, necessary use of conditionalities and various forms of bilateral pressure. The vastly increased vulnerabilities of most of the members of the Group – due to the debt crises that afflicted them since the early 1980s also played a crucial role in the marginalization of the Group.

As the Group muddled its way through the 1990s, the political scene had completely changed. There was no longer a bipolar world and diversity of economic systems. The one single and dominant economic system became the market and a single world dominant power – the United States – dictated the pace. It was the age of globalization and the information society, or rather the digital divide.

Globalization became a household word after the momentous events of 1989, following a period of earlier adulation of market forces and the twin pillars of liberalization and privatization. This newly found enthusiasm for market forces that replaced the search for equity of the turbulent 1970s was to dominate economic "theology" as preached to developing countries in the wake of the Washington Consensus of the 1980s. Developing countries were promised that the new "openness" would bring greater economic growth and unimaginable prosperity.

Developing countries were clearly told to put aside old conceived ideas of a balance between equity and efficiency.[17]

Rubens Ricupero,[18] in his 1999 MOST lecture, said: *"Globalization has been over-sold to the public since 1989, the year of the fall of the Berlin Wall, as a process that would bring greater prosperity and faster economic growth for all. As a matter of fact, the first decade of globalization has a dismal record in terms of economic growth. It has had one of the lowest economic growth rates of the last 50 or 60 years – even more mediocre than that of the 1970s."*

Mr. Ricupero, Secretary-General of UNCTAD, to his credit – out of tune with the new orthodoxy – almost singularly warned against the unfettered adulation of

---

17   Deepak Nayyar explains that progressive international economic integration since 1950 accelerated the process of globalization and its three cutting-edge manifestations – international trade, international investment and international finance. Globalization, however, also entails the expansion of economic transactions and the organization of economic activities across the political boundaries of nation States – in other words it is a process associated with increasing economic openness, growing economic interdependence and economic integration of countries in the world economy, and extends beyond trade, finance and investment flows to encompass flows of services, technology information and ideas across national boundaries. Deepak Nayyar, *Governing Globalization*. UNU/WIDER Studies in Development Economic. New York, Oxford University Press, 2002.

18   Rubens Ricupero, the 1999 MOST Lecture, Paris, 22 February 1999. R. Ricupero, Secretary-General of UNCTAD from 1996 to 2004.

market forces and that globalization brings, not just opportunities but also risks and challenges, many of them insurmountable.

The South Centre in its publication on the occasion of the fortieth anniversary of the Group poignantly described developments of the 1990s as: *"the major powers of the North to have rolled back the international development agenda, which had been laboriously crafted in the U.N. framework during the previous decades, and interrupted the North-South dialogue and keeping the issues of external economic environment and its impacts on development off the agenda, consequently frustrating those processes which the Group of 77 had struggled to achieve."*

In their place, they offered prescriptions to developing countries on how to develop. Structural adjustment, minimizing the role of the state, globalization and liberalization, the Washington consensus, open economies, privatization and foreign investment were the buzzwords of the decade and of a "top down" approach preached to and imposed upon developing countries by the North, which dominated the policy discourse and practice.

The arguments emanating from the power centres of the North, and the multilateral institutions that they controlled or influenced, were pressed forcefully and did not tolerate doubts or any arguing back from developing countries. Indeed, different views were usually ignored, belittled, or systematically discredited. Dissent, opposition or pluralism were not encouraged.

Developing countries were on the defensive. It was a period of survival and "each one for himself", with many countries accepting and following the prescriptions uncritically. The classical negotiations of hard bargain and quid pro quo exchange of concessions between often grossly unequal partners in bilateral and multilateral settings, such as those during the Uruguay Round, were prejudicial to developing countries and yielded highly asymmetrical outcomes. Moreover, this type of negotiation was highly inappropriate when basic policy issues were in question.

Most developing countries did not have internal political or intellectual defences to question or stand up to the neo-liberal model of globalization championed by the North, and to the new world order that it was putting in place. And most were too weak and increasingly dependent on the good will of the major developed countries, and on such institutions as the World Bank and the IMF, to question and express doubt openly on what was being prescribed and required from all.

The "governance" net was cast over the South gradually. This was done initially via structural adjustment programmes (SAPs), to be complemented by WTO trade-related global regimes resulting from the Uruguay Round Agreements, agreements which had neither the development goals nor interests of the developing countries as their inspiration or objective. An underlying message, well known during centuries of colonialism and imperialism, re-emerged into the open during this period, that of the superiority of the North, its models and achievements, and indeed of its culture and civilization which others should follow and emulate.

On the whole, developing countries found their policy space, domestic and external, increasingly circumscribed, a situation which most perceived as erosion of national sovereignty and a shrinking of their hard won political and economic independence."

How this situation came about and who was to blame – if there was blame to share, and who let whom down, UNCTAD or the Group – would be a fascinating story to unravel one day. For the time being, this essay is not the proper venue to address the balance of responsiblities. Nevertheless it does touch upon some of the symptoms:

A.   Solidarity

As stated earlier, the emergence of the developing countries in a group in 1964 was unity, celebrating diversity. As developing countries gained their independence, they sought and joined the Group.[19] The Group became a rallying point in search of economic independence, by uniting forces in political terms. By doing so, the Group would gain a better prospect for more effective and equitable dialogue – they were the "trade union" of the less privileged in the international community.

However, solidarity is indivisible and solidarity meant that the members of the community could not expect equal gains. It was necessary to diversify the agenda and to translate declaratory solidarity into political and economic manifestations. Nevertheless, this was problematic as rhetoric and declarations drowned practical manifestations of that solidarity – which by all means was genuinely proclaimed. Two indicators come to mind which in the author's personal view show the fragility of that solidarity and the manner with which members of the Group dealt with each other, namely the invasion of Afghanistan (1979) by the Soviet Union and the invasion of Iran by Iraq (1981). In both instances the Group failed to take a moral stand.

The second relates to South-South cooperation. Economic cooperation among developing countries was a prominent item on the South agenda. It was the core of collective self-reliance as declared in Arusha in 1978.[20] The Group of 77 had in UNCTAD a major platform for evolving ECDC policies in the fora of the Committee on Economic Cooperation Among Developing Countries. It took some three decades to evolve South-South cooperation from good intentions and declaratory stages to meaningful cooperation for mutual and collective interest and benefit. In mind the GSTP experiences[21] and the cooperation project in the Perez Guerrero Trust Fund administrated by the office of the Group of 77 Chairman in New York.

B.   The Nature of Multilateral Negotiations

Undoubtedly, there was much hope placed on UNCTAD as a forum for negotiations to promote changes demanded by developing countries. The nature of negotiations that took place in UNCTAD, at its inception, tended to be confrontational

---

19   Today the membership of the Group of 77 is 132 countries.

20   Arusha Programme of Action, G77 Ministerial Meeting prior to UNCTAD V, UNCTAD archives.

21   The Global System for Trade Preferences among developing countries was adopted in 1988. It has received new attention as an important element in South-South trade after the Cancun debacle.

in nature with erratic swings from confrontation to accommodation.[22] According to Nayyar this situation was understandable – *"The East West divide, which was responsible for the cold war, shaped what the UN could or could not do in terms of maintaining peace or ensuring security, which was largely in the realm of politics. The North-South divide, which was associated with decolonization and develop-ment, shaped what the UN could or could not do in terms of reducing disparities and promoting development, which was largely in the sphere of economics. In both cases, it was conflict, rivalry and limited, even forced, cooperation, which functioned as checks and balances in the system."[23]*

Evidently it was not an easy task to bridge the gap between those who valued competition and those who valued the role of the State in ensuring equity particu-larly given that both UNCTAD and the Group were conceived out of the desire to change the rules-of-the-game for a more just and equitable economic order. Defence of positions and principles left only few opportunities for accommoda-tions to be seized whenever they arose, particularly in the form of legally binding instruments. UNCTAD served its original purpose so long as it was perceived as an institution empowered as a rule-making body to negotiate on basis of general and specific principles adopted at UNCTAD I, and adopt legal instruments for the purpose of changing the international rules of the game that impact on trade and development. That is why it had such elaborate intergovernmental negotiating machinery.

As explained by Janos Nyerges[24] negotiations that led to the creation of UNCTAD and subsequent negotiations within that framework were genuinely of redistribution or innovative character and were suitable to the group system. However, as issues evolved and increasing resort was made to "soft law" in the form of resolutions, arrangements, common declarations, understandings without any legal binding character while allowing the flexibility in international relations, it was not suited for and in particular to the international trading system. When those "soft" instruments were available for interpretation, the interpretation of the stronger party always prevailed. After the mid 1980s the Group, in UNCTAD, did not negotiate any legally binding instruments on mainstream issues. "Soft law" in-struments such as "agreed conclusions" or resolutions were only legally binding on the secretariat and only resulted in work programmes and occasions for fur-ther meetings. It took some two decades for attitudes to change when civil society saw opportunities, post Seattle, and began to press Governments in the North on instruments of "soft law" nature that were adopted by the United Nations system – particularly in the environmental and social fields. When that happened even outcomes of intergovernmental meetings in UNCTAD – as soft and innocuous as a chairman's summary became unacceptable to some developed countries.

---

22   Diego Cordovez (*op. cit*) page 219.

23   D. Nayyar (*op. cit*) page 359.

24   Statement by Janos Nyerges, The Development Dialogue in the 1980s continuing pa-ralysis or new consensus, UNCTAD/TAD/INF/PUB/85/1.

Clearly, the problem did not lie in the modality of negotiations or whether the group system – much criticized and praised at the same time – was faulty. Its advantages and disadvantages are well documented.[25] It is also a well-known fact that in the dynamics of group negotiations the common denominator may be so low as to become meaningless, or in the extreme may tend to assume a bargaining position that is the highest common denominator in order to satisfy all members. In certain situations this renders dialogue almost impossible.

But what happened in the "transformation" period of the Group and UNCTAD in the mid 1980s and mid 1990s is that developing countries at multilateral fora, instead of accepting political realities of a zero sum gain in the short term, were willing to compromise stands on principles. This was evident in the manner they ultimately accepted to deal with Foreign Direct Investment (FDI), and the attractiveness of short-term flows instead of focussing political attention on issues relating to money and finance where the conditionality and impositions of the Bretton Wood Institutions could be substantively and politically challenged. Similarly, in the area of invisibles – such as shipping – they sought so-called pragmatic consensus for technical assistance in port improvement rather than addressing the systematic issues that were harming their economies.

The Group crossed the point of no return when "forced" to accept defeat in the elaboration of the Code of Conduct for Transfer of Technology, after a decade of negotiations, accepting albeit gradually to transform the TNC code into an open invitation to TNCs to invest in their countries without the safeguards of corporate social responsibilities. The developing countries thus retreated to the battlefield in stages and left it to bureaucrats to sort out.

At the same time, the agenda of GATT was developing and taking shape in which developing countries were proponents and to which they began directing their attention.

It may be rather harsh to place all the blame on developing countries when the real culprits were those powerful vested interests in developed countries that dictated the policies and the feebleness of institutions in which the Group had put their trust. Those institutions, under the guise of pragmatism, felt it more important to save their organizations as they came under increasingly accusatory criticism from countries of the North.

C.   Reform

By the mid 1980s the Group came under increasingly heavy criticism, as did UNCTAD. In fact, during this period, detractors did not differentiate between the two. Their complaints were addressed equally and without distinction to the UNCTAD secretariat and the Group.

Both the UNCTAD secretariat and the Group were set on addressing their "methods of work" – a process that was never destined to end. Reform, rationalization and restructuring of UNCTAD were to be the daily bread of the organization

---

25   See Behnam, The Group System (op. cit).

for two decades, just as the reform of the United Nations itself has been an ongoing endeavour. This is in no way an implied criticism but a statement of fact that international bureaucracies when faced with difficult choices and political stalemate resort to inner surgeries if that is which it takes to keep management in place.

Reform in the Group and UNCTAD appeared to have passed through three stages, namely reform based on developing countries' higher expectations for result, through stages of frustration and finally into transformation.

The nature and consequence of reform in the last two decades is very much part of the history of the evolution of development diplomacy in UNCTAD and the United Nations system.

In 1974, ten years after the creation of UNCTAD as the principal organ of the General Assembly to deal with development as a transitional measure, the question of the establishment of a Comprehensive International Trade Organization was once more on the agenda.

The question of the establishment of a comprehensive international organization was initially considered at the first session of the Conference in 1964, but it was decided that UNCTAD would "review, in the light of experience, the effectiveness and further institutional arrangements with a view to recommending such changes and improvements as necessary".[26]

The matter was considered inclusively at the third session of UNCTAD. The Secretary-General of UNCTAD addressed member States on this issue in the light of Resolution 81(III), entitled "Further evolution in the institutional machinery of UNCTAD". While that resolution was adopted by vote, 27 developed countries voted against it and their position remained unchanged.

The Secretary-General of UNCTAD lamented in his report of December 1974[27] that while the question was well known to UNCTAD and Governments and despite compelling arguments in favour of institutional change, the question remained for discussion rather than action. The situation was considerably more favourable than in 1948 when the first attempt was made to establish an International Trade Organization (ITO) as a specialized agency in relationship with the United Nations.[28]

---

26   General Assembly Resolution 1995(XIX) establishing UNCTAD «to this end it will study all relevant subjects, including matters relating to the establishment of a comprehensive organization based on the entire membership of the United Nations system of organizations to deal with trade and with trade in relation to development.

27   TD/B/535, question of the establishment of a comprehensive International Trade Organization, December 1974.

28   The Havana Charter was drawn up by the United Nations Conference on Trade and Employment and annexed to its Final Act, which was signed on 24 March 1948 by the representatives of 53 Governments. That Charter did not enter into force; nearly all the signatories made their ratification dependent on that of the United States, which did not materialize, and the process of ratification was abandoned in 1951, a victim of the difficulty of reconciling the conflicting claims of trade liberalization and of the direction of national economic activity, for example to ensure full employment.

In his report, the Secretary-General of UNCTAD presented strong argument on the need for new arrangements to deal with trade and development in a comprehensive manner, on basis of response to the need for universality agreed objectives and agreed code of behaviour and framework for intergovernmental agreement and cooperation on trade and development.

The developing countries had a historic opportunity to capture the momentum, then and there, to redefine UNCTAD. The case for changes in institutional arrangements for dealing with trade and development was founded on the need for such arrangements to take into account certain basic realities of the then existing international situation, namely the dominant trend towards universality in international relations with the addition of some 100 nations since 1945 to the community of nations. These nations brought to the fore the problem of development as priority. Consequently, the interrelationship of the welfare of all members of the world community was increasingly recognized. Added to this was the growing readiness to question the code of behaviour that was drawn up, essentially by and for developed market economy countries as the basis of post-war institutional framework for international economic relations. This compromised the principles of non-discrimination, reciprocity and mutual advantage founded on non-State intervention with emerging interdependence as a reality in both a communal and conceptional sense of binding nations and people in economic and welfare pursuits.

None of the then existing institutions, UNCTAD, GATT, IMF, World Bank satisfied the criteria. Developing countries had a golden opportunity at UNCTAD IV in 1976 to transform UNCTAD, but failed to do so. The Conference adopted Resolution 90(IV), Institutional Issues, in May 1976, which focussed on the strengthening of UNCTAD as a step forward. In that resolution developing countries recognized the General Assembly decision on the establishment of a New International Economic Order (NIEO) and recalled Resolution 3362(S-VII) of the General Assembly which decided "the process of restructuring the United Nations System so as to make it more fully capable of dealing with problems of international economic cooperation and development and make it responsive to the requests of the provision of NIEO." This was very telling as to where developing countries finally took the debate and the political decision. It certainly went against UNCTAD's evolution and earlier potential.

If developing countries took action when they had both the opportunity and the voting majority at the time to change the course of history, one cannot help but wonder what kind of world economic relations would exist today, particularly if UNCTAD was indeed transformed into the ITO and if GATT did not evolve into the WTO. In hindsight, one point of view is that developing countries did not act, for they did not know what they wanted. As they first sought to strengthen UNCTAD, they were simultaneously weakening it by pushing New York into the debate and negotiations on NIEO and were also engaged in the restructuring of the United Nations system.

By 1978, there was a major shift in the position of UNCTAD, primarily linked to the increasing role, which the General Assembly had assumed in the field of development. Development politics and development dialogue became inseparable from world politics and was vested in a number of fora, thus placing UNCTAD in an ambiguous and unsatisfactory position. It was difficult to distinguish and ascertain whether UNCTAD's mandate was lacking or rather political will to use the institution was disappointing.

Developing countries thus began to address the symptoms that were beginning to haunt UNCTAD – the institution they called their own. They called for greater resources, fuller administrative, financial autonomy and flexibility, improved negotiating intergovernmental machinery, its rationalization, and the strengthening of its technical assistance capacity. This was the slippery slope path developing countries were encouraged to take either consciously or subconsciously by developed countries.

Soon enough, with frustrations in the implementation of the mandate, developing countries, as well as UNCTAD secretariat, were slowly shifting focus away from strengthening UNCTAD toward the rationalization, reform and finally transformation of UNCTAD in stages responding to pressure and political changes engendered by the powerful and dominant groups of countries.

It is also pertinent to point out that while the earlier rationalization and reform of UNCTAD was driven by the Group with the intention of strengthening the institution, in the years following the mid 1980s, reform measures were driven by the secretariat.

In 1986, UNCTAD and the Group perhaps made the first major break with the past when its third UNCTAD Secretary-General left under pressure from the developed market economy Group countries. UNCTAD's leadership arrangements were composed of an interim arrangement of an officer-in-charge for one year pending the appointment of the fourth Secretary-General from the African region.

In 1986, the Group itself began to view the reform process through the purpose of improving their own methods of work as well as that of UNCTAD. The Group mandated a sub-group of 15 member countries to prepare a working paper for the conduct of such reform measures.

The Group, while declaring that the absence of progress in UNCTAD was directly related to the negative will of the most important member countries of Group B (market economy group), conceded that there was ample scope for improving the working methods of the Group in Geneva with the aim of ensuring quality and coherence of the their positions. They identified their main problems as pertaining to lack of leadership, lack of continuity, lack of discipline and the need to respond to fast moving international economic developments. They also called upon UNCTAD secretariat to improve its efficiency. To achieve these objectives they proposed a set of constitutive and managerial measures.

This was the beginning of a series of sequential events under the rubric of rationalization and restructuring that would change the nature and relationships of both institutions – UNCTAD and the Group in Geneva.

In 1987, the seventh session of UNCTAD (UNCTAD VII) was held in Geneva with very disappointing results. It was also the time of sweeping political change, of dominant global influence (Reagan/Thatcher conservative revolution) in the aftermath of the collapse of the Socialist camp and resurrection and dominance of the market orthodoxy as the universal economic system. The work programme pursued by the Group in UNCTAD was an anathema to everything the free marketers were advocating.

After practicing defensive policies of stalemate and rejection, developed countries moved to active offensive methods to dismantle those programmes not to their liking, but went about it mostly in a subtle and nuanced manner.[29]

With the increasing spread of liberalization and privatization in the world economy, the focus of development dialogue and issues under negotiation began to shift from those concerning external economic environment to those of domestic policies. Domestic policies were "taboo" words inside the Group in the 1970s and early 1980s. The 1980s came to a close without issues of "hard negotiations" on the table and with developing countries witnessing, a rollback of the international development agenda.

Sooner rather than later, the prescription being offered by developed countries (structural adjustment, minimal role for the State, privatization and liberalization, foreign direct investment, the imposition of the Washington Consensus and acceptance of the widely proclaimed promise of globalization) soon began to have an adverse effect on the solidarity of the Group and its ability to resist or maintain its stand on earlier conceived principles.[30]

By the first Gulf War in 1991, cracks were clearly visible. Voices inside the Group began to seriously question and challenge the credibility of the Group and its capacity to represent the interest of all developing countries.[31] The secretariat of UNCTAD was also under pressure from the developed member countries and from powerful private sector lobbies and the media. Calls for more reform, and this time of a surgical nature, were being fervently expressed from all sectors.

Furthermore, the Group's methods of work, in Geneva had become untenable –coordination on procedures was replacing serious substantive discussions, time was wasted on endless meetings and there was an evident absence of enlightened leadership. The Group's reliance on UNCTAD secretariat for substantive input had become tantamount to chemical dependency. While the secretariat had evolved and changed considerably and was more interested in its own survival and with its own preferred work programmes, the Group in Geneva had not evolved out of that "earlier partnership".[32]

---

29   See A. Behnam, "The Unfulfilled Promise of the Seventies", *Ocean Yearbook*, No. 18, University of Chicago Press, Chicago 2004, page 453.

30   See The Group of 77 at Forty, Document of South Centre, June 2004, pages 4 and 5.

31   The calls for reform were heard loudest in the Latin American group of the Group of 77 led by its spokesman, the representative of Chile in 1991.

32   The main institutional reform that was carried through related to the introduction of greater democracy and flexibility in the Group System. For example, it is now possible for any delegation to dissent publicly and in the course of negotiations if it is national intent and position different from that of the majority. Also the Group agreed to relax the need for one spokesman to articulate the position of the Group of 77 thus allow-

The work methods of the Group began to change dramatically as did their span of attention to UNCTAD as the Uruguay Round got under way. In 1996, developed market economy countries declared they would no longer coordinate on substance and would not engage in collective negotiations. Moreover, the European Union perfected coordination to surpass that of developing countries and adopted and strengthened methods, they had themselves criticized so vehemently, particularly those employed by the Group in securing single coordinated and negotiating stands. The Socialist countries that were represented in the group system in Group D melted away from the multilateral scene.

In order to ensure its survival UNCTAD secretariat had to accept difficult impositions. With examples of the United States withdrawing from ILO, UNESCO and UNIDO, the secretariat pressured developing countries to accept and thus end certain programmes and intergovernmental fora including main committees – Committee on Shipping, Committee on Transfer of Technology and Economic cooperation among Developing Countries (ECDC) were abolished. Consequently developing countries lost important fora where they could articulate their problems and seek international solutions. The amazing aspect of this was it was passed without vociferous outcry and went almost unnoticed by developing countries. This may be explained by the fact developing countries were otherwise preoccupied by their and their policy-makers attention toward the Uruguay Round.

Post 1996 and during the ninth UNCTAD Conference it became clear that the institution had been transformed for ever, from one of consensus-building negotiations and rule-making, from one that was to evolve into the ITO into one of a knowledge based institution devoted almost entirely to policy dialogue and capacity building.

Today, no negotiations take place in UNCTAD. There is resistance even to any form of "soft agreement" such as agreed conclusions or chairman's summary. Rule making on trade is exclusively vested in WTO. Nevertheless, UNCTAD has maintained certain intellectual independence and through its flagship publications challenges orthodoxy, as demonstrated only recently in UNCTAD XI in Sao Paulo in June 2004.[33]

UNCTAD has also enjoyed courageous intellectual leadership in the person of its Secretary-General Rubens Ricupero, who continuously challenged the vested interest and the exercise of absolute economic power to oppress the poor. He challenged the legitimacy of certain actions by the WTO at Seattle, the relevance of development in the Development Round of Doha, the cotton and agricultural sub-

---

ing for greater regional representation and spokesmanship. The new reforms placed greater emphasis on substantive regional coordination and less on the coordination at the Group of 77 level for the purposes of a single spokesman system. A. Behnam, The Group System (*op. cit*)

33   On 14 September 2004, UNCTAD, in celebration of its 40th anniversary, issued a publication entitled Beyond Conventional Wisdom in Development Policy: An Intellectual History of UNCTAD 1964-2004 (UNCTAD/EDM/2004/4) Geneva. The publication provided a contrasting view to this essay.

sidies that had devastated many economies in Africa and called for policy space for developing countries. He made efforts to focus policies on the productive sectors of developing countries and strove for solution to the debt burden of developing countries.

However, the UNCTAD secretariat that existed in the 1960s and 1970s evolved and the Group could no longer depend on the secretariat to act as if it was its own, responding to developing countries needs, even in the pursuit of legitimate mandates. UNCTAD after all is an international bureaucracy subject to the pressure of its universal membership.

8.   A Perspective for the Future

A.   An Emerging Trend

The multilateral system is being strained as it comes under constant attack. The centres of power are scorning multilateral solutions. In place of consensus building resort to coercion is often prevalent. There has been a major shift in the development agenda. The issue of security, justified as it is, is taking centre stage and emerging concepts of humanitarian intervention and preventive attack is replacing the development dialogue. While these are serious and worrying trends, there are nevertheless voices of optimism being championed despite a most depressing decade of unfulfilled promises and dashed hopes.

Two eminent leading figures and practitioners of development in the South Centre, Muchkund Dubey and Branislav Gosovic, who despite their concern, are convinced that the current world situation is highly propitious for the Group to resume its traditional role of creating a global economic environment supportive of development and establishing a just and equitable world economic order. They point out that a number of the Group's members have performed extremely well in the field of development and as a result have acquired significant clout in the world economy, thus augmenting the collective strength of the Group. These members have also shown awareness that even their enhanced economic clout gives them, individually, very limited bargaining power and that this power is enhanced exponentially if they negotiate collectively. The association of China on practically all issues of fundamental importance to the Group has further enhanced the bargaining strength of the Group. This was reflected in the abortive WTO Ministerial Conference in Cancun where the effective functioning of issue-centre coalitions of developing countries (G20) exposed the obduracy and unreasonableness of the negotiating positions of the North and prevented the damage that their successful pursuit would have inflicted upon developing countries. This was particularly true of their position on agricultural protection and their objective of extending the mandate of WTO to additional non-trade related areas, with a view mainly to limit the space for policy options for developing countries in these areas.

In the face of unilateral threats, there is now a strong desire to strengthen the United Nations. The revival of multilateralism under the United Nations will inevitably result in the revival of the currently dormant negotiating process in the United Nations, in which the Group will come to play its indispensable role.

This will come at a time when there are much higher stakes involved in multilateral negotiations. Present-day negotiations are not so much about seeking trade concessions or getting technical and financial assistance, but rather about putting in place new regimes and new rules-of-the-game, designed to limit the sovereign economic space available to developing countries and their choices for macro-economic policy making. As the Cancun experience has demonstrated, developing countries can meet this challenge only by acting collectively.

UNCTAD very recently referred to a quiet transformation that is reshaping the global economic and trade landscape.[34] Accordingly, the centuries-old international trade geography, where the South served as hinterlands of resources and captive markets for finished goods of the North, is slowly changing. The share of the South in global trade and financial flows has grown dramatically during the last two decades. Not all the countries in South have been able to take part in this journey, yet even amongst some of the poorest ones there are indications of improved performance, which gives rise for optimism.

The old geography of international trade had been much defined by the colonial era. The Industrial Revolution helped colonial powers attain decisive technological superiority in both civil and military spheres and enabled them to occupy the central position in international economic relations *vis-à-vis* developing countries – an asymmetric pattern that continued into the post-colonial era.

Today, forty years since the founding of UNCTAD, a new geography of trade appears to be emerging, in which the South is moving steadily away from the periphery of the world economy and trade, reflecting changes in the traditional pattern of the international division of labour. This augurs well for trade to be able to play the role of a genuine locomotive for sustained economic growth, diversification, employment generation and poverty reduction in developing countries.

The founding fathers of UNCTAD stressed that what was good for the South was also good for the North. This remains valid since future domestic demand growth potential in some of the developed countries is likely to level off, reflecting their long-term demographic trends and the high degree of consumption saturation. Developing countries, which constitute a vast reservoir of untapped demand, could provide a steady boost to the growth of international trade and expansion of the world economy, with beneficial effects for the welfare of developed country economies, consumers, shareholders and businesses.

The impact China has had on demand, the potential growth of India, Brazil and South Africa as centres of new demand makes for augmenting South-South trade at the same time enhancing growth and prosperity for developing and developed countries alike also deepens North-South complementarities. Therefore,

---

34   UNCTAD/TD/404, New Geography of International Trade, 4 June 2004. In an issues note for the Heads of State Round Table at Sao Paulo in June 2004 on the occasion of UNCTAD XI.

in order to take advantage of this emerging new geography of trade, developing countries need greater policy space.

At its conception, the Group represented unity celebrating diversity. Today, perhaps it represents diversity celebrating unity. Gone forever is the principle of equal gain, or that the interests of individual nations or sub-groups are sacrificed at the expense of political unity. No longer applicable is the highest or lowest common denominators. Countries and sub-groups can coalesce along lines of enlightened self-interest. No longer are sub-groups of interested countries on sectoral or thematic issues of debt, agriculture or subsidies held back awaiting a full G77 position as the emergence of the G20, G15, G30 and G90 have demonstrated.

Cancun was a point of departure where the G20 with the support of the other members emerged as stakeholders. It signified that members of the Group could differentiate their demands and negotiate on sectors of interest where they are ready to do so, accepting legally binding commitments. This meant the emergence of new forms of South-South cooperation.

The North, in current circumstances, is likely to respond in manner that is more benevolent as was the case in the past when South-South cooperation was perceived as countervailing power to pressure the North on the negotiating agenda for development.

Perhaps as the new geography of trade unfolds we may also witness a new geography of an emerging multilateral diplomacy.

B.   Reviewing the Development Agenda

Several of the items on the original agenda of the Group remain valid and unfulfilled. These include adequate resource flows, strong and stable commodity markets, and reduction of the debt burden and dismantling of protectionist barriers. However, these issues have now to be pursued in a drastically changed global economic environment – basically in the context of the current process of globalization and its handmaiden, liberalization. Moreover, new issues such as the protection of the environment, sustainability of development, social justice, equity and inclusion as goals by themselves as well as pre-conditions for development, and the issue of governance both at national and international levels, have appeared on the agenda of multilateral negotiations, often at the cost of the still valid old agenda. These issues are highly complex and are amenable only to an interdisciplinary approach. They call for a thorough grasp of the details, a specialist's approach and extraordinarily high negotiating skills.

It took the Group of 77 thirty-five years before they held their first Summit in Havana in 2000. The Havana Summit did raise hopes and gave some new directions and political impulse to the Group. Unfortunately the follow up to the Summit was not commensurate with the event itself.[35]

The time has come to update and restructure the agenda of the Group and infuse it with new sense of purpose and orientation. The focus should be on world

---

35   An update on the Second Summit is annexed.

order issues and not on seeking concessions of a once-and-for-all nature. Greater attention should be paid to the implications for developing countries of new regimes, new systems and new rules-of-the-game. In analysing such implications, full advantage should be taken of the capacity recently built in the think tanks of developing countries. However, this capacity still remains utterly inadequate and is not at all commensurate with the tasks lying ahead. Besides, the Group so far has not built any capacity of its own. It is yet to put in place an institutional support mechanism.[36]

The Group also needs to work closely and collaborate actively with other stakeholders in development. There should be active consultation with civil society organizations for evolving national positions as well as the common position of the Group. A more intelligent and apt use of the international media is desperately required to advocate the group's mission. Like-minded civil society organizations of developed countries should be brought on a common platform to bolster the position of the South. It is also the opportune time to forge new significant and far-reaching links of South-South cooperation as a means of imparting greater credibility to the platform of the Group. The enhanced economic and technological capabilities of individual members of the Group have opened up new opportunities in this crucial area.

The Group does not have to "reinvent the wheel"; it already has an institution of the South and can very easily, with the necessary political will, evolve into an institution of its own which can serve the Group's interest. The United Nations Secretariat is neither capable of nor willing, let alone permitted to provide the required support. There are institutions in the South that can provide the nucleus for institution building for example the South Centre has been tested over time and has proved its worth substantively, intellectually and institutionally. South institutions have the institutional memory and the intellectual capacity to provide both support and leadership for the Group as it embarks on its new agenda of "South-South cooperation in a world in which the major economic and military powers use the UN system to serve national security interests." The challenge for the South institutions is how to encourage and prepare for change that is founded in true interdependence of interests of all nations. The current global problems of security, injustice, hunger and abject poverty are indivisible. These challenges are interrelated and intertwined. They are integrated and comprehensive in global character and solutions.

In concluding this chapter, it may be most appropriate to quote Rubens Ricupero's concluding paragraph of his masterful lecture at the Fernando H. Cardoso Institute: *"To renew international life, the alliance needed is not an alliance inspired on the splits of the past, such as North-South, or of the present, such as the shock of*

---

36 The Group of 77 at Forty, South Centre *op. cit.* Full and continuous institutional support of the highest professional quality is essential for any multilateral endeavour, especially at the global level where the G77 operates, confronting a complex, overlapping and interrelated agenda, which moreover is scattered between different institutions and world capitals.

civilizations, religions, and cultures. On the contrary, it is imperative that we start from the understanding that the various aspects of human security – political, economic, social, environment – form an inseparable unity not only for each human being individually but also for each human being in relation to all others. This should be the basis of genuine interdependence in addressing new and old threats. Globalization has come to be seen as the mother of all threats precisely because the conviction has been abandoned that all of us, North and South, depend on each other both for combating terrorism and weapons proliferation and for fighting to eradicate poverty and to promote prosperity. The construction of an interdependent, solidarity-based globalization should be the central objective of a new cosmopolitan order, not on moral or idealist grounds but as dictated by realism and enlightened self-interest."

Annex

Update – South Summit II 2005

The Second Summit of Heads of State and Government was held in Doha, Qatar on 12-16 June 2005. It provided an opportunity to review the progress made since the first summit in 2000 (Havana) on the implementation of that summit's decisions.

The Group of 77 were aware that since the last summit the international multilateral environment had considerably changed. Crucial issues they had addressed in 2000 were now outside the multilateral agenda and the need to develop a clear vision of the goals to be achieved

The Summit identified three priority areas: the first being South-South cooperation, namely the move away from rhetoric and lip service to action in implementation of agreed policies on South-South cooperation.

The second was to bring back development on the multilateral agenda and to refocus the work of the UN on economic and social development needs of developing countries. In this regard the reform of the United Nations and the report of the UNSG "In larger freedom: towards development, security and human rights for all", on the reform of the United Nations, figured high in the Summits debates.

The third Review of the Millennium Development Goals in preparation for the September 2005 UN Summit in New York. The Group of 77 made their own assessment of the measures needed to bring about the achievement of the targets set in the MDGs.

These and other more traditional issues of concern to developing countries were addressed in the two documents adopted by the Summit, the Doha Declaration and the Doha Plan of Action (available on <www.G77.org>).

The most outstanding event in the Summit was the announcement of the Emir of Qatar to establish a Fund for Development and Humanitarian Affairs to which Qatar contributed 20 million US dollars and India and China 2 million US dollars each. It may be a modest gesture but it signals a change in the Group of 77 that they are willing to move from dialogue to action in promoting South-South cooperation.

14. America's Doctrines: The Monroe and Bush Doctrines Compared

Alfred P. Rubin

Whether the "United States" or "America" is used to refer to the North American state just south of Canada presumably makes a difference to other states in the Western Hemisphere, or other states of the Americas, but I propose to use "America" and "United States" interchangeably in this chapter. I cannot defend that usage other than by custom and changing patterns of formal usage, like the earlier practice of referring to the United Kingdom as Great Britain. Similarly, I have used the word "state" to refer to the fundamental units of international law. Many political leaders think in terms of ethnic or other groups as the fundamental units, but those groups are much better seen as their constituents; the word "state," meaning the whole, regardless of its ethnic or other composition, seems to be a European/American imposition on others and on parts of themselves.[1] I am not ignorant of the anomalies in that situation, but for the moment stick to the hallowed vocabulary of the United Nations (UN) and its Charter, which refer to members of the UN as "states" (indeed, "peace- loving states"[2]) whatever else the hypocrisies of the Charter and the current membership of the UN may be.

---

1   Cf. ANNE APPLEBAUM, *Pulling the Rug Out from Under*, 5(2) NEW YORK REVIEW OF BOOKS 9 (2004); KAREN KNOP, DIVERSITY AND SELF-DETERMINATION IN INTERNATIONAL LAW (Cambridge, 2002) esp. pp. 132 sq (analyzing the ICJ's opinion in the Western Sahara Case – ICJ, Western Sahara, Advisory Opinion, 1975); one might ask if Belgium, a state with both Walloon and Flemish constituents, is a single "state," or the United Kingdom, with Scottish, Welsh, Irish and English constituencies. Yet some politicians do indeed think in these terms.

2   UN Charter Articles 3 and 4. It might be noted that the original members of the UN are merely "states which, having participated in the United Nations Conference on International Organization at San Francisco ... or [a] ... Declaration ... of 1 January 1942, [then] sign the present Charter and ratify it..." whether or not "peace-loving." "Peace-loving states" may be admitted to the organization later, but only after a recommendation by the Security Council and decision by the General Assembly. That recommendation and that decision are surely colored by political factors. The original members

Ronald St. John Macdonald & Douglas M. Johnston (eds.), Towards World Constitutionalism, *pp. 381-397.*
© *2005 Koninklijke Brill NV. Printed in The Netherlands.* ISBN 90 04 14612 1.

The so-called Monroe Doctrine was part of President James Monroe's State of the Union address to the American Congress on 2 December 1823. It affirmed the interest of the United States in friendship with the Russian Imperial Government and the Government of Great Britain, but continued by stating that the American continents "are henceforth not to be considered as subjects for future colonization by any European [apparently including Russia] powers." Recognizing that there were existing European colonies in the Western Hemisphere's continents (both Northern and Southern) and that several Western Hemisphere colonies of Spain had fought for and achieved independence, Monroe went on to point out, not entirely accurately, as shall be noted below, that:

> With the existing colonies or dependencies of any European power we have not interfered and shall not interfere. But with the Governments who have declared their independence and maintain it, and whose independence we have, on great considerations and on just principles, acknowledged, we could not view any interposition for the purpose of ... controlling ... their destiny, by any European power in any other light than as the manifestation of an unfriendly disposition toward the United States.

He continued:

> It is impossible that the allied powers [apparently meaning those states comprising the Holy Alliance – Prussia (nominally Lutheran Protestant), Russia (nominally Eastern Orthodox Catholic) and Austria (nominally Roman Catholic)] should extend their political system to any portion of either continent without endangering our peace and happiness ...

The United States certainly had interfered in the government of Great Britain in Canada as recently as ten years before the announcement of the Doctrine, and invited the Government of Great Britain to assume responsibility for the governance of the Malvinas/Falkland Islands within ten years after this announcement.[3]

It seems noteworthy that the word "Doctrine" appears nowhere in the speech by President Monroe. But it would appear that the Monroe Doctrine was rhetoric designed to cover a particular situation, in which several southern hemisphere colonies of Spain had successfully fought for their independence, and the United States was prepared to make its own decisions regarding its interventions in those struggles for independence. The word "just" does appear in the declaration by

---

of the UN included the parties' notions of who were the victor states of the Second World War; surely some were not "peace-loving" by any rational definition.

3   On Canada, see S.E. MORISON, OXFORD HISTORY OF THE AMERICAN PEOPLE . (1965) ch. 24, esp. pp. 380, 382. On the United States manipulation of the Malvinas/Falklands situation, see A.P. RUBIN, *Historical and Legal Background of the Falkland/Malvinas Dispute*, in ALBERTO COLL AND ANTHONY AREND, THE FALKLANDS WAR (1985) 9-21. For the Argentine view, see ROBERTO LAVER, THE FALKLANDS/MALVINAS CASE (2001). But the volume of literature on both these situations is huge.

President Monroe. But who is to define what is "just" is left unclear. Apparently, as with most moral terms, the decision is to be made by the user of the word (in this case, the United States) alone, hoping that the rest of the world agrees . There is an assumption that whatever we (Americans – I am one; on both my parents' sides, my family has lived here for over a century) decide to be "just" will be taken by all others also to be "just." But that assumption seems unwarranted. It could well be that to Spain (or the Holy Alliance) "just" would mean the continuation of prior authority regardless of the lack of military dominance. After all, this was the period of Metternich's "legitimacy," which, in those days, apparently meant the continuation of existing governments satisfactory to the Holy Alliance, whatever normative order the word "legitimacy" has been used to refer to since then.[4]

In fact, the United States did intervene at least once (and probably more than once) in those struggles to maintain local independence. In Mexico, during the American Civil War of 1861-1865, France attempted to create a colony under the leadership of Maximilian, an Austrian Archduke who was a favorite relative of the French Emperor.[5] It failed, not because of the Monroe Doctrine and French docility, but because the balance of military force in the Western Hemisphere just South of the United States, had shifted to favor the American Union at the time.

This is not the place to review American involvement in various Western Hemisphere struggles. The United States did intervene many times in them, but not with regard to European attempts to assert an unwarranted (by American standards) authority except the French attempt in Mexico during the American Civil War. The anxieties of the United States with regard to European entanglements in the Western Hemisphere surfaced during the Cuban struggle against Spain in 1898[6] and, indeed, in many other situations, but the proximity of the United States to these events, and the preponderance of American military force[7] made the outcome of these affairs pretty clear, at least in retrospect.

---

4   Whether the word "legitimacy" refers to being "legitimate" in the legal order, the moral order, the historical order, the political order or whatever other order the user intends, remains unclear. The word itself derives from the Latin and seems cognated with the word from which English speakers derive "legislation." But its usage has been much broader than the legal order.

5   France had several claimants to a French crown at that time, tracing their descent from different ousted monarchs, from the Bourbons to the Bonapartes. The particular claimant in Mexico during the early 1860s was favored by the French ruler, Napoleon III. The French used Mexican debts as their excuse for taking over the country in 1863. President Andrew Johnson sent the American Union's General William T. Sherman to the border in 1865, and the Mexicans executed Maximilian themselves. Again, the story has been told often and in many places. A valuable summary is in MORISON, *op.cit.*, chs. 41 and 44, at pp. 661-662 and 706.

6   See WALTER MILLIS, THE MARTIAL SPIRIT (1931) for an account of the Spanish American War and Cuba's role in it.

7   It might be worth mentioning in this place that during the nineteenth century American military force was growing substantially. One result of the Spanish-American War of 1898-1899 was indeed the acquisition of American territory in the Pacific Ocean

One major result of these entanglements was the growth ever more strongly in the United States of a sense that America's sense of "justice," *i.e.*, what was "just," was infallible. Theodore Roosevelt, American President from 1901 to 1909, made it explicit when pronouncing his "corollary" to the Monroe Doctrine in a Speech to the United States Congress on 6 December 1904. He repeatedly praised the sense of "justice" of the United States and used that sense as the basis for saying that "... the other nations of the Western Hemisphere" need have no concerns over the ambitions of the United States "save such as are for their welfare" (presumably that "welfare" was also to be determined by the United States).

> Chronic wrongdoing or an impotence which results in a general loosening of the ties of civilized society, may in America, as elsewhere, ultimately require intervention by some civilized nations, and in the Western Hemisphere the adherence of the United States to the Monroe Doctrine may force the United States, however, reluctantly, in flagrant cases of such wrongdoing or impotence, to the exercise of an international police power.[8]

Again, various key words (not only "justice" and "welfare" but also "civilized" and, indeed, many other key words) are undefined. In the normal moral way of doing things, the decision as to what is justifiable or civilized or otherwise "moral" is left to the actor him/herself. It is the product of a complex weighing process in which various values are considered and given weight. Very few decisions with any moral basis are easy; nearly all have detriments to some values in the moral order of the weigher. In the American legal sphere, this weighing process is well-known, and well-known to be complex and to raise nearly as many questions as it purports to answer.[9] Indeed, for a President of the United States to be fair (another moral-value-laden word) s/he should consult with a lawyer, a military person, an economist, an historian, a political scientist (specializing in local elections and another specializing in international values) and many other specialists, then double or triple the number because such specialists frequently disagree among themselves as to the relative weights to be given the values at stake and very few achievements are possible in any sphere without a loss of some values which seem important to some people both in that very sphere and in other spheres. But I could find no mention of this inevitable lack of clarity in documents relating to the Monroe Doctrine or the Roosevelt corollary.

(The Philippines, Guam *et al.*) where American proximity was only a relative matter, but American military force was substantial.

8   <www.uiowa.edu/~c030162/Common/Handouts/POTUS/TRoos.html> of 6 December 1904.

9   See, e.g., Timberlane Lumber Co. v. Bank of America (Ct. App. 9th Cir. 1984) for a United States example of this weighing process. Nearly all international law cases decided by the International Court of Justice or other bodies, including arbitral tribunals or individuals, involve value-weighing and include dissents by judges or arbitrators whose personal or national value system differs from that supported by the majority. It is not proposed to analyze these many decisions in this place.

Another noteworthy feature of the corollary is that by 1904 it took much more space, many more words, to express a point than had been taken by President Monroe in 1823, when the original Monroe Doctrine was pronounced. That increase in the verbal complexity of an assertion is not merely the result of the evolving usages of the English language (although that might have something to do with the fact). It (also) reflects the increasing perception of the complexity of the "real" world and the increasing complexity of the ideas sought to be expressed in it. On the other hand, it is a frequent illusion of writers (and Presidents) that the world for them is more complex than the world was for Aristotle, Grotius and the many others who have written on the topic of moral ambiguity and international affairs. It may be doubted that the world is increasingly complex; only that whatever stage we are in seems complex to us. A final point that seems appropriate for this place is the persistence of the illusion that whatever we are saying is original in us, that nobody else has previously had the insights we are claiming. I know of many later works saying the things that I have said, but not citing any of my writings. I doubt the authors' knowledge of my writings as much as I doubt the authors' originality.[10] The lack of citation is too common to be new, and I am as guilty as others of failing to cite the originator of some thought I have expressed as if original in me (I hope and think it has been mere ignorance). Indeed, this ignorance was noted even biblically, there being nothing new under the sun according to Ecclesiastes 1:9.

An example of the American use of force in Latin America in the period between the Roosevelt corollary and the first world war was the invasion and occupation of Vera Cruz, Mexico, under President Woodrow Wilson.[11] Wilson, often seen as a champion of self-determination, was not really so when it came to supporting the theories that appealed to him.[12] Not only did he send a fleet to resolve a diplomatic incident by occupying Mexican territory in April 1914, but his doctrine of "recognition" involved his evaluation of the moral standing of the "government" of the "state" involved. President Woodrow Wilson of the United States refused to "recognize" Huerta's government as the government of Mexico even though by 1913 it had certainly achieved the degree of authority that to others seemed to

---

10   One example that comes to hand readily is the mention in O'CONNELL AND SHEARER, THE LAW OF THE SEA (1984), pp. 969-970, of the illogic of the definition of Piracy in the 1982 Convention on the Law of the Sea. Notably lacking is a reference to a Comment in a widely read journal, making exactly the same point with regard to the draft from which the article was taken: RUBIN, *Is Piracy Illegal?* 70 AM. J. OF INT'L L. 92-95 (1976).

11   This example is analyzed in ROBERT E. QUIRK, AN AFFAIR OF HONOR; WOODROW WILSON AND THE OCCUPATION OF VERACRUZ (1962, 1967). There are unfortunately many other examples.

12   Porfirio Diaz, President of Mexico, is reported to have remarked "Poor Mexico, so far from God and so close to the United States." Bartlett's Familiar Quotations (14th ed., 1968), 734a. Diaz was elected President of Mexico 1877-1880 and 1884-1911. He ruled as a dictatorial liberal. See the brief biography by STANLEY R. ROSS in 9 ENCYCLOPEDIA AMERICANA (1974) 71-72.

"justify" such "recognition." On the other hand, President Thomas Jefferson of the United States (and many of his successors) apparently felt that the internal policies of a foreign government were of no concern to the United States as long as that government in fact exercised internal authority. Various attempts to bring these two trains of thought together[13] have failed.

Skipping by various other American Presidential "Doctrines," like the so-called "Truman Doctrine" by which the assistance of the United States was given to the states of Eastern Europe to help defeat supposed Russian communism there, the third "Doctrine" that is the subject of this essay is the so-called "Bush Doctrine."[14] It is called a "doctrine" in Part IV, paragraph 2 of the President's statement. It seems to have been pronounced in President George W. Bush's speech of 17 September 2002.[15] In it, President Bush said:

> We will:
> Cooperate with other nations to deny, contain, and curtail our enemies' efforts to ac-
> quire dangerous technologies. And, as a matter of common sense and self-defense,
> America will act against such emerging threats before they are fully formed.

He also spelled out various steps the United States seems committed to take. For example, he said that:

> We will:
> Speak out honestly about violations of the nonnegotiable demands of human dignity
> using our voice and vote in international institutions to advance freedom;

---

13   The Central American Treaty of 1907 and of 7 February 1923 both seem to provide a "legitimacy" test, but were abandoned by various administrations in the United States and others. Mexico at one time adopted the "Estrada" doctrine under which "recognition" was not a prerequisite for any trade matters. See HERBERT BRIGGS, THE LAW OF NATIONS (2d ed., New York 1952), pp. 123-124. In general, this all involves *de jure* and *de facto* "recognition" and is far too large a topic to be discussed in this place. The disputes about it are endless. On the Wilsonian v. the Jeffersonian inconsistencies in United States foreign policy, and the "recognition" of the Communist Government of China, see the documents collected in WILLIAM W. BISHOP, JR., INTERNATIONAL LAW (Boston and Toronto, 3rd ed., 1971) pp. 337-342, 351-354. There are many questions left unanswered by the official documents, and many cases (like that of Tibet) not dealt with.

14   The word "Doctrine" is used (uncapitalized) by President Bush in Part IV of his state-ment: "No doctrine can anticipate every circumstance in which U.S. (*sic*) action – direct or indirect – is warranted. We have finite political, economic, and military resources to meet our global priorities." The word "Doctrine" is used only in one other place that I could find in the statement and that is clearly irrelevant to this discussion: "Counter-proliferation must also be integrated into the *doctrine* (emphasis added), training, and equipping of our forces and those of our allies..."

15   <http://www.whitehouse.gov/nsc/nssall.html.> The paper runs about 21 pages in length.

use our foreign aid to promote freedom and support those who struggle non-violently for it, ensuring that nations moving toward democracy are rewarded for the steps they take;

make freedom and the development of democratic institutions key themes in our bi-lateral relations, seeking solidarity and cooperation from other democracies while we press governments that deny human rights to move toward a better future; and

take special efforts to promote freedom of religion and conscience and defend it from encroachment by repressive governments.

We will champion the cause of human dignity and oppose those who resist it.

In so saying, he seems to have adopted the moralistic line taken by Samantha Power,[16] erecting American moral standards to the legal level of universal jurisdiction in criminal matters and a legal obligation of states to seek out and try those foreigners whose acts in foreign territory shock the conscience of Americans.

More significantly for present purposes, President Bush defined "terrorism" with the phrase: "premeditated, politically motivated violence perpetrated against innocents."

In doing so, he joined many others in ignoring the definition suggested by the world-wide International Law Association.[17]

"Preempt" or its derivative words (like preemptively, preemptive and preemption) is mentioned once in Part III and six times in Part V of the National Security Strategy document from which the preceding excerpts were taken. Part III is labeled "Strengthen Alliances to Defeat Global Terrorism and Work to Prevent Attacks Against Our Friends." Part V is labeled "Prevent Our Enemies from Threatening Us, Our Allies, and Our Friends with Weapons of Mass Destruction." Rather than analyze the entire document (it is 21 pages long), only those passages of particular interest to international lawyers will be discussed.

The first of the uses of the word "preempt" or its cognates is in a passage in Part III that says:

---

16   SAMANTHA POWER, A PROBLEM FROM HELL (2002). In this book, which won many prizes, including a Pulitzer for non-fiction, Ms. Power makes many errors of law in order to make her moral point. For example, neither "piracy" nor the international traffic in slaves is a matter for universal jurisdiction (p. 22). Although many lawyers have said that they are, some research shows that they are wrong. See RUBIN, THE LAW OF PIRACY (1988), *passim*; RUBIN, ETHICS AND AUTHORITY IN INTERNATIONAL LAW (1997) pp. 97 sq., 183-185. But this is not the place to review all the evidence collected in those books or repeat their conclusions.

17   INTERNATIONAL LAW ASSOCIATION, REPORT OF THE SIXTY-FIRST CONFERENCE, PARIS (1984), *Resolution No. 7 of 1984*, pp. 6-8; see also explanation at pp. 313-322, esp. p. 314-315. See also the REPORT of the *International Law Association Committee on Legal Problems in Relation to Terrorist Offences* in INTERNATIONAL LAW ASSOCIATION, REPORT OF THE SIXTY-THIRD CONFERENCE, WARSAW (1988), *Resolutions I and II* at p. 39 and explanations at pp. 1032-1054.

... We will disrupt and destroy terrorist organizations by:

... defending the United States, the American people, and our interests at home and abroad by identifying and destroying the threat before it reaches our borders. ... we will not hesitate to act, alone, if necessary, to exercise our right of selfdefense [spelling *sic*] by acting *preemptively* [emphasis added] against such terrorists to prevent them from doing harm against our people and our country ...

This raises a number of questions. The assertion that defense of the American people abroad appears to be included in the assertion of America's rights presumes that the law, being the same for all within its contemplation, affirms such rights. But it might be supposed that we (Americans) would strongly object on the basis of international law to the equivalent assertion by anybody else of a "right" at international law to defend by military force their nationals abroad. Since at least the days of the Permanent Court of International Justice and its famous "Lotus" Case, territorial sovereignty has been deemed to be exclusive in the territorial sovereign, and no exercise of "passive personality" jurisdiction has been permitted.[18] It is not at all clear whether this Doctrine is an attempt to assert such jurisdiction by the United States. More important from a lawyer's point of view is the assertion that America has a "right" (presumably a right under international law) of self-defense in the absence of an armed attack regardless of Article 51 of the UN Charter, a Treaty to which the United States is party. Article 51 of the UN Charter says:

Nothing in the present Charter shall impair the inherent right of individual or collective self-defence (spelling *sic*) if an armed attack occurs against a Member of the United Nations, until the Security Council has taken measures necessary to maintain international peace and security. ...

It is highly debatable whether this language precludes action prior to an armed attack, but it does seem clear that only action in self-defense is legally authorized. Self-defense is defined for many international lawyers by the Webster-Ashburton correspondence of 1842, in which Daniel Webster, as Secretary of State of the United States, defined self-defense as justifiable only when a state is confronted with a situation in which the "necessity of that self-defence [spelling *sic*] is instant, overwhelming, and leaving no choice of means and no moment for deliberation."[19] This definition has been challenged often, both as a matter of practice under the UN Charter[20] and as a matter of teleology. The practice under the UN Charter seems

---

18   The Lotus Case, PCIJ Ser. A, No. 10 (1927).

19   J.B. Moore, International Law Digest 412 (1906). The letter from Daniel Webster as Secretary of State of the United States, to Lord Ashburton, the British Minister Plenipotentiary to he United States, is dated 6 August 1842. In it the quoted language is attributed to a letter from Webster to Mr. Fox, Lord Ashburton's predecessor in the United States, cited to 6 Webster's Works 250, 261. I have not been able to check the original.

20   See Goodrich, Hambro and Simons, Charter of the United Nations (3rd ed., Columbia University Press, 1969) 344-348. See also my own analysis of this provi-

clearly broader than the Webster formulation, including the American invasion of Grenada. As to teleology, Article 51 appears as the last article of Chapter VII of the UN Charter and seems to provide an exception for state action when the Security Council has failed to act to maintain international peace and security as it is bound to do under Article 39 of the Charter, the first article in Chapter VII. The issue seems to be whether the silence of the Security Council can authorize action denominated "self-defense" by the state taking the action. In practice, it seems that it can despite the vigorous arguments of those who take a more Webster-oriented view.[21]

As to Part V of the Doctrine, two paragraphs seem to spell out the Bush approach. In one, he says:

> For centuries, international law recognized that nations need not suffer an attack before they can lawfully take action to defend themselves against forces that present an imminent danger of attack. Legal scholars and international jurists often conditioned the legitimacy of preemption on the existence of an imminent threat – most often a visible mobilization of armies, navies, and air forces preparing to attack.

Aside from pointing out that international law as expressed in state practice (*i.e.*, international common law) has been superseded by treaties and has moved on from the views expressed here as if still current, the statement is entirely correct in pointing out that the position of international jurists has been "often" conditioned; often is not always. Moreover, the "legitimacy" mentioned in this text might refer to moral legitimacy, legal legitimacy, military legitimacy, political legitimacy and even economic legitimacy. The word "legitimacy" seems hopelessly confusing as the basis for any firm commitment. It seems to be forgotten that in the early 19th century, "legitimacy" was frequently used as an argument for stability at the expense of popular rule. But that is another argument not to be analyzed in this place.

Several paragraph further on, the Doctrine uses the word to refer to an "option" and action by the United States to "forestall" threats:

> The United States has long maintained the option of *preemptive* actions to counter a sufficient threat to our national security. The greater the threat, the greater is the risk of inaction – and the more compelling the case for taking anticipatory action to defend ourselves, even if uncertainty remains as to the time and place of the enemy's attack. To forestall or prevent such hostile acts by our adversaries, the United States will, if necessary, act *preemptively* (emphasis added).

---

sion in a Review Essay of GERSON, THE KIRKPATRICK MISSION... (1991), in 19(1) THE FLETCHER FORUM 171 (1995) at pp. 172-173. In it, I cited a prior opinion (by Alf Ross, a Dane, in ROSS, THE UNITED NATIONS: PEACE AND PROGRESS (1966) 99, 103-104, 201) that seems to be the same as mine. Many scholars have differed with us and I am not quite certain of Professor Ross's opinion.

21   See the debate among representatives of the American Government set out in GERSON, *op.cit.* note 20 *supra* pp. 14-17. The teleological argument was apparently not made by anybody at that time or place.

In the immediately following paragraph, the statement goes on:

> The United States will not use force in all cases to *preempt* emerging threats, nor should nations use preemption as a pretext for aggression. Yet in an age where the enemies of civilization openly and actively seek the world's most destructive technologies, the United States cannot remain idle while the dangers gather. We will always proceed deliberately, weighing the consequences of our actions. To support *preemptive* options, we will ...

Do various things involving action to enhance intelligence capabilities, enhance military cooperation with our allies, and continue to transform our own military forces to enable them to react quickly and decisively "to eliminate a specific threat to the United States or our allies and friends." The section concludes by noting that: "The reasons for our actions will be clear, the force measured and the cause just."

Again, it is possible to cavil at just about every noun. Who determines the "justice" of the cause of the United States? American statesmen primarily concerned with re-election? Who determines what is "civilization" and what barbarism? The Bush "doctrine" thus represents the continuation of a line of thought about American superior perceptions of moral values; not only are they binding in the United States, but apparently binding on all the world. What begins as President Monroe's statement of American national interest in keeping European influence in the Western Hemisphere to a minimum without getting into an actual squabble with any European power, continues through President Theodore Roosevelt's "corollary" and its assertion of superior United States perceptions of "justice" and "civilization" as if our moral value weighing were somehow objectively superior to that of any other actor and carried legal consequences in an objective legal order reflecting those values. Forgetting that our own Constitution was the product of a revolution in which the ideas of our English (and other) forebears were as deeply held as our own notions of moral superiority, the Roosevelt corollary and the Bush doctrine seem to adopt the view of Sherard Osborn, one of the British empire-builders of the later nineteenth century:

> [P]oliticians at home maunder about the unjust invasion of native rights, and preach against the extension of our rule, as if our Government ... would not be a blessing in such a region, and as much, if not more, our duty to extend, as a Christian people, than to allow them to remain under native rulers.[22]

An opposing moral view was expressed by Sydney Smith in England at least as early as 1823:

> I must think a little of myself. I am sorry for the Spaniards – I am sorry for the Greeks – I deplore the fate of the Jews; the people of the Sandwich Islands are groaning under

---

22   SHERARD OSBORN, THE BLOCKADE OF QUEDAH (2d ed., 1860) 193. The "region" Osborn mentions is, of course, what is now Malaysia or Southeast Asia generally.

the most detestable tyranny; Baghdad is oppressed ... the world is bursting with sin and sorrow. Am I to be champion of the Decalogue and to be eternally raising fleets and armies to make all men good and happy?[23]

Clearly, President Bush, whom I had once thought a convinced "Smithite," has recently adopted Sherard Osborn's point of view, and the bulk of Americans seems to agree with him, although just how large that bulk is remains a matter of some dispute.

It is interesting to note that as convinced a Democrat as William O. Douglas once argued that:

> We in America are apt to think that the world is choosing sides between private enterprise and communism. Vast portions of the world – notably the Middle East and southeast Asia – feel no such compulsion. They seek solutions best suited to the genius of their people. Their way will not necessarily be our way when it comes to economic organization. This does not mean it will be any the less devoted to democratic standards or any the less respectful of human rights and the dignity of man.[24]

The problem for the United States seems to be complicated by many states taking a more or less formal position that some wicked acts, called violations of "human rights," are now also called violations of international criminal law. The criminal law consequences of that belief are rather hard to understand, since many states otherwise adopt the pattern of law based on Roman precedents and now common in Continental Europe and the former colonies of the Netherlands, France and others, that criminal law must be based on legislation.[25] Apparently, many lawyers now believe that agreement to various treaties, normally analogous to contracts rather than legislation, specifying some acts to be made "criminal" by the legislation of the parties to those treaties or made criminal specifically for tribunals erected by the treaties themselves thus binding only on the treaty parties, represents international legislation making those acts universally criminal as violations of the rules of the international community. It is not believed that this assertion will stand either close examination[26] or the truer test of application. When political factors get in the way, the law often proves not to be as "objective" as is frequently asserted.

---

23 *Sydney Smith to Lady Grey, 1823,* in HESKETH PEARSON, SMITH OF SMITHS (1984) 159.

24 W.O. DOUGLAS, STRANGE LANDS AND FRIENDLY PEOPLE (1951) 279.

25 Indeed, the United States, fundamentally a "common law" country, early on refused to accept "common law crimes" in its federal courts, although they continue in at least one state court as they do in England. See U.S. v. Hudson & Goodwin, 11 US (7 Cranch) 32 (1812) and U.S. v. Coolidge, 14 U.S. (1 Wheaton) 415 (1816). These cases and others supporting the assertions made in the text above are cited many places, including RUBIN, *Is International Criminal Law "Universal"?,* 2001 THE UNIVERSITY OF CHICAGO LEGAL FORUM, note 20 at p. 358.

26 See RUBIN, ETHICS AND AUTHORITY IN INTERNATIONAL LAW, cited note 16 *supra.*

And political factors are always in the way. After all, the first priority of an American President is to be re-elected or have his or her favorite candidate elected. In order to do that, it is not the idea of some foreigners as to what is "just" or "criminal" that matter, but the views of the American electorate. And lest one presume that the American perception is more biased than others', there is ample evidence that the perception of Canadians (among others) is equally biased by Canadian (and other) conceptions of their own history and values.[27] What it all means is that the various American "Doctrines" are expressions of American national interest as perceived by American officials, elected by their own constituents, who reserve to themselves the judgment as to whether "truth," "justice" and other values are being served abroad; whether the United States has the will and strength to enforce its own interests and values there, and whether the politicians' constituents will support with money and the lives of their children and friends, the insights of their elected representatives.

Lest it be supposed that these values are applied blindly, it should be recalled that the United States intervened to help determine the governments not only in various Latin American (to use a common phrase not entirely correctly; their heritage is not really or solely Latin) countries (like Panama[28]) but also elsewhere in the world (like Vietnam, Iran and Iraq). Now, under the American Constitution, only the American Congress, supposedly representing the views of the American electorate, has the authority to appropriate funds necessary for these military and diplomatic ventures.[29] Of course, whether the Congress actually represents the views of the American electorate is much debated also.[30] The dispute appears to have centered originally on whether debtors ought to vote on representatives in the American Congress as well as property-holders, and the answer appears to have been in the affirmative, although the matter was left to the various states. Many states of the American union deprive felons of their vote, but none of them pose property

---

27   E.g., HOWARD NORMAN, THE BIRD ARTIST (1994), written by an American and published simultaneously in Canada, presents a view of Canadian society in Newfoundland that seems quite similar to that of American society; yet the book was not only a National Book Award finalist in the United States, but also received encomia from the (London) Times Literary Supplement and Howard's works have been translated into twelve languages other than English. I forbear citing other books, like those of Umberto Eco, originally published in other languages.

28   A.P. RUBIN, *The Panama Canal Treaties: Locks on the Barn Door*, THE YEAR BOOK OF WORLD AFFAIRS 1981, 181-193 (1982).

29   US Constitution Article I.7 ("All bills for raising revenue shall originate in the House of Representatives..."), 8.1 ("The Congress shall have power – to ... provide for the common defence [spelling *sic*] and general welfare of the United States") and 9.6 ("No money shall be drawn from the treasury, but in consequence of appropriations made by law ..."). There are many disputes about the meaning of these articles and there are other provisions of the Constitution that some scholars perceive as pertinent.

30   See 2 MAX FARRAND, THE RECORDS OF THE FEDERAL CONVENTION OF 1787, 123-125 (rev'd ed. 1966). There are many other places recording the original and later understandings of our Constitution and its relationship to constituency views.

restrictions on those elected. There seems to be little question that the elected representatives of whoever is permitted to vote should have the leisure to consider the implications of their votes, including implications regarding expenses and "justice."

Another point to consider is whether these selected "Doctrines" represent American foreign policy at all. There are many statements by high officials in the United States, including Presidents, that are not followed by the Congress or by other high officials; indeed, a distinction has already been mentioned between the recognition policies of President Jefferson, reflecting an "objective" theory under which the United States should not be passing judgment on the legality or "justice" of the selection or election of foreign leaders, and the more subjective theories of President Woodrow Wilson. The notion that the Roosevelt corollary to the Monroe Doctrine remains American foreign policy towards Latin America has a checkered career. Occasionally, arguments are made that America follows a foreign policy favoring "just" governments as determined by some objective standard, but then America did favor the Pinochet government of Chile and others that did achieve stability at the expense of what are now regarded as human "rights" [although "rights" in which order (legal, moral, political, historical etc.) seems to be left unclear]. Whether support of the government of General Pinochet was consistent with American professions of objectivity and "justice" I leave to others to decide. It seems clear that views in the United States have varied as to this and similar matters, and the Presidents and Congresspeople of the United States were much more swayed by the views of an ignorant but voting and deeply convinced electorate than by any objective evaluations of "justice".

This raises yet another question. If a policy is not followed consistently, should it be labeled a "Doctrine" at all? I doubt that language has been so much cheapened over time; there have always been disputes as to the meaning of words. Lawyers like specificity and try to make words definite and certain. Politicians prefer flexibility in their definitions, leaving difficult questions of precision to judges and others in the legal realm. So it is now with words like "terrorism" and "piracy," which are used by politicians freely and even by lawyers, hoping that nobody asks what precisely is intended. The presumption is that the speaker expects everybody to agree with his/her definition(s); a patently untrue presumption. But very few seem to ask, as each commentator seems to presume that his/her favorite definition is intended and those who ask are ignored by the constituents who continue to vote for the deceptive politician. This puts a major burden on the selection process for judicial appointment, each value-laden voter[31] wants to vote for a judicial appointee who shares his/her values with regard to issues s/he regards as essential to the adminis-

---

31   Each State of the American Union has its own procedures for selecting or electing judges; each has its own Bar Examination for selecting lawyers capable of representing clients before the State bar. In the Federal Government, the appointment of "judges of the Supreme Court" and various other inferior court judges normally requires the "advice and consent" of the Senate of the United States. US Constitution, article II.2.2. But the members of the Senate might disagree as to the qualifications of any particular candidate for judicial appointment.

tration of "justice." But "justice" is defined differently by different people. A villain who destroys a kindergarten class may regard him/herself as acting "justly" if the children are of the "wrong" ethnic, religious or other group identity as seen by the villain. Society might regard "justice" as served only by the death of the villain's own family (who might be quite innocent of villainy) in the ground that society should do unto others what was done unto them. Others would regard the death penalty as appropriate only for the villain and his/her aiders. Others would exempt at least the aiders from that penalty. Yet others regard the death penalty as too severe, or at least irreversible in case of error, and we are all fallible, in any case and would incarcerate the villain. Some would want that incarceration to allow for freedom on parole, others would like to prevent any release, whether on parole or not – and the decision as to whether a villain should be paroled should be made by a selected body of people subject to some other unclear law. Theories based on deterring others from similar villainy depend on evidence of deterrence that is not usually available. But the variations on these themes are endless. And this only deals with a legal order in which there are some shared values, and in the world today it is not clear that the values involved in the American "Doctrines" are shared even within the American electorate, not to mention those outside that select group who might nonetheless be affected by the exercise by the United States of its power under one doctrine or another.

This leaves us with a rather dismal picture. My own preference is for a struggle in the realm of ideas, to be resolved temporarily by some arbitrary rule, like majority voting. But that solution must be seen as temporary at best because majorities change and ideas that seem to work for a while frequently prove not to work over a longer period. Moreover, majority rule is at best arbitrary, since majorities are frequently wrong or self-seeking. Plato's suggestion for guardians was answered long ago by the Latin question, *Quis custodet custodiens* – Who guards the guardians? Moreover, there is no suggestion in Plato's writings as to whose judgment is to be determinative of how the "guardians" are to be selected – by whom they should be selected and what considerations should be used in determining those best fitted to rule. It seems clear that anybody whom Plato would regard as fit to be a guardian or be selected by the guardians to be the leader of a community would refuse the selection and would have to be compelled by asking who the refusing candidate would suggest in his/her place.[32] I have no suggestion to make in an area in which Plato himself did not tread.

In international affairs, the problem is even greater. There are few common threads holding us all together, however much people would like their own value systems to be seen as universal, at least among lawyers and judges. Thus there are few "Doctrines" that bind us together.[33]

---

32   PLATO, 1 THE REPUBLIC, Stephanus 347b-d, in JOHN M. COOPER, ED., PLATO, THE COM-PLETE WORKS, (Indianapolis, 1997) p. 991. See also Plato's *Letters VII* and *VIII*, in *id.*, pp. 1646-1671, Stephanus 324a-357d,, explaining Plato's notion of why the idea failed in Sicily.

33   One book making this point among many others is, EVAN LUARD, TYPES OF INTERNA-TIONAL SOCIETY (New York, 1976), reviewed in 72 AM. J. OF INT'L L. 430 (1978).

Among the doctrines that do not bind us together seem to be the Monroe Doctrine, its Roosevelt corollary and the Bush Doctrine that purport to "justify" American intervention by American discretion. It is certainly possible to ask whether "justify" (like "rights" in the phrase "Human Rights" so popular today) refers to a legal system or, as Aristotle proposed, to a moral order. I incline to the Aristotelian (moral) view – an easy choice to make even if wrong. What seems "justifiable" to Americans or Canadians seems unjust to those whose selections seem to us to be improper. In the moral realm, "justice" is determined by each individual for him/herself as a matter of value weighing, and there are very few choices indeed that do not involve some detriments. To those brought up in a tribal or ethnic context, the moral choice might involve selecting as leader a person with the "right" bloodlines. Lest Europeans sneer at this, it might be wise to remember that "legitimacy" in the early 19th century meant precisely that in Europe, and today the word "legitimacy" is used without any reference to the order (legal, moral, political, historical or other) that is assumed (usually falsely) to be understood by the hearer.[34] For an American to argue that the right bloodlines (or military force, as in Liberia, or other value-laden systems) might lead to a corrupt ruler whose decrees are, by our standards, unjust, the answer must be that the ruler chosen by those closest to his/her rule must govern, subject to the authority of a society threatened by that ruler or his/her followers, to resist the encroachment. To label all "unjust" rulers (by our standards) to threaten an encroachment is to threaten a counter-encroachment which must strike the other society as unjust.

To focus this argument on current events is to condemn the American invasion of Iraq in so far as that invasion is not a response to a threatened encroachment by Iraq on the political system of the invading states. Since all known states possess germs capable of being used against an enemy (a Petri dish in a closet is probably enough, and to argue that no country possesses deadly germs but those who have openly declared their possession is so unlikely as to be rejected out of hand) and the use of poison gases by non-state fanatics has been demonstrated (for example, in Japan by a religious group convinced of its righteousness), and nuclear weapons involve massive investments and factories that are very hard indeed to conceal and seem not to have been concealed in Iraq, it is very hard to find Iraqi possession of some of these weapons as morally justifying an invasion. And even that rejection assumes that poison gases or deadly germs will eventually be found in Iraq. Nor is the violation of "law" a justification for invasion.[35] Nor is it clear

---

34   Herodotus wrote, some 2,450 years ago:

> For, if anyone, no matter who, were given the opportunity of choosing from amongst all the nations in the world the set of beliefs he thought best, he would inevitably, afer careful consideration of their relative merits, choose that of his own country. Everyone without exception believes his own native customs, and the religion he was brought up in, to be the best...

HERODOTUS, THE HISTORIES (A. de Sélincourt, transl., A.R. Burn ed., Penguin, 1954, 1972), p. 219 (III.38). There is much else that is wise in Herodotus.

35   RUBIN, *Enforcing the Rules of International Law* 34(1) HARV. INT'L L. J. 149-161 (1993);

that the United Nations has the authority to saddle obligations on Iraq except as a condition for Iraqi representation within the United Nations, and even then, the authority of the Security Council of the UN to make law rests on the legal interpretation of Chapter VII of the UN Charter and Article 25 of that Charter,[36] neither of which is free from doubt.

Indeed, the closer one looks at the invasion and the reasons given for it, the more dubious the entire enterprise. On the other hand, President Bush seems now to have the support of the American electorate, whatever the doubts about his original elevation to office. It is an Osborn moment, a moment in which some Americans, of varied ethnic backgrounds, seem to feel that the United States is unsafe unless we rule the world, and by ruling the world , the use of military force as the ruling instrument is meant. Other Americans (but not the American President as yet) seem to feel that "human rights" are important enough so that, despite Sydney Smith's letter of 1823,[37] American tax money and young lives should be spent to help achieve them in strange parts of the world (although not in the many other parts of the world in which torture and political harassment seem to be routinely used by whoever has achieved authority and remains friendly towards the United States).

The conclusion is rather depressing but borne out by history: Nobody is entirely secure unless possessing unmatched force; rival groups will always exist to challenge that use of force and the use of force alone, whatever its rationale, cannot achieve complete security. It is also incompatible with "democratic" values. The electorate can always select a villain as its leader, and the villain need not always

---

a slightly revised version is also in FESTSKRIFT TILL JACOB W.F. SUNDBERG 267-283 (Juristförlaget, Stockholm, 1993). The article argues that the violation of a treaty has different legal results than invasion, and that the dominant international law penalty for violation of the law under which a state's word is binding, is loss of trust and inability to deal in the modern world. In a sense, a reputation for being a state that does not take its treaty obligations seriously is to make life for that state (to paraphrase THOMAS HOBBES, LEVIATHAN (1651, 1962, 1969) 100) "solitary, poor, nasty, brutish" and expensive (although not necessarily "short"). Interestingly, 27(3) American Journal of International Law features an "Agora" section to which contributors, including some members of the current American Administration, like William H. Taft IV, and some of their apparent sympathizers, like Professors John Yoo and Ruth Wedgwood, disagree with some currently popular scholars, like Professors Richard A. Falk and Thomas M. Franck, about the legality of the United States invasion of Iraq under the terms of the UN Charter. The discussion is sophisticated, but it is clear that eminent scholars do in fact disagree about matters of interpretation and the role of the law in international affairs.

36   UN Charter, Article 25: "The Members of the United Nations agree to accept and carry out the decisions of the Security Council in accordance with the present Charter." But whether the "decisions" of the Security Council with regard to Iraq are made in accordance with the Charter depends on an interpretation of Articles 39 and 51 of the Charter, neither of which is wholly clear, and whether the actions of Iraq conform to the Charter is also open to question.

37   See note 23 *supra*.

hide his villainy. Thus the great dilemma of "democracy" and the reasons for Plato's silence on the point.

I would propose some suggestions to alleviate this problem, convinced, as I am, that the alleviations are not satisfactory to many and that they are not original in me.

First, I would abandon the use of "Doctrines" as a basis for national policy. None seems to be consistent or to be free of subjective evaluation – even the Truman Doctrine rested on the assumption that death (of others than the propounders of the Doctrine) was preferable to Communist rule, and Communist rule rests on the assumption that economics is the bottom line of international affairs. Both assumptions are patently false.

Second, I would encourage each society, whether organized on a patriarchal, matriarchal, aristocratic, democratic, monarchic, tribal or other system, to engage in internal rumination; "truth and reconciliation" commissions might be a step in this direction for some societies.

Third, I would encourage the use of external national remedies (embargoes, refusals to trade on a national basis) to deal with regimes which each state does not like. That will not necessarily change the villainous regime, but it will be a moral answer to a moral problem.

Fourth, I would encourage individual remedies (refusals to trade regardless of the national consensus) as a moral step to achieving the moral goal of what each of us regards as his/her own notion of a more "just" society.

Fifth, I would recognize that there are some situations in which nothing is possible for an outside power other than to refuse to grant a visa or other privilege.

Sixth, I would recognize that in some situations nothing, even the refusal of a privilege, is feasible on the overall national interest and that a degree of hypocrisy is inevitable in any system.

Seventh, and most controversial, I would note that many societies in the world today are ethnically or tribally oriented, and that my own preference for an "open" society might not be feasible or even desirable world-wide. Yet the migration of peoples and the oppression (even killing) of minorities is an atrocity with which I do not wish to be involved. Depending on the numbers involved and the space available in my own country, I would open the door to unrestricted immigration.

Part 4
The Historical Development of International
Legal Institutions

15. Basic Principles of UN Charter Law

Karl Zemanek

1.   Principles of Law

A.   General Theory

i.   The Notion of Legal Principle

In view of the complexity of the subject and the doctrinal disputes surrounding some of its aspects it is useful to clarify the central term first. What, for instance, distinguishes a legal principle from a legal rule?

They differ in their normative structure. A legal rule prescribes a definite conduct in defined circumstances; if the command is disobeyed, it may be enforced. A legal principle, on the other hand, is the expression of a meta-legal value which the law-giving community wishes to observe, but its abstract formulation does not order a *specific* conduct for its implementation. The decision how to implement a legal principle is left to the persons or the state agency applying it to a given situation. Thus, while a legal rule has a more or less self-executing structure, even if it should require interpretation to determine its exact meaning, a legal principle needs an intellectual operation for determining the conduct required by it in a concrete situation. Because of its abstract nature, a legal principle may offer options for the permissible course of action.

To illustrate the point: What the principle of "justice" means may be determined by reference to a specific legal order. But that clarifies only "justice" as understood in the context of that specific legal order; other legal systems may adopt a different solution. In other words: it is a frame of reference which gives the maxim "justice" substance. Ultimately, it is only by reference to the cultural values of the civilization which generates the legal order in question that the meaning of "justice" can be determined. In an ideal society "justice" provided by its legal order would mirror the cultural value of "justice" which that society endorses. In reality that balance is not always achieved, as occasional public criticism of judgments, especially in criminal cases, shows.

Ronald St. John Macdonald & Douglas M. Johnston (eds.), Towards World Constitutionalism, *pp. 401-430.*
© *2005 Koninklijke Brill NV. Printed in The Netherlands.* ISBN 90 04 14612 1.

The value system of the international society is even more complex. That society includes more than one civilization and several sets of cultural values compete in the understanding of its principles. It is not infrequent that, when a legal principle is expressed in the short form of a maxim – like "justice" in the foregoing example – different civilizations do have different expectations of what it means, and may make different choices when called upon to apply it.

Leaving this uncertainty aside for the moment, legal principles may be defined as deductions from meta-legal values which are expressed as abstract guides in a legal order. That may be done explicitly, or implicitly by shaping the rules accordingly. In the latter case the underlying principle(s) can be made explicit by induction from the corpus of rules of that legal order.

The main function of legal principles within a legal order – especially of those which are considered "fundamental" or "basic" – is to act as directives in the process of construing, applying and developing the legal rules in that order. Lawyers, scholars, state organs, but foremost courts and tribunals in the day by day administration of justice, apply legal principles when clarifying obscure provisions of the law.[1] Since basic principles express societal values any change in these affects their sense. They are the dynamic element of a legal order and are often responsible for the review of laws (or treaties), or the preparation of new ones, to give better effect to the values expressed in the principles. The role as ultimate guide makes them an essential element in constitutionalizing a legal order.

ii.   Principles of Law in International Law

In international law the term "principle" has been used in more than one sense. In common use is the expression "general principles of law recognized by civilized nations", taken from Article 38 para. 1(c) of the Statute of the International Court of Justice, but there is little agreement about the meaning of the phrase. Some hold that it means general principles of *international* law; others maintain that it refers to general principles of *national* law, which opinion commands the more numerous support. Yet it is not clear why it should not mean both.[2] Some basic principles, like sovereign equality, are obviously not derived from national law but are proper to international law.

Some authors have used the term in a different sense. Hans Kelsen chose *Principles of International Law*[3] as title of his textbook, which suggests a meaning similar to the German *"Grundzüge des Völkerrechts"*. The same seems to be true for Ian Brownlie's *Principles of Public International Law*.[4] In Georg Schwarzenberger's

---

[1]   With good reason A. Verdross thus gave his Hague lectures of 1953, which dealt with basic principles of UN Charter law, the title "Idées *directrices* de l'Organisation des Nations Unies" (emphasis added); see 83 *Recueil des Cours*, Hague Academy of International Law (henceforth *RdC*) (1953, II), 1-74.

[2]   See P. Malanczuk, in: *Akehurst's Modern Introduction to International Law*, 7th ed. London 1997, 48-49.

[3]   New York 1952. 2nd ed. by R.W. Tucker, New York 1967.

[4]   5th ed. Oxford 1998. Significantly, Brownlie describes the book in the preface as "...

course in the Hague Academy on "The Fundamental Principles of International Law,"[5] on the other hand, the term is used in the sense given at the beginning of this chapter.

Since the task of the present writer is the examination of the basic principles of UN Charter law, this chapter will be limited to "principles" as defined above; no *"Grundzüge"* of UN law will be attempted.

B.   *Legal Principles in the UN Charter*

i.   The Texts

The Charter announces principles in several articles. It states in Article 1, para.1:

> ... and to bring about by peaceful means, and in conformity with the principles of justice and international law, ..."

And in Article 1, para.2:

> To develop friendly relations among nations based on respect for the principle of equal rights and self-determination of peoples, ...

Most principles are proclaimed in Article 2. which reads in its relevant parts:

> The Organization and its Members, in pursuit of the Purposes stated in Article 1, shall act in accordance with the following Principles.
> 1.   The Organizations is based on the principle of the sovereign equality of all its Members.
> 2.   All Members, in order to ensure to all of them the rights and benefits resulting from membership, shall fulfil in good faith the obligations assumed by them in accordance with the present Charter.
> 3.   All Members shall settle their international disputes by peaceful means in such a manner that international peace and security, and justice, are not endangered.
> 4.   All Members shall refrain in their international relations from the threat or use of force against the territorial integrity or political independence of any state, or in any other manner inconsistent with the Purposes of the United Nations.
>
> ...
>
> 7.   Nothing contained in the present Charter shall authorize the United Nations to intervene in matters which are essentially within the domestic jurisdiction of any state ...

---

a study in one volume of the *more significant* aspects of the law of peace" (emphasis added).

5   87 *RdC* (1955, I), 195-383. He identifies seven principles (sovereignty, recognition, consent, good faith, self-defence, international responsibility, freedom of the seas) as tools for ordering the course.

Except in para.1 the term "principle" is not used, but the introductory phrase of the Article and their categorical statement suggest that the text intends to state principles.

Principles in the socio-economic and human rights fields are formulated less imperatively. Article 1, para. 3 states:

> To achieve international co-operation in solving international problems of an economic, social, cultural, or humanitarian character, and in promoting and encouraging respect for human rights and for fundamental freedoms for all without distinction as to race, sex, language, or religion;

Article 55 repeats in more detail:

> ... the United Nations shall promote:
> a.   higher standards of living, full employment, and conditions of economic and social progress and development;
> b.   solutions of international economic,social, health, and related problems; and international cultural and educational co-operation; and
> c.   universal respect for, and observance of, human rights and fundamental freedoms for all without distinction as to race, sex, language, or religion.

To which Article 56 adds:

> All Members pledge themselves to take joint and separate action in co-operation with the Organization for the achievement of the purposes set forth in Article 55.

It is debatable whether more than the confirmation of the principles of "solidarity" and "protection of human rights" can be inferred from these texts, and whether the enumeration of economic, social and cultural purposes gives the principle of solidarity some sort of substance. It is particularly unclear, whether the enumeration is exhaustive or just exemplary.

ii.   Is the Charter the Exclusive Source of Principles?

Since these principles, some of which predate the Charter, have been solemnly proclaimed in it, nearly six decades have passed. In the meantime the membership of the United Nations has grown and is now truly universal. Major political, social and economic changes have taken place and, in answer, UN organs have given a new sense to many of its regulations, including the principles. Their present meaning, not the historical sense of 1945, is the subject of this analysis,

Yet, how far may innovations go? Can they only modify the sense of established principles, or may we assume that *new* principles, or *derived* principles developed in the application of established ones, have emerged in UN Charter law?

That question refers to the concept of UN Charter law. If societal changes and evolutions are reflected in the practice of UN organs it is to be expected that corresponding principles, or subsidiary principles, may have been generated, reflecting those changes. The common heritage of mankind, sustainable development, or the protection of the environment, come to mind as examples.

The formulation of principles in the Charter is not uniform, it varies in degrees of precision and imperativeness.

Some principles state a *maxim*, without detailing its content in the Charter, which is apparently considered self-evident in view of the long existence of these principles in international law. Good faith, justice, sovereign equality, domestic jurisdiction, observance of international law belong to this group.

Other principles are stated in the form of a legal rule and prescribe the conduct which they require, while other sections of the Charter establish procedures for their administration and eventual enforcement against a member state. Principles in this group are the peaceful settlement of disputes, non-use of force and non-intervention. Their common denominator is the maintenance of international peace and security.

And, finally, there exists a third group of principles which are formulated as programmes that UN organs are to implement with the co-operation of states. This is the case with the protection of human rights, with equal rights and self-determination, or with solidarity in socio-economic matters in general.

Do all these principles have the same normative value? Apparently not. There is a difference between a principle that is expressed in a maxim, like "justice" or "sovereign equality" and a principle which states that "all Members shall settle their international disputes by peaceful means..." The latter principle is formulated as a legal obligation, similar to a legal rule. The former, on the contrary, requires an intellectual operation to determine which conduct is required by "justice" in a given situation. Members of the United Nations, drawing inspiration from their own value system, may come to quite different conclusions. In those circumstances a weighty interested state (or states) may be able to impose its understanding on others. Only a third party, a court or an independent international organ, could arrive at an authoritative determination.

Moreover, some of the most fundamental principles straddle the fuzzy borderline between politics and law and have their roots in both, sometimes more in the former than in the latter. Since the political aspects of these principles are governed by the interplay of states interests, their legal side is often relegated to second place. Politics dominate their application in a given situation, and the legal implications, while sometimes used as a convenient argument, are rarely a determining factor. A powerful state, when it achieves a hegemonial or even imperial position, may thus adopt a quite unconventional sense of a principle and defend it successfully against the mainstream. In its most extreme form this attitude may induce a state to invoke a principle, even if its pretended sense was unorthodox, for legitimizing a conduct which would be illegal under existing positive legal rules.

The normative value is even less certain when principles are formulated as exhortations, like those introduced by "shall promote" or "shall encourage", which implies the necessity of institutional action to implement them. Whether in the process of implementation new or derived principles may be generated is a controversial issue. Assuming that the function of law is to stabilize developments in a human society, the former needs to take account of these developments and adjust to them. In this sense, the answer to the question should be affirmative. That answer does, however, not decide the normative value of derived principles. Since they are often the fruit of spontaneously advocated new values, they remain "soft" principles until they are implemented in widely accepted multilateral treaties or in general state practice. Hence it is the reaction of states which may eventually transform a "soft" principle of persuasive value into a principle of law.

The undifferentiated conglomeration of "principles" in the Charter is unfortunate. Collecting principles of different normativeness without clearly indicating their difference carries the risk of deluding lay opinion. When people cannot distinguish between imperative and hortative principles, they may develop uniform expectations warranted only by the former, which reality will almost necessarily disappoint. That may, in turn, lead to a cynical attitude towards the United Nations in general.

iii.   How Do the Principles Interrelate?

The danger of an undifferentiated enumeration of principles becomes particularly apparent when one considers how the principles interrelate. Neither the place of a principle in the Charter, nor its formulations, nor even its derived nature, suggest a hierarchy among principles. It is therefore unclear how a conflict among them should be resolved. And such conflicts do occur. They were and are at the root of some troublesome international crises and pose vexing problems in international law.

Decolonization was one such problem. During the process liberation movements used sometimes force against the respective colonial power and were supported – and often aided – in their fight by sympathetic neighbour states. Nonaligned members of the United Nations argued in the General Assembly that if there was a conflict between "justice" and the "non-use of force" it was "justice" that should prevail.

Humanitarian intervention is a current problem of this sort. If a state commits massive violations of human rights like "ethnic cleansing", should it remain protected by Article 2 para. 7 of the Charter as long as its actions do not amount to a threat to international peace? Or should the principle of humanity (protection of human rights) be considered as having overriding force under such circumstances? And should that also apply when the Security Council fails to take an appropriate decision and one state, or a group of states, feels impelled to act in its stead?

It is evident that under present circumstances such conflicts will not be settled on a rational basis. Political and economic interests, cultural preferences, and emotions, will dictate the choice while systematic considerations of the function of the respective principles in the system as a whole will be relegated to the background or dismissed altogether. Although it must be admitted that a seemingly rational approach may not always yield a better result. Witness the findings of the International Court of Justice in its Advisory Opinion on *Certain Expenses of the United Nations*, that "[t]he primary place ascribed to international peace and security is natural, since the fulfilment of the other purposes will be dependent upon the attainment of that basic condition."[6] Although presented as a rational conclusion, it is a value judgment and, moreover, at odds with reality since the United Nations is achieving some of its purposes in spite of its inability to secure global peace.

The problem could be solved by establishing an authoritative hierarchy among the principles or, at least, a conflict of values/principles regime in which precedence could be determined without recourse to intuitive interpretation. Yet, at the present stage of development of the international society that proposition is hopeless. What one may realistically expect is an *ad-hoc* preference depending on the moral sensibility of the international community at a given moment and in a given situation.[7]

iv. The Friendly Relations Declaration

Some of the principles of UN Charter Law have been explained in greater detail in the "Declaration on Principles of International Law Concerning Friendly Relations and Co-operation Among States in Accordance with the Charter of the United Nations,"[8] a typical product of the "peaceful co-existence" era.[9]

In 1962, at the latter's apex, the General Assembly of the United Nations resolved in Resolution 1815/(XVII):

> to undertake, pursuant to Article 13 of the Charter, a study of the principles of international law concerning friendly relations and co-operation among States in accordance with the Charter with a view to their progressive development and codification so as to secure their more effective application ...

Incidentally, whether intended or not, the Resolution implies that the previous application of these principles had left much to be desired. Contrary to the apparent expectation however, their solemn proclamation has not materially changed that, at least as far as one can see.

In the year following that Resolution, the General Assembly set up a "Special Committee" for its implementation and, by Resolution 1966(XVIII), referred to it the following four principles for consideration: (a) non-use of force; (b) peaceful settlement of disputes; (c) non-intervention; and (d) sovereign equality. Two years later, Resolution 2103 A(XX) added three further principles to the agenda of the Committee: (e) equal rights and self-determination; (f) co-operation; and (g) good faith. As directed, the Committee finished its work in time for the 25th Jubilee Ses-

---

6   ICJ, *Reports* 1962, 151-179, at 168.

7   Witness the failure of the UN to act in Rwanda.

8   Annex to General Assembly Resolution 2625(XXV), of 24 October 1970.

9   For a comprehensive analysis of the genesis and the substance cf. G. Arangio-Ruiz, "The Normative Role of the General Assembly of the United Nations and the Declaration of Principles of Friendly Relations", 163 *RdC* (1972), 419-742; and the volume ed. by M. Sahovic, *Principles of International Law Concerning Friendly Relations*, Beograd 1972.

sion of the General Assembly in 1970, during which the Friendly Relations Declaration, as it has become known, was adopted by consensus.

Because of an unforeseen incident the principle of non-intervention was not elaborated by the Special Committee but by the General Assembly itself. During the 20th Session of the General Assembly (1965) the Soviet Union proposed an agenda item on the inadmissibility of intervention to embarrass the United States which had intervened in the Dominican Republic earlier that year. During the proceedings, however, the initiative shifted from the Soviets to a non-aligned/Latin American draft resolution which was adopted by Plenary with 109 votes against none with one abstention (United Kingdom) as Resolution 2131(XX).

The Special Committee decided in 1966 that Resolution 2131(XX) "by virtue of the number of States which voted in its favour, the scope and profundity of its contents (sic) and, in particular, the absence of opposition, reflects the universal legal conviction which qualifies it to be regarded as an authentic and definite principle of international law", wherefore the Committee would abide by its text.[10] Resolution 2131(XX), with only minor drafting changes and with the deletion of its more glaring ideological ornaments[11] became the text of the definition of non-intervention in the Friendly Relations Declaration and was, in the conciliatory spirit during the 25th Jubilee of the United Nations, adopted with the rest of the principles by consensus.

At the time of its adoption the legal status of the declaration may have been doubtful although, having been adopted by consensus, it was supposed to reflect the shared opinion of the community of states at the time. It the meantime it has been confirmed by the International Court of Justice in the *Nicaragua* case as having become a part of customary international law. The Court held:

> The effect of consent to the text of such resolutions cannot be understood as merely that of 'reiteration and elucidation' of the treaty commitments undertaken in the Charter. On the contrary, it may be understood as an acceptance of the validity of the rule or set of rules declared by the resolution by themselves.[12]

The foregoing permits the conclusion that the fundamental principles of the Charter treated in the Friendly Relations Declaration were part of the general corpus of customary international law of the time in the understanding given to them in that Declaration and have remained so, provided that the practice of States still confirms the *opinio juris* expressed.

On the other hand, the Declaration appears in many respects dated – it was, after all, adopted nearly 35 years ago. Evidences of that are its ideological ornamentation and sometimes lurid language; the many controversial issues which were simply left out; and the emphasis on decolonization which has been eclipsed

---

10   See Report of the Special Committee, UN Doc A/6230, of 27 June 1966, paras. 292-300 and 334-352.

11   The Drafting Committee deleted paras. 4 and 6 of Resolution 2131(XX).

12   ICJ, *Reports* 1986, 14-150, para. 188.

by more recent matters of concern. Moreover, state practice which, for a while, seemed to confirm the *opinio juris*, has taken a new turn with respect to certain principles since the United States began emerging as imperial power.

Nevertheless, stripped of the nonessentials the Declaration is still a useful elucidation of the principles dealt with in it. Yet it is equally clear that the Declaration is non-exhaustive. The fact that a principle of UN Charter law is not dealt with in it (e.g. justice or solidarity) does not affect its quality.

2. Principles Subject to Change

An encyclopaedic examination of all principles proclaimed in the Charter of the United Nations would, in view of the host of existing studies,[13] hardly lead to surprising new discoveries nor could it be undertaken in a reasonable manner in the confines of this essay.

A different approach is, therefore, required and reflects – that goes without saying – the subjective preference of the author. During the last couple of decades the basic principles governing two important parts of UN activity have particularly been affected by developments which modified their sense. These two parts are the maintenance of international peace and security and the socio-economic development of world society. The modifications of the relevant principles will be studied in some detail below.

A. *The Prohibition to Use Force*

i. The Erosion of the Security Council's Monopoly to Legalize the Use of Force

The concept of collective security underlying the Charter entrusted the maintenance of international peace and security and, consequently, the supervision of compliance with the non-use of force and other related principles primarily, but also effectively, to the Security Council. Except in a case of self-defence, the Council alone would have the authority to decide on the use of force. Articles 43 to 48 of the Charter establish the procedures which should provide the Council with the military means necessary to carry out its task.

Regrettably, this ambitious programme was never implemented. Obvious political reasons, which need not be discussed here, have caused the failure.

Because of these reasons, the Military Staff Committee (MSC), which was so important to the founding members that they made it the only subsidiary organ to be regulated in the Charter and attributed crucial functions to it, could not fulfill its task. The Security Council directed it in February 1947 to examine the provisions of Article 43 *et seq.* of the Charter from the military point of view. In 1947 the MSC

---

13   Besides the authors cited in note 9 see the relevant parts of the commentaries ed. by J.-P. Cot and A. Pellet, *La Charte des Nations Unies*, 2nd. Ed. Paris 1991; and by B. Simma, *The Charter of the United Nations*, Oxford 1995 (both with further references to literature).

submitted a report[14] that revealed the irreconcilable dissent among the permanent members of the Security Council on the issue, which prevented the MSC from reaching conclusions on a basic plan. Following a fruitless exchange of letters in August 1948 about the wisdom of further work without agreement on the basic principles, the project was not pursued, although the MSC still meets regularly.[15]

Without a basic military plan, the conclusion of agreements foreseen by Article 43 para.1 of the Charter, whereby member states would make "available to the Security Council, on its call....armed forces..." became impossible. In their absence, the Security Council does not dispose of troops, save those which are eventually provided voluntarily. Even in the latter case, however, the Security Council does not have the operational capability to conduct military campaigns on a larger scale.

Since decision-making in the Security Council concerning security matters was paralyzed during the Cold War, problems that would arise, once the Council would be in a position to discharge its functions properly, were not given much attention. And that despite peace-keeping operations, which the UN began undertaking on a bigger scale in 1956 with the establishment of UNEF, gave a forewarning of the eventual problems.

Peace-keeping operations were not *expressly* provided for in the Charter. But through functional interpretation of the latter they emerged pragmatically in situations where both parties to a conflict wished for the UN's assistance in preventing its aggravation or in policing a cease-fire while they kept negotiating.[16] Over the years the demand on the UN grew, and more – and more sophisticated – operations had to be sustained. The financial side was settled by the Advisory Opinion of the International Court of Justice on *Certain Expenses of the United Nations*[17] and currently all relevant operations safe UNFICYP (in part only) are considered expenses of the organization. But as for obtaining the necessary troops, the UN had and has to rely on contingents which states provide on a voluntary basis, a method that causes severe operational problems. This became strikingly obvious in the case of Somalia. When the situation of UNOSOM deteriorated militarily, the Security Council had to accept the offer of the United States to establish a secure environment with its forces.[18] But when the newly created UNITAF also failed and the United States withdrew its troops, UNOSOM had shortly afterwards to be given up altogether.

---

14   "General Principles Governing the Organization of the Armed Forces Made Available to the Security Council by Member Nations of the United Nations", UN Doc S/336, *UN Yearbook* 1946-47, 424-434.

15   Cf. B.-O. Bryde in Simma, *op.cit.* (note 13), "Commentary to Article 47", MN 11-16 and 28.

16   For more details see K. Zemanek, "Peace-keeping or Peace-making?", in: N. Blokker and S. Muller (eds.), *Essays in Honour of Henry G. Schermers*, Vol. I: "Towards More Effective Supervision by International Organizations", Dordrecht 1994, 29-47.

17   Source note 6.

18   See Resolution 794, of 3 December 1992.

In his Report "An Agenda for Peace"[19] the then Secretary-General of the United Nations Boutros-Ghali proposed certain remedies, in particular improved stand-by agreements for peace-keeping forces, to make them more readily available, but nothing came of these proposals and the new Secretary-General Kofi Annan was still faced with the same problem. In March 2000 he set up a "Panel on United Nations Peace Operations" which reported in the same year[20] but whose recommendations did again not lead to a noticeable improvement, although the Report had dryly remarked: "It is therefore incumbent that the Council members and the membership at large breath life into the words that they pronounce…*res, not verba.*"[21]

It is against this background that the slow erosion of the Security Council's monopoly on the legitimate use of force has to be seen. Milestones are Iraq and Kosovo.

When on 2 August 1990 Iraq attacked Kuwait, the Security Council reacted swiftly. On the same day it determined that the invasion was a breach of international peace and security, condemned it, and demanded the immediate and unconditional withdrawal of Iraqi forces.[22] And when Iraq announced the annexation of Kuwait on 8 August, the Security Council declared it null and void.[23]

In between the Council had ordered an economic embargo under Chapter VII against Iraq in Resolution 661 of 6 August. It had, however, no military means at its direct disposal, either for assistance or for enforcement, and owing to the requirement of ratification for agreements under 43 of the Charter, that lack could not have been remedied quickly even if there had been a wish to do so.

The United States, which had considerable interests in the area, filled the gap by organizing a group of states, later to be known as "Member States co-operating with the Government of Kuwait", to assist Kuwait militarily. From then on the initiative shifted to that group and, through it, more specifically to the United States. This already became apparent in Resolution 665, which called upon the group to police the maritime embargo on Iraq and requested all states to render them assistance.

In Resolution 678 of 29 November 1990 the Security Council finally authorized the group "to use all necessary means to uphold and implement resolution 660(1990) and all subsequent relevant resolutions and to restore international peace and security in the area", requesting to be regularly informed on the actions. It further requested all states to provide appropriate support.

Scholars are divided as to the nature of the subsequent operations.[24] Some consider them an act of collective self-defence rather than a measure of collective

---

19   UN Doc S/24111 and A/47/277 of 17 June 1992.

20   UN Doc S/2000/809 and A/55/305, of 21 August 2000.

21   *Ibid.*, para.276.

22   Security Council Resolution 660, of 2 August 1990.

23   Security Council Resolution 662, of 9 August 1990.

24   *Cf. e.g.* Th.M. Franck and F. Patel, "UN police action in lieu of war: The old order changeth" 85 *AJIL* (1991), 63-74; O. Schachter, "UN Law in the Golf Conflict", *ibid.*, 452-473; E.V. Rostow, "Until What? Enforcement Action or Collective Self-defense?", *ibid.*, 506-516; B.H. Weston, "SCR 678 and Persian Gulf Decision-making: Precarious Legitimacy", *ibid.*,

security. But joining in collective self-defence does not need the approval of the Security Council and hence leaves Security Council Resolution 678(1990) unexplained. What is more, Article 51 of the Charter expressly limits the exercise of the right of self-defence in time "until the Security Council has taken measures necessary to maintain international peace and security". Such measures were the purpose of Resolution 678(1990). Thus, while organizing the "member states cooperating with the Government of Kuwait" may originally have been an exercise of collective self-defence, the group's operations after Resolution 678(1990) are of a different nature: they are enforcement measures in accordance with Article 42 of the Charter. Since Article 48 empowers the Council to determine the states which shall carry out its decisions, arguing *a majore ad minus* that it therefore also has the power of authorizing some of them to do so is conclusive.

This manner of reacting to a situation which demands a military answer lessens, however, the degree of control which the Security Council exercises over the operation, because it is merely informed of it, and not in command of it. But, as explained above, the Council would anyway be incapable of commanding an operation under present circumstances. If it is not to be left powerless when a military response is required, its only option is to authorize a state or a group of them which are ready to use the necessary means. An option for which it has to pay the price of merely supervising rather than directing the operation. Nevertheless, an operation authorized in this manner remains within the confines of the Charter.

The next milestone was the 1999 NATO operation "Allied Force" against Yugoslavia (Serbia), undertaken with intent to force Yugoslavia into ending the massive human rights violations against the Albanian majority population of Kosovo.

The United Nations had tried for years to prevent or end the violence which accompanied the disintegration of the Socialist Federal Republic of Yugoslavia with peace-keeping operations [25] – albeit with modest success. Ultimately it had to enlist NATO's help[26] for the tough task of achieving peace in Bosnia-Hercegovina after the Dayton Agreement of 1995.

In Kosovo, a part of Yugoslavia (Serbia), the situation had continued to deteriorate until 1998. The Security Council observed the situation for some time

---

516-535; P. Weckel, "Le chapitre VII de la Charte et son application par le Conseil de Sécurité", 37 *AFDI* (1992), 165-202; Th.M. Franck, "Who is the Ultimate Guardian of UN Legality?", 86 *AJIL* (1992), 519-523; J.A. Frowein, "Enforcement in Case of Security Council Inaction", in J. Delbrück (ed.), *The Future of International Enforcement*, Berlin 1993, 111-124; D. Sarooshi, *The United Nations and the Development of Collective Security: The Delegation by the UN Security Council of its Chapter VII Powers*, Oxford 1999, 33-34 and 178-185; T. Sato, "The Legitimacy of Security Council Activities Under Chapter VII of the Charter since the End of the Cold War", in: J.M. Coicaud and V. Heiskanen (eds.), *The Legitimacy of International Organizations*, Tokyo 2001, 323-324.

25   For details see Zemanek, *loc.cit.* (note 16), 38-42. The relevant UN Documents are collected by D. Bethlehem and M. Weller (eds.), *The Yugoslav Crisis in International Law: General Issues*, Part. I, Cambridge International Documents Series, Vol. 5, 1997.

26   The NATO-led "Implementation Force" (IFOR), established by Security Council Resolution 1031 of 15 December 1995.

and addressed three resolutions under Chapter VII to Serbia on the issue, none of which was obeyed. In Resolution 1160 of 31 March 1998 the Council decided "… that the failure to make constructive progress towards the peaceful resolution of the situation in Kosovo will lead to the consideration of additional measures", a clear reference to eventual further Security Council action. In Resolution 1199 of 23 September 1998 it threatened "… should the concrete measures demanded in this resolution and resolution 1160(1998) not be taken, to consider further action and additional measures to maintain or restore peace and stability in the region". This was again a reference to the intentions of the Council which cannot be construed as delegation of authority to member states. Hence none of these resolutions decided to use force or to authorize the use of force. Nevertheless, when NATO used force against Serbia, none of the resolutions adopted while the NATO operation was in course, neither Resolution 1203 of 24 October 1998 nor subsequent resolutions,[27] referred to the operation or to any intended measure by the Council. Quite the contrary happened: Russia failed in having the Council condemn NATO's operation as "flagrant violation of the UN Charter."[28]

Scholarly reaction to the operation was contradictory,[29] depending on whether the author supported the legality of humanitarian intervention by a group of states or opposed it. This aspect will be examined later.[30]

Subject of the examination in the present context is the Security Council's exercise of its power to decide on the use of force. Defenders of the legality of NATO's operation have argued[31] either that Resolutions 1160(1998) and 1199(1998) implicitly authorized the use of force by states, or that the Security Council had tacitly validated NATO's operation by its subsequent resolutions.[32] Neither of the arguments bears scrutiny. An examination of the text of the resolutions shows that

---

27   Resolution 1239(1999) of 14 May 1999 and Resolution 1244(1999) of 16 June 1999.

28   The respective draft resolution failed by 12 votes against and 3 (including China and Russia) in favour. See UN Doc S/1999/328 of 26 March 1999.

29   An immediate discussion took place in 19 *European Journal of International Law* (1999), No.1; cf. the contributions of B. Simma, A. Cassese and K Ambros.
For further examinations see F. Francioni, "Of War, Humanity and Justice: International Law after Kosovo", *Max Planck UNYB* 4 (2000), 107-126; Ph. Weckel, "L'emploi de la force contre la Yougoslavie ou la Charte fissurée", 104 *RGDIP* (2000), 19 – 35; M. Brenfors and M. Petersen, "The Legality of Unilateral Humanitarian Intervention – A Defence", 69 *Nordic JIL* (2000), 449-500; A. Buzzi, *L'intervention armée de l'OTAN en République Fédérale de Yougoslavie*, Paris 2001, 67-78; V.-D. Degan, "Humanitarian Intervention (NATO Action Against the Federal Republic of Yugoslavia in 1999)", in: L.Ch. Vohrah *et.al.* (eds.), *Man's Inhumanity to Man*, Essays in International Law in Honour of Antonio Cassese, The Hague 2003, 233-259.

30   *Infra*, 2.A.ii.

31   *Cf.* The references by Buzzi, *op.cit.* (note 29), 70-72; and Degan, *loc.cit.* (note 29), 236.

32   So Sh. Murase, "The Relationship Between the UN Charter and General International Law Regarding Non-Use of Force: The Case of NATO's Air Campaign in the Kosovo Crisis of 1999", in N. Ando *et al.* (eds.), *Liber Amicorum Shigeru Oda*, The Hague 2002, Vol. 2, 1543-1554, at 1563.

the first contention is simply unfounded. The second contention imputes a motive to the Security Council that is not plausible. It is more probable to assume that the Security Council was faced with a situation which it could not alter but which it had to take into account if it was to address the ensuing problems. It does not follow conclusively that it thereby put the stamp of legality on the manner in which the situation was brought about. However, leaving the dispute over legality aside, the fact remains that for the first time after the end of the Cold War, the aggressive use of force by a group of states against a member of the United Nations had not provoked an appropriate Security Council reaction. With hindsight this seems to have been the first step towards the war on Iraq in 2003.[33]

ii. Humanitarian Intervention

In media language the term humanitarian intervention is used for a broad range of events, *inter alia.* also for peacemaking operations of the UN, like those in the Congo (1960) or in Somalia (1992). In the present context, however, only such humanitarian interventions are considered which are carried out by a state, a group of states, or an international organization, as an armed military incursion into the territory of a state, to prevent or end systematic violations of human rights which this state perpetrates against its entire population or against a part of it (genocide); or to end atrocities committed by factions competing for power in a state whose government machinery has broken down (failed state).[34]

Humanitarian intervention in this form highlights a conflict between two sets of basic principles of UN Charter law: On the one hand, the principles of sovereign equality, non-intervention, and non-use of force prohibit *prima facie* the interference (although the argument may be weak in respect of a failed state); the principles of humanity and human rights protection seem, on the other hand, to require it. As explained in the first part of this paper,[35] the Charter does not institutionalize a mechanism for resolving such a conflict in an authoritative and objective manner. Such conflicts are rather dealt with *ad hoc*, in a case to case approach, and with unpredictable results. For many decades the United Nations and its member states followed the reasoning of the International Court of Justice in the *Certain Expenses of the United Nations* Opinion[36] which had given primary place to the maintenance of international peace and security and thus precedence to the principles of non-use of force and non-intervention over all other principles of UN Charter law. Only quite recently a tendency has emerged to revise this position in favour of preferring, at least occasionally, the protection of human rights.[37]

---

33   See *infra*, 2.A.iii.

34   For a more ample discussion of the problem in general see K. Zemanek, "Intervention in the 21st Century", V *Cursos Euromediterráneos Bancaja de Derecho Internacional* (2001), 619-666, at 648-650.

35   *Supra*, 1.B.iii.

36   See source in note 6.

37   This particular aspect is examined more closely by K. Zemanek, "Human Rights Protection vs. Non-Intervention: A Perennial Conflict?", in: L.Ch. Vohrah *et al.* (eds.),

This is reflected in UN practice. Scholars were always divided on the questions if and why the United Nations should intervene in civil wars,[38] and the member states seemed unable to make up their mind. In most cases the prohibition in Article 2 para.7 of the Charter was construed by the organization in its widest sense possible. There were and are, of course, obvious cases where a civil war is also a threat to international peace, like when there is a danger of the fighting spilling over to a neighbouring country, either intentionally or through more or less uncontrollable events; or when other countries might be provoked to intervene in the fighting in support of the warring party with which they ethnically or religiously identify.

But it took the United Nations a long time to realize that a gravely impaired humanitarian situation could itself be or become a threat to international peace.[39] When, however, in the 1990ies atrocities perpetrated in civil wars were, albeit selectively, shown in the media, public opinion around the world reacted with horror and put pressure on governments to do something about it. When governments urged the Security Council into action, it sometimes responded by invoking the danger to international peace and thus Article 39 of the Charter – as it did in the Kosovo case – but it was, for the reasons explained above,[40] not in a position to act effectively with the means at its disposal; it had to content itself with resolutions. *Verba*, not *res*.

This failure stimulated the rediscovery of the idea of humanitarian intervention by states, an idea which scholars, particularly in the United States, had been discussing for some time. Concerned about the state of human rights in some parts of the world and the apparent inefficiency of the United Nations to protect these rights in extreme situations, they argued[41] that in the face of Security Council inaction the rights of states under traditional customary international law, including the right to intervene for humanitarian purposes, revived. These scholars did not doubt that such a "right" existed in international law and so saw no need to prove it. Other defenders of humanitarian intervention had recourse to prepositive moral

---

Man's Inhumanity to Man, Essays on International Law in Honour of Antonio Cassese, The Hague 2003, 953-975.

38   See *e.g.* L.B. Sohn, "The Role of the United Nations in Civil Wars", *Proceedings of the ASIL* 1963, 208-215; and H. McCoubrey and N.D. White, *International Organizations and Civil Wars*, Aldershot 1995, 31-50.

39   *Cf.* the Council decisions concerning the security areas in Iraq (1991), Liberia (1992), Somalia (1992), and the Former Yugoslavia (1992). On the issue see Y. Kerbrat, *La référence au Chapitre VII de la Charte des Nations Unies dans les résolutions à caractère humanitaire du Conseil de Sécurité*, Paris 1995; H. Gading, *Der Schutz grundlegender Menschenrechte durch militärische Maßnahmen des Sicherheitsrates – Das Ende staatlicher Souveränität?*, Berlin 1996.

40   2.A.i.

41   For a carefully researched summary of the different schools of thought and their arguments in well balanced form see W.D. Verwey, "Humanitarian Intervention and International Law", 32 *Netherlands ILR* (1985), 357-418.

precepts in support of their proposition, undeterred by the received doctrine that moral imperatives, though they may vindicate individual conduct in certain extreme situations, do not make it legal and do not change the law.

None of the proposed justifications of humanitarian intervention is a convincing argument for invalidating the obligation in Article 2 para.4 of the Charter. To achieve that, a customary modification of Charter law[42] would be required, and may even have taken place, considering the permissive attitude of the world community towards humanitarian interventions in the recent past. And yet, the result of a fairly recent research in that direction by Abiew[43] is inconclusive. The author claims on the one hand that "[t]he advent of the UN Charter suggests that the customary institution of humanitarian intervention still exists, and is not inconsistent with the purposes of the UN. Thus, in the event of failure of collective action under the Charter, there is a revival of forcible self-help measures to protect human rights. This is buttressed by doctrinal writings.[44] It is not clear whether this is a statement of fact or one of law, because the author admits, on the other hand: "It is apparent that although support for humanitarian intervention is gaining currency, there are still various actors opposed to its use. In order to get closer to an international consensus, a clearer articulation of principle is necessary to further enhance the legitimacy of humanitarian intervention.[45] This latter statement argues against a successful modification of the norms of *jus cogens* concerning the use of force and of non-intervention, since that modification would require acceptance by the international community *as a whole*.

On the basis of the available material it is probably too early to pronounce definitively on the existence of a customary exemption of humanitarian intervention from the obligation of Article 2 para.4 of the Charter.[46] On the other hand, there is no denying the fact that states which undertook humanitarian interventions in disregard of the principles of non-use of force and of non-intervention did so with impunity and without provoking the Security Council into taking measures. This has certainly undermined the absolute force of those principles. If in the future humanitarian intervention should become legal, which does not seem unlikely, especially in relation to failed states, the crucial point will be the mode of selecting the object state. If this is left in the hands of a single state, selective arbitrariness

---

42   On the possibility of this process, particularly in respect of peremptory norms, see G. Cahin, *La coutume internationale et les organisations internationales*, Paris 2001, at 598-604 and 613-621.

43   F.K. Abiew, *The Evolution of the Doctrine and Practice of Humanitarian Intervention*, The Hague 1999.

44   *Ibid.*, at 132; see also 222 and 246. Critical P. Hipold, "Humanitarian Intervention: Is there Need for a Legal Reappraisal?", 12 *EJIL* (2001), 437-467.

45   Abiew *ibid.*, at 256.

46   For the same view see S. Rao Pemmaraju, "International Organizations and the Use of Force", in: N. Ando *et al.* (eds), *Liber Amicorum Judge Shigeru Oda*, The Hague 2002, Vol. 2, 1575-1608, at 1608 (conclusion no. 6).

cannot be excluded. Only an international procedure would guard against abuse – but there we are back at the Security Council and its impotence.

iii. Pre-Emptive Self-Defence

Article 51 of the Charter reserves "the inherent right of individual and collective self-defence" if an armed attack on a member of the United Nations occurs, until the Security Council takes the necessary decision. This provision is an exception to the monopoly of the Security Council to decide on the use of force[47] and allows states to exercise, at least temporarily, their own judgment. This makes it attractive for states to invoke when they wish to use force beyond the paradigmatic case of defence against an armed attack on their territory or instrumentality.[48]

Scholarly opinion concerning the interpretation of Article 51 and, more specifically, the scope and the modality of self-defence was divided from the beginning.[49] One question, in particular, gave rise to controversy, namely whether the right of self-defence existing previously under customary international law ("inherent right") was modified or not by its incorporation into the Charter.[50]

The conflict of academic opinion was reflected in the position of states. The United States for one has always preferred the most extensive understanding of the right of self-defence,[51] especially when defending its nationals abroad,[52] thereby giving the term "members of the United Nations" a personal rather than the customary territorial meaning.

The little common ground in interpreting the content of Article 51 was further weakened by the terrorist attack of September 11, 2001. None of the scenarios previously elaborated for clarifying the modalities of self-defence included the hideous form which that attack actually took and thus no appropriate lawful means to answer it were suggested. Equally unforeseen was an "attack" by a non-state organization with "arms" which defied conventional thinking.

The United States nevertheless informed the Security Council that it was exercising its right of self-defence.[53] It was for the first time that this right was claimed

---

47   For a thorough though slightly over-optimistic analysis of the antagonism between the two concepts cf. N. Krisch, *Selbstverteidigung und kollektive Sicherheit*, Berlin 2001.

48   See O. Schachter, "Self-Defense and the Rule of Law", 38 *AJIL* (1989), 259-277, at 271-272; and L.-A. Sicilianos, *Les réactions décentralisées à l'illicite – Des contre-mesures à la légitime défense*, Paris 1990, 366-426, 456-494.

49   The writings are numerous: St.A. Alexandrov, *Self-Defense Against the Use of Force in International Law*, The Hague 1996 and A. Constantinou, *The Right of Self-Defence Under Customary International Law and Article 51 of the UN Charter*, Brussels 2000, give a good overview of previous writings.

50   See Constantinou, *ibid.*, 53-56, who argues modification.

51   See Schachter (note 48).

52   See K. Zemanek, "The Legal Foundations of the International System", General Course in Public International Law, 266 *RdC* (1997), 23-335, at 53-54.

53   In a letter by the Permanent Representative of 7 October 2001, reprinted in 40 *ILM* (2001), 1281.

against a state – Afghanistan – which had not itself carried out the attack but was accused of harbouring the terrorist organization which had, and that it was exercised in a prolonged campaign.[54] Thus, the traditional understanding that defensive action is allowed only against an ongoing attack, was converted into the right to eliminate the source of the attack. In the particular case this meant the elimination of the Al-Qaeda organization and the Taliban regime in Afghanistan which housed it. Since the Security Council – and one may safely say: nearly all states – accepted the claim of self-defence under these circumstances, the right of self-defence has acquired new dimensions, especially by its extension to attacks by non-state organizations and, thus, to the fight against terrorism on the territory of a host state. Since the forms which future terrorist activities may take are unforeseeable, further modifications of the principle cannot be excluded.

The next step in a new direction was the war against Iraq. Since September 11 the fight against international terrorism has become a primary aim of United States security policy, some may even say an obsession. It has inspired a new "National Security Strategy" which proclaims pre-emptive intervention as new variant of self-defence: "To forestall or prevent such hostile acts by our adversaries, the United States will, if necessary, act pre-emptively."[55] The motive of this ingenious invention is expressed in the heading of the respective section of the security strategy which announces: "Prevent Our Enemies from Threatening Us, Our Allies and Our Friends with Weapons of Mass Destruction".

And this was indeed the first rationale of attacking Iraq put forward by the US administration: that Iraq possessed weapons of mass destruction; although it is difficult to comprehend how such weapons could be a *direct* threat to the territory of the United States on the American continent. Later, however, the rationale was supplemented by a reference to the risk of Iraq making such weapons available to Al-Qaeda. Yet neither of these accusations is supported by the evidence hitherto discovered in Iraq. Which means that even if one were to consider "pre-emptive self-defence" a lawful concept, invoking it in this case was unjustified.

Thus only the third rationale of the attack, a further late addition, remains – to overthrow the dictatorial regime of Saddam Hussein and to introduce democracy in Iraq. In view of the unsavoury Iraqi regime one may sympathize with the noble aim, but it can hardly be subsumed under the concept of legitimate self-defence. Nor does it seem that "democratic governance" can yet be claimed as a principle of general international or UN Charter law. Although most states pay it lip service as a common value, reality tells a different story, and the results of the efforts to es-

---

54   The US air strikes against Libya on 14 April 1986 are no real precedent because they were a response to claimed terrorist attacks on US nationals and installations abroad and, moreover, did not lead to a sustained operation. See K. Zemanek, "Self-Defence Against Terrorism: Reflexions on an Unprecedented Situation", in: F.M. Marino Menéndez (ed.), *El Derecho internacional en los albores del siglo XXI*, Homenaje al profesor Juan Manuel Castro-Rial Canosa, Madrid 2002, 695-714, at 697.

55   The National Security Strategy of the United States of America, September 2002, section V, 15.

tablish democracy in Iraq have so far not been encouraging. It is apparently easier for an imperial power to defeat a state than it is to build a nation afterwards. The remaining reason for attacking Iraq suggests that the United States has a bent for intervening in the domestic affairs of any state whenever the US administration believes this to be required by American interests or by its concept of world society. The manner in which the war on Iraq was prepared further suggests that the United States is determined to act eventually alone, with little or no regard for obligations under the UN Charter. In view of the dominant role of the United States in world affairs this tendency puts the whole complex of principles which derive from and support the concept of collective security in jeopardy. The consequences for the future should be a matter of some concern.

B.   Principles Guiding the Socio-Economic Development of World Society

In the first part of this chapter it has been argued that the Charter proclaims only few and vaguely formulated principles for the socio-economic development of world society. They are mostly worded in the form of programmes directing the activities of UN organs, primarily the General Assembly or ECOSOC and its subsidiary organs. An essential aspect of these programmes consists in the creation of a normative framework for the conduct of states in the socio-economic field, be it in their territories or, to a lesser degree, in inter-state relations. To guide this quasi-legislative task new principles are from time to time announced, frequently in resolutions of the respective organs. Sometimes this is followed by a draft convention implementing the principle, although these drafts do not always find favour with all members of the United Nations in which case the fate of the principle is determined by state practice. Because of the process in which they are generated, the principles are at the beginning "soft", and only growing acceptance by states in their actual conduct can transform them into "hard" – or better: "ordinary" – principles of UN Charter law. Principles which have emerged in the process fall thus in three different categories: Those which have undisputedly acquired the status of legal principle; those which are still in the process of transformation; and finally those which have not lost their "soft" character.

Since the task of developing international law in this field is entrusted to a number of UN organs and sometimes to other organizations, and even the views of one body may change with time, contradictions between new principles,[56] or with classical principles, may occur. This makes the observations concerning the regrettable absence of an institutional mechanism to resolve such conflicts, which were made in the first part of this essay, all the more relevant.

It would exceed the scope of this essay to examine all principles which have appeared in this field since 1945. A choice was, therefore, necessary and, as in the section on the prohibition to use force, that choice reflects the subjective preference of the author. It is, however, hoped that the few examples are sufficiently

---

56   Cf. e.g. R. Wolfrum and N. Matz, Conflicts In International Environmental Law, Berlin 2003.

representative to give a general insight into the mechanism which generates the principles and in the latters' legal value.

i.   Human Rights

Guided by the vaguely formulated programme in the Charter of "promoting universal respect for, and observance of, human rights and fundamental freedoms", the United Nations – and in their wake some regional organizations – have strengthened the underlying principle by developing an impressive array of multilateral conventions for the protection of human rights, gradually enlarging the programme beyond what the founding members of the United Nations presumably had in mind, by adopting special conventions on women, children, or the prohibition of discrimination or torture.[57] Although the number of ratifications of or of accession to these conventions is not in every case what one would hope for, and the relevant instruments are often qualified by sweeping reservations,[58] the process of building an appropriate consciousness has, nevertheless, been successful. Hence a worldwide standard of reference by which to judge the conduct of states in these matters is becoming firmly established. This has persuaded some writers to claim that the "core" of human rights, in other words the basic or most fundamental human rights, are now part of the general corpus of customary international law beyond the circle of contracting parties,[59] although it is difficult to prove a worldwide consensus on the rights which form that "core".

So, by and large, the picture is positive but there are also set-backs. One such originates in the UN system itself. It comes in the much debated but unresolved question whether the Security Council is bound by – at least certain – norms of international law when ordering sanctions and, hence, whether sanctions against a state may or may not impair fundamental human rights of the latter's inhabitants, especially women and children.[60] This is a typical conflict caused by the absence of

---

57   For an overview cf E. Lawson (ed.), *Encyclopedia of Human Rights*, 2nd ed. New York 1996; and H.J. Steiner and Ph. Alston, *International Human Rights in Context: Law, Politics, Morals*, Oxford 1996.

58   See *e.g.* L. Lijnzaad, *Reservations to UN Human Rights Treaties. Ratify and Ruin?*, Dordrecht 1995.

59   See *e.g.* O.Schachter, "International Law in Theory and Practice". General Course in Public International Law, 178 *RdC* (1982, V), at 334-338; El Kouhene, *Les garanties fondamentales de le personne en droit humanitaire et droits del'homme*, Dordrecht 1986, at 109; and Th. Meron, *Human Rights and Humanitarian Norms as Customary Law*, Oxford 1989.

60   See the General Comment 8 (1997) of the Committee on Economic, Social and Cultural Rights, UN Doc E/C.12/1997/8 of 5 December 1997, para.1. And *cf.* D. Starck, *Die Rechtmässigkeit von UNO-Wirtschaftssanktionen in Anbetracht ihrer Auswirkungen auf die Zivilbevölkerung*, Berlin 2000; M.-J. Domestici-Met, "Les sanctions peuvent-elles se heurter à des normes concernant le système des Nations-Unies lui-même?", in: V. Gowland-Debbas (ed.), *United Nations Sanctions and International Law*, The Hague 2001, 167-195; and A. Reinisch, "Developing Human Rights and Humanitarian Law Accountability of the Security Council for the Imposition of Economic Sanctions", 95 *AJIL* (2001), 851-872.

an established hierarchy among principles, which leaves the choice of precedence, security over human rights or *vice versa,* to a subjective value judgment.

Even more disturbing is the risk of regression in the course of the fight against international terrorism. The problem is not limited to the status of detainees on Guantanamo, it appears everywhere where national governments tighten security to prevent terrorist attacks and concomitently restrict certain human rights. It is not surprising that governments play the predicament down. It should, however, be discussed openly because a consensus has to be reached on how much of its freedom a hitherto open society is prepared to sacrifice for the illusion of safety. And that can only be decided by the affected people.

On the other hand there is also reason for hope. The principle of *individual international accountability* for gross violations of fundamental human rights which has emerged during the last decade[61] is a most encouraging development.

Although some attempts in this direction had been made in the past, the new development was promoted by the Security Council when it established the *International Tribunal for the Prosecution of Persons Responsible for Serious Violations of International Humanitarian Law Committed in the Territory of the Former Yugoslavia since 1991* in 1993.[62] Article 5 of its Statute penalizes crimes against humanity directed against the civilian population, irrespective of whether the acts are committed in an international or an internal armed conflict. Punishable crimes are murder, extermination, enslavement, deportation, imprisonment, torture, rape, persecution on political, racial or religious grounds, and other inhuman acts. This is an important step because it recognizes that "crimes against humanity" are, in fact, another term for gross violations of fundamental human rights.[63]

A further stage was reached when the Security Council established the *International Tribunal for Rwanda* by Resolution 955(1994) of 8 November 1994. As far as crimes against humanity are concerned, Article 3 of its Statute follows basically the pattern of article 5 of the Yugoslav Tribunal. But, because of the peculiarity of the Rwandan situation to which it applies, it brakes for the first time the link between crimes against humanity and armed conflict. This position has also influ-

---

61   *Cf.* G. Abi-Saab, "International Criminal Tribunals and the Development of International Humanitarian and Human Rights Law", in: E. Yakpo and T. Boumedra (ed.), *Liber Amicorum Judge Mohammed Bedjaoui,* The Hague 1999, 649-658; and M. Cherif Bassiouni, "The Philosophy and Policy of International Criminal Justice", in: L.Ch. Vorah *et al.,* (eds.), *Man's Inhumanity to Man,* Essays on International Law in Honour of Antonio Cassese, The Hague 2003, 95-126.

62   By Resolution 808(1993) of 22 February 1993 the Security Council established the Tribunal and requested the Secretary-General to submit a draft Statute, which he did in his Report Doc. S/25704 (reprinted in 32 *ILM* (1993), 1192-1201) together with a commentary. The Statute was adopted by the Council in Resolution 827(1993) on 25 May 1993.

63   For the impact of the Tribunal on the protection of these rights cf. A. Rodrigues, "Apport de la pratique du Tribunal pénal international pour l'ex Yougoslavie à la protection des droits fondamentaux de la personne hummaine", in: L.Ch. Vorah *et al.* (eds.), *op. cit.* (note 61), 791-826, particularly at 798-800.

enced the Yugoslav Tribunal, as the celebrated *Tadic* jurisdictional decision of its Appeals Chamber testifies.[64]

The development culminated in the Statute of the *International Criminal Court*,[65] adopted in Rome on 17 July 1998. Having been ratified by 60 states it entered into force on 1 July 2002. Its Article 7 codifies the evolution in the definition of crimes against humanity[66] which states in paragraph 1: "For the purpose of the Statute 'crime against humanity' means any of the following acts when committed as part of a widespread or systematic attack directed against any civilian population..." This is followed by a list of eleven punishable acts which is more sophisticated but basically similar to that in article 5 of the Statute of the Yugoslav Tribunal. Paragraph 2(a) of Article 7 explains further that "'[a]ttack directed against any civilian population' means a course of conduct involving the multiple commission of acts referred to in paragraph 1 against any civilian population, pursuant to or in furtherance of a State or organizational policy to commit such acts". These texts make it clear that crimes against humanity, and the attaching individual criminal responsibility for them, do not require the existence of an international armed conflict, nor even of a military attack. The essential condition is that they are part of a systematic policy by the state or an organized non-state actor. That makes the perpetrators of organized massive violations of those fundamental human rights which are listed in Article 7 of the Statute criminally responsible before an international forum.

Regrettably this step towards improving the effectiveness of international law met with obstruction by the United States. One would have supposed that the United States was sympathetic to the purpose of the ICC not to leave genocide or crimes against humanity unpunished because the relevant national authorities did not prosecute them. But the United States communicated its intention not to ratify the Rome Statute – which it had signed – in a letter to the Secretary-General of the United Nations of 6 May 2002, ostensibly on the ground that it wants to protect its military and civilian personnel abroad from spurious, politically motivated indictments before the ICC. Concern that decisions taken by senior officials in the framework of "pre-emptive self-defence" might lead to prosecutions seems a more realistic explanation.

But that is not all. According to Article 89, paragraph 1 of the Statute of the ICC parties must surrender accused persons arrested on their territory to the Court on its request. Invoking an exception to this obligation, recognized in Article 98, paragraph 1, namely the existence of conflicting other "obligations under international

---

64   *Prosecutor v. Tadic* (Case No. IT-94-1-AR72), Decision on the Defence Motion for Interlocutory Appeal on Jurisdiction, 2 October 1995. Reprinted in 35 *ILM* (1996), 32-74.

65   Text: UN Doc A/CONF.183/9. Here the text is quoted from W.A. Schabas, *An Introduction to the International Criminal Court*, Cambridge 2001.

66   Although at Rome a number of delegations still argued that crimes against humanity could only be committed during an armed conflict. See H. von Hebel and D. Robinson, "Crimes Within the Jurisdiction of the Court", in: R. Lee (ed.), *The International Criminal Court, The Making of the Rome Statute, Issues, Negotiations, Results*, The Hague 1999, 79-126, at 92.

law", the United States solicits parties to the Statute to conclude bilateral agreements in which they undertake not to surrender American personnel requested by the ICC. These bilateral agreements would supply a conflicting "obligation under international law". 30 June 2003 was set as the date after which states which had not adhered to the American request would loose any military aid. As far as the present writer knows, 51 bilateral agreements of this kind have been signed. It has yet to be seen how the ICC will react to the argument once it deals with a relevant case, the crucial point being that the agreements were concluded after the entry into force of the ICC Statute, which *prima facie* violates the obligation which parties to the Statute have under Article 26 of the Vienna Convention on the Law of Treaties.

ii.   The "Common Heritage of Mankind"

It is uncertain when the idea of a common heritage of mankind was first invented, whether in the context of devising a regime for Antarctica, Outer Space, or the deep seabed. Yet it is obvious that it owes some debt to the concept of *res communis (omnium)*, derived from Roman law and since the 19th century applied to the High Seas.[67] Yet, while prohibiting the appropriation of parts of the High Seas, that principle establishes but the freedom for all to navigate and fish on the High Seas and does not regulate their exploitation.[68] In contrast the principle of common heritage embraces four elements: non-appropriation, equal participation, equal share in the benefits of exploitation, and exclusive peaceful use.[69] It focusses thus on exploitation and is designed to limit the previous freedom. To some extent one could call the principle a child of the quest for a "New International Economic Order."[70]

The principle finds its most detailed expression, accompanied by implementing regulations for the exploitation of the deep seabed, in the 1982 *United Nations Convention on the Law of the Sea*.[71] The idea originated in a request by Malta to include a supplementary item in the agenda of the twenty-second session of the General Assembly (1967), proposing that the resources of the seabed and the ocean floor should be used "in the interest of mankind."[72] The initiative led to the es-

---

67   Cf. K. Zemanek, "Was Hugo Grotius Really in Favour of the Freedom of the Seas?", 1 *J of the History of International Law* (1999), 48-60.

68   The first general limitation on the freedom of fishing was introduced by the 1993 FAO Agreement to Promote Compliance with International Conventions and Management Measures by Fishing Vessels on the High Seas; text 33 *ILM* (1994), 968-980.

69   See R.St.J. Macdonald, "The Common Heritage of Mankind", in: U. Beyerlin *et al.* (eds.), *Recht zwischen Umbruch und Bewahrung*, Festschrift für Rudolf Berhardt, Berlin 1995, 153-171, at 154-155; and R. Wolfrum, "The Principle of the Common Heritage of Mankind", 43 *Zeitschrift für ausländisches öffentliches Recht und Völkerrecht* (1983), 312-337. Cf. Also B.E. Helm, "Exploring the last Frontiers for Mineral Resources: A Comparison of International Law Regarding the Deep Seabed, Outer Space, and Antarctica", 23 *Vanderbilt J of Transnational Law* (1990), 819-849.

70   Cf. GA Resolutions 3200(S-VI) and 3201(S-VI) of 1 May 1974, adopted by consensus.

71   Text 21 *ILM* (1982), 1261-1354.

72   UN Doc A/6695, 18 August 1967.

tablishment of the "Seabed Committee" but also generated two pertinent General Assembly resolutions: The so-called "Moratorium" resolution of 1969[73] which suspended potential claims to part of the deep seabed or ocean floor beyond the limits of national jurisdiction; and, one year later, the *Declaration of Principles Governing the Seabed and the Ocean Floor, and Subsoil Thereof, Beyond the Limits of National Jurisdiction*,[74] which declared the area to be the common heritage of mankind and subject to a future international regime. Article 136 of the *Law of the Sea Convention* incorporates the principle and establishes such a regime.[75] Scholars differ in the evaluation of its perspective, opinions ranging from the optimistic view of its possible extension to living resources[76] to the pessimistic view of it having been virtually invalidated[77] by the 1994 *Agreement Relating to the Implementation of Part XI of the UN Law of the Sea Convention of 1982*.[78]

In the context of Outer Space law the principle appeared first in the 1963 *Declaration of Legal Principles Governing the Activities of States in the Exploration and Use of Outer Space*[79] which used the same uncertain formula as the later Maltese proposal for the seabed: "The exploration and use of outer space shall be carried on for the benefit and in the interest if all mankind". The incorporation of the principle in the 1967 *Treaty on Principles Governing the Activities in the Exploration and Use of Outer Space, including the Moon and other Celestial Bodies*[80] is a little more precise and shows the connection with the NIEO clearly when Article 1 states: "The exploration and use of outer space, including the Moon and other celestial bodies, shall be carried out for the benefit and in the interests of all countries, irrespective of the degree of economic or scientific development, and shall be the province of all mankind". That text does not allude to a future international regime nor does it suggest elements of one. It was only in the *Agreement Governing the Activities of States on the Moon and Other Celestial Bodies* of 1979[81] that the principle was explicitly incorporated. Article 11 para.1 states that "[t]he Moon and its resources are the common heritage of mankind, which finds its expression in the provision of this Agreement, in particular paragraph 5 of this article". The paragraph referred to binds states parties to establish an international regime once resource exploitation becomes feasible, which is not yet the case. The provision is, however, the main

---

73 GA Resolution 2574(XXIV), adopted 62:28:16.

74 GA Resolution 2749(XXV), adopted 104:0:16.

75 Articles 137-191 and annexes III and IV regulate the regime.

76 E. Mann Borgese, "The Common Heritage of Mankind: From Non-living to Living Resources and Beyond", in: N. Ando *et al.* (eds.), *Liber Amicorum Judge Shigeru Oda*, The Hague 2003, 1313-1334.

77 V.-D. Degan, "The Common Heritage of Mankind in the Present Law of the Sea", *ibid.*, 1363-1376.

78 Adopted by General Assembly Resolution   48/263 of 28 July 1994.

79 GA Resolution 1962(XVIII) of 13 December 1963, adopted unanimously.

80 Text 6 *ILM* (1967), 386-390.

81 18 *ILM* (1979), 1434-1441.

reason for the refusal of a number of states to ratify the treaty.[82] Even so a German scholar[83] has recently argued that the common heritage of mankind principle is an *"allgemeines Strukturprinzip des Weltraumrechts"* (general structural principle of the law of Outer Space) which, in view of the opposition of important states, somewhat overstates the case.

In the Antarctic regime the principle is only partly and weakly manifest. Before the *Antarctic Treaty* of 1959[84] several states had laid claims to various areas of Antarctica, but the area claimed by one state sometimes overlapped with the area claimed by another state, and none of the areas was effectively controlled by the state concerned. The treaty suspended these claims for the time of its duration but thereby admitted implicitly that appropriation of parts of Antarctica was not prohibited in principle. The first element of a common heritage of mankind regime is therefore missing. On the other hand, the treaty permits only the peaceful use of Antarctica, confirms the freedom of scientific research, and mandates the sharing of the latter's results, touching thus other elements of the concept. The basic treaty was supplemented by specialized agreements, of which the most important in the present context, the *Convention on the Regulation of Antarctic Mineral Resource Activities*[85] did not enter into force and was rendered obsolete by the *Protocol to the Antarctic Treaty*[86] concerning the protection of its environment, which prohibits the exploration of mineral resources other than for scientific purposes. Although not all elements of a common heritage of mankind regime are thus present in the Antarctica regime and the number of participating states is limited, the area is nevertheless viewed as belonging to the "international commons" governed by the principle.[87]

Even in its most elaborate form in the Law of the Sea Convention the principle has been criticized as not being exactly defined and furthermore translated into feeble language in the implementing provisions of the treaty.[88] Others argue that the legal content of the principle has remained obscure because the laying down of its consequences is left to the discretion of states.[89] The fact that some developed countries with the greatest capacity to exploit the resources of the deep seabed have not accepted the principle contained in the Law of the Sea Convention and that none of the leading space powers has ratified the Moon Treaty, argues against a general acceptance of the principle. Its status is best expressed in the conclusion

---

82   See Macdonald (note 69), at 162.

83   D. Woller, *Grundlagen 'Gemeinsamer Sicherheit' im Weltraum nach universellem Völkerrecht*, Berlin 2003, at 215-258.

84   Text 54 *AJIL* (1960), 477-483.

85   Wellington 1988; text 27 *ILM* (1988), 868-900.

86   Madrid 1991; text 30 *ILM* (1991), 1461-1486 (Article 7).

87   See A. Watts, *International Law and the Antarctic Treaty System*, Cambridge 1992, 291-292; and Malanczuk, *op.cit.* (note 2), at 150.

88   See G. Hafner, *Die seerechtliche Verteilung von Nutzungsrechten*, Wien 1987, at 98.

89   Malanczuk (note 2), at 208. For an early criticism see Sh. Oda, *International Law of the Resources of the Sea*, Alphen aan den Rijn 1979, at 116.

of Macdonald[90] which has not lost its relevance in the nearly ten years which have passed since it was stated: "Perhaps the most that can be said is that the development of the principle of common heritage of mankind is a continuing process and that much remains to be done to ensure that it becomes a useful unifying, quasi-constitutional concept within the international legal order."

iii.   International Solidarity

The principle of international solidarity reflects in UN law and international law the moral value of *bonum commune*, or common good. It signifies "the acknowledgment by all States that they have a responsibility to the general global welfare", as Macdonald has put it.[91] He states further:

> Solidarity is neither charity nor welfare; it is an agreement among formal equals that all will refrain from actions that would significantly interfere with the realization of common goals and fundamental interests. Solidarity requires an understanding that every member of the community must consciously and constantly conceive of its own interests as being inextricable from the interests of the whole. No State may choose to use its power to undertake actions that might threaten the integrity of the community.[92]

It would be overstating the case to maintain that the principle is already fully accepted and globally applied to all relevant instances. Its realization requires rethinking the concept of international law,[93] since the latter traditionally was – and in some parts still is –extremely individualistic, focussed on the sovereignty of states[94] and their jealously guarded (formal) independence. But in reality the principle has already made inroads on many aspects of international relations, from the fight against terrorism to the fight against AIDS, sometimes perhaps without the actors being aware that they are, in fact, applying the principle.

This is one reason why the implementation of the principle in multilateral treaties, customary international law, but more often in "soft" law, is poorly coordinated, sometimes even contradictory.[95] This disappointing situation will be examined below by considering together three apparently separate but highly interrelated fields: development, protection of the environment, and free trade.

Economic development as a means to eradicate or at least alleviate the inequality of the international economic system to the advantage of the "Third World"

---

90   *Loc. cit.* (note 69), at 171.

91   R.St.J. Macdonald, "The Principle of Solidarity in Public International Law", in: *Etudes de droit international en l'honneur de Pierre Lalive*, Basel 1993, 275-301, at 295.

92   *Ibid.*, 301.

93   An excellent example of this rethinking is B. Simma, "From Bilateralism to Community Interests in International Law", 250 *RdC* (1994, IV), 229-376.

94   On the conflict between the concepts see Ch. Tomuschat, "International Law: Ensuring the Survival of Mankind on the Eve of the New Century", General Course on Public International Law, 281 *RdC* (1999), at 262-265.

95   See Wolfrum and Matz, *op. cit.* (note 56).

has been a concern of the United Nations since decades. Championed by the non-aligned movement and supported by the Soviet bloc, the policy peaked 1974 in three resolutions of the General Assembly which called for a "New International Economic Order" (NIEO).[96] Various factors, not the least the disintegration of the Soviet Union and the following change in the power structure of the world, contributed to the breakdown of the ambitious but somewhat unrealistic strategy.[97] Other ideas began to influence the concept of economic development, the most important being environmental protection which accounts for the new formulation of the principle as "sustainable development."[98] That idea was promoted by the so-called Brundtland Commission which in 1987 had defined "sustainable development" as "development that meets the need of the present without compromising the ability of future generations to meet their own needs."[99]

Roughly parallel in time, environmental law took a turn in the same direction. Principle 21 of the 1972 Stockholm Declaration on the Human Environment[100] had still echoed traditional international law by stressing the "sovereign rights" of states. But twenty years later, the United Nations Conference on Environment and Development (UNCED) recognized the close relationship between the two principles already in its title. In Principle 7 of the *Rio Declaration on Environment and Development* it stressed that " States shall co-operate in a spirit of global partnership to conserve, protect and restore the health and integrity of the Earth's ecosystem. In view of the different contributions to global environmental degradation, States have common but differentiated responsibilities."[101]

---

96   Resolutions 3200(S-VI) and 3201(S-VI) of 1 May 1974, "Declaration on the Establishment of a New International Economic Order"; and Resolution 3281(XXIX) of 12 December 1974, "Charter of Economic Rights and Duties of States".

97   See Th.M. Waelde, "A Requiem for the 'New International Economic Order'", in: G.Hafner *et al.* (eds.), *Liber Amicorum Ignaz Seidl-Hohenveldern*, The Hague 1998, 771-803; for a more optimistic perspective see P. Slinn, "The International Law of Development: A Millenium Subject or a Relic of the Twentieth Century?", in: W. Benedek *et.al.* (eds.), *Development and Developing International and European Law*, Essays in Honour of Konrad Ginther, Franfurt am Main 1999, 299-318.

98   For the concept see K. Ginther, "Sustainable Development: Development of a Concept and a New Set of Principles", in: N. Steytler (ed.), *Democracy, Human Rights and Economic Development in Southern Africa*, Cape Town 1997, 109-142. The role of the Rio Conference in the integration of environmental policy and development policy is examined by P. Malanczuk, "Die Konferenz der Vereinten Nationen über Umwelt und Entwicklung (UNCED) und das internationale Umweltrecht", in: U. Beyerlin *et al.* (eds.), *Recht zwischen Umbruch und Bewahrung*, Festschrift für Rudolf Bernhardt, Berlin 1995, 984-1002, at 986-988.

99   The World Commission on Environment and Development, Our Common Future, 1987, at 43.

100   Text reprinted in B. Rüster and B. Simma (eds.), *International Protection of the Environment: Treaties and Related Documents*, Vol. I, Dobby Ferry 1975, at 120.

101   Text reprinted in 31 *ILM* (1992), 876-880, at 877.

Contrary to this manifestation of community spirit the translation of the lofty principles into legal obligations, and compliance with them once they are established, leaves much to be desired.[102] The efforts of the international community to combat climate change are an example.

In 1985 the *Vienna Convention for the Protection of the Ozon Layer*[103] was adopted and two years later supplemented by the *Montreal Protocol on Substances that Deplete the Ozon Layer*,[104] In 1992, the Rio Conference added a *Framework Convention on Climate Change*,[105] but nearly six years of intensive negotiations were needed to agree on more precise obligations in the *Kyoto Protocol*[106] which aims at setting quantified limitations and reductions to the emission of greenhouse gases not controlled by the Montreal Protocol.

But the impressive array of international instruments for combating climate change is deceptive. Shortsighted domestic economic interests incite many states – and the United States is just one of them, though the most important – either to refuse ratification of them, or to implement them in a random fashion if they become parties, or to delay implementation with flimsy arguments, and that in spite of a supposedly effective compliance control.[107]

This tends to show that there is an inherent conflict between the principles of sustainable development and environmental protection on the one hand, and the principle of free trade on the other. States, when invoking domestic economic interests in justifying their reluctance to accept obligations to protect the environment, argue nearly always that these would harm the competitiveness of their industry in global trade,[108] which would cause recession in their domestic economy and endanger jobs.

The fact that the guardian of the principle of free trade is the *World Trade Organization* (WTO), and thus an organization formally outside the UN system, does not favour the reconciliation of the two sets of principles. Particularly so because WTO has its own dispute settlement mechanism with rules governing a conflict

---

102   For the reasons cf. W. Lang, "Negotiations on the Environment", in: V. Kremenyuk (ed.), International Negotiations, San Francisco 1991, 343-356; and U. Beyerlin, "Staatliche Souveränität und internationale Umweltschutzkooperation", in: U. Beyerlin *et al.* (eds.), *op.cit.* (note 98), 937-956.

103   22 March 1985; reprinted 26 *ILM* (1987), 1529-1540.

104   16 September 1987; reprinted *ibid.*, 1550-1560.

105   Text reprinted in 31 *ILM* (1992), 849-873. Cf. R. Dolzer, "Die internationale Konvention zum Schutz des Klimas und das allgemeine Völkerrecht", in U. Beyerlin *et al.* (eds.), *op.cit.* (note 98), 957-973.

106   Kyoto Protocol to the United Nations Framework Convention on Climate Change, 10 December 1997; reprinted in 37 *ILM* (1998), 32-43.

107   On the latter cf. W. Loibl, "Compliance with International Environmental Law – The Emerging Regime Under the Kyoto Protocol", in: W. Benedek *et al.* (eds.), *op. cit.* (note 97), 263-283.

108   States use the same argument for refusing to accept certain international labour standards.

of norms that do not encourage the admission of non-WTO international legal instruments in legal disputes before its panels.[109] Conflicts are inherent in the relation of the two sets of principles,[110] for instance when states enact trade restrictions in compliance with their obligations under multilateral environmental agreements. To entrust the protector of one principle with the solution of the conflict is not a suitable remedy.

3. Conclusions

The foregoing enquiry confirms that the basic principles of UN Charter law which were considered in this essay have indeed changed their content in the last couple of decades. It is not unreasonable to assume that the same has happened to other basic principles which were not examined closer. This corroborates what has been argued in the introduction, that the evolution of societal values reflects in the content of corresponding principles, and this evolution has been rapid and profound during the period.

The system of collective security has lost much of its significance and that impairs also the basic principles which underpin it, namely sovereign equality, non-intervention and prohibition to use force. The hope that, after the end of the Cold War, the Security Council would begin to function properly, as was suggested by its reaction to Iraq's aggression against Kuwait, and would effectively use and defend its monopoly to legalize the use of force, was disappointed. This happened partly under the impact of United States practice, characterized by an increasingly assertive policy towards the outside world and a penchant for unilateral action – features which the European Union may try one day to emulate. But it is also the fault of the United Nations – and that does not mean the legal superstructure but its member states – which are unable or unwilling to live up to the noble principles proclaimed in the Charter and fail to effectively support the organization in achieving its purposes.

States have looked on with indifference as economic globalization, which is rapidly expanding into social and cultural globalization, bypassed the UN system and thereby the constraint of its basic principles. Within the United Nations some of the pressing concerns of the world were recognized, initially "soft" principles proclaimed, and appropriate international instruments adopted. But the "soft"

---

109   See J. Pauwelyn, *Conflict of Norms in Public International Law – How WTO Law Relates to Other Rules of International Law*, Cambridge 2003. The author provides a strictly legal solution to the problem (321-324), compares it with the practice of the WTO panels (459-472), and suggests the adaptations required by his solution (472-478). *Cf.* also P. Mengozzi, "The World Trade Organization Law: An Analysis of its First Practice", in: *Divenire sociale e adeguamento del diritto*, Studi in onore di Francesco Capotorti, Vol. I, Milano 1999, 271-315, at 277-283.

110   *Cf.* G. Loibl, "Trade and Environment. A Difficult Relationship – New Approaches and Trends: The Kyoto Protocol and Beyond", in: G. Hafner *et al.* (eds.), *op. cit.* (note 97), 419-443.

principles are often not taken into account and the instruments remain ineffective because the players who dominate the world economy – the United States together with some others – oppose them and refuse to cooperate. This indicates a dialectical tension between the power structure of the world and the concerns of a large majority of the international community.

The United Nations are, therefore, at a crossroads. If they cannot regain the impetus of the founding members and establish themselves firmly in the role which they were assigned by the Charter, and defend the basic principles of the Charter more vigorously, they will increasingly loose influence in security matters and further damage their ability to advance the socio-economic wellbeing of world society. The need for action is clear but the prospect of it dim. Orientating the focus of states from self-interest towards community values cannot be achieved by legal instruments alone, nor by utopian academic schemes. Social engineering in the international community is a laborious task. For its success it needs the improved awareness of the peoples of this world and their engagement in civil society to put pressure on governments from below – and that is a slow process.

Should the United Nations fail in that reform, the system risks to deteriorate into an imperial order governed by the United States.

16. The Legislative Powers of the United Nations Security Council

Munir Akram and Syed Haider Shah

1. Introduction

The role of the Security Council is quite relevant in the discourse on world constitutionalism. The ability of the Council to lay down or reinforce rules of international law, though controversial, is widely accepted.[1] Its actions affect not only states, but also non-state actors and individuals. Not the least is the impact of the Councils' action on other organs and bodies of the UN system.

Any discussion of the actions or powers of the Security Council must refer to the conception of this body in the Charter, its actual practice, and the need for accountability and reform. However, such discussions run the risk of being dominated either by too much legalism or pragmatism. Both approaches fall short of fully understanding the dynamics of a body, which has evolved since its creation and continues to do so. Premising the discourse on Security Council powers on purely academic and legalistic bases runs the risk of underestimating the realities of international politics. On the other hand, too much focus on pragmatism, may translate into resignation to the status quo leaving little room for reform or innovation. Over-emphasizing the role and powers of the permanent members of the Council, reduces the system to a mere product of what these members wish to do[2]

---

[1] O. Schachter, "Law-Making in the United Nations", in *Perspectives on International Law*, Edited by Nandasiri Jasentuliyana, 1995 Kluwer Law International, London, p. 119.

[2] I. Brownlie, "International Law in the Context of the Changing World Order", in *Perspectives on International Law*, Edited by Nandasiri Jasentuliyana, 1995 Kluwer Law International, London. Brownlie quoted from his earlier work, "The United Nations as a Form of Government", 13 *Harvard International Law Journal*, 421, 423 (1972) "If by a political accident the permanent members were a firm faction, the Security Council could launch a variety of violent actions to shape the world in the image shared by the coalition; the European directorate of the nineteenth century would be but a mild precedent for such a new order." p. 60.

Ronald St. John Macdonald & Douglas M. Johnston (eds.), Towards World Constitutionalism, *pp. 431-455.*
© *2005 Koninklijke Brill NV. Printed in The Netherlands.* ISBN 90 04 14612 1.

and fails to take into account the changes that have taken place since 1945, as well as the emergence of new actors on the international scene.

The Security Council is an important actor in international affairs. The impact of its decisions on international law, states and other subjects is growing. It is therefore, quite relevant to discuss the role of this organization in order to develop a clearer appreciation of the scope of its functions, especially those of a legislative nature.

This chapter focuses on the legislative powers of the Security Council, taking into account the role envisaged for it under the UN Charter, its evolving practice and its implications. It also discusses ways to bring the Council's role in conformity with the expectations of the international community.

2.   The Security Council and the International Legal System

A.   *International Legal System*

As the Security Council operates in and contributes to the "international legal system" in different ways, it is useful to explain this term. The international legal system denotes the whole constellation of rules, laws, treaties, customs and practices, which states and other actors follow, observe, or are, expected to observe in their interaction with one another. The system is constantly evolving and normative shifts are not uncommon just as they are in the domestic legal systems.

The discussion of international law is closely linked to its subjects and objects and sources.[3] The Westphalian system of international law, to which the origins of the modern international community are traced, was concerned with states.[4] Therefore, classical international law was limited to governing relations between independent states and considered its rules to emanate from the free will of such states expressed in conventions or by usage.[5] The scope of international law has considerably expanded during the last century due to the emergence of new issues and other developments[6] since World War II. As a result, there has been a transi-

---

3   Rosalyn Higgins, "Fundamentals of International Law", in *Perspectives on International Law*, Edited by Nandasiri Jasentuliyana, 1995, Kluwer Law International, London. According to Higgins, "the fundamentals of international law cannot be discussed without asking to whom it applies and what its sources are." p. 3.

4   E. Brown Weiss, "The New International Legal System in World Order", in *Perspectives on International Law*, Edited by Nandasiri Jasentuliyana, 1995, Kluwer Law International, London, p. 63.

5   *Ibid.*, quoting the Permanent Court of International Justice in the S.S. Lotus Case, 1927 PCIJ (ser.A) No.10, 18, p. 63.

6   *Ibid.*, Weiss refers to issues such as economic welfare, trading relationships, human rights, banking, securities, environment and communications and other developments, such as rapid population growth, rising expectation of material welfare, communication advances and a revolution in information technology, transportation improvements, and rising education levels globally, p. 65.

tion from a hierarchic international system led by states to a non hierarchic system composed of networks of states, non state actors and individuals.[7]

The international legal system is, however, still dominated by states since they continue to be its primary subjects. The system is based on two fundamental principles, state sovereignty and equality of states. Article 2 of the UN Charter refers to "sovereign equality of states".[8] However, the system is also constantly evolving. There has been a growth over time in the range and diversity of the international legal system. The process of international law-making has also evolved. It is no longer the product of treaties or state practice alone. It is not possible to ignore the contribution of soft law,[9] the jurisprudence and practices of international organizations, their decisions or resolutions, and international public opinion to the fabric of international legal framework.

The Statute[10] of the ICJ lays down certain sources of international law to be followed by the ICJ in making decisions on issues before the court. These sources are broad enough to include rules and laws which govern international or inter-state relations including treaties, conventions, agreements, judicial pronouncements of the International Court of Justice or other international courts, tribunals or bodies. Since its establishment in 1945, a substantial body of international law has emerged through United Nations' processes.[11]

Although the UN Charter does not clearly list UN resolutions amongst the sources of international law,[12], these resolutions often have important implications for international law, state[13] practice and behavior. The resolutions of the UN Se-

---

7   *Ibid.*, Weiss.

8   Georges Abi-Saab, "Some thoughts on the principle of non-intervention" in *International Law: Theory and Practice, Essays in Honour of Eric Suy*, edited by Karel Wellens, Kluwer Law International, 1998, p. 225.

9   See Weiss, *supra* note 4, pp. 72-73.

10   Article 38 (1) of the ICJ Statute provides:

    1.   The Court, whose function is to decide in accordance with international law such disputes as are submitted to it, shall apply:

        a.   international conventions, whether general or particular, establishing rules expressly recognized by the contesting states;

        b.   international custom, as evidence of a general practice accepted as law;

        c.   the general principles of law recognized by civilized nations;

        d.   subject to the provisions of Article 59, judicial decisions and the teachings of the most highly qualified publicists of the various nations, as subsidiary means for the determination of rules of law.

11   Schachter *supra* note 1, p. 119.

12   *Ibid.* Schachter was referring to General Assembly resolutions, which he said, are not a formal source of law recognized in Article 38 of the ICJ Statute or by international law doctrine.

13   One cannot afford to ignore the fact that SC resolutions also address non-state actors as well as individuals. See, for example, Resolutions 1267, 1333, 1390, 1455 and 1526 regarding sanctions against Osama bin Laden, Al Qaida and Taliban and their associates including individuals as well as entities.

curity Council, particularly those adopted under Chapter VII of the Charter, may impose binding obligations upon UN members.[14] UN resolutions[15] can also provide evidence of a state practice for which there is sufficient *opinio juris* to represent customary international law.[16] However, UN resolutions have not yet won universal recognition as an independent source of law.[17] Questions remain about the legality, status and impact of UN resolutions, and more so, about the legislative powers of the UN Security Council.

B.   Role of the Security Council

The creation and evolution of the UN system is also instructive in appreciating the role of the Security Council. The creation of the United Nations system was deeply influenced by the experience of its predecessor organization, the League of Nations. Although, the UN system inherited some of the institutions of the League system, such as the Permanent Court of International Justice, there were some key differences[18] between the two organizations. One of the notable differences relates to the maintenance of international peace and security: the Covenant of the League of Nations provided a decentralized system of collective security in which the Council of the League merely had a recommendatory role while member states were to act first and foremost in case of war; the Charter, on the other hand, having a "clear universalist orientation"[19] provides for a centralized system of collective security.[20] Moreover, the Covenant contained obligations mostly for member states, while the Charter attributes most of its powers to the Security Council.[21] The UN Charter

---

14   Higgins *supra* note 3, p. 17.

15   Schachter *supra* note 1. Schachter wrote, "… many resolutions (of the General Assembly) which do not express rules of law serve to generate law since they may often contribute to the emergence of custom or new general principles of law …. Resolutions also help to generate law by expressing policies that call for future law; they also recommend standards of conduct that may, in due course, become customary law or embodied in treaties." p. 129.

16   Higgins *supra* note 3, p. 17.

17   *Ibid.*, p. 18.

18   James Crawford, "The Charter of the United Nations as a Constitution" in *The Changing Constitution of the United Nations*, The British Institute of International and Comparative Law, London, 1997. These differences relate to the use of force/outlawing war, relationship with the post-war peace-making process, collective security system and its trigger mechanism, decision making/veto, and membership. There was also a terminological difference, "covenant" and "charter", pp. 3-5.

19   Abi-Saab *supra* note 8. Abi-Saab says that the Charter "institutionalizes" the "alliance of victorious nations" and projects it into the future. p. 20.

20   Niels Blokker, "Is the Authorization Authorized? Powers and Practice of the UN Security Council to Authorize the Use of Force by 'Coalitions of the Able and Willing'" in *EJIL* (2000), Vol.11 No.3, 541-568. p. 550.

21   *Ibid.*

obliges member states to carry out the decisions of the Security Council.[22]

The non-participation of the United States in the League of Nations had been widely considered to be one of the reasons for the failure of the League system. In order to avoid similar fate for the UN, the founders of the new system were keen on including all the major players who had emerged victorious from World War II. At the time of the establishment of the UN system, the permanent members of the Security Council, representing the victorious powers, were expected to play an important role in the organization. There was therefore, little doubt about the influence of the permanent membership on the future work of the Council. This partly explains the inequality in the voting powers of the permanent and non-permanent members of the Council.[23] Even a change in the size of the Council from 11 to 15[24] has not affected this inequality.

The Security Council[25] is not, strictly speaking, a legal or a judicial body. It is simplistic to describe the UN system as an international government or to treat the Security Council merely as the executive arm of the UN membership. The Council has a predominantly political character. The primary purpose of the UN Charter is to maintain international peace and security[26] and the primary responsibility for maintaining international peace and security is conferred on the Security Council.[27] The Council "shall determine the existence of any threat to the peace, breach of peace, or act of aggression and shall make recommendations, or decide what measures shall be taken in accordance with Articles 41 and 42, to maintain or restore international peace and security."[28]

However, it is difficult to rely only on the textual reading of the Charter to ascertain the powers and functions of the Security Council. There is a growing gap between the letter of the Charter and the powers actually exercised or claimed by the Security Council. Moreover, the language of the Charter is quite vague and

---

22   Article 25 of the Charter, which reads, "The Members of the United Nations agree to accept and carry out the decisions of the Security Council in accordance with the present Charter."

23   Carl-August Fleischhauer, *The Changing Constitution of the United Nations*, The British Institute of International and Comparative Law, London, 1997. Fleischhauer says in the Preface that this inequality may also be described as "weighted voting according to status as permanent or non-permanent member". p. xix.

24   Abi-Saab *supra* note 8. The initial composition of the Council included five permanent and six non-permanent members. By GA Resolution 1991 (XVIII) of 17 December 1963, (which came into force on 31 August 1965), six new non-permanent seats were added to the Security Council. This was in the wake of the "Package deal" and de-colonization, which had more than doubled the membership of the UN since its establishment in 1945. p. 32.

25   See Chapter V (Articles 23-32) of the UN Charter about the functions, composition and procedures of the Security Council. See also Chapter VI, VII, VIII and XII about the powers of the Security Council.

26   Blokker supra note 20, p. 549. Also see Article 1(1) of the UN Charter.

27   *Ibid.*, p. 550. Also see Article 24 (1) of the UN Charter.

28   See Article 39 of the UN Charter. See also Article 41 and 42 of the Charter providing for measures (including use of force) to give effect to its decisions.

open to varying interpretations. The Charter does not provide a clear mechanism for its interpretation, leaving it to each organ to interpret its own powers.[29]

Notwithstanding the wide powers and pre-eminent position granted to the Security Council under the Charter, during the first four and a half decades of its existence this body could not utilize most of its powers due to the East-West Cold War rivalry. In this period, the Security Council authorized use of force under Chapter VII only on two occasions; during the 1950 Korean War and in 1966 regarding the situation in Southern Rhodesia.[30] The Council adopted 646 resolutions between 1945 and 1989. In the last fifteen years the Council has adopted over 900 resolutions, many of them under Chapter VII of the Charter and thus legally binding. Several of these resolutions authorized or contemplated the use of its enforcement powers under Articles 41 and 42 of the Charter.

Thus, the end of Cold War helped release the Security Council from the inactive mode. The end of East-West rivalry was marked by a greater convergence of positions, especially among the five permanent members as most post Cold War crises and conflicts arose in the developing world where the vital national interests of the five were not involved or did not conflict. However differences of interest and approach have at times come to fore such as in the run up to the recent war in Iraq. The Council's inability to authorize the use of force, which was the norm during the Cold War, and the subsequent unilateral intervention by the United States, were perceived by some commentators as indications of the "irrelevance" of the Security Council (and the UN).

3.   Law-making Capacity of the Security Council

A.   Law-making and the UN Charter

The Charter is silent about the legislative powers[31] of the Security Council or of any other UN organ.[32] While this has complicated the task of finding the legal basis of

---

29   Mohammed Bedjaoui, *The New World Order and the Security Council, Testing the Legality of its Acts*, Martinus Nijhoff, 1994, p. 10. According to Bedjaoui the San Francisco Conference decided to "renounce setting up a specific mechanism for interpreting the provisions of the Charter" and to "recognize that ... each organ would inevitably interpret from day to day those provisions of the Charter which concerned its activities". Bedjaoui was quoting from UNCIO, Vol. 13, pp. 709-710 (Commission IV, Judicial Organization, Doc. 873, IV/2/37(1), 12 June 1945, p. 831 (Doc. 750, Iv/2/B/1, p.1). See also Bernd Martenczuk, in "The Security Council, the International Court and Judicial Review: What Lessons from Lockerbie?" in *EJIL* (1999), Vol. 10 No. 3, 517-547. Bernd refers to "decentralized" approach to Charter interpretation followed by the drafters of the Charter, p. 526.

30   Blokker *supra* note 20, p. 543.

31   Legislation can be defined as "the exercise of the power and function of making rules (as laws) that have the force of authority by virtue of their promulgation by an official organ of a state or other organization." *Merriam-Webster Online Dictionary* at <http://www.m-w.com/cgi-bin/dictionary?book=Dictionary&va=legislation>.

32   Schachter *supra* note 1. According to Schachter "Nowhere does the Charter expressly refer to "law-making" by UN organs". p. 120.

actions of UN organs of legal or legislative nature, it has not prevented, especially the Council from assuming functions of legislative nature. Such assumptions of legislative powers have been facilitated by the fact that the Charter does not prohibit UN organs from law-making per se. In some cases it requires general rules of a binding character.[33]

Does the Charter's failure to confer clearly powers of law making on the Security Council render actions of the Council of legislative nature illegal? To be precise, the Council does not "legislate": it enforces Charter obligations.[34] However, the powers given to the Security Council under articles 39, 41 and 42 for the maintenance of international peace and security could be used for taking actions, which may have a legislative effect. Thus, the lawfulness of decisions of the Council which are not in accordance with the provisions of the Charter remains questionable. The Council can spell out, or particularize, the obligations of member states that arise from the Charter but it cannot create totally new obligations.[35]

B.   Forms of Law-making Actions

Law-making by the Security Council through its resolutions, decisions or other actions can result in giving effect to an existing law or amending or modifying an existing law. Some resolutions or statements may provide for the main action to be undertaken by another body or organ. Thus, it could delegate its functions to a subsidiary body to make rules and regulations to be complied by the states.

The Security Council also plays a role in setting norms or endorsing norms evolved by other organizations. A typical resolution of the Security Council consists of decisions of a binding nature and non-binding recommendations. Thus it can influence the behavior of states in accepting, following, and implementing its own recommendations or non-binding pronouncements as well as those emanating from other sources. Legally and technically, such exhortations are not binding on member states. But often these distinctions are blurred to give a binding appearance to a recommendation. A case in point is Resolution 1373 (2001) adopted within a couple of weeks of the events of 11 September 2001 terrorist attacks against the United States. Some of its provisions are only recommendations asking states to

---

33   *Ibid.* Schachter refers to rules governing the UN organization, Security Council resolutions mandating peacekeeping forces, the statutes of the High Commissioner for Refugees, UN Financial Regulations, the regulations governing personnel. p. 120. "The Charter also opens the way to international law-making through Article 13 (1) by requiring General Assembly to undertake studies and make recommendations to encourage the progressive development of international law and its codification .... The Charter also authorizes the Economic and Social Council to prepare draft conventions within its competence for submission to the General Assembly and, presumably to Governments." p. 121

34   D.W. Bowett QC, "Judicial and Political Functions of the Security Council and the International Court of Justice", in *The Changing Constitution of the United Nations*, The British Institute of International and Comparative Law, London, 1997, pp. 73-88, p. 80.

35   *Ibid.*, p. 82.

become parties to relevant international conventions and protocols relating to terrorism.[36] The fact that the resolution was adopted under Chapter VII of the Charter has been used to impress upon states to become parties to the different UN conventions against terrorism. The Counter Terrorism Committee set up under Resolution 1373 (2001) to monitor the implementation of provisions of this resolution, engages in a regular dialogue with states and impresses on them the need for ratifying these conventions. As a result, there has been an increase in the ratifications by states of the UN conventions against terrorism following the adoption of Resolution 1373.[37]

In a more generalized way, the Council also encourages states to follow international best practices and codes and standards in different fields. Calls made by the Council are not easily ignored and are generally followed by states. Similarly, through its reporting requirements under various resolutions particularly Resolution 1373 (2001), the Council receives information about the legal practices of states in different fields, which can be used to influence domestic law-making.

The predominantly political character of the Security Council coupled with its discretionary powers, lack of accountability, and inconsistent and selective practice make its legislative powers a source of concern, particularly, if those powers are not subjected to clear limitations. These constitutional weaknesses make the Council vulnerable to the hegemony of a small group of States.[38]

The Security Council's actions for the maintenance of international peace and security can take different forms such as:

a.   Expression of concern, recommendations to parties for maintenance of international peace and security.
b.   Sending fact-finding missions, appointing a special representative of the Secretary General, asking member states to submit compliance reports.
c.   Imposing obligations under Chapter VII including enforcement action (authorizing use of force), humanitarian intervention, enforcement of no fly zones.
d.   Setting up of subsidiary organs or committees (Sanctions Committees, CTC, Counter Terrorism Committee Executive Directorate) special bodies (UN-MOVIC, International Tribunals, Compensation Commissions, Boundary Commissions).
e.   Norm-setting role, for example, by calling for ratification of UN conventions against terrorism.
f.   Peace keeping[39] and peace enforcement missions.[40]

---

36   See paragraphs 3 (d) of Resolution 1373(2001) and 2(a) of the Declaration annexed to Resolution 1456 (2003).

37   Report by the Chairman CTC to the Security Council, on 19 July 2004, contained in document S/PV.5006, p. 3, available at <http://ods-dds-ny.un.org/doc/UNDOC/PRO/N04/430/00/PDF/N0443000.pdf?OpenElement>.

38   Brownlie *supra* note 2, pp. 55-56. Also see José E. Alvarez, "Hegemonic International Law Revisited", in *American Journal of International Law*, Vol. 97 No. 4, October 2003.

39   As of June 2004, there were 16 peacekeeping operations in different parts of the world. Source: DPI/1634/Rev.37, June 2004.

40   The concept of peacekeeping operations is not mentioned in the UN Charter.

States generally comply with the decisions of the Security Council, although there are major exceptions. The reasons for compliance can range from commitment to Charter obligations to fear of sanctions and other punitive measures. However, such compliance has not been unquestioned and concerns have been expressed about inconsistent application, discrimination and reporting fatigue by the developing countries.

C.   Legal Basis and Constraints

Identification of the legal basis of Security Council actions has merit in lending greater legitimacy to its actions and clarifying its role vis-à-vis other UN organs, international and regional organizations and member states. It is also important amidst concerns of rising unilateralism, abuse of its authority by a few powerful states and its representative credentials. And not the least, it is important due to the frequent failure of the Council to indicate the legal basis or the precise Charter provision, under which it takes a particular action and its tendency to interpret expansively its powers.

The legislative powers of the Security Council are thus closely linked to the Council's interpretive powers. However, the question is whether the Council is obliged to observe certain limitations in the exercise of its powers? If so, what are those limitations and how could they be enforced?

The argument that the Council has a political character and should therefore not be subjected to legal or judicial standards is not tenable especially because its actions have legal effect and are challenged in judicial tribunals. It goes against the principle of accountability and general principles of international organizations, which the UN is bound to respect. It also goes against the doctrines of constitutional powers and limitations.[41] In fact, the assertion of political character reinforces the argument that the Council should not dispose of questions of legal right with finality.[42] Moreover, unreviewable exercise of power translates into unlimited authority.[43] Had it not been for these concerns, the Charter would not have laid

---

41   Eric Suy, "The Role of the United Nations General Assembly", in *The Changing Constitution of the United Nations*, The British Institute of International and Comparative Law, London, 1997, p. 64. In respect to Charter interpretation, the statement of the ICJ remains obviously true that, "The political character of an organ cannot release it from the observance of the treaty provisions established by the Charter when they constitute limitations on its powers or criteria for its judgment. To ascertain whether an organ has freedom of choice for its decisions, reference must be made to the terms of its constitution." Quoting from Conditions of Admission of a State to Membership in the United Nations (Article 4 of the Charter), Advisory Opinion, 1948, I.C.J. Reports 1948, p. 57. This naturally should apply to the UN Security Council.

42   Derek Bowett, "The Impact of Security Council Decisions on Dispute Settlement Procedures", in 5 *EJIL* (1994) 1-101 p. 3.

43   Faiza Patel, "Sensible Scrutiny: the Yugoslavia Tribunal's Development of Limits on the Security Council's Powes"., in *Emory International Law Review*, Vol. 10, Winter 1996, pp. 509-591, p. 522.

down that legal disputes should as a general principle be referred to judicial settlement procedures under Article 36 (3).

The powers given to the Council under Article 39 of the Charter are limited to determining the threats to or breaches of the peace or acts of aggression. However, the vagueness of the conception of peace and security makes it difficult to determine the *ultra vires* of its actions.

From a legalistic perspective the assertion that the Security Council is above the law is unsustainable.[44] It is bound by, among others, the constitutive document which created it. Defining the nature, scope and enforcement of these constraints is important as these also offer standards for review of Council's actions. These constraints may vary depending on their source, descriptive accuracy and normative appeal.[45] Differences persist about the exact nature and scope of constraints on the powers of the Security Council. Given below are some of the constraints which may apply to, and influence, Security Council actions particularly those of a legislative nature. It is worth considering that some of these constraints may have more than one source, for example as a general principle of international law, the UN Charter or treaty law.

i.   General Principles of International Law

1.   The Council cannot be absolved from its obligation to respect the Charter and general principles of international law.[46] The Charter could not be used to justify actions or situations which are patently unlawful and go against internationally accepted principles.[47]

2.   The Council cannot ignore principles of international law such as state sovereignty and territorial integrity which are part of the UN Charter. The Charter

---

44   *Ibid.* Also see Prosecutor v. Dusko Tadic a/k/a "DULE", Decision on the Defence Motion for Interlocutory Appeal on Jurisdiction, of 2 October 1995, para 28, available at <http://www.un.org/icty/tadic/appeal/decision-e/51002.htm>. Also see Suy *supra* note 41 who quoted the statement of Egyptian delegation at the plenary meeting of the General Assembly while discussing the Annual Report of the Security Council for the period 1991-1992 in document A/47/PV.106 p. 71; p. 68.

45   Anthea Elizabeth Roberts, "Traditional and Modern Approaches to Customary International Law: A Reconciliation" in *American Journal of International Law*, Vol. 95: 757, pp. 761-770. It may be noted that Anthea was discussing modern and traditional custom, which may have a limiting power on international actors, including the Security Council.

46   In his dissenting opinion in the Lockerbie Case, Judge Weeramantry noted "The history of the United Nations Charter thus corroborates the view that a clear limitation on the plenitude of the Security Council's powers is that those powers must be exercised in accordance with the well-established principles of international law." Questions Of Interpretation And Application Of The 1971 Montreal Convention Arising From The Aerial Incident At Lockerbie (Libyan Arab Jamahiriya v. United States Of America) available at <http://www.icj-cij.org/icjwww/idocket/ilus/ilusframe.htm>.

47   For example regarding human rights, use of force, outlawing of war, treatment of prisoners of war etc.

refers to sovereign equality of states and treats peace and security as a common good for all peoples. Similarly the prohibition of use or threat of use of force against the territorial integrity or political independence of a state inconsistent with the Purposes of the Charter[48] sets the normative standards for ordering international relations among the United Nations. These principles are *lex lata* and could not be dismissed as merely *lex ferenda*. The Council does not have a choice but to observe these principles. These principles serve as a constraint on the powers of the Security Council and inconsistency of Council's practice with respect to the observance of these principles cannot detract from their legal character.

ii.   Peremptory norms of international law, or *jus cogens*

1.   Some human rights are generally treated as non-derogable or *jus cogens*.[49] Similarly some principles of international humanitarian law, particularly Geneva Conventions on the conduct of wars, armed conflict and treatment of prisoners of war, have come to reflect the common moral values of the international community and are generally considered to be part of international customary law.[50] It is not possible to ignore these norms.

iii.   Limitations of the Charter of the United Nations

1.   The Council is limited by the principles, and purposes and other provisions of the Charter, which can also serve as the standard of review for its resolutions.[51] The Council could not use its competence inconsistently with the Charter's

---

48   Article 2 (4) of the Charter reads, "All Members shall refrain in their international relations from the threat or use of force against the territorial integrity or political independence of any state, or in any other manner inconsistent with the Purposes of the United Nations."

49   Article 53 of the 1969 Vienna Convention on the Law of Treaties provides that, "A treaty is void if, at the time of its conclusion, it conflicts with a peremptory norm of general international law. For the purposes of the present Convention, a peremptory norm of general international law is a norm accepted and recognized by the international community of States as a whole as a norm from which no derogation is permitted and which can be modified only by a subsequent norm of general international law having the same character."

50   In its recent Advisory Opinion in the ICJ Wall Case, the Court held that the provisions of the Hague Regulations concerning Laws and Customs of War on Land annexed to the Fourth Hague Convention of 18 October 1907 have become part of customary law. (Legal Consequences of the Construction of a Wall in the The Occupied Palestinian Territory, General List No. 131, paras 87 and 89, available at <http://www.icj-cij.org/icjwww/idocket/imwp/imwpframe.htm>.

51   Bernd Martenczuk, "The Security Council, the International Court and Judicial Review: What Lessons from Lockerbie?" in *EJIL* (1999), Vol.10 No.3, pp. 517-547, pp. 536-537. See also Faiza Patel *supra* note 43 in the context of the Tadic Case wherein the ICTY held that the Security Council must "'act in accordance with the Purposes and Principles of the United Nations." p. 552.

primary objectives. The Council cannot act in an arbitrary manner or for an ulterior purpose.[52]

2.   The Council is entrusted with functions of an executive nature for the maintenance of international peace and security through such means as issuance of directives of an executive nature. It cannot use its powers to formulate rules and regulations especially when they do not have a direct bearing on international peace and security. It is interesting to note the Security Council was conceived as a 'policeman who will say, when anyone starts to fight, "Stop fighting" Period. And then it will say, when anyone is all ready to begin to fight, "You must not fight. Period."[53] The analogy of the Council as a policeman is quite interesting and revealing insofar as it shows that the drafters of the Charter had not intended the Security Council to be a lawmaker. In the performance of its policing functions, it can devise some rules specific to the nature of its functions but not become a lawmaker.

3.   The interpretive powers of the Council under Article 39 are also not unlimited. It cannot interpret international peace and security in a manner, which amounts to an amendment of the Charter. [54] An interpretation, which has the effect of amending the Charter, is beyond the competence of the Council. Thus the provision in the Charter[55] regarding a conflict between Charter obligations versus treaty obligations cannot be interpreted to mean the abandonment or replacement of general principles of international law. It would be anarchic to read such a conclusion into the Charter. The process of international lawmaking was not sought to be replaced by the Security Council. It should not use its powers to undermine the rights of member states and individuals[56] under international law.

The articulation of most of the above and other limitations in the decisions and opinions of international adjudicative bodies reflects the ideal and belief of most of the international community that the Council's actions should conform to certain

---

52   Patel *supra* note 43, p. 555.

53   Bernd *supra* note 51, p. 545, quoting US delegate Stassesn at the San Francisco Conference, 6 UNCIO (1945) 29.

54   Nicolas Angelet, "Protest Against Security Council Decisions", in *International Law: Theory and Practice, Essays in Honour of Eric Suy*, edited by Karel Wellens, Martinus Nijhoff Publishers, 1998, pp. 277-285, p. 281.

55   See Article 103 of the UN Charter.

56   Hazel Fox, Introduction, in *The Changing Constitution of the United Nations*, The British Institute of International and Comparative Law, London, 1997. The Council may also be charged with a lack of respect or protection for the position of the individual member state. In undertaking demarcation of boundaries, adjudication of compensation for war damage and punishment of war crimes the Security Council extends its mandate from an executive organ to legislate and judicial functions, and in the process runs the risk of inadequate protection of the rights of individuals members States, whether wrongdoer or victims or the individual persons who are brought for the first time under international criminal jurisdiction. pp. xxvii, xxix.

rules and standards of evaluation to lend them greater predictability and certainty. A blanket presumption of validity to all Council actions without any possibility of accountability is not justifiable. These limitations are thus based on legal as well as moral and political principles. Notwithstanding the fact that these limitations do not enjoy universal acceptance, it is not politically wise for the Council to treat them lightly much less violate them.

Recent jurisprudence of international adjudicative bodies has attempted to fill the legal vacuum of the Charter in terms of judicial control of Council actions. However, it is still a policy question whether Council itself should formulate limitations on its powers or should it be left to international judicial bodies such as the ICJ? It requires a political commitment to put in place a mechanism to regulate the exercise of powers by the Security Council. Such a commitment would have to address issues such as the need to preserve Council's efficiency in maintaining international peace and security and consistent and objective enforceability of these limitations.

The Council can hardly fail to match its words with deeds especially in areas such as democracy, human rights, justice and rule of law. The Council should not be viewed merely as a forum for imposing obligations on "other" members and entities and individuals but also one that obliges its own membership to conform to accepted international norms and laws.

D.   Accountability and Judicial Review

Judicial review can be defined as "review by a court of law of actions of a government official or entity or of some other legally appointed person or body or the review by an appellate court of the decision of a trial court."[57] In the case of Security Council it could mean the review of actions of the Security Council or its subsidiary bodies. The crucial question is who would carry out judicial review of Council's actions?[58]

Does the ICJ possess the power to review Council's decisions?[59] This question has led to sharply divergent views as to the nature and scope of judicial review of the Council decisions. It appears that the Charter does not directly provide for judicial review of Council's actions.[60] The Court itself acknowledged this situation in the Expenses[61] case. The absence of a clear enumeration of a review mechanism

---

57   The Free Dictionary.com at <http://www.thefreedictionary.com/Judicial%20review>.

58   Bedjaoui *supra* note 29, p. 105.

59   Bernd *supra* note 51. 'Despite the fact that the Court, according to Article 92 of the Charter, is the "main judicial organ" of the United Nations, it has not been endowed with competences similar to those of a national constitutional court." , p. 525.

60   Bowett *supra* note 34, p. 73.

61   *Ibid.*, Bowett. The Court noted that "In the legal system of States, there is often some procedure for determining the validity of even a legislative or governmental act, but no analogous procedure is to be found in the structure of the United Nations," quoting from Certain Expenses of the United Nations etc. Advisory Opinion of 29 July 1962: ICJ Reports, 1962, at 168, p. 77.

in the Charter does not mean the International Court of Justice or other judicial bodies could not undertake it. However, in the absence of inbuilt mechanisms to ensure compliance with Charter provisions, it is difficult to determine conclusively the *ultra vires* of a Council action.

The Charter provides that legal disputes should as a general rule be referred by the parties to the International Court of Justice.[62] However, this provision has not been made much use of.[63] Similarly, the Court's Advisory Opinion as provided under Article 96(1) of the Charter has not been used much. The Court can also use its incidental competence, in the course of an inter-state dispute, to pronounce on the validity and effect of a Security Council resolution.[64] However, the utility of such competence, which depends on the acceptance by both parties of the Court's jurisdiction, remains questionable.[65]

Notwithstanding the controversy surrounding the notion, scope and modalities of judicial review, the recent actions of the Court in the Lockerbie case, have raised hopes of judicial review of Council actions in future. Other instances in the past also point towards this trend. [66]

i.   Lockerbie Case

This case between Libya and United Kingdom and United States related to the bombing of a Pan Am flight 103 from London to New York over Lockerbie on 21 September 1988. Libya refused to comply with the UN Security Council Resolution 731 (1992) which asked it to surrender two Libyans suspected of the bombing and filed an application[67] in the ICJ under Article 14 (1) of the Montreal Convention.[68]

---

62   See Article 36 (3) of the UN Charter.

63   Bowett *supra* note 34. Bowett mentions that this provision has been used only once by the Security Council in the 1947 Corfu Channel Case between the United Kingdom and Albania. p. 74.

64   *Ibid*, p. 77.

65   *Ibid*., pp. 77-78.

66   See Bardo Fassbender, Reforming the United Nations, in *Die Friedens Warte, Blätter für internationale Verständigung und zwischenstaatliche Organisation*, Herausgeber: Knut Ipsen, Volker Rittberger, Christian Tomuschat, Band 73, Heft 4, 1998, pp. 427-442. It may also be noted that in the Nicaragua case and the recent ICJ Advisory Opinion on the construction of Wall, the Court rejected objections to its jurisdiction.

67   Bernd *supra* note 51. Libya asked the Court to find that it had complied with all of its obligations under the Montreal Convention, that the United Kingdom and United States were in violation of their obligations under that Convention and that they were obliged to desist from the use of any force or threats against Libya, quoting from Questions Of Interpretation And Application Of The 1971 Montreal Convention Arising From The Aerial Incident At Lockerbie (Libyan Arab Jamahiriya v. United Kingdom), p. 520.

68   Article 14 (1) of the Convention For The Suppression Of Unlawful Acts Against The Safety Of Civil Aviation, Montreal, 23 September 1971 reads: "Any dispute between two or more Contracting States concerning the interpretation or application of this Convention which cannot be settled through negotiation, shall, at the request of one of them, be submitted to arbitration. If within six months from the date of the request

The Security Council adopted Resolution 748 (1992) on 31 March 1992 against Libya again calling on the latter to comply with the American and British request for surrender of Libyan suspects. On 14 April 1992, the Court dismissed the Libyan application for provisional measures on the ground that the parties were obliged to accept and carry out Security Council resolutions in accordance with Article 25 of the Charter, and that this obligation *prima facie* also applied to Resolution 748 (1992). For this reason, the Court considered the rights of Libya, under the Montreal Convention as inappropriate for protection by means of provisional measures.[69] Resolution 883 (1993) repeated its finding that Libya's refusal to extradite the suspects constituted a threat to the peace.[70]

In its decision on the preliminary objections raised by the respondents, the Court found that it had jurisdiction[71] in the case. The Court dismissed the objection regarding the effect of Resolutions 748 (1992) and 883 (1993) on the ground, besides others, that since these resolutions had been adopted after the filing of the application, they could not affect the jurisdiction of the Court.[72] It was thus reasserting the position it had taken in the Advisory Opinion in the Namibia case[73] implying that its judicial functions included the power of judicial review covering also the resolutions of the Security Council.[74] Accordingly in the Lockerbie case Article 7 and 14 of the Montreal Convention could have formed the jurisdictional basis for judicial review of Security Council Resolutions 748 (1992) and 883 (1993).[75] It also reaffirmed that the competence of the Security Council for the maintenance of international peace and security is not exclusive[76] and that there is no rule which

---

for arbitration the Parties are unable to agree on the organization of the arbitration, any one of those Parties may refer the dispute to the International Court of Justice by request in conformity with the Statute of the Court."

69   Bernd *supra* note 51, p. 521.

70   *Ibid.*, p. 522.

71   *Ibid.*, p. 523.

72   *Ibid.*, p. 524 quoting from the Lockerbie, Preliminary Objections, para. 37.

73   *Ibid.*, p. 527 quoting from Legal consequences for States of the Continued Presence of south Africa in Namibia (South West Africa) Notwithstanding Security Council Resolution 276 (1970), Advisory Opinion, ICJ Reports (1971) 16, at 45. In the Namibia case the Court held, "Undoubtedly, the Court does not possess powers of judicial review or appeal in respect of the decisions taken by the UN organs concerned. However, in the exercise of its judicial function and since objections have been advanced the Court, in the course of its reasoning, will consider these objections before determining any legal consequences arising form those resolutions."

74   *Ibid.* Bernd clarifies that this is an incidental review function and not an independent power of judicial review. p. 527.

75   *Ibid.* As Bernd points out had Article 7 of the Montreal Convention been construed so as to guarantee Libya a right not to surrender the alleged offenders, then a conflict would exist between Article 7 and Security Council resolutions 748 (1992) and 883 (1993), which require the surrender of the suspects. pp. 530-531.

76   *Ibid.*, p. 531.

prohibits simultaneous proceedings before Court and the Council even if the latter is seized of an affair under Chapter VII of the Charter.[77]

These findings could have far-reaching implications for the relationship between the Court and the Security Council. Although the Court could not go into the merits stage in the Lockerbie case,[78] where it could have pronounced on the validity of the Security Council resolutions, it did indicate that it could undertake such an enterprise should the necessary conditions for it be present. It could also consider whether a Security Council resolution is *ultra vires* of the Charter and that the Council cannot be regarded as the ultimate interpreter of its own bases of jurisdiction.[79] The presumption of validity of Security Council resolutions does not absolve the Court from the fundamental duty that follows from its judicial function and it does not affect the standard of legal scrutiny for Security Council resolutions.[80]

The wording of Article 39 of the Charter does not imply that the Council's determinations of the existence of a threat to the peace, breach of the peace or act of aggression would have preclusive effect. [81] It would be difficult to find in the drafting history of the Charter convincing evidence for a discretionary competence of the Council under Article 39.[82] An unlimited discretion under Article 39 would on the one hand eliminate differences between Chapter VI and VII, it would also allow the Council to have unlimited involvement in the affairs of member states.[83] The terms used in Article 39 are thus, within the ambit of legal interpretation.[84]

The Lockerbie Case is significant as it serves as a paradigm for the conflict between law and politics in international relations.[85] The Court resisted all attempts to remove Chapter VII of the Charter from the ambit of legal interpretation.[86] However, this issue remains politically charged as it involves a check on the authority of the Security Council. There is palpable resistance[87] among those who favor a strong Security Council, to seeking legal advice from ICJ and subjecting Council's decisions to judicial control. Moreover, the Council could not discharge its functions if member states were able to question its decisions.

---

77   *Ibid.*, p. 532.

78   In April 1999, Libya surrendered the two accused to stand trial in The Netherlands.

79   Bernd *supra* note 51, p. 536.

80   *Ibid.*, Bernd *supra* note 51, p. 539.

81   *Ibid.*, p. 541.

82   *Ibid.*, p. 542.

83   *Ibid.*, p. 542.

84   *Ibid.*, p. 543.

85   *Ibid.*, p. 546.

86   *Ibid.*, p. 546.

87   Bowett *supra* note 34. Bowett says that the "real reason for ... reluctance to seek the Court's opinion ... lies in the attitudes of the Members, particularly the permanent Members, of the Security Council." p. 76.

One can anticipate legal challenges to the decisions or actions of the Council from states, as well as from other subjects of Council's actions[88] if they are not strictly in accordance with the principles of the Charter.[89] The Charter does not seem to have prohibited member states from doing so.[90] The challenges could be triggered by the impact on the rights and obligations of these subjects flowing from Council's actions, such as freezing of assets, imposition of sanctions or inclusion in the list of terrorists by the Council. However, it is not clear how such challenges could be made effectively and what could be their political implications including impact on the rights and obligations of the challenger.[91]

3.   Changing Role of the Security Council

The functions of the Council under the Charter are limited to maintaining international peace and security. It has not been invested with absolute powers in all fields. However, the Council has been quite innovative in venturing into areas which are not necessarily linked to imminent threats to peace and security. It has been involved in recent years in peacekeeping missions with more emphasis on the humanitarian aspects,[92] use of force and imposition of sanctions under Chapter VII,[93] determination of boundaries without the consent of affected states,[94] humanitarian interventions, non-proliferation of weapons of mass destruction[95] and terrorism.[96] It has also started creating bodies such as the International Criminal Tribunals for the Former Yugoslavia[97] and Rwanda[98] and the Special Court for Sierra Leone.[99] The Council is also involved in nation building tasks especially in Afghanistan and Iraq.

---

88   See Patel *supra* note 43 about the Dusko Tadic Case.

89   Bedjaoui *supra* note 29. Quoting Henri Rolin who refers to the "jurisdictional necessity of modern society" to institute a means of control over majority decisions affecting the rights and obligations of states. "Les principes de droit international public", *Recueil des cours de l'Académie de droit international de la Haye*, Vol. 77, 1950-II, p. 458, p. 59.

90   Nicolas Angelet *supra* note 54.

91   Mathias J. Herdegen, "The 'Constitutionalization' of the UN Security System, in 27 *Vand. J. Transnat'l L.* 135 (1994), at p. 159. The writer remarks, "a Member State will deny the validity of a mandatory Security Council resolution always at its own risk, a risk only mitigated by the speculative hope of subsequent vindication by the ICJ."

92   Higgins *supra* note 3, p. 3.

93   Blokker *supra* note 20. Blokker cites instances of authorization of force by the UN between 1990-1999. pp. 543-544.

94   Crawford *supra* note 18, p. 11.

95   See UNSCR 1540 adopted on 28 April 2004.

96   See UNSCR 1267 (1999), 1333 (2000), 1363 (2001), 1368 (2001), 1373 (2001), 1377 (2001), 1390 (2002), 1455 (2003), 1456 (2003), 1526 (2004).

97   Established under UNSCR 827 (1993).

98   Established under UNSCR 955 (1994).

99   Established under UNSCR 1315 (2000).

Like the United Nations itself, the Security Council has undergone changes since its establishment. These changes relate to its composition, mandate, functions and working methods. Thus the evolution of the Security Council has entailed the following changes:

a. Subject: Initially the Council addressed mostly international (or inter-state) conflicts and disputes. This has changed. The majority of the Council's resolutions in the post-Cold War period have dealt with internal rather than inter-state conflicts. Also, in the past, only states were subjects of Council's actions and decisions. Now, the Council directs its actions and decisions to states as well as non-state actors[100] and even individuals.[101]

b. Scope: With the end of the cold war, the Council has been able to play an active role in terms of an increasing use of Chapter VII, and greater involvement[102] in international issues. This activism has been helped by a greater understanding among the permanent members and an expanded interpretation of threats to international peace and security.

c. Composition: As mentioned above the size of the Council was increased from 11 to 15. This increase did have an effect on the voting patterns of the Council but could not change the decisive powers of the permanent members over non-procedural decisions.[103]

d. The decision-making process of the Security Council, particularly the instrument of veto, remains controversial but omnipresent. The use or threat of use of veto can prevent or delay decisions, force 'compromises', dilute or strengthen language used in a resolution or a presidential statement of the Council. It constrains the ability of the Council to treat all situations uniformly and consistently and subjects it to the 'control' or overwhelming influence of the five permanent members. The veto is conceptually, in conflict with democratic principles. The power to 'veto' a decision of the Council is one of the most striking symbols of inequality sanctioned by the Charter. The instances

---

100   See P.H. Kooijmans, "The Security Council and Non-State Entities as Parties to Conflicts", in *International Law: Theory and Practice, Essays in Honour of Eric Suy*, edited by Karel Wellens, Martinus Nijhoff Publishers, 1998, pp. 333-346. Kooijmans refers to the Palestinian war of 1948 wherein the Security Council was confronted for the first time with a non-state entity. See also Security Council Resolutions 43 (1948) of 1 April 1948 and 46 (1948) of 17 April 1948. According to Kooijmans the "conclusion of an *internationalized* peace-agreement may lead to a restricted, temporary international legal personality for non-state parties to an internal armed conflict." p. 340.

101   *Ibid.* Kooijmans points out the emphasis on individual responsibility placed by the Security Council for the violations of international humanitarian law in Resolution 941 (1994), p. 339.

102   In 1988 the Council held 55 formal meetings and 62 informal consultations. In contrast, the corresponding figures for 2002 were 259. Website of the Global Policy Forum at <http://www.globalpolicy.org/security/data/secmgtab.htm>.

103   Helen Leigh-Phippard, "Remaking the Security Council: The Options", in *Documents on Reform of the United Nations*, Edited by Paul Taylor, Sam Daws and Ute Adamczick-Gerteis, Dartmouth Publishing Company Ltd, 1997. pp. 427-8.

of abuse of this power have strengthened calls for its elimination or regulation at least to make it more objective and predictable.

e.   Implementation of Council decisions: The Council uses different methods to implement its decisions including authorization of force, imposition of sanctions, humanitarian intervention, creation of judicial tribunals, demarcation of boundaries, appointment of special representatives, inspection and monitoring teams, field visits, sanctions committees, reporting requirements, compensation commissions etc. Not all of these measures are derived from the specific language of the Charter.

f.   Collective security and self-defence: A limited right of self-defense is also granted under Article 51 of the Charter, 'until the Security Council has taken measures necessary to maintain international peace and security.' However, there have been increasingly expansive claims by some powerful states to utilize and extend the right of self-defence accorded under Article 51.[104] Other, less powerful, states have tended to interpret the provision more narrowly. Security Council resolutions have been used to expand the concept of self-defence. Thus the reaffirmation of right of individual and collective self-defense in the Preamble of Resolution 1373 (2001) facilitated the armed attack on Afghanistan by the United States in 2001. But many questions remain regarding the exact contours of the Charter based right to self-defense.[105]

g.   Authorization of use of force: The power of the Security Council to adopt resolutions authorizing member states to take enforcement action is not clearly supported by the UN Charter.[106] Such authorizations also make it difficult to distinguish actions taken under Article 51 from actions under Article 42.[107] It is clear that the Security Council does not have the means to enforce its decisions except such means as are provided by member states under Article 43 and 45 of the Charter. Therefore, the Council has to rely on such states to provide the armed forces when needed for enforcement purposes. Despite the emergence of UN peacekeeping, the Council has, in practical terms, to rely on the armed forces of states. This allows such states to plan, initiate and carry

---

104   Rosalyn Higgins, "The UN Security Council and the Individual State", in *The Changing Constitution of the United Nations*, The British Institute of International and Comparative Law, London, 1997. Higgins has aptly remarked about Article 51 of the Charter "As the only category available for the legitimate use of force by the individual State, its definition had to be expansive." p. 43.

105   Article 51 of the UN Charter, which provides, "Nothing in the present Charter shall impair the inherent right of individual or collective self-defence if an armed attack occurs against a Member of the United Nations, until the Security Council has taken measures necessary to maintain international peace and security. Measures taken by Members in the exercise of this right of self-defence shall be immediately reported to the Security Council and shall not in any way affect the authority and responsibility of the Security Council under the present Charter to take at any time such action as it deems necessary in order to maintain or restore international peace and security."

106   Blokker *supra* note 20, p. 547.

107   Higgins *supra* note 104, p. 45.

on military actions. Naturally, this reliance advantages the powerful states. However, conferring total discretion on a state or states to act on behalf of the Council would be *ultra vires*[108] of the Charter. The possibility of abuse of such authorizations cannot be ruled out, especially in the absence of an effective oversight mechanism. It naturally raises the question about the scope of Council's powers to authorize use of force. And it blurs the UN's 'control' of the process of the use of force.[109]

h.   The developing thesis of so-called humanitarian intervention, utilized in some recent situations, is also increasing the tensions between Council action and the general principles of international law, including sovereignty and territorial integrity of states. The Charter provides for the use of force only in accordance with the purposes of the UN Charter. However, states have at times resorted to the use of force on various grounds, some of which could be construed not to be in accordance with the "purposes" of the UN Charter.

i.   Impact of Security Council's activism: Security Council's post Cold War activism is raising concerns among states, particularly smaller states, international and regional organizations, individuals and not the least the UN system.[110] The Council's decisions can frequently erode their rights and obligations and they have no established means by which to secure remedies for such erosion since the Council is, at present, not legally or politically accountable to any other body or forum.

j.   The UN Charter invests the Security Council with the primary, *not* exclusive, responsibility for the maintenance of international peace and security. However, the increasing activism of the Security Council, accompanied by an expanded conception of international peace and security, seems to have evolved at the cost of role of other UN organs and bodies, including ECOSOC and General Assembly.[111] The Council is adopting an exclusivist stance, par-

---

108   Bowett, *supra* note 34, p. 86

109   Fox *supra* note 56, pp. xx, xxv, xxvi and xxvii.

110   Laurence Helfer, *Constitutional Analogies in the International Legal System*, available at the website of the Social Science Research Network Electronic Paper Collection at: <http://ssrn.com/abstract=437180>, "Where treaty obligations are dynamic and evolve through institutional processes outside of any one state's control, compliance with those obligations may clash with domestic preferences and raise trenchant legitimacy concerns. The formal rules of state consent to treaties do little to ameliorate these concerns, suggesting the need for alternative sources of legitimacy to support adherence to international agreements and institutions."

111   Abi-Saab *supra* note 8. According to Abi-Saab, the function of the General Assembly in 1960s and the 1970s as the "oracle" of the international community and its norm-setting contributions in the fields of human rights, the environment and development of international law has been completely reversed with the end of cold war. p. 31. The Council has also attempted to exercise financial powers reserved to the General Assembly. See Eric Suy in "The Role of the United Nations General Assembly", in *The Changing Constitution of the United Nations*, The British Institute of International and Comparative Law, London, 1997, p. 60.

ticularly towards General Assembly, not only in areas where they have concurrent jurisdiction but also in areas where General Assembly has exclusive
jurisdiction.[112] The General Assembly is thus reduced to retaining importance
only in budgetary matters and the election of non-permanent members of the
Security Council.[113] Ironically, during the cold war paralysis of the Security
Council, the General Assembly had been sought to be invested with powers
to offset the inaction of the Security Council through such moves as the Uniting for Peace resolution mechanism[114] which attempted to shift the "*locus* of
action within the Organization" to the General Assembly.[115]

k.   The absence of checks and balances in the Charter has led to the concentra-
tion of real decision-making powers within the Council's permanent members
making the process less and less representative and transparent. The decision
making process of the Council raises issues of accountability, transparency,[116]
and consistent application.[117] It has also led to the blurring of delineation of
responsibilities among different UN organs.

l.   The changing role of Security Council also raises issues of constitutional weaknesses within the UN system such as absence of separation of powers, lack of
accountability[118] and "an almost total lack of institutional means for implementing the principle of rule of law on the part of individual Member States
(other than the permanent members of the Security Council)."[119] Not the least
are issues of internal administration and recurring fiscal weaknesses[120] within
the UN system brought to the fore as a result of the changes in the Council's
role. This has necessitated a new focus on procedural accuracy and transparency of Council's actions.

m.   The adoption by Security Council of Resolution 1373 (2001) on counter terrorism and Resolution 1540 (2004) on terrorism and weapons of mass destruction
points to a new kind of rule making by the Security Council. These resolutions

---

112   *Ibid.*, pp. 37-38.

113   Eric Suy *supra* note 41, p. 56.

114   Bardo Fassbender *supra* note 66, p. 433.

115   Abi-Saab *supra* note 8, p. 29.

116   Abi-Saab *supra* note 8. According to Abi-Saab transparency became an issue in the
1970s when the Council "suddenly became secretive". pp. 37-38.

117   Fox *supra* note 56. According to Fox, the decision-making equation of the Council
scarcely conforms to the requirement of either accountability or transparency. It flouts
the rights of participation of non-permanent members and in a broader sense the
parliamentary supervision which the assembly should exercise. The selective, as well
as intermittent, application of forcible measures to some but not all situations which
might objectively qualify as a threat to the peace or a breach of peace, disregards, as the
requirements of consistency, and introduces double standards which undermine the
credibility of the Organization. p. xxviii.

118   Crawford *supra* note 18, p. 11.

119   *Ibid.*, p. 12.

120   *Ibid.*, p. 11.

deal with generic issues and amorphous threats, not specific threats to international peace and security. The provisions of these resolutions are prescriptive, rather pre-emptive, and not limited to addressing imminent threats. The resultant creation of new obligations on member states in the form of countering terrorism and non proliferation of weapons of mass destruction raises serious questions about the future of international law making. Needless to say that such law making is beyond the competence of the Council, and raises issues of procedural and substantive normativity.[121] In fact attempts to transform the Security Council into a law making chamber contrary to the spirit and language of the Charter reduces its role as an apologist for power.[122]

4.   Security Council's Future Orientation

The UN system in general, and the Security Council in particular, have an important role to play in the international system. The Council has to provide a credible system of collective security to minimize the resort to use of force and enable the peoples of the world to live in peace and harmony. Its task would be facilitated if it is representative, consistent and objective in its actions and promotes a participative and inclusive approach to allow its wider membership to contribute to its work. It cannot afford to ignore the wishes and aspirations of the United Nations. The powers vested in the Council under the Charter are in the nature of a trust and a delegation from the entire membership of the UN. And they should be able to claim a right of supervision on how this responsibility is exercised on their behalf.[123]

The Council is bound to respect the mandate of other UN bodies. It cannot assume a legislative or judicial role. Its recent actions belie a tendency on the part of the Council to interpret its powers expansively at the cost of other UN bodies. However, the emerging jurisprudence from different judicial sources is reassuring in that it has given a cue to the Security Council that its actions could be subjected to review if the need arose. The Council need not expedite a showdown with the ICJ or other international adjudicative bodies by curbing its tendency to overstep its competence or pretending to be a lawmaker. In the final analysis self restraint by the Council and introduction of internal reforms to address its democratic deficit and procedural deficiencies would be the most desirable course of action.

There is no disagreement over the need for reform of the UN system, particularly the reform of its Security Council. A change in the composition and voting powers of the Council could promote pluralism, curb unilateralist tendencies and also affect the powers of the Security Council. It could be a step towards greater democratization of the decision-making process of the Council by making it more representative. However, this objective would be defeated if the Changes in the

---

121   See Anthea *supra* note 45, pp. 761-770.

122   *Ibid.*

123   Suy *supra* note 41, p. 64.

Council left the veto in place, and enlarged the number of UN Members entitled to the more "privileged" position of permanent membership of the Security Council.

Reform of the Council, especially changing the privileged position of its permanent members, may not be feasible as long as they do not consent to such changes. The Charter itself does not provide an alternative method for a Charter revision that would not entail the opposition of any one of the five permanent members. Unless some mechanism for change is evolved, there is a danger that the Security Council's authority, if applied unequally and unjustly, could be questioned and challenged by a growing number of aggrieved states or parties, thus eroding the stability and predictability of international relations and eroding international peace and security.

Thus, the reform of the Council coupled with a commitment to follow a principled, objective, and consistent position, in accordance with principles of international law and justice would help promote cooperative multilateralism which remains the best paradigm for the future in finding peaceful, just and durable solutions to conflicts and disputes.

A reformed Security Council may be entrusted the task of framing rules and regulations within the realm of maintenance of international peace and security subject to certain clearly defined provisos. Thus, the Council's powers should be:

a.   Limited to the maintenance of international peace and security and should not be used for replacing international law-making processes.
b.   Limited to giving effect to existing rights and obligations and avoid creating new rights and obligations.
c.   Subject to clear guidelines.
d.   Used in an objective and consistent manner.
e.   Used only for situations of imminent threats to international peace and security and not for making general rules and regulations of a long-term nature.
f.   Subject to the judicial review of the International Court of Justice and other international adjudicatory bodies. The subjects of Council actions should have the right to challenge the decisions of the Council.

In a more general vein, the powers of the Council should be subject to Charter principles, and international law and justice. It should respect human rights and *jus cogens*. The Council should also meet the following expectations of the international community expressed from time to time:

a.   The Council should be made more representative and democratic in its composition procedure and practice. It should not, through its actions, sideline the parliaments of the world. It should be more responsive to the need to safeguard the interests and rights of the developing countries.
b.   In order to promote objective and non-discriminatory approach, the Security Council should support efforts to limit the use of force strictly within the ambit of Articles 42 and 51 of the Charter.
c.   The Council should avoid facilitation, in any way, of preemptive wars or humanitarian interventions which are likely to result in "multilateral unilateral-

ism" by the powerful and erode, not enhance, international peace and security.

d.   Internal reform of the Security Council, including transparency, is indispensable. The use of veto power needs to be regulated and subjected to objective criteria to make it more predictable. Consideration could also be given to abolishing veto and replacing it by majority voting.

e.   The United Nations role in peace making, peace keeping and preventive diplomacy cannot be underestimated. The Security Council should intensify its efforts in ensuring provision of assistance to conflict ridden and war torn societies. It should also redouble its role in promoting the pacific settlement of international disputes.

f.   The Council should work in a complementary manner with other UN organs and bodies and strengthen the role of international and regional organizations in different fields. The proposal of establishing "*ad hoc* composite committees"[124] of the three principle organs of the United Nations, the Security Council, the General Assembly and the ECOSOC could be pursued further to effectively address complex crises and emergencies.

g.   The power of judicial review of Council decisions should be clearly delineated to the ICJ and other international adjudicative bodies in a manner that it does not constrain the Council's powers to take immediate action while ensuring accountability.

h.   A mechanism should be evolved to enable states, organizations and individuals to seek redress if their rights have been affected by the Council actions or decisions. In particular, the affected state(s) should be enabled to petition the General Assembly for soliciting an opinion from the ICJ on an impugned decision(s) of the Security Council. In accordance with Article 94 of the Charter, the Security Council should comply with the decisions of the ICJ.

i.   The Powers and practices of the Security Council should be studied closely by the International Law Commission to assist states in the reform of this institution.

5.   Conclusion

The Preamble to the UN Charter expresses the determination of the peoples of the United Nations to save the succeeding generations from the scourge of war. The Charter is also premised on other common interests such as international peace and security. These interests would be ill served if the Council were to be handed a *carte blanche* to do what it deems fit without any accountability. Worse still would be its actions which seek to replace international law making and concentrate this

---

124   The proposal was made by Pakistan at the Wrap-up Session of the Security Council on Conflicts in Africa: Security Council missions and United Nations mechanisms to promote peace and security, held on 30 May 2003, S/PV.4766 (Resumption 1), p. 23, and at the Open meeting of the Security Council on Complex Crises and United Nations Response, held on 28th May 2004, See S/PV.4980, p. 30.

power in a body which continues to be un-democratic in its decision making and suffers from representational problems. The Security Council is an instrument of power and often its actions are cloaked in legality. In the absence of effective accountability, the powers of the Security Council to make international law would license a powerful minority to dominate the rest in addition to undermining the very foundation of the Charter.

In order to maintain the confidence and trust of the international community in the United Nations system, the Security Council should refrain from assuming law making functions. It could exercise its functions for the maintenance of international peace and security subject to certain clear and unambiguous limitations under the judicial control of the ICJ and other international adjudicatory bodies. If there is a need to improve the process of international law making, it could be done by strengthening forums which have the necessary representational credentials like the UN General Assembly. This would be facilitated by promoting harmony and complementarity among different UN organs. Last but not the least, the potential of international parliaments should be fully realized in the progressive development of international law through the timely adoption of international agreements and harmonization of national legislations in accordance with international treaties and agreements. These steps could be facilitated if the process of UN reform were to be completed[125] expeditiously.

Through its involvement in diverse fields in different parts of the world, the UN presence has raised hopes that it could provide support and alternate leadership where national institutions have failed to do so. Its potential in promoting cooperative multilateralism to address challenges common to mankind need not be underestimated. Nor could one dispute its contribution to the normative development of international law. As one of the most important organs of the UN system, the Council could immensely contribute to UN's efforts to realize the ideals of the United Nations. If the Council could conform its actions to the spirit and letter of the Charter as well as other principles of international law, it could be sure to have contributed to the march of the international community towards constitutionalism and rule of law.

---

125   Abi-Saab *supra* note 8, pp. 31-32. At its 47th Session, the General Assembly added to its agenda an item entitled, "Question of equitable representation on and increase in the membership of the Security Council". The Report of the Secretary General as requested by Resolution 47/62 was submitted to the 48th Session of the General Assembly. By Resolution 48/26, the General Assembly established an open ended working group to consider all aspects of the question in the light of the Report and the discussions in the Assembly. The UN members are currently discussing reform of the United Nations against the backdrop of reports by the High Level Panel of the UN Secretary General on Threats, Challenges and Change (*A More Secure World: Our Shared Responsibility*), by the UN Secretary General (*In Larger Freedom: Towards Development, Security and Human Rights for All*) and by the President of the UN General Assembly (*Draft Outcome Document for the High-level Plenary Meeting of the General Assembly, 14-16 September 2005*).

17. Legislative Powers of the Security Council

Axel Marschik *

1. Introduction

The years 2003 and 2004 were not kind to the United Nations. The inability of the Security Council to agree on a strategy for Iraq in 2003 frustrated those who had demanded authorization to intervene as well as those who had counted on the UN to prevent war. The terrorist attack against the UN Mission in Baghdad traumatized the organization and its staff. Allegations of corruption and fraud in connection with the UN's Oil-for-food program, charges of sexual misconduct of peacekeepers, the helplessness of the UN in the Darfur crisis and in regard to other emerging threats fuelled doubts as to the future effective role of the organization and resulted in a severe negative campaign by some UN critics.[1] In an interview, Secretary General Kofi Annan designated 2004 as *"annus horribilis"* for the UN.

To the chagrin of its critics, however, the UN asserted itself in those same two years as more relevant than ever. The public debates on Iraq had brought unprecedented attention to the organization and created a new public awareness about its work. The high-level debates in the General Assembly in 2003 and 2004 demonstrated near universal support for multilateralism and the UN. The relevance of the organization was particularly evident in the relentless activity of the much maligned Security Council.[2] In early 2004, Secretary General Annan had to warn

---

*   The author is the Deputy Permanent Representative of Austria to the United Nations in New York. The views expressed in this article cannot be attributed to the Austrian Foreign Ministry. Sincere thanks are due to Ambassador Andrew Jacovides for supplying much inspiration for this article.

1   Rosett, The UN Needs Regime Change, The Wall Street Journal Europe, 29 December 2004, A/7. Some believed the time had come to celebrate the demise of the United Nations; see Perle, Thank God for the Death of the UN, The Guardian, 21 March 2003, 1/26; The Wall Street Journal (editorial), Au Revoir, Security Council, The Wall Street Journal, 21 March 2003, A/14. For a more nuanced analysis see Glennon, Why the Security Council Failed, Foreign Affairs 82 (2003), Number 3 (May/June), 16.

2   Each year the Council adopted more resolutions than, for instance, in 2000 or 2001.

Ronald St. John Macdonald & Douglas M. Johnston (eds.), Towards World Constitutionalism, *pp. 457-492.*
© *2005 Koninklijke Brill NV. Printed in The Netherlands. ISBN 90 04 14612 1.*

the Council that it was establishing so many peacekeeping missions that, by the end of the year, the UN's capacities would be severely over-extended.[3] The creation of a prominent high level panel launched a serious effort to improve the UN and invigorated the debate on Council reform. Several States declared their interest in becoming permanent or semi-permanent members.[4] Contrary to many expectations, the UN's Security Council apparently managed to gain, rather than lose, in attractiveness and relevance.

There are several reasons for this. The Iraq-crisis solidified the Security Council as the principle world stage for international political debate. Even after the negotiations broke down, the major powers remained committed to the UN and continued their cooperation in the Council. States have also noted the Council's increasing interest in addressing issues of general concern, an exercise normally deemed a function of the General Assembly. Relying on a broader analysis of the factors influencing international peace and security and the recognition of the need to address these issues, the Council initially restricted itself to general debates.[5] Since 2001, however, it has begun using its powers to create binding obligations on the Member States to regulate general areas of international relations. In a lecture in 2003 Judge Guillaume of the International Court of Justice characterized this activity of the Security Council as follows:

> By a broadened interpretation of its mandate, it is now assuming not only powers of action but also legislative powers in the interest of international peace and security.[6]

The creation of general international norms is not a task the Security Council was conceived for. The Council's activism after the Cold War and its interest in assuming functions beyond its primary mandate had already generated unease in the mid-1990s. The limited membership and the decision-making procedures raised doubts whether it was an appropriate body to represent the international community in areas beyond the narrow field of peace-enforcement. Lawmaking by the Security Council raises these concerns again. The principles of legal equality and consent are vital principles in the creation of international law. A shift to lawmaking by binding decree would have considerable consequences for the current in-

---

3   Statement of the Secretary General at the 4970th meeting of the Security Council on 17 May 2004; UN-Doc. S/PV.4970 at 4; see also Powers, Business as usual at the UN, Foreign Policy 144 (2004), (September/October), 38.

4   Interest in the non-permanent category also rose dramatically. Candidatures for elected membership have been announced for terms almost 30 years in the future. Oman, for example, has announced its candidature for a non-permanent seat of the Asian Group for the period 2030-2031.

5   See the examples listed in Wallensteen and Johansson, Security Council Decisions in Perspective, in Malone (ed.), The UN Security Council – From the Cold War to the 21st Century (2004), 17 at 29.

6   Guillaume, Terrorism and International Law, Grotius Lecture at the British Institute of International and Comparative Law, held on 13 November 2003, 8.

ternational order. Some international lawyers and States are trying to dissuade the Council from transforming this trend into regular practice. Others are prepared to accept the legislative role in principle but strive for safeguards to protect the rights and interests of States and individuals.

Faced with new global threats, such as terrorism and the proliferation of weapons of mass destruction, the international community needs to consider all reasonable options of effective reaction, including the possible advantages and disadvantages of having the Security Council assume the role of world legislator. Seeking to facilitate such a discussion this chapter will analyze the Council's relevant practice and determine whether such a legislative function would be lawful and legitimate. It will attempt to establish the formal parameters of lawmaking, its potential content and limitations. The chapter seeks to contribute to the efforts to secure a role for the Council that is accepted and supported by the international community in order to enable it to successfully and legitimately fulfill its functions in maintaining international peace and security.

2.   Points of Departure

A.   *Context and Methodology*

The legal setting for the present analysis is the UN Charter. Irrespective of whether one regards the Charter a constitution or a multilateral treaty,[7] the legal regime of the United Nations is a sub-system of general international law: It contains primary norms (obligations on States) and secondary norms, norms that regulate the primary norms (creation, modification, implementation, etc.).[8] Questions regarding the existence of legislative powers of one of the organs of a sub-system must first be examined in the light of the rules of the sub-system itself.[9] Should those not suffice, recourse may be taken in open subsystems to the rules of interpretation of general international law to determine the organ's competences. This necessitates an analysis of the practice of the organ and the reaction thereto by the Members States.

---

7   Regarding this distinction see Macdonald, Fundamental Norms in Contemporary International Law, CYIL 25 (1987), 115 at 119 – 128. With emphasis on socialist literature: Macdonald, The United Nations Charter: Constitution or Contract, in Macdonald and Johnston, (eds.) *The Structure and Process of International Law* (1983), 889.

8   To the distinction between primary and secondary norms, proposed by Hart, The Concept of Law (1961), 92, and to sub-systems in international law see Zemanek, The Legal Foundations of the International System, Offprint from the *Recueil des Cours* 266 (1997), 63 and 233-36; Marschik, Too much Order – The Impact of Special Secondary Norms on the Unity and Efficacy of the International Legal System, in EJIL 9 (1998), 212.

9   The ICJ stated in the advisory opinion on the admission of new members: "The political character of an organ cannot release it from the observance of the treaty provisions established by the Charter when they constitute limitations on its powers or criteria for its judgement. To ascertain whether an organ has the freedom of choice for its decisions, reference must be made to the terms of its constitution."; Admission of a State to the United Nations (Advisory Opinion of 28 May 1948), ICJ Reports (1948) 64.

Consequently, this article will briefly examine the UN Charter to determine whether it can serve as the legal basis for law-making functions and competences. In the absence of such a basis in the Charter, the competences will be sought in general international law, especially in the concepts of implied powers and subsequent practice. Much attention will be given to the practice of the Security Council and to the reaction of the States. The chapter will not confine itself to descriptions of practice. It is believed, however, that both analysis and theory regarding the question of legislative powers of the Council would benefit from reliance on empirical evidence. The final section will be devoted to the possible consequences of legislative powers of the Council on the UN and international law and propose procedures or conditions to ensure the legitimacy of future lawmaking efforts.

B.   Definitions and Use of Terms

Normally used in the context of rule-making processes within a State, the terms "legislation" and "legislative powers" are not directly transferable to international law, which lacks similar structures or decision-making processes. In the literature on the issue the terms "legislative" or "law-making" powers of the Security Council have been used in very different ways. Some authors who understand the UN Charter as a more or less coherent legal sub-system or "constitution" with organs acting in many ways similar to State organs accept most binding decisions as "laws" or "norms".[10] Others deduce from the political enforcement functions of the Council a general lack of powers to enact real "legislation".[11] A fairly wide approach is adopted by Alvarez in his analysis of the Security Council's acts from the perspective of their legal relevance for the International Court of Justice (ICJ): Legal acts that the ICJ would have to take into account in its findings are understood as "Council-generated law".[12]

---

10   Franck, The "Powers of Appreciation": Who is the Ultimate Guardian of UN Legality, AJIL 86 (1992), 519 at 520; Kirgis, The Security Council's first Fifty Years, AJIL 89 (1995), 506 at 520. Some authors focus predominantly on the effect of the decision-making process by the Council on the rights of the Member States to determine whether the underlying powers are legislative or executive in nature; Arangio-Ruiz, On the Security Council's Law-Making, Rivista di Diritto Internazionale 83 (2000), 609 at 610. Harper also regards the determination by the Council that the possession of certain chemicals is a threat to the peace in SC-Res. 687 as a legislative act; Harper, Does the United Nations Security Council have the competence to act as Court and Legislature? New York University Journal of International Law and Politics 27 (1994) 103 at 128.

11   Perrin de Brichambaut, The Role of the United Nations Security Council in the International Legal System, in Byers (ed.) *The Role of Law in International Politics* (2000), 269 at 272, 275; Bowett, Judicial and Political Functions of the Security Council and the International Court of Justice, in Fox (ed.) *The Changing Constitution of the United Nations* (1997), 73 at 79-80, 82.

12   This includes the determination of a breach of international law, its attribution and consequences, the existence and content of *ius cogens*, the status and interpretation of humanitarian law and its application for personnel of UN-authorized missions, the

This chapter will use a narrow definition of "legislative powers" as the powers of the Security Council to enact general, abstract norms that are directly binding on all the Member States of the UN. The ensuing norms do not enforce the peace in a specific political crisis, but regulate rights and obligations of States on a wider issue with long-term or indefinite effect. This definition tries to distinguish legislative competences from "executive" or "enforcement powers" of the Council, which enable the adoption of directly binding measures to regulate a specific crisis for political reasons.[13] Such "police actions" are short-term, usually coercive measures against a particular State in order to redress a wrong or mitigate the threat of an impending wrong. Obviously, grey areas exist, especially when the Security Council, in addressing a specific situation, declaratorily refers to "norms" not (yet) part of international law. In this case interpretation will determine whether the Council intended to enact general rules or make a (possibly erroneous) legal determination in enforcing the peace.

3.   Legal Basis

A.   The UN Charter

The general functions and powers of the Security Council are defined in Article 24 of the Charter. The specific powers are laid down in several provisions, predominantly in Chapters VI, VII and VIII. There is no provision conferring the right to the Council to enact general legislation or to adopt a decision that could be understood as general lawmaking.[14] A provision of the Charter that could implicitly exclude legislative powers is Article 2(7). This provision prohibits the UN to inter-

---

status of terrorism as an international crime, the scope and limits of immunity and extradition, etc. While it is true that all these instances are relevant for international law, in many cases they rather seem to be examples of the Council applying and interpreting international law, as executive organs do in the exercise of their functions. Alvarez, Judging the Security Council AJIL, 90 (1996), 1 at 20 – 22, with many further examples.

13   See Szasz, The Security Council Starts Legislating, AJIL 96 (2002), 901. A similar distinction is used by Wood, The Interpretation of Security Council Resolutions, *Max Planck Yearbook of United Nations Law* 2 (1998), at 77.

14   The Charter contains no reference to the legal form and nature of the acts of its organs. Articles 25 and 27 indicate that the Security Council shall make "decisions". Chapters VI and VII envisage "recommendations" and "decisions", Articles 34 and 39 foresee the possibility of making a "determination". Article 83 envisages the Council "performing functions". The rules contained in the Security Council's Provisional Rules of Procedure refer to "resolutions" (eg. Rule 31), "decisions" (Rules 37, 48, 51, 59) and "recommendations" (Rule 60). Though the procedure is clearly set out (Article 27), neither the Charter nor the Provisional Rules of Procedure determine the legal form and nature of the decisions. This is not rare for international organizations; see Zemanek, The Legal Foundations of the International System, Offprint from the *Recueil des Cours* 266 (1997), 201.

vene into matters essentially within the domestic jurisdiction of any State except for "enforcement measures under Chapter VII". It could be argued that the creation of general binding norms by the Council does not fall under "enforcement" and would thus be prohibited. On the other hand, the term "enforcement" is not defined in the Charter and the practice of the Council would rather imply that any act legally adopted under Chapter VII can pierce the *domaine réservé* of the States, irrespective of its nature.

Even if not explicitly foreseen, legislative powers could be deduced from the form and nature of the decisions that the Council may adopt.[15] In the case of legislative powers a decision would have to be general, abstract, long-term and legally binding on the States. Among these elements, only the binding character of the decision helps to narrow down the search. Though there are several provisions in the Charter that enable the adoption of binding decisions, the central competence is contained in Chapter VII of the Charter.[16] Article 39 requires a determination of the existence of a threat to the peace, breach of the peace or act of aggression before any act is taken. In conjunction with Article 2(4) such a determination is a legal decision.[17] But it is not an act of creating law but rather one of applying the law, similar to when an executive organ determines the existence of a breach of the law before taking action. After a determination according to Article 39 the Security Council can adopt measures not involving force, such as economic sanctions, rupture of lines of communication and severance of diplomatic relations (Article 41) or measures involving force, which could include "demonstrations, blockade and other operations" by armed forces (Article 42). Though not exhaustively enumer-

---

15   Article 34, for instance, gives the right to determine whether a crisis is likely to endanger the maintenance of international peace and security. In connection with Article 33 such a determination must be a decision devoted exclusively to the individual crisis under investigation; Delbrück, Article 25, in Simma (ed.), *The Charter of the United Nations* (2nd edition; 2002), 457-8.

16   There are other provisions in the Charter pursuant to which the Council can decree binding obligations on the States, such as Articles 34, 94(2) or Chapter VIII. However, none of these are suitable for creating general, abstract rules. Article 34 foresees investigations into a dispute to determine whether it could endanger international peace. Relying on Article 94(2) the Council decides on measures to implement a judgement of the ICJ. Chapter VIII deals with the role of regional arrangements in the maintenance of peace and security. Kelsen also understood recommendations as binding as long as they were accompanied with a threat of sanctions in case of non-compliance; Kelsen, *The Law of the United Nations* (1951), 96 and 293. This view, based on the theory that obligations equipped with adequate enforcement mechanisms can be subsumed under the category of binding legal obligations, fails to take into account that the enforcement action by the Council is a separate decision adopted under Chapter VII. The recommendation itself is not binding.

17   Graefrath explains: "Since peace is the law, such a decision necessarily includes a determination that a State has violated a basic international norm"; Graefrath, International Crimes and Collective Security, in Wellens (ed), *International Law: Theory and Practice*, 237 at 242.

ated, they all have the character of individual enforcement measures.[18] A literal interpretation of the Charter therefore shows no evidence of a legislative function of the Security Council.[19] After an extensive analysis of the *traveaux préparatoires* Arangio-Ruiz comes to the conclusion that it was also not the intention of the drafters of the Charter to endow the Council with such competences.[20] Literal and historic interpretations, however, are not the only means to identify the competences of organs of organizations. These powers can be deduced by other means, in particular by recourse to the concepts of implied powers or subsequent practice.

B.   Implied Powers

The concept of implied powers rests on the idea that organizations or their organs must have the powers and competences, which are necessary or essential for the execution of their functions.[21] A high degree of necessity or essentiality are not necessary, especially since a determination as to whether this criterion is fulfilled is subjectively interpreted by the beholder.[22] Nevertheless, the interpretation must be strictly based on the legal order of the sub-system. Legislative powers of the Security Council could thus arise from the need to enact legislation in order to fulfill its functions. The Charter has designated the Council as executive enforcer of peace, which makes recommendations to the parties of a conflict or adopts, under Chapter VII, binding decisions for specific situations. These tools have never been deemed inadequate for its function. Lawmaking competences do not appear

---

18   Frowein/Krisch, Chapter VII in Simma (ed.), *The Charter of the United Nations* (2nd edition; 2002), 705. Harper initially seems to conclude from the lack of an explicit exclusion of legislative powers that the Council has these powers; Harper, Does the United Nations Security Council have the competence to act as Court and Legislature? New York University Journal of International Law and Politics 27 (1994) 103 at 149. He later claims, however, that the "framers of the Charter" did not intend the Council to use Chapter VII in a legislative sense; at 153.

19   Nolte, The Limits of the Security Council's Powers and its Functions in the International Legal System: Some Reflections, in Byers (ed.) *The Role of Law in International Politics* (2000), 315 at 320-321.

20   Arangio-Ruiz, On the Security Council's Law-Making, Rivista di Diritto Internazionale 83 (2000) 609 at 628, 643, 660-682, 688. Though a proposal for an amendment submitted by Ecuador that the "Security Council shall not establish or modify principles or rules of law" was rejected, the argument *e contrario* that the founders therefore did not want to exclude that option would go too far. The Ecuadorian proposal is quoted in Bedjaoui, The New World Order and the Security Council – Testing the Legality of its Acts (1994), 30.

21   The ICJ stated: "Under international law, the Organization must be deemed to have those powers which, though not expressly provided in the Charter, are conferred upon it by necessary implication as being essential to the performance of its duties."; Reparations for Injuries, 1949 ICJ, 182.

22   Skubiszewski, Implied Powers of International Organizations, in Dinstein (ed.), *International Law at a Time of Perplexity* (1989), 855 at 861.

necessary for the Council to fulfill its mandate. There is thus little support for the deduction of legislative powers of the Security Council based on the concept of implied powers.[23]

C.   Subsequent Practice

The concepts of "established practice of the organization" and "subsequent practice of the parties" are used to bring in line the practice of organs that act in ways not foreseen in their founding instruments. A good example is the practice of the permanent members of the Council (P5) of abstaining during votes on non-procedural matters. In respect to the clear contradiction to Article 27 (3) of the Charter the ICJ noted in the Namibia Case:

> This procedure followed by the Security Council, which has continued unchanged after the amendment in 1965 of Article 27 of the Charter, has been generally accepted by members of the United Nations and evidences a general practice of that Organization.[24]

Two factors are thus necessary: repetition and the acceptance by the general membership of the UN.[25] The first, while simple to verify, has the inherent problem that the very first such act is justified only retroactively, once a pattern has emerged. The need for acceptance depends to a large extent on the functional and institutional setting of the organ in question within the organization and its constituent treaty. In the case of the Security Council, acceptance by the P5, who have special rights in the context of an amendment of the Charter, can be understood to be inherently included in a Council decision because it would not have been taken without the consent of the permanent member. Acceptance by the wider membership must, however, be clearly established, because the Council has limited and unequal membership and can take decisions binding on all States. Though this consent may also be given tacitly, an expansion of powers of the Council requires a clear indication of the will of the States.[26] Acquiescence to an *ultra vires* act of an organ does not automatically imply that the States accept the formation of a rule empowering the organ to act in that way in the future. Obviously, their reaction has to be closely

---

23   Arangio-Ruiz, On the Security Council's Law-Making, Rivista di Diritto Internazionale 83 (2000) 609 at 689. See, however, Kirgis, The Security Council's first Fifty Years, AJIL 89 (1995), 506 at 522-524.

24   Legal Consequences for States of the Continued Presence of South Africa in Namibia (South West Africa) Notwithstanding Security Council Resolution 276 (1970), 1971 ICJ 16, 22.

25   Herdegen, referring to the modification of Article 27(3) of the Charter correctly to the affinity to the creation of customary international law; Herdegen, The "Constitutionalization" of the UN Security System, Vanderbilt Journal of Transnational Law 27 (1994), 135 at 155.

26   Buehler, *State Succession and Membership in International Organizations – Legal Theories versus Political Pragmatism* (2001), 294.

examined to determine whether the act in question is approved as a singular aberration or whether they consent to both the act and the general competence to take similar acts in the future. The consequence of the recurring acceptance of the use of the powers is, as Zemanek points out, that the constituent treaty of the organization is formlessly amended to include the powers or competences.[27] Whether the UN Charter has been amended to give the Security Council legislative powers depends on the reaction of the States to its relevant practice.

4.   Practice of the Security Council

A.   Practice before 2001

In 1965 the Security Council declared the Government of Rhodesia "illegal".[28] The occupation of Namibia by South Africa was also determined to be "illegal" in 1970, and the acts of the occupier "illegal and invalid".[29] In 1983 the Council considered the Declaration of a Turkish Cypriot State legally "invalid."[30] These resolutions created obligations for States not to legally recognize a certain development, but they are not general abstract primary norms that go beyond an individual situation. After the end of the Cold War the Council became more active – with mixed results.[31] Though most resolutions are clearly individual enforcement actions, some contain legal determinations, necessary for the justification of a decision or relevant for subsequent measures.[32] A few instances, however, demonstrate the Council's interest in legislative and adjudicative action and merit closer inspection.

i.   SC-Res. 687 and SC-Res. 692 – Iraq 1990/1991

One of 13 resolutions adopted in response to the invasion of Kuwait by Iraq in 1990, SC-Res. 687[33] contains several noteworthy elements. Section A demands respect of the boundary contractually agreed upon by Iraq and Kuwait in 1963 and decides

---

27   Zemanek, The Legal Foundations of the International System, Offprint from the *Recueil des Cours* 266 (1997), 96.

28   SC-Res. 216 (1965) of 12 November 1965.

29   SC-Res. 276 (1970) of 30 January 1970.

30   SC-Res. 541 (1983) of 18 November 1983; reaffirmed by SC-Res. 550 (1984) of 11 May 1984.

31   See Freudenschuss, Article 39 of the UN Charter Revisited: Threats to the Peace and the Recent Practice of the UN Security Council, Austrian Journal of Public and International Law 46 (1993), 1; Higgins, Peace and Security – Achievement and Failures, EJIL 6 (1995), 445.

32   SC-Res. 1054 (1996) of 26 April 1996 adopted sanctions against Sudan to enforce extradition of three suspects. All States had to reduce the number and level of the staff at Sudanese diplomatic missions and restrict or control the movement of the remaining staff, without doubt a restriction of the freedom envisaged in the Vienna Convention on Diplomatic Relations.

33   SC-Res. 687 (1991) of 3 April 1991.

that the Security Council will "guarantee the inviolability of the boundary". Section E determines the responsibility of Iraq and decides to create a Compensation Commission.[34] It has been argued that the Council acted as a judicial organ regarding the border-settlement because it decided on the conflicting claims regarding the validity of the 1963 Agreement after a judicial analysis.[35] It could also be understood as having acted legislatively by determining the border and guaranteeing its inviolability. The relevant provisions could, however, also be understood as a demand that both parties refrain from violating a boundary they had previously agreed on (para. 2) and that this would be enforced (para. 4).[36] Even if one were to accept the act as a legal determination of a border, it would not fall under the definition of general legislative act, since it is an individual decision for a specific case. Though all States have to respect the decision, it only affects the territorial rights of the two countries parties to the conflict.

In "reaffirming" the legal consequences of the invasion, SC-Res. 687 referred to the general norms of State responsibility.[37] Although the Council's interpretation of the content of Iraq's liability may have been progressive, it did not directly create new general obligations in the field of State responsibility and liability. In fulfilling its functions it has the authority to make decisions of legal relevance, for example the determination of a breach of the peace, and to conclude that the State has the duty to make reparation. The establishment of a subsidiary body to determine the amount of compensation would seem legally justified.[38] Nevertheless, the creation of the Compensation Commission as a sub-organ of the Council was criticized by many authors as *ultra vires*.[39] Indeed, there is a significant difference between a

---

34   The Commission was formally established by SC-Res. 692 (1991) of 20 May 1991.

35   Harper, Does the United Nations Security Council have the competence to act as Court and Legislature? New York University Journal of International Law and Politics 27 (1994) 103 at 115-118.

36   The resolution does not indicate that the Security Council intended to delimit the border for all eternity and would prevent any future agreement between the two States on a different border. See in this regard Sur, Sécurité collective et rétablissment de la paix: la résolution 687 (3 avril 1991) dans l'Affaire du Golfe, in Dupuy (ed), The Development of the Role of the Security Council, Workshop 21-23 July 1992 (1993), 19 at 26.

37   Wood, The Interpretation of Security Council Resolutions, *Max Planck Yearbook of United Nations Law* 2 (1998), at 77. Kirgis understands this as a "quasi-judicial" determination; Kirgis, The Security Council's first Fifty Years, AJIL 89 (1995), 506 at 529. Alvarez writes: "Making law, both in interpreting the Charter and in developing the doctrine of state responsibility, has always been part of the Council's job."; Alvarez, Judging the Security Council AJIL 90 (1996), 1 at 22.

38   Some derive this from inherent powers of the Council, Gattini, The UN Compensation Commission: Old Rules, New Procedures on War Reparation, EJIL 13 (2002), 161 at 165.

39   Graefrath, International Crimes and Collective Security, in Wellens (ed), *International Law: Theory and Practice,* 237 at 245. See also Zemanek, Is the Security Council the Judge of its own Legality? In Yapko, Boumedra (ed), *Liber Amicorum Mohammed Bedjaoui* (1999), 629 at 630.

declaratory pronouncement on the existence of an obligation to pay compensation as a consequence arising from state responsibility and the actual complex judicial process of adjudicating claims and rights of individuals and the defendant.[40] While it may be within the functions of the Security Council to determine the existence of a violation of international law and to reaffirm the general consequences of such a violation, interpretation of the Charter, even with recourse to the concept of implied powers, does not provide evidence of a function to adjudicate individual claims.[41] Article 29 of the Charter stipulates that the Security Council may create only those sub-organs necessary for the performance of its functions. It can only delegate such rights to a sub-organ that it possesses itself. Lack of judicial procedural rights seems to exclude the possibility of establishing a judicial sub-organ of the Council under the Charter.

Even if the establishment of a subsidiary body with judicial competences were *ultra vires*, this does not necessarily invalidate the establishment of the Commission. Acquiescence of the States, as witnessed by the consistent cooperation of the States with the Commission, healed the illegality of the act. The establishment of a judicial body could also be seen as the first instance of a practice, which could, if repeated in similar fashion and accepted by the States, be an indication of "subsequent practice". This argument will be further explored under Section III below.

ii.   SC-Res. 748 – Libya 1992

In the course of the investigations into the crash of PanAm flight 103 in Lockerbie in 1988 and of UTA flight 772 in the Ténéré desert in 1989, France, the UK and the US had unsuccessfully demanded from Libya the extradition of nationals, official recognition of responsibility and compensation. Libya refused to comply but expressed its willingness to settle the dispute peacefully and requested arbitration under Article 14 of the 1971 Montreal Convention. Early in 1992 the Council urged Libya to immediately provide a "full and effective response to the requests so as to contribute to the elimination of terrorism".[42] Libya instituted proceedings against the UK and US before the ICJ, arguing *inter alia* that, under the Montreal Convention, it had the choice of *aut dedere aut iudicare*, and requested provisional measures to prevent the defendants from taking coercive measures against Libya. Shortly after the oral hearings on this request, SC-Res. 748[43] was adopted to force Libya to comply with the requests.

---

40   In his report the Secretary General remarked that the major part of the work of the Commission would not be judicial in nature; Report of the Secretary General, UN Doc. S/2259 (1991) 8-9. This is convincingly disputed by Kirgis, The Security Council's first Fifty Years, AJIL 89 (1995), 506 at 525.

41   Arangio-Ruiz, On the Security Council's Law-Making, Rivista di Diritto Internazionale 83 (2000) 609 at 691; Graefrath, International Crimes and Collective Security, in Wellens (ed), *International Law: Theory and Practice*, 237 at 245.

42   SC-Res. 731 (1992) of 21 January 1992.

43   SC-Res. 748 (1992) of 31 March 1992.

This resolution, adopted under Chapter VII, contains a number of significant legal determinations and consequences. The preamble "reaffirms" that Article 2(4) of the Charter applies to acquiescence in terrorist activities within a state's territory and that the failure of Libya to convincingly renounce terrorism and to respond to the requests was a threat to international peace and security. Para. 1 decides that Libya must comply with the requests of France, the UK and the US. The resolution then decrees various sanctions, the termination of which depended on a Council decision.[44]

The Council's conduct resulted in much criticism. No reasons had been provided why Libya's right to decide to try the suspects instead of extraditing them was denied or how the non-extradition and non-payment of compensation amounted to a threat or breach of the peace. Prescribing a legal duty to extradite negated not only the right of Libya under the Montreal Convention but also the customary principle that, without specific contractual obligations to that effect, national citizens do not have to be extradited. The support of the requests of the three States, each one a permanent Council member, without bothering to establish their legitimacy or even to identify the obligations, alienated not only international lawyers but also some Members of the Council.[45] The issue criticized the most, however, was the fact that SC-Res. 748 had been adopted shortly after the ICJ-hearings on the request for provisional measures. By adopting the resolution under Chapter VII, the Council confronted the Court with a determination binding on Member States and thereby influenced the further judicial proceedings.

The question whether the ICJ has or should have the powers to review acts of the Council has been thoroughly discussed in literature.[46] The Charter contains no provisions to that effect. Among legalists there is some sympathy for the scenario that the Court by way of its practice – similar to US Supreme Court in the case *Marbury v. Madison*[47] – establishes parameters of legality for Council action and, eventually, acquires review power.[48] Others refute the idea of judicial control

---

44   This decision was taken in September 2003, after the extradition and prosecution of two Libyan suspects by a special court, the payment of compensation and confidential negotiations between Libya, the UK and US on weapons of mass destruction had improved bilateral relations. The sanctions had included an air-traffic embargo, arms-embargo, prohibition of military assistance, reduction of Libyan diplomatic personnel, etc. They had been suspended in 1998 after the extradition of two suspects and were formally lifted with SC-Res. 1506 (2003) of 12 September 2003.

45   The resolution was adopted with only 10 votes, 5 States abstained (Cape Verde, China, India, Morocco and Zimbabwe).

46   See Macdonald, Changing Relations between the International Court of Justice and the Security Council of the United Nations, *CYIL* 31 (1993), 3; Martenczuk, The Security Council, the International Court and Judicial Review: What Lessons from Lockerbie?, *EJIL* 10 (1999), 517 at 525-528; Alvarez, Judging the Security Council AJIL 90 (1996), 1, with many further references.

47   5 US (1 Cransh) 137 (1803).

48   Franck, The "Powers of Appreciation": Who is the Ultimate Guardian of UN Legality, AJIL 86 (1992), 519 at 523. Alvarez points out that, irrespective of legal consequences,

of the Security Council.[49] An examination of the extent of the review powers of the ICJ goes well beyond the scope of this article. Here, the relevant acts were the legal determinations that Libya had no right under the Montreal Convention to try the suspects itself and was required to pay compensation as claimed by the three Council Members. Whether or not these acts were *ultra vires*, it suffices to conclude that the Security Council did not, nor intended to, enact general legislation. The resolutions contained specific obligations on one State to achieve the specific goals of extradition and compensation.

iii.   SC-Res. 827 and SC-Res. 955 – Yugoslavia and Rwanda 1993/1994

Seeking to compensate its failure to prevent the crimes committed during the conflicts in Yugoslavia and Rwanda, the Security Council established, with SC-Res. 827,[50] the International Criminal Tribunal for the former Yugoslavia (ICTY), and, with SC-Res. 955,[51] the International Criminal Tribunal for Rwanda (ICTR). Some authors regard the creation of the tribunals as lawful due to the Council's competences to establish subsidiary bodies.[52] Others rely on implied powers under Chapter VII.[53] A third position regards the establishment as *ultra vires*, healed by the acquiescence of the States.[54] The Trial Chamber of the ICTY found that the decision to establish the Tribunal was a political question and could not be reviewed, though it subsequently gave a number of reasons why the act was, in any event, appropriate and lawful.[55] The Appellate Chamber found itself competent to review the legality of the establishment of the Tribunal and concluded that the Security Council had the competence to create a judicial tribunal under Article 41.[56]

It is hardly surprising that the Tribunal itself found that it had been legally established and the reasoning is not unconvincing. The Council certainly has the right to decide, under Chapter VII, that punishment of the gravest crimes will contribute to establishing peace. It is also correct that Article 29 gives the Council the right to freely create sub-organs "for the performance of its functions". However, as demonstrated in connection with the establishment of the Iraq Compensation Commission above, it may not establish sub-organs to carry out functions and rely

---

the effects of the Court order and the arguments presented in the separate and dissenting opinions in the Lockerbie case constitute a clear political warning to the Council to take the "cues" of the Court and its members seriously for any future action; Alvarez, Judging the Security Council AJIL 90 (1996), 1 at 30.

49   Reisman, The Constitutional Crisis in the United Nations, AJIL 87 (1993), 83 at 87, 95.

50   SC-Res. 827 (1993) of 25 May 1993.

51   SC-Res. 955 (1994) of 8 November 1994.

52   Pellet, Le Tribunal criminel international pour l'ex-Yougoslavie, Revue Générale du droit international public 98 (1994), 7 at 28-29.

53   Kirgis, The Security Council's first Fifty Years, AJIL 89 (1995), 506 at 520.

54   Arangio-Ruiz, On the Security Council's Law-Making, Rivista di Diritto Internazionale 83 (2000), 609 at 724.

55   *Prosecutor v. Tadic*, Decision of 10 August 1995, Case IT-94-1-T.

56   *Prosecutor v. Tadic*, Decision of 2 October 1995, Case IT-94-1-AR72, paras 28-38.

on rights that it does not possess itself. There is no evidence in the Charter of judicial functions of the Council or of the right to decide on the criminal responsibility of individuals.[57] Urgency alone cannot confer powers on an organ. It was also not the only means to achieve the goals.[58] The subsequent examples of tribunals established for Sierra Leone and Cambodia demonstrate that the UN has alternative means of creating tribunals to try individuals for crimes.[59]

After a decade of practice, the position that the Tribunals are legally invalid would, of course, be untenable. It would also be wrong, because the lack of basis in the Charter would have healed by acquiescence. Moreover, the theory of subsequent practice could indicate that the Council rightfully assumed the powers to establish judicial sub-organs. As a judicial body that decides on individual claims the Iraq-Compensation Commission is a relevant precedent. Together with the ICTY and the ICTR the requirement for repetitive practice could be fulfilled. The necessary condition of acceptance by the States is easy to document: Though there have been individual instances of States expressing doubts regarding the legality of the tribunals or not cooperating with them, the practice of the general UN-membership demonstrates an overwhelming acceptance of these bodies. This is documented not only in the resolutions of the General Assembly supporting and financing the tribunals but also in the practical cooperation between States and the Tribunals.[60]

It thus seems arguable that the Security Council has attained the powers to establish specific judicial sub-organs. This is not, however, an indication of general legislative powers to enact primary norms as this article has defined. All three bodies were designed to fit a specific individual crisis. The jurisdiction of the Commission and the Tribunals is very narrowly defined with strict temporal and regional limitations. The statutes of the Tribunals, trying to reflect customary humanitarian international law, were limited specifically to the crimes committed in the two

---

57   Zemanek, The Legal Foundations of the International System, Offprint from the *Recueil des Cours* 266 (1997), 204-209. Lamb believes that the SC did not delegate its own functions but the powers that the tribunals needed; Lamb, Legal Limits to United Nations Security Council Powers, in Goodwin-Gill / Talmon eds, *The Reality of International Law: Essays in Honour of Ian Brownlie* (1999), 361 at 376-377. She does not explain, however, how the Council could legally transfer functions or rights that it did not possess.

58   The Council could have recommended the establishment of the tribunals by means of a GA-resolution or requested a regional organisation under Chapter VIII to set up such a body, though it would have had to relinquish effective control.

59   Indeed, the fact that they were not established as subsidiary bodies suggests some unease among Council Members as to legality of the establishment of the ICTY and ICTR. See the doubts expressed by Brazil, China and Venezuela on the legality of the establishment of the ICTY, UN Doc. S/PV.3175 (25.02.93) and S/PV.3217 (25.05.93). At the adoption of SC-Res. 955 China abstained and Rwanda voted against (though for political reasons).

60   As to the practice of the European States see Marschik, The Politics of Prosecution: European National Approaches to War Crimes, in McCormack and Simpson (eds.), *The Law of War Crimes* (1997), 65 at 93.

conflicts. They were not designed as indefinite generally applicable norms.[61] Even if the Security Council had attained certain powers in the context of determining individual responsibility, there is no indication that it has assumed general legislative competences in a primary-law field, in particular humanitarian law.

iv.   SC-Res. 1209 – Arms in Africa 1998

In view of the deteriorating security situation in Africa and the apparent lack of effectiveness of specific embargoes, the Security Council chose to address one of the central causes of the conflicts by promoting national legislation prohibiting or limiting illegal arms flow. SC-Res. 1209[62] called on African States to "enact legislation on the domestic possession and use of arms, including the establishment of national legal and judicial mechanisms for the effective implementation of such laws, and to implement effective import, export and re-export controls, …". Though the resolution clearly has the intention to initiate general, albeit regional, binding legislation, it is not, itself, of legislative nature. It is a recommendation to the States and contains no binding primary norms.

v.   SC-Res. 1267 – Afghanistan 1999

In 1999 the Security Council addressed the support of the Taliban regime in Afghanistan for suspected terrorists and the refusal to extradite Osama bin Laden. During the subsequent five years, the scope of SC-Res. 1267[63] was gradually expanded to establish one of the most complex sanctions regimes of the UN.[64] Today, the regime relies, in essence, on a list of persons (former Taliban dignitaries and members of Al Qaeda) and private companies or associations against whom the States must implement sanctions, such as travel restrictions, freezing of funds and arms embargos. Targeting individuals was hailed as an improvement over conventional sanctions against the State as a whole. It has, at the same time, resulted in effects that go beyond initial intentions. Under the absolute obligation to implement the resolutions, States are unable to guarantee due process and procedural rights to the individuals concerned, though some are required by international or regional conventions to respect these rights.[65] The sanctions would thus derogate

---

61   Report of the Secretary General UN Doc 25704 (1993), 8.

62   SC-Res. 1209 (1998) of 19 November 1998.

63   SC-Res. 1267 (1999) of 15 October 1999.

64   The most important resolutions are: SC-Res. 1333 (2000) of 19 December 2000, SC-Res. 1363 (2001) of 30 July 2001, SC-Res. 1390 (2002) of 16 January 2002, SC-Res. 1452 (2002) of 20 December 2002, SC-Res. 1455 (2003) of 17 January 2003, SC-Res. 1526 (2004) of 30 January 2004, SC-Res. 1535 (2004) of 26 March 2004.

65   To address this problem, the 1267-committee adopted a "de-listing procedure" in 2002. States can request review of the listing of a citizen or resident. Ideally the State should submit a joint request together with the State that had requested the listing of the individual, but it can also submit a request alone. The Committee decides by consensus or refers the case to the Council. Though an improvement, the de-listing procedure does not solve the problem of persons whose rights a State – for whatever reason – chooses not to protect.

the individual's human rights. Derogation could theoretically be based on Article 103 of the Charter. However, if the rights in questions are *ius cogens*, derogation seems, at least, questionable (see Chapter 5.i below).

The 1267-regime has many other problems: The possibility of "listing" persons without justification has enormous potential for misuse.[66] National authorities have difficulties enforcing an arms embargo against individuals and entities. The inflexibility of the sanctions regime prevents quick adaptation to new developments, such as the change in Al Qaeda's financing methods to circumvent the original controls.[67] Implementation by the States has been unsatisfactory for several reasons, such as lack of political will, complexity of the Committees guidelines, lack of resources and technical capacity and coordination difficulties on a national level. International cooperation has been inadequate because States are hesitant to share confidential information on individual terrorists in a UN-sanctions committee.[68] The system also suffers from the general belief that non-compliance will not be sanctioned.

In sum, SC-Res. 1267 and the subsequent amendments are an enlightening example of how the Security Council establishes a complex legal regime. As such, the experience gives little confidence in its abilities. The 1267-regime evolved from the original localized conflict and now contains more general obligations but it is still closely confined to the source of terrorism emanating from Al Qaeda.[69] Though not an example of general, non-specific legislation, it is a useful example for the difficulties that arise when the Council creates a regime that interferes directly into the rights of individuals.

vi. Conclusions

The resolutions examined were tools to establish or enforce peace in response specific localized threats. In some instances the Security Council established the existence or the violation of a legal obligation and declared the consequences of state responsibility. In one case it recommended regional legislation. None of the resolutions were examples of general binding legislation in the sense understood in this article. They did show however, the readiness of the Council to enlarge its scope of secondary-law powers or assume new competences. It could, by means

---

66   States can request the placement of any individual on the list. Dissidents or the political opposition could be tempting targets. If the Council agrees (practice shows that requests for listing are rarely questioned), the individuals are included in the list without any realistic chance for legal recourse.

67   The travel restrictions demand border controls between States, yet they are almost impossible to implement due to a lack of required identifiers.

68   One problem that has been partly solved arose from the duty to freeze all financial assets of the individuals on the list. States that grant assistance to citizens in need had the domestic obligation to assist those persons whose financial assets they had frozen. Aiding persons on the list, however, is prohibited by the 1267-regime. SC-Res. 1452 (2002) of 20 December 2002 enabled States to request for permission to give social aid.

69   Lavalle, A novel, if awkward exercise in international law-making: Security Council Resolution 1540 (2004), NILR 51 (2004), 411 at 414.

of subsequent practice accepted by the Member States, have been endowed with competences to establish judicial sub-organs. The reliance on Chapter VII requires, however, that the establishment of such an organ is preceded by a breach of the peace. There is no indication that the Council has received powers to establish judicial organs with general jurisdiction for future conflicts.[70]

B.   Practice after 2001

After the terrorist attacks in 2001 the relations among the P5, strained by the NATO-interventions in the Balkans, improved. Every permanent Member had suffered terrorism. The severity of the attack against the US showed the vulnerability of even the most powerful State. Though this harmony soon gave way to political tensions over how to proceed with Iraq, it laid the foundation for continued effective cooperation on a technical level in the field of counter-terrorism.[71] The close cooperation can be seen in two resolutions, both extraordinary in scope and legal consequences.

i.   SC-Res. 1373 – Terrorism 2001

Based on Chapter VII, SC-Res. 1373[72] contains wide-ranging obligations for the States to prevent and combat terrorism.[73] Para. 2 obliges States *inter alia* to:
- Prevent and suppress the financing of terrorist acts.
- Criminalize the provision or collection of funds for terrorism by their nationals or in their territories; prohibit that any such act is committed and ensure that any perpetrator is brought to justice.
- Freeze funds and other financial assets or economic resources of terrorists or of persons or entities that attempt, participate in or facilitate acts of terrorism, including funds generated from property owned or controlled by them.
- Refrain from active or passive support for persons involved in terrorist acts and deny them safe haven and use of their territory for terrorist purposes.
- Prevent the movement of terrorists or terrorist groups by effective border controls and secure travel documentation.
- Take necessary steps to prevent the commission of terrorist acts including international cooperation and exchange of information, criminal investigations and proceedings.

---

70   The Council would thus not have the competences to create its own general "Criminal Court" as competition to the International Criminal Court established by the Statute of Rome.

71   In early May 2003 US Ambassador Negroponte stated: "Clearly, with resolution 1373 (2001) the Security Council got something right."; 4752nd meeting of the Security Council on 6 May 2003; S/PV.4752, provisional, 5.

72   SC-Res. 1373 (2001) of 28 September 2001.

73   See to content, scope and consequences of the resolution Rosand, Security Council Resolution 1373, The Counter-Terrorism Committee, and the Fight against Terrorism, AJIL 97 (2003), 333.

The resolution further calls on States to intensify the exchange of information, become parties to the UN's anti-terrorism conventions and protocols, take appropriate measures to ensure that asylum seekers have not been involved in terrorism and that refugee-status is not misused (para. 3). A special subsidiary organ of the Council, the Counter-Terrorism-Committee (CTC), monitors the implementation by the Member States (para. 6).

Even a cursory examination of the resolution shows that it is fundamentally different from its predecessors. Though it contains a brief condemnation of the terrorist attacks of 11 September 2001, the resolution does not respond to any specific act of terrorism. The preamble reaffirms that "such" acts (not "these" acts), like any act of international terrorism, constitute a threat to international peace and security (para. 3). Chapter VII is thus triggered not by an individual crisis but by the general threat of international terrorism. SC-Res. 1373 also does not foresee any "sunset clause" and is therefore in effect until formally revoked. The provisions of para. 2, fundamentally different from normal language of resolutions, were taken from anti-terror conventions, especially the Convention for the Suppression of the Financing of Terrorism.[74] The resolution makes these provisions binding on all States, even though the Convention had, at that time, been ratified by merely four States.[75] The implementation of the obligations – typical for treaty provisions – requires significant domestic legislative measures. The provisions of the resolution are not directed towards (re)establishing peace in an individual crisis but abstract and general obligations designed to impose primary norms. In sum, SC-Res. 1373 is not an act of peace-enforcement but a measure to create legal obligations for the States in an area of international law.[76] The resolution thereby falls precisely under the definition of "legislative acts" proposed in this chapter.

Since the Charter does not foresee legislative powers for the Security Council, such an act would be *ultra vires*. It could have healed, however, if acquiesced to by the States. It could also serve as the first point of reference that the Council has received these powers under the concept of subsequent practice, if further such acts are accepted by the Member States. Indicators for acceptance are formal statements, cooperation between the States and the CTC and domestic implementation of the resolution. The rapid adoption of SC-Res. 1373 after the terrorist attacks prevented

---

74   The Convention had been adopted by the General Assembly and was opened for signature in December 1999; GA-Res. 54/109 of 9 December 1999.

75   Botswana, Sri Lanka, the UK and Uzbekistan. SC-Res. 1373 urged States to ratify the Convention. It entered into force in 2002.

76   Lavalle, A novel, if awkward, exercise in international law-making: Security Council Resolution 1540 (2004), NILR 51 (2004), 411 at 416; Szasz, The Security Council Starts Legislating, AJIL 96 (2002), 901 at 904-905. The insinuation that the Council Members were unaware of the pioneering nature of the resolution is unfounded. Though delegations might not have considered all potential consequences of the resolution, the debriefings outside the Council Chamber during the consultations and after the adoption of the resolution made clear that the delegations were fully aware that SC-Res. 1373 was a radically new type of Council action with considerable consequences.

an in depth debate on the issue. Yet the statements of the Council members and the States at subsequent public debates on terrorism in the Security Council give evidence of strong support for the resolution.[77] At the UN, declaratory support does not always result in corresponding supportive practice. In this respect, however, the 1373-regime is an exception. By the end of May 2003, every State of the UN had submitted a first implementation-report to the CTC. By August 2004, more than 500 reports had been submitted in four rounds of reporting. Though the effectiveness of the regime will depend on the Council's ability to improve its monitoring and enforcement capacity, the regime has already lead to substantial capacity building and information-sharing in the wider UN membership.[78] For this analysis, however, the relevant question is not the effectiveness of the regime but the acceptance of the legislative role of the Council by the States. In this respect, the practice proves a clear and continued acceptance of the 1373 regime. Whether this practice leads to general powers to legislate depends on additional Council practice accepted by the States.

ii.   SC-Res. 1540 – Weapons of Mass Destruction 2004

In view of the success of the 1373-regime, the US initiated negotiations on a draft resolution on the non-proliferation of weapons of mass destruction in the fall of 2003 among the P5. While considerable differences of opinion on scope, definitions and monitoring mechanisms existed, the P5 agreed on the need to counter the proliferation of weapons of mass destruction, especially to non-state actors. The non-permanent members of the Council informally received a draft text on 23 December 2003 but the consultations continued strictly among the P5 until a new version of the draft was circulated at the end of March 2004. After a public debate in late April the Council adopted SC-Res. 1540[79] unanimously.

---

77   See for example the open debate on 15 April 2002, S/PV.4512 (provisional). At the adoption of SC-Res. 1377 of 12 November 2001 France said in regard to the UN role in combating terrorism: "It must, first, provide the international community with strengthened legal instruments enabling it to fight terrorism, including by depriving terrorists of all financing and by ensuring that they can nowhere find support or refuge. The Security Council responded to that urgent need by unanimously adopting resolution 1373 (2001)."; Statement by Mr. Védrine (France) at the 4413th meeting of the Security Council on 12 November 2003, UN Doc S/PV.4413 at 7. In early 2002, before the cooperation was demonstrated in the States' reporting, Szasz found the reception of SC-Res. 1373 by the General Assembly "tepid" because it had referred only once to the resolution in its annual resolution on terrorism; Szasz, The Security Council Starts Legislating, AJIL 96 (2002), 901 at 903. The hesitancy in the General Assembly was, however, mainly due to the concern that the activity of the Security Council in the field of terrorism would reduce the interest of some States to finalize the comprehensive convention on terrorism in the Sixth Committee – a project that still awaits completion three years later.

78   The Council has tried to improve the CTC's monitoring capabilities by means of SC-Res. 1535 of 26 March 2004. The operational work of the CTC is now the responsibility of the CTC Executive Directorate (CTED). The reform will i.a. enable CTED to "visit" (i.e. inspect) States, albeit with their consent, to discuss implementation.

79   SC-Res. 1540 (2004) of 28 April 2004.

In structure, language and legal scope this resolution is similar to SC-Res. 1373. Primary focus is the non-proliferation of weapons of mass destruction to non-State actors. Member States are obliged to:

–   Refrain from providing any form of support to non-State actors that attempt to develop, acquire, manufacture, possess, transport, transfer or use nuclear, chemical or biological weapons and their means of delivery (para. 1).
–   Adopt and enforce appropriate laws to prohibit any non-State actor to do the above (para. 2).
–   Take and enforce effective measures to establish domestic controls to prevent the proliferation of weapons of mass destruction, including by establishing controls over related materials (para. 3).

The resolution establishes a Monitoring Committee for two years, to which the States must report (para. 4). Para. 5 contains a safeguard to ensure the continuing validity of the relevant international disarmament and non-proliferation treaties.[80]

Similar to its predecessor, SC-Res. 1540 does not refer to any specific situation but relies on the general threat of the proliferation of weapons of mass destruction to non-state actors. Though the establishment of the SC-committee to monitor implementation is formally limited to two years, the obligations on the States are permanent. The provisions, drafted in treaty language, contain abstract legal obligations taken from existing international conventions.[81] Obligations under para. 3 go beyond the problem of non-state actors; they are general non-proliferation provisions. Compliance with the resolution requires significant implementing legislation by the States. In sum, SC-Res. 1540 is no individual peace-enforcement measure but a binding legislative act establishing abstract international norms.

As a second instance of legislation after SC-Res. 1373, this development could constitute subsequent practice and establish general legislative powers of the Council if accepted by the wider UN-membership. Due to the recent adoption of the resolution, the cooperation of the States with the Committee or the extent of national implementation cannot yet be evaluated. The delegations' positions expressed before and after the adoption of the resolution will therefore serve as key indication of acceptance.

A public debate in the Council on 22 April 2004, scheduled only after significant pressure of non-members, gives a good picture of the diversity of positions on the issue. On the whole, the project was well received by the western States. Can-

---

80   States are further called upon to strengthen and implement the existing treaty regimes and to cooperate, especially within the framework of the relevant multilateral regimes, i.e. the International Atomic Energy Agency, the Organization for the Prohibition of Chemical Weapons and the Biological and Toxin Weapons Convention (para. 8).

81   Though co-sponsors declared their intention not to alter rights and obligations of existing non-proliferation treaties, para. 5 decides that the provisions shall merely not be *interpreted* so as to conflict with these treaties.

ada welcomed the Council's "leadership in addressing a new challenge".[82] Strong support also came from Ireland speaking on behalf of the EU and its associated countries, as well as Albania, Australia, New Zealand, Singapore and Tajikistan.[83] Sweden did not pursue concerns raised only a month earlier in a "non-paper" but supported the resolution.[84] General support albeit with some reservations was expressed by Jordan, Kuwait, Liechtenstein, Norway, and Thailand.[85] Some States, like Japan and the Republic of Korea, accepted the legislative role of the Council for the issue at hand but urged caution.[86] Mexico was concerned that the resolution could become a precedent. Switzerland stressed the special circumstances authorizing the Council to act:

> In principle, legislative obligations, such as those foreseen in the draft resolution under discussion, should be established through multilateral treaties, in whose elaboration all States can participate. It is acceptable for the Security Council to assume such a legislative role only in exceptional circumstances and in response to an urgent need.[87]

---

82 Statement of Mr Laurin (Canada) at the 4950th meeting of the Security Council on 22 April 2004; UN-Doc. S/PV.4950 at 19.

83 Australia asserted: "It is entirely appropriate that the Council should do so now, consistent with its mandate to maintain international peace and security."; Statement of Mr Dauth (Australia) at the 4950th meeting of the Security Council on 22 April 2004; UN-Doc. S/PV.4950 (Resumption 1) at 7.

84 Sweden "warmly welcomed" the Council's active involvement and considered the resolution a "most welcome step in fulfilling the responsibility of the Council"; Statement of Mr Schori (Sweden) at the 4950th meeting of the Security Council on 22 April 2004; UN-Doc. S/PV.4950 at 27. The non-paper (on file with the author) had pointed to the danger of an evolving practice in which the Council drafts "new horizontal national legislation for global application". This development was regarded as possibly undermining the legitimacy of the Security Council.

85 Kuwait associated itself with the NAM-statement but went on to lend its "moral and political support to the resolution". The resolution was seen as an interim solution: "We agree that a gap exists within the international treaty regime, which does not address the nexus between weapons of mass destruction and non-State actors. This draft resolution could be an interim solution until that gap is addressed fully at a later stage. We also believe that the nature of this draft resolution, as well as possible future actions, should be based on a broad consensus in the international community."; Statement of Ms Al-Mulla (Kuwait) at the 4950th meeting of the Security Council on 22 April 2004; UN-Doc. S/PV.4950 (Resumption 1) at 17.

86 Japan stated: "In adopting a binding Security Council resolution under Chapter VII of the United Nations Charter, the Security Council assumes a lawmaking function. The Security Council should, therefore, be cautious not to undermine the stability of the international legal framework."; Statement of Mr Hamaguchi (Japan) at the 4950th meeting of the Security Council on 22 April 2004; UN-Doc. S/PV.4950 at 28.

87 Statement of Mr Staehelin (Switzerland) at the 4950th meeting of the Security Council on 22 April 2004; UN-Doc. S/PV.4950 at 28.

With some exceptions, the Members of the Non-Aligned-Movement (NAM) were critical of the legislative role of the Council.[88] Addressing the need for broad support from the UN-Membership, Nepal stated:

> To ensure such support, the Council should work within its mandate and be seen to be doing so. Therefore, it should resist the temptation of acting as a world legislature, a world administration and a world court rolled into one.[89]

Some NAM-delegations based their criticism on the fact that the Council was structurally inappropriate to legislate for the UN. Indonesia pointed to the need of consensual participation of the wider membership in the legislative process:

> Indeed, we are of the opinion that legal obligations can only be created and assumed on a voluntary basis. Any far-reaching assumption of authority by the Security Council to enact global legislation is not consistent with the provisions of the United Nations Charter. It is therefore imperative to involve all States in the negotiating process towards the establishment of international norms on the issue.[90]

India was the most outspoken critic, rejecting a legislative role of the Council and threatening to disregard the resolution. India reiterated its concerns in a letter circulated at the adoption of the resolution:

> India is concerned at the increasing tendency of the Security Council in recent years to assume legislative and treaty-making powers on behalf of the international community, binding on all States, a function not envisaged in the Charter of the United Nations.
>
> India has taken note of the observation of cosponsors that the draft resolution contained in document S/2004/326 does not prescribe adherence to treaties to which

---

88   Egypt stated: "We note a growing trend towards granting the Security Council additional legislative powers. Here, we wish to make it very clear that membership of the United Nations and the common desire to strengthen its role places a number of responsibilities on our shoulders in conformity with the provisions of the Charter as drafted by the founding Members. Thus, in defining the role of the Security Council in terms of the maintenance of international peace and security and of guaranteeing compliance by Member States with international law, the Charter does not give the Council legislative authority; it gives it the authority to safeguard the Charter and to monitor compliance with its provisions."; Statement of Mr Aboul Gheit (Egypt) at the 4950th meeting of the Security Council on 22 April 2004; UN-Doc. S/PV.4950 (Resumption 1) at 3.

89   Statement of Mr Sharma (Nepal) at the 4950th meeting of the Security Council on 22 April 2004; UN-Doc. S/PV.4950 (Resumption 1) at 14.

90   Statement of Mr Jenie (Indonesia) at the 4950th meeting of the Security Council on 22 April 2004; UN-Doc. S/PV.4950 at 31. See also the Statement of Mr Requeya Gual (Cuba) at the 4950th meeting of the Security Council on 22 April 2004; UN-Doc. S/PV.4950 at 30.

a State is not party. India cannot accept any obligations arising from treaties that India has not signed or ratified. This position is consistent with the fundamental principles of international law and the law of treaties.

India will not accept externally prescribed norms or standards, whatever their source, on matters within the jurisdiction of its Parliament, including national legislation, regulations or arrangements, which are not consistent with India's national interests or infringe on its sovereignty.[91]

India was the only non-member of the Council that reacted formally at the adoption of the resolution. The statement expresses concern at the legislative role of the Security Council but it does not categorically reject it. The refusal to accept "obligations arising from treaties" cannot be interpreted to mean that India refuses the provisions of the resolution containing similar obligations. The third paragraph of India's statement, however, is a clear rejection of any SC-decision containing norms and standards that India, subjectively, decides not to be in her national interest. This general statement, held in future tense, does not indicate whether it applies to SC-Res. 1540 and seems to be in contradiction to Article 25 of the Charter. It contains some ambiguous formulations and conditions. Its true meaning and consequences will have to be determined in light of the future practice. Nevertheless, the position of India certainly does not amount to "acceptance" of general legislative competences of the Council.

Considering the intense discussion of the Security Council's powers in the public debate, it is surprising that Council Members hardly addressed the issue at the adoption of the resolution on 28 April 2004. The unanimous vote made clear that all Members accepted the legal competence to adopt the resolution. Only Pakistan had reservations:

Pakistan shares the general view expressed in the Council's open debate that the Security Council cannot legislate for the world. The sponsors have assured the Council that this resolution is designed to address a gap in international law to address the risk of terrorists and non-State actors acquiring or developing weapons of mass destruction, and that it does not seek to prescribe specific legislation, which is left to national action by States. ... Pakistan shares the general view of the United Nations Membership that the Security Council cannot assume the stewardship of global non-proliferation and disarmament issues. The Council, composed of 15 States, is not a representative body. It cannot enforce the obligations assumed by five of its members which retain nuclear weapons since they also possess the right of veto in the Council.[92]

---

91   Letter dated 27 April 2004 from the Permanent Representative of India to the United Nations addressed to the President of the Security Council; UN-Doc. S/2004/329 of 28 April 2004.

92   Statement of Mr Akram (Pakistan) at the 4956th meeting of the Security Council on 28 April 2004; UN-Doc. S/PV.4956 at 3.

Pakistan could accept the resolution only as an exceptional measure with precise conditions: there existed an urgent threat, a legal *lacuna* and participation of the wider UN-membership in elaborating the norms. Pakistan made clear that it would not accept general legislative powers of the Security Council without conditions.

iii.   Conclusions

The resolutions discussed in this chapter are significantly different in form and function from the examples before 2001. Though SC-Res. 1373 has obvious roots in the terrorist attacks on 11 September 2001, it does not exclusively regulate that specific event. SC-Res. 1540 is directed at all States without any individually identifiable and locatable breach or threat to the peace. Both resolutions contain provisions that are clearly designed to be general legislation.

The concept of subsequent practice could enable the Security Council to acquire general legislative competences, if there is evidence of recurrence of similar acts and acceptance by the wider membership. The fact that SC-Res. 1540 followed closely the example of its predecessor in form and function implies recurrence. The temporal element is further substantiated by the fact that the regimes both aim at continuity without time limits. SC-Res. 1373 was thus not a unique aberration, an *ultra vires* act remedied by acquiescence, but the beginning of a continuing practice.

Since the Security Council is an executive organ in which not all UN-Members are represented and whose members have different legal rights, the condition of acceptance by the wider membership is particularly relevant. In the case of SC-Res. 1373 the examination of practice has provided substantial evidence of support for the measure and the procedure. Every single UN-member State cooperated with the CTC in the implementation of the resolution. No State considered the Council incompetent to adopt the resolution. The practice in respect to SC-Res. 1373 must be considered as evidence of acceptance not only of the resolution in question but also of the competence to enact such wide, binding rules, at least in the field of terrorism.

The States' reaction to SC-Res. 1540 was very different. While there was general support for both the appraisal of the threat of proliferation of nuclear weapons to non-state actors and, in general, for the Security Council taking action to counter this threat, many delegations proclaimed their dissatisfaction with the Council's assumption of legislative powers. This criticism could imply lack of acceptance. Close reading of the statements shows, on the other hand, that the reservations were mainly raised either in regard to those situations, in which the area targeted by the Council is already regulated by existing treaties, or in cases when the wider membership does not participate in the elaboration of the norms, a condition that, it could be argued, was fulfilled by enabling all States to express their views at the public debate. It is essential, moreover, not to overlook that the interventions at the public debate are not the definite reactions of the States to SC-Res. 1540. The public debate took place almost a week before the resolution was adopted. It was understood and used by the States to present their positions in general or on specific issues of the proposed resolution. As is the practice at the UN, States used the opportunity of a public debate to convey a political message in strong terms, especially if they hoped that a clear message would influence the final deliberations on the resolution. But the interventions in the public debate are not and were not intended to be formal declarations of acceptance or refusal of the resolution or the Council's action.

Valid indications are, however, the statements made at and after the adoption of the resolution. Obviously, the unanimous adoption of the resolution is a clear indication that the 15 Council Members considered the resolution *intra vires*. Pakistan voiced opposition to unrestricted general legislative powers but accepted them under certain conditions. As regards the wider membership, it is surprising that of all the critical voices at the public debate only India formally reiterated its reservations at the adoption of the resolution. It could be argued, that all States – with the sole exception of India – did, in the end, accept the resolution and that the wider Membership has thereby accepted the Council's legislative role for exceptional circumstances. At the time of writing, however, the 1540-regime has only been in force for a few months. It is possible that States use future public debates to elucidate their position. As in the case of the 1373-regime, the most important indication for the acceptance or non-acceptance will be the States' readiness to cooperate with the Committee and to implement the obligations domestically. A final conclusion thus requires further evaluation of State practice.

The practice of the Security Council, on the other hand, shows the increasing determination, especially among the P5, to use the unique powers under Chapter VII to prescribe general and abstract norms for those areas for which they can identify a common interest to establish such norms with immediate and universally binding effect.[93] In October 2004, the Security Council, acting under Chapter VII "recalled" an abstract definition of terrorist acts and instructed States to apply this definition.[94] It is highly likely that the Security Council will make increasing use of its legislative powers in the future. Practice indicates that the P5 are particularly inclined to use this new tool to address "new threats". Terrorism and weapons of mass destruction are just two of these. Similar threats, such as organized crime,

---

93   Considering the intensity of the debate on the legislative authority of the Council, the steadfastness of the permanent Members in ignoring the issue was, if not unexpected, at least remarkable. In the public debate the representative from the UK merely stated: "My delegation believes that, in such circumstances, not only is it appropriate for the Security Council to act, it is imperative that it do so."; Statement of Mr Thomson (UK) at the 4950th meeting of the Security Council on 22 April 2004; UN-Doc. S/PV.4950 at 11. Russia made at similar point, cf. Statement of Mr Gatilov (Russian Federation) at the 4950th meeting of the Security Council on 22 April 2004; UN-Doc. S/PV.4950 at 16. At the adoption of the resolution France observed: "With regard to proliferation, the Security Council draws its legitimacy to act from the Charter of the United Nations."; Statement of Mr De La Sablière (France) at the 4956th meeting of the Security Council on 28 April 2004; UN-Doc. S/PV.4956 at 2.

94   SC-Res. 1566 of 8 October 2004.

trafficking of drugs and arms, etc., could be taken up next. It seems appropriate to therefore examine the scope of the powers the Council would rely on and the consequences of its law-making on the UN and international law.

5.   A New World Order?

A.   *Legislative Powers of the Security Council*

i.   Content and Scope

The practice of the Security Council gives limited information on the form, structure and restrictions of its abstract legislative powers. The norms are abstract and formulated in typical treaty language (SC-Res. 1540 even contains definitions), precise but subject to (mis)interpretation. They apply to a general field of international relations, not to a localized crisis. They are legally binding for all States; they are not retroactive. There is no indication of substantive limits. Before the adoption of SC-Res. 1540 many States stressed the need for a "gap" in treaty-law as a condition for its lawfulness.[95] Though the notion of a "gap" is in itself problematic (there could be different opinions whether it is an omission or a deliberate non-regulation), the underlying concerns regarding the relevance of international law, the UN Charter or *ius cogens* for the Security Council are certainly valid. Kelsen's understanding of Article 24 and its reference to Article 1 result in almost unlimited freedom to act under Chapter VII.[96] Others have rejected this interpretation.[97] Kelsen is correct inasmuch as the sub-system gives the Council powers to authorize acts that would otherwise be violations of the Charter and international law.[98] But this is a systemic

---

[95]   *Cf.* the statement of Pakistan quoted above. At the public debate the Philippines, a SC-Member at the time, stated: "This resolution deviates from time-tested modes of creating multilateral obligations but my delegation essentially regards it as an exceptional measure to address a new and urgent potential threat not covered by existing treaty regimes."; Statement of Mr Baja (Philippines) at the 4950th meeting of the Security Council on 22 April 2004; UN-Doc. S/PV.4950 at 3.

[96]   The restricting referral to the "principles of international law" foreseen in Article 24 only applies to "peaceful means" envisaged under Chapter VI; Kelsen, *The Law of the United Nations* (1951), 96, 275 and 295.

[97]   See Bedjaoui, *The New World Order and the Security Council – Testing the Legality of its Acts* (1994), 32-36; Gowland-Debbas, The Functions of the United Nations Security Council in the International Legal Order, in Byers (ed.) *The Role of Law in International Politics* (2000), 277; Lamb, Legal Limits to United Nations Security Council Powers, in Goodwin-Gill / Talmon eds., *The Reality of International Law: Essays in Honour of Ian Brownlie* (1999), 361 at 370-374.

[98]   Such as, for instance, military sanctions, which would otherwise constitute violations of Article 2(4) and the customary principle of the non-use of force. Similar Macdonald, Changing Relations between the International Court of Justice and the Security Council of the United Nations, *CYIL* 31 (1993), 3 at 18. Writing before the Council adopted its two legislative resolutions Nolte stressed limits arising from the preliminary and

exception. The States' acceptance of the 1267-regime could be interpreted as an indication that, under Chapter VII, the Council is also not bound by essential human rights law, possibly even *ius cogens*.

On the other hand, the justification for special powers to deviate from existing norms has usually been seen in the exceptional and temporary nature of police enforcement measures. This reasoning does not apply to a legislator creating indefinite law. Here, the rules for creating law by treaties could be a guideline. Violations of *ius cogens* would thus be prohibited. Furthermore, an organ of the sub-system creating new norms indefinitely applicable in the sub-system should, in principle, act within the legal parameters of its legal basis or constitution.[99] Both the UN Charter and *ius cogens* are also recognized by some as hierarchically superior to general international law and particularly worthy of protection because of their importance and universal scope and recognition.[100] It would thus seem arguable that the Security Council has to respect these norms in lawmaking. Regarding regular treaties or customary rules of general international law, however, the alleged requirement for a "gap" as a prerequisite for lawmaking by the Council is not convincing. These rights are neither hierarchically superior nor in need of special protection.[101] Should the legislative functions of the Council be accepted, there is no reason why its norms should not be able to supervene existing general international law by means of the *lex specialis* and *lex posterior* rules or by virtue of Article 103. This is supported by practice: Resolutions 1373 and 1540 created rules irrespective of the existence of treaty norms regulating the same issues. Neither resolution relied on the premise that it served only to fill a *lacuna*. At the adoption of SC-Res. 1373 it was underlined that language of the Terrorist Financing Convention was used to assuage fears of legislative inexperience. The fact that the Convention was not yet in force would seem to support the gap-theory. However, the resolution continued to be valid after the Convention entered into force in 2002 and contains

---

situation-specific enforcement function of the Council; Nolte, The Limits of the Security Council's Powers and its Functions in the International Legal System: Some Reflections, in Byers (ed.) *The Role of Law in International Politics* (2000), 315 at 321.

99   Franck, Fairness in the International Legal and Institutional System, *Recueil des Cours* 240 (1993), 190.

100   Macdonald, Fundamental Norms in Contemporary International Law, CYIL 25 (1987), 115 at 128, 134; Pellet, La formation du droit international dans le cadre des Nations Unies, EJIL 6 (1995), 401 at 423-424. The question whether the Council is bound by peremptory norms is dealt with by Frowein/Krisch, Chapter VII in Simma (ed.), *The Charter of the United Nations* (2nd edition; 2002), 705 at 711, with further references.

101   Martenczuk, The Security Council, the International Court and Judicial Review: What Lessons from Lockerbie?, EJIL 10 (1999), 517 at 544-546. However, he does not believe the Council is bound by *ius cogens* when acting under Chapter VII. Schweigman believes that the Security Council is bound to respect the Vienna Convention of the Law of Treaties because it is a treaty organ and, whenever it exercises its "quasi-judicial" authority, customary international law; Schweigman, *The Authority of the Security Council under Chapter VII of the UN Charter* (2001), 203.

provisions found in other terrorism conventions already in force in 2001.[102] Though SC-Res. 1540 refers to the existing validity of the relevant non-proliferation treaties and introduces the new element of non-state actors in its first two paragraphs, para. 3 contains non-proliferation obligations also found in existing conventions.

ii.   Procedure

As regards procedural limitations and conditions, the central requirement for the council's lawmaking is exceptionality. Both legislative resolutions were not adopted merely for the sake of regulating international relations but to address a general threat. At the public debate on non-proliferation Algeria, a Council Member in 2004, emphasized that the Security Council

> ... is acting in an exceptional manner, since, clearly, the Charter does not give it a mandate to legislate on behalf of the international community, but simply gives it the principle responsibility for the maintenance of international peace and security.[103]

The position does not explain how the "exceptional situation" could give the Council this authority. Indeed, the condition of a threat merely arises from its reliance on Chapter VII. It thereby limits, however, the powers to exceptional situations of general crisis. It is true that the Security Council is very free in determining the existence of a threat or breach.[104] Yet, the use of abstract legislation not limited in time implies that the threat must be significant, international and of indefinite duration.

A central question in the public debate was the necessity of participation of the wider membership of the UN. Iran stated:

> The United Nations Charter entrusts the Security Council with the huge responsibility to maintain international peace and security, but it does not confer authority on

---

102   Guillaume stated in reference to the adoption of SC-Res. 1373: "In so acting, the Council rendered certain purely treaty rules binding on all Member States of the United Nations and thus assumed the role of a true international legislator."; Guillaume, Terrorism and International Law, Grotius Lecture at the British Institute of International and Comparative Law, held on 13 November 2003, 8.

103   Statement of Mr Baali (Algeria) at the 4950th meeting of the Security Council on 22 April 2004; UN-Doc. S/PV.4950 at 5.

104   According to Combacau the determination by the Security Council itself actually constitutes the existence of a threat; Combacau, Le Chapitre VII de la Charte des Nations Unies: Résurrection ou Métamorphose ?, in Ben Achour, Laghmani (eds.), Les nouveaux aspects du droit international, Colloque des 14,15 et 16 Avril 1994 (1994), 139 at 45 and 47. The main limitation is self-constraint out of concern for the Council's credibility; Brownlie, International Law at the Fiftieth Anniversary of the United Nations, Recueil des Cours (1995), 9 at 226. The veto serves as a procedural tool to prevent abuse of powers; Herdegen, The "Constitutionalization" of the UN Security System, Vanderbilt Journal of Transnational Law 27 (1994), 135 at 152-153.

the Council to act as a global legislature imposing obligations on States without their participation in the process.[105]

The elected Members of the Council, some of which shared these sentiments, were much more cautious. The Spanish delegation presented its position carefully phrased:

> We believe that, since the Council is legislating for the entire international community, this draft resolution should preferably, although not necessarily, be adopted by consensus and after consultation with non-members of the Council.[106]

Practice corroborates the lack of a requirement to involve the wider membership. In the case of SC-Res. 1373, the non-permanent Members were informed late and had hardly any influence. The non-participation of the wider membership was not criticized. Until late March 2003 the negotiations on SC-Res. 1540 took place almost exclusively within the P5. The elected Council Members had little influence on the text. The public debate a few days before the adoption of the resolution was perceived as an occasion to vent off steam in the face of an impending and unalterable decision.

The two resolutions may be inadequate sources from which one can derive final predicaments on an issue with significant consequences. The evolutionary nature of subsequent practice can lead to the development of a more refined system of checks and balances to limit negative effects. Current practice, however, indicates merely the following requirements for legislation: The Council must identify a significant, international and indefinite threat under Chapter VII, prescribe precise, legal obligations with a wide and general field of application and legally bind the States for the future without time-limit. Though neither resolution directly involved questions of *ius cogens* or the UN Charter, it appears consistent with the law-making functions of the Council that it does not have the competences to derogate peremptory norms or the Charter. Existing regulation by treaties or custom, however, is irrelevant. Participation of wider membership in the elaboration of the norms is not required.

B.   *Consequences*

Should the Security Council have assumed, additionally to its executive functions, the powers of legislation, consequences will arise not only for the UN-system but also for international law. Traditionally, the creation of international law is under-

---

105   Statement of Mr Danesh-Yazdi (Islamic Republic of Iran) at the 4950th meeting of the Security Council on 22 April 2004; UN-Doc. S/PV.4950 at 32. Cf. also the statement of Indonesia quoted above.

106   Statement of Mr Arias (Spain) at the 4950th meeting of the Security Council on 22 April 2004; UN-Doc. S/PV.4950 at 7.

stood to be based on consent.[107] The main traditional sources are custom, in which a State can opt out by being a persistent objector, and treaties, which a State has the freedom to join or to abstain. Under the scenario of a world legislator, bound by hardly any limitations, States would lose that freedom. In becoming members of the UN, States had accepted the competence of the Council to bind them in peace enforcement exercises. They are now confronted with an evolution that threatens their freedom of lawmaking.

Equally significant is the impact on the principle of equal rights of States, embodied in Article 1 of the Charter. States accepted permanent membership and the veto-right of five States in the Council for the sake of exceptional peace enforcement. A general legislative role, however, transfers the inequality into a much larger domain. Practice shows that the inequality goes far beyond permanent membership and veto-right. The P5 effectively control the Council.[108] Should the recent trend of targeting individuals by means of sanctions be taken up in legislation, the inequality could extend to the creation of rights and obligations of the States' nationals.[109] The practice of equipping the primary norms with special monitoring mechanisms, as evidenced in both legislative resolutions, could threaten to extend the inequality further from norm creation to the monitoring phase and into enforcement. The scenario of an unrestrained Security Council with supreme legislative, executive and judicial powers would surpass the most dire predictions of an impending autocratic world order.[110]

It is important to stress that the Council's current practice provides no evidence that it is moving in this direction or that this would be the intention of the P5. Certainly, the P5 have the most incentive to promote furtherCouncil legislation. Their influence enables them to determine the content and scope of the norms and to control enforcement. At the same time, the P5 realize that measures going beyond recognized police enforcement might entail States to reject them and, if

---

107   Henkin, International Law: Politics, Values and Functions, *Recueil des Cours* 216 (1989), 46. See also the judgment of the Permanent Court of International Justice in the Lotus Case (*France v. Turkey*), PCIJ Series A Number 10 (1927), 18.

108   Pellet, La formation du droit international dans le cadre des Nations Unies, EJIL 6 (1995), 401 at 418-419. The recent practice is described by Mahbubani, The Permanent and Elected Council Members, in Malone (ed.), *The UN Security Council – From the Cold War to the 21st Century* (2004), 253.

109   The Security Council could attempt to create norms that benefit nationals that the permanent members want to reward, such as their own, more than other nationals.

110   See, generally, to the potentially negative consequences of increasing powers of the Security Council Koskenniemi, The Police in the Temple – Order, Justice and the UN: A Dialectical View, EJIL 6 (1995), 325 at 338-339, 341 – 348; Arangio-Ruiz, On the Security Council's Law-Making, Rivista di Diritto Internazionale 83 (2000), 609 at 630, 686-688, 700. In 1950 Kelsen wrote: "The veto right of the five permanent members of the Security Council, which places the privileged powers above the law of the United Nations, establishes their legal hegemony over all the other members of the Organisation and thus stamps on it the mark of an autocratic or aristocratic regime."; Kelsen, *The Law of the United Nations* (1951), 276.

that proved inadequate to protect their rights, to leave the sub-system.[111] Since it is doubtful – at least for some of the permanent members – that any new international organized system would give them comparable rights, influence and power, it is in their highest interest to maintain and protect the *status quo*. The P5 have been careful to accompany the expansion of Council powers since 2001 with measures aimed at making its work more accessible and transparent.[112] The permanent members therefore would take every precaution to prevent a development that creates the impression of the emergence of an absolutist regime.

The Security Council developing into an unrestrained tyrant is one extreme scenario. Legislative powers of the Council could also significantly benefit the UN and international law. A Council enacting binding universal norms could be an efficient instrument in a global world and strengthen the UN considerably in an area where its current structures do not enable quick and decisive action.[113] Replacing the tedious and imperfect multilateral norm-creating process by a single binding decision would be welcomed by some, especially practitioners.[114] In practice, however, caution and concern regarding the misuse of the Council's legislative powers will likely outweigh any interest in improving international norm-creation. States will focus on instances of perceived bias, arrogance, ineptitude, double standards and hypocrisy in the past practice of the Council. Lack of confidence in the institution will lead many States to defy and resist any expansion of its functions. However, the current reform process at the UN, aiming *inter alia* at increasing

---

111   Though rare, States will oppose Council decisions: The Organization of African States decided in 1998 not to implement the flight ban against Libya. See also the reaction of India to SC-Res. 1540 discussed above.

112   The P5 have, over the past years, supported measures to increase transparency and the participation of the wider membership in Council activity. Briefings of Special Representatives of the Secretary General are now regularly held in open meetings to enable the passive participation of the wider membership. See also Hulton, Council Working Methods and Procedure, in Malone (ed.), *The UN Security Council – From the Cold War to the 21st Century* (2004), 237 at 242-243.

113   In rejecting the pessimistic appraisals of the Security Council as a danger to the international rule of law and the independence of States Fassbender writes: "At the end of the twentieth century, the world clearly requires an exercise of more, not less authority on a global level; and international lawyers, this reviewer believes, should encourage this development rather than warn against it. For the alternative is either inertia or unilateral action taken by a State or group of States without assuring the target State and the general membership of the international community of that minimum of participation and procedural justice which is characteristic of the decision-making process of the Security Council."; Fassbender, Quis iudicabit? The Security Council, Its Power and Its Legal Control, EJIL 11 (2000), 219 at 220.

114   Szasz, The Security Council Starts Legislating, AJIL 96 (2002), 901. Though not comparable to the creation of international law for States, the experience in localized UN-administrations like those in Kosovo and East Timor shows that the UN is, in principle, capable of enacting legislation. See von Carlowitz, Crossing the Boundary from the International to the Domestic Realm: UNMIK Lawmaking and Property Rights in Kosovo, Global Governance 10 (2004), 307.

legitimacy of its organs, is a window of opportunity for an alternative constructive approach. The potential advantages for the UN and the international community as a whole make an examination worthwhile, whether conditions could be devised to adequately reduce the risk to the legal equality of States and the freedom of consent in the creation of international law.

C.   Quest for Legitimacy

In order to protect the rights of the States and to enhance the legitimacy of the Security Council acting as world legislator various conditions and limitations could be introduced. They could focus on content or procedure.

i.   Content

While limitations of substance primarily come to mind in connection with the competence to create norms that prevail over existing law (section 5.I. above), some authors have focused on the need to protect States from excessive content of the obligations. Kirgis emphasizes the need to respect the "proportionality principle", by which the interference into the rights of the States must not be excessively disproportional to the aims pursued.[115] Macdonald stresses that the Security Council must comply with standards of procedural fairness and may not interfere into rights that may be temporarily suspended by a decision under Chapter VII but that cannot be extinguished, such as the determination of boundaries, human rights and rights concerning extradition examined in the Lockerbie case.[116] For Szasz the legal basis in Chapter VII limits the substance amenable for legislation to issues relevant for the maintenance of peace, such as terrorism, violations of the obligation to maintain friendly relations, disarmament and arms-control, extreme violations of human rights or humanitarian law, or massive assaults on the international environments.[117] Since almost all areas of international law could constitute the setting for a threat to international peace, this restriction is of little practical effect.

One limitation of substance seems advisable in view of the experience with SC-Res. 1267. This sanctions regime demonstrates the limited capacity of the Council to ensure adequate respect for human rights and appropriate treatment of individuals. Though there is currently no indication of any legislative projects directly affecting individuals, the tendency to target private persons and entities in sanctions regimes and the lack of adequate safeguard mechanisms advises caution.[118] In view of the

---

115   Kirgis, The Security Council's first Fifty Years, AJIL 89 (1995), 506 at 517. This applies also to norms that demand States to sacrifice their existence; Herdegen, The "Constitutionalization" of the UN Security System, Vanderbilt Journal of Transnational Law 27 (1994), 135 at 156.

116   Macdonald, Changing Relations between the International Court of Justice and the Security Council of the United Nations, *CYIL* 31 (1993), 3 at 31.

117   Szasz, The Security Council Starts Legislating, AJIL 96 (2002), 901 at 904.

118   Article 2(7) serves as the principal safeguard protecting the domestic jurisdiction of the States. However, it is not applicable under Chapter VII-enforcement. As explained

criticism by States and international and non-governmental organizations that the Council had to endure in respect to the 1267-regime, it would also seem to be in its own interest that the legislative powers are understood not to include the right to create norms of private law, especially inter-personal law, directly affecting the rights of nationals of the Member States.

ii.   Procedure

Protection of the principle of consent in the creation of international norms does not require changes of substantive law but of procedure. At first glance, the attempt to reconcile the principle of consent with the mandatory system under Chapter VII seems impossible. It is precisely the unique binding nature of lawmaking under Chapter VII that would be the main incentive to develop the legislative role of the Council. Nevertheless, with some imagination procedures could be devised to enable States to protect their sovereign rights without undermining the authority of the Council. A procedure could be developed to enable States to request exemption from the application of the resolution as a whole or in part, for instance, by determining in advance the content and scope of such requests. This would be in accordance with Article 48(1) of the Charter. Though the binding character of the resolution would not be affected, the formal procedure enabling States to request exemption could help maintain an element of free consent.

A realistic accommodation of the concerns about inequality of States and individuals is more difficult, although in a time, when the principles of equality of human beings, freedom and democracy are postulated as supreme values, it would seem appropriate that all lawmakers and subjects of the law have equal rights. A simple, though unrealistic solution would be for the P5 to relinquish their right of veto in all legislative acts. An alternative solution would be an understanding that legislative acts require consensus. This would correspond to the practice so far. However, it is doubtful whether an "understanding" on procedure would be accepted as an adequate safeguard by the wider membership. Many States also believe that the current composition of the Council de-legitimizes its decisions even if they are adopted unanimously. Most importantly, however, the inequality in the Council is not only present at the time of adoption of the decisions but especially influential during the preparatory consultations.[119] A satisfactory safeguard of equal rights of States would thus necessitate participation of the wider membership.

---

above, the term "enforcement" is not defined in the Charter and, if legislation is possible under Chapter VII, it could also be applied to all fields of the law.

119   Pellet, La formation du droit international dans le cadre des Nations Unies, EJIL 6 (1995), 401 at 420. Zemanek writes: "It seems that, since the Council started working properly after 1989, its permanent members, once they come to an understanding among themselves, feel not really constrained in their decision-making by provisions of the Charter or by rules of international law if it suits their combined interests; and they are apparently able to persuade other Council members to fall into line."; Zemanek, The Legal Foundations of the International System, Offprint from the *Recueil des Cours* 266 (1997), 93.

Some possibilities of interaction between the Council and the wider member-ship are foreseen in the Charter, such as public debates or submission of annual reports, but none enable true cooperation.[120] Some authors have developed insti-tutional power-sharing solutions. Reisman proposed the formation of a "Chapter VII Consultation Committee" of the General Assembly that would be consulted whenever the Security Council plans to act under Chapter VII.[121] Though not con-ceived for legislative decisions, such a mechanism would be adaptable. In practice the Council scrupulously protects its independence from the other UN-organs but instances of power-sharing exist that even concern such sensitive issues as the use of the veto. The General Assembly established a catalogue of "procedural deci-sions" for Article 27(2) that exclude the applicability of the veto, which has, so far, been complied with.[122] The General Assembly could take the initiative of adopting a resolution laying out the parameters and conditions of legislative action.[123]

---

120   See to the Charter provisions Fassbender, Uncertain Steps into a Post-Cold War World: The Role and Functioning of the UN Security Council after a Decade of Measures against Iraq, EJIL 13 (2002) 273 at 288-292.

121   The Council would notify the Committee, share information on which the delibera-tions were based and solicit the Committee's views; Reisman, The Constitutional Cri-sis in the United Nations, AJIL 87 (1993), 83 at 99. Franck suggested a power-sharing arrangement between the organs before the establishment of peace-keeping opera-tions; Franck, The United Nations as Guarantor of International Peace and Security in Tomuschat (ed.), *The United Nations at Fifty – A Legal Perspective* (1995), 25 at 36. An advisory role could also be foreseen for the International Law Commission, a body that assists the General Assembly in the creation of international law, but its working methods are hardly compatible with the urgency required under Chapter VII.

122   GA-Res. 267 (III) of 14 April 1949.

123   Most proposals focus on the General Assembly not only because it is the only organ comprising all Member States of the UN but also because Article 13(a) gives it the competence in the field of progressive development of international law. Another UN-organ that could serve as guardian of the equal rights of the States in the creation of international norms is the ICJ. The difficult relationship between the executive and the judicial organ of the UN has been dealt with in detail in literature, especially after the Lockerbie incident. The main concern is that review by the ICJ would undermine the authority of the Council; Alvarez, Judging the Security Council AJIL 90 (1996), 1, with many further references. Currently, any inter-institutional procedure or review-func-tion is entirely unrealistic. With adequate imaginative spirit two possible functions come to mind: The ICJ could assist the Council by means of an advisory opinion on the legal implications of the legislative project before the decision is taken; or the resolu-tion could provide a mechanism by which an Advisory Opinion is requested whenever a dispute concerning the scope, content and, possibly, even the applicability of the norms arises. The Court would thus assist the Council in interpreting the norms but would not interfere in questions of enforcement. The States would be reassured that a body mandated to ensure respect for international law would be available to protect their interests.

If an inter-organ solution is too ambitious, the recent practice of opening the Council meetings to non-members could be the basis for alternative procedures. In this respect SC-Res. 1540 is a deterrent example. At the time of the public debate, the P5 had been consulting for half a year and the project had reached the stage of near finality. The adjustments in the draft resolution after the debate were less motivated by the intention to accommodate the concerns raised by the wider membership but rather to enable all Council Members to join consensus. Effective participation of all States would require a public debate at the beginning of the deliberations and a procedure that gives them confidence that their contributions are truly registered and be taken into consideration.[124] Regular information about the negotiating process (briefings by the Security Council President) would be appropriate. Proposals submitted in writing should receive a substantive response. The different opinions expressed could be reflected in a report of the President before the adoption of the resolution. Essentially, from the many possibilities to include the wider membership in the legislative process, those creating the subjective impression on the part of the States that attention was devoted to their concerns and that their proposals were seriously considered will be successful in enhancing the legitimacy of the Council's decisions.

D.   Conclusion

Since the end of the Cold War the Security Council has been increasingly active and has assumed functions beyond those enumerated in the Charter. With SC-Res. 1373 and SC-Res. 1540 it adopted the role of a world legislator, enacting binding general legal norms to address issues of urgent concern. Should the Council have been endowed with the powers to make law, which could be argued on the basis of the concept of subsequent practice, its competences would be greatly enhanced, – especially since practice indicates there are few limitations of content or procedure. Perhaps, such powers are useful or even necessary to deal with the de-localized "new threats" of our time.[125] In view of the potential effects on international law and the UN system, however, the States and the international legal community will have to devise means to ensure that the legislative powers of the Security Council are not seen as a threat in itself, a threat for a stable, equal and legitimate international order.

The evolutionary nature of subsequent practice facilitates revision of an organ's competences. This article has examined limitations and conditions of content and procedure destined to minimize negative effects of Security Council legislation. Since they curtail the Council in its freedom of action or contain work- and time-

---

124   The experience of Ambassadors, who wait for hours to declare their States' vital concerns to a gradually diminishing group of visibly bored Third Secretaries seated around the Council table, increases the level of frustration of non-Council Members with every public debate.

125   Hume, The Security Council in the Twenty-First Century, in Malone (ed.), *The UN Security Council – From the Cold War to the 21st Century* (2004), 607 at 613.

consuming procedures, it is uncertain whether the gain in legitimacy would be an adequate trade-off to convince the Council Members, especially the P5, to provide the necessary support. An important factor would be the interest of the Council in the effectiveness of its decisions. If States believe a resolution is not legitimate, compliance with the obligations and cooperation with the Council will be limited. The debate preceding the adoption of SC-Res. 1540 showed serious reservations on the part of the wider membership regarding unrestricted legislative powers. Legislative acts not deemed legitimate face the risk of unsatisfactory implementation. To ensure effectiveness, the Council is well advised to adopt measures that indicate an honest commitment to abide by strict limitations and conditions in lawmaking. The extent of safeguards and limitations, however, will essentially depend on the determination of the States, civil society and scholarship to continue striving for more legitimacy of Council action.

Should a process emerge that enables the Security Council to use its legislative powers effectively with the approval and support of the States, the benefits for the UN organization and for the international community could be substantial. Lawmaking by the Council may become the international community's method of choice to counter decentralized international threats, such as terrorism, non-proliferation or trafficking of arms, drugs or persons. The combination of legitimate legislative powers and enforcement competences under Chapter VII could become a powerful stimulus for the UN. In appraising SC-Res. 1373 Szasz wrote in 2002:

"Now that this door has been opened, however, it seems likely to constitute a precedent for further legislative activities. If used prudently, this new tool will enhance the United Nations and benefit the world community, whose ability to create international law through traditional processes has lagged behind the urgent requirements of the new millennium."[126]

Not even two years later, SC-Res. 1540 proved Szasz correct as regards his prediction of the 1373-regime becoming a precedent for further legislative acts of the Council. It remains to be seen whether his optimism regarding the enhancement of the UN and the benefit for the world community will also prove prophetic.

---

126   Szasz, The Security Council Starts Legislating, AJIL 96 (2002), 901 at 905.

18. Contribution of the General Assembly to the Constitutional Development and Interpretation of the United Nations Charter

Manuel Rama-Montaldo

1. Introduction

After an examaination of a number of representative examples indicative of the pattern followed in practice by the General Assembly of the United Nations in interpreting the UN Charter provisions, the present chapter will consider the role played by the notion of "constitution" as applied to the Charter, in the development of such interpretative practice, and what are the interactions of such a notion with the norms on interpretation of treaties contained in the 1969 Vienna Convention on the Law of Treaties elaborated and adopted under the auspices of the General Assembly. The chapter will also examine the limits, if any, to which such interpretative practice may be subjected.

2. The General Assembly and its Special Position to Influence the Interpretation of the Charter Provisions

Commentators of the United Nations Charter have often stressed the special position of the General Assembly within the system created at San Francisco. To a large extent this special position of the General Assembly is rooted in some specific hallmarks of its organic nature, such as its aspiration to universality, the breadth of its competences, and its interaction with other United Nations organs. Through the interplay of these characteristics the Assembly has succeeded in becoming over the years a universal forum for discussion of practically every issue of worldwide interest, transforming itself, as it has often been said, in the "town-meeting of the world" and in the "consciousness of mankind". This process, which also implies a democratization of international relations, has also often led, notwithstanding the recommendatory nature of the Assembly's decision making powers, to a process of creation or consolidation of new norms of international law through unanimous or consensus recommendations which the subsequent practice of States has shown to reflect what they consider to be the international law on a given subject matter.

Ronald St. John Macdonald & Douglas M. Johnston (eds.), Towards World Constitutionalism, *pp. 493-513.*
© *2005 Koninklijke Brill NV. Printed in The Netherlands.* ISBN 90 04 14612 1.

What was, at the inception of the Organization, an "aspiration" to universality has today been almost fully realized with the Organization's practically universal membership. Since all members of the Organization are represented in the General Assembly, the Assembly is the only principal organ of the United Nations which benefits from the input which such broad membership entails in terms of a full reflection of the world's political, social and cultural spectrum.

Also contributing to the above-mentioned special role of the General Assembly is the broad scope of this main organ's functions and powers which are, for the most part, described in Chapter IV of the United Nations Charter. The Assembly, under Article 10, has the power to discuss any question or any matter within the scope of the Charter or relating to the powers and functions of any organs therein provided, and to make recommendations on such questions or matters to the UN members or to the Security Council or to both. This generic provision is further detailed and specified in Articles 11 to 17 of the Charter. Thus, under Article 11, and subject to the limitations of Articles 11 (2) (in fine) and 12 (1), the Assembly has the power to discuss and make recommendations on general questions or specific situations regarding the maintenance of international peace and security. Under Article 14, it further has the power to recommend measures for the peaceful adjustment of international situations. Under Article 13 it is mandated to initiate studies and make recommendations for the purpose of promoting international co-operation in the political, economic, social, cultural, educational and health fields, of assisting in the realization of human rights and fundamental freedoms and of encouraging the progressive development of international law and its codification. It also has, under Articles 15 and 17, the power to receive and consider reports from the Security Council and other organs of the United Nations as well as to consider and approve the budget of the Organization.

This amplitude of the General Assembly's competence, together with its almost universal membership and its interaction with other United Nations organs, has placed it in a unique position to also influence in a decisive manner the constitutional development of the United Nations Charter through its own practice in the interpretation or application of the relevant provisions of the Charter. As is well known, there is no organ in the United Nations structure charged with the "authentic" interpretation of the UN Charter provisions for all organs. Even the advisory opinions of the International Court of Justice, although conveying a special weight and exercising a great influence in the subsequent practice of the organs concerned, have not in themselves binding character. It was clarified in the San Francisco Conference that "in the course of the operations from day to day of the various organs of the Organization, it is inevitable that each organ will interpret such parts of the Charter as are applicable to its particular functions. This process is inherent in the functioning of any body which operates under an instrument defining its functions and powers."[1]

The above notwithstanding, the General Assembly, because of its special features in the UN structure, has been in a position to lead the way into a dynamic, ev-

---

[1]   United Nations Conference on International Organization (UNCIO), Vol. 13, p. 709.

olutive and purpose-oriented interpretation of the Charter provisions which has to a large extent attenuated the rigidity of the articles dealing with the amendments to the Charter. This it has done in direct and indirect ways. Directly, through its own practice in resolutions concerning its own substantive competence, or procedural or internal matters. Indirectly through its interaction with other principal organs such as the Security Council and ECOSOC, through the activity of its subsidiary organs or of international conferences convened by the Assembly, and through the request of advisory opinions to the International Court of Justice on matters relating to the Assembly's competence.

3.   Brief Review of the General Assembly's Practice in Interpreting Charter Provisions

The dynamic, evolutive and purpose-oriented character of the interpretation or application of the Charter provisions by the Assembly may be perceived in numerous areas of its competence. The present review will refer to some of the most telling examples in areas of a very diverse nature.

A.   *Number of Representatives*

Thus, for instance, Article 9 (2) of the Charter states that each member shall have not more than five representatives in the General Assembly. A strict and to the letter application of this provision, while it would ensure a "formal" equality between all members of the United Nations in the General Assembly, would also create a factual inequality given the different involvement of the members in the various activities of the General Assembly. Paradoxically, by giving to the word "representative" a restrictive sense, the Assembly, through its Rules of Procedure and actual practice, has succeeded in providing the article with a flexible application which permits its adaptation to the actual needs of delegations.

Thus, Rule of Procedure 25 clarifies that "the delegation of a member shall consist of not more than five representatives and five alternate representatives and as many advisors, technical advisors, experts and persons of similar status as may be required by the delegation" and Rule 26 that "an alternate representative may act as a representative upon designation by the delegation". Furthermore, Rules 100 and 101 allow that advisors, technical advisors, experts and persons of similar status be assigned as members of the main Committees and other Committees of the Assembly, the only limitation being that they cannot be members of the Bureau of the Committee or seat in plenary meetings, unless designated as alternate representatives.[2] By confining the scope of paragraph 2 of Article 9 of the Charter to a

---

[2]   In practice, the prohibition to seat in plenary meetings appears to be hardly enforced, even during the voting process, *cf.* André Levin, in Cot and Pellet, *La Charte des Nations Unies, Commentaire*, Paris, Second Edition, p. 240; Siegfried Magiera, in *The Charter of the United Nations. A Commentary*. Edited by Bruno Simma, Second Edition, Oxford University Press, Vol. I, p. 250.

strict concept of "representative" the Assembly has, without incurring in a breach of the article, adopted an interpretation which ensures the effectiveness of the work of the delegations in the pursuit of the purposes of the Organization.

B.   *Participation of Observers*

The participation of observers in the work of the General Assembly is another case in point. The only mention the Charter makes of participation by non members in the work of the General Assembly is contained in Articles 11 (2) and 35 (2), according to which the General Assembly may discuss and make recommendations on any dispute brought to it by a State which is not a member of the United Nations if such a State is a party to the dispute and it accepts in advance for the purposes of the dispute, the obligations of pacific settlement provided in the Charter. Yet, notwithstanding the silence of the Charter and the Rules of Procedure of the Assembly, the latter has developed a practice whereby a number of entities of different nature have been granted the right to participate, in various degrees and under the broad designation of "observers", in the work of the Assembly, its committees, subsidiary bodies and conferences convened by it. These observers may be States not members of the United Nations, national liberation movements, specialized agencies contemplated in Article 57 (of an intergovernmental nature), which under Article 63 are brought, by agreement, into relationship with the United Nations (such as FAO, UNESCO, etc.), other intergovernmental organizations in the regional, social, economic and cultural fields, as well as non-governmental organizations.

The source of their status as "observers" may be an agreement which brings the entity into relationship with the United Nations, a resolution of the General Assembly or even the practice of the Assembly in conjunction with a decision of the Secretary General. As for their actual rights of participation in the work of the Assembly, they may also vary depending on the source on which they are based[3] and they can range from attending the meetings of the organs concerned, having access to its documentation, distributing documentation in such organ to making oral statements.[4] The exercise of some of these rights occasionally may be dependent on a decision of the chairman or Bureau of the organ concerned subject to the

---

3   For instance, Resolution 52/160 of 15 December 1997 defines "participation" of non-governmental organizations in the Diplomatic Conference for the establishment of an international criminal court as "attending meetings of its plenary and, unless otherwise decided by the Assembly in specific situations, formal meetings of its subsidiary bodies except the drafting group, receiving copies of the official documents, making available their materials to delegates and addressing, through a limited number of their representatives, its opening and/or closing sessions, as appropriate, in accordance with the rules of procedure to be adopted by the Conference" (para. 9) *cf.* also Rama-Montaldo, *Manuel. La codification du droit international*, Colloque d´Aix-en-Provence, Société Française pour le droit international, Pedone, Paris, 1999 pp. 198-199.

4   Aside from Member States, the only provision contained in the Rules of Procedure for making oral or written statements is for the Secretary General or a member of the Secretariat designated by him as his representative, (*cf.* Rule 112).

approval of the plenary. Perhaps the common denominator to the legal status of all the "observers" may be defined negatively, by asserting that they cannot participate in the decision-making process of the organ concerned, whether substantively or procedurally.

What is most relevant here is to stress the fact that the participation of observers, as briefly described above, has been developed by the General Assembly in the silence of the Charter provisions and even of its Rules of Procedure.[5] This silence has been interpreted rather than as a prohibition, as a door open to organize the Assembly's work in the manner most conducive to carry out the purposes of the Charter, in particular to achieve international cooperation in solving international problems of an economic, social, cultural or humanitarian character and to be a centre for harmonizing the actions of nations in the attainment of the common ends laid down in the Charter.

Further examples of this purpose-oriented interpretation of the Charter provisions by the General Assembly over the years, may be found in connection with its decision-making process and with the creation of subsidiary organs by the Assembly.

C.   *Decision-Making Process*

As regards the decision-making process, the Charter, in Article 18, contemplates a voting process where a distinction is made between decisions on "important questions" which require a majority of at least two thirds of the members present and voting, and decisions on "other questions", including the determination of additional categories of questions to be decided by a two thirds majority, which require just a majority of the members present and voting. Paragraph 2 of Article 18 as well as Rules 83, 84, 81 and 19 of the Rules of Procedure, rather than giving a definition of "important questions" provide an enumeration of such questions.

Notwithstanding this clear decision-making procedure set out in the Charter and in the Rules of Procedure, the Assembly, from its 19th session onwards, has increasingly adopted its resolutions and decisions without resorting to a formal vote. This "no vote" or "consensus" procedure was originally devised in order to avoid the application of article 19 on suspension of vote, to a number of States which were in arrears of their contribution to the Organization because of their resistance to accept as expenses of the Organization the expenditures authorized by the Assembly to cover the costs of the United Nations operations in the Congo (ONUC) and of the operations of the United Nations Emergency Force in the Middle East (UNEF). Yet, subsequently, this "no vote", "no objection" or "consensus" procedure became a standard rule for decision-making in the Assembly. Delegations would consider it desirable to seek consensus first, and only if the reaching of such consensus proves to be impossible would a vote be taken. By resorting to consensus, the contents of a

---

5   In the case of subsidiary organs of the General Assembly the point could be made that under Rule 161, the subsidiary organ being the master of its own procedure, this is also the basis for the status of observers in that organ.

resolution or decision would then represent the minimum common denominator attainable on a given subject matter.

The legitimacy of this procedure would be ensured by the fact that any delegation can, if it so wishes, ask for a vote in accordance with the Rules of Procedure. This practice of the General Assembly concerning its decision-making has been justified initially on the need to ensure the continuity of the Assembly's work at a time of crisis. Subsequently, once the crisis was over, on the perceived enhanced acceptability enjoyed by a resolution or decision when adopted by a non objection or consensus procedure, which would presumably lead to an increased effectiveness of the work of the Organization.

D.   Establishment of Subsidiary Organs

The power of the General Assembly to establish subsidiary organs as it deems necessary for the performance of its functions is expressly laid down in Article 22 of the Charter. Many subsidiary organs have been created by the Assembly under the umbrella of this provision to the point that the proliferation of such organs has come under criticism and has been pointed out as one of the aspects of the Organization needing reform.[6] But there are two aspects of the interpretation of this article by the Assembly over the years which deserve special mention in this brief review.

The first was the creation by the General Assembly in 1949 (Resolution 351 A(IV) of 24 November 1949) of the Administrative Tribunal of the United Nations, competent to hear and pass judgment upon applications alleging non-observance of contracts of employment of staff members of the UN Secretariat or of the terms of appointment of such staff members. Faced with the need to provide for funds to cover some substantial awards of compensation made by the Tribunal and given the resistance of some member States to comply with such awards, the Assembly decided to request an advisory opinion from the International Court of Justice asking whether the Assembly had the right on any grounds to refuse to give effect to an award of compensation made by the Tribunal and, in the affirmative, what would be the legal grounds upon which the Assembly could lawfully exercise such a right.

The opinion of the Court is of relevance here not so much because of the reply it gave to the questions above but rather, because in doing so, it had to give a rationale justifying the establishment of the Tribunal by the Assembly and provide a purpose-oriented criterion for the interpretation of the Charter. The Court recalled its dictum in the Reparation Advisory Opinion[7] that "under international law, the Organization must be deemed to have those powers which, though not expressly provided in the Charter, are conferred upon it by necessary implication as being essential to the performance of its duties". It went on to find that, under article 101 of the Charter, to establish regulations for United Nations staff was one of the functions of the General Assembly. Taking into account also article 22 which provides

---

6   *Cf.* for instance, Meinhard Hilf and Daniel-Erasmus Khan, in Bruno Simma, *op. cit.*, commentary to Article 22, p. 432.

7   Advisory Opinion on Reparation for Injuries, ICJ Reports 1949, p. 182.

that the Assembly may establish such subsidiary organs as it deems necessary for the performance of its functions, the Court found that "the power to establish a tribunal to do justice between the Organization and the staff members may be exercised by the General Assembly". In the view of the Court "the power to establish a tribunal to do justice as between the Organization and the staff members was essential to ensure the efficient working of the Secretariat, and to give effect to the paramount consideration of securing the highest standards of efficiency, competence and integrity. Capacity to do this arises by necessary intendment out of the Charter."[8]

The second aspect concerning subsidiary organs which deserves special mention in this review is the participation by the Assembly in the setting up of joint subsidiary organs with other principal organs such as ECOSOC and with the UN specialized agencies. An example of the first is the Committee on Programme and Coordination. An example of the second is the Joint Inspection Unit.[9] Neither Article 22 dealing with subsidiary organs of the Assembly, nor Article 68 relating to subsidiary bodies of ECOSOC nor Article 7 dealing in general with subsidiary bodies of the UN principal organs, expressly provide for the joint establishment of such bodies. Their creation, which is not precluded either by such articles, appears to respond to an application of the principle of effectiveness in discharging the functions of the Organization as well as to a perception that the possibility of resorting to them is implied in expressions such as, "necessary" or "necessary for the performance of its functions" contained in those articles.[10]

E.   Maintenance of International Peace and Security

The provisions of the Charter dealing with the interaction of the General Assembly and the Security Council in the maintenance of international peace and security, namely Articles 11, 12, 34 and 35, are of particular importance in the global context of the purposes of the United Nations, raise significant issues concerning the balance of powers as contemplated in the Charter between two of the principal organs of the Organization and have been among the most commented upon provisions of the Charter, particularly since the adoption by the General Assembly on 3 November 1950 of Resolution 377 (V), known as the Uniting for Peace resolution. In

---

8   Effects of Awards of Compensation made by the UN Administrative Tribunal, ICJ Reports 1954, reproduced in LC Green, *International Law through the Cases*, London 1959, Chapter 41, pp. 848-849.

9   The Committee on Programme and Coordination jointly established by the General Assembly and ECOSOC is in charge of planning, programming and co-ordination of UN activities with financial implications. The Joint Inspection Unit is a subsidiary body of the General Assembly and the legislative bodies of the UN specialized agencies which become party to its statute and has the function of examining the management methods of the international organizations within the UN system and of making recommendations to their competent legislative organs for the most economical and optimal use of available resources. *Cf.* Janicke, in Bruno Simma, *op. cit.*, commentary to Article 7, p. 227.

10   *Ibid.* pp. 227-228.

the light of the purpose of this brief review, their examination here will only seek to bring out some particular aspects of their interpretation or application by the Assembly in which a specific purpose-oriented or dynamic approach are manifest.

One such aspect to be noted is the interpretation the Assembly made early in its application of paragraph 2 of Article 11 to the effect that its competence to "discuss any questions relating to the maintenance of international peace and security brought before it by any member of the United Nations, or by the Security Council, or by a State which is not a member of the United Nations in accordance with Article 35 paragraph 2" and "to make recommendations with regard to such questions to the State or States concerned or to the Security Council or to both" necessarily implied for the General Assembly the power to investigate such question brought before it in order to be in a position to properly discuss and recommend on such matter. Thus, for instance, an investigation commission to make findings on the field was created in connection with the Palestine question. A similar commission was also established in connection with the problem of the relations between Greece and its northern neighbors, namely Albania, Bulgaria and Yugoslavia.[11]

Another aspect worth mentioning concerning the evolutive interpretation of these provisions, is the use the Assembly has made of two features of Article 11 paragraph 2. The first feature is that the State which brings the question to the Assembly for discussion does not necessarily have to be involved in or be a part concerned in that question. The second feature is that the paragraph does not require that the recommendation be addressed to the State which brings the question to the Assembly. Consequently, the Assembly has interpreted the provision in a manner enabling it to make recommendations to a broad range of addressees not expressly contemplated in the paragraph. As one commentary to the Charter puts it, these addressees have covered "member States", "specific member States", "all States", "governments", "the people of a specific member State", "the parties concerned", "subsidiary or special agencies", "the Security Council", "the Secretary General", and "non-State actors" such as "the Afghan parties, in particular the Taliban" or "the Kosovar Serb and Albanian leaderships" or "representatives" and "all others concerned."[12]

A development of particular importance in the history of the interpretation of the articles dealing with the Assembly's competence in the maintenance of international peace and security was the adoption by the Assembly of Resolution 377 (V) (Uniting for Peace). Its importance arises from the fact that it touches upon the interpretation of the relevant Charter provisions in those parts establishing the balance of powers between the Assembly and the Security Council in the field of maintenance of international peace and security. The two provisions concerned in this balance are the second clause of paragraph 2 of Article 11 and Article 12. According to the first "any such question on which action is necessary shall be referred to the Security Council by the General Assembly either before or after discussion".

---

11   *Cf.* Jiménez de Aréchaga, Eduardo, Derecho Constitucional de las Naciones Unidas, Madrid, 1958, p. 181.

12   *Cf.* Kay Hailbronner and Eckart Klein, in Bruno Simma, *op. cit.*, commentary to Article 11, p. 283.

According to the second, "while the Security Council is exercising in respect to any dispute or situation the functions assigned to it in the present Charter, the General Assembly shall not make any recommendations with regard to that dispute or situation unless the Security Council so requests". These two provisions constitute a manifestation of the fact that, according to Article 24, in the field of international peace and security, the Security Council has the "primary" responsibility.

The Uniting for Peace resolution comes into operation when, "because of a lack of unanimity of its permanent members", the Security Council "fails to exercise its primary responsibility for the maintenance of international peace and security". In such a case the overriding character of "maintenance of peace and security" as the fundamental purpose of the United Nations comes to the forefront and the Assembly assumes the competence which the Council cannot exercise. Consequently, the two criteria for the delimitation of the sphere of competence contemplated in Articles 12 and 11 (2) are overridden. First, since the Council is paralyzed by inaction, it can no longer be considered as "exercising in respect to any dispute or situation the functions assigned to it in the present Charter". Second, the Assembly can recommend "action" or, as the resolution puts it "the General Assembly shall consider the matter immediately with a view to making appropriate recommendations to members for collective measures, including in the case of a breach of the peace or act of aggression the use of armed force when necessary, to maintain or restore international peace and security".

Therein lies the ground-breaking character of this resolution of the Assembly: to put the main purpose of the Organization in the forefront and to interpret the relevant provisions of the Charter in such a manner that such purpose is effectively implemented. The "emergency special sessions" to which the resolution refers (namely, "if not in session at the time, the General Assembly may meet in emergency special session within twenty four hours of the request therefor") are in reality a sub-species of the "special sessions" contemplated in Article 20 of the Charter, a sub-species to be convened in the special circumstances described in the resolution.

Aside from the cases covered by the Uniting for Peace resolution referred to above, the interpretation of Article 12, in particular of the words "the Security Council is exercising" as a limit to the competence of the General Assembly in the field of the maintenance of international peace and security, has undergone an evolution over the years. Initially the Assembly interpreted the mere presence of a dispute or situation in the agenda of the Security Council as enough to prevent the Assembly from making any recommendation thereon. Subsequently, the practice evolved and the words of article 12 have been taken to mean, "is exercising at this moment", as corroborated by a legal opinion from the Legal Counsel of the United Nations.[13] The evolution in the interpretation appears to continue, to the point that one commentator has noted that nowadays, with regard to major issues, it has become usual and al-

---

13   See for this evolution, Kay Hailbronner and Eckart Klein, in Bruno Simma, *op. cit.*, commentary to Article 121, p. 290. Also Philippe Manin, in Cot and Pellet, *op. cit.*, commentary to Article 12, paragraph 1, pp. 297-301.

most to be expected that the Assembly and the Council deal with the same question "in a parallel manner."[14] The reasons for this evolution in practice are probably to be found in the increased political role that the Assembly has been led to play over the years as a result of its membership having acquired an almost universal character, the shifting balance of forces in its midst, the increased perception on the part of third world countries of the composition of the Security Council as reflecting a world reality frozen in the past and, in contrast, of the Assembly as a world body which, because of its almost universal representation, reflects present day reality.

F.   *Evolutionary UN Reform*

This process of dynamic evolutive and purpose-oriented interpretation or application of the Charter provisions by the General Assembly, summarized in the present review, constitutes an example of what has been considered one of the most interesting characteristics of the United Nations, namely "its capability to initiate reform processes below the level of the Charter amendments" thus showing "an organization which is open to new demands from its environment and capable of adapting its structure and methods to a changing environment" in keeping with "the open and dynamic nature of the principles and purposes of the United Nations."[15]

Occasionally over the years, the Assembly also undertook more systematic and sustained efforts at reform short of amending the UN Charter, particularly in the economic and social sectors of the United Nations system and in the administrative and financial functioning of the United Nations.

As regards the economic, social and related fields the Assembly, on 20 December 1977, adopted Resolution 32/197 entitled "Restructuring of the economic and social sectors of the United Nations system" whereby it endorsed and annexed to the resolution the conclusions and recommendations of the Ad Hoc Committee it had established earlier on the topic referred to above, with a view to initiating the process of restructuring the United Nations system so as to make it more fully capable of dealing with problems of international economic cooperation and development in a comprehensive and effective manner. Such conclusions and recommendations encompassed measures relating to the General Assembly itself, the Economic and Social Council, other United Nations Forums in the field, the structures for regional and interregional co-operation, the operational activities of the United Nations system, the planning, programming, budgeting and evaluation, interagency coordination and the Secretariat support services. Furthermore, by its Resolution 45/264 of 13 May 1991 entitled "Restructuring and revitalization of the United Nations in the economic, social and related fields", the General Assembly adopted and annexed to the resolution further basic principles and guidelines, goals and measures relating to the topic referred to above.

---

14   Philippe Manin, *loc. cit.*, p. 300.

15   Quotations from Klaus Dicke. Reform of the United Nations, in *United Nations: Law, Policies and Practice*, edited by Rüdiger Wolfrum, Verlag CH Beck and Martinus Nijhoff Publishers, Vol. 2, p. 1012.

As regards the administrative and financial functioning of the United Nations, the Assembly, by its Resolution 21/213 of 19 December 1986 entitled "Review of the efficiency of the administrative and financial functioning of the United Nations", decided that the recommendations agreed upon and contained in the report of the Group of High-Level Intergovernmental Experts it had created earlier on the topic above should be implemented by the Secretary General and the relevant organs and bodies of the United Nations. It also decided that the planning, programming and budgeting process of the United Nations would be governed, inter alia, by a number of principles spelt out in the resolution.[16]

G.   *Codification and Progressive Development of the Law of Treaties*

Still another manifestation of the General Assembly's dynamic and evolutionary approach towards the purposes and principles of the United Nations Charter is the process of codification and progressive development of international law.

We have dealt extensively elsewhere with the efficient manner in which the General Assembly has carried out, through the establishment of permanent or ad hoc subsidiary bodies, the mandate contained in Article 13 (1) (a) of the Charter to "initiate and make recommendations for the purpose of ... encouraging the progressive development of international law and its codification."[17] Our purpose here is just to stress that, as part of that process, the Assembly has had a significant role in the codification, development and crystallization of the law of treaties which had traditionally been the domain of customary law and doctrine. Such role was played first trough its permanent subsidiary organ, the International Law Commission, which studied the subject of the Law of Treaties from 1950 to 1966 culminating in the adoption in 1966 of a set of draft articles with commentaries. Secondly, through the convening in 1967 [Resolution 2287 (XXII)] of the Vienna Conference on the Law of Treaties to consider the draft articles recommended by the Commission. After two

---

16   For a number of useful observations on Resolutions 32/197, 45/264 and 41/213, see Klaus Dicke, *loc. cit.*, pp. 1016 to 1021. A number of proposals for evolutionary UN reform (next to a few others calling for amendments to the UN Charter) are also contained in two reports recently published by the UN Secretariat, for consideration by the General Assembly; namely "Report of the High-Level Panel on Threats, Challenges and Change", which Panel had been convened by the Secretary-General (doc. A/59/565) and "In Larger Freedom: Towards Development, Security and Human Rights for All", a report by the Secretary-General (doc. A/59/2005).

17   *Cf.* Manuel Rama-Montaldo
    –   La codification du droit international comme instrument de la justice internationale, *Les cahiers de droit*, Vol. 42, n° 3, septembre 2001, Quebec, Canada, pp. 722-723.
    –   La codification du droit international, "L'exemple des autres organismes des Nations Unies", Colloque d'Aix en Provence, Société Française pour le droit international, Editions Pedone Paris, 1999, pp. 193-206.
    –   The International Law Commission in *The United Nations system at Geneva. Scope and practices of multilateral diplomacy and cooperation*, edited by Boisard and Chossudovsky, UNITAR, 1991, pp. 412-415.

sessions, in 1968 and 1969, the Conference adopted the Vienna Convention on the Law of Treaties on 23 May 1969, which came into force on 27 January 1980.[18]

Actually the role of the General Assembly in the codification and progressive development of the Law of Treaties has been twofold. First through the creation or convening of the bodies charged with the elaboration of the draft articles which culminated in the adoption of the Vienna Convention in 1969. Secondly, and this applies specially to the interpretation of treaties, by having become the source of a dynamic practice of constitutional development in the interpretation of the relevant Charter provisions, which practice was duly taken into account by the International Law Commission and the Vienna Conference at the time of drafting the relevant provisions on the interpretation of treaties. Section 3 of this chapter will further examine this aspect of the Assembly's role.

4.   Legal Basis for the General Assembly's Practice: The Notion of "Constitution", the United Nations Charter and the Interpretation of Treaties

The preceding brief review of the dynamic, evolutive and purpose – oriented manner in which the General Assembly has, in practice, interpreted and applied the provisions of the Charter concerning the exercise of its own powers and functions brings up the question of the legal basis for such interpretation. This, in turn, elicits the question of the nature of the United Nations Charter as an international instrument and the issue of how all this relates to past and present doctrine, practice and legal texts regarding the interpretation of treaties.

A.   The Notion of "Constitution" in Connection with the United Nations Charter

The question concerning the legal nature of the basic instrument of the United Nations, namely its Charter and, in particular, whether it is a multilateral treaty or a "constitution" or both, was raised by commentators early in the life of the Organization and it has given rise, since then, to differing views.

Thus, for Jiménez de Aréchaga, "the exact answer [to that question] is that the Charter is the constitution of the international community, a constitution which entered into force by means of an international treaty with the formalities and techniques of conventional law."[19] On the other hand, for Goodrich and Hambro "the concluding words of the Preamble ... make it clear that the Charter is not a constituent act of the peoples of the United Nations, but rather an agreement freely entered into between governments. In this respect it does not differ from the covenant of the League of Nations. The contractual character of the Charter is further emphasized by the recognition given in Article 2 to "the principle of the sovereign equal-

---

18   Cf. *The Work of the International Law Commission*, fourth edition, United Nations, New York, 1988, pp 53-39 and 260-286.

19   Jiménez de Aréchaga, Eduardo, *op. cit.*, p. 621 (our translation from the Spanish text).

ity" of all members of the Organization and by the provision that an amendment to the Charter shall come into force only when it has been ratified "in accordance with their respective constitutional processes by two thirds of the members of the Organization, including all the permanent members of the Security Council."[20]

These diverging views have continued to this day. Just to give an example, two recent members of the International Law Commission of the United Nations have reacted in very different ways as regards the application of the concept of "constitution" to the international community. Thus, in an article written in connection with the fiftieth anniversary of the United Nations, Arangio Ruiz strongly criticizes the analogy drawn by some authors between the Charter of the United Nations and the constitution of States, in particular of federal States.[21] On the other hand, Tomuschat, in an article entitled "International Law as the Constitution of Mankind" when examining what he terms "the features of the constitution of mankind under positive international law", points out that "the Charter of the United Nations has laid down the guiding principles of the present-day world order which has emerged from the ruins of the Second World War."[22]

There is no denying that the word "constitution" has more than one meaning. One way by which the Charter of the United Nations can be referred to as "constitution" is by giving to that word the meaning of "constituent instrument"[23] of the world Organization. However this acceptation of the word is not one likely to arouse much controversy since it would in essence refer to the multilateral treaty which serves as a basis to the Organization. Actually when authors try to characterize the UN Charter as a "constitution" or when they oppose such characterization, they are thinking of the concept of "constitution" as it applies to States, extending or refusing to extend, as the case may be, to the international community, a concept which, in its origin, applied only to States and referred to "the basic legal framework of a given human community, its essential structures, and the ties that hold it together."[24] As Burdeau points out, "as soon as the State makes a distinction between the power and the holder of the power, every State has necessarily a constitution" ... [containing] "rules relating to the way the holders of the political power are designated and to the organization and functioning of such power."[25] To this "legal" and "neuter" meaning of the word "constitution" he also adds a "politi-

---

20   Leland M. Goodrich and Edvard Hambro, *Charter of the United Nations, Commentary and Documents*, Boston 1949, p. 20.

21   Gaetano Arangio Ruiz, *Nazione Unite e Legalità Internazionale in L´ONU: Cinquant´anni di attività e prospettive per il futuro*, Roma, 1996, pp. 387-415.

22   Christian Tomuschat, International Law as the Constitution of Mankind, in *International Law on the Eve of the 21st Century*, United Nations, New York, 1997, pp. 37-50.

23   *Cf.* James Crawford, The Charter of the United Nations as a Constitution, in *The Changing Constitution of the United Nations*, edited by Hazel Fox, The British Institute of International and Comparative Law, London 1997, p. 8.

24   *Cf.* Christian Tomuschat, *loc. cit.*, p. 37.

25   Georges Burdeau, *Droit Constitutionnel et Institutions Politiques*, Paris 1962, pp. 48-49 (our translation from the French text).

cal" meaning stemming from the French Revolution which "equates the constitution with a certain form of political organization namely, one which safeguards individual freedoms by placing restrictions to the activity of the rulers."[26] He goes on to indicate as hallmarks of a constitution, the existence of rules relating to governmental technique, of rules containing a declaration of rights and freedoms as well as the supremacy of the constitution's norms vis a vis other State norms as regards their respective hierarchical position as well as the special way in which constitutional rules are enacted and amended.[27]

Writing in 1958, in a book entitled "Constitutional Law of the United Nations", Jiménez de Aréchaga found in the UN Charter some of the characteristics of a "constitution" in this second meaning to which we were just referring. In his view, the Charter contains both a "dogmatic" section and an "organic" one, its first chapter and specially its article 2 ensuring a number of reciprocal rights and obligations among the members. Furthermore the Charter creates a detailed system of organs charged with the implementation of such rights and obligations. He also points out as constitutional characteristics the "universal calling" of the Organization established by the Charter and in particular the provision of article 2 (6) of the Charter whereby the Organization shall ensure that non-members act in accordance with the principles of the Charter so far as may be necessary for the maintenance of international peace and security. Further arguments he found in article 103 of the Charter laying down the prevalence of obligations under the Charter over obligations under any other international agreement, as well as in articles 108 and 109 setting up special procedures for Charter amendments.[28]

B.   The Interpretation of the UN Charter in the Light of Doctrine Preceding the 1969 Vienna Convention on the Law of Treaties

The main reasons which would prompt authors to discuss the contractual or constitutional character of the UN Charter were not of a theoretical nature alone. The main practical reason to prompt those discussions was the method of interpretation to be applied to the Charter provisions. However, the question whether the Charter is preponderantly a contractual text or a constitutional text had a much greater significance for its interpretation before the adoption of the 1969 Vienna Convention on the Law of Treaties, than it has now.

Before the adoption of the Vienna Convention there were two main schools of thought as regards the interpretation of treaties. The first school of thought, which could be labeled as the subjective method, would look to the common intention of the parties to the treaty as the keystone for the interpretation.[29] Clive Parry,

---

26   *Ibid.,* p. 49.

27   *Ibid.,* pp. 57-84.

28   Jiménez de Aréchaga, Eduardo, *op. cit.,* pp. 622-636. See also Crawford, James, *loc. cit.,* pp. 10-11.

29   *Cf.* Jiménez de Aréchaga, Eduardo, *op cit.,* p. 636. Also, LA Podestá Costa and José María Ruda, *Derecho Internacional Público.* Vol. 2, Buenos Aires 1985, p. 103. In ad-

writing in 1968 just before the adoption of the Vienna Convention, states that "it is common ground amongst all authorities that the ultimate test of the meaning of a treaty is the common intention of the parties."[30]

The second school, which could be termed the "textual or objective method", would seek to establish what the text means according to the ordinary meaning of the words.[31]

Actually these two schools correspond to the two basic methods of interpretation usually existing in domestic law depending on whether the text to be interpreted is one emanating from the State (of a constitutional, legal or administrative nature) (textual or objective method) or, by contrast, the text of a contract (subjective method looking to the intention of the parties).

As regards the interpretation of State constitutions, the textual or objective method also gave rise, by logical extension, to a fuller interpretative tool, based on the principle of effectiveness, whereby the authorities established by the constitution are understood to have the power to apply the necessary means to attain the goals expressly stated in the constitutional text, provided such means are not expressly forbidden by the Constitution.

Typical of this interpretative mechanism is clause 18 of Section 8 of the Constitution of the United States of America, according to which "The Congress shall have power ... [t]o make all laws which shall be necessary and proper for carrying into execution the foregoing powers, and all other powers vested by the Constitution in the government of the United States, or in any Department or Officer thereof."

This clause of the American Constitution has been called the coefficient or elastic clause and the powers based thereon have been termed "incidental powers" or "implied powers". A leading commentary on the United States Constitution points out that it was Marshall's classic opinion in McCullock v. Maryland which established that "this clause ... enables the lawmakers to select any means reasonably adapted to effectuate those powers." "[L]et the end be legitimate", he wrote, "let it be within the scope of the Constitution, and all means which are appropriate, which are plainly adapted to that end, which are not prohibited, but consistent with the letter and spirit of the Constitution, are constitutional."[32]

Not very far from the above mentioned method of interpretation, doctrine preceding the adoption of the Vienna Convention on the Law of Treaties also developed a third method of interpretation of treaties, the so called "functional" or "teleological" approach to interpretation, which takes into account the object and

---

dition to Sorensen, they group Swarzenberger, Guggenheim and Verdross under this school.

30   Clive Parry in *Manual of Public International Law* edited by Max Sorensen, New York 1968, Section 4, p. 210.

31   Jiménez de Aréchaga, citing Fitzmaurice, *op. cit.,* p. 637. Also, Podestá Costa and Ruda, *op. cit.,* pp. 102-103, who group Cavaré, McNair, Beckett and Huber under this school.

32   *The Constitution of the United States of America – Analysis and Interpretation*, Library of Congress, Washington 1987, Commentary to Section 8, clause 18, pp. 370-371.

purpose of the treaty in the light of the moment in which it needs to be interpreted.[33]

C.   The Interpretation of the UN Charter in the Light of the 1969 Vienna Convention

The 1969 Vienna Convention on the Law of Treaties, which picked up the draft provisions on interpretation of treaties prepared by the International Law Commission, adopted a very balanced solution. Although starting from the textual or objective method of interpretation, it also takes into account the criteria defended by the other schools of thought. Article 31 of the Convention, entitled "general rule of interpretation" states in its paragraph 1 that "A treaty shall be interpreted in good faith in accordance with the ordinary meaning to be given to the terms of the treaty in their context and in the light of its object and purpose".

The first part of the paragraph clearly adopts the textual or objective approach. Yet, the reference to the "context" of the treaty is, to some extent, a tribute paid to the "subjective approach". This becomes clearer when account is taken of the definition of "context" given by paragraph 2 of Article 31, namely:

> The context, for the purpose of the interpretation of a treaty shall comprise, in addition to the text, including its preamble and annexes:
> i.   any agreement relating to the treaty which was made between all the parties in connection with the conclusion of the treaty;
> ii.   any instrument which was made by one or more parties in connection with the conclusion of the treaty and accepted by the other parties as an instrument related to the treaty,

The "intentional" or subjective element is further enhanced by paragraph 4 of Article 31, which reads:

> A special meaning shall be given to a term if it is established that the parties so intended

Specially relevant for the application of this first part of Article 31 is Article 32 of the Convention whereby recourse may be had to supplementary means of interpretation, including the preparatory work of the treaty and the circumstances of its conclusion, in order to confirm the meaning resulting from the application of Article 31, or to determine the meaning when the interpretation according to Article 31 leaves the meaning ambiguous or obscure or leads to a result which is manifestly absurd or unreasonable.

By means of the expression "in the light of its object and purpose," the Vienna Convention also incorporates the functional or teleological method into the con-

---

33   *Cf.* Podestá Costa and Ruda, *op cit.*, p. 103, who group Castberg, Bartos and Alvarez under this school.

solidated method of interpretation contemplated in the general rule of Article 31. This notion of "object and purpose" encompasses both the effectiveness rule or principle (*principe de l'effet utile, ut res magis valeat quam pereat*) whereby if more than one interpretation is possible, the one permitting a better implementation of the object and purpose of the treaty should be applied, as well as the "incidental" or "implied" powers principle of constitutional law to which we referred above. This arises clearly from the introduction to the commentary of the International Law Commission to Articles 27 and 28 of the draft [which later became Articles 31 and 32 of the Vienna Convention]. In it the Commission noted that "as far as the maxim *ut res magis valeat quam pereat* reflects a true general rule of interpretation, it is embodied in Article 27 [later 31] paragraph 1 which requires that a treaty shall be interpreted in good faith in accordance with the ordinary meaning to be given to its terms in the context of the treaty *and in the light of its object and purpose*. When a treaty is open to two interpretations one of which does and the other does not enable the treaty to have appropriate effects, good faith and the objects and purposes of the treaty demand that the former interpretation should be adopted. Properly limited and applied, the maxim does not call for an "extensive" or "liberal" interpretation going beyond what is expressed *or necessarily to be implied* in the terms of the treaty" (emphasis added).[34]

Finally, the Vienna Convention also includes, as a relevant factor in the interpretation of a treaty, the subsequent practice by the parties in the interpretation or application of its provisions, by laying down in paragraph 3 of Article 31 that:

> there shall be taken into account together with the context (a) any subsequent agreement between the parties regarding the interpretation of the treaty or the application of its provisions;
> (b) any subsequent practice in the application of the treaty which establishes the agreement of the parties regarding its interpretation and (c) any relevant rules of international law applicable in the relations between the parties".

It is important to note that the various criteria contained in the "general rule of interpretation" provided in Article 31 do not constitute rungs in a hierarchical ladder but elements to be taken into account in a single operation pursuing to determine the true contents and the full extent of the text to be interpreted. As the International Law Commission put it in the introduction to its commentary to Articles 27 and 28 of the draft [which became Articles 31 and 32 of the Vienna Convention] "by heading the article "General rule of interpretation" in the singular and by underlining the connection between paragraphs 1 and 2 and again between paragraphs 3

---

34   *Cf.* United Nations Conference on the Law of Treaties, Official Records, Documents of the Conference, Draft articles on the law of treaties, with commentaries, adopted by the International Law Commission at its eighteenth session, introduction to the commentary to Articles 27 and 28, paragraph (6) [United Nations, New York, 1971]. See, also in this connection, Ress, G. "Interpretation of the Charter" in Bruno Simma, *op. cit.*, Vol. I, pp. 30-31.

and the two previous paragraphs, [the Commission] intended to indicate that the application of the means of interpretation in the article would be a single combined operation. All the various elements, as they were present in a given case, would be thrown into the crucible, and their interaction would give the legally relevant interpretation. Thus, Article 27 [later 31] is entitled "General <u>rule</u> of interpretation" in the singular, not "General rules" in the plural, because the Commission desired to emphasize that the process of interpretation is a unity and that the provisions of the article form a single, closely integrated rule."[35]

It is also relevant to stress the fact that, in accordance with Article 5 of the Convention, the latter also applies "to any treaty which is the constituent instrument of an international organization". This would then mean that the rules of interpretation of the Vienna Convention apply now to the provisions of the Charter of the United Nations.

It is true however, that Article 4 of the Convention provides that .... "the Convention applies only to treaties which are concluded by States after the entry into force of the present Convention with regard to such States". This part of Article 4, which lays down the principle of non-retroactivity of the Convention, might lead some to believe that the provisions on interpretation contained in Part III Section 3 are not applicable to the UN Charter.

Yet, when considering this question it is also necessary to take into account the first part of Article 4 according to which the principle of non-retroactivity contemplated in the article is "without prejudice to the application of any rules set forth in the present Convention to which treaties would be subject under international law independently of the Convention". As has been rightly pointed out, "legal rules concerning the interpretation of treaties constitute one of the sections of the Vienna Convention which were adopted without a dissenting vote at the Conference and consequently may be considered as declaratory of existing law."[36] "Notwithstanding the fact that not all member States and permanent members of the Security Council have yet ratified the Convention, its rules of interpretation are part of customary international law."[37]

Consequently if the rules of interpretation contained in the Vienna Convention are part of general international law they also apply to the Charter of the United Nations. And this conclusion is by no means cancelled by the last part of Article 5 stating that the applicability of the Convention to the constituent instrument of an international organization is "without prejudice to any relevant rules of the organization". In the case of the United Nations Charter there are not such rules contradicting the rules of the Convention. On the contrary, to a large extent the articles on interpretation contained in the Convention reflect the practice of United Nations organs, in particular the General Assembly, in interpreting the Charter provisions, a practice which has often been reaffirmed by the jurisprudence of the Inter-

---

35   *Ibid.*, paragraph 8.

36   Eduardo Jiménez de Aréchaga, International law in the past third of a century, *Recueil des Cours*, Hague Academy of International Law, 1978 (I), Vol. 159, p. 42.

37   *Cf.* Ress, G. in Bruno Simma, *op. cit.*, Vol. 1, p. 18.

national Court of Justice, particularly as regards the textual approach, the principle of effectiveness and the theory of implied powers.[38] It has rightly been noted that "the four articles devoted to the interpretation of treaties are based on the jurisprudence of the World Court and distil the essence of such fundamental principles as could properly be treated as rules of international law on the subject."[39]

To sum up, while in the past the notion of "constitution" applied to the United Nations Charter has been instrumental in providing a legal basis for a dynamic, evolutive and purpose – oriented interpretation of the Charter by the Assembly, this interpretation can also be supported today by a proper application to the Charter of the notion of "object and purpose" as enshrined in the rule of interpretation of the Vienna Convention on the Law of Treaties.[40]

5.   Constitutional Development and *ultra vires* Acts

The concept of dynamic, evolutive and purpose-oriented interpretation to which we referred earlier and which led to the constitutional development of the United Nations Charter is of course not synonym with "arbitrary", "extensive or liberal" interpretation, which may raise the question of ultra vires acts.[41] The first test which should prevent a decision from being ultra vires is that it must be demonstrably adopted to carry out one of the purposes of the Organization. As the International Court of Justice put it in the Advisory Opinion on "Certain expenses of the United Nations" "in determining whether the actual expenditures authorized constitute "expenses of the Organization within the meaning of Article 17 paragraph 2 of the Charter", the Court agrees that such expenditures must be tested by their relationship to the purposes of the United Nations in the sense that if an expenditure were

---

38   The San Francisco clarification on interpretation referred to in paragraph 5 under Section 2 above, according to which "each organ shall interpret such parts of the Charter as are applicable to its particular function" does not refer to criteria or methods of interpretation but to the agent of the interpretation.

39   Jiménez de Aréchaga, *loc. cit.*, p. 42. This can easily be verified by means of an examination of the commentary of the International Law Commission to Articles 27, 28 and 29 of the draft (see note 34 above).

40   The foregoing renders statements such as the following made in 1996, rather anachronistic and obsolete: "The doctrine of implied powers is consequently inapplicable. It is inapplicable not only as a means of interpretation of the powers of the Security Council, but also as a means of interpretation of the powers of the General Assembly or of any other organ of the United Nations" cf. Arangio Ruiz, *loc. cit.*, p. 387 (our translation from the Italian text).

41   In paragraph (6) of its introduction to the commentary to Articles 27 and 28 [which later became Articles 31 and 32 of the Vienna Convention], the International Law Commission noted that "properly limited and applied the maxim [*ut res magit valeat quam pereat* embodied in the expression "and in the light of its object and purpose"] does not call for an "extensive" or "liberal" interpretation in the sense of an interpretation going beyond what is expressed or necessarily to be implied in the terms of the treaty" (see note 34 above).

made for a purpose which is not one of the purposes of the United Nations, it could not be considered an expense of the Organization."[42]

In the case of the United Nations Organization the broad character of its purposes reduces substantially the risk of an act of the Organization being considered ultra vires, but as the Court itself put it in the same Advisory Opinion referred to above, "these purposes are broad indeed, but neither they nor the powers conferred to effectuate them are unlimited. Save as they have entrusted the Organization with the attainment of these common ends, the Member States retain their freedom of action."[43]

The second test which should prevent a decision from being ultra vires is that it should be "necessary" or "appropriate" to achieve a purpose of the Organization. Again, in the case of the United Nations, and in particular, of decisions taken by the General Assembly, because of its almost universal composition and the consensus procedure adopted for its decision-making, the risk of a decision being considered as not "necessary" or not "appropriate" for the attainment of one of the purposes of the United Nations is considerably reduced. Furthermore, as the Court put it in the Advisory Opinion quoted above, "when the Organization takes action which warrants the assertion that it was appropriate for the fulfillment of one of the stated purposes of the United Nations the presumption is that such action is not ultra vires the Organization."[44]

However, the possibility remains open that an act or decision may be considered beyond the purposes of the Organization or not necessary or appropriate to attain them. In such a case Member States could avail themselves of the means of redress, however imperfect at the present time, provided by international law as regards illegal acts of international organizations.[45]

6. Conclusions

The preceding paragraphs show that, over the years, the General Assembly, when faced with problems which could compromise or even paralyze the effective per-

---

42   Certain expenses of the United Nations (Article 17, paragraph 2, of the Charter) Advisory Opinion of 20 July 1962: ICJ Reports 1962, p. 167. For the circumstances which led to the request for this Opinion, see paragraphs 15-16 above, under Section 3.C.

43   *Ibid.*, p. 168.

44   *Ibid.*, p. 168.

45   *Cf.* E. Lauterpacht, The legal effect of illegal acts of international organizations, in *Essays in Honor of Lord McNair* (Cambridge Essays in International Law) London – New York, 1965, pp. 115-121. The International Law Commission has recently initiated consideration of the topic: "Responsibility of international organizations" and, consequently, further developments are to be expected on the issues here addressed. For the latest on these matters see, in particular Reports of the International Law Commission on the work of its fifty-sixth session (1994) and of its fifty-seventh Session (1995), General Assembly, Official Records, A/59/10 and A/60/10, as well as First, Second and Third reports on responsibility of international organizations, by Mr. Giorgio Gaja, Special Rapporteur, United Nations documents A/CN4/532 and A/CN4/541 and A/CN4/553*.

formance of its functions, chose a dynamic and evolutive interpretation of the relevant Charter provisions, which would facilitate rather than hamper the effective accomplishment of the purposes for which the Organization was created.

The concept of "constitution" applied to the Charter of the world Organization proved historically instrumental for providing a legal basis for the dynamic and evolutive interpretation of the Charter provisions. This development of interpretative practice, in its turn, had an influence on the codification and progressive development of the norms of interpretation contained in the Vienna Convention on the Law of Treaties, particularly through the incorporation of the notion of "object and purpose" into the set of criteria contemplated in the "general rule of interpretation" of treaties enshrined in the Convention. This "general rule of interpretation" is applicable today to the Charter of the United Nations and it confirms the practice followed by the Assembly, providing the basis for further constitutional developments.

This notion of constitutional development of the Charter has in practice, through the notion of evolutionary Charter reform, provided in the past a palliative to the difficulties inherent in any proposed Charter amendment, and it may usefully continue to do so in the future.

While the Assembly, because of its almost universal composition, amplitude of its competence and interaction with other United Nations organs, has been in a privileged position within the UN structure to lead the process of constitutional development of the Charter, such process is also open to other organs of the United Nations in the task of interpretation of the provisions relevant for their own spheres of competence.

In the case of the United Nations Organization, and in particular of the General Assembly, the broad nature of their purposes and competence, the almost universal character of their composition as well as the consensus decision-making procedure adopted, substantially reduce, while not entirely eliminating, the risk of a decision being considered *ultra vires*.

19. The Relevance of International Adjudication Revisited: Reflections on the Need and Quest for International Compulsory Jurisdiction

Antonio Augusto Cançado Trindade

1. International Rule of Law Beyond Peaceful Settlement of Disputes

Most of the classic works on international adjudication date from a time when one counted only on, besides the Permanent Court of Arbitration and international arbitral tribunals, the Hague Court – the Permanent Court of International Justice (PCIJ) followed by its successor, the International Court of Justice (ICJ). In recent years international adjudication has experienced a considerable expansion, with the emergence of new international tribunals. This phenomenon appears to acknowledge that judicial settlement of international disputes has come to be seen as retaining a superiority, at least at the conceptual level, in relation to political means of settlement, to the extent that the solution reached is based on the rule of law, and no State is to regard itself as standing above the law.

International jurisdiction seems nowadays to go beyond the framework of methods of peaceful settlement of international disputes. Its expansion in contemporary international law responds and corresponds to a need of the international community of our times. The international rule of law finds expression no longer only at national, but also at international level. At this latter, the idea of a *préeminence* of international law has gained ground in recent years, as acknowledged, *e.g.*, by the Advisory Opinion of the ICJ on the *Obligation to Arbitrate by Virtue of Section 21 of the 1947 U.N. Headquarters Agreement* (1988); this *idée-force* has fostered the search for the realization of justice under the rule of law at international level, and has stressed the universal dimension of a new *jus gentium* in our days.[1]

It has been suggested, in this respect, that the growth of international adjudicative organs transcends peaceful settlement of disputes, and points to the gradual

---

[1]   J.-Y. Morin, "L'état de Droit: émergence d'un principe du Droit international", 254 *Recueil des Cours de l'Académie de Droit International de La Haye* (1995) pp. 199, 451 and 462.

Ronald St. John Macdonald & Douglas M. Johnston (eds.), Towards World Constitutionalism, *pp. 515-542.*
© 2005 *Koninklijke Brill NV. Printed in The Netherlands.* ISBN 90 04 14612 1.

formation of a judicial branch of the international legal system.[2] There is great need for a law-abiding system of international relations, and, in this respect, it is important that the trend in the last decades is maintained, of growing acceptance of international judicial and arbitral decisions (rather than individual State practice) as "the best evidence of international law."[3] It has further been contended that, bearing in mind this evolution towards a true international rule of law, nowadays "any progress in international law passes through progress in international adjudication."[4]

Beyond the confines of strict settlement of successive individual cases, lies the imperative of building a true law-abiding international system. Those jurists who have the privilege and honor to integrate the emerging judicial branch of that system have also the responsibility of securing the prevalence of international law and the consolidation of an international legal order capable of fulfilling the need of realization of justice. Judicial settlement bears testimony to the superiority of law over will or pressure or force. The applicable legal norms pre-exist the dispute itself. The final outcome of such means of settlement will much depend on the belief that the law applied is just. Such belief, in turn, makes a case for international compulsory jurisdiction.

Despite the growth of international jurisdiction, there remains the old ambivalence between the duty of peaceful settlement of international disputes and the freedom left to the contending parties of the choice of the means of settlement. This has subsisted, throughout the years, as a true *vexata quaestio* permeating this whole chapter of public international law. Yet, some advances have been achieved in recent years in this domain, although there appears to remain still a long way in pursuance of international compulsory jurisdiction at universal level. A current reassessment of international adjudication can thus be appropriately undertaken, in my view, in historical perspective and in the context of the growth of international jurisdiction, bearing in mind the recurring need and quest for compulsory jurisdiction, in pursuance of the realization of international justice.

---

2   J. Allain, "The Future of International Dispute Resolution – The Continued Evolution of International Adjudication", in *Looking Ahead: International Law in the 21st Century / Tournés vers l'avenir: Le droit international au 21ème siècle* (Proceedings of the 29th Annual Conference of the Canadian Council of International Law, Ottawa, October 2000), The Hague, Kluwer, 2002, pp. 65, 67, 69 and 71, and *cf.* pp. 61 and 64.

3   Bin Cheng, "Whither International Law?", in *Contemporary Issues in International Law* (eds. D. Freestone, S. Subedi and S. Davidson), The Hague, Kluwer, 2002, pp. 56 and 35.

4   J. Allain, *A Century of International Adjudication: The Rule of Law and Its Limits*, The Hague, T.M.C. Asser Press, 2000, p. 186, and *cf.* p. 185.

2.   International Rule of Law: The Saga of the Optional Clause of Compulsory Jurisdiction

A.   *From the Professed Ideal to a Distorted Practice*

In this respect, one may initially recall the legislative history of the provision of the optional clause of compulsory jurisdiction, as found in Article 36(2) of the Statute of the International Court of Justice (ICJ), which is essentially the same as the corresponding provision of the Statute of its predecessor, the old Permanent Court of International Justice (PCIJ). The aforementioned Article 36(2) establishes that

> The States Parties to the present Statute may at any time declare that they recognize as compulsory *ipso facto* and without special agreement, in relation to any other State accepting the same obligation, the jurisdiction of the Court in all legal disputes concerning:
> a)   the interpretation of a treaty;
> b)   any question of international law;
> c)   the existence of any fact which, if established, would constitute a breach of an international obligation;
> d)   the nature or extent of the reparation to be made for the breach of an international obligation.

Article 36(3) adds that "the declaration referred to above may be made unconditionally or on condition of reciprocity on the part of several or certain States, or for a certain time."[5]

The origin of the provision quoted above is found in the *travaux préparatoires* of the original Statute of the PCIJ. This latter was drafted in 1920 by an Advisory Committee of Jurists (of 10 members),[6] appointed by the Council of the League of Nations, and which met at The Hague, in the months of June and July of 1920. On that occasion there were those who favored the pure and simple recognition of the compulsory jurisdiction of the future PCIJ, to which the more powerful States were opposed, alleging that they had gradually to come to trust the international tribunal to be created, before conferring upon it compulsory jurisdiction *tout court*. In order to overcome the deadlock within the Committee of Jurists referred to, one of its members, the Brazilian jurist Raul Fernandes, proposed the ingenuous formula which was to become Article 36(2) of the Statute – the same as the one of the present Statute of the ICJ – which came to be known as the "optional clause of

---

5   And Article 36(6) determines that "in the event of a dispute as to whether the Court has jurisdiction, the matter shall be settled by the decision of the Court."

6   Namely: Mr. Adatci (Japan), Altamira (Spain), Fernandes (Brazil), Baron Descamps (Belgium), Hagerup (Norway), De La Pradelle (France), Loder (The Netherlands), Lord Phillimore (Great Britain), Ricci Busatti (Italy) and Elihu Root (United States).

the compulsory jurisdiction."[7] The Statute, approved on 13 December 1920, entered into force on 1 September 1921.[8]

At that time, the decision that was taken constituted the initial step that, during the period of 1921-1940, contributed to attract the acceptance of the compulsory jurisdiction – under the optional clause – of the PCIJ by a total of 45 States.[9] This principle was firmly supported by the Latin-American States, and, in bearing it in mind, the formula of Raul Fernandes,[10] incorporated into the Statute of the PCIJ, was acclaimed as a Latin-American contribution to the establishment of the international jurisdiction.[11] Such a formula served its purpose in the following two decades.

At the San Francisco Conference of 1945, the possibility was contemplated to take a step forward, with an eventual automatic acceptance of the compulsory jurisdiction of the new ICJ; nevertheless, the great powers – in particular the United States and the Soviet Union – were opposed to this evolution, sustaining the retention, in the Statute of the new ICJ, of the same "optional clause of compulsory jurisdiction" of the Statute of 1920 of the predecessor PCIJ. The *rapporteur* of the Commission of Jurists entrusted with the study of the matter at the San Francisco Conference of 1945, the French jurist Jules Basdevant, pointed out that, although the majority of the members of the Commission favored the automatic acceptance

---

7   *Cf.* R.P. Anand, *Compulsory Jurisdiction of the International Court of Justice*, New Delhi/Bombay, Asia Publ. House, 1961, pp. 19 and 34-36.

8   For an account, *cf.*, *inter alia*, J.C. Witenberg, *L'organisation judiciaire, la procédure et la sentence internationales – Traité pratique*, Paris, Pédone, 1937, pp. 22-23; L. Gross, "Compulsory Jurisdiction under the Optional Clause: History and Practice", *The International Court of Justice at a Crossroads* (ed. L.F. Damrosch), Dobbs Ferry/N.Y., ASIL/Transnational Publs., 1987, pp. 20-21.

9   *Cf.* the account of a Judge of the old PCIJ, M.O. Hudson, *International Tribunals – Past and Future*, Washington, Carnegie Endowment for International Peace/Brookings Institution, 1944, pp. 76-78. That total of 45 States represented, in reality, a high proportion, at that epoch, considering that, at the end of the thirties, 52 States were members of the League of Nations (of which the old PCIJ was not part, distinctly from the ICJ, which is the main judicial organ of the United Nations, and whose State forms an organic whole with the United Nations Charter itself).

10   In his book of memories published in 1967, Raul Fernandes revealed that the Committee of Jurists of 1920 was faced with the challenge of establishing the basis of the jurisdiction of the PCIJ (as from the mutual consent among the States) and, at the same time, of safeguarding and reaffirming the principle of the juridical equality of the States; *cf.* R. Fernandes, *Nonagésimo Aniversário – Conferências e Trabalhos Esparsos*, vol. I, Rio de Janeiro, M.R.E., 1967, pp. 174-175.

11   J.-M. Yepes, "La contribution de l'Amérique Latine au développement du Droit international public et privé", 32 *Recueil des Cours de l'Académie de Droit International de La Haye* (1930) p. 712; F.-J. Urrutia, "La Codification du Droit International en Amérique", 22 *Recueil des Cours de l'Académie de Droit International de La Haye* (1928) pp. 148-149; and *cf.* M. Bourquin, "Règles générales du droit de la paix", 35 *Recueil des Cours de l'Académie de Droit International de La Haye* (1931) pp. 195-196.

of the compulsory jurisdiction, there was no political will at the Conference (nor in the Dumbarton Oaks proposals) to take this step forward.[12]

Consequently, the same formulation of 1920, which corresponded to a conception of international law of the beginning of the 20th century, was maintained in the present Statute of the ICJ. Due to the intransigent position of the more powerful States, a unique opportunity was lost to overcome the lack of automatism of the international jurisdiction and to foster a greater development of the compulsory jurisdiction of the international tribunal.[13] It may be singled out that all this took place at the level of purely inter-State relations. The formula of the optional clause of compulsory jurisdiction (of the ICJ) which exists today, is nothing more than a scheme of the twenties, stratified in time,[14] and which, rigorously speaking, no longer corresponds to the needs of the international *contentieux* not even of a purely inter-State dimension.[15]

Such is the case that, in 1997, for example, of the 185 member States of the United Nations, no more than 60 States were subject to the compulsory jurisdiction of the ICJ by acceptance of the optional clause of Article 36(2) of its Statute[16] – that is, less than a third of the international community of our days. And several of the States which have utilized it, have made a distorted use of it, denaturalizing it, in introducing restrictions which militate against its *rationale* and which deprive it of all efficacy. In reality, almost two thirds of the declarations of acceptance of

12   *Cf.* the account of R.P. Anand, *op. cit. supra* n. (8), pp. 38-46; and *cf.* also, on the issue, S. Rosenne, *The Law and Practice of the International Court*, vol. I, Leyden, Sijthoff, 1965, pp. 32-36; Ian Brownlie, *Principles of Public International Law*, 4th. ed., Oxford, Clarendon Press, 1995 (reprint), pp. 715-716; O.J. Lissitzyn, *The International Court of Justice*, N.Y., Carnegie Endowment for International Peace, 1951, pp. 61-64.

13   As human unreasonableness seems to have no limits, the chapter of international law pertaining to the peaceful settlement of international disputes continued to suffer from the old ambivalence – a true *vexata quaestio* – which has always characterized it, also in our days, namely, the ineluctable tension between the general duty of peaceful settlement and the free choice by the States of the methods of settlement of the dispute.

14   For expressions of pessimism as to the practice of States under that optional clause, at the end of the seventies, *cf.* J.G. Merrills, "The Optional Clause Today", 50 *British Yearbook of International Law* (1979) pp. 90-91, 108, 113 and 116.

15   One decade ago, a former President of the ICJ, after pointing out that "nowadays a very considerable part of international law directly affects individuals, corporations and legal entities other than States", and of recalling that, nevertheless, the Statute of the ICJ still sustains – according to a conception of international law proper of the twenties – that only the States can be parties in cases before the Court (Article 34(1)), admitted and regretted that this outdated position has insulated the Hague Court from the great *corpus* of contemporary international law. R.Y. Jennings, "The International Court of Justice after Fifty Years", 89 *American Journal of International Law* (1995) p. 504.

16   International Court of Justice, *Yearbook 1996-1997*, vol. 51, The Hague, ICJ, 1997, p. 84, and *cf.* pp. 84-125.

the aforementioned clause have been accompanied by limitations and restrictions which have rendered them "practically meaningless."[17]

One may, thus, seriously question whether the optional clause keeps on serving the same purpose which inspired it at the epoch of the PCIJ.[18] The rate of its acceptance in the era of the ICJ is proportionally inferior to that of the epoch of its predecessor, the PCIJ. Furthermore, throughout the years, the possibility opened by the optional clause of acceptance of the jurisdiction of the international tribunal became, in fact, the object of excesses on the part of some States, which only accepted the compulsory jurisdiction of the ICJ in their own terms, with all kinds of limitations.[19] Thus, it is not at all surprising that, already by the mid-fifties, one began to speak openly of a *decline* of the optional clause.[20]

Those excesses occurred precisely because, in elaborating the Statute of the new ICJ, one failed to follow the evolution of the international community. One abandoned the very basis of the compulsory jurisdiction of the ICJ to a voluntarist conception of international law, which prevailed at the beginning of the last century, but was subsequently disauthorized by its harmful consequences to the conduct of international relations – such as vehemently warned by the more authoritative contemporary international juridical doctrine. There can be no doubt whatsoever that the distorted and incongruous practice, developed under Article 36(2) of the Statute of the ICJ, definitively does not serve as an example or model to be followed by the States Parties to treaties of protection of the rights of the human being such as the European and American Conventions on Human Rights, in relation to the extent of the jurisdictional basis of the work of the European and Inter-American Courts of Human Rights.

---

17   G. Weissberg, "The Role of the International Court of Justice in the United Nations System: The First Quarter Century", *The Future of the International Court of Justice* (ed. L. Gross), vol. I, Dobbs Ferry N.Y., Oceana Publs., 1976, p. 163; and, on the feeling of frustration that this generated, *cf. ibid.*, pp. 186-190. Cf. also *Report on the Connally Amendment – Views of Law School Deans, Law School Professors, International Law Professors* (compiled under the auspices of the Committee for Effective Use of the International Court by Repealing the Self-Judging Reservation), New York, [1961], pp. 1-154.

18   *Cf.* statistic data in G. Weissberg, *op. cit. supra* n. (18), pp. 160-161; however, one ought to recall the *clauses compromissoires* pertaining to the contentious jurisdiction of the ICJ, which, in the mid-seventies, appeared in about 180 treaties and conventions (more than two thirds of which of a bilateral character, and concerning more than 50 States – *ibid.*, p. 164).

19   Some of them gave the impression that they thus accepted that aforementioned optional clause in order to sue other States before the ICJ, trying, however, to avoid themselves to be sued by other States; J. Soubeyrol, "Validité dans le temps de la déclaration d'acceptation de la juridiction obligatoire", 5 *Annuaire français de Droit international* (1959) pp. 232-257, esp. p. 233.

20   C.H.M. Waldock, "Decline of the Optional Clause", 32 *British Yearbook of International Law* (1955-1956) pp. 244-287. And, on the origins of this decline, *cf.* the Dissenting Opinion of Judge Guerrero in the *Norwegian Loans* case (Judgment of 06.07.1857), *ICJ Reports* (1957) pp. 69-70.

B.   *International Compulsory Jurisdiction: Reflections* Lex Lata

Contemporary international law has gradually evolved, putting limits to the manifestations of a State voluntarism which revealed itself as belonging to another era.[21] Much progress has here been achieved due to the impact of the international law of human rights upon public international law. The methodology of interpretation of human rights treaties,[22] to start with, has been developed as from the rules of interpretation set forth in international law (such as those formulated in Articles 31-33 of the two Vienna Conventions on the Law of Treaties, of 1969 and 1986), comprise not only the substantive norms (on the protected rights), but also the clauses that regulate the mechanisms of international protection.

The optional clauses of recognition of the contentious jurisdiction of both the European Court of Human Rights (prior to Protocol nr. 11 to the European Convention)[23] and the Inter-American Court of Human Rights found inspiration in the model of the optional clause of compulsory jurisdiction of the ICJ – a formula originally conceived more than 80 years ago (*cf. supra*). Despite the common origin, in search of the realization of the ideal of international justice, the *rationale* of the application of the optional clause has been interpreted in a fundamentally distinct way, on the one hand in inter-State litigation, and on the other hand in that of human rights. In the former, considerations of contractual equilibrium between the Parties, of reciprocity, in the light of the juridical equality of the sovereign States have prevailed to date; in the latter, there has been a primacy of considerations of *ordre public*, of the collective guarantee exercised by all the States Parties, of the accomplishment of a common goal, superior to the individual interests of each Contracting Party. (*cf. infra*)

---

21   When this outlook still prevailed to some extent, in a classic book published in 1934, Georges Scelle, questioning it, pointed out that the self-attribution of discretionary competence to the rulers, and the exercise of functions according to the criteria of the power-holders themselves, were characteristics of a not much evolved, imperfect, and still almost anarchical international society; G. Scelle, *Précis de droit des gens – Principes et systématique*, part II, Paris, Rec. Sirey, 1934 (reed. 1984), pp. 547-548. And *cf.*, earlier on, to the same effect, L. Duguit, *L'État, le Droit objectif et la loi positive*, vol. I, Paris, A. Fontemoing Ed., 1901, pp. 122-131 and 614.

22   As can be inferred from the vast international case-law in this respect, analysed in detail in: A.A. Cançado Trindade, *El Derecho Internacional de los Derechos Humanos en el Siglo XXI*, Santiago/Mexico/Buenos Aires/Barcelona, Editorial Jurídica de Chile, 2001, pp. 15-58.

23   Protocol nr. 11 to the European Convention of Human Rights entered into force on 1 November 1998. On the original optional clause (Article 46) of the European Convention, *cf.* Council of Europe/Conseil de l'Europe, *Collected Edition of the `Travaux Préparatoires' of the European Convention on Human Rights/Recueil des Travaux Préparatoires de la Convention Européenne des Droits de l'Homme*, vol. IV, The Hague, Nijhoff, 1977, pp. 200-201 and 266-267; and vol. V, The Hague, Nijhoff, 1979, pp. 58-59.

The two aforementioned international human rights Tribunals have found themselves under the duty to preserve the integrity of the regional conventional system of protection of human rights as a whole. In their common understanding, it would be inadmissible to subordinate the operation of the respective conventional mechanisms of protection to restrictions not expressly authorized by the European and American Convention, interposed by the States Parties in their instruments of acceptance of the optional clauses of compulsory jurisdiction of the two Courts (Article 62 of the American Convention, and Article 46 of the European Convention before Protocol nr. 11). This would not only immediately affect the efficacy of the operation of the conventional mechanism of protection, but, furthermore, it would fatally impede its possibilities of future development.

By virtue of the principle *ut res magis valeat quam pereat*, which corresponds to the so-called *effet utile* (sometimes called principle of effectiveness), widely supported by case-law, the States Parties to human rights treaties ought to secure to the conventional provisions the proper effects at the level of their respective domestic legal orders. This principle applies not only in relation to the substantive norms of human rights treaties (that is, those which provide for the protected rights), but also in relation to the procedural norms, in particular those relating to the right of individual petition and to the acceptance of the contentious jurisdiction of the international judicial organs of protection.[24] Such conventional norms, essential to the efficacy of the system of international protection, ought to be interpreted and applied in such a way as to render their safeguards truly practical and effective, bearing in mind the special character of the human rights treaties and their collective implementation.

The European Court of Human Rights had the occasion to pronounce in this respect. Thus, in its Judgment on Preliminary Objections (of March 23rd, 1995) in the case of *Loizidou versus Turkey*, it warned that, in the light of the letter and the spirit of the European Convention the possibility cannot be inferred of restrictions to the optional clause relating to the recognition of the contentious jurisdiction of the European Court,[25] by analogy with the permissive State practice under Article 36 of the Statute of the ICJ; under the European Convention, a practice of the States Parties was formed precisely *a contrario sensu*, accepting such clause without restrictions.[26]

---

24   *Cf.*, to this effect, the decision of the old European Commission of Human Rights (EComHR) in the case *Chrysostomos et alii versus Turkey* (1991), *in* EComHR, *Decisions and Reports*, vol. 68, Strasbourg, C.E., [1991], pp. 216-253; and *cf.*, earlier on, the *obiter dicta* of the Commission, to the same effect, in its decisions in the *Belgian Linguistic Cases* (1966-1967) and in the cases *Kjeldsen, Busk Madsen and Pedersen versus Denmark* (1976).

25   Article 46 of the European Convention, prior to the entry into force, on 1 November 1998, of Protocol nr. 11 to the European Convention.

26   To that it added, moreover, the fundamentally distinct context in which international tribunals operate, the ICJ being "a free-standing international tribunal which has no links to a standard-setting treaty such as the Convention"; *cf.* European Court of Human Rights (ECtHR), *Case of Loizidou versus Turkey* (Preliminary Objections), Strasbourg,

In the domain of the international protection of human rights, there are no "implicit" limitations to the exercise of the protected rights; and the limitations set forth in the treaties of protection ought to be restrictively interpreted. The optional clause of compulsory jurisdiction of the international tribunals of human rights makes no exception to that: it does not admit limitations other than those expressly contained in the human rights treaties at issue, and, given its capital importance, it could not be at the mercy of limitations not foreseen therein and invoked by the States Parties for reasons or vicissitudes of domestic order.[27]

In their classic studies on the basis of the international jurisdiction, C.W. Jenks and C.H.M. Waldock warned, already in the decades of the fifties and the sixties, of the grave problem presented by the insertion, by the States, of all kinds of limitations and restrictions in their instruments of acceptance of the optional clause of compulsory jurisdiction (of the ICJ).[28] Although those limitations had never been

---

C.E., Judgment of 23.03.1995, p. 25, para. 82, and *cf.* p. 22, para. 68. On the prevalence of the conventional obligations of the States Parties, *cf.* also the Court's *obiter dicta* in its previous decision anterior, in the case *Belilos versus Switzerland* (1988). The Hague Court, in its turn, in its Judgment of 04.12.1998 in the *Fisheries Jurisdiction* case (Spain *versus* Canada), yielded to the voluntarist subjectivism of the contending States (*cf. ICJ Reports* (1998) pp. 438-468), the antithesis of the very notion of international compulsory jurisdiction – provoking Dissenting Opinions of five of its Judges, to whom the ICJ put at risk the future itself of the mechanism of the optional clause under Article 36(2) of its Statute, paving the way for an eventual desertion from it (*cf. ibid.*, pp. 496-515, 516-552, 553-569, 570-581 and 582-738, respectively). On more than one occasion the undue emphasis on the consent of States led the ICJ to incongruous decisions, as its Judgment of 1995 in the case of *East Timor*; *cf.* criticisms in, *e.g.*, J. Dugard, "1966 and All That: the *South West African* Judgment Revisited in the *East Timor* Case", 8 *African Journal of International and Comparative Law* (1996) pp. 549-563; A.A. Cançado Trindade, "O Caso do Timor-Leste (1999): O Direito de Autodeterminação do Povo Timorense", 1 *Revista de Derecho de la Universidad Católica del Uruguay* (2000) pp. 68-75. As well pointed out by Shabtai Rosenne, the international judicial procedure of the Hague Court unfortunately continues to follow nowadays the model of bilateralism in international litigation, proper of the XIXth century; S. Rosenne, "Decolonisation in the International Court of Justice", 8 *African Journal of International and Comparative Law* (1996) p. 576.

27   *Cf.* Inter-American Court of Human Rights, case of *Castillo Petruzzi and Others versus Peru* (Preliminary Objections), Judgment of 04.09.1998, Series C, n. 41, Concurring Opinion of Judge A.A. Cançado Trindade, paras. 36 and 38.

28   Examples of such excesses have been the objections of domestic jurisdiction (*domestic jurisdiction/compétence nationale exclusive*) of States, the foreseeing of withdrawal at any moment of the acceptance of the optional clause, the foreseeing of subsequent modification of the terms of acceptance of the clause, and the foreseeing of insertion of new reservations in the future; *cf.* C.W. Jenks, *The Prospects of International Adjudication*, London, Stevens, 1964, p. 108, and *cf.* pp. 113, 118 and 760-761; C.H.M. Waldock, "Decline of the Optional Clause", *op. cit. supra* n. (21), p. 270; and for criticisms of those excesses, *cf.* A.A. Cançado Trindade, "The Domestic Jurisdiction of States in the Practice of the United Nations and Regional Organisations", 25 *International and Comparative Law Quarterly* (1976) pp. 744-751.

foreseen in the formulation of the optional clause, the States, in the face of such legal vacuum, have felt, nevertheless, "free" to insert them. Such excesses have undermined, in a contradictory way, the basis itself of the system of international compulsory jurisdiction. As well pointed out in a classic study on the matter, the instruments of acceptance of the contentious jurisdiction of an international tribunal should be undertaken "on terms which ensure a reasonable measure of stability in the acceptance of the jurisdiction of the Court"[29] – that is, in the terms expressly provided for in the international treaty itself (cf. infra).

The clause pertaining to the compulsory jurisdiction of the international tribunals of human rights constitutes, in my view, a fundamental clause (cláusula pétrea) of the international protection of the human being, which does not admit any restrictions other than those expressly provided for in the human rights treaties at issue. This has been so established by the Inter-American Court in its Judgments on Competence in the cases of the Constitutional Tribunal and Ivcher Bronstein versus Peru (1999):

> Recognition of the Court's compulsory jurisdiction is a fundamental clause (cláusula pétrea) to which there can be no limitations except those expressly provided for in Article 62(1) of the American Convention. Because the clause is so fundamental to the operation of the Convention's system of protection, it cannot be at the mercy of limitations not already stipulated but invoked by States Parties for reasons of domestic order.[30]

The permissiveness of the insertion of limitations, not foreseen in the human rights treaties, in an instrument of acceptance of an optional clause of compulsory jurisdiction,[31] represents a regrettable historical deformation of the original conception of such clause, in my view unacceptable in the field of the international protection of the rights of the human person.

It is the duty of an international tribunal of human rights to look after the due application of the human rights treaty at issue in the framework of the domestic law of each State Party, so as to secure the effective protection in the ambit of this latter of the human rights set forth in such treaty.[32] Any understanding to the con-

---

29   C.W. Jenks, op. cit. supra n. (29), pp. 760-761.

30   IACtHR, case of the Constitutional Tribunal (Competence), Judgment of 24.09.1999, Series C, nr. 55, p. 44, para. 35; CtIADH, case of Ivcher Bronstein (Competence), Judgment of 24.09.1999, Series C, nr. 54, p. 39, para. 36.

31   Exemplified by State practice under Article 36(2) of the ICJ Statute (supra).

32   If it were not so, there would be no juridical security in international litigation, with harmful consequences above all in the domain of the international protection of human rights. The intended analogy between the classic inter-State contentieux and the international contentieux of human rights – fundamentally distinct domains – is manifestly inadequate, as in the latter the considerations of a superior order (international ordre public) have primacy over State voluntarism. The States cannot count on the same latitude of discretionality which they have reserved to themselves in the traditional context of the purely inter-State litigation.

trary would deprive the international tribunal of human rights of the exercise of the function and of the duty of protection inherent to its jurisdiction, failing to ensure that the human rights treaty has the appropriate effects (*effet utile*) in the domestic law of each State Party.

The case of *Hilaire versus Trinidad and Tobago* (Preliminary Objections, Judgment of 1st September 2001) before the Inter-American Court led one to a more detailed examination of that specific point. Article 62(1) and (2) of the American Convention on Human Rights provides that:

> A State Party may, upon depositing its instrument of ratification or adherence to this Convention, or at any subsequent time, declare that it recognizes as binding, *ipso facto*, and not requiring special agreement, the jurisdiction of the Court on all matters relating to the interpretation or application of this Convention.
>
> Such declaration may be made unconditionally, on the condition of reciprocity, for a specified period, or for specific cases. It shall be presented to the Secretary General of the Organization, who shall transmit copies thereof to the other member States of the Organization and to the Secretary of the Court.[33]

In fact, the modalities of acceptance, by a State Party to the Convention, of the contentious jurisdiction of the Inter-American Court, are expressly stipulated in the aforementioned provisions; the formulation of the optional clause of compulsory jurisdiction of the Inter-American Court, in Article 62 of the American Convention, is not simply illustrative, but clearly *precise*. No State is obliged to accept an optional clause, as its own name indicates. Thus, a "reservation" to the optional clause of compulsory jurisdiction of the Inter-American Court of Article 62 of the American Convention would amount simply to the non-acceptance of that clause, what is foreseen in the Convention. But if a State Party decides to accept it, it ought to do so in the terms expressly stipulated in such clause.

According to Article 62(2) of the Convention, the acceptance, by a State Party, of the contentious jurisdiction of the Inter-American Court, can be made in four modalities, namely: a) unconditionally; b) on the condition of reciprocity; c) for a specified period; and d) for specific cases. Those, and only those, are the modalities of acceptance of the contentious jurisdiction of the Inter-American Court foreseen and authorized by Article 62(2) of the Convention, which does not authorize the States Parties to interpose any other conditions or restrictions (*numerus clausus*).

In my Concurring Opinion in the aforementioned *Hilaire versus Trinidad and Tobago* case, I saw fit to ponder that:

---

33   Paragraph 3 of Article 62 of the Convention adds that: "The jurisdiction of the Court shall comprise all cases concerning the interpretation and application of the provisions of this Convention that are submitted to it, provided that the States Parties to the case recognize or have recognized such jurisdiction, whether by special declaration pursuant to the preceding paragraphs, or by a special agreement."

In my understanding, in this matter, it cannot be sustained that what is not prohibited, is permitted. This posture would amount to the traditional – and surpassed – attitude of the *laisser-faire, laisser-passer*, proper to an international legal order fragmented by the voluntarist State subjectivism, which in the history of Law has ineluctably favoured the more powerful ones. *Ubi societas, ibi jus* ... At this beginning of the XXIst century, in an international legal order wherein one seeks to affirm superior common values, among considerations of international *ordre public*, as in the domain of the International Law of Human Rights, it is precisely the opposite logic which ought to apply: *what is not permitted, is prohibited.*

If we are really prepared to extract the lessons of the evolution of International Law in a turbulent world throughout the XXth century, if we intend to keep in mind the endeavours of past generations to construct a more equitable and just world, if we believe that the same norms, principles and criteria ought to apply to all States (juridically equal despite factual disparities), and if we are really prepared to advance the ideals of the true international jurists who preceded us, – we cannot abide by an international practice which has been subservient to State voluntarism, which has betrayed the spirit and purpose of the optional clause of compulsory jurisdiction, – to the point of entirely denaturalizing it, – and which has led to the perpetuation of a world fragmented into State units which regard themselves as final arbiters of the extent of the contracted international obligations, at the same time that they do not seem truly to believe in what they have accepted: the international justice.

Not every practice consubstantiates into custom so as to conform general international law, as a given practice may not be in conformity with Law (*ex injuria jus non oritur*). Thus, it is not the function of the jurist simply to take note of the practice of States, but rather to say what the Law is. Since the classic work of H. Grotius in the XVIIth century, there is a whole trend of international law thinking which conceives international law as a legal order endowed with an intrinsic value of its own (and thereby superior to a simply "voluntary" law), – as well recalled by H. Accioly,[34] – as it derives its authority from certain principles of sound reason (*est dictatum rectae rationis*). (paras. 24-26)

In its Judgment in the case of *Hilaire versus Trinidad and Tobago*, the Inter-American Court rightly observed that, if restrictions interposed in the instrument of acceptance of its contentious jurisdiction were accepted, in the terms proposed by the respondent State in the *cas d'espèce*, not expressly foreseen in Article 62 of the American Convention, this

(...) would lead to a situation in which the Court would have as first parameter of reference the Constitution of the State and only subsidiarily the American Convention, situation which would bring about a fragmentation of the international legal order of protection of human rights and would render illusory the object and purpose of the American Convention. (para. 93)

---

34   H. Accioly, *Tratado de Derecho Internacional Público*, volume I, Rio de Janeiro, Imprensa Nacional, 1945, p. 5.

And the Court, furthermore, in that Judgment correctly added that:

> (...) The instrument of acceptance, on the part of Trinidad and Tobago, of the contentious jurisdiction of the Tribunal, does not fit into the hypotheses foreseen in Article 62(2) of the Convention. It has a general scope, which ends up by subordinating the application of the American Convention to the domestic law of Trinidad and Tobago in a total way and pursuant to what its national tribunals decide. All this implies that this instrument of acceptance is manifestly incompatible with the object and purpose of the Convention. (para. 88)

This conclusion of the Court found clear support in the precise, and quite clear, formulation of Article 62(2) of the American Convention. Bearing in mind the three component elements of the general rule of interpretation *bona fides* of treaties – text in the current meaning, context, and object and purpose of the treaty – set forth in Article 31(1) of the two Vienna Conventions on the Law of Treaties (of 1969 and 1986), it could be initially inferred that the text, in the current meaning (*numerus clausus*), of Article 62(2) of the American Convention, fully corroborated the decision taken by the Inter-American Court in that Judgment.

In the theory and practice of international law one has sought to distinguish a "reservation" from an "interpretative declaration,"[35] in conformity with the legal effects which are intended to be attributed to one and the other:[36] thus, if one intends to clarify the meaning and scope of a given conventional provision, it is an interpretative declaration, while if one intends to modify a given conventional provision or to exclude its application, it is a reservation. In practice, it is not always easy to draw the dividing line between one and the other,[37] as illustrated by the controversy which has surrounded, in the last decades, the question of the legal effects of

---

[35] *Cf.* U.N./International Law Commission, "Draft Guidelines on Reservations to Treaties", in: U.N., *Report of the International Law Commission on the Work of Its 51st Session* (May/July 1999), *G.A.O.R.* – Suppl. n. 10 (A/54/10/Corr.1-2), 1999, pp. 18-24, item 1.3; and in: *Report of the International Law Commission on the Work of Its 52nd Session* (May/June and July/August 2000), *G.A.O.R.* – Suppl. nr. 10 (A/55/10), 2000, pp. 229-272, item 1.7; and *cf.* also, more recently, A. Pellet (special *rapporteur*), *Sixth Report on Reservations to Treaties* (*Addendum*), U.N./I.L.C. doc. A/CN.4/518/Add.1, of 21.05.2001, pp. 3-31, paras. 38-133.

[36] For an examination of the question, *cf., e.g.*, F. Horn, *Reservations and Interpretative Declarations to Multilateral Treaties*, The Hague/Uppsala, T.M.C. Asser Instituut/ Swedish Institute of International Law, 1988, pp. 98-110 and 229-337, and *cf.* pp. 184-222; D.M. McRae, "The Legal Effect of Interpretative Declarations", 49 *British Yearbook of International Law* (1978) pp. 155-173.

[37] It may be recalled that in the well-known case of *Belilos versus Switzerland* (1988), the European Court of Human Rights considered that a declaration interposed by Switzerland amounted to a reservation – of a general character – to the European Convention on Human Rights, incompatible with the object and purpose of this latter. European Court of Human Rights, *Belilos versus Switzerland* case, Judgment of 29.04.1988, Series A, nr. 132, pp. 20-28, paras. 38-60.

declarations inserted into the instruments of acceptance of the optional clause of compulsory jurisdiction, given the *sui generis* character of such clause.

In any way, in considering the meaning and scope of a declaration of acceptance of an optional clause of compulsory jurisdiction – such as the one presented by Trinidad and Tobago under Article 62 of the American Convention and interposed as preliminary objection in the present case *Hilaire* – one has to bear in mind the *nature* of the treaty in which that clause appears. This corresponds to the "context", precisely the second component element of the general rule of interpretation of treaties set forth in Article 31 of the two Vienna Conventions on the Law of Treaties. In the *Hilaire versus Trinidad and Tobago* case (*supra*), the Inter-American Court had duly done so, in stressing the special character of the human rights treaties (paras. 94-97).

Likewise, the Inter-American Court has kept constantly in mind the third component element of that general rule of interpretation, namely, the "object and purpose" of the treaty at issue, the American Convention on Human Rights (paras. 82-83 and 88). Thus, the understanding advanced in the *cas d'espèce* by the respondent State of the scope of its own acceptance of the optional clause of compulsory jurisdiction of the Inter-American Court, does not resist the proper interpretation of Article 62 of the American Convention, developed in the light of the canons of interpretation of the law of treaties.

As I saw fit to point out in my Separate Opinion in the case *Blake versus Guatemala* (Reparations, 1999) before the Inter-American Court:

> (...) In contracting conventional obligations of protection, it is not reasonable, on the part of the State, to assume a discretion so unduly broad and conditioning of the extent itself of such obligations, which would militate against the integrity of the treaty.
>
> The principles and methods of interpretation of human rights treaties, developed in the case-law of conventional organs of protection, can much assist and foster this necessary evolution. Thus, in so far as human rights treaties are concerned, one is to bear always in mind the objective character of the obligations enshrined therein, the autonomous meaning (in relation to the domestic law of the States) of the terms of such treaties, the collective guarantee underlying them, the wide scope of the obligations of protection and the restrictive interpretation of permissible restrictions. These elements converge in sustaining the integrity of human rights treaties, in seeking the fulfillment of their object and purpose, and, accordingly, in establishing limits to State voluntarism. From all this one can detect a new vision of the relations between public power and the human being, which is summed up, ultimately, in the recognition that the State exists for the human being, and not vice-versa.
>
> The juridical concepts and categories, inasmuch as they enshrine values, are a product of their time, and, as such, are in constant evolution. The protection of the human being in any circumstances, against all the manifestations of arbitrary power, corresponds to the new *ethos* of our times, which is to be reflected in the postulates of Public International Law. (...).[38]

---

38   IACtHR, case *Blake versus Guatemala* (Reparations), Judgment of 22.01.1999, Series C, n. 48, Separate Opinion of Judge A.A. Cançado Trindade, pp. 114-115, paras. 32-34.

C.   *International Compulsory Jurisdiction: Reflections* De Lege Ferenda

A further line of reflections, *de lege ferenda*, on international compulsory jurisdiction, is here called for. The "judicial decisions", referred to in the enumeration of the formal sources and evidences of International Law, set forth in Article 38(1)(d) of the Statute of the ICJ,[39] certainly are *not* limited to the case-law of the ICJ itself.[40] They likewise comprise, nowadays, the judicial decisions of the international tribunals (Inter-American and European Courts) of human rights, of the *ad hoc* International Criminal Tribunals (for ex-Yugoslavia and for Rwanda), of the International Tribunal for the Law of the Sea, of other international and arbitral tribunals, as well as of national tribunals in matters of international law.[41] This expansion of international jurisdiction has been contributing, in my understanding, to enlarge the aptitude of international law to encompass legal relations in distinct domains of human activity.

In this sense, in my aforementioned Separate Opinion in the case of *Blake versus Guatemala*, in warning as to the necessity to establish the juridical bases of a minimally institutionalized international community, I pointed out that:

> (...) With the evolution of the International Law of Human Rights, it is Public International Law itself which is justified and legitimized, in affirming juridical principles, concepts and categories proper to the present domain of protection, based on premises fundamentally distinct from those which have guided the application of its postulates at the level of purely inter-State relations. (...) The norms of the law of treaties (...) can greatly enrich with the impact of the International Law of Human Rights, and develop their aptitude to regulate adequately the legal relations at inter-State as well as intra-State levels, under the respective treaties of protection. (...).[42]

The Inter-American Court of Human Rights, by means of the Judgments on Preliminary Objections in the cases of *Hilaire*, *Benjamin*, and *Constantine*, as well as

---

39   As "subsidiary means for the determination of rules of law".

40   As this latter itself has acknowledged, *e.g.*, in its Judgment of 18 November 1960 in the case of the *Arbitral Award of the King of Spain of 1906* (Honduras *versus* Nicaragua), *ICJ Reports* (1960) pp. 204-217.

41   I. Brownlie, *Principles of Public International Law*, 4th. ed., Oxford, Clarendon Press, 1990, pp. 19-24; A.A. Cançado Trindade, *Princípios do Direito Internacional Contemporâneo*, Brasília, Editora Universidade de Brasília, 1981, pp. 19-20; R.A. Falk, *The Role of Domestic Courts in the International Legal Order*, Syracuse University Press, 1964, pp. 21-52 and 170; J.A. Barberis, "Les arrêts des tribunaux nationaux et la formation du droit international coutumier", 46 *Revue de droit international de sciences diplomatiques et politiques* (1968) pp. 247-253; F. Morgenstern, "Judicial Practice and the Supremacy of International Law", 27 *British Yearbook of International Law* (1950) p. 90.

42   IACtHR, case *Blake versus Guatemala* (Reparations), Judgment of 22.01.1999, Series C, nr. 48, Separate Opinion of Judge A.A. Cançado Trindade, pp. 110 and 112, paras. 23 and 27-28.

its earlier Judgments on Competence in the cases of the *Constitutional Tribunal* and *Ivcher Bronstein*, safeguarded the integrity of the American Convention on Human Rights, remained master of its own jurisdiction and acted in accordance with the high responsibilities accorded to it by the American Convention. The same can be said of the European Court of Human Rights, by means of its Judgment on Preliminary Objections in the case *Loizidou versus Turkey*, in so far as the European Convention on Human Rights is concerned. Thus, the two existing international Tribunals of human rights to date, in their converging case-law on the question, have refused to yield to undue manifestations of State voluntarism, have fully performed the functions attributed to them by the human rights treaties which created them, and have given a worthy contribution to the strengthening of the international jurisdiction and to the realization of the old ideal of international justice.[43]

There is a pressing need for States to be convinced that the international legal order is, more than voluntary, *necessary*. In the ambit of general international law, in my view, the time has come to advance decidedly in the improvement of the judicial settlement of international disputes. In the last 80 years, the advances in this field could have been much greater if State practice would not have betrayed the purpose which inspired the creation of the mechanism of the optional clause of compulsory jurisdiction (of the PCIJ and the ICJ), that is, the submission of political interests to Law by means of the development in the realization of justice at international level.

The time has come to overcome definitively the regrettable lack of automatism of the international jurisdiction. With the distortions of their practice on the matter, States face today a dilemma which should have been overcome a long time ago: either they return to the voluntarist conception of international law, abandoning for good the hope in the primacy of law over political interests,[44] or they

---

43   A.A. Cançado Trindade, *Tratado de Direito Internacional dos Direitos Humanos*, vol. III, Porto Alegre/Brazil, S.A. Fabris Ed., 2003, ch. XV-XVI, pp. 60-83 and 147-168.

44   In fact, more advances have not been achieved in the judicial settlement of international disputes precisely because States have shown themselves reluctant with regard to it, paying more attention to political factors; Ch. de Visscher, *Aspects récents du droit procédural de la Cour Internationale de Justice*, Paris, Pédone, 1966, p. 204; and *cf.* also L. Delbez, *Les principes généraux du contentieux international*, Paris, LGDJ, 1962, pp. 68, 74 and 76-77. Subsequently, a former President of the ICJ criticized as unsatisfactory the bad use made by the States of the mechanism of the optional clause (of the compulsory jurisdiction of the ICJ) of the Statute of the Court; in his words, the States may consider that "there is some political advantage in remaining outside a system which permits States to join more or less on their own terms at an opportune moment". R.Y. Jennings, "The International Court of Justice after Fifty Years", *op. cit. supra* n. (16), p. 495. *Cf.* also the criticisms of another former President of the ICJ: E. Jiménez de Aréchaga, "International Law in the Past Third of a Century", 159 *Recueil des Cours de l'Académie de Droit International de La Haye* (1978) pp. 154-155; and *cf.* also the criticisms *in*: H.W. Briggs, "Reservations to the Acceptance of Compulsory Jurisdiction of the International Court of Justice", 93 *Recueil des Cours de l'Académie*

retake and achieve with determination the ideal of construction of an international community with greater cohesion and institutionalization in the light of law and in search of justice, moving resolutely from *jus dispositivum* to *jus cogens*.[45]

As I concluded in my Concurring Opinion in the *Hilaire versus Trinidad and Tobago* before the Inter-American Court of Human Rights:

> The time has come to consider, in particular, in a future Protocol of amendments to the procedural part of the American Convention on Human Rights, aiming at strengthening its mechanism of protection, the possibility of an amendment to Article 62 of the American Convention, in order to render such clause also *mandatory*, in conformity with its character of fundamental clause (*cláusula pétrea*), thus establishing the *automatism*[46] of the jurisdiction of the Inter-American Court of Human Rights.[47] There is pressing need for the old ideal of the permanent international compulsory jurisdiction to become reality also in the American continent, in the present domain of protection, with the necessary adjustments in order to face its reality of human rights and to fulfil the growing needs of effective protection of the human being. (para. 39)

3.   The Recurring Need and Quest for Compulsory Jurisdiction

Despite the undeniable advances experienced by the idea of compulsory jurisdiction in the domain of the international law of human rights (*supra*), the picture

---

de Droit International de La Haye (1958) p. 273. And *cf.* also: P. Guggenheim, *Traité de Droit international public*, vol. I, Genève, Georg, 1967, p. 279; and, in general, J. Sicault, "Du caractère obligatoire des engagements unilatéraux en Droit international public", 83 *Revue générale de droit international public* (1979) pp. 633-688. Such distorted State practice cannot, definitively, serve as model for the operation of the judicial organs created by human rights treaties.

45   And always bearing in mind that the protection of fundamental rights places us precisely in the domain of *jus cogens*. In this respect, in an intervention in the debates of March 12th,1986 of the Vienna Conference on the Law of Treaties between States and International Organizations or between International Organizations, I saw it fit to warn as to the manifest incompatibility with the concept of *jus cogens* of the voluntarist conception of international law, which is not able even to explain the formation of the rules of general international law; *cf.* U.N., *United Nations Conference on the Law of Treaties between States and International Organizations or between International Organizations (Vienna, 1986) – Official Records*, volume I, NY, UN, 1995, pp. 187-188 (intervention of A.A. Cançado Trindade).

46   Which became a reality, as to the European Court of Human Rights, as from the entry into force, on November 1st, 1998, of Protocol nr. 11 to the European Convention on Human Rights (*cf. infra*).

47   With the necessary amendment – by means of a Protocol – to this effect, of Article 62 of the American Convention, putting an end to the restrictions therein foreseen and expressly discarding the possibility of any other restrictions, and also putting and end to reciprocity and the optional character of the acceptance of the contentious jurisdiction of the Court, which would become compulsory to all the States Parties.

appears somewhat distinct in the sphere of purely inter-State relations: it is hard to escape the assessment that, herein, compulsory jurisdiction has made a rather modest progress in recent decades. As pointed out by C.W. Jenks over forty years ago, the foundation of compulsory jurisdiction is, ultimately, the confidence in the rule of law at international level.[48] While full confidence is still lacking, not much progress is bound to be achieved in the present domain. It is most unfortunate that statesmen and those responsible for the conduct of the external affairs of States have not displayed sufficient confidence in compulsory jurisdiction to date. The need for such compulsory jurisdiction has, however, been felt, and calls for it have been expressed for a long time.

In this respect, *e.g.*, the *Institut de Droit International*, in its Neuchâtel session of 1959, adopted unanimously a resolution in support of the compulsory jurisdiction of international courts and tribunals. Noting with concern that the evolution of international jurisdiction was already lagging behind the needs of international justice, the resolution pondered that:

> (...) submission to law through acceptance of recourse to international courts and arbitral tribunals is an essential complement to the renunciation of recourse to force in international relations.[49]

In order to overcome the unsatisfactory situation, the resolution *inter alia* called for the development of the practice of insertion into general conventions of a clause, binding on all States Parties, of submission of disputes, relating to the interpretation or application of the respective conventions, to international courts and tribunals.[50]

The plea for compulsory jurisdiction has been duly expressed in expert writing along the last eight decades. In a monograph published as early as in 1924 (four years after the adoption of the Statute of the old PCIJ), Nicolas Politis, in recalling the historical evolution from private justice to public justice, advocated the evolution, at international level, from optional justice to compulsory justice.[51] Subsequently, despite the alleged "decline" of the optional clause of the ICJ Statute (*cf. supra*), one decade after the adoption by the *Institut de Droit International* (in 1959) of the aforementioned resolution, C.W. Jenks wrote that:

> The problem of compulsory jurisdiction (...) remains one of the central problems of world organization. (...) A larger measure of compulsory jurisdiction remains a funda-

---

48   C.W. Jenks, *The Prospects of International Adjudication*, London, Stevens/Oceana, 1964, pp. 101, 117, 757, 762 and 770.

49   *Annuaire de l'Institut de Droit International* (1959), *cit. in* C.W. Jenks, *op. cit. supra* n. (49), pp. 113-114.

50   *Annuaire de l'Institut de Droit International* (1959), *cit. in ibid.*, p. 115.

51   *Cf.* N. Politis, *La justice internationale*, Paris, Libr. Hachette, 1924, pp. 7-255, esp. pp. 193-194 and 249-250.

mental element in the progress of the rule of law among nations. There can be no solid progress in the matter of jurisdiction without a relaxation of world tension and mutual suspicion reflected in a fuller confidence in the substantive law. The progress of compulsory jurisdiction presupposes a parallel progress of the substantive law in adjusting itself to the changing needs of a changing society.[52]

International jurisdiction is becoming, in our days, an imperative of the contemporary international legal order itself, and compulsory jurisdiction responds to a need of the international community in our days; although the latter has not yet been fully achieved, some advances have been made in the last decades.[53] The Court of Justice of the European Communities provides one example of supranational compulsory jurisdiction, though limited to community law or the law of integration. The European Convention of Human Rights, after the entry into force of Protocol nr. 11, affords another conspicuous example of automatic compulsory jurisdiction. The newly-established International Criminal Court is the most recent example in this regard; although other means were contemplated throughout the *travaux préparatoires* of the 1998 Rome Statute (such as cumbersome "opting in" and "opting out" procedures), at the end compulsory jurisdiction prevailed, with no need for further expression of consent on the part of States Parties to the Rome Statute.[54] This was a significant decision, enhancing international jurisdiction.

The system of the 1982 UN Law of the Sea Convention, in its own way, moves beyond the traditional regime of the optional clause of the ICJ Statute. It allows States Parties to the Convention the option between the International Tribunal for the Law of the Sea, or the ICJ, or else arbitration (Article 287); despite the exclusion of certain matters, the Convention succeeds in establishing a compulsory procedure containing coercive elements; the specified choice of procedures at least secures law-abiding settlement of disputes under the UN Law of the Sea Convention.[55]

---

52   C.W. Jenks, *The World Beyond the Charter*, London, G. Allen and Unwin, 1969, p. 166.

53   H. Steiger, "Plaidoyer pour une juridiction internationale obligatoire", *in Theory of International Law at the Threshold of the 21st Century – Essays in Honour of K. Skubiszewski* (ed. J. Makarczyk), The Hague, Kluwer, 1996, pp. 818, 821-822 and 832. It has been argued that it is quite possible to bear in mind national interests while at the same time accepting and enhancing international compulsory jurisdiction; R.St.J. MacDonald, "The New Canadian Declaration of Acceptance of the Compulsory Jurisdiction of the International Court of Justice", 8 *Canadian Yearbook of International Law* (1970) pp. 21, 33 and 37. In support of the need for "a system of general compulsory and binding dispute settlement procedures", *cf.* further M.M.T.A. Brus, *Third Party Dispute Settlement in an Interdependent World*, Dordrecht, Nijhoff, 1995, p. 182.

54   H. Corell, "Evaluating the ICC Regime: The Likely Impact on States and International Law", The Hague, T.M.C. Asser Institute, 2000, p. 8 (internal circulation).

55   L. Caflisch, "Cent ans de règlement pacifique des différends interétatiques", 288 *Recueil des Cours de l'Académie de Droit International de La Haye* (2001) pp. 365-366 and 448-449; J. Allain, "The Continued Evolution ...", *op. cit. supra* n. (3), pp. 61-62; S. Karagiannis, "La multiplication des juridictions internationales ...", *op. cit. infra* n. (60), p. 34; M. Kamto, "Les interactions des jurisprudences internationales ...", *op. cit. infra* n. (61), p. 424.

These illustrations suffice to disclose that compulsory jurisdiction is already a reality – at least in some circumscribed domains of international law, as indicated above. International compulsory jurisdiction is, by all means, a juridical possibility. If it has not yet been attained on a worldwide level, this cannot be attributed to an absence of juridical viability, but rather to misperceptions of its role, or simply to a lack of will to widen its scope. Compulsory jurisdiction is a manifestation of the recognition that international law, more than voluntary, is indeed necessary.

In addition to the advances already achieved to this effect, reference could also be made to endeavors in the same sense. One such example is found in the Proposals for a Draft Protocol to the American Convention on Human Rights, which I prepared as *rapporteur* of the Inter-American Court of Human Rights, which *inter alia* advocates an amendment to Article 62 of the American Convention so as to render the jurisdiction of the Inter-American Court in contentious matters automatically compulsory upon ratification of the Convention.[56]

Furthermore, several international treaties[57] foresee a compulsory resort to the jurisdiction of the International Court of Justice (ICJ). To the extent that they do so, States Parties would be under the Court's jurisdiction to settle disputes pertaining to those treaties, and that paves the way for a broader acceptance of compulsory jurisdiction on a worldwide basis. In fact, the optional clause (of the ICJ Statute) is not the only source of compulsory jurisdiction of the ICJ; another source consists precisely of jurisdictional clauses inserted into treaties conferring jurisdiction on international tribunals to settle disputes concerning their interpretation and application.

Although not as often invoked as they possibly could be, a more systematic inclusion in treaties of such jurisdictional or arbitration clauses would contribute to widen the scope of compulsory jurisdiction.[58] The expansion of compulsory jurisdiction is bound to occur to the extent that States realize that it is ultimately in their own interest, and the common or general interest, to have their disputes normally settled by judicial means. This latter is the most perfected way of peaceful settlement, for all that it affords: pre-existing rules, rigor and juridical security. Beyond such settlement, compulsory jurisdiction is an expression of the rule of law at international level, conducive to a more cohesive international legal order inspired and guided by the imperative of justice.

---

56   A.A. Cançado Trindade, *Informe: Bases para un Proyecto de Protocolo a la Convención Americana sobre Derechos Humanos, para Fortalecer Su Mecanismo de Protección*, vol. II, 2nd. ed., San José of Costa Rica, Inter-American Court of Human Rights, 2003, pp. 1-64.

57   *E.g.*, *inter alia*, the 1957 European Convention on Peaceful Settlement of Disputes, Article 1.

58   C.W. Jenks, *The Prospects of International Adjudication*, London/N.Y., Stevens/Oceana, 1964, p. 761, and *cf.* pp. 109 and 111.

4.   International Rule of Law: The Growth of International Jurisdiction

It is well-known that the international community counts nowadays on a multiplicity of international tribunals (*e.g.*, besides the ICJ, the International Tribunal for the Law of the Sea, the permanent International Criminal Court, the international tribunals – Inter-American and European Courts – of human rights, the *ad hoc* International Criminal Tribunals – for ex-Yugoslavia and for Rwanda – the Court of Justice of the European Communities, among others). This is symptomatic of the way contemporary international law has evolved, and of an increasing recourse to international adjudication. Throughout the last years the old ideal of international justice has been revitalized and has gained ground, with the considerable expansion of the international judicial function, reflected in the creation of new international tribunals; the work of these latter has been enriching contemporary international case-law, contributing, as already indicated, to assert and develop the aptitude of International Law to regulate adequately the juridical relations in distinct domains of human activity (cf. *supra*).

Disputes submitted to international adjudication in our days are no longer vested with strict inter-State dimension; hence the creation and co-existence of multiple specialized international tribunals of our times, reflecting a decentralized international legal order.[59] Still more significantly, in expanding international jurisdiction, contemporary multiple international tribunals have enlarged the access to international justice of the subjects of international law (other than States).[60] They have done what the ICJ alone has not been capable of doing (by force of the constraints of its Statute). They are responding to a pressing need of the contemporary international community. The human person has at last been granted access to justice, no longer only at national level, but likewise at international level.

Specialized international tribunals, such as the European and Inter-American Courts of Human Rights, and the *ad hoc* International Criminal Tribunals for ex-Yugoslavia and Rwanda, have asserted universalist principles, and the primacy of humanitarianism over traditional techniques of inter-State litigation.[61] Their work

---

59   S. Karagiannis, "La multiplication des juridictions internationales: un système anarchique?", *in* Société française pour le Droit international, *in La juridictionnalisation du Droit international* (Colloque de Lille), Paris, Pédone, 2003, pp. 61 and 156; E. Jouannet, "La notion de jurisprudence internationale en question", in *ibid.*, p. 365; M. Bedjaoui, "La multiplication des tribunaux internationaux ou la bonne fortune du droit des gens", *in ibid.*, pp. 530 and 539.

60   H. Ascensio, "La notion de juridiction internationale en question", *in La juridictionnalisation du Droit international* (Colloque de Lille), Paris, Pédone, 2003, p. 198; M. Kamto, "Les interactions des jurisprudences internationales et des jurisprudences nationales", *in ibid.*, pp. 414 and 459; J.-P. Cot, "Le monde de la justice internationale", *in ibid.*, pp. 517 and 521; M. Bedjaoui, "La multiplication des tribunaux internationaux ou la bonne fortune du droit des gens", *in ibid.*, pp. 541-544.

61   M. Koskenniemi and P. Leino, "Fragmentation of International Law? Postmodern Anxieties", 15 *Leiden Journal of International Law* (2002) pp. 576-578. It may be recalled that the International Tribunal for the Law of the Sea, in the *M/V Saiga* case

has thus proved to be complementary to that of the ICJ, and they have contributed to erect contemporary international adjudication into a new universalist dimension, beyond peaceful settlement of international disputes on a strictly inter-State basis. They have thereby enriched contemporary public international law.

The multiplication of international tribunals is, thus, a reassuring phenomenon, in providing additional forums for the access to, and realization of, justice at the international level. Attention should be focused on this healthy substantial development which is a reflection of the expansion of the application of international law in general and of judicial settlement in particular,[62] instead of attempting – as some international lawyers have tried to do – to create a "problem" with the traditional concern with delimitation of competences. The issues arising from the co-existence of international tribunals can be properly addressed by means of dialogue among international judges, not by self-assertions of alleged supremacy.

As rightly reminded by L. Caflisch, there is currently no basis in any international instrument for asserting the supremacy of the ICJ, or any other international tribunal, over the other international courts; nowhere is such "supremacy" set forth in any text whatsoever.[63] Contemporary international tribunals, working in a cooperative and complementary way, have the common mission of realization of justice at international level. With this same spirit, some international specialized tribunals are entrusted with the task of deciding on highly specific or technical matters, giving also their contribution to the evolution of an expanded international law.

As recently recalled with pertinence, nowadays

(...) we are confronted not only with a quantitative development of dispute settlement bodies but also with a qualitative expansion and transformation of the nature and competence of those bodies which are not only aimed at the settlement of disputes but also at ensuring and monitoring compliance with international law. Thus, international dispute settlement is no longer restricted only to resolve inter-State disputes; the number

---

(1999), also evoked basic considerations of humanity; in considering, within the framework of the applicable rules of international law, the force used by Guinea in the arrest of the ship *Saiga*, it was of the view that although the 1982 U.N. Convention on the Law of the Sea did not contain express provisions on the use of force in the arrest of ships,"international law, which is applicable by virtue of Article 293 of the Convention, requires that the use of force must be avoided as far as possible and, where force is unavoidable, it must not go beyond what is reasonable and necessary in the circumstances. Considerations of humanity must apply in the law of the sea, as they do in other areas of international law." ITLS, *M/V Saiga* (nr. 2) case (Saint Vincent and the Grenadines *versus* Guinea), *Reports of Judgments, Advisory Opinions and Orders* (1999) pp. 61-62, paras. 155-156.

62   *Cf.* J.I. Charney, "Is International Law Threatened by Multiple International Tribunals?", 271 *Recueil des Cours de l'Académie de Droit International de La Haye* (1998) pp. 116, 121, 125, 135, 347, 351 and 373.

63   L. Caflisch, "Cent ans de règlement pacifique...", *op. cit. supra* n. (56), p. 431.

of judicial bodies granting standing to non-State entities outnumber meanwhile the traditional jurisdictions limited to disputes between sovereign States.[64]

The co-existing international human rights Tribunals to date, the European and the Inter-American Courts of Human Rights, have succeeded in setting forth approximations and convergences in their respective case-law, despite the distinct factual realities of the two continents in which they operate.[65] This converging case-law has generated their common understanding that human rights treaties are endowed with a special nature (as distinguished from multilateral treaties of the traditional type); that human rights treaties have a normative character, of *ordre public*; that their terms are to be autonomously interpreted; that in their application one ought to ensure an effective protection (*effet utile*) of the guaranteed rights; that the obligations enshrined therein do have an objective character, and are to be duly complied with by the States Parties, which have the additional common duty of exercise of the collective guarantee of the protected rights; and that permissible restrictions (limitations and derogations) to the exercise of guaranteed rights are to be restrictively interpreted.[66] The work of the European and Inter-American Courts of Human Rights has indeed contributed to the creation of an international *ordre public* based upon the respect for human rights in all circumstances.

Moreover, the dynamic or evolutive interpretation of the respective human rights Conventions (the intertemporal dimension) has been followed by both the European Court[67] and the Inter-American Court.[68] In its sixteenth and pioneering Advisory Opinion, on the *Right to Information on Consular Assistance in the Framework of the Guarantees of the Due Process of Law* (1999), of the greatest importance (which has inspired the international case-law *in statu nascendi* on the matter), the Inter-American Court clarified that, in its interpretation of the norms

---

64   K. Oellers-Frahm, "Multiplication of International Courts and Tribunals and Conflicting Jurisdiction – Problems and Possible Solutions", 5 *Max Planck Yearbook of United Nations Law* (2001) p. 69.

65   A clear example of such convergence of outlook can in fact be perceived in the tackling of fundamental issues of interpretation and application of the two regional Conventions on Human Rights. The rich case-law on methods of interpretation of the European Convention is a major historical contribution of the European Court to the International Law of Human Rights as a whole; the Inter-American Court has also, in the settlement of cases which reflect the realities of human rights in the American continent, had the occasion to construct its own case-law on methods of interpretation of the American Convention, disclosing, as already indicated, a reassuring convergence with that of the European Court.

66   A.A. Cançado Trindade, *Tratado de Direito Internacional dos Direitos Humanos*, vol. II, Porto Alegre/Brazil, S.A. Fabris Ed., 1999, ch. XI, pp. 23-58 and 185-194.

67   Cases *Tyrer versus United Kingdom*, 1978; *Airey versus Ireland*, 1979; *Marckx versus Belgium*, 1979; *Dudgeon versus United Kingdom*, 1981, among others.

68   Sixteenth Advisory Opinion, on *The Right to Information on Consular Assistance in the Framework of the Guarantees of the Due Process of Law*, 1999; and eighteenth Advisory Opinion, on *Juridical Condition and Rights of Undocumented Migrants*, 2003.

of the American Convention, it should extend protection in new situations (such as that concerning the observance of the right to information on consular assistance) on the basis of pre-existing rights.[69] The same vision has been propounded by the Inter-American Court in its most recent and forward-looking eighteenth Advisory Opinion, on the *Juridical Condition and Rights of Undocumented Migrants* (2003).

At procedural law level, one of the basic issues dwelt upon by both Courts has been precisely that of the access to justice at international level, achieved under the two Conventions by means of the operation of the respective provisions on the international jurisdiction of the two Human Rights Courts and on the right of individual petition. I regard those provisions of such a fundamental character – as true fundamental clauses (*cláusulas pétreas*) of the international protection of human rights – that any attempt to undermine them would threaten the functioning of the whole mechanism of protection under the two regional Conventions. They constitute the basic pillars of the mechanism whereby the emancipation of the individual *vis-à-vis* his own State is achieved. This outlook grows in importance for having come at a time when the establishment of a new international human rights Tribunal (an African Court on Human and Peoples' Rights) under the 1998 Protocol to the African Charter on Human and Peoples' Rights appears forthcoming.

Despite the challenges that the two human rights Tribunals nowadays face, particularly with the increasing overload of cases (the European Court to a far greater extent than the Inter-American Court), individuals have been raised as subjects of the international law of human rights, endowed with full procedural capacity, and have recovered their faith in human justice when it appeared to fade

---

69   The Inter-American Court of Human Rights was the first international tribunal to affirm the existence of an individual right to information on consular assistance in the framework of the guarantees of the due process of law; *cf.* Advisory Opinion nr. 16 (OC-16/99), of 01.10.1999, Series A, nr. 16, pp. 3-123, paras. 1-141 [Spanish text]. This historical Advisory Opinion revealed the impact of the International Law of Human Rights in the evolution of Public International Law itself, specifically for having the Inter-American Court been the first international tribunal to warn that non-compliance with Article 36(1)(b) of the Vienna Convention on Consular Relations of 1963 took place to the detriment not only of a State Party but also of the human beings at issue (as the ICJ has subsequently also admitted, in the case *LaGrand*). This contribution by the case-law of the Inter-American Court has been promptly acknowledged by cotemporary expert writing on the subject. *Cf., e.g.,* G. Cohen-Jonathan, "Cour Européenne des Droits de l'Homme et droit international général (2000)", 46 *Annuaire français de Droit international* (2000) p. 642; M. Mennecke, "Towards the Humanization of the Vienna Convention of Consular Rights – The *LaGrand* Case before the International Court of Justice", 44 *German Yearbook of International Law/Jahrbuch für internationales Recht* (2001) pp. 430-432, 453-455, 459-460 and 467-468; Ph. Weckel, M.S.E. Helali and M. Sastre, "Chronique de jurisprudence internationale", 104 *Revue générale de Droit international public* (2000) pp. 794 and 791; Ph. Weckel, "Chronique de jurisprudence internationale", 105 *Revue générale de Droit international public* (2001) pp. 764-765 and 770; M. Mennecke and C.J. Tams, "The *LaGrand* Case", 51 *International and Comparative Law Quarterly* (2002) pp. 454-455.

away at domestic law level. This significant procedural development, with the automatism of the international jurisdiction of the European Court and recent developments to this effect as regards the Inter-American Court, strongly suggests, as far as our two international human rights Tribunals are concerned, that the old ideal of the *realization of international justice* is finally seeing the light of the day.

I saw fit to single out, as guest speaker, in my address at the ceremony of the opening of the judicial year of 2004 of the European Court of Human Rights (on 22 January 2004, at the *Palais des Droits de l'Homme* in Strasbourg), as follows:

> This is a point which deserves to be stressed on the present occasion, as in some international legal circles attention has been diverted in recent years from this fundamental achievement to the false problem of the so-called "proliferation of international tribunals". This narrow-minded, unelegant and derogatory expression simply misses the key point of the considerable advances of the old ideal of international justice in the contemporary world. The establishment of new international tribunals is but a reflection of the way contemporary international law has evolved, and of the current search for, and construction of, an international community guided by the rule of law and committed to the realization of justice. It is, furthermore, an acknowledgement of the superiority of the judicial means of settlement of disputes, bearing witness of the prevalence of the rule of law in democratic societies, and discarding any surrender to State voluntarism.
>
> Since the visionary writings and ideas of Nicolas Politis and Jean Spiropoulos of Greece, Alejandro Álvarez of Chile, André Mandelstam of Russia, Raul Fernandes of Brazil, René Cassin and Georges Scelle of France, Hersch Lauterpacht of the United Kindgom, John Humphrey of Canada, among others, it was necessary to wait for decades for the current developments in the realization of international justice to take place, nowadays enriching rather than threatening international law, strengthening rather than undermining international law. The reassuring growth of international tribunals is a sign of our new times, and we have to live up to it, to make sure that each of them gives its contribution to the continuing evolution of international law in the pursuit of international justice."[70]

In the domain of the protection of the fundamental rights of the human person, the growth and consolidation of international human rights jurisdictions in the European and American continents indeed bear witness to the notorious advances of the old ideal of international justice in our days. Both the European and Inter-

---

[70]   A.A. Cançado Trindade, *Speech on the Occasion of the Opening of the Judicial Year of the European Court of Human Rights (Thursday, 22 January 2004) / Discours dans l'audience solennelle à l'occasion de l'ouverture de l'année judiciaire de la Cour Européenne des Droits de l'Homme (le jeudi 22 janvier 2004)*, Strasbourg, Council of Europe/ECtHR doc. nr. 926464, of 22.01.2004, p. 11, paras. 10-11; and *cf.*, forthcoming, A.A. Cançado Trindade, "The Merits of Coordination of International Courts on Human Rights", 2 *Journal of International Criminal Justice* (2004) nr. 1, pp. 1-4 (in print) (revised and abridged version of the author's aforementioned Strasbourg address).

American Courts have rightly set limits to State voluntarism, have safeguarded the integrity of the respective human rights Conventions and the primacy of considerations of *ordre public* over the will of individual States, have set higher standards of State behavior and established some degree of control over the interposition of undue restrictions by States, and have reassuringly enhanced the position of individuals as subjects of the international law of human rights, with full procedural capacity.

In so far as the basis of their jurisdiction in contentious matters is concerned, eloquent illustrations of their firm stand in support of the integrity of the mechanisms of protection of the two Conventions are afforded, for example, by recent decisions of the European Court[71] as well as of the Inter-American Court.[72] The two international human rights Tribunals, by correctly resolving basic procedural issues raised in such recent cases, have aptly made use of the techniques of public international law in order to strengthen their respective jurisdictions of protection of the human person. They have decisively safeguarded the integrity of the mechanisms of protection of the American and European Conventions on Human Rights, whereby the juridical emancipation of the human person *vis-à-vis* her own State is achieved.

As to substantive law, the contribution of the two human rights Courts to this effect is illustrated by numerous examples of their respective case-law pertaining to the rights protected under the two regional Conventions. The European Court has a vast and impressive case-law, for example, on the right to the protection of liberty and security of person (Article 5 of the European Convention), and the right to a fair trial (Article 6). The Inter-American Court has a significant case-law on the fundamental right to life, comprising also the conditions of living, as from its decision in the paradigmatic case of the so-called *"Street Children"* (*Villagrán Morales and Others versus Guatemala*, Merits, 1999).

The two human rights Tribunals have achieved a remarkable jurisprudential construction on the right of access to justice (and of obtaining reparation) at the international level. In its historical Judgment in the case, concerning Peru, of the massacre of *Barrios Altos* (2001), the Inter-American Court warned that provisions of amnesty, of prescription and of factors excluding responsibility, intended to impede the investigation and punishment of those responsible for grave violations of human rights (such as torture, summary, extra-legal or arbitrary executions, and forced disappearances) are inadmissible; they violate non-derogable rights recognized by the international law of human rights. This case-law has been reiterated by the Court (with regard to prescription) in its recent decision in the *Bulacio versus Argentina* case (2003).

---

71   In the *Belilos versus Switzerland* case (1988), in the *Loizidou versus Turkey* case (Preliminary Objections, 1995), and in the *I. Ilascu, A. Lesco, A. Ivantoc and T. Petrov-Popa versus Moldovia and the Russian Federation* case (2001).

72   In the *Constitutional Tribunal* and *Ivtcher Bronstein versus Peru* cases, Jurisdiction (1999), and in the *Hilaire, Constantine and Benjamin and Others versus Trinidad and Tobago* (Preliminary Objection, 2001).

The extensive case-law of the European Court covers virtually the totality of the rights protected under the European Convention and some of its Protocols. The growing case-law of the Inter-American Court, in its turn, appears innovative and forward-looking with regard to reparations in its multiple forms, and provisional measures of protection, these latter sometimes benefiting members of entire human collectivities (particularly in the present situation of armed conflict in Colombia).

It is not surprising that the interpretation and application of certain provisions of a given human rights treaty are at times utilized as a guide for the interpretation and application of corresponding provisions of another human rights treaty. Thus, in the pursuit of their common cause and ideal, the European and the Inter-American Courts have had no difficulty to refer to each other's case-law whenever they have deemed it pertinent. The Inter-American Court has referred to the case-law of its European counterpart constantly, throughout the whole of its case-law to date. The European Court, for its part, is increasingly doing the same, particularly in recent years: until last July 2003, for example, the published Judgments of the European Court contained references to the case-law of the Inter-American Court in no less than 12 cases.

Human rights treaties such as the European and American Conventions have, in this way, by means of such interpretative interaction, reinforced each other mutually, to the ultimate benefit of the protected human beings. Interpretative interaction has in a way contributed to the universality of the conventional law on the protection of human rights. This has paved the way for a *uniform* interpretation of the *corpus juris* of contemporary international human rights Law. Such uniform interpretation in no way threatens the unity of international law. Quite on the contrary, instead of threatening "to fragment" international law, our two Tribunals have helped to develop and achieve the aptitude of international law to regulate efficiently relations which have a specificity of their own – at intra-State, rather than inter-State, level, opposing States to individuals under their respective jurisdictions, – and which require a specialized knowledge from the Judges.

The European and Inter-American human rights Tribunals have helped to secure, in the domain of protection of the rights of the human person, compliance with the conventional obligations of protection of the States *vis-à-vis* all human beings under their respective jurisdictions. With the evolution of the international law of human rights, it is public international law itself which is thereby justified and legitimized, in affirming juridical principles, concepts and categories proper to the present domain of protection, based on premises fundamentally distinct from those which have guided the application of its postulates at the level of purely inter-State relations.

One could not pretend to foster the development of the international law of human rights to the detriment of the law of treaties. But nor could one pretend to hinder the evolution of the international law of human rights by making abstraction of the specificity of human rights treaties. By means of the application of human rights treaties, within the framework of the law of treaties, and also resorting to general international law, one can perfectly develop the aptitude of international law to regulate adequately the legal relations at inter-State as well as intra-State levels, under the respective treaties of protection. The unity and effectiveness of public international law itself can be measured precisely by its aptitude to regulate legal relations in distinct contexts with equal adequacy.

From all the aforesaid one can detect the current historical process of *humanization* of international law (a new *jus gentium*), disclosing a new outlook of the relations between public power and the human being – an outlook which is summed up, ultimately, in the recognition that the State exists for the human being, and not vice-versa. In operating, and constructing their converging case-law, to that effect, our two international human rights Tribunals, the European and the Inter-American Courts, have indeed contributed to enrich and humanize contemporary public international law. They have done so as from an essentially and necessarily anthropocentric outlook, as aptly foreseen, since the 16th century, by the so-called founding fathers of the *law of nations* (the *droit des gens*).

20. The Legal Ordering of International Trade: From GATT to the WTO

Donald M. McRae*

1. Introduction

Fifty years ago it would have been a novelty to have included a chapter on international trade law in a volume on international legal ordering. The mammoth contributions of Falk and Black on the international legal order dealt only marginally with international trade,[1] and the series that came out of Yale on law and minimum public order did not devote a volume to trade or other economic issues.[2] Trade and often economic issues more broadly, were simply outside of the mainstream of international law.[3] In 1969, John Jackson's *World Trade and the Law of the GATT*[4] was unique in the field, and Jackson and Robert Hudec stood out in North America as two legal scholars in a field that was generally absent of public international lawyers. There was interest in the private transactional side of international trade, in international commercial arbitration, even in the international aspects of competition policy.[5] But the public international law side of the cross border movement of

---

*   I am grateful for the research assistance of Robin Hansen.

1   See Cyril E. Black and Richard A. Falk, eds., *The Future of the International Legal Order*, (Princeton, N.J.: Princeton University Press, 1969), c.1 Wolfgang Friedmann, "The Relevance of International Law to the Processes of Economic and Social Development".

2   The first volume in this series was Myres S. McDougal and Florentino P. Feliciano, *Law and Minimum World Public Order: The Legal Regulation of International Coercion* (New Haven: Yale University Press, 1961). Other works dealt with law of the sea, human rights and treaty interpretation. Feliciano was subsequently to become one of the first members of the WTO Appellate Body.

3   Donald M. McRae, "The Contribution of International Trade Law to the Development of International Law" (1996) 260 *Recueil des Cours, Collected Courses of the Hague Academy of International Law*, 111-123.

4   John Jackson, *World Trade and the Law of GATT* (New York: The Bobbs-Merrill Company, 1969).

5   D.H.W. Henry, "International Aspects of Competition Policy" in R. St. J. Macdonald, Gerald L. Morris and Douglas M. Johnston, eds., *Canadian Perspectives on International Law and Organization* (Toronto: University of Toronto Press, 1974) 756.

Ronald St. John Macdonald & Douglas M. Johnston (eds.), Towards World Constitutionalism, *pp. 543-566.*
© *2005 Koninklijke Brill NV. Printed in The Netherlands. ISBN 90 04 14612 1.*

goods and services was limited to the international minimum standards relating to the treatment of aliens, the basis for a modern international investment law.

The GATT, then, as a legal framework for international trade, had a kind of twilight existence. It was based on and embodied legal principles, as Jackson's book demonstrated. But was it a treaty, or as "GATT insiders"[6] would have preferred at the time, just a "contract"? And, in public international law-making terms, GATT was different. Historically, public international law was based on customary international law; the principles set out in GATT were not. Law-making treaties tended to codify public international law and in some instances progressively develop it. GATT was not a codification. Law-making treaties that were widely accepted tended to be creative of new customary international law. The principles in GATT never emerged through general acceptance to become customary international law.[7]

So for a discipline whose centre was the nation-state, and which saw the practice of nation-states at its foundation, GATT sat rather uncomfortably. The nation-state had at its core the defence of its integrity and the security of its citizens. This would be accomplished by developing strength to maintain internal order and to defend against threats from outside. Peace and security was at the centre of public international law. Institution-building based on the core ideas of sovereign equality, freedom from aggression and attack, and more recently, respect for the rights of the individual, were some of the central developments of the 20th century.

In some respects, international trade law stood apart from the rest of public international law.[8] It did not derive from any inherent rights of the nation to protect itself, or from any idea of equality of states, or from ideas about the inherent dignity or the economic autonomy of individuals. The links between sovereignty and trade, symbolised by the freedom of states to raise their tariffs at will, led to the "beggar-thy-neighbour" policies of the inter-War years and disastrous economic outcomes. Instead, GATT had a simple economic rationale implemented through a principle of non-discrimination, although a principle of non-discrimination that was not based on the equality of states.

The economic rationale of "free trade", which underlies the GATT, is that of comparative advantage. If instead of seeking to produce everything needed to supply all of its own needs a state produces what it can produce most efficiently and trades for what it produces less efficiently, it will produce more. If all states produce more in this way, global production and hence global welfare will be enhanced. The core principles of the GATT were designed to limit what states could do that would interfere with the operation of comparative advantage. The non-discrimination principle that was key to giving effect to this was in two parts; treat all foreign

---

6   Robert Howse, "From Politics to Technocracy – and Back Again: The Fate of the Multilateral Trading Regime (Symposium: The Boundaries of the WTO)." (2002) 96:1 Am. J. Int'l L. 94 at 98.

7   Stephen T. Zamora, "Is There Customary International Economic Law?" (1990) 32 German Yearbook of International Law 9-42.

8   For a criticism of this view, see Joost Pauwelyn, *Conflict of Norms in Public International Law*, (Cambridge: Cambridge University Press, 2003), 29-33.

goods equally at the border (the MFN principle) and do not discriminate between domestic and foreign goods within the domestic market (the national treatment principle). There were corollaries: the lowering of tariffs and the avoidance of other border restrictions that were an essential part of GATT also served to implement this economic rationale. At the same time, GATT included certain provisions that ran counter to that rationale, including the right to take action against "dumping" and the right to continue preferential regional trade agreements.[9] But overall, the provisions of GATT pursued a core economic objective which entailed limitations on states that seemed to run counter to the political objectives of reaffirming and strengthening statehood that was an important part of the institution-building of the post-War era.[10]

The economic objective of GATT is central to an understanding of the international trading regime although promoting economic liberalization was a political as well as an economic objective particularly during the Cold War. But its economic orientation was part of the reason that GATT stood apart in the international legal order. Other areas of the "international law of cooperation"[11] – human rights, environmental law – made intuitive sense. Trade law did not. The clash between the desire of states to do what they felt they were entitled to do as nation-states, through protectionist measures, through trade remedy laws, even though these might undermine the economic objectives of GATT, and in some cases even violate GATT's express provisions, was a constant part of the history of the GATT and it continues with the WTO. GATT obligations require states to do what intuitively is contrary to what citizens' believe their states should be doing for them. Citizens expect to be given priority over foreigners; that is the point of being a citizen. Trade laws require that no preference should be given. Citizens expect the state to use its revenues to assist their economic activities. Trade laws say this should not be done.

All of this has helped to add to the obscurity of GATT. To say that it had an economic rationale during the Cold War era was to identify GATT with a capitalist ideology, which continues today with the easy identification of the WTO with uncontrolled and environmentally harmful activity by multinational corporations. There is a perceived clash between the principles of trade regulation and principles from other areas of international law – an incompatibility between the protection of the environment and the protection of human rights and the rules of the WTO.

---

9   For a discussion of the "embedded liberalism" bargain under which states sought to accommodate notions of free trade with their commitment to an interventionist welfare state, see Pauwelyn, at 35-36; Howse, *op.cit*, 97-98.

10   Article 2(7) of the UN Charter sought to preserve the domestic jurisdiction of states. GATT obligations all involved limitations on domestic jurisdiction. *Charter of the United Nations*, 26 June 1945, Can. T.S. 1945 No. 7 (entered into force 24 October 1945).

11   Pauwelyn, *op.cit.*, at 31, drawing on Wolfgang Friedmann's classic distinction between the international law of coexistence and the international law of cooperation; *The Changing Structure of International Law* (Stevens: 1964) 60-64.

The result is that today, far from being outside the mainstream of international law, international trade law is central to many key debates in the field of international law. Dispute settlement between states in the field of international trade law under the mechanism established in the WTO, is perhaps the most advanced dispute settlement mechanism in any area of international law. And unlike the obscure GATT, the WTO is one of the most readily recognizable names of international institutions. In short, international trade law has now become recognized as an essential part of any legal ordering of the world community.

In this chapter I shall trace the development of the GATT and the development of international trade law within the international legal community and consider the role that it now plays within that legal order.

2.   GATT as an International Institution

A.   *The ITO and Its Failure*

The twilight existence of GATT owed much to the rather accidental way that it came into existence. The grand design for an economic future at the end of the Second World War had three pillars; an International Monetary Fund (IMF), an International Bank for Reconstruction and Development (IBRD) and an International Trade Organization (ITO). The ITO (known as the Havana Charter)[12] was crafted as a public international law institution, covering a wide range of cross border activity, including commercial policy (tariffs, quotas, subsidies, state trading activities) restrictive business practices, commodity agreements, investment, and even the linkages between trade and employment. It provided for an international organization, with a plenary conference, an executive board, commissions and a Director-General. It provided for a variety of ways to resolve disputes and even contemplated references to the International Court of Justice. It was to be brought into relationship with the United Nations under Article 57 of the Charter and become a specialized agency. It was to be an integral part of the UN system.

Of course, none of this happened. The ITO was never ratified by the US Senate and without US support the regime it provided for could not come into existence. What remained was an interim agreement, put together a year before the signing of the Havana Charter to provide the necessary commercial framework for the tariff concessions that had been agreed to in Geneva. It contained "general clauses" of obligation that would ensure that the agreed tariff arrangements would function effectively and it was intended that it would be taken over and would function within the ITO once that organization came into existence.[13]

---

12   The Havana Charter was signed on 24 March 1948. For text of the *Havana Charter for an International Trade Organization* see *United Nations Conference on Trade and Employment, Final Act and Related Documents,* E/CONF.2/78, 1948, United Nations publication, Sales No. 1948.II.D.4. online: WTO <http://www.wto.org/english/docs_e/legal_e/havana_e.pdf> [hereinafter *Havana Charter*].

13   John H. Jackson, *The World Trading System: Law and Policy of International Economic*

B.   The Institutional Basis of GATT

Although in multilateral treaty form, the GATT was styled as an "agreement", and it came into effect provisionally on 1 January 1948 by a "Protocol of Provisional Application".[14] This device enabled states, particularly the United States, to apply the provisions of the GATT without having to seek congressional or parliamentary approval for them. Moreover, not all of the provisions of the GATT were implemented fully. Part II of the GATT dealing with most of the core obligations was, with the exception of MFN, to be implemented "to the fullest extent not inconsistent with existing legislation."[15] All of this cast GATT as an arrangement of complexity, and helped contribute to the myth that GATT was a contract, not a treaty, and thus had to be dealt with differently.

GATT was an agreement recording tariff concessions and providing general obligations on states. It was not an international organization. This was essential for US participation because any organization would require Senate approval. To emphasize this, the parties were referred to as Contracting Parties throughout the Agreement. The Contracting Parties were, however, not to be limited to governments. Governments could sign on behalf of their metropolitan territories and other territories for which they were responsible. They also had to notify the Executive Secretary of any separate customs territory for which they were responsible. They could then or subsequently notify the Executive Secretary that their acceptance of the GATT applied to that separate customs territory.

However, if the separate customs territory was to possess or acquire "full autonomy in the conduct of its external commercial relations and of the matters provided for in this Agreement,"[16] it could become a contracting party in its own right. In this way, Hong Kong became a full member of GATT. GATT membership was, thus, not limited to sovereign states. This reinforced the economic objective of the agreement. The necessary parties were those entities which are responsible for external commercial relations. The agreement was providing a series of rights and obligations and a framework that would facilitate trade, not reinforcing ideas of sovereignty.

No institutions were provided for in the GATT; any action taken under the Agreement was to be taken by the "Contracting Parties". Article XXV:1 provided:

> Representatives of the contracting parties shall meet from time to time for the purpose of giving effect to those provisions of this Agreement which involve joint action and,

---

Relations (Cambridge, Mass.: MIT Press, 1989) at 32-33.

14   *Protocol of Provisional Application of the GATT,* 30 October 1947, 55 UNTS 308 (entered into force 1 January 1948).

15   This was the source of the claims to "grandfather rights"; Jackson, *supra* note 13 at 34-37.

16   *General Agreement on Tariffs and Trade,* 30 October 1947, 58 U.N.T.S. 187, Article XXVI: 5(c) (entered into force 1 January 1948) [hereinafter *GATT 1947*].

generally with a view to facilitating the operation and furthering the objectives of this Agreement.

Article XXV also provided for voting at such meetings, normally by majority and a two-thirds majority in the case of waivers of obligations.[17]

Although not expressly provided for in the Agreement itself, the text of the GATT assumed that there would be an "Executive Secretary" because functions are assigned to such an entity. However, no secretariat is provided for in the Agreement. Following the signing of the Havana Charter an interim commission (ICITO) was established to prepare for the coming into effect of the ITO and it provided services to the GATT as well. The head of ICITO became the executive secretary of the GATT. Since the ITO came to nothing, the ICITO continued to act as the secretariat for the GATT.[18] In 1965 the Contracting Parties gave the title of Director-General to the person holding the office of Executive Secretary, although the references in the GATT itself to Executive Secretary were not changed.

From this inauspicious start, the GATT continued and developed for the next 50 years of its existence. It was born from a pragmatic need and it functioned pragmatically, acting where it had to and allowing practice rather than regulation to be its *modus operandi*. The power given to the Contracting Parties to take "joint action" to further the objectives of the Agreement was potentially very broad, although it was exercised moderately. The hallmark of the GATT was pragmatism and "trial and error.[19]

Operating in this way, the GATT was able to make several important institutional developments. The meeting of the Contracting Parties became the "GATT Council". Committees, commissions and working groups were established, and regardless of the specific rules in Article XXV on voting, GATT developed a practice of taking decisions by consensus. This latter approach was facilitated by the fact that GATT membership in its early years involved a limited number of either western developed states or states linked to them through former colonial ties, and all with varying forms of with market economies.

Perhaps most importantly, a dispute settlement process evolved under GATT. The institutional basis for this process is found in Articles XXII and XXIII. Article XXII provides for consultation between contracting parties over any matter affecting the operation of the Agreement. It also provides that the Contracting Parties as a whole may consult with a particular contracting party where consultations have not been successful. This is taken further in Article XXIII which relates specifically to claims by a Contracting Party that benefits accruing to it under the Agreement have been "nullified or impaired" by the actions of another party either through failing to carry out its obligations under the Agreement or otherwise. Article XXIII contemplates that where the parties themselves are unable to resolve the issue, the

---

17   *Ibid.*, Article XXV:5.

18   Jackson, *supra* note 4 at 320.

19   Jackson, *supra* note 13 at 38.

Contracting Parties may investigate the matter and make "appropriate recommendation" to the parties "or may give a ruling on the matter as appropriate".[20]

This power to make rulings was coupled with a power to impose sanctions. Article XXII:2 provided that if the Contracting Parties considered that "the circumstances are serious enough to justify such action" they could authorize a contracting party "to suspend the application to any other contracting party or parties of such concessions or other obligations under this Agreement that they consider appropriate in the circumstances." In short, this non-organization, GATT, had the institutional power to authorize retaliation against states, something that was practically unheard of amongst "real" international organizations.[21]

From this basis, GATT developed a dispute settlement process based on the appointment of "panels" of individuals, five members initially and later three, who would receive written submissions, meet with the parties twice in a form of hearing, and then make recommendations to the GATT Council on how the dispute should be resolved. That recommendation could then be adopted or rejected by the Council. If the Council adopted the recommendation of the panel and the party concerned failed to implement that recommendation (usually by withdrawing the measure that caused "nullification or impairment") the GATT Council could authorize retaliation against the contracting party through the withdrawal of concessions of equivalent benefit.

This dispute settlement process, founded in practice and in "trial and error", developed from informal beginnings to more and more formality. And it was surprisingly successful.[22] But it could not overcome some of the institutional limitations of the GATT system. The GATT Council, which made the decision whether or not to establish a panel and whether to adopt its recommendation, was a plenary body. This meant that the disputing parties on any issue were both involved in the decision to send the matter to a panel and the decision to adopt or reject the panel's recommendations. And, since the GATT Council operated by consensus, a disputing party could prevent a consensus to allow a panel to be established and prevent a consensus for the adoption of the recommendations of a panel. Ultimately, these and other institutional limitations were major factors influencing the amendment of the trading system in the new WTO.[23]

The institutional role of the GATT was not limited to dispute settlement. The GATT Council, the committees and working groups were important for the dis-

---

20   The Havana Charter (Article 93) envisaged that this stage would be one of arbitration, but provided also for the Executive Board to investigate the matter and authorize the withdrawal of concessions (Article 94). *Havana Charter*, *supra* note 8.

21   The major exception was the power granted to the UN Security Council in respect of the use of force.

22   See generally Robert E. Hudec, *Enforcing International Trade Law: The Evolution of the Modern GATT Legal System* (Salem, N.H.: Butterworth Legal Publishers, 1993).

23   For a discussion of the institutional deficit of the GATT see John H. Jackson, "The Crumbling Institutions of the Liberal Trade System" (1978) 12 Journal of World Trade Law 93.

cussion of trade policy issues and for determining where possibilities might exist for further trade liberalization. More importantly, GATT, which owed its origin to a tariff negotiating round, became the sponsor of eight successive tariff negotiation rounds. Initially these rounds involved the negotiation of tariff reductions. They then moved to include non-tariff measures and by the Tokyo Round began the development of new agreements or codes, elaborating on the provisions of the GATT and sometimes covering new areas. Finally, with the Uruguay Round institution-building occurred and the GATT was transformed into the WTO.

Thus, the GATT, the non-institution, became the base for one of the most important examples of international legal institution-building to occur in the latter part of the 20th century.

C.   The Relationship of GATT with the UN

The negotiators of the ITO envisaged that the organization would become a specialized agency of the UN. Since GATT was interim and provisional, such a relationship was never contemplated for it. Nor was the GATT ever brought into any formal relationship with the UN. Indeed, the conclusion of any agreement by the GATT with another international organization would have implied some form of international organizational status, and perhaps a legal personality – something that the Contracting Parties were anxious to avoid.

Nevertheless, the GATT was not totally divorced from the UN system. The United Nations Conference on Trade and Employment, which led to both the GATT and the Havana Charter, resulted from a resolution of ECOSOC in 1946,[24] and ECOSOC continued as a presence in the minds of the GATT negotiators. ECOSOC is specifically mentioned in GATT Article XXIII as a body with which the Contracting Parties might consult in seeking to resolve disputes. The UN Secretary General was to be the depositary for the original copies of the Agreement in English and in French,[25] but not for the instruments of acceptance of the Agreement, which were to go to the GATT Executive Secretary.[26] The UN was authorized to register the Agreement once it came into force[27] and the Secretary-General was given responsibility for convening the first meeting of the GATT Contracting Parties. The UN Secretary-General was also to receive any instruments of acceptance of subsequent amendments to the Agreement.[28]

The authority of the UN in respect of peace and security issues was given explicit recognition in the GATT. Article XXI provides that nothing in the Agreement prevents a contracting party from taking action in pursuance of its obligations

---

24   *Economic and Social Council. Report Of The Drafting Subcommittee On The Trade Conference Resolution*, UN ECOSOC Res. 13, 1st Sess., UN Doc. E/22 (16 February 1946).

25   *GATT 1947, supra* note 16, Article XXVI:3.

26   *Ibid.*, Article XXVI:4.

27   *Ibid.*, Article XXVI:7.

28   *Ibid.*, Article XXX:2.

under the UN Charter for the maintenance of international peace and security.[29] Cooperation with the UN was also contemplated in Part IV of the GATT, which was added in 1966, in respect of trade and development. GATT Article XXVII:2(b) provided for "appropriate collaboration" on trade and development issues between the Contracting Parties and the UN, its organs and agencies, including any institutions resulting from the United Nations Conference on Trade and Development.[30] Apart from these formal references and links, the GATT stayed outside of the UN system. Members of the GATT secretariat continued to be employed by ICITO, and were not UN staff members. Moreover, in a Cold War era, GATT was not seen as having the attribute of universality that UN organs and agencies had. Communist regimes did not operate economies that fitted within the framework of GATT rules, and developing countries, although increasingly becoming GATT contracting parties, did not believe that the rules of the GATT were always for their benefit. Their reaction against GATT was a significant factor in the convening of the United Nations Conference on Trade and Development and the creation of the permanent organ UNCTAD that resulted from it.[31] As long as GATT was seen as representing a specific economic ideology, by both communist states and developing countries, it was difficult for it to be recognised as part of an international legal order that aspired to be universal in values and aspirations.

D.   The Legal Regime of GATT

The original reason for the GATT was to secure tariff reductions, and the negotiated tariff concessions are included in each contracting party's schedule and made binding.[32] The benefits of these tariff concessions are made available to all contracting parties by virtue of the MFN principle. Indeed, MFN is one of the two pillars of the principle of non-discrimination under the GATT. Article I provides that, "any advantage, favour, privilege or immunity granted by any contracting party to any product originating in or destined for any other country shall be accorded immediately and unconditionally to the like product originating in or destined for the territories of all other contracting parties."

The second pillar of non-discrimination is the principle of national treatment found in GATT Article III. The national treatment principle requires Contracting Parties to treat imported products in their domestic market no less favourably than "like" domestic products. This applies to taxation[33] as well as to "any laws, regulations and requirements, affecting their internal sale, offering for sale, purchase, transportation, distribution or use."[34]

---

29   *Ibid.*, Article XXI.

30   *Ibid.*, Article XXVII:2(b).

31   UNCTAD was created by General Assembly Resolution 1995(XIX), 30 December 1964.

32   *Ibid.*, Article II. These are often referred to as tariff "bindings".

33   GATT Article III:2.

34   GATT Article III:4.

The final central or core obligation of the GATT system is to prohibit other, non-tariff restrictions, such as quotas or import licences, at the border on imports and exports. Article XI:1 makes the prohibition absolute, but the remainder of Article XI carves out important exceptions, particularly in the field of agriculture.

The fundamental objective of these provisions is, as has been mentioned, economic. If products can compete across borders freed from restriction, or at least operating under the same restrictions, then countries will be able to produce what they really are more efficient at producing; hence comparative advantage will work and world production will be enhanced.

This, of course, provides a very simple view of both the operation of comparative advantage and the full extent of GATT obligations. The ability of goods to compete are affected by a variety of other factors, including subsidies and dumping. States need to provide indications of the origins of their products and they need to impose restrictions on goods at their borders for health and safety reasons, they also need to have laws and institutions affecting economic issues that are transparent and accessible. GATT provides a legal framework for all of these things. GATT provisions contain a mix between the hortatory – encouraging states not to provide export subsidies,[35] and the facilitative – indicating how contracting parties are to act domestically when imposing countervailing duties.[36] And, of course, being a compromise between the economic and the political, GATT was riddled with exceptions and exclusions. Notwithstanding its overall success particularly in lowering tariffs on industrial products, the practice of the Contracting Parties over the years of GATT's existence was marked by permitted waivers of obligations and by deviation without any waiver from its provisions.

E.   The Contribution of GATT to International Law

In spite of its tenuous origins and existence and the informal and "trial and error" nature of practice under it, the GATT played an important role in the development of post-War legal institutions and in providing an orderly basis for facilitating international trade. Few could have anticipated that it would become the foundation for essentially a universal regime for the regulation of international trade. Much of what GATT did has been subsumed into and became an essential part of the new international trading regime under the WTO.

The contributions of GATT to international law are of two kinds. First, there are the concepts that are used in the GATT which are particular applications of what can be found elsewhere in international law. Their importance is not that they bring new concepts into international law, but rather that they bring a new and sometimes different way of thinking about international law concepts. Second, there is the contribution to the process of international law. Here one finds both new mechanisms and new applications of processes that exist under international law.

---

35   *Ibid.*, Article XVI.
36   *Ibid.*, Article VI.

Two concepts will be mentioned here. First, there is the expression of loss or harm in terms of "nullification and impairment", which is unique to GATT.[37] It reflects the fact that GATT was founded on the negotiation of tariffs where concessions were arrived at reciprocally. Anything that "nullified or impaired" negotiated benefits was a loss because the payment for those benefits had been wasted. Thus, nullification or impairment could occur through a breach of a provision of the GATT itself, or it could arise through action that did not constitute a breach but nevertheless deprived a contracting party of a negotiated benefit – hence the concept of "non-violation" nullification and impairment.

Non-violation nullification or impairment has no direct analogue in public international law. Responsibility under international law is generally based on breach of an international obligation.[38] Where liability is sought to be found in the absence of a breach of an international obligation, it is based on absolute liability.[39] By contrast, non-violation nullification and impairment is based on disappointed expectation, a contractual rather than a tortious measure of loss, but not based on a breach of contract. The need for such a remedy may be specifically a response to the GATT tariff negotiating process, and in fact under the WTO its use seems less likely.[40]

The second GATT concept is that of non-discrimination, which applies both at the border (MFN) and within the domestic market (national treatment). MFN was not a historically a principle of non-discrimination. It was a principle of preference. It was included in bilateral treaties of friendship, commerce and navigation as a means of getting a party the best that the other party gave to anyone else. There was no guarantee that all states would receive that treatment. Only when it was included in a multilateral treaty and in an unconditional form, as it did in GATT, did it become a principle of non-discrimination, a principle that opposed rather than provided preference.[41]

---

37   *Ibid.,* Article XXIII.

38   *Case Concerning the Factory of Chorzow (Germany v. Poland)* (1928), P.C.I.J. (Ser. A) No. 17; *Draft articles on Responsibility of States for Internationally Wrongful Acts,* Article 2(b) in *Report of the International Law Commission on the work of its fifty-third session,* UN GAOR, 56th Sess., Supp. No. 10, U.N. Doc. A/56/10. (2001) chp.IV.E.1. online: UN. <http://www.un.org/law/ilc/texts/State_responsibility/responsibilityfra.htm>.

39   "Text of the draft articles on international liability for injurious consequences arising out of action not prohibited by international law (Prevention of transboundary damage for hazardous activities) provisionally adopted by the Commission on first reading" in *Report of the International Law Commission on the work of its fiftieth session,* UN GAOR, 53rd Sess., Supp. No. 10, U.N. Doc. A/53/10. (1998) chp. IV.C.1. online: UN <http://www.un.org/law/ilc/reports/1998/98repfra.htm>.

40   In the one case in which it has been raised under the WTO, the claim has been rejected: *Japan-Measures Affecting Consumer Photographic Film and Paper,* WT/DS44/R, 30 March 1998, Report of the Panel.

41   D.M. McRae and J.C. Thomas, The Development of the Most-Favoured-Nation Principle: Treaties of Friendship, Navigation and Commerce and the GATT" in Irish and

The reason for denying preference was economic. Preference distorts competition in the market. Comparative advantage does not work when the price of the products of one country reflect a tariff that the same products from another country did not have to pay. And when domestic goods are taxed at a lower rate than imported goods, once again the economic benefits of free trade are obscured. Because almost all of the GATT contracting parties are states, the GATT principle of non-discrimination can easily be seen as a principle based on the equality of states. But, in a sense, the coalescence between the GATT principle of non-discrimination and the principle of non-discrimination in Article 2(1) of the UN Charter is fortuitous. Under GATT, Hong Kong, which was not a sovereign state, but still a GATT contracting party, was equally entitled to receive the treatment that a state was entitled to. Articles I and III are in the GATT because they help maximize the economic benefits of trade, not because they reflect the entitlement of sovereign and equal states.

The most obvious way in which GATT has contributed to the process of international law is through its dispute settlement process.[42] The "panel" process was the basis on which dispute settlement was structured in Chapters 18 and 19 of the Canada-US Free Trade Agreement[43] and in Chapters 19 and 20 of NAFTA.[44] It also became the model for a variety of bilateral and regional free trade agreements. And, of course, it formed the basis of a much more structured dispute settlement process in the WTO.

More broadly, the GATT constitutes an early and important example of the interaction between international and domestic law. GATT obligations required domestic action. Negotiated tariffs had to be implemented into domestic law. Import and export restrictions and import licensing had to be adapted to GATT obligations. Taxation and laws affecting the sale of imported products had to conform to GATT obligations. Dumping and countervailing duty regimes had to be in conformity with the provisions of GATT. Thus, GATT obligations have a direct impact on the nature and content of domestic law and on domestic legal and administrative processes. And, to the extent that compliance with GATT resulted in states following similar procedures or adopting similar laws, GATT had potentially a

Carasco, eds., *The Legal Framework for Canada-United States Trade* (Carswell: 1987) 225-247.

42   The particular negotiating process of tariff negotiating rounds also provides insight into international negotiations: see Fen Osler Hampson with Michael Hart, *Multilateral Negotiations: Lessons from Arms Control, Trade, and the Environment* (Baltimore: Johns Hopkins University Press, 1995) c. 3 at 125-254.

43   Free Trade Agreement between the Government of CANADA and the Government of the UNITED STATES OF AMERICA (with Exchange of Note), Ottawa, December 22, 1987 and January 2, 1988 and Washington and Palm Springs, December 23, 1987 and January 2, 1988, Can. T.S. 1989 No. 3 (entered into force 1 January 1989).

44   North American Free Trade Agreement Between the Government of Canada, the Government of Mexico and the Government of the United States, 17 December 1992, Can. T.S. 1994 No. 2, 32 I.L.M. 289 (entered into force 1 January 1994).

harmonizing role in respect of domestic law. Although they were not fully realized under the GATT, the implications of international trade obligations for domestic law were far-reaching.

3.   The New Order of the WTO

A.   *The Institutional Regime*

The negotiations for a new trade negotiating round were launched at Punta del Este in Uruguay in September 1986. The negotiations promised to be the most ambitious in the history of the GATT, and they more than fulfilled their promise. What emerged was an international trading regime that was broader in coverage and deeper in the detail of the obligations undertaken than had hitherto been seen. It was a rules-based system anchored by a comprehensive dispute settlement process and an international organization that would quickly take on a prominence greater than what the negotiators might have anticipated.

The WTO agreements constitute an expansion and transformation of the old GATT regime. The complex set of agreements making up the WTO system consist of the GATT and twelve related multilateral agreements on trade in goods, a general agreement on trade in services, an agreement on trade-related aspects of intellectual property, an agreement relating to dispute settlement and an agreement establishing a "trade policy review mechanism", all annexed to the foundational "Agreement Establishing the World Trade Organization" (WTO Agreement). These agreements are a single package and a state that is party to the WTO Agreement is bound by them all.[45]

The first important development is that the WTO remedies the institutional deficit of GATT. The WTO is an international organization, explicitly so. The WTO Agreement grants the organization legal personality and contemplates privileges and immunities for itself and its employees. It also contemplates the conclusion of a headquarters agreement.[46] The Agreement provides for a ministerial conference, a general council and councils to oversee all of the major areas covered by the WTO.[47] It provides for a secretariat, headed by a Director-General,[48] and sets out rules for decision-making by the Ministerial Conference, although it affirms and continues the GATT practice of reaching decisions by consensus.[49]

Alongside this major institutional development is the fact that the WTO agreements cover a far wider range of areas than did GATT. GATT was an agree-

---

45   *Agreement Establishing the World Trade Organization,* 14 April 1994, MTN/FA II, Article II.2, online: WTO: <http://www.wto.org/english/docs_e/legal_e/legal_e.htm> [hereinafter *WTO Agreement*]. Four further "plurilateral" agreements were available for states to become party to as well. Only two of these agreements remain in force.

46   *Ibid.,* Article VIII.

47   *Ibid.,* Article IV.

48   *Ibid.,* Article VI.

49   *Ibid.,* Article IX.

ment about trade in goods. The WTO goes beyond this. It covers services and some aspects of investment, and brings obligations relating to intellectual property into the international trading regime. Moreover, even in the area of trade in goods, the WTO agreements both elaborate in detail on some basic GATT obligations, building on what was included in the Tokyo Round codes, and also extend GATT disciplines into areas that either GATT had not covered or had dealt with only in a very general way. Thus, agreements were included on subsidies and countervailing measures, on safeguards and on sanitary and phytosanitary measures and an Agreement on Agriculture brought important disciplines into agricultural trade.

Consisting as it does a set of separate agreements under the umbrella of the core WTO Agreement, the WTO has its own form of constitutional problems. GATT is retained unchanged, but many of the multilateral agreements on trade in goods take particular provisions of GATT and elaborate on them in more detail. How are these agreements to be reconciled where conflicts occur?

The negotiators have addressed this problem, although there are still many issues to be worked out. The starting point is that the WTO Agreement itself takes priority over all; in the event of any conflict, it governs.[50] As between GATT and the other multilateral agreements on trade in goods, the latter prevail in the event of conflict.[51] However, in the case of a conflict between a multilateral agreement on trade in goods and the Agreement on Agriculture, it is the Agreement on Agriculture that prevails.[52] This somewhat bewildering complex of options has been clarified in part by decisions of the WTO Appellate Body. The agreements of the WTO system are to be treated as an integrated whole.[53] This has meant that in some cases the provisions of GATT have been superseded by the multilateral agreement,[54] and in other cases GATT provisions supplement those of the multilateral agreement.[55] The priority to be given to the Agreement on Agriculture, it has been said, depends

---

50   *Ibid.*, Article XVI:3.

51   *Ibid.*, Annex 1A: Multilateral Agreements on Trade in Goods, *General interpretative note to Annex 1A*, online: WTO <http://www.wto.org/english/docs_e/legal_e/05-anx1a_e.htm>.

52   *WTO Agreement, supra* note 33, Annex 1A: Multilateral Agreements on Trade in Goods, *Agreement on Agriculture*, Article 21.1., online: WTO <http://www.wto.org/english/docs_e/legal_e/14-ag.pdf>.

53   *Brazil--Measures Affecting Desiccated Coconut (Complaints by the United States and European Communities)* (21 February 1997), WTO Doc. WT/DS22/AB/R at 21 (Appellate Body Report).

54   *Guatemala – Definitive Anti-Dumping Measures on Grey Portland Cement From Mexico (Complaint by Mexico)* (24 October 2000) WTO Doc. WT/DS156/R (Panel Report). (GATT Article VI provides no rights independently of the Antidumping Agreement).

55   *Argentina – Safeguard Measures on Imports of Footwear (Complaint by the European Communities)* (14 December 1999), WTO doc. WT/DS121/AB/R at para. 81 (Appellate Body Report) [hereinafter *Argentina – Footwear*]. (GATT Article XIX's requirement for the existence of "unforeseen developments" as a precondition to taking a safeguards measure continues alongside the requirements of the Safeguards Agreement).

on that Agreement containing "specific provisions dealing specifically with the same matter" as the other agreement.[56] In short, there is a growing jurisprudence concerning the constitutional relationship of the WTO Agreements.

Unlike the ITO which contemplated a specific relationship with the UN, that of a specialized agency, the WTO makes no provision for such a relationship. It provides that the General Council "shall make appropriate arrangements for effective cooperation with other intergovernmental organizations that have responsibilities related to the WTO" which presumably would include the UN. Otherwise, the UN gets scant mention in the WTO Agreement. There is a reference to the Convention on the Privileges and Immunities of the Specialized Agencies, adopted by the General Assembly of the UN on 21 November 1947. Members are to accord to the Organization, its officials and representative of other Members to the WTO "similar" privileges and immunities.[57] The "least developed countries" that are entitled to limit their commitments to the extent consistent with their level of development are described as the "least developed countries recognised as such by the United Nations."[58] And, the WTO Agreement is to be registered in accordance with Article 102 of the UN Charter.[59]

The General Agreement on Trade in Services (GATS), by contrast, does make reference to cooperation with the United Nations. The General Council of the WTO is mandated to "make appropriate arrangements for consultation and cooperation with the United Nations and its specialized agencies as well as with other intergovernmental organizations concerned with services."[60] In addition, modelled on the GATT, the GATS also provides that nothing prevents Members from "taking any action in pursuance of its obligations under the United Nations Charter for the maintenance of international peace and security."[61] A similar exception is found in TRIPS,[62] which also contemplates cooperation with the World Intellectual Property Organization (WIPO).[63]

Initially, the WTO concluded cooperation agreements with the World Bank and the IMF providing for sharing of information and observer status in certain of each other's meetings. It has also concluded cooperation arrangements with UNCTAD and the United Nations Industrial Development Organisation (UNIDO) on technical assistance, but no agreement on cooperation has been concluded with the UN. Yet, even though the WTO remains outside of the UN system at a

---

56   *European Communities – Regime for the Importation, Sale and Distribution of Bananas* (9 September 1997) WTO Doc. WT/DS27/AB/R at para. 155 (Appellate Body Report) [hereinafter *EC – Bananas*].

57   *WTO Agreement, supra* note 33, Art. VIII.5.

58   *Ibid.*, Art. XI.2.

59   WTO Agreement, Art. XVI.6.

60   GATS Art. XXVI.

61   GATS Art. XIV *bis*.

62   TRIPS Art. 73.

63   TRIPS Art. 68.

practical level there are important links. The WTO participates in the work of the UN Administrative Committee on Cooperation (ACC) and utilizes the ILO Administrative Tribunal.

B.   The Dispute Settlement Process

Dispute settlement has clearly been one of the most significant developments under the WTO. One of the agreements under the WTO umbrella is the Dispute Settlement Understanding (DSU) which sets out the institutions and the rules and procedures for dispute settlement. The WTO took the GATT dispute settlement process and improved on it in three critical respects. First, it made dispute settlement compulsory and binding. Second, it made the process expeditions. Third, it established an appellate process.

i.   Compulsory and Binding Dispute Settlement

Any WTO Member can invoke the dispute settlement provisions. First it must seek consultations with the other party. If those consultations are not successful, it can then request the WTO organ administering disputes, the Dispute Settlement Body (DSB)[64] to establish a panel, which the DSB must do unless there is a consensus not to do so.[65] This is known as the reverse consensus rule. Under the GATT one dissent would prevent a panel from being established. Under the WTO the refusal by one Member to join a consensus against setting up a panel will ensure that the panel is established. As a result of this compulsory form of jurisdiction, there is little basis for challenges to the jurisdiction of panels and although in theory a Member could refuse to participate in a panel proceeding to which it objected, in fact this has not happened. WTO Members show up and defend cases brought against them.

Decisions of panels, or of the Appellate Body, are placed before the DSB for adoption. Again the reverse consensus rule applies. Unless there is a consensus to reject the report of a panel or the Appellate Body, then the report must be adopted. Once again, a single Member can assure the adoption of the report. Once adopted, the decision of the panel or Appellate Body is binding on the Member. Failure to implement in accordance with the relevant rulings can lead to further challenges and ultimately, with the authorization of the DSB, retaliation.[66] This takes the form of the suspension by the complaining party of concessions or other obligations owed to the non-complying party of benefits equivalent to the nullification and impairment that non-compliance has caused.

---

64   The DSB is a plenary organ and thus includes representatives of the disputing parties on it.

65   The Member against which the claim is brought can delay the setting up of a panel by one month: DSU Art. 6.1.

66   DSU Arts 21 and 22.

ii. Expeditious Dispute Settlement

Once a panel is established, the process to delivery of the panel's report to the Members is not normally to exceed nine months.[67] Thus, time limits are set for each stage of the process, written pleadings, response, oral hearing, rebuttal submissions, second oral hearing, final submissions, interim review process and delivery of the report, are all set by the panel at the outset, and they are generally adhered to. Equally, if the matter is appealed, even shorter time limits have to be followed, and the Appellate Body is supposed to reach a decision within 60 days and not more than 90 days of the appeal.[68] Once, again, in most instances these timelines are adhered to.

There are opportunities for delay. The selection of panel members, which involves discussions between the disputing parties and the secretariat, can be prolonged, although after 10 days from the DSB decision to establish the panel there is the option for the Director General to select the panel members. If the parties accept the decision of the panel, then the matter stops there. If the decision is appealed the process is prolonged, and if a party challenges implementation a further panel and Appellate Body process can ensue. A decision to seek authorization to retaliate can also lead to a further arbitral process on the appropriateness of the retaliation sought. However, each procedure is conducted with its own set of deadlines and time limits. The ability that existed under the GATT to delay or block proceedings has now gone.

iii. An Appellate Process

An appellate process was in part the *quid pro quo* for accepting compulsory jurisdiction. An unfavourable panel decision could be reviewed by a body that would consider "issues of law covered in the panel report and legal interpretations developed by the panel."[69] Although the provisions relating to the appellate process are not articulated in detail in the DSU, the Appellate Body has been able to function extremely effectively. Composed of seven members appointed by the DSB to a four year renewable term and who are broadly representative of the WTO membership, the Appellate Body is to be available at all times and on short notice. The volume of cases has meant that at times the Appellate Body is essentially a full time organ.

Beyond providing the WTO membership with the satisfaction of knowing they can get panel decisions reviewed, the Appellate Body has made a number of significant contributions to WTO dispute settlement, to WTO law and more broadly to the field of public international law.

First, it developed a sophisticated set of working procedures, dealing with such matters as conflict of interest and providing for collegiality in decision-making.[70]

---

67 DSU Art. 12 and Appendix 3.

68 DSU Art. 17.

69 *WTO Agreement, supra* note 33, Annex 2: Understanding on Rules and Procedures Governing the Settlement of Disputes, Article 17.6., online: WTO <http://www.wto.org/english/docs_e/legal_e/28-dsu.pdf> [hereinafter *DSU*].

70 Collegiality in the working procedures means that even though the Appellate Body sits in chambers of 3 members, all members receive the written pleadings and the full membership of 7 discusses each case.

The confidence that this brought was a factor in acceptance by WTO members that Appellate Body members sit on cases regardless of nationality.[71]

Second, the Appellate Body laid down a common interpretative approach to the WTO agreements based on Article 31 of the Vienna Convention on the Law of Treaties.[72] Generally it has been consistent in following this approach and insisting that panels do likewise. In doing so, the Appellate Body has located the WTO agreements clearly within the realm of public international law. In addition, the Appellate Body has had to develop procedural rules designed to make the process function effectively and fairly. This has included such matters as burden of proof, judicial economy,[73] "completing the analysis,"[74] and the submission of *amicus* briefs.

Third, in interpreting the WTO agreements, the Appellate Body has been able in a number of areas to explain and clarify what is often opaque and obscure in the wording of the WTO agreements. The jurisprudence developed by the Appellate Body, and to a lesser extent by panels, is now essential to an understanding of the nature and extent of WTO obligations.

Fourth, the Appellate Body has been conscious of the relevance of principles of public international law to the interpretation of the WTO agreements and has discussed these principles and invoked them where it considers them appropriate. Thus, it has referred to the "precautionary principle"[75] and other principles of international environmental law,[76] to the principle of "good faith"[77] as well as to maxims

---

71   By contrast, panel members are not to be nationals of one of the disputing parties unless the parties agree.

72   DSU Article 3.2 requires that the WTO agreements are to be interpreted in accordance with the "customary principles of interpretation of public international law". The rule in Article 31 has been endorsed by the Appellate Body as a rule of customary international law: *United States - Standards for Reformulated and Conventional Gasoline (Complaints by Brazil and Venezuela)* (29 April 1996), WTO Doc. WT/DS2/AB/R, at 17 (Appellate Body Report).

73   Under the principle of judicial economy panels are not required to rule on submissions of the parties if they have already decided the case on another ground.

74   The concept of "completing the analysis" was developed by the Appellate Body to allow it to decide a case where it overturned the decision of the panel where there were sufficient facts on the record to make a finding. This responded in part to the fact that the Appellate Body has no power to refer a matter back to a panel and the case would otherwise have to be started again by the complaining party.

75   *EC – Measures Concerning Meat and Meat Products (Hormones) (Complaints by the United States and Canada)* (16 January 1998), WTO Doc. WT/DS26/DS48/AB/R at paras.120-125 (Appellate Body Report) [hereinafter *EC – Hormones*].

76   *United States – Import Prohibition of Certain Shrimp and Shrimp Products (Complaints by India, Malaysia, Pakistan and Thailand)* (12 October 1998), WT/DS58/AB/R at paras. 154-155 (Appellate Body Report) [hereinafter *U. S. –Shrimp (AB)*].

77   *United States – Continued Dumping and Subsidy Offset Act of 2000*, WT/DS219/AB/R, 16 January 2003, (Appellate Body Report).

of interpretation that supplement the Vienna Convention rule.[78]

These developments have not escaped criticism. The decision by the Appellate Body to receive amicus briefs[79] was almost universally criticised by the WTO membership, and there is considerable criticism in the United States of Appellate Body decisions on trade remedy law.[80] But the system survives. WTO Members keep bringing cases and keep insisting that decisions in their favour are implemented. Although some cases of non-compliance receive considerable publicity,[81] in fact the general rate of compliance is high.

C.   The Expansion in Legal Scope

The WTO agreements cover existing GATT obligations in more detail and enlarge on the rules applicable to trade in goods. But they go further and extend to areas such as services and intellectual property rights that had not previously been included in multilateral trading regimes. This expansion in the scope and coverage of the WTO agreements affects not only the body of international trade law; it has broader implications for other areas of international law.

At one level the frame of reference of the WTO agreements has expanded. The Agreement on the Trade-Related Aspects of Intellectual Property (TRIPS) incorporates the obligations of intellectual property conventions[82] with the result that these conventions will be interpreted through the process of WTO dispute settlement. At another level, the reach of WTO law into domestic legal systems has expanded. The notion of "prohibited subsidies"[83] which will render illegal sup-

---

78   *Japan – Taxes on Alcoholic Beverages (Complaints by the European Communities, Canada and the United States)* (4 October 1996), WTO Doc. WT/DS8/DS10/DS11/AB/R, at 12 (Appellate Body Report).

79   *United States – Imposition of Countervailing Duties on Certain Hot-Rolled Lead and Bismuth Carbon Steel Products Originating in the United Kingdom (Complaint by the European Communities)* (10 May 2000), WTO Doc. WT/DS138/AB/R at para. 42 (Appellate Body Report).

80   See e.g., John Greenwald, "WTO Dispute Settlement: An Exercise in Trade Law Legislation?" (2003) 6:1 JIEL 113-124.

81   *EC – Hormones, supra* note 75; *EC – Bananas, supra* note 56; *United States – Tax Treatment for "Foreign Sales Corporations" (Complaint by the European Communities)* (24 February 2000), WTO Doc. WT/DS108/AB/R FSC (Appellate Body Report).

82   *WTO Agreement, supra* note 33, Annex 1C: Trade-Related Aspects of Intellectual Property Rights, Footnote 2, online: WTO <http://www.wto.org/english/docs_e/legal_e/27-trips.pdf>. This agreement incorporates the following conventions: *Paris Convention for the Protection of Industrial Property,* 20 March 1883 as revised 14 July 1967; *Berne Convention for the Protection of Literary and Artistic Works,* 9 September 1886 as revised 24 July 1971; *International Convention for the Protection of Performers, Producers of Phonograms and Broadcasting Organizations,* 26 October 1961; *Treaty on Intellectual Property in Respect of Integrated Circuits,* 26 May 1989.

83   SCM Agreement, Art. 3.

port that states have been giving to their exporters, and "actionable subsidies"[84] which will require states to remove the "adverse effects" that the subsidization of their domestic industries is having on foreign exporters, places limits on behaviour that has been a commonplace of domestic policy-making. Equally, the freedom states once had in placing restrictions on imports on health and disease prevention grounds has been curtailed by the obligations under the Agreement on Sanitary and Phytosanitary Measures (SPS Agreement) to base such measures in science, to conduct risk assessments and to choose measures that are the least trade restrictive available.[85]

Beyond this, what is becoming more evident under the WTO, in part as a result of enhanced dispute settlement, is that the disciplines of the WTO intersect with other areas of international legal concern with the potential for conflict between the rules of the WTO agreements and principles of customary international law or other treaty obligations. The spectre of this was raised in the field of trade and the environment. The GATT panel decisions in the *Tuna/Dolphin* cases, where United States restrictions on imports of tuna, claimed to have been adopted in order to enhance the protection of dolphins, were held to be contrary to the GATT Article XI ban on import restrictions, notwithstanding the exception in GATT Article XX(g) which permits contracting parties to derogate from their GATT obligations in respect of measures "relating to the conservation of an exhaustible natural resource."[86] Although the United States did not claim that it was implementing any multilateral agreement, the concern was that multilateral agreements which did use economic measures as a means of enforcement would be undermined by WTO panels or the Appellate Body striking down those measures as contrary to trade law.

In fact, that eventuality has not occurred. The decision of the Appellate Body in *Shrimp-Turtle* indicated that it was predisposed to interpreting WTO obligations in a way that was compatible with international environmental obligations.[87] Furthermore, in the subsequent *Shrimp-Turtle* case on implementation, the Appellate Body upheld the United States measures on the basis that the United States had tried although been unsuccessful, to find a multilateral solution to the protection of sea-turtles.[88] The implication is clear. States that enact measures that

---

84   SCM Agreement, Art. 5.

85   *WTO Agreement, supra* note 45, Annex 1A: Multilateral Agreements on Trade in Goods, *Agreement on the Application of Sanitary and Phytosanitary Measures*, Articles 2 and 5, online: WTO <http://www.wto.org/english/docs_e/legal_e/15-sps.pdf>.

86   *United States – Restrictions on Imports of Tuna ("Tuna/Dolphin I") (Complaint by Mexico)*, (3 September 1991), GATT Doc. DS21/R, 39S/155; *United States – Restrictions on Imports of Tuna ("Tuna/Dolphin II") (Complaint by the European Economic Community)* (16 June 1994), GATT Doc. DS29/R.

87   *US – Shrimp (AB), supra 76* at para. 196.

88   *(United States – Import Prohibition of Certain Shrimp and Shrimp Products (Recourse to Article 21.5 of the DSU by Malaysia)* (22 October 2001),WTO Doc. WT/DS58/AB/RW (Appellate Body Report).

otherwise would be contrary to their WTO obligations will be able to justify such measures if they are implementing the provisions of an international environmental agreement.

But this still leaves many unanswered questions. There are other areas of international law that could potentially conflict with the rules of the WTO agreements, for example, treaties establishing international labour standards or human rights treaties, for neither of which there is any express exclusion in GATT Article XX. Are these matters to be regulated by the rules in the Vienna Convention on the Law of Treaties governing the "application of successive treaties relating to the same subject matter"?[89] Moreover, there are international standards that are governed by customary international law – how are these to be dealt with when they conflict with WTO rules? Although the Appellate Body has recognised the relevance of customary international law to the interpretation of the WTO agreements, it has yet to deal with any direct conflict between the two.

The issue is complicated because of the existence of binding WTO dispute settlement. The conflict between environmental and trade law arose in a WTO forum because it was the only judicial forum where it could be brought. There are no binding environmental or human rights law processes that can offer a competing view. So the issues are dealt with by a body whose mandate derives from a trade agreement. Should tribunals be developed in other areas then the potential for conflict between competing jurisdictions will occur. There is a possibility of an overlap between the jurisdiction of a WTO panel and the United Nations Tribunal on the Law of the Sea but it has yet to materialize.[90]

The Appellate Body has yet to develop the jurisprudence that will reconcile conflicts between WTO norms and other norms of public international law. Moreover, there is controversy over the extent to which public international law is relevant to the interpretation and application of the WTO agreements, one view that the WTO is a self-contained system, another that all of public international law can be incorporated and applied by the Appellate Body.[91] A third view is the public international law is relevant to the extent that it is related to the obligations

---

89   *Vienna Convention on the Law of Treaties*, 23 May 1969, 1155 UNTS 331, Article 30 (entered into force 27 January 1980).

90   A dispute between Peru and the European Communities over swordfish fisheries lead to simultaneous cases at the WTO and the International Tribunal for the Law of the Sea (ITLOS). However, both were suspended following the reaching of a provisional agreement. *Chile – Measures Affecting the Transit and Importation of Swordfish (Complaint by the European Communities)*, "Arrangement between the European Communities and Chile" (6 April 2001), WTO Doc. WT/DS193/3 (Communication from the European Communities); *Case on Conservation of Swordfish Stocks between Chile and the European Community in the South-Eastern Pacific Ocean*, "Provisional Agreement Reached Between Parties – President of the Special Chamber Extends Time-Limits" (21 March 2001), ITLOS/Press 45, ITLOS case no. 7 (Press Release – Issued by the Registrar), online: ITLOS: <http://www.itlos.org/news/press_release/2001/press_release_45_en.pdf>.

91   For a discussion of these views, see Pauwelyn, *op. cit.*, 35-40.

of the WTO agreements, but it provides no independent basis for actions by WTO members under the dispute settlement process.[92]

4.   The Future

The most obvious institutional contribution of the WTO to the international legal order is the model of dispute settlement. Combining an informality of hearing with strictness of timing and deadlines, an orderly approach to interpretation and a hierarchy of authority, WTO dispute settlement is unique. Yet it is not well-known in public international law where the focus is on more traditional international judicial processes such as the International Court of Justice and the International Tribunal on the Law of the Sea. Any increased resort to principles of public international law by WTO dispute settlement bodies or further regime clashes such as was the case with trade and the environment will lead to greater awareness of what the WTO process has to offer.

This is not to argue that the WTO dispute settlement process should be used for the resolution of other, non-trade disputes. Rather it is that a process combining an initial arbitral-type hearing where the parties have input into the selection of arbitrators followed by an appeal on issues of law provides more than an arbitral or a judicial process alone can provide. It is a model that is particularly appropriate where the initial level is often fact intensive. Moreover, an appellate level tends to give more credibility to legal decision-making and provides an opportunity for an orderly development in the law. It is noteworthy that concerns over *ad hoc* arbitration under the investment provisions of NAFTA, has led to calls for the development of an appellate process for those disputes.

Beyond this, the WTO dispute settlement organs have developed jurisprudence not just on the interpretation and application of the WTO agreements, but also on treaty interpretation more broadly and on the procedure of dispute settlement as well as providing insight into other areas of international law. Decisions on disputes over international trade law are no less a contribution to the corpus of international law than decisions on international maritime boundary delimitation are a contribution to the broader field of international law.

Nevertheless, the dispute settlement system has a degree of fragility. The Appellate Body has generally been successful at maintaining a balance between effective interpretation and retaining the confidence of WTO Members. But it has come in for criticism, from the membership broadly over its acceptance of amicus briefs and from the United States in particular over its interpretation of the Antidumping Agreement and the Safeguards Agreement. So far that criticism has not

---

92   Donald McRae, "Claus-Dieter Ehlermann's Presentation on 'The Role and Record of Dispute Settlement Panels and the Appellate Body of the WTO'" Comment (2003) 6:3 J.I.E.L. 709; Debra Steger, "The Jurisdiction of the WTO" (American Society of International Law Annual Meeting, Loews L'Enfant Plaza Hotel, Washington, DC, 2 April 2004) [unpublished].

appeared to have any real impact on its decision-making. But it remains a challenge for the Appellate Body ensure it retains both juridical and political integrity.[93]

There are, however, a number of other challenges that face the WTO and the international legal order more generally. The first is a problem that has been present from the early days of the GATT. How does the international trading regime contribute to international development? Although the WTO agreements presented an image of focusing on development – the opening paragraph of the preamble to the WTO Agreement speaks of raising standards of living and the second paragraph refers specifically to ensuring a share for developing countries in the growth of international trade – the reality has been otherwise. While making special provisions for the least developed countries, the agreements generally did little more than extend time limits for the assumption of obligations by developing countries.[94] Moreover, the failure of agricultural liberalization to provide the benefits that developing countries expected led to significant disillusion and the sense that the bargain that had led to the inclusion of the trade-related intellectual property regime had been broken.

At the same time the numbers of developing countries that are members of the WTO is substantial and increasing. And a system based on consensus gives power to disaffected states. This is evident in the WTO. The current trade negotiating round, the Doha Development Round, is to focus on development. Failure to achieve progress in that round in the Cancun ministerial meeting was a signal of the disaffection of developing countries and an emergence of coalition of developing countries determined to have an influence on the trade negotiations. The Doha Round began to make progress in August, 2004 when a framework for negotiation that focused on issues of concern to developing countries.[95] What could emerge from this is as model for negotiations between the developing and the developed world.

What becomes clear from this is that the days of trade existing in the isolated environment of a GATT "club" are over. The international trading regime is part of a broader international economic regime affecting states, which encompasses such issues as international finance, capital flows and international development. And that links it directly to the international political system that is loosely ordered around the United Nations. Some of this is clearly recognised in the collaboration between the WTO and the IMF and the World Bank. The WTO's relationship with UNCTAD provides also emerging recognition of this broader framework.

In this regard, the continued independence of the WTO from the UN system poses a future challenge. Are states going to pursue their international economic agendas through the WTO by expanding its framework and terms of reference, or will they insist on a closer linking between the WTO and the UN system? The latter approach is evident in proposals to include investment and competition policy

---

93   Donald McRae, "What is the Future of WTO Dispute Settlement?" (2004) 7:1 JIEL 3-21.

94   See, *e.g.*, DSU Art. 24, SCM Agreement Art. 27.

95   Decision of the WTO General Council. 1 August 2004, WT/L/579, 2 August 2004.

within the Doha negotiations, but the rejection of this by developing countries might indicate that expansion of the WTO's mandate is unlikely. But the central question remains, will the UN develop as the core constitutional base for the international system, or will the success of the WTO both through its negotiating process and through its dispute settlement system provide an alternative model for the constitutional development of international law.

21. The Legal Ordering of Environmental Protection

Alexandre Kiss

Since 1994, the creation of the World Trade Organization, the word "globalization" is much used. It is interpreted as meaning that the generalization of the free trade system and its expansion over the whole world create a global human economy. In fact, globalization, the understanding that the whole of humankind has to face the same problem, that of the depletion of natural resources while the number of human beings living on such resources is constantly growing, began much earlier, in the mid-sixties. Very soon after the rise of such awareness the whole international community was engaged in a cooperative action. Today, such action would be called "environmental governance". This term may be considered as meaning that a given community is governed by adequate laws and managed by the most adapted institutions.[1] The international legal ordering of environmental protection includes the two components: on the one hand, legal norms intended to govern the behavior of states and other actors of international law and on the other hand international regulation creating international bodies and determining their functions. The two sides of governance interact: different forms of international cooperation, conferences or permanent institutions create international legal norms the implementation of which needs new forms of international organisms. The cooperation is to be undertaken at a world-wide level as well as in regional frameworks. Such forms can be considered as the world Constitution governing environmental matters.

More than twenty years ago the editors of the present book, Professors R.St. J. Macdonald and Douglas M. Johnston, published a work as editors on the Struc-

---

1   According to the Plan of Implementation of the 2002 World Summit on Sustainable Development, "good governance at the international level is fundamental for achieving sustainable development", being understood that environmental protection is only one of the three pillars of sustainable development, behind economic and social development (Document A/CONF.199/CRP.7, para.122). See also: D.C. Esty and M.H. Ivanova, editors, *Global Environmental Governance*, Yale Center for Environmental Law and Policy, 2002.

Ronald St. John Macdonald & Douglas M. Johnston (eds.), Towards World Constitutionalism, *pp. 567-584.*
© *2005 Koninklijke Brill NV. Printed in The Netherlands. ISBN 90 04 14612 1.*

ture and Process of International Law[2] which also summarized the contemporary state of the international protection of the environment.[3] For the present chapter it seems useful to shortly recall in a first section the different stages of the development of international environmental law since that time, in order to better understand the emergence and the functioning of the world Constitution in this field, which will be the subject of the second section.

1.   Emergence of a World Constitution

While since the beginning of the XXth century a slowly growing number of multilateral international treaties was devoted to the protection of the environment, the first international organism created in this field was established by a bilateral agreement adopted in 1909 respecting boundary waters between Canada and the United States: a mixed commission which has played an important role in pollution control since that time.[4] The initiative was followed between the two world wars by States entering into a growing number of boundary water agreements that included provisions on the problem of water pollution. These efforts continued after World War II: some States concluded a network of bilateral agreements to regulate the utilization of waters through the creation of international commissions. In 1950, Belgium, France and Luxembourg concluded the first treaty entirely dedicated to countering freshwater pollution, one part of which created a tripartite standing committee to tackle the problem.[5]

Several years earlier, the global dimension of environmental problems already had appeared with the 1946 International Convention for the Regulation of Whaling which created the International Whaling Commission. That body can adopt recommendations in this field, organize studies and inquiries on whales and whaling, collects and analyzes statistical information on the current condition and trend of whale stocks and the effects of whaling activities on these populations. An annexed Schedule to the Convention contains regulations on whaling; the Commission has the power to modify it (Art. 5 of the Convention).[6] Progressively, more global conventions related to the world environment appeared showing a growing understanding of the problems raised by its deterioration. Efforts to combat marine pollution appeared during the 1950s. The 1954 International Convention for the Prevention of Pollution of the Sea by Oil concerned for the first time the global commons.[7] It was followed in 1958 by other global conventions prohibiting ocean

---

2   *The Structure and Process of International Law: Essays in Legal Philosophy, Doctrine and Theory*, Martinus Nijhoff, 1983.

3   *Op.cit.*, pp. 1069-1091.

4   Washington, Jan. 11, 1909.

5   Protocol to Establish a Tripartite Standing Committee on Polluted Waters, Brussels, Apr. 8, 1950. All the multilateral treaties related to the environment can be found in the series *International Environmental Law, Multilateral Treaties*, Kluwer Law International.

6   Washington, Dec. 2, 1946.

7   London, May 12, 1954.

pollution by oil or pipelines and radioactive waste, as well as damage to the marine environment caused by drilling operations on the continental shelf.[8] A third convention was entirely dedicated to fishing and the conservation of marine living resources.[9] Less than ten years later, in 1967, the Treaty on Principles Governing the Exploration and Use of Outer Space Including the Moon and Other Celestial Bodies declared that States should avoid contamination as well as harmful modifications of the earth through the introduction of extraterrestrial subtances.[10]

At the end of the 1960s, scientific studies raised general public awareness of dangers threatening the biosphere. Ecological catastrophes such as the 1967 "black tides" off the coast of France, England and Belgium, caused by the grounding of the oil tanker *Torrey Canyon*, and the realization that the environment increasingly was threatened, incited governments to take action. The resulting mobilization of public opinion was unprecedented: it was international from the beginning. It authentified former research by international bodies, such as the studies which the United Nations Economic Commission for Europe started in 1956 about pollution of inland waters and later the dumping of wastes. The year 1968 was the turning point, however. The Council of Europe adopted the first general environmental texts approved by an international organization: a Declaration on Air Pollution Control[11] and the European Water Charter.[12] During the same year, the same organization also adopted the first European regional environmental treaty, the European Agreement on the Restriction of the Use of Certain Detergents in Washing and Cleansing Products.[13] Africa produced the second major initiative : on September 15, 1968 the heads of states and of governments of the Organization of African Unity signed in Algiers an African Convention on the Conservation of Nature and Natural Resources which is a model of comprehensiveness: it concerns virtually the entire environment.

The United Nations joined the actions when the General Assembly convoked a world conference on the human environment to be held in Stockholm in June 1972. The meeting brought together some 6000 persons, including delegations from 113 States, representatives of every major inter-governmental organization, 700 observers sent by 400 non-governmental organizations, invited individuals and approximateluy 1,500 journalists. The result of the conference was the adoption of three texts which are particularly important. A Declaration on the Human Environment affirms the fundamental human right to liberty, equality and adequate conditions of life in an environment of a quality that permits a life of dignity

---

8   Convention on the High Seas, Arts. 24-25, Geneva, April 29, 1958; Convention on the Continental Shelf, Art. 5(7), Geneva, Apr. 29, 1958.

9   Convention on Fishing and Conservation of the Living Resources of the High Seas, Geneva, Apr. 29, 1958.

10   Article IX, Jan. 27, 1967.

11   Res. 60(4) of Mar. 8, 1968, Committee of Ministers.

12   May 6, 1968, published as a separate sheet, without number.

13   Brussels, Sept. 16, 1968.

and well-being, adding that man bears a solemn responsibility to protect and improve the environment for present and future generations. Similar principles can be found in later national Constitutions, they clearly make the link between environment and human rights. Other principles include that safeguarding the natural resources of the globe – which are also air, water, earth, plants and animals as well as representative samples of natural ecosystems – constitute a major interest of humankind. Among other tools for implementing environmental protection, the Declaration stresses the importance of economic and social development and of integrated, coordinated and rational development planning. Several principles are of particular interest for international law. Principle 21 is generally recognized as expressing a basic norm of customary law:

> States have, in accordance with the Charter of the United Nations and the principles of international law, the sovereign right to expoloit their own resources pursuant to their own environmental policies, and the responsibility to ensure that the activities within their jurisdiction or control do not cause damage to the environment of other states or of areas beyond the limits of national jurisdiction.[14]

The Declaration further affirms that states should cooperate to develop international law regarding liability and compensation for victims of pollution and other environmental damage produced outside their boundaries. They should define criteria and norms in environmental matters, taking into consideration the system of values prevailing in each country, in particular in developing countries. States should cooperate to protect and improve the environment and ensure that international organizations play a coordinated, effective and dynamic role in this field. (Principles 22-25). The final principle condemns nuclear weapons and all other means of mass destruction.

The second main result of the Stockholm Conference an "Action Plan for the Human Environment" composed of 106 recommendations, addresses various issues such as pollution, wastes, the protection of the marine environment, that of wildlife and natural species, and stresses the importance of planning, including the development of international plans of action. The third major result of the Stockholm Conference was a recommendation proposing the creation of a central organ to be charged with environmental matters. On the basis of that recommendation the United Nations General Assembly in 1972 created a specialized subsidiary organ, the United Nations Environment Program (UNEP).[15]

The vision of Stockholm and its implications characterize the subsequent evolution of environmental law until the following conference, held in 1992 in Rio de

---

14   See, in particular, Principle 2 of the Declaration on Environment and Development adopted by the Conference of Rio de Janeiro on June 13, 1992 which only added the words "and developmental" before "policies". The same form was used in Article 3 of the Convention on Biological Diversity adopted on June 13, 1992, at Rio de Janeiro.

15   UN General Assembly Resolution 2995(XXVII) Concerning Cooperation Betwen States in the Field of the Environment, December 15, 1972.

Janeiro. International environmental law substantially increased during those two decades. The dominant approach of the 1970s concentrated on protecting specific sectors of the environment: oceans, inland waters, atmosphere, wild plants and animals. In all of the four sectors numerous global and regional treaties were concluded, according to the necessities and the possibilities. Such evolution still continues, although later two other approaches emerged. Specific norms, global or regional, created in each of the four sectors, can now be considered as parts of a coherent regulation, since in each of them a global convention sets the general principles and rules framing special agreements. For the oceans Part XII and several other provisions of the UN Convention on the Law of the Sea of 1982 set the main principles;[16] for continental waters the 1997 Convention on the Law of Non-Navigational Uses of International Watercourses codified international law;[17] for the atmosphere the Framework Convention on Climate Change[18] can be considered as the synthesis of the main principles goverrning this sector and, finally, for all forms of life – and not only wildlife – the Convention on Biological Diversity[19] reaffirms or sets the main principles.

As mentioned earlier, a new approach to environmental problems resulted in a second stage in the development of international environmental law. During the 1980s, it became increasingly evident that a sectoral approach was insufficient to address environmental deterioration because generally it failed to regulate the causes or sources of harm that could affect more than one or several sectors. Thus, a second approach, which aimed at regulating sources and risks of harm, became a common complement to sectoral regulation. Correspondingly, a new series of international conventions appeared, involving the creation of treaty-specific institutions in different fields, such as the elimination of substances that deplete the ozone layer,[20] the control of transboundary movements of hazardous wastes and their disposal,[21] or the limitation of the production and use of persistent organic pollutants.[22]

A new, very important stage was reached in the normative development of international environmental law which, of course, produced a major effect on its institutional aspects. Building on its 1980 resolution, the UN General Assembly voted in 1983 to create the World Commission on Environment and Development,

---

16   Montego Bay, December 10, 1982.

17   Adopted in New York on May 21, 1997, this instrument, prepared by the UN Commission of International Law, is not yet in force, but is generally considered as expressing international customary law rules. As such, it was invoked by the International Court of Justice in the case of the Gabçikovo-Nagymaros Project, judgment of September 25, 1995, para 147.

18   New York, May 9, 1992.

19   Rio de Janeiro, June 5, 1992.

20   Vienna Convention for the Protection of the Ozone Layer, March 22, 1985 and Montreal Protocol on Substances that Deplete the Ozone Layer, September 16, 1987.

21   Convention of Basel of March 22, 1989.

22   Stockholm Convention on Persistent Organic Pollutants, May 22, 2001.

an independent body linked to, but outside the UN system and more commonly known as the Brundtland Commission. The report issued by the Commission[23] stressed the need for an integrated approach to developmental policies and projects which, if environmentally sound, should lead to sustainable economic development in both developed and developing countries. The report emphasized the need to give higher priority to anticipating and preventing problems. It defined "sustainable development" as development that meets the needs of the present and future environment and development objectives and concluded that without an equitable sharing of the costs and benefits of environmental protection within and between countries neither social justice nor sustainable development can be achieved. The Brundtland Report led the UN to convene a second global conference, held in Rio de Janeiro under the title United Nations Conference on Environment and Development (UNCED). The very name of the conference reflected a new approach starting a period where integrated environmental protection appeared in two senses: environmental protection was to be integrated on the one hand in almost all human activities and, on the other hand, in the development of human society in general.

The instruments adopted by the Conference of Rio de Janeiro on Environment and Development in which the participation was even higher than in that of Stockholm, twenty years before, reflect the new orientation. The central concept of the Declaration on Environment and Development is sustainable development which integrates development and environmental protection. At the same time, different aspects of human activities are touched upon. Principle 7 of the Declaration proclaims common but differentiated responsibilities "in view of the pressures their societies place on the global environment". Principle 8 adds that States should reduce and eliminate unsustainable patterns of production and consumption and promote demographic policies. Principle 12 advocates a "supportive and open economic system" and international consensus, and condemns discriminatory trade measures or disguised restrictions on international trade, as well as unilateral actions. Public participation is largely recognized: Principle 10 proclaims for individuals the rights to information, to participation in the decision-making process and to remedies in environmental matters. Several principles of the Declaration have a major legal significance: they call for the development of liability rules (Principle 13) and for the notification of other States about emergencies and projects which may affect their environment (Principles 18 and 19). Several then-emerging principles are also formulated: the precautionary principle (Principle 15), the "polluter pays" principle which requires internalization of environmental costs (Principle 16) and the general requirement of environmental impact assessment (Principle 17).

The second general document adopted by the Rio Conference is Agenda 21, a program of action consisting of forty chapters with 115 specific topics. There are four main parts: socio-economic dimensions, conservation and resource management, the role of non-governmental organizations and other social groups and mesures of implementation. Chapter 38 on international institutional arrange-

---

23   Our Common Future, 1987.

ments declares in its introduction that "the intergovernmental follow-up of the Conference process shall be within the framework of the United Nations system, with the General Assembly being the supreme policy-making forum that would provide overall guidance to Governments, United Nations system and relevant treaty bodies". At the same time, governments, as well as regional economic and technical cooperation organizations, have a responsability to play an important role in the follow-up of the Conference. Their commitments and actions should be adequately supported by the UN system and multilateral financial institutions. All agencies of the UN system have a key role to play in the implementation of Agenda 21, there should be an effective division of labor between them based on their terms of reference and comparative advantages. The overall objective is the integration of environment and development issues at national, sub-regional and international levels.

The impact of the Rio conference on the whole of international law was important. Quite a few of its areas evolved in new directions because of insistence that they take into account environmental considerations. The result was an infusion of environmental norms into nearly every branch of international law : trade, control of weapons systems, rules concerning new technologies, the control of substances which can harm the environment, the management of landscapes. Ten years later, between August 26 and September 4, 2002, the representatives of more than 190 countries met in Johannesburg in order to "reaffirm commitment to the Rio Principles, the full implementation of Agenda 21". At the end of this World Summit for Sustainable Development the participating governments adopted a declaration affirming their will to "assume a collective responsibility to advance and strenghten the interdependent and mutually reinforcing pillars of sustainable development – economic development, social development and environmental protection – at local, national, regional and global levels".[24] The Declaration mainly focuses on development and poverty eradication, especially in the poorest countries. Despite proposals advocating the creation of a specialized global institution for environmental protection, it less ambitiously supports the leadership role of the UN. The lengthy Plan of Implementation provides concrete suggestions of measures to implement the Declaration. It is dominated by the economic pillar. Its section on institutional development proposes to strenghten collaboration within and between the UN system, and international financial institutions, the Global Environment Facility and the World Trade Organization, mainly in the perspective of sustainable development (paragraphs 121-137). It states that strenghtening of the international institutional framework for sustainable development is an evolutionary process. It is necessary to keep under review relevant arrangements, identify gaps, eliminate duplication of functions, and to continue to strive for greater integration, efficiency and coordination of the economic, social and environmental dimensions of sustainable development aiming at the implementation of Agenda 21 (para 139). Action should also be pursued at the regional and subregional levels, through the regional commissions and other regional and subregional institutions

---

24   A/CONF./L.6/Rev.2.para. 5.

and bodies (para. 140). A short paragraph at the end of the Plan invites partner-ships between governmental and non-governmental actors for the achievement of sustainable development at all levels (para. 151).

After 36 years of development and even of real existence of international en-vironmental law can we speak of a world constitutionalism in this field ? Certainly not in the usual sense of the term: there is neither a global instrument nor an in-dependent global institution overarching the whole area and even environmental protection is integrated into a vast complex: sustainable development. Still, there are international functions which have to be ensured and there are corresponding institutions to satisfy such needs. It is thus necessary to analyze first the functions which derive from the necessity to protect the environment and in a last stage to make an attempt to present shortly the responses which the international com-munity elaborated.

2.   Environmental Functions in International Law

The importance of international institutional cooperation derives from several rea-sons. Environmental protection is inevitably based on scientific knowledge. Rapid evolution in such knowledge makes necessary permanent assessment of the envi-ronment, in most cases on an international level or in cooperation with research-ers of other countries. In this regard international organizations are indispensable, because effective assessment requires coordinated monitoring to fully obtain and evaluate information on global environmental trends. Elaboration of and adherence to international norms and standards are the elementary conditions of preventing deterioration of the environment. By itself, however, entry into force of regulations usually does not and cannot ensure resolution of the problems addressed. There must be mechanisms to supervise application of the rules. In addition, evolution of the state of the environment and knowledge of it requires virtually constant revi-sions of the rules, adapting existing instruments and their application. More and more often it is also recognized that natural resources should be managed, quite frequently on an international level, which means in fact a subregional, regional or even global level. For this, as well, international organizations are crucial, the more so since they represent the common interest of mankind. These various tasks and the importance of developing international environmental law rules necessitate a continuity of cooperative structures that can be assured only by permanent institu-tions.

The multiplicity of aspects of environmental problems and the proliferation of environmental agreements has resulted in increased duties for existing interna-tional organizations. In addition, most of the major multilateral conventions estab-lish a governing structure, generally consisting of a conference or meeting of the parties, a secretariat, and often a scientific and other subsidiary committees. While these institutions have taken on considerable importance, problems of coordina-tion and duplication have been raised and in some cases exacerbated, the more so since they can arise on different international levels according to the conventions: global, regional or subregional.

The necessity to protect the environment on the international level creates specific functions for international bodies.

a. Research plays a particularly important role. While international organizations rarely carry out their own scientific resarch, their specialized organs often undertake comparative legal studies of national or international measures prior to drafting international treaties, recommendations, directives and model laws. Where research programs do require scientific analysis, the member States generally undertake the resarch with international organizations assuring coordination of the tasks delegated to one or more States and disseminating the results. In certain cases, international institutions may give financial assistance or may conclude research contracts with experts or groups.

b. Exchange of information based on national and international studies, research and projects is another important aspect of cooperation. Nearly all international organizations collect and exchange information with and among member States. Some of them also prepare a synthesis of information received concerning a given problem, such as reports prepared by the UN Economic Commission for Europe, or may address the whole state of the environment as do the annual reports of the UN Environment Program.

c. Regulatory functions consist in adopting recommendations, or, more rarely, obligatory decisions or drafting treaties. Often texts which are intended to become binding are elaborated by a group or groups of experts followed by submission to a diplomatic conference which should adopt them. Numerous environmental agreements create their own organs invested with responsibility for elaborating rules for implementation or application of the treaty or for modification of existing norms, sometimes contained in detailed appendices. Very often, two different procedures are foreseen for the modification of a same environmental treaty. The rules applicable for the modification of appendices to treaties allow an easier adaptation of the existing text than those which govern amendments to the treaty itself. The reason is that environmental data can change quite often and the technical provisions, generally included in appendices, need to be updated, while the general rules establishing the cooperation among the contracting States do generally not need such adaptation.

    When such power is conferred, as a rule participating States maintain their right to object to changes and thus to withhold acceptance of them.

d. Supervising implementation of the norms generally does not extend to coercive action, such as policing the high seas to catch polluters, but such power may be granted either to the organization or, more commonly, to its member States. The use of such coercive measures may be increasing in respect to common resources. Article 24 of the 1980 Canberra Convention on the Conservation of Marine Living Resources establishes an international system of observation and inspection.[25] The 1995 UN Convention on Straddling Stocks also provides for boarding, inspecting, and even potential seizure of vessels il-

---

25   May 20, 1980.

legally fishing in regulated high seas fishing areas.[26] Supervision is much more common, however, through review by designated international organs of periodic state reports about national implementation of international norms.

e.   Management of natural resources by an international organization is the most developed form of international cooperation. Shared natural resources are in fact increasingly coming under international management agreements, such as those governing fish stocks and freshwaters. It flows from the nature of the concerned resources that management is most often adopted in regional or subregional frameworks by the most adapted institutions. An important exception is the management system for mineral resource activities on the deep seabed created by Chapter XI of the Law of the Sea Convention, in which protection of the marine environment holds an important place.[27]

3.   The Response of International Institutions

Efforts to protect the environment touch most activities of public agencies and institutions. In addition, most multilateral treaties adopted in this realm need permanent cooperation among the contracting parties and thus create their proper organs. A division is to be operated between environmental activities of existing institutions which can be global, regional or subregional, and those created by conventions related to specific aspects of environmental protection. An additional point is that more and more non-governmental entities or even private persons appear in this field and their quality of actors of international environmental law was progressively recognized.

The first criteria of the division of tasks among existing international organizations is geographic. Certain environmental questions are best treated at a global level, such as the protection of the marine environment, the problems raised by the threats to biological diversity or to the stratospheric ozone layer, while others concern the countries of a region, such as the pollution of a watercourse or a lake involving the need to protect its whole catchment area, or the protection of endemic species of wild fauna and flora. The general principle to be applied in this regard could be inspired by the European Union which largely applies the principle of subsidiarity. Decisions for resolving a problem should be made at the lowest effective level of governance: local, then subregional, then regional and at the end, when global interests are at stake, global.

A.   Global Organizations

Despite attempts made by groups and even by governments at the Conference of Rio de Janeiro and later at the World Summit on Sustainable Development of Jo-

---

26   Agreement for the Implementation of the UN Convention on the Law of the Sea relating to the Conservation and Management of Straddling Fish Stocks and Highly Migratory Fish Stocks, New York, August 4, 1995, Art.34.

27   Montego Bay, December 10, 1982.

hannesburg, no specialized institution for environment was created, neither as a specialized agency like FAO or UNESCO, nor as a High Commission like those which exist for the protection of human rights or for refugees. The United Nations Organization is thus the central organism for environmental protection. Its General Assembly made several specific recommendations in this field[28] adopted the Word Charter for Nature.[29] and approved treaties such as the Convention on the Law of the Non-Navigational Uses of International Watercourses.[30] It also recommended convening the 1972 Stockholm Conference, set up the Brundtland Commission and convened the 1992 Rio Conference and the 2002 Johannesburg Summit on Sustainable Development. The General Assembly also created two special organs for environmental cooperation, in 1972 the United Nations Environment Program (UNEP) and in 1992 the Commission on Sustainable Development. While the second is a functional commission of the Economic and Social Council, originally charged with monitoring the progress in implementing Agenda 21, often focusing its interest on economic development, UNEP is the organ which really acts for environmental protection. A subsidiary body of the General Assembly, established in Nairobi, Kenya, UNEP's secretariat is the central organ of action and coordination for environmental matters within the UN system as well as for regional organizations outside the UN. Its role is generally that of a catalyst for action by other institutions. It studies environmental problems and elaborates programs, but implementation is undertaken by the UN as a whole, with the aid, if appropriate, of regional governmental and non-governmental organizations as well as individual states. Specific projects are encouraged by utilizing the Environmental Fund which operates with voluntary contributions of States. UNEP's working method largely consists of programming. Its programs, based on the gathering of information and the definition of strategies, are presented to interested international organizations, governmental or non-governmental, as well as to governments. Activities which are chosen may receive support from the Environment Fund and UNEP can provide the secretariat for multilateral environmental conventions. The contribution of UNEP to the development of international environmental law is very important, not only by stimulating the conclusion of conventions, and often helping to draft their texts, as well as of non-binding instruments, but also by adopting specific programs for the development and periodic review of environmental law. In 1982 it adopted a first program, renewed successively by two others, in 1990 and in 2001. On the whole, over the last 25 years more than 40 multilateral environmental treaties have been negiotiated under UNEP's guidance. In addition, UNEP has the task to enhance coordination across the UN system and improve coordination and coherence between multilateral environmental agreements and the organs which they created.

---

28   See the long series of resolutions adopted by the General Assembly on Large-Scale Pelagic Driftnet Fishing and its Impact on the Living Marine Resources of the World's Oceans and Seas between 1989 and 1999: Resolutions 44/207, 45/197, 46/215, 47/443, 48/445, 49/436, 50/25, 51/36, 52/29 and 53/33.

29   October 28, 1982, Resolution 37 /7.

30   New York, May 21, 1997.

Owing to the integrating character of environmental problems and their inclusion into development, almost all other UN bodies are stakeholders in the protection of the environment, such as the Security Council,[31] the International Law Commission,[32] the Human Rights Commission and the UN Development Program. The International Court of Justice, principal judicial organ of the UN, indicated its readiness to accept environmental cases, in particular by establishing, in 1993, a seven-member Chamber for environmental matters. The Chamber, however, was not used so far. Still functioning in its usual composition, the Court recognized in an Advisory Opinion[33] and in a judgment concerning a dispute between Hungary and Slovakia that States have the obligation to respect and protect the natural environment.[34]

Regional commissions created by the UN Economic and Social Council were also active in questions concerning the environment; in particular, the UN Economic Commission for Europe played a major role in the preparation and adoption of several regional conventions.

Almost all the specialized agencies of the UN contributed to the governance of environmental matters, each in its special field, either directly, by drafting international conventions devoted to environmental problems or touching such problems (UNESCO, FAO, the International Atomic Energy Agency, the International Maritime Organization) or by contributing to a better knowledge and action in this field (World Health Organization, World Meteorological Organization, International Labor Organization, International Civil Aviation Organization).

International financial institutions can play a role in the monitoring of compliance with international environmental rules. The World Bank decides on certain loans on "technical eligibility criteria" which may take into account environmental considerations.

B.   Regional Organizations

Almost all regional organizations have become engaged in activities in the environmental field. However, the term "regional" has to be clarified. Some non-global institutions have been created not only according to geographical, but also accord-

---

31   The Security Council adopted a series of resolutions concerning the occupation of Kuweit by Iraq also concerning environmental problems and creating, in particular, a UN Compensation Commission in 1991 to hear claims of environmental damage and depletion of natural resources caused by military activities.

32   Several draft conventions tending to codify international law include provisions concerning the environment. See Art.20 Draft Code of Crimes against the Peace and Security of Mankind as well as the Draft Articles on Prevention of Transboundary Harm from Hazardous Activities. The International Law Commission also prepared the 1997 General Convention on the Non-Navigational Uses of International Watercourses.

33   Legality of the Threat or Use of Nuclear Weapons in Armed Conflict, July 8, 1996, para 63.

34   International Court of Justice, September 25, 1997, Case Concerning the Gabçikovo-Nagymaros Project, paras. 140-141.

ing to economic or political criteria. Such is the situation of the Organization for Economic Cooperation and Development (OECD) which now consists of all Western and Central European countries, but also of Australia, Canada, Japan, Korea, Mexico, New Zealand and the United States – in other words, of the industrialized countries. OECD had since 1970 important activities in studying environmental problems and proposing solutions, paying particular attention to economic considerations. It formulated the first legal definition of pollution and enunciated the basic standards applicable to transfrontier pollution, as well as principles, such as the polluter-pays principle and the obligation to inform, consult and to notify emergency situations in transfrontier relations. OECD also reviews the economic performance of its member countries and its reports are regularly published.

In general, among the regional organizations those within Europe have the most comprehensive regulations, for several reasons. First, the process of political and legal integration is most developed in Europe. Second, Europe is very densely populated and highly industrialized, leading to greater risks of pollution. Finally, cooperation in environmental matters is facilitated by the homogeneity of economic structures and the similarity of political conceptions. European institutions include, on the one hand, organizations of cooperation respectful of the sovereignty of their member States, on the other an institution of integration, the European Union which tends to the unification of its member States and which is very different from the general environmental constitutionality in international law. As a consequence, it is not considered in the present chapter.

The most typical example of a regional organization participating in environmental protection is that of the Council of Europe which is the oldest existing European institution, created in London, May 5, 1949 and based in Strasbourg. Today it consists of 46 States, all European countries, except Yugoslavia. It has sufficiently broad jurisdiction to address environmental issues, but its broad competence is not equally accompanied by equally expansive powers. Its main organs, the Committee of Ministers and the Parliamentary Assembly, can only adopt recommendations, but both reflect European political consensus and can be considered as laboratories of ideas where many initiatives began. The Council of Europe was among the first organizations to take action and had a constant activity in the field of environmental protection since the 1960s by adopting a considerable amount of non-obligatory texts such as resolutions, recommendations, reports and programs of action. It also drafted an important number of international environmental conventions submitted to the adoption of its member States, mainly in the field of nature protection, and transfrontier cooperation. It also drafted the first international conventions related to civil liability for environmental damage[35] and to the protection of the environment through criminal law.[36] The institution of Strasbourg is thus mainly a legislative authority and plays a role of contact within European civil society.

---

35   Convention on Civil Liability for Damage Resulting from Activities Dangerous to the Environment, Lugano, June 21, 1993.

36   Convention on the Protection of the Environment through Criminal Law, Strasbourg, November 4, 1998.

C.   Institutions Established by Multilateral Environmental Conventions

Many multilateral environmental agreements present common features and procedures they establish. The pattern of the institutions includes a plenary Conference
or Meeting of the Parties, (COP or MOP), a Secretariat, and scientific committees
or other subsidiary commissions. The Conference is generally the supreme body of
the convention and designates the others. It acts in a quasi-legislative capacity, making decisions, interpreting the principal agreement and adopting recommendations
and plans of action. Several conventions invest their conferences of the Parties with
the power to adopt amendments to the convention according to a special procedure, allowing the convention to be adapted to new circumstances to enhance its effectiveness. In addition, a COP often may draft and adopt additional protocols. This
function can constitute one of the most important contributions to achieving the
goals of the treaty concerned, since the original provisions may only create a frame
for the cooperation among the parties, while the detailed rules of the cooperation
must be drafted later and adopted in the form of protocols. The role of the 1987
Montreal Protocol which established the norms, standards and technical aspects of
the control of ozone-depleting substances,[37] building on the principles established
by the 1985 Ozone Convention,[38] is the most developed example. Similarly, the COP
established by the 1992 Framework Convention on Climate Change drafted the 1997
Kyoto Protocol in order to make it possible to progress towards the implementation
of the principles of the convention by requiring certain countries to meet quantified emission limitation and reduction commitments with respect to six greenhouse
gases. When such protocols are adopted, the instruments can have separate plenary
bodies, as is the case with the Conference of the Parties of the Vienna Ozone Convention and the separate meeting of the Parties of the Montreal Protocol.

A crucial function of bodies created by treaties is the reviewing of compliance
with the obligations accepted by the contracting Parties. Most often this function
is ensured by the discussion of reports submitted by each Party as well as other
information concerning measures that it has taken in order to ensure the effectiveness of the provisions of the agreement. COPs generally discuss such information
which in most cases is submitted to them by the Secretariat, sometimes after a preliminary examination. In some cases COPs discuss information provided by NGOs
and even by individuals. COPs can adopt recommendations for the guidance of all
the contracting Parties and in some cases address recommendations to individual
state Parties. The meetings of COPs are often open to participants other than representatives of the contracting Parties and the trend is towards greater openness
and transparency of their work. The Basel Convention on Transboundary Movement of Hazardous Wastes and Their Elimination[39] is particularly progressive in
this regard; it foresees that the UN, its specialized agencies, as well as States not
party to the convention may participate as observers in COP meetings. Any other

---

37   Protocol on Substances that Deplete the Ozone Layer, September 16, 1987.

38   Convention for the Protection of the Ozone Layer, Vienna, March 22, 1985.

39   Basel, March 22, 1989.

body or agency, whether international or national, governmental or non-governmental, such as industry associations, that are qualified in the matter of hazardous wastes or other wastes, and having given notice of their interest in attending the COP can participate as observer unless one-third of the states Parties objects. Other COPs also admit observers: more than 200 governmental and non-governmental organizations were represented in Kyoto in 1997.

COPs usually create subsidiary bodies to ensure the functioning of the treaty between sessions and to facilitate state implementation of the Convention. Secretariats in most cases either created or designated by the basic convention, assist the COPs. Their services may be provided by existing international bodies, like the UNEP which provides the secretariat for the Convention of Biological Diversity,[40] the Washington Convention on the International Trade in Endangered Species of Wild Fauna and Flora (CITES)[41] and the Basel Convention.[42] The Ozone Treaties refer to other international bodies such as UNDP and the World Bank. More frequently, however, environmental agreements establish their own secretariat, sometimes after a transitory period. Secretariats can play an important role in supporting the implementation of the relevant conventions by collecting national reports on compliance by domestic authorities. In some cases they can also accept information on compliance submitted by other governments, non-governmental organizations and/or individuals. They transmit to the COP such reports and information, but sometimes they elaborate a synthesis of the national reports and information on implementation. Often they also act as an information clearing-house.

Secretariats may assist states Parties to implement the convention. The secretariat of Convention on Biological Diversity, for example, facilitates technology and information transfer, and the development of cross-border projects, and in certain cases works to enhance the capacity of officials regarding information. The Secretariat of the Convention on Hazardous Wastes contributes to capacity-building and development of appropriate legislation by States in order to prevent and monitor illegal traffic. For this purpose it compiled existing national legislation and drew up a draft model law on the management of hazardous wastes and their disposal. It prepared a manual for the implementation of the Convention and a number of technical guidelines on related issues for the practical management of wastes. The UNEP-administered secretariat for CITES has published Guidelines for Legislation to Implement CITES.

COPs usually also create other subsidiary bodies to ensure the functioning of the treaty between sessions and to facilitate state implementation of the convention. The Convention on Biological Diversity, for example, has a Subsidiary Body on Scientific, Technical and Technological Advice (SBSTTA) whose members meet annually to draft proposals for adoption by the COP. Each Party to the Convention may designate a governmental representative, but the representatives must have expertise in one or more of the relevant fields. The SBSTTA has drafted

---

40   Rio de Janeiro, June 5, 1992.

41   March 3, 1973.

42   See footnote 38.

many important guidelines that the COPs have adopted, such as on access to genetic resources, and on integrated coastal management. Similar bodies exist for the Ramsar Convention on Wetlands of International Importance,[43] the UNESCO Convention Concerning the Protection of the World Cultural and Natural Heritage[44] and others.

Implementation of the obligations flowing from a convention is one of the most important tasks, but not all the conventions foresee means for ensuring it. The Montreal Protocol's Implementation Committee of the Non-Compliance Procedure is the most advanced body in this field. A Party that cannot meet its obligations may report its compliance problems to it, but any Party or Parties that has concerns about another Party's implementation of its obligations under the Protocol may communicate the concerns in writing, supported by corroborating information, to the Secretariat. After having the possibility to gather more information, the Implementation Committee reports to the Meeting of the Parties which may decide about steps to bring about full compliance with the Protocol. Different measures can be decided by the MOP, including technical or financial assistance and the issuing of warnings and, as an ultimate sanction, the suspension of specific rights and privileges under the Protocol.

COPs/MOPs also can facilitate compliance by creating financial bodies. A Multilateral Fund was established by a decision of the Second Meeting of the Parties to the Montreal Protocol[45] with a view of assisting developing country parties to comply with the control measures of the Protocol. UNEP, UNDP, the World Bank and the United Nations Industrial Development Organization (UNIDO) have contractual agreements with the Executive Committee to assist such countries.

These examples, which are far from constituting an exhaustive list, only concern institutions created in the framework of global international agreements. Several dozens of other international bodies created by the Parties to regional treaties could be added to give a complete picture, but the main characteristics of all of them are rather alike.

The proliferation of environmental agreements and new treaty bodies combined with the generalized attention to environmental matters within international organizations result in a vast array of international entities working on similar issues, raising the problem of coordination and cooperative action. While by no means resolved, several actions have been taken to increase coordination. Secretariats of some treaty bodies have concluded Memoranda of Understanding to provide mutual assistance. The Secretariat of the Ramsar Convention on Wetlands of International Importance[46] has been particularly proactive in seeking cooperation with other treaty bodies like the secretariat of the Convention on Biological Diversity.

---

43   February 2, 1971, Scientific and Technical Review Panel.

44   Paris, November 23, 1972, Inter-Governmental Committee for the Protection of the Cultural and Natural Heritage of Outstanding Universal Value ("World Heritage Committee").

45   London, June 1990.

46   February 2, 1971.

In other actions, the complex problems raised by hazardous substances in international trade led to the establishment of an Inter-Organizational Program for the Sound Management of Chemicals, whose participating members are the World Health Organization, the International Labor Organization, UNEP, FAO, UNIDO, OECD and the United Nations Training and Research Institute. Particular areas of coordination include harmonizing the classification of chemicals, information exchange on toxic chemicals and chemical risks, pollutant release and transfer registers and chemical accident prevention and response. The UN General Assembly also has acted, creating by Resolution 53/242 an overarching Environmental Management Group that includes specialized agencies, funds and programs of the UN system and the secretariats of multilateral environmental agreements.

D. Non-State Actors

As was mentioned earlier, non-state actors, non-governmental organizations and in some cases also individuals can participate as observers in the meetings of certain intergovernmental institutions. One of the non-state actors, the World Conservation Union (IUCN from its earlier name) has a special status. On the one hand, it is composed of national and international associations, on the other, also of State members and public or private scientific institutions. Its activities include recommendations to governments and the participation in the drafting of environmental treaties. The Union played an essential role in the elaboration of half a dozen of the major international conventions relating to the conservation of nature and natural resources, such as the 1968 African Convention on the Conservation of Nature and Natural Resources[47] to be replaced by a new instrument adopted in 2003,[48] the 1973 Convention on Trade in Endangered Species (CITES) already mentioned and the 1979 Convention on the Conservation of Migratory Species of Wild Animals.[49]

Individuals can play a role as far as they are entitled to protect their rights related to the environment. A series of international environmental treaties recognized them the right to environmental information, some others also the right to participation in the decision-making process and the right to remedies. Following Principle 10 of the Declaration on Environment and Development of the Conference of Rio de Janeiro, a specific treaty proclaimed such rights in the framework of the UN Economic Commission for Europe, making of individuals possible environmental actors, not only in the domestic sphere, but also as far as international rules are concerned.[50] However, there is no international jurisdiction in which they could bring environmental cases, with the exception of the Permanent Court of

---

47   Algiers, September 11, 1968.

48   African Convention on the Conservation of Nature and Natural Resources, Maputo, July 21, 2003.

49   Bonn, June 23, 1979.

50   Convention on Access to Information, Public Participation in Decision-Making and Access to Justice in Environmental Matters, Aarhus, June 25, 1998.

Arbitration as far as the State which they want to sue accepts its jurisdiction.[51] Several decisions of international human rights courts also recognize rights directly or indirectly related to determined aspects of the environment.[52]

4.   Final Considerations

One of the main trends in the international law of the last thirty-five years is the proliferation of rules tending to protect the environment. Areas of international law that developed during earlier periods are now also evolving in new directions because of insistence that they take into account environmental considerations. Such proliferation raises the problem of overlapping or even conflicting obligations and could possibly lead to choices in implementation and should impose rationalization. International environmental agreements also increasingly include detailed provisions for monitoring, implementation review, compliance verification, and non-compliance mechanisms. Accordingly there is a corresponding increase in the number and variety of international mechanisms to supervise national implementation of and compliance with international environmental obligations. Where there are multiple institutions, each with specific and sometimes competing agendas, their contribution however becomes diffuse and less effective. One of the issues for the future will be evaluating the effectiveness of such institutions, their possible reform, and harmonization. There is a need for overall policy coordination that is currently lacking. States appear to prefer a case-by case approach to international environmental policy-making, but there is still a need for coherence. With the enormous growth in international environmental law, the opportunity missed at the 1992 Rio Conference on Environment and Development and at the 2002 Johannesburg Summit on Sustainable Development should be seized in the future. It is appropriate to consider the possible development of a specialized agency or institution with comprehensive authority over environmental matters. A single institution can enhance public attention to environmental problems and to failures by States to comply with international obligations and better coordinate the collection and dissemination of environmental information and be a focal point of cooperation among States and between States and other international actors.

The necessary two-fold approach to environmental protection, normative and institutional, in the form of good governance, seems to be the way to enhance the protection of one of the most important common values of the present humankind, the environment and of its resources which must be safeguarded for future humanity.

---

51   See the Optional Rules for Arbitration of Disputes Relating to Natural Resources and/ or the Environment adopted on June 19, 2001 by 94 member states of the Permanent Court of Arbitration.

52   See, for example, European Court of Human Rights, *Lopez-Ostra v. Spain*, 303C Eur. Ct.H.R. (ser.A), December 9, 1994; African Commission on Human and Peoples Rights, Decision Regarding Communication 155/96, *Social and Economic Rights Action Center/Center for Economic and Social Rights v. Nigeria*, Case Nr. COMM/A044/1, May 27, 2002.

22. Accountability of International Organizations – A Critical View

Gerhard Hafner

1. Introduction

In recent times, the topic "accountability of international organizations" has gained wider attraction as can be seen from the increasingly frequent references in the international literature. Whereas classical textbooks on international organizations only a few years ago did not contain any reference to this expression,[1] recent articles and textbooks deal with it in an extensive manner.[2] This development seems to be the follow-up of the generally wider use of the term "accountability" in international relations and by several actors in this field, starting from States to non-governmental organizations (NGOs),[3] and reaching to transnational corporations (TNCs).[4] As far as international organizations (IOs) are concerned, it is in particular the work of the International Law Association (ILA), which applied this term to international organizations: it established a Committee on this topic and expects a final report in 2004.[5]

---

1   See *e.g.* Henry G. Schermers, Niels M. Blokker, *International Institutional Law*, The Hague, London, Boston, 1995, *passim*.

2   August Reinisch, Governance without Accountability?, *GYIL* 2001, vol. 44, 270-306, 273.

3   Simon Zadek, In defense of non-profit accountability, *Ethical Corporation Magazine*, September 2003, 34-36, at 34.

4   Vincenzo Franco, FDI Regulation and Corporate Accountability: A Discussion of Policy Options, Friends of the Earth-US, Washington, DC, November 1998, *passim*; See also *e.g. Minding Our Business: The Role of Corporate Accountability in Sustainable Development. An NGO report to the UN Commission on Sustainable Development*, Revised March 28, 1997; <http://www.corporate-accountability.org/docs/tobistat.htm>; Simon Zadek, In defence of non-profit accountability, *Ethical Corporation Magazine* September 2003, 34.

5   The First Report was presented to the 68th Conference of the ILA at Taipei, see The International Law Association, Report of 68th Conference, Taipei 1998, 584; the second was submitted to the 70th Conference in New Delhi, see: The International Law Association, Report of 70th Conference, New Delhi 2002, 772.

Ronald St. John Macdonald & Douglas M. Johnston (eds.), Towards World Constitutionalism, *pp. 585-630.*
© 2005 *Koninklijke Brill NV. Printed in The Netherlands. ISBN 90 04 14612 1.*

However, despite its wider use, the term "accountability" escapes *prima facie* any clear definition. One reason for this is that this term cannot be translated in other languages. Neither in the Romanic languages such as French, Italian, Romanian, Spanish, nor in Slavic languages such as Russian or in German or languages like Korean or Thai[6] can an equivalent expression be found. The lack of such expressions in other languages than English seems to indicate the absence of a generally shared understanding except that which originates from, and is guided by, the Anglo-American political environment.[7] Any further search for a clearer meaning has to proceed from the approach suggested by Wittgenstein in whose view "the meaning of a word is its use in the language."[8]

It is for this reason that the further inquiry is based on:
– the origin of this concept;
– the motivation and reasons of its usage;
– cognate concepts;
– its substance if applied to international organizations;
– the reflection in existing international law.

But, before dealing with the individual sub-items, a further clarification has to be added insofar as the present discussion is focused on international organizations that are of intergovernmental nature and encompasses such institutions of most different kinds, regional as well as universal ones. It does not cover other actors in international relations, neither States nor multi- or TNCs or NGOs, despite the vast quantity of ink that has been spilled over this subject.[9]

2.   The Origin of the Concept of Accountability

As can be seen from the linguistic usage, the concept of accountability of States, from which accountability of IOs derives, stems from the Anglo-American political world. According to Rosenbaum, its origin can be traced back to the concept of public accountability of government officials and civil servants of the United States more than 220 years ago.[10] In his view, the American citizens had a different relation to the State than the Europeans: whereas to the European citizens the State was a source of authority, superimposed on the individuals, the American civil servant was seen, in particular since the "Jacksonian Revolution" in the 1830's, as a person who simply happens to work for the government. These civil servants have been considered as persons working in the interests of the citizens and therefore

---

6   See the UNDP "PARAGON" Generic Training Module on Public Service Ethics and Accountability, 2 <http://unpan1.un.org/intradoc/groups/public/documents/eropa/unpan002622.pdf>.

7   Allan Rosenbaum, Good Governance, Accountability and the Public Servant, 2. <http://unpan1.un.org/intradoc/groups/public/documents/nispacee/unpan005698.pdf>; rosenbaum.

8   Ludwig Wittgenstein, *Philosophical Investigations*, New York 1953, Sect. 43.

9   See *supra*, fn. 4.

10   Rosenbaum, *op. cit.*, fn. 7, 2.

particularly accountable to them. Governmental information has to be made available to the individuals, generating increased transparency of governmental activities.[11] This basic concept has been backed by the requirement of openness of the meetings of governmental bodies. The citizens should also be enabled to resort to effective redress against the government which resulted in the creation of institutions of the kind of the European Ombudsman.[12]

According to these explanations the American concept of the State follows a bottom-up approach whereas, in contrast, the European conception of the State corresponds to a top-down approach built on the authority of the State; accountability is a result rather of the former concept than of the latter. Accountability in this sense is more typical of the common law system, and less of the civil law system. This distinction parallels the different attitudes to legal positivism which is characteristic for the civil law system, but less for the common law system. This difference explains why this concept of accountability can be married with legal positivism only with certain difficulties as this concept requires State officials and civil servants to comply not only with positive norms, but also with ethical codes and standards.

As such, accountability is defined as a desire to "make public sector staff more accountable for their decisions and actions". According to Heek, it means in more detail:

> that some set of recipients receives information about the outcomes of decisions made by identified individuals who are source decision makers that those sources can be made to explain their decisions and that some sanctions can be imposed if the explanations are unsatisfactory.[13]

This duty to respect accountability is owed to different addressees. Thus, for instance, one could distinguish external accountability which is the requirement to

---

11   *Ibidem.*

12   The Ninth report of the European Ombudsman describes its function in the following way: "The office of European Ombudsman was established by the Maastricht Treaty as part of the citizenship of the European Union. The Ombudsman investigates complaints about maladministration in the activities of Community institutions and bodies, with the exception of the Court of Justice and the Court of First Instance acting in their judicial role. With the approval of the European Parliament, the Ombudsman has defined "maladministration" in a way that includes respect for human rights, for the rule of law and for principles of good administration.

   As well as responding to complaints from individuals, companies and associations, the Ombudsman launches inquiries on his own initiative and reaches out to empower citizens by informing them of their rights and of how to exercise their rights." Executive summary and statistics from the annual report 2003, at 3; <http://www.euro-ombudsman.eu.int/report03/pdf/en/short03_en.pdf>.

13   Richard Heeks, Information Systems and Public Sector Accountability, Information Systems for Public Sector Management; Working Paper Series; Paper No. 1 July 1998, 6. <http://www.man.ac.uk/idpm/idpm_dp.htm#isps_wp>.

answer to external groups of persons and internal accountability which is owed to internal groups. Other distinctions concern the basis of the accountability, i.e. whether it is based on political, ethical or legal commitments.

3.   The Application to International Relations

This America-oriented concept of State accountability was transferred to international relations as a result of the fundamental change that international law underwent in the last decades of the 20th century. The objective of classical international law, based on the Westphalian system, was still to guarantee the power of the State as a single entity. In Schwarzenberger's concept, the power relations or at best the relations of cooperation were dominating; their objective was to separate and delimit the claims of the States for increasing influence as was clearly reflected in the judgment of the Permanent Court of Justice in the *Lotus* Case,[14] which perceived the rules of international law as rules of delimitation of State power and jurisdiction as its legal manifestation. The interests that the States tried to assert in their relations with other States were defined by the foreign policy bureaucracy belonging to the executive branch of the individual States.

Even at the end of the Second World War, States remained the only actors in international relations;[15] international organizations served as transmission belts for the assertion of State interests.[16] The IOs were to a certain extent paralyzed by the two dominating conflicts: the East-West conflict and the North-South conflict. The opponents in these conflicts were only States that remained the main actors in the relations governed by international law.

But soon after the end of the Second World War, the situation changed: the individual gained a better standing in international relations to challenge States as a result of new developments in international law, such as the development of human rights, the global expansion of concepts like democracy and the rule of law, the request for good governance with regard to developing countries and the materialization of the civil society.[17]

---

14   This conclusion is reflected in the judgment: "Now the first and foremost restriction imposed by international law upon a State is that – failing the existence of a permissive rule to the contrary – it may not exercise its power in any form in the territory of another State. In this sense jurisdiction is certainly territorial; it cannot be exercised by a State outside its territory except by virtue of a permissive rule derived from international custom or from a convention"; *France v Turkey*, PCIJ, Ser. A, No. 10 (1927).

15   *Cf* The new discussion on the role of sovereignty in international law: John H. Jackson, Sovereignty-Modern: A New Approach to an Outdated Concept, *AJIL* 2003, vol. 97, 782-802, 801.

16   Barnett, Michael N, Finnemore, Martha, The Politics, Power, and Pathologies of International Organizations, *International Organization* 1999, vol 53, 699-732, 700.

Jon C. Pevehouse, Democracy from the Outside-In? International Organizations and Democratization, *International Organization*, Summer 2002, vol. 56, 515-549.

17   See Jackson, *op. cit.* fn. 15, 801.

Already with the growing number of international instruments for the protection and guarantee of human rights, in particular with the increased establishment and use of mechanisms to which individuals could resort in order to protect human rights against States, a considerable change occurred. First, the legal status of individuals became a direct subject-matter of international law insofar as their rights were directly protected by norms of international law and, later, they were given the instruments to enforce their rights against States. Europe played a pivotal role in this development through the Council of Europe and the European Convention for the Protection of Human Rights and Fundamental Freedoms.[18] Although the European approach to Human Rights as reflected in the European Convention did not entail directly the concept of democracy, the Council of Europe made first steps in this direction through Article 3 of its Statute and the requirement of the adherence to the rule of law for States that wished to accede to it.[19] Only later, in particular through the work of the Venice Commission, as was stated in the opinion regarding Liechtenstein,[20] democracy as such became an explicit commitment within the framework of the Council of Europe.

However, it cannot be denied that through these developments regarding human rights a new actor has entered the field of international law: the individuals who were enabled even to make and enforce international claims against States. This development was no longer confined to Europe, but went beyond this region *stricto sensu* already by the development of the instruments of the CSCE/OSCE and encompassed other world regions albeit with a reduced intensity and received a global vocation through the International Covenant on Economic, Social and Cultural Rights[21] and the International Covenant on Civil and Political Rights of December 16, 1966.[22]

By the end of the Cold War by the late 80's and beginning of the 90's this development was expanded: it was no longer required to prove the infringement of specific human rights as defined in the relevant conventions. Consequently, individuals could make complaints against States for breaches of the obligations owed to them, but States were considered responsible for certain conduct towards the entity of their citizens even if no specific individual human rights were infringed. The best evidence of this development is provided by a comparison of the Final Act of Helsinki of 1975[23] with the Charter of Paris for a New Europe which committed

---

18   ETS No. 5.

19   Article 3 of its Statute reads as follows:

> Every member of the Council of Europe must accept the principles of the rule of law and of the enjoyment by all persons within its jurisdiction of human rights and fundamental freedoms, and collaborate sincerely and effectively in the realisation of the aim of the Council as specified in Chapter I.

20   Avis no. 227/2002; Doc. CDL-AD (2002) 32 of 7 January 2003, §§ 6.

21   UNTS vol. 993, 3.

22   UNTS vol. 999, 171.

23   Principle VII reads:

States no longer only to the respect of human rights as contained in the Universal Declaration of 1948, but to principles of democracy and the rule of law. This Charter establishes a direct link already between democracy and accountability: "Democracy, with its representative and pluralist character, entails accountability to the electorate, the obligation of public authorities to comply with the law and justice administered impartially."[24]

The rise of the role of individuals in international relations finally benefited also from the growing role of NGO's in various fields where formerly only States could become active: the elaboration of international law and the enforcement of international commitments. By the end of the State-centred Cold War, NGOs received greater leeway for their participation in international activities.[25] They in-

---

"VII. Respect for human rights and fundamental freedoms, including the freedom of thought, conscience, religion or belief

The participating States will respect human rights and fundamental freedoms, including the freedom of thought, conscience, religion or belief, for all without distinction as to race, sex, language or religion.

They will promote and encourage the effective exercise of civil, political, economic, social, cultural and other rights and freedoms all of which derive from the inherent dignity of the human person and are essential for his free and full development.

Within this framework the participating States will recognize and respect the freedom of the individual to profess and practice, alone or in community with others, religion or belief acting in accordance with the dictates of his own conscience.

The participating States on whose territory national minorities exist will respect the right of persons belonging to such minorities to equality before the law, will afford them the full opportunity for the actual enjoyment of human rights and fundamental freedoms and will, in this manner, protect their legitimate interests in this sphere.

The participating States recognize the universal significance of human rights and fundamental freedoms, respect for which is an essential factor for the peace, justice and well-being necessary to ensure the development of friendly relations and co-operation among themselves as among all States.

They will constantly respect these rights and freedoms in their mutual relations and will endeavour jointly and separately, including in co-operation with the United Nations, to promote universal and effective respect for them.

They confirm the right of the individual to know and act upon his rights and duties in this field.

In the field of human rights and fundamental freedoms, the participating States will act in conformity with the purposes and principles of the Charter of the United Nations and with the Universal Declaration of Human Rights. They will also fulfil their obligations as set forth in the international declarations and agreements in this field, including inter alia the International Covenants on Human Rights, by which they may be bound.

Text in: <http://www.osce.org/docs/english/1990-1999/summits/helfa75e.htm>.

24   Text in: <http://www.osce.org/docs/english/1990-1999/summits/paris90e.htm>.

25   Christopher C. Horner, Modern developments in the treaty process: Recent Developments Regarding Advice and Consent, Withdrawal, and the Growing Role of Nongovernmental Organizations in International Agreements With Particular Examination of the 1997 Kyoto Protocol, 9; <http://www.fed-soc.org/Intllaw&%20AmerSov/Treatypaper.pdf>.

tensified their activity in international conferences dedicated primarily to the protection of the environment, human rights and development. In particular NGO's claimed to represent the "civil society", the unorganized society of man outside the State structure.

A different source for a development in this direction stems from the developing countries: in view of the difficulties on their way from the colonial regime to modern States, the request for a certain kind of government was couched in terms like good governance, democracy and accountability.[26]

These developments culminated finally in the use of more informal mechanisms of international relations, in particular outside legal devices like tribunals or courts, such as negotiations, in order to face the States with requests for a certain conduct not in the interest of State power, but in the interest of individuals. It is for this reason that the Millenium report of the Secretary General emphasizes the preambular reference of the Charter to the individuals:

> For even though the United Nations is an organization of states, the Charter is written in the name of "we the peoples". It reaffirms the dignity and worth of the human person, respect for human rights and the equal rights of men and women, and a commitment to social progress as measured by better standards of life, in freedom from want and fear alike. Ultimately, then, the United Nations exists for, and must serve, the needs and hopes of people everywhere.[27]

As a result of these developments the whole fabric of international law became more individual-oriented; States were seen no longer as the power centres of international relations, but as legal devices to serve the interests of the individuals instead of instrument to preserve or increase State power. A recent result of this development was the elaboration of individual responsibility in international law and finally the establishment of the International Criminal Court (ICC),[28] which to a certain extent released the individual from the unavoidable involvement into State responsibility. Although both kinds of responsibility are still declared not to affect each other,[29] it cannot be excluded that in a given case international bodies that de-

---

26   Committee on Human Development and Civil Society, Second Meeting; Ethics And Accountability For Enhanced Public Service Delivery In Africa, 26-27 May 2003, Addis Ababa, Ethiopia; <http://www.uneca.org/chdcs/chdcs_main.htm>.

27   Kofi Annan, *"We the peoples", The Role of the United Nations in the 21st Century*, New York 2000, UN Doc. A/54/2000, 6.

28   Text: <http://www.un.org/law/icc/statute/romefra.htm>.

29   Article 25 (4) of the ICC Statute reads: "No provision in this Statute relating to individual criminal responsibility shall affect the responsibility of States under international law." The corresponding provision is included in the Article on Responsibility of States for internationally wrongful acts; Article 58 reads as follows:

> These Articles are without prejudice to any question of the individual responsibility under international law of any person acting on behalf of a State.

UN Doc. A/RES/56/83.

cide on State responsibility will also take into account any individual responsibility decided upon in a given case. The first step in this direction has already been made by the adoption of targeted sanctions by the Security Council, which evade the dilemma caused by the former economic sanctions that affected the entirety of the population of the target State, irrespective of whether or not the individuals shared the political orientation of the political leaders of the target State.[30]

Accordingly, accountability has been understood mainly as a commitment of the State to act in the interest and for the benefit of the citizen even without their concrete human rights being affected. An example where this understanding has already been translated into legal terms is the UN Convention against Corruption of 2003,[31] the Preamble of which frequently refers to concepts closely related to accountability. Article 1 states as the purpose of the Convention "(t)o promote integrity, accountability and proper management of public affairs and public property."

Understood in this sense, accountability could also be seen as – in the first instance – a political device through which the population of a State, which does not directly participate in the political decision-making, *i.e.* in a representative democracy the constituency may claim a certain kind of behavior of the State organs in their interest and to their benefit without them being directly affected in their individual rights or, at least, have to prove it. The recent international developments envisage the application of this original municipal concept to the field of international relations and international law and its enforceability through international actions.

4.   The Application to International Organizations

In recent years, the concept of accountability was increasingly applied to international organizations,[32] in particular to different concepts which surfaced in the literature. The one examines up to which extent IOs serve as a means to increase accountability in States,[33] the other discusses how far IOs themselves correspond to the standard of accountability. This paper focuses on the second approach.

This latter application of accountability to IOs resulted from the fear that IOs could be and indeed were used by States as a tool to escape responsibility and accountability by transferring the decision-making competences to IOs. In con-

---

30   Jürg Burri, Introductory Paper for the Expert Seminar on Targeting United Nations Sanctions, Interlaken, 1998, 5.

31   UN Doc. A/58/422 of 7 October 2003; The first preambular paragraph reads:
Concerned about the seriousness of problems and threats posed by corruption to the stability and security of societies, undermining the institutions and values of democracy, ethical values and justice and jeopardizing sustainable development and the rule of law.

32   See *e.g.* August Reinisch, Securing the Accountability of International Organizations, in: *Global Governance. A Review of Multilateralism and International Organizations,* vol. 7, No. 2, 2001, 131-151, at 131.

33   So *e.g.* Jon C. Pevehouse, Democracy from the Outside-In? International Organizations and Democratization, in: *International Organization,* vol. 56, 2002, 515-549, 516.

nection therewith, IOs started to gain growing influence on international relations and to replace States concerning decisions that have a direct impact on the social, political, economic and legal status of individuals. This growing power of IOs in international relations was combined with the lack of democracy from which IOs have been alleged to suffer.[34]

These two tendencies generated the increase of the demand for more accountability of IOs, primarily expressed in the question of the limits of their powers and respect of the interests of individuals. Whereas formerly the constituent instruments were considered as limiting the powers of IOs, the development based on the implied theory concept seemed to confirm Seyersted's view on the "sovereignty" of IO.[35] Accordingly, IOs were seen as legally capable to do everything that their constituent instrument did not prohibit. A perusal of the doctrine and international instruments reveals that first of all those IOs were addressed by this demand, which adopted decisions and carried out activities that have a direct and indirect effect on this status of individuals. This question was directed particularly to the United Nations where the powers of the Security Council were questioned,[36] but also to the conditionality of the financial institutions such as the IMF,[37] to the WTO with particular regard to the developing countries[38] and the European Union (mostly in the form of the European Community) that increasingly engaged in the field of human and social rights affecting the position of individuals.[39]

5. Cognate Concepts

Accountability is frequently connected with other concepts and expressions between which, however, no clear relation can be established: These expressions are *e.g.* good governance, democracy, rule of law, responsibility, eliminating corruption, transparency in public services.

It is impossible to state whether these concepts form a constituent part of accountability and *vice versa* or whether they are separated from accountability, and

---

34   Robert O. Keohane, International Institutions: Can Interdependence work? In: *Foreign Policy*, 1998.

35   Finn Seyersted, International Personality of Intergovernmental Organizations, Reprinted from *The Indian Journal of International Law*, vol. IV, 1964, 42.

36   *Cf.* Seyersted, *op. cit.*, fn. 35, *passim*; Erika de Wet, The Role of Human Rights in Limiting the Enforcement Power of the Security Council: A Principled View, in: Erika de Wet, André Nollkaemper, *Review of the Security Council by Member States*, Antwerp, Oxford, New York, 2003, 7-30, 24.

37   Leo Van Houtven, Governance of the IMF, Decision Making, Institutional Oversight, Transparency and Accountability, IMF 2002, 54, 56, 63.

38   Gabrielle Marceau, WTO Dispute Settlement and Human Rights, *EJIL* vol. 13 No. 4, 2002, 753-814, 757 *seq.*

39   *Cf.* in particular European Commission, European Governance-A White Paper, Doc. COM(2001) 428 final, Brussels, 25.7.2001, *passim*; Carol Harlow, Problems of Accountability in the European Union, National Europe Centre Paper No. 53 <http://www.anu.edu.au/NEC/harlow.pdf>.

opinions in literature considerably vary in this regard. However, it seems worthwhile to have a look at them with a view to clarifying these relations. Not all of the various expressions used in this context are scrutinized here concerning their relation to accountability, but only those which are of a more general scope, whereas others of a more specific nature, such as combat of corruption or transparency, are dealt with in the course of the discussion of the alleged content of accountability.

A.   *Good Governance*

The closest ally of accountability is governance. As Reinisch rightly points out, this is not to be confused with government.[40] According to Sakiko Fukuda-Parr and Richard Ponzio's the following definitions could be ascertained:[41]

> World Bank: Governance is defined as the manner in which power is exercised in the management of a country's economic and social resources. The World Bank has identified three distinct aspects of governance: (i) the form of political regime; (ii) the process by which authority is exercised in the management of a country's economic and social resources for development; and (iii) the capacity of governments to design, formulate, and implement policies and discharge functions. (World Bank, 1997);
>
> UNDP: Governance is viewed as the exercise of economic, political and administrative authority to manage a country's affairs at all levels. It comprises mechanisms, processes and institutions through which citizens and groups articulate their interests, exercise their legal rights, meet their obligations and mediate their differences. (UNDP 1997);
>
> OECD: The concept of governance denotes the use of political authority and exercise of control in a society in relation to the management of its resources for social and economic development. This broad definition encompasses the role of public authorities in establishing the environment in which economic operators function and in determining the distribution of benefits as well as the nature of the relationship between the ruler and the ruled. (OECD DAC, 1995);
>
> Institute of Governance, Ottawa: Governance comprises the institutions, processes and conventions in a society which determine how power is exercised, how important decisions affecting society are made and how various interests are accorded a place in such decisions.
>
> Institute of governance, 2002, Commission on Global Governance: Governance is the sum of the many ways individuals and institutions, public and private, manage their common affairs. It is a continuing process through which conflicting or diverse interests may be accommodated and co-operative action may be taken. It includes formal institutions and regimes empowered to enforce compliance, as well as informal

---

40   August Reinisch, Governance Without Accountability? *GYIL* vol. 44, 2001, 270-306, 272.

41   Sakiko Fukuda-Parr and Richard Ponzio, Governance: Past, Present, Future. Setting the governance agenda for the Millennium Declaration, 2. <http://www.undp.org/governance/docsaccount/gov-past-present-future.pdf>.

arrangements that people and institutions either have agreed to or perceive to be in their interest.

These authors come to the conclusion that governance

> is about the process by which power and authority is exercised in a society by which government, the private sector, citizens' groups articulate their interests, mediate their differences, and exercise their legal rights and obligations.

The epithet "good", however, escapes any objective definition and leaves open the perspective under which it could be defined. "Good" can mean different things to States and to individuals. Whereas States could interpret it in the sense of beneficial to the State interests based on power politics; individuals could and will have a totally different view on this, putting more emphasis on issues like human rights, human dignity and protection of the environment. It is therefore not surprising that even other qualifiers are also used such as "human governance"[42] or democratic governance, depending on the particular rules (human rights or participatory rights) on which emphasis is put.

The origin and the usage of this term points towards an interpretation from the standpoint of individuals. If good governance in this sense means conduct of the government (in the wide sense of the word), which serves the interests of the collective of the individuals, it may be queried by whom these interests are defined. Two actors could be called for this purpose: the political parties according to the concept of representative democracy which is based on the representation of the individuals through them, on the one hand, and, on the other, NGO's that claim the right to represent the interests of the civil society.

But if taken in this sense, one may doubt any distinction between accountability and governance. The confusion becomes even greater if one refers to the explanation within the EU according to which "Five principles underpin good governance and the changes proposed in this White Paper: openness, participation, accountability, effectiveness and coherence."[43]

According to Reinisch, the difference can be couched in the following way, although a certain overlapping cannot be excluded. Accountability refers in particular to the tasks of governing and exercising power and influence, whereas accountability encompasses political, administrative, and various informal, non-legal mechanisms by which someone may be held answerable for something.[44]

The distinction can be seen in the difference between primary and secondary rules insofar as the primary rules relate to good governance whereas the accountability rather refers to the rules which guarantee the possibility to invoke good governance and to establish a duty to comply with these primary rules. However, this distinction is not consistently maintained in the literature where accountability is

---

42   Richard Falk, *On Humane Governance*, University Park, 1995, 1.

43   White Paper, *op. cit.* fn. 39, 10.

44   Reinisch, *op. cit.*, fn. 40, 277.

also deemed to encompass primary rules. For the further discussion it is therefore necessary to keep in mind this broad understanding.

Irrespective of which of the two understandings corresponds more closely to the concept of good governance, it seems to be applicable to IOs only with great difficulties. The application of "good governance" to IOs suffers in particular from the uncertainty to which such good governance should be owed: either to the Member States or – piercing the veil of statehood – directly to the individuals. The latter understanding raises fewer problems if it is applied to IO's that adopt legal instruments having a direct effect on individuals. Good governance is therefore an issue within IOs such as the EC the legal order of which has a direct effect on individuals. As the ECJ stated, the subjects of community law are not only States, but also individuals[45] so that individuals are also entitled to enforce their rights against organs of the relevant IO.

But even outside the EC, one cannot deny presently the increase of activities of IOs which also otherwise have a direct effect on the status of individuals; so, for instance, peace- keeping operations, administration of territories or the work of criminal tribunals. Financial organizations are often criticised for the negative effect of their activities on the well-being of individuals through the application of the "conditionality" under which loans and credit have been granted to States.[46] If good governance is understood in this sense as owed to individuals, presently a wide range of IOs could become candidates for requests or complaints regarding the interference with the rights of individuals.

B. *Democracy*

A further concept or standard of conduct that is frequently applied to IOs is that of democracy. It is well established that IOs suffer from the democratic deficit,[47] an issue which is often addressed particularly with regard to the EU.[48] The core of this assertion of democratic deficit is connected with the fact that, generally, foreign policy is a prerogative of the executive power of the State. The assertion of this deficit is extended to IOs since the collective organs of IOs are traditionally composed of representatives of the executive power of the State.

---

45   *Van Gend and Loos v. Nederlandse Administratie der Belastingen*, case 26/62, 1963, ECR 1.

46   Morris Goldstein, IMF Structural Conditionality: How Much Is Too Much? Revision of paper presented at NBER Conference on "Economic and Financial Crises in Emerging Market Economies" Woodstock, Vermont, 19-21 October 2000, 8; <http://www.iie.com/publications/wp/2001/01-4.pdf>.

47   Joseph S. Nye, Jr., Globalization's Democratic Deficit: How to Make International Institutions More Accountable, *Foreign Affairs*, July/August 2001 Vol. 80, Number 4, James Crawford, Democracy and the body of international law, in: Gregory H. Fix, Brad R. Roth (eds.), *Democratic Governance and International Law*, Cambridge, 2000, 91-122, 112.

48   See *e.g.* Harlow, *op. cit.*, fn. 39, 8.

The democratic deficit is reduced in organizations that are provided with parliamentary organs and their democratic standard can best be measured by the scope of the power such organs possess. Through such organs, individuals, represented by their political parties, can have a larger influence on the decision-making process within organizations even outside the area where their rights are immediately affected. But only few organizations, interestingly enough mostly Europe-centred ones, are furnished with parliamentary organs, such as the Council of Europe or the European Union.[49] It could be long discussed why these organizations are mostly located in Europe, but even where this is the case, the parliamentary organs are only of limited competence.[50]

Within the European Union, the term "democracy" was elaborated in Council Regulation (EC) No 975/1999 of 29 April 1999.[51] This regulation deals in more detail with "the general objective of developing and consolidating democracy and the rule of law and to that of respecting human rights and fundamental freedoms." Where Article 3 of this regulation refers to the objective of democratization, it defines it, in addition to the protection of human rights, in particular by the reference to an independent judiciary, separation of powers, political pluralism, free press, participation in political decision-making, free election and separation of the civil sector from the military sector.

However, democratic standards are also applied in a different context within the framework of international organizations; under this catchphrase States attempt to ascertain participatory rights in IOs and ask for an expanded opportunity to participate in organs with decision-making power.[52] They consider this standard affected in particular by organs with limited membership. In their view, the principle of democracy requires that all member States of an IO should be offered access to such organs. The discussions of the increase of membership of the UNCITRAL in 2001 and 2002 or the permanent discussion on the composition of the Security Council are the best evidence of these claims. Such claims have been raised irrespective of the disadvantage of an open-ended composition of such organs, which requires balancing carefully between the solution of problems according to the lowest common denominator and the need of an increased acceptability.[53]

---

49 Schermers, *op. cit.* 1, fn. 383 *seq.*

50 *Ibidem*, 397; the only exception is the European Parliament.

51 Council Regulation (EC) No 975/1999 of 29 April 1999 laying down the requirements for the implementation of development cooperation operations which contribute to the general objective of developing and consolidating democracy and the rule of law and to that of respecting human rights and fundamental freedoms, OJ L 120/1 of 8 May 1999.

52 See in this sense Christopher W. Pinto, Democratization of International Relations and Its Implications for the Development and Application of International Law, in: *Proceedings of the United Nations Congress of Public International Law*, New York 13-17 March 1995, *International Law as a Language for International Relations*, The Hague, London, Boston 1996, 250-264, 250.

53 Gerhard Hafner, Certain issues of the work of the Sixth Committee of the 56th General Assembly in 2001, *AJIL* 2003.

The only conclusion that can be drawn from these divergent conceptions is a great variety of understandings so that a certain vagueness concerning the meaning and its relation to accountability cannot be avoided.

C.   *Rule of Law*

A further standard applied to IOs is frequently that of the compliance with the "rule of law" (*Rechtssicherheit*). Originally applied to States, this requirement amounts to a standard that States have to meet before they are admitted to IOs or are granted certain benefits from the organization. The best example is Article 3 of the Statute of the Council of Europe although it demonstrates the blurred distinction between the different standards. The Council of Europe used the commitment to the rule of law as the germ for the emergence of other standards like that of good governance or democracy.[54] Other usages by IOs include conditions imposed on States receiving loans and credits from the International Monetary Fund (IMF). According to the declaration *Partnership for Sustainable Global Growth*,[55] the objective of the concept of rule of law was identified as "promoting good governance in all its aspects, including ensuring the rule of law, improving the efficiency and accountability of the public sector, and tackling corruption."

The application of this standard to IOs could be seen as leading to the obligation of IOs to comply with the law applicable to them as transpires in the statement relating to the EU that the

> Union is built on the rule of law; it can draw on the Charter of fundamental rights, and it has a double democratic mandate through a Parliament representing EU citizens and a Council representing the elected governments of the Member States. Monitoring closely the application of Community law is an essential task for the Commission if it is to make the Union a reality for businesses and citizens.[56]

Beside the Commission, the European Court of Justice is called as a guarantor of the rule of law of the EU.[57]

Conceived in this perspective, as the duty to comply with the applicable law, it is a corollary to the principle of "*pacta sunt servanda*" with the sole difference that the constituent treaties are in relation to the IOs rather constitutions than treaties, as IOs are created by international treaties and not parties to their own constituent treaties.

This commitment does not only restrict the freedom of activity of organs of the organizations, which are independent like the Secretariat and likewise bodies, it indirectly also obliges the Member States of an IO not to expand the activities of

---

54   See *supra,* text at fn. 19.

55   Partnership for Sustainable Global Growth, Interim Committee Declaration, Washington DC, September 29, 1996, <http://www.imf.org/external/np/exr/dec.pdf>.

56   See White Paper, *op. cit.,* fn.39, 7.

57   *Ibidem,* 8.

the IO beyond the limits drawn by the applicable law so that it addresses not only the IO, but also the Member States.

6.   The Ramification of Accountability and Elements of Accountability of IOs

Although the discussion on these terms on the one side and accountability on the other induces a distinction between them, the actual usage of these terms does not sustain it. By some authors, in particular by the report of the ILA, accountability is seen as the totality of all the commitments and standards to which IOs should be subject, irrespective of whether they rely on rules of primary or of secondary nature. Such an approach risks ending in a vague mass of different prescriptions the sense of which it is hardly possible to grasp.

In order to obtain a greater amount of clarity of these different commitments, some distinctions could be made in various ways.

One distinction could separate those commitments that are clearly of a legal nature from those outside the black letter law structure; the second should make a distinction between those standards that rather are of a primary nature and those that are of a secondary nature,[58] the latter comprising the rules that govern the emergence, alteration, termination and enforcement of the former ones. Of course, it must not be ignored that these distinctions are often difficult to perform. The first because it is often difficult to recognize precisely which of the commitments have already been converted into black letter law or belong still to the soft law category (if at all), the second because whether a rule belongs to one or the other category is a matter of their function and less one of their content.

A further distinction can be inferred from the various categories of actors to whom accountability is owed. First, these are the individuals who are affected by activities of IOs. Secondly, they are individuals that enjoy a particular status in this respect as belonging to the personnel of the organization. As part of the staff they are directly affected by the activities of the organization and frequently have a direct resort to judicial remedies against the organization. The third category of addressees comprises the States, either Member States or third States, to which the organizations owe a conduct of a certain kind. Although the States are the first candidates becoming directly affected by the activities of the organizations and the IO's primarily act in relation to them and not to the individuals (with the exception of the personnel), the genesis of the term accountability puts more emphasis on the individuals than on States.

Of course, one must not neglect the fact that the commitments or obligations owed to the different categories of actors differ: so, for instance, the commitments towards States differ from the obligations owed to the staff members. Nevertheless, there are some general commitments which relate to the general structure and are applicable to the relations to all of these actors.

---

58   The distinction originates from Hart's legal theory; see H.L.A. Hart, *The Concept of Law* (1961).

As shown above, a certain difficulty arises as to the definition of the precise meaning of accountability; it is hardly possible to identify the elements composing this concept although Patel concluded that "scholars have been able to identify certain elements that constitute accountability."[59] However, this conclusion is to be doubted since the views expressed so far are too diverse and divergent to permit a clear guidance supported by the authors concerning the elements of accountability. Patel himself does not divulge which elements constituted accountability; he implicitly refers to the legal personality of IOs or the presence of review mechanisms with the IOs.[60]

The broadest record of elements of accountability is presented by the ILA report. It distinguishes various levels of accountability and derives certain more concrete requirements from general principles.[61] This inventory of different aspects and elements which are ascribed to accountability by the Report of the ILA do not necessarily follow the above-mentioned distinctions so that they suffer from a certain unorganized structure which intermingles commitments resulting from existing legal rules with those that are nothing more than exhortatory aspirations, those which are owed to the staff members with those owed to States. It can hardly claim to present a generally applicable record of the various elements of accountability: For instance, the taking of economic enforcement measures or peace-keeping op-

---

59   Bimal N. Patel, The Accountability of International Organisations: A Case Study of the Organisation for the Prohibition of Chemical Weapons, 13 *Leiden Journal of International Law*, 2000, 571-597, 575.

60   *Ibidem*, 577.

61   First level of accountability:
Objectives, principles and concepts common to all IO
Good governance (Transparency, Participatory decision making, Access to information, Well functioning international civil service, Sound financial management, Reporting and evaluation), Good faith, Constitutionality and institutional balance, Supervision and control, Stating reasons for decisions or a particular course of action, Procedural regularity, Objectivity and impartiality, Due diligence and Promoting justice
Relationship between IO's and NGO
Responsibility and Liability of IO:
Applicable Law, Relations between IO's and MS, Relations between IO's and staff, Relations between IO's and third parties, Contractual relations between IO's and third party, Non-contractual liability, Non-contractual liability for significant harm, Human Rights and Humanitarian Law (Temporary administration of territory, Economic coercive measures, Peace-keeping and peace-enforcement), Monitoring and verification of IO, Rule of Law for IO's and MS
Responsibility of IO: State responsibility and responsibility of IO, Dilemmas, General Rules and Recommended Practices on responsibility, Attribution of wrongful acts, Attribution in case of delegation and authorisation (In case of delegation, In case of authorisation)
(Concurrent or residual liability of MS for non-fulfilment by IO's of their obligations toward third parties)
Remedies against IO.
The International Law Association, Report of the Seventieth Conference, New Delhi, London 2002, 774 *seq*.

erations are reserved to few IOs. Neither is this record embedded in international law. Elements derived from applicable principles of international law are mixed with political demands or simply wishful thinking. Thus, impartiality seems hardly reconcilable with a right to apply economic sanctions against one State. It is also hard to define the addressees of the requirements presented in this list. The call for a well-functioning international civil service must be addressed to the Member States since they are to a wide extent responsible for the composition of the staff of the IO, irrespective of certain provisions in the constituent instrument.

A totally different view is presented by the EU. Proceeding from the discussion of good governance the White paper[62] "accountability" as one of its elements is declared to require that "(r)oles in the legislative and executive processes need to be clearer. Each of the EU Institutions must explain and take responsibility for what it does in Europe. But there is also a need for greater clarity and responsibility from Member States and all those involved in developing and implementing EU policy at whatever level."[63] Hence, this understanding reflects a much narrower view referring in particular to more transparency in the decision-making process and the duty to assume responsibility combined with corresponding duties incumbent upon the Member States. It has already met with criticism because of its narrowness.[64]

Other definitions are even more restrictive as, for instance, that delivered by Ratner: in his view, accountability "refers to a process for holding individuals personally responsible for human rights abuses they have committed"[65] so that his concept is exclusively rooted in the field of the protection of human rights.

It is therefore suggested to put aside the claims raised under the heading of accountability, which purport to subject the performance of IOs to standards which are neither rooted in hard law nor can be generalized, and to start the further discussion from the original objectives of the claims for accountability, namely to limit activities of IOs by the applicable law and to hold them answerable for violations of this law in particular in relation to individuals. What remains under this heading of accountability is that IOs are bound to comply with applicable rules of international law in the widest sense and that they are answerable for their activities by assuming international responsibility. But so understood, no separate label such as "accountability" would be required since both aspects, the duty of compliance and responsibility, are traditional concepts of international law. IOs in their quality as subjects of international law would automatically become subject to these concepts.

However, despite the emphasis put on these rather traditional elements of accountability, some new elements seem to emerge.

---

62   See *supra*, fn. 39.

63   *Ibidem*, 10.

64   Harlow, *op. cit.*, fn. 39, 5.

65   Steven R. Ratner, Democracy and accountability: the criss-crossing paths of two emerging norms, in: Gregory H. Fox, Brad R. Roth (eds.) *Democratic Governance and International Law*, Cambridge, 2000, 449-492, 449.

First, they result from the fact that IOs consider themselves frequently as *"legibus solutae"* insofar as they themselves frequently define the applicable law. It is to be doubted that States by creating such organizations or adhering to them intended to confer upon them such wide competences.

Secondly, new elements of accountability are prompted by the fact that IOs escape any judicial control, either due to the lack of appropriate institutions or by referring to their immunity.

Thirdly, they result from the fact that individuals have no access to judicial remedies against IOs in order to protect their rights. This issue arises because either the individuals are not directly affected by the activities of international organizations or no judicial means exist by which proceedings against IOs could be instituted.

Accordingly, some elements of accountability can indeed by identified which seem to find a certain degree of common support:

- The limits of the powers of IOs;
- The duty of compliance with international law, including the definition of the applicable law as well as the question of the protection of the rights of individuals;
- The responsibility of IOs;
- The means and instruments available to protect the rights of the individuals against activities of IOs.

These issues represent certain claims addressed to IOs according to which they should conform to a certain standard of accountability in these fields. As such, they are to be spotted rather in the area of political claims than of legal obligations. From an international law perspective, what can be done is only to measure how far the existing legal structure of IOs meets the claims raised under the heading of accountability.

A.   The Powers of IOs as Subjects of International Law

The limitation of the powers of IOs has been a source of permanent discussion having arisen out of the fear of the absence of any legal impediment to the uncontrolled extension of their powers as well as of the uncertainty about *ultra virus* activities.[66] IOs are undoubtedly subjects of IL and as such immediate addressees of the norms of IL. Their powers are based on two levels of rules that are applicable to IOs: the constituent instrument of the IOs *lato sensu* on the one side and general international law on the other.

The IOs as subjects of international law are a creation of their constituent instruments that serve not only as a treaty but also as the constitution of the relevant organization[67] and as legal basis of its powers. In this respect, there is no doubt

---

66   Karl Zemanek, The legal foundations of the international system. General Course on Public International Law. Academy of International Law, *Recueil des Cours*, vol. 266, 1997, 91.

67   See *e.g.* Seyersted, *op. cit.*, 35, 25.

that they are bound by their constituent instruments. However, the scope of the constituent instrument already raised concern since the limits of the powers of IOs were increasingly extended, starting from the application of the implied powers doctrine by the ICJ[68] to the view that the powers of IOs are unlimited unless they are excluded under the constituent instruments.[69] The implied powers doctrine widened the field of activities of IOs beyond the wording of the constituent instruments by endowing the IOs with the powers "essential to the performance of its duties."[70] Irrespective of the distinction between implied and inherent competences,[71] this doctrine enabled IOs to develop activities which justified Seyersted even to attribute sovereignty to IOs.[72]

But according to Bowett this widening through the implied powers doctrine "cannot extend to powers which are not provided for in the Charter, were never in contemplation when the Charter was drafted, and do not flow from the express powers by necessary or reasonable interpretation."[73] Arangio Ruiz connects this doctrine directly with the problem of the rule of law. He discards the applicability of the doctrine of implied powers as "an interpretive tool of the Charter for the determination of the powers of the political organs of the UN." In particular in the case of the Security Council, he considers it "more dangerous for the preservation and development of the rule of law in the 'organized international community'".[74]

The extent of the power of IOs was tested during the Vienna Conference on the law of treaties between States and international organizations or between international organizations in 1986 when the conference had to decide on the scope of the treaty-making power of international organizations. According to former Communist views an IO enjoyed only those powers that were explicitly provided in its Statute.[75] This view was motivated by the emphasis on the sovereignty of States and by the risk of being overruled in IOs due to the small numbers of States belonging to this group. This position was juxtaposed to the view according to which IOs enjoyed powers not explicitly provided in the Statute pursuant to the implied powers doctrine. The Convention attempts to make a compromise: whereas its Pream-

---

68 Advisory Opinion of the International Court of Justice on Reparation for Injuries suffered in the Service of the United Nations, *ICJ Reports*, 1949, p. 174.

69 See *e.g.* Seyersted, *op. cit.*, fn. 36, 23.

70 See the advisory opinion, *op. cit.*, fn. 68.

71 Seyersted, *op, cit.*, fn. 35, 19; N.D. White, *The Law of International Organisations*, Manchester, New York, 1996, 131.

72 *Ibidem*, 42.

73 Derek William Bowett, Crimes of State and the 1996 Report of the International Law Commission on State Responsibility, *EJIL* vol 9 No. 1, 1998, 163-173, 166.

74 Gaetano Arangio-Ruiz, The Federal Analogy and UN Charter Interpretation: A Crucial Issue, *EJIL* vol. 8 No. 1, 1997, 29, 2 .

75 See *e.g.* F.I. Kozhenikov, V.M. Koretskii, D.V. Levin, G.I. Tunkin, N.A. Ushakov, V.M. Tchikvadze, V.M. Shurshalov (eds.), *Kurs mezhdunarodnogo prava v shesti tomakh, tom V: Osnovnye instituty i otrasli sovremennogo mezhdunarodnogo prava*. Moskva 1969, 59.

ble states that IOs possess the treaty-making power,[76] Article 6 limits this power by the rules of that organization. As a consequence, a discussion arose about the definition of the "rules of the organization"; Article 2 defines them as, "in particular, the constituent instruments, decisions and resolutions adopted in accordance with them, and established practice of the organization." Since this text does not contain an exhaustive enumeration of the different kinds of rules of the organizations it does not confine the activity of an organization only to those explicitly authorized by the constituent instruments[77] and accepts a certain leeway the organization could use so that no clear solution as to the limits of the treaty-making power can be inferred therefrom.

But quite often the constituent instruments themselves open the door for a widened activity. The striking example is the Security Council whose powers are under permanent challenge. In the *Tadic* case[78] in particular counsels for defence queried whether the resolution which established the ICTY (S/RES/827) was still within the powers of the Security Council and received an affirmative answer.

This Security Council resolution reflects various motives behind it. The expansion of powers of the IOs as reflected by this resolution is not only caused by the wish to endow such institutions with the authority of the United Nations, it also permits Member States to hide behind the veil of the organization in order to pursue certain objectives they want to ascribe to the entire community of Member States.[79]

As far as the power to take sanctions is concerned, the Bossuyt report,[80] submitted to the Fifty-second Session of the Sub-Commission on the Promotion and Protection of Human Rights of the Commission on Human Rights, already elaborated the legal framework for taking sanctions under Chapter VII of the Charter which not only addresses the issue of the power to take sanctions, but also the legal regime applicable to them. It starts from the assertion that this power is not unlimited, but

---

76   This passage reads: "Noting that international organizations possess the capacity to conclude treaties which is necessary for the exercise of their functions and the fulfillment of their purposes", UN Doc A/CONF. 129/15.

77   Hubert Isak, Gerhard Loibl, United Nations Conference on the Law of Treaties between States and International Organizations or between International Organizations, *Österreichische Zeitschrift für Öffentliches Recht und Völkerrecht* vol. 38, 1987, 49-78, 55.

78   *Prosecutor v. Dusko Tadic A/K/A "Dule"*, Decision on the Defence Motion on Jurisdiction of 10 August 1995; Tadic (IT-94-1) "Prijedor" <http://www.un.org/icty/tadic/trialc2/decision-e/100895.htm>; the decision was upheld by the appeal chamber: *Prosecutor v. Dusko Tadic A/K/A "Dule"*, Decision on the Defence Motion for Interlocutory Appeal on Jurisdiction of 2 October 1995; Tadic (IT-94-1) "Prijedor", <http://www.un.org/icty/tadic/appeal/decision-e/51002.htm>.

79   *Cf* Michael Barnett and Martha Finnemore, "The Politics, Power, and Pathologies of International Organizations" *International Organization* vol. 53, No 4, 1999, 699-732, 704.

80   "The Adverse Consequences of Economic Sanctions on the Enjoyment of Human Rights", Working paper prepared by Marc Bossuyt, UN Doc. E/CN.4/Sub.2/2000/33.

subject to several legal restraints; such sanctions must not only aim at maintaining or restoring international peace and security, but also depend on the existence of a threat to or breach of the peace, or an act of aggression.[81] Further restraints are said to result from Article 24 of the Charter so that they must be in conformity with the Purposes and Principles of the Charter, from Article 1(1) insofar as they must be "in conformity with the principles of justice and international law" as well as from Article 1 (2), which requires that sanctions or other measures "respect the principle of equal rights and the self-determination of peoples." In the spirit of Article 1(3) sanctions have to respect human rights such as the right to life, the rights to security of the person, health, education or employment. According to Article 1(4) sanctions or other measures should facilitate the harmonization of national or international action. These limitations are considered as reinforced by Article 55.[82] According to this report, sanctions would have even to respect certain resolutions of the General Assembly such as the Declaration on Principles of International Law Concerning Friendly Relations and Cooperation among States in Accordance with the Charter of the United Nations, the Charter of Economic Rights and Duties of States, the Resolution on the Permanent Sovereignty over Natural Resources and the Universal Declaration on the Eradication of Hunger and Malnutrition.[83]

However, already the reference to these resolutions raises doubts as to whether the Security Council, in particular its permanent Members, consider themselves subject to all these legal regulations if they feel a need to adopt a resolution under Chapter VII. Seen in a more general perspective, the legality or illegality of such expanded activity by collective organs of the majority of IOs finally depends only on the will of the Member States. The competences of the organization can be expanded only if such expansion is either authorised by the constituent instrument and the rules of the organization, by general international law or subsequently sanctioned by the Member States so that eventually any expansion of activities of the powers of an IO depends on the anticipated or subsequent explicit or implicit consent of States. Seen as such, fears concerning an unlimited exercise of power cannot be addressed towards IOs but to the Member States which supplied the IOs with such powers.

B.   The Duty of Compliance with Applicable Law, Including the Definition of the Applicable Law as well as the Question of the Protection of the Rights of Individuals

i.   The Scope of Applicable International Law

As can also be seen from the Bossuyt report, the exercise of the powers of IOs raises the question as to whether and to which extent they are bound by general international law. The general answer results from their status as subjects of in-

---

81   *Ibidem*, 7.

82   *Ibidem*.

83   *Ibidem*, 9.

ternational law, which makes them addressees of general international law. Consequently, their activities are governed by those rules of international law which generally apply to such activities.

The first legal basis for these activities is the constituent instrument as their legal foundation. Its interpretation pursuant to the general rules of treaty interpretation as laid down in Article 31 VCLT enlarges the scope of the applicable law insofar as it requires the interpretation of any treaty, including constituent instruments of IO, in accordance with "relevant rules of international law applicable in the relations between the parties."

This reference to rules outside the constituent instruments raises the problem of the definition of the rules applicable to IOs. As far as treaties concluded by IOs are concerned there is not doubt of the binding effect on the organizations.[84]

A different situation arises in regard of rules of general international law: The simple conclusion could be that insofar as these rules are compatible with the constituent instruments, IOs are certainly bound by them. Whatever the discussion and the interpretation of the limitations of the powers of the Charter produces, even such a powerful organ as the Security Council cannot be considered as *legibus solutus* since it is not immune against the systematic rules of general international law including those on international responsibility or *pacta sunt servanda*.[85] It cannot be argued that the organizations are excluded from the application of these rules because they did not take part in the creation of the latter so that the content of such rules would not address IOs. On the contrary, the States that founded an IO did so with the intention to subject it to international law so that general international law is applicable to the activities of IOs as far as more specific rules such as those embodied in the constituent instruments do not contradict it.[86] Within the parameters of their activities IOs are subject to general international law to the extent that no other rule exists which has gained priority due to the *lex specialis* or *lex posterior* rule and insofar as the rules of general international law are applicable to the activities. The question, however, remains open to which extent IOs may be empowered by Member States to amend such rules.

It is, however, impossible to develop the full scope of this issue in this context; it should rather be illustrated by different topical issues, namely the application of human rights to the staff members, the respect of human rights in the context of the targeted sanctions and finally, the observance of humanitarian law by the military forces of the UN.

---

84   See Christoph Schreuer, Die Bindung internationaler Organisationen an völkerrechtliche Verträge ihrer Mitgliedstaaten, in: K. Ginther, G. Hafner, W. Lang, H. Neuhold, L. Sucharipa-Behrmann, *Völkerrecht zwischen normativem Anspruch und Wirklichkeit*, Berlin , 1994, 223-250, *passim*.

85   A problem however arises insofar as these rules are inconsistent with these instruments since the Member States could then become subject to conflicting obligations resulting from international law, a conflict that would however have to be resolved by the States and not by the IO.

86   Patel, *op. cit.*, fn. 59, 577.

ii.   The Respect of the Rights of Individuals: Human Rights and IOs

Even if Member States concur in the intention to expand the powers of the IO, they still have to reckon with the resistance of individuals, in particular if the rights of individuals are directly infringed. This problem arose in connection with the targeted sanctions of the SC since they were already examined against the background of a possible breach of human rights as embodied in the International Covenant on Civil and Political Rights (ICCPR). In this respect, the claim for more accountability of IOs stems from the feeling that the rights and interests of the individuals are ignored by the IOs. Although the latter frequently act as promoter, *spiritus rectores* and defenders of human rights, it has been asked in the context of the accountability discussion whether they consider themselves bound by human rights obligations as far as their own activities are concerned.[87] This issue has already gained wider attention not only with respect to the staff members, but also regarding individuals outside the IO.[88]

In particular in recent time, IOs became increasingly subject to complaints that their activities directly infringed upon rights of individuals. Such complaints addressed in particular the UN with regard to the sanctions adopted by it[89] and the WTO concerning economic measures.[90]

In the case of European Union, the Treaty on the European Union (EUT) explicitly obliges the EU to respect human rights as they are derived from the European Convention on Human Rights and Fundament Freedoms (ECHR) and the constitutional traditions of the Member States.[91] The obligation to respect human

---

87   Erika de Wet, The Role of Human Rights in Limiting the Enforcement Power of the Security Council: A Principled View, in: de Wet, Nollkaemper, *op. cit.*, fn. 36, 8; August Reinisch, Developing Human Rights and Humanitarian Law Accountability of the Security Council for Imposition of Economic Sanctions, in: *AJIL* vol 95, 2001, 851-872, 854.

88   See *e.g.* Vera Gowlland-Debbas, The Domestic Implementation of UN Sanctions, in: de Wet, Nollkaemper, *op. cit.*, fn. 36, 63-76, 64; Erika de Wet, André Nollkaemper, Review of Security Council Decisions by National Courts, in: *GYIL* vol. 45, 2002, 166-202, 171.

89   See fn. 88.

90   See *e.g.* the Report of the High Commissioner to the Fifty-second session of the Commission on Human Rights, Sub-Commission on the Promotion and Protection of Human Rights: The impact of the Agreement on Trade-Related Aspects of Intellectual Property Rights on human rights, UN Doc E/CN.4/Sub.2/2001/13 of 27 June 2001.

91   Article 6 of the Treaty on the European Union reads:

1.   The Union is founded on the principles of liberty, democracy, respect for human rights and fundamental freedoms, and the rule of law, principles which are common to the Member States.

2.   The Union shall respect fundamental rights, as guaranteed by the European Convention for the Protection of Human Rights and Fundamental Freedoms signed in Rome on 4 November 1950 and as they result from the constitutional traditions common to the Member States, as general principles of Community law.

3.   The Union shall respect the national identities of its Member States.

4.   The Union shall provide itself with the means necessary to attain its objectives and carry through its policies.

rights was confirmed *e.g.* in the case *JCB Service v Commission* where the Court 1st Instance explicitly referred to the need to comply with human rights as laid down in the Charter of Nice.[92]

However, this is not generally the rule; unlike this situation of the EU where a specific provision of the Treaty obliges the EU in this respect, IOs are not explicitly made subject to human rights. Although the UN is a focal point for the elaboration and enforcement of human rights, starting from the adoption of the Universal Declaration to the work of the Human Rights Committee, its own activities are not made subject to human rights. Thus, in the case of the ICTY, a subsidiary organ of the Security Council, concern was already voiced on the consistency of the procedure related to this body with the UN Covenant on Civil and Political Rights[93] despite its Article 21 which embodies the minimal rights of the accused several inconsistencies with the Covenant were already identified.[94]

---

92   Case T-67/01, Judgment of the Court of First Instance (First Chamber) of 13 January 2004 .

93   See *e.g.* Johan G. Lammers, Challenging the Establishment of the ICTY before the Dutch Courts: *The Case of Slobodan Milosevic v. The Netherlands*, in: de Wet, Nollkaemper, *op. cit.*, fn. 36, 107-112, 108; A. Reinisch, "Das Jugoslawien-Tribunal der Vereinten Nationen und die Verfahrensgarantien des II. VN-Menschenrechtspaktes. Ein Beitrag zur Frage der Bindung der Vereinten Nationen an nicht-ratifiziertes Vertragsrecht", *ÖZÖRV* 47 (1995), pp. 173-213, at pp. 177-182.

94   Article 21 reads:

Rights of the accused
1.   All persons shall be equal before the International Tribunal.
2.   In the determination of charges against him, the accused shall be entitled to a fair and public hearing, subject to article 22 of the Statute.
3.   The accused shall be presumed innocent until proved guilty according to the provisions of the present Statute.
4.   In the determination of any charge against the accused pursuant to the present Statute, the accused shall be entitled to the following minimum guarantees, in full equality:
    (a)   to be informed promptly and in detail in a language which he understands of the nature and cause of the charge against him;
    (b)   to have adequate time and facilities for the preparation of his defence and to communicate with counsel of his own choosing;
    (c)   to be tried without undue delay;
    (d)   to be tried in his presence, and to defend himself in person or through legal assistance of his own choosing; to be informed, if he does not have legal assistance, of this right; and to have legal assistance assigned to him, in any case where the interests of justice so require, and without payment by him in any such case if he does not have sufficient means to pay for it;
    (e)   to examine, or have examined, the witnesses against him and to obtain the attendance and examination of witnesses on his behalf under the same conditions as witnesses against him;
    (f)   to have the free assistance of an interpreter if he cannot understand or speak the language used in the International Tribunal;
    (g)   not to be compelled to testify against himself or to confess guilt.

The main argument militating in favour of being subject to human rights would result from the legal personality of IOs since as such they are considered to be bound by general customary international law[95] insofar as they develop activities for which human rights become relevant. From a theoretical point of view one could therefore conclude that the IOs are subject to human rights so far as they result from general customary international law being applicable to all subjects of international law which perform activities addressed by these rules.[96] This argument becomes primarily pertinent if human rights are provided with a *ius cogens* character; any other rule would be open to any change through explicit rules of the organizations.

In this respect the issue of succession of the IOs into the treaties of human rights concluded by their Member States has also been raised.[97] From a purely dogmatic point of view, the accession to an IO cannot be compared with the succession into treaties since, contrary to the case of State succession, the State retains its competence in the issues dealt with by the relevant treaty. It is to be distinguished whether a State could become subject to contradictory obligations or ceases to dispose of its powers that are conferred to a different subject of law. The well known case *International Fruit Company* before the ECJ[98] cannot serve as an example to the contrary. In this case, the ECJ relied on the argument that with the transferral of exclusive competences upon the EC, the EC also inherited the obligations which the MS had assumed under the GATT.[99] This solution was dictated by the fact that, within GATT, the Member States could no longer act on their own, but only on behalf of the EC. In the field of human rights, however, the EU explicitly declared itself bound by the ECHR so that the question of succession into this convention did not arise. Contrary to this situation where all Member States are concerned, the ECT itself provides also a different solution for the situation relating only to individual Member States since, as far as treaties concluded by such States before their becoming member of the EC with third States are concerned, these treaties precede the obligations under the ECT according to Article 307 ECT.[100]

---

95   So the ICJ in the Advisory Opinion on the *Interpretation of the Agreement of 25 March 1951 between the WHO and Egypt, ICJ Reports* 1980, 80.

96   See *e.g.* Reinisch, *op. cit.*, fn. 87, 858 *seq.*

97   See Schermers, *op. cit.*, fn. 1, 983.

98   Joined Cases 21/72 to 24/72 *International Fruit Company and Others* [1972] ECR 1219, paragraphs 6 and 7

99   See also Schreuer, *op. cit.*, fn. 84, 227.

100   Article 307 reads:

The rights and obligations arising from agreements concluded before 1 January 1958 or, for acceding States, before the date of their accession, between one or more Member States on the one hand, and one or more third countries on the other, shall not be affected by the provisions of this Treaty.

To the extent that such agreements are not compatible with this Treaty, the Member State or States concerned shall take all appropriate steps to eliminate the incompatibilities established. Member States shall, where necessary, assist each other to this end and shall, where appropriate, adopt a common attitude.

This issue can be tested not only with regard to the application of human rights standards to sanctions of IOs , but goes even further as to encompass also whether members of the staff of IOs were entitled to invoke human rights with regard to their labor conditions within the IO; in this regard it could be asked whether the staff regulations have to respect human rights.

a. The Labor Regulations Concerning the Staff Members

Although according to Schermers the legal position of the civil servant is well regulated,[101] problems can nevertheless arise as to whether these persons can invoke human rights against the relevant organization. So far, the UN staff regulations are not considered as being subject to such commitments resulting for instance from the UN Covenants, despite the fact that these Covenants were elaborated under the auspices of the UN. One could, however, argue that staff regulations must at least correspond to customary human rights or must not contradict them. A deviation therefrom could only occur with the explicit or implicit consent of the Member States.

The question of human rights that can be invoked against an organization became crucial at the moment when the staff of several IOs claimed the right to strike, which was considered as a basic human right and was already frequently invoked.[102] Without pronouncing on the real issue of the applicability of human rights, the practice recognized such a right and it was confirmed by the ILOAT: although no payment is made during the time,[103] the ILOAT did not consider a strike as a violation of the service contracts.[104]

Although so far, human rights have not been expressly acknowledged as applicable to staff members within the context of their labor conditions, the UNAT and ILOAT developed certain principles that apply to staff regulations and limit even the discretionary power of those that are responsible for the elaboration of the staff rules.[105] These principles are deemed to meet the requirements under a gener-

---

In applying the agreements referred to in the first paragraph, Member States shall take into account the fact that the advantages accorded under this Treaty by each Member State form an integral part of the establishment of the Community and are thereby inseparably linked with the creation of common institutions, the conferring of powers upon them and the granting of the same advantages by all the other Member States.

101 Schermers, *op. cit.*, fn. 1, 364.

102 *Ibidem,*; see also Alain Pellet, La grève des fonctionnaires internationaux, *RGDIP* vol 79, 1975, 932-971.

103 See the resolution of the General Assembly A/31/193.

104 See See the judgments In re *Cook* (No. 4), Judgment 1612 of 30 January 1997, <http://www.ilo.org/public/english/tribunal/fulltext/1612.htm>; In re *Franks* (No. 2) *and Vollering* (No. 2), Judgment 1333 of 31 January 1994, <http://www.ilo.org/public/english/tribunal/fulltext/1333.htm>; In re *Lammineur*, Judgment 1041 of 26 June 1990; In re *Aras, Conreaux, Davison, Fisher, Kettle, Kraanen* (No. 2), *Kruijdenberg, Mijnders* (No. 2), *De Roo, Van Rosmalen, Rossi, Schuurmans and Watchman*, Judgment 805 of 13 March 1987, <http://www.ilo.org/public/english/tribunal/fulltext/0805.htm>.

105 Schermers, *op. cit.*, fn. 1, 366; see also the Report (Rapporteur: Mr Giuseppe Aleffi): Nature and scope of the contractually acquired rights of Council of Europe staff, Council

ally applicable human rights regime. In the *Waite and Kennedy* case, the European Court of Human Rights concluded that the staff regulations of the relevant IOs amounted to a guarantee of human rights as reflected in Article 6 of the European Convention on Human Rights so that the State that denied its own jurisdiction did not breach the Convention.[106] According to the report submitted in the Parliamentary Assembly of the Council of Europe, a general conclusion can be drawn from an overview of case-law. It is the concept of acquired rights, which gained in the law of international organizations a greater significance than in the law of national civil services. "In the international civil service, the concept of acquired rights refers in particular to inviolable situations or qualities, i.e. which are not affected by the passing of time."[107] It seems therefore that these acquired rights serve as a substitute for the reluctance to apply human rights derived from general international law.

Although an assessment generally applicable to all IOs is hardly possible, it seems that the regime governing the status of civil servants of IOs corresponds to the general human rights standards, subject, however, to individual cases where this conclusion might be contested. It is only quite interesting to note that the applicability of human rights as part of general international law is not asserted, but that instead a separate set of principles has been developed.

b.   Sanctions of the United Nations

Within the UN, the call for accountability is particularly prompted by the recent sanction practice of the Security Council. As the ECHR argued "any measures imposing sanctions has, by definition, consequences which affect the right to property and the freedom to pursue a trade or business, thereby causing harm to persons who are in no way responsible for the situation which led to the adoption of the sanctions."[108] The increase of the number of these resolutions imposing economic

---

of Europe, Parliamentary Assembly, Doc. 8868 of 11 October 2000; according to this report "Acquired rights" are explicitly protected in the staff regulations of the following organizations: the World Health Organisation (WHO), the International Labour Organisation (ILO), UNESCO, the International Atomic Energy Agency (IAEA), the International Maritime Organisation (IMO) and the FAO. Among the coordinated organizations, the staff regulations of OECD and the European Space Agency contain rules of this type; the NATO Civilian Personnel Regulations establish the concept of "contractual rights" ; *ibidem*, para. 12.

106   *Case Waite and Kennedy v. Germany,* 18 February 1999, Application no. 26083/94, § 73 (*Case Beer and Regan v. Germany,* Application no. 28934/95, of the same date): "Taking into account in particular the alternative means of legal process available to the applicants, it cannot be said that the limitation on their access to the German Courts with regard to ESA impaired the essence of their right to a court or was disproportionate for the purposes of article 6 § 1."

107   *Supra,* fn. 105, para. 19.

108   Case C-317/00 P(R), Order of the President of the Court of 13 November 2000 on Appeal against the order of the President of the Second Chamber of the Court of First Instance of the European Communities of 2 August 2000 (Case T-189/00 R *'Invest' Import und Export and Invest Commerce* v *Commission* [2000] ECR II-2993, No. 59.

sanctions exacerbates the problem of their effect on the individuals. This issue has become particularly pertinent since, in particular as a means to combat terrorism, the Security Council moved away from its former practice of imposing sanctions only on States by which the entire population was addressed and started to adopt sanctions addressing individuals, first called smart sanctions, now targeted sanctions.[109] This change is motivated by the intention to reduce the negative effect of sanctions on individuals[110] so that only those will be affected who are allegedly involved in terrorist activities. An illustrative example of this kind are Resolutions S/RES/1267 (1999), S/RES/1333 (2000) as modified by Resolution S/RES/1390 (2002) and S/RES/1455 (2003): These resolutions taken under Chapter VII of the Charter oblige States to take measures against individual persons contained in a list drawn up by the 1267 Committee,[111] such as freezing of their accounts without any procedural guarantees offered to them.

Two different issues have to be dealt with separately: the problem of whether IOs themselves have to respect general human rights in the adoption of sanctions and the question how far States are obliged to apply such sanctions irrespective of their human right obligations which can result either from general international law or specific human right treaties to which they are parties.

As to the first issue, the Bossuyt report[112] even subjects the sanctions, apart from the general obligations under the Charter referred to above,[113] to certain human right obligations already derived from the Universal Declaration of Human Rights such as the right to life (art. 3), the right to freedom from inhuman or de-

---

109   As to the development of the sanction regime see: J. Stephanides, *A Brief Overview of United Nations Sanctions*; Informal Background Paper prepared by the United Nations Sanctions Secretariat in: Swiss Federal Office for Foreign Economic Affairs, Department of Economy; Expert seminar on targeting UN financial sanctions; March 17-19, 1998; Interlaken, Switzerland, 53; Koenraad Van Brabant, *Can Sanctions be Smarter? The Current Debate*. Report of a conference held in London, 1998, 10.

110   "In that respect, sanctions should be used not as a tool for collective punishment but as a device aimed at facilitating the solution of a particular crisis.", Stephanides, *op. cit.*, fn. 109, 65.

111   The Security Council Committee, called 1267 Committee, was established pursuant to paragraph 6 of Resolution 1267 (1999); its function is to watch over the implementation by States of the sanctions imposed by the Security Council on individuals and entities belonging or related to the Taliban, Usama Bin Laden and the Al-Qaida organization and to maintain a list of individuals and entities for this purpose. Resolutions 1267 (1999), 1333 (2000), 1390 (2002) and 1455 (2003) oblige all States to freeze the assets, prevent the entry into or the transit through their territories, and prevent the direct or indirect supply, sale and transfer of arms and military equipment with regard to the individuals/entities included on the list. See <http://www.un.org/Docs/sc/committees/1267/1267ListEng.htm>.

112   See fn. 80; see also Resolution 1997/35 of the Sub-Commission on Prevention of Discrimination and Protection of Minorities, Commission of Human Rights: "Adverse consequences of economic sanctions on the enjoyment of human rights", 28 August 1997.

113   See *supra* fn. 80.

grading treatment (art. 5), and the right to an adequate standard of living, including food, clothing, housing and medical care (art. 25). According to the report, the two International Covenants on Human Rights are likewise to be taken into account, in particular the International Covenant on Economic, Social and Cultural Rights concerning the right to an adequate standard of living (article 11); the right to health (article 12) and the right to education (article 13), the International Covenant on Civil and Political Rights concerning the right to life (article 6). The report quotes, beside these two instruments, the Convention on the Rights of the Child, the Declaration of the Principles of International Cultural Cooperation, the Standard Minimum Rules for the Treatment of Prisoners as further human rights instruments relevant to sanctions. The problem is, however, that not all of these instruments have a binding force and, insofar as they are treaties, the UN itself is not party to them so that hardly any legal obligation incumbent upon the UN can be deduced. The only legal effect on the UN can be derived from general international law; the reference of the Charter to human rights in Article 1(3) does not suffice to impose legal obligations on the organization so that, as also stated by Alvarez,[114] human rights do not constitute a limit to the sanctions taken by the Security Council, unless they can be qualified as *ius cogens* norms. It is therefore futile to raise the question whether the emergency clause in the human rights instruments are an appropriate legal device permitting the deviation from these instruments.[115]

A different issue is the question whether States have to disregard their human rights obligations when they apply such sanctions. The States so addressed are pursuant to Article 103 of the Charter under the strict obligation to comply with the resolution irrespective of their human rights obligations, such as the duty under Article 6 of the ECHR,[116] which ensures a fair and public hearing for the

---

114   José E. Alvarez, The Security Council's War on Terrorism: Problems and Policy Options, in: de Wet, Nollkaemper, *op. cit.*, fn. 36, 119-146, 125, 128.

115   De Wet, *op. cit.*, fn. 36 , 17.

116   Article 6 reads as follows:

> In the determination of his civil rights and obligations or of any criminal charge against him, everyone is entitled to a fair and public hearing within a reasonable time by an independent and impartial tribunal established by law. Judgement shall be pronounced publicly by the press and public may be excluded from all or part of the trial in the interest of morals, public order or national security in a democratic society, where the interests of juveniles or the protection of the private life of the parties so require, or the extent strictly necessary in the opinion of the court in special circumstances where publicity would prejudice the interests of justice.
>
> Everyone charged with a criminal offence shall be presumed innocent until proved guilty according to law.
>
> Everyone charged with a criminal offence has the following minimum rights:
>
> (a) to be informed promptly, in a language which he understands and in detail, of the nature and cause of the accusation against him;
>
> (b) to have adequate time and the facilities for the preparation of his defence;
>
> (c) to defend himself in person or through legal assistance of his own choosing or, if he has not sufficient means to pay for legal assistance, to be given it free when the interests of justice so require;

determination of the civil rights and obligations or of any criminal charge against an individual. But Article 103 of the United Nations Charter[117] is not an appropriate device to solve this issue in all respects since it precludes the States to invoke their conventional obligations only within the framework of the UN so that, if the matter arises outside the UN, the conflict between contradicting obligations cannot be settled by reference to this Charter provision.

Insofar as judicial institutions, in particular international ones like the European Court of Human Rights and the ECJ, have dealt with this issue they tried to strike a balance of interests weighing the interests of the individual against the overriding interest of the community. The practice of the ECJ reflects the difficulty of applying human rights to the activities of IOs. Presently, the EU implements Security Council resolutions through the adoption of a common position within the framework of the Common Foreign and Security Policy according to Article 15 of the Treaty on the European Union[118] followed by a regulation within the framework of the first pillar, based on Article 301 ECT.[119] In practice, this procedure converts the Security Council resolution that is not considered as self-executing, into a directly applicable regulation. If proceedings were instituted before the ECJ against the EC for the breach of human rights obligations to which the EC is explicitly committed under its own treaty, caused by such regulations, the Court dismissed these actions by referring to the binding effect of EC resolutions and denied any responsibility of the EC for such implementing regulations, obviously qualifying them as being in conformity with international law. In the *Dorsch* case, the Tribunal of first Instance made it quite clear that no responsibility could be imposed on the EC:

    (d) to examine or have examined witnesses against him and to obtain the attendance and examination of witnesses on his behalf under the same conditions as witnesses against him;

    (e) to have the free assistance of an interpreter if he cannot understand or speak the language used in court.

117   Article 103 reads as follows:

In the event of a conflict between the obligations of the Members of the United Nations under the present Charter and their obligations under any other international agreement, their obligations under the present Charter shall prevail."

118   Article 15 reads:

The Council shall adopt common positions. Common positions shall define the approach of the Union to a particular matter of a geographical or thematic nature. Member States shall ensure that their national policies conform to the common positions.

119   Article 301 ECTZ reads:

Where it is provided, in a common position or in a joint action adopted according to the provisions of the Treaty on European Union relating to the common foreign and security policy, for an action by the Community to interrupt or to reduce, in part or completely, economic relations with one or more third countries, the Council shall take the necessary urgent measures. The Council shall act by a qualified majority on a proposal from the Commission.

In that regard, the Court observes that, under Article 25 of the United Nations Charter, only the 'Members of the United Nations' are required to accept and carry out the decisions of the Security Council of that organisation. Whilst it is true that the Member States of the UNO were required, in that capacity, to take all necessary measures to give effect to the trade embargo against Iraq imposed by Resolution No 661 (1990), the fact remains that those of them which were also Member States of the Community were able to take action to that effect only under the Treaty, since any measure of common commercial policy, such as the imposition of a trade embargo, falls, by virtue of Article 113 of the Treaty, within the exclusive competence of the Community. It was on the basis of those considerations that Regulation No 2340/90 was adopted, its preamble stating that 'the Community and its Member States have agreed to have recourse to a Community instrument in order to ensure uniform implementation, throughout the Community, of the measures concerning trade with Iraq and Kuwait decided upon by the United Nations Security Council'. The Court therefore considers that, in the circumstances of this case, the alleged damage can be attributed not to the adoption of Regulation No 2340/90 but only to United Nations Security Council Resolution No 661 (1990) which imposed the embargo on trade with Iraq. It follows from the foregoing that the applicant has not demonstrated the existence of a direct causal link between the alleged damage and the adoption of Regulation No 2340/90.[120]

It further referred to "the objective of general interest so fundamental for the international community of bringing to an end the invasion and occupation of Kuwait by Iraq and maintaining international peace and security in the region, the damage alleged by the applicant, even if it were capable of being classified as substantial cannot render the Community liable in this case".

Generally, in the cases before the EJC, either the causal link between the damage and the activity of the EC was denied and the general interest was declared as overwhelming as demonstrated in the *Dorsch* case[121] or the plea for urgency was dismissed.

Another example is the Dispute Settlement Body (DSB) of the WTO where the issue arose under the question whether the DSB under the heading "other applicable law" as referred to by Article 31 Vienna Convention on the Law of Treaties of 1969[122] had to apply, in combination with the applicable WTO law, human rights

---

120   Case T-184/95, *Dorsch Consult Ingenieurgesellschaft mbH, v. Council of the European Union, and Commission of the European Communities*; the judgment of the Court of first instance was confirmed by the Court in C-237/98 P, Dorsch Consult Ingenieurgesellschaft mbH, on Appeal against the judgment of the Court of First Instance of the European Communities (Second Chamber) of 28 April 1998 in Case T-184/95 *Dorsch Consult v. Council and Commission* [1998] ECR II-667.

121   See also Case T-220/96, *Elliniki Viomichania Oplon AE (EVO), v. Council of the European Union and Commission of the European Communities*.

122   Article 31 reads:
        General rule of interpretation
        1.   A treaty shall be interpreted in good faith in accordance with the ordinary meaning

rules by which the relevant Member States were bound. Arguments have been put forward in both directions,[123] referring in particular to the statement that WTO rules must not be applied in clinical isolation.[124] In any case, even if human rights considerations are included in the legal reasoning and interpretation of the WTO rules, they can under no circumstances derogate from the applicable WTO rules: at best, they can supplement them.[125]

The reluctance, for instance, of the European Court of Human Rights as well as other international instances to decide on questions whether IOs are bound by human rights must not be interpreted as an absolute denial of any application of the human rights on IOs. As far as human rights form part of general international law, IOs as subjects of international law are bound by them as far as they are not authorized by the Member State to deviate therefrom either through the constituent instruments or other authorization by the Member States. This power is only insofar not unlimited as the ultimate limits are the rules of general international law which have the quality of *ius cogens*. The appeal for accountability of IOs in this respect purports to raise the awareness of IOs of their obligations under general international law.

The problem which remains is whether the Member States of an IO may authorize the IO to take measures in contradiction to general obligations of human rights. Here again, the request for respect of human rights has to be addressed to the States as was reflected in the *Matthews* case before the European Court of Human Rights[126] where a certain protection was granted insofar as the complaint was

---

to be given to the terms of the treaty in their context and in the light of its object and purpose.

2. The context for the purpose of the interpretation of a treaty shall comprise, in addition to the text, including its preamble and annexes:
   (a) any agreement relating to the treaty which was made between all the parties in connection with the conclusion of the treaty;
   (b) any instrument which was made by one or more parties in connection with the conclusion of the treaty and accepted by the other parties as an instrument related to the treaty.
3. There shall be taken into account, together with the context:
   (a) any subsequent agreement between the parties regarding the interpretation of the treaty or the application of its provisions;
   (b) any subsequent practice in the application of the treaty which establishes the agreement of the parties regarding its interpretation;
   (c) any relevant rules of international law applicable in the relations between the parties.
4. A special meaning shall be given to a term if it is established that the parties so intended."

123   Marceau, *op. cit.*, fn. 38, 779.

124   *Ibidem*, referring to the Appellate Body Report, *United States – Standards for Reformulated and Conventional Gasolines* ("US-Gasoline"), WT/DS2/AB/R, adopted on 20 May 1996, DSR 1996:1, 18

125   Marceau, *op. cit.*, fn. 38, 797.

126   *Case Of Matthews v. the United Kingdom* (Application no. 24833/94), Judgment of 18 February 1999 ; this case dealt with the exclusion of Gibraltar from the franchise for the

addressed against the Member States of the relevant international organization; this case perfectly illustrates that this kind of action is the only one that could offer a certain guarantee against the disrespect of human rights by IOs proceeding from the assertion that by creating an international organization States cannot escape their human rights obligations.

iii. The Application of International Humanitarian Law to Military Forces of the UN

Another illustrative situation where the problem of application of general international law to personnel of IOs is of certain relevance results from the problem of whether military forces under UN command are bound to respect international humanitarian law. In order to remove any doubt on the applicability of humanitarian law to UN actions, the Secretary General promulgated certain principles "for the purpose of setting out fundamental principles and rules of international humanitarian law applicable to United Nations forces conducting operations under United Nations command and control."[127] These include the fundamental principles and rules of international humanitarian law relating to the Protection of the civilian population, means and methods of combat, the treatment of civilians and persons *hors de combat*, the treatment of detained persons as well as to the protection of the wounded, the sick, and medical and relief personnel. In view of this bulletin, it could quite easily have been argued that the UN forces are subject to customary international law and that this bulletin of the SG only had the purpose to clarify the scope of this law. A different view would consider only this bulletin as the legal basis of the applicability of humanitarian law to UN operations. However, the approach taken in this report speaks in favour of the first view insofar as the operations of the UN are subject to general customary international law applicable *ratione materiae* unless the UN had the power to deviate therefrom and made use of this power.

European parliamentary elections. This exclusion was based on the EC legislation, but claimed to be a breach of Article 3 of Protocol No. 1, which provides: "The High Contracting Parties undertake to hold free elections at reasonable intervals by secret ballot, under conditions which will ensure the free expression of the opinion of the people in the choice of the legislature." The Court declared that there was "no difference between European and domestic legislation, and no reason why the United Kingdom should not be required to "secure" the rights in Article 3 of Protocol No. 1 in respect of European legislation, in the same way as those rights are required to be "secured" in respect of purely domestic legislation. In particular, the suggestion that the United Kingdom may not have effective control over the state of affairs complained of cannot affect the position, as the United Kingdom's responsibility derives from its having entered into treaty commitments subsequent to the applicability of Article 3 of Protocol No. 1 to Gibraltar, namely the Maastricht Treaty taken together with its obligations under the Council Decision and the 1976 Act." For this reasons, the United Kingdom was declare of having breached its human rights obligation.

127 Secretary-General's Bulletin: Observance by United Nations forces of international humanitarian law, UN Doc ST/SGB/1999/13 of 6 August 1999.

This bulletin of the Secretary General can therefore be seen as serving a double purpose: on the one hand, as a clarification of the applicable law, on the other as an impediment to the application of rules that would contradict them.

C. *Responsibility*

The issue of the responsibility of IOs regularly figures on the agenda of accountability since it is considered as one of its major elements. There is no doubt that IOs could come in the position of assuming international responsibility for wrongful acts and this result has already been confirmed by judicial decisions. The issue of international responsibility of international organizations has presently aroused certain attention, in particular since it has been dealt with by the International Law Commission (ILC), the main codification body of the United Nations. That the Commission inscribed the issue of responsibility of international organizations on its agenda was prompted by two developments, namely, on the one hand, by the successful completion of the elaboration of the articles on the international responsibility of states for wrongful acts,[128] and, on the other, by the former works of ILC on the legal status of international organizations; as reflected in the Vienna Convention on the Representation of States in Their Relations with International Organizations of a Universal Character, adopted in 1975 and 1986 Vienna Convention on the Law of Treaties Between States and International Organizations or Between International Organizations of 1986.[129]

Despite the relative clarity of the legal regime of responsibility, the issue undeniably still raises a number of problems if applied to IOs because IOs themselves are already a complex legal phenomenon that is difficult to grasp. In this respect, IOs can hardly be assimilated with States that, in the ultimate effect, act through individuals, natural or juridical persons, which are not subjects of international law and as such cannot become internationally responsible. Contrary to it, IOs are composed by States that are subject to their own international responsibility, irrespective of whether performed inside or outside the framework of IO. It will be necessary to draw a clear distinction between those acts for which IOs and States have to bear their own responsibility separately and those where a joint one would arise. For instance, difficulties arise over attributability: in view of the different structures and functions of IOs, there might be solutions that differ from that applicable to States. It is also hard to distinguish between the responsibility to be

---

128   UN Doc. A/RES/56/83.

129   The text of the Convention is reproduced in: *United Nations, The Work of the International Law Commission*, New York 1996, 464. The ILC had also discussed other issues within the general topic of relations between states and international organizations (IOs); one was the status, privileges, and immunities of IOs, but the ILC decided in 1992 not to pursue consideration of it. Still, it seems that the existence of IOs and their growing importance in international relations require a closer look at their legal status or at last at legal questions connected with them. This may be why the ILC has now embarked on the issue of the responsibility of international organizations.

assumed by the Member States of IOs and that to be assumed by the organization itself. In this respect, for instance, particular problems could arise in cases where state organs were seconded to organizations.[130] As regards the UN military forces, the Secretary-General's Bulletin[131] states clearly that military personnel seconded to the UN for peace-keeping operations remain bound throughout the operation by their national law (Sec 2) and that in case of violations of international humanitarian law, members of the military personnel of a United Nations force are subject to prosecution in their national courts (Sec 4). This legal situation or one where States may be held responsible for the activities of IOs of which they are members could generate issues such as joint and several responsibility.

The need for a clear separation of the responsibility of IOs from that of States became already manifest in the framework of the Law of the Sea Convention[132] that had to provide for the possibility of the EC becoming party to it. Annex IX obliges the EC and their Member States to indicate clearly which matters regulated by the Convention fall within the competence of the EC and to assume also responsibility for them.[133]

---

130   See International Law Commission, Report on the work of its fifty-fourth session, General Assembly, Official Records, Fifty-fifth Session, Supplement No 10 (A/57/10), 2002, 228 *seq.*

131   See *supra* fn. 127.

132   UNTS No. 31363; <http://www.un.org/Depts/los/convention_agreements/convention_agreements.htm>.

133   Article 4 of Annex IX to the Convention reads:
Extent of participation and rights and obligations
   1.   The instrument of formal confirmation or of accession of an international organization shall contain an undertaking to accept the rights and obligations of States under this Convention in respect of matters relating to which competence has been transferred to it by its member States which are Parties to this Convention .
   2.   An international organization shall be a Party to this Convention to the extent that it has competence in accordance with the declarations, communications of information or notifications referred to in article 5 of this Annex.
   3.   Such an international organization shall exercise the rights and perform the obligations which its member States which are Parties would otherwise have under this Convention, on matters relating to which competence has been transferred to it by those member States. The member States of that international organization shall not exercise competence which they have transferred to it.
   4.   Participation of such an international organization shall in no case entail an increase of the representation to which its member States which are States Parties would otherwise be entitled, including rights in decision-making.
   5.   Participation of such an international organization shall in no case confer any rights under this Convention on member States of the organization which are not States Parties to this Convention.
   6.   In the event of a conflict between the obligations of an international organization under this Convention and its obligations under the agreement establishing the organization or any acts relating to it, the obligations under this Convention shall prevail." The EC and its Member States made the necessary declaration indicating, in particular, how far the matters regulated in the Convention on the Law of the Sea fall within the exclusive competence of the EC. The EC made one declaration upon

The *MOX Plant* case between Ireland and the United Kingdom[134] is not only the best illustration for the need for a clear distinction, but also highlights the legal problem which may arise in connexion with any responsibility arising for breaches of those provisions of the Convention which fall within the ambit of the exclusive competence of the EC.[135] Even if the breach was committed by a MS, a third country would have to invoke the responsibility of the EC.

It could be futile to ascribe the term responsibility as regards IOs a particular meaning within the topic of accountability. Nevertheless, it has to be borne in mind that the term responsibility of IOs as discussed in the framework of accountability is given a broader meaning than that used by the ILC. It includes all kinds of responsibility to be assumed by IOs, not only that towards States (members or not), which seems to be the main focus of the ILC work. It includes also responsibility towards the IOs' staff members as well as other individual persons, irrespective of the legal order governing the responsibility, which can be general international law, the particular legal order of the organization or even national law.

Two conclusions can be drawn form these considerations: first, since it is generally recognized that IOs can become subject of international responsibility as well as responsibility under the national legal order, the problem is not the possible failure of the IOs to assume responsibility but the question of the definition of the substantive rules applicable to IOs, for the breach of which they have to answer. Seen in this perspective, the claim for more accountability does not add anything to the responsibility IOs could incur. Second, the responsibility of IOs in the perspective of accountability includes a broader scope as it can arise not only towards

---

signature on 7 December 1984 and on upon formal confirmation on 1 April 1998: "Declaration concerning the competence of the European Community with regard to matters governed by the United Nations Convention on the Law of the Sea of 10 December 1982 and the Agreement of 28 July 1994 relating to the implementation of Part XI of the Convention"; http://www.un.org/Depts/los/convention_agreements/convention_declarations.htm#European%20Community%20Upon%20signature.

134   <http://www.pca-cpa.org/PDF/MOX%20%20-%20Day%204.pdf>.

135   In this case Ireland instituted proceedings against the United Kingdom under the Law of the Sea Convention because of alleged pollution of the Irish Sea caused by the installation of the MOX plant at Sellafields. The International Tribunal for the Law of the Sea issued an order on provisional measures (http://www.worldlii.org/int/cases/ITLOS/2001/2.html); the further proceedings were conducted before an arbitral tribunal. The latter, however, suspended its proceedings because of the question of the exclusive competence of the ECJ over the matter. In the meantime, the Commission of the European Union instituted proceedings against Ireland for non-compliance with the exclusive jurisdiction of the ECJ. In the meanwhile an action was brought on 30 October 2003 by the Commission of the European Communities against Ireland (Case C-459/03) where it was claimed that, by instituting dispute settlement proceedings against the United Kingdom under the UN Convention for the Law of the Sea concerning the MOX Plant located at Sellafield, Ireland has failed to fulfil its obligations under Article 10 and 292 EC and Article 192 and 193 Euratom; *Official Journal of the European Union* C 7/24 of 10.1.2004.

States, but also towards individual civil servants as well as towards other individuals affected by the activities of the organization. This second aspect provides a new feature to the issue of responsibility of IOs.

D.   The Absence of Judicial Means

The second main issue addressed by the request for increased accountability of IOs stems from the request for instruments to guarantee the legal protection against measures of IOs, which are not in compliance with international law or some institutional control. In this regard different issues are involved: the inner organizational control concerning in particular financial matters, the control with regard to the protection of the rights of the staff members and the control concerning the external effects of activities of IOs. A further distinction must also be drawn with regard to judicial or similar means within the relevant organization whose acts should be challenged on the one hand, and such legal devices outside the relevant organization. Accordingly, these instruments are of a different kind: they can consist of instruments of the internal review of an IO, of instruments that are accessible to individuals and, finally, albeit to a certain extent outside the scope of accountability, to States. It must be admitted from the outset that judicial means outside the relevant organization, which have the power to control or review the activity of an IO, are presently generally not available; very limited exceptions are arbitral tribunals empowered to deal with disputes between States and IOs.

i.   The Internal Review Mechanisms

The internal review has in particular the function of "overseeing compliance by an international organization with its own acts". IOs have already reacted to the appeal for increased control in particular with regard to financial but also other misuse of power and have developed a great variety of bodies entrusted with such functions. They do not only deal with financial issues, but also with other matters of compliance with the legal framework.

The UN provides different mechanisms to this effect: as far as financial matters are concerned, the Joint Inspection Unit which forms a comprehensive institution and was a consequence of one of the most serious financial crises in the UN carries out the relevant review. It provides an independent view through inspection and evaluation, aiming at improving management and methods and achieving greater coordination between organizations; its further task is to monitor that the activities undertaken by the UN and the specialized organizations are carried out in the most economical manner and that the optimum use is made of resources available for carrying out these activities.[136]

---

136   Wolfgang Münch, The Joint Inspection Unit of the United Nations and the Specialized Agencies, in: Jochen A. Frowein, Rüdiger Woflrum (eds.), *Max Planck Yearbook of United Nations Law*, vol. 2, 1998, Kluwer, 287-306, 288; Fatih Bouayad-Agha, Homero L. Hernández, Administration of Justice at the United Nations, Joint Inspection Unit, Geneva 2000.

Based on Article 274 ECT, the EU activities are under scrutiny by the the European Anti-Fraud Office (OLAF); its duty is to fight fraud, corruption and any other irregular activity, including misconduct within the European Institutions.[137] In the field of financial organizations the IMF has established the World Bank Inspection Panel (WBIP) as an innovative mechanism for accountability and governance.[138]

Usually the financial activities of IOs are subject to an audit, either by an internal audit like the court of auditors of the EC[139] or by an external auditor of recognized competence. So for instance, the International Seabed Authority has established a Finance Committee as well as providing that the budget must be made subject to an annual audit by external auditors.[140]

Although its legal nature as an IO may be questioned, even the OSCE has established a relevant review and control mechanism in the "Ad Hoc Committee on Transparency and Accountability in the OSCE" in order "to monitor and promote the implementation of the Parliamentary Assembly's policies on strengthening the OSCE parliamentary dimension and, in particular, enhancing transparency and accountability in the OSCE."

Other means to control the use of the financial resources are the setting of priorities among the planned activities.

In sum, IOs are regularly furnished with different bodies to review the performance of their obligations. The common characteristic is that insofar as they are more regularly involved in the review process they normally do not end up with an obligatory result stating clearly the breach.

What remains to be questioned is whether the efficiency of IOs is guaranteed by such internal review bodies and mechanisms. On the one hand, the efficiency certainly depends on the composition of the competent bodies, the right to resort to them and the legal value of its outcome. If, on the other, problems still remain they result from the tension between the IOs and the States insofar as the legal nature of the IO, which is derived from the States, make them dependent on the States and largely reduce their autonomy, including their power to control the use of their financial resources and to direct them so as to achieve the optimum use.

---

137   Commission Decision of 28 April 1999 establishing the European Anti-fraud Office (OLAF); *Official Journal of the European Communities* L 136/20 of 31. 5. 1999.

138   <http://wbln0018.worldbank.org/IPN/IPNWeb.nsf?OpenDatabase>; the WBIP was established by resolution Resolution No. IBRD 93-10 and Resolution No. IDA 93-6: "The World Bank Inspection Panel" of 22 September 1993.

139   Article 246-248 ECT.

140   Article 175 of the United Nations Convention on the Law of the Sea.

ii.   The Institutions Accessible to the Staff Members to Protect their Rights

The IOs usually provide adequate means to protect the rights of the staff members,[141] for instance, the UNAT[142] and ILOAT[143] are the best illustrations, as well as the ECJ being competent to hear staff cases. If the request for accountability also includes the availability of judicial means to protect the rights of staff members, it is only of rhetorical nature in view of the existence of a great variety of organs to this effect.

iii.   The Institutions Accessible to Other Individuals for the Protection of Their Rights

Contrary to the situation of staff members, other individuals suffering from activities of IOs hardly dispose of any access to judicial or other means to seek redress for their injuries. This issue has become particularly virulent in connection with the targeted sanctions that single out particular individuals.[144]

However, any attempt of individuals who are affected by these sanctions to institute proceedings against the relevant IOs before a national court would be doomed to failure because of the immunity of the organization.[145] The only remaining possible judicial means would be proceedings against the State as member of the IO. While, in the case of a proceeding because of sanctions adopted by the Security Council, the effect of Article 103 of the Charter would give priority to any obligation under the Charter, it has already been stated that the States remain nevertheless bound by their human rights obligations.[146] But we must also not be loose sight of the fact that any reaction resulting in a declaration of illegality of the Security Council resolution would incur international responsibility of States.[147] A different solution could only be achieved by proceedings against the relevant States for a breach of the human rights obligations by measures implementing the

---

141   Other similar bodies are for instance the Administrative Tribunal of the International Labour Organisation (ILOAT), the NATO Appeals Board, the World Bank Administrative Tribunal, the Administrative Tribunal for the International Monetary Fund, the Council of Europe Appeals Board, the Administrative Tribunal of the Bank for International Settlements, the Inter-American Development Bank Administrative Tribunal, Administrative Tribunal of the Organization of American States ("OASAT").

142   It was established by General Assembly Resolution A/RES/351 (IV) on 24 November 1949.

143   It was already established under the League of Nations on 26 September 1927.

144   *Cf* the Swedish statement: "The United Nations must develop a system that better safeguards the legal rights of individuals in cases where sanctions affect individual people", quoted by: Per Cramér, Recent Swedish Experiences with Targeted UN Sanctions: The Erosion of Trust in the Security Council, in: de Wet, Nollkaemper, *op. cit.*, fn. 36, 85-106, 102.

145   August Reinisch, *International Organizations before National Courts*, Cambridge, 2000, 127 *seq.*

146   So in the *Matthews* case, *supra* fn. 126.

147   Cramér, *op. cit.*, fn. 144, 96.

resolution.[148] A similar situation exists if proceedings are being instituted against the implementing measures of the EC: several cases were instituted,[149] the ECJ did not deny the admissibility, but in none of these cases did it annul the implementing measure and the chances of an annulment are rather slight.[150]

However, recent practice proves that hardly any resort to judicial means would be available even if the plea is directed against the implementing legislation of the relevant State. Hence, Gowlland-Debbas can quite rightly assert, "courts have tended to pass the buck."[151]

The only remaining legal device is to institute proceeding against the States on the ground that they are bound by human right conventions and must not confer rights upon an IO, which were inconsistent with the obligations under these conventions. In this way the European Court of Human Rights argued in the *Matthews* case where it decided that the United Kingdom had to assume responsibility for breaches of the HR conventions when it gave its consent to a restriction of the rights resulting from such conventions within the framework of the EC.[152]

But as far as the access to international courts is concerned, individuals suffer from the restricted access to such institutions with the exception of the EC where Article 230 ECT offers individuals a right to institute proceedings against acts of the EC itself.[153] However, even in this case, the individual would always have to

---

148   Such cases were instituted for instance in Sweden (see Cramér, *op.cit.*, fn. 144, 96).

149   So for instance Case T-184/95, *Dorsch Consult Ingenieurgesellschaft mbH, v Council of the European Union, and Commission of the European Communities*; the judgment of the Court of first instance was confirmed by the Court in C-237/98 P, *Dorsch Consult Ingenieurgesellschaft mbH*, on Appeal against the judgment of the Court of First Instance of the European Communities (Second Chamber) of 28 April 1998 in Case T-184/95 Dorsch Consult v Council and Commission [1998] ECR II-667; Case T-220/96, *Elliniki Viomichania Oplon AE (EVO), v Council of the European Union and Commission of the European Communities*; Case T-306/01 R, *Abdirisak Aden, Abdulaziz Ali, Ahmed Yusuf, Al Barakaat International Foundation v Council and Commission of the European Communities*; Case T-189/00 R *'Invest' Import und Export and Invest Commerce v Commission* [2000] ECR II-2993.

150   P.J.G. Kapteyn, The Role of the ECJ in Implementing Security Council Resolutions, in: de Wet, Nollkaemper, *op. cit.*, fn. 36, 57-62, 61.

151   Vera Gowlland-Debbas, The Domestic Implementation of UN Sanctions, in: de Wet, Nollkaemper, *op. cit.*, fn. 36, 63-76, 75.

152   See *supra* fn. 126.

153   Article 230 ECT reads:

The Court of Justice shall review the legality of acts adopted jointly by the European Parliament and the Council, of acts of the Council, of the Commission and of the ECB, other than recommendations and opinions, and of acts of the European Parliament intended to produce legal effects vis-à-vis third parties.

It shall for this purpose have jurisdiction in actions brought by a Member State, the Council or the Commission on grounds of lack of competence, infringement of an essential procedural requirement, infringement of this Treaty or of any rule of law relating to its application, or misuse of powers.

prove that it is individually directly affected by the challenged decision so that only under exceptional circumstances could it enjoy a *locus standi* before the Court. A further, but less powerful device to protect the interests of the individuals outside judicial instruments is the ombudsman established by the EC,[154] whose task is "to uncover maladministration in the activities of the Community institutions and bodies, with the exception of the Court of Justice and the Court of First Instance acting in their judicial role."[155]

The need for similar institutions for the protection of human rights is corroborated by the fact that the World Bank Inspection Panel (WBIP) of the IBRD was created not only as a mechanism for accountability and governance,[156] but also as a body for the protection of individual interests. According to its own explanation, the panel "provides a means for ensuring that World Bank policies and procedures are implemented by addressing the concerns of people who might be affected by Bank projects – particularly communities and individuals who simultaneously are among the ostensible beneficiaries of Bank-funded projects and at the same time are often vulnerable and politically marginalized groups who may otherwise not be heard in development discussions." Accordingly, it provides the opportunity for local citizens to challenge the activities of the IMF.

These cases, where the individuals could resort to international institutions to protect their interests against an IO are restricted to situations where the judicial institution seised belongs to the organization whose acts are challenged. By contrast, the access of individuals to the European Court of Human Rights in proceedings against a different international organization is totally excluded since no organization is party to the ECHR.

Despite these relatively sparse cases, one cannot ignore that individuals have hardly any judicial means at their disposal to protect their rights against activities of IOs even if these activities negatively affect their rights. One reason is that legal

---

The Court of Justice shall have jurisdiction under the same conditions in actions brought by the European Parliament, by the Court of Auditors and by the ECB for the purpose of protecting their prerogatives.

Any natural or legal person may, under the same conditions, institute proceedings against a decision addressed to that person or against a decision which, although in the form of a regulation or a decision addressed to another person, is of direct and individual concern to the former.

The proceedings provided for in this Article shall be instituted within two months of the publication of the measure, or of its notification to the plaintiff, or, in the absence thereof, of the day on which it came to the knowledge of the latter, as the case may be.

154   It is based on Article 195(4) of the Treaty establishing the European Community, Article 20d(4) of the Treaty establishing the European Coal and Steel Community and Article 107d(4) of the Treaty establishing the European Atomic Energy Community; its statute is contained in the Decision of the European Parliament on the regulations and general conditions governing the performance of the Ombudsman's duties of 9 March 1994, *Official Journal* L 113, 4.5.1994, p. 15.

155   Article 2 of the Statute.

156   See *supra*, fn. 138.

acts adopted by IOs normally are not directly applicable so that they cannot be challenged by the individuals before domestic and accessible international courts or tribunals, but need implementation by legislative or administrative acts of the Member States. Another reason for the dissatisfaction is the immunity IOs enjoy before the judicial institutions of States. And finally, individuals mostly lack any access to international institutions where they could institute proceedings against IOs.

For this reason, other actors, in particular the NGOs, started to defend the interests of the individuals,[157] and made their case their own, pretending to act in the name of the civil society. Although they have already obtained certain recognition in international relations and achieved a legal status in the form of a consultative status or of observers at international conferences,[158] such as the Rome Conference on the International Criminal Court,[159] they nevertheless lack access to judicial means[160] so that they voice their concern mainly through political means.

iv.   Judicial Means Available to States

Although the demand for accountability focuses mainly on the interests and rights of individuals, which could be affected by acts of IOs, it is nevertheless worthwhile to address also the right of States to resort to judicial means against IOs. In this regard, States differ from individuals not very much. In more integrated organizations, such as the EC, a highly developed system is available, which culminates in jurisdiction of the EC, in particular Article 230 ECT[161] which entitles States and, under certain conditions also individuals, to institute proceedings against the organs of the EC for breach of communitarian law.

As far as the UN is concerned, judicial instances can hardly be resorted to by States in order to challenge acts of the UN. The ICJ does not provide the *ius standi* to IOs, so that they cannot be sued. Only the Headquarter Agreements or agreements on the privileges and immunities of IOs normally provide the possibility of arbitration that is nevertheless contingent upon the explicit consent of the organization.[162] A more general competence *ratione personae*, however limited *ratione*

---

157   See *e.g.* Ratner, *op. cit.*, fn. 65, 477; Reinisch, *op. cit.*, fn. 40, 291.

158   As to the participation of NGO's in the international law creating process see Horner, *op. cit.*, fn. 25.

159   William R. Pace, Mark Thieroff, Participation of Non-Governmental Organizations, in: Roy S. Lee (ed.), *The International Criminal Court*, The Hague, London. Boston, 391-398.

160   Only exceptionally the enjoy a limited access to similar bodies, in particular by acting as amicus curiae; see Dinah Shelton, The Participation of Nongovernmental Organizations in International Judicial Proceedings, *AJIL* vol. 88, 1994, 611-642, 640.

161   See *supra*, fn. 153.

162   As far as the Immunities of IOs are concerned a recent example is the Protocol on the Privileges and Immunities of the International Seabed Authority of 1998; its Article 14 reads:

materiae, to deal with disputes in which IOs are involved by institutions outside the relevant IO is provided by the Vienna Convention on the Law of Treaties between States and international organizations or between international organizations of 1986.[163] Article 66 of this Convention stipulates that either an advisory opinion with final effect could be sought or arbitration could be resorted to in the case that a question of *ius cogens* is involved in the relevant dispute out of Part V of the Convention.[164]

Settlement of disputes
1. In connection with the implementation of the privileges and immunities granted under this Protocol, the Authority shall make suitable provision for the proper settlement of:
   (a) disputes of a private law character to which the Authority is a party;
   (b) disputes involving any official of the Authority or any expert on mission for the Authority who by reason of his or her official position enjoys immunity, if immunity has not been waived by the Secretary-General.
2. Any dispute between the Authority and a member of the Authority concerning the interpretation or application of this Protocol which is not settled by consultation, negotiation or other agreed mode of settlement within three months following a request by one of the parties to the dispute shall, at the request of either party, be referred for a final and binding decision to a panel of three arbitrators:
   (a) one to be nominated by the Secretary-General, one to be nominated by the other party to the dispute and the third, who shall be Chairman of the panel, to be chosen by the first two arbitrators;
   (b) if either party has failed to make its appointment of an arbitrator within two months of the appointment of an arbitrator by the other party, the President of the International Tribunal for the Law of the Sea shall proceed to make such appointment. Should the first two arbitrators fail to agree upon the appointment of the third arbitrator within three months following the appointment of the first two arbitrators, the third arbitrator shall be chosen by the President of the International Tribunal for the Law of the Sea upon the request of the Secretary-General or the other party to the dispute."

163 Text in: International Law Commission, *op. cit.*, fn. 129, 464.

164 The article reads:

Procedures for judicial settlement, arbitration and conciliation
1. If, under paragraph 3 of article 65, no solution has been reached within a period of twelve months following the date on which the objection was raised, the procedures specified in the following paragraphs shall be followed.
2. With respect to a dispute concerning the application or the interpretation of article 53 or 64:
   (a) if a State is a party to the dispute with one or more States, it may, by a written application, submit the dispute to the International Court of Justice for a decision;
   (b) if a State is a party to the dispute to which one or more international organizations are parties, the State may, through a Member State of the United Nations if necessary, request the General Assembly or the Security Council or, where appropriate, the competent organ of an international organization which is a party to the dispute and is authorized in accordance with Article 96 of the Charter of the United Nations, to request an advisory opinion of the International Court of Justice in accordance with article 65 of the Statute of the Court;

Apart from this possibility, the instrument of advisory opinion provided by the ICJ does not really serve as an appropriate substitute since the States have no right to request it and the ICJ is legally not obliged to accept such request by the General Assembly or other organs or organizations.[165] The idea to entitle the Secretary General with a power to request advisory opinions once advanced, was immediately rejected,[166] obviously for the reason that this right would endow this organ with too great power that it could use against organs such as the Security Council. Similar reasons seem to motivate the discussion of whether the ICJ should be entitled to review resolutions of the Security Council, which met with a different reaction in the literature[167] and was seen even as having a detrimental effect on the powers of the Security Council.[168]

Although the access of States to courts in cases against IOs is also relatively limited, again with exception of the EC, their status differs from that of individuals insofar as they participate in the shaping, elaboration and formation of the activities of IOs so that they can control them and prevent an infringement of their rights. Since any such action can be taken only with their direct or indirect consent

---

(c) if the United Nations or an international organization that is authorized in accordance with Article 96 of the Charter of the United Nations is a party to the dispute, it may request an advisory opinion of the International Court of Justice in accordance with article 65 of the Statute of the Court;

(d) if an international organization other than those referred to in sub-paragraph (c) is a party to the dispute, it may, through a Member State of the United Nations, follow the procedure specified in sub-paragraph (b);

(e) the advisory opinion given pursuant to sub-paragraph (b), (c) or (d) shall be accepted as decisive by all the parties to the dispute concerned;

(f) if the request under sub-paragraph (b), (c) or (d) for an advisory opinion of the Court is not granted, any one of the parties to the dispute may, by written notification to the other party or parties, submit it to arbitration in accordance with the provisions of the Annex to the present Convention.

3. The provisions of paragraph 2 apply unless all the parties to a dispute referred to in that paragraph by common consent agree to submit the dispute to an arbitration procedure, including the one specified in the Annex to the present Convention.

4. With respect to a dispute concerning the application or the interpretation of any of the articles in Part V, other than articles 53 and 64, of the present Convention, any one of the parties to the dispute may set in motion the conciliation procedure specified in the Annex to the Convention by submitting a request to that effect to the Secretary-General of the United Nations.

165 Nevertheless, the ICJ regularly declared its willingness to accept such a request.

166 See Mohammed Bedjaoui, Les resources offerts par la fonction consultative de la Cour International de Justice: Bilan et perspectives, in: Proceedings, *op. cit.*, fn. 52, 117-143, 142.

167 See for instance a more positive view in: Vera Gowlland-Debbas, The Relationship between the International Court of Justice and the Security Council in the Light of the *Lockerbie* Case, *AJIL* vol. 88, 1994, 643-677, 676.

168 Anthony Aust, The Role of Human Rights in Limiting the Enforcement Powers of the Security Council: A Practitioner's View, in: de Wet, Nollkaemper, *op. cit.*, fn. 36, 31-38, 36.

in accordance with the derivative nature of the IO, the appeal for more accountability should not address the IOs, but the Member States themselves. It has to be borne in mind that acts of IOs are mainly the result of the conduct of State representatives acting in double capacity, as State organs and as a part of the collective organ of IO. It seems rather unlikely that States would like to challenge acts which were created by their own representatives.

A slightly different situation would occur where States institute proceedings against an organ in which not all States are represented, such as in the case of the Security Council, or which is composed of independent individuals, such as the European Commission. This conclusion is confirmed by statistics: The cases under Article 230 ECT[169] instituted by States against acts of the Council, *i. e.* the organ consisting of State representatives, are minimal in comparison with the number of cases brought by States or individuals against the Commission, the independent body.[170]

7.   Conclusions

The demand or even request to raise the accountability of IOs results from the increase in the power and significance of IOs in today's international relations, where competences are increasingly shifted from States to IOs. The accountability should define, eventually limit the ways these organizations exercise the powers they obtain from States and overcome the deficit of democracy in IOs. The treaty law of IOs can no longer be seen as the sole legal basis of their activities so that recourse must be made to customary international law or general principles of law. These deficiencies increase with the growing significance of IOs for international relations.

For this reason, solutions are sought under the heading of accountability that reaches beyond the traditional understanding of the law of international organizations as consisting mainly of treaty law. However, this claim for increased accountability of IOs is rather a political concept than a legal one; under this motto claims are raised to make IOs aware of their obligations under international law and to endow IOs with appropriate mechanisms being aimed at protecting the rights in particular of individuals. In this perspective, this claim is raised on behalf of the civil society and is connected with the rise of the individual in international relations becoming an independent actor; its primary aim is to protect the rights and interests of individuals against the growing power of IOs. If the existing legal structures of IOs as well as those relating to IOs are measured against the claim of accountability one cannot avoid the impression of an inadequacy of legal means to protect the rights and interests of individuals against infringements by IOs; only to a certain very limited extent do the appropriate mechanisms exist. It has to be

---

169   See *supra*, fn. 153.

170   See Proceedings of the Court of Justice; Synopsis of the judgments delivered by the Court of Justice in 2001, <http://curia.eu.int/en/instit/presentationfr/rapport/act/act01/tab01cj.pdf>.

acknowledged that in some regard, in particular the awareness of the applicable law and the mechanisms to protect the rights of the individuals are not yet sufficiently developed in order to make such appeals redundant.

On the whole, the standard labelled as the accountability of international organizations is a political response to the growing actual or potential impact of IOs on international relations. But it would be wrong to direct this complaint to the IOs themselves; the Member States as being those responsible for the structures of IOs, must be the first addressees, as IOs can hardly develop activities which reach beyond the will of the States.

23. Forging a Multilayered System of Global Governance*

Charlotte Ku

1. Introduction: International Law's Challenge to Global Governance

The 1648 Peace of Westphalia marked the beginning of the system of sovereign states that remains a part of global governance today. By opting for this voluntarist system more than 300 years ago, the major powers of the day rejected a "juridical order founded on a common respect for law" in favor of a system where law operated "between rather than above states."[1] International lawyers have worked for centuries to move the international system to one of an order based on a common respect for law, and have made great progress. Indeed, the twentieth century surely will be remembered as one of the most significant in the development of international law.

During the twentieth century:

- The coverage of international law expanded to embrace both new subject matters and forms of interaction. Issues are no longer exclusively local or global, they are now often both.[2]
- The players in international law expanded both in numbers and types with the number of states tripling and private entities like corporations and non-governmental organizations gaining prominence as recognized international actors.
- The volume and pace of cross-border activity has increased.

---

* Portions of this chapter are drawn from Charlotte Ku, *Global Governance and the Changing Face of International Law,* 2001 John W. Holmes Memorial Lecture (Academic Council on the United Nations System: ACUNS Reports & Papers, 2001) and Charlotte Ku, "When *Can* Nations Go to War? Politics and Change in the UN Security System," 24 *Michigan Journal of International Law* (Summer 2003), pp. 1077-1120.

1   See Leo Gross, "The Peace of Westhpalia, 1648-1948," 42 *American Journal of International Law* (1948), p. 29.

2   See David Held, "From Executive to Cosmopolitan Multilateralism," in *Taming Globalization: Frontiers of Governance,"* edited by David Held and Mathias Koenig-Archibugi (Cambridge, UK: Polity Press, 2003), p. 162.

Ronald St. John Macdonald & Douglas M. Johnston (eds.), Towards World Constitutionalism, *pp. 631-651.*
© 2005 *Koninklijke Brill NV. Printed in The Netherlands. ISBN 90 04 14612 1.*

–   The standards of international behavior particularly in the treatment of individuals have changed so that states now ignore human rights standards at some cost to their international reputation. Although inconsistently applied as happened in Rwanda, if the violations are widespread enough, states may even risk war to correct the perceived transgression as happened in the former Yugoslavia.

A major contributing factor to this horizontal expansion has been the increased number of private actors entering into the public sphere. As an academic subject, much pioneering work to draw attention to this phenomenon of shifting boundaries can be linked to feminist scholarship that sought to raise awareness of the experience of women whose lack of public status and identity often precluded pursuit of their individual rights and the political engagement to correct that.[3] Another area that encouraged thinking about the relationship between the public and the private is in the area of international economic and trade law.[4] The public/private relationship that needed a basis for operation was in dispute settlement where the investment and trade agreements would be made by states, but the disputes often occurred between private corporations and the public authorities in the countries where trade or investment was taking place. Such innovations as the International Centre for the Settlement of Investment Disputes were created so that private parties could directly pursue a dispute against a state to resolve issues arising from investments.

In like manner, we have seen a vertical development where the international and the national systems of governance are converging to perform legislative and administrative functions for international law. This occurs because:
–   of the limited capacities of international institutions;
–   of the more developed institutional, political and legal processes that are available at the national level; and
–   working within a less institutionalized international framework can provide the opportunity for cooperation and coordination without developing a hierarchy that may make such cooperation more politically costly for states.[5]

Ensuring that the elements of such a mixed system of governance remain appropriately synchronized to support international law is the challenge that these developments have created. Taken individually, each of the developments listed above could be seen as a positive development. It is the cumulative effect of these developments that may be responsible for a sense of system-wide stress and dysfunction causing some to wonder if we are heading into a "World of Disorder."[6]

---

3   See Hilary Charlesworth and Christine Chinkin, *The Boundaries of International Law: A Feminist Analysis* (Manchester: Manchester University Press, 2000).

4   See, for example, Ronald A. Brand, "Sovereignty: The State, the Individual, and the International Legal System in the Twenty First Century," 25 *Hastings International and Comparative Law Review* (Summer 2002).

5   Anne-Marie Slaughter, "Courting the World," *Foreign Policy* (March-April 2004), p. 79.

6   See ASIL 2005 Annual Meeting Theme Statement, "New World Order or World in Disorder? Testing the Limits of International Law," available at www.asil.org.

In a 2001 lecture titled "Global Governance and the Changing Face of International Law," I observed that one of the enduring themes of international relations was expansion and diffusion. I further remarked that "[h]ow well international law has expanded its framework to address this diffusion is a key test of international law's relevance to global governance questions in the future."[7] In fact what we seem to be witnessing since the mid-twentieth century is normative growth without a related increase in the capacity of international institutions and frameworks to implement these norms. What has therefore resulted is something of a potpourri approach to governance where *ad hoc* partnerships may be formed to perform functions that the formal institutions seem unable to carry out either effectively or adequately. And what adds to the complexity of understanding governance today is that those playing important governance roles are no longer exclusively from the public sector, but also increasingly from the private sector. David Held described this situation:

> … [W]e live with a challenging paradox – that governance is becoming increasingly a multilevel, intricately institutionalized and spatially dispersed activity, while representation, loyalty and identity remain stubbornly rooted in traditional ethnic, regional and national communities.[8]

The number of governance elements in question today can be potentially destabilizing because of the number of possible disconnects among them. Or as Robert Keohane observed: "Since there is no global government, global governance involves strategic interactions among entities that are not arranged in formal hierarchies. Since there is no global constitution, the entities that wield power and make rules are often not authorized to do so by general agreement."[9] Such a multilevel system could work, but only if it has adequate capacity to govern effectively and if all elements at all levels are willing to cooperate. The role of states has therefore also changed from being one of problem solving to one of interdependence manager.[10] Working towards a juridical order with a common respect for law could provide all these elements with common purpose and direction to enhance coordination and to contribute to a generally stable governing structure. But accomplishing this may require a fundamentally changed view of world order where states remain major actors, but where the

---

7   Charlotte Ku, "Global Governance and the Changing Face of International Law," 2001 John W. Holmes Lecture, ACUNS Reports and Papers 2001 No. 2 (Academic Council on the United Nations System: 2001), p. 7.

8   David Held, "From Executive to Cosmopolitan Multilateralism," in *Taming Globalization: Frontiers of Governance*, edited by David Held and Mathias Koenig-Archibugi (Cambridge, UK: Polity Press, 2003), p. 166.

9   Robert O. Keohane, "Global Governance and Democratic Accountability," in *Taming Globalization: Frontiers of Governance*, edited by David Held and Mathias Koenig-Archibugi (Cambridge, UK: Polity Press, 2003), p. 131-2.

10 Paul Kennedy, Dirk Messner, and Franz Nuscheler, eds. *Global Trends & Global Governance* (London: Pluto Press, 2002), p. 59.

supplements to state authority and capacity may come from a wider pool of public and private institutions at both the international and national levels.

2. Strategic Interactions to Bolster Governance

Looking into the future at the end of the twentieth century, Louis Henkin wrote that the world was moving away from an emphasis on state values to a growing concern for human values.

> State autonomy remains a powerful value, but the distinction between state and human values continues to converge. The right of a state "to be let alone" subsumes the rights of its inhabitants to be let alone, to maintain their traditions and culture, as well as their ways of life.[11]

Table 1 shows the growth in multilateral treaty activity in the areas of human rights and more broadly in human welfare over 300 years of treaty activity. (Human welfare includes items like health and food safety that do not fall directly under human rights and are included in the table as "Other Human Welfare.") Although increasing in numbers, multilateral treaties that address human rights and human welfare still generally account for less than 15% of overall multilateral treaty activity.

Table 1: Multilateral Treaty Subjects by Period 1648-1995[12]

	1648-1750		1751-1850		1851-1899		1900-1925		1926-1950		1951-1975		1976-1995	
	#	%	#	%	#	%	#	%	#	%	#	%	#	%
Political/ Diplomatic	72	84	64	64	162	48.0	249	38	292	25	508	25	315	19
Military	13	18	8	8	17	8.0	55	8	99	8	80	4	59	4
Economic	1	1	13	13	143	42.0	241	36	546	46	885	43	719	44
Human Welfare			13	13	11	3.0	68	10	144	12	158	8	111	7
Cultural			1	1			7	1	17	1	34	2	24	1
Environment			1	1	3	0.8	20	3	56	5	134	7	209	13
Other					2	0.6	23	3	29	2	248	12	182	11
Period Total	86	100	100	100	338	100.0	663	100	1,183	100	2,047	100	1,619	100

The diversity of issues represented above and now managed by states has created opportunities for private entities willing to work with governments in specific ar-

---

11   Louis Henkin, Chapter XV: Politics, Values and Functions at the Turn of the Century, in *International Law: Politics and Values* (Dordrecht: Martinus Nijhoff Publishers, 1995), p. 284.

12   This table was derived from the Comprehensive Statistical Database of Multilateral Treaties (CSDMT), a project of the Honors Programs at Pennsylvania State University at Erie directed by Professor John Gamble. It originated in 1998 with a review of Christian Wiktor, *Multilateral Treaty Calendar*, 1648-1995 (1998) that Gamble prepared for

eas. This has happened as states seek to increase their resources and capacities. Power today therefore is not only in the hands of 191 states and governments and the international institutions they have created, but also in those of private entities – multinational corporations, networks of individuals, and nongovernmental organizations (NGOs).[13]

NGOs were particularly effective in areas such as human rights and the environment where states needed political support and capacity "on the ground." Private organizations had an advantage in pursuing these activities within countries that no foreign government could. But the political power and experience gained in securing the promulgation of various new portions of international law continued beyond the enactment of specific obligations to monitoring their ongoing development and implementation. Given their familiarity with the issues and the players, NGOs may in fact be more expert at monitoring and overseeing development of norms than the formal organizations created to do so on an official basis. Robert Keohane and Joseph Nye observed that in addition to the formal governance provided by states and the intergovernmental organizations that they created, governance now also takes place through networks of agents that can be both public and private, that derive credibility from their flexibility and dynamism to address new issues with the fewest start-up costs.[14]

At first glance, one would think that the intensified transborder activity and increased international regulation needed in a globalized world would be a great boost to international law. Instead, what we have seen are increased challenges to the institutional frameworks that were developed to support specific international agreements and obligations. And these challenges to institutions are often perceived as challenges to the international law and legal order that created them. The challenges to these frameworks have come from various levels – from states that act unilaterally, to individuals who organize to demonstrate against the perceived negative effects of globalization, to private terrorist networks that appear dedicated to destroying much of the world order established following World War II because of the power and value structure that the present order represents and supports. States have therefore sought to bolster their ability to govern although through strategic partnerships that may not fit the current formal institutional structure.

Several factors are responsible for this shift:

–   The increased number of individual rights and responsibilities now recognized by international law some of which can be more effectively addressed by private rather than public entities.

---

the *American Journal of International Law* (v. 93, pp. 565-6, 2000). Wiktor and other sources are being used to develop a comprehensive listing of all multilateral treaties from 1500-1999.

13   Paul Kennedy, Dirk Messner, and Franz Nuscheler, eds. *Global Trends & Global Governance* (London: Pluto Press, 2002), p. 54.

14   Robert O. Keohane and Joseph S. Nye, Jr., "Introduction." *Governance in a Globalizing World* edited by Joseph S. Nye and John D. Donohue (Brookings Institution, 2000), pp. 18-20.

–   The need for private resources to address the complex of issues that make up international law today and the perceived greater agility of the nongovernmental sector to focus on issues particularly in a media contest.[15]

–   The general acceptance that broad public participation is part of good international governance and the technology that not only makes such broad participation possible, but encourages it. As Jessica Mathews wrote: "In every sphere of activity, instantaneous access to information and the ability to put it to use multiplies the number of players who matter and reduces the number who command great authority."[16]

States seeking such strategic partnerships do so in order to strengthen the likelihood that they will remain the sovereign authorities in their territories even though they no longer "monopolize institutions of global governance, even those that they have formally established, such as the World Bank, International Monetary Fund, and World Trade Organization."[17]

The burgeoning influence of nongovernmental organizations has generated a rich literature. Although the character of their long-term influence is not fully understood, there seems little disagreement that nongovernmental organizations are now a permanent feature of the international political landscape. Fewer than 300 NGOs were represented at the 1972 UN Environment Conference in Stockholm. At the 1992 environment conference in Rio, there were 1,400 NGOs attending the parallel NGO forum. In the area of human rights, at the 1993 UN World Human Rights Conference in Vienna, 248 NGOs were registered with 593 participants. At the Mexico City UN Women's Conference in 1975, 6,000 people attended the NGO forum. In 1985, there were 13,500 individuals registered for the Nairobi UN Women's Conference. And at the 1995 UN Women's Conference in Beijing, over 300,000 individuals attended.[18]

The NGO "cottage industry" has grown to such an extent that an intergovernmental gathering can now be overshadowed by the activities of NGOs. NGOs increasingly have their own venues and activities. But their presence has created an additional source of political pressure that, if linked to other issues or to state sponsors, can develop into a potent political force. The prominence of women's issues on the international agenda today and the adoption of treaties like the Landmines

---

15   Robert O. Keohane, "Global Governance and Democratic Accountability," in *Taming Globalization: Frontiers of Governance*, edited by David Held and Mathias Koenig-Archibugi (Cambridge, UK: Polity Press, 2003), p. 131.

16   Jessica T. Mathews, "Power Shift," *Foreign Affairs* (January/February 1997), pp. 50-1.

17   Robert O. Keohane, "Global Governance and Democratic Accountability," in *Taming Globalization: Frontiers of Governance*, edited by David Held and Mathias Koenig-Archibugi (Cambridge, UK: Polity Press, 2003), p. 131.

18   Ann Marie Clark, Elisabeth J. Friedman, Kathryn Hochstetler, "The Sovereign Limits of Global Civil Society," 51 *World Politics* (October 1998), p. 9.

Convention and the Statute for an International Criminal Court, are examples of strategic NGO-state alliances that resulted in highly effective political lobbying.[19]

One study of NGO influence at world conferences concluded that: "[t]heir importance resides in their role as monitors of governments perceived as unlikely or unable to resolve global problems."[20] Another observer of UN conference activity wrote that: "The expertise and experience of NGOs are invaluable inputs in decisionmaking processes, and UN conferences have significantly helped legitimize the participation of civil society in international arenas."[21] The ongoing work of NGOs will depend somewhat on the opportunities states and state institutions (including intergovernmental conferences) provide for direct or parallel activities from NGOs and how able NGOs are to seize these opportunities or to create additional ones. The 1999 demonstrations in Seattle during the World Trade Organization summit and subsequent protests during economic summits are examples of efforts – not all successful – to create new opportunities. NGOs have demonstrated their capacities as political forces and information resources and now draw on a growing coterie of individuals experienced in the related functions of international diplomacy and communication at high profile venues.

Voluntary networks have also demonstrated their power to influence states in the monitoring of state conduct in the treatment of their own citizens. "Principled issue networks," as agents for change in state behavior and even in international standards, are a force for social change that appear to have emerged from the increased level of private transnational activity. Made possible through resources provided by foundations, spurred on by the commitment of individuals, and held together by new technologies, these transnationally linked organizations have had some notable achievements particularly in the protection of human rights.[22]

The technical character of many of the problems requiring international attention and the multi-sector cooperation needed to address them are also part of the explanation for the prominence and recognition of the power of the nongovernmental sector. Technology has also "broken governments' monopoly on the collection and management of large amounts of information."[23] Events leading up to the signing of the convention to ban the use of anti-personnel landmines (Ottawa Convention, 1997) provided an example of the new power that individuals linked by technology, organized into a political network, and working in alliance

---

19   Charlotte Ku (with John King Gamble), "International Law – New Actors and New Technologies: Center Stage for NGOs?" *Law and Policy in International Business*, Volume 31, No. 2, (Winter 2000), pp. 221-62.

20   Ann Marie Clark, Elisabeth J. Friedman, Kathryn Hochstetler, "The Sovereign Limits of Global Civil Society," 51 *World Politics* (October 1998), p. 21.

21   Jacques Fomerand, "UN Conferences: Media Events or Genuine Diplomacy?" 2 *Global Governance* (1996), p. 372.

22   Kathryn Sikkink, "Human Rights, Principled Issue-Networks, and Sovereignty in Latin America, " 47 *International Organization* (Summer 1993), pp. 411-41.

23   Jessica T. Mathews, "Power Shift," 76 *Foreign Affairs* (January/February 1997), p. 57.

with governments can wield.[24] The Internet-based campaign spearheaded by Jody Williams gained sufficient recognition for its efforts to win the Nobel Prize for Peace in 1997.

NGO involvement in the drafting of the Statute for the International Criminal Court and its role at the 1998 Rome intergovernmental conference on the ICC shows another kind of NGO role. The two year run-up to the Rome conference gave NGOs the opportunity to organize and to build relationships with UN secretariat staff and other key players in the drafting. This careful cultivation by the NGO coalition of opportunities for participation and influence paid off. At the end of the process, one NGO participant concluded that: "Governments and the team from the [UN] Office of Legal Affairs came to accept NGOs as indispensable consultants and worthwhile advocates."[25] That there may be as many ways for NGOs to be influential as there are issues does not diminish the general conclusion that they have become a political force on the international scene that is not likely to vanish.

Even decades ago, the kind of "people power" generated by Helsinki Watch, Charter 77, Solidarity and other nongovernmental groups eventually created pressures for human rights and an end to the Cold War from within the Warsaw Pact countries themselves. Yet, while it seems clear that the public sector can no longer function effectively without the cooperation and participation of the private sector and the involvement of individual citizens, it remains true that the private sector cannot solve all problems without the infrastructure and coordination that states and international institutions provide. The 1975 Helsinki Final Act of the Conference on Security and Cooperation in Europe was, after all, an intergovernmental agreement that fostered an important "human dimension" through its system of follow-up conferences. The follow-up conferences also provided opportunities for NGOs seeking to liberalize the political institutions of the Warsaw Pact countries to gain political legitimacy and for their leaders to gain confidence in political activism and in the support of the international media for their efforts. The entire process fostered nothing less than a quiet and largely bloodless revolution.[26]

These examples show the promise of such strategic partnerships. Indeed, they might even be viewed as essential in today's globalized environment. UN Secretary-General Kofi Annan expressed such views in his millennium report, "We the Peoples: The Role of the United Nations in the 21st Century." He wrote:

---

24   See Stephen Greene, "A Campaign to Sweep Away Danger," 60 *Chronicle of Philanthropy* (20 October 1997). See also Richard Price, "Transnational Civil Society Targets Land Mines," 52 *International Organization* (Summer 1998), pp. 613-44.

25   Fanny Benedetti and John L. Washburn, "Drafting the International Criminal Court Treaty: Two Years to Rome and an Afterword on the Rome Diplomatic Conference," 3 *Global Governance* (1999), p. 25.

26   See Thomas Buergenthal, "CSCE Human Dimension: The Birth of a System," in *Collected Courses of the Academy of European Law* (1992).

… while the post-war multilateral system made it possible for the new globalization to emerge and flourish, globalization, in turn, has progressively rendered its designs antiquated. Simply put, our post-war institutions were built for an inter-*national* world, but we now live in a *global* world.[27]

Annan further noted that: "We must also adapt international institutions, through which states govern together, to the realities of the new era. We must form coalitions for change, often with partners well beyond the precincts of officialdom."[28] But the *ad hoc* and selective character of these partnerships have caused concern about the effectiveness and reliability of such arrangements as durable pillars of global governance.

3. The Multiple Forms of Legal Obligation

Further adding to the complexity of the contemporary governing environment are the forms legal obligations can now take. Although the reasons for accepting obligations under international law may vary, a growing body of empirical work shows that both formal and informal obligations can influence behavior.[29] In an illuminating essay on the emergence of soft law, Christine Chinkin points to the challenges posed by the concept to global governance, but nevertheless concludes that it be maintained for the contribution that it can make. She writes:

> There is a wide diversity in the instruments of so-called soft law which makes the generic term a misleading simplification. Even a cursory examination of these diverse instruments inevitably exposes their many variables in form, language, subject matter, participants, addressees, purposes, follow up and monitoring procedures. These variables, coupled with the inherent contradictions in any concept of soft law, highlight the challenges presented to the structure and substance of the traditional legal order by the increasing use of soft law forms.[30]

Why, then adopt such a potentially confusing form of obligation? There are a number of reasons:

---

27   Kofi A. Annan, "We the Peoples: The Role of the United Nations in the 21st Century," (New York: United Nations Office of Public Information, 2000), p. 11.

28   Kofi A. Annan, "We the Peoples: The Role of the United Nations in the 21st Century," (New York: United Nations Office of Public Information, 2000), p. 7.

29   See Dinah Shelton, ed., *Commitment and Compliance: The Role of Non-Binding Norms in the International Legal System* (Oxford: Oxford University Press, 2000); Antonia Handler Chayes and Abram Chayes, *The New Sovereignty* (Cambridge: Harvard University Press, 1995), Edith Brown Weiss and Harold K. Jacobson, *Engaging Countries: Strengthening Compliance with International Environmental Accords* (Cambridge, MA: The MIT Press, 1998).

30   C.M. Chinkin, "The Challenge of Soft Law: Development and Change in International Law," 38 *International and Comparative Law Quarterly* (October 1989), p. 850.

- It is a form that can move domestic issues into the international realm for ex-ample as seen in commodity agreements or marketing specific products like breast milk substitutes.[31]
- It is a vehicle to link international law to private entities regulated principally by domestic law like individuals and transnational corporations.[32]
- It may provide states a way to come to terms without the political difficulty of undertaking a full scale legal obligation. Examples of such important "politi-cal" agreements are the Yalta agreement of 1945 and the Helsinki Final Act of 1975.
- Different forms of obligation may be combined as can be seen in environ-mental law-making where a framework convention can be followed by proto-cols that generate soft law or practice to supplement the original text. Dinah Shelton explained that: "Typically, the framework convention establishes a structure for further co-operation between the parties through monitoring and implementation procedures, exchanging data, and facilitating regulation. They also permit ease of response to changed scientific knowledge and cir-cumstances."[33]

The specific governance problem created by soft law on the international level is how to identify it as an international obligation, i.e. can it be considered to be *jus cogens* or customary international law?[34] Despite the challenges, Professor Chinkin observed that soft law is also a phenomenon that is here to stay because interna-tional affairs have outpaced the ability of the traditional law-making machinery "through international organizations, specialized agencies, programmes, and pri-vate bodies that do not fit the paradigm of Article 38(1) of the Statute of the ICJ."[35] At its best, soft law can bridge the gap "between the formalities of law-making and the needs of international life by legitimating behavior and creating stability." On the other side of the ledger, soft law can produce incoherent standards and multiple legal regimes. On balance though, Professor Chinkin argues favorably for soft law as a means to "allow for the incorporation of conflicting standards and goals and provide States with the room to manoeuvre in the making of claims and counter-

---

31   C.M. Chinkin, "The Challenge of Soft Law: Development and Change in International Law," 38 *International and Comparative Law Quarterly* (October 1989), p. 853.

32   C.M. Chinkin, "The Challenge of Soft Law: Development and Change in International Law," 38 *International and Comparative Law Quarterly* (October 1989), p. 854.

33   Christine Chinkin, "Normative Development in the International Legal System" in Di-nah Shelton, ed., *Commitment and Compliance: The Role of Non-Binding Norms in the International Legal System* (Oxford: Oxford University Press, 2000), p. 27.

34   C.M. Chinkin, "The Challenge of Soft Law: Development and Change in International Law," 38 *International and Comparative Law Quarterly* (October 1989), p. 857.

35   Christine Chinkin, "Normative Development in the International Legal System" in Di-nah Shelton, ed., *Commitment and Compliance: The Role of Non-Binding Norms in the International Legal System* (Oxford: Oxford University Press, 2000), p. 42.

claims."³⁶ We may also find that over time, soft law may harden through practice or through implementation by international or national institutions that are hard governing or regulatory regimes.

International law's challenge to global governance is therefore to provide effective regulation and problem-solving for the newly enlarged international and transnational political space that has been one of the great successes of the twentieth century. As Mary Kaldor observes, the elements of civil society – voluntary associations, movements, parties, and unions for example, enable individuals "to act publicly."³⁷ But, what about the public institutions charged with important governance functions? In many respects, these units of global governance seem out of step with the world we now live in. Several reasons help explain why this has occurred:

–   International law and the institutions it creates are state-based and therefore generally voluntary. This makes undertaking change difficult whenever a state and even more so if an important state's interest are affected by such change. A prominent example is the difficulty now faced to revise the permanent membership of the United Nations Security Council. None of the privileged states that are presently permanent members would willingly give up that privilege. On the other hand, the very voluntary character of these institutions may also make it difficult to regulate or to control powerful states that do not wish to be controlled. Examples of this are the failure of France and Germany to comply with the deficit levels set by the Maastricht Treaty for countries using the euro and the US use of force in Iraq in 2003.

–   The capacities of international institutions are limited and remain at the mercy of member states that may withhold resources for programs and operations as may suit these instincts rather than the objectives of the institutions or the programs. See, for example, the sobering conclusion of a report prepared for Congress by the General Accounting Office concluding that it may be difficult to use any results-oriented measures in state-building because donor states may pull out regardless of whether objectives have been met or not.³⁸

–   That the ability to respond to new situations can be further constrained by the need to achieve consensus among a wide range of views and interests. Indeed, the perceived need to put the most positive face on a situation in order to avoid political embarrassment was thought to be a problem for adequate preparation and training for troops assigned to UN peace-building operations.³⁹

---

36   C.M. Chinkin, "The Challenge of Soft Law: Development and Change in International Law," 38 *International and Comparative Law Quarterly* (October 1989), p. 866.

37   Mary Kaldor, "The idea of global civil society," 79 *International Affairs* (2003), p. 585.

38   See U.S. General Accounting Office, "U.N. Peacekeeping: Transition Strategies for Post-Conflict Countries Lack Results-Oriented Measures of Progress," (September 2003).

39   See UN Report of the Panel on United Nations Peace Operations (August 2000).

- That the effectiveness of international institutions may be constrained by the preceding three factors causing states to reduce further support because of a concern that the institution is no longer effective and can no longer serve their interests. This was clearly the message delivered by U.S. President George W. Bush when he addressed the United Nations General Assembly on September 12, 2002.[40]
- And finally that international institutions may not be regarded as accountable for their conduct because officials serving in these institutions are too far removed from the political processes that could bring about their dismissal.

Reflecting this development, John Rawls envisions a more explicit role for civil society as he writes: "… it may turn out that there will be many different kinds of organizations subject to the judgment of the Law of Peoples and charged with regulating cooperation among them and meeting certain recognized duties."[41] But what does such a governing system look like and what role might international law play in such a diffused and only partially institutionalized system?

4.   Elements of a Multilayered and Mixed System of Governance

As the above suggests, international law and global governance have become multilayered in part because political power has become multilayered. David Held noted that: [Political power] became diffused below, above and alongside the nation-state."[42] To address this, the state has undertaken informal governing partnerships that may not be readily identifiable, accountable or even long-lasting. Nevertheless, international lawyers should readily recognize that "norms do not operate automatically but through the activities of agents in networks."[43] These networks and *ad hoc* arrangements do not replace the formal institutionalized governing mechanisms such as the UN system, but exist alongside it.

International lawyers have long recognized the partially institutionalized character of international law and note it as a fundamental difference from domestic law when describing the nature of international law. A great effort was made through the nineteenth and twentieth centuries to institutionalize international legal activities at the international level. The effort began with the regulatory unions of the nineteenth century that were the predecessor organizations of many of the UN's specialized agencies today. The effort continued with the establishment of the League of Nations and the United Nations to provide a centerpiece for inter-

---

40   George W. Bush, Address to the UN General Assembly, September 2002.

41   John Rawls, *The Law of Peoples* (Cambridge: Harvard University Press, 1999), p. 36.

42   David Held, "From Executive to Cosmopolitan Multilateralism," in *Taming Globalization: Frontiers of Governance*, edited by David Held and Mathias Koenig-Archibugi (Cambridge, UK: Polity Press, 2003), p. 180.

43   Robert O. Keohane and Joseph S. Nye, Jr., "Introduction." *Governance in a Globalizing World* edited by Joseph S. Nye and John D. Donohue (Brookings Institution, 2000), p. 25.

national activity. The organizations were set up with a plenary body, a governing council, a secretariat and a court. The United Nations added economic and social concerns to its principal responsibilities and dedicated one of its six principal organs to those responsibilities.

The existence of this universal organization, however, did not quell the effort to develop regional organizations in the European Union and in less integrationist efforts like the Organization of American States or the African Union. And as we now move into the twenty-first century, we see that the partially institutionalized character of international law may in fact provide an advantage for its ongoing effectiveness by making it possible to work in a number of institutional settings. This means that states can join forces with each other, with sub-national components of states, with NGOs or with intergovernmental organizations in order to carry out their obligations. What may be presently lacking in this mixed system of governance is cohesion and coordination among all possible governing units and processes. Within such a non-hierarchical and partially institutionalized structure, such cohesion and coordination could be provided by a common and broad commitment to governance on the basis of respect for law. Three elements of such governance already exist and are described below. Each is tied to an institutional framework although it may not be an international one. The more institutionalized and formal framework may in fact be a national one working informally at the transnational or international level. At the same time, the transnational and international may offer the national something that it does not have operating alone – the ability to reach outside its borders. Given the globalized character of many regulatory problems today, this ability to reach beyond one's own borders and to be able to count on the assistance of counterparts in other countries is one of the incentives for cross border cooperation.

5.   Transnational Networks: Governing through Transgovernmentalism

More than 20 years ago in 1983, Harold Jacobson wrote:

> What we have … is a global political system that is already complex and growing even more complex. Nation-states retain sovereignty and consequently remain the principal actors in international politics. But all states are enmeshed in complex webs of international organizations, both governmental and nongovernmental, and their societies, rather than being sealed from one another, are linked by growing transnational connections. Although political authority continues to be centered in governments of nation-states, in reality it is widely dispersed. With respect to countless issues, to be effective governments must act together, but different issues elicit cooperation by different combinations of states. States entangled in webs of international organizations is the proper simile to describe the contemporary global political system, and international organizations, both IGOs and INGOs, are best seen as sophisticated communication devices, instruments for transmitting and relaying messages and coordinating actions. The global political system continues to consist of multiple sovereign centers

of decision making, but effective power is increasingly being organized in a non-hierarchical manner.[44]

Given the effects of globalization, this view of a non-hierarchic multi-centered political system in which both states and international institutions play roles in governance certainly seems an accurate depiction of the world today.

Fifteen years later in 1997, reflecting on similar issues, Anne-Marie Slaughter published "The Real New World Order," where she concluded that the international governance model of a multipurpose international institution like the United Nations at its center had built in limits because "it requires a centralized rule-making authority, a hierarchy of institutions, and universal membership."[45] In place of this, she observes that governance has moved into a transgovernmental order of "courts, regulatory agencies, executives, and even legislatures…networking with their counterparts abroad, creating a dense web of relations … ."[46] She argues that this can provide a much more expandable and flexible system of governance than is available through the classic system of states and intergovernmental organizations.

Transgovernmental governance works by adopting "rules concerning issues that each nation already regulates within its borders: crime, securities fraud, pollution, tax evasion," for example. Examples of such networks are the Basle Committee on Banking Supervision, the International Organization of Securities Commissioners, and the International Association of Insurance Supervisors. Another form of transgovernmental governance occurs through bilateral and plurilateral regulatory agreements in the form of Memoranda of Understanding and Mutual Legal Assistance Treaties.[47] The incentive for national regulators to use these transgovernmental rules is the transnational nature of many of the issues they now address. And working transnationally provides regulators the benefits of coordinating actions with other countries.[48] The advantage for states is the flexibility and decentralization that this approach provides. The shortcoming is in any formal accountability or oversight of such actions until or unless a conflict occurs.

An example of where a country's security may be very much dependent on activities outside that country is the effort to address the post September 11, 2001 security needs in the United States. Dean Slaughter explained:

---

44   Harold K. Jacobson, *Networks of Interdependence: International Organizations and the Global Political System,* 2nd edition (New York: Alfred A. Knopf, 1984), p. 387.

45   Anne-Marie Slaughter, "The Real New World Order," 76 *Foreign Affairs* (September/October 1997), p. 183.

46   Anne-Marie Slaughter, "The Real New World Order," 76 *Foreign Affairs* (September/October 1997), p. 184.

47   See Anne-Marie Slaughter, "Governing through Government Networks," in Michael Byers, ed., *The Role of Law in International Politics* (Oxford: Oxford University Press, 2000), pp. 177-205 and Anne-Marie Slaughter, *A New World Order* (Princeton: Princeton University Press, 2004).

48   Anne-Marie Slaughter, "The Real New World Order," 76 *Foreign Affairs* (September/October 1997), p. 191-2.

Public attention focused on military cooperation, but the networks of financial regulators working to identify and freeze terrorist assets, of law enforcement officials sharing vital information on terrorist suspects, and of intelligence operatives working to preempt the next attack have been equally important. Indeed, the leading expert in the "new security" of borders and container bombs insists that the domestic agencies responsible for customs, food safety, and regulation of all kinds must extend their reach abroad, through reorganization and much closer cooperation with their foreign counterparts....Networked threats require a networked response.[49]

For international law, this approach means a "nationalization of international law." In this vision, "[r]egulatory agreements between states are pledges of good faith, that are self-enforcing, in the sense that each nation will be better able to enforce its national law by implementing the agreement if other nations do likewise. Laws are binding or coercive only at the national level. Uniformity of result and diversity of means go hand in hand, and the makers and enforcers of rules are national leaders who are accountable to the people."[50] This is clearly a piece of the contemporary governance picture although its operation and implications for a common respect for the law may still be developing.

6.   Transnational Legal Process and Legal Internalization

Another approach that relies on national systems to implement international law is Harold Koh's view of transnational legal process. He sees the process as threefold: interaction, interpretation, and internalization.[51]

> Legal internalization occurs when an international norm is incorporated into the domestic legal system through executive action, judicial interpretation, legislative action, or some combination of the three....Judicial internalization can occur when domestic litigation provokes judicial incorporation of human rights norms either implicitly, by construing existing statutes consistently with international human rights norms, or explicitly, through what I have elsewhere called "transnational public law litigation." Legislative internationalization occurs when domestic lobbying embeds international law norms into binding domestic legislation or even constitutional law that officials of a noncomplying government must then obey as part of the domestic legal fabric.[52]

---

49   Anne-Marie Slaughter, *A New World Order* (Princeton: Princeton University Press, 2004), pp. 1-2.

50   Anne-Marie Slaughter, "The Real New World Order," 76 *Foreign Affairs* (September/ October 1997), p. 192.

51   Harold Honjuh Koh, "Why Do Nations Obey International Law?" 106 *The Yale Law Journal* (June 1997), p. 2649.

52   Harold Honjuh Koh, "Why Do Nations Obey International Law?" 106 *The Yale Law Journal* (June 1997), p. 2657.

Such internalization has given rise to a visceral backlash against the use of foreign law in U.S. courts. The editors-in-chief of *The American Journal of International Law* in an introduction to the "Agora: The United States Constitution and International Law" put it this way:

> On the docket of the United States Supreme Court in 2004 is a substantial cluster of cases at the intersection of constitutional and international law. In the previous two Supreme Court Terms, the Court had adverted to sources of law and practice outside the United States, in its treatment of constitutional claims involving the death penalty and same-sex relationships. The apparent willingness of the Court to consider international and foreign authorities in reaching its conclusions on contested issues of international law has raised to new prominence the debate over the relationship between constitutional and international law. It is not yet clear whether the new (or newly rediscovered) interest of the Court in international sources presages a long-term trend towards a more cosmopolitan constitutional jurisprudence. On the assumption that this represents more than a passing fad, advocates before the Court in the current Term—for example, in the cases involving the "enemy combatant" detainees at Guantanamo Bay—have vigorously pressed arguments concerning international and foreign law in connection with the constitutional issues at stake. The Court's acceptance of quite a few cases raising a mixture of international and constitutional questions for decision in 2004 may signal that the Court is preparing for a new era of engagement with legal developments external to the United States, or, alternatively, that it seeks to limit (or in any event to delimit) the relevance of such developments for the U.S. legal system.[53]

The tenor of the above comment suggests that the process of internalization is underway. And indeed, while controversy may rage on the appropriate use of international law at the level of the U.S. Supreme Court, the Chief Justice of the Supreme Court of Texas noted that:

> ... both state courts and federal courts have, since the inception of the Republic, applied and developed international law. The constitutional framers could have structured the government so that most of this authority would lodge in the federal system, but they declined to do so. Congress could have used the jurisdictional grant in the Constitution to place most international questions in federal court, but it has likewise declined to do so. Thus the state courts remain vital partners in the interpretation and application of both formal and customary international law.[54]

---

53   Lori Fisler Damrosch and Bernard H. Oxman, "Editors' Introduction to Agora: The United States Constitution and International Law," 98 *American Journal of International Law* (January 2004), p. 42.

54   Thomas R. Philips, "State Supreme Courts: Local Courts in a Global World," 38 *Texas International Law Journal* (Special 2003), p. 558.

Justice Philips further predicted that in certain areas, international cases would increase and particularly for state courts because of the nature of those cases in the criminal and family law areas that have traditionally been the province of state courts. At the same time, Justice Phillips noted that there may be an overall decline of international cases as mediation and extra-judicial proceedings are used more frequently even for family law and trade matters. But, he concludes that as long as courts retain a role in handling international matters, state courts in the United States will be among them.[55]

A special example of internalization comes from the European Union. Anne-Marie Slaughter and Walter Mattli described this:

> Until 1963 the enforcement of the Rome treaty [the constituent treaty of the European Union], like that of any other international treaty, depended entirely on action by the national legislatures of the member states of the community. By 1965, a citizen of a community country could ask a national court to invalidate any provision of domestic law found to conflict with certain directly applicable provisions of the treaty. By 1975, a citizen of an EC country could seek the invalidation of national law found to conflict with self-executing provisions of community secondary legislation, the "directives" to national governments passed by the EC Council of Ministers. And by 1990, community citizens could ask their national courts to interpret national legislation consistently with community legislation in the face of undue delay in passing directives on the part of national legislatures.[56]

The pioneering work in the development of a regional human rights system that the jurisprudence of the European Court of Human Rights represents is a further important example of the interactions between extra-national and national systems of law.

One of the more sweeping recent examples of incorporation is that of the British incorporation of the European Convention on Human Rights into its domestic law that "marks a dramatic shift in how individual rights are conceptualized under British law ….The Human Rights Act, which puts courts and other public authorities under a positive duty to 'give effect' to the rights enumerated in the European Convention in their day-to-day activities, marks a shift in the perception of civil liberties from residual freedoms to positive rights."[57]

States undertake such dramatic changes because of the advantages to being part of a regional system. It may be worth remembering that the genesis of the European human rights system was the desire to create normative and institutional safeguards against the atrocities and genocide committed by Nazi Germany. These safeguards

---

55   Thomas R. Philips, "State Supreme Courts: Local Courts in a Global World," 38 *Texas International Law Journal* (Special 2003), pp. 564-5.

56   Anne-Marie Burley (Slaughter) and Walter Mattli, "Europe Before the Court: A Political Theory of Legal Integration," 47 *International Organization* (Winter 1993), p. 42.

57   Douglas W. Vick, "The Human Rights Act and the British Constitution," 37 *Texas International Law Journal* (2002), p. 330.

called for transnational oversight and monitoring of national actions as represented by the investigations of the European Commission on Human Rights and subsequent adjudication before the European Court of Human Rights. The system, however, does not mandate homogeneity. Indeed, it provides for a structure in which differences can be recognized and accepted as a tolerable difference that does not stand in the way of the protection of human rights that is the Convention's primary objective.

7.   Global Governance through Coordination

Perhaps one of the most serious apparent inadequacies of the present governance system is in the area of the use of force. Whether it has been understanding the appropriate normative approach to the concept of humanitarian intervention or of preemptive action in the face of some other perceived threat, the UN Charter system dealing with the use of force has come under increasing stress since the end of the Cold War in 1989.[58] But, if the current structure of international institutions does not effectively address these questions, does this necessarily mean the return to a self-judging and unregulated international security system?

Implicit in that question is the assumption that without international regulation by international institutions, state behavior is essentially unregulated. Such a conclusion would overlook the considerable number of national safeguards that can exist at the state level to protect against the wanton loss of lives and resources through military operations that do not serve a state's interests. This is relevant to international regulation because the international system also tries to eliminate the unregulated use of force in order to minimize destruction and loss of life and as such, is consistent with the purposes of many national safeguards.

National safeguards are not a substitute for international regulation, but when international regulation fails or proves inadequate, regulation can and does move to the national level. National safeguards further come in two forms – the formal and the informal. Formal safeguards are found in constitutions and national institutions such as legislatures, courts, and budgets.[59] Informal safeguards operate through political culture and public opinion.[60] The effectiveness of these safeguards varies widely depending on the strength of the domestic political system including whether it is democratic and how open it is to public debate or not.

---

58   See Boutros Boutros-Ghali, *An Agenda for Peace* (New York: United Nations Department of Public Information, 1995).

59   For examples of constitutional restraints, see Lori Fisler Damrosch, "The interface of national constitutional systems with international law and institutions on using military forces: changing trends in executive and legislative powers," in Charlotte Ku and Harold K. Jacobson, *Democratic Accountability and the Use of Force in International Law* (Cambridge: Cambridge University Press, 2003), pp. 39-60.

60   For examples of such political factors, see Karen A. Mingst, "Domestic political factors and decisions of use military forces," in Charlotte Ku and Harold K. Jacobson, *Democratic Accountability and the Use of Force in International Law* (Cambridge: Cambridge University Press, 2003), pp. 61-80.

National political and legal processes may also take on more prominent roles in cases when international law appears inadequate to address particular circumstances. When existing international standards and structures are under stress, national debate and political process may help to fill the gap and set the criteria for action as well as the limits for such operations.[61] The closer the use of military force gets to war, the more will national systems play a role in the decision to take part in such operations and in overseeing their operation. This process in turn contributes to shaping both the practice and scope of international action. As the Panel on UN Peace Operations concluded in 2001: "[T]he United Nations does not wage war. Where enforcement action is required, it has consistently been entrusted to coalitions of willing States, with the authorization of the Security Council acting under Chapter VII of the Charter."[62]

The interactions of international and domestic decision-making processes have been well recognized in international organization studies like Robert Cox and Harold Jacobson who concluded in their classic study of decision-making, *The Anatomy of Influence,* that the significance of international organizations is better judged "not as how independent they are of states, but how far they involve the effective policy-making process of governments."[63] What debates over the 2003 war in Iraq now tell us is that involving the effective policy-making processes of national governments is no longer adequate in all cases. National decision-making processes require certain levels of legitimacy that may now include appropriate international authorization and standards.

Another example of the current influence of international institutions is the generalized move towards multilateralism as the basis for foreign policy. This view has been most publicly advanced by two of the principal powers of the European Union, France and Germany. The French view has been described as stemming from:

> … its opposition to any kind of domination or hegemony of the world scene by a single state; France has a preference for multipolarity, of which the Security Council is an institutional component and safeguard. The UNSC remains the only international institution able to legitimize the use of force. In the Kosovo crisis…France was keen to find a legal basis for action by NATO in the previous resolutions of the Security Council, even if this justification was difficult to sustain. When urgency prevents such authorization beforehand, France still insists on having the Security Council ratify *a posteriori* an intervention. The continuous efforts made by France to get the UNSC involved in the Kosovo crisis, after the military intervention started in the spring of 1999, derived directly from this opposition to *ad hoc* multipolarity.[64]

---

61   See Adam Roberts, "NATO's 'Humanitarian War,'" *Survival* (Autumn 1999), p. 107.

62   UN Report of the Panel on United Nations Peace Operations (August 2000).

63   Robert W. Cox and Harold K. Jacobson, *The Anatomy of Influence: Decision Making in International Organization* (New Haven: Yale University Press, 1974), p. 428.

64   Yves Boyer, Serge Sur, and Olivier Fleurence, "France: Security Council legitimacy and executive primacy," in Charlotte Ku and Harold K. Jacobson, *Democratic Accountabil-*

And even in the United States, poll after poll showed that Americans prefer that their government work under a UN or other multilateral mandate whenever possible. Those surveyed, however, also indicated that they looked for effectiveness in these mandates.[65] The coordinated approach therefore meshes the international and national with increased prominence of the international at certain levels of activity like the initial authorization of the use of force.

8. Conclusion: Imagining a Multilayered System of Governance

The pressures on international institutions created by the growth in international law in the twentieth century coupled with the economic, social, and political forces collectively known as globalization have produced gaps in global governance. These gaps have created concern about the viability of any global order if individual states begin to act on their own and revert to the voluntarist system of international relations that existed prior to the twentieth century. But as we review some of the innovations that have developed to increase the capacity of states and international institutions to regulate and to manage the issues they face, the future of global governance may not be as dire as one might imagine. States are seeking ways to address problems and to manage issues in ways that can also contribute to global governance over time.

The ability of these new governance channels to operate in a coordinated way, however, will depend in part on the ability of international lawyers to think in a global and transnational way. In other words, we must begin to develop an awareness of states as part of a globalized system of governance system that does not consist only of international institutions. States may contribute to global governance by working with each other, and with the private and NGO sectors, not only through international institutions. The means by which states contribute to governance may differ. They include informal relations, incorporation, and coordination to pursue common goals, implement international standards, and carry out international obligations.

This is not a return to some form of early Westphalianism where multiple units compete without regard to the general order. It is rather recognition of a complex governing system in which elements of global governance act in less formal and less hierarchical ways in order to increase the flexibility and speed with which they can address new developments. Even though the existing system of institutionalized global governance may be under stress, this does not mean a return to unregulated state behavior. But if states cannot be made to act in the collective interest through international institutions, how can they be expected to do so when regulating activities through informal structures and processes? This is where some

---

ity and the Use of Force in International Law (Cambridge: Cambridge University Press, 2003), p. 287.

65   Chicago Council on Foreign Relations, Worldviews 2002 Survey of American and European Attitudes and Public Opinion on Foreign Policy: American Public Opinion & Foreign Policy available at htto://www.worldviews.org/index.html.

broad general principles with a common objective of establishing a juridical order with a common respect for law might be helpful. Such principles might include:

1. A commitment to a rule-based, but not necessarily institutionalized international system that is sufficiently robust to address the myriad challenges and issues that now face states and that is effective in addressing a state's interests and responsibilities.
2. A commitment to creating the conditions that will compel states to close the economic, political, and social gaps that presently exist within societies and throughout the world. A rule-based system cannot work unless the rules appear to provide all with equal opportunity and the means to pursue interests within the system.
3. A commitment to effective management of transnational problems through strategic public and private sector partnerships.
4. A commitment to "consultation and active assistance" in the place of "unilateral action and noninterference."[66]
5. A commitment to broad participation by all who are affected by an issue.

The effective operation of a multilayered system of governance will require the commentary and insight of jurists around the world. Article 38, paragraph 1 of the Statute of the International Court of Justice recognizes such a function since it includes "judicial decisions and the teachings of the most highly qualified publicists of the various nations, as subsidiary means for the determination of the rules of law." This will ensure effective interaction of the disparate elements of a global governance system.

This multilayered system is already in operation, but perhaps not yet well understood by international lawyers. It is one where additional forms of governance, some of which might be *ad hoc*, will work alongside existing international institutions to carry out international obligations. This will provide greater flexibility and increase the resources available to address problems as they arise and provide a means to harness global resources for local problems. Globalization has created a world where local problems and issues have far reaching and sometimes global effects. Globalization has also provided the means for broad participation in the resolution of such issues. The measure of international law's success will be its effectiveness in addressing issues and creating the means to formulate solutions. International lawyers will need to think and work beyond existing institution-centered concepts to encompass a wider variety of processes and agents to give life and meaning to international legal obligations. Present conditions provide international law with an opportunity to take center stage as the hub of a multilayered and multidimensional system of global governance.

---

66 Anne-Marie Slaughter, *A New World Order* (Princeton: Princeton University Press, 2004), p. 30.

Part 5

Confrontations with Established Principles of
International Law

24. Security Concerns and National Sovereignty in the Age of World-Wide Terrorism

Vaughan Lowe

For many States, the security concerns in the age of world-wide terrorism are much the same as they have been for many years. Some States have faced terrorist threats for decades: others face practically no serious terrorist threats. Almost all States maintain military and security forces whose responsibilities may range from constant readiness to repel invasion of the State, to assistance for the civil authorities in the maintenance of law and order and coping with natural disasters. It is doubtful whether the world at large has made fundamental adjustments in the disposition or tasking of its military forces in the wake of the Al Qaida attacks of 11 September 2001, which are widely regarded as marking the beginning of the age of world-wide terrorism.

There are changes in the military environment, notably those propelled by the spiralling costs of modern military hardware and the social costs of maintaining large military forces. These changes are evident in the changing security regime in Europe, for example. The structure and capabilities of NATO have been streamlined in the wake of the ending of the Cold War and the changing demands for military interventions in the Balkans and elsewhere, and in accordance with the procedures of agreements such as the treaty on Conventional Forces in Europe ("CFE").[1] There have been changes in the laws of war, with the outlawing (or, more properly, the agreed multilateral abandonment) of certain types of weapon, such as anti-personnel landmines.[2] Other parts of the world have seen comparable developments. For instance, in May 2004, the African Union launched its Peace and Security Council, which it aims to reinforce with a 15,000-strong rapid reaction force by 2010.[3] These developments are important; but, with the exception of the major developments in regional organizations, they are largely evolutionary. They

---

[1] See <http://www.nato.int/>.

[2] See, e.g., <http://www.armscontrol.org/treaties/>.

[3] See <http://africa.iafrica.com/c2cnews/324941.htm>. And see the African Union website, <http://www.africa-union.org/home/Welcome.htm>.

Ronald St. John Macdonald & Douglas M. Johnston (eds.), Towards World Constitutionalism, *pp. 655-679.*
© 2005 *Koninklijke Brill NV. Printed in The Netherlands.* ISBN 90 04 14612 1.

are not radical changes resulting primarily from the emergence of world-wide terrorism as a new phenomenon.

This paper focuses not upon those evolutionary developments, but upon the
changes that are linked to the world-wide terrorist threat and to responses to it.
The novelty of that threat must not be overstated. In Sri Lanka and Peru, in the
United Kingdom and Spain, in Russia and Indonesia, to name but a few, terrorist
activity has been a feature of life for very many years. It may be said that the terrorism that has been faced by those States is different from the current "global"
terrorist threat, being largely an expression of separatist or other internal political
conflicts; and that the exceptional groups that did have larger political agendas,
such as the Baader-Meinhof group and the Red Brigades, had relatively little impact. The threat exemplified by Al Qaida, on this view, is of a quite different order:
a world-wide terrorist conspiracy that threatens all States.

It is far from clear that such an analysis is correct. First, there is the obvious
point that one terrorist attack is much like another: as physical events they do not
vary according to the motives behind them. It may, however, be objected that the
geographical scope of contemporary terrorism is a new factor and does render it
a threat to each and every State. That would be correct if terrorists could properly
be regarded, as pirates have traditionally been regarded, as *hostes humani generis*
– the common enemies of humankind. In that case every State would have an
interest in repressing their activity. In fact, terrorists tend not to be *hostes humani
generis* in the way that, say, pirates are. The difference is that pirates are, by definition, acting for private ends,[4] and everyone (and every State) wants to hold on to
their own money. Terrorists, on the other hand, use terror as an instrument for
advancing a political, religious or ideological cause, which is necessarily a sectional
interest. It is almost inevitable that *some* States, even if not actively supporting the
cause in question, will at least have a very much lesser interest in repressing any
given terrorist group than do other States, if only because of the tendency to be
tolerant of the behaviour of one's enemy's enemies.

There are exceptions. Anarchists have traditionally been regarded as the enemies of all governments;[5] but it is now a century since anarchists have presented
anything like a sustained terrorist threat to governments. Currently, the most plausible candidates for the *hostes humani generis* label are probably the handful of
people prepared to use extreme violence in defence of animal rights. But even they
are not in fact a threat to all States, but only to those States in which experimentation on animals, or maltreatment of animals, is prominent. Certainly Al Qaida and
the groups said to be allied to it are not threatening all States. Their primary targets
are very obviously the States and communities that make up that curious politico-
economic grouping 'the West'. Some aspects of the activities of some groups linked
to Al Qaida may threaten to destabilise other States, notably those with communities within which militant Islam might be thought to be a cause, catalyst or vehicle
for discontent with the ruling State authorities. But it is hard to see a real qualita-

---

4   See the 1982 UN Convention on the Law of the Sea, Article 101.

5   See, *e.g.,* the English case of *Meunier*, [1894] 2 QB 415.

tive change in the nature of the terrorist threat, beyond the change in the scale of the threat that the events of 9/11 signified.

Moreover, it is far from clear that the groups responsible for the September 11th, Bali, Madrid and other terrorist outrages are linked so closely that they should be regarded as parts of the same organization, rather than as separate manifestations of the same underlying problem. The *modus operandi* of terrorist groups does not easily lend itself to formation of organs such as the Comintern. If, as I believe, this is correct, the term "world-wide terrorism" in the title of this paper must be understood as referring not to a world-wide conspiracy but rather to a world-wide (or at least, a widely spread) phenomenon.

It is, then, unhelpful to think in terms of a world-wide terrorist conspiracy that threatens all States. Nonetheless, even if terrorism is not qualitatively new, and is not a universal threat, the scale of the violence that terrorists now employ, the weapons (including weapons of mass destruction) now available to them, and the geographical range over which they may be deployed, have undoubtedly effected a significant change in the dimensions of the phenomenon. This was the theme of a speech by the British Prime Minister, delivered in March 2004. It is such a clear statement of this view, from the leader of a State that is likely to act upon it, that it is worth quoting at some length:[6]

> Everything about our world is changing: its economy, its technology, its culture, its way of living.
>
> If the 20th century scripted our conventional way of thinking, the 21st century is unconventional in almost every respect.
>
> This is true also of our security.
>
> The threat we face is not conventional. It is a challenge of a different nature from anything the world has faced before. It is to the world's security, what globalisation is to the world's economy.
>
> It was defined not by Iraq but by September 11th. September 11th did not create the threat Saddam posed.
>
> But it altered crucially the balance of risk as to whether to deal with it or simply carry on, however imperfectly, trying to contain it.
>
> Let me attempt an explanation of how my own thinking, as a political leader, has evolved during these past few years.
>
> Already, before September 11th the world's view of the justification of military action had been changing.
>
> The only clear case in international relations for armed intervention had been self-defence, response to aggression.
>
> But the notion of intervening on humanitarian grounds had been gaining currency. I set this out, following the Kosovo war, in a speech in Chicago in 1999, where I called for a doctrine of international community, where in certain clear circumstances, we do intervene, even though we are not directly threatened.

---

6   The speech appears at <http://news.bbc.co.uk/2/hi/uk_news/politics/3536131.stm>.

I said this was not just to correct injustice, but also because in an increasingly inter-dependent world, our self-interest was allied to the interests of others; and seldom did conflict in one region of the world not contaminate another.

We acted in Sierra Leone for similar reasons, though frankly even if that country had become run by gangsters and murderers and its democracy crushed, it would have been a long time before it impacted on us. But we were able to act to help them and we did.

So, for me, before September 11th, I was already reaching for a different philosophy in international relations from a traditional one that has held sway since the treaty of Westphalia in 1648; namely that a country's internal affairs are for it and you don't interfere unless it threatens you, or breaches a treaty, or triggers an obligation of alliance.

I did not consider Iraq fitted into this philosophy, though I could see the horrible injustice done to its people by Saddam. However, I had started to become concerned about two other phenomena.

The first was the increasing amount of information about Islamic extremism and terrorism that was crossing my desk. Chechnya was blighted by it. So was Kashmir. Afghanistan was its training ground.

Some 300 people had been killed in the attacks on the USS Cole and US embassies in East Africa.

The extremism seemed remarkably well financed. It was very active. And it was driven not by a set of negotiable political demands, but by religious fanaticism.

The second was the attempts by states – some of them highly unstable and repressive – to develop nuclear weapons programmes, CW and BW materiel, and long-range missiles.

What is more, it was obvious that there was a considerable network of individuals and companies with expertise in this area, prepared to sell it.

All this was before September 11th. I discussed the issue of WMD with President Bush at our first meeting in Camp David in February 2001.

...

September 11th was for me a revelation. What had seemed inchoate came together.

The point about September 11th was not its detailed planning; not its devilish execution; not even, simply, that it happened in America, on the streets of New York. All of this made it an astonishing, terrible and wicked tragedy, a barbaric murder of innocent people.

But what galvanised me was that it was a declaration of war by religious fanatics who were prepared to wage that war without limit. They killed 3000.

But if they could have killed 30,000 or 300,000 they would have rejoiced in it.

The purpose was to cause such hatred between Moslems and the West that a religious jihad became reality; and the world engulfed by it.

That is a good summary of a view which appears to be current in many western States. It sees the new terrorism as a serious threat even to distant States, threatening massive international instability, and death and destruction on a massive scale. The old international law, which forbids unilateral interventions by one State in another sovereign State except for the purposes of self-defence (to which State practice is arguably adding the additional exception of humanitarian intervention), is inadequate to deal with this threat. International law must change.

This view has become encapsulated in the phrase, "the war against terrorism." That phrase signals a new approach to international law, permitting armed interventions in foreign States which the 'traditional' international law (that is, international law as it was generally understood to be prior to 11 September 2001, and is still understood by most international lawyers to be) would condemn as violations of sovereignty and of the prohibition on the use of force in international relations. The central argument of this paper is that it is unhelpful, and perhaps even dangerous, to frame the legal response to terrorism in such terms, and particularly in terms of a "war against terrorism." There are three reasons why this is so. First, it is wrong as a matter of law to characterize terrorist attacks as "wars", and to do so leads to unhelpful consequences; second, the conflation, which underlies and sustains the error, of the ordinary law-enforcement powers of a government with the wholly exceptional emergency powers that governments arrogate to themselves in war-time creates a risk, already eventuating, of the serious erosion of established legal principles and of fundamental human rights; and third, the error impedes proper consideration of what does need to be done to address the very serious threat that is undoubtedly constituted by the new wave of 'global' terrorism. I shall address these three points in turn in this chapter.

1.   The Non-War Against Terrorism

A.   The Definition of "War"

First, the question of the "war against terror". For international lawyers, "war" is a term of art. It signifies a condition, a state of affairs, in relations between two or more States that is quite distinct from the usual state of "peace" (itself a term of art in this context). "War" as a legal term has a particular meaning, and it does not extend to what are often called 'asymmetric' conflicts between States and terrorist groups. This fact may become obscured by the used of the term "armed conflict" to describe the situations in which what used to be called the Law of War, and is now (since the renunciation of war as an instrument of national policy in the 1928 Kellog-Briand Pact[7]) more usually called the Law of Armed Conflict or Humanitarian Law, applies. The "armed conflict" label was, however, designed to meet a specific problem; and properly understood it did not effect the radical change in the scope of the legal state of war that is sometimes supposed.

For most of its history, public international law permitted recourse to war as an instrument of foreign policy. The movement from the state of Peace to the state of War, in legal terms, was traditionally signalled by the making of a formal declaration of war, which brought into operation the Law of War between the States concerned. The sheer scale of the futile waste of the Great War of 1914-1918 generated

---

7   <http://www.yale.edu/lawweb/avalon/kbpact/kbpact.htm>.

an unprecedented willingness on the part of States to contemplate the acceptance of formal and legally-binding limitations upon their right to wage war. The international community sought to outlaw the use of war as an instrument of foreign policy. Restrictions on recourse to war accepted under the Covenant of the League of Nations, and the renunciation of war in the 1928 Kellog-Briand Pact, were the most significant steps in this regard. During the 1930s, however, there were several international conflicts which were not preceded by declarations of war and which were argued to be not acts of "war", but rather uses of armed force (or the threat of armed force) that fell short of what was, in law, "war". The hostilities between Japan and China in the 1930s, and the Italo-Ethiopian conflict of 1935-36, are the best-known examples. If, as a matter of law, those conflicts were indeed not "wars", they escaped the constraints imposed by the League Covenant and the Pact of Paris on the waging of war.

The legal loophole was obvious; and although no-one would argue that that those who sought to argue their way through it were blind to the inconsistency between the armed attacks of the 1930s and the spirit of the internationally-agreed constraints, it was plainly desirable that the loophole be blocked. Accordingly, when the UN Charter was drafted, it prohibited not simply recourse to "war" but *all* uses of armed force. Article 2(4) of the UN Charter, reads as follows:

> All Members shall refrain in their international relations from the threat or use of force against the territorial integrity of political independence of any state, or in any other manner inconsistent with the Purposes of the United Nations."

It was intended to establish a comprehensive prohibition on the use of armed force in international relations, against other States. It was not intended to widen the scope of the Charter so as to regulate the way in which States dealt with internal threats to their security. The use of force otherwise than against other States was not prohibited. The use of force internally to repress non-State actors falls outside Article 2(4). The point is reinforced by Article 2(7) of the Charter, which forbids the UN to interfere in matters within the domestic jurisdiction of its Member States. Similarly, Article 2(4) of the Charter imposes its obligation upon "Members" – that is, States, which alone are eligible for membership of the UN: uses of force *by* non-State actors were not addressed by Article 2(4).

The change in focus from "war" to "use of force" was reflected in the 1949 Geneva Conventions, which state in Common Article 2 that they apply to "all cases of declared war or of any other armed conflict." Undeclared wars are one "other" category of armed conflicts. Civil wars, or "non-international armed conflicts" in the terminology of the 1977 Protocols to the Geneva Conventions, are the other.[8] There is no agreed international definition of "war or other armed conflicts" in this context; but there are well-established criteria that mark out those conflicts that do fall within this category of conflicts that are regulated by international law

---

8   The Geneva Conventions and their Protocols appear at <http://www.icrc.org/Web/Eng/siteengo.nsf/html/genevaconventions>.

from those that do not. As might be expected of criteria generated by "the Law of Nations", they are aimed at identifying wars that might be said to be wars between "nations". The criteria relate to the organized nature and the territorial bases of the parties to the conflict, and to the intensity of the conflict.

B.   The Organization Nature and Territorial Bases of the Combatants

War is normally thought of as a matter between two or more States. States exemplify the "organized" parties to an armed conflict; but they are not the only grouping that may be a party to what is in law an armed conflict. That is clear from the fact that colonial wars of independence and civil wars are included in the category of armed conflicts. The rebel forces may wish to become a State, or to take over the State: but while the conflict continues, they are not a State. Nonetheless, it is necessary that the rebels be organized and have control over areas of territory.[9] Organization does not mean simply that they must have a command structure, although that is a necessary element. It means that they must be assuming and discharging responsibilities for running the territory. That is, they must maintain a minimal public order, exercising quasi-governmental authority within the area that they control.[10] This characteristic is reflected in the long-established principle that once insurgents secure control over an appreciable area of territory within a State they are entitled to recognition as belligerents in a civil war, so that third States fall under a duty to remain impartial in relation to the warring parties.[11] For violence to amount to an armed conflict as a matter of international law, the crucial requirement is thus that each of the combatant parties be organized and have a territorial base.[12]

It is this requirement for organization and a territorial base that distinguishes entities that can qualify as parties to what is in law an armed conflict from "bandits" or "terrorists" and so on. Terrorists do not have a territorial base –or at least, they cannot qualify as parties to an armed conflict unless they do. As the Belgian Cour de Cassation put it:

> War is a collection of military operations or hostilities between regular or irregular troops. Acts of terrorism having no connection with acts of war cannot be considered as war, irrespective of the fact that the terrorism in question was directed against persons considered as enemies by the perpetrators of that terrorism.[13]

---

9   See, *e.g.*, *Prosecutor* v. *Blaškić* (ICTY, 2000), 122 ILR 2 at 40 paragraph 64; *Prosecutor* v. *Tadić (Judgment)*, 112 ILR 2, at 180 and 181, paragraphs 564, 566.

10   *Cf.*, the approach to the recognition of acts of rebel governments: *Texas* v. *White*, 74 US 700 (1868) at 733.

11   See, *e.g.*, the *Spanish Civil War Pension Entitlement* case (F. R. Germany, Federal Social Court. 1978), 80 ILR 666 at 668-669.

12   See, *e.g.*, *Prosecutor* v. *Blaškić* (ICTY, 2000), 122 ILR 2 at 40 paragraph 64; *Prosecutor* v. *Tadić (Judgment)*, 112 ILR 2, at 180 and 181, paragraphs 564, 566.

13   *Fonds des Accidents du Travail* v. *Société Anonyme 'Compagnie d'Assurances Urbaine / UAP*, (1988), 91 ILR 256 at 258.

This distinction between acts of war and terrorist acts has been adopted in the decisions of municipal courts, in cases such as the *Spanish Civil War Pension Entitlement* case (Germany, Federal Social Court, 1978),[14] *End Conscription Campaign* v. *Minister of Defence* (South Africa, Supreme Court, 1988);[15] and *Fonds des Accidents* v. *Cie d'Assurances*, (Belgium, Cour de Cassation, 1988).[16] It is true that acts of terrorism may be committed in the course of an armed conflict: that is recognised in the Geneva Conventions.[17] If terrorists do control territory and have an organization, the conflict in which they are involved may amount to a war or armed conflict despite the fact that it involves the commission of terrorist acts. But acts of terrorism alone, unconnected with a territorially-based armed conflict, do not amount to a war.

The essence of the matter is that there should be an armed contest for control of the government of all or part of the State.[18] The French attack on the *Rainbow Warrior* in a New Zealand harbour,[19] for example, was plainly an attack in a foreign State by agents of a "group with significant attributes of sovereignty" (*viz.*, France), but it was equally clearly not part of a sustained attempt to take over any part of New Zealand. It was an isolated (but deplorable) act of violence. This is the approach that was adopted by the Appeals Chamber of the International Criminal Tribunal for the former Yugoslavia ("ICTY") in the case of *Prosecutor* v. *Tadić (Jurisdiction)*. It referred to the "intensity requirements applicable to both international and internal armed conflicts"[20] and said:

> ... we find that an armed conflict exists whenever there is resort to armed force between States or protracted armed violence between governmental authorities and organized armed groups or between such groups within a State. International humanitarian law applies from the initiation of such armed conflicts and extends beyond the cessation of hostilities until a general conclusion of peace is reached; or, in the case of internal conflicts, a peaceful settlement is achieved. Until that moment, international humanitarian law continues to apply in the whole territory of the warring States or, in the case of internal conflicts, the whole territory under the control of a party, whether or not actual combat takes place there.[21]

This approach was elaborated in the case of *Prosecutor* v. *Tadić (Judgment)*, where Trial Chamber II of the ICTY said that:

---

14   80 *International Law Reports* 666.

15   87 *International Law Reports* 257.

16   91 *International Law Reports* 256.

17   See Article 33 of the Fourth Geneva Convention.

18   See, *e.g.*, *Société Purfina Française* v. *Compagnie d'Assurances la Nationale* (France, Cour de Cassation. 1962), 44 ILR 439 at 440; *Bull.* Civ.1962, I, p. 396.

19   See 74 ILR 241.

20   105 ILR 420 at 489, paragraph 70. Cited with approval in *Prosecutor* v. *Nikolić (Rule 61)*, 108 ILR 21 at 35.

21   105 ILR 420 at 488, paragraph 70.

The test applied by the Appeals Chamber to the existence of an armed conflict for the purposes of the rules contained in the Common Article 3 focuses on two aspects of a conflict: the intensity of the conflict and the organization of the parties to the conflict. In an armed conflict of an internal or mixed character, these closely related criteria are used solely for the purpose, as a minimum, of distinguishing an armed conflict from banditry, unorganized and short-lived insurrections, or terrorist activities, which are not subject to international humanitarian law.[22]

The same view has been taken by municipal courts. The question was subjected to a lengthy analysis in two US cases, *Pan American*[23] and *Holiday Inns.*[24] "War" or "armed conflict", they held, can be conducted only by territorially-based organized political entities. As the *Pan American* court put it:

> war is a course of hostility engaged in by entities that have at least significant attributes of sovereignty.[25]

C.   *The Intensity of the Conflict*

The second element in the definition of a "war" or "armed conflict" is the requirement, referred to by the ICTY in the passages just quoted, that the violence has reached a certain level of intensity. The requirement of intensity is sometimes described in terms of the "scope and extent" of the conflict.[26] This criterion aims to determine whether an outbreak of violence is, to put it crudely, "big" enough to amount to a war or is, on the other hand, an isolated attack or a low-level skirmish. This is important in the context of inter-State conflicts, where it is necessary to distinguish between isolated acts of violence and all-out war. An incident that consists in firing across the border by an ill-disciplined platoon is clearly an attack on the other State; but it does not of itself precipitate a state of war. The distinction between the generalized violence of an "armed conflict" and isolated acts of violence

---

22   112 ILR 2, at 179 paragraph 562, citing Jean Pictet (gen. ed.) *Commentary, Geneva Convention for the Amelioration of the Condition of the Wounded, Sick and Shipwrecked Members of Armed Forces at Sea*, Convention II (ICRC, Geneva, 1960), 33 ("*Commentary*, Geneva Convention II"); Jean Pictet (gen. ed.) *Commentary, Geneva Convention Relative to the Treatment of Prisoners of War*, Convention III, (ICRC, Geneva, 1960), 37 ("*Commentary*, Geneva Convention III"). 47. (ICRC, Geneva, 1952) 49-50.

23   *Pan American World Airways, Inc.* v. *Aetna Casualty & Surety Co.*, 505 F.2d 989 (1974).

24   *Holiday Inns Inc.* v. *Aetna Insurance Company*, 571 F.Supp. 1460 (1983).

25   *Pan American World Airways, Inc.* v. *Aetna Casualty & Surety Co.*, 505 F.2d 989 at 1012. Cited with approval in *Holiday Inns Inc.* v. *Aetna Insurance Company*, 571 F.Supp. 1460 at 1465. See also *Spinney's (1948) Ltd* v. *Royal Assurance* [1980] 1 Lloyd's Rep 406.

26   *Dalmia Cement Ltd* v. *National Bank of Pakistan* (Lalive, sole arbitrator. 1976), 67 ILR 611 at 613.

that do not amount to armed conflict is made clear in the 1977 Additional Protocol II to the Geneva Conventions. Article 1(2) of that Protocol excludes from its scope of application (albeit in a slightly different context) "riots, isolated and sporadic acts of violence and other acts of a similar nature, as not being armed conflicts." Unless that distinction is maintained, the possibility of containing low-level violence and maintaining reasonably normal relations between the States is lost.

D.   The Significance of the Shift from the Law of Peace to the Law of Armed Conflict

The most important reason for avoiding a premature determination that a war or armed conflict exists is that once the determination is made the legal relations between the combatants *inter se*, and between the combatants and third States, are radically altered. The Law of Peace is replaced by the Law of Armed Conflict. This has a dramatic effect on the legal rights and duties of States and of their nationals. Indeed, it is a primary characteristic of war that it comprehensively dislocates normal life in the State. Legal authorities refer to the purpose of war "which is always the same— namely, the overpowering and utter defeat of the opponent."[27] In time of war, nationals of the enemy State are regarded as being inherently suspect. There is a real and imminent risk of an attack by the enemy at any place in the territory and at any time. Exceptional measures are necessary to preserve public safety and public order. The Law of Armed Conflict provides powers to deal with those threats. For example, under the 1949 Geneva Conventions enemy nationals may be interned for the duration of hostilities; enemy combatants may be taken prisoner, or killed if they do not surrender; enemy military facilities may be attacked. On the other hand, there are limitations upon what States may do in their dealings with the enemy. If enemy combatants are captured, they may not be punished for simply participating in the war, even if they have killed or destroyed property in doing so. Hostilities must be conducted in accordance with the rules of international humanitarian law.

Relations with third States are radically affected, too. They are immediately obliged, subject to whatever obligations might be imposed by treaty or by the UN Security Council, to remain neutral in the conflict, withholding all militarily useful aid and assistance from both sides. This is a complete reversal of the position in time of peace, when (again subject to obligations such as the implementation of mandatory sanctions decided upon by the Security Council) States may assist foreign governments in repressing internal unrest.

The requirements concerning the organized nature and territorial basis of the combatants, and the scope and intensity of the attack, are firmly established in international law. It follows that terrorist attacks, such as those on the World Trade Centre in September 2001, on the Bali nightclub in October 2002, and the Madrid

---

27   *Dalmia Cement Ltd* v. *National Bank of Pakistan* (Lalive, sole arbitrator. 1976), 67 ILR 611 at 620 paragraph 30, citing Oppenheim-Lauterpacht (vol. 2, 7th ed., p. 202) and Westlake, *International Law*, II, (1913), p. 1.

railway station bombing of March 2004, are not acts of war. It could scarcely be otherwise. With whom would the USA have been at war in September 2001? Not, presumably, the national States of all those persons alleged to have been involved in the attacks, which included States such as Saudi Arabia and the United Kingdom. Nor with Afghanistan; nor even, initially, with the Taliban. In his address to Congress, on 21 September 2001, President Bush made demands of the Taliban, but indicated that if those demands were met the Taliban would not be attacked by the USA.[28] That is not compatible with the view that the USA was then 'at war' with Afghanistan.

Terrorist attacks such as these are not part of a sustained armed contest for the control of the whole or part of a State. Terrorists involved in such attacks are accordingly not entitled to prisoner of war status. Unlike soldiers, they are also liable to prosecution in respect of the violence in which they engage. Third States are not obliged to remain neutral or impartial in the "war against terrorism". States may join in the fight to repress it.

Similarly, those who fight against terrorism are not engaged in something that is in law a war. They are engaged in the fight to repress violent criminal behaviour; and they will ordinarily do so within the framework of domestic criminal law and procedures for international co-operation in criminal matters.

There may, it is true, be occasions when the fight against terrorism involves States in actions that do indeed constitute armed conflict in the strict legal sense of the term. There was an armed intervention in Afghanistan in 2001, justified by the fact that the Taliban regime in Afghanistan appeared to be harbouring Al Qaida terrorists who were engaged in the planning and execution of attacks against foreign States, and to be unable or unwilling to act to repress that terrorist activity. That intervention was a full-scale military invasion, which eventually aimed to topple the Taliban regime and succeeded in doing so. It was undoubtedly in law a "war" or armed conflict, and regulated by the rules of the law of armed conflict. That was, however, exceptional. Other actions against Al Qaida have not involved military operations of that kind. It is simply incorrect as a matter of law to say that terrorist suspects picked up in, say, Germany or The Gambia have been arrested in the course of a "war" against terrorism.

Incorrect it may be to speak of the "war against terrorism"; but should the point concern anyone other than pedants? I think that it should, because the elision of routine criminal law enforcement and exceptional wartime measures creates a serious risk of undermining legal principles that have set the framework for international rights and duties in time of conflict, and of eroding fundamental human rights. That is the "internal" aspect of national security. There is also an external aspect of the matter. The "war" focus diverts attention away from the areas where international co-operation is most needed, and likely to be most fruitful, in countering the terrorist threat. The remaining two sections of this chapter deal with these aspects.

---

28   <http://www.johnstonsarchive.net/terrorism/bush911c.html>.

2.   Why We Should Keep Crime and War Distinct?

One might think that, having determined that terrorist attacks do not amount to a "war", and that ordinarily the fight against terrorism does not do so either, it would be axiomatic that terrorism should be dealt with through the mechanisms of the criminal law that are used to fight other forms of serious organized crime and violence. But that is not what is happening in practice.

The most notorious, and scandalous, example is the use of US naval base in Guantanamo Bay, leased from Cuba, for the detention of suspected terrorists.[29] The detainees, who number around six hundred and forty, include not only persons captured in Afghanistan, who may be entitled to prisoner of war status if they were engaged in the armed hostilities in Afghanistan, but also others who were arrested far from the battlefield and played no part whatever in the hostilities. There are, for instance, people who were arrested in The Gambia and handed over to US authorities without, it appears, going through any formal extradition procedure, and then transported to Guantanamo.[30] (The detainees had already been questioned and released by British authorities before they flew to The Gambia.) There appears to be no basis for holding them as prisoners of war, in order to prevent them returning to participate in the armed conflict, because they were not participants in the conflict. Even if there had been some semblance of a basis, the question of their status should have been put before a competent tribunal for determination, which it was not. They are not charged with criminal offences; and if they had been, they should have been handed over through a normal extradition procedure, and detained in a normal prison in the United States. In some ways the closest analogy to their position might seem to be that of the enemy nationals, detained not because of what they have done as combatants or as criminals but because of what it is feared that they might do during the conduct of hostilities. But the analogy is utterly inappropriate – a State may detain only those enemy civilians who are found in its territory during the hostilities: it has no right to ship them back to its territory in order to imprison them. And even putting that objection to one side, the analogy is inexact. One has the clear impression that many of the detainees are held, not because of anything that they themselves might have done or might do in the future, but because of what they might know.

The detainees have been kept at Guantanamo, in metal cages under the Caribbean sun, sometimes chained and blindfolded,[31] in conditions in which have caused grave concern, despite the crass reassurances offered by US Defense Secretary Donald Rumsfeld ("To be in an 8-by-8 cell in beautiful, sunny Guantanamo, Cuba,

---

29   See, *e.g.*, Scott Higham, Joe Stephens and Margot Williams, "Guantanamo – A Holding Cell In War on Terror", *Washington Post*, Sunday, May 2, 2004, page A01; <http://www.washingtonpost.com/ac2/wp-dyn/A58702-2004May1>.

30   See the cases of Bisher Al-Rawi and Jamil Al-Banna, referred to in the statement dated 11 July 2003, made by Amnesty International: <http://www.amnesty.org.uk/deliver?document=14723>.

31   See <http://news.bbc.co.uk/1/hi/world/americas/1766037.stm>.

is not inhumane treatment").[32] Despite all the warnings from intelligence experts about the unreliability of information obtained under duress, it is clear that many of the detainees are held because of information that they might be able to provide. The US Department of Defense has explicitly said (in the context of the release in 2004 of three detainees under the age of 16 years) that it has a "commitment to release detainees when we are able to determine that they no longer pose a threat to our nation, that they are of no intelligence value and that they are not appropriate for criminal prosecution"[33] It is difficult to avoid the awful, Kafkaesque vision of people seized, detained and interrogated in Guantanamo in order to extract from them the names of others who will then be seized, detained and interrogated in order to extract yet more names, in what becomes a self-perpetuating process.

The legal basis for holding such people is unclear. The location of their detention, outside the borders of the United States, appears to have been chosen precisely in order to keep the detainees in a place that was believed to be beyond the reach of *habeas corpus* and other legal remedies that might have allowed them to challenge the legality of their detention by actions in the US courts. The United States Government also attempted to bar them from raising the question in any international forum. Section 7 of the US Military Order of 13 November 2001, concerning the detention at Guantanamo Bay of "international terrorists" stipulated in relation to detained individuals that

> the individual shall not be privileged to seek any remedy or maintain any proceeding, directly or indirectly, or to have any such remedy or proceeding sought on the individual's behalf, in (i) any court of the United States, or any State thereof, (ii) any court of any foreign nation, or (iii) any international tribunal."[34]

The Order is an affront to the Rule of Law. It did not succeed in blocking consideration of the position of the detainees by the Inter-American Commission of Human Rights, which requested the United States to take urgent measures to have the legal status of the detainees at Guantanamo Bay determined by a competent tribunal.[35] But the United States did not accede to that request, either. The detainees remained in what one British Law Lord called a "legal black hole."[36]

The situation is not satisfactory, whether viewed from the perspective of the individual detainee or the perspective of the State. Terrorists are not viewed or treated as criminals, no doubt because terrorist atrocities are regarded as being of a quite different order from the wickedness and destruction of "ordinary" crime.

---

32   <http://www.newsmax.com/archives/articles/2002/1/22/151910.shtml>.

33   The US Department of Defense has said that it has a "commitment to release detainees when we are able to determine that they no longer pose a threat to our nation, that they are of no intelligence value and that they are not appropriate for criminal prosecution": <http://www.defenselink.mil/releases/2004/nr20040129-0934.html>.

34   <http://www.whitehouse.gov/news/releases/2001/11/print/20011113-27.html>.

35   The Inter-American Commission acted anyway: see 41 *ILM* 532 (2002).

36   Lord Steyn, "Guantanamo Bay: The Legal Black Hole", 53 *ICLQ* 1-15 (2003).

Detainees —who are, of course, not "terrorists" but at worst "suspected terrorists", since they have not been convicted of any offences— are denied the basic rights of suspects in ordinary criminal investigations. They have no right to counsel, no maximum period of detention for questioning without charge, no right to challenge their detention. But nor, on the other hand, are they treated as prisoners of war. The United States Government maintains that the detainees "are not prisoners of war in the legal sense."[37] Denied the rights either of criminals or of prisoners of war, the indefinite detention without charge of detainees is a matter of grave concern.

Guantamo has become the by-word for detention outside the Rule of Law, filling a role that earlier generations identified with the Lubyanka. But it is by no means the only instance of the erosion of fundamental rights in the name of the war against terror. In the United Kingdom, the Government derogated from Article 5 (Right to liberty and security) of the European Convention on Human Rights in December 2001,[38] in order to implement the Anti-Terrorism, Crime and Security Act 2001. That Act provides for the indefinite detention of foreign nationals without trial, if they are certified by the British Government to be reasonably suspected of being terrorists or of having links with a terrorist group and to be a risk to national security.[39] They have a right of appeal to the Special Immigration Appeals Commission, but under severe procedural handicaps. Each detainee is assigned a special advocate, approved by the Government and given security clearance to view sensitive evidence against the detainee. Special advocates are not permitted to discuss that evidence with the detainee or with the detainee's own chosen lawyer without permission from the Commission. Nor is the detainee or his chosen lawyer permitted to attend closed sessions of the Commission at which the evidence is discussed, although there are open hearings which the detainee and his lawyer are allowed to attend. The system is ostensibly motivated by humanitarian concerns: the detainees are free to return to their home States, but it is said that they choose not to do so because they face the risk of being tortured;[40] and the United Kingdom is obliged by provisions of international law from which it has no right to derogate not to send them to countries where they do face torture. The indefinite detention of alleged terrorists whom the Government chooses not to prosecute is nevertheless a serious erosion of basic legal rights. This aspect of the British Act has been strongly criticised by the UK Parliament, which noted that other European States had not found it necessary to derogate from the European Convention on Human

---

37   American Forces Information Service, statement, 23 June 2004, "White House, DoD Discuss Interrogation Process": <http://www.globalsecurity.org/military/library/news/2004/06/mil-040623-afps01.htm>. Many of the *amicus curiae* briefs in the cases before the US Supreme Court on this issue address the question of the detainees' legal status. See <http://www.jenner.com/gitmo>.

38   See the Human Rights Act 1998 (Designated Derogation) Order 2001, S.I. 2001, No. 3644. (Entry into force on November 13, 2001).

39   Section 21.

40   In fact, some have left the UK voluntarily: see the Human Rights Watch paper on the Act, at <http://www.hrw.org/backgrounder/eca/uk/1.htm>.

Rights as the United Kingdom had;[41] but, as yet, there is little sign of the system being changed.

The abandonment of the criminal law framework is unlikely in the long run to prove any more satisfactory from the point of view of the States involved, for two main reasons. First, courts in mature democracies are not infinitely tolerant of the erosion of the Rule of Law by the Executive. That is already becoming clear. In one of the most remarkable fortnights on record for international lawyers the US Supreme Court held on 28 June 2004 in the cases of *Rasul* and *Odah* that the Guantanamo detainees had a right of access to US courts to challenge their detention. Significantly, the Court held that the petitioners were "not nationals of countries at war with the United States." That decision of the Supreme Court will at least force a determination of their status. Two days later the Israeli Supreme Court ruled against the legality of the 'anti-terror' wall being built in the Occupied Palestinian Territory, on the ground that it caused hardship disproportionate to any legitimate advantage that could be derived from it.[42] Nine days after that the International Court of Justice, in its Advisory Opinion on the *Legal Consequences of the Construction of a Wall in the Occupied Palestinian Territory*, held that a State's obligations under the International Covenant on Civil and Political Rights and the International Covenant on Economic, Social and Cultural Rights, apply not only within its territory but also to exercises by the State of its jurisdiction outside its territory.[43] The idea that fundamental rights are really benefits to which individuals become entitled by their presence within the territory of the State is, rightly, being rejected in such court decisions. Fundamental rights are entitlements that arise for individuals simply because they are human beings; and they are not simply rights, they are also constraints upon what a government may properly and lawfully do wherever the government may be acting.

---

41 "Anti-Terrorism, Crime and Security Act 2001 Review: Report", HC 100, <http://www.atcsact-review.org.uk/lib/documents/18_12_2003/Report.pdf>.

42 *Beit Sourik Village Council* v. *The Government of Israel and the Commander of the IDF Forces in the West Bank*, HCJ 2056/04 (30 June 2004). For the text see <http://www.mfa.gov.il/MFA/About+the+Ministry/MFA+Spokesman/2004/Statement+on+Fence+Ruling+30-June-2004.htm>.

43 Advisory Opinion of 9 July 2004, paragraphs 108-113. Practice elsewhere supports this view. See, *e.g.*, United Nations Human Rights Committee, *López Burgos* v. *Uruguay*, No.52/1979, Views of the Human Rights Committee, CCPR/C/13/D/52/1979 at para. 12.3, 29 July 1981; *Casariego* v. *Uruguay*, No.56/1979, Views of the HRC, CCPR/C/13/D/56/1979 at paras. 10.1-10.3, 29 July 1981. Cf., the Inter-American Commission on Human Rights, *Coard* v. *United States*, Case 10.951, Inter-Am. CHR Report No. 109/99, OEA/Ser.L/V/II.106, doc. 6 rev. at 1283 (1999) at §§ 37, 39, 41 and 43. And also the European Commission and the European Court of Human Rights, *Cyprus* v. *Turkey*, App. No. 8007/77, 13 DR 85 (1977), *Loizidou* v. *Turkey*, App. No. 14318/89, 23 Eur. HR Rep. 513 (1996); *Bankovic* v. *Belgium and 16 Other Contracting States*, App. No. 52207/99, 12 December 2001, 11 BHRC 435; *Ocalan* v. *Turkey*, App. No. 46221/99, 37 Eur. HR Rep. 10 (2003).

The second main reason why departure from the criminal law model is unlikely to succeed in the long run is that it will almost inevitably impede international co-operation in the fight against terrorism. There will certainly be occasions when armed forces will be called in to use force against terrorist groups, although most occasions will surely arise inside a single State so that the question of the *international* law on the use of force is not engaged. This obvious fact is sometimes overlooked when governments announce the need for more liberal rules of international law permitting the use of force to suppress terrorism. But even where forcible action that does engage international law is necessary, it will usually be taken by agreement with other States concerned. For example, the Proliferation Security Initiative ('PSI'), which involves the interdiction of shipping on the high seas in the search for the transportation of terrorist materiel,[44] is built upon a network of bilateral and multilateral agreements allowing the visit and search of national flag ships.[45] Legally, the consent of the flag State removes the jurisdictional problems that would otherwise exist.

Most counter-terrorist activity will not involve the armed forces at all. Much of it will be long-term monitoring and intelligence gathering, and the collection of information and evidence, by civilian agencies operating within the framework of the ordinary criminal law. International cooperation between these agencies will also need to take place within that framework. While all States are likely to adopt a robust approach to legal niceties when countering terrorist threats, agencies will need to act on the basis that at least some (and very probably the majority) of those involved in terrorism will be brought before the courts, rather than killed in combat with the armed forces or the police. If prosecutions are to succeed, matters such as the acquisition of evidence and the extradition of alleged offenders will have to proceed within the limits set by the criminal law. In the States most likely to be targets of terrorist activity, those limits will include references to human rights standards. Co-operation with any States that disregard those standards may be affected, in the way that the *Soering* case established that States Parties to the European Convention on Human Rights are bound not to extradite alleged offenders to States where they face torture or to inhuman or degrading treatment or punishment.[46] It is, for example, in principle possible that extradition may be resisted on the ground that the individual concerned would face violation of other Convention rights if he or she were extradited.[47] If States detain people in the kind of conditions that have

---

44   See Andrew Prosser, "The Proliferation Security Initiative in Perspective" (June 2004), at <http://www.cdi.org/pdfs/psi.pdf>; *cf.*, the speech of President Bush, "President President Announces New Measures to Counter the Threat of WMD", (11 February 2004), at <http://www.whitehouse.gov/news/releases/2004/02/20040211-4.html>.

45   For an account of the US-Panama Agreement, see <http://www.whitehouse.gov/news/releases/2004/02/20040211-4.html>.

46   *Soering* v. *United Kingdom* (14038/88) [1989] ECHR 14 (7 July 1989).

47   See the discussion in *R (Razgar)* v. *Secretary of State for the Home Department* [2004] UKHL 27, [2004] 3 WLR 58; *R (Ullah)* v. *Special Adjudicator* [2004] UKHL 26, [2004] 3 WLR 23.

prevailed in Guantanamo, they can expect to encounter some difficulty in securing the cooperation of foreign authorities.

Again, much of the effort will be preventive. The tightening of export controls and mechanisms for monitoring the transfer of munitions, the raw materials and technology necessary for the production of weapons of mass destruction, and the money necessary to pay for them, will be at the forefront of counter-terrorist strategies. This is already clear from the work of the UN Counter-terrorism Committee ('CTC'), established under Security Council resolution 1373.[48] This approach, too, requires international cooperation, within the framework of ordinary peacetime relations between States.

Given the very limited role that *international* uses of armed force will play in counter-terrorist activities, it would be perverse to put those activities on the footing of the 'Law of War'. The choice between the criminal law and the 'Law of War' approaches to dealing with terrorism is in effect a choice of ways of organizing society for the foreseeable future, for there is no foreseeable end to the fight against terrorism. The "war against terrorism" is not a war that can ever be objectively won. It is not like a direct attack upon the whole or part of the territory of a State, where it is first necessary to struggle to gain control of the territory, and where the war can be said to be over once the enemy is expelled from the territory and lays down its arms and accepts terms of peace. No government can be confident that terrorist attacks have finally ceased simply because there has been no attack for some time. Terrorists do not generally sign armistice agreements or peace treaties. True, political groups closely allied to terrorist groups may negotiate with the government and lead to the announcement of a cease-fire or something of that sort. That is essentially what was done in the 1998 Belfast Agreement (the "Good Friday Agreement")[49] between the parties to the Northern Ireland conflict, including political groups close to Loyalist and Republican paramilitary groups. But this is possible only when terrorist groups have been brought, even if indirectly through surrogate political representatives, into the political process. Ordinarily, terrorists do not definitively and reliably renounce violence. The consequence is that the war against terrorism can end only when the government chooses to declare that it has ended, at a point where it considers that it has done enough to neutralise the terrorist threat and prevent the threat from reasserting itself.

In practice it will often be extremely difficult, if not impossible, for a government to reach that conclusion. It may be possible to round up all the members of a small and relatively isolated group operating within a limited geographical area, such as the Baader-Meinhof Group: but it is practically impossible to round up all the members of a large, amorphous group linked by strong ideological or religious bonds to many other groups operating in many countries across the globe. How, then, will the current "War Against Terrorism" end? One must be prepared for the possibility that it will have no end in the foreseeable future. Even the more cautious

---

48   See <http://www.un.org/Docs/sc/committees/1373/> for an account of the CTC's work.

49   <http://www.nio.gov.uk/issues/agreement.htm>.

proponents of that "war" stress that it will be a long-term operation.[50] In those circumstances, one must approach the question of how best to deal, in legal terms, with the terrorist threat on the basis that the legal framework chosen might well be a practically permanent framework and not a short-term emergency expedient.

It must be said, too, that the framework has an indisputable social bias. The British Prime Minister's speech, quoted above, described the terrorist threat (or rather, *a* terrorist threat) in terms of a *jihad*, a conflict between Islam and the West. As Ronald Dworkin pointed out in a trenchant analysis of the issue,[51] the fact is that the security of the majority in the western States will be preserved by practices that impact very largely not upon the majority but upon racial and religious minorities. It is unrealistic to suppose that those practices will not be seen by many as discriminatory and oppressive. The social costs of fighting terrorism with laws and practices that circumvent and subvert basic human rights could be very high indeed.

3.   Why We Should Keep Self-Defence and the Maintenance of International Peace and Security Distinct?

There is a further danger in approaching the fight against terrorism as a war: it diverts attention away from the area in which the most productive measures might be taken by the international community to deal with the terrorist threat, and does so in a manner that distorts the basic constitutional allocation of powers that is the foundation of the international order established by the UN Charter.

The principles of the UN order governing the use of force are clear; and they amount to a constitutional allocation of powers within the international law community. The intention was that the UN Charter would forbid the threat or use of force in international relations; that the UN itself would have at its disposal military forces contributed by Member States, to be deployed as necessary for the maintenance of international peace and security; and that in order to protect their rights pending mobilization of UN forces, States would retain the right to use force in self-defence. Self-defence is, as befits a first-aid measure, exercisable unilaterally, by the attacked State or by a group of States exercising collective self-defence. It is subject only to a duty to report to the Security Council on measures taken in self-defence: there is no need to obtain Security Council authorisation in advance. Action for the maintenance of international peace and security, on the other hand, was intended to be a multilateral matter and to be the preserve of the Security Council. The scheme has not worked equally well in every respect. The prohibition on the use of force, in Article 2(4) of the Charter, and the preservation of the right of self defence,

---

50   President Bush has said that "America, and the entire civilized world, will face this threat for decades to come": 'President Announces New Measures to Counter the Threat of WMD', (11 February 2004), at <http://www.whitehouse.gov/news/releas­es/2004/02/20040211-4.html>.

51   Ronald Dworkin, 'Terror and the Attack on Civil Liberties', *The New York Review of Books*, vol. 50, No. 17, 6 November 2003, p. 37.

in Article 51, are effective components of the contemporary international order; but the middle element, the standing UN force, is an unrealised ambition. Equally, the Security Council has not always discharged its responsibilities effectively. There has been Security Council approval of military actions under the auspices of the UN, notably the 1991 action against Iraq; but there have been other episodes, such as the massacres in Rwanda and Burundi and the Former Yugoslavia, that cried out for UN intervention, where the UN remained inactive.

What seems to be occurring in the wake of the September 11 bombings is that the mechanisms of unilateral action in self-defence are being extended to circumstances that are properly cases of action to restore or maintain international peace and security, in order to remedy what are seen as the defects in the UN system. The invasion of Iraq in 2004 is the most prominent example. The Iraq episode, often mixed up in the public mind with the terrorist threat, was quite distinct from the post-September 11 anti-terrorist actions pursued in Afghanistan and elsewhere. Nevertheless, it has much in common with the current counter-terrorist strategy. There was no serious suggestion that the invasion of Iraq was justified by any imminent threat of an attack upon the United States, the United Kingdom or any other State. Indeed, the British Government expressly denied that its participation in the invasion was based upon an assertion of a right of self-defence. The precise rationale for the action remains unclear, but was certainly rooted in the preceding Security Council resolutions, dating back to 1990, requiring Iraq to disarm. Those resolutions, and the calculated ambiguity of Resolution 1441 in 2003, were said to provide sufficient authorisation for the use of force by the United States and its allies if Iraq continued to "defy the international community", as it was put. Iraqi non-co-operation with the demands of the United States and its allies, was accordingly regarded as sufficient justification for the invasion.

A great deal has been written about the precise scope of the Security Council resolutions on Iraq. It seems plain to me that the early resolutions authorised the use of force by the pro-Kuwait coalition of the day in order to rectify the unlawful invasion of Kuwait by Iraq. It strains credibility to interpret them so as to provide a permanent right (either for any State, or for the States that happened to participate in the 1991 coalition) to take armed action to compel Iraq to comply with each and every term of those early resolutions at any time in the future. Similarly, resolution 1441 self-evidently provided no clear authorisation to do anything. But whatever view one takes on that question, two points are surely clear.

First, if the use of force to compel compliance with Security Council resolutions is permissible it can only be on the basis that the Security Council, and not an individual Member State, determines that action is necessary in order to maintain or restore international peace and security. While the UN Charter gives a power to employ non-forcible measures in order to enforce Security Council resolutions, it gives no general power, either to individual States or to the Security Council, to employ armed force in order to enforce Security Council resolutions. The two Articles of the Charter that give the Security Council the power to take, or to authorise the taking, of action read as follows:

Article 41

The Security Council may decide what measures not involving the use of armed force are to be employed to give effect to its decisions, and it may call upon the Members of the United Nations to apply such measures. These may include complete or partial interruption of economic relations and of rail, sea, air, postal, telegraphic, radio, and other means of communication, and the severance of diplomatic relations

Article 42

Should the Security Council consider that measures provided for in Article 41 would be inadequate or have proved to be inadequate, it may take such action by air, sea, or land forces as may be necessary to maintain or restore international peace and security. Such action may include demonstrations, blockade, and other operations by air, sea, or land forces of Members of the United Nations.

The text distinguishes between the power of the Council to call upon Members to take non-forcible measures, and the power of the Council to take armed action itself. Taking action necessarily involves a purposive element. There must be an intention to act, a purpose in acting, and some degree of control and direction of the action, *on the part of the Council.* It is no doubt a valid and reasonable constitutional development to extend the Council's power under Article 42 to include the power to authorise armed action by Member States even in cases where the Security Council itself is not acting, (whether directly using forces at the disposition of the UN or indirectly by commanding forces of Member States), so that the Members are acting alone. But even in such a situation there must be some degree of direction by the Council; and that direction must lie within the limits of the Council's power to act to maintain or restore international peace and security.

Under the Charter system, only the Security Council can make the judgement that action is necessary in order to maintain or restore international peace and security. The decision that action is necessary is not the same as the decision that a threat to international peace and security exists. They are distinct steps, as is evident from the terms of Article 39 of the Charter.[52] The suggestion that States may themselves decide unilaterally that an occasion has arisen on which force should be used to give effect to Security Council resolutions finds no authority in the Charter, even if the Council has determined that the situation constitutes a threat to international peace and security. That is not to say that the Charter may not evolve so as to give such a power: but none exists at present.

The second point is that even if it is determined that an occasion requiring the use of armed force in order to enforce certain Security Council resolutions has arisen, the right to use force would plainly be limited. Even in the hands of the Security Council, it is not a power to do whatever the Council wishes, whenever a situation threatening international peace and security arises. It is a power to do

---

52 "The Security Council shall determine the existence of any threat to the peace, breach of the peace, or act of aggression and shall make recommendations, or decide what measures shall be taken in accordance with Articles 41 and 42, to maintain or restore international peace and security."

what the Council judges to be *necessary* to maintain or restore international peace and security. To return to the example of Iraq, it would be one thing to decide that armed force was necessary to compel Iraq to comply with the proper demands of the Security Council as represented by the UN arms inspectors, but quite another matter to decide to launch an all-out attack on the State, to topple its government, and to occupy it. It is for the Council to decide between such options.

Again, that is not to say that the Security Council may never authorise the replacement of governments and occupation of States. If a particular regime is itself the incontrovertible and irremediable source of the threat to international peace and security, its replacement may in some circumstances be the only way in which the Security Council can act effectively to restore international peace and security. But the determination that such action may be necessary can only properly be made once less extreme measures have been tried and failed, or at least considered and rejected as evidently unlikely to be effective. The weakest part of the argument presented by the 2003 coalition against Iraq is that it gave no indication of how a supposed power to enforce Security Council resolutions, even if the existence of such a power were admitted, would justify the full-scale invasion of Iraq and the toppling not just of its government but of its entire political and economic regime.

Those are arguments: but they did not prevail. Iraq was in fact invaded, and as a result of the continued assertions by the coalition – or at least by the United States and the United Kingdom – that the invasion was lawful, one must conclude that there is at least pressure for a shift in the constitution of the international order. That shift is, in essence, that States (or at least, powerful States) are arrogating to themselves the right to use force to maintain and restore international peace and security when they consider that a particular situation presents a grave threat. That is tantamount to a conflation of the unilateral right of self-defence with the right of the Security Council to take action to preserve international peace and security. Is such a development desirable?

There are arguments in favour of it. In the past fifteen years alone there have been atrocities on a massive scale, in Rwanda, Burundi, the Former Yugoslavia, the Congo, and Sudan, for example, which timely military intervention might have averted or mitigated. If the UN is unable to marshal international action in order to prevent massive killing in circumstances constituting gross violations of international law and of fundamental human rights, there is a very plausible argument that either the UN structure and processes should be changed or an alternative mechanism for mobilising international action should be found.

It may also be said that the nature of the distribution of power has changed significantly since the middle of the last century. Though it is often said that there is now a unipolar world, dominated by a sole superpower, that is not an accurate picture of the position. The United States cannot intervene in every crisis, and it does not try to do so. Indeed, the United States has rarely intervened anywhere without support from allies, such as it had in Iraq, in Yugoslavia, and even in Vietnam. Exceptions, such as the American intervention in Panama, were at the modest end of the range of military operations. Moreover, there are regional powers and regional organizations of considerable power and influence. Their presence is a factor that demands some tempering of the unipolar view of the world. It is, nonetheless, clear that it is possible for States acting alone or collectively to take armed action to preserve international peace and security where that is necessary. There is a viable alternative to the UN as the sole authority on the use of force.

Indeed, it is possible to overstate the importance of the Security Council. While "western" States tend to favour giving the Council a crucial role, at least as long as the Council does not block what they regard as proper and necessary action, it is by no means clear that States in, say, Africa and Asia always welcome the prospect of military interventions even where they are authorised by the Council; and that is likely to remain the case as long as the Council is in practice so heavily influenced by western States. It may be preferable to encourage regional powers and regional organizations to take the initiative, as did ECOWAS in respect of the conflicts in West Africa and NATO in Yugoslavia.

The structural weaknesses of the UN and the availability of effective alternatives have led some to urge the extension of the right to use force without explicit Security Council authorization. There is a further argument in favour of an extension of the right to use force that focuses upon the substantive rights of States.

The right of self-defence, and the Charter mechanisms built upon it, presupposed that the target of an attack was identifiable while the attack was still imminent, so that the target State could act in time to prevent the attack and protect itself. The terrorist threat does not necessarily operate in that way. For example, a group of terrorists might possess a flask containing a biological weapon, and have decided to use it against an underground railway system in a western city. They may not have decided which city; and it is possible that, say, half a dozen members of the group are issued with identical flasks, only one of which contains the genuine biological toxin, and that each of them is directed to release the contents of the flask in a different city in a different State. If the terrorists are gathered in a remote and hilly district in a State that is unable or unwilling to arrest them, and they are about to disperse, so that the only practical chance of seizing or neutralizing all six flasks is to launch a military raid on the group, which State could claim to act in self-defence? Not only would no State know with certainty that it was the real target, each State would know with certainty that it was much more likely than not that it was not the target. In cases such as this it is difficult to say that a State that takes pre-emptive action is acting in *self*-defence.[53] It is more accurate to say that it is acting in a policing capacity to maintain international peace and security. Yet it flies in the face of common sense to deny a State the right to take protective action in those circumstances.

For reasons such as these it may be thought better to circumvent the UN, and permit military action by other international organizations and by individual States, rather than stay with the original UN structure centred upon the unique authority of the Security Council. There is, however, a great difference between those

---

53   And collective self-defence is not a complete answer unless all the States concerned are linked by a collective self-defence agreement.

two options: extending the power of individual States is not the same as extending the power of regional and international organizations.

There is certainly room for an adjustment of the concept of imminence and proportionality as they apply in the context of self-defence, so as to permit individual States to take action unilaterally where it is evident that an attack is about to be put into operation upon one or more of a small number of States, including the State seeking to take the action,[54] and the situation has reached the point of the last practical opportunity to take defensive action with a reasonable assurance of success.[55] Self-defence is practically self-authorising: there is no need to appeal to anything other than the necessity of the action in order to preserve the State (or an individual, or some facility in the State) from attack and destruction.

It is unwise to go further and to entitle States to take preventive policing action, independently of any specific threat to themselves or to a limited group of States of which they are a member, in the way that the United States 2002 National Security Strategy suggested should be done.[56] The key advance during the twentieth century in the international law on the use of force was not the "outlawing" of the use of force, which has proven uneven in its efficacy, but rather the insistence that uses of force must be *legitimate* in the opinion of the international community as reflected in its institutional structures – the League of Nations, the United Nations and so on. It is not enough that a State considers it reasonable and expedient to use force: force is no longer an acceptable instrument of foreign policy. The debates over the invasion of Iraq clearly demonstrated the strength of that requirement of legitimacy. It was considered necessary to discover some kind of legitimate basis for the invasion; and there is little doubt that had it not been for that factor the invasion would have occurred sooner. While much could be said about the detrimental effects of the economic pressures which have largely replaced the use of force as instruments of foreign policy, it is important that the advance represented by the limitations on recourse to armed force not be lost. States need to be able to give a convincing answer to the question, what right do you have to use force in this way?

Single States acting unilaterally have little legitimacy when they use force outside established legal principles. It is self-evident that a State has the right to defend itself. It is not self-evident that it has a right, say, to bomb a building in another State alleged to be housing terrorists or bomb-making equipment, even if an extraordinary combination of circumstances precludes proceeding to deal with the threat with the co-operation, or at least with the consent, of the State where the building is located. That wider action needs to find its legitimation elsewhere.

There is a further point. There is a tendency to think that once it is decided that the use of force is justified, as long as the force used is proportionate no further

---

54   EU lawyers may detect the echo of the test of "direct and individual concern", as used in respect of challenges to Community Regulations.

55   I have argued for this in my paper "'Clear and Present Danger': Responses to Terrorism", [2005] 54 *ICQL* 185-196.

56   Text at <http://www.whitehouse.gov/nsc/nss.html>.

question arises. That is not so. There will (despite the reference in the celebrated *Caroline* formula to there being 'no choice of means'[57]) often be a choice of proportionate responses. The question of *how* force is used is as important as the question of *when* it is used. International disquiet over the strategy of aerial bombing, rather than deployments of ground troops, in Kosovo is one example; the manner of the invasion and occupation of Iraq is another. The question of the means used is a matter of the greatest importance. It is often much more difficult to reach agreement on the answer to that question than on the question whether force should be used at all. To take a domestic analogy, if a child abuser is discovered in a community it may be agreed that something must be done; but the choice between psychological treatment, imprisonment, and breaking his legs with baseball bats may divide the community. Each course may be argued to represent a proportionate and effective response; but the choice between them raises obvious and important issues. In particular, it raises the question of the point at which law enforcement slips over into unacceptable vigilantism and undermines rather than reinforces the Rule of Law. That question also arises when States such as the United States and the United Kingdom take upon themselves the responsibility for enforcing international law. The choice raises the question of the kind of society that should be maintained. Would we want to live in a world where order is maintained by vigilantes rather than by the police?

One way in which States can give a plausible answer to the question, what right do you have to use force in this way? is to appeal to the judgement of the community. The State may say: we discussed this in detail with other States, and we all saw no alternative to using force as we did. The action then becomes an expression of the will of the community, and not simply of the interests of one member of the community. It acquires some legitimacy. That is why, when the Western States sought to articulate the justification for the NATO action in Kosovo, which fell outside the established right to use force, it emphasised not only the substantive evils that would be averted by the action but also the involvement of NATO in the taking of a collective decision to 'authorise' the intervention.[58] The arguments in favour of the Kosovo action were also premised upon the inability of the Security Council to act. The same arguments apply in relation to policing actions against terrorism, in my view. States cannot unilaterally legitimate their own actions in using force in the community interest unless they do something to determine what the views of the community are.

First, it must in principle be for the Security Council to take action. If the Council decides not to act at a particular time, or in a particular way, that does not mean that the Council is stalemated or dysfunctional. It may be that the majority think inaction is the most prudent course for the time being. To the extent that there is a risk of the Security Council becoming paralysed and dysfunctional, the

---

57   For the full text see K.E. Shewmaker (ed.), *The Papers of Daniel Webster. Diplomatic Papers*, vol. 1, 1841-1843, (Hanover, NH, and London. 1983), p. 58 at 67-68.

58   See the discussions in "Kosovo: House of Commons Foreign Affairs Committee 4th Report, June 2000", 49 *ICLQ* 876-943.

better course is plainly to anticipate the problem and take preventive or mitigating action. One such step would be strengthening regional organizations. The Council may be more willing to hand over decisions regarding the precise timing and manner of the use of force to a regional organization than it is to take such decisions itself. And given that regional organizations might be expected to have a better grasp than the Security Council of the circumstances and the practicalities of action, that seems a reasonable position to take. Decisions taken by regional organizations to authorise the use of force offer the cloak of legitimacy, and some assurance that the force is being used for agreed community ends.

The need for unilateral action involving the use of force against terrorists is likely to be very limited indeed: but it could arise. Rogue regimes such as Afghanistan under the Taliban, or failed States such as Somalia in which there is no effective government capable of repressing terrorist activity, may occasionally become safe bases for terrorist attacks on foreign States. In such circumstances it is possible to envisage the need for other States to act; and it is conceivable that the Security Council will be unable to take an effective grip on the situation. But interventions in such circumstances are unlikely to be swift and clinical incisions followed by an equally swift and clinical withdrawal. International operations are as messy as medical operations, and they usually leave the patient in the same need of aftercare and convalescence. If armed intervention in a foreign State is necessary, it is very likely that some re-ordering of the State will be necessary: well-run States are unlikely to require armed interventions in order to remove threats. That is a further reason for strengthening the involvement of regional organizations, which can play a crucial role in nursing the neighbouring State back to health.

For all these reasons it seems to me important that we continue to distinguish between, on the one hand, the right of States to use force unilaterally in self-defence, accepting that the scope of that right must adjust to the changing nature of threats faced by States, and, on the other hand, the use of force in order to maintain international peace and security, which should remain a community responsibility and not a matter for unilateral action by individual States. There is, in my view, no need for fundamental changes in the basic architecture of international law in order to cope with the threats of world-wide terrorism.

25. Terrorism and Non-state Organizations

Bertrand G. Ramcharan

1. Introduction

In the evolving international constitutional and legal order it is imperative to address the new threats that confront humanity. The United Nations Secretary-General has established a high-level panel on future threats and challenges. These will certainly include global terrorism which, if combined with the use of weapons of mass destruction, would bring to the fore dangers that humanity has not had to confront before. The international constitutional and legal order is thus faced with formidable challenges.

Until now the international constitutional and legal order has been called upon to regulate, essentially, the conduct of States – even though, in more recent times, it has also dealt to a certain extent with non-state actors and individuals – as regards international crimes, for example. However, the changing nature of international intercourse will require international law to evolve and accommodate the growing involvement of non-state actors, such as international business and international non-governmental organizations. This is not the angle that concerns us in this chapter. It is rather the special challenges posed to international law by the threat of terrorism from non-state actors and how to deal with it.

In considering the nexus between terrorism and non-state organizations issues that call for attention include the following: the legal criteria to be used in determining what is a non-state terrorist organization; international legal cooperation against terrorist threats from non-state organizations; risk assessments in respect of threats of terrorism by non-state actors; the international criminal responsibility of terrorists; the international responsibility of non-state terrorist organizations; the responsibility of States for terrorist threats by non-state organizations operating in their jurisdictions; the duty of cooperation among States in responding to terrorist threats from non-state organizations. In this chapter we shall try to trace the outlines of the international law of the future on these issues.[1]

---

1   See generally:

Arts, Noortmann and Reinalda, *Non-state Actors in World Politics* (2001).

Ronald St. John Macdonald & Douglas M. Johnston (eds.), Towards World Constitutionalism, *pp. 681-703.*
© *2005 Koninklijke Brill NV. Printed in The Netherlands. ISBN 90 04 14612 1.*

2. Non-state Terrorist Organizations

That global non state-terrorist organizations exist is a matter of record. A Committee of the Security Council has drawn up a list of terrorist organizations. The United States Department of State regularly publishes a list of non-state terrorist organizations and other governments do likewise. From the point of view of international law, the question of interest is: according to what criteria are these organizations listed and what procedural safeguards are necessary in the event that an organization is innocent and wishes to challenge such a designation?

The Security Council Committee established pursuant to paragraph 6 of Resolution 1267 (1999), the 1267 Committee which oversees the implementation by States of the sanctions imposed by the Security Council on individuals and entities belonging or related to the Taliban, Usama Bin Laden and the Al-Qaida organization and maintains a list of individuals and entities for this purpose. In Resolutions 1267 (1999), 1333 (2000), 1390 (2002) and 1455 (2003), the Security Council obliged all States to freeze the assets, prevent the entry into, or the transit through, their territories, and prevent the direct or indirect supply, sale and transfer of arms and military equipment with regard to the individuals/entities included on the following lists:

A.   *Individuals* belonging to or associated with the *Taliban* (143 individuals);
B.   *Entities* belonging to or associated with the *Taliban* (1 entity);
C.   *Individuals* belonging to or associated with the *Al-Qaida* organization (174 individuals);

R. Bernhardt, Individuals in International Law. *Encyclopedia of Public International Law*. Vol. 2 (1995) pp. 957-962.

T. Burch, "Non-State Actors in the Nuclear Black Market: Proposing an International Legal Framework for Preventing Nuclear Expertise Proliferation & Nuclear Smuggling by Non-State Actors," *Santa Clara Journal of International Law*.

Cohen, Samy, *La Résistance des Etats*, (2003).

ICRC, *International Law and Non-State Actors*. Third Annual Colloquium on International Humanitarian Law organised jointly by the College of Europe and the International Committee of the Red Cross. Bruges, 25-26 October 2002.

Josselin and Wallace, *Non-State Actors in International Relations*, (2001).

W. Kälin, "Non-State Agents of Persecution and the Inability of the State to Protect," 15 *Georgetown Immigration Law Journal* (2002).

J. Kellenberger, "International Humanitarian Law at the Beginning of the 21st Century," Address to 26th Roundtable on Current Problems of International Humanitarian Law, San Remo, 5 September 2002.

Non-State Actors and International Law. Journal published by Brill Publishers (Volumes 1-4; latest volume, 2004).

A. Petitpierre, "Relevance of International Law to Non-State Actors," Address to Bruges Colloquium on International Humanitarian Law and Non-State Actors, 25-26 October 2002.

A. Sofaer, "On the Necessity of Pre-emption," *EJIL*, (2003), Vol. 14 No.2, pp. 209-26.

D.   *Entities* belonging to or associated with the *Al-Qaida* organization (111 entities);
     (The figures provided are as given on the website of the Committee, last updated on 6 July, 2004.)

The names and identifying information on the lists have been submitted to the 1267 Committee by United Nations Member States. Some governments would prefer that the Security Council promulgate the list based on national submissions, while others want independently to examine the evidence and make a collective determination to add or remove names from the list.

The absence of an internationally-recognized screening mechanism for identifying terrorist groups has been a particular point of contention. Some, like the United Nations Association of the USA, have expressed concern that if the 1267 Committee does not independently verify and decide what groups are to be suppressed, some countries might simply assert links between homegrown dissident movements and Al-Qaida organizations. Sweden, at one point, sharply contested as unsubstantiated the US designation of three Swedish citizens of Somali origin as terrorist accomplices whose financial business must be suppressed. The three were subsequently removed from the United Nations list in August 2002 following a request to the Security Council by the 1267 Committee.

This issue of the designation of an organization as a terrorist one has given rise to problems within the framework of the United Nations Commission on Human Rights. Some governments have deemed organizations to be terrorist, have issued national arrest warrants against named individuals for allegedly engaging in terrorist acts, have registered these national arrest warrants with Interpol, and, on this basis, sought and obtained the barring of these individuals from the Commission on Human Rights in 2003 and 2004. This led to an outcry from international human rights organizations, which have complained that the national designation of a person or an organization as a terrorist and the registration of a national arrest warrant with Interpol have been used as a way of barring people from bringing their causes to the Commission. At of the time of writing, this is an open issue and will require the most careful handling.

The US State Department's list of Foreign Terrorist Organizations (FTO) was compiled in 1997 as a method of tracking and taking action against terrorist groups around the world. FTOs are groups that allegedly either engage in or have the capacity or interest in carrying out terrorist activity that threatens US nationals or US national security or engage in efforts to disrupt national defence, foreign relations, or US economic interests. The list provides the United States with the legal basis to prosecute people who are under its jurisdiction for aiding, through money or other resources, any designated person. The United States also has the authority to move against US financial institutions with assets linked to an FTO, and report them to the US Department of the Treasury.

In our respectful submission, international law must require that there be a procedure for the determination of what is a terrorist organization and that the basis for such a determination should be periodically communicated to the world at large.

It would also be our submission that there must be the possibility of recourse by an individual or an organization to clear its name. The Guidelines of the 1267 Committee provide that a petitioner (individual(s), groups, undertakings, and/or entities on the Committee's consolidated list) may petition the government of residence and/or citizenship to request review of the case. In this regard, the petitioner should provide justification for the de-listing request, offer relevant information and request support for de-listing. The government to which a petition is submitted should review all relevant information and then approach bilaterally the government(s) originally proposing designation to hold consultations on the de-listing request.

The original designating government(s) may also request additional information from the petitioner's country of citizenship or residency. The petitioned and the designating government(s) may, as appropriate, consult with the Chairman of the Committee during the course of any such bilateral consultations. If, after reviewing any additional information, the petitioned government wishes to pursue a de-listing request, it should seek to persuade the designating government(s) to submit jointly or separately a request for de-listing to the Committee. The petitioned government may, without an accompanying request from the original designating government(s) submit a request for de-listing to the Committee pursuant to a no-objection procedure.

The Committee takes its decision by consensus of its members. If consensus cannot be reached on a particular issue, the Chairman will undertake such further consultations as may facilitate agreement. If, after these consultations, consensus still cannot be reached, the matter may be submitted to the Security Council.

Having looked at issues concerning the designation of terrorist organizations, we turn next to the international constitutional and legal architecture to deal with threats of terrorism from non-state institutions.

3.   The International Constitutional Architecture to Deal with Threats of Terrorism from Non-state Institutions

From the evidence we have it would be reasonable to expect that the international community would have to deal with non-state terrorist threats for some time to come. As of the time of writing, the international community has so far established the following constitutional architecture to deal with threats of terrorism from non-state organizations: There are twelve international conventions that deal with particular terrorist threats. The Security Council has taken the lead in addressing the threat of terrorism. It has adopted a number of resolutions and it has also established the Counter-Terrorism Committee and the 1267 Committee. The General Assembly has also adopted resolutions against terrorism. An *Ad Hoc* Committee of the General Assembly is working on a draft of a comprehensive convention on international terrorism. Bodies like the Commission on Human Rights and its Sub-Commission on the Promotion and Protection of Human Rights regularly examine the protection of human rights in counter terrorism strategy. Treaty Bodies such as the Human Rights Committee have established close working relation with the Counter-Terrorism Committee of the Security Council.

A. The Counter-Terrorism Committee

Resolution 1373 of the Security Council established the Counter-Terrorism Committee (CTC) made up of all fifteen members of the Security Council. The Committee monitors the implementation of Resolution 1373 by all States and tries to increase the capability of States to fight terrorism. The Committee considers information relevant to its work not only from States but also from any other sources in a position to provide such information, including international organizations and institutions, non-governmental organizations and individuals.

B. The 1267 Committee

The Security Council Committee established pursuant to paragraph 6 of Resolution 1267 (1999), now referred to as the 1267 Committee, oversees the implementation by States of the sanctions imposed by the Security Council on individuals and entities belonging or related to the Taliban, Usama Bin Laden and the Al-Quaida organization and maintains a list of individuals and entities for this purpose. The Committee consists of all members of the Security Council. In its latest report (S/2004/281) the Committee indicated that on 10 April, 2003, it had adopted specific guidelines for considering additional information on listed individuals and entities submitted by States and/or regional organizations, which serve to inform Member States of the Committee's procedures for processing and considering such information. The Committee further decided to include as part of its guidelines, the criteria used by the Monitoring Group in reviewing list-related information at the request of the Committee. During 2003, the Committee decided to add the names of 70 individuals and 7 entities to its consolidated list.

C. The United Nations Commission on Human Rights

The United Nations Commission on Human Rights is essentially a political organ from which there may emanate from time to time strands of practice that might help us distill the emerging lines of the law. Recently the Commission has been called upon to deal with some issues and situations on which it has made pronouncements relevant to the issues under consideration in this chapter.

The Commission has adopted a series of resolutions reiterating its unequivocal condemnation of all acts, methods and practices of terrorism, regardless of motivation, in all their forms and manifestations, wherever, whenever and by whomever committed as acts aimed at the destruction of human rights, fundamental freedoms and democracy, threatening the territorial integrity and security of States, destabilizing legitimately constituted governments, undermining pluralist society and the rule of law and having consequences for the economic and social development of the State. The Commission has urged States to fulfill their obligations under the Charter of the United Nations in strict conformity with international law including human rights standards and obligations and international humanitarian law, to prevent, combat and eliminate terrorism in all its forms and manifestations wherever, whenever, and by whomever committed. It has also called upon States to strengthen their legislation to combat terrorism in all its forms and manifestations.[2] The Commission has reaffirmed that "states must ensure that any measures taken to combat terrorism complies with their obligation under international law in particular international human rights, refugee and humanitarian law."[3]

The Commission has consistently taken the view that the use of mercenaries and their recruitment, financing and training are causes for grave concern to all States and violate the purposes and principles of the United Nations Charter. The Commission has urged all States to take the necessary steps and to exercise the utmost vigilance against the menace posed by the activities of mercenaries and to take legislative measures to ensure that their territories, as well as their nationals, are not used for the recruitment, assembly, financing, training and transit of mercenaries.[4] The Commission has strongly condemned the practice of abduction of children for various purposes, for example as soldiers or workers, for purposes of sexual exploitation and or pedophilia, and for the purposes of trade in human organs.[5] As we shall see later in this chapter, the Commission has expressed grave concern over targeted assassinations, liquidation and murder of political leadership by the Israeli armed forces.[6]

The Commission's pronouncements on the situation in Colombia are particularly significant. In an agreed Chairperson's statement adopted at its 60th session in 2004, the Commission condemned all breaches of international humanitarian law arising from the conflict in Colombia and called for respect for the humanitarian principles of distinction, limitation, proportionality and immunity of the civilian population. The Commission strongly condemned all acts of terrorism and other criminal attacks and strongly urged "all illegal armed groups to comply with international humanitarian law and to respect the legitimate exercise by the population of their human rights." The Commission strongly condemned all acts of violence and breaches of humanitarian law committed by paramilitary groups, by other illegal armed groups, especially the revolutionary armed forces of Colombia (FARC), in particular through their attacks on the civilian population. The Commission deplored in particular the latter's frequent indiscriminate attacks with explosive devices and anti-personnel landmines.

---

2   Resolution 2004/44 adopted by 31 votes to 14, with 8 abstentions. The votes against were cast mainly by members of the Western Group which explained that, while deploring acts of terrorism, they could not agree that terrorist groups commit human rights violations *per se.*

3   Resolution 2004/87 adopted without a vote.

4   Resolution 2004/5 adopted y a recorded vote of 36 to 14 with three abstentions.

5   Resolution 2004/47 adopted without a vote.

6   Resolution 2004/1 adopted by 31 votes to 2, with 18 abstentions.

D.   The Human Rights Committee

The Human Rights Committee, which operates under the International Covenant on Civil and Political Rights has sought to develop contacts with the Counter-Terrorism Committee, occasionally sending one or two of its members to brief the CTC and in return receiving a representative of the CTC to exchange views. This process is expected to continue in the future.

4.   International Legal Cooperation to Deal with Threats of Terrorism from Non-state Institutions

In addition to the twelve international conventions,[7] the United Nations Security Council has established an elaborate legal framework to deal with threats of terrorism, including from non-state organizations. In its Resolution 1269 (1999), the Security Council expressed its deep concern over the increase in acts of international terrorism which endangered the lives and well-being of individuals worldwide as well as the peace and security of all States. The Council condemned all acts of terrorism, irrespective of motive, wherever and by whomever committed. The Council unequivocally condemned all acts, methods and practices of terrorism as criminal and unjustifiable, regardless of their motivation, in all their forms and manifestations, wherever and by whomsoever committed, in particular those which could threaten international peace and security.

---

7   The twelve conventions are the following: 1. Convention on Offences and Certain Other Acts Committed on Board Aircraft ("Tokyo Convention", 1963 – safety of aviation); 2. Convention for the Suppression of Unlawful Seizure of Aircraft ("Hague Convention", 1970 – aircraft hijackings); 3. Convention for the Suppression of Unlawful Acts Against the Safety of Civil Aviation ("Montreal Convention", 1971 – applies to acts of aviation sabotage such as bombings aboard aircraft in flight); 4. Convention on the Prevention and Punishment of Crimes Against Internationally Protected Persons (1973-outlaws attacks on senior government officials and diplomats); 5. International Convention Against the Taking of Hostages ("Hostages Convention", 1979); 6. Convention on the Physical Protection of Nuclear Material ("Nuclear Materials Convention", 1980 – combats unlawful taking and use of nuclear material); 7. Protocol for the Suppression of Unlawful Acts of Violence at Airports Serving International Civil Aviation, supplementary to the Convention for the Suppression of Unlawful Acts against the Safety of Civil Aviation (Extends and supplements the Montreal Convention on Air Safety), (1988); 8. Convention for the Suppression of Unlawful Acts Against the Safety of Maritime Navigation, (1988 – applies to terrorist activities on ships); 9. Protocol for the Suppression of Unlawful Acts Against the Safety of Fixed Platforms Located on the Continental Shelf (1988 – applies to terrorist activities on fixed offshore platforms); 10. Convention on the Marking of Plastic Explosives for the Purpose of Detection (1991 – provides for chemical marking to facilitate detection of plastic explosives, e.g., to combat aircraft sabotage); 11. International Convention for the Suppression of Terrorist Bombing (1997); (UN General Assembly Resolution): 12. International Convention for the Suppression of the Financing of Terrorism (1999).

The Security Council called upon all States to cooperate with one another, to prevent and suppress terrorist acts, protect their nationals and other persons against terrorist attacks and bring to justice the perpetrators of such acts. The Council called upon all States to take appropriate measures in conformity with the relevant provisions of national and international law, including international standards of human rights, before granting refugee status, for the purpose of ensuring that the asylum-seeker has not participated in terrorist acts. The Council further urged all States to exchange information in accordance with international and domestic law, and cooperate on administrative and judicial matters in order to prevent the commission of terrorist acts.

Subsequent resolutions of the Security Council have built on this policy foundation. In its Resolution 1377 of 12 November 2001, the Security Council declared that acts of international terrorism constitute one of the most serious threats to international peace and security in the twenty-first century and that terrorism constituted a challenge to all States and to all of humanity. It endangered innocent lives and the dignity and security of human beings everywhere, threatened the social and economic development of all States and undermined global stability and prosperity.

This policy framework of the Security Council is important. The Council can be seen to invoke global stability and the peace and security of all States as well as of human beings everywhere. It can be seen calling on States to cooperate for the prevention of terrorism and in bringing perpetrators to justice. It can be seen calling on States to screen asylum-seekers to ensure that they have not participated in terrorist acts – doing so with due regard to international standards of human rights.

Security Council Resolution 1373 declared that "... acts, methods and practices of terrorism are contrary to the purposes and principles of the United Nations." It called upon Member States to become parties as soon as possible to the relevant international conventions and protocols "to increase cooperation and fully implement the relevant international conventions and protocols."

The Terrorism Prevention Branch of the United Nations Office in Vienna provides guidance to States in legislating and implementing anti-terrorism measures. The Office was specifically requested by the Counter-Terrorism Committee to provide assistance to requesting States.

The Global Programme against Terrorism was launched in October 2002 as a framework for UNODC's operational activities in this field. It works to promote ratification of the twelve universal legal conventions and assists in the preparation of implementation legislation. It also works through technical assistance projects on Strengthening the Legal Regime against Terrorism.

The activities of the Global Programme seek to provide prompt response to requests from Member States and the CTC. The Programme is committed to deliver tailor-made assistance through:

–   Reviewing domestic legislation and providing advice on drafting enabling laws;
–   Facilitating and providing training to national administrations with regard to new legislation;

- Providing in-depth assistance on the implementation of the new legislation against terrorism through the mentorship programme; and
- Maintaining a roster of experts to supplement specific expertise where required.

The tools for technical assistance are:
- The Programme drafted a UN Legislative Guide to the Universal Anti-Terrorism Conventions and Protocols to serve as guidance notes for legislating and implementing the international instruments pertaining to terrorism. A checklist will provide an easy overview for legislators in this field.
- Model laws and examples of relevant legislation are regularly updated to keep abreast of developments in legislating terrorism.

The Programme seeks to build partnerships through activities such as the following:
- The work of the Programme is guided by policy decisions made by the Counter-Terrorism Committee. Activities are coordinated with the CTC and the UN Headquarters Office of Legal Affairs.
- The exchange of expertise and information with other international and regional organizations and national institutions is emphasized.
- Where possible, activities draw on existing in-house expertise, particularly of the Global Programmes against Money Laundering, Organized Crime and Corruption, and the Legal Advisory Programme.

5. Risk Assessment in Respect of Threats of Terrorism by Non-state Institutions

In its recent Advisory Opinion on legal consequences of the construction of a wall ... the International Court of Justice recognized that Israel "has to face numerous indiscriminate and deadly acts of violence against its civilian population. It has the right, and indeed the duty, to respond in order to protect the life of its citizens. Nevertheless, the Court underlined that: "The measures taken are bound nonetheless to remain in conformity with applicable international law."[8]

One of the major legal issues to be thought through in the future legal framework for dealing with the threat of terrorism is the issue of risk assessment and controls thereon. In a democracy, it is generally accepted that it is for the Executive to make a determination of the level of threat and the courts have usually not supervised this assessment by the Executive. The rationale for this has been that the Executive is accountable to the people who will judge them at election time. We have seen in recent experience that the intelligence services of both the United Kingdom and the United States erred in their assessment of the existence of mass destruction in Iraq and that a war was launched to deal with weapons of mass destruction of which there has so far been no sign. The governments of the

8   ICJ Reports, 2004, Paragraph 141.

United Kingdom and the United States of America are effectively accountable to no one for their assessments and for the actions they took on the basis of those assessments.

In Brannigan and McBride v. The United Kingdom, the European Court of Human Rights advanced the principle of European Supervision:

> The Court recalls that it falls to each Contracting State, with its responsibility for 'the life of [its] nation', to determine whether that life is threatened by a 'public emergency' and, if so, how far it is necessary to go in attempting to overcome the emergency. ...

Nevertheless, Contracting Parties do not enjoy an unlimited power of appreciation. It is for the Court to rule on whether *inter alia* the States have gone beyond the "extent strictly required by the exigencies" of the crisis. The domestic margin of appreciation is thus accompanied by a European supervision. At the same time, in exercising its supervision the Court must give appropriate weight to such relevant factors as the nature of the rights affected by the derogation, the circumstances leading to, and the duration of the emergency situation.[9]

The Human Rights Committee, which operates under the International Covenant on Civil and Political Rights has urged that: "constitutional and legal provisions should ensure that compliance with Article 4 of the Covenant can be independently monitored." It has said that it was "concerned that courts do not have the power to examine the legality of the declaration of emergency and of the different measures taken during the state of emergency." How is the international law of the future to deal with this issue?

6.   The International Responsibility of Non-state Terrorist Organizations

Under existing international law, a member of a non-state terrorist organization may be charged with an international crime. Of relevance for present purposes is the Statute of the International Criminal Court which lays down individual criminal responsibility for offences such as genocide, crimes against humanity, war crimes and the crime of aggression.

Genocide covers, with intent to destroy, in whole or in part, a national, ethnical, racial or religious group, killing members of the group or causing serious bodily or mental harm to members of the group. Crime against humanity includes, when committed as part of a widespread or systematic attack directed against any civilian population, with knowledge of the attack, murder, extermination, torture, rape, and other inhuman acts of a similar character intentionally causing great suffering, or serious injury to body or to mental or physical health. War crimes mean grave breaches of the Geneva Conventions of 12 August, 1949 and other serious violations of the laws and customs applicable in international armed conflict. Aggression is not defined in the Statute of the International Criminal Court and it is open to discussion whether members of a non-state organization might be charged with aggression.

---

9   Brannigan and McBride *v.* The United Kingdom, ECHR, 26 May 1993 (para. 43).

The International Criminal Court has jurisdiction only with respect to crimes committed after the entry into force of the Statute. The Court has jurisdiction over natural persons. A person who commits a crime within the jurisdiction of the Court is individually responsible and liable for punishment in accordance with the Statute. A State which becomes a Party to the Statute of the Court thereby accepts the jurisdiction of Court with respect to the crimes referred to above. The Court may exercise its jurisdiction in cases of referrals by the Prosecutor or by a State Party if the State on the territory of which the conduct in question occurred has accepted the jurisdiction of the Court or, if the crime was committed on board a vessel or aircraft, the State of registration of that vessel or aircraft has accepted the jurisdiction of the Court. The Court may also exercise its jurisdiction if the State of which the person accused of the crime is a national has accepted the jurisdiction of the Court.

7. The International Responsibility of States for Non-state Terrorism Institutions Operating in Their Jurisdiction

Under the international law of State Responsibility a State is internationally liable for conduct in breach of its international obligations. This may be for acts which are directly imputable to it or for acts of private individuals, whether nationals, or aliens in the state's territory. In respect of the latter, in particular, the State's responsibility calls for it to take certain preventive measures and requires it to secure that as far as possible the wrongdoer makes suitable reparation, and if necessary to punish him.[10]

International law thus requires a State to take measures to prevent international terrorist acts from being planned, organized or executed from within its territory or jurisdiction. A State which has knowingly or culpably failed to act against such acts would be internationally responsible for its failure. In certain areas responsibility may arise without fault. Absolute or strict responsibility has been adopted by treaty for some particularly dangerous activities. The Ninth Edition of Oppenheim's *International Law* offers the comment that absolute or strict responsibility probably does not yet attach to any conduct by virtue of customary international law.[11] World-wide revulsion after the terrorist attacks of 11 September 2001, and the various resolutions adopted by the Security Council thereafter would, in our submission, make the duty to prevent terrorist acts from being committed in one's territory an obligation under international customary law the breach of which would entail the responsibility of the State.

8. Self-defence

A major legal question that arises for consideration is whether the right of self-defence under Article 51 of the United Nations Charter is applicable to terrorist threats by non-state organizations. Article 51 of the Charter states "Nothing in the

---

10   Oppenheim's *International Law*, Ninth Edition, Vol. I, Peace, Chapter 4
11   *Ibid*, p. 511.

present Charter shall impair the inherent right of individual or collective self-defence if an armed attack occurs against a Member of the United Nations, until the Security Council has taken measures necessary to maintain international peace and security. Measures taken by Members in the exercise of this right of self-defence shall be immediately reported to the Security Council and shall not in any way affect the authority and responsibility of the Security Council under the present Charter to take at any time such action as it deems necessary in order to maintain or restore international peace and security."

In its Advisory Opinion on Legal consequences of the construction of a wall in the Occupied Palestinian Territory, the International Court of Justice concluded that Article 51 had no relevance in that case. The Court stated:

> Article 51 of the Charter thus recognizes the existence of an inherent right of self-defence in the case of armed attack by one State against another State. However, Israel does not claim that the attacks against it are imputable to a foreign State.[12]

The position of the Court on this issue has been strongly criticized inside and outside of the Court. In his dissenting opinion Judge Buergenthal criticized this finding on the following grounds:

> There are two principal problems with this conclusion. The first is that the United Nations Charter, in affirming the inherent right of self-defence, does not make its exercise dependent upon an armed attack by another State, leaving aside for the moment the question whether Palestine, for purposes of this case, should not be and is not in fact being assimilated by the Court to a State. Article 51 of the Charter provides that 'Nothing in the present Charter shall impair the inherent right of individual or collective self-defence if an armed attack occurs against a Member of the United Nations...' Moreover, in the resolutions cited by the Court, the Security Council has made clear that 'international terrorism constitutes a threat to international peace and security' while '*reaffirming* the inherent right of individual or collective self-defence as recognized by the Charter of the United Nations as reiterated in resolution 1368 (2001)' (Security Council resolution 1373 (2001)). In its resolution 1368 (2001), adopted only one day after the September 11, 2001 attacks on the United States, the Security Council invokes the right of self-defence in calling on the international community to combat terrorism. In neither of these resolutions did the Security Council limit their application to terrorist attacks by State actors only, nor was an assumption to that effect implicit in these resolutions. In fact, the contrary appears to have been the case.
> (See Thomas Franck, "Terrorism and the Right of Self-Defence", *American Journal of International Law*, Vol. 95, 2001. p.p. 839-840.)

In his Separate Opinion Judge Kooijmans took the following position on the right of self-defence:

---

12   *Loc. Cit*, para. 139.

The Court starts its response to this argument by stating that Article 51 recognizes the existence of an inherent right of self-defence in the case of an armed attack by one State against another State (para.139). Although this statement is undoubtedly correct, as a reply to Israel's argument it is, with all due respect, beside the point. Resolutions 1368 and 1373 recognize the inherent right of individual or collective self-defence without making any reference to an armed attack by a State. The Security Council called acts of international terrorism, without any further qualification, a threat to international peace and security which authorizes it to act under Chapter VII of the Charter. And it actually did so in resolution 1373 without ascribing these acts of terrorism to a particular State. This is the completely new element in these resolutions. This new element is not excluded by the terms of Article 51 since this conditions the exercise of the inherent right of self-defence on a previous armed attack without saying that this armed attack must come from another State even if this has been the generally accepted interpretation for more than 50 years. The Court has regrettably by passed this new element, the legal implications of which cannot as yet be assessed but which marks undeniably a new approach to the concept of self-defence.

The argument which in my view is decisive for the dismissal of Israel's claim that it is merely exercising its right of self-defence can be found in the second part of paragraph 139. The right of self-defence as contained in the Charter is a rule of international law and thus relates to international phenomena. Resolutions 1368 and 1373 refer to acts of *international* terrorism as constituting a threat to *international* peace and security: they therefore have no immediate bearing on terrorist acts originating within a territory which is under control of the State which is also the victim of these acts. And Israel does not claim that these acts have their origin elsewhere. The Court therefore rightly concludes that the situation is different from that contemplated by resolutions 1368 and 1373 and that consequently Article 51 of the Charter cannot be invoked by Israel.

Judge Higgins, in her Separate Opinion, disagreed with the majority on the law of self-defence. "There is", she wrote, "nothing in the text of Article 51 that *thus* stipulates that self-defence is available only when an armed attack is made by a State." She also found unpersuasive the Court's contention that, as the use of force emanated from occupied territory it was not an armed attack "by one State against another": "The question is surely where responsibility lies for the sending of groups and persons who act against Israeli civilians and the cumulative severity of such action."

United States representatives for their part have considered the Court's conclusions that the inherent right of self-defence contained in Article 51 of the Charter was not applicable to the situation was an inconsistent interpretation of Article 51. It is our view that the Court had wrongly concluded that the inherent right of self-defence was applicable solely in the case of an armed attack by one state against another state. If Article 51 were applicable only to attacks by another State it would ignore the present dangers caused by non-state entities.

9. Prevention

The issue of pre-emption to head off terrorist threats has been much discussed recently. It has an internal and an international dimension.

As far as the internal dimension is concerned, there is significant guidance to be obtained from international human rights law. In Delgado Paez *v.* Colombia, the Human Rights Committee, which functions under the International Covenant on Civil and Political Rights, discussed Article 9 of the Covenant on personal security and took the view that, as a matter of law, a State cannot ignore known threats to the life of persons under their jurisdiction. States parties are under an obligation to take reasonable and appropriate measures to protect them.

In Kilic *v.* Turkey, the European Court of Human Rights held that a State party to the European Convention had a primary duty to secure the right to life by putting in place effective criminal-law provisions to deter the commission of offences against the person, backed up by law enforcement machinery for the prevention, suppression and punishment of breaches of such provisions. It also extends in appropriate circumstances to a positive obligation on the authorities to take preventive operational measures to protect an individual or individuals whose life is at risk from the criminal acts of another individual.[13]

In the case of Ascencios Lindo *et al.*, the Inter-American Commission on Human Rights expressed the view that the State's national and international obligation to confront individuals or groups who use violent methods to create terror among the populace, and to investigate, try, and punish those who commit such acts means that it must punish all the guilty but only the guilty. The State must function within the rule of law.[14]

International human rights law specifies binding commitments for all States. However, it recognizes that some rights can be derogated from in times of public emergency. Article 4 of the International Covenant on Civil and Political Rights requires a number of substantive and procedural safeguards regarding the declaration and implementation of a state of emergency. These are that:

–   the nature of the emergency must threaten the life of the nation;
–   the existence of a state of emergency must be officially declared;
–   measures adopted are necessary to the extent strictly required by the exigencies of the situation;
–   derogations are not incompatible with the derogating State's other obligations under international law;
–   the derogating State notifies other States parties, through the Secretary-General of the UN, of the provisions it has derogated from and the reasons for such derogation, as well as of the date when the derogation has ceased to apply.

---

13   ECHR, 28 March 2000, para. 62.
14   Annual Report of the IACHR (1999) para. 58.

Article 4 also lists provisions that may not be derogated from even in times of public emergency. These are: Article 6 (right to life), Article 7 (prohibition of torture or cruel, inhuman or degrading punishment, or of medical or scientific experimentation without consent), Article 8, paragraphs 1 and 2 (prohibition of slavery, slave-trade and servitude), Article 11 (prohibition of imprisonment because of inability to fulfil a contractual obligation), Article 15 (the principle of legality in the field of criminal law, *i.e.* the requirement of both criminal liability and punishment being limited to clear and precise provisions in the law that was in place and applicable at the time the act or omission took place, except in cases where a later law imposes a lighter penalty), Article 16 (the recognition of everyone as a person before the law), and Article 18 (freedom of thought, conscience and religion).

On 24 July 2001, the UN Human Rights Committee adopted General Comment No 29 concerning Article 4 of the ICCPR.[15] The Committee suggested that even during an armed conflict, measures derogating from the Covenant are allowed only if and to the extent that the situation constitutes a threat to the life of the nation. Even then, States should carefully consider the justification of why such a measure is necessary and legitimate in the circumstances. The Committee also clarified the list of elements that cannot be subject to lawful derogations. These elements include the following: all those deprived of liberty must be treated with respect for their dignity; the prohibition of hostage taking, abductions, or unacknowledged detention; the protection of persons belonging to minorities; the prohibition of unlawful deportation or transfer of population; and that "no declaration of a state of emergency … may be used as justification for a State party to engage itself … in propaganda for war, or in advocacy of national, racial or religious hatred that would constitute incitement to discrimination, hostility or violence."

The General Comment also outlines some important principles with regard to the right to a fair trial. It stresses that any trial leading to the imposition of death penalty during a state of emergency must conform to the provisions of the Covenant including those on fair trial. It also emphasises that as the right to a fair trial is explicitly guaranteed under international humanitarian law during armed conflict, these rights cannot be derogated from during other emergency situations.

Article 2 of the Convention Against Torture and Other Cruel, Inhuman or Degrading Treatment or Punishment states: "No exceptional circumstances whatsoever, whether a state of war or a threat of war, internal political instability or any other public emergency, may be invoked as a justification of torture."[16]

Finally, Article 3 of the same Convention, which is also of absolute character provides:

> No State party shall expel, return (refouler) or extradite a person to another State where there are substantial grounds for believing that he would be in danger of being subjected to torture.

---

15   CCPR/C/21/rev.1/Add.11. Available on OHCHR Website, under Treaty-Bodies Data Base.

16   There are 126 States that have ratified or acceded to the Torture Convention.

As it was emphasized earlier, the States have a duty to protect the rights of all individuals residing on their territory or subjects to their jurisdiction, including against acts of terrorism.

Within the Council of Europe, the *European Court* has acknowledged the duty of States Parties to fight terrorism and protect its citizens and also recognized the essential values in the non-derogable provisions in Article 15 of the European Convention on Human Rights (ECHR). In Klass and Others *v.* Germany (1978), the Court emphasized that some compromise between the requirements for defending democratic society and individual rights was inherent in the system of the Convention. Accordingly, the Court was prepared to take into account the background to the cases submitted to it, particularly problems linked to the prevention of terrorism. States parties, however, did not enjoy an unlimited discretion to subject persons within their jurisdiction to special measures.[17]

Article 2 of the European Convention on Human Rights related to the *right to life* does not exclude the possibility that a deliberate use of a lethal solution can be justified when it is "absolutely necessary" to prevent some sorts of crimes. This must be done, however, in very strict conditions in order to respect human life as much as possible, even as regards persons suspected of preparing a terrorist attack.

In the "Murray" case (1994), the European Court admitted that the *use of confidential information* was essential to fight terrorist violence and threats to citizens and the democratic society as a whole. This did not mean, however, that the investigating authorities had "*carte blanche*" under Article 5 (art. 5) to arrest suspects for questioning, free from effective control by the domestic courts or by the Convention's supervisory institutions, whenever they choose to assert that terrorism was involved.

Confronted with the need to estimate the conformity to the Convention of certain forms of inquiries and proceedings, the European Court admitted, for example, that the use of *anonymous testimony* was not always incompatible with the Convention (Doorson *v.* The Netherlands). In some cases, indeed, as those linked to terrorism, the witnesses needed to be protected against the eventual risk of retaliation that could bring into play their life, liberty or security: The Court had recognized in principle in Mechelen *v.* The Netherlands that, provided that the rights of the defence are respected, it might be legitimate for the police authorities to wish to preserve the anonymity of an agent deployed in undercover activities, for his own or his family's protection and so as not to impair his usefulness for future operations.

On 14 July, 1999 the *Organization of African Unity (OAU)*, motivated by the desire to establish a coordinated legal framework for combating terrorism in Africa, adopted the OAU Convention on the Prevention and Combating of Terrorism (The OAU Convention on terrorism). The Convention recognizes that "terrorism constitutes a serious violation of human rights and, in particular, the rights to phys-

---

17   ECHR, 6 September 1978, para. 49.

ical integrity, life, freedom and security, and impedes socio-economic development through destabilization of States."

Moreover, following the 11 September events, some African leaders felt the need to renew their collective efforts to fight terrorism and adopted the Dakar Declaration which expressed concern that the development of terrorism continued to constitute an unacceptable infringement of the most essential human rights and democracy, as well as a threat to world peace and security.

When it comes to the international dimensions of prevention, there are formidable new challenges for international law. As we have seen earlier, the International Court of Justice has taken the view in one Opinion that the right of self-defence is applicable in respect of threats of an armed attack by one State against another State. Nowadays, however, terrorist groups present serious dangers to the security of targeted States and it is feared that non-state terrorist groups could resort to use of a weapon of mass destruction.

If a government has solid evidence of such a threat posed by a non-state actor, it is surely entitled to act for the protection of its security and that of its citizens. In such a case, it would be our submission that the proper course of action would be for the State perceiving the threat to approach the State from which the group is operating and ask it to act to remove the threat. In the event that this is not possible, or the danger is so great, it would be our submission that the government at risk has a duty of consultation with the United Nations Security Council.

10. Proportionality

In its Advisory Opinion on the legal consequences of the construction of a wall the International Court of Justice took the following position "The Court, from the material available to it, is not convinced that the specific course Israel has chosen for the wall was necessary to attain its security objectives. The wall, along the route chosen, and its associated régime gravely infringe a number of rights of Palestinians residing in the territory occupied by Israel, and the infringements resulting from that route cannot be justified by military exigencies or by the requirements of national security or public order. The construction of such a wall accordingly constitutes breaches by Israel of various of its obligations under the applicable international humanitarian law and human rights instruments."

Dealing with the argument of "necessity" the Court, recalling its earlier jurisprudence, declared the following: "the state of necessity is a ground recognized by customary international law" that "can only be accepted on an exceptional basis"; it "can only be invoked under certain strictly defined conditions which must be cumulatively satisfied: and the State concerned is not the sole judge of whether those conditions have been met." (ICJ Reports 1997, p. 40, para.51).

11. International Human Rights Law

The principal questions that arise here are: how are international human rights and humanitarian law applicable to non-state terrorist organizations? And then there is the issue of whether terrorists commit crimes only or whether they also commit violations of human rights.

A legal advisor in the Legal Division of the International Committee of the Red Cross wrote recently:

> The essential humanitarian function of humanitarian law is carried out through the parties to the conflict. They have rights and responsibilities. There can be no humanitarian law conflict without identifiable parties."

"Terror" or "terrorism" cannot be a party to the conflict. As a result, a war on terror cannot be a humanitarian law event. It has been suggested that wars against proper nouns (*e.g.* Germany and Japan) have advantages over those against common nouns (*e.g.* crime, poverty, terrorism), since proper nouns can surrender and promise not to do it again. Humanitarian law is not concerned with the entitlement to engage in hostilities or the promise not to do so again (the *"jus ad bellu"*). Rather, it concerns the conduct of hostilities and the treatment of persons in the power of the enemy (the *"jus in bello"*). But there is still a strong connection to humanitarian law in this observation. The concept of a "party" suggests a minimum level of organization required to enable the entity to carry out the obligations of law. There can be no assessment of rights and responsibilities under humanitarian law in a war without identifiable parties.

A terrorist group can conceivably be a party to an armed conflict and a subject of humanitarian law, but the lack of commonly accepted definitions is a hurdle. What exactly is terrorism? What is a terrorist act? Does terrorism include state actors? How is terrorism distinguished from "mere" criminality? How has the international community's reaction to terrorism differed from its treatment of mere criminality; from its traditional treatment of international and non-international armed conflict?"[18]

The second issue, namely whether terrorists commit violations of human rights, has been the subject of extensive discussion as well as of study by the Special Rapporteur of the Sub-Commission on the Promotion and Protection of Human Rights, Mrs. K. Kouffa. In her final report to the Sub-Commission submitted in the summer of 2004 she crystallized her view that modern trends in human rights practice indicated some modification of the traditional position that private individuals or groups do not have the legal capacity to violate human rights. She notes that resolutions of the General Assembly, the Commission on Human Rights and the Sub-Commission itself speak of terrorism as a violation of human rights. Nevertheless, she observes:

> Notwithstanding the adverse consequences for the enjoyment of human rights of all acts, methods and practices of terrorism, the exact meaning, scope, pertinence and

---

18   G. Rona, "International Law under Fire: Interesting Times for International Humanitarian Law: Challenges from the 'War on Terror'", *Fletcher Forum of World Affairs Journal*, Summer/Fall 2003.

legal implications of an assertion that terrorists and other non-State actors are bound by human rights law and may be held accountable for violating it remain very controversial.

The major argument she cites against application of human rights obligations to non-state actors stresses that this would carry the risk that States might defer their responsibility to these actors, which might diminish existing State obligations and accountability. The counter argument was that there was reasonable concern about preventing the scrutiny by the international community of actions by armed insurgencies and individuals that would, within the present interpretations of international human rights and humanitarian law, clearly constitute massive violations of human rights if committed by a State. She added:

> Furthermore, ... the international human rights movement may have been concentrating, possibly for too long, on the repressive measures adopted by the governments only, without paying much attention to the means used by those opposing them. (... para. 55)

11. International Humanitarian Law

The major issue that recent practice has thrown up for consideration in international law is the legal status of persons accused of terrorist acts. If the terrorist act takes place within the jurisdiction of the State of nationality of the terrorist, then this issue will be dealt with by the relevant provisions of national criminal law and by international human rights law. If, however, there is an international dimension to the issue, problems may arise. In the case of the Guantanamo detainees, the United States detained and transferred to Guantanamo over 600 persons who allegedly fought on the Taliban side, but were not members of armed forces in the sense of the Geneva Conventions. In at least two other instances, United States military authorities took into their custody and removed abroad persons alleged to have committed terrorist acts, or considered to pose terrorist threats. In one instance, United States military forces took into their custody and removed from Sarajevo six persons said to pose terrorist threats and, in another instance, some alleged terrorists were also taken into custody and removed from Zambia.

The persons taken from Sarajevo and Zambia were clearly not members of an armed force and were not engaged in military activities. They were clearly not combatants and must be considered to benefit from the protection of international human rights law. The Bosnia/Herzegovina Human Rights Chamber, in a trenchant Opinion, called for respect for due process and of the provisions of international human rights law in the treatment of these persons.

The United States has asserted that the persons detained in Afghanistan and taken to Guantanamo were "illegal combatants" who did not satisfy the requirements of Article 4 of the Third Geneva Convention regulating the status of a prisoner of war. Article 4 of the Third Geneva Convention provides that a prisoner of war is a person who has fallen into the power of the enemy and is a member of the armed forces of a party to the conflict or of militias or volunteer corps forming part of such armed forces. However, in respect of militias, volunteer corps, or organized resistance movements, it is necessary to show that it is being commanded by a person responsible for his subordinates; that it has a fixed distinctive sign recognizable at a distance; that it is carrying arms openly; and that it is conducting operations in accordance with the laws and customs of war. Terrorists clearly do not meet these requirements.

It would be our submission that the status of "unlawful combatant" is unacceptable in international humanitarian law, which recognizes categories such as combatants, civilians, protected persons, civilian detainees, and persons who have fallen in combat and are therefore entitled to protection. To admit the concept of an "unlawful combatant" would be to place people outside of the regime of international humanitarian law, and leave them without the protection of that body of law. If the person is not a combatant in the sense of the Geneva Convention, then the person is a civilian subject to international criminal law and entitled to the protection of international human rights law.

12. Reprisals: Targeted Assassinations

One of the issues that have emerged in practice in recent years concerns the question of targeted assassinations of persons deemed, by one or more governments, a terrorist. In a rather well-known incident, the United States, using a Drone aircraft, launched a missile attack against alleged terrorists in Yemen and killed a number of people. The United States claimed the right to do this in the war against terrorism. This case, while discussed in the media, did not come up for consideration in any international body.

Israel's policy of targeted assassinations has however come in for comments within the United Nations. A case in point was that of Sheikh Ahmed Yassin who was killed with eight others (with more than a dozen wounded, some critically) when an Israeli helicopter gunship fired on them in their vehicles early in the morning as they were leaving a Mosque in Gaza on 22nd March 2004. Yassin was one of the founders of Hamas in 1978 and was considered its "spiritual leader". In 1989, he was arrested by Israeli forces and sentenced in 1991 to life imprisonment for ordering the killings of Israelis and Palestinians who had allegedly collaborated with the Israeli Army. He was released in 1997 in an exchange of prisoners. Israel had been open about its intention to kill him and narrowly missed doing so in September 2003.

The Israeli position was that Yassin was the dominant authority of the Hamas leadership which was directly involved in planning, orchestrating and launching terror attacks carried out by the organization. According to Israel, Yassin had personally given his approval for the launching of Kassam rockets against Israeli cities, as well as for the numerous Hamas terrorist bombings and suicide operations. Israel claimed that in his public appearances and interviews Yassin had repeatedly called for a continuation of the "armed struggle against Israel and for an intensification of attacks against its citizens." Israel considered the successful operation against Yassin a significant blow to a central figure of the Hamas organization and a major setback to its terrorist infrastructure.

The Secretary-General of the United Nations, in a statement issued on 22 March 2004, strongly condemned Israel's assassination of Yassin. He reiterated that extrajudicial killings are against international law and called on the government of Israel to immediately end this practice.

This case raises serious issues of principle and of law. The right to life is guaranteed in international human rights law and there may be no derogation from it. The Human Rights Committee, which monitors the implementation of the International Covenant on Civil and Political Rights, has expressed concern about targeted killings of those identified as suspected terrorists. In its comments following consideration of a report by Israel, the Committee stated: "the State party should not use 'targeted killings' as a deterrent or punishment...before resorting to the use of deadly force, all measures to arrest a person suspected of being in the process of committing acts of terror must be exhausted."[19]

Under international humanitarian law, civilians under occupation are protected persons under the Geneva Conventions and its Protocols. They may lose their protected status if they engage in military activities, but while a person could lose his protected status for the duration of his armed engagement, does proof or suspicion that a person participated in an armed attack at an earlier point justify targeting him for death later on?

The Commission on Human Rights, which has a known reputation for being critical of Israel, has condemned the "practice of liquidation" and "extrajudicial executions" carried out by the Israeli army against Palestinians. The Commission similarly condemned the killing of Sheikh Yassin.

The issue of law and policy that is presented for consideration in cases such as those we have mentioned above is: in an age of global terrorism by non-state actors, is it a legitimate act of self-defence for a state to kill someone against whom it has solid evidence that he has committed acts of terrorism and is planning to do so in the future. Is it realistic, for example, to expect the United States or other countries to wait until they can arrest Osama bin Laden and bring him to trial? This would be an absurd proposition.

At the same time, it cannot be left simply to the security forces of a country to deem a person a terrorist and then to proceed to kill that person. For the international constitutional and legal architecture of the future, we would advance the following propositions: First, there should be a procedure within the framework of the Security Council for a State to present evidence in its possession about the international terrorist activities of an individual and for there to be scrutiny of such information before any intervention to eliminate the terrorist can be accepted. Likewise at the national level there should be a procedure whereby there is a judicial or quasi-judicial process for the designation of a person as a terrorist before any fatal action can be taken against that person.

---

19   CCPR/CO/78/ISR, 21 August 2003.

13. Conclusion

We would conclude this chapter by noting that non-state terrorist organizations pose a major threat to humanity, especially when one considers the dangers of their use of weapons of mass destruction. Whereas, when it comes to state behavior, one can develop rules and codes of conduct, terrorist non-state actors are outside the law. The international constitutional and legal architecture of the future must come to terms with this unfortunate reality.

As far as the determination of a non-state terrorist organization is concerned, it is not easy to put down rules because, by their very nature, they are hidden, nefarious organizations. Nevertheless, there cannot be a free-for-all, otherwise there would be no law. It would be our submission that it is for the "1267 Committee" of the United Nations Security Council to determine what is a terrorist organization. It must do this on the basis of pre-announced criteria and with the possibility of recourse by an individual or an organization to clear its name.

From this perspective it would be our submission that the future international constitutional and legal architecture to deal with threats of terrorism from non-state organizations should include a legal advisory board of the "1267 Committee" to which issues of legality and human rights might be referred for advice.

The issue of risk-assessment in respect of threats of terrorism by non-state organizations presents particular challenges. To leave the determination of risk solely to a national authority carries serious dangers of arbitrariness and unlawfulness. It therefore must be right to insist on a role for the United Nations Security Council when it comes to the determination of risk insofar as *international* terrorism is involved.

The international criminal responsibility of terrorists must be reinforced. One must also insist on the international responsibility of states to prevent international terrorist organizations from operating within their territories or jurisdiction.

The issue of self-defense against international terrorism is an important one. It surely cannot be correct to hold, as the International Court of Justice did, that the right of self-defence under Article 51 of the United Nations Charter exists only in respect of threats from another State. The threat of the use of weapons of mass destruction is as great, if not greater, from terrorist organizations. How then, can one say that a State has the right of self-defence against another State, but not against an international terrorist organization ...?

The duty to act to prevent terrorism is an international as well as a national one. In its future deliberations, the Counter-Terrorism Committee of the Security Council would do well to give regular consideration to the preventive aspect.

The principle of proportionality must remain a basic pillar of the law in the fight against terrorism and everything must be done to uphold international human rights and humanitarian law. It would be our submission that targeted killings of known international terrorists cannot be excluded, but there must be legal and procedural safeguards.

From the foregoing it will be seen that challenging new issues arise for consideration in the international constitutional and legal architecture of the future that would be required to deal with international terrorist threats particularly combined with the use of weapons of mass destruction. It is a riskier and even more dangerous world that we face.

26. The Doctrine of "Just War" and Contemporary International Law

Benedetto Conforti *

An outstanding Italian scholar, Rolando Quadri, wrote in his textbook on public international law, a text wherein many opinions are still up to date and extremely interesting indeed: "No doubt the distinction between *just and unjust wars* was rejected and considered as a mere historical curiosity in the 19th and in the first decades of the 20th century".[1]

As it is known, the rejection was due to the adoption of positivism in legal doctrine and, in the realm of international law, the idea that war was *in all cases* legal, that it pertained to the *physiology* of the international community. War being legal and inevitable, no other task was to be performed by States than that of making humanitarian rules regarding the conduct of hostilities. Centuries and centuries of speculations about war, particularly the right to resort to war (*jus ad bellum*) and the notion of just war, were cancelled in a very short time. The doctrine of just war – a doctrine professed in the first instance by theologians and experts in canon law, from St. Augustine and St. Thomas Aquinas to Francisco De Vitoria, followed by international lawyers, from Hugo Grotius to the last representatives of the School of natural law in the 19th century – has never been resurrected as a current legal doctrine. It is my firm opinion, however, that its study would be very useful in contemporary times, when the resort to war is tragically increasing. I will show in a moment how, and to what extent, the knowledge of such doctrine is to be taken into account today. First, and although very quickly and superficially, it may be useful to recall the principal opinions expressed in the past on the subject of just war.

Although some precedents of the doctrine of just war can be found among the ancient Greek and Roman authors, it is only in the pre-medieval literature that it

---

* The author is grateful to Brill Academic Publishers and the Board of Editors of the Italian Yearbook of International Law for allowing him to publish this article, which first appeared in the Yearbook, Volume XII (2002), in this book.

1 QUADRI, *Diritto internazionale pubblico*, 5th ed., Napoli, 1968, p. 284.

Ronald St. John Macdonald & Douglas M. Johnston (eds.), Towards World Constitutionalism, *pp. 705-713.*
© *2005 Koninklijke Brill NV. Printed in The Netherlands.* ISBN 90 04 14612 1.

was expressed in its most complete and precise form.[2] Understandably, the question was raised within the Christian community as to whether war, with its tragic consequences, was a sin or not. St. Augustine gave a thorough answer to this question. His opinion remained authoritative for a very long time. What he had written about the just war was expanded and developed, but not rejected, by subsequent scholars.

In Augustine's opinion, war can be resorted to only in cases of extreme necessity. It is just when it aims at avenging or repelling an injustice (*"ulcisci injurias"*), or at punishing a people or a State (*"gens vel civitas"*) whose members have committed heinous crimes, or at recovering what has been unjustly taken (*"quod per injurias ablatum est"*). War is just also whenever it is ordered by God, as in the case of the biblical war of the Jews against the Cananeis and the Amalechites.[3] Posterity has discussed at length what the word *"ulcisci"* means; particularly it has been discussed whether it has a criminal law meaning, *i.e.* the punishment for a negligent or intentional wrongful act, or if it refers to the mere reaction against an objective wrong. As we shall see, two different streams of thought are linked to the one or the other meaning. Lastly, according to Augustine, just war must provoke peace and order (*"tranquillitatis ordinis"*) as well as the redemption of the enemy who should be persuaded of the necessity of peace (*"ut eos quos expugnas ad pacis utilitatem vincendo perducas"*): when these are the consequences, war can be compatible with Christian religion and the love for others.

There are other aspects of Augustine's doctrine, such as, for instance, the opinion that war must only be made by rulers (*"princeps"*), not by private persons, but these can be set aside since they are not relevant in relation to the wars of today.

Also worth noting is the fact that Augustine does not expressly and clearly deal with self-defence as a justification for war. However, still in the pre-medieval epoch, the matter was treated, before and after him, by other scholars, such as Saint Ambrose, bishop of Milan (340-397) and St. Isidore of Seville (560-636), who adds the counter-attack on the enemy (*"propulsandorum hostium causa"*) to the reparation of an injustice as a cause of just war.

In the Middle Ages, all the theologians and experts in canon law essentially followed Augustine's doctrine, with few additions or modifications. Among these, worthy of note is the expanded treatment of self-defence. Gratianus, the compiler of the famous *Decretum* or *Concordantia discordantium canonum* (about 1150), has to be quoted in this regard, since he thoroughly deals with what we call today collective self-defence: those who do not help the attacked ally – he says – become accomplices of the enemy (*"jniurias sociorum est propulsanda... Hoc qui non facit, consentit"*).

---

2   With regard to the pre-medieval and medieval authors who are quoted in the present paragraph, references are taken from the very precise and detailed book by Regout, *La doctrine de la guerre juste de Saint Augustin à nos jours*, Paris, 1934, Parts 1 and 2.

3   On the war directly ordered by God, which should not be identified with the (unjust) war for making proselytes, see Gentili, *De jure belli* (1612), in Scott, *The Classics of International Law*, Oxford, 1933, Vol. I, Chapter VIII, p. 56 ff., with quotations from Augustine and many others authors.

Notwithstanding the monumental philosophical work contained in the *Summa theologica*, the contribution of St. Thomas Aquinas to the doctrine of just war does not depart in essence from Augustine's thoughts either. For him, the just cause of war is the fault of the enemy ("*illi qui impugnantur propter aliquam culpam impugnationem mereantur*"), so that just war acquires the form of a true punishment. As rulers can punish criminals who trouble the internal order, so too they can protect their communities against external enemies. Expressly, Thomas interprets in such a way the Augustinian "*ulcisci jniuria*".

An important new idea appears with Thomas Aquinas however, that being the idea that war should pursue the general interest, the common good ("*pugna quae est licita fit pro commune utilitate*" and "*Homo defendit bonum commune per justum bello*"). The common good Thomas refers to in this quotation is without qualification, so that it may be interpreted as the interest of mankind as a whole. In other parts of the *Summa*, however, it becomes the good of Christianity exclusively, when it is necessary to react against anybody who wants to prevent the spread of the Christian faith: to prevent the spread of the Christian faith – it must be clear – not to convert the unbelievers ("*fideles Christi frequenter contra infideles bellum movent, non quidem ut eos ad credendum cogant...sed propter hoc ut eos compellant ne fidem Christi impediant*"). In fact, Thomas clearly condemns war aimed at gaining proselytes. Conversion to the Christian faith is a question of persuasion, not of war. This statement is maintained by subsequent scholars, and with particular force by Francisco De Vitoria and Alberico Gentili.

Francisco De Vitoria (1483-1546), the great Spanish scholar who can be considered half theologian and half lawyer or, better, a kind of bridge between medieval scholars and the founders of the modern science of international law, takes the pre-medieval and medieval doctrines of just war as the basic ingredients of his re-elaboration of the natural law of war.[4] Although, like Thomas Aquinas, Vitoria holds that, generally speaking, the cause of just war is the wrongful injustice of the enemy, he admits that in exceptional circumstances a war can be made even when the fault is not attributable to the enemy, if the use of force is necessary for obtaining the respect of a right. Examples of such exceptions are war which aims at recovering property ("*ad repetendas res*") or at repelling unjustified but not wrongful attacks from barbarian people.[5] It is worth noting that the idea that war

---

4   The re-elaboration is contained in two out the twelve "*Relectiones theologicae*", entitled respectively "*De indis recenter inventis – Relectio prior*" (hereinafter *De Indis*) e "*De Indis, sive de jure belli Hispanorum in barbaros – Relectio Posterior*" (hereinafter *De jure belli*), both in SCOTT, *cit. supra* note 3, Washington, 1917.

5   "*In bello licet omnia facere, quae necessaria sunt ad defensionem boni publici... Licet recuperare omnes res perditas et illarum partem. Haec etiam est notior quam ut indigeat probatione. Ad hoc enim vel infertur vel suscipitur bellum*", (*De jure belli, cit. supra* note 4, p. 430). On the war against the Indians as self-defence, see for instance *De Indis*, Sect. III, *cit. supra* note 4, p. 394 ("*Postquam autem, ut dictum est, licet Hispanis bellum suscipere, vel etiam, si necesse sit, inferre, ergo licet omnia facere necessaria ad finem belli, scilicet ad obtinendam securitatem et pacem*").

is exceptionally justified when a right is infringed, and no other means are available to restore the previous situation, anticipates the theory of war as an extreme means of protecting a right (*"juris executio"*), which was later professed by Grotius as a general rule of the right to make war. It is only an anticipation, however, since in Vitoria, unlike in Grotius, war is still considered as a punishment.

Like Thomas Aquinas, Vitoria does not consider a war to be just when used for spreading the Christian faith. On the contrary, as it is well known, the larger part of his work was devoted to the defence of the Indians' rights, and to the rejection of the justifications for their subjection to Spanish domination.

Perhaps one of the most important and new elements of Vitoria's doctrine on just war is proportionality. For him, the resort to war becomes unjust if it is not proportionate to the aims pursued, if there is not a correct balance between the use of force and the utility sought (a balance, it must be clear, between the use of force and the utility sought, not between the war and the injustice suffered). He says textually:

> If the recovery of one town entails heavy damages, such as the devastation of others towns, the justification for other wars, the death of numerous persons, the irritation of other rulers (*"irritatio principum"*)... then the ruler must give up his right and abstain from the use of force....[6]

Vitoria's answer to the question of whether war can be considered just when it entails the death of innocent people, like women and children, is also to be recalled here, although it pertains rather to the limits to the hostilities (*"jus in bello"*) – a subject which is beyond the scope of this study – than to the right to make war (*"jus ad bellum"*). According to him, war is just only when such deaths are intentionally provoked (*"nunquam licet per se et ex intentione interficere innocentem"*).[7]

Another question answered by Vitoria – a question already treated before him but more frequently treated after him – is whether war can be just from the point of view of both belligerents. Objectively – he says – this is impossible, since the injustice and its victim cannot be confused. It may happen, however, that people on the wrong side are in good faith and erroneously and inflexibly believe that they are right (*"ignorantia invincibilis"*). In this case both sides are excused, one for objective and the other for subjective reasons.[8]

The additions and modifications to the ideas and opinions on just war, which can be found in the works of international lawyers between the 16th and the 19th centuries, *i.e.* in the epoch characterized by the School of Natural Law, are very few. Even the founders of the modern science of international law, Alberico Gentili

---

6   *De jure belli, cit. supra* note 4, p. 445: "... *si ad recuperandam unam civitatem necesse est quod sequantur maiora mala..., ut vastatio multarum civitatum, caedes magna mortalium, irritatio principum, occasiones novorum bellorum...indubitatum est quin teneatur princeps potius cedere iuri suo et abstinere se bello"*.

7   *Ibid.*, p. 446.

8   *Ibid.*, p. 443 f.; *De Indis*, Sect. III, *cit. supra* note 4, p. 396.

and Hugo Grotius, to whom we are indebted for so many developments in a wide range of topics of international law, lack originality on the subject we are dealing with. They, and all the authors after them, repeat what had already been said in the past. However, they do this by adopting more accurate terminology, a more legal approach and more modern categories. For instance, injustice as a cause of just war becomes once and for all the violation of a right ("*bellum justum* – says Grotius – *est juris executio*");[9] self-defence is divided into different kinds by Gentili, in particular into subsequent self-defence ("*necessaria defensio*"), preventive self-defence ("*utilis defensio*") and collective self-defence ("*honesta defensio*").[10] The consideration of war as *extrema ratio* is accompanied by the theory of the friendly and peaceful solution of disputes, particularly by the German philosopher and lawyer Christian Wolff (1679-1754)[11] and his pupil, the great Swiss international lawyer, Emerich De Vattel (1714-1767).[12]

I have given nothing more than a very general idea of the doctrine of just war, a doctrine extremely rich in details and developments. By contrast, the *jus ad bellum* is treated in a very poor way by positivists pertaining to the different streams of thought, including the so-called "normativist" stream of the Wiener School. From the beginning of the 20th century until the end of the Scond World War, war was considered by international lawyers as almost legal, with very few exceptions – very soon abandoned in practice – embodied in the Covenant of the League of Nations. The use of force was considered to be a natural and physiological event within the international community. It is interesting to remind ourselves of the opinion of the authoritative Italian scholar and judge at the ICJ, Gaetano Morelli, who taught in Naples and Rome before and after the Second World War. He wrote in his textbook, developing ideas already expressed by Dionisio Anzilotti at the beginning of the 20th century:

> The rule of international law according to which every State has the right [*potere giuridico*] to make war ... is adherent to the structure of the international legal order ... Such a rule gives a flexibility to the international legal order which is unknown within the domestic legal orders... The use of force is permitted in international law as a way to ensure the necessary renewal of international law when this cannot happen by means of agreements....[13]

---

9   Grotius, *De jure praedae* (1604), in HAMAKER (ed.), The Hague, 1868, p. 66.

10   *De jure belli, cit. supra* note 4, Vol. I, Chapter XIII, p. 92 ff.

11   *Jus gentium methodo scientifica pertractatum* (1764), in SCOTT, *cit. supra* note 3, Oxford, 1934, p. 205, § 572.

12   PRADIER FODÉRÉ (ed.), *Le droit des gens ou principes de la loi naturelle appliqués à la conduites et aux affaires des Nations et des souveraines*, Paris, 1863, Vol. II, p. 303 ff, § 326 ff.

13   MORELLI, *Nozioni di diritto internazionale*, 7th ed., Padova, 1967, p. 50 f. See also ANZILOTTI, *Corso di diritto internazionale*, Vol. III, Part I, Roma, 1915, p. 183 ff.

After the Second World War a radical change of opinions among international lawyers gradually occurred. As it is known, the UN Charter considers war as a "scourge ... which has brought untold sorrow to mankind" (Preamble) and declares that member States shall refrain from the threat or the use of force (Article 2, n. 4) with the exception of the right of individual or collective self-defence if an armed attack occurs against a member State (the *necessaria defensio*, according to the terminology of Alberico Gentili) (Article 51). It is also known that the prohibition of the use of force by States has its *pendant* in the system of collective security, headed by the Security Council (Articles 39 ff.) and includes the possibility for the Council to decide on military interventions (Article 42).

In fact, before the United Nations achieved universality, the obligation to refrain from the use of force was considered as limited to member States and not imposed on *all* States by a general principle of international law. This is the reason why the opinion of G. Morelli we have quoted above was even maintained by him in the last edition of his textbook, which appeared in 1967. By contrast, when the UN became a truly universal organization, and many solemn declarations and opinions (unfortunately only declarations and opinions, not facts!) were expressed by States in favour of peace, the idea that the use of force was prohibited even by general international law, apart from the cases authorised by the Charter, became generally accepted. Perhaps the peak of this idea was the opinion held by the International Court of Justice in 1986 in the *Military and Paramilitary Activities* case (*Nicaragua v. United States*), wherein Article 2(4) of the Charter was considered as corresponding not only to a customary principle of international law but also as a fundamental and essential principle of such law.[14]

Then, in no more than fifty years, the unilateral use of force (i.e. the use of force not permitted by a universal organization especially competent in maintaining international peace and security) passed from full legality to full illegality! Of course, attempts have been made to find justifications and exculpations for wars made outside the UN system, both during the Cold War (suffice it to remember the interventions of the two super powers in countries within their sphere of influence, or wars made by Israel, India and South Africa against their neighbours) and after the fall of the Berlin Wall (such as air strikes against the Republic of Yugoslavia, use of force against Afghanistan until the recent war against Iraq). In each case many arguments have been put forward, for instance by enlarging the notion of self-defence or inventing new customary exceptions. By contrast, the principle of the prohibition of unilateral use of force has been strongly defended. I do not intend to deal in depth with those arguments or counter-arguments. In my opinion, looking at the practice, that is, at what States do and not at what they say, a fundamental

---

14   ICJ Reports, 1986, para. 187 ff. *Inter alia* the Court says that a "... confirmation of the validity as customary law of the principle of the prohibition of the use of force expressed in Article 2(4) of the Charter of the United Nations may be found in the fact that it is frequently referred to in statements by States representatives as being not only a principle of customary international law but also a fundamental or cardinal principle of such law" (*ibid.*, para. 190).

question remains open and is the following: do indisputable and general principles of international law on the use of force really exist, irrespective of whether they prohibit or permit war? I have serious doubts that it is possible to give an affirmative answer to this question.

In my opinion, the prohibition of the use of force is strictly linked to the UN system of collective security under the direction of the Security Council: if and when the system does not work, if and when the United Nations is unable to prevent a crisis or to intervene by military operations or other means provided for by Chapter VII of the Charter, then the prohibition does not work. When force is used, and the United Nations is unable to control it, the result is that international law is unable to govern the *jus ad bellum*. A war that is not authorized or controlled according to the Charter is neither illegal nor legal; it is beyond right and wrong in the international legal order; legally speaking it pertains to the realm of indifference.[15] International law has not been able to express an evaluation whatsoever of the use of force outside the UN system.

By saying that there is a kind of "lacuna" in international law as far as the evaluation of war is concerned, I do not want to embark on a discussion of the completeness of legal orders, nor to discuss the question of whether everything which is not forbidden is legally permitted. These are theoretical speculations that can be left to the philosophers. What I want to say is that, up to now, international law has not been able to govern the right to use force, and that the United Nations has quite unsuccessfully tried to fill this gap.

If no legal rules exist, the way is opened to discuss the problem of war by resuming the old debate on just war, by placing the debate in its proper context, *i.e.* in the context of the old and eternal principles of natural law. The alternative now suggested by positivists in the sense that the war is legal if made within the system of the United Nations and illegal if not, is a radical opinion which has stifled such a rich debate. Even in the public opinion the dispute among peace-loving and non peace-loving peoples is focused on the alternative between wars authorized or not authorized by the Security Council. I do not understand such an alternative. For me, even a war that is authorized by the Security Council is no less a tragedy for the innocent people involved than a war which, perhaps thanks to a clever diplomatic game, succeeds in being supported by the majority of the Council. Assuming that the United States and the United Kingdom succeeded in getting the authorization for the war against Iraq in March 2003, can we say that such an event was able, by itself, to alleviate the suffering of the Iraqi people?

The resumption of the old debate does not mean that all the opinions of the scholars of natural law and even the opinions of the medieval theologians can be adopted *sic et simpliciter* today. It is rather the case that we must develop and adapt

---

15   As a precedent, see McNair, "Collective Security", *BYIL*, 1936, p. 152, according to whom the war is "extra-legal". This word is interpreted by Tucker ("The Interpretation of War Under Present International Law", *ICLQ*, 1961, p. 13) as meaning that war is not authorized by the law, yet at the same time it is not legally forbidden "since the law attaches no specific consequences, especially a sanction, to the commission of the act".

to new circumstances the eternal verities contained in the doctrine of just war; *i.e.*, using the words of an Italian scholar of the end of the 19th century, "those supreme rules all moral individuals must abide by in order to ensure their coexistence."[16]

Of course, some of the old opinions cannot be used today: it would be absurd, for instance, to resume St. Thomas' doctrine on war as a punishment, or the Augustinian theory on war "*ad repetendas res*". By contrast, some other ideas could be very usefully resumed and made up-to-date. This is the case, for instance, of the common idea that war is an extreme means to resort to when all other peaceful means have been exhausted, or Vitoria's idea that a balance should always exist between war and the utility which is sought by using such force. Perhaps, by applying these ideas, it could be possible to justify humanitarian interventions when all attempts at convincing a government not to commit genocide and other atrocities against innocent people have proved useless.[17] By the same token, I wonder whether the reaction against the crime of terrorism can consist in the use of force *against States*, involving the death of innocent people, instead of the adoption of all the appropriate preventive and repressive measures *against the individuals* committing such crimes. Moreover, can we justify a war that, according to Augustine's formula, neither provokes peace and order nor the redemption of the enemy, with the sole consequence of increasing the hatred for war-making? On the other hand, by applying the doctrine of just war, can preventive self-defence (the "*utilis defensio*", according to Alberico Gentili) be excluded in any case? Can it be excluded when it is proved that an attack with weapons of mass destruction is absolutely imminent and there are no other means to avoid it?

I have no precise answer to these and similar questions. A precise list of the cases wherein war may or may not be considered as a just war is out of the scope of this chapter. My only purpose is a methodological one, that is, to affirm that the problem of the right to make war cannot be solved unless we resort to natural law. Having said that, the debate is open and the opinions are varied. What is necessary is to prove that a certain opinion corresponds to the universal conscience: in particular, evidence can be drawn *pro* or *contra* a certain war from the attitude of the international community as a whole, as is expressed by the General Assembly of the United Nations and/or public opinion in the world. From this point of view, and taking into account that not every war is rejected by the common opinion as unjust – this is true for instance as far as humanitarian interventions are concerned – even the doctrine of just war, upheld today by the Catholic Church, according to which self-defence is the only permitted use of force, seems too restrictive. How-

---

16   FIORE, *Trattato di diritto internazionale pubblico*, 4th ed., Torino, 1904, p. 118.

17   Humanitarian interventions are justified in the volume *The Responsibility to Protect – Report of the International Commission on Intervention and State Sovereignty*, International Development Research Center, 2001, particularly the part entitled *Synopsis, Principles for Military Intervention*, (1) *The Just Cause Threshold*. The reasons for justifications are very close to the just war doctrine. The volume is also on line: http://www.idrc.ca/booktique.

ever the notion of self-defence adopted by the Catholic Church seems to be very broad.[18]

It should be clear that my attempt at resurrecting natural law principles and doctrines is limited exclusively to the right to make war. I am and remain a positivist in all other sectors of international law. In fact, natural law may work, and has worked, when positive law is no longer able to work. In national law it serves when anarchy and confusion are predominant. For instance natural law was applied in Germany and in Japan by the Nuremberg and Tokyo Tribunals after the Second World War. Natural law can justify even the retroactive application of criminal law in post-war conflicts, in order to punish individuals who have committed atrocities not considered to be a crime in their country at the time they were committed. Moreover, the famous doctrine known as the Radbruch formula, expressed in post-Nazi Germany and resumed by some German courts after the reunification of the country in the nineties, is also based on natural law principles. According to this doctrine, national positive law must be set aside when it becomes absolutely intolerable from the point of view of common justice.[19] If anarchy and confusion entails the application of natural law in national legal orders, it is understandable why I attempt to resort to natural law in order to evaluate the war within the international community wherein anarchy and confusion are unfortunately endemic.

---

18   See rules 2308 and 2309 of the Catechism issued from the Council Vatican II, under the fifth commandment (Do not kill). Self-defence is not restricted to the response to an armed attack, like in Article 2(2) of the Charter, but is justified when "the damage" inflicted by the aggressor on the nation or the community of nations is "lasting, grave and certain". On the other hand, even the action in self-defence is subject to "strict conditions" which, as the text of the Catechism itself says, are "the traditional elements enumerated in what is called the "just war" doctrine", *i.e.*: "... – all other means must have been shown to be impractical or ineffective; – there must be serious prospects of success; – the use of arms must not produce evils and disorders graver than the evil to be eliminated ...".

19   The doctrine, expressed for the first time in 1946, can be found in RADBRUCH, *Rechtsphilosophie*, 5th ed., Stuttgart, 1956, p. 135 ff. For applications by German courts after the reunification, in order to avoid the rule contained in the Reunification Treaty, according to which the crimes committed in the DDR had to be judged by applying DDR criminal rules, see VASSALLI, *Formula di Radbruch e diritto penale (Note sulla punizione dei "delitti di Stato" nella Germania postnazista e nella Germania post-comunista)*, Milano, 2001, p. 68 ff.

27. *Hostes Humani Generis*: Piracy, Territory and the Concept of Universal Jurisdiction

Hilario G. Davide, Jr.

1. Introduction

Any standard textbook on public international law includes some entry on piracy in the law of nations. While this chapter will inevitably take us through piracy as the current state of international law deals with it, I propose to review international law on piracy as the progenitor of the controversial doctrine of "universal jurisdiction" which, although received with enthusiasm by many States, is approached with great trepidation by others. I will, therefore, be concerned with the question why, for several centuries now, piracy has been almost unanimously accepted as a ground for the exercise of "universal jurisdiction" or for the application of the "universality principle." I will argue in the main that the less we think of international law as a corpus of fixed rules – a position resulting from what to me is a transposition of domestic law to international law thinking – the less we will be inclined to think of universal jurisdiction as a "derogation" to the general legal principle on jurisdiction; and the more we will be disposed to accept it as an evolving legal mechanism by which States cope with such notions as the "freedom of the high seas" and the universal interest in keeping the sea-lanes free of predators.

Even as I consider piracy more than a problem of historical interest, I will likewise examine the law on piracy itself and invite closer attention to the provisions on piracy in the 1982 *United Nations Convention on the Law of the Sea* (UNCLOS). Interestingly, the UNCLOS includes aircrafts while previous international law instruments dealt only with maritime vessels.

Finally, drawing from the current reception of international law in Philippine law, I propose to discuss what domestic jurisdictions may do towards the application of universal jurisdiction principally in piracy and, by extension, to other cases that current international law may recognize to be susceptible to the application of universality.

Ronald St. John Macdonald & Douglas M. Johnston (eds.), Towards World Constitutionalism, pp. 715-736.
© *2005 Koninklijke Brill NV. Printed in The Netherlands.* ISBN 90 04 14612 1.

2.   Piracy: The Facts

In some corner of almost any child's imagination is the swashbuckling band of pi-rates in the immortal childhood literature *Peter Pan*. The trouble, however, is that pirates refuse to be consigned to memory, or to the charming pages of children's books. They remain a live and pressing concern, as they continue to plague the high seas and visit terror on their prey. Neither is piracy a historical issue.

In an article in *National Geographic*, Zoltan Istvan reports that pirates had attacked 335 vessels in 2001 and 338 vessels in 2002. The year 2003 saw yet an in-crease in the number of piracy cases: 344, the highest number since 1991, resulting in 20 deaths to crew.

If 95 percent of the world's commerce is aboard marine vessels and if pov-erty in the Third World goes unabated, then the stage is set for the dangerous and deadly play of piracy. Many cases of piracy have for their object cash or anything of value. Some are highly-organized enterprises. While the highly-advertised lux-ury cruise liners have undoubtedly very wealthy passengers on board, they are not likely targets of pirates because of the huge contingent of crew on board. Ships with less crew, such as oil and chemical tankers, as well as fishing trawlers, are more likely the targets. Marine experts bewail the fact that a ship at sea is most of the time a "sitting duck" for pirates. Sadly, less than one percent of pirates are caught. This dismal rate may be attributed to problems of jurisdiction, limitations to hot pursuit, or the lack of patrol ships on the high seas.[1]

One report notes that pirates keep up with technological developments. With the increased sophistication in gadgetry available to them, their attacks conse-quently grow more lethal. The report notes the waters around Indonesia, Bangla-desh, and Somalia to be particularly dangerous. It also mentions improved condi-tions in some previously notorious pirate havens.[2]

The 1994 Report of the Secretary General of the United Nations identifies the South China Sea as the part of international waters most plagued by pirates. It notes, however, a drastic reduction of piracy incidents in the Malacca Strait, which it attributes to strict and resolute implementation of countermeasures by the lit-toral States concerned. Likewise, it identifies a new, albeit troubling, phenomenon that does not easily lend itself to characterization: Ships at sea are asked to yield to boarding parties who loot and plunder right after boarding. The Report suggests, quite correctly to my mind, that whether the acts constitute piracy will depend in a large measure on whether the boarding parties in fact have the legal right to board. In international law, there are stringent requirements for the exercise of the "right of visit" – including a strict liability clause that indemnifies vessels boarded without sufficient justification.[3]

---

1   Zoltan Istvan, "Piracy Rises Again on the High Seas, Study Says" *National Geographic Today,* December 19, 2002; Web Version.

2   CBBC Newsround, Web Version, updated October 31, 2003.

3   *Reports on Piracy,* 49th Session (1994), Report of the Secretary-General, Chapter IX, "Crime at Sea," § 190-194.

Government vessels have not been spared. In the past, seafarers were enticed and rewarded for seizing enemy vessels. This practice had very little to distinguish itself from State-sponsored piracy and "letters of marque," which gave private persons commission to plunder the maritime commerce of the enemy. Understandably, an enemy, whether man-of-war or government vessel, was a particularly prized catch. But in more placid times like ours, pirates do not seem prepared to grant concessions to government vessels. On 31 January 1985, *The San Francisco Chronicle* reported that days before, pirates boarded an American cargo ship leased to the Navy as it was passing through the notorious Strait of Malacca. While the sum they made off with, $19,471, may seem paltry today, the event was no less telling for its audacity. It was the second incident involving a Navy-chartered ship in the same Strait in two years. The pirates were armed with knives and bayonets, and traveled on a speedboat. Quite disturbingly, the report observes that piracy attacks in the area "have become almost routine since 1981."[4]

These are, of course, modern-day renditions of an age-old phenomenon. The venerable vintage of rules belonging to *jus gentium* on piracy attests to the terrifying encounter with pirates that could very well be part of the "rime" of *any* ancient mariner.

3.   Defining the Crime of Piracy: Municipal Law

It is usual for authors to distinguish between the crime of piracy that may be defined and punished by domestic legislation and piracy *juris gentium* that is properly the concern of international law. Equally important, however, is to endeavor to understand the relation, if any, between piracy that municipal law deals with and that for which customary international law has evolved some settled principles. Most likely, States would prosecute pirates apprehended on the high seas under domestic legislation on piracy.

For obvious reasons, I shall start by examining Philippine penal law on piracy. The *Revised Penal Code* of the Philippines, which took effect on 1 January 1932, and is among the earliest of Philippine law codes, classifies piracy as a crime "against national security and the law of nations." The fact that the very first category of crimes that it defines reflects sensitivity to the demands of "the law of nations" should not be missed. I am sure that this is true not only of Philippine penal law, but also of those of other jurisdictions.

4.   Piracy under Philippine Law

Article 122 of the Revised Penal Code of the Philippines provides:

> Art. 122. *Piracy in general and mutiny on the high seas.* – The penalty of *reclusion temporal* shall be inflicted upon any person who, on the high seas, shall attack or seize a

---

4   In Joseph Sweeney, Covey Oliver and Noyes Leech, *The International Legal System: Cases and Materials*, 3rd Edition, 235-236.

vessel or, not being a member of its complement nor a passenger, shall seize the whole or part of the cargo or said vessel, its equipment or personal belongings of its complement or passengers.

Under Article 27 of the Code, the penalty of *reclusion temporal* is imprisonment with a range of 12 years and 1 day to 20 years.

There are two ways of committing piracy under Article 122: (1) by attacking or seizing a vessel on the high seas; and (2) by seizing the whole or part of its cargo, its equipment, or the personal belongings of its complement or passengers while on the high seas.[5]

Since the taking of cargo or equipment, in whole or in part, is piracy, how does one distinguish between robbery on the high seas and piracy? The question draws attention to what, for Philippine law, is the defining element of piracy. What makes an act piratical is, therefore, not the taking or seizure of equipment, property or baggage on the high seas, but the attack or depredation by "those who are not members of the complement of the vessel."[6] The succeeding article, Article 123, "considers piracy as 'qualified,' warranting the penalty of *reclusion perpetua* (imprisonment from 20 years and 1 day to 40 years) to death, when the pirates 'seize' a vessel by boarding or firing upon the same." Quite importantly, the motives for the attack or the seizure are irrelevant to the domestic definition of piracy. Thus, an attack of a vessel by a member of a rebel group or insurgency movement for political purposes would constitute piracy under Philippine law. Similarly, should an activist group, like "Greenpeace," seize a vessel believed to be engaged in polluting the marine environment, it could be charged with piracy as presently defined.

Former Philippine President Ferdinand E. Marcos, exercising what he claimed to be his right to legislate as the Commander-in-Chief, enacted *Presidential Decree No. 532* including within the definition of piracy attacks on, or seizures of, vessels even in Philippine waters and even when perpetrated by the passengers or members of the complement of a vessel. The Decree was, however, meant to mete out heavier penalties on such assaults, rather than to modify the legal concept of piracy.

Ten years before the *Revised Penal Code* took effect, the Supreme Court of the Philippines had occasion to rule on piracy in *People v. Lol-lo.*[7] The accused, who were residents of the southernmost islands of the Philippines, plundered a vessel in the waters surrounding Dutch possessions and repeatedly raped two women. Charged with piracy, they filed a demurrer to evidence, claiming that the crime occurred outside Philippine territory. In upholding the trial court's denial of the demurrer, the Supreme Court, through Mr. Justice Malcolm, held:

It cannot be contended with any degree of force as was done in the lower court and as is again done in this court, that the Court of First Instance was without jurisdiction

---

5   2 Luis Reyes, *The Revised Penal Code: Criminal Law*, 13th Ed., 28-30.

6   2 Ramon Aquino, *The Revised Penal Code*, 1987 Ed., 42-44; 2 Reyes, 29.

7   43 Phil. 19 (1922).

of the case. Pirates are in law *hostes humani generis*. Piracy is a crime not against any particular state but against all mankind. It may be punished in the competent tribunal of any country where the offender may be found or into which he may be carried. The jurisdiction of piracy unlike all other crimes has no territorial limits. As it is against all so may it be punished by all. Nor does it matter that the crime was committed within the jurisdictional 3-mile limit of a foreign state, "for those limits, though neutral to war, are not neutral to crimes.[8]

Not only did the Court rule that the prosecution and punishment of piracy observe no territorial limits; it went even further to identify the piracy that domestic law contemplates and that dealt with by the law of nations, thus:

> The opinion of Grotius was that piracy by the law of nations is the same thing as piracy by the civil law, and he has never been disputed. The specific provisions of the Penal Code are similar in tenor to statutory provisions elsewhere and to the concepts of the public law. This must necessarily be so, considering that the Penal Code finds its inspiration in this respect in the *Novelas*, the *Partidas*, and the *Novisima Recopilacion*.[9]

While modern-day documents, such as the *UNCLOS*, have refined the concept of piracy as international law deals with it, fundamentally, there is a justified persuasion that domestic legislation on piracy embodies that scourge of marine travel with which the law of nations has meant to deal.

Article 2 of the *Revised Penal Code* of the Philippines, however, bears closer examination.

> Art. 2. *Application of its provisions.* – Except as provided in the treaties and laws of preferential application, the provisions of this Code shall be enforced not only within the Philippine Archipelago, including its atmosphere, its interior waters and maritime zone, but also outside of its jurisdiction against those who:
>
> ...
>
> 5. Should commit any of the crimes against national security and the law of nations, defined in Title One of Book Two of this Code.

Piracy, being one of the crimes against the law of nations defined by the Code, is a crime that may be punished when perpetrated even outside the jurisdiction of the Philippines. In fact, by its definition in Philippine law, it is a crime committed on the high seas. No requirement for jurisdiction is set forth that the accused or the victim be a national or a resident of the Philippines. My position then is that as Philippine law on piracy presently stands, it allows for the exercise of universal jurisdiction in the case of piracy. The only reason available to us for this peculiarity of piracy in Philippine law is what comes down to us from Justice Malcolm – which echoes common teaching in international law. The only jurisdictional requirement

---

8   *Id.*, 22-23. *Citing* U.S. *v.* Furlong [1820], 5 Wheat., 184.

9   43 Phil. 25 (1922).

is that provided for in criminal procedure: the arrest of the accused. Whatever is the nationality or domicile of the accused or the victims, whatever is the registry of the vessel attacked or seized, wherever on the high seas the pirate may have struck, all that is required is that the accused be arrested and "bound to answer for the commission of an offense."[10] This generally requires that the accused be within the Philippine territory for purposes of a valid arrest.

The Philippine law never alludes to piracy as an exception to its rules on jurisdiction, as its very definition is such as to admit the application of "universality." Undoubtedly, however, the characterization of piracy as an offense "against the law of nations" goes into shaping the treatment it receives in Philippine law.

I find an excursus on the "extraterritorial" reach of Philippine penal law necessary. Significantly, the law identifies the cases of such reach against those who:

1. Should commit an offense while on a Philippine ship or airship;
2. Should forge or counterfeit any coin or currency note of the Philippine Islands or obligations and securities issued by the Government of the Philippine Islands;
3. Should be liable for acts connected with the introduction into these Islands of the obligations and securities mentioned in the preceding number;
4. While being public officers or employees, should commit an offense in the exercise of their functions; or
5. Should commit any of the crimes against national security and the law of nations, defined in Title One of Book Two of this Code.[11]

The first case is explained by the traditional fiction that considers a maritime vessel as an extension of the territory of the State whose flag it flies. The second, third, and fourth cases are varying expressions of the protective principle, as they deal with offenses deleterious to the Republic of the Philippines in one way or the other, though not necessarily perpetrated within its territorial confines. Crimes against national security are understandably punished even if committed abroad obviously because of their detrimental effects on national security. Piracy concerns not only the security of the Philippines and its citizens but that of humankind. Hence, the extraterritorial reach of Philippine penal law in its regard is consistent with the entire treatment that Philippine law gives to offenses enumerated above. Commentators, however, acknowledge that the origin of the domestic treatment of piracy is in the law of nations.[12]

The United States has maintained that piracy, as defined by the law of nations, punishes "robbery on the high seas." However US Federal law also includes within the ambit of piracy a sailor's act of laying violent hands upon his commander, preventing the latter from defending the vessel and the goods entrusted to his care, as

---

10   *Rule 113, Section 1*, Revised Rules of Criminal Procedure.

11   *Article 2*, Revised Penal Code.

12   1 Aquino, The Revised Penal Code (1987), 32.

well as robbing on shore while on a piratical cruise.[13] The amplitude of jurisdiction exercised over cases of piracy is justified in the following terms:

> The operation of the acts of Congress respecting piracy is not limited to offenses committed by or upon the citizens of the United States; when persons on board any vessel throw off their national character by cruising piratically and committing piracy on other vessels, they become amenable to our laws punishing piracy. In other words, piracy committed by persons on board a vessel not at the time belonging to the subjects of any foreign power but in the possession of a crew acting in defiance of all law and acknowledging obedience to no government whatever is punishable in the courts of the United States. Persons of this description are proper subjects for the penal codes of all nations and general words of a statute applying to all persons whatsoever, although they are not construed so as to extend to persons under acknowledged authority of a foreign state, ought to be construed to comprehend those who acknowledge the authority of no state.[14]

According to this disquisition, pirates submit to, and act under, no authority. It is the odiousness of persons acknowledging no authority and cruising predatorily on the high seas that makes the United States assert the jurisdiction of its courts over them – and not only for itself, but for "the penal codes of all nations." Importantly, it seems to be the position of American law that a pirate is subject to, and prosecuted under, the laws of the United States which are doubtlessly rooted in the law of nations. Elsewise stated, US courts apply US laws to fill in the void that pirates themselves create by acting without authority of any State and subjecting themselves to none.

Pursuant to the characterization of pirates as "common enemies of all humanity," American law allows the capture of pirates on the ocean "by the public or private ships of every nation."[15] This authority to arrest pirates can be reasonably considered to arise from the right of all to defend humankind against a common enemy. More than just a tag of opprobrium *enemy of humankind* is legal entitlement to the vessels of any State to protect humankind by seizing a common enemy when the opportunity presents itself. Significantly, under US law, pirates need not wander into US territory or stray into territorial waters before they can be rightfully seized. Public or private ships, acting in behalf of humankind, may seize pirates on the ocean.

In sum, both Philippine and American law codify or incorporate the rules of customary international law on piracy, specifically (1) the characterization of pirates as *hostes humani generis*; and (2) the susceptibility of pirates to the criminal jurisdiction of any State. That pirates are "the enemies of humankind" is the reason that Philippine and American courts exercise jurisdiction over them even if their

---

13   61 Am Jur 2d, *Piracy*, § 3.

14   *Id.*, § 4.

15   61 Am Jur 2d, *Piracy*, § 11.

acts are committed on the high seas. What we then have are laws of States first, hewing to customary international law, and enabling the States to cope effectively with the scourge that piracy is. Without always using the term "universal juris-diction" or "universality," the laws of both jurisdictions assert the competence of their courts over cases of piracy on the high seas in large measure as a pragmatic response to the common threat that piracy poses. Likewise clear is that the varying forms of domestic adoption of the universality principle rest on customary inter-national law. In other words, the municipal laws both of the Philippines and of the United States have incorporated customary international law as it had evolved at the time both countries wrote their relevant codes or laws.

One discerns a similar application of the principle of universality in Italian law. Under *Article 1135* of its Code of Navigation, a commander or an official of an Italian or a foreign ship who commits acts of depredation endangering an Italian or a foreign ship or its cargo, or who in connection with acts of depredation commits violence to the peril of persons on board an Italian or a foreign ship is punished with a prison term of ten to twenty years. Pursuant to a policy of repressing piracy, Italy likewise punishes as a crime the unauthorized arming of a vessel.[16] The assail-ant ship and the victim ship may either be an Italian or a foreign ship. In every case, Italian law provides for a penalty.

Notably, while the municipal law systems to which we have referred draw from customary international law (*the law of nations*) the rights to seize pirate vessels and arrest pirates, prosecute and try them, it is the municipal penal law that speci-fies the penalty to be meted out. In this regard, it is the domestic law that enforces the policy of international law outlawing piracy and pirates.

5.   Piracy in International Law

Exegetically, it is important that *Article 100* of the UNCLOS precedes the legal defi-nition of piracy *juris gentium*. The article obligates States to cooperate towards the repression of piracy whether "on the high seas or in any other place outside of the jurisdiction of any State." Current treaty law thus premises the power of any State to seize a pirate ship (or aircraft) on the high seas or in any other place outside the jurisdiction of any State on the common obligation to repress piracy.

Piracy is defined by the *High Seas Convention of 1958* and the *UNCLOS*. The definitions, it is claimed, reflect customary international law on piracy.[17] It might be well to dissect *Articles 101* and *102* of the *UNCLOS* according to the following scheme:

---

16   Lefebvre, Pescatori e Tullio, *Manuale di diritto della navigazione*, Settima Ed., 954-955.

17   "Universal Jurisdiction," Chapter II, *Amnesty International Index*: IOR 53/004/2001 (1 September 2001).

I.   **The acts covered**:
1.   Illegal acts of violence or detention,
2.   Depredation,
3.   Voluntary participation in the operation of a pirate ship or aircraft, and
4.   Facilitation of any of the illegal acts, or voluntary participation therein.
II. **Motive**: For private ends.
III. **By whom piracy is committed**:
1.   By the crew or passengers of a private ship or a private aircraft, or
2.   By the crew of a government ship, government aircraft or warship that has mutinied.
IV. **Against whom piracy is directed**:
1.   When on the high seas:
   a.   Against another ship or aircraft, or
   b.   Against persons or property on board such ship or aircraft.
2.   When outside the jurisdiction of any State:
   a.   Against a ship or aircraft, or
   b.   Against persons or property.

The definition itself provides the bases for the following initial observations:
1.   The ambit of piracy, as defined by current treaty law, is considerably more restricted than that contemplated either by Philippine or American domestic law.
2.   To be an act of piracy, the motive must be private. While obviously robbery and plunder are of private motives, so is the desire to exact vengeance or merely to sow terror. Textually unclear is whether political motives, such as advancing the cause of a liberation or secessionist movement, are included. Clearly excluded are State-directed or State-sponsored attacks.
3.   Piracy now expressly includes acts against an aircraft.
4.   On the high seas, piracy contemplates at least two vessels: marine or air. Thus, an attack directed against a ship, aircraft, persons or property outside the jurisdiction of a State would be piratical. The provisions then suggest the query: Would an attack by passengers of a private ship on explorers on *terra nullius* constitute piracy?
5.   Intentionally facilitating or inciting the commission of piracy is itself piracy.

The UNCLOS's definition does not completely codify the notion in customary international law that piracy is violence on the high seas visited by one private ship against another where such violence is not authorized by the flag-state of such a ship, with intent to plunder (*animus furandi*).[18] While one who, aboard a private vessel, plunders another vessel on the high seas is doubtless a pirate, any act of violence or detention for private ends also constitutes piracy. Thus, piracy is committed when a spurned lover and his band of sympathizers on their own vessel

---

18   *See* Mario Giuliani, Tullio Scovazzi and Tullio Treves, *Diritto Internazionale*, Vol. II, 2ⁿᵈ Edizione, 294.

overtake a yacht carrying the woman who is the object of his love and the husband to whom she has just been wed, and then subsequently detain the two without harming them.

Importantly, all that treaty-law currently requires is that the piratical acts be for private ends. Nowhere in the current definition of piracy is *animus furandi* an indispensable element, and sensibly so, for the terror, damage and injury that marauders with private ends other than plunder may visit on a ship on the high seas is not necessarily any more benign than that which plunderers are capable of. Earlier I raised the question of whether attacks in the name of some secessionist, liberation, independence or ideological movement fall within the concept of "private ends." Some authorities are of the belief that the law, as it currently stands, excludes hijacking and taking over for political reasons from the scope of piracy.[19]

Of greater moment, however, is the exclusion of acts of violence, detention or depredation committed by warships or government ships or aircraft from the scope of piracy. Issues arising out of such incidents properly fall within the scope of the rules on State responsibility. Similarly acts of the crew or passengers directed against the ship itself, although mutinous under the common notion of mutiny, do not constitute piracy under the UNCLOS.[20] What a mutiny can result in, however, is the conversion of a warship or a government ship into a pirate ship.

Similarly excluded from the contemplation of piracy *ratione loci* are otherwise piratical acts perpetrated within the territorial waters of a State. Philippine law, as I have earlier pointed out, has broadened its penal definition of piracy to cover the same acts committed within the territorial waters of the Philippines. Why the *UNCLOS* has not done so is obvious: Municipal law suffices to deal with the matter. *Article 100* and the succeeding articles thereof that deal with piracy fall within Part VII of the treaty that deals with the High Seas. Clearly then, what we have here is international regulation on the high seas.

While identifying the "high seas" seems easy enough, it has ceased to be a simple matter owing to the institutionalization of such a vast area of water as the Exclusive Economic Zone (EEZ). The United States and other States maintain the position that the EEZ is part of the high seas, subject to the special rights that the coastal State enjoys.[21] There is good reason for this position: The EEZ, sometimes called the "patrimonial sea," lies well beyond the reach of the territorial sea, and ships on the EEZ enjoy the freedoms of the high seas except over marine resources. *Article 86* of the *UNCLOS*, however, makes it clear that while the freedoms ships enjoy on the EEZ are preserved, the provisions on the high seas apply only to the portion of ocean *beyond* the EEZ. Piracy then can be committed only beyond the EEZ.

It is at once apparent that this poses problems for hot pursuit. *Article 111* of the *UNCLOS* provides for rules on hot pursuit. Should a piratical act be committed

19   Malcolm Shaw, *International Law*, 3rd Ed., 269.

20   Ian Brownlie, *Principles of Public International Law*, 4th Ed., 239-240.

21   Louis Sohn and Kristen Gustafson, *The Law of the Sea*, Nutshell Series, 1984 Ed., 122-123.

on the EEZ against a ship that flies the flag of a coastal State, the authorities of the coastal state would be unable to commence hot pursuit against the pirate ship, for under *paragraph 1* hot pursuit "must be commenced when the foreign ship or one of its boats is within the internal waters, the archipelagic waters, the territorial sea, or the contiguous zone of the pursuing State." While hot pursuit for violations in the EEZ is allowed by *paragraph 2*, only violations of the rules involving the EEZ, principally on the exploitation and conservation of marine and aquatic resources by the coastal State, constitute the exclusive bases for pursuit. I think that what we have here exemplified is a juxtaposition of doctrines taken over from customary law – the first on the notion of the "high seas" and its freedoms, the second on "hot pursuit" – that do not serve each other's purposes optimally.

Piracy may be committed "in a place outside the jurisdiction of any State." This was not introduced by the *UNCLOS*, but is found in an antecedent document *The Convention on the High Seas*, dated 29 April 1958 at Geneva. *Article 15* of the latter document uses identical terms as those of *UNCLOS*. This phrase then would include an island that is *terra nullius* or the shore of unoccupied territory.[22] Piracy then need not take place at sea. An attack by the passengers or crew of a private ship on scientists conducting experiments on an island that has just emerged from the ocean floor through volcanic activity would be piracy.

Under *sub-paragraph "b"* of *Article 101* of the UNCLOS, the crew of a pirate ship become pirates themselves when they operate the vessel "with knowledge of facts making it a pirate ship or aircraft." That they took no direct part in the acts of assault, depredation, looting or murder will not exculpate them. However, when they operate under duress, the general principles of law exempt them from liability.

As early as 26 July 1934, when the judgment of the Judicial Committee of the British Privy Council in *In re Piracy Jure Gentium* was made, there have been suggestions that the definition of piracy in international law be broad enough to encompass "frustrated acts or attempts at piracy."[23] Obviously, it serves the international legal order to punish not only consummated acts but also attempted and frustrated acts of piracy. While, in some way, this is taken care of by *sub-paragraph "c"* of the same article that includes within the definition of piracy "any act of inciting or intentionally facilitating an act described as piratical" still, it seems that the acts contemplated in *Article 101* are consummated acts. Consonant with the general principle of law on the restrictive interpretation of penal provisions, "acts of violence or detention, or any act of depredation" cannot assimilate attempted or frustrated acts.

Interestingly, however, the *UNCLOS* provides for the possibility of there being a pirate ship *without* an act of piracy. Its Article 103 provides:

> *Article 103.* A ship or aircraft is considered a pirate ship or aircraft if it is intended by persons in dominant control to be used for the purposes of committing one of the

---

22   Brownlie, 239-240.

23   Giuliani, *et al.*, 295.

acts referred to in Article 101. The same applies if the ship or aircraft has been used to commit any such act, so long as it remains under the control of the persons guilty of that act.

When the crew or complement of a ship or aircraft is discovered to have an intention to attack another vessel, then the ship is considered a pirate ship even if there has as yet been no piratical activity. Of course, a ship, regardless of its nature, whether a cruise ship, oil tanker, yacht, etc., and irrespective of what flag it flies, is a pirate ship when it has been used to commit a piratical act. This, in fact, is the complication that international lawyers point to in the law on piracy: that a pirate ship may in fact be marked with nationality, insofar as it flies a flag.[24] A pirate ship then is not necessarily flagless. When manned by persons intending to commit acts of piracy, or when it has been used to commit piracy, it is a pirate ship, and the significance of its characterization as a pirate ship is found in *Article 105* that lays down the rules on the seizure of pirate ships.

I would like to argue, pursuant to the position I proposed at the beginning of this paper, that whatever rights are granted other States by international law in regard to a pirate ship need not be considered a "derogation" or a diminution of the sovereignty that a State exercises over ships that fly its flag, but a companion norm crafted by the international community to deal with the scourge of piracy. It is less a matter of other States operating by a norm derogating from the rule on sovereignty over vessels as of protecting themselves from depredation by using a norm on piracy and pirate ships that has emerged.

Significantly, *Article 104* of the UNCLOS separates the issue of the nationality of a vessel and its characterization as a pirate ship. As already mentioned earlier, a pirate ship need not be flagless. The treaty leaves it to the domestic legislation of the flag-State to determine whether the ship's engagement in piracy entails loss of its nationality. Professor Ian Brownlie points out that this, as well as the last clause of *Article 105* that preserves the rights of third parties acting in good faith, reflects the principle *pirata non mutat dominium* (a pirate does not bring about a change in ownership).[25]

To be considered a pirate ship, however, its involvement in piratical attacks should not be at the behest or on orders of the flag-State. Otherwise, the ends cease to be private, and what we have is a case of State responsibility rather than a case of piracy. When a pirate ship flies the flag of a State, the flag-State, pursuant to Article 29(1), "effectively exercise[s] its jurisdiction and control in administrative, technical and social matters," and can then be expected to take action against the ship. I submit that a flag-State that is indifferent to the reported piracy of a vessel flying its flag can be held responsible for its inaction. The least that it can do is to strip the pirate ship of nationality, this being a matter left by the treaty to the competence of domestic law.

---

24   Giuliani, *et al.*, 294.

25   Brownlie, 240.

I wish to stress the point that an exigency – created by the predatory activities or intent of a pirate ship – is what triggers the exercise of that jurisdiction that is peculiar to cases of piracy. It is then not because a pirate ship is flagless that it is fair game for other States, but because it is a pirate ship – a vessel at the service of the *enemies of humankind*.

Articles 105 and *107* of the UNCLOS should be read together.

> *Article 105.* On the high seas, or in any other place outside the jurisdiction of any State, every State may seize a pirate ship or aircraft, or a ship or aircraft taken by piracy and under the control of pirates, and arrest the persons and seize the property on board. The courts of the State which carried out the seizure may decide upon the penalties to be imposed, and may also determine the action to be taken with regard to the ships, aircraft or property, subject to the rights of third parties acting in good faith.

Article 107 limits the right of seizure to "warships or military aircraft, or other ships or aircraft clearly marked and identifiable as being on government service and authorized to that effect." The essential provisions may be thus parsed:

1.   The seizure can take place on the high seas, or in any other place outside the jurisdiction of any State, and therefore even on land.
2.   Pirate ships or a ship taken by piracy and under the control of pirates may be seized. A ship commandeered by pirates and used by them in one foray, but later restored to the control of its rightful crew cannot, however, be so seized.
3.   The seizing State may be any State, even if not a party to the U.N. Charter or to the *UNCLOS*. This is so because the concession of authority to seize is owed not really to treaty-provision but to customary law of which the treaty is a codification.
4.   The right to seize also includes the right to arrest the persons and seize the property on board.
5.   Seizure is consequent upon the status of a ship being a pirate ship, or a ship taken by piracy, not upon a piratical act. A pirate ship is then liable to be seized even if no piratical act has as yet been perpetrated.
6.   The provision is permissive, and so there is nothing to prevent a State from yielding jurisdiction to another, or from extraditing the accused for prosecution and trial in another jurisdiction. Any State thus enjoys jurisdiction over the offense of piracy, insofar as the right of any State "to decide upon the penalties to be imposed" is provided for.

The arrest contemplated by this provision of *UNCLOS* is arrest on the high seas or in any place outside the jurisdiction of any State. Clearly, the arresting State does not have to await the presence of the pirate within its territory. The arrest that the Article provides for is arrest *incidental* to seizure. Furthermore, the State may decide to arrest without deciding to seize. This can be gleaned from the permissive term "may." The State may decide to seize or to arrest, but in so doing it must respect the rights of third parties acting in good faith.

May a State arrest an identified pirate who is not on board a pirate ship but is found, vacationing perhaps, within the territory of another State? This question is not addressed by *UNCLOS*. The matter may be resolved by referring to the general principles of international law (or customary international law) and to domestic legislation.

Professor Brownlie characterizes the act of boarding even when reasonable ground exists as a *privilege*. Thus, if no act has been committed on the boarded ship that triggers a suspicion, strict liability attaches and the flag-State of the warship must compensate for loss or damage caused by the seizure. This "strict liability clause" is deemed necessary to prevent abuse of the right of visit.[26] What makes a boarding State liable is "seizure without adequate grounds." Therefore, it is not the boarding that yields negative results, but rather the unjustified seizure that gives rise to liability on the part of the boarding State. Before a vessel is seized, there should be sufficient opportunity to determine whether there is enough basis to seize. To be free of liability, the boarding State must have had "adequate grounds" to seize. The seizure need not be justified by the ultimate finding of fact that the vessel is in fact a pirate ship.

What then constitute "adequate grounds"? No guidance is provided by the treaty itself, nor by the rules for the interpretation of treaties. Under Section 2 of Article III (Bill of Rights) of the Philippine Constitution, no search warrant or warrant of arrest shall issue except upon probable cause to be determined personally by the judge after examination under oath or affirmation of the complainant and the witnesses he may produce, and particularly describing the place to be searched and the persons or things to be seized. In the 1914 case of the *United States vs. Addison*[27] the Philippine Supreme Court defined *probable cause* "as such reasons, supported by facts and circumstances, as will a warrant a cautious man in the belief that his action, and the means taken in prosecuting it, are legally just and proper." Stated differently by the Court in a recent case,[28] *probable cause* is evidence showing that more likely than not a crime has been committed and was committed by the suspect. *Probable cause* does not therefore require clear and convincing evidence, or proof beyond reasonable doubt. I suggest this to be a useful concept for determining the adequacy of grounds to seize.

A final note on the liability clause: Liability is not to the ship-owner but "to the State the nationality of which is possessed by the ship or aircraft." No matter how wrongful or capricious the seizure is, the ship-owner has no cause of action against the boarding and seizing State unless the claim is espoused by the flag-State.

I have reserved for now the discussion on the inclusion of "aircraft" in the articles of *UNCLOS* on piracy. Without a doubt, piracy, under the present treaty law, may be committed against an aircraft as against maritime vessels. For some time, the issue was debated whether the unlawful seizure of aircraft constituted piracy,

---

26   Brownlie, 244.

27   28 Phil. 566, *cited* in 1 Bernas, The Constitution of the Republic of the Philippines (1987), 86.

28   *Serapio v. Sandiganbayan*, G.R. 148468, 28 January 2003.

and whether customary international law sufficiently covers attacks on an aircraft. In fact, "hijacking," as commonly understood, is still outside the provisions of *UN-CLOS* on piracy for the following reasons:

1. Hijacking takes place when one or more passengers illegally seize control of an aircraft. This is not the factual situation contemplated by the *UNCLOS* provisions on piracy.
2. Many cases of hijacking occur over the airspace of one State, usually a State friendly to the hijackers.
3. Most hijackers are politically motivated or, at least, announce political reasons or ends.[29]

The result is that whatever jurisdiction is vested in States is the result of treaty law, aside from the operation of the principles of municipal penal law. It remains significant, however, that *UNCLOS* has made applicable also to aircraft the provisions of customary law formerly applicable only to maritime vessels.

The Hague Convention, which addresses the illegal seizure of an aircraft, expands jurisdiction by conferring concurrent jurisdiction on

1. The State of registration of the aircraft,
2. The State of landing if the offender is on board the aircraft,
3. Any party to the Convention within whose boundaries the alleged offender is present, and
4. Passive nationality, where national laws allow the exercise of such jurisdiction.[30]

The closest the Convention comes to universality is conferring jurisdiction on any party to the Convention. But this, of course, is not itself an exercise of universal jurisdiction because the condition precedent for such exercise of jurisdiction is accession to the Convention.

In several respects, *UNCLOS* confines the exercise of jurisdiction by any State over pirate vessels and pirates. First, the Treaty situates its provisions on piracy within the set of rules on the high seas. Whenever the need for construction arises, reference must be made to the regime of the high seas that the Treaty wishes to safeguard. Otherwise stated, this section of *UNCLOS* should not be construed as a chapter of an international penal law code. Consequently, what States do about pirate ships or pirates that stray into their territories is beyond its purview. Second, *UNCLOS* attempts a precise definition of piracy and excludes much of what municipal law considers piracy. It also excludes the most common cases of hijacking of an aircraft. Third, it limits the right of seizure to warships or government vessels, and provides for strict liability in case of unjustified seizure.

---

29   M. McDougal and M. Reisman, *International Law in Contemporary Perspective* (1981 Ed.), p. 1422.

30   M. McDougal and M. Reisman, *International Law in Contemporary Perspective* (1981 Ed.), p. 1423.

In a relatively recent House of Lords case reviewing a lower court judgment on a petition for *habeas corpus* by one charged with conspiring with Osama Bin Laden for different acts of terrorism, Lord Rodger of Earlsferry analyzed the concept "within English jurisdiction." He then cited Viscount Sankey LC when giving advice to the Privy Council on a special reference *In re Piracy Jure Gentium* [1934] AC 586,589. For Viscount Sankey, a paramount consideration was that international law had no way of trying or punishing crimes defined by international law itself, leaving it to the municipal law of each country to vindicate the international legal order. A pirate places himself beyond the protection of any State. He is no longer a national but an enemy of humankind, and as such he is subject to the jurisdiction of any State. From this reference to Viscount Sankey, Lord Rodger concludes that piracy on the high seas is a crime committed *within the jurisdiction* of the apprehending and trying State.[31]

In contrast to such sweeping claims for the exercise of jurisdiction by any State over piracy, *UNCLOS* is a refinement as well as a codification of the fundamental convictions of the community of nations on piracy. There has thus evolved over the centuries a set of norms adopted by the consensus of States for coping with piracy. The rights of each State to seize pirate ships and to try and punish pirates are among these norms. Treaty law has rendered precise the parameters of the claims made under customary international law. I do not see how one can argue that the jurisdiction that the courts of all nations have over pirates is a "derogation" of an existing norm of international law on territorial sovereignty. It seems more accurate rather to say that the norms of territoriality in international law and of universal jurisdiction in regard to piracy emerged side by side. It appears to be that the assertion of territorial sovereignty never excludes the exercise of universality over pirates. What happens is that the international community develops norms by which it addresses common concerns that do not ascribe to themselves rigidity or absoluteness but are meant to enable States, in a normative manner, to cope with varying challenges, without being any less normative on the conduct of States.

In this respect, "jurisdiction" as municipal law deals with it may not be a very useful analogy for "jurisdiction" in international law. While the extent, source, and the entailments of jurisdiction are rather fixed and determinate within a municipal law system, "jurisdiction" in international law is a coping mechanism that expands and contracts in accordance with the exigencies of particular challenges of international co-existence. I find support for my position in this regard in the positions many writers on international law today take. Puente Egido, for one, contrasts internal law with international law by differentiating their sources of obligation:

Si prescindimos de las demas fuentes de las obligaciones para fijarnos exclusivamente en la ley y los contratos, un conocimiento elemental del derecho interno, permite afirmar que la gran fuente de obligaciones es la ley, en menor grado, aunque importante,

---

31   *In re Al-Fawwaz* [2001] UKHL 69 (17 December 2001), nos. 140-142.

las que nacen de los acuerdos libremente concertados por los sujetos de Derecho; y en todo caso sometidas a las disposiciones imperativas de la ley.

En el derecho internacional la situacion cambia radicalmente. El consensualismo omni-presente, incluso cuando se enmascara con formulas mas flexibles, permite afirmar que las obligaciones internacionales so nacidas en principio, ex contractu *y no* ex lege.³²

Interestingly, however, Puente Egido also argues the thesis that international law has undergone an evolution so that there are now aspects of law – subsumed by the category *jus cogens* – that are not at the free disposition of States. I agree with the refreshing view advanced by Professor Rosalyn Higgins that international law is a *process* of decision-making, a system, rather than a set of rules or commands.³³

6.   Universal Jurisdiction

Jus gentium, it appears to me, is not interested in crafting a theory of universal ju-risdiction as it is in devising a response to the common scourge of pirates. Pirates are subject to the jurisdiction of the courts of whichever State got hold of them. The principal reason for this is the lack of effective state control over the area in which they operate, as well as the resulting impunity from justice of leaving them unpunished for want of jurisdiction.³⁴ Plying the high seas – beyond the reach of the jurisdiction of any State – pirates could forever wreck havoc and destruction unchecked unless they could be dealt with effectively by whichever State could lay its hands on them. ³⁵

The argument is likewise frequently made, quite reasonably to my mind, that piracy violates a universal interest – the freedom of the high seas – and is a grave offense for its plunder and violence. Pirates have been *hostes humani generis* who threaten the international order. They may not have such grand design, but by mak-ing the international sea lanes places of peril, they do assault the international legal order. Being offensive to the international community, whoever or whichever the particular victim might be, piracy is dealt with by the international community.³⁶

It is important to be clear about what universal jurisdiction is. In its most common acceptation, universal jurisdiction is that basis of competence by which the courts of any State try persons whose alleged offenses are committed outside the boundaries of the prosecuting and trying State. It is the competence granted by international law to a State in regard to certain offenses to exercise its jurisdic-tion to apply its laws, even if the act has occurred outside its territory, and even

---

32   J. Puente Egido, *Lecciones de derecho internacional publico.* Vol. I.1, 1997 Ed., 127-129.

33   Rosalyn Higgins, *Problems and Process: International Law and How We Use It.*, 1994 Ed, 10 and ff.

34   "Universal Jurisdiction," *Amnesty International*, 1-3.

35   See for example Giuliani, *et al.*, 293.

36   Shaw, 411.

if the offender and the victim are non-nationals.[37] The connection with the crime and the offender is neither the territory nor the nationality of the offender or the victim, nor the protection of any domestic interest (protective principle), or passive personality, but the interest of the global community in dealing resolutely with the crime and in punishing the offender. Often cited in discussions today on universal jurisdiction is Augusto Pinochet's extradition sought by a Spanish judge principally for crimes against Spanish citizens on Chilean soil.

A multilateral treaty that vests jurisdiction on State-parties does not confer universal jurisdiction because the latter is enjoyed by all States regardless of accession or non-accession to a treaty. Thus, when the International Criminal Court (ICC) tries an accused haled before it, it is not exercising universal jurisdiction. It does so by virtue of a multilateral treaty binding State-parties where the crimes are committed, or of which the accused may be a national, to recognize the ICC's jurisdiction. Likewise, the *ad hoc* tribunals for former Yugoslavia and Rwanda drew their competence not from universal jurisdiction but from an express grant of jurisdiction by the Security Council, invoking the UN Charter.

In almost all cases, the exercise of universal jurisdiction by domestic courts will depend on whether the offenses the accused are charged with are defined as crimes in municipal legislation. The United States and Belgium have enacted legislation expressly allowing the exercise of universal jurisdiction in respect to certain crimes. The Philippine Constitution incorporates as part of the law of the land the "generally accepted principles of international law" – the customary international law, in other words. Hence, it would be possible for a person to be prosecuted for "genocide" or "crimes against humanity" before Philippine domestic court, even if these crimes are nowhere defined in municipal legislation. The more practical recourse of both the prosecution and the courts in the Philippines in regard to international crimes is to focus on one or the other key predicate act of internationally defined crimes and charge the accused under the appropriate heading of the Philippine *Revised Penal Code* or special penal legislation.

Once more, I find myself sharing the thesis of Professor Higgins, who is less inclined to think of universal jurisdiction as an exception to the general principles on jurisdiction and to approach it rather as a well-established norm standing alongside other norms of jurisdiction.[38] The interest of the international community, as well as of courts and jurists, is dealing with pirates, and thus arose the consensus that an effective way of keeping the high seas free of the loathsome predators is to allow any State to deal with them.

Were there any other situations with which the community of States had to deal which were similar to piracy and, therefore, warranted the application of analogous rules? Some see in the *jus militaire* of the 14th century the application of universal jurisdiction to war crimes. The reason advanced for the exercise of this kind of jurisdiction was that in the place where the crime was committed there was

---

37   Higgins, 56-57.

38   Higgins, 58.

no adequate judicial system.[39] The 1922 Treaty of Washington, in fact, expressly provides that violators of the agreement against the use of submarines and asphyxiating gases in times of war would be treated as pirates. Article III thus provides:

> *Les Puissances signataires ... declarent ... que tout individu au service de quelque puissance que ce soit, agissant ou non sur l'ordre d'un superieur heirarchique, qui violera l'une ou l'autre des dites regles, sera repute avoir viole les lois de la guerre et sera susceptible d'etre juge **comme s'il avait commis un acte de piraterie**.* (Emphasis supplied)

We then discern two bases for the exercise of "universal jurisdiction" over war crimes. The first, which we may call "idealistic," although "vindicative" is, to my mind, the more appropriate term. It is the view that such offenses assault the fundamental values of civilized co-existence, and the abhorrence therefore provokes the exercise of jurisdiction by all States. The second is more pragmatic: Before the advent of an international criminal court – and even with one – it is not too difficult for the war criminal to escape penal sanctions by evading (or fleeing from) the States having jurisdiction on the basis of territoriality or protective exercise.

The disposition of the issue of the jurisdiction of the District Court of Jerusalem to try Eichmann for the offenses with which he was charged espoused these two bases:

1. But we have also perused the sources of international law, including the numerous authorities mentioned by learned Counsel in his comprehensive written brief upon which he based his oral pleadings, and by the learned Attorney General in his comprehensive oral pleadings, and have failed to find any foundation for the contention that Israeli law is in conflict with the principles of international law. On the contrary, we have reached the conclusion that the Law in question conforms to the best traditions of the law of nations.

   The power of the State of Israel to enact the Law in question or Israel's "right to punish" is based, with respect to the offences in question, from the point of view of international law, on a dual foundation. The universal character of the crimes in question and their specific character as being designed to exterminate the Jewish People. In what follows, we shall deal with each of these two aspects separately.

2. The abhorrent crimes defined in this Law are crimes not under Israeli law alone. These crimes which offended the whole of mankind and shocked the conscience of nations are grave offences against the law of nations itself (*delicta juris gentium*). Therefore, so far from international law negating or limiting the jurisdiction of countries with respect to such crimes, in the absence of an International Court, the international law is in need of the judicial and legislative authorities of every country, to give effect to its penal injunctions and to bring criminals to trial. The jurisdiction to try crimes under international law is universal.[40]

---

39   "University Jurisdiction," *Amnesty International*, 2.

40   In the District Court of Jerusalem, Criminal Case No. 40/61; The Accused: Adolf, son of Karl Adolf, Eichmann.

The judgment calls attention to a limitation of international law: the absence of efficient mechanisms in the enforcement of international penal law. For this, the Israeli court argues, it needs the legislatures and judiciaries of each State. Malcolm Shaw echoes the "idealistic basis" when he argues that universal jurisdiction applies to those crimes deemed offensive to the international community, such as piracy and war crimes.[41] More pragmatically, Higgins finds the juridical basis for the exercise of universal jurisdiction in the importance of the rights involved, as well as in the legal interest all States have in their protection. The obligations thus violated by the crimes that provoke the exercise of universal jurisdiction are obligations *erga omnes*.[42]

While warning of the pitfalls of the abuse of universal jurisdiction, Alan Baker advances a reason for the enhancement of universal jurisdiction in international criminal law:

> Several reasons may be posited to explain what lies behind the marked progress and enhancement of universal jurisdiction in international criminal law. One is clearly a growing international awareness and genuine concern as to the importance of preventing situations of impunity in which political and military leaders, perpetrators of particularly gross violations of human rights, terrorists and the like will not be permitted to 'get off scot free' – whether within their own respective home jurisdictions or within other foreign jurisdictions.[43]

Clearly the acceptability of the exercise of universal jurisdiction depends in a large measure on the correctness of the premises on which its exercise is claimed to rest. Universal jurisdiction in piracy is not difficult to explain: It emerged by consensus as a coping mechanism considering (1) the factual constellation of the high seas; (2) the very serious threat that pirates pose to all sea-going vessels of all States; (3) the interest that all have in maintaining the freedom of the high seas; and (4) the fact that there is no other way one could deal with sea-faring, crest-riding predators. One does not have exactly the same confluence of circumstances in regard to war crimes, and less, in regard to other offenses for which universal jurisdiction is currently claimed. Stated otherwise, the world seems to have other means at its disposal of dealing with violators of international penal laws that make claims to universality less plausible. In fact, I do not myself subscribe to the proposition that the violation of an obligation *erga omnes* justifies the application of universality.

Henry Kissinger's frequently-cited critical remarks on universal jurisdiction are less a juridical analysis than a justification for American reticence towards the International Criminal Court and dire predictions about the misuse of universal jurisdiction. Kissinger voices the well-known fear of the United States: The exercise

---

41   Shaw, 411.

42   Higgins, 57.

43   Alan Baker, "Universal Jurisdiction in International Criminal Law," *20th Biennial Conference on the Law of the World*, Dublin, Ireland, September 30 – October 5, 2001.

of universal jurisdiction will be used to hinder it at what it considers its "role" in the world. The roots of Kissigner's misgivings are clear:

> For example, can any leader of the United States or of another country be hauled before international tribunals established for other purposes? This is precisely what Amnesty International implied when, in the summer of 1999, it supported a "complaint" by a group of European and Canadian law professors to Louise Arbour, then the prosecutor of the International Criminal Tribunal for Former Yugoslavia (ICTY).[44]

For his part, Kenneth Roth invokes the "impunity" reason in arguing for universal jurisdiction and against Kissinger. He asserts that tyrants commit atrocities when they calculate they can get away with them. Domestic courts exercising universal jurisdiction effectively break this pattern of impunity. He believes that the availability of universality to domestic courts as a basis for the exercise of jurisdiction is a deterrent to would-be tyrants.[45]

7. Conclusion

The jurisdiction of all States over pirates did not emerge as a theory of jurisdiction, but rather, out of necessity. The community of States needed to cope with the threat of pirates, who are indeed "enemies of all humankind." From an obviously descriptive phrase, *hostes humani generis* became a juridical characterization, as well as an assertion of entitlement on the part of all States to exercise jurisdiction over them. There is no need to convince States to accept or to exercise universal jurisdiction because it is not the issue. The protection of the high seas, ridding the sea-lanes of swashbucklers, is the world's primordial concern. Crucial as well in the evolution of the doctrine of universality was the fact that the high seas are subject to the jurisdiction of none and, therefore, pirates who perpetrated their hideous crimes on the high seas were free of the jurisdiction of any particular State. Directly related to the exercise of universal jurisdiction in the case of pirates is the fact that piracy has been a universal concern, harming universal interests and striking at universal values.

Unlike domestic legislatures that can conjure legislation at will and even borrow concerns from other jurisdictions to make them the subject matter of legislation, the world community contends with the problems and challenges of co-existence. States, by communicative action, identify their values and enshrine them in rules that draw strength from a consensual response to a defined problem. That international law is a set of coping mechanisms of the global community does not make it any less law, but this fact about international norms does broaden our understanding of law and its variegated forms.

---

44   Henry Kissinger, "The Pitfalls of Universal Jurisdiction: Risking Judicial Tyranny," *Foreign Affairs*, July/August 2001.

45   Kenneth Roth, "The Case for Universal Jurisdiction," *Foreign Affairs*, September/October 2001.

To enjoy the same acceptance as that accorded it in the case of piracy, any claim to universal jurisdiction must be premised on that same conjunction of necessity, value, and pragmatic responsiveness that has allowed the exercise of universality in piracy cases to be a general principle of law adopted as we have seen by municipal legal systems, and not a derogation of the general principles on jurisdiction. "Impunity" may indeed sound like an idealistic basis for claims to universal jurisdiction, but it is pragmatic as well. Where there are ways of coping with war criminals and even terrorists – such as the adoption by domestic legislatures of common legislation, the resoluteness of domestic judiciaries in dealing with perpetrators, and the establishment of a functional international criminal justice system of which the ICC is doubtless a promising start – "impunity" will be a less compelling argument for the exercise of universal jurisdiction. When these are not present, however, impunity remains a motive force for claims at universal jurisdiction. In the wake of the "9/11 tragedy" in the United States and the constant dread of the latest visitation of terror that has darkened our days, we have not heard the last of appeals for the exercise of universal jurisdiction on the grounds of impunity.

28. Sovereign Equality of States and the Legitimacy of "Leader States"

Sienho Yee *

One can easily agree that the principle of sovereign equality of States and the role and place of the "leader States"[1] concern nothing less than the organizing principles for the international community. For example, Brownlie says, "The sovereignty and equality of states represent the basic constitutional doctrine of the law of nations, which governs a community consisting primarily of states having a uniform legal personality."[2] It is thus fitting or even obligatory to address this topic and the related issues when one contemplates world constitutionalism.

The topic and the related issues have caught the attention of many scholars.[3] The common discussion of the topic normally recounts the history of the develop-

---

*   I thank the distinguished Editors for their invitation to participate in this important project and for assigning me this topic, particularly Judge Macdonald with whom I have had many conversations on the topic and the project. This assignment has forced me to consider the various issues more carefully than I would otherwise have. I am grateful despite the fact that I have had to write this chapter under considerable pressure and stress. This chapter was completed on December 27, 2004.

1   The term "leader States" is given to me by the Editors. I am using it to denote States that exhibit leader qualities, not in the sense of *Führerstaat* (a State under the control of the leader). See Part 5 of this paper for further analysis.

2   Ian Brownlie, *Principles of Public International Law* (6th ed., 2003), 287.

3   Useful literature includes: Bardo Fassbender & Albert Bleckmann, Article 2(1), in: Bruno Simma (ed.), *The Charter of the United Nations: A Commentary* (2002), 68; Michael Byers & Georg Nolte (eds.), *United States Hegemony and Foundations of International Law* (2003); Michael Cosnard, Sovereign equality – "the Wimbledon sails on", *ibid.*, 117; Nico Krisch, More equal than the rest? – Hierarchy, equality and US predominance in international law, *ibid.*, 135; GAO Feng, China and the Principle of Sovereign Equality in the 21st Century, in: Sienho Yee & WANG Tieya (eds.), *International Law in the Post-Cold War World: Essays in Memory of Li Haopei* (2001), 224; Athena Debbie Efraim, *Sovereign (In)equality in International Organizations* (2000); Christian Tomuschat, International Law: Ensuring the Survival of Mankind on the Eve of a New Century, General Course on Public International Law, 281 *Recueil des cours* (1999), 161-202; Thomas

Ronald St. John Macdonald & Douglas M. Johnston (eds.), Towards World Constitutionalism, *pp. 737-772.*
© *2005 Koninklijke Brill NV. Printed in The Netherlands. ISBN 90 04 14612 1.*

ment of the doctrine, and comments on its current status. The common analysis involves (1) treating the doctrine of State equality as having two components, equality or equal protection before the law, and equal rights, and (2) emphasizing the former. While such a distinction has contributed to the understanding of the doctrine, there is still much to be desired, as was pointed out already in 1944 by Kelsen.[4]

I shall not "reinvent the wheel," so to speak, by repeating the fine work that has already been done, but will only touch upon some aspects that are of particular interest to me. I will take a slightly different course. I will discuss these issues one by one: (1) the phenomenon of the State and equality of States; (2) the current authoritative statements on sovereign equality of States; (3) understanding sovereign equality of States: its maximum, its minimum, and the continuum; (4) safeguarding the irreducible minimum and promoting greater equality while justifying differences fairly; and (5) leader States' legitimacy. My focus is on conceptual, and, to some extent, philosophical inquiries, and thus I will not deal with all aspects of the topic, particularly those that fall within the sphere of application of the various types of arguments. As it is rather difficult to summarize the arguments made here, I will not attempt to rehash them at the end of my chapter, except that in the final paragraph I will summarize what I consider to be the qualifications for the status of the strong State, the great State and the leader State.

One may find some of my arguments disagreeable. I simply would like to say, at the outset, that these arguments are presented here as an earnest effort to participate in the consideration of some tough issues, a venture that could provide fertile ground for mistakes by all participants.

Franck, *Fairness in International Law and Institutions* (1995); Manfred Lachs, Some Thoughts on Equality, in: Ronald St. John Macdonald (ed.), *Essays in Honour of Wang Tieya* (1994), 483; Alan Branthwaite, The Psychological Basis of Independent Statehood, in: Robert H. Jackson & Alan James (eds.), *States in a Changing World: A Contemporary Analysis* (1993), 46; R.P. Anand, Sovereign Equality of States in International Law, 197 *Recueil des cours* (1986-II), 9; Vratislav Pechota, Equality: Political Justice in an Unequal World, in: Ronald St. John Macdonald & Douglas M. Johnston (eds.), *The Structure and Process of International Law: Essays in Legal Philosophy Doctrine and Theory* (1983), 453; Hans Kelsen, The Principle of Sovereign Equality of States as a Basis for International Organizations, 53 *Yale Law Journal* (1944), 207; P.J. Baker, The Doctrine of Legal Equality of States, 4 *British Yearbook of International Law* (1923-24), 1. For an examination of equality regarding individuals, see Amartya Sen, *Inequality Reexamined* (1992). I would like to note that the idea of equality was the subject of some stinking trade-off at the Paris Peace Conference. See Robert A. Klein, *Sovereign Equality Among States: the History of an Idea* (1974), 76-83. As I was finalizing this paper, the useful document called "A more secure world: our shared responsibility: Report of the High-Level Panel on Threats, Challenges and Change" ("High-Level Panel Report"), A/59/565 (2004; http://www.un.org/secureworld/) was released on December 2, 2004.

4   As already detailed by Kelsen, n. 3 above (1944).

1. The State and the Equality of States

As the concept of sovereign equality of States has the phenomenon of the State at its root, our understanding of the need for and the meaning of the concept of sovereign equality of States must be based on our perception of the value of the State. By now probably we must be content with the fact that the world is organized along State lines, with the State as the primary end unit.[5] Yet, many people probably also would not believe in the existential or mysterious indispensable value of the phenomenon called "State". After all, the world was once not organized this way – witness, for example, the pre-Westphalia world. Some philosophers have also argued that in due course the State would wither away. In addition, many people also believe that in the final analysis, human values are the end goal of all societal organizations.[6] Naturally one would ask, consistent with pursuing human values as the end goal of all social organizations and with the historical record of and sensible future projections for the world, why our society has to be organized as it is? If it need not be organized around States as the primary end units, then we do not need to speak of sovereign equality of States at all.

Such a question apparently is not susceptible of any definitive answer. At least we can perhaps say that such is the world as a matter of historical fact or accident, and the fact that it has been so may prove that it is better than what it might have once been historically and, perhaps, better than what philosophers have projected for it in the future. It is difficult to argue with such success.

One can say probably that as a matter of efficiency or instrumental value, the world must be organized in a way so as to assure certain efficiency in social activities in an all-encompassing way, politically, economically and culturally. Organizing the world along State lines, despite its wide variety, has proven to be tolerable for the purposes of efficiency, in its totality, at least we perhaps may conclude that a better arrangement has not been found. The pre-Westphalia world apparently removed the authorities from the realities of life, too far, and blinded them to the pains and suffering of the local denizens. The projected withering away of the State in the future assumes the noble character of all individuals, and thus may never take place.

If the State were just about a matter of economic activities, one perhaps could imagine nicer arrangements for the world, such as regions, blocks, unions, and the like. However, the phenomenon of the State involves more, and other aspects of social activities may have to be premised on the phenomenon of the State. For example, political life and democracy only thrive within a manageable community. We have been told that "all politics is local". One can imagine what a task it would be to organize world democracy without borders, if it is possible at all. Indeed, if

---

5   See High-level Panel Report, n. 3 above.

6   See, *e.g.*, Charles de Visscher, *Theory and Reality in Public International Law* (3d ed. (1960), P.E. Corbett tran., 1968); Sienho Yee, *Towards an International Law of Co-progressiveness* (2004), 23-26.

Aristotle had to suffer his fate the way he did in the hands of democracy even in a small city republic in ancient Greece, should we have greater confidence in world democracy without borders?

More important, although normally we tend to think of the State as more or less a matter of political function, psychologists have demonstrated that there is more to the phenomenon.[7] Certain intrinsic value may be inherent in the phenomenon. There is certain psychological basis for statehood that consists of citizens or nationals identifying themselves with the State, together with the assorted cultural, traditional, and other folklore, which serves as the unifying force connecting citizens and nationals and provides one of the bases for their solidarity. The sense of belonging to the State adds to the personality or personhood of the citizens. In fact, these factors may be the moving forces in the establishment of many States. Thus, the existence of the State furthers the end goal of social organizations by making human values fuller and richer.

Such are the virtues of the phenomenon of the State that it is only natural for the organized entities to strive to become States in the pursuit of self-determination and, ultimately, sovereignty, and equality of dignity – or more formally called equality of States. These further dimensions of statehood afford great value to the world at large. Self-determination means being one's own master. Equality means a State is being its own master in the same way that another is. These two aspects of statehood were felt most strongly in the leaders and citizens of those States which were previously not considered to be equals to the other States. No one has savored this better than the citizens of those States who finally have managed to throw away the colonial yoke and become masters of their destiny.[8] To this extent, the equality of States has intrinsic value; it is a virtue to be pursued in and of itself.

These values of the State should have moved the world to promote strong States and strong cultures. However, the post-Cold War history until now has been largely one of dismantling the big States. And the values of strong States seem to have been appreciated by some only recently, perhaps somewhat unfortunately. Thus, the deadliness of failed or weak States to their own citizens, as well as to the outside world, was pointed out in the National Security Strategy of the United States.[9] It is to the credit of the statesmen that the importance of the State as the primary end unit of the international system was emphasized in December 2004 by the High-level Panel on Threats, Challenges and Change convened by the United Nations Secretary-General.[10] Indeed, the failure of one State is now the national security problem of another. One hopes that such "recent" revelations would move States to stop the practices that were originally intended to prevail over their enemies in the ideological contest between the communist and capitalist systems, which have resulted in the breakup of some States or in serious tension within

---

7   See Alan Branthwaite, n. 3 above (1993); Sienho Yee, n. 6 above.

8   See, *e.g.*, Wang Tieya, The Third World and International Law, in: R. St. J. Macdonald and D.M. Johnston (eds.), *The Structure and Process of International Law* (1983), 955.

9   See <http://www.whitehouse.gov/nsc/nss.html>.

10   See High-Level Panel Report, n. 3 above.

some States almost to a point of breaking up. These practices including selling arms to secessionist movements or generally fanning the fervency of secessionist sentiments. Such practices go against the need to promote strong States and strong cultures, and can lead to chaos in the affected States and greater national security crises for other States. On the other hand, a tendency or bias in favor of holding States together would be beneficial to all concerned.

Such a view of the world consisting of States as the primary end units would require us to evaluate all sorts of problems, such as the challenges posed by non-State actors,[11] in the framework of States. That is to say, ultimately almost all issues of the world can be dealt with, to a large extent, as issues relating to the State. Such a view of the world would also make it a meaningful exercise for us to consider the topic of sovereign equality of States and the role of the leader States in the present world.

2.   Current Authoritative Statements on Sovereign Equality of States

Such are the virtues of the phenomenon of the State and equality of States that we should not be surprised by the strenuous pursuit of sovereignty and equality of States. Many years' efforts have culminated in the current scene of more than 190 sovereign States in the world and in some more or less authoritative statements on the idea of equality of States. By now the idea has become recognized as one of the foundations of the modern international political and legal system.

The Charter of the United Nations, in Article 2(1), declares that "[t]he Organization is based on the principle of sovereign equality of all its Members." That is to say, the new United Nations Organization was built upon this principle. Article 2(4) provides that "All Members shall refrain in their international relations from the threat or use of force against the territorial integrity or political independence of any state, or in any other manner inconsistent with the Purposes of the United Nations." Article 2(7) declares that "Nothing contained in the present Charter shall authorize the United Nations to intervene in matters which are essentially within the domestic jurisdiction of any state or shall require the Members to submit such matters to settlement under the present Charter; but this principle shall not prejudice the application of enforcement measures under Chapter VII."

These provisions are given some concretization in the subsequent elaboration of the term "sovereign equality," in the United Nations Declaration of Principles of International Law Concerning Friendly Relations and Cooperation of States (the "Friendly Relations Declaration"):

The principle of sovereign equality of States

All States enjoy sovereign equality. They have equal rights and duties and are equal members of the international community, notwithstanding differences of an economic, social, political or other nature.

---

11   As my inquiry focuses on States, issues relating to non-State actors can only be mentioned in passing.

In particular, sovereign equality includes the following elements:

(a)   States are juridically equal;
(b)   Each State enjoys the rights inherent in full sovereignty;
(c)   Each State has the duty to respect the personality of other States;
(d)   The territorial integrity and political independence of the State are inviolable;
(e)   Each State has the right freely to choose and develop its political, social, economic and cultural systems;
(f)   Each State has the duty to comply fully and in good faith with its international obligations and to live in peace with other States.[12]

This elaboration no doubt has gone a long way in giving meaning to the concept of "sovereign equality of States". Still different readers may see different things in this elaboration. In the next section, I shall present a reading of the concept, more or less according to me, without taking account of all views because of the abundance of literature on point.

3.   Understanding Sovereign Equality of States: Its Maximum, Its Minimum, and the Continuum

The normal discussion of the issue speaks of "the equality of States." Immediately the term "sovereign equality of States" presents something of an enigma. According to researchers, the term first appeared in the Moscow Declaration of October 13, 1943,[13] in which the United States, the United Kingdom, the Soviet Union and China declared that "they recognize the necessity of establishing at the earliest practicable date a general international organization, based on the principle of sovereign equality of all peace-loving States, and open to membership by all such States, large and small, for the maintenance of international peace and security." The term has ever since been shrouded in mystery. Efforts have been made to understand it in different ways.[14] It is not clear whether such efforts have been successful, or whether the term is really meant to be rhetorical – meaning no more than "equality of states" – and was used to better galvanize the support of all States to participate in the new world organization.

To some extent, putting "sovereign" and "equality" together appears to be awkward at least, if not oxymoronic. Two kinds of difficulty may present themselves when we try to understand the phrase in its ordinary meaning. The first is that "equality" may be meaningless. "Sovereign" appears to refer to a certain "supreme quality". If so, what does "equality" add? This is the normal difficulty in understanding the term "equality" in general: the term may often be tautological; nothing that

---

12   UNGA Res. 2625 (SSV) (1970). See Aleksandar Magaršević, The Sovereign Equality of Sates, in Milan Šahović (ed.), *Principles of International Law concerning Friendly Relations and Cooperation* (1972), 171.

13   *UNYB* 1946-47, 3.

14   See Fassbender & Bleckmann, n. 3 above (2002); Kelsen, n. 3 (1944).

it conveys seldom cannot be ascertained through another substantive criterion. For example, if legality is assured, equality is simply its resulting corollary.[15] A second difficulty is that equality may mean "equally supreme" or "equally minimal", and if the latter version of "equality" is adopted, the juxtaposition of "sovereign" and "equality" together would lead to a logical difficulty: something of "supreme quality" may yet be a minimal equal to others.

The prevailing international realities, however, may reduce the difficulty to some extent, so that we can find some meaning in the phrase "sovereign equality of States". Following the understanding of the phrase sketched above, I think we can find evidence that the phenomenon has been understood as having a maximum, an irreducible minimum and a vast continuum from the minimum to the maximum.

A.   The Flawed Vision of the Maximum

It seems that when the equality of States idea first came into the picture, it was envisioned as having a maximum: each State has the same rights and obligations in every respect and is entitled to participate in international life equally. Championing this view were theoreticians as well as politicians. The basis for this view was apparently the attempt to analogize the phenomenon of the State to the individual and to resort to the principle that one individual is equal to another.

This approach crumbled immediately when it got into contact with two important objections. The first objection was put forward by none other than Elihu Root, a very international-law-friendly United States statesman, in the context of discussing the necessity for some kind of permanent representation of the big powers in the new Permanent Court of International Justice that was being proposed in 1920. He said that every individual in a democracy would like to have his or her vote carry the same weight as that of the citizen of another State. Therefore:

> [I]t would be impossible to put forward a plan in which, for instance, the hundred million inhabitants of the United States would have to consent to have the sovereign rights of their country limited by a Court on which the vote of the half-million inhabitants of Honduras might decide a case against the United States.[16]

While this understanding of the judicial character of the Court might not be perfect, the message against the absolute equality of States is powerfully devastating to any attempt to base that equality on an analogy of the State to the individual.

The mistake in such an analogy is explicable this way: while the individual is the end unit for many things, or almost everything, the State is not necessarily such an end unit for so many things. An attempt to build perfect equality of States by analogizing the State to the individual, with the ostensible goal of promoting

---

15   See Kelsen, n. 3 above (1944).

16   Permanent Court of International Justice Advisory Committee, *Procès-verbaux of the Proceedings of the Committee, June 16th – July 24th, 1920* (1920), 134-35.

democracy, would simply turn democracy on its head: it would treat individuals differently simply on the basis of which State he or she belongs to.

The second objection was epitomized by that given by one of the main drafters of the Covenant of the League of Nations, Mr. David Hunter Miller. After paraphrasing a statement on equality of States as "The rights and obligations of Albania as a member of the League are no more and no less than those of the British Empire", he proceeded:

> As to such a statement my view is that what it suggests is nothing but a form of words having no meaning whatever in the actual world in which human beings live. Of course the doctrine of equality of states means that a small and insignificant and feeble state is entitled to fair and just treatment on a footing of equality before the law with larger neighbors; but to say that in any international organization or in international affairs however conducted or in international relations either of the present or of any past whatever, the influence or moral or political authority in the world of a few thousand backward people organized as an independent unit or state entity has been or should be the same as that of a country like the United States, for example, is simply to shut one's eyes to everything except a few words of print.[17]

This objection speaks from experience and reality. And there is logic to this argument, although the coldness of that logic is not appetizing. However, the insistence on equality in the face of such realities will quickly yield if the equal obligations are also imposed on the small States which would have trouble fulfilling them.

Perhaps for these reasons, one can find only a grand statement on this point in the "chapeau" of the section on the principle of sovereign equality of States in the Friendly Relations Declaration, which states, in part, that all States "have equal rights and duties and are equal members of the international community".[18] The elaboration of the detailed content of this concept seems to have a different emphasis. One might have reason to think, then, the maxim of sovereign equality is a slogan, a catchphrase, an ideal that we put on the pedestal to look at, to look to, or even to be drawn to, yet unrealizable.

B.   The Irreducible Minimum of Sovereign Equality of States

If one cannot find concrete elaboration on the maximum of sovereign equality of States in the Friendly Relations Declaration, one can find one on the minimum of it. After the grand statement in the chapeau of that section, the Declaration proceeds to spell out what States consider to be most important elements by prefacing them with the phrase "In particular". These elements have been considered to be essential to the concept so as to warrant such a treatment of being singled out for

---

17   David Hunter Miller, 1 *The Drafting of the Covenant* (1928, reprinted 1969), 23 (footnote omitted).

18   Text to n. 12 above.

elaboration. They can be distilled into two concretizable points: (1) juridical equality and (2) inviolable territorial integrity and political independence.

The first guarantees the equal juridical status to each State. This formulation of equality is a slightly narrower and more precise than "equality before the law", as commonly used. Juridical equality, to my mind, only means the status that a State enjoys before the law, probably only in the sense of capacity, procedure, and pomp and appearance. As such, it has a dignity dimension that many States care about, particularly before international courts and tribunals. On the other hand, "equality before the law" may have a broader scope in the minds of the ordinary people. Still, this aspect of the concept is not that useful in practical terms.

The second element is the core of sovereignty/independence, as time and again affirmed by States and international judges, and as embodied in Article 2(4) of the United Nations Charter. As Judge Huber explained in *Island of Palmas*, "Sovereignty in the relations between States signifies independence. Independence in regard to a portion of the globe is the right to exercise therein, to the exclusion of any other State, the functions of a State."[19] As recognized by Judge Anzilotti, sovereignty/independence is the "normal condition of States according to international law",[20] meaning that "the State has over it no other authority than that of international law".[21] As a result, one can clearly tell that its content does not derive from "equality", but from "sovereignty", and in this sense one can see the merits to Kelsen's argument that equality may be really legality.[22] However, precisely because of this one can make sense of the phrase "sovereign equality": "Sovereignty" leads to "equality" in the minimum sense of the latter term in this context.

While limiting and constraining to some extent, sovereign equality in this minimum sense has its beauty: Small though a territory may be, there is no other place like it for the sovereign over it. At least there is one piece of space within which the sovereign people may express themselves and realize their value and virtues to the full, without outside interference. For this reason, if this minimum of sovereign equality can be safeguarded, the world would still be in a good shape.

C.   The Continuum from the Irreducible Minimum to the Maximum

Beautiful though the minimum of sovereign equality may be, it seems to fit the isolated co-existence of States best. This irreducible minimum can be said to be the crowning achievement of the international law of co-existence. As soon as States interact with each other, as soon as they start to jointly conduct international activities, they will have to go out of their "castles", so to speak, realizing that such a way of seeing the world will not be adequate to the tasks of taking account of different issues and situations.

---

19   2 RIAA 829, 838 (decision of 1928).

20   *Autro-German Customs Regime, PCIJ*, Series A/B, No. 41 (1931), 57 (individual op. Anzilotti).

21   *Ibid.*

22   See Kelsen, n. 3 above.

Unreachable though the maximum of sovereign equality may be, it is an ideal that holds certain attraction for many. It makes people – generally, and particularly those in smaller countries – feel that their dignity is respected, that their worth is being appreciated and recognized. As a result, it would be easier to obtain their support for any views and projects under such a condition of maximum equality.

Since the early 1960s, the world has moved into the sphere of co-operation, where solidarity of peoples and interactions between and among them are the highlight of the day. It has now entered the sphere of co-progressiveness after the end of the Cold War, where international law has become all encompassing (hence "co"), preoccupied with advancements in moral and ethical terms more than in other respects and, in my view, having human flourishing as its ultimate goal (hence "progressiveness"). The advancements in international law continue unabated, despite the aberrations such as those that manifested as the September 11 attack and its aftermath.[23]

In order for co-operation and co-progressiveness to be realized to the fullest, States must, while preserving the irreducible minimum of sovereign equality, go beyond it. The need to galvanize as many people as possible from around the world to promote peace, security, prosperity and progressiveness would militate in favor of moving towards the maximum scope of sovereign equality, to the extent possible, though we know that we will never reach that point. As explained, that maximum point is not necessarily a good point to reach, but the movement towards it is of value. Accordingly, the best scope of sovereign equality under current conditions and in anticipation of a better future, has to be a continuum from the irreducible minimum to the maximum. Within the continuum, there is an infinite variety of diverse States, peoples and rights and obligations. Thus, differences and inequalities are inevitable, and we must be content with the fact that it is not possible to please everyone in the world.

4.   Safeguarding the Irreducible Minimum and Promoting Greater Equality while Justifying Differences Fairly

A.   *Background Considerations*

Given the essential importance of the irreducible minimum of sovereign equality and the central place that it holds in the hearts and minds of the people around the world, it requires no stressing that the most important task of international law is to safeguard the irreducible minimum of equality from being eroded. In my view, this is taken as granted and axiomatic, without any further need for justification. Thus, when there are breaches of this cardinal principle, such breaches present themselves not as the result of a direct attack on this principle; rather, other creative, though not necessarily successful, arguments were presented to justify such breaches. For example, the United States had to attempt to justify its use of force against Nicaragua as an exercise of the right of collective self-defense, rather than saying that there was no rule on point or that there was a rule but it did not care

---

23   See Sienho Yee, *Towards*, n. 6 above, 1-26.

about it.[24] So there is no need for me to defend the need to safeguard the irreducible minimum of sovereignty equality.

The appeal that the vision of the maximum of sovereign equality has to the world, its value as a slogan and as something to put on the pedestal, is the reason why we may want to realize it. The inevitable differences and inequalities convince us that we simply cannot achieve it; they do not, however, prevent us from moving in that direction. Naturally, our task is how to promote equality to the greatest extent and to deal with or manage such differences and inequalities in a way that is satisfactory to the greatest number of States and people possible.

Accordingly, one can see the task of international law as threefold: to safeguard the irreducible minimum of sovereignty equality, to promote greater equality to the extent possible, and to try our best to promote equality, while justifying the differences and inequalities in a fair way.

To a great extent, the idea of a rule of law itself has a certain equalizing effect: at least consistency is achieved in the application of a rule. As human behavior almost always is oriented around certain rules or customs – whether moral, social or legal, a certain minimum level of equality in the form of consistency in their application obtains. Consistency applies horizontally to all subjects of law (i.e., the same law applies to everyone unless valid exceptions apply – famously described by Anatole France as "the majestic equality of the laws, which forbid rich and poor alike to sleep under bridges, to beg in the streets, and to steal their bread"[25]) and vertically to the conduct of one subject of law over a period of time. We shall refer to this as the "minimal consistency" condition.

Because of this minimal consistency, often both equality and differences are present in one and the same argument: equality is usually equality according to one criterion, while differences often result from the application of some criteria equally. As a result, it is not easy for one to separate equality and differences in a discussion, and I will touch upon both issues often. However, as we often agree on the attractiveness of equality, I will focus on the tougher task of justifying differences and inequalities.

Without going into all the details, there can be two kinds of differences: (1) the law provides for the same treatment for each State, but that law is applied differently; or (2) the law provides for different treatment for different States, and it is applied consistently. Many arguments can be considered to be relevant to our inquiry as to how each kind of differences can be justifiable or legitimate. In this section, I will attempt to provide a list of the main arguments and critique them only briefly. These arguments may apply only to *some* players in the world and only to *some* circumstances, rather than to all and for all seasons. For the sake of simplicity, I will refer to these arguments as "difference arguments". I choose this phrase rather than the more grandiose "difference principles" because I am not sure about the validity of, nor do I agree with, some, or even many, of these arguments. I will simply present them here for the appreciation of the reader.

---

24   See *Case concerning Military and Paramilitary Activities in and against Nicaragua (Nicaragua v. United States), ICJ Reports 1986*, 14.

25   Anatole France, *The Red Lily* (Winifred Stephens trans., 1930), 95.

B.   Meta-Arguments

There are several arguments that can be categorized as "meta-arguments" attempting to justify differences generally. Ordinarily these meta-arguments appear to operate at the law-making stage. At the law-application stage their relevance is not clear, although a rule of law that does not pass muster under these arguments can potentially be considered invalid. As such, these arguments may have a corrective function in favor of equality. Probably they do not, however, function in a way at the law-application stage so as to require different applications of the same law.

These meta-arguments include the age-old "treat like cases alike" principle which touches upon both kinds of differences as described above. Obviously this principle has a strong equality component, and it acts as a meta-principle so that whatever happens this principle may still be applied. To this extent it is part of minimal consistency. However, embedded in this principle is a fundamental difference principle: the corollary of "treat like cases alike" is "treat different cases differently". While "treat like cases alike" is not difficult to apply, "treat different cases differently" may prove difficult to struggle with: one still needs to find criteria for defining what cases are different and how differently to treat them. So in the final analysis, this principle may help to justify or explain the need for different treatment of different cases, it does not provide further guidance.

Another meta-argument is Thomas Franck's formulation of the criteria for the legitimacy of a rule of international law, which I shall call "the secondary rule meta-argument". To his mind, a primary rule of conduct's legitimacy can be measured through several criteria that relate to the secondary rules (such as law-making) showing the "associative" nature of the community. These criteria include: determinacy, symbolic validation, coherence, and adherence.[26] One can accept these criteria in general, so that if these criteria have been met and if differences still exist, then they will be considered fair to some extent.

One wonders, however, whether this approach – focusing on the secondary rules – is sufficient. To some, no matter how fair the process may be, how determinate the rules may be, what matters at the end of the day is whether the substantive content of the rules is fair and acceptable. That is to say, any differences must pass the test of substantive fairness. Although the "coherence" criterion in Franck's sketch could include an element of substantive fairness, his discussion seems to focus on the even-handed or uniform application of the law such as the "treat like cases a like" principle.[27] In any event, the unmistakable focus of Franck's formulation is on the "associative" secondary rules, not the substantive primary rules of conduct. As a result, Franck's sketch of legitimation is incomplete.

One meta-argument that clearly has primary rule in mind comes from a social scientist in an attempt to formulate a rule to justify power. Power in this sense can be generalized as the ability to assert a role that overwhelms others in a way that does not include the use of force. On this view:

---

26   Thomas Franck, *Fairness in International Law and Institutions* (1995), 30 ff.

27   *Ibid.*, 38-41.

Power can be said to be legitimate to the extent that:
i)   it conforms to established rules,
ii)   the rules can be justified by reference to beliefs shared by both dominant and subordinate, and
iii) there is evidence of consent by the subordinate to the particular power relation.[28]

Such a justification would thus be all encompassing, drawing upon established rules, shared beliefs and consent. If all these obtain, the justification can be almost perfect. However, such conditions are often difficult to establish. As a result such a perfect justification may be impossible most of the time. While this argument applies *prima facie* to both primary and secondary rules, its emphasis is on primary rules, and I shall call it the "primary rule meta-argument".

As can be seen, each of these meta-arguments would serve to promote equality and to help to justify differences and inequalities, to a great extent. However, meta-arguments often work well in terms of general direction; they cannot take account of many micro-issues. Nevertheless, perhaps one may say that an equality that satisfies the primary rule and secondary rule meta-arguments would probably be a virtue, and a difference that satisfies both would probably be fair.

C. Specific Arguments

In addition to meta-arguments, human intelligence has also produced many specific arguments targeting particular issues, although they do not work well once taken out of the particular contexts. In this section, I will briefly describe and critique some of these specific arguments, in an illustrative manner only. I will put them in two broad categories: (1) arguments for exceptions to a rule of law and (2) arguments for differing rights and/or obligations. While I will explain the reasons for this categorization, I do not attempt here to provide any systemic rationalization for them, as that would be a difficult task, though a very interesting one. Nor will I attempt to evaluate the potential success of each argument, although I will comment on its merits, and will mention, where appropriate, their compatibility with the meta-arguments discussed above.

i. Arguments for Exceptions to a Rule of Law

Arguments sometimes are made for a general exception to a rule of law or an *ad hoc* exception to a rule of law "just this once", for the benefit of one or more, but not all, subjects of law, while affirming the force of the existing rule itself. As such, the arguments for exceptions to rules of law address the scope of application of the rules of law. They deal with issues surrounding "equality" or "inequality" before the law.

---

28   David Beetham, *The Legitimation of Power* (1991), 16.

These arguments are not the same as those for exceptions to a rule of law that are available to any subject of law. For example, the right to self-defense is an exception to the prohibition against the use of force. These exceptions are not for some subjects of law only, but for all. They serve to delimit the content of the general rule, not the scope of its application only.

These arguments for exceptions do not include, of course, the attempts to make a new rule of customary international law. As the perennial debates on this issue show us, sometimes when a new customary international law rule is being made, the very first attempts to do so may not be consistent with existing rules of law.[29] Before a new rule formally solidifies, there is a period of time during which there is uncertainty as to whether a certain course of conduct is lawful or not. This situation differs from attempts to claim an exception to a rule of law: the attempt to make a new rule does not recognize the existing rule as proper (as regards all), while the attempts to claim exceptions recognize the existing rule of law, but claim that it does not apply to the claimant only. If the attempts to make a new rule succeed, then the new rule would apply to all.

(a)   Arguments for a general exception to a rule of law. Such an argument proceeds this way: We agree that there is a rule of law (such as each coastal State is entitled to a territorial sea of 12 miles from the baseline), but it does not apply to us at all. In the law of treaties, a State can achieve this result by making a valid reservation to a treaty.

In customary international law, currently a State can achieve this result by attempting to establish its status as a persistent objector to an emerging rule of customary international law. The persistent objector rule is probably a widely accepted rule of law. The International Court of Justice in the *Fisheries Jurisdiction (United Kingdom v. Norway)* case[30] seemed to support this concept and this approach.

However, sometimes one encounters an argument that proceeds from a simple assertion of national interest: because this rule harms our national interest, therefore, we will not follow it. We shall call this a "national interest argument". To some extent such an argument constitutes the origin of the persistent objector rule. The difference between this argument and the persistent objector rule is that the persistent objector rule has been accepted generally by the international community, and is available to a State that has met the requirement of having made objections to a rule when it emerges and has persisted in objecting to it. The national interest argument ignores these requirements, and uses national interest as the sole criterion for behavior.

---

29   See Sienho Yee, The News that Opinio Juris "Is Not a Necessary Element of Customary [International] Law" Is Greatly Exaggerated, 43 *German Yearbook of International Law* (2000), 227, reprinted in: Sienho Yee, *Towards*, n. 6 above, 27.

30   *ICJ Reports 1951*, 116, 131 ("In any event the ten-mile rule would appear to be inapplicable as against Norway inasmuch as she has always opposed any attempt to apply to the Norwegian coast."). See also *Asylum, ICJ Reports 1950*, 277-278.

In addition, while it is difficult to require a State to forego its national interest for the sake of complying with international law, several difficulties may arise from such a way of justifying exceptions from the law. Because of the need for minimal consistency, the predominantly national interest argument would lead to undesirable consequences both vertically – within one State – and horizontally, across the world. One serious problem with this argument is the difficulty in defining national interest. Vertically within one State, different sectors may have a different definition and the same sector may have different definitions at different times. Then there are different versions of how national interest yearnings can be satisfied: Morgenthau may think that a nation is an extension of a relentlessly power-hungry individual; Mearsheimer may think that nations are under the spell of "offensive realism" so that their survival mandates aggressive behavior, without any stopping until the State becomes "the hegemon in the system".[31] So painted, every State is a scary, insecure creature constantly fearing being cornered.

No doubt horizontally different States, if allowed the same national interest argument, may have an equal or greater number of different definitions of national interest. There is simply an infinite variety of the argument, defying any meaningful response to it. The only way out seems to be to build up one's own military force. Certainly an enlightened leader would appreciate that a peaceful and stable world is in the best interest of any State in the long term at least, yet history has shown time and again that a short-sighted assessment of the immediate national interest has driven leaders down the ugly path.

Because of these difficulties, the national interest argument normally is not compatible with the primary rule and secondary rule meta-arguments discussed. However, in the extreme circumstance, this argument may still have some value, particularly in the extreme circumstance of self-defence where the very survival of the State is at stake. This has been recognized by the International Court of Justice in the *Nuclear Weapons* advisory opinion.[32]

Sometimes one can see an even more blatant form of the argument: this rule does not apply to us because we have the power to prevent it from being applied to us. As this argument does not even attempt to find justification in any principle other than the proponent's perceived overwhelming power to get its way, we shall called this argument "raw power argument". While this argument is seldom made in plain language, it may have been the basis for military action many times. Recently there is a streak of this argument in the debate regarding the justification for the use of force against Iraq in March and April of 2003. This argument was described in the media as this: because the United States was the only remaining superpower, and because the United States could use force to defeat Saddam Hussein, it might just as well put that power to use.[33] This argument has the beauty of simplicity, and an appeal from its straightforwardness. These qualities of this argument become

31   John J. Mearsheimer, *The Tragedy of Great Power Politics* (2001), 21 and generally.
32   *ICJ Reports 1996* (Generally Assembly request), 226.
33   See, *e.g.*, William Bunch, Invading Iraq Not a New Idea for Bush Clique, <http://www.philly.com/mld/dailynews/2003/01/27/news/local/5025024.htm?1c>.

more obvious when this argument is compared to the other strained justifications such as previous authorization by the Security Council or Iraq presenting a threat to the United States or even its neighbors, often contorted to such an extent that they show either disingenuousness or an inability to understand the world.

However, by giving up all pretense to legitimacy based on principle and by basing its conduct on the perceived ability or raw power to get its way, the sole superpower will return the world to its state of nature where, as the ancients have told us, "the strong do what they can and the weak suffer what they must."[34] In such a world, one cannot be sure whether the status of power will be immutable and what the consequences will be when there is a change in that status.

Second and more important, such an argument with express resort to raw power and overwhelming force normally breeds resentment and provokes strong reaction against it. Normally the overwhelming power that the superpower enjoys would make it suicidal for any State to attempt to put up a fight with the superpower, and, therefore, the superpower almost always gets its way. However, there may be some objectors, normally non-State actors, who may internalize their objection to this form of exercise of raw power as their cause to pursue, and persist in pursuing, their objection despite sacrifices. Such "internalization", according to social scientists, is the strongest form of motivational force.[35] It can lead to strong compliance with norms, or, one may add, to horrendous devastation on the scale of the September 11 attacks. So the world may be that on the one hand, the superpower may exert its overwhelming power on sovereign States, but, on the other hand, it may have to face retaliation by determined non-State actors who take up the cause of the "oppressed" State or group as their own. Whether this is a good price to pay is better left to the appreciation of the decision-makers.

(b)   Arguments for an *ad hoc* exception to a rule of law. Such an argument proceeds this way: We agree that there is a rule of law and it applies to us, too, generally but not in this instance. Such an argument does not appear to be supportable under general international law as we know it today. Therefore the proponent normally would resort to morality or other considerations. Such arguments can hardly meet the "legitimacy" conditions laid down in the primary rule and secondary rule meta-arguments described above.

One prime example of this is the attempt to deal with the aftermath of the Kosovo war waged by the NATO. The resort to morality was made by some of the

---

34   Thucydides, *The Peloponnesian War* (Modern Library ed., 1951), 331.

35   Alan Branthwaite, The Psychological Basis of Independent Statehood, in: Robert H. Jackson & Alan James, n. 3 above, at 62, said that there were three levels of motivation for compliance with norms: (1) Compliance, produced by social pressure, and maintained by rewards and punishments; (2) Identification, conformity out of a desire to be like other people whom they admire (inwardly and personally motivated; also maintained by social incentives); and (3) Internalization, strongest personal commitment to group norms and standards – conformity to norms because they make sense, and are believed by the individual to be right and worthy.

NATO members when attempting to justify the alleged humanitarian intervention in Kosovo in 1999. At least officials from Germany and the United States have said that the Kosovo approach does not apply elsewhere and that others should not try it either.[36]

One can imagine that the different formulations of "national interest argument" and the "raw power argument", as described above, would be made even more often or with stronger voice when arguing for an *ad hoc* exception than for a general exception. As the evaluation of national interest varies, so does the need for exceptions. As a result, *ad hoc* exceptions may be of greater value to those who would resort to this argument.

ii. Arguments for Differing Rights and Obligations

The arguments for exceptions to rules of law deal with equality or inequality before the law, focusing on the application of the existing rules and principles. They do not argue with the content of the rules and principles themselves directly, although the disagreement with the content of these rules and principle may have motivated some of the arguments. If indeed disagreement with the content of the rules and principles is of the essence, the rules and principles may themselves be under pressure for a reformulation so that they provide for differing rights and obligations, leading to the result that, while these rules and principles apply equally to all the subjects of law, the outcome varies with each of them.

The arguments for differing rights and obligations seem to succeed more often in treaties and conventions than in general customary international law. The reason for this discrepancy is probably thus: treaty making depends on consent and the parties may make compromises and delimit their rights and obligations in any way they deem fit, while in general customary international law the ideal of equality of all subjects of law exerts greater influence. Still we can find instances of differing treatments that have been provided in customary international law. Examples can be found in the law of the sea where some States are allowed a straight baseline system, and some States are given the archipelagic State regime. In my discussion here, I will not make a distinction between the two categories in a strict fashion, but will address these arguments in a more or less general way. This is reasonable because, although we have the impression that differing treatments in customary international law are based on generalizable reasons, while those in treaties are based on ad hoc horse-trading consent, we often can see that even consent in treaty-making is further based on generalizable reasons or is informed by them to a large extent.

Some of the varied arguments for differing rights and obligations are as follows:

---

36   See the analysis on this point in Vaughan Lowe, International Legal Issues Arising in the Kosovo Crisis, in: Sienho Yee & Wang Tieya (eds.), n. 3 above (2001), 278, 282 (quoting statements by the German Foreign Minister and the US Secretary of State).

(a) Argument from retribution. This is an argument to tie responsibility to past behavior as, for example, those who polluted more in the past must now contribute more to clean up the environment. This in fact is one strand of the justification for the commonly accepted "different but common responsibility" in international environmental law.[37] This argument has moral appeal and, perhaps for this reason, has led to the general acceptance of the "different but common responsibility" principle, although its concretization is still to be found.

(b) Argument from capability. This is an argument that attempts to tie responsibility to capability. It is simply this: We will contribute what we can. It is not that easy to justify such argument, but we know that it is impossible to demand more of a State than it can give. Perhaps this is more a resignation to the inevitable than anything else. This is also a strand of the justification for commonly accepted "different but common responsibility" in international environmental law.[38]

Another form of this argument can be made to tie right to capacity: because we are able to do this, therefore we have the right to do it. The right to over-flight in outer space may have received support from this argument, and *vice versa*. Originally, the *usque ad coelum* ("all the way up to heaven") rule provides for State sovereignty over territorial airspace to an unlimited extent. The launch of the satellites and other spacecrafts by the Soviet Union and the United States in 1950-60s immediately brought a modification to this rule, with the acquiescence of other States, so that the sovereignty of States over their airspace is now limited in height to the point where airspace and outer space meet.[39] This is perhaps the best example of the assertion by some States of a right based on capability and the resignation of other States because of inability.

Tying right to capacity can often be abused. For example, a State may make an argument for a right in a neutral way, knowing that only itself or a small number of powerful States similarly situated may be able to avail themselves of the right. For example, in the *Corfu Channel* case the United Kingdom argued that it had the right to intervene in the territory of another State to "secure possession of evidence in the territory of another State, in order to submit it to an international tribunal and thus facilitate its task".[40] The International Court of Justice resoundingly rejected this argument:

---

37   For an analysis, see Sienho Yee, *Towards*, n. 6 above, 16-17.

38   For an analysis, see *ibid.*; Michael Weisslitz, Rethinking the Equitable Principle of Common but Differentiated Responsibility: Differential versus Absolute Norms of Compliance and Contribution in the Global Climate Change Context, 13 *Colorado Journal of International Environmental Law and Policy* (2002), 473.

39   See, *e.g.*, Malcolm N. Shaw, *International Law* (4th ed., 1997), 381-82; Bin Cheng, United Nations Resolutions on Outer Space: "Instant" International Customary Law?, 5 *Indian JIL* (1965), 23.

40   *ICJ Reports 1949*, 4, 34.

The Court cannot accept such a line of defence. The Court can only regard the alleged right of intervention as the manifestation of a policy of force, such as has, in the past, given rise to most serious abuses and such as cannot, whatever be the present defects in international organization, find a place in international law. Intervention is perhaps still less admissible in the particular form it would take here; for, from the nature of things, it would be reserved for the most powerful States, and might easily lead to perverting the administration of international justice itself.[41]

As is clear, the argument criticized by the Court is really an argument based on power or raw power, but under camouflage. The same kind of logic may be present in the arguments for making a new rule of law or for making a general exception to a rule of law, and should be rejected for the same reasons.

(c)   Argument from need. This is an argument that ties rights to need. Its logic is simple: we should have this right simply because we need it. This is even harder to justify, but traces of it can be found in Kant's concept of an "imperfect duty" on the part of us to help those in need.[42] Of course, the ideal distribution of goods in communism would be done on this principle. At this moment the arguments for foreign aid are closer to Kant's imperfect duty than to the ideal distribution of goods.

(d)   Argument from democracy. This argument can take two forms. One is that, because we are a democracy, we should have more rights. This idea at this moment is not yet generally accepted, although democracies may grant to each other more rights than to non-democratic States.

Another form of the argument from democracy is based on the "one man, one vote" ideal, so that we will have "one man, one right", leading to a greater collective sum of rights for a State with a bigger population than for a State with a smaller population. In international relations this argument would favor a State with a large population.

The importance of this principle is obvious. The world has generally agreed that the will of the people is the basis of government.[43] The emphasis on the "human ends" of power and international order goes to the very root of the principle.[44] Its importance is becoming greater still day by day as the bugle of democracy has been sounding very loudly and the bandwagon of democracy has promised to leave no one behind. If one is to be faithful to what one preaches, this principle must be given serious effect.

---

41   *Ibid.*, 35.

42   See I. Kant, *The Metaphysics of Morals* (1797, M. Gregor tran. 1991), 241-42.

43   See Univ. Declaration of Human Rights, UNGA Res. 217(A) (1948), art. 21 ("The will of the people shall be the basis of the authority of government"); Int'l Covenant on Civil & Political Rights, 999 UNTS 171, art. 25. See also James Crawford, Democracy and International Law, 64 *British Yearbook of International Law* (1993), 113.

44   Charles de Visscher, n. 6 above, 124-34.

On the other hand, giving this argument unfettered effect would lead to a situation where a big State such as China or a small number of the big States would control the decision-making in the world. While such an outcome is not necessarily unfair in itself (indeed, if the argument from democracy is a fair one, such an outcome is a corollary of it), it would still be unseemly, so to speak, and it would impede the efforts to promote greater sovereign equality. So some form of compromise is in order.

(e)   Argument from economic power or GNP. This argument is simply that the rights and obligations of a State should be decided upon its economic power or GNP. Needless to say, there is some logic to this argument, and it can be grounded generally on capacity, need, or retribution/reward. But such an argument can only be good up to a point, and cannot be carried to its extreme, just as the argument from democracy. In addition, there can be some controversy as to whether economic power in itself should be given such weight. If so, it is not certain that GNP should be the proper measure for economic power.

(f)   Argument from comprehensive national strength. This argument would base a State's rights and obligations on that State's comprehensive national strength, including population, national economic power, military power, possession of nuclear weapons, etc. This argument would operate in a way similar to the argument from economic power or GNP, and is supported by the same reasoning and open to similar challenges. However, comprehensive national strength would seem to be a better basis upon which rights and obligations are grounded. In the customary international law-making process, the special weight that the big powers possess has long been recognized. Charles de Visscher noted long ago that the more powerful an actor was the heavier its footprint would be in the development of customary international law.[45] One may characterize these States as the "heavy footprint" States. The smaller States were not well-endowed enough to be contenders in this process.

The argument from economic power or comprehensive national strength may be perceived as a resort to raw power. Yet power cannot be ignored. For this reason, neither argument is easily accepted; each is usually swallowed with a sense of resignation.

(g)   Argument from efficiency. This argument would base a State's rights and obligations on some index of efficiency. Such an argument has great appeal, which takes on a greater dimension in some particular areas such as the utilization of resources. The argument is that since we are faced with scarcity of resources in the world, we must let the most efficient user of resources take the best advantage

---

45   See Charles de Visscher, n. 6 above, 155. See also generally M. Byers, *Custom, Power and the Power of Rules* (1999); contra, M. Chemillier-Gendreau, *Humanité et souverainetés: Essai sur la fonction du droit international* (1995).

of the limited supply. However, whether efficiency is a virtue itself, so that greater efficiency is our pursuit, is not a settled question; if one were to be able to find a formula to produce a balanced mix of happiness and a lower level of efficiency, I suppose that formula should be the basis for decision-making, not the pursuit for the greatest efficiency. Such a possibility would counsel against resorting to efficiency in a strong manner.

(h)   Argument from the nature of the function at issue. This argument attempts to base rights and obligations on the particular function at issue: (1) the distribution is made on a function-by-function basis rather than across the board, and (2) the rights and obligations are closely tailored to the particular function at issue so that those who are better in performing the function will be in a privileged position. Such a distribution of rights and obligations can be grounded on moral reward as well as efficiency – in fact, sophisticated efficiency. Thus, those who are peace-loving and strongly interested in safeguarding peace and security of the world are normally placed in some privileged position in the performance of such a function such as permanent membership in the United Nations Security Council, an organ entrusted with the primary responsibility to maintain peace and security in the world. Conversely, one who aspires to permanent membership in the United Nations Security Council should have the qualities for performing that function – being peace-loving themselves and being capable of performing the tasks entrusted to them. So when Japan – whose leaders annually go to worship at a shrine where former Class A war criminals convicted of most heinous international crimes including war of aggression and crimes against humanity were buried – pleads for permanent membership in the United Nations Security Council, one wonders whether such a plea for privilege was intended as a mockery of the very function of the United Nations Security Council.

(i)   Argument from potential effects on certain States. This is the argument that the rights and obligations may be determined, to a large extent, on the effects that a State may have to shoulder. Reasonably enough, this reasoning would apply to States big or small. While not directly dealing with this issue, the International Court of Justice appeared to give special weight to the practices of "specially affected" [46] States in the search for the trajectory of customary international law formation. While its import is not completely clear, this concept of "specially affected State" stands in contrast to what may be termed the "heavy footprint State" concept as intimated by de Visscher,[47] because even a diminutive State can be specially affected under some circumstances.

However, it has been accepted that the big powers would be affected most by the disturbances in the world, although this point does not appear to have been perfectly explained. And the big powers relied upon this for their privileged status

---

46   *North Sea Continental Shelf, ICJ Reports 1969*, 3, paras. 73-74.

47   Text to n. 45 above (idea of "heavy footprint" States).

in the League of Nations and then United Nations. As related by David Miller, a chief drafter of the Covenant of the League of Nations, Woodrow Wilson supported the primacy of the great powers on the ground that:

> [T]he chief physical burdens of the League will fall on the great powers whether these burdens are military or economic ... It is desirable to make the plan acceptable that the powers should be in Executive Council. ... The general idea is that the Executive Council will consist of those other powers whose interests are affected. The scheme is to have the Executive Council consist of the interested parties. The great powers are always interested.[48]

Subsequently this logic was affirmed by the Permanent Court of International Justice:

> [I]t is hardly conceivable that resolutions on questions affecting the peace of the world could be adopted against the will of those amongst the Members of the Council who, although in a minority, would, by reason of their political position, have to bear the larger share of the responsibilities and consequences ensuing therefrom.[49]

Similarly, the Joint Statement of the big powers stated eloquently at San Francisco:

> In view of the primary responsibilities of the permanent members, they could not be expected, in the present condition of the world, to assume the obligation to act in so serious a matter as the maintenance of international peace and security in consequence of a decision in which they had not concurred. Therefore, if a majority voting in the Security Council is to be made possible, the only practicable method is to provide, in respect of non-procedural decisions, for unanimity of the permanent members plus the concurring votes of at least two of the non-permanent members.[50]

Accordingly, it seems that it is generally accepted that being affected gives one the right to participate in decision-making; being affected substantially entitles one to substantial weight in the decision-making. Big powers are always affected most and therefore they are always entitled to special privilege in the decision-making, so goes the argument. That is to say, big powers have big powers' burdens, big powers' perils and, therefore, should have big powers' privileges.

(j)   Argument from contribution. This is a general argument formulated as follows: the rights a State enjoys in the international community are to be determined by the contribution it makes to that community. Thus formulated, there is a ring

---

48   David Miller, n. 17 above, 146.

49   *Interpretation of Article 3, paragraph 2 of the Treaty of Lausanne*, Advisory Opinion, *PCIJ*, Series B, No. 12 (1925), 29.

50   As quoted in: Report to the President on the Results of the San Francisco Conference by the Chairman of the US Delegation (Dept of State, pub. No. 2349, 1945), 76.

of reasonableness to it, as a general consideration. It can be grounded on retribution or reward. As they say, one who pays the piper calls the tune. However, the specific formulations of this argument can encounter several problems such as the difficulty in comparing different types of contribution, the frequent mismatches between the function at issue and the contribution, and the possible over-privileging of contribution to an extent well above the proportion of the contribution. The difficulty in comparing different types of contribution is easy to appreciate and needs no elaboration.

The mismatches between the function at issue and the contribution are illustrated by the recent debate on whether Japan should be given permanent membership with veto power at the United Nations Security Council because Japan is among the biggest financial contributors to the United Nations. One response was that the Security Council was not a "board of directors".[51] The High-level Panel on Threats, Challenges and Change convened by the United Nations Secretary-General seemed to believe that increased involvement in the decision-making of the United Nations Security Council should be based on contributions to the United Nations, "financially, militarily and diplomatically",[52] a position that appears to be reasonable, at least better than focusing on financial contributions alone.

The over-privileging of contribution can occur when the biggest contributor or contributors manage to exact a veto over the decision-making of an organization, at least on some issues, although the contribution is not necessarily very big in absolute terms. For example, at the International Monetary Fund and the World Bank this phenomenon may exist at the moment because the voting is weighted so that a *de facto* veto obtains.

5.   Leader States' Legitimacy

Given the inevitable differences and the great variety of arguments justifying such differences, it is easy for one to imagine that there is inevitably a great spectrum of differing positions in the world for different States to occupy. At what point does a State achieve the leader State position, and what constitutes the basis for its legitimacy?

As neither the term "leader States" nor "legitimacy" has received official definition, I shall take these as encompassing several possible understandings.[53] Before we examine these possibilities, let me state my assumptions and explain, in general, how I will address these two issues.

As I set out in the beginning of this paper, I stress the intrinsic and instrumental value of the phenomenon of the State and territorial integrity and political independence as the irreducible minimum for sovereign equality. These two positions

---

51   See news report at: <http://www.chinadaily.com.cn/english/doc/2004-09/22/content _376639.htm> (financial contribution).

52   High-level Panel Report, n. 3 above, 66-67.

53   It is clear that we are not here dealing with the domestic order, and we will exclude from the term the sense of *Führerstaat* (a State under the control of the leader).

will serve as the starting point for our analysis, and they are treated as axiomatic without any need for legitimatizing.

As a State moves from this starting point to another place, it may achieve another position in the spectrum of States, and there is an index of legitimacy that accompanies this movement. This index will be deemed to have included the respect for the irreducible minimum of sovereign equality. Any violation of this minimum would make the changed position of a State illegitimate.

A.   The Strong State

One obvious possibility would be to treat a State that has managed to achieve a privileged position or a strong position in the spectrum as a "leader State". Such a State would be in the part of the spectrum that would indicate that it is stronger or better than many other States. The index of legitimacy for such a position would include, in addition to respect for the irreducible minimum of sovereign equality, all the difference arguments[54] that result in a privileged position if these arguments can be applied in a way that does not offend the minimum consistency condition and can meet, to the best, the conditions of fairness either in the meta-arguments or in each individual arguments. Of course, as the above analysis shows, this can be a Herculean exercise, and, at the end of the day, one can only achieve an approximate assessment. Such an assessment may be a virtue in itself, and may exert an influence on State behavior.

In my view, however, if a State manages to achieve a privileged or strong position legitimately, it is only a "strong State", not yet a "leader State". This is so because *most* of the difference arguments, as described in Part IV above, all proceed from the perspective of the particular State itself; they are self-centered arguments. Several arguments have the potential of being more, such as the argument from the potential effects on particular States, but they are asserted from a self-centered perspective. Viewed this way, such a State is simply one that is fending for itself; it is acting like an individual elbowing to make a living, not to make a difference. For a strong State to secure a better status, it must adopt a course of action and an outlook that are "other-regarded", and must also reason from the perspective of other States.[55]

B.   The Great State

Another possibility would be to treat the big powers, such as the permanent members of the United Nations Security Council or States with almost the same power (other than the veto) in international governance, as the leader States. The claim to such a status can be based on the fact that they are big powers, sufficient to move

---

54   As described in Part 4 above.

55   This is similar to the Confucianist understanding of human nature as "being conscious of others". See Sienho Yee, *Towards*, n. 6 above, 293 (chapter 14, The Concept of Human Rights in Asia).

mountains, and on their index of legitimacy, including all the components as in-cluded in the index of legitimacy for a "strong State". To this extent, the big powers in the United Nations Security Council and their influence serve as a proxy, not a perfect reflection, of a fair result if most of the "difference agreements" including the argument from democracy are given effect in as fair a way as possible.

In my view, however, if a State manages to achieve the big power status legiti-mately, it is only a "great State", not necessarily a "leader State". The big powers are "great States" for the reasons given here; they are not necessarily "leader States" for the reasons to be given below. As Phillip Jessup noted, "Great powers have power because they are great".[56] I can say that great powers are great not simply because they have power. Their greatness comes from their respect for the value of, and their responsibility toward, the international system as a whole – maintaining peace and security and generally contributing to the health of the system – and their success in fulfilling this responsibility. The responsibility and success are both necessary components of the "great State" status. No doubt a State that shoulders a hefty responsibility toward the international system as a whole can be said to have paid the dues for that status. However, responsibility alone would not suffice; a State which bears such a responsibility but frequently leaves a mess behind in any venture would be simply doing a disservice to the international system. Substantial success in acquitting oneself of the responsibility is a necessary condition for great-ness, as one can infer from the fact that international law has always placed great weight on the idea of effectivity.[57] Success is, perhaps, the ultimate qualification for the great State status: one simply cannot argue with victory. Of course, a single State will not be able to fulfill such a responsibility; collective action is required.

Such a way of seeing the world is reasonable. Systemic value and the respon-sibility toward the system as a whole have always weighed heavily on the hearts and minds of great statesmen and great States in history. For example, the Confu-cianist ideal includes several stages of achievement: cultivating oneself, regulating the family, ordering the State and bringing peace to the world.[58] The United States participated in both World Wars, which were fought far away from its own shores, because the international system could not survive the victory of the other side.

At the end of World War II, the great States took upon themselves the "pri-mary responsibility for the maintenance of international peace and security" under

---

56   See P.C. Jessup, Introduction to the Equality of States as Dogma and Reality, LX *Politi-cal Science Quarterly* (No. 4, Dec. 1945), 530 ("Great powers have power because they are great and not because a skillful draftsman has invented an ingenious formula"), as quoted in Lachs, n. 3 above, 486.

57   This seems to inform the ICJ's view on the so-called objective personality of the United Nations vs. non-members. See *Reparation for Injuries Suffered in the Service of the United Nations*, Advisory Opinion, *ICJ Reports 1949*, 174, especially 185. For a succinct general analysis on effectivity, see de Visscher, n. 6 above, 318-32.

58   The maxim is from *Daxue* (大學, The Great Learning), and appears in Chinese as "修身齊家治國平天下", pronounced as "xiushen qijia zhiguo pingtianxia". I have trans-lated the maxim slightly differently than the normal translation.

Article 24 of the United Nations Charter.[59] The word choice of "maintenance" was deliberate; it was meant to convey the systemic nature of world peace and security and the nature of the responsibility of the big powers. The Chairman of the United States Delegation to the San Francisco Conference put it elegantly this way: "We realize, in short, that peace is a world-wide problem and that the *maintenance* of peace, and not merely its *restoration*, depends primarily upon the unity of the great powers".[60] As a result, the "provisions for the Security Council recognize the special responsibilities of the great powers for maintaining the peace and the fact that the maintenance of their unity is the crucial political problem of our time".[61]

Even in times of peace, statesmen often remind themselves of the great States' responsibility toward the international system. For example, Hu Jintao, when introducing President Bush to students at Tsinghua University, said that China and the United States had many things in common, among which was their common responsibility to the world.[62] I am sure the list of examples is very long, and I shall not attempt to complete it.

Such a responsibility sometimes entails selfless self-sacrifice, at least if an accounting is done for the *immediate* cost and benefit arising from a certain course of action, although in the long term a properly functioning international system always redounds to the benefit of all, including the self-sacrificing great States. To a great extent, this self-sacrifice was exhibited to its best by the United States' participation in the two World Wars.

It was also illustrated by the Chinese government's decision to refrain from devaluating the Chinese Yuan during the height of the Asian financial crisis back in the late 1990s in order to make Chinese products competitive with those from the other Asian States whose currencies had devalued dramatically. A devaluation of the Chinese Yuan then, so it was commonly thought, would have sent the already distressed Asian economies into a tailspin, which possibly could send the entire world into a depression, and would definitely have delayed the possible Asian recovery, if ever. Currently, in the debate as to whether the Chinese Yuan should be appreciated in value, the Chinese leaders again have been acting very cautiously. In the face of the dropping dollar, the Chinese leaders are calling upon the United States to fulfill its historic responsibility toward the international system, by adopting the same attitude that China did during the Asian crisis, which would mean beefing up the dollar.[63] It remains to be seen how this battle of currencies will play out in the future.

---

59   See also Hans Kelsen, *The Law of the United Nations: A Critical Analysis of Its Fundamental Problems*, with Supplement (1964), 272-73.

60   Report to the President, n. 50 above, 66.

61   *Ibid.*, 67.

62   "Chinese Vice-President Welcomes US President at Tsinghua University", *Xinhua News Agency* (22 February 2002) online: China Internet Information Centre <http://www.china.org.cn/english/27348.htm>.

63   See news report on the dispute: <www.forbes.com/home_asia/currencies/2004/12/02/cz_rm_1202chinadollar.html>.

So far the record of the great States in acquitting themselves of their responsibility toward the international system has been good overall. Since World War II, there has been no worldwide or systemic war. While the Cold War created tension and separation between the socialist and capitalist camps, systemic peace was assured, perhaps as result of that tension, ironically enough. In addition, overall economic development and the improvement of livelihood have been remarkable. For these reasons, perhaps the great State status that the big powers enjoy has been earned.

However, the international system is faced with serious challenges at present. The High-level Panel on Threats, Challenges and Change convened by the United Nations Secretary-General is of the view that

> [T]he biggest security threats we face now, and in the decades ahead, go far beyond States waging aggressive war. They extend to poverty, infectious disease and environmental degradation; war and violence within States; the spread and possible use of nuclear, radiological, chemical and biological weapons; terrorism; and transnational organized crime. The threats are from non-State actors as well as States, and to human security as well as State security.[64]

Serious indeed are these challenges, and hefty is the responsibility of the great States toward the international system. As to how the great States may fulfill their responsibility, the High-level Panel has a great deal to say, and it is not my intent to deal with the details here.

However, I would like to say that the alleged right of humanitarian intervention and the exaggerated right to self-defense have the potential of disturbing the existing system, if the minimal consistency condition were to apply to these alleged rights. The chaos created in the world system, as a whole, by the alleged right of humanitarian intervention and the almost inevitable result of causing greater sudden and dramatic sufferings than non-intervention (which could result in more slow sufferings), would seem to make such an alleged right suspect, to say the least, if not outright unlawful and immoral.[65] An exaggerated right to self-defense of one State against another or of one State against non-State groups in another State can also lead to inroads into the current regime of sovereign equality. It would seem that, at least in the long term, the best antidote to the problems created by non-State groups is to promote strong States around the world and the cooperation between and among them.

C.   The Leader State

A further possibility would be to identify a "leader State" by identifying what is the function at issue and assessing how a particular State is carrying out that function, with a view to ascertaining whether certain "leader qualities" are exhibited or not.

---

64   High-level Panel Report, n. 3 above, 11.

65   See Sienho Yee, *Towards*, n. 6 above, 21-22.

In the context of our inquiry here and in order to make the inquiry manageable, I have in mind only the function that the great States perform in the international system – maintaining peace and security in the world and generally contributing to the health of the system as a whole.[66] Obviously, in order to be a contender as a "leader State", a State must be a big power or something close to it; otherwise, it would not have the wherewithal to perform this important function.

With this in mind, let us inquire into what would constitute the index of legitimacy for a "leader State". This index must include the entire index of legitimacy for "great States", although the measure of success need not be as substantial as that for a great State. Slightly weaker States too can be leaders if they have also contributed, to a significant extent, to maintaining international peace and security and to meeting the interconnected, serious challenges that the world is facing.

Second, and more importantly, this index must include a component dealing with how such a contribution is made. Current understanding of "leadership" seems to be saying that leadership is based on a position of authority, the ability to receive deference from the followers.[67] Different philosophers and sociologists have given us different formulations of leadership. Its essence has remained the same: Leaders are not leaders because they manage to get ahead of the pack, but because they lead the pack, and are followed by the pack.

Several factors may help one earn deference from others. First of all, the existence of a body of legitimate rules and the leader's own good faith efforts to follow them are among the most important factors that give rise to authority and leadership in modern societies.[68] The international community is no different and those big powers that make good faith efforts to follow the existing legitimate rules will no doubt receive the deference from other States. Thus, it would seem that the prevailing of the general state of the rule of law[69] and the potential leaders' good faith efforts in contributing to that general state of affairs are important minimal bases for the leader State status.

Second, in addition to good faith efforts, sometimes potential leader States may have to make exemplary efforts to comply with the existing rules, in order to induce deference from others or voluntary compliance with the rules by others. Dissenting in a case on a point of domestic law, Justice Louis D. Brandeis of the United States Supreme Court put it this way:

---

66   No doubt there is an infinite variety of functions and of the ways and means of performing those functions. Limiting our inquiry this way does not mean slighting other important functions; it is simply a resignation to the inability to deal with all of them here.

67   See generally, Thomas Carlyle, *On Heroes, Hero-Worship, and the Heroic in History* (1900); From Max Weber: *Essays in Sociology* (H.H. Gerth & C. Wright Mills eds., 1991), Part II.

68   Max Weber, *ibid.*

69   For a formulation of such a state of affairs, see Sienho Yee, *Towards*, n. 6 above, 41-58.

Decency, security and liberty alike demand that government officials shall be subjected to the same rules of conduct that are commands to the citizen. In a government of laws, existence of the government will be imperilled if it fails to observe the law scrupulously. Our Government is the potent, the omnipresent teacher. For good or for ill, it teaches the whole people by its example. Crime is contagious. If the Government becomes a lawbreaker, it breeds contempt for law; it invites every man to become a law unto himself; it invites anarchy. To declare that in the administration of the criminal law the end justifies the means – to declare that the Government may commit crimes in order to secure the conviction of a private criminal – would bring terrible retribution. Against that pernicious doctrine this Court should resolutely set its face.[70]

What Brandeis said about the "teacher" role of the United States Government can also be said about any State in a potential leadership position. Such a State too is an "omnipresent teacher" to the world. Inducing deference by exemplary efforts applies with greater force to the international community because of its existing disorganized and semi-anarchical nature. Otherwise, the anarchy that Brandeis feared would be visited upon the world.

Sadly enough, some major powers are still sticking to their mentality held over from a beyond era called the Cold War and attempt to produce "deference" or compliance through deterrence and coercion. Needless to say, such an approach has not produced any deference or good results.

In no other area than in the non-proliferation and elimination of nuclear weapons have the pitfalls of this approach been shown clearly. Without going into the details and without attempting to be meticulous in details, one can say that the reality of the current regime of non-proliferation and elimination of nuclear weapons consists of basically two points: (1) the "haves" shall keep what they have for now, and the "have-nots" shall wash their hands of them; and (2) the "haves" shall in due course eliminate what they have. Obviously this regime is born of a concession to reality. It also serves, however, to magnify the injustice that inheres in a world consisting of haves and have-nots. Exacerbating this feeling is the lack of genuine efforts on the part of the haves to move towards eventual elimination, the nice promise notwithstanding, because without complete elimination, the injustice becomes permanent, rather than only temporary. Thus, the commentator David Scofield reported that when South Korean President Roh Moo-hyun visited California, he "stunned many in the audience of foreign-policy experts with his assertion that the central argument underpinning North Korea's nuclear-weapons program – that it is a necessary defense in the face of hostility and threat – is not entirely illogical."[71] Appropriate inducement in the form of promises of reward sometimes may work wonders, such as in the case of Libya's elimination of its pro-

---

70   *Olmstead v. United States*, 277 U.S. 438, 485, 48 S.Ct. 564, 575 (Brandeis, J., dissenting).

71   David Scofield, Seoul rows against the US tide, *Asia Times*, 24 Nov. 2004, <http://www.atimes.com/atimes/Korea/FK24Dg03.html>.

gram of weapons of mass destruction. But, in the nature of things, such wonders will be limited if minimal logic or fairness is not assured.

Furthermore, the policy of nuclear deterrence or coercion is still a tool that has been resorted to by some nuclear powers. For example, some nuclear powers, such as, the United States, have not made the "no first strike" pledge. Some are making efforts to neutralize the nuclear capability of others, in the name of building a "National Missile Defense" system. While dressed upon in the garb of self-defence, such a system becomes an offensive system when coupled with the failure of some nuclear powers to make the "no first strike" pledge. Such efforts obviously can only lead to an arms race, and the recent Russian pronouncement[72] that it is working on a new nuclear system is prime proof of that.

So it would seem that unless the nuclear powers start to make genuine and exemplary efforts to move towards eventual elimination of nuclear weapons, one can understand why there would be dogged and clandestine attempts to obtain the forbidden fruit. For the sake of the world, any State that aspires to the leader State status should act like a leader in the non-proliferation effort.

One wonders whether the possibility that that non-State groups may attempt to obtain nuclear weapons would serve as the saving grace for the nuclear deterrence policy propounded by some States. I do not believe so. First of all, the victims of the execution of the deterrence policy will probably be innocent bystanders, not the culprit groups. Second, so far the lowest-tech, not high-tech, has been used by such groups, and evidence shows that it is difficult for such groups to obtain nuclear weapons without the assistance of States. Accordingly, the possibility that non-State groups may manage to obtain nuclear weapons should be cause for the world to promote strong States capable of controlling such non-State groups, and, more important, for the nuclear powers to move as soon as possible to complete elimination of nuclear weapons so that it would be impossible for non-State groups to obtain them.

In other areas, the behavior of some potential leader States seems to paint a picture of strong States elbowing for their own advantages only or even simply for the sake of throwing their weight around, demonstrating who is the boss, showing pride or moral superiority, punishing others for spite, or simply ensuring that one can have his or her way. Clearly such behavior is no leader's style. It epitomizes the kind of behavior that starts with a self-regarded perspective, without regard to others,[73] a tendency that can lead to untold misery in the future. Clearly such behavior will not induce any positive results for the world. It serves only as a source for bad examples.

Against the background of use of force or deploying force to settle disputes, an exemplary effort to settle disputes by peaceful means was made by France and the Republic of Congo. On December 9, 2002, the Republic of the Congo (the Congo) filed an application against France, alleging that in attempting to prosecute a Congolese Minister and to seek to examine the Congolese President as a witness,

---

72   Putin Says Russia Working on New Nuclear Systems, Reuters News, Moscow, 17 November 2004, <http://www.washingtonpost.com/wp-dyn/articles/A56417-2004Nov17.html>.

73   See paragraph accompanying n. 52 above ("other-regardedness").

France violated the principle of sovereign equality and the criminal immunity of a foreign Head of State. The Congo sought to found the jurisdiction of the International Court of Justice (ICJ), pursuant to Article 38, paragraph 5,[74] of the Rules of Court, "on the consent of the French Republic, which will certainly be given."[75] This is normally considered an attempt by the Congo to employ the doctrine of *forum prorogatum*.[76] Such an attempt can be described as a "naked attempt" for the reason that when the application was filed there was *plainly* no basis for jurisdiction over the other State. And yet it can be successful, sometimes. By a letter dated April 8, 2003 and received on April 11, 2003 in the Registry, the French Republic stated that it "consent[ed] to the jurisdiction of the Court to entertain the Application pursuant to Article 38, paragraph 5".[77] This marks "the first instance since the adoption in 1978 of Article 38, paragraph 5, of the Rules of Court in which a State has thus accepted another State's invitation to recognize the jurisdiction of the International Court of Justice to deal with a case against it",[78] and thus the return of the doctrine of *forum prorogatum* to the International Court of Justice since probably the *Haya de la Torre* case.[79] The ICJ has now entered this case in the General List as "the case concerning *Certain Criminal Proceedings in France (Republic of Congo v. France)*."[80]

By any standards, the French acceptance of the Congo's invitation, which it need not accept, is exemplary. The Agent for France made clear before the Court that France had done so because of the following reasons: the importance of the good faith search for peaceful settlement of international disputes in international relations; the confidence France has in and the respect it has for the Court; and its belief that neither its laws nor the acts of its judiciary in this particular case violated any rules of international law.[81] Not directly addressed by the French Agent is the question whether, at the particular moment when the Iraq War was going on, France intended to provide a counter-example to the unilateral use of force by the United States. Yet this question might be on the minds of many. One wishes

---

74   Article 38(5) of the 1978 Rules of Court states:

   When the applicant State proposes to found the jurisdiction of the Court upon a consent thereto yet to be given or manifested by the State against which such application is made, the application shall be transmitted to that State. It shall not however be entered in the General List, nor any action be taken in the proceedings, unless and until the State against which such application is made consents to the Court's jurisdiction for the purposes of the case.

75   ICJ Press Release 2002/37 (9 December 2002).

76   See Sienho Yee, *Forum Prorogatum* Returns to the International Court, in: Yee, *Towards*, n.6 above, 85.

77   ICJ Press Release 2003/14 (11 April 2003).

78   *Ibid.*

79   *ICJ Reports 1951*, 71.

80   ICJ Press Release 2003/15 (23 April 2003). See also ICJ Verbatim Record CR 2003/20 (28 April 2003), 1.

81   ICJ Verbatim Record CR 2003/21 (28 April 2003, un-corrected version), 6-7.

that the exemplary urge would move France soon to re-accept the Court's "compulsory jurisdiction" by filing a declaration under Article 36(2) of the ICJ Statute. That would be the ultimate example for France to set and for other States to follow. Judicial settlement of disputes no doubt will redound to benefit of the parties to the dispute and the world at large; it is far better to go to court than to go to war.

The ultimate leader State is, however, a leader State that has not only been making good faith or even exemplary efforts to comply with the existing legitimate rules, but, more importantly, has helped to formulate or refine substantially a good vision of the international system and to build it up. That is to say, the ultimate leader State is not only a vision purveyor and promoter or a system maintainer and promoter, but also a vision originator or refiner and a system builder. The ultimate leader State helps to mold the world. While some might believe that the destiny of history has already been predetermined, great leaders and great leader States have never given up their efforts to formulate better visions for the international system and to build up the system according to their visions.

The United States has been a most powerful leader in this regard. In the aftermath of both World Wars, the United States devoted considerable time and energy to formulating better visions for the world system and building it up. This great story has been told many times, and need not be repeated here.[82] This leadership role may be changing. One can see evidence of this, for example, in the recent brouhaha surrounding the International Criminal Court (ICC), such as the "unsigning" of the Rome Statute and making the weak and meek States sign the so-called "Article 98 agreements". These agreements were thought to be capable of ensuring that United States nationals would not end up as defendants before the ICC, after the proposed control of the United Nations Security Council over the ICC's activities (under Article 23 in the draft statute proposed by the International Law Commission) was overridden by subsequent developments.[83] I can see that the erstwhile moral leader has now become the persistent objector in the progressive development of international law. I can only sigh: what a reversal of roles. I also see something unseemly in asking the weak and meek States to be the henchmen in one's own fight. If I were to coax anyone, I would choose the big and strong as my targets. Even a neighborhood bully will get bored with bullying the little ones, and will pick on the stronger and stronger for a fight.[84]

---

82   See, *e.g.*, David Miller, n. 17 above; Report to the President, n. 50 above; Ruth B. Russell, *A history of the United Nations Charter : The role of the United States 1940-1945* (1958); Mary Ann Glendon, *A World Made New: Eleanor Roosevelt and the Universal Declaration of Human Rights* (2001).

83   See my paper, A Proposal to Reformulate Article 23 of the ILC Draft Statute for an International Criminal Court, 19 *Hastings Int'l & Comp. Law Review* (1996), 523, reprinted in Sienho Yee, *Towards*, n. 6 above, 105.

84   It is not my goal here to give an assessment of the US arguments against the ICC; other scholars have done so. Nevertheless, I would like to mention that the normal commentaries published in the US media regarding the expansive jurisdiction of the ICC or the possible loss of US sovereignty do not seem to have been well-informed. The

Of course, the vision that a leader State helps to formulate must be a good and fair one. There can be many such visions, all focusing on international peace and security, friendly relations and economic development. This can be seen in the Friendly Relations Declaration, which embodies a vision that has commanded the general support of the world community, and in the "Five Principles of Peaceful Coexistence" championed by China and India.[85] The High-level Panel convened by the United Nations Secretary-General has also presented in its report a vision of a solidly multilateral system for the world for decades to come, focusing on security challenges.[86] Such an emphasis is of course appropriate, as peace is the foundation for all, whether it is human rights or development. Without peace and security, one will only see a mirage of idealism.

In the National Security Strategy of the United States,[87] a vision of a proper world order was also presented. The interconnected nature of the world and the importance of eliminating poverty and promoting economic development were appreciated. To this extent, the National Security Strategy embodies an integrated approach, and has much to commend it. However, a strong unilateral approach to security has also been asserted. This is commonly called the Bush doctrine of preemption. It would seem that one generally has sympathy for the perception of threat, particularly after the threat came true on September 11, 2001. Yet, a proper response in a pre-emptive manner must answer the question "how much in advance can the response be" in a balanced and proper fashion. If this question is dealt with improperly, the world may return to the state of nature. Another question to consider is how to distribute State responsibility for any mistakes in conducting pre-emptive strikes, on a *post-facto* examination of the situation, although the mistakes appear reasonable immediately before such strikes occur.

It remains to be seen how the Bush vision may affect the world both externally and internally, and whether this vision may become the vision for the world. The recent events that have resulted from the execution of this vision have led to hardship and reduced liberty for many, although my assessment may be wrong. One only hopes that if justice in the world can only be an ideal, life would be at least bearable – not too much a comedy for those who think, and not too much a tragedy for those who feel.

Rome Statute in fact implements a version of the jurisdictional principle that is narrower than is permissible under international law, and the complementarity principle and other safeguards more than protect the sovereignty of any reasonable State.

85   See generally the 50th Anniversary celebration symposium in 3 *Chinese Journal of International Law* (2004), 363 *et seq.*

86   High-level Panel Report, n. 3 above.

87   See <http://www.whitehouse.gov/nsc/nss.html>. For commentaries, see Edward McWhinney, President Bush and the New U.S. National Security Strategy: The Continuing Relevance of the Legal Adviser and International Law, 2 *Chinese Journal of International Law* (2002), 421; Christine Gray, The US National Security Strategy and the New "Bush Doctrine" on Pre-emptive Self-defence, *ibid.*, 437.

The wide variety of visions for the world would seem to make it fruitless for one to evaluate them one by one. Still I cannot resist presenting what I consider to be the best one in general and abstract terms.

In my view, any proper vision would have to take human flourishing as the ultimate goal. Any proper international system must be one that would provide the playground for the flowering of individuals, keeping in mind that the personhood of any individual may include belonging to a particular community and a particular State. Under such a vision, life cannot simply be bearable; life must be beautiful. It should include making firecrackers out of gunpowder, and not gunpowder out of firecrackers. Under such a vision, leadership does not mean the power to use bows to shoot, guns to destroy, or lasers to fry, but the intelligence to lead, the strategy to guide, and the prowess to inspire all to achieve the flourishing of humanity.[88]

This would require the world, particularly the leader States, to place an emphasis on winning the minds and souls of all players in the world to move towards that goal. My assessment, which can be wrong, is that currently there is a strong tendency, at least in some quarters, in idolizing overwhelming force, or superiority, or the appearance thereof. Such a culture normally leads to over-moralization of, and antagonism in, international relations. This needs to be changed, and it can be changed only by immersing everyone in the world in an atmosphere of idolizing refinement and the pursuit of excellence in airing differences orally rather than violently, in arts and sciences, and in culture generally. Or, as Montesquieu would have

---

88   Commenting on historical Chinese figures, Chairman Mao Zedong muses in a poem that many of them knew only power and force; they lack "literary inspiration". Mao Zedong, Qinyuan Chun, Snow (1936), in: *Selected Poems of Mao Zedong* (Lao Chi, ed., 1993), 143. The poem is in a classic form of Chinese poetry, and reads in part as follows: "江山如此多娇，引无数英雄竞折腰。 惜秦皇汉武， 略输文采；唐宗宋祖， 稍逊风骚。 一代天骄， 成吉思汗， 只识弯弓射大雕。 " (Here is my own English rendition of this: "Motherland, you are so beautiful; you move countless heroes to compete to serve you selflessly. Pity Qin Emperor the First and Han Emperor Wudi: they lacked the literary inspiration for civilian governance; Pity Tang Emperor Tangzong and Song Emperor Taizu: they lacked the poetic prowess for civilian success. Too bad too, the chosen Son of Heaven, of one time, Ghenghis Khan, only knew how to shoot the big birds with his magic bow. All this is now passé; if one is to count outstanding figures, one must take a look at those living now".) From this one can see the Chinese ideal of "literary king" and the Chinese dislike of use of force. In fact, if one were to substitute "The world" for "Motherland", the poem could similarly apply to the world. One might wonder how much this had been put into practice by Mao Zedong, particularly in the Cultural Revolution. First of all, such an inquiry is beyond the scope of my paper; as mentioned earlier, my goal is not to survey practice, but to focus on conceptual and philosophical inquiries, perhaps in an idealist fashion. In any event, the very name of "Cultural Revolution" itself reflects Mao's philosophy – a revolution of culture – and the actual events that took place during the course of the Cultural Revolution no doubt diverged, for whatever reason, from the original intent. In any event, one may simply consider the Cultural Revolution an aberration from the general course of the unfolding of the normal Chinese philosophy or pursuits.

it, everyone should be immersed in a culture of "soft manners and morals".[89] He said that such "softness" would naturally help to promote commerce and elevate humanity.[90] Perhaps he was right; he could find support in the earlier teachings of Confucius on the "middle way" as the ideal way of managing things,[91] as well as of those of many others following him.

Previously,[92] I have explained that having human flourishing as the ultimate goal of any society is nothing new, and that freedom or liberty in its negative and/or positive form might not be enough for this purpose, and that a third form of "induced liberty" may be important. The web of relations and responsibility serves as an important force to induce liberty. Furthermore, general achievements in human rights and a properly functioning democracy will also promote human flourishing. Diversity to the widest extent possible will serve to produce richness that would form the basis for human flourishing.

To some extent, the High-level Panel Report[93] can be faulted for only focusing on security challenges and peace-building, and not paying sufficient attention to the need for better education, cultural and spiritual enrichment and a general atmosphere conducive to human flourishing and conducive to inducing human flourishing, which in the long term will be more important. A glance at the table of contents of the Report reveals this. Perhaps a second report focusing on the ways and means of inducing human flourishing will be of value. Leader States have a substantial responsibility in providing such ways and means and generally in building up the international system that would support and promote human flourishing. I hope in due course the work of UNESCO will be recognized as important in this regard, although the term "UNESCO" was reported by my computer as "not found" in this High-level Panel Report.[94]

Such a vision of human flourishing, in the final analysis, would present the best strategy for eliminating terror and threat to security, by inducing the various players into performing tasks that would enrich their lives, thus eradicating the roots for terrorism. One fully understands that it will take time to achieve this. The States feeling threatened now may believe that they would not have the luxury to wait for that to happen, and may resort to high-pressure tactics in order to prevent terrorism, which may then turn the world into a spiral of horror. An alternative view can be that precisely because of this situation and this possibility, the leader

---

89   Montesquieu, *The Spirit of Laws*, XX.i (T. Nugent tran. 1823).

90   *Ibid.* See also T. Pangle & P. Ahrensdorf, *Justice among Nations* (1999), 160.

91   See Confucius, *The Analects*, especially Bk. VI, Chp. XXVII (William E. Soothill tran. Dover ed. 1995), 32.

92   See generally Sienho Yee, *Towards*, n. 6 above, 24-26.

93   High-level Panel Report, n. 3 above.

94   I must say that I do not vouch for my computer search skills. The absence of UNESCO from the Report may have resulted from the fact that the Report had a narrow scope in mind: only the UN agencies themselves are examined, not the specialized agencies. Then one can disagree with such a narrow scope, given the title of the Panel.

States shall feel a greater urgency to make stronger efforts to win the minds and souls of everyone.

In conclusion, let me say to the States:

(1)   When you (a) have respected the irreducible minimum of sovereign equality and (b) have managed to reach a privileged or strong position legitimately under the difference arguments, you are merely a strong State;

(2)   When you (a) have respected the irreducible minimum of sovereign equality, (b) have become a strong State legitimately and have achieved the big power status, and (c) have paid respect to the value of, and shouldered, with substantial success, the hefty responsibility toward, the international system, you are merely a great State;

(3)   When you (a) have respected the irreducible minimum of sovereign equality, (b) have respected the value of, and shouldered, with success, substantial responsibility toward, the international system, (c) have not only been making good faith efforts or even exemplary efforts to comply with the existing legitimate rules, but also, more important, (d) have helped to formulate or refine a proper vision of the international system and to build it up so that the flourishing of humanity can be achieved to the greatest extent, you are a leader State.

Part 6

Idealism and the Arena: International Law under Stress

29. Solidarity as a Constitutional Principle: Its Expanding Role and Inherent Limitations

Karel Wellens

1. Introduction

The notion of solidarity has evolved in recent times to become a principle of international law. In various branches of international law it has reached different stages of development. The purpose of this contribution is to explore how in this process the principle of solidarity has acquired and performed a constitutional role towards the international legal order at large because it operates across various branches and it has permeated both primary and secondary rules.

This chapter squarely places itself within the *constitutionalist approach* to international law, which is based upon "a concern for collective goals and a belief in community rather than State-oriented values transcending the aggregate interests of the subjects of international law (*i.e.* principally the States)," and upon the "assumption that substantive, universal, community values exist, implementation of which must be guaranteed by international mechanisms."[1]

2. Solidarity: From Notion to Principle

Societal consensus over common interests and thus their prioritisation against the interests of individual States distinguishes a community from its components, and from a society, and it constitutes the precondition for the formation of and the respect for legal rules.[2]

---

1   Anne Peters, "There is Nothing More Practical than a Good Theory; An Overview of Contemporary Approaches to International Law", *German Yearbook of International Law*, 2001, pp. 25-38, at pp. 35 and 36. See the same volume for a broad overview of international theories of international law, pp. 25-201.

2   Bruno Simma, From Bilateralism to Community Interest in International Law, *Recueil des Cours de l'Académie de La Haye*, vol. 250, 1994, VI, pp. 217-384, at p. 245. See also Charles De Visscher, *Théories et Réalités en Droit International Public*, 4th Edition, Paris, Pedone, 1970, 450 pp., at p. 111.

Ronald St. John Macdonald & Douglas M. Johnston (eds.), Towards World Constitutionalism, *pp. 775-807.*
© *2005 Koninklijke Brill NV. Printed in The Netherlands. ISBN 90 04 14612 1.*

Solidarity within society may be considered to be one of the cornerstones upon which each particular domestic legal order inevitably has to be built not only as a given, holding together the members of such a national society, but more importantly as the expression of the basic values shared by all of its members. As a foundation common to the constitutional traditions it may be recognized as a general principle of law.

Rooted in the phenomena of international interdependence[3] and globalization,[4] solidarity has recently[5] become the expression of a philosophy inherent to the international order without any need to further prove its axiomatic authority.[6]

The essence of the concept of solidarity is that "it links the factual and legal interdependence of states."[7]

The UN General Assembly recently described solidarity as "a fundamental value, by virtue of which global challenges must be managed in a way that distributes costs and burdens fairly in accordance with basic principles of equity and social justice and ensures that those who suffer or who benefit the least receive help from those who benefit the most."[8]

While maintaining its political nature the notion of solidarity has become a principle proper to the international legal order because it has given rise to the creation, modification or confirmation of rights and obligations,[9] and this to vary-

---

3   Described as "a condition which for all practical purposes must be regarded as unchangeable ..." by Paul Weithman, "Natural law, solidarity and international justice", in Brian Berry and Robert Goodin, (Eds.), *Free Movement*, New York, Harvester Wheatsheaf, 1992, 300 pp., pp. 181-202, at p. 190.

4   Depicted as "a process of denationalisation of markets, politics and law on the international as well as national levels" by Jost Delbrück, "Prospects for a 'World (Internal) Law?': Legal Developments in a Changing International System", in *Indiana Journal of Global Legal Studies*, 2002, pp. 401-431, at p. 401.

5   On the pre-20th century presence of the notion/idea of solidarity see *inter alia* Ulrich Scheuner, "*Solidarität unter den Nationen als Grundsatz in der gegenwärtigen Internationalen Gemeinschaft*", in J. Delbrück (Ed.), *Recht in Dienst des Friedens, Festschrift für Eberhard Menzel*, Berlin, Duncker und Humblot, 1975, 660 pp., pp. 251-277, at pp. 256-270. Particularly relevant were Vattel and Wolf, although they were referring to a moral duty of solidarity: *ibid.*, at pp. 266-267.
    In his *Theory of Moral Sentiments* (1759) Adam Smith emphasized sympathy as a motivating factor in human society: referred to by R.St.J. Macdonald, D. M Johnston and G. L. Morris, "The International Law of Human Welfare; Concept, Experience, and Priorities", in *The International Law and Policy of Human Welfare*, Alphen aan den Rijn, Sijthoff and Noordhoff, 1978, 690 pp., pp. 3-79, at p. 68, note 24.

6   Michel Virally, *Le rôle des "principes "dans le développement du droit international*, in *Recueil d'études de droit international en hommage à Paul Guggenheim*, Faculté de Droit de l'Unversité de Genève and IUHEI de Genève, 1968, 901 pp., pp. 531-554, at pp. 542-543.

7   Malgosia Fitzmaurice, International Protection of the Environment, *Receuil des Cours de l'Académie de La Haye*, Vol. 293, 2001, pp 13-488, at p. 441.

8   General Assembly Resolutions 56/151, para. 3 (f) and 57/123, para. 4 (f) adopted on 19 December 2001 and 18 December 2002.

9   Michel Virally, *op. cit.*, at pp. 532, 534-535.

ing degrees and a wide range of modalities. Solidarity has evolved, gradually and not without difficulty, from an ideological principle of law into a principle of existing law.[10] It has evolved from the realm of justice into the domain of law.

Although the notion itself of solidarity is of a rather general nature and does not present itself in a normative way, it does qualify both as a framework concept *of* international law and as a perspective concept relating *to* international law:[11] it is capable of governing, either on a structural or on an *ad hoc* basis, a wider range of cases and circumstances than other international law concepts, and its relevance to the solution of pertinent interdisciplinary questions has been successfully tested.

Solidarity became a concept with a normative aim, a substrate for rules of law.

Solidarity went through a "spontaneous social process generating general principles of international law, part of custom, general principles of Article 38, c or a *sui generis* source."[12] As to the *sui generis* origin, solidarity can be found as a binding principle "by looking at general international law" and its legal basis "must be assumed to exist as (an) associative obligation(s) of the international legal community."[13]

Solidarity is a multifaceted principle. Although in a number of cases it is instrumental in combating or responding to dangers or events threatening the international community or larger parts of it (negative), it normally operates through the creation of joint rights and obligations (positive). These obligations may in turn contain measures of abstention such as, pursuant to Article 41 of the ILC Articles on state responsibility, non-recognition of situations created by a serious breach of an obligation arising under a peremptory norm of general international law.

Although initially in a fragmented and piecemeal way solidarity has now more fully penetrated into the international legal order, it has claimed a particular place within that order and its content has been clarified over time.[14] It is now firmly a part of the analytical and legal framework for the 21st century.

---

10   *Ibid.* at pp. 544-545.

11   Georg Schwarzenberger, "The Conceptual Apparatus of International Law", in R.St. J. Macdonald, (Ed.), *Essays in Legal Philosophy, Doctrine and Theory. The Structure of International Law,* The Hague, Boston, Lancaster, Martinus Nijhoff, 1983, 1234 pp., pp. 685-712, at pp. 692-693.

12   Which the ICJ seems to recognize: Vera Gowlland-Debbas, "Judicial Insights into Fundamental Values and Interests of the International Community", in A. Muller, D. Raic and J. Thuranszky (Eds.), *The International Court of Justice. Its Future Role after Fifty Years,* Martinus Nijhoff Publishers, The Hague, Boston, London, 1997, 433 pp., pp.327-366, at p. 344.

13   Marcel Brus, *Third Party Dispute Settlement in an Interdependent World. Developing a Theoretical Framework,* Martinus Nijhoff Publishers, Dordrecht, Boston, London, 1995, 275 pp., at p. 149.
     For a critique of the idea of an international community see Dino Kritsiotis, "Imagining the International Community", *European Journal of International Law,* 2002, pp.961-992.

14   Michel Virally, *op. cit.,* at p. 546.

3.   The Principle of Solidarity in Various Branches of International Law

The complexity of the problems global society is facing is unlimited. In an almost natural way this has led to the creation within the overall international legal order of a variety of branches of international law each claiming not only the need for a particular set of primary rules but also the right to utilize secondary rules in a way best adapted to the issues it is dealing with. These processes of creation, interpretation, implementation and dispute settlement vary accordingly.[15]

It is not surprising that the principle of solidarity has reached different stages of development in various branches of international law. International human rights, humanitarian law, disaster and refugee law, and development law constitute the natural habitat for the notion of solidarity to come to fruition: its core is perfectly suited to address the fundamental needs these branches are coping with.

The penetration of the principle of solidarity in various branches did occur at different moments in time and not in a uniform way. One relevant factor is the "tradition" within a particular branch: the actors involved may be willing to let solidarity enter in a direct way through treaties (*e.g.* international environmental law) or by unilateral acts (*e.g.* pledges to provide development or reconstruction assistance) or they may opt for a more indirect entrance through custom (*e.g.* disaster law).

Contemporary international law demonstrates that once applied in one branch of international law the principle of solidarity easily lends itself to be applied in an increasing number of other branches.[16]

Whereas in many branches the principle of solidarity was, in the mid 1970s and 1980s, considered to constitute progressive development, it may now safely be concluded that it has gradually become more codified.

4.   The UN Law on the Maintenance of International Peace and Security

A.   *A Collective Responsibility*

The Preamble of the Charter leaves no doubt that, as a community commitment, the peoples of the United Nations have united their "strength to maintain international peace and security." The "acceptance of the principles and the institution of methods" has to ensure that "armed force shall not be used, save in the *common interest.*" The maintenance of international peace and security is the first purpose of the UN and it "can be understood as the cornerstone of modern international law and the United Nations Charter."[17]

---

15   See for instance the 25th anniversary volume of the *Netherlands Yearbook of International Law*, 1994, pp. 3-333.

16   Michel Virally, *op. cit.*, at p. 542.

17   Bruno Simma, *op. cit.*, at p. 236.

Through the creation of the UN States have not only internationalized their obligation to provide for peace and security in their international relations,[18] but it is in the UN law on the maintenance of international peace and security that the principle of solidarity has reached its highest degree of constitutionalization. Solidarity is not only a fundamental principle upon which the Charter is ultimately based but it is also a duty accepted by Member States by the mere fact of their adherence to the Charter.[19]

Because issues "like the environment, development, and human rights embody, in the last instance, also essential aspects of security,"[20] the maintenance of international peace and security is a public good of such a global nature that only the principle of solidarity is capable of providing a permanent and reliable basis for its preservation. It is thus not surprising that in recent resolutions on the promotion of a democratic and equitable international order the General Assembly included solidarity as one of the principles "enshrined in the Charter."[21]

The principle of solidarity forms the political and legal foundation for the collective security system established by the UN Charter.

The collective security "window" created by the Charter was "intended to make the peace and security of each the responsibility of all states."[22] Articles 43 and 48 are designed and aimed at securing the necessary mutual assistance between Member States and towards the organization in the carrying out of that collective responsibility.

Mutual trust and solidarity would be called into question in case of concurrent powers between Member States and the Security Council. This explains the temporary exercise of the individual or, solidarity-based, collective right of self-defence until institutionalised solidarity rightfully claims its operational role through the exercise of its powers by the Security Council on behalf of the entire membership as the trustee of the international community.

Council practice to guarantee and implement solidarity has clarified and sanctioned "the Charter based and customary legal obligation *erga omnes* for Member States not to commit, acquiesce in or support, directly or indirectly acts or courses of conduct which may constitute or result in a threat to international peace and

18   Jost Delbrück, "Structural Changes in the International System and its Legal Order: International Law in the Era of Globalization", in *Revue Suisse de Droit International*, 2001, pp. 1-36, at p. 2.

19   Epaminondas Marias, "Solidarity as an Objective of the European Union and the European Community", in *Legal Issues of European Integration*, 1994, pp. 85-114, at p. 91, but with regard to EC membership. Also outside the UN framework solidarity may provide the foundation for the establishment of a common defence policy and organization, *e.g.* NATO.

20   Bruno Simma, *op. cit.*, at p. 237.

21   Resolutions 56/151 adopted on 19 December 2001 and 57/213 adopted on 18 December 2002.

22   Thomas Franck, *Fairness in International Law and International Institutions*, Clarendon Press, Oxford, 1995, 500 pp., at p. 286.

security."[23] This obligation has, through the constitutionalization of the principle of solidarity in the Charter, acquired a universal customary value to the extent it did not have prior to 1945.[24]

B.   The Scope of Articles 49 and 50

The overall picture of the collective security system has for long been exclusively based upon the negative aspect of solidarity *i.e.* to protect the international community from threats to the peace, breaches of the peace and acts of aggression. It is only recently that more attention has been paid to the positive aspect of solidarity.

Economic coercive measures taken by the Council pursuant to Article 41 are factual expressions of the principle of solidarity: consequently Member States cannot apply them in a selective manner, and, in case of difficulties they cannot unilaterally opt out.[25]

As a substantive way of expressing solidarity the duty of Member States mutually to assist each other in *carrying out the measures* decided upon by the Security Council is the central concern of Article 49.[26] Although at first glance this Article seems to cover both the positive and negative aspects of solidarity, probably no more than a general duty not to obstruct the measures by the Council can be deduced from it, as its application to military enforcement actions is subject to the conclusion of the agreements pursuant to Article 43.[27]

As a result of an unsuccessful attempt to do otherwise at San Francisco, Article 49 does "not form a meaningful basis for regulating the bearing of costs of preventive and enforcement measures."[28] The conclusion that assistance under Article 49 might only in a general way "serve a more equitable distribution of the burden, depending on the use the SC makes of it"[29] applies also to Article 50 which deals with potential assistance *on the occasion* of carrying out measures of the Council. Both articles institutionalise, albeit to a limited extent, one of the modalities to enact the principle of solidarity *i.e.* burden sharing and equitable distribution of costs.

---

23   Karel Wellens, "The UN Security Council and New Threats to the Peace: Back to the Future", in *Journal of Conflict and Security Law*, 2003, pp. 15-69, at p. 54.

24   Michel Virally, *op. cit.*, at p. 547.

25   Epaminondas Marias, *op. cit.*, at p. 89, but in relation to EC Regulations.

26   Under the regime of state responsibility the former Special Rapporteur Riphagen "seems to have considered this the minimum degree of solidarity required amongst States in the face of an international crime, and that a greater degree of solidarity might be required in relation to particular crimes": D. Hutchinson, "Solidarity and Breaches of Multilateral Treaties", *British Yearbook of International Law*, 1988, pp. 151-215, at p. 209, note 249.

27   Bryde/Reinisch, Article 49 in B. Simma, (Ed.), *The Charter of the United Nations. A Commentary*, Second edition, Oxford University Press, 2002, Vol. I, 895 pp., at p. 782.

28   *Ibid.*, at p. 782.

29   *Ibid.*, at p. 783.

They also share a common objective: to maximize the potential of solidarity with regard to the maintenance of international peace and security by reducing as far as possible potential disincentives. States should be insulated from collateral damage both as "matter of equity and as a means of encouraging States to cooperate with the decisions of the Security Council."[30]

As a proposal to provide for a right to assistance was unsuccessful at San Francisco, it was only one of the weaker modalities of solidarity, *i.e.* the possibility to request consultations,that found its way into Article 50. It covers both difficulties arising from the requesting State's participation in the measures and difficulties resulting from application by other States.[31]Although Article 50 could not be construed to be "merely of a procedural nature"[32] a correct interpretation makes it clear that there is no duty on the part of the Council to provide a specific remedy. The collective solidarity to be channelled through the Council's procedures and troubled waters could in principle take the form of a (*de facto*) exemption from further participation in the measures, or of financial assistance.

C.   *The Practice under Article 50: The Need for Reform*

Although the Secretary-General has stressed that States "should have a realistic possibility of having their difficulties addressed,"[33] in practice the Council has limited itself to invite States and financial institutions to contribute a voluntary assistance to States that have invoked Article 50.

A thorough and detailed study of that practice until the spring of 2000 has produced the following conclusions. There had certainly not been consistency in the practice, some problems have received a more effective response from the Council, no panacea had been devised to insulate neighbouring States[34] from the inevitable economic damage and in many cases the collateral damage is not simply the result of the implementation of the sanctions themselves.[35] The lessons of experience to be drawn from the practice so far concern improvement of both the consultation procedure and the adequacy of the assistance.

---

30   An Agenda for Peace, UN Document A/47/277, para. 41.

31   Bryde/Reinisch, Article 50 in Bruno Simma, (Ed.), *op. cit.* note 27 at pp. 784-785.

32   Report of the Special Committee on the Charter of the United Nations and on the Strengthening of the Organization, UN Document A/56/33, p. 5, para. 41.

33   An Agenda for Peace, UN Document A/47/277, para. 41.

34   They "usually bore a disproportionate burden while carrying out their duties on behalf of the international community": Report of the Special Committee on the Charter of the United Nations and on the Strengthening of the Organization, UN Document A/55/33, p. 5, para. 39.

35   Jeremy Carver and Jenine Hulsmann, "The Role of Article 50 of the UN Charter in the Search for International Peace and Security", *International and Comparative Law Quarterly*, 2000, pp.528-577, at pp. 529-530.

With regard to the consultation procedure a uniform and internationally recognised methodology for identifying and quantifying the direct impact of sanctions seems essential.[36]

An impact assessment should take place not only prior to the imposition of
the sanctions but throughout their entire lifetime.[37]

Furthermore there should be a mechanism for independent verification of
losses and implementation of sanctions.[38]

As to the adequacy of assistance, it has proven difficult "to identify the assistance specifically intended to address the problems caused by sanctions."[39] On the
institutional side there is "no realistic prospect of a trust fund being established
on assessed contributions,"[40] and there has "been little appetite on the part of the
international financial institutions to develop" a special procedure either.[41]

The UN "has yet to develop an effectively functioning institutional response to
assist third States affected by sanctions".[42] Proposals here do include "a permanent
mechanism that could be activated automatically to address the issue of assistance
to third States affected by sanctions."[43]

In a series of successive resolutions the General Assembly has invited the Security Council to consider the establishment of further[44] mechanisms and procedures for consultations under Article 50 and also to ensure the inclusion of likely
and unintended impact on third States in its pre-assessment and ongoing assessment reports[45] and to continue developing an assessment methodology.

---

36   In the summer of 1997 an Ad Hoc Expert Group considered such a methodology. Eco-
      nomic costs were identified "resulting from (a) embargoes on trade with the target
      country, (b) restrictions on financial transactions, including foreign aid, and the freez-
      ing of financial assets, and (c) other costs associated with special links with the target
      country": Jeremy Carver and Jenine Hulsmann, *op. cit.*, p. 571.

37   *Ibid.*, p. 576.

38   *Ibid.*, pp. 572-573: the Ad hoc Expert Group had recommended that a Special Repre-
      sentative of the Secretary-General would deal only with the assessment of the losses.

39   *Ibid.*, p. 573.

40   *Ibid.*, p. 574.

41   *Ibid.*, p. 575.

42   Bryde/Reinisch, *op. cit.*, at p. 788.

43   Report of the Special Committee on the Charter of the United Nations and on the
      Strengthening of the Organization, UN Document A/56/33, p. 3, para. 20.

44   In January 1999 the Security Council reached agreement on a number of special meas-
      ures: Sanctions Committees should establish appropriate arrangements to improve the
      monitoring of the economic consequences on neighbouring States and other States. This
      may include visits to the regions concerned by the Chairpersons of the Committees: UN
      Document S/ 199/92 of 29 January 1999. Note by the President of the Security Council.

45   General Assembly Resolutions 54/107 adopted on 9 December 1999; 55/157 adopted on
      12 December 2000; 56/87 adopted on 12 December 2001; 57/25 adopted on 19 Novem-
      ber 2002 and 58/80 adopted on 9 December 2003. This is in line with recommenda-
      tions made by the Secretary-General in the 1995 Supplement to an Agenda for Peace

It is not merely because of the complexity of the problem but because of the lack of effort on the part of the Security Council that the radical changes needed have not been made.[46]

Whether in case the Council would recognise a right to financial assistance to a State as a result of the consultations under Article 50 such assistance would be considered by the membership as expenses of the organization remains to be seen.

5.   International Humanitarian Law

It has to be noted that the "only situation in respect of which there is a coherent international legislation on humanitarian assistance are armed conflicts,"[47] although the degree to which the principle of solidarity has given rise to hard law obligations is more limited in the 1977 Protocols than in the case of the 1949 Geneva Conventions.

Solidarity clearly belongs to those "principles of the law of nations as they result from the usage established among civilised peoples, from the law of humanity and the dictates of the public conscience" and by virtue of which the parties to a conflict shall remain bound to the ensuing obligations even in case they denounce one of the conventions.[48]

Parties to an international armed conflict have clear obligations concerning humanitarian assistance to the populations in occupied territories.[49]

From the wording of the relevant provisions Schindler rightly deduced that there is furthermore the "duty of parties to an armed conflict to accept international relief which may be offered to them by States or by impartial humanitarian organizations." [50] Although the provision of humanitarian assistance to civilian victims is subject to the consent of the State concerned, the extent of the principle of

---

that a mechanism should be established to fulfil a series of Article 50-related functions: the assessment prior to the imposition of sanctions of the potential impact on target and third countries, to measure their effects in order to minimize collateral damage, to explore ways of assisting Member States suffering such damage and to evaluate claims submitted pursuant to Article 50: Bryde/Reinisch, *op. cit.*, at p. 787.

In the same resolutions the General Assembly requested the Special Committee on the Charter of the UN and on the Strengthening of the Role of the Organization to continue on a priority basis the question of the implementation of the provisions of the Charter related to assistance to third States affected by the application of sanctions.

46   Report of the Sixth Committee, A/C.6/56/SR.6, p. 13, para. 35: delegate from Belarus.

47   Budislav Vukas, "Provisional Report on Humanitarian Assistance", *Annuaire de l'Institut de Droit International*, Vol. 70, Part I, p. 466.

48   Military and Paramilitary Activities in and against Nicaragua (Nicaragua *v.* United States of America), Merits, Judgment, *ICJ Reports 1986*, p. 14, at pp. 113-114, para. 218 referring to various articles of the Four Geneva Conventions.

49   Articles 55, 56 and 60 of the Fourth Geneva Convention and Article 69 of the First 1977 Protocol.

50   Dietrich Schindler, "Humanitarian Assistance, Humanitarian Interference and International Law", in R.St.J. Macdonald, (Ed.), *Essays in Honour of Wang Tieya*, Martinus Nijhoff Publishers, Dordrecht, Boston, London, 1994, 964 pp., pp. 689-701, at p. 696.

solidarity manifests itself even with regard to this exercise of territorial sovereignty: "States may not arbitrarily refuse their consent", as the relevant provisions "have in practice been understood as implying an obligation to accept outside assistance."[51]

If a "party to a non-international armed conflict refuses to admit outside relief in favour of a starving population" the prohibition of starvation of civilians is violated.[52]

The principle of solidarity thus prevents an abuse of right by a party consisting in a refusal to accept an offer of humanitarian assistance.

Finally there is a duty of all States to facilitate humanitarian assistance.[53]

According to David, the above rules may *a fortiori* be invoked to justify the right of these states to provide humanitarian assistance to victims of armed conflict.[54]

6. International Disaster Law

The principle of solidarity sometimes puts aside normally governing rules and it can thus interfere with consistency and predictability in international relations. A prime area for this to happen is that of peacetime provision of humanitarian assistance in case of natural or man-made disasters.

The prime responsibility to provide humanitarian assistance in case of natural disasters lies clearly with the territorial State,[55] but the scale and duration of many emergency situations in peacetime risk to be beyond the capacity of many victim States.[56] A State may find itself incapable of carrying out its normal responsibilities under international law such as to protect the population of its territory from the consequences of man-made or natural disasters. This is fertile ground for the principle of solidarity to become operational, even if this takes place in a subsidiary way.[57]

Third States may limit themselves to conveying their sympathy with the victims of an earthquake[58] or a terrorist attack; outside the context of an armed conflict, they may provide humanitarian assistance because of a sense of moral duty;

---

51 *Ibid.* On the scope of this duty to accept depending on the situation of the potential beneficiaries and the kind of assistance offered see Eric David, *Principes de Droit des Conflits Armés*, Bruylant, Bruxelles, 1994, 792 pp., p. 393, para. 2.256.

52 Dietrich Schindler, *op. cit.*, at p. 696.

53 *Ibid.*, at p. 697.

54 Eric David, *op. cit.*, at p. 403, para. 2.270.

55 UN General Assembly Resolutions 43/131 adopted on 8 December 1988 and 45/100 adopted on 14 December 1990, Resolution 46/182, Annex, point 4, adopted on 19 December 1991, and Resolutions 56/103 adopted on 14 December 2001 and 57/152 adopted on 16 December 2002.

56 Resolution 46/182, I, 5.

57 Carrillo Salcedo, "Preliminary Report on Humanitarian Assistance", *Annuaire de l'Institut de Droit International*, Vol. 70, Part I, p. 405.

58 See for instance GA Resolution 56/99 on emergency response to disasters, adopted on 14 December 2001, para. 1.

they may do so because of a legal duty in case of an armed conflict; or they even may, in case solidarity within the international community is not forthcoming, on a unilateral basis but as trustees of that same community, carry out a humanitarian intervention to prevent or stop a man-made disaster such as genocide.

The elaboration of the principle of solidarity in the area of disaster law has given rise to three separate but of course connected rights: the right to be assisted, the right to offer humanitarian assistance and the right of access to the victims.[59]

A.   *The Right to Receive and Provide Humanitarian Assistance*

The existence of a right to receive humanitarian assistance the articulation of which was recommended in 1988 by the Independent Commission on International Humanitarian Issues[60] appears now to be widely accepted.[61] This recognition does "not depend upon the identification of the international subject(s) responsible for its realization."[62]

The (Draft) Resolution of the Institute of International Law recognises that humanitarian assistance provided in accordance with the principles of neutrality, humanity and impartiality[63] does not represent an act of interference in internal affairs of States and, according to the ruling of the International Court of Justice, it is a concept in accordance with international law.[64] All States have the right to offer humanitarian assistance.[65] The (Draft) Resolution further confirms that the right to humanitarian assistance implies the right to request and to receive such assistance.[66]

B.   *The Duty to Admit Humanitarian Assistance*

The consent of the territorial State as a precondition for the delivery of humanitarian assistance was reconfirmed by the General Assembly in the relevant resolutions mentioned earlier and in the Institute's (Draft) resolution.[67]

---

59   Carrillo Salcedo, *op. cit.*, at p. 404. The guiding principles on the provision of emergency humanitarian assistance, formulated by the UN General Assembly in 1991 and which were originally limited to the UN system have recently been given a much wider scope of application by the General Assembly: compare Resolution 46/182 with para. s 5 of Resolutions 56/103 and 57/152.

60   Badislav Vukas, *op. cit.*, at pp. 553-554.

61   *Ibid.*, at pp. 554-555.

62   *Ibid.*, at p. 555.

63   The importance of these principles has also been stressed by the UN General Assembly in its Resolutions 56/103 and 57/152.

64   *Annuaire de l'Institut de Droit International*, Vol. 70, Part I, p. 571, Preamble.

65   *Ibid.*, at p. 574, V.1.

66   *Ibid.*, at p. 573, II.1.

67   *Ibid.*, at p. 574, V.2.

These and other principles aimed to be applied by the United Nations system in providing humanitarian assistance to victims of natural disasters and other emergencies "have proven to be at the basis of all the activities of humanitarian assistance."[68]

In contrast to the provisions of international humanitarian law, the General Assembly resolutions on humanitarian assistance are "less explicit with respect to the duty of States to accept external assistance."[69]

According to the Institute's (Draft) resolution the affected State may be obliged to seek and to accept aid from competent international organizations and/or from third States.[70]

The affected State even has the duty to admit humanitarian assistance.[71] Refusal of such an offer may lead to States taking all necessary measures to ensure access to the victims, in conformity with international humanitarian law and human rights and to inform the Security Council.[72] As far as the latter's intervention is concerned, the proposal to consider the refusal to allow humanitarian assistance as a threat to international peace and security in order to open the way for an institutionalised action by the international community[73] is reflected in the (Draft) resolution.[74]

C.   A Duty to Provide Humanitarian Assistance?

The proposed rules attached to Salcedo's Preliminary Report on humanitarian assistance to the Institute made it clear that the obligation of States which have been affected by a natural or man-made disaster to provide assistance to the victims was considered to be an obligation *erga omnes* which implied, in conformity with Articles 1, paragraph 3, 55 and 56 of the UN Charter a duty of solidarity among all States.[75]

In the replies to the Preliminary Report it was pointed out on the one hand that Article 1, paragraph 3 of the UN Charter does not provide a duty for the UN to give humanitarian assistance.[76] On the other hand, the view was expressed that "a general duty to help should be one of the basic principles of our approach to humanitarian assistance in the world of today."[77]

---

68   Badislav Vukas, *op. cit.*, at p. 544.

69   Dietrich Schindler, *op. cit.*, at p. 697.

70   *Annuaire de l'Institut de Droit International*, Vol. 70, Part I, p. 574, III.3.

71   *Ibid.*, at p. 575, VII.1.

72   *Ibid.*, at p. 576, VII.2.

73   Henry Schermers, *Annuaire de l'Institut de Droit International*, Vol. 70, Part I, p. 448.

74   *Ibid.*, at p. 576, VII.3.

75   Carrillo Salcedo, *op. cit.*, at p. 435, rule 5.

76   Dietrich Schindler, *Annuaire de l'Institut de Droit International*, Vol. 70, Part I, p. 414.

77   Badislav Vukas, *Annuaire de l'Institut de Droit International*, Vol. 70, Part I, p. 417.

Salcedo admitted that de *lege ferenda* the ideal should be the existence of a right *erga omnes* of victims to be assisted and a corresponding universal obligation to provide assistance;[78] such an obligation would not go too far on the road of progressive development.[79] Of course the Rapporteur was right in pointing out that at present the right to be assisted is only opposable to the territorial State and that an institutionalised action was only possible if the Security Council has determined the situation to constitute a threat to international peace and security.[80]

In his provisional Report submitted in June 2002 the new Rapporteur Vukas tentatively suggested that, based on provisions in penal codes of many States, there might be, in the sense of Article 38, paragraph 1, c of the Statute of the ICJ, a general principle of law to provide humanitarian assistance.[81]

Subsequently the Rapporteur proposed that the Institute could take the first steps towards a direction suggesting such a duty in cases where large groups of human beings are confronted with starvation, torture, humiliation, illness, and death. The obligation would rest upon all the neighbouring States and all other States that are in a position to provide assistance.[82]

According to the (Draft) resolution all States should provide humanitarian assistance whenever they are in a position to do so.[83]

D.   Duty of States to Facilitate the Provision of Humanitarian Assistance by Third States

Humanitarian assistance is aimed at protecting fundamental human rights such as the right to life which is an *erga omnes* right, to be respected by all States.[84] It is thus not surprising to find convergence, at this juncture, between the operational implications of the principle of solidarity in the law of armed conflict and in disaster law: relevant General Assembly resolutions fix duties for States to facilitate humanitarian assistance which correspond to the Geneva provisions.[85]

---

78   Carrillo Salcedo, *op. cit.*, at pp. 431-432.

79   *Ibid.*, at p. 443.

80   *Ibid.*, at p. 432.

81   Badislav Vukas, *op. cit.*, at p. 467. Schindler referred to provisions of international criminal law as an additional legal basis of such a duty: *Annuaire de l'Institut de Droit International*, Vol. 70, Part I, p. 494.

82   Badislav Vukas, *op. cit.*, at p. 475. When the situation as a consequence of the implementation of coercive measures imposed by the Security Council renders the State incapable to provide the basic needs to its population, then the request for assistance under Article 50 of the Charter changes into a right to receive humanitarian assistance and the duty arises for other States to facilitate the provision of such assistance.

83   *Annuaire de l'Institut de Droit International*, Vol. 70, Part I, p. 575, V.4.

84   Badislav Vukas, *op. cit.*, at p. 555.

85   Dietrich Schindler, *op. cit.*, at p. 697.

Modalities of implementing the duty of solidarity would include granting rights of transit for States delivering humanitarian assistance[86] or giving victims from a neighbouring State access to one's territory.[87]

Recent practice of humanitarian assistance has demonstrated that solidarity has not only become an essential component of the foreign policy of States[88] as a value or a concept invoked and operationalised on *ad hoc* basis, but also how it has evolved into a principle that has penetrated into the realm of disaster law. The degree of penetration has succinctly but correctly been described by Vukas: "Rules on humanitarian assistance in various situations of emergency in peacetime are mostly *in statu nascendi*."[89] The Resolution adopted by the Institute thus reflects both the potential and the limitations of implementation of the principle of solidarity in this area.

Finally one should never forget that because of the intrinsic humanitarian aspect of the principle of solidarity donors should "consider the importance of ensuring that assistance in the case of higher-profile disasters does not come at the expense of those that may have a relatively lower profile,"[90] and that problems of distributive justice remain after the relief of an emergency.[91]

7.   International Refugee Law

One of the predictable consequences of both man-made and natural disasters is the occurrence of massive flows of refugees.

The recurring tragedies in Central Africa have brought into sharp focus "the paramount moral duties of the international community in terms of international solidarity and burden-sharing."[92]

International solidarity is a basic principle of international refugee law.[93] Its articulation makes clear that a refugee is a person of concern to the international community, that there is an obligation to extend refugee status or at least to accord protection to those compelled to flee persecution or communal violence and that States have an obligation to share the responsibility to find durable solutions.[94]

---

86   Oscar Schachter, *Annuaire de l'Institut de Droit International*, Vol. 70, Part I, at p. 523.

87   Badislav Vukas, *op. cit.*, at p. 462.

88   Carillo Salcedo, *op. cit.*, at p. 402.

89   Badislav Vukas, *op. cit.*, at p. 489.

90   UN General Assembly Resolution 57/152, para. 21.

91   B.A. Wortley, "Reflections by an International Lawyer on Distributive Justice", *Tulane Law Review*, 1974-1975, pp. 358-365, at p. 359.

92   Guy Martin, "International Solidarity and Co-operation in Assistance to African refugees: Burden-Sharing or Burden-Shifting?" , in *International Journal of Refugee Law*, 1995, pp. 250-273, at p. 251.

93   *Ibid.*, at p. 253.

94   *Ibid.*

The various actors may well recognise that solidarity is legally justified, and a consensus may have emerged that it is the responsibility particularly of the most developed countries to alleviate the burden of the neighbouring states facing mass influx.[95] The OAU *Convention* even "creates joint responsibility of the OAU member States in relation to the refugee problem in that, in the name of 'African solidarity', those States endeavour to ease the burden of some of their members who have difficulty in coping with the refugees crossing their borders." [96]

Harsh reality proves that it is the actual implementation of the solidarity that encounters difficulties.[97]

8.   International Environmental Law

As globalization is also partly a subjective phenomenon, there is a growing realization that "challenges like the threat to the human environment have to be met in the common interest of mankind."[98] The protection of the planetary environment thus became another area of international law where community interests have been incorporated.[99]

The solemn declarations of relevant principles and the subsequent first generation of environmental agreements were characterized by the negative aspect of the principle of solidarity, *i.e.* not to cause damage to the environment of other States or to areas outside national jurisdictions.

Later on the focus shifted towards the positive aspect of solidarity once it became clear that non-compliance with environmental agreements was quite often caused by the lack of technical and financial resources on the part of developing countries. The next class of agreements were "based on the commitment to mutual assistance in the implementation of the treaty."[100]

It is at this juncture that the concept of sustainable development "which attempts to integrate environmental considerations into economic and other development and which takes into account other than environmental needs while formulating the principle of environmental protection"[101] becomes relevant.

The concept[102] embodies two core elements which are both related to equity and are powerful tools towards further development and clarification of the principle of solidarity: common but differentiated responsibilities and intergenerational equity.

---

95   *Ibid.*, at p. 254.

96   *Ibid.*, at p. 259.

97   *Ibid.*, at p. 254.

98   Jost Delbrück, *op. cit.* note 18, at p. 16.

99   Bruno Simma, *op. cit.*, at p. 243.

100   Jost Delbrück, *op. cit.* note 4, at p. 426.

101   Malgosia Fitmaurice, *op. cit.*, at p. 47.

102   Fitzmaurice rightly pointed out that the ICJ in the Gabcikovo judgment merely considered it to be a concept: *op. cit.*, at p. 57.

The Rio Declaration and the UN Framework Convention on Climate Change confirm "a specific facet of the principle of solidarity in as far they distinguish between the responsibility of developed and developing countries."[103] Different environmental standards constitute at present "the heart of many environmental conventions"[104] and they are accompanied by an obligation for developed States to render financial assistance and to transfer technology for the benefit of less developed economies[105] in order to achieve the environmental goals.

Common but differentiated responsibilities in international environmental law may thus be seen to "define an explicit equitable balance between developed and developing countries in at least two senses: it sets lesser standards for developing states and it makes the performance of those standards dependent on the provision of solidarity assistance by developed states."[106]

Intergenerational equity, which is based upon the concept of the wealth of the earth held in trust[107] gives expression to the principle of solidarity between present and future generations.[108]

As intergenerational equity has woven itself "into international law through major treaties, through juristic opinion and through general principles of law recognized by civilised nations,"[109] it may have reached the stage where it may reflect universal values[110] although it may still be legally too elusive "to be justiciable."[111]

9.   International Development Law

In the context of present international relations the discussion of international economic inequality between North and South is not only unavoidable but it undoubtedly is a major issue to be resolved in order to maintain international peace

---

103   Bruno Simma, *op. cit.*, at p. 240.

104   Malgosia Fitzmaurice, *op. cit.*, at p. 66.

105   Malgosia Fitzmaurice, *op. cit.*, at p. 61 referring to the Ozone Layer Convention, the Climate Change Convention and the Kyoto Protocol. She is right in pointing out that the aspect of sharing benefits and burdens may also be derived from certain features of the concept of common heritage of mankind; *op. cit.*, at p. 159.

106   P. S. Rao, "Multiple International Judicial Forums: A Reflection of the Growing Strength of International Law or its Fragmentation?", original paper for the 25th anniversary Symposium of the *Michigan Journal of International Law*, March 2004: Diversity or Cacophony? New Sources of Norms in International Law, note 7: referring to P. Bernie and A. Boyle, *International Law and the Environment*, 2002, pp. 100-101.

107   Malgosia Fitzmaurice, *op. cit.*, at p. 187.

108   The concept of sustainable development as it was originally presented in the Brundlandt Report was limited to this aspect; M. Fitzmaurice, *op. cit.*, at p. 48.

109   Judge Weeramantry as cited by Malgosia Fitzmaurice, *op. cit.*, at p. 200.

110   Gilbert. Guillaume, "*Les thèmes favoris de la Communauté internationale ont-ils en droit une valeur universelle?*" in G. Guillaume, *La Cour Internationale de Justice à l'aube du XXIè Siècle*, Paris, Editions Paris, 2003, 331 pp., pp. 189-197, at p. 197.

111   Malgosia Fitzmaurce, *op. cit.*, at p. 199.

and security as "a world split into extremely poor and extremely rich States simply cannot remain a peaceful place."[112] The degree of consensus on a general political level that greater equity in north-south economic relations is called for, may thus be not that surprising.[113]

Principles of justice are ethical principles that normally adjudicate conflicting claims on scare goods and are aimed at securing a balance of reciprocal advantage.[114] The history of international development law is replete with controversy as to how this objective had to be brought closer. International development law may be said to have drawn upon and wavering between sometimes conflicting elements of both the social good theory and the natural right theory in political and legal philosophy.[115]

A.   Development Law in the 1970s and 1980s

Development law has been marked by tidal waves, especially in the mid-1970s of unbridled invocation of corrective justice "concerned with restitution and the award of compensation within an existing framework."[116] In this particular sense the "goal of anti-colonialist scholarship (was) a solidary reconstruction of the international community."[117]

A "one-sided concept of solidarity" giving rise to a "unilateral obligation" to compensate "for the wrongs of the colonial period" was still underlying the Charter of Economic Rights and Duties of States.[118] The common resolve in the mid-1970s to establish a New International Economic Order presupposed "the recognition of the principle of solidarity,"[119] but when it joined the traditional liberal principles of freedom and legal equality the purpose was to prevent them "from harming the particular interests of the less developed members of the international com-

---

112   Bruno Simma, *op. cit.*, at p. 237.

113   Richard Falk, "The domains of law and justice" *International Journal* (Toronto), 1975-1976, pp. 1-13, p. 1, note 2: in the mid-1970s he considered the consensus to be surprising.

114   David Richards, "International distributive justice", in *Nomos*, 1982, pp. 275-299, at p. 276.

115   Douglas Johnston, "The Foundations of Justice in International Law", in *The International Law and Policy of Human Welfare, op. cit.* note 5, pp. 111-146, at p. 113: the social good theory: "justice is doing what is useful for the common good" and the natural right theory: "justice is rendering to each what is his due by right."

116   B.A. Wortley, *op. cit.*, referring to Aristotle, at p. 358.

117   Anne Peters, *op. cit.*, at p. 34.

118   Bruno Simma, *op. cit.*, at p. 237. When proposing the elaboration of the Charter President Echeverria of Mexico called to "separate the economic co-operation from the framework of goodwill and crystallize it into the realm of law."

119   Wil Verwey, *The principle of solidarity as a legal cornerstone of a new international economic order*, Thesaurus Acroasium, Vol. XII, Thessaloniki, 1982, pp. 487-518, at p. 489.

munity."[120] It was thus predominantly limited to both the negative and corrective aspects of solidarity.

In the mid-1980s divergent views were still being held. Some argued that "the principle of reciprocity has to be replaced, at least for a longer period, by the principle of preferential treatment,"[121] while others strongly defended the view that the principle of duality of norms has to be superseded by the right to development as that principle left untouched "the fundamental structure of international economic problems, especially relating to international trade, and the liberal principles which underlie that structure."[122]

B.   Recent Trends

In any case, the notion of corrective justice "presumes a more ultimate conception of distributive justice."[123]

Although Weithman is right in claiming that "few of the great philosophers of the natural law tradition gave sustained attention to questions of international distributive justice"[124] there seems to be no more room for today's international relations to further enjoy "blanket exemption" from "requirements of distributive justice."[125] In the view of some there is nothing more than just a "dawning recognition" of distributive justice,[126] while others are convinced that it has become "a novel principle in the international context."[127]

In more recent practice it is to this aspect of justice that international development law has turned. The shift already cautiously present in the 1980s towards a more balanced view of solidarity culminated in the adoption in 1990 by the UN General Assembly of the Declaration of International Economic Co-operation,[128] in which all States acknowledged that they "all have a responsibility to the general global welfare."[129]

---

120   *Ibid.*

121   Wil Verwey, "Preferential treatment of developing countries", in K. Wellens (Ed.), *Peace and Security: Justice and Development, Report of a Congress held on the occasion of 40 years United Nations*, T.M.C. Asser Institute, The Hague, 1986, 99 pp., pp. 29-32, at p. 32.

122   Mohammed Bedjaoui, "Some unorthodox reflections on the 'right to development'", in F. Snyder and P. Slinn, (Eds.), *International Law of Development: Comparative Perspectives*, Professional Books, Abingdon, 1987, 322 pp., pp. 87-116, at p. 101.

123   Andrew Walter, "Distributive Justice and the Theory of International Relations", *Australian Outlook*, 1983, pp. 98-103, at p. 99.

124   Paul Weithmann, *op. cit.*, at p. 182.

125   David Richards, *op. cit.*, at p. 292.

126   *Ibid.*, at p. 294.

127   David Armstrong, "Law, justice and the idea of a world society", in *International Affairs*, 1999, pp. 547-561, at p. 549.

128   Bruno Simma, *op. cit.*, at p. 238.

129   R.St.J. Macdonald, "The Principle of Solidarity in Public International Law", in Christian Dominice (Ed.), *Etudes de Droit International en l'honneur de Pierre Lalive*, Fac-

It has to be said however that after the turn of the century the attitude of the UN General Assembly appears to have become ambivalent in some respects. The General Assembly recalls its 1975 determination to work for the establishment of a new international economic order, with all the controversial connotations such a reference might incite, and includes the right to an international economic order based *inter alia* upon solidarity in the list of realizations a democratic and equitable order would require.[130]

On the other hand when the need was stressed to establish a new system of international economic relations, based on the principles of the UN Charter, and that would promote economic development, coordinate economic cooperation, ensure justice and promote equitable access to goods and distribution of wealth for all States in a globalized world, the General Assembly merely noted that this question could be considered in the future. [131]

If the view is correct that international development law has come to a standstill[132] and that the greater part of it has "remained in form of soft law, if not of *lex ferenda*,"[133] then formal elaboration of the principle of solidarity into norms and rules is required "to specify a fair distribution of the benefits and burdens which global interdependence entails"[134] as obviously the limits of the traditional law of co-operation have been reached in this area.[135]

The calling into action of a correctly interpreted principle of solidarity – and thus not merely entailing one-sided obligations[136] – is part of a systematic approach to global poverty that has to recognize that the claim to economic fairness cannot possibly be satisfied "solely or even primarily by redistributive means."[137] The vali-

---

ulté de Droit de l'Université de Genève and the IU HEI, Genève, Helbing and Lichtenhahn, Basel, 1993, 790 pp., pp. 275-307, at p. 295.

130   Resolution 57/213, paras. 9 and 4 (e). When in 2000 the General Assembly resumed consideration of the legal aspects of international economic relations the item was entitled "Progressive development of the principles and norms of international law relating to the new international economic order", while the item which, with some intervals, had been on its agenda since 1975 was entitled "Consolidation and progressive evolution of the norms and principles of international economic development law."

131   GA decision 58/522, adopted on 9 December 2003: A/58/PV.72, p. 6.

132   Nico Schrijver, *"De verankering en betekenis van duurzame ontwikkeling in het internationale recht"*, in *Mededelingen van de Nederlandse Vereniging voor Internationaal Recht*, 2003, pp. 1-92, at p. 8.

133   Georges Abi-Saab, "Whither the International Community?", in *European Journal of International Law*, 1998, pp. 248-265, at p. 263.

134   Beits cited by Andrew Walter, *op. cit.*, at p. 100.

135   Ulrich Scheuner, *op. cit.*, at pp. 254-255.

136   As the 1974 declaration on the NIEO and the CERDS, but also the 1986 ILA Seoul Declaration on the right to development appear to do: R.St.J. Macdonald, "Solidarity in the practice and discourse of public international law", *Pace International Law Review*, 1996, 259-302, at pp. 265-266.

137   Thomas Franck, *op. cit.*, at p. 415.

dation and implementation of this interpretation of the principle of solidarity then could become the true instrument and powerful tool for the reactivation of the international debate on the unequal distribution on wealth on the globe, a situation called "global apartheid" by the President of South Africa.

10. International Trade Law

"Underdevelopment is a structural phenomenon linked to a given model of international economic relations, and to a certain international division of labour."[138]

So if "the general international legal system has little redistributive capacity,"[139] because there is "... no general obligation to offer economic assistance in international law,"[140] and the "trade system must not be seen to stand in the way of poverty reduction,"[141] then perhaps international trade law could show the way and offer solutions based upon the principle of solidarity, because of the "shared responsibility of the nations of the world for managing worldwide economic and social development."[142]

A.   The Potential Role of Primary Rules

The most-favoured nation treatment embodied in Article I-1 of the GATT is a "cornerstone of the GATT" and "one of the pillars of the WTO trading system."[143]

Solidarity is thus not the foundation of the most-favoured nation treatment in GATT: trade liberalization is.

The view, put forward in the 1970s and 1980s, that developed countries have actually an obligation to grant tariff preferences is now very much a minority position. Most developing countries accept the voluntary nature of the system,[144] a position that recently has been confirmed by the Panel's decision in the EEC GSP case.[145] The Panel found that the Enabling Clause does not provide "positive rules establishing obligations in themselves" while the Appellate Body understood the

---

138   Mohammed Bedjaoui, *op. cit.*, at p. 91.

139   Joel Trachtman, "Legal Aspects of a Poverty Agenda at the WTO: Trade Law and 'Global apartheid'", *Journal of International Economic Law*, 2003, pp. 3-21, at p. 4.

140   Kemper as referred to by R.St.J. Macdonald, *op. cit.* note 129, at p. 279.

141   Joel Trachtman, *op. cit.*, at p. 21.

142   General Assembly Resolution 56/151, para. 3 (n).

143   European Communities – conditions for the granting of tariff preferences to developing countries, Report of the Appellate body, WT/DS246/AB/R, Report of 7 April 2004, para. 101.

144   Lorand Bartels, "The WTO Enabling Clause and positive conditionality in the European Community's GSP Program", *Journal of International Economic Law*, 2003, pp. 507-532, at p. 513.

145   European Communities – conditions for the granting of tariff preferences to developing countries, Report of the Panel, WT/DS246/R, Report of 1 December 2003, para.7.38.

enabling Clause as one of the positive efforts called for in the Preamble to the WTO Agreement "to be taken by developed-country Members."[146]

Although the idea of "*inégalité compensatrice*", is clearly reflected in the General System of Preferences set up "to effect greater distributive justice in the international trading system"[147] the promotion of free world trade is also served by a set of principles that have been included in the system.[148]

It is then no surprise that from the perspective of the effectiveness of the principle of solidarity, the GSP in terms of preferential market access, is assessed to have produced "modest benefits."[149] And even "the most ambitious scheme to support developing countries' trade" the EEC's STABEX which was also based upon "*inégalité compensatrice*", "has not lived up to expectations with its developing country members' share of EU trade actually declining since the scheme was established."[150]

Since the modified Part IV of the GATT based upon non-reciprocity was unable to "enact the principles of solidarity" there was a need to rethink the concept of solidarity as "preference."[151]

There is a clear and distinct need for radical non-reciprocity in this branch of international law[152] and the question has rightly been raised "why the NIEO of the 1970s was less fair than the present economic system, given the NIEO's emphasis on redistributive outcomes."[153]

According to the WTO Agreement there is a "need for positive efforts designed to ensure developing countries, and especially the least developed among them, secure a share in the growth in international trade commensurate with the needs of their economic development" as one of its objectives is that the expansion of trade must be accompanied by the "optimal use of the world's resources in accordance with the objective of sustainable development."[154]

The WTO established a "unified legal framework" for the world economic order which "reflects not only the individual rights and interests of the WTO members, but also their common collective interest in promoting the general welfare."[155]

The 1994 Marrakech Agreement however does not affect MacDonald's 1978 assessment, admittedly limited to UN membership, that there is no sign that Mem-

---

146   Appellate Body Report, para.s 10 and 92.

147   Thomas Franck, *op. cit.*, at p. 58.

148   *Ibid.*

149   Joel Trachtman, *op. cit.*, at p. 11.

150   David Armstrong, *op. cit.*, at p. 557.

151   R.St.J. Macdonald, *op. cit.* note 136, at p. 270.

152   David Richards, *op. cit.*, at p. 276.

153   Gerry Simpson, "Is International Law Fair?", in *Michigan Journal of International Law*, 1996, pp. 615-642, at p. 639.

154   Nico Schrijver, *op. cit.*, at p. 33.

155   Jost Delbrück, *op. cit.* note 18, at p. 18.

ber States "have accepted a legal obligation to participate in international welfare programmes."[156]

Although the issue of poverty "should, and will, transform the international economic system, and with it, the field of international economic law," the special and differential treatment within the Doha Development Agenda has limited utility "at least as applied so far,"[157] although some of its aspects are without doubt beneficial.

If the primary rules of international trade are deficient in terms of successfully implementing the principle of solidarity, could one then perhaps turn to the functioning of secondary rules to provide part of the solution?

B.   *The Role of Secondary Rules*

As one of the policy goals underpinning international judicial institutions is to help redress asymmetries of power, it is important to note that the WTO dispute settlement system is not only to "build jurisprudential predictability" but also "to level the playing field for parties of different wealth and power structure."[158]

A particular light on the issues before us was shed on 7 April 2004 when the WTO Appellate Body issued its Report in European Communities – Conditions for the granting of tariff preferences to developing countries.[159]

Preferences additional to the general arrangements were provided for by the EC for the protection of labour rights and the environment but they were restricted to developing countries the EC determined were complying with certain standard in those areas.

According to the EC, the words "generalized, non-reciprocal and non-discriminatory" in footnote 3 of the Enabling Clause "are" distinct from and intended to replace the most-favoured-nation ("MFN ") obligation in Article I-1.[160] Part IV of the GATT 1994 and the enabling Clause constitute a special regime for developing countries "to address inequalities among the WTO membership."[161]

---

156   R.St.J. Macdonald, *op. cit.*, note 5, at p. 60.

157   Joel Trachtman, *op. cit.*, at p. 10.

158   John Jackson, "Policy Underpinnings of International Juridical Institutions", original paper for the 25th anniversary Symposium of the *Michigan Journal of International Law*, March 2004: Diversity or Cacophony? New Sources of Norms in International Law, p. 2. That smaller or less developed countries can bring a case against larger, wealthier countries and win was illustrated by Costa Rica against the US in a case about underwear, paper p. 4.

159   See *supra* note 143. For a brief overview of the history of the GSP system see most recently Lorand Bartels, *op. cit.*, at pp. 510-513. The article was written prior to the Appellate Body's Report, which also contains a brief history of the GSP system in paras. 107-108.

160   Appellate Body Report, para. 12.

161   *Ibid.*, para. 13.

Special and differential treatment, the EC continued, is "the most basic principle of the international law of development" and is *lex specialis* to the exclusion of more general WTO rules on the matter.[162]

The EC also maintained that the enabling Clause and Article I-1 exist "side-by-side and on an equal level."[163]

India's main argument was that the MFN principle is a "fundamental norm of the rules-based multilateral trading system of the WTO" and that developing countries did not waive their rights to MFN treatment between themselves in agreeing to the Enabling /Clause.[164]

The Appellate Body upheld the Panel's finding that the Enabling Clause does not exclude the applicability of the MFN principle.[165]

11. The Principle of Solidarity at Work with Regard to Both Primary and Secondary Rules

A. *The Case of Primary Rules*

In the previous sections we have examined how the principle of solidarity operates in its "substantive" mode, when it occupies itself with primary rules. Before we turn to its "procedural" component when secondary rules become the focus of its attention,[166] it has to be noted that the principle of solidarity provides the irreducible and fundamental foundation for and the channel through which the primary norms of *ius cogens* and obligations owed to the international community as a whole may be brought into existence. It is also interesting to note that the term "mutual benefit" is absent from the text of the Vienna Convention on the Law of Treaties despite its frequent use in a variety of instruments to express the basic purpose of treaty-making.[167] The same goes for the principle of solidarity.

One of the various legal modes to render the principle of solidarity operational is to use common but differentiated responsibilities. The term "common but differentiated responsibilities" is somewhat misleading as it may cover either or both of the following modalities.[168]

---

162   *Ibid.*, para. 14.

163   *Ibid.*, para. 85.

164   *Ibid.* para. 47.

165   *Ibid.*, para. 103.

166   Epaminondas Marias, *op. cit.*, at pp. 98 and 101.

167   Douglas Johnston, *op. cit.*, at p. 142, note 74

168   Alastair Iles, "Rethinking Differential Obligations: Equity Under the Biodiversity Convention", *Leiden Journal of International Law*, 2003, pp. 217-251, at pp. 225-226: differential obligations may indeed consist of quantified target goals for different categories, differing access to finance, technology, different timescales and special funding to assist developing countries in implementing the treaty obligations.

One option for States is to formulate, on a temporary basis[169] a different set of rules and norms to be complied with by previously identified particular categories of states because of their distinctive features in terms of wealth and/or capacity towards compliance.

The concept of asymmetric obligations may be a "powerful, but controversial means of changing the normative basis"[170] of the branch of international law concerned.

Differential obligations "could defuse equity-related complaints by developing countries and therefore ensure universal participation"[171] in treaties. They can "deal with the structural dimensions of development."[172]

Given the limited number of cases of application however, Dupuy is right in concluding that duality of norms cannot be held to constitute a general principle of contemporary international law, not even of international development law.[173]

The concept of differential obligations is not yet either "part of customary international law, nor it is likely to be for some time."[174]

Another possible mode to operate with the principle of solidarity is to maintain uniformity of applicable rules and norms but to introduce a differentiation on the level of responsibility in case of non-compliance by previously identified particular categories of States for the reasons mentioned above *e.g.* through "different time frames and standards of compliance under the rubric of the same obligation,"[175] taking into account the development level of States.[176]

Practice in the field of international environmental, development and trade law illustrates that also a combination of both approaches may be called for: differentiated norms and differentiated responsibility.

A further, pre-existing example of such a combination may be found in Article 19 of the UN Charter with regard to the collective financial responsibility. The principle of solidarity finds its expression both in the scale of the assessments for the apportionment of the expenses of the Organization and in the role attached to conditions beyond the control of the Member State in case of failure to pay its contributions.

---

169 "… as a state's relative weight should not be allowed to influence a permanently applicable legal finding." Fuentes, referring to the ICJ 's 1982 judgment in the Tunisia-Libya continental shelf case, and referred to by David Armstrong, *op. cit.*, at p. 555.

170 Alastair Iles, *op. cit.*, at p. 220.

171 *Ibid.*, at p. 222.

172 *Ibid.*, at p. 243.

173 Pierre-Marie Dupuy, *Droit International Public*, 5th edition, Dalloz, Paris, 2000, 731 pp., at p. 614, para. 608.

174 Alastair Iles, *op. cit.*, at p. 223. The concept has also been referred to by the WTO Appellate Body in the Shrimp-Turtle case: WT/DS58/AB/RW, of 22 October 2001.

175 P. S. Rao, *op. cit.*, at p. 3.

176 Pierre-Marie Dupuy, *op. cit.*, at p. 614, para. 608, referring to the major environmental agreements mentioned earlier.

Although the idea of common but differentiated responsibilities "could be misunderstood as a threat to the unity and development of universal international law" it "is an advance in the law."[177]

Several branches of international law in particular international development and environmental law have also "institutionalised dissimilar eligibilities" for States in order to obtain solidarity according to their status.[178]

Referring to the WTO preamble the Appellate Body in the EC GSP case stressed that developing countries may have different needs according to their levels of development and particular circumstances and that as a result the application of the Enabling Clause may vary accordingly,[179] but without however imposing "unjustifiable burdens on other Members."[180]

According to the Appellate Body the non-discriminatory nature of the GSP schemes does not require the granting of identical tariff preferences, but subjects the possibility of additional preferences to developing countries with special needs to the condition that they are "generalized" and "non-reciprocal."[181] The Appellate Body reversed the Panel's finding that identical preferences under GSP schemes should be provided to all developing countries without differentiation.[182]

From the perspective of the implementation of the principle of solidarity it is clear that once developed countries have opted for the granting of a generalized system of preferences under the Enabling Clause the Panel's interpretation would have secured maximal impact of the voluntary act of solidarity carried out by developed countries. In a more differentiated interpretation of the principle of solidarity the Appellate Body protected the interests of the least-developed countries of the third world.

B.   The Case of Secondary Rules

The solidarity underpinning the creation of primary conventional obligations in the first place, is in a natural way carried over into the situation of serious non-compliance by any of the parties.[183]

---

177   Sienho Yee, "Towards an international law of co-progressiveness", in Sienho Yee and Wang Tieya, (Eds.), *International Law in the Post-Cold-War World. Essays in Memory of Li Haopeii*, London, Routledgde, 2001, 529 pp., pp. 18-39, at p. 31.

178   Epaminondas Marias, *op. cit.*, at p. 105, but in relation to the EC.

179   Paragraphs 161-162.

180   Paragraph 167.

181   Paragraph 169.

182   Paragraph 190, (e).

183   For other traces of the principle of solidarity becoming operational in the law of treaties see, such as the States Parties explicitly ruling out the possibility of reservations being made see D. Hutchinson, *op. cit.*, at pp. 190-192. For a strong expression of mutual solidarity see also Common Article 1 of the 1949 Geneva Conventions: the obligation for States Parties not only to respect but also to ensure respect for international humanitarian law. Jost Delbrück, *op. cit.*, note 18, at p. 28.

Whereas bilateral treaties may be considered to be potentially the perfect expression of solidarity between parties, different degrees of solidarity may have led a larger group of States to formulate integral or differentiated obligations as the most articulated expression of their mutual solidarity. It is also in the name of the same principle of solidarity that "public interest related universal conventions"[184] are claiming *erga omnes* effect for certain basic principles they embody.

The possibility for any of the parties, pursuant to Article 60(2) c of the Vienna Convention on the Law of Treaties to invoke a material breach of an integral obligation as a ground for suspension of the treaty in whole or in part with respect to itself[185] is justified because such a breach threatens the structure of the treaty as a whole, as its performance is intentionally of an interdependent nature.[186]

As an injured State may not have at its disposal the necessary means to enforce its rights (the) other States parties may be coming to its aid in a spirit of solidarity *stricto sensu* through the exercise of second-level rights of an auxiliary nature[187] *i.e.* in order to help the injured State to enforce its remedial rights against the defaulting State.[188] Although in the regime of state responsibility a certain parallelism is maintained with the Vienna Convention, Article 42 (b) (ii) of the ILC Articles reflects a narrower definition of integral obligation.[189] Article 48 (1) (a) "does not exclude the possibility of a group of States undertaking an obligation which is in the common interest of a larger group or of the international community as a whole."[190]

Articles 48 (2) and 54 make it possible for any other State than the injured State, in a spirit of solidarity *senso latu*[191] to invoke responsibility of a State and to take lawful measures against the State having committed a breach of such an obligation: here the second-level rights are not of an auxiliary nature but are originally vested in each party "in recognition of its own individual and independent interest, severable from that of every other party, in upholding the legal regime which the treaty creates."[192] Hutchinson rightly pointed out that the same notion of solidarity *sensu lato* may be found at work in Article 63 of the Statute of the International Court of Justice.[193]

---

184   *Ibid.*

185   And thereby withholding from the defaulting State the benefits which the agreement affords; Hutchinson referring to Special Rapporteur Waldock, *op. cit.*, at p. 187.

186   James Crawford, *The International Law Commission's Articles on State Responsibility. Introduction, Text and Commentaries,* Cambridge University Press, 2002, p. 41.

187   D. Hutchinson, *op. cit.*, at pp. 159-164.

188   *Ibid.*, at p. 184.

189   James Crawford, *op. cit.*, at p. 42.

190   *Ibid.*, at p. 43 and see also Christian Walter, "Constitutionlaizing (Inter) national Governance- Possibilities for and Limits to the Development of an International Constitutional Law", *German Yearbook of International Law,* 2001, pp. 170-201, at p. 176, note 33.

191   D. Hutchinson, *op. cit.*, at pp. 164-174.

192   *Ibid.*, at p. 171.

193   *Ibid.*, at p. 178.

In case of obligations *erga omnes partes* all States parties are entitled to invoke responsibility, although *e.g.* an obligation "not to emit excess CFCs into the atmosphere" is a "purely solidary obligation, and there will never be a demonstrable connection with any particular breach and the impact on any particular State party".[194]

In these cases "solidarity *stricto sensu* has no role to play".[195]

In the 2001 compromise with regard to serious breaches of obligations under peremptory norms of general international law, no "provision on solidarity measures remained in the text,"[196] in spite of the efforts by the Special Rapporteur in the course of 2000 to provide for such measures in the case of a breach of an obligation established for the protection of collective interests, of an obligation owed to the international community as a whole, or of a serious breach of an obligation *erga omnes* that had been essential to the protection of fundamental interests of the international community.[197] Article 48 (2) substantially reduced the potential scope of application of solidarity measures.

As far as solidary responsibility is concerned, Article 47 "neither recognizes a general rule of joint and several responsibility nor does it exclude the possibility that two or more States will be responsible for the same internationally wrongful act."[198]

The circumstances and the international obligations of each of the States concerned will be determinative in this respect.[199]

In both the regimes of treaties and state responsibility it is "the very deficiencies of organization in the international legal system which create the pressure to recognize solidarity rights,"[200] while at the same time precluding the need for such rights being met in a satisfactory way.[201] A combined reading of Articles 40-41 and the without prejudice clause of Article 59 on state responsibility can only partly remedy this deficiency.

Solidarity measures "should be taken in accordance with institutional procedures, principles of due process, transparency, and the possibility of administrative or perhaps judicial review."[202] In a fully integrated, quasi-constitutional legal system as the EC the principle of solidarity prohibits States from taking the law into their own hands.[203]

---

194 Malgosia Fitzmaurice, *op. cit.*, at pp. 178 and 179, quoting James Crawford.

195 D. Hutchinson, *op cit.*, at p. 197, note 182.

196 Martti Koskeniemmi, "Solidarity measures: state responsibility as a new international order?" *British Yearbook of International Law*, 2001, pp.337-356, at p. 342, note 19.

197 See *ibid.* at pp. 344-346 for an overview of the proposals. On the solidarity underpinning the earlier approach of the ILC with respect to international crimes see also D. Hutchinson, *op. cit*, at pp. 196-212.

198 James Crawford, *op. cit.*, at p. 273.

199 *Ibid.*, at p. 274.

200 D. Hutchinson, *op. cit*, at p. 214.

201 *Ibid.*, at p. 215.

202 Martti Koskeniemmi, *op. cit.*, at p. 355.

203 Epaminondas Marias, *op. cit.*, at p. 97.

12. Solidarity as a Constitutional Principle

As an ideological and political notion and principle solidarity encompasses a natural potential for an overarching role in international relations. Distributive justice based upon solidarity calling for a fair international economic order is an essential element for the effective promotion of human rights which in turn is an important prerequisite for the maintenance of international peace and security.

This overarching role of solidarity has not been kept within the constraints of the political order but it has also found its way into the realm of law.

There is no doubt that contemporary international law "has entered into a process of constitutionalization."[204]

A principle of law may acquire a constitutional status within a particular order in various ways. It may have been included into a written constitutional document.

The UN Charter has "almost universally been recognized as the constitutional document of the international community of States."[205] In the pivotal area of the maintenance of international peace and security the principle of solidarity has clearly reached its full constitutional status through the collective security system elaborated in Chapter VII and endowed with an institutional mechanism to guarantee its permanent functioning.

A principle may also claim constitutional status because of its accepted particular role within the legal order, by "protecting fundamental values shared"[206] by the community .The principle of solidarity has not followed a different course.

As part of the irreversible process of humanisation of international law solidarity is increasingly perceived as a basic principle that protects fundamental values of the international community. It has joined the protection of human dignity as a constitutional principle.[207]

As such solidarity works at both the level of the IOs and the international community and at the level of individual states.[208]

Solidarity is one of the "distinct and different *Grundnorms* of World public Order" that emerged since the Second World War.[209]

It is a basic norm because it "restrains the use of power and force, (it) offer(s) orientation and (it) integrate(s) its members around basic values … ."[210] Solidarity

---

204   Jost Delbrück, *op. cit.*, note 4, at p. 430. See also Christian Walter, *op. cit.* Philip Allott once described international society as a "constitution-free zone", "The Concept of International Law", *European Journal of International Law*, 1999, pp. 30-50, at p. 35.

205   Bruno Simma, *op. cit.*, at p. 260.

206   Jost Delbrück, *op. cit.*, note 18, at p. 35.

207   Badislav Vukas, *op. cit.*, at p. 432. .

208   Ulrich Scheuner, *op. cit.*, at p. 272.

209   Edward McWhinney, "Shifting paradigms of international law and world order in an era of historical transition", in *International Law in the Post-Cold-War World, op. cit.* note 177, pp. 3-17, at p. 4.

210   Anne Peters, *op. cit.*, at p. 36.

runs in the opposite direction of the New *Approaches* to international law that "have highlighted the impact of power and hierarchy on the formation and application of international law."[211]

Another role for a constitutional principle is to enhance, ensure and protect the internal cohesion and consistency within a legal system.

The principle of solidarity is "infectious, travelling freely from one area of international law to the next."[212]

The slow, but clearly discernible proliferation and acceptance of the principle of solidarity throughout various branches of international law has made it gradually become one of the "basic constitutional norms that serve as the integrating foundation of the composite new legal order."[213] It is one of the cohesive factors in maintaining the systemic unity of the international legal system over and beyond the variety of its component branches.[214] In doing so, the principle of solidarity allows the process of constitutionalizing to reach the international community as a *whole*.[215]

The principle's constitutional role becomes apparent for instance through the notion of intergenerational equity which as part of the concept of sustainable development links environmental and development law, in the debate over assistance to States facing difficulties in carrying out sanctions[216] and in the more frequent use of differential obligations in an increasing number of branches as one technique to flesh out the principle.

A principle's constitutional role also demonstrates itself through the functions it performs with regard to both primary and secondary rules of a legal system. The previous section has demonstrated how the principle of solidarity has operated in that respect. The underpinning and moulding by the principle of solidarity of both primary and secondary rules may vary considerably from one branch to another but this does not basically affect either its instrumental or substantive role: it merely demonstrates the "infinite variety" of its impact in different branches of international law, and throughout the international legal system.

The global picture of contemporary international law shows a still cautious but undeniable awareness that the principle of solidarity may rightfully claim a

---

211   *Ibid.*, at p. 33.

212   Gerry Simpson, *op. cit.*, at p. 638, but with regard to fairness.

213   Jost Delbrück, *op. cit.*, note 4, at p. 430.

214   See the 25th anniversary Symposium of the *Michigan Journal of International Law*, March 2004: Diversity or Cacophony? New Sources of Norms in International Law, *Michigan Journal of International Law*, 2004, pp. 845-1375.

215   According to Christian Walter the process only occurs within the various sectoral regimes: *op. cit.*, at p. 195.

216   Such assistance eventually becoming available should be supplemented by non-financial measures in the area of international trade such as special tariff preferences and special commodity purchase agreements as UN sanctions should not affect a State's right to development: Reports Special Committee on the Charter of the United Nations and on the Strengthening of the Organization, UN Document A/56/33, p. 4, para. 29 and Document A/55/33, p. 5, para. 38.

hierarchically higher status *vis-à-vis* normal (or even fundamental) primary norms and rules of international law because of its constitutional role.

13. The Changing Structure of International Law: Law of Solidarity, Final Destination?

The above picture of both the constitutional and substantive role recently played by the principle of solidarity justifies the view that we are witnessing a process of transformation in the structure of international law from the mere law of co-operation [217] to a law of solidarity.

Just as there were "mere islands of the law of cooperation in an ocean of the law of coexistence,"[218] islands of the law of solidarity have surfaced in an ocean of the law of cooperation.

Interdependence and globalization have most probably initiated this, perhaps final, stage in the changing structure of international law, a process that has rather to be understood as a continuum where the law of coexistence[219] and the law of co-operation are not superseded by the law of solidarity. Indeed, the law of coexistence continues to occupy a central place because of the persistence of the central role of the state[220] and elements of the law of co-operation such as the "relative normativity"[221] are also present in the era of the law of solidarity through the phenomenon of differentiated obligations and responsibilities.

The law of co-operation, the law of coexistence and the law of solidarity will continue to "coexist" for the foreseeable future, but their mutual interrelationship will gradually change over time and the law of solidarity will influence the respective and combined role and impact of the two pre-existing approaches to international law.

The law of co-operation was more ambitious than the law of coexistence with regard to the role and task attributed to law,[222] and reciprocity under that law, may have been perceived as a "practical, if inadequate, step towards the ultimate goal

---

217   On the evolution of the international legal system from the Westphalian era to the era of the institutionalised co-operation see *inter alia* Jost Delbrück, *op. cit.*, note 18, at pp. 3-13. The present stage of international law referred to by others as the law of integration (replacing a horizontal structure mainly serving the purpose of regulating the relations between different sovereign states: Christian Walter, *op. cit.*, at p. 188) or more aptly the law of co-progressiveness in the post-cold-war era: Sienho Yee, *op. cit.*, at p. 19.

218   Georges Abi-Saab, *op. cit.*, at p. 255.

219   See the seminal article by Lazar Focsaneanu, *"Les 'Cinq Principes' de coexistence et le droit international",* Annuaire Français de Droit International, 1956, pp. 150-180.

220   Pierre-Marie Dupuy, "International Law: Torn between Coexistence, /cooperation and Globalization. General Conclusions", *European Journal of International Law*, 1998, pp. 278-286, at p. 283, note 6.

221   Sienho Yee, p. 24.

222   Georges Abi-Saab, *op. cit.*, at p. 256.

of distributive justice."[223] In a similar fashion the law of solidarity may now, as it permeates the international discourse and becomes institutionalized in legal instruments, be seen as a further, perhaps final step towards the same goal. In fact it is already playing a crucial role in solving key problems it inherited from the law of co-operation such as "equitable distribution of the benefits and burdens of effective environmental protection, and the mediation between environment and development."[224] Under the law of co-operation partial solidarity was invoked every single time a common need or interest was felt,[225] in the present era the solution of global issues requires solidarity's global dimension.

The notion of solidarity has already replaced some of the "preconceived ideas" from which, in customary law, a "limited set of norms for ensuring the coexistence and vital co-operation of the member of the international community" have been deduced.[226]

14. The Era of the Law of Solidarity: Challenges Ahead

The above review has demonstrated how the notion of solidarity became a legal principle that has gradually assumed a constitutional role in the international legal order. It has been at the origin of a paradigm shift towards the law of solidarity.

The process took long, it has not been straightforward and smooth, and it is clear that it has not reached its completion yet.

The major deficiency of both separate branches and the overall international legal system that has been brought to light by the penetration of the principle of solidarity is of an institutional nature. "The international legal order has been unable to crystallize an institutional basis for upholding shared interest."[227] The question has to be raised whether it is useful "to assign authority centrally in order to achieve" the goal of distributive justice.[228]

There is no "special system of tribunals to administer a branch of remedial justice in an unequal world."[229]

---

223 Douglas Johnston, *op. cit.*, at p. 125.

224 Georges Abi-Saab, *op. cit.*, at p. 262.

225 Georges Abi-Saab, *Cours Général de Droit International Public, Recueil des Cours de l'Académie de La Haye*, Vol. 207, 1987-VII, pp. 9-464, at p. 97.

226 Vera Gowlland-Debbas, *op. cit.*, referring to the Gulf of Maine case, at p. 345.

227 Richard Falk, *op. cit.*, at p. 3.

228 Joel Trachtman, "Review Essay. The Law and Economics of Global Justice", *American Journal of International Law*, 2002, pp. 984-995, at p. 993.

229 Douglas Johnston, *op. cit.*, at p. 137, note 26.
As the ICJ "has clearly endorsed the notion of elementary considerations of morality only whether these can be seen as an integral element of the international legal order" (Vera Gowlland-Debbas, *op. cit,* at p. 345), the principle of solidarity may now be considered to qualify in that respect.

With regard to the problem of refugees there is "no international relief system *per se*, as the diverse sets of actors display little structural interdependence and rarely share a set of common institutional goals."[230]

In international disaster law the key question is the establishment of a system of institutionalized public action to face cumulative processes of major humanitarian crises whatever their origin,[231] and this should be "a system bringing together States and NGOs, and only loosely linked with the United Nations."[232]

Even in the area of the maintenance of international peace and security "fair burden-sharing commends the proposal towards the establishment of a permanent volunteer force to be called in emergencies,"[233] while the institutional gap under Article 50 of the Charter still awaits to be properly addressed.

15. Conclusion

International law is always "supposed to reflect contemporary societal needs and expectations."[234]

In recent times the societal basis of international law has been shifted from a limited association to a more fully developed community, which is nowadays developing from a rule-oriented community to one based upon the existence of shared- values [235]and principles.[236]

Solidarity as a value[237] positioned itself at the heart of a theory of international justice required on the long way towards a coherent set of solutions to the problems the international community is facing.[238] Solidarity became a coherent and powerful idea providing strength and direction to the process towards the prosperous survival of the international community.

As part of a "renewed injection of moral content in the legal norms governing the world community,"[239] the notion of solidarity developed itself from the realm of justice into a "fundamental and a fundamentally sound principle"[240] of international law and it became the ultimate foundation of the international legal system in this era of globalization.

---

230   Guy Martin, *op. cit*., at p. 257.

231   Carillo Salcedo, *op. cit.*, at p. 431.

232   Badislav Vukas, *op. cit.*, at p. 442.

233   Thomas Franck, *op. cit.*, at p. 315.

234   Edward McWhinney, *op. cit.*, at p. 13.

235   Terry Nardin, "International ethics and international law", in *Review of International Studies*, 1992, pp. 19-30, at p. 22.

236   Marcel Brus, *op. cit.*, at p. 150.

237   As a "unity or accordnesses of feeling, action, especially among individuals with common interest, sympathies or concerns", *Oxford English Dictionary*.

238   Paul Wheitman, *op. cit.*, at p. 184.

239   Guy Martin, *op. cit.*, at p. 253.

240   R.St.J. Macdonald, *op. cit.* note 136, at p. 259.

The law of solidarity has gradually and increasingly penetrated into the structure and the normative content of international law[241] as did the law of cooperation before it[242] and it has acquired a more precise operational meaning. In most branches of international law reviewed here it has occupied a prominent rather than subsidiary role, also as a result of the irreversible humanisation of international law.

Apart from its functional, constitutional role, solidarity also has to operate as a material principle containing rights and duties.[243] In this respect Macdonald pointed out that solidarity *rights* have been recognized "only in situations where there are obligations on *both* sides, including, for example, the duty of developing countries to supply natural resources, to use financial resources efficiently and to realize specific development projects."[244]

It is more a *"balance of long-term interests* between developed countries, who give assistance and developing countries, who receive it" than a relationship of equal obligations.[245]

In this respect international environmental law is at the forefront of an unfolding process towards the recognition of the principle of solidarity as a material principle of universal international law.[246] The UN Climate Change Convention is a prime example: under the same principle of solidarity industrialized states fulfil their obligations by measures of technology transfer and contributions to the fund, while developing countries have a corresponding obligation to cooperate and participate in the common efforts to protect the environment.[247]

"Solidarität bedeutet Verantworting und Pflicht für alle Glieder der internationalen Gemeinschaft"[248] and also developing countries will have to recognize that solidarity they expect from others does bring with it obligations and duties.[249]

The further proliferation of solidarity as a material principle includes the recognition of some joint obligations of all States and some broadening of duty bearers beyond states.[250]*

---

241   As a "form of obligation involving joint and several responsibilities or rights", *Oxford English Dictionary*.

242   See George Abi-Saab, *op. cit.* note 133, at p. 256.

243   R.St.J. Macdonald, *op. cit.* note 136, at p. 266.

244   *Ibid.*, at p. 280, referring to the conclusions of Raimond Schütz.

245   *Ibid.*, at p. 281.

246   *Ibid.*, at pp. 282 and 301.

247   *Ibid.*, at p. 289.

248   Ulrich Scheuner, *op. cit.*, at p. 273: solidarity means responsibility and obligation for all members of the international community.

249   *Ibid.*, at p. 275.

250   Carl Wellman, "Solidarity, the Individual and Human Rights", in *Human Rights Quarterly*, 2000, pp. 639-657, at p. 657.

*   This study was completed on 30 April 2004.

30. Straddling Law and Politics: Judicial Review in International Law

Jan Klabbers

1. Introduction

It has been remarked that there is a "central paradox" at the heart of the operations of the US Supreme Court. On the one hand, all the important issues in US politics tend to come, sooner or later, before the Supreme Court; the Court therewith plays an important political role. On the other hand, however, the jurisdiction of the Court is limited to situations arising out of concrete "cases and controversies", and in deciding, the Court often (though obviously not always[1]) adopts a minimalist attitude, interfering as little as possible with political processes.[2]

It is indeed this paradox (or, better perhaps, dichotomy) which any account of judicial review, in whatever setting, has to overcome.[3] On the one hand, it would generally seem clearly desirable that basic legal guarantees be maintained, even (or especially) in the face of a political decision having broad support yet tending to undermine the position of a minority. On the other hand, however, there is the desideratum, generally thought wise, to leave politics to the politicians. Absent a specific grant of political decision-making powers to the courts, there is no reason why the courts should engage in political decision-making beyond the point where

---

1   Complaints about judicial activism are a fundamental staple of US constitutional discourse. See generally, *e.g.*, Duncan Kennedy, *A Critique of Adjudication {Fin de Siècle}* (Cambridge MA: Harvard University Press, 1997).

2   The observation was made by Paul A. Freund, "The Supreme Court", in Harold J. Berman (ed.), *Talks on American Law* (Washington DC: Voice of America, 1972, rev. edn.) 81-94, at 83.

3   Grimm can write without blushing that judicial review answers to the need to have "an independent system specialising in political matters". See Dieter Grimm, "Constitutional Adjudication and Democracy", in Mads Andenas & Duncan Fairgrieve (eds.), *Judicial Review in International Perspective: Liber Amicorum in Honour of Lord Slynn of Hadley* (The Hague: Kluwer, 2000) 103-120, at 106.

Ronald St. John Macdonald & Douglas M. Johnston (eds.), Towards World Constitutionalism, *pp. 809-835.*
© 2005 *Koninklijke Brill NV. Printed in The Netherlands.* ISBN 90 04 14612 1.

all adjudication is somehow political decision-making.[4] After all, there is no particular reason to suppose that judges (or lawyers generally) are better qualified or
in a better position to take political decisions than, say, a college of obstetricians,
or a gathering of truck drivers or, perish the though, a grouping of talk radio hosts.
Nor would a body of lawyers, no matter how brilliant, necessarily be more representative of the values and opinions in the relevant political community. As the
inimitable John Hart Ely put it with respect to the US, "Our society did not make
the constitutional decision to move to near-universal suffrage only to turn around
and have superimposed on popular decisions the values of first-rate lawyers."[5]

The present chapter aims to explore this difficult relationship between law
and politics by studying the possibilities and limits of judicial review in public international law, more in particular in the UN system. As will transpire below, I will
not simply posit the need or desirability of some form of judicial review; following
Crawford,[6] I take it that a limited form of judicial review is already in existence,
although not often recognized as such perhaps. Nor will I make or endorse the
argument that judicial review, because so widely used in domestic legal systems, is
therefore part of customary international law or, more subtle perhaps, an emerging
general principle of law.[7] I will also refrain from making or endorsing the argument
that constitutional review is inherent in a democracy or a state governed by the
rule of law. The examples of The Netherlands and the United Kingdom, where review testing the constitutionality of legislation is not engaged in, suggest that there
is no such necessary connection.[8]

Instead, I hope to sketch a limited possibility for judicial review, informed by
the law-politics dichotomy.[9] In doing so, I will occasionally have a look at how judicial review is manifested in European Community law, not so much with a view to

---

4   This refers to the somewhat crude position that simply by interpreting relatively inde-
     terminate provisions, courts engage in political decision-making; the argument might
     neglect some of the constraints on interpretation identified from various directions.
     See, *e.g.*, Benjamin N. Cardozo, *The Nature of the Judicial Process* (New Haven CT: Yale
     University Press, 1921); Stanley Fish, *Doing What Comes Naturally* (Oxford: Claren-
     don, 1989).

5   See John Hart Ely, *Democracy and Distrust: A Theory of Judicial Review* (Cambridge
     MA: Harvard University Press, 1980), at 59.

6   See note 57 below and accompanying text.

7   A careful argument to that effect is made by Erika de Wet, "Judicial Review as an
     Emerging General Principle of Law and Its Implications for the International Court of
     Justice", 47 *Netherlands International Law Review* (2000) 181-210.

8   The case of The Netherlands is, however, somewhat distorted, as the Dutch system
     does allow for testing the legality of legislation in light of the European Convention on
     Human Rights, the contents of which are by and large reflected in the Constitution. For
     further discussion, see Tim Koopmans, *Courts and Political Institutions* (Cambridge:
     Cambridge University Press, 2003) 76-84.

9   For an illuminating recent study, see Martin Loughlin, *Swords & Scales: An Examina-
     tion of the Relationship Between Law and Politics* (Oxford: Hart, 2000).

positing this as the only, or even the best, possible way of organizing judicial review beyond the state, but rather in order to pick up pointers.

I will limit this borrowing from EC law to the EC's most direct judicial review mechanism: the action for annulment envisaged in article 230 TEC. In other words: I will not take into account the preliminary ruling procedure of Article 234 TEC (whereby the legality of an EC act can be challenged in defense before a domestic court[10]), or the "prosecutorial" procedure of article 226 TEC,[11] or the advisory procedure of article 300 TEC.[12] The reason for this is largely practical: the case-law of the ECJ has become too vast. Besides, since article 230 TEC is drafted with a view to laying down the possibility of judicial review, it would stand to reason to expect that it offers the most interesting lessons, even if the form judicial review may take within the UN system is, as will be discussed, not of the same nature.[13]

2.   Law, Politics, Procedure

There is a second paradox at work with judicial review. Not only does judicial review have to straddle the law-politics dichotomy in that somehow a compromise or balance has to be found between the two, but the same dichotomy also plays out on a different level. On the one hand, it is often thought desirable that political organs be kept in check by the law; left to their own devices, political bodies may be tempted to engage in "the end justifies the means" type of activities. On the other hand though, it is often unclear what exactly the law says and why the law would be binding on international actors to begin with. It is one thing to hold that, for example, the World Bank ought to respect human rights (and, consequently, that decisions or policies violating human rights ought not to be implemented). There is controversy, however, about whether the Bank is bound by human rights to begin with; if so, by what human rights in particular;[14] and whether the Bank's own constitution even allows it to have human rights considerations enter the decision-making process.[15]

---

10   A typical scenario could be that in which a trader is prosecuted for violating a regulation, and in defense argues that the regulation itself violates a higher norm. In such a case, the member state court can (or must) refer the case to the ECJ for an opinion on the EC law aspects.

11   Under this procedure, the Commission can initiate proceedings against a member state for violating EC law.

12   This procedure allows the Court, upon request, to test in advance the compatibility of a treaty to be concluded between the EC and third parties with Community law.

13   See section 4 below.

14   See generally Sigrun Skogly, *The Human Rights Obligations of the World Bank and the International Monetary Fund* (London: Cavendish, 2001), or the brief but thoughtful analysis in Koen de Feyter, *The International Financial Institutions and Human Rights – Law and Practice* (discussion paper, Institute of Development and Policy Management, University of Antwerp, 2002).

15   The Bank's former Vice President and General Counsel, Ibrahim Shihata, argued that in order for the Bank to take human rights seriously, its mandate would require revi-

The paradoxical circumstance, then, is this: judicial review aims to hook up to strict positivism. It is often connected to the rule of law, and one element of the rule of law, it would seem, is that actors know in some detail what sort of behavior can be expected of them.[16] And this, in turn, would be greatly facilitated by positivism. Yet, if positivism be taken seriously, there may not be all that much law to apply to the acts of international organizations and their organs. Much of this law is uncertain, not so much in its scope or substance – although it is that too – but on issues of whether positivism would have it apply to organizations to begin with. It might often fail to satisfy the standards that positivism would set, and is thus often forced to resort back to more naturalist notions. To stick to the World Bank example: many would hold that it simply must be the case that the Bank is bound by human rights law because the alternative would be unthinkable. It cannot be the case that the World Bank is free to disregard human rights completely and with impunity; hence, it follows that it must be bound.[17] That may be a plausible proposition, of course, but not on any positivist conception of international law.[18]

One of the motivations (amongst quite a few others) behind the call for judicial review in international law resides in the circumstance that political agreement is often lacking. States disagree – in much the same way as reasonable individuals disagree – on what constitutes the good life. As a result, political decisions may be taken which may not be to everyone's liking or which may be seen by some to be in discord with other notions. In particular where "dissident" actions are the work of powerful actors, the prevailing sentiment would seem to be that power cannot be fought with power; that the only thing capable of fighting "might" would be "right".

That is, to some extent, a misguided notion, in that it is based on too simple a dichotomy between law and politics (with law being the good guy, and politics being the bad guy). It fails to acknowledge that the contents of much law – and international law can hardly claim to be an exception – is (or aims to be) itself the result of political agreement. One of the more obvious ways out, then, is to enter-

---

sion. See Ibrahim Shihata, "Human Rights, Development and International Financial Institutions", 8 *American University Journal of International Law and Policy* (1992) 27-37.

16   See, *e.g.*, the requirements formulated (albeit not under the explicit heading of Rule of Law) by Lon L. Fuller, *The Morality of Law* (New Haven CT: Yale University Press, 1969, rev. edn.), ch. 2.

17   For a recent formulation of the thesis that international law originates in social necessity, see Jonathan I. Charney, "Universal International Law", 87 *American Journal of International Law* (1993) 529-551.

18   In a similar vein, Dyzenhaus – who associates judicial review with antipositivism – observes that "[p]ositivism cannot supply a foundation for judicial review since it is politically committed to minimising the role of judges in legal order." See David Dyzenhaus, "Form and Substance in the Rule of Law: A Democratic Justification for Judicial Review?", in Christopher Forsyth (ed.), *Judicial Review and the Constitution* (Oxford: Hart, 2000) 141-172, at 159.

tain the flight into procedure,[19] and as will be seen, this is perhaps the only way in which some form of judicial review can be engaged in on the international level: testing measures not so much for their concord with substantive norms and values, but rather on how they came about, or are applied, procedurally.[20]

The aim of this chapter will be, accordingly, to sketch a process-oriented judicial review. The one drawback, of course, is that the separation between procedural and substantive notions is itself arbitrary, and that both shade into each other. While undoubtedly correct, there would still seem to be a difference between testing against substance, and testing on procedural issues, provided there is widespread agreement on the procedural issue at stake. And often widespread agreement is possible precisely because an issue is perceived to be (for ill or good) procedural rather than substantive.

This approach finds considerable justification in neo-republican political theory. While liberal individualists tend to conceptualize social relationships in terms of individual rights, to the point of ignoring anything social, and communitarians tend to think in terms of group relations at the risk of undermining the position of individuals,[21] neo-republican political thought stresses the importance of procedure; not so much procedure for its own sake, but procedures as the proper methods of channelling political debate.[22] In the neo-republican view, the point of politics is not so much to reach agreement on the good life; indeed, this would be deemed well-nigh impossible in light of the plurality of human existence, and most likely undesirable as well. Nor is the point of politics the acquisition of power for the sake of power, as impoverished political science doctrine would hold. Instead, the point of politics is to engage in free and open debate, unimpeded by everyday concerns if at all possible, between equals.[23] It follows, that a premium

---

19   As such, this is hardly a novel phenomenon, associated as it is with the increased reliance on general principles which in itself results from the vast expansion of regulatory ambition. See, *e.g.*, Roberto Unger, *Law in Modern Society: Toward a Criticism of Social Theory* (New York: Free Press, 1976), *e.g.* at 196-197, or, in Dutch, the brief classic by Gerard J. Wiarda, *Drie typen van rechtsvinding* (Zwolle: Tjeenk Willink, 1972).

20   Thus, I try to avoid being typecast as one of those "incurable judicial romantics who look to courts as a type of *deus ex machina*, ready to descend, upon the mere utterance of some juridical incantations that summon forth mysterious powers inherent in the law, to bring order and justice to the most untidy, even violent political situations." See W. Michael Reisman, "The Constitutional Crisis in the United Nations", 87 *American Journal of International Law* (1993) 83-100, at 94 (emphasis in original).

21   A fine overview of the debate is Shlomo Avineri & Avner de-Shalit (eds.), *Communitarianism and Individualism* (Oxford: Oxford University Press, 1992).

22   This is inspired by a variety of works (not all of them self-consciously neo-republican), including Hannah Arendt, *The Human Condition* (Chicago: University of Chicago Press, 1958); Benjamin R. Barber, *The Conquest of Politics* (Princeton: Princeton University Press, 1988); Dana R. Villa, *Arendt and Heidegger: The Fate of the Political* (Princeton: Princeton University Press, 1996), and Jeremy Waldron, *Law and Disagreement* (Oxford: Oxford University Press, 1999).

23   Politics for politics' sake, as it may be put. The classic objection is that people might be less than interested in engaging in politics for its own sake. For a (sympathetically criti-

is to be placed on the background conditions facilitating such political debate, *i.e.* procedures relating to decision-making processes: freedom of speech and freedom of assembly come to mind, as do such things as transparency and a right to be informed.[24] And from this, it is but a short step (although rarely taken[25]) to also insist on the importance of procedural guarantees in the implementation of policies.[26]

3.   The Call for Review

The call for judicial review of the acts of international organizations is, with the possible exception of the EC, of relatively recent origin, and probably started only to blossom after the Security Council had imposed sanctions on Libya for its failure to hand over two suspected terrorists,[27] and had been accused before the ICJ of contributing to the ethnic cleaning of the Bosnians, and therewith violating, however inadvertently, the prohibition of genocide.[28] These incidents appeared to suggest that, even if working on the basis of noble intentions (fighting terrorism, aiming to prevent the further eruption of a bloody conflict), the Council could do wrong.[29]

---

cal) discussion in Dutch, see Ido de Haan, *Zelfbestuur en staatsbeheer: Het politieke debat over burgerschap en rechtsstaat in de twintigste eeuw* (Amsterdam: Amsterdam University Press, 1993).

24   Elsewhere I have argued that much human rights law can be seen as deriving its force from facilitating and guaranteeing the political process. See Jan Klabbers, "Glorified Esperanto? Rethinking Human Rights", 13 *Finnish Yearbook of International Law* (2002).

25   The most sophisticated account that I am aware of is Trevor Allan's which is, however, presented as grounded in liberal individualism à la Dworkin. See T.R.S. Allan, *Constitutional Justice: A Liberal Theory of the Rule of Law* (Oxford: Oxford University Press, 2001).

26   This should not be confused with the liberal procedural republic so famously complained of by Sandel, in that neo-republicanist proceduralism cherishes the integrity of the political process and therewith the communal aspects of human existence. See Michael Sandel, "The Procedural Republic and the Unencumbered Self", reproduced in Avineri & De-Shalit (eds.), note 21 above, 12-28. See also Michael Sandel, *Democracy's Discontent: American in Search of a Public Philosophy* (Cambridge MA: Harvard University Press, 1996).

27   See Resolution 748 (1992) jo. 731 (1992).

28   See *Case Concerning Application of the Convention on the Prevention and Punishment of the Crime of Genocide* (Bosnia and Herzegovina v. Yugoslavia (Serbia and Montenegro)), Further Request for the Indication of Provisional Measures, [1993] *ICJ Reports* 325, in particular the separate opinion of ad hoc judge Lauterpacht.

29   Surprisingly perhaps, the proposition that "it is inherent in government that it must continually generate discontent", took some time to settle down with respect to international organizations. The phrase is taken from Charles L. Black, *The People and the Court: Judicial Review in a Democracy* (New York: Macmillan, 1960), at 42. Note also that the Dutch system (absence of constitutional review) is based on the idea that, as Koopmans puts it, "a decent government and a decent parliament would never act in violation of the constitution". See Koopmans, note 8 above, at 76.

Since the mid-1980s, the World Bank had established its Inspection Panel in response to complaints that its policies would be so single-minded as to ignore the plight of groups of people affected by them altogether.[30] The European Court of Human Rights started to wonder whether the activities of international organizations could give rise to human rights ramifications, both in the setting of employees of organizations,[31] and in respect of activities of organizations more generally.[32] The collapse of the International Tin Council suggested that organizations could fail in their tasks, leading to investigations into the responsibility or accountability of organizations under international law, both academic[33] and by professional organizations of international lawyers.[34] The controversial bombing of Belgrade by NATO made clear that organizations can actually kill people.[35] And the transformation of the GATT into the WTO brought with it an increasing realization that decisions of international bodies can possibly affect domestic law, even, so the realization dawned, domestic constitutional law.[36]

Much of this can no doubt be traced back to the end of the Cold War, and the concomitant rise in activism and activities on the part of international organiza-

---

30   See Daniel D. Bradlow & Sabine Schlemmer-Schulte, "The World Bank's New Inspection Panel: A Constructive Step in the Transformation of the International Legal Order", 54 *Zeitschrift für ausländisches öffentliches Recht und Völkerrecht* (1994) 392-415; Ellen Hey, "The World Bank Inspection Panel: Towards the Recognition of a New Legally Relevant Relationship to International Law", 2 *Hofstra Law & Policy Symposium* (1997) 61-74.

31   See *Waite & Kennedy* v. *Germany* and *Beer & Regan* v. *Germany*, judgments of 18 February 1999, reproduced in 118 ILR 121. Earlier, the European Commission of Human Rights had declined such a suggestion in *Spaans* v. *Netherlands*, reproduced in 107 ILR 1.

32   In *Matthews* v. *United Kingdom*, reproduced in 30 *European Human Rights Reports* (1999) 361, it held that the EU member states retain responsibility for free elections, including the organization of elections to the European Parliament.

33   The seminal article is Romana Sadurska & Christine Chinkin, "The Collapse of the International Tin Council: A Case of State Responsibility?", 30 *Virginia Journal of International Law* (1990) 845-890. On the topic more generally, see August Reinisch, "Securing the Accountability of International Organizations", 7 *Global Governance* (2001) 131-149.

34   See the reports by Rosalyn Higgins to the Institut de Droit International, in 66 *Annuaire de l'Institut de Droit International* (1995/I) and (1996/II); the third report of the Committee on Accountability of International Organizations of the International Law Association, complete with a set of Recommended Rules and Practices, in International Law Association, *Report of the Seventieth Conference: New Delhi* (London: International Law Association, 2002) 772-806, and the two reports by ILC Special Rapporteur Giorgio Gaja, UN Docs A/CN.4/532 of 26 March 2003, and A/CN.4/541 of 2 April 2004.

35   See in particular Martti Koskenniemi, "'The Lady Doth Protest Too Much': Kosovo, and the Turn to Ethics in International Law", 65 *Modern Law Review* (2002) 159-175.

36   See generally Mark Tushnet, *The New Constitutional Order* (Princeton: Princeton University Press, 2003), ch. 5.

tions. There is, however, a deeper change at work as well, which may help explain why constitutionalism broadly speaking, and more narrowly judicial review, have come to be regarded as somehow appropriate for international organizations. International organizations have fallen from grace. The image of organizations, in the eyes of statesmen, courts, and observers alike, has undergone a fundamental change.[37] Where once international organizations were seen to embody the "salvation of mankind", as Nagendra Singh could strikingly put it in 1958,[38] at present the insight has gained momentum that organizations, endowed with the task to exercise official authority, must be held to standards that generally apply to official authority. Organizations are no longer regarded as the "benign", inherently good alternatives to states.[39] Instead, they are increasingly taken for what they are: alternatives to states perhaps, but also created by states and doing things that make them indiscernible from states.[40] It follows, that there is no particular reason, so we tend to think,[41] to single them out for special treatment: to the extent that they exercise public authority, their acts should be subject to control. This takes the broad form of constitutionalism and respect for human rights,[42] and the more specialized form of calls for judicial review.[43]

As H.L.A. Hart once suggested, it is of the utmost importance in liberal jurisprudence that punishment follows the perpetrator, and preferably one who intends to perpetrate at that: strict liability is something we are generally reluctant to install, and the idea of punishing an individual for something committed by someone else is, save perhaps in modified form in cases of command responsibility, generally considered to be abhorrent.[44]

---

37   See Jan Klabbers, "The Changing Image of International Organizations", in Jean-Marc Coicaud & Veijo Heiskanen (eds.), *The Legitimacy of International Organizations* (Tokyo: United Nations University Press, 2001) 221-255.

38   See Nagendra Singh, *Termination of Membership of International Organisations* (London: Stevens & Sons, 1958), at vii.

39   This role has, by and large and for the moment, been taken over by non-governmental organizations, as embodiments of civil society.

40   For a broad overview of the shifts in our thinking about international organizations, see Jan Klabbers, "The Life and Times of The Law of International Organizations", 70 *Nordic Journal of International Law* (2001) 287-317. On the identity between states and organizations, see also Jan Klabbers, *An Introduction to International Institutional Law* (Cambridge: Cambridge University Press, 2002).

41   Or rather: we no longer tend to think that there is such a special reason.

42   Elsewhere, I discuss this phenomenon in greater depth. See Jan Klabbers, "Constitutionalism Lite", 1 *International Organizations Law Review* (2004) 31-58.

43   See also Jan Klabbers, "Introduction", in Jan Klabbers (ed.), *International Organizations* (Aldershot: Dartmouth, Library of Essays in International Law, 2005, forthcoming).

44   See generally the essays collected in H.L.A. Hart, *Punishment and Responsibility: Essays in the Philosophy of Law* (Oxford 1967). As Fletcher puts it (while defending collective guilt but not necessarily also collective punishment): the idea of collective guilt "disturbs liberal individualists". See George P. Fletcher, "Collective Guilt and Collective Punishment", 5 *Theoretical Inquiries in Law* (2004) 163-178.

Many notions of (liberal) criminal law would seem to follow. Thus, an accused should have a right to defend himself, should have access to justice and a fair trial, should be informed about the charges made against him, *et cetera*.[45] These notions have become so ingrained in our thinking that they are part and parcel of human rights instruments such as the European Convention on Human Rights and Fundamental Freedoms, and it is probably no accident that the Convention's article dealing with the right to a fair trial and all that entails (Article 6) is the article most often invoked.[46]

The rule of law is generally thought to contain similar elements: fairness of procedure, equality of treatment, absence of favourable or disfavourable *ad hominem* treatment, all those things are usually considered to form part and parcel of the rule of law. As Loughlin formulates it concisely: the modern notion of the rule of law "reflects the belief that citizens are equal in the eyes of the law, that the rule structure should be insulated from gross manipulation and that, as an operative system of rules, legal judgment is quite distinct from political decision-making."[47] Yet, this general acceptance of notions such as the legality principle in criminal law, or more generally the recognized relevance of the rule of law, the *Rechtsstaat*,[48] or any variation thereon, is not reflected within the United Nations system.

Take, for instance, the Security Council which, as the main political organ of the UN, is in the position to impose sanctions on states, which can be implemented by means of Sanctions Committees without paying much attention to procedural niceties, and without there being any mechanisms for fighting the imposition of sanctions. And if sanctions are to be regarded as a form of punishment (which, at least in part, would seem eminently plausible), then the entire sanctions system seems difficult to reconcile with modern conceptions of both criminal law and human rights law.

An example, taken from many, may illustrate the gravity of the issue. On May 22, 2003, at its 4761st meeting, the Security Council adopted Resolution 1483 (2003) which, among other things, "affirm[ed] the need for accountability for crimes and atrocities committed by the previous Iraqi regime".[49] Under paragraph 23 of the Resolution, funds and other assets of the former Iraqi government and of Saddam Hussein, former senior officials and immediate family members shall be frozen and transferred to the Development Fund for Iraq.

Official Guidelines suggest that the Committee established in 1990 to oversee Resolution 661 shall identify the individuals and entities concerned on the basis of

---

45   See generally George P. Fletcher, *Basic Concepts of Criminal Law* (Oxford: Oxford University Press, 1998).

46   See Iain Cameron, *An Introduction to the European Convention on Human Rights* (Uppsala 1998, 3d edn.), at 71.

47   See Loughlin, note 9 above, at 79.

48   The term is sometimes translated as "law-state", signifying a state-under-law. For a brief discussion, see Neil MacCormick, *Questioning Sovereignty: Law, State, and Practical Reasoning* (Oxford: Oxford University Press, 1999), at 9.

49   Preamble, 11th consideration.

whatever relevant information it may receive. The Guidelines specify though, that if persons or entities are proposed for identification, such proposal "should be accompanied by, to the extent possible, a narrative description of the information that forms the basis or justification for taking action".[50] The Committee works, so it says, on the basis of consensus, and does allow for a written "no objection" procedure amongst its members. In case consensus remains elusive, the Security Council can be activated.[51] Yet further details are set out in what is sadly called a "non-paper" which reflects the common understanding of the Committee Members, which is deemed to serve as indication only, and which is supposed not to be legally binding.[52]

For anyone concerned with the rule of law, in whichever guise and with whatever political sympathies, this system raises some serious questions. A legal regime, with possibly grave consequences for the individuals concerned, is created by invisible and democratically unaccountable bureaucrats, with the details based on instruments of elusive status, such as guidelines and non-papers. And this is only one of a growing list of examples of the expanding activities, and expanding reach of activities, of the United Nations. The more active the UN becomes, involving itself with detailed sanctions regimes, extensive peace-keeping and peace-enforcement operations, and even the administration of entire territories such as Kosovo and East Timor, the greater the need for procedural and substantive clarity.[53] In this light, it is no surprise that increasingly, some form of judicial review is advocated within the UN system.

4.   A System of Review

Discussions on whether judicial review could possibly exist within the UN system used to be (to a large extent still are, in all likelihood) based on either rather straightforward normative considerations, or derived through the technique of interpreting past judgments of the ICJ. Thus, Thomas Franck holds that the World Court's opinion in *Lockerbie* presupposes that at least the Court itself holds there to be a possibility for judicial review of Security Council decisions: "The majority and dissenting opinions seem to be in agreement that there are ... limits and that they cannot be left exclusively to the Security Council to interpret."[54] Suggestive of a more (or more overtly) politicized approach is the rejection of judicial review by Nolte as too risky. There may well be limits to what the Security Council can do, but to ask the ICJ to police those limits would politically be unwise: a judgment declaring a Council resolution *ultra vires* might well be disregarded by the Council,

---

50   Guidelines, point 1(b).

51   *Ibid.*, point 2.

52   See Press Release SC/7831 IK372 of 29 July 2003.

53   See, *e.g.*, Frédéric Mégret & Florian Hoffmann, "The UN as a Human Rights Violator? Some Reflections on the United Nations Changing Human Rights Responsibilities", 25 *Human Rights Quarterly* (2003) 314-342.

54   See Thomas M. Franck, *Fairness in International Law and Institutions* (Oxford: Oxford University Press, 1995), at 244.

which "would put the international legal system into far greater jeopardy than if the question of the lawfulness of Security Council action remained unresolved."[55]

James Crawford recently presented a different type of argument – a more systemic argument – when he argued that, in a modest form, judicial review can and does indeed exist in international law.[56] Crawford's reasoning goes as follows: the ICJ is endowed with the task to apply international law in cases between states. International law consists not solely of treaties between states or rules of customary international law, but also consists of such things as Security Council resolutions. Part of applying the law is, no doubt, assessing the validity of the legal arguments invoked, and the legal instruments relied on. Hence, it follows that, in applying international law, the ICJ is perfectly at liberty to assess the validity of Security Council resolutions (or decisions of other organs or organizations), if and when appropriate, and if that is not judicial review, then nothing is.[57]

That is a compelling line of argumentation, but it will be obvious that it allows for judicial review only to a limited extent. It does not, *e.g.*, allow for review in other than contentious proceedings; it does not allow for review on the basis of individual complaints; it does not, in and of itself, allow for review before courts or tribunals other than the ICJ; and it says nothing about the possible legal effects following review.

If Crawford's analysis is correct, then the question is not (or no longer) whether judicial review is at all possible at the international level, but the question is to what extent it is limited. And this, in turn, breaks up into a number of smaller questions of a more or less conceptual nature, into such things as the sort of acts that can be reviewed, the desirability of judicial review outside the context of interstate proceedings, the problem of standing, and the connections between judicial review and public law.

It has been observed that judicial review in public law will inevitably be limited. Sedley J., in a case decided in 1997, put it succinctly: "Public law is not at base about rights ...; it is about wrongs – that is to say misuses of public power."[58] Or as the constitutional theorist Trevor Allan notes in greater depth:

> Since there is usually no right to any particular outcome, but a right to fair treatment in the light of the reasonable requirements of public policy, as settled by the relevant

---

55 So, *e.g.*, Georg Nolte, "The Limits of the Security Council's Powers and its Functions in the International Legal System: Some Reflections", in Michael Byers (ed.), *The Role of Law in International Politics* (Oxford: Oxford University Press, 2000) 315-326, at 318. See also Reisman, note 20 above, esp. at 88-89.

56 Crawford's argument was to some extent foreshadowed by Geoffrey R. Watson, "Constitutionalism, Judicial Review, and the World Court", 34 *Harvard International Law Journal* (1993) 1-45.

57 See James Crawford, "Marbury v. Madison at the International Level", 36 *George Washington International Law Review* (2004) 505-514.

58 Sedley J. in *R. v. Somerset County Council and ARC Southern Ltd, ex parte Dixon*, as quoted in Michael J. Beloff, "Who Whom? Issues in Locus Standi in Public Law", in Andenas & Fairgrieve (eds.), note 3 above, 275-291, at 278.

authority, the court's judgment of the merits of an administrative decision is of a strictly limited kind. In determining the plausibility and propriety of the public authority's judgment, in so far as is necessary to assess the fairness of the citizen's treatment, the court must rely on the reasons and evidence that the litigants adduce. But since it does not question the wisdom of the underlying policy, but only the fairness of its application in the circumstances of the case, no further inquiry is either necessary or legitimate.[59]

The passage nicely encapsulates a number of important considerations relating to judicial review in general. First, when speaking of administrative decisions, Allan brings to light the obvious (but sometimes ignored) distinction between reviewing the validity of legislation, and the legality of administrative decisions based on legislation. Second, the passage suggests that judicial review is almost by definition linked to public acts taking place under the aegis of public law. Third, Allan's passage underlines the difference between questioning a policy and the application of that policy. In addition, at least two more issues must be addressed. The first of these relates to the identity of those who can instigate judicial review; the second concerns the effects of judicial review. The remainder of this chapter is devoted to a discussion of these five issues in light of the law-politics dichotomy.

A.   Judicial Review of What?

Testing the validity of legislation presupposes two things. It presupposes, first, that there is such a thing as legislation in the normal meaning of the word; in international law, there is some doubt as to this. While admittedly the Security Council came close in Resolution 748 to creating a new rule on extradition ("thou shalt extradite people, including thy own citizens, even in the absence of an extradition agreement and even in the face of contrary constitutional provisions if it is terrorism they are suspected of"), by and large it would seem that to speak of international legislation is either evidence of wishful thinking, or simply a misnomer – needless to say, the two may shade into each other. Lacking a legislature, international "legislation" is still generally based on the specific consent of states, and therewith closer to contractual notions.

Second, testing the validity of legislation presupposes that there are standards of validity in existence which, moreover, are to be given preference over ordinary norms. This too is not a certainty in international law. International lawyers have attempted to posit the existence of such norms by means of concepts of *jus cogens* norms or *erga omnes* obligations, but the ICJ, for one, has been less than forthcoming on the former and seemed even to have buried the latter,[60] at least until its recent resurrection in the opinion on the wall built by Israel.[61]

---

59   See Allan, note 25 above, at 191.

60   See Jan Klabbers, "The Scope of International Law: *Erga Omnes* Obligations and the Turn to Morality", in Matti Tupamäki (ed.), *Liber Amicorum Bengt Broms* (Helsinki, Finnish ILA Branch, 1999) 149-179.

61   See *Legal Consequences of the Construction of a Wall in the Occupied Palestinian Territory*, advisory opinion, International Court of Justice, 9 July 2004.

In addition (but this adds to the complexity of the issue, rather than its simplification), there is article 103 of the UN Charter. Yet, instead of making it possible to submit practices under the Charter to higher norms, article 103 does the opposite: as the ICJ suggested in its 1992 *Lockerbie* opinion,[62] Article 103 UN Charter might have the effect of isolating anything based on the Charter from further scrutiny, and it would seem to be that this was precisely what article 103 was intended to achieve, on the apparent theory that the Security Council could do no wrong.

The general law of treaties too is not terribly keen on creating a hierarchy between norms, and to the (relatively limited) extent that it does aim to solve conflicts between norms, its solution is the neutral one (and again, counterproductive for those wishing to think of there being a higher law[63]) of favouring the later in time.[64] This again has the effect of depriving later acts from a standard of review.

In short, it would seem that even if the ICJ were entitled or authorized to engage in the review of the legality of legislation, there is not much legislation in existence, and not many standards to test this legislation against either. The absence of legislation as such would not preclude testing the legality of contractual engagements entered into (although the difficult existence of higher standards might prove an obstacle), but it is doubtful whether such testing should properly go by the name of judicial review.

The law-politics dichotomy makes an overt appearance here. Surely, any attempt to undo "legislation" (such as it is) runs into the countermajoritarian problem familiar from US constitutional discussions: if a majority democratically reaches a decision, then why should a minority be allowed to interfere and obstruct? The only good response would be: to protect its rights, but that is often thought difficult to reconcile precisely with democracy. Still, put like this, the unlikelihood of judicial review of international legislation is brought to the fore: terms like "democracy" or even "majority" hardly apply on the international level in the context of binding norms.

A different option, however, would be administrative review. This presupposes that rules are in place, and that these rules are applied by some sort of public authority. Not much more is required (and here's the rub) than that those rules are applied with fairness, or consistency, or equality, or so as to protect individu-

---

62   See *Case Concerning Questions of Interpretation and Application of the 1971 Montreal Convention Arising From the Aerial Incident at Lockerbie* (Libya v. UK), order, [1992] *ICJ Reports* 3.

63   Lauterpacht's position was, perhaps, more receptive of judicial review: for him, a later treaty conflicting with an earlier one would normally be void. This alone evidences the persistence of the law-politics dichotomy: Lauterpacht's position prefers legal certainty (the older treaty) over a more accurate reflection of current political configurations (the newer treaty). See Hersch Lauterpacht, "First Report on the Law of Treaties", in *Yearbook of the International Law Commission* (1953/II) 90-166, esp. at 156-159.

64   See generally Article 30 VCLT which, however, provides little relief when the conflict is not one between the same parties. The most sophisticated analysis is no doubt Guyora Binder, *Treaty Conflict and Political Contradiction: The Dialectics of Duplicity* (New York: Praeger, 1988).

als. In short, here the problem is, again, the standard to apply or, perhaps, the aim of review: what is review supposed to guarantee? The strict positivist might note here that the UN Charter, to name one example, at no point spells out that Security Council decisions ought to take individual rights into account, or that their application ought to be based on equality, or take place with consistency. The less strict positivist might rebut, however, that the same holds true with respect to many domestic legal systems (which may not be all too precise in instructing judges what to take into account) and, moreover, is required not just by a sense of propriety, but follows from the rule of law[65] and is of the utmost importance with a view to the legitimacy of, in our example, Security Council activities: if not done with respect for individual rights, or on the basis of equality, the Council's decisions and their application will lack legitimacy.[66]

Either way, if judicial review means review of the way in which administrative decisions are applied, then there surely is room for such an approach in the UN system. The Security Council and other UN organs, suborgans and temporary organs and agencies, are bound to act within the limits of the law, however vague and undefined these themselves may be (and are). The important thing to realize, however, is that what matters is not even so much that the Security Council respects those limits (it may be, that they are too ill-defined to be conclusively respected to begin with – reasonable people may come to different conclusions on, *e.g.*, such issues as to whether proclaiming a duty to extradite,[67] or creating a temporary legal regime,[68] or distributing territory,[69] properly fall within the scope of what the Council can do) but that when and where the Council acts, it does so while respecting procedural requirements, taking equality into account, that sort of thing. At least part of the call for Security Council reform, after all, finds its origin not so much in what the Council does, but rather in what it does not do, therewith provoking critiques of unequal treatment and clientelism: how it failed to act in Rwanda and, at the time of writing, threatens to fail to act in Sudan; how the veto protects Israel, or how the veto protects Serbia, or how, indeed, the veto shields the five permanent members from closer scrutiny. As long as the veto system is in

---

65   See generally Allan, note 25 above.

66   Note, however, that legitimacy itself is a contested concept and is often used in the service of other contestations. For an incisive critique, see Martti Koskenniemi, "Legitimacy, Rights, and Ideology: Notes Towards a Critique of the New Moral Internationalism", 7 *Associations* (2003) 349-373.

67   See *Lockerbie*, note 62 above.

68   Thus, UNMIK declared that in Kosovo, the European Convention on Human Rights would apply, despite the circumstance that Yugoslavia nor Serbia had become parties to the Convention. On post-conflict governance generally, see Outi Korhonen & Jutta Gras, *International Governance in Post-Conflict Situations* (Helsinki: Erik Castrén Institute, 2001).

69   The boundary between Iraq and Kuwait comes to mind. For a brief analysis, see Jan Klabbers, "No More Shifting Lines? The Report of the Iraq-Kuwait Boundary Demarcation Commission", 43 *International & Comparative Law Quarterly* (1994) 904-913.

place, it would be unrealistic to expect the total disappearance of clientelism, but in the meantime the Council can still adhere more closely than it presently does to requirements of procedural fairness.

B.   Whose Acts Should Be Reviewed?

Within the UN system, it is common to connect the possibility or desirability of judicial review to the Security Council. It is the Council's activities which often give cause for concern, more so than the acts of the other principal organs of the UN, including the General Assembly.

This preoccupation with the Security Council stems from two factors. One is, that the Council's composition is often considered to be far from representative or, alternatively, that to the extent that it is representative, it represents global power configurations rather than, say, the people. In particular the permanent membership of China, the US, Russia, France and the UK, in conjunction with the veto, is often deemed to be a bone of contention. Decision-making within the Council often follows naked interests rather than principle, humanitarian concerns, or some conception of the common good, is not terribly transparent and is, in the end, the result of the interplay of fifteen individuals on the proverbial powder keg.

In addition to being a thoroughly unrepresentative body, the Council has the power to actually order the UN's member states what to do. Some of its decisions (perhaps depending on their wording and perhaps depending on their legal basis) are legally binding. Others, if not legally binding, are at least procedurally required.[70] As a result, the important political issues of the day (if not vetoed) tend to end up before the Council, and as the Council actually has the power to do something about them, it should come as no surprise that the Council is often singled out for criticism.

Yet, to the extent that their decisions can be binding on states, there seems to be no particular reason to exclude the other principal organs from the scope of judicial review. Surely, the General Assembly is as capable as the Security Council of taking bad decisions (or non-decisions); the circumstance that the Assembly's opportunism may rest on a broader, more representative base of support would seem to be, for purposes of judicial review, rather irrelevant. After all, often judicial review finds as one of its justifications precisely the idea that it should serve in order to protect against "the tyranny of the majority".

Obviously, such assessments depend strongly on one's political views; while a resolution portraying zionism as racism may represent deep wisdom to some, it may represent silly opportunism in the eyes of others. Likewise, a resolution endorsing an advisory opinion on the legality of certain types of weaponry may be opportunistic to some and wise to others. But that is hardly the point.

---

70   Think of decisions on admission of new member states; see *Competence of the General Assembly for the Admission of a State to the United Nations*, advisory opinion, [1950] ICJ Reports 4. With membership being near-universal nowadays, this particular issue has lost some of its urgency.

The point is, rather, that some of the decisions of the Assembly give rise to immediate legal effects. A decision to reject a state's application for membership; a decision to suspend the rights of a member state; a decision to reject the credentials of a state's representatives, or a decision on the budget, all these engender immediate legal consequences, and the theory of judicial review (any theory of judicial review) would hold as a minimum[71] that where legal effects are immediately resulting, review ought to be possible.[72]

Article 230 of the EC Treaty is instructive perhaps. It posits that the Court of Justice shall review the legality of acts "other than recommendations and opinions" (these, so article 249 TEC says, "shall have no binding force"), and as far as acts of the European Parliament are concerned, the Court's jurisdiction comprises only those of its acts which are "intended to produce legal effects *vis-à-vis* third parties". While one may quarrel about the requirement of intent (in that legal effects may also come about through good faith, reliance or estoppel, quite independently of intent[73]), nonetheless the basic idea is clear: judicial review in the EC covers acts which have legal effects.[74]

There would, therefore, seem to be no special reason to exclude acts of organs other than the Security Council from the scope of judicial review. Acts of the General Assembly, the Economic and Social Council, the Secretariat, even, hypothetically, acts of the defunct (but still extant) Trusteeship Council, and all their subsidiary organs (ranging from temporary territorial administrations to the United Nations Administrative Tribunal[75]) would, hence, be susceptible to review.

---

71   One can think of expanding review so as to cover non-binding acts (although this would not seem to make too much sense except on the view that non-binding acts are as authoritative as binding ones), but it would be quite inconceivable to have judicial review but have it refrain from covering binding acts generally.

72   This might benefit also the organization itself, as became clear after the messy treatment of Serbia. Stripping Serbia of its UN membership (which some maintain is what happened) resulted in the claim that the ICJ lost much of the basis of its jurisdiction to address complaints against Serbia. See *Application for the Revision of the Judgment of 11 July 1996 in the case Concerning Application of the Convention on the prevention and Punishment of the crime of Genocide (Bosnia and Herzegovina v. Yugoslavia), Preliminary Objections* (Yugoslavia v. Bosnia and Herzegovina), International Court of Justice, judgment of 3 February 2003.

73   And indeed, the European Court of Justice has given this a rather broad interpretation, *e.g.*, in Case 22/70, *Commission v. Council (ERTA)*, [1971] ECR 263 (finding the proceedings of a Council meeting to be reviewable). See more generally Jan Klabbers, "Informal Instruments Before the European Court of Justice", 31 *Common Market Law Review* (1994) 997-1023.

74   This is confirmed by the Court's anti-trust case-law, which makes a decisive distinction between binding communications and non-binding ones. The seminal case is Case 60/81, *IBM v. Commission*, [1981] ECR 2639.

75   Curiously perhaps given the general trend towards judicialization that is sometimes observed, in 1996 the General Assembly terminated the possibility for UNAT to ask for an advisory opinion.

C. Judicial Review and Public Law

Judicial review is inevitably bound up with public authorities exercising public authority. Too argue that public international law is by definition public law (as many law schools do by implication, incorporating international lawyers in their departments of public law) is too facile perhaps: much of public international law is, the adjective "public" notwithstanding, more in the nature of private law – albeit between public actors -, based as much of it is on bilateral or bilateralized relations (or bipolar, as Bleckmann helpfully calls them[76]), where often reciprocity between singular actors is considered to be an important element.[77] This applies most obviously to many bilateral treaties, but also to quite a few multilateral treaties which even if multilateral in form, tend to predominantly create bilateral relations (a multilateral extradition treaty is a good example, as it will normally govern relations between dyads of states: the requesting and requested states).[78]

This holds true even with respect to some of the more important international organizations, such as the WTO. The three largest trading blocs view the WTO not as some public legislator for international trade, but as essentially an organization which happens to manage bundles of bilateral relations. While on the one hand a notion such as the Most-Favoured-Nation obligation (which demands that concessions to one trading partner should be extended to all[79]) aims to create something of a public law backdrop, developments such as the emergence of regional trading arrangements (which de-activate MFN treatment), or the refusal of the US, the EU and Japan to have WTO be self-executing within their domestic legal orders, can be traced back to considerations of reciprocity and bilateralism.[80]

Nonetheless, it would also seem clear that international law contains a growing body which is more in the nature of public law; indeed, the typical example would be precisely the sort of example which causes the call for judicial review to

---

76   See Albert Bleckmann, "Zur Wandlung der Strukturen der Völkerrechtsverträge", 34 *Archiv des Völkerrechts* (1996) 218-236.

77   See on reciprocity also Lon L. Fuller, "The Forms and Limits of Adjudication", 92 *Harvard Law Review* (1978) 353-409.

78   This is of course to some extent in the eye of the beholder, in that one could argue, from a different perspective, that groups of bilateral undertakings end up being multilateral: bilateral extradition relations, to stick to the example, end up creating a multilateral regime, albeit organized in bilateral fashion. The point is not to enter into such debates; the point, quite simply, is not to overemphasize the public law nature of public international law. As Craven once suggested, international law's methodology begins and ends with individual states, resulting in "a palpable lack of epistemic access to collective interests". See Matthew Craven, "Legal Differentiation and the Concept of the Human Rights Treaty in International Law", 11 *European Journal of International Law* (2000) 489-519, at 506 (inverted commas omitted).

79   See Article I GATT.

80   For an overview of the discussion, see Jan Klabbers, "International Law in Community Law: The Law and Politics of Direct Effect", 21 *Yearbook of European Law* (2002), 263-298.

begin with: the acts of organs of international organizations, such as the Security Council. Put differently, if all international legal relations would still be bipolar, the call for judicial review would have been unlikely to arise: judicial review, after all, does not, in the normal sense of the term, apply to contractual disputes or tort cases.[81]

While it would be overstating the case to say that acts of international organizations and their organs are pure public law acts (in the sense that, for example, Security Council acts often contain traces of bargaining between the permanent Five: support me on this resolution, and I will support you on yours, or veto mine and surely I will veto yours), nonetheless such decisions do aspire to exercise some form of public authority and that, it would seem, might be more relevant than whether they are based on reciprocal bargaining or on other considerations.

Still, this too is a highly charged political debate: to find traces of public law in international law would imply that no single state can afford to ignore the system altogether or limit itself to purely consensual obligations. To claim that there is an international public law is to claim the existence of authority higher than the mightiest state; and while such may have limited practical effects, the symbolic force of such a claim should not be underestimated.[82]

EC law too is based on the assumption that review concerns public acts: article 230 TEC allows an action of annulment against public acts by the institutions, but does not provide the Court with jurisdiction in cases involving acts of the member states, precisely because those would not, in the framework of the EC, qualify as public EC acts.[83]

D. *Marginal Review*

Judicial review is perhaps most acceptable as "marginal review", so to speak (the Dutch speak of "*marginale toetsing*"), or low-level scrutiny, as some would have it.[84] The basic idea behind judicial review would be not to test the wisdom behind a certain policy, but rather to test whether that policy is applied in accordance with certain requirements. As a result, judicial review will, almost inevitably, be procedural in nature.

Several sorts of disputes, it would seem, are generally unsuitable for adjudication in any serious form (that is, anything involving more than the throwing

---

81   It may of course arise incidentally in such disputes, but that is a different matter altogether.

82   See generally Murray Edelman, *The Symbolic Uses of Politics* (Urbana Ill: University of Illinois Press, 1964).

83   That is not to say that no legal action can be taken against member state acts; it is just to say that those do not come under the heading of judicial review by the Community courts.

84   This is the term used by Mark Tushnet, "Judicial Review of Legislation", in Peter Cane & Mark Tushnet (eds.), *The Oxford Handbook of Legal Studies* (Oxford: Oxford University Press, 2003) 164-182, at 175.

of dice). Most predominantly, as Lon Fuller has pointed out, this would apply to what he referred to as "polycentric disputes": disputes with, literally, many centers, where a decision on a dispute between A and B might end up affecting C, D, E and F as well. The standard example would be the composition of a football team:[85] a decision to cast A as the centre forward might only make sense if B plays in midfield to provide A with clever passes, but if B is to play in midfield, he needs F on his side to do defensive duties. Et cetera; the permutations are too complicated, so Fuller argues, to be solvable by means of adjudication.[86]

Another example offered by Fuller might be more immediately recognizable:

> In allocating $100 million for scientific research it is never a case of Project A v. Project B, but rather of project A v. Project B v. Project C v. project D.... bearing in mind that Project Q may be an alternative to Project B, while Project M supplements it, and that project R may seek the same objective as Project C by a cheaper method, though one less certain to succeed, etc.[87]

It follows (although Fuller does not spell it out) that to the extent that the above example could be submitted to judicial review, it could hardly be substantive review: a court, one may assume, would not be in a position to assess the respective skills and potential for playing together of a number of football players, or to weigh the relative merits of the various project proposals, and none of the players can have a legal right to be fielded, in much the same way as none of the project proposals can have a legal right to be awarded research funds. At best, then, it could be submitted to review on the procedural aspects; review would be limited (and would have to be limited) to procedural aspects, not to substance.[88]

It is perhaps no coincidence, as Fuller suggests, that attempts to have the courts solve polycentric disputes are most prevalent in administrative law, that is, precisely in the field where judicial review would be most appropriate.[89] This, then, creates a paradoxical situation: judicial review is mostly conceivable in disputes of an administrative nature, yet such disputes may often be too polycentric to be adjudicated. The case of the football team's composition would best be addressed by a team manager; the case of competing research proposals by a committee of experts, presumably. The best one may hope for, as far as judicial review is concerned, is procedural review: the team manager systematically ignoring a would-be centre

---

85   Americans should think of soccer here.

86   It is this sort of conception which may help explain the ICJ's judgment in the *Case Concerning East Timor* (Portugal v. Australia), [1995] *ICJ Reports* 89.

87   See Fuller, Forms and Limits, note 77 above, at 401.

88   Which is not to say that substance plays no role whatsoever: the procedural standards will themselves contain conceptions of substance. Equal treatment, *e.g.*, presupposes a conception of equality, but this conception of equality itself would not be up for review. For an extensive and sophisticated discussion, see Allan, note 25 above.

89   See Fuller, Forms and Limits, note 77 above, at 400.

forward would be vulnerable to criticism, not for not fielding the player, but for not taking him seriously.

This is, odd as it may seem, something of a jurisprudential issue in human rights law as well. Far from being rights in the traditional sense of the term (as, say, contractual rights are rights[90]), human rights typically, if not invariably perhaps, turn on procedural elements. Much of the case-law of the European Court of Human Rights dealing with so-called positive obligations takes on this form:[91] the right to life, *e.g.*, enshrined in Article 2 of the European Convention on Human Rights, can not literally be guaranteed, but what the states parties do their utmost to prevent is unnecessary deaths,[92] and what they should guarantee is that suspicious deaths are properly investigated (there is, in other words, a positive obligation to investigate which can be derived from the right to life);[93] failure to investigate would result in a violation of the right to life. At least in part, this can be explained by a desire to make the rights at issue "practical and effective":[94] this suggests that the substantive core of rights can only come to life by being surrounded by procedural notions, or perhaps consists exclusively of bundles of procedural rights. It follows, that much of the review engaged in by the Strasbourg court is, indeed, marginal review: the Court does not place itself in the position of the domestic agency or court whose acts are complained of; instead, it reviews whether the procedural issues have been properly taken into account.[95]

The most prominent manifestation is the development of the doctrine of the margin of appreciation: the Court accepts the idea that the state parties are generally better placed to decide whether a certain practice offends widely held moral notions or not; the Court will not take the place of the state party.[96] Likewise, as the Court will not re-conduct domestic legal proceedings claiming violations of the right to a fair trial, much of the Court's case-law on this issue, again, tends to focus on elements of procedure. Or, put differently, the right to a fair trial is a procedural

---

90   The analogy would seem too facile to be of much use, although it is occasionally invoked. See, *e.g.*, Harold Hongju Koh, "Transnational Public Law Litigation", 100 *Yale Law Journal* (1991) 2347-2403.

91   And such positive obligations form the answer of international human rights law, so far at any rate, to claims that human rights should also apply between individuals. See generally Andrew Clapham, *Human Rights in the Private Sphere* (Oxford: Oxford University Press, 1993).

92   See, *e.g.*, *McCann & others* v. *United Kingdom*, 21 *European Human Rights Reports* (1996) 97.

93   See, *e.g.*, *Kaya* v. *Turkey*, 28 *European Human Rights Reports* (1998) 1.

94   See generally Alastair Mowbray, *The Development of Positive Obligations under the European Convention on Human Rights by the European Court of Human Rights* (Oxford: Hart, 2004).

95   See generally Clare Ovey & Robin C.A. White, *Jacobs & White European Convention on Human Rights* (Oxford: Oxford University Press, 2002, 3d edn).

96   The leading case is *Handyside* v. *United Kingdom*, 1 *European Human Rights Reports* (1979-80) 737.

right, almost (if not completely perhaps, since the very notion of fairness demands some substantive contents) by definition: the right to have trials proceed fairly.[97]

Less surprisingly perhaps, recent developments with regard to economic and social rights, often considered to be less obviously enforceable than civil and political rights,[98] would tend to confirm this picture. The celebrated *Grootboom* decision of South Africa's Constitutional Court,[99] found the right of access to adequate housing (as contained in Article 26 of the South African Constitution) to consist of, amongst other things, a duty on authorities to develop housing programmes which would encompass the position of those in desperate need of housing;[100] more generally, it conceptualized the right of access to adequate housing consistently as a set of procedural norms.

Likewise, in one of its more recent general comments, the Committee on Economic, Social and Cultural Rights considered the core obligations in relation to the right of water to consist not just of a right of access to water, but to include also non-discrimination, equitable distribution, the adoption of a water strategy and plan of action, personal security on the way to water, monitoring of the realization of the right, low-cost targeted water programmes, and measures related to diseases. In short, much (though perhaps not all) of the right to water consists of procedural notions; the substance of the right is given teeth by insisting on procedural elements.[101]

EC law too recognizes that much administrative review is, indeed, review of procedural niceties. While empirical research may be hard to come by, it would seem that many of the cases involving article 230 TEC can be classified as procedural cases. Article 230 TEC lists four grounds for annulment, of which three would be classified by most as being not overly substantive. Actions brought on grounds of lack of competence, infringement of an essential procedural requirement, and abuse of powers, are essentially actions not going into the substance of EC law.

It is, hypothetically at any rate, different with the remaining ground for annulment: infringement of the EC Treaty or of any rule of law relating to its application.

---

97   As good an example as any is *Benthem* v. *the Netherlands*, 8 *European Human Rights Reports* (1986) 1. Mr Benthem had applied for a license to operate a small industry; his application was denied, and in the end, the Court found that the Dutch proceedings had been unfair. This did not result in Mr Benthem getting his license, after all; instead, it resulted in the Dutch law on administrative proceedings being amended. Whatever substance was discussed related to the fairness of proceedings, not to the fairness of him receiving or not receiving a license.

98   See, *e.g.*, E.W. Vierdag, "The Legal Nature of the Rights Granted by the Covenant on Economic, Social and Cultural Rights", 9 *Netherlands Yearbook of International Law* (1978) 69-105.

99   Case CCT 11/00, *Republic of South Africa and others* v. *Irene Grootboom and others*, decided on 4 May 2000. For commentary, see, *e.g.*, Cass Sunstein, *Designing Democracy: What Constitutions Do* (Oxford: Oxford University Press, 2001), ch 10.

100   *Grootboom*, note 99 above, para. 69.

101   See UN Doc. E/C.12/2002/11, of 20 January 2003, para. 37.

This is, potentially, a broad category – a group of Dutch authors summarize is, conveniently, as "infringement of the law", comprising notions such as proportionality[102] – and the Court has indeed interpreted this to encompass also public international law, including customary international law.[103] Yet, in practice, it would seem that here too, many cases revolve around more or less procedural issues. Put differently, it is not all that often the case that EC legislation is being annulled because it directly violates a substantive rule; instead, it may do so by means of violating a principle of proportionality, or a principle of legitimate expectations, or a principle of legal certainty.[104] In short, the grounds for review tend to be procedural rather than substantive. Typically, what the Court will test is whether the authorities, in applying the substantive rule, have taken an intermediary principle such as proportionality into account, and such testing, while not strictly procedural, is not best classified as strictly substantive either.

There is, of course, a certain logic to this limited review. Lest judicial review becomes the continuation of politics by other means (and this danger always looms largely), what ought to be reviewed is not the wisdom of a policy itself, but its application. The temptation is always great to overextend the use of judicial review, and have the courts take the place of professional politicians (always assuming that judges are not). As Koopmans puts it, "[l]itigation is becoming a form of protest against political decisions."[105] And, it might be added, litigation is also being used as a mode to overcome political stalemates.[106] The problem with this, of course, is that judicial review ceases to be judicial review, and becomes political review, a way to undo political decisions by using the courts, with the unhappy result that both the integrity of the courts and of the political process are undermined. Its possible justification (something to the effect that courts engage in politics at any rate, and might as well be candid about it), while not without rhetorical force, tends to be self-defeating: if courts are political agencies anyway, there is no point in insisting on review being somehow "judicial". Or, differently put, there is no particular rea-

---

102   See J.H. Jans, R. de Lange, S. Prechal & R.J.G.M. Widdershoven, *Inleiding tot het Europees bestuursrecht* (Nijmegen: Ars Aequi, 1999), at 269. It covers, in addition to proportionality, notions such as legal certainty, good faith, *et cetera*. All of these, it would seem, are by themselves non-substantive: proportionality, *e.g.*, does not in itself indicate whether, say, trade restrictions are permitted. It merely specifies that when such restrictions are introduced, they must be introduced proportionally, which may often mean that no less-intrusive alternatives are available, or that their effects do not exceed the goal for which they are introduced.

103   See, e.g., case 181/73, *Haegeman* v. *Belgium*, [1974] ECR 449.

104   The leading study is Takis Tridimas, *The General Principles of EC Law* (Oxford: Oxford University Press, 1999).

105   See Koopmans, note 8 above, at 262.

106   The leading example in international law might be the *Nuclear Weapons* opinion: see *Legality of the Threat or Use of Nuclear Weapons*, advisory opinion, [1996] *ICJ Reports* 226. For a discussion, see Martti Koskenniemi, "Faith, Identity, and the Killing of the Innocent: International Lawyers and Nuclear Weapons", 10 *Leiden Journal of International Law* (1997) 137-162.

son why precisely courts would be endowed with the task of reconsidering political decisions. If political decisions need to be second-guessed to begin with, it would seem more obvious to leave this second-guessing to representative political bodies.

E.   Who Can Instigate Judicial Review?

At present, contentious proceedings can only be brought before the ICJ by states against other states; Article 34 of the ICJ Statute permits of no other conclusion. This is often deplored, with many advocating that, for instance, international organizations ought to be given standing before the ICJ.

Whatever the merits of that particular proposition, there is some room for the thought of leaving the possibilities for review limited. Apart from considerations of judicial economy (the ICJ, most likely, would lack the infrastructure to deal with many more cases than it does at present[107]), there is the additional risk that access to tribunals, unless completely open, tends to include some and exclude others. At the very least, there ought to be a clearly established basis as to why some would be excluded whereas others are not.

On a deeper level, limited access serves to underline the limited functions of judicial review: broad access for groups not themselves affected (or whose members are not themselves affected) by the measure at hand might tend to turn litigation into a political spectacle. Public interest litigation, with standing granted on ideological grounds alone, would easily transform litigation into a political meeting or a planning activity.[108]

The EC system perhaps can serve as something of a model (without this suggesting full support for the EC position). Article 230 TEC, in effect, creates three classes of complainants. The first is the so-called privileged class, consisting of the member states, the Council (the plenary organ of the EC), the Commission and, since the Nice Treaty, the European Parliament as well. These can bring complaints on a general basis, and it is not uncommon for a member state that found itself outvoted during the decision-making process to later contest the validity of the measure.[109] Likewise, a member might complain in order to safeguard its prerogatives (or those of the Council, in which all member states are represented) against the Commission.[110]

---

107   It might not be overly realistic to envisage a court other than the ICJ to be engaged with judicial review within the UN system; there are some attractions though to thinking of something like, *e.g.*, the French Conseil Constitutionnel.

108   See further Allan, note 25 above, at 194-199.

109   See, *e.g.*, *Germany* v. *European Parliament and Council (Tobacco Advertising)*, [2000] ECR I-8419.

110   See, *e.g.*, case C-327/91, *France* v. *Commission*, [1994] ECR I-3641 (where France claimed that the Commission lacked the competence to conclude international agreements. The Court agreed.)

A second class of applicants under Article 230 consists of the European Central Bank and the Court of Auditors. Their standing is limited to those cases where their own prerogatives are at issue, and is the result of a hard-fought battle instigated by the European Parliament in the 1980s. The EP was somewhat miffed about the circumstance that it could not apply for judicial review even in cases where its own position was at stake. While the Court was, at first, reluctant to agree, pointing out that several other mechanisms existed to protect the EP's position,[111] in 1990 it finally agreed with the EP's position, albeit in a limited way.[112] It held that the lack of power on the part of the EP to initiate an action under article 230 TEC might "constitute a procedural gap", which was to be closed. However, it ought to be closed in light of the institutional balance created by the treaties[113], and thus would be admissible "provided that the action seeks only to safeguard its [the EP's – JK] prerogatives and that it is founded only on submissions alleging their infringement."[114] Hence, while the EP itself has been "promoted" and joined the privileged class, the case-law would continue to apply to the European Central Bank and the Court of Auditors.

Finally, article 230 recognizes a third (some would say underprivileged) class of complainants, consisting of natural and legal persons. These can complain only about administrative acts (so-called decisions; the other classes can also attack regulations or directives, which are instruments of a more legislative nature[115]) which are addressed to them or, if not literally addressed, which nonetheless are "of direct and individual concern" to the applicant. A serious body of case-law has evolved over the years concerning this phrase, the gist of which is that the Court of Justice adopts a restrictive attitude.[116] A recent opening appearing in the case-law of the Court of First Instance (which argued that the narrow interpretation of article 230 TEC on standing of individuals would be difficult to reconcile with the right of access to courts, and thus advocated a broader interpretation[117]) was rapidly closed by the Court itself.[118]

Public interest litigation too has, hitherto, been rejected by the ECJ, with the leading recent illustration being the *Greenpeace* case.[119] Here, Greenpeace Inter-

---

111   Case 302/87, *European Parliament* v. *Council (Comitology)*, [1988] ECR 5615.

112   Case 70/88, *European Parliament* v. *Council (Chernobyl)*, [1990] ECR I-2041.

113   *Ibid.*, para. 26.

114   *Ibid.*, para. 27.

115   What is decisive here though is the contents of the measure: the case-law makes clear that a regulation can be a bundle of decisions in disguise, in which case applicant may have standing if he can show direct and individual concern. See, *e.g.*, case 6/68, *Zuckerfabrik Watenstedt* v. *Council*, [1968] ECR 409.

116   The classic case is case 25/62, *Plaumann & Co.* v. *Commission*, [1963] ECR 95.

117   See case T-177/01, *Jégo-Quéré & Cie SA* v. *Commission*, Judgment of 3 May 2002.

118   See Case C-263/02 P, *Commission* v. *Jégo-Quéré & Cie SA*, judgment of 1 April 2004, not yet reported. Part of the justification is that access to justice remains possible through other procedures, including through the courts of the member states.

119   Case C-321/95 P, *Stichting Greenpeace Council (Greenpeace International) and others* v. *Commission*, [1998] ECR I-1651.

national, a non-governmental organization devoted to environmental protection, acted as applicant claiming that the decision to finance, with Community funds, two power stations in the Canary Islands was made without the compulsory environmental impact assessment having taken place. Greenpeace's action was dismissed for lack of standing by the Court of First Instance, a decision affirmed on appeal by the ECJ. The position upheld by both tribunals is "that an association formed for the protection of the collective interests of a category of persons could not be considered to be directly and individually concerned ... by a measure affecting the general interests of that category."[120] The message will be clear: the integrity of the judicial review mechanism is protected by limiting access, with public interest litigation by and large being the preserve of the privileged class of complainants.[121]

F.   The Consequences of Review

There are three main consequences to be attached to judicial review: a court may have either the power to declare the contested measure invalid (in whole or in part), or it may have the more limited power to declare it inapplicable to the case at hand or, even softer, it may have the power to observe that the contested measure is not in conformity with the law against which it is tested, yet be powerless to do more than this. This latter option is exemplified by the United Kingdom's Human Rights Act, which leaves the power to actually repeal the contested measure to Parliament and so aims to reconcile parliamentary sovereignty with the rule of law.[122]

The power to invalidate is a rather strong power, and thus, arguably, should be based on an explicit grant to that effect. After all, it would allow a court the possibility to change the law, something usually (under democratic rule of law, at any rate) reserved for elected and accountable officials. Absent a specific grant to invalidate measures, perhaps a court's possibilities should be limited to declaring the contested measure inapplicable in the case at hand. Otherwise, the court would be certain to become a political player, with the tag "judicial" becoming increasingly less applicable.

This resonates well with international law generally. International courts and tribunals, generally speaking, do not have the power to invalidate any legal rules: they may declare, *e.g.*, that domestic law is incompatible with international law, but it is usually for domestic authorities to remedy the situation, for instance by repealing a law held to violate international law.

More specifically, the notion of legal validity is not automatic in international law. The Vienna Convention on the Law of Treaties envisaged an entire mechanism

---

120 *Ibid.*, para. 14.

121 For it is not excluded that a member state takes up a case out of altruistic or public interest considerations.

122 A very useful collection of essays on the Human Rights Act generally is Tom Campbell, K.D. Ewing & Adam Tomkins (eds.), *Sceptical Essays on Human Rights* (Oxford: Oxford University Press, 2001).

to decide on the possible invalidity of treaties, including treaties which would violate *jus cogens* norms. While it can hardly be plausibly argued that the establishment of the machinery envisaged, despite its non-functioning nature, pre-empts other courts from declaring treaties invalid, nonetheless it suggests that the conclusion of invalidity should not lightly be drawn, and should be reached only with some guarantees of fair and equal treatment along the way.

The consequence of inapplicability would also seem to be the major result under Article 103 UN Charter. The article itself merely provides that in case of conflicting obligations under the Charter and under other treaties, the obligations under the Charter shall prevail; it would seem that this is akin to a grant to leave contested measures inapplicable, rather than a grant to invalidate them. The ICJ also seemed to suggest as much in its 1992 *Lockerbie* opinion, merely giving preference to UN sanctions over obligations arising under other agreements.

Still, not too much ought to be read into the *Lockerbie* case and Article 103 UN. One reason for reticence is that it concerned a request for provisional measures: to invalidate anything at all would have been inappropriate at that stage. More importantly, though, the typical article 103 scenario is a short-term scenario: obligations arising out of the Charter, such as sanctions, tend to be temporary in design (if not always in practice); as a result, a conflict with obligations under other agreements will also, by definition, be a temporary conflict only. In those circumstances, declaring those other obligations invalid is not a wise option.

The EC Court does have the power to invalidate measures, in whole or in part, and does use this power. It is here, however, that the distinction between the EC and other international organizations assumes its most prominent features: the EC does have a legislature, albeit one of varying compositions[123] and characterized, some would say, by a democratic deficit. In other words: the institutional machinery is in place to provide a declaration of invalidity with some follow-up: a measure annulled due to a defect may be introduced later with the defect cured.[124]

The Court is also empowered to declare measures invalid in part (something which works better when the invalidity results from a substantive defect; if the defect is procedural, it is more likely to affect the entire measure), or to limit the temporal scope of invalidity, at least when it concerns regulations.

5.   By Way of Conclusion

Judicial review will inevitably sit uncomfortably between the twin demands of politics and law; it could hardly be otherwise. The above has been an outline of a sketch of a few possible characteristics judicial review could possibly take on in the UN system, ever mindful of the difficulties of navigating between law and politics. An

---

123   Depending on the issue, the European Parliament either plays a co-legislative role, or an advisory role, or even, in rare circumstances, no formal role at all. The latter option applies in particular to the conclusion of some agreements.

124   Article 233 TEC obliges the institutions whose acts have been declared void to "take the necessary measures to comply with the judgment of the Court of Justice".

overly politicized version of judicial review tends to undermine the rule of law, and ends up substituting one "rule of man" by another. Too legalistic a conception, however, may result in a political community of lawyers, where political debate is either precluded or takes the form of legal argument alone – neither would seem to be terribly desirable.

The resulting straddling of the law-politics dichotomy is bound to be considered less than satisfactory, but that in itself is only evidence of the ever-present law-politics dichotomy: it is well-nigh impossible to argue about judicial review on legal grounds alone. Indeed, as the present paper hopes to have indicated, taking a stand on issues related to judicial review, be it the identity of complainants, or the sort of measures to be reviewed, or the consequences to be attached to findings of illegality, will always have to come to terms with the law-politics dichotomy.[125]

For some, the notions sketched above may be too conservative; international law, so the argument could go, would require bolder, more daring, visions. The rule of law in international affairs would imply, so the argument might continue, ruthless adherence to legal concerns, a broad concept of standing, and a wide notion of the sort of thing to be reviewed. To this, the reply would be that the rule of law is, despite what its name suggests, also the rule of man; to be overly generous with judicial review would tend to undermine the very idea of judicial review.

Others though, more sensitive perhaps to political configurations, might find the above rather too progressive: the rule of law, so the argument could go, is after all nothing but the rule of man, and man's quest for power cannot be tamed by putting legal institutions in place. Developing judicial review would at best be pointless, at worst counterproductive, in that disregard of judicial pronounciations might further damage whatever credibility international law has to begin with.

In the end, it is perhaps not so much a matter of either/or, but rather of a different style of politics. As Ivor Jennings remarked a long time ago, what matters is not so much the form of government, but the style of government:[126] if leaders and authorities could be trusted to act with fairness, reasonableness, moderation and wisdom, then there would be fairly little room for judicial review except perhaps, as Black once put it, as the "ritual symbolization of a great idea".[127] But trust in authorities, alas, cannot be created by institutions alone.

---

125   And then there is the more general, overtly political point that judicial review may, in the words of Duncan Kennedy, serve "the interest of the intelligentsia as a whole in the stability of the regime, as well as the interest shared by each particular intelligentsia and its constituency in 'freedom from' the other side's majoritarian excesses." See Kennedy, note 1 above, at 234.

126   See W. Ivor Jennings, *The Law and the Constitution* (London: University of London Press, 1943, 3d edn.), at xxxi, contrasting the psychology of government with the forms of government.

127   See Black, note 29 above, at 32.

31. The Meaning of International Constitutional Law

Bardo Fassbender

1. Two Faces of a Problem: Sovereignty and Constitutionalism in International Law

At the end of an article about the concept of sovereignty in international law,[1] I quoted Hans Kelsen and Wolfgang Friedmann. In spite of all their differences, both scholars were strong supporters of an international constitutional order. In the late 1920s, Kelsen referred to his time as a transitional period in the history of international law, and saw this character reflected in the "contradictions of an international legal theory which in an almost tragic conflict aspires to the height of a universal legal community erected above the individual states but, at the same time, remains a captive of the sphere of power of the sovereign state."[2] Almost forty years later, Wolfgang Friedmann arrived at a very similar conclusion when he said: "In terms of objectives, powers, legal structure and scope, the present state of international organisation presents an extremely complex picture. It reflects the state of a society that is both desperately clinging to the legal and political symbols of national sovereignty and being pushed towards the pursuit of common needs and goals that can be achieved only by a steadily intensifying degree of international organisation."[3] What Kelsen described as a shortcoming of legal science – its inability to climb over the mental walls of the sovereign state – Friedmann extended to the state of the international order as such.

The contradictions Kelsen spoke of and the dilemma outlined by Friedmann are also, I think, characteristic features of this volume's theme – issues and perspectives of world constitutionalism. Sovereignty, which the two authors ad-

---

1   See Bardo Fassbender, "Sovereignty and Constitutionalism in International Law", in Neil Walker (ed.), *Sovereignty in Transition* (2003) 115, at 142.

2   See Hans Kelsen, *Das Problem der Souveränität und die Theorie des Völkerrechts. Beitrag zu einer Reinen Rechtslehre* (2nd ed. 1928), at 320.

3   See Wolfgang Friedmann, *The Changing Structure of International Law* (1964), at 293 *et seq.*

Ronald St. John Macdonald & Douglas M. Johnston (eds.), Towards World Constitutionalism, *pp. 837-851.*
© *2005 Koninklijke Brill NV. Printed in The Netherlands. ISBN 90 04 14612 1.*

dressed, and constitutionalism in international law are closely related issues. It was, in fact, Friedmann who first produced a sketch of international constitutional law as a "new field of international law."[4] To speak, in our time, about the international constitutional order means approaching the same subject from the opposite side. But what, exactly, is that subject? In other words: What is, and to which ends do we study, international constitutional law?

That discipline is not to be confused with comparative constitutional law which recently has become the subject of a new journal.[5] Instead, we are searching for a sub-discipline of public international law, namely the constitutional law of the international community which may be influenced by constitutional ideas and practices developed in a national context but stands on its own feet.

2. Constitutional Arguments in International Law

To use the notion of constitution in the context of public international law is today, it seems, much less problematic than it was five or, in any case, ten years ago. In an article published in 1998, I devoted substantial space to showing that there is no compelling reason to reserve the term constitution for the supreme law of a (sovereign) state[6] but that, instead, the fundamental legal order of any autonomous community or body politic can be addressed as a constitution.[7] With the words of Philip Allott, a scholar who has profoundly reflected on the meaning of constitutionalism in national societies and in the international society, "[a] constitution is a structure-system which is shared by all societies."[8] This understanding entails a certain demystification of the institution of the (etatist) constitution and, with it, of the "sovereign state" as the former constitutional monopolist.[9]

---

4   *Ibid.* at 152-159.

5   See *I•CON (Int'l J. Const'l L.)*, founded in 2003.

6   For a thoughtful analysis of the relationship of state and constitution, which reflects much of the great tradition of the German *Staatslehre* of the nineteenth and twentieth centuries, see Josef Isensee, "Staat und Verfassung", in *Idem* & Paul Kirchhof (eds.), 2 *Handbuch des Staatsrechts der Bundesrepublik Deutschland* (3rd ed. 2004), 3.

7   See Bardo Fassbender, "The United Nations Charter as Constitution of the International Community", 36 *Col. J. Transnat'l L.* (1998) 529, at 532-38, 555-61.

8   See Philip Allott, *Eunomia: New Order for a New World* (1990), at 164. See also *Idem*, "The Concept of International Law", in Michael Byers (ed.), *The Role of Law in International Politics: Essays in International Relations and International Law* (2000), at 72-76.

9   But see Dieter Grimm, "Ursprung und Wandel der Verfassung", in Isensee & Kirchhof (eds.), 1 *Handbuch des Staatsrechts der Bundesrepublik Deutschland* (3rd ed. 2003), 3, at 36 *et seq.* (arguing that the international order is characterized by a plurality of unconnected institutions and legal sources, and that there is so far, on the international level, no entity which could be constitutionalized ("*kein konstitutionsfähiger Gegenstand*")), and Ulrich Haltern, "Internationales Verfassungsrecht?", 128 *Archiv des öffentlichen Rechts* (2003) 511 (arguing that there is a fundamental difference between the "aesthetic-symbolic meaning" of national law on the one hand, and European and international

It is not entirely clear why in the meantime this transfer of the constitutional idea into the sphere of international law, which had had only few advocates, has become largely uncontroversial – many differences of opinion about how exactly such transfer should be understood or constructed notwithstanding.[10]

To some extent, the discussion about the future legal order of the European Union has contributed to that result. In the case of the EU, a gradual "constitutionalization" of a treaty-based order has been generally accepted.[11] In the summer of 2003, the European Convention adopted by consensus the "Draft Treaty Establishing a Constitution for Europe"[12] which in an amended version was signed by the Heads of State or Government of the EU member states on October 29, 2004 in Rome as the "Treaty Establishing the Constitution for Europe."[13] If a text is officially called a "constitution", lawyers tend not to contradict. Some of the ideas developed in the context of European Community law were then carried over to the law of other organizations, especially the GATT and WTO.[14] Secondly, it was understood that one can apply the notion of constitution in the realm of universal international law without necessarily being a proponent of a "world state", something which to many is still the epitome of horror. Also, and thirdly, as it happens, some writers jumped onto a wagon which appeared to be increasingly popular, content with

---

law on the other, leading to fundamentally different "imaginations of the political"). For reasons not to be discussed here, German legal culture has produced both the strongest supporters and opponents of the idea of a constitution beyond the nation-state.

10   For a recent review of the literature and a re-evaluation of issues like the traditional dichotomy between international and constitutional law (see Fassbender, *supra* note 7, at 532-538 and 555-561), "constitution" as a contested notion (*ibid.* at 553 *et seq.*) or the use of constitutional language (*ibid.* at 538 *et seq.*), see Thomas Cottier & Maya Hertig, "The Prospects of 21ˢᵗ Century Constitutionalism", 7 *Max Planck UNYB* (2004) 261.

11   Of the extensive literature, I only mention Jörg Gerkrath, *L'émergence d'un droit constitutionnel pour l'Europe* (1997); Ingolf Pernice, "Multilevel Constitutionalism and the Treaty of Amsterdam: European Constitution-Making Revisited", 36 *Common Market Law Review* 703 (1999); Christian Joerges, *Das Recht im Prozess der Konstitutionalisierung Europas* (EUI Working Paper LAW No. 2001/6); Anne Peters, *Elemente einer Theorie der Verfassung Europas* (2001); Neil Walker, "The EU and the WTO: Constitutionalism in a New Key", in G. de Burca and J. Scott (eds.), *The EU and the WTO: Legal and Constitutional Issues* (2001), at 31; *Idem*, "The Idea of Constitutional Pluralism", 65 *Modern Law Review* (2002) 317; *Idem*, "Postnational Constitutionalism and the Problem of Translation", in J.H.H. Weiler & M. Wind (eds.), *European Constitutionalism Beyond the State* (2003), at 27; Bruno de Witte, "The Closest Thing to a Constitutional Conversation in Europe: The Semi-Permanent Treaty Revision Process", in Paul R. Beaumont *et al.* (eds.), *Convergence and Divergence in European Public Law* (2002), at 39.

12   See European Convention Doc. 850/03 of 18 July 2003.

13   For text, see *Official Journal of the EU* 2004/C 310 of 16 Dec. 2004.

14   See, in particular, Ernst-Ulrich Petersmann, *Constitutional Functions and Constitutional Problems of International Economic Law* (1991). For a critical discussion, see Armin von Bogdandy, "Law and Politics in the WTO–Strategies to Cope with a Deficient Relationship", 5 *Max Planck UNYB* (2001) 609, at 653-656.

the general "progressive" ring of the words "constitution" and, especially, "constitutionalization". Or, to put it in a friendlier way: Those writers seized upon a notion which, albeit blurry, still seems to capture at least a great part of the fundamental changes in the international legal order which we all are sensing but cannot easily express in the language of (international) law we have learned.[15]

However, this growing popularity of the use of the constitutional argument in international law has rather increased the terminological confusion. For instance, the different issues of a constitutionalization of the law of a particular intergovernmental organization or international regime on the one hand, and of the existence of a constitution of the international community as such, on the other, are often not sufficiently distinguished.[16] Recent scholarship based on the work of Niklas Luhmann has argued against a "state-centered constitutionalism" (both on a national and an international level) and produced a new notion of "global civil constitutions" meant to express a "constitutionalization of a multiplicity of autonomous subsystems of world society."[17] Such an inflationary use of the word "constitution" entails the danger of its devaluation. Not every increase in legal regulation, and not even every evolution of a hierarchical system of rules, equals a "constitutionalization."[18]

A few years ago, I argued that the constitutional rhetoric I had analyzed was rarely based on a coherent idea of constitutionalism, and that only few writers had made an effort systematically to explain both the reasons and the consequences of the adoption of constitutional ideas.[19] This situation has not changed much since. I identified three schools of thought to which such systematic efforts can be attributed: *first* the school founded by the Viennese jurist Alfred Verdross,[20] who started out from Kelsen's legal theory but later both approached and influenced the mainstream,

---

15   For a systematic review of scholarly efforts to understand the changed international landscape, and for the place of the idea of "constitutionalization" in the current debate, see Armin von Bogdandy, "Demokratie, Globalisierung, Zukunft des Völkerrechts – eine Bestandsaufnahme", 63 *Zeitschrift für ausländisches öffentliches Recht und Völkerrecht* (2003) 853, at 864 *et seq.*, 869 *et seq.*

16   But see Christian Walter, "Constitutionalizing (Inter)national Governance – Possibilities for and Limits to the Development of an International Constitutional Law", 44 *German YB Int'l L.* (2001) 170, at 191 *et seq.*, who understands the statutes and basic rules of such organizations and regimes as *Teilverfassungen*, or "partial constitutions", of the international community.

17   See Gunther Teubner, "Globale Zivilverfassungen: Alternativen zur staatszentrierten Verfassungstheorie", 63 *Zeitschrift für ausländisches öffentliches Recht und Völkerrecht* (2003) 1. See also Andreas Fischer-Lescano, "Die Emergenz der Globalverfassung", *ibid.* at 717.

18   See Grimm, *supra* note 9, at 4 and 7.

19   See Fassbender, *supra* note 7, at 538. For a thoughtful recent re-examination, focusing on the constitutional character of the UN Charter, see Pierre-Marie Dupuy, "L'unité de l'ordre juridique international", Cours général de droit international public, 297 *RdC* (2002) 9, at 215-244, 286 *et seq.*, 303-307.

20   See, in particular, Alfred Verdross, *Die Verfassung der Völkerrechtsgemeinschaft* (1926), and Alfred Verdross & Bruno Simma, *Universelles Völkerrecht: Theorie und Praxis* (3rd

second (and partially influenced by the first) a group of scholars, led by the late judge of the ICJ Hermann Mosler, his successor Bruno Simma and Christian Tomuschat, advocating what I named the "doctrine of international community,"[21] and *thirdly* the New Haven School (or "policy-science approach")[22] with Myres McDougal and Michael Reisman being the most prolific authors for the subject under discussion. Today, in the literature of international law, in particular the European, the second mentioned school, is by far the most influential one of the three. The term "the international community" has become commonplace, but more so in continental Europe than in Great Britain or the United States.[23] (At the founding conference of the European Society of International Law in May 2004, Martti Koskenniemi critically discussed the international community school as an example of the European imagination of an international order modeled on European values and ideas: "We Europeans have one goal in common: International law shall be like we are.")[24]

A fourth approach, championed by Ernst-Ulrich Petersmann, insists on the need for integrating human rights into the law of the United Nations: "As long as international law and the UN Charter focus on state sovereignty without effective protection of human rights and without judicial safeguards against the frequent abuses of government powers and violations of the rule of law, it seems misleading to denote the UN Charter as the 'constitution' of 'the peoples of the United Nations.'"[25] A related critique emphasizes the "democratic deficit", or lack of democratic participation, in international organizations.[26]

---

ed. 1984). See also Bruno Simma, "The Contribution of Alfred Verdross to the Theory of International Law", 6 *EJIL* (1995) 33.

21   See, in particular, Hermann Mosler, "The International Society as a Legal Community", 140 *RdC* (1974, IV) 1, revised version published as *The International Society as a Legal Community* (1980); Christian Tomuschat, "Obligations Arising for States Without or Against Their Will", 241 *RdC* (1993, IV) 195; *Idem*, "Die internationale Gemeinschaft", 33 *Archiv des Völkerrechts* (1995) 1; Bruno Simma, "From Bilateralism to Community Interest in International Law", 250 *RdC* (1994-VI) 217.

22   See, in particular, Myres S. McDougal, Harold D. Lasswell and W. Michael Reisman, "The World Constitutive Process of Authoritative Decision", in Myres S. McDougal & W. Michael Reisman, *International Law Essays: A Supplement to International Law in Contemporary Perspective* (1981) 191.

23   For respective writings see, in particular, Christian Tomuschat, "Die internationale Gemeinschaft", 33 *Archiv des Völkerrechts* (1995) 1, Daniel Thürer, "Recht der internationalen Gemeinschaft und Wandel der Staatlichkeit", in *Idem et al.* (eds.), *Verfassungsrecht der Schweiz–Droit constitutionnel suisse* (2001) 37, and Andreas L. Paulus, *Die internationale Gemeinschaft im Völkerrecht* (2001).

24   See Martti Koskenniemi, "International Law in Europe–Between Tradition and Renewal", Keynote Address at the ESIL Inaugural Conference, 14 May 2004.

25   See Ernst-Ulrich Petersmann, "Constitutionalism, International Law and We the Peoples of the United Nations", in Hans-Joachim Cremer *et al.* (eds.), *Tradition und Weltoffenheit des Rechts: Festschrift für Helmut Steinberger* (2002) 291, at 303.

26   See Hauke Brunkhorst, "Globalizing Democracy without a State", 31 *Millenium-Journal of International Studies* (2002) 675.

Most recently, this array of approaches has been supplemented by an important contribution from political philosophy. Re-examining the Kantian vision of a world republic, Jürgen Habermas has outlined the structure of a "political constitution of a decentralized world society as a multi-level system of governance."[27] Based on a dispassionate analysis of the present global situation, Habermas sees "a conceptual possibility of a political multi-level system which, as a whole, is not a state but nevertheless able to safeguard, without a world government, on a supranational level peace and human rights … and to solve on a transnational level the many practical problems of 'global domestic politics' (*Weltinnenpolitik*)."[28] He describes a "post-national constellation" of international affairs as supportive of a constitutionalization of public international law[29] and agrees with this writer that in that process the UN Charter is of central importance.[30]

3. Different Constitutions: Fundamental Rules, Rules Not Based on State Consent, *Jus Cogens*

In what seems to be the book that established the notion of constitution in international law, Alfred Verdross in 1926 used the word to describe "those norms which deal with the structure and subdivision of, and the distribution of spheres of jurisdiction in, a community."[31] Accordingly, Verdross held that the constitution of the international legal community was composed of the fundamental rules and principles of international law determining its sources, subjects and application, and the jurisdiction allocated by that law to the individual states. Similarly, Christian Tomuschat said much later, in 1993: "Together with the rules on discharge of the executive and the judicial functions, the rules on law-making form the constitution of any system of governance. All these sets of prescriptions can be logically characterized as meta-rules, rules on how the bulk of other rules are produced, how they enter into force, how they are implemented and who, in case of differences over their interpretation and application, is empowered to settle an ensuing dispute."[32]

---

27   See Jürgen Habermas, "Hat die Konstitutionalisierung des Völkerrechts noch eine Chance?" [Does the constitutionalization of international law still have a chance?], in *Idem, Der gespaltene Westen* (2004), 113, at 134. This translation and the following are provided by me, B.F.

28   Habermas, *ibid.* at 143. See also *ibid.* at 159 *et seq.* For the possibility of a global constitution without a (global) state, see Fassbender, *supra* note 7, at 558: "Having untied the bond between state and constitution, one may also apply the term in the realm of universal international law without necessarily being a proponent of a 'world state'. An international constitution so understood is not bound to put an end to interstate relations based on international law."

29   See Habermas, *supra* note 27, at 176.

30   See *infra* text accompanying note 56.

31   See Verdross, *Die Verfassung der Völkerrechtsgemeinschaft, supra* note 20, at v.

32   See Tomuschat, "Obligations", *supra* note 21, at 216. See also Allott, "The Concept of International Law", *supra* note 8, at 75 *et seq.*: "International constitutional law is what

Clearly, this definition was influenced by H.L.A. Hart's distinction between "primary" and "secondary" rules, the latter being understood as "rules about rules."[33]

In that perspective, international constitutional law embodies rules of international law distinguished by their fundamental character. Those rules are either formal in nature (like the rules defining the subjects and sources of international law), or substantive (like the principle of sovereign equality of states, the principle of self-determination of peoples, or the ban on the use of force).[34] The exact delimitation of a constitutional law so perceived varies from author to author. More or less, the respective rules belong to what, in analogy to the structure of civil codes like the German enacted in 1896, we could call the "general part" of international law. They address issues pertinent to the "foundation of the law of nations", as the first chapter of the introduction to Oppenheim-Lauterpacht's treatise was entitled,[35] as opposed to specific issues of, for instance, the law of the sea, the law of diplomatic relations, or environmental law.

However, what is the specific value of such a terminology? What does it tell us apart from what we all know by intuition – that some rules of international law are more important than others? Or does it mainly serve an instructive purpose, helping us to distinguish various types of rules and thereby better to understand the substance of the international law of our time?

Some authors do not stop here but emphasize, as the principal feature of international constitutional rules, their non-consensual character. Consider this statement by Professor Tomuschat: "States live, as from their birth, within a legal framework of a limited number of basic rules which determines their basic rights and obligations *with or without their will* …. One may call this framework … the

---

some older writers called the 'necessary' law of nations. It contains the structural legal relations which are intrinsic to the coexistence of all kinds of subordinate societies. It confers on artificial legal persons, including the State-societies, the capacity to act as parties to international legal relations. … The geographical and material distribution of constitutional authority among subordinate legal systems cannot finally be determined by those legal systems themselves, but only by a superordinate legal system, namely international constitutional law. … International constitutional law determines the legal relationship of the subordinate public realms."

33   See H.L.A. Hart, *The Concept of Law* (1961), ch. V: "Law as the Union of Primary and Secondary Rules", at 92: "Thus they [the secondary rules] may all be said to be on a different level from the primary rules [of obligation], for they are all *about* such rules; in the sense that while primary rules are concerned with the actions that individuals must or must not do, these secondary rules are all concerned with the primary rules themselves. They specify the ways in which the primary rules may be conclusively ascertained, introduced, eliminated, varied, and the fact of their violation conclusively determined."

34   The principles in question are also being addressed as "the founding principles of the international legal order". See Christian Tomuschat, "International Law: Ensuring the Survival of Mankind on the Eve of a New Century", 281 *RdC* (1999) 9, at 161 *et seq.*

35   See L. Oppenheim, *International Law*, vol. I: Peace (8th ed. 1955, H. Lauterpacht ed.), at 3.

constitution of the international community."[36] According to that view, the international constitution is the entirety of those basic rules – whether formal or substantive – which every state is bound to observe irrespective of its own will. Those rules shall be distinguished from so-called "contingent" (*i.e.* accidental or nonessential) prescriptions that "in the same way as traffic rules on left-hand or right-hand driving, must be determined for the sake of legal clarity and avoiding disorder."[37] In the case of "contingent" rules, state consent is said to be still the relevant basis of obligation, whereas constitutional prescriptions are determined by community interests which may allow for some degree of majoritarianism.

This concept borders on another which sees the rules of *jus cogens* (or peremptory norms of international law) as the heart of an international constitution – *i.e.*, in the words of the Vienna Convention on the Law of Treaties, rules "accepted and recognized by the international community of States as a whole ... from which no derogation is permitted and which can be modified only by subsequent norm[s] of general international law having the same character."[38] Rules of *jus cogens* are "meta-rules" as described by Tomuschat. They are rules about rules because they control the admissibility and validity of rules states want to insert in a treaty concluded by them. At the same time, *jus cogens* rules are "higher law" (a feature characteristic of national constitutional law in comparison with other, "ordinary" law) because they place certain norms beyond the reach of states when states, bilaterally or multilaterally, exercise their law-making function. In that sense, Antonio Cassese noted that with *jus cogens* "a body of supreme or 'constitutional' principles was created."[39]

It is well known that in recent years the concept of *jus cogens* has gained importance in fields other than the law of treaties, in particular in international criminal law,[40] the law of sovereign immunity of states and state officials,[41] the determination of universal criminal jurisdiction[42] and the law of state responsibility.[43] Switzerland is the first country which has incorporated the concept into its constitutional law. Articles 193 and 194 of the revised Swiss Federal Constitution of 1999 provide that amendments to the Constitution may not violate peremptory norms of international law.

---

36   See Tomuschat, "Obligations", *supra* note 21, at 211 (emphasis added).

37   *Ibid.* at 286. – Similarly, Allott, "The Concept of International Law", *supra* note 8, at 75, distinguished between "international constitutional law" and "international public law".

38   See Vienna Convention on the Law of Treaties, opened for signature May 23, 1969, art. 53.

39   See Antonio Cassese, *International Law* (2001), at 141.

40   *Ibid.* at 141, 144 *et seq.*

41   *Ibid.* at 145. See also Oliver Dörr, "Staatliche Immunität auf dem Rückzug?", 41 *Archiv des Völkerrechts* (2003) 201, at 214 *et seq.*

42   *Ibid.*

43   See arts. 26, 40, 41 and 50 of the ILC Draft Articles on the Responsibility of States for Internationally Wrongful Acts of July 26, 2001, UN Doc. A/CN.4/L.602/Rev.1.

The *jus cogens* perspective of international constitutional law is particularly value-oriented because all the rules presently recognized as *jus cogens* (in the first place, the prohibitions of genocide, aggression, slavery and of trading in human beings, and the right of peoples to self-determination) are substantive in nature and have a human rights dimension, the latter mainly accounting for the use the International Criminal Tribunals for the former Yugoslavia and for Rwanda have made of *jus cogens* arguments.[44] *Jus cogens*, one could say, is a sort of Decalogue of a secularized world, a minimal code of behaviour that can be condensed into one rule: Thou shalt not do other human beings terrible wrongs! While this decalogue is in accordance with contemporary "Western" values, the criticism that it is *only* reflecting such values is unfounded. It was after all the developing countries and the socialist states who advocated the concept of *jus cogens* against the opposition or skepticism of the West.[45]

There is a partial substantive identity of *jus cogens* and obligations *erga omnes* which, as is well known, the ICJ described as obligations "towards the international community as a whole."[46] The category of obligations *erga omnes* was advanced to give states who, according to traditional international law, were not affected by a certain breach of rules, "a legal interest in their protection."[47] This way, pivotal community values should be safeguarded in the absence of effective community organs. The Court gave a number of examples of such obligations *erga omnes*, including the prohibition of acts of aggression and genocide, "the principles and rules concerning the basic rights of the human person, including protection from slavery and discrimination,"[48] and the right of self-determination.[49] A related third concept, "international crimes of states", which once had been supported by the ILC,[50] was

---

44   See Bardo Fassbender, "Der Schutz der Menschenrechte als zentraler Inhalt des völkerrechtlichen Gemeinwohls", 30 *Europäische Grundrechte Zeitschrift* (2003) 1, at 5 *et seq.*

45   See Cassese, *supra* note 39, at 139.

46   See *Barcelona Traction*, 1970 ICJ Reports 3, at 32, paras. 33-34, and *East Timor* (Portugal *v.* Australia), 1995 ICJ Reports 90, at 102, para. 29. See also art. 48, para. 1(b), and art. 54 of the ILC Draft Articles, *supra* note 43.

47   See *Barcelona Traction*, 1970 ICJ Reports at 32, para. 33.

48   *Ibid.*, para. 34.

49   See *East Timor*, *supra* note 46, para. 29.

50   Art. 19(2) of the draft articles on state responsibility (part 1) adopted by the ILC on first reading on July 25, 1980, defined an "international crime" as follows: "An internationally wrongful act which results from the breach by a State of an international obligation so essential for the protection of fundamental interests of the international community that its breach is recognized as a crime by that community as a whole constitutes an international crime." Report of the ILC, UN General Assembly Official Records, Supp. No. 10, UN Doc. A/35/10 (1980); 2 ILC Y.B. (1980), pt. 2, 30, 32. For discussion, see Joseph H.H. Weiler *et al.* (eds), *International Crimes of States: A Critical Analysis of the ILC's Draft Article 19 on State Responsibility* (1989), and André de Hoogh, *Obligations Erga Omnes and International Crimes: A Theoretical Inquiry into the Implementation and Enforcement of the International Responsibility of States* (1996).

eventually abandoned by the Commission when it accepted the proposals of its special rapporteur Professor James Crawford.[51]

What do the different approaches I mentioned have in common? The international constitutionalism supported by them is, one can say, a "progressive" movement – "progressive" in the sense the UN Charter speaks of the "progressive development of international law" (Art. 13(1a)) – which aims at fostering international cooperation by consolidating the substantive legal ties between states as well as the organizational structures built in the past. The idea of a constitution in, or of, international law is summoned as an abbreviation for an increasingly differentiated and hierarchical law, and as a symbol of a (political) unity which eventually shall be realized on a global scale. This implies that he or she who is basically satisfied with the present state of affairs or who insists on preserving the independence of the individual state *vis-à-vis* the international community as much as possible has no reason to refer to the notion of an international constitution.[52]

The relative success of the "international community school" is understandable because this school (unlike, for instance, the New Haven approach) stays within the limits of "mainstream" legal thought. Rooted in positivism and determined not to lose touch with actual state practice, but at the same time cautiously idealistic, it seeks to develop the international legal system towards greater cohesion and effectiveness. This tension causes a certain doctrinal improvisation that cannot satisfy those looking for a clear and convincing theoretical foundation upon which the concept of an international constitution could rest. The contents of a constitutional law as a part of international law remain indistinct, and so do the legal consequences, if there are any, of characterizing a rule as a constitutional rule. In particular, the supremacy of international constitutional law in a hierarchy of norms of international law is only a vague concept. Indeed, for the authors of the "international community school" the symbolic value of the constitutional terminology prevails, "constitution" implying the high degree of interdependence and integration of peoples and states which is regarded as a reality or, at least, a necessity.

Perhaps this indistinct and vague character of what is addressed as international constitutional law is a true representation of the law as it stands. In that case, international constitutional law would essentially belong to an international law of the future, with only certain beginnings and forerunners being discernible in our time.

4.   The UN Charter as Constitution of the International Community

In my own work, I have tried to give the idea of an international constitutional law a clearer and more concrete meaning by closely associating it with the United Nations Charter. Drawing especially on the writings of Verdross, I suggested that the Charter, although it was formally created as a treaty, is characterized by a consti-

---

51   For an analysis of the 2001 draft articles by the special rapporteur, see James Crawford, *The International Law Commission's Articles on State Responsibility: Introduction, Text and Commentaries* (2002).

52   The last sentences have partly been taken from my 1998 article, *supra* note 7, at 552.

tutional quality which in the course of the last fifty years has been confirmed and strengthened in such a way that today the instrument must be referred to as the constitution of the international community.[53] I argued that the Charter shows a number of strong constitutional features.[54] In particular, the Charter includes rules about how the basic functions of governance are performed in the international community, that is to say, how and by whom the law is made and applied, and how and by whom legal claims are adjudicated.[55] The Charter also establishes a hierarchy of norms (Article 103). I further tried to demonstrate that by understanding the Charter as a constitution we gain a standard allowing adequate (legal) solutions of issues such as the interpretation of the Charter, the relationship between its law and "general international law", the reform of the UN Security Council, or the question to what extent the Security Council is bound by international law.

In his recent book *The Divided West*, Jürgen Habermas has taken up this analytical effort by identifying three "normative innovations" which primarily provide the UN Charter with a constitutional quality and make it possible to interpret the Charter as a global constitution: (1) the explicit combination of the goal of safeguarding world peace and a human rights policy, (2) the connection of the prohibition of the use of force with a realistic threat of sanctions and criminal prosecution, and (3) the inclusiveness of the United Nations and the universality of UN law.[56] Habermas concluded that the UN Charter "is a framework in which UN member states no longer *must* understand themselves exclusively as subjects bringing forth international treaties; they rather can now perceive themselves, together with their citizens, as the constituent parts of a politically constituted world society."[57]

Today, the outstanding importance of the UN Charter in the international legal order is generally accepted in legal literature. As R.St.J. Macdonald already remarked in 1988, "the majority of international lawyers would probably classify the Charter as something more than a treaty yet less than a world constitution."[58] Recently Pierre-Marie Dupuy called the Charter *"un traité sans equivalent"*, *"un acte*

---

53   See *ibid.* at 531 *et seq.*

54   See *ibid.* at 573-84. For a similar analysis with much the same results, see Thomas M. Franck, "Is the U.N. Charter a Constitution?", in Jochen A. Frowein *et al.* (eds), *Negotiating for Peace: Liber Amicorum Tono Eitel* (2003), 95. Franck concluded: "Perpetuity, indelibleness, primacy, and institutional autochthony: these four characteristics of the U.N. Charter relate that unique treaty more proximately to a constitution than to an ordinary contractual normative arrangement" (*ibid.* at 102).

55   For an exposition of the "main functions of governance" of the international community, see Tomuschat, *supra* note 34, part III (pp. 305-433).

56   See Habermas, *supra* note 27, at 159.

57   *Ibid.* (*"Nach meiner Auffassung stellt die UN-Charta einen Rahmen bereit, worin sich die Mitgliedstaaten nicht länger nur als Subjekte völkerrechtlicher Verträge verstehen müssen; zusammen mit ihren Bürgern können sie sich nun als die konstituierenden Träger einer politisch verfassten Weltgesellschaft erkennen."*)

58   See R. St. J. Macdonald, "The Charter of the United Nations and the Development of Fundamental Principles of International Law", in Bin Cheng & E. D. Brown (eds.), *Con-*

fondateur, constitutif d'un nouvel ordre international."[59] Also, almost all authors who use constitutional language refer in one way or another to the Charter. There is a tradition in political speech and legal writing of speaking of the Charter as a constitution. Consider, for instance, the following quotation from Lord McNair's *Law of Treaties* of 1961: "[T]he Charter ... is the nearest approach to legislation by the whole community of States that has yet been realised. Our submission is that those of its provisions which purport to create legal rights and duties possess a constitutive or semi-legislative character, with the result that member States cannot 'contract out of' them or derogate from them by treaties made between them, and that any treaty whereby they attempted to produce this effect would be void."[60] This statement draws our attention to the problem of the legal consequences of attributing to the Charter a constitutional quality. In that respect, Lord McNair did not go beyond what is expressly provided for in Article 103 of the Charter. He did not suggest, as in fact I do, that the Charter is the supporting frame of all international law and the highest layer in a hierarchy of norms of international law leaving no room for a category of "general international law" existing independently beside the Charter.[61]

A principal reason for my suggesting that the UN Charter must be understood as *the* constitution of the international community was the intention to get out of the fog of the indistinct constitutional rhetoric by turning to one visible document as an authoritative statement of the fundamental rights and responsibilities of the members of the international community and the values to which this community is committed, as well as the basis of the most important community institutions.[62] I pointed out that there is no irreconcilable contradiction between the idea of such a written constitution and that of a more inclusive constitutional process. I also did not overlook the shortcomings of the Charter as a constitution, in particular its limitations with respect to a definition of the rights of the individual, and the concomitant necessity to see the Charter together with other customary and treaty law of a fundamental nature which I called the "constitutional by-laws" of the international community.[63] Further, I tried to explain that addressing the UN Charter as a constitution does not mean to equate the Charter with a state constitution like that of the United States of America or the French Republic, but that instead the constitutional idea in international law must be understood as an autonomous concept rather than an extrapolation of the constitutional law of a particular state.[64] At the same time, an

---

    temporary Problems of International Law: Essays in Honour of Georg Schwarzenberger on his Eightieth Birthday (1988), 196, at 197.

59   See Dupuy, *supra* note 19, at 217.

60   See Lord Arnold D. McNair, *Law of Treaties* (1961), at 217. See also I. Brownlie, "The United Nations Charter and the Use of Force, 1945-1985", in Antonio Cassese (ed.), *The Current Legal Regulation of the Use of Force* (1986), 491, at 495.

61   See Fassbender, *supra* note 7, at 585.

62   See *ibid.* at 616 *et seq.*

63   See *ibid.* at 588 *et seq.*

64   See *ibid.* at 572.

established notion like "constitution" is malleable only up to a certain degree; it cannot be extended or adapted at will. Since the American and the French Revolution, and notwithstanding the English exception, Western political thinking associates that notion not only with a system of fundamental principles according to which a state is governed but also with the document embodying these principles. Therefore, it is doubtful whether a concept of a fragmented international constitution – a constitution not unified by a central text like the UN Charter – has a chance of success.

One may add that a certain gap between constitutional rules and constitutional reality is not unusual in the case of state constitutions too. For that reason, the argument that, for instance, the Security Council actually has not played the role provided for in the Charter, or the Economic and Social Council did not become the center of international economic and social cooperation envisaged by Chapters IX and X of the Charter, is not refuting the Charter's constitutional quality.

Lastly, it is a profound misunderstanding to equate the advancement of the constitutional idea in international law with a weakening of the institution of the independent state. To assume the existence of a constitution of the international community does not mean to put the state in new, more restraining chains of law. On the contrary, it is that constitution which protects the legal authority and autonomy of every state against unlawful interventions by other states and international organizations, similar to the protection of the fundamental rights and freedoms afforded to individual citizens by a state constitution.[65] It is the constitution of the international community which safeguards the entitlement of a state, and the people constituting it, to autonomous development and self-responsibility within the limits set by international law.

However, so far most legal scholars favouring the idea of international constitutionalism prefer to stay in conceptually vaguer worlds. Some of them seem to suffer a sort of reality shock when encountering a United Nations so far away from their ideals of pure theory. Others, while acknowledging the necessity of a steadily intensifying degree of international organisation, remain captives of a legal training based on the cornerstone of the "sovereign state." In the legal map of the world that is on their minds they cannot find a proper place for a global constitution. This is also the reason for the comparative attractiveness of *jus cogens*. In its quality as customary international law it can easily be fit into the traditional system of sources of international law and, what is more important, the traditional idea of international law as a system of rules based on the consent of states. Accordingly, Charter law is ranked below *jus cogens*[66] – as if those peremptory norms, all of which are based on rules and values of the Charter, could survive without the Charter. The true relationship between the UN Charter and *jus cogens* is turned on its head.[67] Besides,

---

65   See Fassbender, *supra* note 1, at 128 *et seq.*

66   See Application of the Convention on the Prevention and Punishment of the Crime of Genocide (*Bosnia & Herzegovina v. Yugoslavia* (Serbia & Montenegro)), 1993 ICJ Reports 407, at 440 para. 100 (E. Lauterpacht, J., separate opinion). For critical discussion, see Fassbender, *supra* note 7, at 589 *et seq.*

67   See also Dupuy, *supra* note 19, at 307.

as Professor Cassese has reminded us, "the fact remains that, at the level of State to State relations, peremptory norms have largely remained a potentiality."[68]

But the hesitancies to give the UN Charter a central place in a constitutional structure of the international community are also politically motivated. At the beginning of the twenty-first century, the position and role of the United Nations in international affairs find themselves under great stress.[69] In turbulent times, the organization faces an environment which is partly openly hostile, partly disinterested, and partly friendly but not decisively supportive. Fundamental rules of the Charter, such as the ban on the use of force, are challenged,[70] and the legitimacy of the Security Council, as the organization's institutional backbone, is called into question. And yet, and in my opinion deplorably, the members of the international community are far away from uniting their strength in an effort to give new life and vigor to the Charter system of international governance.[71] To many, the Charter looks more and more like a monument of a distant past – an embodiment of an idea of collective security whose days are over. In this situation, can one dare to regard the Charter as the foundation of the entire house of contemporary international law?

Philip Allott once remarked: "Failing to recognize itself as a society, international society has not known that it has a constitution."[72] The future of the constitutional understanding and effectiveness of the UN Charter – which is, I suggest, tantamount to the foreseeable future of constitutionalism in international law in general – will not depend on the interpretive and constructive efforts of legal science but on the fate of the United Nations itself. Only a strong political move, comparable to the founding of the UN in the constitutional moment of 1944-45, could reaffirm the Charter's claim to be the constitution of the international community. Perhaps the UN era is drawing to a close,[73] and only now, looking back, the peoples of the United Nations realize that they had a constitution. But the idea of a constitution of the international community will survive because it is both indispensable as a legal device and unrivalled as a symbol of unity of humankind realizing its existence in *one world*. If the future landscape of international relations

---

68   See Cassese, *supra* note 39, at 147.

69   For an analysis of "anti-constitutionalist trends" in international law, see Anne Peters, "Global Constitutionalism Revisited" (2004) (on file with author).

70   See Bardo Fassbender, "Die Gegenwartskrise des völkerrechtlichen Gewaltverbotes vor dem Hintergrund der geschichtlichen Entwicklung", 31 *Europäische Grundrechte-Zeitschrift* (2004) 241.

71   See Bardo Fassbender, "All Illusions Shattered? Looking Back on a Decade of Failed Attempts to Reform the UN Security Council", 7 *Max Planck UNYB* (2003) 183.

72   See Allott, *supra* note 4, at 418.

73   For a description of possible alternatives to a constitutionalization of international law as a continuation of the "Kantian project," see Habermas, *supra* note 27, at 178 *et seq.* As such alternatives, the author identifies (1) a US "hegemonic liberalism," (2) a "neoliberal global market society" with marginalized states, (3) a "postmarxist scenario of a scattered imperial rule without a capital," and (4) a global *Grossraumordnung* based on the ideas of Carl Schmitt.

will know a legal order at all, as an order based on the principles of self-determination, autonomy and equality of all nations, a universal constitution will be an essential element of that order. And just as much as the idea of a constitution of the international community will survive, the contribution the UN Charter has made to this idea's development will be unextinguishable in the book of world history. As Jürgen Habermas said, "the League of Nations and the United Nations are great, even though risky and reversible, achievements on the arduous way to a political constitution of world society."[74]

---

74   See Habermas, *supra* note 27, at 145.

32. The International Community as a Legal Community

Ronald St. John Macdonald *

1. Introduction

The Charter of the United Nations is one of the most important treaties ever created. It provides a system of governance, a rudimentary form of separation of powers, and a hierarchy of norms. Its objectives are so important that they are binding even on the few remaining non-members of the United Nations and on other subjects of international law as well. The Charter is a constituting document in the sense that it creates organs for a collectivity and outlines principles, processes and procedures to be followed. Its universal nature can be implied from the virtually universal participation of states in the United Nations organization.

The chapter that follows is intended to draw attention to the increasingly constitutional characteristics of the Charter of the United Nations, the great law-making treaties inextricably related to the Charter, and the timeliness of efforts to consider how the values and principles of world constitutionalism can be promoted and protected more effectively. Learned opinion will be reviewed and suggestions made as to specific areas in which the international constitutional regime anchored in the Charter can be strengthened.[1]

*   The author wishes to recognize with pleasure and gratitude the contributions of Ian Rennie, Richard Jordan and Eric Myles to the content of this chapter. The title of the chapter is a slight adaptation of Hermann Mosler's famous lecture at The Hague: 140 *Recueil de Cours* 2 (1974).

1   Bruno Simma (ed.), *The Charter of the United Nations: A Commentary* (Oxford U.P., 2nd ed., 2002); J.P. Cot and A. Pellet, *La Charte des Nations Unies, Commentaire Article par Article* (Paris: Economica Bruylant, 1958); Bengt Broms, *The United Nations* (Helsinki: Suomalainev Tiedeakatemia, 1990); Benedetto Conforti, *The Law and Practice of the United Nations* (The Hague: Kluwer Law Int., 1969); Hans Kelsen, *The Law of the United Nations* (London: Stevens 19); R.St.J. Macdonald, "The United Nations Charter: Constitution or Contract?," in Macdonald and Johnston (eds.), *The Structure and Process of International Law: Essays in Legal Philosophy Doctrine and Theory* (Dodrecht: Martinus Nijhoff, 1986) p. 889; R.St.J. Macdonald, "The Charter of the United

Ronald St. John Macdonald & Douglas M. Johnston (eds.), Towards World Constitutionalism, *pp. 853-909.*
© *2005 Koninklijke Brill NV. Printed in The Netherlands. ISBN 90 04 14612 1.*

Before turning to the international constitutional order represented by the Charter of the United Nations and the pioneering international legal documents of the second half of the 20th century, most of which are juridically linked to the Charter, it will be instructive to look briefly at the European Union, a phenomenon already qualified by the European Court of Justice as constitutional in nature, and at the draft constitution of Europe, the most complete and complex international constitution under construction in the world today. Since the same constitutional tendencies appear at both regional and global levels, the legal architecture and essential content of the *Draft Treaty Establishing a Constitution for Europe*, indeed its very language, is of great interest for purposes of sharpening our appreciation of the strengths and weaknesses of the global constitutional system.

The rest of this chapter is divided into two parts. Part 2 reviews a few of the familiar principles of the international constitutional order, Part 3 addresses present-day problems of the two principal institutions of the United Nations, the Security Council and the General Assembly. The purpose of the chapter is to emphasize the accelerated rate at which legal constitutionalism is developing in the world community, the rising interest in designing a comprehensive and effective constitution for humankind, and the pressing need for jurists the world over to join in concerted efforts to give shape and substance to enlightened international constitutionalism in the early decades of the 21st century.

2.   The Draft European Constitution

When the *Draft Treaty Establishing a Constitution for Europe* enters into force it will provide Europe with a single constitutional system affirming the dual nature of the European Union, a union of European peoples and a union of European States. Before entering into force the European Constitution must be approved and ratified in the form of referenda in some countries and parliamentary approval in others.

The great historic originality of the European Constitution, and one reason it is relevant to any reconsideration of the Charter of the United Nations, is that it represents a major effort to devise a democratic structure that goes beyond the nation state. The nation state model fails to adequately address the reality of the double legitimacy of the member states and of the populations. The European Constitution, embedded in a draft treaty, strikes a balance between the representation of states and of peoples.[2]

Nations in Constitutional Perspective," 20 *Australian Y.B. of Int. Law* 205 (2000); James Crawford, "The Charter of the United Nations as a Constitution" in Hazel Fox (ed.), *The Changing Constitution of the United Nations* (1997), p. 12; Robert Kolb, "La structure constitutionelle du droit international public," 29 *Canadian Y.B.I.L.* 69 (2001); Karl Zemanek, *The Legal Foundations of the International System*, 1997; Thomas Franck, *Fairness in International Law and Institutions* (Oxford: Clarendon Press, 1995); Bardo Fassbender, "The Meaning of International Constitutional Law", Chapter 31, *infra*; and in 36 *Colombia J. Int. Law* 528 (1998); Blain Sloan, "The United Nations Charter as a Constitution," 1 *Pace Yearbook of International Law* 237 (1996).

2   "Consolidated Version of the Treaty on European Union," *Official Journal* C340, 10.11.1997, at 145-172. For a summary of the Draft Constitution see: European Un-

The text of the Constitution, a compromise between different bodies, perspectives and interests, is based on a number of essential elements: the incorporation of a Charter of Fundamental Rights; the stating of a clearer distinction of powers between the Union and the Member States; the introduction of mechanisms to ensure respect for the principle of subsidiarity; and the adoption of new procedures to bring about the involvement of national parliaments in the work of the Union and to facilitate the citizens' right of legislative initiative.

In the paragraphs that follow I will draw attention only to a few of the many provisions of the European Constitution that are particularly suggestive for improving the quality of constitutionalism at the level of the Charter of the United Nations. Unfortunately, it is not possible at this time to describe the reflexive and pragmatic form of governance being developed within and alongside the formal structures of the EU, a form of constitutionalism less top-down than usual, that emphasizes intersecting roles for national and EU actors at various stages. It is a strategy which "blends the setting of guidelines or objectives at EU level with the elaboration of member state action plans or strategy reports at national level in an interactive process intended to bring about greater coordination and national learning in policy fields."[3] This emerging system of complex multilevel governance, "which defies ready classification along the traditional polar lines," is of great relevance to reconsiderations of the role and functioning of the organs of the United Nations.[4]

---

ion, *Draft Constitution Citizens' Guide – Presentation to Citizens* (Brussels: European Commission Secretariat General, 2003) online: <http://european-convention.eu.int/docs/Treaty/cv00850.en03.pdf> (accessed 22 November 2003). Also see the website of the Intergovernmental Conference Group for information at <http://ue.eu.int/igc/index.asp?lang=EN> (accessed 22 November 2003). See too Dimitris N. Triantafyllou, *Le project constitutionnel de la Convention européenne* (Bruxelles: Bruylant, 2003); Christian Philip et Panayotis Soldatos (eds.), *La Convention sur l'avenir de l'Europe* (Bruxelles: Bruylant, 2004); J.H.H. Weiler and Marlene Wind (eds.), *European Constitutionalism Beyond the State* (Cambridge: Cambridge U.P., 2003); and the very useful summaries of text and debates in the European Parliament in 24 *Human Rights Law Journal* (Strasbourg), pp. 1-148 (2003).

3   Grainne de Burca, "The Constitutional Challenge of New Governance in the European Union," 56 *Current Legal Problems* 403, 418 (2003).

4   *Ibid.*, p. 423. Rich insights into the complex, unprecedented and idiosyncratic nature of EU legal developments (on pre-accession and implementation) are revealed in Marise Cremona, *The Enlargement of the European Union* (Oxford: Oxford U.P., 2003).
For Anne-Marie Slaughter, the extensive web of horizontal networks and international agencies, as evidenced especially by the EU, not only encourages cooperation and convergence but makes a global system of governance based on juridical, especial quasi-federal and confederal ideas, unnecessary and undesirable. This limited perspective minimalizes the structural, ordering, educational and psychological roles of international legislative planning, legal logic and internal coherence so prominent in the European experiment and so essential an element in the construction of a liberating universal legal system. For related discussion see Dr. Charlotte Ku's excellent chapter in this volume, "Forging a Multilayered System of Global Governance," Chapter 23, *infra*.

Let us start with the Preamble of the European Constitution, which is somewhat more extensive than the Preamble of the Charter of the United Nations. The EU Preamble is written in the third person and changes from the present to past tenses. It is similar to the Charter principally in the importance it attaches, in the first paragraph, to human rights, specifically "values underlying humanism, equality of persons, freedom, respect for reason" and, subsequently, "the central role of the human person and his or her inviolable or inalienable rights and respect for law." Although pledging that Europe wishes to "strive for peace, justice and solidarity throughout the world," the Preamble makes only limited reference to Europe's violent past. The peoples of Europe, while remaining proud of their national identities and history, are determined to transcend their ancient divisions and, united ever more closely, to forge a common destiny. Unity is a major theme in the Preamble. The penultimate, forward-looking paragraph states that: "united in its diversity, Europe offers [its peoples] the best chance of pursuing, with due regard for the rights of each individual and in awareness of their responsibilities to future generations and the Earth, the great venture which makes of it a special area of human hope."

Debate over the contents of the Preamble provoked a debate in Europe as to whether reference should be made to the Judea-Christian tradition in general and the word "God" in particular. This potentially divisive question was sidestepped by resort to the phrase "drawing inspiration from the cultural, religious and humanist inheritance of Europe."

The Preamble also referred to the Constitution having been prepared on behalf of the citizens and States of Europe. By referring to citizens first, it can be argued that peoples rather than States were recognized as the source of power, a view that is strengthened by the quotation from Thucydides at the very start of the document: "Our Constitution ... is called a democracy because power is in the hands not of a minority but of the greatest number."

The Preamble to the EU constitution contains no glaring omissions, save for a renunciation of the use of armed force similar to that contained in the UN Charter. This exclusion is noticeable in light of the historical propensity of Europeans to resort to force. Though it can be argued that the rejection of force is implicit in the contents of the Preamble, it would be interesting to know more about this particular omission.

Can the Charter of the UN learn anything from the Preamble of the EU Constitution? The principal item missing from the Charter is a reference to the "responsibilities to future generations and the Earth", a reference to environmental concerns contained in the European document. However, the Charter should not be too hard on itself. A dynamic document written nearly sixty years ago, it was fully adequate to meet the challenges of the period in which it was drafted. It has stood the test of time and it will be intriguing to see if we can say the same about the Preamble to the European Constitution in 2065.

Article I-1, on the establishment of the Union, reflects "the will of the citizens and States of Europe to build a common future." Article I-2 says the Union is founded on the values of respect for human dignity, liberty, democracy, equality, the rule of law and respect for human rights. The Union's aim is "to promote peace, its values and the well-being of its peoples."

The Constitution draws clear lines between the jurisdiction of member states and the jurisdiction of the EU. Article 1-9 enumerates the fundamental principles of Union competences:

1. The limits of Union competences are governed by the principle of conferral. The use of Union competences is governed by the principles of subsidiarity and proportionality.

2. Under the principle of conferral, the Union shall act within the limits of the competences conferred upon it by the Member States in the Constitution to attain the objectives set out in the Constitution. Competences not conferred upon the Union in the Constitution remain with the Member States.

3. Under the principle of subsidiarity, in areas which do not fall within its exclusive competence the Union shall act only if and insofar as the objectives of the intended action cannot be sufficiently achieved by the Member States, either at central level or at regional and local level, but can rather, by reason of the scale or effects of the proposed action, be better achieved at Union level.

    The Union Institutions shall apply the principle of subsidiarity as laid down in the Protocol on the application of the principles of subsidiarity and proportionality, annexed to the Constitution. National Parliaments shall ensure compliance with that principle in accordance with the procedure set out in the Protocol.

4. Under the principle of proportionality, the content and form of Union action shall not exceed what is necessary to achieve the objectives of the Constitution. The Institutions shall apply the principle of proportionality as laid down in the Protocol referred to in paragraph 3.

The principle of conferral serves as a reminder that the collective consciousness of the Union and its expression in the treaty-constitution stems from the Member States themselves. Provisions for secession from the Union (Article I-59) reinforce this message in a way that prior versions of the treaty did not. There were no such prior provisions.

In areas which do not fall within its exclusive competence the Union can act only if and insofar as the objectives of the intended action cannot be sufficiently achieved by the Member State but can "rather by reason of the scale or effects of the proposed action, be better achieved at Union level" and then, under the principle of proportionality, only to the extent necessary to achieve the objectives in question. (Article 1-9, 1-10).

Under Article 1-11, if the subject matter is in the exclusive competence of the Union only the Union may legislate and adopt legally binding acts, the Member States being able to do so themselves "only if so empowered by the Union or for the implementation of acts adopted by the Union." If the subject matter is within a shared competence then both the Union and the Member States shall have the power to legislate and adopt legally binding acts in the area concerned. The Member States exercise their competence to the extent that the Union has not exercised or has decided to cease exercising its competence. Under Article 1-9(4), the content and form of Union action shall not exceed what is necessary to achieve the objectives of the Constitution. The manner in which the principles of subsidiarity and proportionality are to be applied is outlined in the Protocol on the application of the principles of subsidiarity and proportionality annexed to the text of the constitution. The opening words of this Protocol state that the High contracting Parties wish to ensure "that decisions are taken as closely as possible to the citizens of the Union."

Gráinne de Búrca distinguishes between "democratic subsidiarity" and "executive subsidiarity." "Democratic subsidiarity" is a form of subsidiarity aimed at protecting the rights of individuals. It is tied to the classical definition of subsidiarity in the TEU (Article 5) and at Article I-9(3) of the Constitution. An example of democratic subsidiarity is Union legislation protecting mobility rights of migrant workers crossing the borders of Member States. "Executive subsidiarity" aims at protecting the rights of Member States. An example of executive subsidiarity is the right to derogate from individual mobility rights on grounds of public policy, public security or public health.[5]

As to whether the Member State can sufficiently achieve the Union objectives in question, the presumption is that the Member is "willing and capable", but that presumption can be rebutted.

Legislating: The Protocol annexed to the text of the Convention outlines a very important consultative procedure under which national parliaments and the organs of the Union (Commission, European Parliament, Council of Ministers, and the Committee of the Regions) work together to achieve unanimity or, failing that, a majority of 67 per cent based on equal representation by Member States. Bringing notice of non-compliance to the attention of the Member State concerned is the first stage in securing respect for the obligations involved, the presumption being that the Member State can reach the objectives of the intended action on its own.

Under Article 1-10, "the Constitution, and law adopted by the Union's Institutions in exercising competences conferred on it, shall have primacy over the law of the Member States." Member States shall take "all appropriate measures, general or particular" to ensure fulfillment of their obligations under the Constitution "or resulting from the Union Institutions' acts". Students of the United Nations will be interested to observe that, under the principle of loyal cooperation in Article 1-5, the Union and the Member States shall assist each other in carrying out the tasks which flow from the Constitution. Members must "facilitate the achievement of the Union's tasks and refrain from any measure which could jeopardize the attainment of the objectives set out in the Constitution." It is assumed that the Member State must at all times retain an overarching commitment to interpret community law in accordance with the purposes and principles of the Draft Treaty. The principle of

---

5   Grainne de Burca, "Reappraising Subsidiarity's Significance after Amsterdam, "*Harvard Jean Monnet Working Paper 7/99* (Cambridge, Massachusetts: Harvard Law School, 2000) at 12. See also the useful papers in Charles B. Blankart and Dennis C. Mueller, *A Constitution for the European Union* (Cambridge, Mass.: The MIT Press, 2004).

solidarity (in the international context) or of loyal cooperation (in the EU context) is thus integrated into the complementary relationship between the principles of conferral and subsidiarity.

The foregoing features of the Draft Treaty Establishing a Constitution for Europe clearly indicate that the EU constitutional system, like the global system, contains "a tension between the intergovernmentalism – supranationalism dichotomy that has long characterized the political debate over federalism and ... multi-level governance."[6] What is relevant for present purposes is that the European Constitution is replete with provisions worthy of serious attention by jurists engaged in the on-going task of further developing an effective constitution for the world at large. With that in mind, we can now turn to a few of the familiar principles of world constitutionalism as reflected in the Charter of the United Nations.

3.   The Global Constitution

Philip Allot's theoretical description of a constitution represents a useful conceptualisation to keep in mind when considering the international legal order. A constitution is a high-level abstraction of policy, not a detailed direction. It is a generalization of society's vision of its past, present and future. In the Charter of the United Nations this vision is to be found in the Preamble and the institutional Purposes and Principles.[7]

The Preamble: Generally speaking, it is inherent in a constitution that it goes back to an act taken by or at least attributed to the people, an act in which the people attribute political capacity to themselves. From a strictly formal, textual point of view the Charter of the United Nations lacks this usual characteristic of a constitution: the legitimating basis of the Charter is the written agreement of the Member States. However, since 1945 the basis of the Charter has come to be seen as the identity of the peoples of the world; they have been recognized as standing at the top of the hierarchical structure of norms and the starting point for formal institutional power relating to the people. Resort to the phrase "We the peoples of the United Nations", was prophetic at the time and rightly indicative of where power originates.[8]

---

6   Grainne de Burca, note 3 above, at 418.

7   Philip Allott, *Eunomia: New Order for a New World* (New York: Oxford University Press, 1990) at 133.

8   Simma suggests that these words were originally intended to express a democratic basis for the New Organization but that such a meaning was quickly rejected. See especially Ruth B. Russell, *A History of the United Nations Charter: The Role of the United States 1940 – 1945* (Washington, D.C.: The Brookings Institution, 1958) p. 910; H. Kelsen, *The Law of the United Nations*, 1950, pp. 3-11. See too Eric Suy, "*Le Préambule*," in Emile Yakpo and Tahar Bourmedra (eds.), *Liber Amicorum Judge Mohammed Bedjaoui* (The Hague, Netherlands: Kluwer Law International, 1999) at 253. Suy compares the usefulness of preambles of international treaties to the role of preambles of Security Council

The question of the origin of power is critical to an understanding of the Preamble. If one considers the Charter primarily as an international treaty, the power allocated to the United Nations would seem to flow formally from Member States. If one considers the Charter as something more, a constitutional-like document, power may be said to flow from citizens of the Member States, indeed from citizens of the world. Adopting one view or the other inevitably leads to a regionalist (deference to the state) or a universalist (deference to the United Nations) approach. Important as the original source of the power may be, its legitimate delegation and exercise is also highly relevant. How power is delegated and the accountability of those who exercise it matter. Legitimate delegation and exercise of power is caught up with principles of administrative law, accountability, transparency, procedural fairness, judicial review and constitutionality.

The Preamble contains an assertion of identity: there are references to "We, the Peoples of the United Nations" and to "... our respective Governments, through [diplomatic] representatives assembled in the city of San Francisco ..." There are references to the past, notably "the scourge of war." There is a reaffirmation of current beliefs, the maintenance of peace and security, fundamental human rights, the dignity and worth of the human person, equal rights of men and women, and of nations. A plan for the future is adumbrated – to establish justice and respect for the obligations of treaties, to promote social and economic progress, respect for self-determination of peoples, and to achieve economic cooperation. In short, the Preamble of the Charter is an expression of collective identity in space and time. As a statement of the highest importance, introducing the substantive provisions of the document establishing the world's leading international organization, the Preamble is obviously of great significance for purposes of interpreting the meaning and purport of the Charter's specific provisions.

The aims of the Preamble reflect the experiences of the international community in the First and Second World Wars: i) determination to save future generations from war; ii) reaffirmation of human rights and the rights of nations; iii) respect for international treaties and other sources of international law; and, iv) promotion of social progress and better standards of living. Broadly speaking, the Preamble is a statement of collective willing by a society and therefore an expression of constitutionalism present, past, and future.

While the Preamble is a statement of identity and aims, the Purposes and Principles of the Charter are concerned primarily, although, as we shall see, not exclusively, with the rights of states *inter se* and within the United Nations Organization itself. Purposes are described in Article 1 and Principles in Article 2. In

---

Resolutions. Security Council Resolutions necessarily imply that the Preamble to the Charter is operative. Nevertheless, such preambles represent statements of intention and the "general concept of operations;" they are crucial in adopting a purposive approach to legal interpretation. See too the excellent paper by Michiel Brand, "Affirming and Refining European Constitutionalism: Towards the Establishment of the First Constitution for the European Union," (Florence: European University Institute, 2004), p. 48.

line with a constitution, Article 1 enunciates broad abstractions of a collective will, while Article 2, though still broad and abstract, begins to be more specific in terms of articulating basic rules.

Purposes: The purposes of the Organization, outlined in Article 1, include: the maintenance of international peace and security, the development of friendly relations among nations, the achievement of international cooperation in solving problems of an international scope (economic, social, cultural and humanitarian), and to serve as a centre for "harmonizing the actions of nations in the attainment of these common ends." While the last four provisions of Article 1 are directory, the first is mandatory:

> To maintain international peace and security, and to that end: to take effective collective measures for the prevention and removal of threats to the peace, and for the suppression of acts of aggression or other breaches of the peace, and to bring about by peaceful means, and in conformity with the principles of justice and international law, adjustment or settlement of international disputes or situations which might lead to a breach of the peace ...

This provision is at the core of what the United Nations is about. Its overarching purpose is to maintain international peace and security. Article 1(1) authorizes the Organization to deal with threats to the peace, acts of aggression or other breaches of the peace *and* the pacific settlement of disputes in conformity with justice and international law.

Principles: To effect its aims and purposes, Article 2 of the Charter sets out fundamental principles in accordance with which the Organization and its Members must act: (i) sovereign equality of all States; (ii) fulfillment in good faith of obligations assumed in accordance with the Charter; (iii) settlement of disputes by peaceful means; (iv) refraining from the threat or use of force against the territorial integrity or political independence of any other state or in any other manner inconsistent with the purposes of the United Nations; (v) giving the UN every assistance in any action taken in accordance with the Charter and refraining from assisting any state against which the UN is taking preventive or enforcement action; (vi) ensuring that non-member states act in accordance with these principles; and, (vii) respecting the sovereignty of all states by not authorizing the UN to intervene in matters which are essentially within the domestic jurisdiction of any state with the exception of the application of enforcement measures under Chapter VII.

Membership: Under Articles 3 through 6 membership is restricted to "peace-loving states" who have accepted the obligations of the Charter and, in the judgment of the Organization, are able and willing to carry out those obligations. Significantly, the provisions on membership contain no references to individuals despite the fact that later Articles contain seven important references to fundamental human rights, dignity and worth of the human person, and equal rights for men and women. The exclusivity of the standing of states is further reflected in the Statute of the International Court of Justice, the principal judicial organ of the United Nations.

Today of course it is incorrect to say that only states have standing in international law and international organizations. As we shall see, a number of non-state entities enjoy observer status in the General Assembly and individuals have standing in various international legal jurisdictions, for example, as defendants before the International Criminal Tribunal for the Former Yugoslavia, a subsidiary organ of the Security Council, and the International Criminal Court, a non-United Nations body, arguably a regional-like organization based upon a multilateral treaty. An increasing number of international courts and tribunals provide individuals with standing in international law. International democratic subsidiarity is rapidly evolving at international law.

Primacy of the Charter: Article 103 provides that, "In the event of a conflict between the obligations of the Members of the United Nations under the present Charter and their obligations under any other international agreement, their obligations under the present Charter shall prevail." As early as 1946, Leland M. Goodrich and Edvard Hambro rightly said that, owing to Article 103, "The Charter thus assumes the character of basic law of the international community. Nonmembers, while they have not formally accepted it, are nevertheless expected to recognize this law as one of the facts of international life and to adjust themselves to it."[9] Article 103 does not apply to obligations under customary law. In order to protect the doctrine of *jus cogens*, states cannot agree by treaty to violate peremptory norms of customary international law.

Article 103 represents one of the most persuasive arguments in favour of the view that the Charter is in fact a constitution. Dan Ciobanu compared Article 103 with Article 20 of the Covenant of the League of Nations and found that, though the wording of the former is weaker than the latter, Article 103 nevertheless permits us to characterize the Charter, in the language Lauterpacht used to describe the Covenant, as higher law.[10] Michael Virally agreed that Article 103 defines the constitutional character of the Charter but expressed the view that there is not an equivalency between the notions of a constitutional norm and a norm *"jus cogens."*[11]

Article 25 says that Members agree to accept and carry out the decisions of the Security Council *in accordance with the Charter*. Chapters VI (Pacific Settlement of Disputes) and VII (Action with Respect to Threats to the Peace, Breaches of the Peace and Acts of Aggression) are based on the idea of peaceful resolution of conflict and, failing that, a limited and legitimate use of force only in regulated and temporary circumstances as properly authorized and supervised by the Security Council.

---

9   Leland M. Goodrich and Edvard Hambro, *Charter of the United Nations* (Boston: World Peace Foundation, 1946), p. 281.

10   Dan Ciobranu, "Impact of the Characteristics of the Charter Upon Its Interpretation," in Antonio Cassese (ed.), *Current Problems of International Law* (Milan, 1975), pp. 3-80.

11   Michael Virally, "La rôle des Principes ...", Faculté de Droit et IUHEL de Genève, 1968, pp. 531 ff.

Institutional Administration: The Charter establishes the organs of the United Nations and serves as the constitution of the Organization. Details pertaining to the establishment of the General Assembly, Security Council, Economic and Social Council, Trusteeship Council, International Court of Justice, and Secretariat are set forth in Chapter III. Those provisions reflect the formal constitutional authority by which power is delegated from the peoples to their governmental representatives, from governmental representatives to the United Nations, and from the United Nations to these organs. For example, Chapter XIV (Articles 92 through 96) is the basis on which the Statute of the International Court of Justice is founded and the Court empowered. Much like a parliamentary Act, these articles are supplemented by additional statutory instruments, such as the Rules of Court, practice directions, and declarations accepting the compulsory jurisdiction of the Court. A similar line of reasoning can be applied to other organs.

Limitations: Limitations on the exercise of a power reflect the trichotomous balance between the ideal, actual and legal aspects of a constitution. The limitations imposed by the Charter on the Security Council were noted by Judge Antonio Cassese in 1995 when he considered the power of the Council under Chapter VII to establish the International Tribunal for the Former Yugoslavia:

> It is clear … that the Security Council plays a pivotal role and exercises a very wide discretion under this Article. But this does not mean that its powers are unlimited. The Security Council is an organ of an international organization, established by a treaty which serves as a constitutional framework for that organization. The Security Council is thus subjected to certain constitutional limitations, however broad its powers under the constitution may be. Those powers cannot, in any case go beyond the limits of the jurisdiction of the Organization at large, not to mention other specific limitations or those which may derive from the internal division of power within the Organization. In any case, neither the text nor the spirit of the Charter conceives of the Security Council as legibus solutus (unbound by law).[12]

Ideally and legally the Charter imposes its Purposes and Principles on all organs of the United Nations and on all Members. At the same time, the ideal aspect is restrained by limitations of jurisdiction as set out in the Charter and by the realities of divisions of power between the organs and the Members including non-Members.

Delegation: In the nation state, the task of implementing broad policy directives is left to policy statements and declarations, departmental directives, statutory instruments, and judicial interpretations. A constitution, rightly, does not establish a scheme for micro-managing; it authorizes the delegation of authority and power. Constitutional law may indeed be likened to the high-level, abstract language of

---

12   *Prosecutor v. Tadic* (1994), Case No. IT-94-1, (International Criminal Tribunal for the Former Yugoslavia, Appeals Chamber, Decision), 5 October 1994 at paragraph 28.

mathematics. Administrative law, founded upon *"des règles ponctuelles et détaillées,"* represents the "machine code" of how constitutional aspirations are implemented. As in the domestic order, international law embodies symbiotic relationships between laws in both constitutional and administrative domains. In the draft European Constitution, but not in the Charter of the United Nations, delegation is expressly provided for in Article I-35. That Article rightly provides that the objectives, content, scope and duration of any delegation must be explicitly defined.[13]

Regional Organizations: Particularly in the absence of reforms of the Security Council and the General Assembly, resort to regional arrangements under Chapter VIII offers attractive possibilities.[14] Chapter VIII gives the Charter unique flexibility. Recognition of the dichotomy between universal and regional approaches translates into a "softening" of the centralization of power, perhaps not a completely realistic idea in the first place, in relation to the maintenance of peace and security. Through the use of regional arrangements, delegation is achieved.

The principle of subsidiarity (or complementarity) represents a useful possibility within the United Nations scheme of operations. The concept of subsidiarity is that actions should be undertaken not on the level of the state as a whole but rather, if possible, at regional and lower levels. Arguments for this approach are pragmatic: costs are lower, knowledge of the problem is usually more comprehensive at the local level, and the realization of effectiveness is often more likely. Provisions on regional organizations in the Charter of United Nations could and should be interpreted in the light of this principle. It would mean, in the first instance, a preference for regional and local problem-solving rather than resort to universal solutions and reliance on foreign personnel and resources.

In my opinion, the recognition of regional arrangements and agencies within the UN system, and the need to work out compromises between universalism and regionalism in the economic, cultural and social fields, as well as in military matters, is a striking example of an important, under-used constitutional feature of the Charter of the United Nations. Indeed, if we compare the functioning of federal constitutions in the large land-mass states of the world, including the European Union, we will see that they all recognize and rely on the principle of subsidiarity. It is heartening to observe that the recent report (2005) of the Secretary General's high level panel places heavy emphasis on regional organizations and arrangements.

Regional agencies or arrangements are mentioned in the Charter. Article 33(1) refers to them as one of the means by which states are to resolve disputes whose

---

13   Danesh Sarooshi, *The United Nations and the Development of Collective Security: The Delegation by the U.N. Security Council of its Chapter VII Powers* (Oxford: Clarendon Press, 1999).

14   See Michael Schweitzer, "Chapter VIII Regional Arrangements" in Bruno Simma, (ed.), *The Charter of the United Nations: A Commentary* (New York: Oxford University Press, 1995), p. 679, and, A., "Regional organization without big-power participation: a suggestion for a total world development system," 30 *International Journal* (Toronto) 768 (1975).

continuance is likely to endanger the maintenance of international peace and security. Article 52 states that nothing in the Charter precludes the existence of regional arrangements or agencies for dealing with matters relating to the maintenance of international peace and security that are appropriate for regional action, provided such arrangements or agencies and their activities are consistent with the Purposes and Principles of the United Nations. Article 53 provides that no enforcement action can be taken under regional arrangements or by regional agencies without the authorisation of the Security Council.

In order to rely on Article 53(1) there is a need to define the organizations that qualify as regional organizations. The term regional implies a distinctive feature about the members of the organization, which is understood to be of a geographic nature. It might refer to: the geographic region from which the members of the organization come; the geographic region in which the organization operates; or a combination of both. These organizations thus differ from regional "defence" organizations whose primary purpose is defence. Alliances fall under Article 51 whereas regional organizations operate under Chapter VIII. NATO, as the classic "defence" organization, operates under Article 51. The Security Council was thus unable to authorize NATO's presence in the former Yugoslavia in terms of Article 53(1).

But the principle of subsidiarity also touches on the delicate question of the division of competences between a "supranational" organ (the whole organisation) and member states belonging to it. The idea of subsidiarity is embedded in the Charter itself: Article 53(1) leaves to the Security Council a subjective assessment as to whether recourse to regional structures is "appropriate." The presumption is that member states and regional organizations are willing and capable of acting properly and sufficiently.

Article 43 indicates the extent to which member states or regional organizations are obliged to participate in a military operation of the United Nations. It does not indicate whether the Security Council may authorize regional organizations to execute military measures on its behalf. Article 53(1), on the other hand, says the Council shall, where appropriate, utilize regional arrangements or agencies for enforcement action under its authority.

Enforcement: In the administration of the international legal system through the Charter, the implementation of democratic subsidiarity is and has been comparatively weak. Democratic subsidiarity certainly exists in the Charter system but the overall tone of the Charter favors executive subsidiarity and the protection of the rights of states. Democratic subsidiarity occupies a secondary role; it appears, if at all, in delegated legislation, in, for example, the myriad of human rights treaties, declarations, and resolutions ranging from the Geneva Conventions to the Genocide Convention.

If we are correct in our belief that the Charter is a constitution-like document, then the mechanism of how it works needs to be understood. This is the point at which constitutional law and administrative law tend to merge. The presumption is that states are willing and capable of carrying out the Purposes and Principles of the Charter and that they have established procedures and processes to enable them to do so. Only in exceptional cases, through acts or omissions by states flagrantly contrary to the Purposes and Principles of the UN will this presumption be formally challenged by organs of the UN. Threats to the maintenance of international peace and security are within the purvue of the Security Council. Other acts and omissions can be challenged by resorting to the increasing range of national and international administrative, bureaucratic, and legal processes through which the municipal and international legal systems are interlocked.

In practice, the Security Council has not established a Military Staff Committee to advise and assist it as mandated by Articles 46 and 47 of the *Charter*. The Military Staff Committee was originally envisaged as a United Nations' General Staff but it never amounted to anything in practical terms. The Military Staff Committee has repeatedly been by-passed by a Security Council acting directly on peace-keeping activities. Some commentators say this is evidence that peace-keeping activities are contrary to the *Charter*, others say peace-keeping is within the Purposes and Principles of the Charter, a view endorsed by the International Court of Justice in the *Expenses Case*.[15] Despite the Committee's continued existence and renewed interest in its work after the Persian Gulf War of 1991, it performs no meaningful function.[16]

Instead of the United Nations running the Military Staff Committee, the Security Council has delegated this power to Member States willing to provide forces to participate with the consent of all parties involved. The Canadian International Peacekeeping Training Centre describes this as "peacekeeping by proxy:"

> Peacekeeping by Proxy... refers to a situation in which the Member States of the United Nations Security Council, which has 'responsibility for the maintenance of international peace and security,' decides, for some reason, that they cannot establish a needed peacekeeping mission. In that case, the Council gives its proxy to an individual country, a group of countries or an organization. With this proxy and linked to the UN by an authorizing resolution, the acceptor of the proxy organizes and carries out the operation. Some examples are Multi-national Force and Observers (MFO), the Italian-led operation with regard to Albanian re[f]ugees and, of course, IFOR, SFOR and the OSCE Kosovo Verification Mission."[17]

Or, in the words of Hans Haekkerup, Danish Minister of Defence: "The limitations in the UN's capabilities are particularly pronounced in operations at the higher end of the peace support spectrum. The UN does not have the capacity or the experience to manage such complex military operations. Therefore, such operations will

---

15   *Certain Expenses Case* [1962], ICJ Reports 157.

16   On the whole problem, see Charlotte Ku and Harold K. Jacobson (eds.), *Democratic Accountability and the Use of Force in International Law* (Cambridge U.P., 2003), ch. 15.

17   Alex Morrison (ed.), *Peacekeeping by Proxy*, (The Lester B. Pearson Canadian International Peacekeeping Training Centre: Clementsport, NS, 1999).

have to be carried out by proxy, as we have seen recently in the former Yugoslavia and with the liberation of Kuwait in 1991 …. Proxies should be used for operations beyond the UN's capability and capacity. Nonetheless, such operations must still be carried out under a UN mandate …"[18]

While this proxy may make practical sense in terms of allowing an immediate response to a perceived threat to international peace and security, the problem remains as to what authorization is needed. Is a unanimous resolution supported by all members of the Security Council required? What if approval is not forthcoming? Can authorization be implied if the draft resolution is neither adopted nor rejected? Do abstentions amount in reality to rejections?

The problem arising in the case of NATO's intervention in Kosovo in 1999 was a contemporary one. Both Simma and Cassese argue that threats by NATO to use force followed by recourse to air strikes could not be supported by the Charter, either under Chapter VII or the inherent right to self-defence under Article 51. It is here that what exists in terms of a "legal constitution", namely the *Charter*, is in fact divergent as to what exists in the "actual constitution", namely, the practice of states in matters of conflict resolution, and, in this case, intervention in the territory of another sovereign state in support of humanitarian concerns.[19]

Cassese suggests that humanitarian intervention may even be an emerging international doctrine, perhaps a new exception to the Charter along the lines of Article 51. However, the implementation of such a doctrine would completely by-passes the Charter system, unless one can accept the strained construction that the absence of a prohibition by the Security Council means that the action in question may still be in accordance with the Purposes and Principles of the Charter. Such an argument seems contrary to at least one of the aims of the Charter, namely, the "acceptance of principles and the institution of methods, that armed force shall not be used, save in the common interest." The divergence is not unique. Legal fictions give rise to deviation – whether it is the lack of efficacy of the Military Staff Committee, the authorization of peace-keeping as a Chapter VII action, or the doctrine of humanitarian intervention.

Legal fictions are used to adapt the Charter to current events, to achieve what Allot calls constitutional principles of transformation. Through this tool, the Charter reveals itself not as a static but as a dynamic instrument. Provided legal fictions are consistent with the Purposes and Principles of the Charter, it is not fatal that they diverge from the more administrative provisions of the Charter.

Withdrawal: The Charter does not contain an explicit textual provision guaranteeing a right to secede or withdraw. Whether the Indonesian case indicates the existence of an implicit understanding that the Charter contains that right is not clear. Fortunately, however, the potentially destabilizing effects of even a serious threat to secede have thus far not arisen. American withdrawal from UNESCO was temporary.

---

18   Comments by the Hans Haekkerup are cited in Alex Morrison, (ed.), *Peacekeeping by Proxy* (Toronto: Brown Book Company, 1999), p. vii-viii.

19   Cassesse and Simma.

In 1956, the Government of Indonesia, led by Dr. Sukarno, informed Secretary General U Thant that Indonesia would be withdrawing from the United Nations Organization, including all principal and subsidiary organs. Indonesia's intent was to bring about the collapse of the United Nations, apparently with the support of the Peoples' Republic of China, and to create a rival organization. The General Assembly omitted Indonesia from its annual scale of assessments for the financial years 1965 to 1967. The Sukarno regime was overthrown and in 1966 the new regime immediately reversed the withdrawal. Rather than view the situation as a formal withdrawal followed by the admission of a new member, the General Assembly created the fiction that Indonesia had not withdrawn from the Organization but had simply ceased to cooperate. The President of the General Assembly stated it thus:

> It would ... appear that the Government of Indonesia considers that its recent absence from the Organization was based not upon a withdrawal from the United Nations but upon a cessation of co-operation. The action so far taken by the United Nations on this matter, would not appear to preclude this view. If this is also the general view of the membership, the Secretary-General would give instructions for the necessary administrative actions to be taken for Indonesia to participate again in the proceedings of the Organization.[20]

In contrast to the Charter's silence on this fundamentally important question, the European Constitution provides, in Article I-59, for voluntary withdrawal from the Union under a withdrawal agreement between the Union and the withdrawing state.

4.   Principles of Global Constitutionalism

Constitutional principles of the international legal order are basic statements identifying and safeguarding the collective identity, underlining the purposes and principles of the society and organization concerned, providing a framework for reinforcing and from time to time revising those purposes and principles, and indicating the manner in which the trichotomy between ideal, legal and actual constitutional practice is balanced, that is, the manner in which power is delegated.

In the international constitutional order, three kinds of principle are addressed, all designed to protect the rights of certain members of the international legal system: (A) classical state rights, principles and rules that exist to preserve the rights of states in relations between themselves in a society of states. This is the realm of classical international law; (B) international rights, principles and rules that exist to preserve the stability and existence of the international order itself. This is a relatively novel category intricately tied into the expression of a collective international will; (C) individual rights, perhaps the newest and most controversial category. It

---

20   For full discussion see Henry G. Schermers and Niels M. Blokker, *International Institutional Law* (Boston / Leiden: Martinus Nijhoff Publishers, 4th revised ed., 2003), p. 92 ff.; and for an argument against including a right to secede in a constitution see Cass R. Sunstein, *Designing Democracy: What Constitutions Do* (Oxford U.P., 2001), ch. 4.

is here that we see the traditional international legal order undergoing profound change. Just as the European legal order is being transformed as a result of the European Union, the international legal order, nominally based on constitution-like treaties or treaty-like constitutions, is also being transformed and strengthened as a constitution-like system.

A.   *Classical State Rights*

The traditional model of the international legal order is centred on the principles of state sovereignty and equality. These are indeed the first principles of the United Nations. As stated in Article 2(1) of the Charter, "The Organization is based on the principle of the sovereign equality of all its Members." As to sovereignty, the feature thought necessary for the creation and success of statehood and its supremacy, suffice it to say that the question of how to deal with state sovereignty, in a world that has become increasingly interdependent, is answered pragmatically by saying that sovereignty is capable of limitation with a state's consent. Whether state sovereignty, a phenomenon of the Westphalian past, has become a fiction, is a matter that must be demonstrated in the particular case at hand.

B.   *International Rights: Provisions* **jus cogens** *and* **erga omnes**

These norms have a collective character; they are not unique to any one state but to all states: the international community of states. Peremptory norms include those aimed at suppressing the unlawful use of force, aggression, genocide, many categories of human rights and fundamental freedoms, crimes against humanity, discrimination, slavery, piracy, and other types of trans-national criminal activity. International courts have repeatedly held that the right to life is a fundamental human right the exercise of which is essential for the exercise of all other human rights.

Article 53 of the Vienna Convention on the Law of Treaties 1969 provides that treaties are void if they conflict with peremptory norms of general international law. A peremptory norm is defined as a norm accepted and recognized by the international community of states as a whole as a norm from which no derogation is permitted and which can be modified only by a subsequent norm of general international law having the same character. In order to determine that a norm is a peremptory norm, there should exist the consent of a "very large majority" of states or of their totality. Article 53 provides that a rule of *jus cogens* can invalidate a treaty if the rule meets the "double consent" test; if it is accepted and recognized by the international community of states as a whole as a norm from which no derogation is permitted and which can be modified only by a subsequent norm of general international law having the same character. As the Drafting Committee made clear, a persistent objector cannot prevent the emergence of a norm of jus cogens binding upon itself as a member of the international community of states.

Discussions leading up to the adoption of the Vienna Convention show that norms of *jus cogens* can be derived only from treaty or custom. There was no consensus as to whether they can arise from general principles of law.

These famous provisions clearly reveal the existence of supra-international norms recognized as norms superior to other rules or principles contained either within international treaties or state constitutions.

If we consider the Charter of the United Nations as a document containing *jus cogens* norms binding *erga omnes*, would not this presumption, by itself, justify our attribution of constitutional characteristics to the Charter? Norms prevailing over other norms, including those contained in national constitutions, should be perceived as constitutional in the material sense. And the documents containing them should be seen as constitutional. As Charles Cadoux said long ago, the Charter is placed "at the summit of the juridical order, as it is the fundamental norm to which are subject all other rules of law, be they conventional or legislative."[21]

The usual definition of *jus cogens* places the main stress on the interest to be protected: the criterion for these rules consists in the fact that they do not exist to satisfy the needs of the individual states but the higher interest of the whole international community. "By their very nature", observed the International Court of Justice, these norms "are the concern of all states. In view of the importance of the rights involved all states can be held to have a legal interest in their protection; they are obligations erga omnes."[22] We see then that *jus cogens* comprise norms aimed at protecting the public interest of international society as such, not the particular interests of individual states.

Almost all the principles listed in Article 2 of the Charter have achieved the status of *jus cogens*: sovereign equality of all members; the duty of member states to fulfil the Charter's obligations in good faith; the use of peaceful means to settle international disputes; the prohibition of the threat or use of force against the territorial integrity or independence of any state; the duty to assist the United Nations in any action it takes in accordance with the Charter – Article 2(5) (principle of loyalty); the obligation of non-members to act in accordance with the principles laid down in the Charter – Article 2(6). The formulation of Article 2(6) indicates, as I have said, that the whole of Chapter 1 of the Charter is to be considered as binding on all participants of international society.

In an early and influential article, the eminent jurist Georg Schwarzenberger, said that the seven principles of Article 2, which he described as "the seven pillars", occupied a higher place in the system of the Charter because they constitute a consensual *jus cogens* of the organization. These norms are "peremptory and overriding in the relations of those subjects in the law of the UN." By assuming that the rules in the Charter are consensual *jus cogens* the author implies that the nature of the Charter is derived from a contract or a treaty binding on the parties to it. The rules in question represent a major part of the constitution of the organization, a legal framework within which the institution operates.[23]

Schwarzenberger thus seems to be limiting the impact of the Charter to member states of the United Nations. That, however, is too narrow an interpretation.

---

21 *Jus cogens* general.

22 *Barcelona Traction Case*, ICJ Reports 1970, p. 32; 46 *Int. Law Reports* 178, 206.

23 Georg Schwarzenberger, "International Jus Cogens" 45 *Texas L.R.* 455 (1965).

Jus cogens norms contained in the Charter, even if effectively expressed by the consensual text of the Charter, are binding regardless of the document from which they stem. Their content makes them constitutional and the text containing them constitutional in character. The fundamental treaty containing basic norms of *jus cogens* should be seen as not only binding the parties to this very treaty but as inspiring the whole of international society.

In summary, we can say, with Juan Carrillo Salcedo, "that we can no longer defend an exclusively voluntarist conception of international law ... since the existence of norms of international jus cogens and of obligations erga omnes show that it has to an extent been transcended .... The notion of jus cogens has introduced a hierarchy into contemporary international law."[24] What is needed now is a new and more complete articulation of the rights of the international community and the obligations of the members to protect and promote the community as such.

Principles of Solidarity and Cooperation

Collective rights manifest themselves in many areas. The duty of a state not to defeat the object and purpose of a treaty which it has signed or approved (though not yet ratified or become a party thereto) represents a duty of solidarity to other states parties. It also represents a duty of collective solidarity to the international collectivity of states and to the institutional framework created by the treaty. Several solidarity-related concepts are already well established in national and international judicial systems and even a brief reference to a few examples helps us acquire a sense of the emerging constitutional nature of the international legal system.

i.   *Bundestreue* in German Constitutional Law

The principle of "*Bundestreue*", which translates into English as "fidelity to the federation", has a long history in German constitutional law. It expresses a duty of loyalty to the federation and to the idea of cooperation between the federal government and the Länder and it influences the strict interpretation and application of the letter of the Basic Law.[25]

The German Constitutional Court first elaborated the principle of *Bundestreue* in the 1950s and used it most aggressively in the 1960s. It was first mentioned in 1952 in a case where the Constitutional Court held that a legislative provision requiring the *Länder* to agree to the allocation of federal funds demanded unanimous consent of all *Länder*. The Court emphasized, however, that a duty of fidelity obligated the Länder to cooperate and work together in good faith to reach a common understanding with the federal government. Other cases involved salaries of Länder employees, restriction of confessional education by the *Länder* and obligations of

---

24   Juan Antonio Carrillo Salcedo, "Reflections on the Existence of a Hierarchy of Norms in International Law," 8 *European Journal of International Law* 583 (1997).

25   R.St.J. Macdonald, "Solidarity in the Practice and Discourse of Public International Law," 8 *Pace International Law Review* 259 (1996); K. Wellens, "Solidarity as a Constitutional Principle: Its Expanding Role and Inherent Limitations," Chapter 29, *supra*.

international treaties, and the establishment of a second television channel by the federal government. The court also applied the doctrine of *Bundestreue* to protect the power of the federal government, for example, in the case of a referendum on nuclear armament organized by a local authority.

In addition to *Bundestreue*, which, though now less prominent than it was in the 1960s, remains a relevant principle in the context of German federalism, it is important to bear in mind that German constitutional law also incorporates major obligations on mutual cooperation, loyalty and assistance in the financial chapter of the Basic Law (*Das Finanzwesen* Articles 104(a) to 115 GG). The structure of the financial system of federalism in the Basic Law seeks to reconcile the budgetary and fiscal autonomy of the *Länder* and local authorities with sound finance and an equal level of resources and social provision throughout Germany.

ii.   The Duty of Mutual Cooperation in the Jurisprudence of the European Court of Justice

The concept of solidarity is also echoed in the jurisprudence of the European Court of Justice. Article 5 of the European Economic Community Treaty says that "Member States shall take all appropriate measures, whether general or particular, to ensure fulfilment of the obligations arising out of this Treaty or resulting from action taken by the institutions of the Community. They shall facilitate the achievement of the Community's tasks. They shall abstain from any measure which could jeopardize the attainment of the objectives of this Treaty." Article 5 thus imposes two general duties on states parties to the treaty: to honor commitments growing out of the treaty or Community actions and to promote the realization of the aims of the Community. The jurisprudence of the European Court of Justice (ECJ), especially in recent years, has developed these general duties.

Three applications of Article 5 can be distinguished. Originally the court used Article 5 to reinforce the application of other more specific provisions in the treaty. A second application uses Article 5 as an independent basis of obligations of states party to the treaty. For example, in *Factortame and Others*, a case involving new British requirements for the registration of fishing vessels, the ECJ held that "it is for the national courts, in application of the principle of cooperation laid down in Article 5 of the EEC Treaty, to ensure the legal protection which persons derive from the direct effect of provisions of Community law." While in the *Factortame case* the ECJ required the national court to "invent" injunctions against Acts of the Crown (measures that were unknown to British law up to that moment) the *Francovich case* went even further. Based on Article 5, the court laid down the principle that member states that violate their treaty obligations must compensate individuals who suffer damage as a consequence thereof. This application of Article 5 thus seeks to ensure the full implementation of Community law by creating positive obligations for member states.

The third application of Article 5 most closely resembles the concept of solidarity in international law in that it establishes a duty of mutual cooperation or loyalty in interstate federalism. Under this case law, a state may have failed to comply with its Article 5 obligations if it "adversely affected the interests of another Member State" without good reason. Since the prosperity of all member states is an aim of the treaty, one state may not harm another without reason or justification. Member states may also be obliged to take positive action to harmonize their legislation and policies to conform with those of other member states.

This duty of mutual cooperation also obtains between Community institutions and member states in a manner analogous to the principle of Bundestreue on the domestic level. In fact, Judge Ole Due, President of the ECJ, recently observed that *"[L]'article 5 a pris, dans la jurisprudence de la Cour, une importance qui dépasse de loin celle du principe 'Pacta sunt servanda'dans le droit international et qui se rapproche de celle du principe de droit fédéral qui, dans le droit constitutionnel allemand, s'appelle la 'Bundestreue'".*

iii.   The Principle of Cooperation

But the principle of solidarity is to be found not only in the jurisprudence of the European Court of Justice in relation to Article 5 of the EC Treaty. As early as 1953, the preamble of the ECSC Treaty, which was concluded before the EEC Treaty and the Euratom Treaty, referred to solidarity by recognizing that Europe could be built "only through practical achievements which will first of all create real solidarity, and through the establishment of common bases for economic development." After the adoption of the *Maastricht Treaty*, a reference to the principle of solidarity was included in the EC Treaty (the former EEC Treaty): "The Community shall have as its task ... the promotion ... of ... the economic and social cohesion and solidarity among member States."

Article 18 of the Vienna Convention, the obligation not to defeat the object and purpose of a treaty prior to its entry into force, is carried a step farther in Article I-5(2) of the European *Constitution*:

> Following the principle of loyal cooperation, the Union and the Member States shall, in full mutual respect, assist each other in carrying out tasks which flow from the Constitution.
>
> The Member States shall facilitate the achievement of the Union's tasks and refrain from any measure which could jeopardise the attainment of the objectives set out in the Constitution.

This important concept, expressed at least as clearly as similar provisions in the Charter of the United Nations, is balanced by the idea of state sovereignty at Article I-5(1):

> The Union shall respect the national identities of the Member States, inherent in their fundamental structures, political and constitutional, inclusive of regional and local self-government. It shall respect their essential State functions, including those for ensuring the territorial integrity of the State, and for maintaining law and order and safeguarding internal security.

In other words, the principle of loyal cooperation applies (mainly) in so far as it does not fundamentally interfere with basic prerogative powers of the state concerning territorial integrity, law and order, and internal security. The European Constitution quite rightly recognizes the need for an essential balance between the collective interest and the singular state interest.

iv.   Other Examples

It is possible to find expressions of collective rights beyond the Charter. The ancient principle of *pacta sunt servanda*, reaffirmed by the Preamble and Article 2(2) of the Charter, thought by Kelsen to be a *grundnorm*, does not bind individual states to treaties agreed upon by other states but nevertheless it represents a protection of state interests and has a collective component in that it involves a principle of the free will of states and a requirement for consent in treaty matters. Other examples may be mentioned. The "common heritage of humanity" is a collective concept re-iterated frequently in constitution-like treaties such as the United Nations Law of the Sea Convention.[26] The 2001 Convention on the Protection of the Underwater Cultural Heritage requires States Parties to "preserve underwater cultural heritage for the benefit of humanity in conformity with the provisions of this Convention."[27] Not only is a collective interest (and a collective identity) identified but the role of states parties is defined: they are *trustees on behalf of the collective*. We see here evidence of the law of equity in operation – for example in the idea of sustainability so that resources or heritage are shared fairly. Inherent in such a regime would be good faith dealings, proportionality, and reasonableness.

C.   *Individual Rights*

(i)   In the Charter*:* Despite its positivist orientation, the Charter contains ex-tremely important provisions on international human rights. The Preamble men-tions the rights of individuals both in terms of the ultimate source of its authority ("We the Peoples of the United Nations") and in its determination: "To reaffirm faith in fundamental human rights, in the dignity and worth of the human person, in the equal rights of men and women and of nations large and small ... [and] To employ international machinery for the promotion of the economic and social advancement of all peoples...". Article 1(3) includes among the purposes of the organization "pro-moting and encouraging respect for human rights and fundamental freedoms for all without distinction as to race, sex, language or religion." Article 13(1)(b) mandates

---

26   United Nations Convention on the Law of the Sea, Dec. 10, 1982, 1833 UNTS 397; 21 ILM 1261 (1982) at Article 119. Frank Biermann, "Common Concerns of Humankind and National Sovereignty," in *Globalism: People, Profits and Progress*. Canadian Coun-cil on International Law, 30th Annual Conference, 2001 (The Hague: Kluwer, 2002), p. 158. See too Maurizio Ragazzi, "*The Concept of International Obligations Erga Omnes* (Oxford: Clarendon Press, 1997).

27   UNESCO, UN Educational, Scientific and Cultural Organization (UNESCO): Conven-tion on the Protection of the Underwater Cultural Heritage, Text of Convention, ILM 41 (2002), 40; also on UNESCO website <http://www.unesco.org/culture/laws/under-water/html_eng/convention.shtml> (accessed 30 November 2003).

the General Assembly to initiate studies and make recommendations to promote international cooperation in the economic, social, cultural, educational, and health fields, and to assist in the realization of human rights and fundamental freedoms for all without distinction as to race, sex, language or religion. Article 55 similarly mandates the United Nations to promote economic, social, health, cultural and educational interests and to promote universal respect for, and observance of, human rights and fundamental freedoms. In brief, the Charter represents a major step forward in the process of articulating and establishing internationally recognized standards of human rights. It reaffirmed the commitment to promoting individuals' rights that appeared in many major instruments from the mid-nineteenth century onwards and provided the foundation on which was built the modern process of rendering individuals responsible for their violations of international law.

(ii) **International Instruments**: Direct reference to individual rights outside the *Charter* abound in a series of constitution-like treaties some of which have standing as jus cogens and customary international law. The rightly famous Universal Declaration of Human Rights, adopted by the General Assembly in 1948, establishes a "common standard of achievement for all peoples and nations." Over time the ratification of "supplementary" conventions on specific aspects of human rights gave greater weight to the general standards of the Universal Declaration. Support for these conventions range from near unanimity (the Genocide Convention) to the sporadic (the Mercenary Convention).[28] Generally speaking, the rights so itemized affect individuals indirectly, though it can be argued that some of these treaties, for instance the Geneva Conventions of 1949, have acquired standing as customary international law. Thus Protocol II of the Geneva Conventions of 1979 was applied (arguably) to both France and the United States – even though they were not signatories – during the Kosovo conflict of 1991.

(iii) **Statute of the International Criminal Tribunal**: Perhaps the greatest advance in terms of the standing of individuals in the international legal order occurred in the domain of international criminal law. Under Article 1 of the Statute of the International Criminal Tribunal for the former Yugoslavia, created by Security Council Resolution, the Tribunal has power to prosecute persons responsible for serious violations of international humanitarian law committed in the territory of the former Yugoslavia since 1991, in accordance with the provisions of the Statute.[29]

---

28   Convention on the Prevention and Punishment of the Crime of Genocide, December 9, 1948, 78 UNTS 277, reprinted in 28 ILM 763 (1989); and International Convention against the Recruitment, Use, Financing and Training of Mercenaries, 4 December 1989, GAOR UN Doc. A/RES/44/43 online: UNTS Official Records of the General Assembly, Forty-Fourth Session, Supplement No. 49 (A/44/49) <http://www.un.org> (accessed 5 May 2002).

29   ICTY, *Statute of the International Tribuna*, SC Res. 827 (1993), UN Doc. S/RES.827 (1993) (25 May 1993) last amended by UN Doc. S/RES 1534 (2004) (26 March 2004). ICTY Office of the Prosecutor, *Final Report to the Prosecutor by the Committee Estab-*

The Tribunal recognizes the individual through its provisions on personal jurisdiction and individual criminal responsibility. Individuals who are victims are also recognized. In brief, a direct link to individuals is established in an international jurisdiction by a subsidiary organ of the Security Council. We see here a radical departure from the traditional positivist perspective that states are the sole intermediary between individuals at the national level and international institutions at the global level.

Articles 9 and 10 of the Statute deal with "concurrent jurisdiction" and "ne bis in idem." Article 9 provides, first, that the Tribunal and national courts shall have concurrent jurisdiction, yet, in a following sub-paragraph, the Tribunal is said to enjoy primacy over national courts at any stage of the procedure; it can request that a case be deferred to it. In Article 10, the Security Council asserts that the Tribunal can try a case previously tried by a national court but only if the act or crime was mischaracterized as an ordinary crime or "the national court proceedings were not impartial or independent" and were essentially sham proceedings. Article 9 is curious in that there is no presumption that the state is willing and capable of carrying out the trial: it is entirely up to the Prosecutor to determine if a *prima facie* case exists and for the Trial Chamber judge to review it for confirmation. Since the Statute was adopted under a Security Council Resolution 827(1993), Article 103 of the Charter and Article 29 of the Statute require its compliance by all Member States.

The approach adopted for the International Criminal Tribunal for the former Yugoslavia was also adopted for the International Criminal Tribunal for Rwanda and, to a lesser extent, the Special Court for Sierra Leone. Perhaps the reason for the absence of a presumption of state capability and willingness is that, in all these countries, there was no doubt that the state was incapable and unwilling to prosecute serious crimes contrary to international humanitarian law. Nevertheless, the international standing of individuals within those states represents an unparalleled achievement in the modern era.

(iv) The Rome Statute of the International Criminal Court: This Statute marks the establishment of another direct link between international law and institutions and individuals within the States Party to the Statute, a treaty. Article 1 of the Statute says that:

> An International Criminal Court ('the Court') is hereby established. It shall be a permanent institution and shall have the power to exercise its jurisdiction over persons for the most serious crimes of international concern, as referred to in this Statute, and shall be complementary to national criminal jurisdictions. The jurisdiction and functioning of the Court shall be governed by the provisions of this Statute.

---

lished to *Review the NATO Bombing Campaign Against the Federal Republic of Yugoslavia* (The Hague: 13 June 2000). This report is contentious; it represented the views of the Office of the Prosecutor but it was never formally endorsed (or rejected) by the Chambers of the Tribunal or by the Security Council.

The Court is described as being "complementary" rather than having "primacy", as in the case of the International Criminal Tribunal. Unlike the Statute of the ICTY, the Rome Statute is not based on a Security Council Resolution; it is founded on a multilateral treaty of "like-minded states." Importantly, there exists a presumption that Member States are capable and willing to investigate and prosecute an individual alleged to have committed international crimes that fall within the jurisdiction of the International Criminal Court. Only after this presumption is rebutted is the case deemed admissible. Article 17(1) says that a case is inadmissible when:

a.   The case is being investigated or prosecuted by a State which has jurisdiction over it, unless the State is unwilling or unable genuinely to carry out the investigation or prosecution;

b.   The case has been investigated by a State which has jurisdiction over it and the State has decided not to prosecute the person concerned, unless the decision resulted from the unwillingness or inability of the State genuinely to prosecute.

Some commentators (including a former Chief Prosecutor of the ICTY) think that Article 17 amounts to a reversal of the "primacy approach" adopted in the Statute of the ICTY: the ICC, it is said, may only supplement national criminal justice systems when there is inadequate domestic will or inability to prosecute. This assessment may not be entirely fair. In the ICTY context, the assessment was made in 1993 that the successor state to the former Yugoslavia was no longer capable and willing to investigate or prosecute in good faith. Presumably the Security Council was fully aware of the situation when it gave the Tribunal primacy over this limited group of national jurisdictions.

In 2001, Tribunal President Claude Jorda (now a judge at the ICC) grappled with the issue of primacy and the complementary relationship between the Tribunal and national courts. The issue arose over a Bosnian proposal to establish a Truth and Reconciliation Commission in Bosnia and Herzegovina:

... I consider it my duty to ensure that this national initiative not run counter to the mission of the Tribunal and that it be consonant with the powers conferred on the Tribunal by the Security Council. I also believe it appropriate to reflect on a system for reconciliation which complements the work of the International Tribunal and which allows for a more effective contribution to the reconstruction of national unity without which democracy and deep-rooted lasting peace are impossible ...[30]

This mode of thinking is consistent with the way the ICC asserts its jurisdiction over states that are unwilling or incapable and on how the EU accomplishes the same thing when a Member State cannot sufficiently achieve the objectives of an intended action of the Union. In this sensitive, potentially controversial and divisive area, we see practical limitations at work on the powers of an international

---

30   ICTY, Press Release JL/P.I.S./591-e, "President Claude Jorda: The ICTY and the Truth and Reconciliation Commission in Bosnia and Herzegovina" (17 May 2001).

institution to override the preferences of a reluctant or recalcatrant state. An equilibrium is sought between international democratic subsidiarity and national executive subsidiarity.

In bringing these brief remarks on a few of the principles of global constitutionalism to a close, it is appropriate to emphasize that the United Nations, as a constitutional legal order, confers juridically enforceable rights and obligations on individuals and associations as well as on states themselves. While it is apparent that there are insufficient mechanisms closely linking international institutions, which represent the values and power of the international community, with the peoples of the world, the fact remains that there are essential doctrines of interconnection, such as those on supremacy, direct effect, self execution, and implied powers, assuring the enforceability of individual rights and obligations by the national courts and tribunals. It is highly important to recognize that normal relations between the constitutional orders of nation states and the constitutional order of the United Nations are not in conflict but are complementary, cooperative and coexistent. When conflict does arise, the state (or UN) has deviated from the Purpose and Principles.

In continuing our search for ways and means of effectively connecting national institutions with institutions of international government, a possibility meriting renewed attention is the familiar but neglected idea of allowing national courts to request advisory opinions of the International Court of Justice. In this regard, it is intriguing to recall that even before the Permanent Court of International Justice took shape, some scholars (Von Bar, Anzilotti) recognized that it would be useful to allow individual States to seek advisory opinions on matters of international law from a world tribunal. This idea received scholarly support towards the end of the First World War and during the interwar years, notably from Lauterpacht, but it found no expression in the statute of the Permanent Court of International Justice. When the San Francisco Conference convened in the spring of 1945 to define the post-World War Two international order, British and Venezuelan representatives proposed that the new world court be authorized to provide advisory opinions to individual States; the Committee of Jurists declined to adopt the proposal and it lapsed temporarily into obscurity.

However, when the United Nations General Assembly examined the role of the International Court of Justice in the early 1970s, such a proposal attracted renewed attention. The representatives of Argentina, Austria, Belgium, Cyprus, Denmark, Finland, Guatemala, Iraq, Madagascar, Senegal, Sweden, Switzerland and Turkey stated that a proposal to allow States to request advisory opinions of the International Court of Justice deserved consideration.

In 1976 the United States Department of State went a step further: it agreed that the International Court's statute might be amended to permit it to issue preliminary opinions on international legal issues submitted by national appellate courts. A 1982 resolution of the House of Representatives invited President Reagan to explore whether a special committee might be instituted under United Nations auspices to seek advisory opinions from the International Court further to a national court's request. As the 1980s advanced, American enthusiasm for the proposal dwindled: a contributory factor was doubtless the International Court's judgment in *Nicaragua v. United States*, [1986] 1 ICJ Reports 14. In the mid-1990s, though, former President Guillaume of the International Court, in line with earlier suggestions by Judges Lauterpact and Schwebel, expressed the opinion that references to the International Court by national courts of vexed issues of public international law might be appropriate in some circumstances.

5.   The Institutions: Security Council and the General Assembly

Bearing in mind that it is not the word "constitution" that gives to some legal texts greater importance than others, it is apparent from the foregoing that the material content of the Charter of United Nations is indeed constitutional and that we are fully justified in treating the Charter as the constitution of the international community. Reassuring as this is, we must nevertheless recognize that even if the material framework of an international constitution is in place the institutional and procedural guarantees that would provide realistic and effective application of those provisions have yet to be realized. While the present state of world affairs does not make one wildly optimistic, a gradual reform of the legal-constitutional structure created by the Charter is in the common interest. While it remains to be seen whether this idea can be translated into concrete political decisions it is highly relevant to promote informed discussion of two of the principal institutions that require attention at the present time.

A.   *The Security Council* [31]

i.   The Problems

Under Article 24(1) of the Charter of the United Nations, signed in San Francisco in 1945, Members of the United Nations conferred on the Security Council primary responsibility for the maintenance of international peace and security, and agreed that in carrying out its duties under this responsibility the Security Council acts on their behalf. The fifty-one original members have now become 191, with just two states, Taiwan and the Vatican, outside the UN family. Despite this overwhelming increase in membership, reform of the organs of the UN has not kept apace. The only alteration to the composition of the Security Council occurred in 1963, when the eleven members, comprising the permanent five (P-5) and the elected six, agreed to increase the number of elected members by four. Since then, the "executive" of the UN, or what former British Prime Minister Harold Macmillan memorably called "the Cabinet of the world,"[32] has frustratingly remained unchanged.

---

31   "The [Security] Council must work effectively, but it must also enjoy unquestioned legitimacy. Those two criteria define the space within which a solution must be found." Kofi A. Annan, *We the Peoples: The Role of the United Nations in the 21ˢᵗ Century*, (New York: United Nations, Department of Public Information, 2000), p. 69.

32   Quoted in Kishore Mahbubani, "The Permanent and Elected Council Members," in David M. Malone (ed.), *The UN Security Council: From the Cold War to the 21ˢᵗ Cen-*

The end of the Cold War, the collapse of the former USSR, and the consensus achieved by the Security Council in ensuring that military force was used against Iraq in the first Gulf War, caused many to forecast a central role for the UN in what President George Bush described as the "new world order." The fact that it has not taken this opportunity cannot be said to be due to any lack of political will on the part of the majority of the member states or indeed the officials within the organization. In 1992, former Secretary-General Boutros Boutros-Ghali called for "the application of the principles of democracy within the World Organisation itself"[33] and in September 2002, Kofi Annan observed that "a formula that would allow an increase in Council membership is still eluding Member States, [notwithstanding that] in the eyes of much of the world, the size and composition of the Security Council appear insufficiently representative."[34]

In December 1993, the General Assembly established the Open-ended Working Group (OEWG), a body that continues to meet to this day, on the Question of Equitable Representation on and increase in the Membership of the Security Council. Shortly after its formation, the OEWG organised its work into two main topics. Cluster I would discuss "equitable representation on and increase in the membership of the Security Council" and Cluster II would concentrate on Other Matters related to the Security Council, particularly measures and practices to enhance the Council's transparency and to improve its working methods. I will address only those proposals brought up in the context of Cluster I.

Relevant problems are essentially threefold and are all interlinked. First, how large should an enlarged Security Council be? Second, should it be made up of new permanent or non-permanent members, or a mixture of both, and by what criteria should these be determined? Finally, what should be the future status of the veto? Should the veto be given to any new permanent members and should its application be limited?

ii.   The Size of an Enlarged Security Council

Perhaps the only issue on which all member states unanimously agree is that the Security Council must increase in size. As many delegations and scholars have noted, "Council membership [in 1945] represented 21.56% of the membership of the Organisation, or a ratio of one Council member to every five Member States [whereas] .... Today, with a total membership of 191 Member States, the Council represents 7.85% of the UN membership, or a ratio of 1 Council member to every 12.5 Member States."[35]

---

tury, (Boulder: Lynne Rienner, 2004), pp. 253-266, at p. 255.

33   Boutros Boutros-Ghali, *Agenda for Peace*, (2nd edition, New York: United Nations, 1995), para. 82.

34   Quoted in Bardo Fassbender, "Pressure for Security Council Reform," in David Malone, *supra* note 32, pp. 341-356, at p. 341.

35   Chairman's Summary of the Open-Ended Working Group on the Question of Equitable Representation on and Increase in the Membership of the Security Council and

The problem is difficult to address without considering how the divide between permanent and non-permanent members can be fairly resolved. Many of the developing countries stress Article 23(1) of the Charter, which confirms that non-permanent members should be elected with due regard being specially paid, in the first instance to the contribution of Members of the United Nations to the maintenance of international peace and security and to the other purposes of the organization, and *also to equitable geographical distribution.* Although amendments to the Charter in the 1960s helped ensure that underrepresented areas, including Africa, Latin America, and Asia, were better represented in the Security Council, the feeling persists that until the Security Council considers electing permanent members from some or all of these continents the imbalance between North and South will endure. Abdulmejid Hussein, the representative of Ethiopia, on behalf of the African Group, ominously warned the General Assembly in 2002 that, "An expansion of the Council, particularly of the permanent members, would only occur if Africa were included."[36]

One of the more difficult challenges is to reconcile Article 2(1) of the Charter, which provides for "the sovereign equality of all members", with the Security Council's representativeness. Bardo Fassbender defines the latter as "a function of its composition and the relative participatory rights of its members," adding that "a body can only be called representative if due regard is paid to the dissimilarity of its constituent members."[37] Understandably, the developing countries stress the lack of equality, contending that a 15-seat body representing 191 states is unfair, especially considering that the P-5 are permanently guaranteed representation and all possess the right of veto.

On the other hand, the P-5 and some other developed countries, particularly Germany and Japan, who are seeking permanent seats on the Council, argue that they contribute most resources to international peace and security as per Article 23(1), including troops where necessary, and UN budget assistance. Indeed, in 1998 in regard to the latter, "only 14 of the 185 Member States contributed more than 1% each; together, they raise more than 80% of the budget."[38] Perhaps this debate is best surmised by Kishore Mahbubani, the Permanent Representative of Singapore to the UN: "the structural weakness in the Council has resulted from a dichotomy. In the Council, the P-5 have been given power without responsibility; the E-10 have been given responsibility without power."[39]

The other principal claim advanced by developed countries for limiting the reform of the Security Council is the 'efficiency and effectiveness' argument. Fass-

---

Other Matters Related to the Security Council, [hereafter Chairman's Summary] 6 May 2004, paras. 4 & 5.

36   Quoted in Bardo Fassbender, *supra* note 34, at p. 352.

37   Bardo Fassbender, *UN Security Council Reform and the Right of Veto*, (The Hague: Kluwer Law International, 1998), pp. 296, 298.

38   *Ibid.*, 206.

39   Bardo Fassbender, *supra* note 34, at 346.

bender again provides the definition: Efficiency "is meant to describe the Council's ability to deal swiftly with a situation that falls within its sphere of competence, that is to say, to adopt necessary measures without delay.... Effectiveness characterizes the degree to which the Council's decisions are actually implemented. The more 'players' there are...the less efficient and effective the work of the Council will be."[40] One could also point out that pursuit of national interests by the P-5 prevents the decision-making processes of the Security Council from working more efficiently than any expansion of its membership. A lack of UN action in the Balkans, in Rwanda in 1994 and in Darfur, a region of Sudan in 2004, is evidence of the weaknesses of the Council that prevent it from reaching resolutions quickly and effectively. Nonetheless, national interests or not, it is probably true that more members would make the decision-making processes of the Council more unmanageable.

Before considering a few of the proposals for dividing the permanent and non-permanent members, it is useful to review the proposals of some members for the potential size and composition of a future Security Council. In its last public statement on the subject in July 1997, the United States declared that it could "agree to a maximum of 20 to 21 members" However, the most recent summary from the OEWG in April 2004 held that "a majority of those speaking in favour of an expanded Security Council proposed numbers ranging from 24 to 26 members, which would involve an increase of between 9 and 11 members respectively."[41] Britain's most recent proposal for UN Security Council reform, published in June 2003, calls for a 24-seat body, as does the most recent Japanese submission (see below). Among other permanent members, China, in its self-professed role as leader of the developing world, would probably be happiest to see a Council made up of a number of members in the mid-20s, whereas Russia and France, who fear their global influence may wane, are likely to favour a number in the low-20s rather than around 25.

iii.   The Structure of a Future Security Council and a "Third Category" of Members

Potential candidates for permanent membership of the Security Council include Germany in Europe, Japan and India in Asia, Brazil and Argentina in Latin America, and Egypt, South Africa and Nigeria in Africa. By permanent membership, it is important to note that we mean a permanent seat on the Security Council. There is a great deal of controversy as to whether new permanent members should be granted the right of veto, a matter that will be discussed below.

Attempts to reform have consistently been obstructed. As Ambassador Mahbubani explains, "the usual gridlock of competing national interests, in which each new aspirant state is strongly blocked by a jealous or threatened neighboring state, has stymied all efforts to change the composition."[42] This criticism extends to the P-5 as well. From 1995 onwards, the United States has maintained that it "enthusiasti-

---

40   Bardo Fassbender, *supra* note 34, at 341.

41   Chairman's Summary, *supra* note 35, paragraph 6.

42   Kishore Mahbubani, *supra* note 32, at p. 261.

cally endorse[s] the candidacies of Japan and Germany and that it could not agree to a Council enlargement that did not result in their permanent membership."[43] The latest British proposal is for an expansion to ten permanent members, including Germany, Japan, India as well as one Latin American and African country, yet to be decided.[44] However, it seems Moscow and Beijing may object to Germany and Japan. As Fassbender acknowledges in relation to Russia, "strong resentments against enhancing the status of the former enemies Germany and Japan must be presumed" and, regarding China, "it will not be easy to win China's support for any improvement in the position of Western capitalist states on the Council."[45] China and Japan, moreover, have a long-running dispute over the absence of Japanese apologies for atrocities committed during the Second World War and Russia is unlikely to wish to broker a deal with America's foremost ally in the Asia-Pacific without the resolution of the dispute over the Kurile Islands.

Germany and Japan have both indicated their "willingness" to become permanent members. Germany has advanced "a 2 + 3" proposal, which would see Germany and Japan join as permanent members at the same time as one representative from Asia, Latin America and Africa. The Germans argue that this arrangement would shift the balance more favourably from developed to developing countries from the present 4:1 ratio, to a 6:4 ratio in the future.

An interesting feature of the German suggestion is the proposal for the adoption, under Article 23 of the Charter, of a "periodic review clause," which would only be applied to new permanent members, who would not be permitted to veto its results. According to the Germans, this review, "compulsorily taking place after fifteen years, 'shall guarantee that an increase in both membership categories is not irreversible.'"[46] It could be argued that this plan should be made applicable to the permanent members as well, but that is simply fanciful.

One of the problems with the review aspect of the German proposal is the potential for blackmail. Although completely against the spirit of the UN, the review clause would need to be passed by a two-thirds majority of the General Assembly. It is not inconceivable that a group of nations, from Africa for example, though the group could easily come from other areas as well, could come together to insist that it would not support continued German membership until Germany fulfilled certain conditions, such as pledging to increase aid to Africa or refusing to participate in humanitarian interventions in Africa, which many African countries continue to view as an infringement of sovereignty and thus contrary to international law.

The United States has never said so explicitly, but it is nevertheless in favor of the "2 + 3" proposal. In July 1997, America agreed with the principle of granting three new permanent seats to the continents proposed by Germany, adding that

---

43   Bardo Fassbender, *supra* note 34, p. 346.

44   Ewen MacAskill, "Straw Plan to Boost UN Security Council," *The Guardian*, June 11th 2003, available online at <http://www.globalpolicy.org/security/reform/cluster1/2003/0611straw.htm>, (accessed 12 May 2004).

45   Bardo Fassbender, *supra* note 34, p. 346.

46   *Ibid.*, 242.

"the regions themselves ought to decide how these seats will be filled."[47] However, the "gridlock of competing national interests" to which Ambassador Mahbubani referred, makes this unlikely. Argentina refuses to accept Brazil's candidature on the ground that it would be wrong for a non-Spanish speaking country to represent Latin America; Pakistan dismisses Indian claims for the right to a seat, and in Africa it is far from clear whether Nigeria, the largest country by population, is sufficiently stable politically to represent the continent; South Africa and Egypt maintain that they would be more suitable applicants.

The one method of resolving these competing and, some would argue, seemingly irresolvable claims would be for a rotation of members from each region; such members would then represent their continent on the Security Council for a specified length of time, probably around five years. This proposal of "permanent regional rotating seats" has found particular favour with the African Union, formerly the Organization for African Unity (OAU), which demands at least two permanent seats on any reformed Council. The selection of rotating members would be made by the region itself, according to criteria that it establishes. As Fassbender notes, "what is meant by this was made clear in a statement by Tunisia on May 10, 1996: 'the country which occupies that seat will have to enjoy the veto right and would not have to consult with other states of that region before exercising it.'"[48]

While the African Union is more or less united behind this proposal, it remains to be seen whether it could work in other regions. India, for example, rejects any rotation scheme, arguing that it deserves permanent membership outright. Moreover, it is not certain that Latin American nations would agree with the rotating proposal, although the Organization of American States (OAS) is a political body through which decisions about selection could be filtered.

The rotation plan is unlikely to be achieved because it is inimical to the interests of the current permanent members, for reasons that will be explained.

Many states have advanced the idea of establishing criteria within Article 23 that members must satisfy if they wish to serve on the Security Council. This however has simply stirred up more debate about what the most important criteria should be. Large countries, such as India and Nigeria, say that population is critical, whereas others, such as Japan, say that contributions to the UN budget are major considerations. Other countries, including the United States, argued that the 'best way' to make sure the Security Council is truly representative is "to ensure that democratic countries serve on it."[49] China, for one, would be unlikely to support such a statement. Other states emphasize other factors, including economic

---

47   Statements by a spokesman of the Department of State, July 17-18, 1997; US Department of State, Daily Press Briefing nos. 108-109 (quoted in Fassbender, *supra* note 34, at p. 347).

48   *Ibid.*, p. 349.

49   Kim R. Holmes, "The Challenges Facing the United Nations Today: An American View," Speech to the Council on Foreign Relations, October 21st 2003, Washington DC, available online at <http://www.state.gov/p/io/rls/rm/2003/25491.htm> (accessed 22 June 2004).

power, a country's size, and differing interpretations of the language of Article 23, such as "the contribution of Members of the United Nations to the maintenance of international peace and security and to other purposes of the Organization". Some states interpret this to mean financial support whereas others stress the provision of troops and/or peacekeepers.

As mentioned above, almost every state has committed to increase the number of non-permanent/elected members, although by what number is dependent on how many new permanent members are admitted. It is probable that membership would be extended on the basis of the geographical representation established by the previous enlargement in the 1960s. Although they are more than happy to consider the principle of "equitable geographical distribution" in Article 23 in relation to new elected or non-permanent members, the P-5 appear reluctant to pay due attention to that principle when pondering new permanent members. The current distribution of elected seats is two for the Western Europe and Other Group (WEO), one for Eastern Europe, five for Africa and Asia and two for Latin America and the Caribbean.[50]

If, as it should be, the goal is to have true equitable geographical distribution, it may be appropriate to extend the number of regions by two so as to include both East Asia and Oceania and either a Middle East or League of Arab States representative. In the 1990s, Italy submitted a paper arguing that members of the United Nations are not evenly rotating the non-permanent seats and claiming that 77 out of the 185 members of the UN (at that time) had never sat on the Security Council. However, the Czech Republic countered that this number could be reduced to 17 since the others had obstacles preventing their inclusion. For example, they

> became members of the organization only after 1990, they have a population of less than 0.5m and are therefore likely to lack the resources needed for an effective participation in the work of the Security Council; they are themselves coping with serious problems concerning peace and security; they are chronically in arrears in the payment of their financial contributions to the United Nations (Article 19 of the Charter); or they do not belong to any of the regional groups.[51]

Another idea that has received a measure of support is to create a "third category" of members. This idea stems from a perceived inability to find solutions that will be acceptable to both the P-5 and a majority of other countries. There are varying forms that such an idea could take. One is the concept of quasi or semi-permanent members, who would have the same rights as permanent members, except the right of veto. The positive and negative implications of this suggestion will be explored below. Turkey has proposed "ten new seats to be rotated among a specific

---

50   As established by GA Res. 1991A (XVIII), eighteenth session (1963); the amendments did not come into force until 1965 after a two-thirds ratification by Assembly members. See David M. Malone, "Eyes on the Prize: The Quest for Non-permanent Seats on the UN Security Council," 6 *Global Governance* 3 at p. 4 (2000).

51   Fassbender, *supra* note 37, 201.

number of states determined by population, geopolitical situation, military capacity, economic potential, [and] 'history of working within the Charter,'" in addition to the two principles under Article 23. This submission appears too unwieldy, based as it is on broad categories and without guidance as to which measures are most important.

One other suggestion that has gained considerable attention, particularly among "middle powers", who sense an opportunity for more frequent representation, is a joint proposition by Italy and Spain. They advocate "10 new non-permanent seats, each of which rotates among three states, making a total of 30…. [This would mean] two years on, four years off, based on objective criteria determined by the General Assembly and subject to revision every 10, 12 or 15 years."[52] Although the flexibility this proposal offers in the form of a review clause is welcome, it nonetheless reeks of a proposal that would serve only to further the interests of so-called "middle powers" who feel that they are underrepresented on the Security Council vis-à-vis smaller nations.

iv.   The Veto

Since the establishment of the OEWG in the early 1990s, the veto probably ranks as the principal source of disagreement. Many developing countries view it as an anachronism contrary to the principle of "sovereign equality" laid out in Article 2(1) of the Charter. As Richard Hiscocks stated in 1973, "The veto accurately reflected the divided world in which it was so often used. It reflected also the deliberate choice of the great powers to pursue methods of diplomacy based on national power rather than to cultivate the high principles of international cooperation and tolerance on which the United Nations Charter is based."[53]

Since the end of the Cold War, the veto has been used less frequently than in the earlier period. Nonetheless, it is often the threat of the use of the veto, rather than a veto itself, that is effective in preventing action from being taken and resolutions adopted by the Security Council. As Thomas Schindlmayr points out, "while there has been a significant increase in the number of resolutions adopted, and a marked decline in the use of the veto … the decision-making has moved away from public meetings of the Security Council to closed-door consultations, with presumably a greater use of closet vetoes."[54] An excellent example of this in practice is the lack of a UN resolution to either condemn or intervene in Russia's involvement in Chechnya. Though this is clearly a threat to international peace and security, there will not be any action taken by the Security Council due to Russian membership of the P-5.

Abolishment of the veto is the first of three principal options open to members of the Security Council. It is also the least likely. As George Monbiot, an award-

---

52   *Ibid.* p. 259.

53   Kishore Mahbubani, *supra* note 32, p. 254, quoting Richard Hiscocks.

54   Thomas Schindlmayr, "Obstructing the Security Council: The Use of the Veto in the Twentieth Century," 3 *Journal of the History of International Law* 218-234, at p. 234 (2001).

winning British Journalist and author, has noted, "the veto powers [that the] permanent members possess are a constitutional guarantee against reform: no change can be made without the consent of those whom we would seek to change. No one, at the international level, guards the guards."[55] It follows that the lack of a provision in the Charter for the abrogation of the veto makes it extremely improbable that any of the P-5 will voluntarily surrender or limit this right.

Several of the P-5, led by the United States, have repeatedly refused even to discuss the issue. American policy has not changed since Madeline Albright's famous statement as US Permanent Representative to the UN: "Because we have the veto at the Security Council, we can block any mission that is contrary to our interests, and I don't need to assure you that our continued right to the veto is not negotiable."[56] Others, such as Jeffrey Laurenti, consider any plan to alter the right of veto enjoyed by the P-5 to be futile: "American policymakers chafe at, and will bypass or breach, a system in which "has-been" powers that can't contribute to solutions nonetheless enjoy the artificial power to block solutions."[57] Furthermore, as the OEWG Vice-Chairmen wrote in their 1995 report, the P-5 continue to insist that it serves a useful function:

> Supporters of the veto asserted that it was never intended to be democratic, but rather had been a useful device which had helped to preserve unanimity among the Permanent Members, and had ensured the continued participation of the major powers in the Organization. The veto was viewed as useful in helping to guarantee that the decisions taken by the Council were balanced, as well as providing stability, preventing conflicts between major powers which could undermine UN collective security.[58]

The second option is to retain the veto for the current permanent members and refuse to extend it to new permanent members. This is the option that would be most likely to succeed, since it would not require the P-5 to weaken their status on the Council in any way. This was an integral part of the "Ismail plan" for UN reform in March 1997 by former General Assembly president Razali Ismail of Malaysia, which was arguably the closest the UN has come to reform in the past ten years. He contended that "as sustained and virtually universal condemnation has been expressed against the veto, I find it inconsistent and unacceptable both logically and morally to extend such a power to new permanent members of the Security

---

55 George Monbiot, "Who Guards the Guards?" The Guardian, December 10th 2002, available online at <http://www.globalpolicy.org/reform/1211 tyrannical. htm> (accessed 17 May 2004).

56 Fassbender, *supra* note 37.

57 Jeffrey Laurenti, "Reforming the United Nations Security Council: Will its Time Ever Come?" Conference speech in Tokyo on "The U.N Security Council and Japan," March 17th 2003, available online at <http://www.globalpolicy.org/security/reform/cluster1/2003/0513reforming.htm> (accessed 13 May 2004).

58 OEWG Vice Chairmen Report, 15 September 1995, UN Document A/49/965.

Council. To do so would be to compound an inequity."⁵⁹ However, the Singaporean Foreign Minister, Wong Kan Seng, highlighted the stubbornness of the problem of not granting the right of veto to these members when he said that, "No country that is capable of making a contribution as a new permanent member will accept such second class status for long."⁶⁰

However, the P-5 and the proposed new permanent members from every continent are deadlocked. Germany has expressed the views of the latter group in a nut-shell, maintaining that if it is to become a new permanent member, "this has to be on an equal footing with the other permanent members, without discrimination, i.e. with the same rights and the same obligations."⁶¹ This appears unlikely to garner even the support of the "P-1," let alone the P-5. As Fassbender acknowledges, "the United States intimated that it could also agree to a permanent membership of other states if they were to enjoy universal support [but] the United States has ... strictly opposed the idea of granting any developing country the right of veto."⁶² With the exception of France, the rest of the P-5 agrees with that position.

The final option, on paper the fairest solution, would be to grant all new permanent members the right of veto, but this appears improbable. The P-5 has two responses to this proposal, both of which fall under their preferred "efficiency and effectiveness" argument.

The first reflects the P-5's unwillingness to negotiate over permanent regional rotating seats. This scheme is a non-starter as far as the P-5 is concerned, because the states enjoying the right of veto would not be known in advance. Secondly, the P-5 insists that the extension of the veto to other members would undermine the ability of the Security Council to function effectively. Bill Rammell, the British Foreign Office minister responsible for the UN, acknowledged as much about Britain's proposal for Security Council reform in 2003; Britain's plan advocated no extension of the veto to new permanent members; "If we went for 10 countries with permanent vetoes, we might as well shut up shop."⁶³ This view is supported by a number of states and some NGOs, including those, such as the Global Policy Forum, which promote UN reform. As its Executive Director, James Paul, points out, "If you add another five permanent members, all of them casting vetoes, forget about anything being accomplished .... It's not just casting a veto, but the threat of casting a veto that keeps the whole issue off the agenda."⁶⁴

---

59   Statement by Razali Ismail: UN Press Release GA/9228, 20th March 1997, available online at <http://www.un.org/News/Press/ docs/1997/ 19970320. ga9228.html> (accessed 23 June 2004).

60   Bardo Fassbender, *supra* note 32, p. 350.

61   *Ibid.*

62   *Ibid.*, 346.

63   Ewen MacAskill, note 44 above.

64   Michael J. Jordan, "Who's In, Who's Out: UN Security Council Mulls Reform," *Christian Science Monitor*, October 16th 2002, available online at <http://www.globalpolicy.org/security/reform/cluster1/2002/1016who.htm> (accessed 16 May 2004).

There have been three other proposals to limit the use of the veto. The first is to limit its application to resolutions under Chapter VII of the Charter. There has been much discussion about how the Security Council has attempted to extend its powers and mandate and how its members are threatening to use the veto for matters that are inappropriate, such as the election of the Secretary-General. One journalist, citing the views of diplomatic observers, recently claimed that the P-5 "might accept a diminished veto if pressed by the main body of UN representation, the General Assembly ... [since its] resolutions are not legally binding but they carry considerable moral weight."[65]

Secondly, the African Union, in particular, has pushed the idea of a "double veto", under which it would be necessary for two countries to utilize the veto in order that it be effective. Unsurprisingly, the P-5 rejected this plan out of hand. Finally, some states have proposed that if a country exercises its veto, a majority decision on whether that exercise was justified should be taken in the General Assembly. If the Assembly found the use of the veto to have been unfair it could overrule the use of the veto with a two-thirds majority. Either way, it is apparent that the controversy surrounding the veto, which has been on the agenda in one way or another since the formation of the UN, is no nearer to being resolved.

B.   *The General Assembly*[66]

i.   The Problems

The General Assembly is the United Nations' most important but not always most relevant body. It is the first organ described by the Charter and the principal institution of the organisation, guaranteeing representation for all member states on the basis of sovereign equality. Therein lie many of its difficulties as well as strengths. With 191 delegations, a mandate that permits the Assembly to discuss any questions or any matters within the scope of the present Charter but only with the ability to "initiate studies" or "make recommendations", it is hardly surprising that the General Assembly is frequently derided as a "talking shop". In the pages that follow, I will examine alternatives to the one-member, one-vote (OMOV) policy of the Assembly and indicate how the organization could be strengthened.

The problem with OMOV can be linked to the method of voting. Although the practice is not explicitly laid down in the Charter, which states in Article 18 that

---

65   Alan Boyd, "India, Japan Still Shooting for Security Council," *Asia Times*, 26th February 2004, available online at <http://www.globalpolicy.org/security/reform/cluster1/2004/0226shooting.htm> (accessed 16 May 2004).

66   "The parliamentary voice – the voice of the people – must be an integral component of the work of the United Nations." Kofi Annan, 4th December 2001. Senator Douglas Roche, "The Case for a UN Parliamentary Assembly," in Saul Mendlovitz & Barbara Walker, (eds.), *A Reader on Second Assembly and Parliamentary Proposals*, (Wayne, NJ: Center for UN Reform Education, 2003), available online at <http://www.unreformcenter.org/Reader%20Articles.htm> (accessed 11 June 2004).

decisions should be made on the basis of a simple majority, except on "important questions," where a two-thirds majority is needed, the General Assembly likes to vote on the basis of consensus. Nations that object to an Assembly resolution are thus encouraged to abstain from voting or not to attend the vote. The reason for this procedure is the desire to show strength of will in the international community. UN officials, and more powerful states, however, often decry this process, arguing that it creates cumbersome or watered-down decisions and resolutions that are not in the interests of the international community. It is possible that "by adopting resolutions on the basis of one nation-one vote, coalitions unrepresentative of the world's population or of the political/economic/military reality are able to dominate the Assembly's work and exploit it for propaganda purposes."[67] A measure may be passed by a two-thirds vote consisting of some 122 members who represent but 6 or 7 percent of the population of the membership.[68] Thus it is difficult to disagree with Martin Rochester, who says that

> No amount of informal adjustment of UN General Assembly decision-making procedures can compensate for the absurdity of the Assembly's formal arrangements that permit a two-thirds majority to be constructed by a coalition of states paying less than 2 percent of the organisation's assessed budget, that gives the residents of one state (Liechtenstein) more than 39,000 times the influence of those of another state (China) and that defy almost any reasonable criteria.
>
> The two principal organs of the United Nations therefore suffer contrasting fates. On the one hand, excessive power in the Security Council is concentrated in the hands of the non-elected five members to the exclusion of the rest of the membership, and yet, on the other hand, in the General Assembly, excessive power resides with groups of nations that contribute little financially to the UN and groups of mini-states that represent a tiny fraction of the world's population. I will propose a reform in my conclusion, but, first it is necessary to examine proposals to alter the voting system of the General Assembly.[69]

ii.   Voting Proposals for the General Assembly

There have long been calls for the General Assembly to adopt a system of weighted voting, in line with the procedures of other organizations, such as the World Bank, the International Monetary Fund (IMF), and the European Council, and there are many suggestions for the criteria that should be used. These include measures of military and economic power (measured by GDP), proportional to population or relative population, the physical size of a country, and contributions to the UN

---

67   *Cf*: Manuel Rama-Montaldo, "Contribution of the General Assembly to the Constitutional Development and Interpretation of the United Nations Charter," in this volume, Chapter 18, *supra*.

68   Excerpts from the Conclusions and Recommendations of Robert K. Morrow, Proposals for a More Equitable General Assembly Voting Structure, available online at <http://www.unreformcenter. org /orgs.htm> (accessed 8 June 2004).

69   J. Martin Rochester, *Waiting for the Millennium: The United Nations and the Future of World Order*, (Colombia: University of South Carolina Press, 1993), p. 147.

budget or an objective assessment of each nation's commitment to the UN's principal goals of international peace and security.

Many of these ideas can be ruled out immediately. Neither military and economic power alone or the territorial size of a state should be overriding considerations in determining representation in an assembly that represents the peoples of the world. Similarly, an objective assessment is unlikely to be acceptable, because it begs the question, who could carry out such an unbiased appraisal? It is almost certain that some states would reject the recommendations of an assessing body, thus delegitimising the creation of the new assembly. As the late Paul Szasz observed in relation to weighted voting; "Only two possible factors commend themselves: population and contributions. However as both of these would, if based on raw data, lead to apparent inequities in the opposite direction (i.e. to excessive power to the most populous and richest states), some formula for compressing the raw figures should be developed."[70]

Although the literature on weighted voting for the General Assembly dates back to the 1970s, more recent scholarship has been scarce, with UN officials and NGOs more focused on reforming the Security Council.[71] Nevertheless, the foremost weighted voting proposal, known as the Binding Triad system, has been under discussion since it was conceived in 1964 by Richard Hudson, who is now the Executive Director of the Center for War/Peace Studies in New York. In his evaluation of weighted voting proposals in 2001, the respected UN official, Paul Szasz, concluded that although the Binding Triad "may not be adoptable in precisely its present form; it should be used to stimulate discussion on this most important subject."[72]

The Binding Triad scheme would, in effect, create a global legislature. Hudson suggests that,

> By an amendment to Article 13 of the United Nations Charter, the Binding Triad system could be introduced into the global decision-making process. This amendment would enable the General Assembly to make binding decisions by resolutions which receive concurrent majority votes based on three factors: 1) one-nation-one-vote, 2) population, 3) contributions to the UN budget. The rationale behind the Binding Triad concept is this: The one-nation-one-vote system is deeply rooted in diplomatic tradition, and this voting leg gives the smaller countries an important voice in global decisions. The population leg introduces a strong element of democracy into UN decision-making. The leg based on contributions to the UN budget, roughly based on GNP,

---

70   Excerpts from the Conclusions and Recommendations of Paul C. Szasz, "Alternative Voting Systems in International Organizations and the Binding Triad Proposal to Improve U.N. General Assembly Decision-Taking," available online at <http://www.unreformcenter.org/orgs.htm> (accessed 8 June 2004).

71   Despite negative conclusions about the feasibility of weighted voting, the most comprehensive review of this scholarship is still worth studying: see William J. Dixon, "The Evaluation of Weighted Voting Schemes for the United Nations General Assembly," 27 *International Studies Quarterly* 295-314 (1983).

72   Excerpts from the Conclusions and Recommendations of Paul C. Szasz, *supra* note 70.

allows the more important donor countries to have increased influence on decisions involving projects for which they will have to pay most of the bills.[73]

Under this plan, the General Assembly would be endowed with capacity to make international law binding on all UN member states, if a resolution was passed that was supported by delegations from a majority of member states, representing a majority of the world's population and representing states that contributed a total of 51% or more of the UN budget, roughly based on GDP. Currently, only the Security Council, under Article 25, has the power to make binding decisions, but Hudson's proposal would alter this. The Binding Triad, though, does not address how its binding resolutions would be enforced, nor whether there would be any limits on its powers.

In March 2004, Hudson updated the Binding Triad proposal to campaign for the Tobin-Triad (or T^2) resolution. This, a proposal even more ambitious than others, envisages the creation of a World Regulatory Agency whose mandate would be to "lay down the rules for the establishment of a global system that will seek to guarantee peace and security for every inhabitant of the planet, assuring the integrity of all states, large and small, rich and poor."[74] The Assembly would vote on the basis of the Binding Triad system and acquire the additional funds needed to help fund this proposal by imposing the "Tobin tax" of a quarter or twentieth of one percent on all global currency transfers.

However, just as the non-elected five are unwilling to countenance reform of the Security Council, so a majority of African and Asian countries and "mini-states" from all over the globe refuse to discuss a watering down of their voting rights in the General Assembly. Indeed, the ambassador of one developing country stated that "'his small country stood nothing to gain by a weighted vote,' [arguing] that 'as a country that has gone to considerable lengths to cede some of our sovereignty, he looks at other countries and sees that no others have ceded any part of theirs.'"[75] As an example, he cites the unwillingness of the United States to accept the compulsory jurisdiction of the International Court of Justice and refusal to join the International Criminal Court. Overall, the advocates of the Binding Triad still have a number of obstacles to come.

Another innovative proposal in the present-day picture of General Assembly reform is provided by George Monbiot. He recommends that each nation should be weighted on the basis of the number of people it represents in addition to its degree of democratisation. The results would be dramatic:

---

73   Richard Hudson, "How the Binding Triad Would Work," available online at <http://www.cwps.org/bt.html> (accessed 27 May 2004).

74   Richard Hudson, "The Tobin-Triad Resolution," 15th March 2004, available online at <http://www.cwps.org/ttresolution.html> (accessed 29 May 2004).

75   Pat Orvis, "United Nations Reform and Article 109," 29th January 2004, available online at <http://www.fpa.org/newsletter_info2489/newsletter _info_ sub_list.htm?section= United%20Nations%20Reform%20and%20Article%20109> (accessed 15 July 2004).

The government of Tuvalu, representing 10,000 people, would, then, have a far smaller vote than the government of China. But China, in turn, would possess far fewer votes than it would if its government was democratically elected. Rigorous means of measuring democratisation are beginning to be developed by bodies such as Democratic Audit. It would not be hard, using their criteria, to compile an objective global index of democracy. Governments, under this system, would be presented with a powerful incentive to democratise: the more democratic they became, the greater their influence over world affairs.[76]

Obviously, there is a danger that this proposal would be thought too "Western" by many member states who would see it as imposing a value judgement on the type of political system a nation could adopt. It is hard to believe that China, for example, would not regard this proposal as an attempt to interfere in its domestic affairs and perhaps a "hegemonic" plot to topple its government. The proposal has merit but the results of its application would be far from pleasing to everyone. Would the United States, for example, wish India to possess more than double America's number of representatives?

The European Council, which has pioneered successful negotiations on weighted voting for an organization that has expanded from 6 to 25 members, and whose population sizes and relative power are totally incongruent, is a useful model to study. The Council took decisions based on a simple majority (for procedural matters), qualified majority voting, (QMV) for many decisions concerning economics and the internal EU market, and unanimity in areas such as taxation, social and foreign policy, where each country effectively has the right of veto. Under the Treaty of Rome, smaller nations, such as Luxembourg, (population 2,000,000) were overrepresented with two seats on the Council, in comparison to Germany (population 80m) with ten seats. The Treaty of Nice in 2000 altered this by ensuring that the relative weight of the size of smaller and medium-sized countries was not out of proportion to their total population. From November 2004 until the European Constitution comes into force, any decision must receive a "set" number of votes, which will change, dependent on the number of members (but will be around 70%) as well as be agreed upon by a majority of member states. In addition, a member state may request that the qualified majority represents at least 62% of the population (a proposal known as the "demographic safety net"); otherwise the decision cannot be adopted.

The proposed EU constitution will have decisions made on the basis of the double majority rule of 55% of the members of the Council, including at least 15 members and representing states comprising at least 65% of the population. This scheme certainly has merit, but it would appear that the Binding Triad system would be slightly fairer, given that it is also based on contributions to the UN budget. Nonetheless, supporters of the Binding Triad proposal could be forced to move

---

76   George Monbiot, "How to Stop the United States of America II," 11th June 2003, available online at <http://www.dailytimes.com.pk/default.asp? page= story_11-6-2003_ pg4_12> (accessed 17 July 2004).

towards "double majority" if they are not able to produce a formula that can fairly and accurately assess contributions to the UN budget by 191 nations with completely disparate GDPs.

Given that securing unanimity in several areas could prove to be impossible in the expanded EU, the concept of a "reinforced qualified majority" has been floated. This would require a compromise that retains the population requirement, but sets the bar so that the percentage of votes will be higher than normal for double majority (and reinforced qualified majority). Such a system could be transferred to the UN where, as in the EU, different issues would require either a simple majority, double majority, reinforced double majority or unanimity as appropriate. Although the extensive array of views from 191 countries would make the categorization of issues an extremely difficult proposition, it is quite possible that solutions could be found.

On the other hand, Kamil Idris and Michael Bartolo recommend that the General Assembly should be reinvented as "the supreme organ", of the UN, by convening year-long sessions organized around special topics and meeting at the level of permanent representative and at summit [executive] level as necessary. They conclude that,

> It is crucial that the most important decisions should be taken at the level of the General Assembly. It is, therefore, this organ that needs to be strengthened above all others to give the United Nations a new credibility and relevance.... It would be more appropriate to rename it the Global Assembly. The reconstituted Global Assembly would have a very broad-based and diverse membership. This would enable its moral authority to extend beyond that provided by the conventional representation of national governments.[77]

The authors believe that, in order to ensure wider representation "in the spirit of the Charter", the Global Assembly should include representatives from civil society and national parliaments in addition to national governments. This tripartite representation would be similar to that of the International Labour Organisation (ILO), whose executive is made up of representatives of government, employers, and workers. It is envisaged that this proposal would ensure that UN delegations are comprised equally of representatives of national governments, national parliaments, and civil society, for example two of each, and that, therefore, each nation's vote would represent a joint decision taken by this eclectic mix. Idris and Bartolo freely admit, though, that getting each nation to embrace this ideal may be difficult:

> Some governments may not feel comfortable sharing their decision-making responsibilities at the United Nations with either nongovernmental organisations or with members of parliament not forming part of the government. The important point

---

77   Kamil Idris & Michael Bartolo, *A Better United Nations for the New Millennium*, (The Hague: Kluwer Law International, 2000), p. 187.

in this wider representation is to give the opportunity of consultation with a greater number of people. The question of the role in the decision-making process of civil society and parliaments should at this stage be left to the individual delegations, who can best interpret the national consensus on this very delicate matter.[78]

The foregoing is probably the most promising of the proposals aimed at countering the vicious circle of representation at the global level. It is understandable that ordinary citizens may not have an interest in the work of the United Nations because it is usually remote from their lives. Critics go on to say there is not sufficient interest amongst citizens for electing representatives to the United Nations as evidenced by the falling participation rates for national elections in almost all Western democracies. Thus, we are left in the classic catch-22 situation; do nothing to change the system and the disconnect between the UN and the people grows wider, or, attempt to change the system and risk turnout rates for direct elections to the UN that are embarrassingly low. The second option is undoubtedly preferable and the results may not be as bad as some detractors claim. An October 2000 poll in the United States asked the following question:

> An increasing number of important decisions are made in international institutions such as the United Nations, the World Bank or the World Trade Organization. The people making the decisions are either representatives of national governments or employees of the international organizations. There have been proposals for a People's Assembly at the United Nations, directly elected by the world's citizens, to hold those international organizations democratically accountable to the public. Would you favor or oppose the creation of such a UN People's Assembly?' Fifty-seven percent favored the idea and 30 percent opposed it. [Hence] even in a powerful country already capable of representing its interests well throughout the world, a majority of the public favored the idea.[79]

Before I consider proposals for improving the effectiveness of the General Assembly, it is relevant to refer to the selection process preferred by the majority of member states for approving their delegations to the United Nations. Even if states do not move to direct election of their UN representatives in the near future, a more transparent process of selection could be initiated without difficulty. Too often, the representative is simply selected by the executive, thereby propagating the trend to guard the "national interest" at all costs. Smaller and middle-size states could take the lead by encouraging participation from civil society in the selection of delegates to the United Nations, thus promoting a kind of representation more amenable to the interests of the wider international community rather than (usually) the narrower national interest of a particular country.

---

78   *Ibid.*, at 145.

79   Robert C. Johansen, "An E-Parliament to Democratise Globalisation," in Saul Mendlovitz & Barbara Walker, *supra* note 66.

iii.   Other Reform Proposals for the General Assembly

In a not inaccurate description, one scholar observed that the General Assembly, "like a herd of grazing cattle that moves as it chews, head down, gets through its day … without any particular drive, yet not without a certain vaguely diffused sense of purpose."[80] The problem is that even this vaguely diffused sense of purpose is seldom translated into action. Like many national legislatures, the General Assembly deals with too many subjects: it adopts at each session more than two hundred resolutions on topics from arms control to international waterways, from Albania to Zimbabwe.

Proposals to improve the functioning of the General Assembly are under consideration at the present time.[81] Mr. Julian Hunte, Foreign Minister of St Lucia, and President of the 58th Session of the Assembly, has been proactive in pushing for reform. He secured the passage of General Assembly Resolution 58/126 of December 19th 2003 which introduced regular monthly meetings between the Presidents of the General Assembly and Security Council, in order to try to close the perceived gap that had opened between these two organs. At the beginning of July, 2004, the Assembly adopted draft resolution A/58/L.66, entitled Further Measures for the Revitalisation of the Work of the General Assembly. The measures referred to are: (i) to ensure that Main Committees adopt a provisional programme of work at the end of each session for the next session, (ii) to introduce "Question Time" periods into the work of the Main Committees, and, (iii) to increase the number of interactive debates and panels in the General Assembly from September 2004.

Hunte has signalled that the work of the six main committees (Disarmament, Economic and Financial, Social, Humanitarian and Cultural, Decolonisation and Special Political Questions, Budget and Legal) should be split, with the budget committee continuing to meet all year round and the Second and Third committees meeting in the northern autumn with the remainder meeting in the northern spring.[82] Whilst consideration of this proposal has been delayed until the 59th session, Hunte remains optimistic as to the outcome. As he noted with reference to the period September to December in 2003, "We considered 276 items and sub-items, had submitted to us 347 reports totalling 5,500 pages, and adopted 287 resolutions. It is not clear to me why we should continue to operate in this fashion."[83]

---

80   H.G. Nicholas, quoted in J. Martin Rochester, *supra* note 69, p. 137.

81   Louis B. Sohn, "Important Improvements in the Functioning of the Principal Organs of the United Nations That Can Be Made Without Charter Reform," *American Journal of International Law*, (October 1997), available online at <http://www.globalpolicy.org/reform/sohn.htm> (accessed 18 July 2004).

82   UN News Centre, "Proposal Would Break UN General Assembly Main Session into Two Parts," 19th March 2004, available online at <http://www.globalpolicy.org/reform/topics/ga/2004/0319break.htm> (accessed 18 July 2004).

83   Remarks of Julian R. Hunte, following the Adoption of Draft Resolution A/58/L.66, 1st July 2004, available online at <http://www.un.org/ga/president/58/speeches/040701-2.htm> (accessed 20 July 2004).

Although proposals for reform within the General Assembly are mainly confined to its working practices, a number of commentators are promoting the idea of establishing a global parliament or a United Nations People's Assembly alongside the General Assembly. Three authors have made the case for such a body. Dieter Heindrich thinks it would raise the level of democracy and accountability in the United Nations:

> The UN Charter begins with the words, 'We the peoples of the United Nations...' In practice, the UN is a meeting place not of the peoples but of the governments – and only the executive branch of governments at that. One of the first reforms might best be to establish, finally, the citizen dimension at the UN, and give the UN back to the world's people. This would help ensure that any expansion in the UN's authority will be accompanied by an increase in democratic accountability.[84]

For Richard Falk and Andrew Strauss, the implications of establishing such a body would be positive in the realm of international cooperation. "Because elected delegates would represent individuals and society instead of states, they would not have to vote along national lines. Coalitions would likely form on other bases, such as world-view, political orientation, and interests."[85] Finally, George Monbiot believes that a new assembly "would be a body which possesses something no other global or international agency possesses: legitimacy. Directly elected, owned by the people of the world, our parliament would possess the moral authority which all other bodies lack. And this alone, if effectively deployed, is a source of power."[86]

What role would a People's Assembly play? It might be useful if it were consultative, at least initially. Consultative status would remove concerns about the powers of a global legislative assembly and serve as a basis on which additional responsibilities might be built from the bottom up. There is a lesson to be learned from the operation of the European Parliament, which is perceived as remote and boring by many of the people it represents, largely because it was imposed from above by national governments."[87]

The European Parliament provides an instructive example of how a supranational organization, like a UNPA, might develop. From its formation in 1957 until the first direct elections in 1979, the European Parliament was composed of members of national parliaments. If the UN were to follow this example, "a UN parliamentary chamber could to be created easily and inexpensively in a way which nevertheless creates a valid democratic link between the UN and the world's citi-

---

84   Dieter Heindrich, "Extension of Democracy to the Global Level," in Saul Mendlovitz & Barbara Walker, *supra* note 66, p. 69.

85   Richard Falk & Andrew Strauss, "Toward Global Parliament," 80 *Foreign Affairs* 212-220, at p. 216 (2001).

86   George Monbiot, *supra* note 76.

87   George Monbiot, "A Parliament for the Planet," in Saul Mendlovitz & Barbara Walker, *supra* note 66, at p. 79.

zens through their representatives in the national legislatures."[88] Falk and Strauss observe that:

> As with the early European parliament, a relatively weak assembly initially equipped with largely advisory powers could begin to address concerns about the democratic deficit while posing only a long-term threat to the realities of state power. Systemic transformation of world order that would largely affect successors would not significantly threaten those political leaders who are inclined to embrace democratic ideals. Indeed, it might even appeal to them.[89]

The major benefit of a new body is that representatives, for the first time, would be free to pass non-binding resolutions on the basis of their consciences, free from the influence of national governments. However, fair and public financing mechanisms would be required unless the selection of 1000 or 3000 parliamentarians is to be "unduly controlled by governments and trans-national business interests."[90] In other words, how could your average man on the Clapham omnibus find enough money to run for election to a UNPA? And how are the six billion people of the world to be fairly represented. There seem to be only two main possibilities: a parliamentary assembly comprising national parliamentarians or a parliamentary assembly that is selected independently."[91]

As Roche concedes, there are also a number of open questions on the criteria and method of selection of independent candidates: "Should they be selected by a universal electoral system or by nationally based systems? What would the electoral calendar be? Who would supervise elections? Would variances in election practices damage overall UNPA credibility? How many representatives should each member-state have, etc.? These questions have no ready answers."[92]

In addition, Joseph Schwartzberg is among the first to study the actual practical difficulties of creating a completely new UNPA;

> The House of Commons, perhaps the largest of all such bodies, presently has a membership of 659, more than half again as many as the 435 in the US House of Representatives. But in both the Commons and in Congress all representatives speak the same language. This condition could not be met in a global parliament and simultaneous translation would go only so far in alleviating the problem. Somewhat arbitrarily, I shall assume that the maximum size of a global parliamentary assembly would be set at 1,000. Given the world's present population total of roughly 6.1 billion persons, this means that, on average, one representative would have some 6.1 million constituents

---

88   Dieter Heindrich, *supra* note 84, p. 70.

89   Richard Falk & Andrew Strauss, *supra* note 85, at p. 218.

90   William R. Pace, "Foreword," in Saul Mendlovitz & Barbara Walker, *supra* note 66, at p. 41, vi.

91   Douglas Roche, *supra* note 66, p. 40.

92   Roche, *supra* note 66, p. 45.

if an assembly with universal membership were already in existence. This is far greater than in any existing or past parliament. (In the Lok Sabha, the lower house of the Indian Parliament, one legislator represents, on average, about 2 million constituents, which is probably the world record for a democratic polity.) This presents a problem in that 94 of the soon to be 192 members of the UN had fewer than 6 million inhabitants (as of the year 2000). Of these, 39 had populations below one million, while more than a third of those had populations ranging from 10,000 to 100,000. From these figures it follows that, for purposes of representation, if one tries to adhere to the one person – one vote principle, two or more political entities (whether independent states or dependencies), would sometimes have to be clubbed together in a single parliamentary constituency.[93]

These conclusions suggest that a UNPA should be based, at least initially, on existing parliamentarians. This procedure would not only remove the issue of elections and the question whether those concerned speak for the people; it would also mean that UN parliamentarians would bring to the new body parliamentary experience and their own parliamentary staff. The parliamentarians would not occupy full-time positions; the new organ would ideally meet three times a year; at the beginning and end of each session of the General Assembly and probably sometime in the northern spring. The number and the question of representation of parliamentarians would still need to be determined, although a sliding scale by population is probably the fairest means with the number capped at one thousand.

As a number of authors have noted, the UNPA could easily be established under Article 22 of the Charter, which gives the General Assembly power to "establish such subsidiary organs as it deems necessary for the performance of its functions." Another suggestion, made by Heindrich, is that "A UN Parliamentary Assembly might rather consider an important modification to our precedents by having national parliaments send non-parliamentarian delegates. These might be former parliamentarians, or distinguished citizens-at-large. In this way, a full-time global body could be created."[94] This would be useful in attracting media attention to the new organ and publicity for its decisions, but that advantage could be offset by the unelected nature of these non-parliamentarian delegates and the lack of both a need and a role for a full-time assembly.

An additional problem is what to do about non-democratic countries. If the purpose of a new body is to move away from representation by national governments, what measures could one take to ensure that delegates from non-democratic states are sufficiently detached from the will of their governments?

It would be possible, no doubt, to have non-democratic countries excluded from participation in a UNPA through ingenious criteria only democracies could satisfy. But a case can be made for admitting parliamentarians of all countries. A parliamentary as-

---

93   Joseph E. Schwartzberg, "Overcoming Practical Difficulties in Creating a World Parliamentary Assembly," in Saul Mendlovitz & Barbara Walker, *supra* note 66, p. 83.

94   Dieter Heindrich, *supra* note 84, p. 72.

sembly with only consultative status is not yet a parliament, after all, and so the inclusion of even a large number of dubious members may be of little practical consequence in the short term. Parliamentarians, unlike diplomats, could be directly challenged to defend their views or change them. Collegial persuasion might have an educational effect on non-democratic representatives, and so hasten the spread of new ideas to non-democratic countries. The fear of this might keep some dictatorships from participating, thus solving the problem in another way. A UNPA, as a consultative body, would have no formal powers initially. Its resolutions, however, would have a moral influence on governments' the way today's General Assembly have.[95]

More outlandish is the idea of basing the UNPA on Donella Meadows' famous quote about the global village of 1000, out of which "584 would be Asians, 123 would be Africans, 95 would be East and West Europeans, 84 Latin Americans, 55 Soviets, 52 North Americans [and] 6 Australians and New Zealanders."[96] Although proportionally the fairest, this scheme would exclude a number of mini-states, which would be without representation. A slightly more feasible proposal might be Robert Johansen's idea of an E-Parliament. He says that the long-term mission of this design is to give,

> Every person on Earth an equal vote and equal opportunity to be represented in solving problems that affect their lives. The immediate purpose of the proposed e-Parliament is to enable all those legislators throughout the world who have been democratically elected to their national legislatures to deliberate with one another, primarily over the Internet, and to engage with citizens in a joint search for effective solutions to global problems.[97]

The idea of an "e-Forum," attached to the e-Parliament, which all citizens could use to spread ideas about important issues should not be excluded out of hand. However, until equal access to the internet is available on every continent, it is hard to see how this tool would adequately represent, for example, the people of Africa.

Not everyone is in favor of a United Nations Parliamentary Assembly. Jeffrey Laurenti, Director of the United States United Nations Association, claims that "imaginings of a global parliament are almost certain to founder on their own internal contradictions. Particularly treacherous are the questions of a proposed parliament's inclusivity, its authority, and its efficiency."[98] If the proposed body "has no authority over the activities of even the scarecrow agencies of the United Nations, why, he asks "should serious politicians invest serious time in it?" adding that, "an unanticipated consequence of "democratising" the international policy debate

---

95   *Ibid.*, 73.

96   David Taub, "The Originator and Story behind the Global Village," available online at <http://members.aol.com/UKpoet/global1.htm> (accessed 20 July 2004).

97   Robert C. Johansen, *supra* note 79, at p. 97.

98   Jeffrey Laurenti, "An Idea Whose Time Has *Not* Yet Come," in Saul Mendlovitz & Barbara Walker, *supra* note 66, at p. 120.

by election of a global assembly might be its capture by intensely passionate niche interests in the electorate."[99]

Many of these criticisms are well founded but they do not preclude the usefulness of continuing to study the possible design of a UNPA. Politicians will be increasingly inclined to take an interest in the idea because of the need for a body that can oversee unrepresentative global institutions and express an opinion in international affairs with strong moral authority. The Inter Parliamentary Union (IPU) could play a role in conducting a feasibility study into a UNPA and, using its newly achieved special observer status at the General Assembly, working more closely to establish more effective links with national parliaments.

Interest in discussing the possibility of a new body continues. The 1995 UN-funded Commission on Global Governance proposed the creation of a Global Civil Society Forum. The Millennium Forum followed in 2000 with a five-day conference which "represented the dress rehearsal of such a Forum.... It is not an exaggeration to state that it represented the first babble of global democracy .... The Forum was an assembly representing as closely as possible the peoples of the world or at least the most active part of them."[100] The Forum principally comprised members of NGOs, and its radical conclusions were released as an official document of the General Assembly. In June 2004, the Secretary General's Panel of Eminent Persons on United Nations and Civil Society Relations produced a report on how to enhance interaction between the UN and civil society, including parliamentarians and the private sector. The Panel concluded that a four-pronged strategy was needed: 1. Take United Nations issues to national parliaments more systematically, 2. Ensure that parliamentarians coming to United Nations events have more strategic roles at those events, 3. Link parliaments themselves with the international deliberative processes [and] 4. Provide an institutional home in the United Nations for engaging parliamentarians.[101]

The Panel further recommended the trial and formation of global public policy committees and the creation of an Elected Representatives Liaison Unit to provide a dedicated information service for parliaments and parliamentarians and to create more attention to United Nations processes in national parliaments. The Secretary-General has indicated that he will take steps to initiate those recommendations in 2004.

C.   Conclusions and Recommendations

The issues touched on in the two previous sections of this chapter are too complex to be explored in detail in one chapter of a large book devoted to world constitution-

---

99   *Ibid.*, pp. 122, 128.

100   Lucio Levi, "Globalisation, International Democracy and a World Parliament," in Saul Mendlovitz & Barbara Walker, *supra* note 66, at pp. 61-2.

101   Report of the Panel of Eminent Persons on United Nations-Civil Society Relations, "We the Peoples: Civil Society, the United Nations and Global Governance," 21st June 2004, UN General Assembly Document A/58/817, paragraph 102, available online at <http://www.un.org/reform/a58_817_ english.doc> (accessed 20 July 2004).

alism. Suffice it to say that the reason for discussing them even in outline is to increase public and professional awareness of existing possibilities for strengthening and rationalizing the international legal order founded on the Charter and the great law-making documents of the 20th century. Although substantial change at the UN is sometimes said to necessitate a "big bang" approach, commentators are correct in saying that "the only deliberate UN institutional reform that is at all possible is piecemeal, minor reform; such reform is virtually inconsequential in its effects, except insofar as it contributes to cumulative change that cannot be planned."[102] Indeed, if one lesson can be learned from the negotiations to alter the structure of the Security Council it is that gradual reform is about all that is possible.

The forthcoming sixtieth anniversary of the United Nations, in June 2005, presents an opportunity for another round of reports on the future of the Organization. This is not necessary. What is needed is that the UN redouble its efforts to achieve its eight Millennium Goals before 2015. The United Nations Millennium Development Goals are (i) to eradicate Extreme Poverty and Hunger, (ii) to achieve Universal Primary Education, (iii) to promote Gender Equality and Empower Women, (iv) to reduce Child Mortality, (v) to improve Maternal Health, (vi) to combat HIV/AIDS, Malaria and other diseases, (vii) to ensure Environmental Sustainability, (viii) to develop a Global Partnership for Development.[103]

This, in addition to international peace and security, should comprise its mission, and General Assembly debates should focus on these objectives. Eradicating world hunger and life-threatening viruses such as HIV-AIDS, as well as working to develop a sustainable environmental framework that adequately addresses regional disparities and the economic development needs of Third World countries, are in the interests of all nations. In the era of globalisation, it is plausible that efforts to combat global disease and problems associated with a deteriorating environment, such as regional water shortages, will represent major challenges for a reformed Security Council concerned with international peace and security.

In my opinion, the resources of the international community must be mobilised through the United Nations to ensure realization of the Millennium Goals. In this respect, it is obvious to all that the UN's chances of success are affected by the attitude of the lone superpower, the United States towards the Organization. As the current lone superpower, the United States, is in a position to strengthen the Council or to undermine it: it can do this by choosing to act within or without the Council. As David Malone observed, "in the post-Cold War world the main issue for the Council is whether it can meaningfully engage the United States on the major security challenges of any given period and restrain its unilateralist impulses."[104]

The primary responsibility of the Security Council is the maintenance of international peace and security, but we need to remember that the Council is also charged with responsibility to participate actively in the positive development of the international community. In addition to their responsibility for "hard" military

---

102   Rochester, *supra* note 69, at p. 190.

103   Available online at <http://www.un.org/millenniumgoals/> (accessed 22 July 2004).

104   Malone, note 32 above.

aspects of peace and security, the P-5 have a responsibility to make the economic system of the world fairer, especially for developing countries. Debate on the role the Council could play in this area is overdue.

i.   Security Council Recommendations

There is little chance that any of the permanent members will voluntarily surrender their right of veto. The one change that might occur is the amalgamation of the UK and French seats under a common EU seat, if a European Common Foreign and Security Policy (CFSP) is ever achieved. Whilst such a prospect is unlikely in the near future, the EU Foreign Policy Chief (likely to be the EU's first Foreign Minister under the new EU constitution) Javier Solana, has already expressed his desire for a common EU seat on the Council.[105]

In my opinion, it would serve the Security Council well to incorporate five additional permanent seats and five new elected seats to bring the full membership up to a total of twenty-five seats (see Table 1). As the largest country in Europe and the third-highest contributor to the EU budget, Germany would certainly be an appropriate member of the Council. Germany's presence would mean that Western Europe is overrepresented, but this would be overcome by three seats for the developing world. Latin America and the Caribbean, Africa, and Asia/Oceania would each be given a permanent regional rotating seat (see Table 2). Japan is the second-highest contributor to the UN budget and its permanent membership would serve to expand geographical representation from Asia.

In respect of the non-permanent seats, the ratios may have to be changed to incorporate representation from the League of Arab States and perhaps from the Non-Aligned Movement (NAM). Suggestions for representation are presented in Table 1, which advocates abolition of the Western European and Other Group, with Canada moving to the American group and Australia and New Zealand, notwithstanding definitional difficulties of establishing the boundaries of Asia, moving into Asia/Oceania. In line with Germany's proposal, provision would be made for periodic review, perhaps every ten years. Periodic review would prevent the paralysis of the 1990s and guarantee that there would be no repeat of the events of 1955. According to Article 109(3) of the Charter, there was to have been a debate, before 1955 at the latest, to analyze the decision-making processes of the UN, but this, as we know, did not occur. If a review under the new procedures indicates that the new seats have not altered the effectiveness and efficiency of the Council, then, after a specified number of years (10-15), Africa could be granted an additional permanent seat (to be decided by a two-thirds majority vote of the General Assembly, rather than the Security Council). If that change impeded the Council's effectiveness, another Working Group could be convened.

The imperative within this plan is that it must be based on the longer-term. What is important is to find a method that is not a "quick fix" but that takes effect

---

105   Honor Mahony, "Solana Considers One EU Seat in UN Solution to Divisions," EUObserver.com, March 24th 2003, available online at <http://www. Global policy.org/security/reform/cluster1/2003/0324eu.htm> (accessed 23 May 2004).

as a fundamental reform during the years ahead. Political leaders need time to persuade their electorates of the need for reform and to protect themselves from charges of weakness.

The question of the veto is harder to settle. On the one hand, it makes little sense to perpetuate an inequality, and yet, on the other, it seems unfair to preserve the status of the P-5, especially when one considers that only the United States and China would qualify if a non-elected five were to be re-evaluated today. It is arguable therefore that the time has come to approve the African plan for permanent regional rotating seats. The applicable criteria would be established by each region before the region's nomination received the approval of two-thirds of the Security Council. The principal objection to a regional rotation plan enabling developing countries to gain a foothold on the Council is the concern of the P-5 that these countries would hold the right of veto.

Table 1 – Recommendations for the Future UN Security Council.

YEAR	CHANGES
2005	5 new quasi-permanent members elected. Germany, Japan and permanent regional rotating seats for Africa, Asia/Oceania & Latin American and the Caribbean. Five new elected seats to bring to a total of fifteen, to be divided 2 – W. Europe, 1 – E. Europe, 4 – Africa, 4 – Asia and Oceania, 2 – Organisation of American States, 1 – League of Arab States, 1 – Non-Aligned Movement.
2010	First rotation of quasi-permanent seats from three continents.
2015	Second rotation of quasi-permanent seats from three continents. First Review of new Security Council. Vote in General Assembly and Security Council about effectiveness of decision-making processes. A two-thirds majority is needed.
2020	Third rotation of quasi-permanent seats. If vote in 2015 is passed, permit the acceptance of an additional quasi-permanent African member. Accept submissions from all continents for 12th and final quasi-permanent seat (the most likely candidate by this stage will probably be India). Establish Working Group on possibility of a permanent EU seat.

Table 2 – Potential Permanent Regional Rotational Members.

YEAR	ASIA	LATIN AMERICA	AFRICA
2005	India	Argentina	Nigeria
2010	Pakistan	Brazil	South Africa
2015	Korea	Colombia	Egypt
2020	Indonesia	Jamaica	Ethiopia & Kenya

Reluctantly therefore, it seems sensible to preserve the present position of inequality: the P-5 would retain their veto and that right would not be extended to new quasi-permanent members. In exchange, Germany, Japan and the developing countries, would seek concessions from the P-5, the most likely being an agreement to limit the use of the veto to matters under Chapter VII, backed up by a resolution of the General Assembly. Another, longer-range possibility, is agreement that a veto could be overruled by a double majority in the Security Council and (two thirds of) the General Assembly. This latter proposal is similar to one by Walter Hoffmann, who contends that "the General Assembly should have the right to block decisions of the Security Council in matters relating to Article 13 or Chapters IX or X, not involving state on state aggression, provided it acts within 15 days of the receipt of the report of such action."[106]

The new non-elected members would essentially represent a third category of members. Although sceptics will argue that non-elected members would have essentially the same role as elected members, there are two important differences. New non-elected members would sit on the Council for a period of five years, a period longer than the two years that elected members currently receive. Secondly, the more equitable geographical distribution will give greater legitimacy to resolutions of the Council.

Another proposal that merits attention is based on a suggestion by the Global Policy Forum. This proposal advocates changing the name from permanent to non-elected members to expose the implication that the status of the P-5 will last forever. As the authors add, "it's time we use terms that are better suited for promoting change. Maybe then one day we'll wake up and say: 'Why do we put up with non-elected members?' and 'When are those non-elected members going to stand for election like everyone else?'"[107] This small step would require a change to Article 23(1) of the Charter but would pay psychological dividends.   Finally, the Security Council needs to be more accountable, a point of major importance expressed eloquently be Ambassador Mahbubani:

> One clear demand that is likely to emerge, [to preserve the assets of legitimacy and compliance] in line with a growing global trend, is that the Council should become more accountable for its actions. Traditionally, in most constitutions and organisations, privileges come with responsibilities. The two are often seen to be opposite sides of the same coin. What is remarkable about the veto privilege accorded to the P-5 members is that it was conferred without an explicit or implicit agreement that this privilege also carried with it significant responsibilities.[108]

This principle is likely to evolve over time and there is little need to precipitate its natural course by attempting to draft or enforce rules. Observing that the Security Council often proves to be unaccountable in "passing unrealistic mandates, making decisions about missions, and serving as an instrument for self interest," many commentators and think tanks have proposed "the creation of a mechanism to serve as a watchdog of the Council. This proposal is unlikely to attract the positive support of the P-5. Nonetheless, if it can be shown that a member wielding the veto, perhaps even threatening its use, is preventing action in a situation in which a large majority of Security Council members wish to act, there should be strategies

---

106   Walter Hoffman, "Security Council Reform and Restructuring," *The Center for UN Reform*, available online at <http://www.unreformcenter.org/orgs.htm> (accessed 22 May 2004).

107   Ellen Paine, "What's in a Name? Proposal for a Change in Membership Terminology for the Security Council," April 1997, available online at <http://www.globalpolicy.org/security/membship/name.htm> (accessed 23 June 2004).

108   Kishore Mahbubani, *supra* note 32, 262.

of accountability and persuasion available for use at the disposal of the General Assembly. Situations like Rwanda must be avoided.

ii.   The UN High-Level Panel Report

The report issued by Kofi Annan's High-Level Panel in December 2004 will hopefully mark a watershed in the ongoing debate about Security Council reform. The Panel proposed two possible models for enlargement, which ably demonstrates the ongoing complexity and controversy which appears to follow this institution. Model A "provides for six new permanent seats with no veto being created and three new two-year term non-permanent seats, divided among the major regional areas as follows."[109]

Table 3 – Model A

Regional Area	No of States	Permanent Seats (Continuing)	Proposed new permanent seats	Proposed 2- year seats (non-re-newable)	Total
Africa	53	0	2	4	6
Asia & Pacific	56	1	2	3	6
Europe	47	3	1	2	6
Americas	35	1	1	4	6
Totals model A	191	5	6	13	24

On the other hand, "model B provides for no new permanent seats but creates a new category of eight four-year renewable-term seats and one new two-year non-permanent (and non-renewable) seat, divided among the major regional areas as follows."[110]

Table 4 – Model B

Regional Area	No of States	Permanent Seats (Continuing)	Proposed Four-year renewable Seats	Proposed 2- year seats (non-re-newable)	Total
Africa	53	0	2	4	6
Asia & Pacific	56	1	2	3	6
Europe	47	3	2	1	6
Americas	35	1	2	3	6
Totals model B	191	5	8	11	24

---

109   Report of the Secretary General's High-Level Panel on Threats, Challenges and Change, General Assembly Document, A/59/565, paragraph 252, available online at <http://www.un.org/secureworld/> (accessed 4 January 2005).

110   *Ibid.*, at paragraph 253.

The Panel "recommend that under any reform proposal, there should be no expansion of the veto," adding that "the institution of the veto has an anachronistic character that is unsuitable for the institution in an increasingly democratic age and we would urge that its use be limited to matters where vital interests are genuinely at stake."[111]

Obviously, neither model is perfect, but Model B is preferable for two principal reasons. First, because of its rotation system after four years, model B is infinitely more likely to appeal to a higher number of nations, especially middle powers, who seek permanent membership of the Council. In short, it is the most likely model to work, providing that the opposition of the big four (Germany, Japan, Brazil and India) can be mollified. This is admittedly a huge condition, although it is less stringent than the terms which would need to be agreed before September 2005 for model A to be a realistic proposition. This is the second difficulty that must be overcome. Reform has constantly foundered for the past fifteen years on jealous national interests between countries and it remains dubious that clashes between Japan and China, Germany and Italy, India and Pakistan and Brazil and Argentina will be resolved by September 2005, not to mention the competition between African countries for representation.

This is not to say that model B is without its faults. Europe appears to be overrepresented in comparison to any other continent, but it is positive that both models have six representatives from each continent. Nonetheless, it is imperative that the debate in 2005 on Security Council reform leads to an international conversation where the emphasis should be on which countries from each continent best fulfil the criteria laid down in Article 23 of the Charter rather than identifying the possible countries and then looking at the criteria second. Finally, although a Security Council of 24 may prove unwieldy, it would nevertheless be a significant improvement on the current format and lead to greater legitimacy in the Security Council's decision-making. Furthermore, the High-Level Panel's call for "a review of the composition of the Security Council in 2020"[112] will ensure that any changes to its function or composition will not necessarily be permanent.

iii.   General Assembly Recommendations

The General Assembly is at the heart of institutional reforms at the UN. It must take the lead in attempting to achieve the Millennium Goals and reforming its main committees and subsidiary agencies to reflect this vital objective. Furthermore, the Assembly should continue to build on the work done by Julian Hunte to increase consultative mechanisms between itself and the Security Council. This will be especially important if the General Assembly manages to find a way to incorporate views, expressed by NGOs and even individuals, into its decisions.

There are two major options for a newly-improved General Assembly, both of which would feature a voting system based on population and contributions to the UN budget. This system would be reviewed, say, every ten years, either by the Gen-

---

111   *Ibid.* at paragraph 256.
112   *Ibid.* at paragraph 255.

eral Assembly or a new United Nations People's Assembly, depending on which scenario is adopted. For the foreseeable future, attempts to give a reformed General or Global Assembly binding legislative powers should be resisted. It is obvious that such a proposal is most unlikely to attract support.

Two alternative scenarios commend themselves. On the one hand, members of the Organization might agree that the Assembly should be based on tripartite representation, by national governments, national parliamentarians, and individuals, in a new Global Assembly as proposed by Idris and Bartolo. This proposal still leaves the Global Assembly at the will of national governments, rather than altering its composition in any meaningful manner.

On the other hand, the General Assembly, under Article 22 of the Charter, could establish a United Nations Peoples Assembly made up of 1000 national parliamentarians, meeting 2-3 times a year. While the exact method of selecting parliamentarians would be based largely on population (with every sovereign nation guaranteed at least one representative), there are two schools of thought as to the best scheme. Whilst Heindrich's argument to base the system entirely on population and extending to national parliaments of all nations, including dictatorships, largely makes sense, it would give the body more legitimacy to reward democracies with proportionally more seats. As Monbiot suggests, this could be done by a group such as Democracy Audit, although the self-proclaimed critic of a UNPA, Jeffrey Laurenti, may have accidentally stumbled across a better means. As he explains:

> The millennium has brought into existence a promising vehicle for separating the democratic wheat from the authoritarian chaff – the Community of Democracies. Constituted in 2000 in Warsaw, the Community has sought to define criteria for membership that would include as many states as possible (and give it the non-Western majority it would need for global credibility) and yet not outrage the human rights nongovernmental organizations that are its principal public constituencies.[113]

However selected, this body would enjoy a largely consultative role, its one power being related to revisions of the weighted voting system. It would enjoy an enormous amount of legitimacy and its role would likely evolve based on the concerns of citizens and any perceived lack of accountability on the part of major international institutions.

Either way, the General Assembly will continue to be the "town-hall" of the world, but one with greater participation by citizens, national parliaments and NGOs, and thus, one that holds greater moral authority. From this position of greater power, a revitalised General Assembly, in either scenario, could use its new dynamic interaction with the Security Council to press for action when the non-elected five are reluctant to carry out their mandate under the Charter.

---

113   Jeffrey Laurenti, *supra* note 98.

iv.   Linking Security Council and General Assembly Reform

While a "big bang" approach to UN institutional reform is unlikely to work there appears to be space for a natural linkage between the Security Council and the General Assembly. Developing countries want a stronger role in the Security Council but the P-5 would prefer the concept of "representativeness" to be applied in the General Assembly. What is needed therefore is an arrangement satisfactory for both parties.

This is a challenge. The P-5 recognize that the Security Council is the predominant UN institution and are therefore reluctant to cede any of its influence, particularly when they contribute the most money towards the UN budget. They also probably realize that "An equitably representative and democratic Council, without sufficient economic and military resources at its disposal is not different from an unrepresentative Council that has the capacity to pursue the narrow objectives of a powerful few. None of the two scenarios can foster the purposes and principles of the UN."[114]

The P-5 could start the reform process and show the international community that they are serious about achieving the Millennium Goals by offering the following three concessions. First, extend the Council to twenty-five members with five quasi-permanent seats and five new elected seats as outlined in Table 1 above. The quasi-permanent members would not enjoy the right of veto. Second, agree to a voluntary pledge to attempt to restrict their use of the veto to matters under Chapter VII of the Charter. If a permanent member used or threatens to use its veto for other matters it must provide written justification of its conduct to the General Assembly. Third, the P-5 should view more favourably a role for the International Court of Justice on questions of the extent of the Council's mandate under Chapters VI and VII.

For their part, mini-states and smaller nations should be encouraged to accept a system of weighted voting in the General Assembly. Based on contributions and population, this system would give the P-5 considerably more power in the Assembly. The new arrangement would be complemented by a resolution stating that the international community recognizes the importance of deploying the leadership, resources and power of the great powers in the General Assembly to work for the achievement of the Millennium Goals. Finally, an option would be given to the P-5 as to whether the new goal of the General Assembly would best be achieved by reforming the Assembly on the basis of tripartite representation or through the formation of a UNPA.

In conclusion, it is heartening, in these times of change, to recall the words of Edvard Hambro, President of the 25th Session of the General Assembly in 1970-71; "We ought not to be satisfied when people tell us that politics is the art of the possible. Politics should be the art to make possible tomorrow what seems impossible today." [115]

---

114   David M. Malone, *supra* note 32, p. 7.

115   Edvard Hambro, quoted in Ramesh Thakur, (ed.), *Past Imperfect, Future Uncertain: The United Nations at Fifty* (New York: St. Martin's Press, 1998), p. 203. See too the many useful suggestions in the excellent collection edited by Christian Tomuschat, *The United Nations at Fifty* (The Hague: Kluwer Law International, 1995).

33. The United Nations and New Threats, Challenges and Change: The Report of the High-Level Panel[1]

Bertrand G. Ramcharan

1. Introduction

The United Nations is at one of the lowest points it has ever been and its Secretary-General has been under attack on issues of leadership, judgment, efficiency of the administration he heads, and charges of financial wrong-doing by senior personnel in the Iraq Oil for Food Programme. The Secretary-General has been embarrassed by revelations relating to the employment of a close family member in a company involved in the Oil for Food programme. It is difficult to recall a time when both the Organization and its Secretary-General were under such wide-ranging attack.

At the same time, two related processes are underway to energise the role of the United Nations in respect of development goals and its ability to deal with new threats, challenges and change. In September 2005 a summit meeting will be held at the United Nations General Assembly to consider recommendations of the Secretary-General on these two sets of issues. It remains to be seen whether these two processes, coming at the twilight of the mandate of the Secretary-General, will develop traction or will have to await the arrival of his successor. Leaving this aside, this chapter will be concerned with the second set of issues namely the role of the United Nations in dealing with new threats, challenges and change.

The background is that in the aftermath of the military intervention in Iraq by a Coalition led by the United States of America, which had involved profound clashes at the United Nations, the Secretary-General felt the need to establish a High-Level Panel to help steady the world organization and to look to its future role in an age of rights as well as an age of terrorism.[2] The High-Level Panel, led by a former Prime Minister of Thailand, reported to the Secretary-General in November, 2004. In a Foreword to the published report, the Secretary-General already

---

1   *A More Secure World: Our Shared Responsibility. Report of the High-Level Panel on Threats, Challenges and Change, United Nations*, New York, (2004).

2   This characterization was used by Professor Louis Henkin of Columbia University at a Conference at the University of Santa Clara Law School in January 2005. Professor Henkin is the author of the widely acclaimed book, *The Age of Rights* (1990).

Ronald St. John Macdonald & Douglas M. Johnston (eds.), Towards World Constitutionalism, *pp. 911-925.*
© *2005 Koninklijke Brill NV. Printed in The Netherlands. ISBN 90 04 14612 1.*

welcomed the report and intimated that he would submit a report of his own in the spring of 2005 providing pointers of his own on how the recommendations of the Panel could be implemented.

The report of the Panel is an important think-piece. Whether it will turn out to be a blueprint for re-energizing the United Nations remains to be seen. Historically, major reports might have inspired the United Nations, but have not necessarily resulted in significant transformation of the organization. The first Secretary-General, Trygve Lie, submitted a (Ten?)-point plan to energize the Organization. It was politely received and then ignored. Dag Hammarskjold saw the United Nations as a body that could help advance the development of the developing countries and helped shape the concepts of conflict prevention and peacekeeping. U Thant sought to develop the role of the United Nations in dealing with humanitarian crises. Kurt Waldheim was a diplomatic helmsman as was Javier Perez de Cuellar. Perez de Cuellar did, however, press hard to develop the capacity of the United Nations for conflict prevention. This was continued by Boutros Boutros-Ghali, whose Agenda for Peace sought to mobilise the forces of the organization for conflict prevention. Even he, however, two years later, issued a Supplement to the Agenda for Peace in which he called into the question whether the very ideas he had advanced could be implemented practically. His subsequent Agenda for Development and Agenda for Democratisation hardly received attention as he exited office shortly after they were published.

Kofi Annan has given voice to the right of humanitarian intervention, a much contested concept that has subsequently been superseded by the concept of the responsibility to protect. He orchestrated the process that led to the adoption of the Millennium Development Goals and has now launched forth in the areas of new threats, challenges, and change, the subjects of the report of the High-Level Panel. Some commentators have commented negatively on the wisdom and practicality of a succession of reports and initiatives by the Secretary-General.

There is much hype and hoopla in and around the report of the High-Level Panel. This chapter will focus on the principal recommendations from the perspective of international law and organization. In short, the question we shall seek to answer is: what is there in the report that international lawyers might be particularly interested in or build upon? We begin with the future of international law, a topic, unfortunately that is not dealt with directly in the report – something we consider a major weakness and a misunderstanding of the role of international organizations in addressing the challenges of international security.

2.   International Law

The key to the security of nations and to the success of the United Nations is the international rule of law. This requires that the United Nations pay special attention to the development, application, modernisation, teaching and dissemination of international law. Following on the start of the League of Nations, the United Nations did foundation work on the codification and progressive development of international law. The International Court of Justice and the Permanent Court of

Arbitration are available to Member States to help them settle their disputes peacefully. The International Law Commission continues to watch over the codification and progressive development of international law, albeit in a conservative rather than a dynamic manner. The United Nations Institute for Training and Research does a limited amount of training in international law for government officials, in conjunction with the annual sessions of the International Law Commission. The ground-rules of international law governing relations among nations are mostly respected in practice, but there are serious problems in practice when it comes to issues, for example, of international peace and security.

Addressing the United Nations General Assembly on 21 September, 2004, Secretary-General Kofi Annan felt it necessary "to remind" Governments "of the all important framework ..., namely the rule of law in each country and in the world." He invoked Hammurabi's code, the vision of "a Government of laws and not of men", and the "principles of justice", including legal protection of the poor; restraints on the strong, so they cannot oppress the weak; and "laws publicly enacted, and known to all." He went on to lament that "today the rule of law is at risk around the world. Again and again, we see fundamental laws shamelessly disregarded – those that ordain respect for innocent life, for civilians, for the vulnerable – especially children."[3]

The Secretary-General went on to urge that "we must start from the principle that no one is above the law, and no one should be denied its protection. Every nation that proclaims the rule of law at home must respect it abroad, and every nation that insists on it abroad must enforce it at home." At the international level, he continued, "... all states – strong and weak, big and small – need a framework of fair rules, which each can be confident that others will obey."[4] Each generation, he counselled, has its part to play in the age-long struggle to strengthen the rule of law for all – which alone can guarantee freedom for all. "Let our generation not be found wanting."[5]

With such a strategic centrality for international law in the mission of the United Nations, how, we might ask, is the United Nations doing when it comes to the reinforcement and further development of international law? We offer a brief assessment next.

I wish to draw particular attention to the present-day atrophy in the codification and progressive development of international law.

The International Law Commission currently has under consideration the topics of: diplomatic protection; responsibility of international organizations; shared natural resources; international liability for injurious consequences arising out of acts not yet prohibited by international law; unilateral acts of States; reservations to treaties. At its fifty-sixth session, in 2004, it decided to include on its long-term

---

3   Secretary-General Kofi Annan's Address to the General Assembly, 21 September, 2004, p. 1.

4   *Idem*, p. 2.

5   *Idem*, p. 4.

programme of work the topics: obligation to extradite or prosecute; expulsion of aliens; and effects of armed conflicts on treaties.[6]

The codification and progressive development of international law is expressly provided for in the United Nations Charter. In the early days of the United Nations, the great Sir Hersch Lauterpacht did a survey of international law to stimulate the work of the International Law Commission. A second survey was prepared by the UN Secretariat in 1973. Thirty years later, no such survey is on the horizon. The International Law Commission is locked in consideration each year of mainly technical issues – albeit important ones – of international law. In the early days of the United Nations, the Sixth (Legal) Committee used to prompt the ILC on topics requiring attention. Great initiatives, such as the Maltese proposal to revise the law of the sea, are now rarely seen. The major national societies of international law organize conferences and sponsor research on some of the contemporary problems but are producing very little that is contributing to shaping the future development of international law. It is as if paralysis has set in sixty years after the establishment of the United Nations. We have serious problems at hand here.

3.   The High-Level Panel on New Threats and Challenges

At the beginning of December, 2004, a High-Level Panel on Threats, Challenges, and Change, which had been established by Secretary-General Kofi Annan, reported to him with its assessment and recommendations. The report is significant for the future of international law and the role of the United Nations therein, as we shall see below.

A.   *International Constitutional Law*

The Panel recommended that all Member States "rededicate themselves to the purposes and principles of the Charter and to applying them in a purposeful way, matching political will with the necessary resources."[7]

The Panel recommended that the United Nations build on the experience of regional organizations in developing frameworks for minority rights and the protection of democratically elected Governments from unconstitutional overthrow.[8]

B.   *Poverty Reduction*

The Panel stressed that all states must recommit themselves to the goals of eradicating poverty, achieving sustained economic growth and promoting sustainable development.[9]

---

6   Report of the International Law Commission. Fifty Sixth Session. General Assembly Official Records. Fifty-Ninth Session, Supplement No. 10 (A/59/10).

7   Recommendation 100.

8   Recommendation 14.

9   Recommendation 1.

C. Responsibility to Protect

The Panel endorsed the emerging norm that there is a collective international responsibility to protect, exercisable by the Security Council authorizing military intervention as a last resort, in the event of genocide and other large-scale killing, ethnic cleansing or serious violations of humanitarian law which sovereign Governments have proved powerless or unwilling to prevent.[10]

The Panel recommended that the United Nations High Commissioner for Human Rights should be called upon to prepare an annual report on the situation of human rights worldwide.[11]

It urged that all combatants must abide by the Geneva Conventions. All Member States should sign, ratify and act on all treaties relating to the protection of civilians, such as the Genocide Convention, the Geneva Conventions, the Rome Statute of the International Criminal Court and all refugee conventions. It is curious that foundation human rights conventions, such as the Convention against Torture, are not specifically mentioned.[12]

D. International Peace and Security: Five Criteria of Legitimacy

The Panel recommended that in considering whether to authorize or endorse the use of military force, the Security Council should always address – whatever other considerations it may take into account – at least the following five basic criteria of legitimacy:

(a) *Seriousness of threat:* Is the threatened harm to State or human security of a kind, and sufficiently clear and serious, to justify *prima facie* the use of military force? In the case of internal threats, does it involve genocide and other large-scale killing, ethnic cleansing or serious violations of international humanitarian law, actual or imminently apprehended?

(b) *Proper purpose:* Is it clear that the primary purpose of the proposed military action is to halt or avert the threat in question, whatever other purposes or motives may be involved?

(c) *Last resort:* Has every non-military option for meeting the threat in question been explored, with reasonable grounds for believing that other measures will not succeed?

(d) *Proportional means:* Are the scale, duration and intensity of the proposed military action the minimum necessary to meet the threat in question?

(e) *Balance of consequences:* Is there a reasonable chance of the military action being successful in meeting the threat in question, with the consequences of action not likely to be worse than the consequences of inaction?

---

10   Recommendation 55.

11   Recommendation 93.

12   Recommendation 66.

E.   Terrorism

The Panel called for the development of better instruments for global counter-terrorism cooperation, all within a legal framework that is respectful of civil liberties and human rights, including in the areas of law enforcement, intelligence-sharing, where possible; denial and interdiction, when required; and financial controls. It called upon the General Assembly to complete negotiations rapidly on a comprehensive convention on terrorism, incorporating a definition of terrorism with the following elements:

(a)   recognition, in the preamble, that State use of force against civilians is regulated by the Geneva Conventions and other instruments, and, if of sufficient scale, constitutes a war crime by the persons concerned or a crime against humanity;

(b)   restatement that acts under the 12 preceding anti-terrorism conventions are terrorism, and a declaration that they are a crime under international law; and restatement that terrorism in time of armed conflicts is prohibited by the Geneva Conventions and Protocols;

(c)   reference to the definitions contained in the 1999 International Convention for the Suppression of the Financing of Terrorism and Security Council Resolution 1566 (2004);

(d)   description of terrorism as "any action, in addition to actions already specified by the existing conventions on aspects of terrorism, the Geneva Conventions and Security Council resolution 1566 (12004), that is intended to cause death or serious bodily harm to civilians or non-combatants, when the purpose of such act, by its nature or context, is to intimidate a population, or to compel a Government or an international organization to do or to abstain from doing any act."[13]

F.   Protecting the Environment

The Panel recommended that States begin to phase out environmentally harmful subsidies, especially fossil fuel use and development.[14] It urged Member States to begin new negotiations to produce a new long-term strategy for reducing global warming beyond the period covered by the Kyoto Protocol.

G.   HIV/AIDS

The Panel recommended that the Security Council host a second special session on HIV/AIDS as a threat to international peace and security, to explore the future effects of HIV/AIDS on States and societies, generate research on the problem and identify critical steps towards a long-term strategy for diminishing the threat.[15]

---

13   Recommendation 44.
14   Recommendation 10.
15   Recommendation 7.

H.   Arms and Conflicts

The Panel recommended that Member States should expedite and conclude negotiations on legally binding agreements on the marking and tracing, as well as the brokering and transfer of small arms and light weapons.[16]

I.   Resources and Conflicts

The Panel recommended that the United Nations work with national authorities, international financial institutions, civil society organizations and the private sector to develop norms governing the management of natural resources for countries emerging from or at risk of conflict.[17]

J.   Cooperation with Regional Organizations

The Panel recommended that consultation and cooperation between the United Nations and regional organizations should be expanded and could be formalized in an agreement, covering such issues as meetings of the heads of the organizations, more frequent exchange of information and early warning, co-training of civilian and military personnel, and exchange of personnel within peace operations.[18]

K.   Disarmament

The Panel recommended that States Parties to the Biological and Toxin Weapons Convention should negotiate a new bio-security protocol to classify dangerous biological agents and establish binding international standards for the export of such agents.[19] It also recommended that the Conference on Disarmament move without further delay to negotiate a verifiable fissile material cut-off treaty that, on a designated schedule, ends the production of highly enriched uranium for non-weapons use, as well as on any serious concerns they have which might fall short of an actual breach of the Treaty on the Non-Proliferation of Nuclear Weapons and the Chemical Weapons Convention.[20]

L.   Transnational Organized Crime

The Panel called for a comprehensive international convention on money-laundering, bank secrecy and financial havens to be negotiated and endorsed by the General Assembly.[21]

---

16   Recommendation 15.
17   Recommendation 13.
18   Recommendation 86(b).
19   Recommendation 34.
20   Recommendation 36.
21   Recommendation 47.

M.   Rule of Law and International Criminal Justice

The Panel urged that the United Nations establish a robust capacity-building mechanism for rule of law assistance.[22]

The Panel urged the Security Council to be ready to use the authority it has under the Rome Statute to refer cases of suspected war crimes and crimes against humanity to the International Criminal Court.[23]

N.   Sanctions

The Panel recommended that the Security Council, in instances of verified, chronic violations, impose secondary sanctions against those involved in sanctions-busting.[24] The Secretary-General, in consultation with the Security Council, should ensure that an appropriate auditing mechanism is in place to oversee sanctions administration.

O.   Security Council

The Panel advised that reform of the Security Council should meet the following principles:

(a)   They should, in honouring Article 23 of the Charter of the United Nations, increase the involvement in decision-making of those who contribute most to the United Nations financially, militarily and diplomatically – specifically in terms of contributions to United Nations assessed budgets, participation in mandated peace operations, contributions to the voluntary activities of the United Nations in the areas of security and development, and diplomatic activities in support of United Nations objectives and mandates. Among developed countries, achieving or making substantial progress towards the internationally agreed level of 0.7 per cent of gross national product for official development assistance should be considered an important criterion of contribution;

(b)   They should bring into the decision-making process countries more representative of the broader membership, especially of the developing world;

(c)   They should not impair the effectiveness of the Security Council;

(d)   They should increase the democratic and accountable nature of the body.[25]

P.   Peace Enforcement and Peacekeeping

The Panel recommended that States with advanced military capacities should establish standby high readiness, self-sufficient battalions at up to brigade level that

---

22   Recommendation 49.
23   Recommendation 12.
24   Recommendation 50 (e).
25   Recommendation 73.

can reinforce United Nations missions, and should place them at the disposal of the United Nations.[26]

Q.   Peacebuilding

The Panel recommended that the Security Council establish a Peacebuilding Commission whose core functions would be to identify countries that are under stress and risk sliding towards State collapse; to organize, in partnership with the national Government, proactive assistance in preventing that process from developing further; to assist in the planning for transitions between conflict and post-conflict peacebuilding; and in particular to marshal and sustain the efforts of the international community in post-conflict peacebuilding over whatever period may be necessary.[27]

4.   The Way Ahead

Unless the United Nations can help uphold the international rule of law it will have no future. The "power", if any, of the United Nations, resides in the principles and rules of international law. From a strategic point of view, therefore, the search to strengthen the United Nations should begin with the application, and development, of international law. Collective security, the prevention of conflicts and the avoidance of humanitarian disasters or gross violations of human rights all depend on upholding the law.

It is a matter of the greatest urgency to refocus the quest for international security in the better application of international law. To begin with, the development of the law must keep up with fast-paced changes in international society. At the present time there is no international body that advises on new challenges requiring legal responses. The International Law Commission is not doing this, nor is the Legal Committee of the General Assembly. There is pressing need for such an advisory body. The United Nations Secretary-General should swiftly designate an Advisory Group on the Strengthening of International Law.

The international law of the future must develop safeguards against the procurement and use of weapons of mass destruction. It must develop stronger safeguards for the protection of the environment. It must insist on the democratic legitimacy of governments. It must be attentive to the realization of economic, social and cultural rights, as well as civil and political rights in a globalizing world. It must contribute to genuine protection of human rights against threatened atrocities. The preventive dimension is crucial here. The international law of the future must help bring about genuine equality and justice for women. The international law of the future must underwrite cultural diversity.

Where in the United Nations are issues such as these being addressed? Alas, nowhere. Atrophy has come about in the progressive development of international

---

26   Recommendation 60.

27   Recommendations 82 and 83.

law. There is need for expert advisers putting out think pieces on new challenges for the law. There is also great need to mobilize the international community about the better application of international law. This would include issues such as more recourse to the International Court of Justice or the Permanent Court of Arbitration: wider ratification of the Statute of the International Criminal Court or of regional human rights courts, such as the African Court of Human Rights: revitalized programmes for the dissemination and teaching of international law.

There is need to rally public opinion across the globe on the side of respect for international law. We must return to the time of the World Peace through World Law movement. What we have in mind is not new blueprints but a simple proposition: let the rules of international law on the books be respected and applied by everyone.

A.   *International Peace and Security*

1.   The report of the High-Level Panel on Threats, Challenges and Change calls for a restructured Department of Political Affairs and looks to a more activist Department in the areas of conflict prevention, support for good offices and mediation, and post-conflict peacebuilding. The Department will need to absorb and implement the report in light of its central analytical and political mission, certain still-present political realities, the most efficient use of its existing resources, the importance of taking on board valuable suggestions of the Panel, and the broader political context in which the report will be followed up.

2.   The *raison d'etre* of the Department of Political Affairs is sound analysis and hard-nosed political judgment and advice. It must always safeguard these two aspects. The USG is the political adviser of the Secretary-General and requires for this solid country and issues-related analysis. The concept of each country covered by a desk officer has to be retained. This would make continued regional or sub-regional divisions a necessity.

3.   It is in the interest of the Department to keep responsibility for servicing the Security Council, which also entails responsibility for servicing its Sanctions Committees.

4.   Member States are likely to react adversely to any suggestion to shift the Division of Palestine Rights from the Department. The same would be the case with regard to the hold-over decolonization unit. A question that arises for reflection, however, is whether these two elements could be merged into a Division of Decolonization and Palestine Rights. This could result in economies and make redeployments possible to new tasks.

5.   The Report advocates a field-oriented, dedicated mediation support capacity, competence on thematic issues that recur in peace negotiations, greater consultation and interaction with partners in peace processes. The Report also has radical proposals in the area of peacebuilding, including the establishment of a Peacebuilding Commission and a support secretariat for it.

6. There are three political factors that would need to be followed closely as the Department responds to the implementation of the Report: first, it is fundamentally intrusive in many instances and one would need to test the waters of Member States reactions prudently before wading in; second, the Report calls in various parts for massive resource outlays and it remains to be seen how the major contributors will absorb this; and third, the Report has pointed criticism in places of the pre-eminent power in the United Nations. One would need to gauge each of these factors carefully in calibrating the DPA strategy of absorbing the report.

7. DPA could pursue a strategy of "starting with what it has and augmenting capacity in light of additional resource allocations". This leads to the question: are there resources within DPA that could be drawn upon to accommodate the key thrusts of the Panel's recommendations and make them sustainable in any event? This question can be answered in the affirmative.

8. For a start, there are the two ASGs and their immediate staff. Directors of regional divisions and their staff have long voiced the view that the ASGs add a layer of supervision that can be lightened. One could study this. Might it be possible, for example, to have the regional directors reporting directly to the Office of the USG and to assign to the two ASGs thematic as well as geographical responsibilities? Could one ASG, for example, be the focal point for conflict prevention and another ASG the focal point for the mediation support capacity? The role of the ASGs could be fundamentally re-configured on the understanding that they form a close working team under the USG. Should a peacebuilding commission be established and resources provided a third ASG could eventually be envisaged as the focal point for peacebuilding activities?

9. An approach such as the above would call for a Director position in the Office of the USG that would help the USG and the ASGs liaise and coordinate with the regional and other divisions.

10. On the reasoning set out above, DPA could be restructured along the following lines:
    A. USG for Political Affairs;
    B. ASG for Early Warning and Prevention (Office would have dedicated staff);
    C. ASG for Mediation and Negotiation Support (Office would have dedicated staff.);
    D. ASG for Peacebuilding (Office would have dedicated staff);
    E. Office of the USG (This would include policy planning and analysis);
    F. Regional Divisions;
    G. Division for Security Council Affairs;
    H. Division for Decolonization and Palestine Rights.

11. The above changes could be brought in immediately (even D if the SG were to redeploy a post). As new resources are granted, capacity could be augmented in particular areas.

12. The above presentation is based on the focal point for peacebuilding being based in DPA. This must be right. DPA is the department that has global coverage. DPKO is the department that deals with particular country situations. In such particular situations the close cooperation between the two departments will continue. However, the global coverage of DPA would make it logical that global peacebuilding responsibilities be located there.

B. Human Rights

The Report of the High-Level Panel on Threats, Challenges and Change advances some sensible recommendations as well as some controversial ones that have attracted significant hostility on the part of human rights non-governmental organizations. This comment does not take a view on the controversial recommendation for a Commission on Human Rights with universal membership. Rather, it focuses on how the recommendations might be taken forward constructively were it decided to implement them.

Recommendation No. 91 suggests that all members of the Commission on Human Rights should designate prominent and experienced human rights figures at the heads of their delegations. This is surely worthy of broad support in the human rights movement. When the current commission was established the ground rules were that Members States on the Commission would submit the names of their nominees to the Secretary-General, that there would be a process of consultation with the Secretary-General, and that the nominee would be subject to confirmation by the Economic and Social Council. The consultations have never taken place. Should the Commission remain as it is, it would be urgent to devise a consultation process and to set down some criteria for being a Head of Delegation on the Commission. Should the Commission become universal, it would be even more important to devise criteria for serving as a Head of Delegation. The Secretary-General may wish to have prepared such a set of criteria and submit it to the Membership for endorsement. That would help develop a consensus on the kind of person who should be a Head of Delegation on the Commission.

Recommendation No. 93 suggests that the High Commissioner for Human Rights should be called upon to prepare an annual report on the situation of human rights worldwide. The High Commissioner has the competence to do so. The basis for such a report could be a recapitulation of the principal findings of the special rapporteurs, representatives, and working groups established by the Commission and reporting to it. The High Commissioner could preface these findings with an Introduction of her own, highlighting issues or situations of particular concern to her. Such a report would be an important step forward in the protection of human rights globally. It would not entail much additional outlay of resources.

Recommendation No.94 suggests that the Security Council and the proposed Peacebuilding Commission should request the High Commissioner for Human Rights to report to them regularly on the implementation of all human rights-related provisions of Security Council resolutions, thus enabling focused, effective monitoring of those provisions. This is surely a sensible recommendation to Members of the Security Council. There are two aspects to this recommendation. In the first place, the High Commissioner could have prepared and publish such a report in any event, say, on a quarterly basis. Such a written report would be at the disposal of the Security Council and, indeed, all other United Nations bodies. The second aspect of this recommendation is that the High Commissioner could present her report personally to the Security Council, as needed. There are many ways of achieving this. In the first place, the Office of the High Commissioner already briefs the President of the Security Council monthly. In the second place, the High Commissioner or her representative could brief the Security Council regularly in informal consultations. In the third place, the High Commissioner, as needed, could be invited by the Security Council to brief it in formal sessions. There is thus much room for the constructive implementation of this recommendation.

Recommendation No.92 suggests that the Commission on Human Rights should be supported in its work by an Advisory Council or Panel. If one takes the Commission as it is, it would seem wise for this Advisory Council or Panel to consist of the rapporteurs, representatives, and chairpersons of working groups, cumulatively called the special procedures. There is a sound rationale for this: they have been mandated by the Commission to monitor the protection of human rights and are therefore in the best position to advise on protection issues. The Advisory Council or Panel could also include the heads of the principal human rights treaty bodies. These two groups already meet annually for a week and then hold a joint meeting. This would be an ideal advisory forum. Making them the Advisory Panel would give them the opportunity to make protection-related recommendations to the Commission, whether in its current composition or enlarged.

This brings us to the last of the five recommendations, Recommendation No. 90 that membership of the Commission should be made universal. There are two groups of views on this recommendation. The first is based on the premise that a Commission on Human Rights presupposes special commitment and responsibility on the part of the members, that protection of human rights should be the primary goal, and that Members of the Commission must be able to take principled positions on issues and situations. On top of this, human rights non-governmental organizations participate in large numbers in the Commission and, by their presence, make it a special body attuned to conditions on the ground in countries. The participation of special rapportuers and other special procedures, the national human rights commission, and regional human rights organizations give the Commission, in the eyes of those loyal to the historic commission, a special place in the United Nations that would be lost were it enlarged to universal membership. Furthermore, it is argued, the Commission has a lead role in the drafting of standards, in supervising the work of the Sub-Commission, particularly its research reports and studies, and the Commission also occasionally commissions studies of its own. Could these all be done, it is asked, in a universal Commission?

On the other side, there are those who argue that the election of Members with questionable human rights records presents a problem of credibility for the United Nations as a whole and the High-Level Panel was obviously moved by this concern in making its recommendation for universal membership. It is further argued that a universal Commission would place on each Member State of the United Nations the responsibility to respond to protection challenges. Even further, it is argued, the majority of Member States of the United Nations – at least those with diplomatic representation in Geneva – participate *en masse* in the Commission, contributing to debates, moving procedural motions, and sponsoring resolutions. The only thing non-members cannot do, it is argued, is vote on resolutions.

It needs to be pointed out that should a decision be taken to move to a universal commission it would probably have to meet in New York where all Member States are represented, otherwise it would be necessary to envisage United Nations financial assistance for Member States who would find the costs of sustaining a delegation in Geneva for several weeks taxing. Even should the Commission meet in New York, it might still be necessary to envisage financial assistance to needy Member States if one would like to have real experts from home participate in the Commission. Without such financial assistance one might well end up in a situation in which the Heads and other members of delegations are mostly coming from diplomatic missions to the United Nations – which would be at cross purpose with the recommendation that heads of delegations should be prominent and experienced human rights figures. There is need for some hard thinking on this issue.

Be that as it may, were the decision taken to move to a universal human rights Commission, how could this be made to work in favor of human rights protection? That would seem to be the crux of the matter.

One could envisage a scenario in which the suggested Advisory Council or Panel, consisting of special procedures mandate holders and chairpersons of human rights treaty bodies, meets twice annually under the chairpersonship of the High Commissioner. They offer recommendations for the Human Rights Commission, which meets biannually for the purpose of responding to protection challenges. Studies, drafting of norms, and advice and technical assistance issues would be considered principally in the Sub-Commission, which would continue to meet annually. Such an arrangement would give a sharper protection focus to the Commission and would bring it, the special procedures, the treaty bodies, and the High Commissioner into better synergy for the more effective protection of human rights.

The Advisory Council or Panel would continue to meet in Geneva. Where the Commission meets would depend on the issues of policy and financing adduced earlier. Realistically it would probably end up meeting in New York. The Commission currently has a session of six weeks. One could envisage this being split into two sessions of three weeks each. The Third Committee of the General Assembly meets usually in October and November. One could envisage the Commission meeting in the spring and in late summer, on the eve of the General Assembly. On the line of reasoning being presented here it is envisaged that the Third Committee of the General Assembly would continue to exist. This would seem to be right for reasons of policy and principle. The General Assembly has an important role under the Charter in the advancement of the universal realization of human rights. It would therefore be essential for the General Assembly itself to be organized in such a manner as to discharge its human rights role. Besides, the Third Committee also deals with social and humanitarian issues and these must remain the focus of considered discussion in the General Assembly. Having said this, it is quite conceivable for the Third Committee to have shorter sessions during which, as far as human rights issues are concerned, it would be acting mainly on recommendations of the High Commissioner and the Commission on Human Rights.

This comment is written from the perspective of how, should it be decided to go forward with a universal Commission, it might possibly be organized. We have sought to rationalize the recommendations of the High-Level Panel for a universal Commission and an Advisory Council or Panel. The line of organization advanced here leaves unanswered a key question: how would the participation of NGOs, one of the key features of the Commission at the present time, be satisfactorily achieved? A six-week session of the Commission is predictable from the point of view of planning and enables NGOs to optimize their participation. Likewise, the participation of national human rights commissions is growing to be an important feature of the Commission and it would be essential to think this through so that their participation is optimized.

Having regard to these considerations it would be highly advisable, before taking a decision on this issue of universal membership, to request the Secretariat to canvass the views of NGOs and national human rights commissions so that the most careful consideration is given to them. It would also be important for the Secretariat to present to the decision-making body a detailed "implementation paper" on what it would entail in delegation costs, meeting costs, and documentation costs, to have a universal Commission, whether it meets once a year or it meets in biannual session, as would seem to be called for to make optimal use of the proposal.

The recommendation for a universal Commission was undoubtedly offered out of a desire to overcome a serious credibility problem for the United Nations. It therefore deserves to be carefully examined from all points of view. At the end of the day, there is a key underlying consideration: change must lead to stronger, not weaker, protection and gains achieved slowly over the years must not be given up in the quest for reform. Reform must contribute to stronger, not weaker protection of human rights. Effective protection is, after all, the mission of the Commission on Human Rights.

About the Contributors

Munir Akram is Permanent Representative of Pakistan to the United Nations in New York (from May 2002). He holds a Master of Arts and a Bachelor of Law. His previous positions include: Ambassador and Permanent Representative of Pakistan to the UN in Geneva, Switzerland (1995–2002); Additional Foreign Secretary (UN) (1992–1995); Ambassador of Pakistan to the European Community, Belgium and Luxembourg (1988–1992); Director-General (UN, Economic Cooperation and Policy Planning), Ministry of Foreign Affairs (1985–1988); Minister-Counsellor, Embassy of Pakistan, Tokyo (1982–1985); Counsellor & Deputy Permanent Representative, Permanent Mission of Pakistan, Geneva (1979–1982); Director (UN), Ministry of Foreign Affairs (1973–1979); Second Secretary, Permanent Mission of Pakistan, New York (1969–1973); Section Officer, Ministry of Foreign Affairs (1968–1969). His conference experience includes: UN General Assembly (16 regular and 3 Special Sessions); UN Security Council, UNDP, UNICEF, UNESCO General Conference, ECOSOC, UN Human Rights Commission, Sub-Commission on Prevention of Discrimination and Protection of Minorities, Committee on Disarmament, World Health Assembly. He has participated in conferences and seminars on Disarmament and International Security, World Trade and Socio-Economic issues. Ambassador Akram was President of the UN Security Council in May 2003 and May 2004.

Philip Allott is Professor Emeritus of International Public Law in the University of Cambridge and Fellow of Trinity College, Cambridge. He was at one time a Legal Counsellor in the British Foreign and Commonwealth Office. He is the author of *Eunomia. New Order for a New World* (Oxford University Press, 1990/2001) and *The Health of Nations. Society and Law Beyond the State* (Cambridge Unviersity Press, 2002). He is a Fellow of the British Academy.

Awni Behnam is President of the International Ocean Institute. From July 1977 to October 2004, he held senior positions in the United Nations Conference on Trade and Development. He was appointed as the Chief of Liaison for the Group of 77 in 1986, subsequently as Director, Secretary of the Trade and Development Board and the Secretary of the Conference of UNCTAD. He was responsible for the preparations and negotiations of several conventions adopted under the auspices of UNCTAD. From 2001 to 2004, he was the Senior Advisor to the Secretary-General in the organization. He had privileged and unique access to the Group of 77, its meetings and provided support to the Group's chapters and in particular to the New York office of the Group of 77. Prior to joining UNCTAD in 1977, he lectured at the University of Wales, Department of Maritime Studies, where he obtained his Masters and Doctorate degrees. He served as a seagoing officer in his earlier career.

Brun-Otto Bryde is a Judge of the German Constitutional Court (since 2001) and Professor of Public Law and Political Science, Justus Liebig-Universität Giessen (from 1987); *Dr. jur.* Hamburg (1971); Habilitation (Hamburg 1980) for Public Law, International Law, Sociology of Law and Comparative Law; 1971–1973 Lecturer, Faculty of Law, Addis Abeba, Ethiopia; 1973–1974 Law and Modernization Fellow, Yale Law School; 1974–1982 Research Fellow and Lecturer, University of Hamburg; 1982–1987 Professor of Public Law, Universität der Bundeswehr München; 1989 and 1994 Visiting Professor at Wisconsin Law School; 1992–1998 chair of the German Sociology of Law Association; 2000–2001 member of the Committee on the Elimination of Racial Discrimination. His publications include *The Politics and Sociology of African Legal Development* (1976), *Verfassungsentwicklung* (1982), and many articles in the fields of (comparative) public law and democratic theory, international law and socio-legal studies; he is co-editor of *Verfassung und Recht in Obersee.*

Benedetto Conforti has been Professor of International Law in the Law Faculties of the Universities of Siena (1963–1969), Padua (1969–1972), Naples (1972–1987), Rome "La Sapienza" (1989–1994) and Naples (1994–present). He was Permanent Visiting Professor of Public International Law at the Law Faculty of the University of Alexandria (1978–1993). He is a member of the *Institut de droit international*, a member of the Curatorium of the Hague Academy of International Law, a member of the Italian Group of the Permanent Court of Arbitration and a former member of the European Commission of Human Rights. He is a former judge of the European Court of Human Rights.

Władysław Czapliński is Jean Monnet Professor of International and European Law, and Director of the Institute of Law Studies of the Polish Academy of Sciences in Warsaw. He is a member of the Advisory Boards with the Prime Minister and Minister of Foreign Affairs. He is a Visiting Scholar of the A. von Humboldt Foundation, FRG (Tuebingen, Heidelberg, Berlin), and Rapporteur of the ILA Committee on State Succession. He has published numerous publications on state succession, state responsibility, and EU law.

Hilario G. Davide, Jr. is the present Chief Justice of the Philippines. He has been with the 15-member Supreme Court since 1991 and was appointed to the pinnacle of the judicial hierarchy in 1998. Born 69 years ago in a remote upland village of the town of Argao in the central Philippine Island of Cebu, he is the twentieth Filipino jurist to hold this position in the Court's 103 years of existence. In 2002, he was conferred the *Magsaysay Award for Government Service*, a singular honor that is the Asian equivalent of the Nobel Prize. His contributions to the propagation of human rights and protection of the environment, in addition to a lifelong career devoted to the law, have been amply recognized and honored by leading universities and colleges in the Philippines and abroad. To date, he has been conferred no fewer than thirteen honorary doctoral degrees in law and the humanities, including those conferred by the country's premiere law schools.

Ahmed Abou-el-Wafa is Chief of the Department of Public International Law of Cairo University. He has the following diplomas: Diploma of the Hague Academy of International Law (1980); *Doctorat d'Etat* (University of Lyon III, France 1981); DEA of European law (Idem); Diploma of higher studies in public law (1976) and in penal law (1977); Bachelor in law, Cairo University (1974). He has published about 15 books and more than 50 articles (in Arabic, English and French) related to public international law, international organizations, law of the sea, diplomatic and consular relations, anti-personal landmines, international protection of human rights, the League of Arab States, the International Court of Justice, international humanitarian law, international negotiations, and the Council for Cooperation of Arab States of the Gulf. He has also published an encyclopaedia of 15 volumes (in about 6300 pages) on: "The rules of international law and relations in Islamic Shari'a" (in Arabic).

Bardo Fassbender is Associate Professor of Law at Humboldt University, Berlin, Germany. He studied law, history and political science at the University of Bonn (Germany) and the Yale Law School. He holds a Master of Law (LL.M.) 1992 (Yale Law School), *Doctor iuris*, 1997, *Privatdozent*, 2004 (Humboldt University). He was a Ford Foundation Senior Fellow in Public International Law at Yale University, a Jean Monnet Fellow at the European University Institute in Florence, and a lecturer in international law at the University of Sankt Gallen, Switzerland. He has taught at Humboldt University from 1998. His principal fields of research are public international law (in particular UN law), German constitutional law, comparative constitutional law and theory, and the history of international and constitutional law. Among his publications is the article "The United Nations Charter as Constitution of the International Community" (*Columbia Journal of Transnational Law vol. 36 (1998)*).

Gerhard Hafner teaches public international law and European law at the Institute of International Law and International Relations, Jurisprudence Faculty of the University of Vienna. His areas of research expertise include international legal regulations for the prevention of transboundary damage and liability in cases of damage, the peaceful settlement of conflicts, codification of public international law, European law, neutrality, governmental succession of states and international criminal law. Professor Dr. Hafner worked for several years in the Austrian Foreign Ministry's legal department, where he ultimately held the position of Director of the Division of Public International Law from 1993 to 1995. Professor Dr. Hafner has also been a member of the Austrian delegation to the United Nations' General Assembly; from as early as 1972, he acted as member of the Austrian delegations to numerous international conferences, sometimes as head of delegation. He was a long-standing member of the United Nations' International Law Commission, where he was primarily concerned with jurisdictional immunities of states and state responsibility. Moreover, he acts as legal expert in numerous other committees and associations, for instance, as President of the Austrian Branch of the International Law Association; he is also a member of the governing board of the German Society for International Law.

Douglas M. Johnston (JSD, Yale University) was born, and received most of his education, in Scotland, but spent his 40-year teaching career at universities in Canada, the United States and Singapore before retirement in 1999. He has taught a variety of subjects in political science and history as well as public and private law. His special interests lie in marine and environmental law and policy, the theory and history of international law, and modern Asian history. His books include works on the law of the sea, marine pollution, international fisheries, maritime boundary making, and treaty-making. He is now Professor Emeritus at the University of Victoria in British Columbia and Adjunct Professor at Dalhousie University in Nova Scotia.

Alexandre Kiss is Director of Research Emeritus at the French National Center for Scientific Research. He has lectured in different universities and institutions in Europe, North and South America, Africa and Asia, and published twelve books and more than 300 articles on general international law, European law, and, for some years, mainly on international human rights law and environmental law. He currently works as a consultant for international institutions and is president of the European Council of Environmental Law.

Jan Klabbers has been professor of International Law at the University of Helsinki since 1996, and is deputy director of the Erik Castrén Institute of International Law and Human Rights. He holds a doctorate in law (with distinction) and a master's degree in political science, both from the University of Amsterdam. His main publications include *The Concept of Treaty in International Law* (1996), and *An Introduction to International Institutional Law* (2002).

Tommy Koh is Ambassador-At-Large at the Ministry of Foreign Affairs; Chairman of the Institute of Policy Studies; Chairman of the National Heritage Board; Chairman of the Chinese Heritage Centre; and Director of SingTel. He is also a Professor of Law at the National University of Singapore. He was Dean of the Law Faculty from 1971–1974. He was Singapore's Permanent Representative to the United Nations in New York from 1968 to 1971 (concurrently accredited as High Commissioner to Canada) and from 1974 to 1984 (concurrently accredited as High Commissioner to Canada and Ambassador to Mexico). He was Ambassador to the

United States of America from 1984 to 1990. Professor Koh was President of the Third UN Conference on the Law of the Sea from 1980 to 1982. He was Chairman of the Preparatory Committee and the Main Committee of the UN Conference on Environment and Development from 1990 to 1992. He served as the UN Secretary-General's Special Envoy to Russia, Estonia, Latvia and Lithuania in 1993. He was Chairman of two WTO dispute panels and was a member of a third panel. Professor Koh received, in addition to his post-graduate qualifications from Harvard and Cambridge universities, an honorary doctorate in law from Yale University and Monash University, and various awards from Columbia, Stanford, Georgetown, Tufts and Curtin universities.

Roman A. Kolodkin graduated with honours from Moscow State University, Law Faculty (1982). He completed his postgraduate studies at Moscow State University, Law Faculty, International Law Chair (1982–85); Ph.D. International Law (1986). He works at the Ministry of Foreign Affairs, Russia (1991–present). He is Director, Legal Department, Member of the Board, MFA, Russia (2001–present). He is a Member of the International Law Commission (2003–present).

Charlotte Ku is Executive Director and Executive Vice President of The American Society of International Law. Her most recent article, "When Can Nations Go to War? Politics and Change in the UN System," was published in summer 2003 in the *Michigan Journal of International Law*. With the late Professor Harold K. Jacobson, she co-authored *Democratic Accountability and the Use of Force in International Law* (Cambridge University Press, 2003), which was awarded the 2004 ASIL Certificate of Merit for a specialized work in international law. Dr. Ku is a former chair of the Academic Council on the United Nations System, a member of the Council on Foreign Relations, and immediate past chair of the International Section of the International Studies Association.

Vaughan Lowe is Chichele Professor of Public International Law, and a Fellow of All Souls College, Oxford University, and a Barrister practising from Essex Court Chambers, London. He appeared as counsel for Palestine in the Case concerning the *Legal Consequences of the Construction of a Wall in the Occupied Palestinian Territory* in the International Court of Justice, and has also acted as counsel in cases in the International Tribunal for the Law of the Sea, the European Court of Human Rights, the Inter-American Commission on Human Rights, and arbitral tribunals hearing cases on international investment disputes, the law of the sea, and other matters. He has published widely on questions of international law.

Ronald St. John Macdonald is Honorary President for Life of the Canadian Council on International Law in Ottawa. A long-time dean and professor of law and a former Judge of the European Court of Human Rights in Strasbourg 1980–1998, he is Honorary Professor in the Law Department of Peking University, a Member Emeritus of the *Institut de droit international*, and an Honorary Member of the American Society of International Law. A former Representative of Canada to the

United Nations, he served as a member of the five-nation drafting committee of the Declaration of Teheran, 1968.

V.S. Mani holds a B.A., M.A., LL.B., and Ph.D. (International Law, Jawaharlal Nehru University (JNU), New Delhi). Currently he is Director of Gujarat National Law University; previously he was Professor of International Space Law, a Chair instituted by the Government of India Department of Space, and Director of the Human Rights Teaching and Research Program, both at JNU. He was Visiting Professor to Tokyo University (2000); Visiting Professor at National University of Juridical Sciences, Kolkata (2001); Visiting Fellow, Max Planck Institute of Comparative Public Law and International Law, Heidelberg (2003); and Rockefeller Research Fellow at the British Institute of International and Comparative Law, London (1969–1970); he presented a paper and chaired a session of the Space Law Technical Forum of UNSPACE III, Vienna (1999). He has published over 90 articles and 7 books. He was Legal Adviser (& Chief Secretary, 1985–1990), Republic of Nauru (1981–1993); he appeared before the ICJ in two cases (*Certain Phosphate Lands in Nauru & The Atlantique*). He was invited to deliver lectures at The Hague Academy of International Law on "Humanitarian Intervention Today" (August 2005). He is Executive President of the Indian Society of International Law, New Delhi (2003–2006).

Axel Marschik is a Master and Doctor of Law at the University of Vienna, Austria. His further studies or courses include: *Université de la Sorbonne* (Paris I), France (1990); Hague Academy of International Law, The Netherlands (1991); Academy of European Law at the European University Institute, Italy (1993); Visiting Scholar at Stanford University, California, USA, (1994). His appointments include: 1989–1996: Assistant Professor at the Institute of International Law and International Relations of the University of Vienna, Austria; 1990–1998: Lecturer of International Law at the University of Vienna; 1996: Entry into the Austrian Ministry for Foreign Affairs, EU division; 1997: Attaché at the Austrian Mission to the UN in Geneva; 1997–1999: Head of General-Affairs-Council-Unit in the EU-Division, Austrian Ministry for Foreign Affairs; 1999–2002: Legal and Political Counsellor at the Austrian Mission to the United Nations in New York; Since 2003: Minister, Deputy Permanent Representative of Austria to the UN in NY. Functions: 2001–2002: Vice-Chairman of the 6th Committee (Legal) of the 56th General Assembly of the United Nations; 2002–2004: Rapporteur of the Assembly of States Parties to the International Criminal Court.

Donald M. McRae is the Hyman Soloway Professor of Business and Trade Law, and former Dean in the Common Law Section of the Faculty of Law, at the University of Ottawa. He has advised the Department of Foreign Affairs and International Trade of the Government of Canada and has been counsel for Canada in fisheries, maritime boundary and investment arbitrations. He was the Chief Negotiator for Canada for the Pacific Salmon dispute. He has also advised the Government of New Zealand on international trade law and other international law matters. Professor McRae has chaired and sat on dispute settlement panels under the Canada-

US Free Trade Agreement, the US-Israel Free Trade Agreement, and NAFTA, and has appeared as counsel before WTO panels and the Appellate Body and been a member of two WTO panels. Professor McRae has published widely on international law, law of the sea and international trade law. He is a member of the Board of Editors of the *Journal of International Economic Law*, and is Editor-in-Chief of the *Canadian Yearbook of International Law*.

Saeid Mirzaee-Yengejeh served as the legal advisor of the Permanent Mission of Iran to the United Nations for two terms (1989–1994 and 1997–2002). Between the two terms (1994–1997) he served as the Director of the legal department of the Ministry of Foreign Affairs of Iran. He was the coordinator of the Non-Aligned Movement during the 1998 Rome Conference on the establishment of an International Criminal Court. He continued to hold that position during the entire life-span of the Preparatory Commission on the establishment of the International Criminal Court, from 1998 to 2002, and coordinated two working groups on the rules of procedure of the Assembly of States Parties, and on the Assembly of States Parties – preparatory documents of the Preparatory Commission of the ICC. He was the Chairman of the Special Committee on the Charter of the United Nations and on the Strengthening of the Role of the Organization, in 2000.

Manuel Rama-Montaldo is Doctor of Law and Social Sciences (Montevideo). He holds a Diploma in International Law (Oxford University). Formerly, he was Associate Professor and *Chargé de cours* of Public International Law, University of the Republic, Montevideo; Secretary of the United Nations Programme of Assistance in the Teaching, Study, Dissemination and Wider Appreciation of International Law; Deputy Director for Research and Studies and Deputy Director, Codification Division, Office of Legal Affairs, United Nations Secretariat. Currently, he is an International Law Consultant, Montevideo, Uruguay. He is the author and/or editor of numerous articles and books in the field of international law.

Onuma Yasuaki is Professor of International Law, University of Tokyo, Graduate School of Law and Politics, and has taught at Paris I, Columbia, Michigan and other universities as visiting professor. His publications include *The Tokyo War Crimes Trial: An International Symposium* (eds., Kodansha International, 1986); *A Normative Approach to War: Peace, War, and Justice in Hugo Grotius* (ed., Clarendon Press, Oxford, 1993); "When was the Law of International Society Born?" *Journal of the History of International Law*, II (2000); "Towards an Intercivilizational Approach to Human Rights," *Asian Yearbook of International Law*, VII (2001); "The ICJ: An Emperor Without Clothes?" N. Ando et al., eds., *Liber Amicorum Judge Shigeru Oda* (Kluwer Law International, 2002); "International Law in and with International Politics: The Functions of International Law in International Society," *European Journal of International Law*, XIV, no.1 (2003).

Alain Papaux completed his studies at the Universities of Lausanne (LL.L.), Geneva (M.A. Philosophy), Heidelberg, Lausanne (LL.D.) and Brussels (LL.M.). Otto

Riese Award, Walter Hug Award. Lector in Private International Law; Lector in Public International Law; *Chargé de cours* of Legal Philosophy and Assistant Professor at the University of Lausanne. He is currently Professor of Legal Philosophy at the European Academy of Legal Theory (*Facultés universitaires Saint-Louis* and Katholieke Universiteit Brussel, Brussels). He has published several books and articles on Legal Philosophy, Ethics, Public International Law, Private International Law, Comparative Law, Epistemology of Law, Legal Semiotics, Legal Hermeneutics, Law and Natural Sciences, Environmental Law. He is project manager for the creation of an Institute of philosophy of environmental law and environmental sciences at the University of Lausanne.

Bertrand G. Ramcharan is Chancellor of the University of Guyana and Professor of International Human Rights Law concurrently in The Netherlands and Sweden. He is a Barrister-at-Law of Lincoln's Inn with a Doctorate in law from the London School of Economics and Political Science (LSE). At the LSE he was International Law Scholar and holds the prestigious Diploma in International Law of The Hague Academy of International Law. He has served as Director of Research at the Academy. He has been a Fellow of the LSE and was UN Fellow at Harvard University's Kennedy School of Government in 2004. He has previously been Adjunct Professor of International Human Rights Law at Columbia University and also taught at the Geneva Graduate Institute of International Studies. He is the author/editor of some 25 books and numerous articles. His latest, edited, book is *Conflict Prevention in Practice*: *Essays in Honour of Jim Sutterlin*.

In a United Nations career of more than three decades he served in the human rights, peacemaking, peacekeeping, political and policy-planning parts of the United Nations. He was Head of the Secretary-General's Speechwriting Service and served for nearly four years with the peace negotiators and peacekeepers in the former Yugoslavia. He carried out the functions of United Nations High Commissioner for Human Rights for fourteen months over 2003–2004 at the level of United Nations Under-Secretary-General. He has written a book about this, the first by any incumbent: *A UN High Commissioner in Defence of Human Rights* (2004).

Alfred P. Rubin is Emeritus Distinguished Professor of International Law at the Fletcher School of Law & Diplomacy. He was for six years (1994–2000) the President of the American Branch of the International Law Association, then (2000–2004) Chairman of its Executive Committee. In 1981–82 he served as the Charles H. Stockton Chair of International Law at the Naval War College in Newport, Rhode Island, and prior to that on the Executive Committee of the American Society of International Law and many other posts. He is the sole author of four books including *The International Personality of the Malay Peninsula* and *Piracy, Paramountcy and Protectorates*, both published by the University of Malaya Press, 1984, *The Law of Piracy* (2nd, Revised Edition, Transnational Publishers, 1998) and *Ethics and Authority in International Law* (Cambridge University Press, 1997). He is also the author of over 100 articles.

Syed Haider Shah is First Secretary, Permanent Mission of Pakistan to the United Nations, New York (from July 2002), covering legal issues (Sixth Committee) and counter terrorism. He represented Pakistan on the Counter Terrorism Committee and the Al Qaida and Taliban Sanctions Committee of the Security Council from 2003–04; participated in the negotiations of a number of Security Council and General Assembly resolutions on counter terrorism and other legal issues; attended three sessions of the United Nations General Assembly; joined the Foreign Service of Pakistan in November 1995, served at Foreign Office Islamabad on different desks including United Nations, Afghanistan and South Asia. He also worked as staff officer to the Foreign Secretary and the Foreign Minister. He served briefly as a Civil Judge-cum-Judicial Magistrate at Swat (NWFP) in 1995.

Christian Tomuschat is Professor of Public Law, in particular International and European Law, Humboldt University Berlin. He is a member of the *Institut de droit international*; *Dr. jur.*, Heidelberg (1964); *Privatdozent*, Heidelberg (1972); Professor of Public Law, in particular International and European Law, Bonn (1972–1995). He was a member of the Human Rights Committee under the International Covenant on Civil and Political Rights (1977–1986); Member, UN International Law Commission (1985–1996); Rapporteur of the UN Human Rights Commission on the situation of human rights in Guatemala (1990–1993); Coordinator, Commission on Historical Clarification, Guatemala (1997–1999); Judge, Administrative Tribunal of the African Development Bank, 1998–2005. Member, International Commission of Jurists, 1980–1995; President, German Society of International Law (1993–1999). He is the author of numerous books and articles, most recently: *Human Rights. Between Idealism and Realism*, Oxford 2003.

Antônio Augusto Cançado Trindade holds a Ph.D. from Cambrige University (Yorke Prize) in International Law. He is Professor of International Law at the University of Brasilia, Brazil; and Judge President of the Inter-American Court of Human Rights. He was formerly Legal Adviser to the Ministry of External Relations of Brazil (1985–1990). He is a member of the *Institut de Droit International*; Member of the Boards of Directors of the Inter-American Institute of Human Rights (Costa Rica) and of the International Institute of Human Rights (Strasbourg). He was invited to give the general course on public international law at the Hague Academy of International Law in August 2005. He is the author of several books and numerous articles on international law published in various countries.

Robert F. Turner holds both professional and academic doctorates from the University of Virginia School of Law, where in 1981 he co-founded the Center for National Security Law. An army veteran of the Vietnam War, he has served in the government as national security adviser to a member of the Senate Foreign Relations Committee, Special Assistant to the Under Secretary of Defense for Policy, Counsel to the President's Intelligence Oversight Board at the White House, Principal Deputy Assistant Secretary of State, and first President of the US Institute of Peace. During 1994–95 he occupied the Charles H. Stockton Chair of International

Law at the US Naval War College. A former three-term chairman of the American Bar Association Standing Committee on Law and National Security and for many years editor of the ABA *National Security Law Report*, he is the author or editor of more than a dozen books and numerous articles.

Karel Wellens graduated, *summa cum laude*, from the Law Faculty of the Catholic University of Leuven in June 1973. He became a junior lecturer in international law at the University of Antwerp (1973–1979), preparing a Ph.D. on "The Charter of Economic Rights and Duties of States" which he defended, *magna cum laude*, in January 1977. In February 1980, Professor Wellens was invited to become a senior lecturer in European Law at the Faculty of Law of the University of Nijmegen, The Netherlands, before his appointment in 1982 at the same faculty as Professor of International Law and the Law of International Organizations.

His writings cover a wide range of areas including international economic law, the law of international organizations and general problems of international law. He was General Editor of the *Netherlands Yearbook of International Law* from 1989 through 1997. He also edited *Resolutions and Statements of the UN Security Council (1946–2000): A Thematic Guide* (2001). His recent publications include *Economic Conflicts and Disputes before the World Court (1962–1995). A Functional Analysis* (1996) and *Remedies against International Organizations*, published by Cambridge University Press in 2002.

He is Chairman of the Advisory Committee on International Legal Issues to the Dutch Foreign Ministry and Co-Rapporteur of the International Law Association's Committee on Accountability of International Organizations.

Eric Wyler is Professor of International Law. He has taught at the following Universities: Neuchâtel, Lausanne, Geneva, Paris II-Pantheon Assas (Visiting Prof.). Currently he is *Chargé d'enseignement* at the Graduate Institute of International Studies (HEI), Geneva. He is a member of the *Société française pour le droit international*, and of the *Société suisse de droit international*. His main research activities are: responsibility of states, the ICJ, the relationship between private and public international law, and philosophy of law. His publications include: *L'illicite et la condition des personnes privées* (1995); *L'éthique du droit international* (1997, with Alain Papaux), *L'extranéité ou le dépassement de l'ordre juridique étatique* (1999, Wyler-Papaux ed.). He is currently consultant for a private lawyers Cabinet (Etude Mudry & Iglehart, Geneva).

Sienho Yee is associate professor of law at the University of Colorado at Boulder. He is Editor-in-Chief of the *Chinese Journal of International Law*, and an Editorial Board member of the *Oxford Reports on International Law in Domestic Courts* (OUP). His research interests are the structural issues of the international legal system and the case law of the International Court of Justice (ICJ). His papers have appeared in journals such as *AJIL, ICLQ* and *Columbia Law Review* and in the syllabi of august universities. He has been both praised and blamed for his proposal that contributed to the subsequent adoption of Article 16 of the Rome Statute of the International Criminal Court. His *ICLQ* paper on Article 35(2) of the ICJ Statute was reproduced as an annex by Germany, described as an "excellent study" by Italy, and quoted from by separate opinions in the *Legality of Use of Force* cases before the ICJ. He has acted as a consultant to governments on international dispute settlement. His homepage is: www.sienhoyee.org.

Karl Zemanek is *Dr. jur.*, Emeritus Professor of International Law and International Organizations. From 1958 to 1998 he was Professor at the Faculty of Law, University of Vienna, Austria. From 1967 to 2003 he was legal consultant to the Austrian Ministry for Foreign Affairs and delegate to eighteen sessions of the General Assembly of the United Nations. He was President of the UN Conference on State Succession to Treaties (1977–78) and of the UN Conference on Agreements of International Organizations (1986). He is a member of the *Institut de droit international* and of the International Court of Arbitration. He has given a general course on public international law at the Hague Academy of International Law (1997).

Index

Accountability
  commitment of state, as, 592
  concept, origin of, 586-588
  duty to respect, 587
  good governance, as element of, 601
  governance as ally of, 594
  International organizations. of. *See* Accountability of international organizations
  international relations, transfer of concept to, 588-592
  meaning, 585-587, 600
  political device, as, 592
  primary and secondary rules, 595-596
  translation, inability, 586
  United States public servants, of, 586
Accountability of international organizations
  actors to whom owed, 599
  application of concept, 592-593
  cases against, judicial means available to states, 626-629
  challenging acts, absence of judicial means for, 621
  cognate concepts,
    democracy, 596-598
    generally, 593
    good governance, 594-596
    rule of law, 598
  demand to raise, 629
  elements of,
    broadest record of, 600
    new, emergence of, 601-602
  focus of demand for, 626
  increase of demand for, 593
  increased, request for, 620
  internal review mechanisms, 621-622

International Law Association Committee, 585
  protection of rights,
    non-staff, 623-626
    staff members, 623
  ramification of, 599
  responsibility, 618-621
  solutions sought under heading of, 629
  standard labelled as, 630
  totality of commitments, as, 599
  wider attraction of topic, 585
  wrongful acts, responsibility for, 618-621
Administrative review
  judicial review, as alternative to, 821-822
  procedural niceties, of, 829
Afghanistan
  United Nations Security Council, reaction to regime by, 471-472
Aggression
  crime of, 690
  definition,
    General Assembly resolution on, 196-198
    Preparatory Commission, work of, 213
    International Criminal Court core crime, as, 197, 212-213
Aircraft
  hijacking, 729
  illegal seizure of, 729
  piracy against, 728-729
Antarctica
  regime, common heritage of mankind, 423, 425
Apartheid
  eradication of, 203
  International Convention on Suppression and Punishment of, 204

International Criminal Court core crime,
    as, 204
violation of international law principles,
    as, 202
Armed conflict
    existence of, 662
    generalized violence, 663
    global reparations, agreements for, 66
    High-Level Panel report, recommenda-
        tion, 917
    human rights derogations in, 695-696
    humanitarian assistance, 783
    law of, shift from law of peace, 664-665
    terrorist group as party to, 698
Armed force
    counter-terrorism, limited role in, 671
Assassination
    targeted, 700-701
Authority-auctoritas
    roots of, 301
Autonomy
    international law, model of, 6
    members of global systems, of, 7
    state, 634

Benevolence
    international law, model of, 7-8
Biological weapons
    prohibition, 51
Brundtland Commission
    creation of, 571-572

Capitalism
    democracy-capitalism, philosophy of,
        146-149
    industrial, rise of, 137
    naturalist theories, 147
China
    formal law, development of, 5
    future world power, as, 25
    Sino-centric view, 156
Civilization
    clash of, 168
    Eurocentric, 164
    European way of life, not requiring, 165
    functional term, as, 163
    influences between, 171
    international law, use of term in, 164
    modern European, 162
    plural, 162

problem of, 154-155
substantive and exclusive notion of, 154
substantive entities, as, 168
theories of, 162
transcivilizational perspectives, 153-163
Colonies, former
    conformity with international law, 201
    foundations for liberation of, 193
    law-making conferences, contribution to,
        generally, 205-206
        International Criminal Court, establish-
            ment of, 211-214
        law of the sea, 206-210
    Trusteeship System, 202
    United Nations, membership of, 192
Common good
    moral value of, 426-429
Conflict resolution,
    international law, model of, 13-14
Constitution
    abstraction of policy, as, 859
    European Union, of. See European Union
    fundamental rules, 842-846
    global, 859
    idealised version, 104
    international community, of, 846-851
    international rules, non-consensual nature
        of, 843
    interpretation, 507
    jus cogens at heart of, 844-846
    malleability of notion, 849
    narrow concept of, 105
    notion of, 504-506
    public international law, in context of, 838
    world, emergence of, 568-574
Constitutional law
    internationalisation of, 120-121
Constitutionalism
    coherent idea of, 840-841
    concept of, 16-19
    consensual basis of,
        common interests of mankind, 107-108
        verticalisation, 108
    constitutio, evolution of, 17
    global,
        classical state rights, 869
        cooperation, 873
        individual rights, 874-879
        international rights, 869-871
        principles of, 868-879

provisions *jus cogens* and *erga omnes*,
    869-871
solidarity and cooperation, principles of,
    871-874
governance, structure of, 241
heterogeneous propositions, 17-18
importance of, 18
institutional,
    conflicts, resolution of, 110
    costs of, 110
    human rights, protection of, 112
    incomplete, costs of, 110
    international governance, 111-112
    main object of, 115
    normative, underpinning, 110
    use of force, of, 113-115
international,
    critics of, 104-106
    defence of, 105
    weak reading of, 105
international governance, control of, 115-
    116
international law, of, 106
    model of, 15-16
meaning, 838
methodology, 109
multifaceted nature of, 18
nation-state, reservation to, 104
progressive movement, 846
ratio, 106
social activists, 20
sovereignty, and, 837-838
starting point of, 113
theory of state, derived from, 16
United States, in, 242
use of force, of, 113-115
world,
    cultural issue, 20
    ethical opponents, 20
    exceptionalism, 21-24
    goal of, 19
    national interests, and, 21
    organisational reform, 28
    political objections, 20
    prospects for, 27-29
    resistance to, 19-21
Cooperation
    international law, model of, 11-12
    multilateralism, and, 32
Corruption

UN Convention against, 592
Cosmopolitanism
    universal justice, model of, 285-288
Council of Europe
    environmental issues, addressing, 579
Court of Auditors
    standing, 832
Crime
    international crimes of state, 845
    transnational, High-Level Panel report,
        917
    war, distinct from, 666-672
Crimes against humanity
    definition, 422
    domestic court, exercise of jurisdiction
        by, 732
    meaning, 690
Criminal law
    international, violations of, 391
    legislation, based on, 391
    liberal, notions of, 817
    political factors, 392
    sanction, threat of, 274
    verticality, 274
Cuba
    delivery of Soviet ballistic missiles, pre-
        vention of, 96
Customary norms
    conflict between, rules for, 260-261
    human rights, 268
    international. *See* International law
    regional,
        existence of, 257
        peremptory nature, whether of, 258

Death penalty
    appropriateness of, 394
Decolonization
    force, use of, 406
Democracy
    a people, link to, 117
    accountability, and, 596-598
    borders, without, 739
    Cicero, development of idea by, 16
    democracy-capitalism, philosophy of,
        146-149
    European Union, within, 597
    international,
        democratic imperative, 116-118
        doctrinal and semantic problems, 116-118

institutions of, 119
international civil society, creation of, 118
national interests, translation to, 118
search for, 116
international organizations, deficit, 596-598
naturalist theories, 147
popular, rise of, 137
Developing countries
application of international law by, 214-218
application of norms of international law, role in, 193
challenges facing, 365
defensive, on, 367
development, seeking redress in issues of, 363
economic development, 426-427
efficiency and equity, debate between, 365
fall of socialist bloc, effect of, 364-365
globalization, advent of, 366-367
government, terms of request for, 591
Group of 77. *See* Group of 77
international conferences, participation in, 193
law-making conferences, contribution to, generally, 205-206
International Criminal Court, establishment of, 211-214
law of the sea, 206-210
negotiation process, influence on, 219-221
meaning, 191
new world order, role in, 219
perspectives of, 161
policy space, shrinking of, 367
political negotiating power, search for, 355-356
solidarity, 368
United Nations, participation in, 192-193
Development
international law, model of, 9
soft law, 793
solidarity, principle of,
inequality, 790
justice, principles of, 791
law in 1970s and 1980s, 791
recent trends, 792-794
unilateral obligation, 791
Diplomacy
exceptionalism in, 21-24

Disarmament
High-Level Panel report, recommendation, 917
Disasters
humanitarian assistance in case of,
duty to admit, 785-786
duty to facilitate provision of, 787-788
duty to provide, 786-787
responsibility for, 784-785
right to receive and provide, 785
institutionalized public action, need for, 806

Empires
colonising, 142
Environment
climate change, 39-40
common interests of mankind, 107
multilateral regime, 39-40
ozone layer, protection of, 39
Environmental protection
Agenda 21, 572-573
aspects of, 574
biosphere, dangers threatening, 569
climate change, combating, 428
compensation law, 570
compliance with obligations, review of, 580
developmental ethic, and, 11
ecological disasters, 569
evolution of law, 570-571
global dimension of problems, 568
governance, 567
High-Level Panel report, recommendation, 916
human environment, world conference on, 569
human rights, link with, 570
individuals, rights of, 583
international bodies, functions of, 575-576
international institutions, responses of,
Council of Europe, 579
division of tasks, 576
global organizations, 576-578
multilateral conventions, established by, 580-583
non-state actors, 583
regional organizations, 578-579
UN bodies, 578
international law, 10-11, 107

functions in, 574-576
international, state of, 568
multilateral agreements,
    Conference or Meeting of the Parties,
        580-583
    financial bodies under, 582
    institutions established by, 580-583
    proliferation of, 582
multilateral treaties, 568-569
new approach to, 571
normative and institutional approach to,
    584
ozone layer, protection of, 428
proliferation of rules for, 584
Rio Conference, instruments adopted at,
    572-573
Rio Declaration, 427
solidarity, principle of, 789-790
Stockholm Declaration, 427
United Nations Environment Programme,
    570
World Commission on Environment and
    Development, creation of, 571-572
European Central Bank
    standing, 832
European Convention on Human Rights
    contents of, 268
    European Court of Justice, application by,
        269
    reservations, 225, 233-236, 258
    UK domestic law, incorporation in, 646
European Court of Human Rights
    access to, 540
    automatism of jurisdiction, 539
    case-law of, 541
    compliance with obligations, securing, 541
    compulsory jurisdiction, optional clause
        of, 521-522
        fundamental nature of, 524
    contentious jurisdiction, 540
    interpretative declaration, 225
    overload, 538
    reservations to treaty, determining validity
        of, 225, 233-234
    State voluntarism, limits to, 540
    substantive law, contribution to, 540
European Court of Justice
    jurisprudence, duty of mutual cooperation
        in, 872-873

natural and legal persons, complainants
    as, 832
public interest litigation, 832-833
standing, bodies with, 831-832
supranational compulsory jurisdiction, 533
European Parliament
    development of, 897-898
European Union
    Constitution,
        effect of, 854
        establishment of Union, 856-857
        historic originality, 854
        jurisdictional provisions, 857-858
        legislating, protocol, 858
        Preamble, 856
        Protocol, 858
        text, basis of, 855
        voting rules, 893-894
    constitutional nature of, 854
    Council, voting in, 893
    democracy within, 597
    differentiation, phenomenon of, 297
    extraterritorial effects of US regulations,
        contention over, 67-68
    future legal order of, 839
    good governance, accountability as ele-
        ment of, 601
    human rights, requirement to respect,
        607-608
    institutional development, 111
    internalization, example of, 646
    law of the sea, competence as to, 619
    legislation, 43
    standing, bodies with, 831-832
    Treaty, infringement of, 829-830
    treaty-based order, constitutionalization
        of, 839
Exceptionalism
    American, 22-24
    Roman precedent, 24-27
    world politics and diplomacy, in, 21-24
Extradition
    US treaties, 55

Fairness
    international law, model of, 8-9
    reciprocity, 8
Force
    armed, 660
    authorization of use of, 449

collective security, prohibition linked to,
    711
decolonization, use in, 406
justified use of, 677
legalization of use, erosion of Security
    Council's monopoly, 409-414
non-use, principle of, 265
obligation to refrain fro use of, 710
proportionate, 678
regional arrangements, qualification of
    coalitions as, 265
regional organizations, use by,
    aspects of, 263
    decision on, 264
    ECOWAS, operations of, 263-264
    Kosovo, intervention in, 263-264
    political and judicial control of, 265
    recognition of power of, 264
    responsibility for, 265
    superpower, domination of, 264, 266
self-defence, use in. *See* Self-defence
settlement of disputes, use for, 766-768
UN Charter, provisions of, 262
unilateral use of, 266, 710
US Security Council resolutions, to com-
    pel compliance with, 673-675
use of, regulation, 261-266
Fragmentation of international law
    autonomous regimes, 236-237
    debate on, 223
    examples of, 232-234
    fragment, meaning, 224
    freedom of action, resulting from, 252-254
    ILC, consideration by, 231-232
    institutional, dangers of, 225
    institutions, activities of, 232
    integrity, loss of, 226
    international courts, proliferation of, 225
    meaning, 224
    new rules, formulation of, 232
    parallel settlement of questions, 226
    process of, 224
    proliferation of rules, 224
    regionalism, contribution of, 238-239
    regionalization and specialization,' 224
    scientific research, as topic of, 223
    threat of, 239-240

General Agreement on Tariffs and Trade
    (GATT)

agreement, as, 547
core principles, 544-545
dispute settlement process, 548-549, 554
economic objective, 545
Executive Secretary, 548
free trade, economic rationale of, 544
institutional basis of, 547-550
international and domestic law, interac-
    tion between, 554
international institution, as, 546-555
international law, contribution to, 552-555
legal framework for international trade,
    as, 544
legal regime, 551-552
most-favoured-nation treatment, 794
national treatment, principle of, 551
non-discrimination, principle of, 544,
    553-554
non-tariff restrictions, prohibition, 552
nullification and impairment, reference
    to, 553
General Agreement on Tariffs and Trade
    obscurity of, 545
    original purpose, 551
    tariff negotiations, 550
    treaty or contract, as, 544
    United Nations, relationship with, 550-551
General Agreement on Trade in Services
    (GARS)
    cooperation, reference to, 557
Genocide
    domestic court, exercise of jurisdiction
        by, 732
    obligation to repress, 297
    scope of, 690
Germany
    Bundestreue, principle of, 871-872
Global legal order
    abode of Islam and abode of War, division
        of world into, 155
    East Asia, division of world in, 156
    elements of, 152
    international perspective, 155-157
    justice, 152
    legitimacy, 152-153. *See also* Legitimacy
    powerful nations, lack of support of, 153
    schisms, 153
    transboundary relations, 169-171
    transcivilizational perspectives, 153-163
    transnational perspective, 157-159

Globalization
  advent of, 366-367
  democracy-capitalism, social phenom-
    enon of, 146-148
  national boundaries, penetrating, 168
  new rules to settle new issues, require-
    ment of, 239
  period of, 271
  process of, 104
  revolutionary effects of, 142
  social transformation, modes of, 146
  UN system, bypassing, 429
  use of term, 567
Governance
  accountability, and, 594-596
  definition, 594
  global,
    coordination, through, 648-650
    effective regulation and problem-solving,
      provision of, 641
    international law, challenge of, 631-634
    public institutions, role of, 641-642
    soft law, effect of emergence of, 639-641
    sovereign states, system of, 631
    state behavior, regulation of, 648
    transnational legal process, 645-648
  good, 594-596
  international,
    control of, 115-116
    legitimacy of, 115-120
  law-making, rules for, 842-843
  mixed system, elements of, 632-633
  multilayered and mixed system, elements
    of, 642-643
  multilayered system, imagining, 650-651
  national and international systems, merg-
    er of, 632
  political constitution as multi-layered sys-
    tem of, 842
  primary and secondary rules, 595-596
  strategic interactions to bolster, 634-639
  transgovernmentalism, 643-645
Grenada
  US troops in, 88
Group of 77
  accommodation, 361-363
  achievements of, 358-359
  coalition of countries, as, 357
  Code of Conduct for Transfer of Technol-
    ogy, defeat on, 370

  confrontation, 361-363
  cracks in, 374
  criticism of, 370
  decisions, adoption of, 360
  decline and weakening of, 364
  development agenda, reviewing, 378-380
  diversity developing unity, celebrating, 378
  Doha Summit, 380
  Dr Prebisch as founding father of, 355
  emergence of, significance, 355
  emotional attachment to, 362
  equity and justice, striving for, 356
  first appearance of, 355
  functioning of UN, contribution to, 359
  future of, 376-380
  globalization, advent of, 366-367
  Havana Summit, 378
  international economic issues, dealing
    with, 356
  joint Declaration, 356-357
  law of the sea negotiations, 208
  methods of work,
    addressing, 370
    change in, 374-375
  multilateral negotiations, nature of, 368-
    370
  Non-Aligned Movement, function in tan-
    dem with, 359
  North-South dialogue, strains in, 363
  oil crises, impact of, 362, 364
  other stakeholders, collaboration with, 379
  reform, 370-376
  success and setback, pendulum of, 360
  transformation period, 370
  UNCTAD, as twin of, 358
  UNCTAD secretariat, reliance on, 360,
    375
  unity in,
    diversity, in, 357-358
    group system, universality of, 359-360
    joint Declaration, 356-357
    multilateral diplomacy, 359-360
    solidarity, effect of, 368
    undermining of, 366
  vulnerability, signs of, 364
  world economic order, shaping, 358

Hazardous substances
  problems of, 583
Hegemony

foundation of, 33
international multilateralism, in,
   historical recollection, 44-45
   Non-Proliferation Treaty, 46-47
   Security Council, 45-46
   world financial institutions, 47
leadership, position of, 34
meaning, 33-34
sovereign equality, and, 34
History
   chance and accident, roles of, 139
   epochs, identification of, 140
   generalisations, 139-140
   human, diversity of, 130
   nature of, 129
   writing, 139
HIV/AIDS
   High-Level Panel report, recommenda-
      tion, 916
Human nature
   re-forming of, 129
Human rights
   access to justice, 538
   African protection system, 269-270
   American protection system, 269-270
   Arab Charter, 270
   armed conflict, derogations during, 695-
      696
   autonomous regimes, 236
   binding force of, 115-116
   codification, 331
   Committee, 235
   common interests of mankind, 107-108
   compliance with applicable law, duty of,
      617
   constitutional protection of, 112
   Conventions, dynamic or evolutive inter-
      pretation of, 537-538
   Council of Europe instruments, 268
   CSCE/OSCE, instruments of, 268
   customary norms, 268
   economic and social, developments, 829
   environment, link with, 570
   Europe, levels of protection in, 269
   European Union, respect by, 607-608
   government policies, scrutiny of, 170
   growth of jurisdictions, 539
   High-Level Panel report, recommenda-
      tion, 922-925
   individual accountability, 421

international concern,
   becoming of, 166
   matters of, 166-167
International Covenant on Civil and Political Rights,
   becoming party to, 42-43
   US, half-hearted ratification by, 51-52
international instruments, 267
   growth in, 589
international law, development of, 107-108
international organizations, respect by,
   argument for, 609
   complaints as to, 607
   requirement, 607-617
   staff members, labor regulations con-
      cerning, 610-611
   treaties, succession to, 609
   UN sanctions, practice as to, 611-617
international tribunals,
   access to, 540
   African Court, 538
   challenges to, 538
   co-existence of, 537
   contentious jurisdiction, 540
   substantive law, contribution to, 540
Islam, contribution of. See Islam
Islamic states, in, 270
jurisprudential issue, 828
jus cogens, 441
life, right to, 701
logic, development of, 284
mass violations, 406
multilateral regime, 42-43
national constitutional law, influences on,
   120-121
non-state terrorism organizations, law
   applied to, 697-699
protected, no implicit limitations, 523
regional plane, protection on, 268
   effectiveness of, 270-271
   problems of, 269
sanctions, effect of imposing, 611-617
serious violations,
   international concern, matters of, 166-
      167
   non-Western countries, in, 167
   Western NGOs, criticism by, 167
States, binding commitments, 694
transcivilization legitimacy, 170
treaties,

interpretative interaction, 541
reservations, 225, 233-236
UN law, integration into, 841
UN treaties, monitoring systems, 112
United States, role of, 52
universal and particular norms, interactions between, 267
Universal Declaration, 267
individual rights, 875
universal justice, model of, 283-285
world society, principles guiding socio-economic development of, 420-423
Humanitarian intervention
developing thesis of, 450
justifications, 416
legal principles, conflict of, 414
non-use of force, principle of, 416
object state, election of, 416-417
rediscovery of idea of, 415
right of, 912
United Nations, by, 415
use of term, 414
Humanitarian law
fundamental rules of, 292
military force of UN, application to, 617
non-state terrorism organizations, law applied to, 697-699
persons accused of terrorist acts, legal status of, 699-700
solidarity, 783-784
unlawful combatants, status of, 699-700

India
dismemberment, threat of, 242
nationhood, constitution of, 241
United Nations founding member, as, 245
Intellectual property
TRIPS Agreement, 561
Inter-American Court of Human Rights
access to, 540
American Convention on Human Rights, safeguarding integrity of, 530
compliance with obligations, securing, 541
compulsory jurisdiction, optional clause of, 521-522
acceptance, modalities of, 525-527
examination of, 525
fundamental nature of, 524
object and purpose of, 528
contentious jurisdiction, 540

State voluntarism, limits to, 540
substantive law, contribution to, 540
Internalization
European Union, example of, 646
legal, occurrence of, 645
process of, 646
international
use of term, 157-158
International community
American turning against, 21-22
concept of, 32-33
constitution, notion of, 505
constitutional by-laws, 848
doctrine of, 841
evolution of, 520
law-making, achievements in, 220-221
minimally instituted, juridical bases of, 529
obligations to, 845
resources, mobilization of, 902
school, relative success of, 846
UN Charter as constitution of, 846-851
International Court of Justice
adjudication, norms of, 177
advisory opinions, 73-74, 215-216, 628
compulsory jurisdiction,
optional clause of,
de lege ferenda reflections, 529-531
declaration of acceptance, meaning and scope of, 528
legislative history, 517-520
lex lata, 521-528
limitations and restrictions on acceptance, 523-524
purpose of, 520
resort to, 534
customary international law, use of notion of, 172-174
International Criminal Tribunal for the Former Yugoslavia, differences in judgments, 225, 232-233
international law, upholding, 72
Lockerbie case, actions in, 444-447
norms applied by, 183
preliminary opinions, proposal for 878
principal judicial organ of UN, as, 72
provisional measures, 69
reference of disputes to, 198
resort to, 215-216
role of, 878

Security Council, judicial review of decisions of, 443-447, 468
standing, bodies with, 831
Statute, laying down sources of international law, 433
supremacy, no basis for, 536
US relationship with, 69, 72-73
International courts
conflict resolution by, 13-14
International Criminal Court
American reticence towards, 734
core crimes,
aggression, 197, 212-213
apartheid, 204
individual responsibility for, 690
nuclear weapons, use of, 214
developing countries, role of, 211-214
establishment of, 211-214
individual responsibility, elaboration of, 591
jurisdiction, 691
operational stage, in, 214
Rome Statute,
crimes against humanity, definition of, 422
drafting, 638
formal adoption of, 53
individual rights, 876-879
parties to, 213
surrender of accused persons under, 422=423
US, attitude of, 53
Security Council, role of, 212
United States, attitude of,
effectiveness, hampering, 56
signature by, 54
Statute, voting against, 53
strategies to combat institution of, 54
test case, as, 56
US citizens, protection of, 53-55
International Criminal Tribunal for Rwanda
establishment of, 53-54, 421, 469-471
International Criminal Tribunal for the Former Yugoslavia
establishment of, 53-54, 469-471
national courts, relationship with, 877
Statute,
foundation of, 877
individual rights, 875-876
individual rights, 876

International institutions
independent, importance of, 72-74
influence of, 649
nature and functioning of, 242
United Nations as, 243
International jurisdiction
automatism, lack of, 530
compulsory,
declaration of acceptance, meaning and scope of, 528
optional clause. See optional clause of compulsory jurisdiction, below
plea for, 532
problem of, 532-533
reality of, 534
recurring need and quest for, 531-534
widening scope of, 534
disputes submitted to, 535
growth of, 535-542
imperative of, 533
international, scope of, 515
optional clause of compulsory jurisdiction,
de lege ferenda reflections, 529-531
ideal and practice of, 517-520
legislative history, 517
lex lata, 521-528
limitations and restrictions on acceptance, 523-524
purpose of, 520
International law
adjudication, norms of, 183
agnosticism, 286
anarchy, organization of, 106
application, role of developing countries, 193
area of regulation, development of, 228
argumentative process, participation in, 183-184
basic principles, reaffirmation of, 194-201
branch principles, 228
Christian origin of, 306
civilization, use of term, 164
civilizational factors, within sovereign state system, 163-166
codification, 15
international conferences for, 205-206
common respect for, 631
comprehensive system, as, 239
conduct of states, regulating, 175-176
conferences,

common group positions, 220
  developing countries, role of, 206-210
  new global issues, emergence of, 220
conflict of systems, 230
constitutional arguments, 838-842
constitutionalization, methodology of, 109
constitutionalism, reflection of features of,
  18. *See also* Constitutionalism
constitutionalist system of, 106
contemporary societal needs and expectations, reflection of, 806
convergence of civilizations, as, 218-221
cooperation, of, 545
creation of, 106
  basis for, 485-485
cultural bias, allegations of, 27
customary,
  cognitive or existential for of law, as, 174
  general and special, 174
  general, equation with, 172-176
  general rules, 185
  International Court of Justice, use of
    notion by, 172
  legal webs, maze of, 253
  legitimacy deficit, 176-181
  mystical theory, 176-181
  tacit consent, abuse of, 185
  traditional theory, persuasive power of,
    184
  treatises and textbooks, norms from, 179
  universal validity, with, 173-175, 177
debate on, 191
developing countries, application by, 214-
  218
diversification, 225
effectiveness of, 180
ending of Cold War, changes on, 261
environmental protection, of, 107
Euro-centric, 192
evolution of, 731
expansion and diffusion, 633
expansion of scope, 432
field of, 3
fons et origo, 308
forces of anarchy, control over, 4-5
forums for discussion, 183-184, 186-187
fragmentation. *See* Fragmentation of international law
fundamental principles, 227, 230-231
gaps in, 228-229, 239

general and customary, equation of, 172-
  176
general norms of conduct, 186
global governance, challenge to, 631-634
global market of ideas, as, 188
globalized world society, in, 103-104
humanization of, 542
idealistic models of,
  autonomy, 6-7
  benevolence, 7-8
  conflict resolution, 13-14
  constitutional authority, 15-16
  cooperation, 11-12
  ecological, 10
  environment, 10-11
  fairness, 8-9
  national development, 9-10
  order, preservation of, 4-5
  regulation, 5-6
  system convergence, 14-15
  war prevention and management, 12
inadequate, where, 649
individual-orientated, becoming, 591
integral system, whether, 226
internal law contrasted, 730
international community, achievements
  of, 220-221
international governance, 111-112
international perspective, 155-157
Islam, contribution of. *See* Islam
judicial-centrism, liberation from, 181-185
juridical values, 3
jurisdiction in, 730
jus cogens. See Jus cogens
law-making, literature on, 191
legal development, process of, 119
legitimacy,
  embodiment of, 153
  mankind as source of, 109
logic of, 299
multiform nature of, 230
national law in conflict with, 120-121
national law, implementation by, 645
national practices, assertion of, 296
Nehru's perception of, 245-246
new norms, codification of, 201-205
new rules, substitution of, 232
non-intervention principle,
  decline of, 166-169
  end of Cold War, effect of, 167

limitations on, 166
significance of, 163-166
non-state actors, involvement of, 186
norms regulating conduct of states, as, 173
norms with universal validity, recognizing,
181-185
origin of, 7-8
partially institutionalized character of, 642
peremptory norms, 253
political use of, 186
potestas, place of, 300
prevailing values, 3-4
principles of law in, 402
progressive development of, 912-914
public law, in nature of, 825-826
realization of lives in peaceful manner, use
for, 187-188
reasserted value, 296
regional norms, notion of, 256-258
remedial function, 4-5
Roman law tradition, 3
Romans, test applied by, 26
rule of law, 912-914
Russian doctrine, in, 226-228
shield, as, 6
sources of, 172-173, 176, 182, 432-433
sovereign state entitlements, 6
sovereignty and constitutionalism in, 837-
838
state-based perspective, 295-296
subjects and objects of, 432
system of rules, as, 226
traditional, 104
transboundary relations, 169-171
transcivilizational perspectives, 153-163,
187
transnational perspective, 157-159
twentieth century development, 631
unforced, consequences of, 84-86
United Nations Decade of, 216-218
universal application, dream of, 255
verticalisation, 108
West-centric, study being, 180
Western States, domestic law model for,
278
Westphalian system, 432
will of states, coincidence of, 247
International Law Commission
fragmentation of international law, consideration of, 231-232

topics under consideration, 913
International law community
controversy within, 3-4
International lawyers
education, tradition of, 3
juridical mode, operating in, 4
practising lawyers, as, 182
problems of international law, dealing
with, 175-176
transnational perspective, adoption of, 187
International legal norms
conflict of, 258-261
hierarchy, 258
regional, 257-258
International legal system
judicial branch of, 516
organisational, 6
states dominating, 433
United Nations Security Council, place of,
432-434
International Monetary Fund
voting power in, 47
International organizations
accountability. *See* Accountability of international organizations
assertion of State interests, transmission
belts for, 588
common agencies for discharge of tasks,
as, 36
complex legal phenomenon, as, 618
compliance with applicable law, duty of,
general international law, rules of, 606
individuals, respect of rights of, 607-617
legal basis for activities, 606
scope of law, 605-606
creation of, 111-112
democratic deficit, 596-598
implied powers, 603
individuals, respect of rights of,
argument for, 609
complaints as to, 607
requirement, 607-617
staff members, labor regulations concerning, 610-611
treaties, succession to, 609
UN sanctions, practice as to, 611-617
intergovernmental, 243-251
internal review mechanisms, 621-622
legal nature, questioning, 622
limitation of powers of, 602

protection of rights,
  non-staff, 623-626
  staff members, 623
public law acts of, 826
regional, 112
rule of law, compliance with, 598
sanctions by, 604-605
staff members,
  labor regulations concerning, 610-611
  rights, institutions for protection of, 623
subjects of as subjects of international law,
  602-605
treaties, succession to, 609
wrongful acts, responsibility for, 618-621
International relations
  threat of use of force, refraining from, 199
International rule of law
  compulsory jurisdiction,
    optional clause. *See* optional clause of
      compulsory jurisdiction,below
    plea for, 532
    problem of, 532-533
    recurring need and quest for, 531-534
  international jurisdiction. *See* International jurisdiction
  optional clause of compulsory jurisdiction,
    de lege ferenda reflections, 529-531
    declaration of acceptance, meaning and
      scope of, 528
    ideal and practice of, 517-520
    legislative history, 517
    lex lata, 521-528
    limitations and restrictions on acceptance, 523-524
    purpose of, 520
  peaceful settlement of disputes, beyond,
    515-516
  security of nations, key to, 912-914
International trade
  dispute settlement, 546
  GATT. *See* General Agreement on Tariffs
    and Trade
  hazardous substances, problems of, 583
  legal ordering, 543
  multilateral regime, 40
  old geography of, 377
  public and private, relationship of, 632
  public international law of, 543-544
  solidarity, principle of,
    poverty reduction, 794
    primary rule, potential role of, 794-796
    secondary rules, role of, 796-797
  South-South, 377
International Trade Organization
  failure of, 546
International tribunals
  human rights,
    access to, 540
    African Court, 538
    challenges to, 538
    co-existence of, 537
    contentious jurisdiction, 540
    substantive law, contribution to, 540
  individuals, access by, 624
  judicial decisions of, 529
  multiplicity of, 535-536
  new, emergence of, 515
  specialized, 535
  universalist principles, 535
Iraq
  American invasion, condemnation of,
    395-396
  humanitarian intervention in, 98
  international democracy, failure to stop
    war, 118
  invasion of, reparations, 66
  Kuwait, invasion of, 411
    Security Council resolutions, 465-467
  legal obligations, failure to comply with,
    96, 101
  Operation Iraqi Freedom, 97-99
  unilateral action, condemnation of, 114
  US attack, justification of, 418-419
  war against, 418
Islam
  allegations against, 305
  appearance of, 305
  clash of civilizations, concept of,
    arguing, rules for, 350-351
    avoidance of, 347-352
    dangerous consequences of, 346-347
    dialogue in order to know each other,
      348-349
    diversity and pluralism, recognition of,
      347-348
    green threat, 345-346
    mode de vie, no imposition of, 351
    other, recognition of, 347-348
    peoples not to mock at each other, 350

principle of good faith, observance of,
352
provocation of evil, prohibition, 351
violation of Shari'a rules not justifying,
349
Western scholars, theory of, 345-346
compensation for loss, payment of, 329-
330
development of global community, contributions to,
clash of civilizations, concept of, 345-352
general principles of international law
and relations, to, 310-318
human rights, 331-340
imperative to respect, 352-353
operative aspects, to, 318-331
scheme of research, 310
war and peace, concerning, 340-345
diplomatic intercourse, contribution to,
322-325
general principles of law,
bad deeds, prohibition of, 311
categories of, 310
cheating, prohibition, 311
collective security, 312-313
good deeds, acceptance of, 311
illegal orders, non-execution of, 311
jurisdiction and laws of other states, respect for, 313-314
negative effects of sanctions related to
civilian population, avoidance of, 313
no harm and no harming, 311
territoriality, principle of, 313-314
global community, aim of establishing,
308-310
human rights,
Al-Shighar, prohibition, 335
child, rights of, 334-335
equality, right of, 337-338
five universals, 331-332
fons et origo, 332
human dignity, 332
inheritance, right of, 336-337
life, right to, 335
non-Muslim authors admitting role of,
333
practice of states, in, 339
principle, history of, 333
property, right of, 335-336
Quran, verses of, 338

ratio legis, 331-332
Sunna, examples in, 338
women's rights, 335
international law,
contributions to, 307
relationship with, 305
international responsibility,
concept of, 327-328
effects of, 329-331
international treaties, contributions to,
bindingness, rules governing, 319-322
non-Muslim authors, sayings of, 319
obligations, carrying out, 320
prefatory remarks, 318-319
violation of, 319
Jihad,
meaning, 340
permitted, 341-243
legal system, principles specific to,
Aman, giving, 314-315
being on a par, 316
end not necessarily justifying the means,
317
La Hissbah, 315
nationalism or chauvinism, no, 318
no Jahilia, 318
non-abuse of rights, 315
Mohamed as messenger of, 305
non-Muslims, dealings with, 306
operative aspects of international law,
contributions to,
diplomatic intercourse, 322-325
international responsibility, in field of,
327-331
international terrorism, combating, 325-
327
international treaties, 318-322
peace,
prefatory remarks, 344
Quran, verses of, 344
Sunna, in, 344-345
principle of good faith, observance of, 352
provocation of evil, prohibition, 351
Quran, rules in, 305
religion and culture, as, 305
reparation, principle of, 329
restituio in integrum, principle of, 329
satisfaction for wrongful acts, 330
Sunna of the Prophet, 305, 310, 338, 344-
345

terrorism,
  fallacy of view, 325-327
  Western view of, 325
war,
  permitted, 341-243
  prohibited, cases of, 341
  scholars, opinions of, 340-341
  study of, 340
  Western international law, impact on, 308
  world religion, as, 308-309

Judicial review
  acts subject to, 823-824
  administrative review, and, 821-822
  application of administrative decisions,
    of, 822
  consequences of, 833-834
  continuation of politics, as, 830
  definition, 443
  General Assembly decisions, of, 823-824
  invalidation, power of, 833
  law-politics dichotomy, 810-811, 821, 834-
    835
  limited access to, 831
  low-level scrutiny, 826
  marginal, 826-831
  motivations behind call for, 812
  neo-republican political thought, 813
  persons or bodies instigating, 831-833
  political organs, keeping in check, 811
  polycentric disputes, of, 827
  process-orientated, 813
  public international law, in, 810
    administrative decisions, of, 820
    call for, 814-818
    existence of, 819
    international organizations, decisions
      of, 825
    limitations, 819
    public law, as, 825-826
  Security Council decisions, of, 818, 823
  strict positivism, and, 812
  subject matter of, 820-823
  system of, 818-834
  UN system, in, 810
  US system, within, 823-824
  validity of legislation, of, 820
Jurisdiction
  international law, in, 730
  multilateral treaty vesting, 732

  municipal law, as, 730
  universal,
    abuse of, 734
    acceptability of, 734
    bases for exercise of, 733
    domestic court, exercise by, 732
    exception to general principles, as, 732
    Kissinger, view of, 734-735
    meaning, 731-732
    piracy. *See* Piracy
    theory of, 731
    war crimes, over, 732-734
    within English, analysis of, 730
Jus cogens
  applications, short of, 290
  constitution rules, at heart of, 844-846
  content of, 296
  definition, 870
  differential normativity, 291
  emergence of, 253
  flaws of, 295
  free determination, overturning idea of,
    294-295
  human rights, 441
  importance of concept, 844
  international constitutional law, perspec-
    tive of, 845
  international law principles, 108, 227, 253-
    254
  location of, 294
  norms of, 869-871
  positive law, as, 290-291
  peremptory norms, as, 253
  process analysis of legal phenomenon, 296
  reinforced authority norm, as, 301
  revolutionary theory of, 295
  shift of perspective, as, 301
  significance of existence of, 299
  state-based and community finalized law,
    as beginning of, 290-299
  type of norm, referring to, 298
Justice
  abstract conception of, 275
  commensurability, 275, 293
  commutative, 302
  determination of principle of, 401
  distributive, primacy of, 302
  general, 276-277
  imperfect world, in, 289
  individuals, determination by, 395

law of the strongest, as, 276
legal order, by reference to, 401
meaning, 273-277
polysemic concept of, 273
reality of world, reflecting, 277
sanctions, 274
search, philosophical meaning of, 289-290
traditional meanings, 276
universal,
  acultural model, 285-288
  ana-logical, 289-302
  authority, reciprocity and recognition,
    299-302
  human rights model, 283-285
  ideal system of, 283
  jus cogens, 290-299
  realistic, 275
  relativity of notions, 278
  social contract model, 278-283
  Utopian, 277-288
varying definitions of, 394

Kosovo
  NATO intervention in, 867
  NATO operation in, 412-413
Kuwait
  defence of, 91-92
  Iraqi invasion of, 411
    Security Council resolutions, 465-467

Law
  disclosure, not, 291
  fundamental notions, relativity of, 293
  juridical values, 3
  medium, as, 296
  objectivist doctrines, 293
  polar conception of, 294
  relationship, in terms of, 294
  social process, as, 3
  ultimate end of, 274
Law of nations
  Jefferson as champion of, 80
Law of the sea
  AALCO, concerns of, 207
  compulsory jurisdiction, 533
  Convention, adoption of, 207, 209
  developing countries, role of, 206-210
  Exclusive Economic Zone, 209
  free market regime, 208
  Group of 77, 206-207

non-ratification of UNCLOS by US, 48-
  50, 77
piracy. *See* Piracy
political and economic changes, effect of,
  210
regime, common heritage of mankind,
  423-424
regional agreements, provision for, 259
Sea-Bed Authority, 209-210
sea-bed, exploration and exploitation of,
  208
Third United Nations Conference, 206-
  210
transfer of technology, 210
Tribunal, 209
UNCLOS regime, 38
League of Nations
  decisions of, 45
  establishment of, 45
  failure of, 255
  United States, non-participation of, 435
  world government, idea of, 255
Legal formalism
  artificiality of, 4
Legal obligation
  multiple forms of, 639-642
  soft law, 639-640
Legal principle
  definition, 402
  innovations, 404
  international law, in, 402
  legal rule distinguished, 401
  main function of, 402
  notion of, 401-482
  options for action, 401
  soft, 429-430
  UN Charter, in,
    change, subject to, 409-429
    content, change of, 429
    exclusive source, whether, 404-406
    force, prohibition on use of, 409-419
    friendly relations Declaration, explana-
      tion in, 407-409
    human rights, observation of, 420-423
    humanitarian intervention, 414-417
    interrelation of, 406-407
    legal rules, 405
    maxims, 405
    non-intervention, 408
    normative value, 405-406

politics and law, roots in, 405
precision and imperativeness, varying
     in, 405
programmes, 405
self-defence, preemptive, 417-419
socio-economic development of world
     society, 419-429
texts, 403-404
Legal systems
convergence, 14-15
Legitimacy
customary International law, deficit of,
     176-181
global legal order, in, 152-153
global norms of conduct, identification of,
     186-189
international law as embodiment of, 153
multilateral treaties, of, 177
UNGA resolution, of, 177-178
Libya
US attacks on, 91

Margin of appreciation
development of doctrine, 828
Mines
anti-personnel, prohibition of, 50
Multiculturalism
international relations, characteristic of,
     277
Multilateralism
action, in, 36-43
environment, problems of, 39-40
hegemony in,
     historical recollection, 44-45
     Non-Proliferation Treaty, 46-47
     Security Council, 45-46
     world financial institutions, 47
human rights regime, 42-43
Inter-American Treaty of Reciprocal As-
     sistance, 38
international cooperation, and 32
international legislation, 43
international trade, framework for, 40
North Atlantic Treaty Organisation
     (NATO), 37
oceans, regime for, 38
security, 37-38
terrorism, fight against, 41-42
treaty-making, reliance on, 43
United States challenge to,

binding majority decisions, failure to
     accept, 72
binding rules of international law, viola-
     tion of, 57-71
conclusions, 71-72
extraterritorial effects, regulations with,
     67-68
Geneva Conventions, refusal to ratify
     Additional Protocols, 51
International Covenant on Civil and Po-
     litical Rights, half-hearted ratification
     of, 51-52
International Criminal Court Statute,
     voting against, 53-56. See also Interna-
     tional Criminal Court
international review of conduct, reluc-
     tance to submit to, 51-53
law of nations, actions concerning, 66-67
non-use of force, as to, 57-63
obligations under International law, fail-
     ure to honour, 68
refusal to play role in, 48
rules applying, 47-48
security, in field of, 50
sovereign equality, respect for principle
     of, 63
state immunity, in field of, 64-66
treaty regimes, remaining aloof from, 56
UNCLOS, non-ratification of, 48-50, 77
world order treaties, distancing from,
     48-56
US hegemony, in age of, 33-35
Warsaw Pact, 38
Multinational enterprises
international law, influences on, 159
trans-boundary issues, addressing, 157
Muslims. See also Islam
abode of Islam and abode of War, division
     of world into, 155
military action not to be taken as against,
     170

Natural law
sovereign equals, notion of state as, 31
Natural resources
permanent sovereignty over, 205
Natural sciences
development of, 136
New International Economic Order
call for, 427

Declaration, 193
national development needs, 9
support, lack of, 153
Nicaragua
arms in, 90
Sandinista Front,
character of, 89
international terrorism, involvement in,
90
US role in, 88
Non-Aligned Movement
Decade of International Law, proposal
for, 216
G77, function in tandem with, 359
international affairs, involvement in, 210
International Criminal Court, statement
on establishment of, 211
Non-governmental organizations
activities of, 635
burgeoning influence of, 636
cottage industry, growth in, 636
creative process of international law, involvement in, 159
economic and social development, involvement in, 160
environmental issues, tackling, 583
focus of, 251
growth in, 590
International Criminal Court Statute, involvement in drafting, 638
international, 251-252
observer status, 118
participation in international affairs, leeway for, 590
partisan role, 251
power of, 635
state conduct, influencing, 637
study of influence, 637
trans-boundary issues, addressing, 157
transnational function of, 251
West-centric, 160
world constitutive process, representing,
251
Non-state actors
environmental issues, tackling, 583
international law, involvement in, 186
nature of, 160-161
public sphere, in, 632
North Atlantic Treaty Organisation
(NATO)

Kosovo, intervention in, 263-264, 867
structure and capabilities, 655
United States, role of, 37
Yugoslavia, operations in, 412-413
North Korea
South Korea, invasion of, 86
Nuclear weapons
non-proliferation and elimination regime,
haves and have-nots, 765-766
Non-Proliferation Treaty, 46-47
non-State groups obtaining, 766
use,
crime of, 214
legality of, 229

Occupied Palestinian Territory
anti-terror wall, 669, 692
Oceans
UNCLOS regime, 38
Order
essence of law, as, 274
preservation, legal function of, 4-5
Organization for Economic Cooperation
and Development
role of, 579

Pacta sunt servanda
principle of, 291-292, 598, 874
Peace
Islam, in. See Islam
law of, 275
Security Council, role of. See United Nations Security Council
ultimate end of law, as, 274-275
Philosophy
affirmation, presence of, 133
collective self-consciousness, 133
democracy-capitalism, of, 146-149
dialectical moment, 133
global revolutionary social transformation, of, 132
gradual accumulation of consciousness,
as, 135
great tradition, in, 150
ideal,
idea of, 144-145
moral imperative, 143
public enlightenment, 145-146
universalism, 144
world-making, 143

moral imperative, 143
new world, 149
scepticism, 133
self-betrayal, 138
self-consciousness of consciousness, as, 135
self-destruction, 134
social conditions, reflecting, 135
social function of, 132
true,
  collective thinking, 132-133
  ideal, idea of, 144-145
  moral imperative, 143
  public enlightenment, 145-146
  universalism, 144
  world-making, 143
unphilosophy,
  ideology of, 134
  meaning, 132, 134
  social factors, 135-138
will, based on, 288
Piracy
acts covered, 723
against whom committed, 723
aircraft, against, 728-729
attempts. 725
cargo or equipment, taking, 718
crime, defining, 717
EEZ, within, 724-725
exercise of jurisdiction, trigger for, 727
facts of, 716-717
frustrated acts, 725
government ships, exclusion of acts of, 724
high seas, on, 724
hot pursuit, rules of, 724-725
intention to attack, 726
international law of,
  customary, codification of, 721-722
  legal definition, 722-723
  review of, 715
Italian law of, 722
law against nations, crime against, 719-720
legal definition, 722-723
liability, 728
motive, 723
municipal law, 717
nationality of vessel, 726
persons committing, 723
Philippine law, under, 717-722

pirate ship,
  acts of piracy, without, 725-726
  boarding, 728
  characterization as, 726
  enemies of humankind, at service of, 727
  involvement in attacks, not at behest of flag state, 726
  seizure of, 726-728
pirates,
  Barbary, 82-83
  common enemies of humanity, as, 721
  crew as, 725
  no authority, acting under. 721
  not on board ship, arrest of, 728
  place outside jurisdiction of any state, in, 725
  private ends, for, 724
  robbery on the high seas, as, 720
  technological developments, 716
  territorial waters, within, 724
  UNCLOS definition, 722-723
  UNCLOS, jurisdiction under, 729-730
  universal jurisdiction,
    argument for, 731
    claim, premise of, 736
    emergence of, 735
    ground for exercise of, 715
    impunity, on grounds of, 736
    meaning, 731-732
    theory of, 731
    UNCLOS, provisions of, 729-730
  US law, 720-721
  use of term without definition, 393
  warships, exclusion of acts of, 724
Politics
  world, exceptionalism in, 21-24

Racial discrimination
  elimination of, 202-203
Refugees
  international relief system, absence of, 806
  solidarity, principle of, 788-789
Regional organizations
  cooperation, High-Level Panel report, 917
  development of, 643
Regulation
  government, role of, 5-6
Religion
  formation of global community, leading role in, 305

nineteenth century crisis, 136
Revolution
  Chinese, 141
  dimensions of, 139-142
  English Civil War, 142
  Japan, in, 141
  Roman, 141
  Russian, 141
  self-constituting of society, reflection of,
    141
Rule of law
  elements of, 817
  exceptions, arguments for,
    ad hoc, 752-753
    general exception, 750-752
    generally, 749-750
  High-Level Panel report, recommenda-
    tion, 918
  international. See International rule of law
  international organizations, applied to,
    598
  terrorism, erosion in case of, 667-669

Search
  philosophical meaning of, 289-290
Security
  Africa and Asia, lack of systems in, 38
  general principles of Islamic law, 312-313
  Inter-American Treaty of Reciprocal As-
    sistance, 38
  members of society, of, 152
  multilateralism, 37-38
    US challenge to, 50
  North Atlantic Treaty Organisation
    (NATO), 37
  regional organisations,
    action by, 262-263
    armed force, use of, 263
    categories of, 262
    recognition of power of, 264
    superpower, domination of, 264, 266
  regional, 259
  Warsaw Pact, 38
Self-defence
  enlarging notion of, 710
  force, right to use, 678
  historical treatment of, 706
  imminence and proportionality, adjust-
    ment of concept, 677

maintenance of international peace and
  security, keeping distinct, 672-679
preemptive, 417-419, 676
preventive policing action, 677
proportionate, 678
right of, 449
single States. by, 677
target of attack, presupposing identification of, 676
threat from non-state terrorist organizations, against, 691-693
types of, 709
unilateral action in, 673
Self-determination
  principles of, 202-203
Settlement of disputes
  disputes unsuitable for, 826-827
  formation of new international law rules,
    arising from, 239-240
  GATT, under, 548-549, 554
  improvement, need for, 530
  International Court of Justice, reference
    to, 198
  international trade. See International trade
  Manila Declaration, 198-199, 215
  means, choice of, 516
  universal and regional level, on, 226
  World Trade Organization, within, 428-
    429. See also World Trade Organization
Shipping
  Proliferation Security Initiative, 670
Social contract
  antagonistic members of same commu-
    nity, between, 302
  homogenizing function, 281
  initial deficiencies, 282
  internal contradiction, 282
  international law, in, 280
  modern version, 280
  paralogism at root of, 279
  political based on legal, doctrine of, 281
  political ontology, 279
  political regime, establishment of, 279
  status of regime, constitution of, 282
  universal justice, model of, 278-283
  rise of, 135
Society
  constitution of, 130-131
  diversity of, 130
  goal of, 771

international,
  plurality of, 297-298
  value system, 402
just, conditions for, 397
legitimate order, 152
solidarity. *See* Solidarity
transformation of, 129
twentieth-century history of, 130
world, principles guiding socio-economic
  development of,
  common heritage of mankind, 423-426
  human rights, 420-423
  international solidarity, 426-429
  UN Charter, in, 419-429
Soft law
  emergence of, 639
  governance problem of, 640-641
  instruments, 369
  international development law, 793
  reasons for, 639-640
Solidarity
  challenges ahead, 805-806
  changing structure of international law, as
    destination of, 804-805
  collective security system, political and
    legal foundation of, 779
  constitutional principle, as, 802-804
  disasters, humanitarian assistance in case
    of,
    duty to admit, 785-786
    duty to facilitate provision of, 787-788
    duty to provide, 786-787
    responsibility for, 784-785
    right to receive and provide, 785
  factual and legal independence of States,
    linking, 776
  general notion of, 777
  global constitutionalism, principle in,
    871-874
  Grundnorm of world public order, as, 802
  international development law,
    inequality, 790
    justice, principles of, 791
    law in 1970s and 1980s, 791
    recent trends, 792-794
    unilateral obligation, 791
  international environment law, 789-790
  international humanitarian law, 783-784
  international justice, at centre of, 806
  international refugee law, 788-789

international trade law,
  poverty reduction, 794
  primary rule, potential role of, 794-796
  secondary rules, role of, 796-797
international, principle of, 426-429
maintenance of international peace and
  security,
  Articles 49 and 50, scope of, 780-781
  collective responsibility, 778-780
  practice, need for reform, 781-783
  UN law, 778-783
material principle, as, 807
notion, evolution of, 775
political nature, 776
principle,
  differential obligations, 798
  international law, in branches of, 778
  maintenance of international peace and
    security, UN law on, 778-783
  multifaceted, 777
  notion, move from, 775-777
  primary rules, practice of, 797-799
  secondary rules, practice of, 799-801
  proliferation and acceptance of, 803
  public interest related universal conven-
    tions, of, 800
  society, within, 776
  structure and content of international law,
    penetrating, 807
  substantive expression of, 780
  sui generis origin, 777
South Africa
  apartheid, 202
Sovereign equality
  authoritative statements on, 741-742
  basic principle of, 31-32
  common analysis of, 738
  components of, 738
  continuum, 745-746
  current world order, cornerstone in, 31
  development of doctrine, 737-738
  differing rights and obligations, arguments
    for,
    capability, from, 754
    comprehensive national strength, from,
      756
    contribution, from, 758-759
    democracy, from, 755
    economic power, from, 756
    efficiency, from, 756

GNP, from, 756
nature of function at issue, from, 757
need, from, 755
potential effects of States, from, 757-758
retribution, from, 754
treaties and conventions, in, 753
exceptions to rule of law, argument for,
    ad hoc, 752-753
    general exception, 750-752
    generally, 749-750
hegemony, and, 34
maximum, 743-744
minimum, irreducible, 744-745
    background considerations, 746-747
    differing rights and obligations, argu-
        ments for, 753-759
    exceptions to rule of law, argument for,
        749-759
    meta-arguments, 748-749
    respect for, 772
    safeguarding, 746-759
    specific arguments, 749-759
notion of, 31-32
ordinary meaning, 742
origin of term, 742
principle of, 737
rogue states, 63
State, phenomenon of, 739-741
strong States, 760
UN Charter provisions, 741-742
Sovereignty
constitutionalism, and, 837-838
Space
International law, regulation of conduct of
    states by, 176
regime, common heritage of mankind,
    423-425
State
behavior, lawfulness of, 229
big, dismantling, 740
dimensions of statehood, 740
economic activities, 739
equality. See Sovereign equality
goodwill of, 290
great, 760-763
independence, restrictions on, 229
leader,
    deference, earning, 764-765
    human flourishing, responsibility for, 771
    identification of, 763

index of legitimacy, 764
legitimacy, 759-772
potential, behavior of, 766
qualities of, 763-764
role and place of, 737
ultimate, 768
United States as, 768
vision formulated by, 769-770
modern, foundation of, 241
nationhood, constitution of, 241
perception of, 739
phenomenon of, 739-741
political function, 740
psychological basis, 740
strong, 760
system, consolidation of, 242
theory of, 16
values of, 740
State equality
principle of, 21
State immunity
civil rights, breach of, 65
customary law, in, 65
derogations, 65
global reparations, agreements for, 66
United States, hegemonic position of,
    64-66
State sovereignty
fragmentation of international law result-
    ing from, 252
historically evolved concept of, 247-248
issue-based concept of, 249
principle, 5
small powers, of, 249-250
weak, protection of, 7

Technology
information, collation of, 637
Territoriality
weak, protection of, 7
Terrorism
acts of war distinguished, 662
Al Qaida, threat from, 656
anarchists, 656
anti-terrorist treaties, 231
arms control, 671
attacks, nature of, 663
Bush, definition by, 387
combating, contribution of Islam to, 325-
    327

Comprehensive Convention, calls for, 238
counter-terrorism activity, 670
Counter-Terrorism Committee, 685
criminal law, dealt with by, 666
  abandonment of framework, 669-670
  law of war, choice of, 671
dimensions, change in, 657-658
fight against, loss of human rights, 421
Global Programme against, 688
Guantanamo Bay, detention of suspects
  at, 666-668
High-Level Panel report, recommendation, 916
Human Rights Committee, role of, 687
Islamic terrorists, dealing with, 82-84
linked groups responsible for, 657
monitoring and intelligence gathering, 670
multilateral action against, 41-42
new, threat from, 658
non-state organizations,
  bilteral consultations, 684
  decisions as to, 684
  designation, 683
  global, 682
  human rights violations by, 698
  identification, 683, 702
  international human rights law, applica-
    tion of, 697-699
  international responsibility, 690-691
  list of, 682-683
  nexus between, 681
  procedure for determining, 683
  recourse for clearing name, 684
  threat from,
  constitutional architecture, 684-687
  international legal cooperation, 687-689
  preemptive action, 694-697
  prevention, 694-697
  proportionality, 697
  risk assessment, 689-690, 702
  self-defence, use of, 691-693
non-war against,
  combatants, organization, nature and
    territorial bases of, 661-663
  conflict, intensity of, 663
  war, definition, 659-661
OAU Convention, 696-697
persons accused of terrorist acts, legal
  status of, 699-700
physical events, 656

political dimension, 161
political groups, negotiation by, 671
preemptive action against, 387-390
religious dimension, 161-162
resort to, 153
rogue states supporting, 96
Sandinista Front, role of, 90
Security Council Committee (1267 Committee), 685
state practising, lack of state immunity,
  64-65
targeted assassinations, 700-701
territorial base, lack of, 661
terrorists, killing, 701
UN Commission on Human Rights, resolutions of, 685-686
unilateral action against, 679
United Kingdom, detention of suspects
  in, 668
United Nations Security Council resolutions, 473-475
universal definition, attempt to work out,
  238
use of term without definition, 393
war against,
  ending of, 671-672
  incorrect use of term, 663
  meaning, 659
  social bias, 672
war against, nature of, 168
way of life, where, 656
within English jurisdiction, analysis of, 730
world-wide,
  conspiracy, 657
  military environment, changes in, 655
  security concerns, 655
Transgovernmentalism
  governing through, 643-645
Transnational law
  constitutionalized systems of, 29
Treaties
  conflict between, rules for, 259-260
  criminal, specifying acts as, 391
  customary rules, modified by, 261
  dangerous, useless or disagreeable obliga-
    tions, 80
  general international law, rules of, 234
  hierarchy between norms, reluctance for,
    821
  interpretation,

consolidated method, 509
context, 508
doctrine preceding Vienna Convention,
    in light of, 506-508
general rule, 509
elements of, 527
intentional element, 508
subsequent practice, 509
Vienna Convention, in light of, 508-511
interpretation,
    principles of, 236
    schools of thought, 506-508
Islam, contribution of. *See* Islam
law of, codification and development of,
    503-504
multilateral,
    defects, 185
    legitimacy of, 177
    subjects of, 634
regional agreements,
    conflict between, rules for, 260
    provision for, 259
regional international law, creation of, 256
self-destructive obligations, 80
Vienna Convention, in light of, 508-511
Trusteeship System
    purpose of, 202
Truth and reconciliation commissions
    use of, 397

United Nations
    accession to, 193-194
    acts, challenging, 626
    administrative and financial functioning,
        reform of, 503
    Administrative Tribunal, 498
    atrocities, failure to prevent, 675
    attacks on, 457
    autonomy, 247-250
    collective security, as system of, 114, 255
    constitutional weaknesses, 451
    corruption and fraud, allegations of, 457
    crossroads, at, 430
    Department of Political Affairs, 920-922
    expenditure, advisory opinion on, 511
    expenses of, 410
    financial obligations, US failure to honour,
        68
    functionalist view, 250-251
    future of, 902

GATT, relationship with, 550-551
General Assembly. *See* United Nations
    General Assembly
High-Level Panel report,
    hype about, 912
    importance of, 912
    models for enlargement, 906-907
    recommendations,
        arms and conflicts, 917
        disarmament, 917
        environment, protection of, 916
        HIV/AIDS, 916
        international constitutional law,914
        international criminal justice, 917
        international peace and security, criteria
            of legitimacy, 915
        peace enforcement and peacekeeping,
            918
        peacebuilding, 919
        poverty reduction,914
        regional organizations, cooperation with,
            917
        resources and conflicts, 917
        rule of law, 918
        sanctions, 918
        Security Council, 918
        terrorism, 916
        transnational organized crime, 917
        responsibility to protect, endorsement
            of, 915
    idealism and realism, mix of, 243-246
    intergovernmental international organiza-
        tion, as, 243
    international system, role in, 452
    juridically enforceable rights and obliga-
        tions, conferring, 878
    League of Nations, replacing, 255
    low point, at, 911
    maintenance of international peace and
        security,
        Articles 49 and 50, scope of, 780-781
        collective responsibility, 778-780
        practice, need for reform, 781-783
    membership,
        growth in, 404
        universal, 494
    military forces, application of interna-
        tional humanitarian law to, 617
    Military Staff Committee, 409
    Millennium goals, 902

multilateralism, revival of, 376-377
nation-building needs, attention to, 9
Nehru's perception of, 245-246
new states, participation by, 192-193
no compunction to join, 31-32
non-use of force, rule of, 57-63
peace-keeping, 410-410
People's Assembly, proposal for, 897-901,
    908
purpose, broad character of, 512
reform, 502
reform of system, need for, 452
resolutions,
    implications of, 433-434
    sources of international law, not, 433
Security Council. *See* United Nations Se-
    curity Council
states liberated from colonial rule, mem-
    bership of, 192
strengthening, desire for, 376
structural weaknesses, 676
treaty-making, 43
UNCTAD,
    absence of negotiations, 375
    criticism of, 370
    establishment of, 358
    forum for negotiation, as, 368
    future of, 376-380
    institutional arrangements, review of, 371
    intellectual leadership, 375
    leadership, 373
    methods of work, addressing, 370
    multilateral negotiations, nature of, 368-
        370
    redefinition, 372
    reform, 370-376
    shift in position, 372
    soft law instruments, 369
    trade policy, call for, 355
    transformation period, 370
use of force, principles governing, 672
war, aim of banning, 36
war prevention and management, 12
way ahead,
    generally, 919
    human rights, 922-925
    international peace and security, 920-922
United Nations Charter
  Asia and Africa, whether representing,
    245

checks and balances, absence of, 451
collective security, concept of, 409, 429
constitution, notion of, 504-506, 513
constitutional characteristics, 853, 855
delegation of authority, 863
drafting, 244
enforcement, 865-867
functions under, 251
identity, assertion of, 860
importance of, 853
individual rights, 874-875
international community, as constitution
    of, 846-851
international legal order, importance in,
    847
interpretation of provisions, role of Gen-
    eral Assembly. *See* United Nations Gen-
    eral Assembly
law, 404
legal principles in. *See* Legal principle
legal regime, legal setting for, 459-460
limitations on exercise of power, 863
membership, 861-862
organs, establishment of, 863
Preamble, 454, 856, 859-861
primacy of, 862
principles, 861
principles of sovereign equality, erosion
    of, 252
provisions *jus cogens* and *erga omnes*,
    869-871
purposes, 861
regional organizations, provision for, 865-
    866
Security Council functions and powers,
    setting down, 461-463
use of force, rule as to, 262
we the peoples, in terms of, 591
withdrawal from, 867-867
United Nations Environment Programme
  creation of, 570
  role of, 577
United Nations General Assembly
  aggression, definition of, 196-198
  Binding Triad system, 891-892
  committees, work of, 896
  competence, 494
  constitution, notion of, 504-506
  decision-making process, 497-498
  decisions, judicial review of, 823-824

declarations, 195
  nature of, 179
disputes and situations threatening peace
  and security, declaration on prevention
  of, 200
Elected Representatives Liaison Unit, proposal for, 901
elimination of racial discrimination, declaration on, 202-203
enhancement of cooperation with regional
  arrangements or agencies, declaration
  on, 200-201
fact-finding in field of maintenance of international peace and security, declaration on, 200
formal votes, absence of, 497
friendly relations declaration, 192, 195-196,
  407-409
functions and powers, 494
global parliament, proposal for replacement by, 897-901, 908
human environment, world conference
  on, 569
inaugural meeting, 244
international peace and security, maintenance of, 499-502
interpretation of Charter provisions,
  constitution, notion of, 504-506, 513
  constitutional developments, 511-512
  context, 508
  doctrine preceding Vienna Convention,
    in light of, 506-508
  dynamic and evolutive, 513
  evolution of, 500
  intentional element, 508
  international peace and security, mainte-
    nance of, 499-502
  review of, 495-504
  Security Council, balance of power with,
    499-502
  special position, 493-495
  ultra vires acts, 511-512
  UN reform, 502
  Vienna Convention, in light of, 508-511
law of treaties, codification and development of, 503-504
Manila Declaration on Peaceful Settlement of Disputes, adoption of, 198-199,
  215
norm-creating process, 181

observers, participation of, 496-497
one-member one-vote policy, 889-890
Open-ended Working group, 880
permanent sovereignty over natural resources, resolution on, 205
practice, legal basis for,
  constitution, notion of, 504-506
problems of, 889-890
reform,
  proposals, 896-901
  recommendations for, 907-908
  Security Council reform, link with, 990
representatives, 894-895
  number of, 495
resolutions, legitimacy of, 177-178, 185
self-determination, resolutions and declarations on, 202
selection process, 895
special position of, 493-495
subsidiary organs, 498-499
threat or use of force, enhancement of
  principle of refraining from, 199
voting in, 178
voting method in, 889-890
voting proposals, 890-895
weighted voting, proposal for, 890-893
United Nations Security Council
accountability, 443
action, power to take, 673-674
activism, impact of, 450
Afghanistan, reaction to regime in, 471-
  472
aggression in Korea, responding to, 86
attack on Iraq, lack of judgment on, 60-61
binding obligations, creation of, 458
changing role of, 447-452
Charter,
  conception in, 431
  powers and functions defined in, 461-463
  principles, powers subject to, 453-454
clashes of views in, 62
Cold War, impotence during, 86-92
collective hegemony, 45-46
composition, 448, 879
constraints on,
  general principles of international law,
    440-441
  jus cogens, 441
  UN Charter, in, 441-443
counter terrorism resolution, 451-452

decision-making in, 410
  process, 448
decisions, 45-46
  compliance with, 439
  judicial review of, 818, 823
end of Cold War, effect of, 436
enlargement, 880-882
executive functions, 442
executive organ, as, 480
future orientation, 452-454
future, structure of, 882-886, 903-906
General Assembly, interaction with, 499-
  502
governments declared to be illegal, 465
High-Level Panel report, recommendation, 918
humanitarian intervention, developing
  thesis of, 450
illegal arms flow, limiting, 471
immunity from international prosecution
  of US nationals, US obtaining, 55
implementation of decisions, 448
importance of, overstating, 676
inaction, deciding on, 678-679
increasing activity of, 491
international affairs, as actor in, 432
international best practices, encourage-
  ment of, 438
International Criminal Tribunals, establishment of, 469-471
international legal system, in, 432-434
international peace and security, maintenance of, 499-502
international system, role in, 452
interpretative powers, 439, 440
Iraq attack on Kuwait,
  reaction to, 411
  resolutions, 465-467
judicial review of decisions, 443-447
judicial sub-organs, establishment of, 470
law-making capacity. *See also* legislative
  powers, below
  forms of action, 437-439
  legal basis and constraints, 439-443
  norms, settling or endorsing, 437
  refraining from assuming, 455
  UN Charter provisions, 436-437
legalization of use of force, erosion of monopoly on, 409-414
legislation, negative effects of, 491

legislative powers,
  benefiting UN, 487
  binding obligations, creation of, 458
  characterization of, 458
  consequences, 485-488
  content and scope of, 482-484, 488
  context and methodology, 459-460
  definitions, 460-461
  effective use of, 492
  equal rights of States, impact on princi-
    ple of, 485, 489
  implied, 463
  justifications, 483
  legal basis for, 461-465
  legal setting, 459
  legitimacy, quest for, 488-491
  norms, 482-483
  procedure, 484-485, 489-491
  subsequent practice, 464
  use of terms, 460-461
Lockerbie case, actions in, 444-447, 467-
  469
maintenance of international peace and
  security, actions for, 438, 450
  criteria of legitimacy, 915
  responsibility for, 879, 902
  way ahead, 920-922
Military Staff Committee, 866
national interest, effect of, 61
non-members, opening meetings to, 491
other UN bodies, respecting mandate of,
  452
permanent members, 45
political character, 435, 439
powers and functions of, 435-436
practice of,
  after 2001, 473-482
  before 2001, 465-473
  subsequent, concept of, 480, 491
reform, 452-453
  General Assembly reform, link with, 990
  recommendations for, 903-906
replacement of governments, authorisation of, 675
resolutions,
  Afghanistan, on, 471-472
  implications of, 433-434
  invasion of Kuwait, on, 465-467
  Iraq, need for accountability for crimes
    and atrocities, 817-818

Iraq, on, 673

legal obligations, establishment of, 472

Lockerbie crash, reaction to, 467-469

terrorism, on, 473-475

use of force to compel complaince, 673-675

weapons of mass destruction, as to, 475-481

role of, 431, 434-436

sanctions, power to impose, 817

sanctions regime, 488

scope of action, 448

self-defence, grant of right of, 449

strategy for Iraq, failure to agree, 457

strict legal criteria, decisions according to, 61

subjects of, 448

third category of members, 882-886

threat to international community, acting on, 61-62

threat to peace, interpretation of, 114

US domination, 55-56

use of force, authorization of, 449

veto, 62, 886-889, 904

voting abstentions, 464

wider membership, interaction with, 490

United States

Alien Tort Claims Act, 66-67

AMB Treaty, withdrawal from, 77-78

American Servicemembers' Protection Act, 54

anti-Communism, 93

anticipatory self-defence, 95

bilateral non-extradition treaties, 55

binding rules of international law, violation of,

  intention of, 57

  non-use of force, as to, 57-63

Bush Doctrine,

  content of, 386-389

  interventions, justification of, 395

  origin of, 386-387

  preemptive action against terrorism, 387-390

  Sherard Osborn, adoption of view of, 390-391

  terrorism, definition, 387

  threat, action to forestall, 389

Canada, relationship with, 94

constitutionalism, progress of, 242

democratic character of, 100

entangling alliances, reluctance to be involved in, 79-81

exceptionalism, 22-23, 100

exemplar nation, as, 22

extraterritorial exercise of jurisdiction, 67

felons, deprivation of vote, 392

financial obligations to UN, failure to honour, 68

foreign law, backlash against use of, 646

foreign policy, place of Doctrines in, 393

frustration over behaviour of, 77

Grenada, troops in, 88

Guantanamo Bay,

  detention of suspects at, 666-668

  situation at, 70-71

hegemon, whether, 74

hegemony, 35-36

human rights, role in, 52

imports, 35

informal world-empire, 25

international community, advancement of, 21

International Court of Justice, relationship with, 69, 72-73

international prosecution of nationals, immunity from, 55

international relations, in, 35-36

intervention in other countries, thinking on, 99

interventions by, 392

invasion of Iraq, condemnation of, 395-396

Islamic terrorists, dealing with, 82-84

isolationalism, 22

judicial appointments, 393-394

justice of cause of, 390

justice, sense of, 384

Kuwait, defence of, 91-92

Latin America, use of force in, 385, 392

leader State, as, 768

League of Nations, non-participation in, 435

Libya, attacking, 91

Mexico, intervention in, 383

military force, use as preemption, 77

military power, 93

Monroe doctrine, 36, 80

  content of, 382

  interventions, as to, 382-383

interventions, justification of, 395
rhetoric of, 382
Roosevelt corollary, 384-385, 393, 395
multilateralism, challenge to,
  binding majority decisions, failure to
    accept, 72
  binding rules of international law, viola-
    tion of, 57-71
  conclusions, 71-72
  extraterritorial effects, regulations with,
    67-68
  Geneva Conventions, refusal to ratify
    Additional Protocols, 51
  International Covenant on Civil and Po-
    litical Rights, half-hearted ratification
    of, 51-52
  International Criminal Court Statute,
    voting against, 53-56. *See also* Interna-
    tional Criminal Court
  international review of conduct, reluc-
    tance to submit to, 51-53
  law of nations, actions concerning, 66-67
  non-use of force, as to, 57-63
  obligations under International law, fail-
    ure to honour, 68
  refusal to play role in, 48
  rules applying, 47-48
  security, in field of, 50
  sovereign equality, respect for principle
    of, 63
  state immunity, in field of, 64-66
  treaty regimes, remaining aloof from, 56
  UNCLOS, non-ratification of, 48-50, 77
  world order treaties, distancing from,
    48-56
national policy, Doctrines as basis of, 397
National Security Strategy,
  fatal flaws of, 61
  Iraq, as blueprint for invasion of, 58-60
  non-use of force, violation of interna-
    tional law of, 57
  preemptive actions, option of, 58
  proper world order, vision of, 769
neutrality laws, 85
Nicaragua, role in, 88-90
North Atlantic Treaty Organisation
  (NATO), role in, 37
obligations under International law, failure
  to honour, 68
Operation Iraqi Freedom, 97-99

opposition within UN system, 21-22
peace and friendship, goal of, 101
peace through strength policy, 81-82, 92-
  93
post World War II, 85
preemption, 95-97
public servants, accountability, 586
Roman Empire compared, 26
Saddam Hussein planning attacks on,
  97-98
Security Council domination, 55-56
self-defence,
  preemptive, 417-419
  right of, 388
State, bottom-up concept of, 587
states, reference to, 381
stress, acting under, 26
Supreme Court,
  central paradox at heart of, 809-810
  jurisdiction, 809
  political role, 809
  terrorist threat to, 23-24
Truman Doctrine, 386
unchecked power, fears of, 93-97
unique position of, 74
Vietnam war, role in, 86-88, 94
war powers laws, 85
Western Hemisphere struggles, involvement in, 383
world peace, as threat to, 78
WTO third-party settlement, submission
  to, 72

Vietnam war
US role in, 86-88, 94

War
acts of terrorism distinguished, 662
Augustine's doctrine of, 706
banning, UN aim, 36
conflict, intensity of, 663
conflicts not being, 660
crime, distinct from, 666-672
definition, 659-661
evaluation, international law lacuna, 711
existence of, 662
extreme necessity, is case of, 706
general interest, pursuing, 707
history, place in, 340
Islam, in. *See* Islam

just,
  both belligerents, from viewpoint of, 708
  cases of, 712
  De Vitoria, doctrine of, 707-708
  doctrine of, 705-709
  injustice as cause of, 709
  natural law principles, 713
  old debate, resuming,711-712
  proportionality, 708
  Radbruch formula, 713
  Thomas Aquinas, contribution to doc-
    trine, 707
  unjust, and, 705
law of, changes in, 655
legality, 705
limitations on, 660
Middle Ages, in, 706
prevention and management, 12
recourse to, law permitting, 659
right to resort to (jus ad bellum), 705, 709
terrorism, against. *See* Terrorism
third states, relations with, 662
treaties renouncing, 84
UK Charter, provisions of, 710
use of force, change in focus to, 660
uses of armed force, and, 660
War crimes
  meaning, 690
  universal jurisdiction, application of, 732-
    734
Water
  right to, 829
Watercourses
  international, uses of, 237
West Africa
  ECOWAS, operations of, 263-264
World Bank
  human rights, respect for, 811
  Inspection Panel, 625, 815

  voting power in, 47
World Commission on Environment and
  Development
  creation of, 571-572
World Trade Organization
  bilateral relations, handling, 825
  challenges facing, 565
  constitutional problems, 556
  cooperation agreements, 557
  developing countries as members of, 565
  Dispute Settlement Body, 236
  dispute settlement process,
    appellate process, 559-561
    compulsory and binding, 558, 563
    expeditious, 559
    fragility, 564
    future of, 564-566
    intersection of disciplines, 562
    jurisprudence, 563-564
    legal scope, expansion, 561-564
    mechanism, 428-429
    panels, decisions of, 558
    potential conflict, areas of, 563
    solidarity, principle of, 796
  free trade principle, 428
  GATT regime, expansion of, 555
  human rights rules, application of, 615-616
  institutional regime, 555-558
  international organization, as, 555
  multilateral regime, 40
  priority of agreements, 556-557
  role of international law, analysis of, 237
  scope of agreements, 555-556
  solidarity, principle of, 795
  third-party settlement, submission of US
    to, 72
  TRIPS Agreement, 561
  US system, independence from, 565